IFIP Advances in Information and Communication Technology 540

IFIP – The International Federation for Information Processing

IFIP was founded in 1960 under the auspices of UNESCO, following the first World Computer Congress held in Paris the previous year. A federation for societies working in information processing, IFIP's aim is two-fold: to support information processing in the countries of its members and to encourage technology transfer to developing nations. As its mission statement clearly states:

IFIP is the global non-profit federation of societies of ICT professionals that aims at achieving a worldwide professional and socially responsible development and application of information and communication technologies.

IFIP is a non-profit-making organization, run almost solely by 2500 volunteers. It operates through a number of technical committees and working groups, which organize events and publications. IFIP's events range from large international open conferences to working conferences and local seminars.

The flagship event is the IFIP World Computer Congress, at which both invited and contributed papers are presented. Contributed papers are rigorously refereed and the rejection rate is high.

As with the Congress, participation in the open conferences is open to all and papers may be invited or submitted. Again, submitted papers are stringently refereed.

The working conferences are structured differently. They are usually run by a working group and attendance is generally smaller and occasionally by invitation only. Their purpose is to create an atmosphere conducive to innovation and development. Refereeing is also rigorous and papers are subjected to extensive group discussion.

Publications arising from IFIP events vary. The papers presented at the IFIP World Computer Congress and at open conferences are published as conference proceedings, while the results of the working conferences are often published as collections of selected and edited papers.

IFIP distinguishes three types of institutional membership: Country Representative Members, Members at Large, and Associate Members. The type of organization that can apply for membership is a wide variety and includes national or international societies of individual computer scientists/ICT professionals, associations or federations of such societies, government institutions/government related organizations, national or international research institutes or consortia, universities, academies of sciences, companies, national or international associations or federations of companies.

More information about this series at http://www.springer.com/series/6102

Paolo Chiabert · Abdelaziz Bouras
Frédéric Noël · José Ríos (Eds.)

Product Lifecycle Management to Support Industry 4.0

15th IFIP WG 5.1 International Conference, PLM 2018
Turin, Italy, July 2–4, 2018
Proceedings

Springer

Editors
Paolo Chiabert
Politecnico di Torino
Torino, Italy

Abdelaziz Bouras
Qatar University
Doha, Qatar

Frédéric Noël
INP Grenoble
Grenoble, France

José Ríos
Polytechnic University of Madrid
Madrid, Spain

ISSN 1868-4238 ISSN 1868-422X (electronic)
IFIP Advances in Information and Communication Technology
ISBN 978-3-030-01613-5 ISBN 978-3-030-01614-2 (eBook)
https://doi.org/10.1007/978-3-030-01614-2

Library of Congress Control Number: 2018957481

This Springer imprint is published by the registered company Springer Nature Switzerland AG
The registered company address is: Gewerbestrasse 11, 6330 Cham, Switzerland

Preface

The rise of the Industry 4.0 paradigm is disruptively changing manufacturing environments: The increasing need for integration across value chains is highlighting the need for smart, powerful information systems. In this field, product lifecycle management (PLM) plays a key role: heterogeneous information concerning product ideation, design, manufacturing, support, recycling and many other trades has to be properly managed. Further, novel approaches such as product-service systems and circular economy are posing new challenges.

IFIP PLM 2018 marked the 15th anniversary of the conference, which continues its progress at an excellent rate both in terms of quality and quantity. The topics covered in the program include ontologies, knowledge and data models, product-service systems approaches, new product development, modular design and products, cyber-physical systems, building information modeling (BIM), educational approaches to PLM, production process simulation, digital factory, CAX tools, knowledge creation and management, the role of lean organization and studies on PLM maturity, adoption, and implementation.

The IFIP International Conference on Product Lifecycle Management (www.plm-conference.org) started in 2003 and since then it has been held yearly around the world and has facilitated the exchange and discussion of the most up-to-date information on product lifecycle management among professionals from academia and industry. This is the official conference of the IFIP Working Group WG 5.1 "Global Product Development for the Whole Lifecycle" (www.ifip-wg51.org), and IFIP PLM 2018 was held in Turin, Italy, during July 2–4, 2018.

One of the objectives of the conference is to provide a platform for experts to discuss and share their success in applying advanced concepts in their respective fields. The IFIP PLM 2018 conference included an outstanding technical program, with distinguished keynote speeches on current developments and future vision, with a special focus on BIM and the industry of the future, from Prof. Jennifer Whyte (Imperial College, London), Prof. André Stork (TU Darmstadt), Eng. Paolo Calefati (Prima Industrie, Italy), and Eng. Alberto Codrino (PLM Systems, Italy). Two insightful visits to manufacturing facilities were also organized: to the Maserati Levante final assembly line and Baladin brewery.

The conference also offered a great opportunity for young and aspiring researchers to present their research proposals and ongoing work during a dedicated PhD Workshop on the preconference day. This regular workshop is designed to support students in their networking activities and help them build their future community.

In line with the conference scientific sessions, IFIP PLM 2018 aimed at encouraging innovation and exchange with industry and digital service providers. A full day was dedicated to industry applications, highlighting some efforts and initiatives related to industry digitalization in the fields of Aerospace and Rail (Airbus, Avio GE, Hitachi Rail), Process and Product industries (TMC, COMAU, Siemens PLM Software, Electrolux),

ICT solutions for data exchange (TIM), digital constructions (Hansen Yuncken), automotive (FCA Group), as well as food and beverage (Baladin, Ferrero) sectors.

This book, organized in 12 chapters, is composed of selected enhanced papers presented at the IFIP PLM 2018 conference. Submissions followed a single-blind peer-review process. From a total of 82 submissions, 72 were accepted to be presented at the conference. This book is part of the IFIP *Advances in Information and Communication Technology* (AICT) series that publishes state-of-the-art results in the sciences and technologies of information and communication.

In addition to this conference, the *International Journal of Product Lifecycle Management* (IJPLM) is the official journal of the WG5.1 (www.inderscience.com/ijplm).

On behalf of the conference, we thank all the authors, session chairs, reviewers, and keynote speakers for their help and support in achieving a great conference. Our gratitude goes to Politecnico di Torino, to the sponsors PLM Systems, FCA Group, Siemens, Autodesk and Electrolux, as well as to Regione Piemonte and Comune di Torino for their great support.

We hope this book serves as a step forward in this exciting area of PLM and we look forward to meeting you at the next PLM conference in Moscow, Russia, during July 10–12, 2019 (www.plm-conference.org).

September 2018

Paolo Chiabert
Abdelaziz Bouras
Frédéric Noël
José Ríos

Organization

Program Chairs

P. Chiabert	Politecnico di Torino, Italy
J. Ríos	Universidad Politecnica de Madrid, Spain
F. Noël	INP Grenoble, France

Conference Chairs

M. Gattiglio	Convergent Photonics, Italy
G. Molina	FCA Group, Italy
K.-D. Thoben	University of Bremen, Germany

Steering Committee

K.-D. Thoben (Chair)	University of Bremen, Germany
R. Bandinelli	University of Florence, Italy
A. Bernard	Ecole Centrale de Nantes, France
A. Bouras	Qatar University, Qatar
D. Dutta	Rutgers University, USA
B. Eynard	UTC Compiègne, France
S. Foufou	Université de Bourgogne, France and New York University Abu Dhabi, UAE
S. Fukuda (Honorary Professor)	Keio University, Japan
B. Gurumoorthy	IISc Bangalore, India
C. McMahon	Technical University of Denmark, Denmark
L. Rivest	ETS Montreal, Canada
L. Roucoules	Arts et Métiers Paris Tech, France
S. Terzi	Politecnico di Milano, Italy

Scientific Committee

S. Altavilla	Politecnico di Torino, Italy
A. Aoussat	Arts et Métiers ParisTech, France
R. Bandinelli	University of Florence, Italy
A. Bernard	Ecole Centrale de Nantes, France
N. Bilalis	Technical University of Crete, Greece
A. Bouras	Qatar University, Qatar
M. Bricogne	University of Technology Compiègne, France
C. Castiglione	Politecnico di Torino, Italy
N. Chakpitak	Chiang Mai University, Thailand

P. Chiabert	Politecnico di Torino, Italy
U. Cugini	Politecnico di Milano, Italy
G. D'Antonio	Politecnico di Torino, Italy
C. Danjou	Ecole de Technologie Supérieure de Montréal, Canada
E. De Senzi Zancul	University of Sao Paulo, Brazil
F. Demoly	University of Technology - Belfort Montbéliard, France
T. Diallo	Superior Engineering Institute of Paris, France
D. Dutta	Rutgers University, USA
G. Egger	Fraunhofer Italia, Italy
B. Eynard	UTC Compiègne, France
E. Filos	European Commission, Belgium
S. Foufou	Université de Bourgogne, France and New York University Abu Dhabi, UAE
S. Fukuda (Honorary Professor)	Keio University, Japan
M. Galati	Politecnico di Torino, Italy
F. Giannini	Consiglio Nazionale delle Ricerche, Italy
J. Gopsill	University of Bath, UK
B. Gurumoorthy	IISc Bangalore, India
R. Harik	University of South Carolina, USA
N. Hartman	Purdue University, USA
P. Hehenberger	Johannes Kepler University Linz, Austria
H. Hiraoka	Chuo University, Japan
P. Hong	University of Toledo, USA
G. Huang	University of Hong Kong, SAR China
J. Jupp	University of Technology Sydney, Australia
H. Karkkainen	Tampere University of Technology, Finland
D. Kiritsis	Ecole Polytechnique Fédérale de Lausanne, Switzerland
B. Koomen	University of Twente, The Netherlands
H. Lampela	Lappeenranta University of Technology, Finland
J. Le Duigou	University of Technology Compiegne, France
J.G. Lim	Samsung Electronics, Republic of South Korea
F. Lu Wen	National University of Singapore, Singapore
J. Malmqvist	Chalmers University of Technology, Sweden
N. Maranzana	Arts et Métiers ParisTech, France
F. Mas	Airbus, Spain
M. Matei	University of Ottawa, Canada
A. McKay	University of Leeds, UK
C. McMahon	Technical University of Denmark, Denmark
M. Messaadia	CESI, France
D. Morales Palma	University of Seville, Spain
S. Myung	Youngsan University, Republic of South Korea
S. Nikolaev	Skolkovo Institute of Science and Technology
F. Noël	INP Grenoble, France

F. Nyffenegger	HSR Rapperswil, Switzerland
Y. Ouzrout	University of Lyon, France
H. Panetto	University of Lorraine, France
H.-J. Pels (Honorary Professor)	Eindhoven University of Technology, The Netherlands
M. Peruzzini	Polytechnic University of Marche, Italy
J. Racero	University of Seville, Spain
S. Rachuri	National Institute of Standards and Technology, USA
J. Ríos	Polytechnic University of Madrid, Spain
L. Rivest	ETS Montreal, Canada
M. Rossi	Politecnico di Milano, Italy
L. Roucoules	University of Technology of Troyes, France
N. Sapidis	University of Western Macedonia, Greece
J. Sauza Bedolla	CERN, Switzerland
M. Schabacker	University of Magdeburg, Germany
F. Segonds	Arts et Métiers ParisTech, France
A. Silventoinen	Lappeenranta University of Technology, Finland
V. Singh	Aalto University, Finland
A. Smirnov	St. Petersburg IFI and A. R. Academy of Sciences, Russia
C. Snider	University of Bristol, UK
D. Stadnicka	Rzeszow University of Technology, Poland
S. Terzi	Politecnico di Milano, Italy
K.-D. Thoben	University of Bremen, Germany
S. Vajna	University of Magdeburg, Germany
D. Vieira	Université du Québec à Trois-Rivières, Canada
C. Vila	Polytechnic University Valencia, Spain
T. Wuest	West Virginia University, USA
R. Young	Loughborough University, UK

Doctoral Workshop Chairs

Y. Ouzrout	University of Lyon, France
M. Rossi	Politecnico di Milano, Italy

Local Committee

K. Aliev	Politecnico di Torino, Italy
S. Altavilla	Politecnico di Torino, Italy
G. Bruno	Politecnico di Torino, Italy
C. Castiglione	Politecnico di Torino, Italy
G. D'Antonio	Politecnico di Torino, Italy
M. De Maddis	Politecnico di Torino, Italy

Contents

Building Information Modeling

Collaborative Environments and New Product Development

PLM for Digital Factories and Cyber Physical Systems

Building Information Modeling

Mixed Reality Tools as an Enabler for Improving Operation and Maintenance in Small and Medium Enterprises

Harry Whiskard[1(✉)], David Jones[1(✉)], Steve Voller[2(✉)], Chris Snider[1(✉)], James Gopsill[3(✉)], and Ben Hicks[1(✉)]

[1] University of Bristol, Bristol, UK
{hw13082, david. jones, chris. snider, ben. hicks}@bristol. ac. uk
[2] Altuity Solutions Ltd, Bristol, UK
steve. voller@altuity. com
[3] University of Bath, Bath, UK
j. a. gopsill@bath. ac. uk

Abstract. The use of Mixed Reality (MR) tools can improve information retrieval, collaboration and decision making, thus aiding the management of buildings within the operation and maintenance (O&M) lifecycle stages. In this paper, we focus on the use of MR in visualising BIM data to aid building lifecycle management.

This paper compares current and emerging MR tools and explores their potential in being applied to O&M of Small and Medium Enterprises (SMEs). MR refers to technology that enhances reality by integrating it with the digital world, such as Augmented Reality (AR), Virtual Reality (VR) and spherical panoramas, known as Photospheres.

Current literature on applications and limitations of MR in the O&M cycle for small businesses is explored and the user requirements for implementation and use are elicited. Key requirements are found to be cost, skill level, interoperability, pre-requisite data, interactivity and time. Using these requirements, the state-of-the-art in VR, AR and Photosphere environments is assessed and the contexts in which they are most appropriate are developed. The paper concludes with a number of recommendations for the selection of an appropriate strategy dependent on the maturity of BIM adoption within an enterprise. A number of theoretical and conceptual implications are also developed.

1 Introduction

The lifecycle of a building comprises four main stages: Design, Build, Operate and Maintain. The first two stages cover a building from its conception, through to construction until hand over to building owners and facility management teams for use. Operation and Maintenance (O&M) is relevant to all assets from infrastructure to high value products and can incur up to 60% of the total lifecycle costs for a building [1]. Thus, effective management is crucial to reduce costs and extend lifespans.

Published by Springer Nature Switzerland AG 2018.
P. Chiabert et al. (Eds.): PLM 2018, IFIP AICT 540, pp. 3–14, 2018.
https://doi.org/10.1007/978-3-030-01614-2_1

Lifecycle management within O&M aims to provide a safe working environment, minimise lifecycle costs and optimise for desired building function. To help achieve these aims, Building Information Modelling (BIM) is employed to improve collaboration, information retrieval and decision making across the entire supply-chain and product lifecycle. BIM is the process of generating, integrating and collaborating on digital models and data to support building management to support design, building, maintenance and operation. BIM is defined by four levels that feature the level of detail, data and collaboration involved in the management of a building. For example, level 0 involves 2D drafting and plans and little to no collaboration, while level 3 requires the sharing and collaboration across the prime contractor, customer and entire market place of all 3D models. Level 3+ BIM can enable, for example, advanced analysis such as clash detection and interrogation of construction plans. In the UK, government projects are generally required to conform to Level 2 BIM, which demands the exchange of models and data using standards such as COBie (Construction Operations Building Information Exchange). While large contractors for major projects endeavour to comply with Level 2 BIM, the majority of small projects achieve Level 1 BIM compliance by documenting some 3D CAD work for concepts, 2D drawings for statutory documentation and some form of common data repository for access and re-use. Given that the majority of projects conform at least to Level 1 BIM standards, the focus of this paper is in enhancing the re-use of this data within O&M. This is achieved by visualising the information and models through a low-cost, lightweight platform suitable for small BIM projects.

Emerging Mixed Reality (MR) technologies can provide superior visualisation through more immersive and interactive environments. MR refers to technology that enhances reality by integrating it with the digital world, such as Augmented Reality (AR), Virtual Reality (VR) and spherical panoramas. AR and VR are becoming increasingly commonplace and research shows they could be effectively applied to support Small and Medium enterprise (SME) O&M [2, 3]. This paper introduces the use of spherical panoramas (a.k.a. Photospheres), which are commonly used within Google Street View, as a means to provide the visual navigation and search of BIM information one would expect from a BIM level 2+ compliant project.

Small and Medium enterprises (SMEs) are generally defined as firms with less than 250 employees and turnover of below €50 million [4]. This limit of company size will in turn have an effect on the building it occupies and the resources dedicated to management of the building lifecycle. Hence some visualisation tools suited to larger facilities may be too expensive, require too much expert knowledge and require technical pre-requisites that are not available within small facilities. Whilst research has been performed into the use of mixed reality tools within Facility Management and O&M, there has been no little to no consideration of their suitability for SMEs.

This paper aims to understand the different requirements for visualisation tools between large and small enterprises (facilities), and present recommendations on the most suited MR tools for smaller companies. Finally, a number of recommendations are developed for the selection of an appropriate strategy dependent upon maturity of BIM adoption.

2 Operation and Maintenance

The purpose of this section is to highlight the need for Mixed Reality tools within the management of the Operation and Maintenance stages, commonly known as Facilities Management (FM). FM is an organisational process focused on maintaining and enhancing building infrastructure within O&M. Typical responsibilities of a facility manager within the O&M cycle focus on three key areas: cost, performance and risk. Through employing Building Information Modelling (BIM), FM tasks can be improved as maintenance data is more readily available, and decision and collaboration with internal and external stakeholders is enhanced.

FM is a complex process, encompassing many cross-organisational activities, many stakeholders and large amounts of data. The potential applications of BIM within FM were highlighted through online user surveys and were found to be: locating building components, facilitating real-time data access, visualisation and marketing, checking maintainability, and creating digital assets [5]. Hence, in this paper, MR tools will be explored based on how they can be used within these scenarios.

To service assets and perform corrective maintenance, important building assets must be frequently located and inspected. Through providing asset location in 3D models, the exact location can be easily visualised, helping reduce maintenance time. Subsequently, asset information, along with repair instructions and maintenance schedules, must be accessed to perform maintenance. Providing this information in an easy to comprehend format and in-situ with the maintenance location can help reduce errors and increase time spent performing repairs. Achieving such interoperability is one of the key tenets of BIM solutions that aim to bring all relevant information into a single platform.

The use of BIM within FM is often limited by the availability of digital models from the design and build phase, which are often either non-existent, not accessible or not up-to-date. For example, 80% of European buildings were created pre 1990, before mainstream BIM software to create building models was available [6]. Further, despite the inception of BIM, not all building projects use digital models and many models are either not kept up-to-date or not transferred to facility managers in the handover process. The lack of pre-existing models to underpin BIM is a major barrier to BIM-enabled FM. Therefore, to start utilising BIM within FM, digital models of assets need to first be created in order to provide traceability. Maintainability is the ease with which a product can be repaired to perform its desired function. Within buildings, assets must be easily accessible so that maintenance teams can perform repairs quickly with minimum cost and where possible, designed sustainably to preserve asset life span.

To evaluate how applicable different visualisation tools are, the stakeholder requirements for implementation and use must first be considered. [2] highlighted the main issues for implementation of BIM and mobile AR in FM. Issues relevant to technology were cost, lack of BIM models, lack of BIM-trained personnel and interoperability. Similarly, [7] review of barriers to BIM adoption highlighted the main issues to be: cost of investment, learning curve for BIM technologies, lack of executive buy-in, poor collaboration among participants and poor interoperability among BIM software. In terms of technology specific requirements, [6] presented the requirements for data capturing techniques within BIM as being: applicability in existing buildings, cost, time, spatial accuracy, level of detail, influence of size and complexity of the scene, influence of environmental conditions, importability into BIM, data volumes, degree of automation, operability, equipment portability, equipment durability and robustness. Through synthesis of these existing studies, this study considers six aspects of MR tool implementation within the context of O&M, these are:

Cost: Must be minimised to be attractive to companies with limited budgets. This includes both initial hardware costs and running costs.

Time: The tool should require as little time commitment as possible. Through increased automation of tasks and faster data retrieval, visualisation tools enable the reduction of time spent performing maintenance tasks.

Interoperability: The ability to integrate with current BIM systems and maintenance information is fundamental for ease of implementation.

Technical requirements: Required skills and expert knowledge should be low, in order to minimise the amount of specific training time and increase the number of staff who can use the tools.

Pre-existing data: BIM data must exist before using visualisation tools; the lower the data requirements (level of detail and completeness), the easier a visualisation tool is to implement and use.

Degree of Interactivity: The level to which the environment can be interacted with and the ease with which relevant information can be retrieved.

3 Operation and Maintenance in Small-to-Medium Enterprises

Large businesses are able to commit more resources to implementing technology to aid processes and are usually the first to benefit from technological advances. BIM is an area which has been primarily focused towards large companies and projects, however SMEs, which contributed £1.8 Trillion to the UK in 2014, can also benefit from implementing it to support O&M [4]. Within FM, the maintenance process is the same as larger companies, where maintenance procedures and extensive collaboration between internal and external stakeholders is necessary. Visualisation tools present a method of improving these collaborations, which includes sharing and modification of data, information and models, and as barriers to entry are lower, they become increasing viable for small companies.

A challenge for smaller firms is the ability to provide cost-effective FM, which when combined with non-adaptive employees and a lack of understanding of the capabilities of BIM, can prevent the adoption of new technologies. Visualisation tools that require specific hardware, perform limited tasks and have high running costs would therefore be unsuitable to SMEs. In a large company, many employees would be committed to maintenance and can afford to spend more time in training and keeping BIM related data and models up-to-date. The creation of visualisation tools that require minimal training and are as time efficient as possible is therefore increasingly important.

As discussed in Sect. 2, implementing BIM and visualisation tools in FM requires pre-existing BIM data and models and is a challenge for small enterprises who would not possess or have access to digital models. Rather, paper-based floor plans are often the main source of documentation on an existing building. In order to create digital models, current data capture technologies are laser scanning, photogrammetry, RFID and Barcode tagging. Laser scanning produces the most accurate 3D models but is very expensive. Photogrammetry is a much cheaper method of creating models but with lower resolution. RFID and Barcodes are used to mark assets to provide quick information retrieval rather than creating digital models. Whilst a lower cost solution, tagging methods are limited to the applications they can be used for and it is time-consuming to mark every asset. For a SME, the cost of creating, curating and marking-up digital models and assets is a major barrier, which limits the visualisation tools that can be implemented to aid the FM process. Thus, the visualisation tool in turn must be suited to the level of BIM adopted by the company, which maybe relatively low (Level 0).

4 Mixed Reality

The following section will cover the state-of-the-art in Mixed Reality (MR) and its suitability for supporting the O&M activities of SMEs. MR refers to technology that involves the merging of real and virtual worlds and can vary from real environments to fully virtual environments [8]. The term incorporates technologies that enhance real environments with virtual objects, known as Augmented Reality (AR), and fully simulated environments, known as Virtual Reality (VR). MR offers benefits in terms of visualisation compared to standard screen based methods. Users are not limited to visualising 3D objects on 2D screens and by integrating the real world with technology data can be linked to real objects. Three different MR technologies will be reviewed in the following sections and appraised based on the maintenance activities they are suited to support and how they satisfy the requirements given in Sect. 2.

4.1 Augmented Reality

Augmented Reality involves the enhancement of the real world by overlaying virtual objects via a computer. Two different types of AR are considered; monitor-based devices and 'See-through' head mounted AR devices.

Research into the use of Augmented Reality for BIM and FM, has mainly looked at the effectiveness of information access using hand-held AR devices and applications in which it can be implemented. Within construction, site inspection and hazard identification can be enhanced by using computer vision to detect, and AR to highlight unsafe environments for workers [9]. Hidden utilities, such as underground pipes can be revealed, to help prevent collisions in laying pipework [10]. Augmenting assembly instructions can help improve construction speeds and reduce mistakes compared to paper-based approaches. A study in electrical construction found mistakes were reduced by 75%, whilst a study in using AR for piping assembly found a time and error reduction of 50% [11, 12].

Using either hand-held or head-mounted devices, AR is suitable for on-site work. Head Mounted devices such as the Microsoft HoloLens use a combination of inertial measurement unit and depth sensors to create basic 3D models, perceive distance of objects and recognise environments. This allows users to walk around and interact with objects, such as marking defective features and retrieve data in-situ. Therefore, AR would be effective in asset tracking, facilitating real-time data access and checking maintainability of assets, as they are on-site tasks.

Locating building components requires the process of the user localising themselves relative to assets within a building. Localising assets can be achieved using SLAM (Simultaneous Localisation And Mapping) or tagging. The current standard method involves either linking RFID or visual markers to assets, meaning users locate assets, and by detecting markers, information and assets can be augmented automatically. This provides a faster method of information access, however, assets must be found initially which can be time consuming. Using localisation methods, AR devices can be used to understand a user's location in a building and provide directions to the desired asset. Through object recognition methods, the asset could be automatically identified, preventing the need to manually install asset tags. Manually installing RFID or visual markers is a very time-consuming process and requires regular servicing to ensure they remain in working condition. A comparison of mobile and head-mounted AR is shown in Table 1.

Table 1. Mobile and Head mounted AR against user requirements

Requirement	Mobile AR	Head Mounted AR
Cost	Readily available on smartphones, so cheap	Microsoft HoloLens costs $3000
Technical Skill	Low skill required as controlled using smartphones/tablets	Hand gesture control and non-screen based visualisation requires training
Interoperability	Web-based	Requires specific software
Pre-requisite data	Requires asset tags or models	Requires asset tags or models
Interactivity	Screen based visualisation, can augment hidden features	3D visualisations in real space, can augment hidden features
Time	Helps reduce time accessing data	Facilitates hands free working

Two types of AR are presented, mobile and head-mounted. Both types are suited for in-situ maintenance, but vary in the cost, hardware requirements and level of interactivity. Mobile AR is the lowest cost and lowest skill solution, but users are limited to screen based visualisation with no spatial understanding capability.

4.2 Virtual Reality

Virtual Reality is the full simulation of an environment allowing a user to interact with it, usually via a head-mounted display. VR aims to fully immerse a user within a virtual world, even providing sensory feedback to enhance the degree of realism. VR headsets comprise two main types from mounted smartphones to more expensive and powerful computer-tethered devices.

A major focus of VR for BIM is within the design stage, before any physical infrastructure exists. Designs can be viewed in actual scale and explored fully, providing a better sense of how users will interact with the building and visually detect any design flaws. Further use of VR lies in training, where users can be put in specific scenarios too dangerous to experience in real settings, such as identifying construction hazards before going on-site [13]. A benefit of VR use in BIM is that within building simulations, user experience can be tested with much greater realism than conventional methods. For example, by using VR to simulate lighting configurations of buildings, the user can visualise room atmosphere and optimum lighting setup, which wouldn't be possible by simply viewing on a computer screen [3]. Within FM, VR has been shown to be able to be used as a multi-user network to allow remotely situated stakeholders to collaborate using virtual building models to aid in maintenance decision-making [14].

Due to VR being a fully simulated environment, digital models are required. Thus, to implement, building models must either be pre-existing or be generated using data capture techniques. The use of head mounted devices is something that is unfamiliar to many people as methods of control are dissimilar to controlling smartphones or computers. Virtual worlds must also be specially designed to consider motion sickness and fatigued eyes. These factors mean that use of VR will need both specialist training and there is likely to be resistance to uptake, as people don't feel confident in using the devices. VR enables off-site inspection; therefore, time can be saved through preventing physical inspections. The suitability of VR with respect to the user requirements is shown in Table 2.

Table 2. Virtual Reality against user requirements

Requirement	Virtual Reality
Cost	Mobile VR <\$100 and Tethered VR \$400–\$800
Technical Skill	3D interactions require training
Interoperability	Requires specific software
Pre-requisite data	Full digital models
Interactivity	3D visualisation, tethered devices capable of movement tracking
Time	Minimal setup time, reduce time spent performing inspections

Mobile and tethered VR have similar capabilities, but tethered VR has higher processing power as they use powerful computer hardware and motion tracking to increase interactivity and allow users to move around virtual environments.

4.3 Photospheres

Spherical panoramas, known as Photospheres, are 360-degree spherical images, most commonly used in Google Street View. They can be created by using specialist cameras, such as the Ricoh Theta S, or by stitching multiple images on smartphones. Although comprised as static images stitched together, Photospheres can be considered to be a sub-set of virtual reality, as a real environment is recreated in a virtual environment. This provides a greater level of immersion than standard images and a higher level of resolution than common Virtual Reality environments.

At present, the use of Photosphere beyond Google Street View remains limited. The capability to better understand an environment has been demonstrated through virtual tours mainly in museums and galleries [15]. The potential in extracting information automatically has also been explored, an example being mapping out road sign location using computer vision within Street View [16]. Within the area of BIM, more advanced 3D models can be generated using photogrammetry and further used as a tool to compare deviation of buildings from the 'as-built' to 'designed as' models [17, 18].

Photospheres have the benefit of a high level of detail, meaning users can easily relate their actual environment to the digital model. If a user was to stand in the same place as the Photosphere, what they observe on their device should be identical to the real world. This easy to understand environment could aid the localisation of maintenance issues by building users. By integrating with building plans, from 2D plans to 3D models, a greater degree of realism to BIM systems can be introduced.

Unlike Virtual Reality, the computing power required to create, view and manipulate Photospheres is very low due to the static image format and ability to be viewed interactively on modern web browsers. Capturing a building with Photospheres is a predominantly manual process. Similar to Street View with cars driving through streets taking photos, a person is required to walk around a desired building and capture the panoramas of each room. However, as only images are taken in rooms, the process is much quicker than taking manual measurements or laser scanning to create digital models. Table 3 shows the suitability of Photospheres to meet the requirements in Sect. 2.

Table 3. Photosphere against user requirements

Requirement	Photosphere
Cost	Readily available on most devices, so cheap
Technical Skill	Low skill required as controlled using smartphones/tablets
Interoperability	Web-based
Pre-requisite data	Can be used with any level of data
Interactivity	Image based visualisation
Time	Reduced time accessing and locating data, high setup time

Photospheres offer a lost cost, low skill visualisation method. Users are constrained to visualisations of buildings based on capture location, but environments are easy to understand as they are photograph based.

5 Discussion

The three visualisation methods vary in their potential applications and their ability to meet the requirements developed in Sect. 2. Table 4 shows the comparison of each MR tool presented against the elicited set of user requirements from Sect. 2.

Table 4. Comparison of MR tools based on user requirements

Requirements	Photospheres	Mobile AR	Head Mounted AR	VR
Cost	Low	Low	High	High
Technical Skill	Low	Low	Medium	Medium
Interoperability	High	High	Medium	Low
Pre-requisite data	Low	Medium	Medium	High
Interactivity	Low	Medium	High	High
Time	High	Medium	Medium	Medium

Both VR and head mounted AR devices require higher technical skill to use, due to methods of control many people are unfamiliar with. Due to the unusual methods of use, cultural resistance to implementation is likely to be greater than the other tools. Both Photospheres and AR are compatible on smartphones and tablets, therefore have low skill requirements and have low initial costs as no specific hardware is required. Further, on-going costs are likely to be low due to open source toolkits and standards. Whilst VR and head mounted AR have the highest skill requirements, they also provide the highest level of interactivity, through 3D environments that can be manipulated and navigated easily. Mobile AR is limited to screen-based visualisations but with a higher degree of interactivity than photospheres. Photospheres are image-based therefore cannot be manipulated and environment visualisation is limited by the number of Photospheres captured. AR and Photospheres are web-based meaning there is higher compatibility across different data types and platforms including desktop and mobile devices [19].

VR has the highest data requirements, as digital models are needed to visualise building information. Companies must have a BIM Level 2+ (detailed CAD models and asset information) or use data capture methods to generate models. AR can be used with either full digital models or with asset tagging, a lower cost solution. Future AR may employ localisation and object recognition to allow building navigation and remove the need for models or asset tagging. Photospheres employ a more manual approach to asset location and information retrieval, therefore have much lower data requirements. Given the capabilities and limitations of each technology, the applications they are suited to varies, which is summarised in Table 5.

AR and Photospheres are generally more portable than VR and can integrate with real environments and thus can be used effectively in in-situ maintenance tasks. VR however, is limited to off-site use only as the visualisation is a full virtual environment.

There is no clear MR tool that would be the most effective in FM, with the most suitable tool being dependent on the company needs, desired application and current

Table 5. Suitability of mixed reality tools to maintenance activities

Mixed Reality	Application
Augmented Reality	Best suited to in-situ maintenance activities. Locating assets can be performed by detecting asset tags or localisation. Asset information can be augmented onto assets themselves to provide greater level of information
Virtual Reality	Best suited to off-site maintenance activities. Virtual environment enables remote inspections, marketing visualisation and checking maintainability
Photospheres	Best suited to in-situ maintenance activities. Appropriate for reporting maintenance and locating assets and facilitating real time data access

level of BIM maturity. For smaller companies with low budgets, the current level of BIM adoption is likely to be low. Without up-to-date 3D building models, use of VR tools would not be advantageous.

Using Photospheres to locate building components requires no extra hardware and can be used with any level of BIM maturity. In buildings, where only 2D plans are present, Photospheres can be integrated to give a level of 3D visualisation without the need for full digital models. Whilst benefits are gained in cost and pre-existing data required, there is a low level of interactivity as Photospheres are image based. The process of setting up Photospheres within a building is also time consuming, as photos must be captured and assets manually linked within each Photosphere.

Where slightly larger budgets and workforces are accessible, locating building assets and data access could be facilitated using AR. Current AR tools require assets being marked using either RFID or visual markers, which along with initial setup time, require regular servicing to ensure markers work correctly.

In a company with an already high level of adoption, the use of VR should be considered. With a high level of maturity already present, using VR can aid in collaboration, training and checking assets off-site.

6 Conclusion

Mixed Reality tools present a method of enhancing the management of buildings within Operation and Maintenance. This paper explored the requirements for implementation and use of mixed reality tools, and the current state of the art in Virtual Reality, Augmented Reality and Photospheres.

VR was found to be best suited for visualisation and collaboration activities, however high cost and high pre-requisite data requirements limit its applicability to SMEs. Both AR and Photospheres could be applied to locating building components, facilitating real-time data access and visualisation activities. Mobile AR and Photospheres are low cost solutions, which can run with both web-based applications and smart phones. Their low cost also relates to their implementation where they have little to no on-going costs. High device compatibility means there are low technical skill requirements and high interoperability, therefore would be well suited to smaller companies. Current AR requires either assets to be tagged or digital models, whereas Photospheres can be used with any level of BIM adoption and buildings can be quickly mapped using smart phones or specific cameras. For a small company with low levels of BIM maturity (level 0 or 1), Photospheres can most easily be implemented to support the O&M process.

Whilst there are benefits to using Mixed Reality tools to support maintenance within small companies, current barriers limit their widespread implementation. Future development in the technologies could see them becoming used regularly within building management.

In terms of the long-term outlook, the conceptual implications of integrating Photospheres with 2D plans may offer the opportunity to leapfrog existing BIM level 0/1 projects to level 4 projects. Further, advanced image processing techniques may allow for automatic asset identification and the construction if 3D models. These aspects are being considered by the Authors in their future research.

References

1. Akcamete, A., Akinci, B., Garrett, J.: Potential utilization of building information models for planning maintenance activities. In: Proceedings of the International Conference on Computing in Civil and Building Engineering (2010)
2. Gheisari, M., Goodman, S., Schmidt, J., Williams, G., Irizarry, J.: Exploring BIM and mobile augmented reality use in facilities management. In: Construction Research Congress, pp. 1941–1950 (2014)
3. Natephra, W., Motamedi, A., Fukuda, T., Yabuki, N.: Integrating building information modeling and virtual reality development engines for building indoor lighting design. Vis. Eng. **5**, 19 (2017)
4. Department for Business Innovation & Skills: Business Population Estimates for the Uk and Regions 2014 (2014)
5. Becerik-Gerber, B., Jazizadeh, F., Li, N., Calis, G.: Application areas and data requirements for BIM-enabled facilities management. Build. Simul. **138**, 431–442 (2012)
6. Volk, R., Stengel, J., Schultmann, F.: Building Information Modeling (BIM) for existing buildings - Literature review and future needs. Autom. Constr. **38**, 109–127 (2014)
7. Won, J., Lee, G., Dossick, C., Messner, J.: Where to focus for successful adoption of building information modeling within organization. J. Constr. Eng. Manag. **139**(11), 04013014 (2013)
8. Milgram, P., Kishino, F.: A taxonomy of mixed reality visual displays. IEICE Trans. Inf. Syst. **77**(12), 1321–1329 (1994)
9. Li, X., Yi, W., Chi, H.L., Wang, X., Chan, A.P.C.: A critical review of virtual and augmented reality (VR/AR) applications in construction safety. Autom. Constr. **86**, 150–162 (2018)
10. Behzadan, A.H., Dong, S., Kamat, V.R.: Augmented reality visualization: a review of civil infrastructure system applications. Adv. Eng. Inform. **29**, 252–267 (2015)
11. Hou, L., Wang, X., Truijens, M.: Using augmented reality to facilitate piping assembly: an experiment-based evaluation. J. Comput. Civ. Eng. **29**, 05014007 (2015)
12. Chalhoub, J., Ayer, S.K.: Using Mixed Reality for electrical construction design communication. Autom. Constr. **86**, 1–10 (2018)
13. Sacks, R., Perlman, A., Barak, R.: Construction safety training using immersive virtual reality. Constr. Manag. Econ. **31**(9), 1005–1017 (2013)

14. Shi, Y., Du, J., Lavy, S., Zhao, D.: A multiuser shared virtual environment for facility management. Procedia Eng. **145**, 120–127 (2016)
15. Napolitano, R.K., Douglas, I.P., Garlock, M.E., Glisic, B.: Virtual tour environment of Cuba's national school of art. In: ISPRS-International Archives of the Photogrammetry, Remote Sensing and Spatial Information Sciences, vol. XLII-2/W5, pp. 547–551 (2017)
16. Balali, V., Ashouri Rad, A., Golparvar-Fard, M.: Detection, classification, and mapping of U.S. traffic signs using Google street view images for roadway inventory management. Vis. Eng. **3**(1), 15 (2015)
17. Kwiatek, K., Tokarczyk, R.: Immersive Photogrammetry in 3D Modelling (2016)
18. Jokinen, O., Kauhanen, H.: Lower bounds for as-built deviations against as-designed 3-D Building Information Model from single spherical panoramic image. Autom. Constr. **84**, 274–291 (2017)
19. Pauwels, P., Zhang, S., Lee, Y.C.: Semantic web technologies in AEC industry: a literature overview. Autom. Constr. **73**, 145–165 (2017)

A Three-Step BIM Implementation Framework for the SME Contractors

Arman M. Kouch(✉)

Oulu University of Applied Sciences, Oulu, Finland
arman.kouch@outlook.com

Abstract. Building information modeling (BIM) is quickly booming while the ICT and digitalization are developing. Still, the BIM implementation particularly for the SME (Small and Medium-sized Enterprises) firms like contractors in the building industry is not efficiently recognized and used. In fact, the SMEs mostly recognize BIM as just a tool to create a 3D model and are not aware of the technology, its implementation and challenges. Therefore, the main aim of this study is to introduce BIM, the factors and challenges related to implementing a basic practical adoption model to employ building information modelling technology for the SME contractors by introducing a basic, easy to implement, practical three-step BIM implementation framework, which can potentially increase their competitiveness and profit.

Keywords: Building information modeling · BIM implementation framework
The building industry · BIM adoption · SME contractors

1 Background: BIM and Its Importance

A building description system (BDS), as the origin of BIM, was introduced in 1975 [1]. However, building information modeling is known as a process [2], a new technology and methodology that provides accurate data and processes for all the involved stakeholders [3] to manage and employ the data and to benefit from its integration during the building lifecycle [4–6]. BIM can represent two different meanings that should be distinguished. As a product, BIM is a building information model possessing geometrical information and non-geometrical data. On the other hand, BIM as building information modeling is a process/technology/methodology including the BIM product. BIM as modeling is a transition from the single sequential process method to a multiple parallel method of data integration, distribution, employment and communication to be used for several tasks and activities from the creation to the demolition of buildings throughout building lifecycle.

Regarding employing new technologies, processes and methods, for instance in comparison with the aviation industry, the building industry and particularly the construction sector are late adopters and have not employed new innovative methods or discovered new opportunities as it happens in other industries [8]. The unwillingness behavior to adopt the latest or new technologies has made difficulties for the industry. The outcome is that productivity, efficiency, quality and profit are decreased and waste, risk, duplicating activities and repeating mistakes are increased [6, 7]. However, due to

Published by Springer Nature Switzerland AG 2018.
P. Chiabert et al. (Eds.): PLM 2018, IFIP AICT 540, pp. 15–24, 2018.
https://doi.org/10.1007/978-3-030-01614-2_2

enormous progress in ICT and digitalization, the industry has started to realize and ask for more data based processes and integrated management that can increase productivity and efficiency not only for the designing phase but also for the execution, operation and maintenance phases. Furthermore, robotics and automation are being recognized more as solution to mass production, quality, time, waste and labors difficulties. Additionally, the NISB report reveals that only in the US capital facility industry the annual cost of insufficient data interoperability is about $15.8 billion dollars [11]. The lack of interoperability can increase the total cost of projects up to 3.1% [5]. Instead, according to the studies [9, 10], BIM increases profit of the firms and return on investment (ROI) in comparison with the traditional approach and creates positive impacts on projects [12, 13]. On the other hand, although BIM is used for the design phase, it is not fully recognized for the execution phase in the construction sector. Thus, one of the aims of this research is to address the gap for firms who are active in the construction section by introducing the key factors of the BIM implementation framework. This research, as the outcome of the framework, expects faster project delivery, higher quality, less duplicate works in the project level and increasing efficiency of the organization.

2 Problem Statement

According to the European Commission, about 90% of the firms are SMEs, including micro, small and medium-sized enterprises with up to 250 employees and 50 million Euros turnover annually. SMEs create about 67% of the jobs [17] consequently their role in the industry is significant and should be addressed.

As it was mentioned previously, the technical and financial benefits of BIM are not efficiently achieved by the firms, specially by the SME contractors, because the building industry and the construction sector hesitate to employ BIM [14, 16]. Additionally, the SME contractors are mainly not aware of the technology as modelling and the key factors that can increase their competitiveness, profit and even save their existence in the future, the era of automation and robotics. One of the reasons for the hesitation could be that the current frameworks are more focused on the theory and the ontology of BIM, are mostly studied for big companies, providing too many details and might not introduce a simple practical framework, which is suitable for the SME contractors. Thus, the main problem that this study attempts to address is that an effective simple BIM implementation framework tailored for SME contractors is still missing.

3 Methodology

First, in order to determine an effective BIM implementation framework, this research reviews and extracts the literatures on the BIM implementation challenges and issues as well as the effective factors. The literature review consists of more than a decade of the previous studies on the BIM implementation and relevant topics. A summary of the review is tabulated in Table 1, followed by the key factors. Then analysis and critical discussions will be provided. In the end, a general practical BIM implementation framework, as a guideline for the SME contractors, will be presented.

3.1 Literature Review

With the aim of improving the processes of design, planning and construction for USACE (the U.S. Army Corps of Engineers), in 2006 a strategic BIM implementation plan was offered by Brucker et al. [15]. The plan is based on current design team and assigning a BIM team who is responsible for an action plan. The team members, aims, processes, tasks, metrics and training are the key factors of the implementation plan. However, in 2009 according to the interviews from the UK and Finland, Arayici et al. [18] studied the factors, challenges and barriers of the BIM implementation. The survey-based research of the construction stakeholders and academics shows that organizational changes and processes are the two significant factors for the implementation while BIM technology, BIM based tools, training, costs, and unclear BIM's technical & financial benefits are highly considered. In 2009, Succar [19] created the BIM domain concepts as a BIM ontology. The domain describes the BIM conceptual parts and the main BIM activity fields as technology, process and policy. The fields share players like designers (architectural, structural, mechanical etc.), contractors, technology developers, manufacturers, operators, legal bodies, researchers and owners). They also share some deliverables such as construction services/products, standards, regulations and equipment (software, hardware). Furthermore in 2010, an interview based research study on focused group of architects, engineers and contractors by Gu and London [20] shows that two main issues of the adoption are technical issues (BIM tools and software) and non-technical issues (processes, strategies and work practices).

However, in 2011, Jung and Joo [21] introduced a BIM framework based on BIM perspective, technology and business model. The BIM perspective indicates three levels of BIM utilization as in projects, organizations and the industry. The technology includes data and standards. The BIM business function refers to such as design, estimation, planning, scheduling, materials, safety, contracts, cost control, sales, research and developments, HR and administrations. In 2012, Khosrowshahi and Arayici [22] described an extensive BIM implementation roadmap with three main factors on training, organizational culture and information management focused on managerial and operational levels. Besides, in 2013 Eadie et al. [12] indicated that BIM could be used in the entire period of building lifecycle and process, stakeholder collaboration, software, BIM experience and training are the most effective factors of the adoption. Furthermore, the study of Takim et al. [23] in 2013 revealed that there could be gaps due to process change, technical supports, product limitation, people acceptance, economic demand, profitability, simple methodology and use. Additionally, in 2014, Miettinen and Paavola [24] published an analytical study, which introduces the important factors such as continuous learning, guidelines, standards and local trialing. In 2014, Morlhon et al. [25], introduced the BIM implementation factors as standards, external stakeholders, process (business and system), education (management and technical). Meanwhile at the same year, Smith [26] found that, training, business impacts, standards (national and global), legal and liability issues, research and governmental support are the main factor of the implementation. Also, in 2015 Son et al. [28] presented the BIM implementation drivers as management support and the computer knowledge in an architectural organization.

Table 1. Literature review summary

Fields	Organization		People		Process	Technology	Policy
Factors/ equivalnt parameters	Investment (costs, ROI)	Risks & Challenges	Training & need (HR, organizatioan)	Resistance to changee	Work process & team collaboration	Tools (software & hardware)	Standards, Regulations, legal issues
Brucker et al, 2006 [15]		○	○		○	○	
Arayici et al, 2009 [18]	○	○	○	○	○		
Succar, 2009 [19]			○		○	○	○
Gu and London, 2010 [20]		○			○	○	
Azhar, 2011 [6]	○	○	○	○	○	○	○
Jung and Joo (2011) [21]	○	○			○	○	○
Eastman et al, 2011 [7]	○	○	○	○	○	○	○
Khosrowshahi and Arayici (2012) [22]	○	○	○	○	○	○	○
Eadie et al (2013) [12]			○		○	○	
Takim et al (2013) [23]	○			○	○	○	
Miettinen and Paavola (2014) [24]			○				○
Morlhon et al (2014) [25]		○	○		○		○
Peter Smith (2014) [26]	○	○	○				○
Lindblad and Vass (2015) [27]					○		
Son et al (2015) [28]		○				○	
Tulenheimo (2015) [29]	○	○	○	○	○	○	
Bui et al (2016) [30]	○		○				○
Cao et al (2016) [31]	○	○	○				
Hosseini et al (2016) [32]	○	○					
Ghaffarianhosein et al (2017) [14]	○	○	○		○	○	

However, in 2015 the key barriers and challenges for the adoption were studied by Tulenheimo [29]. The results are listed as clients demand, managerial vision and strategy, organizational change process and technology (hardware and software).

In 2016, Bui et al. [30] mentioned that in developing countries governmental supports, standards, legal issues, BIM knowledge, business function and BIM benefits are the current BIM adoption factors. Furthermore, Cao et al. [31] suggested a strong relation between the BIM implementation motivation and organizational ownership as well as its economic benefits during maturing of BIM. Meanwhile, Hosseini et al. [32] found that SMEs' lack of interest and higher investment risk are the key factors. Finally, a 2017 study of Ghaffarianhoseini et al. [14] on the BIM implementation revealed the critical factors such as process development (change), business development (demand and ROI), training (skills and experience) and tools (software and hardware). However, the literature review shows that various viewpoints and approaches were used by different studies to address the factors or the equivalent parameters. The summery of the literature review is illustrated in Table 1 where a group of factors is pointed by each field that addresses the vital requirements, issues and challenges that potentially influence the BIM implementation.

3.2 Analysis and Discussion

The literature review verifies a complex nature of the implementation and its broad range of factors as well as their interconnections. In order to build a basic approach of a general practical BIM implementation framework for the SME contractors, this article provides an analysis and discusses common critical issues required for an effective framework. According to Table 1, the most frequently cited factors, indicated in the previous studies, are organization (28 times), people (21 times), process (14) and technology (12 times) followed by policy (9 times) respectively. Figure 1 illustrates the fields, the factors and their linear distribution percentages, which, in this text, are also

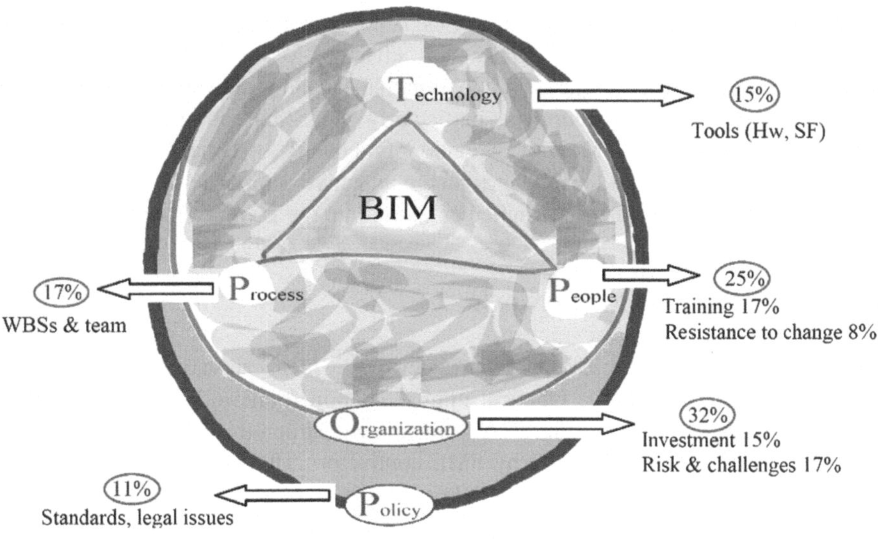

Fig. 1. The BIM implementation key factors and the distribution percentages (Color figure online)

written in the brackets. As it is shown in Fig. 1, the fields are divided into two layers as an inner layer (red circle) that includes organization (32%) that possesses the major role for the implementation, people (25%), process (17%) and technology (15%) and an outer layer (blue circle) as policy field (11%). The inner layer reflects a firm's internal domain of actions and reactions. It is affected by its internal stakeholders, processes and tools. The policy field includes e.g. governments who can affect the firms by legal issues and standards.

This analysis proves the vital role of organization, represented by top managers (plus CEOs & board members), including the business challenges and risks (17%) as well as investments and financial factors (15%) such as the costs and return on investment (ROI). Therefore, the first step of any adoption should consider the top managers' understanding and strong support, which means only utilizing the technology (e.g. employing software) without a long-term/strategic plan, might decrease the effectiveness of the adoption or lead to an unsuccessful implementation. The second major field is people, with a major effect of 17% for training and 8% for employees' resistance to change, indicating the role of the team members and the related challenges. The third field is process field (17%), includes work processes and team collaboration, addressing what should be done and how the processes should be managed. The next important field is technology (15%) that indicates tools, software and hardware that represents all means required for an effective implementation framework. Finally, the external field is policy (11%) that reflects standards, mandates, legal issues and guidelines by governments.

Although the studies have covered various viewpoints, so far finding a general basic consolidated implementation model or a simple practical BIM implementation framework is missing. Furthermore, the studies are mostly focused on theoretical and academic view. In fact, the current BIM implementation frameworks might not effectively provide an easy to follow and a simple practical framework that can help a majority of the SME contractors to harvest the benefits of the studies due to being more theoretical or providing a lot of details with advanced knowledge. Thus, an easy to implement basic approach of the BIM adoption that can almost cover all known aspects and challenges for the practitioners, particularly the SME contractors is required. Actually, this proposed BIM implementation framework systematically attempts to address all the factors and challenges in an effective simplistic and considerably practical model to provide better implementation than the current models.

4 Implementation Framework

A general 3-step BIM implementation framework, which can satisfy all mentioned aspects of an effective simple practical implementation framework, is easy to follow and implement is illustrated in Fig. 2. As it mentioned earlier, this BIM implementation framework is proposed to be used by SME contractors. However, due to similarities between the other firms in the building industry, such as design or maintenance firms, it is feasible for other enterprises to employ the framework with some modifications in the third step. The framework is a three-step model including understanding (step one), planning (step two) and piloting (step three).

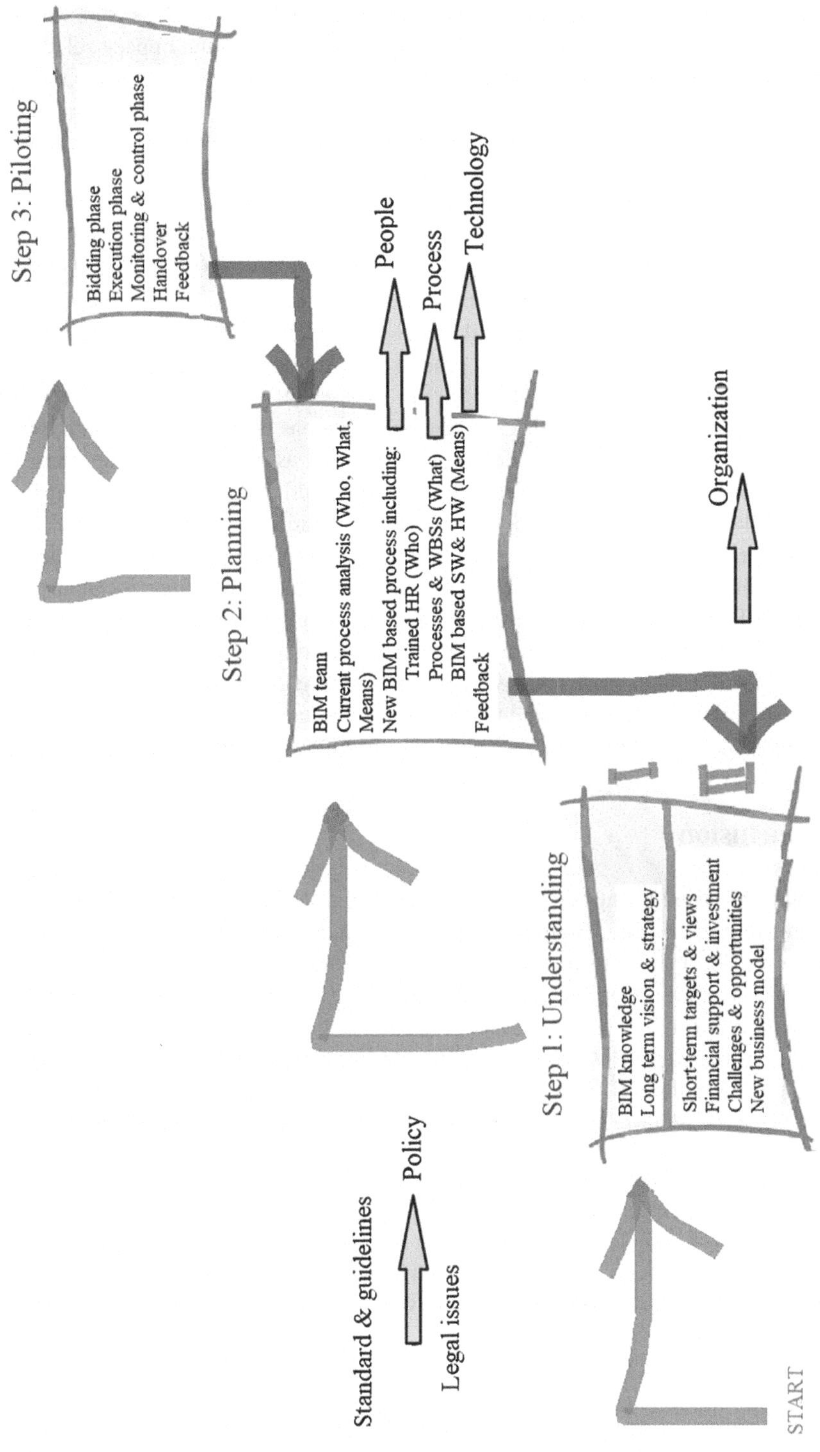

Fig. 2. A general 3-step BIM implementation framework

The first step for implementing BIM is an understanding step. This is an important step for the top managerial level like CEOs and boards to learn the impacts, challenges, benefits and opportunities BIM can provide in short-term and long-term for the firms. Defining a new strategy that possibly can target a longer run, exploring business opportunities and more integrated delivery approach are considered. However, part two of the first step is dedicated to directors and other middle level managers to address challenges, legal issues, BIM teams and short-term strategies.

The second step is the planning step. In this step, assigned BIM teams including the current teams and BIM experts analyze current activities, processes, tools and resources in order to create a new BIM based approach of the processes. Feedbacks of this step will be transferred to the organizational level to amend the short-term and the long-term strategies as well as to support the processes. Additionally, current standards and guidelines can be used in this step.

The third step is called piloting. In this step what has been planned in step two will be executed. This is a practical step thus tools such as software for preparing QTL (quantity takeoff list) and cost estimation in the bidding phase extracted from 3D models will be used. Also, in this step clash detection and constructability will be examined via appropriate tools in order to decrease the time and increase the accuracy of the execution plans and works besides work activities, scheduling, risk management plans etc. VR (virtual reality) and AR (augmented reality) tools can be employed in this step to assist the execution, monitoring and verification of the activities on sites and off sites. The feedbacks from this step will be sent to the BIM teams in step two for future evaluation of the planning step and make it more efficient. Finally, the circulation of the information, data and knowledge will improve productivity and efficiency of the firms.

5 Conclusion

This study has tried to introduce BIM as modelling, the factors and challenges related to implementing an initial framework that can employ BIM technology for the SME contractors. The main aim of this study is to provide a basic and easy to implement BIM implementation framework that is extensively required assisting the SME contractors to harvest the benefits that an effective practical framework can provide. Finally, a three-step BIM implementation framework/guideline is provided for an effective BIM adoption. This study proposes a future research on the presented framework to be employed for different kind of SME contractors to evaluate the results in real cases.

Acknowledgments. The author would like to thank Jyrki Röpelinen, the director of civil engineering department of Oulu University of Applied Sciences (OAMK) for the financial support and the members of the Interrg Nord project, Increasing Competence in Northern Building (ICNB), from Finland, Norway and Sweden for their contributions during the workshops and the meetings.

References

1. Eastman, C.M.: The use of computers instead of drawings in building design. AIA J. **1**(1), 46–50 (1975)
2. Penttilä, H.: Describing the changes in architectural information technology to understand design complexity and free-form architectural expression. J. Inf. Technol. Construct. (ITcon) **11**, 395–408 (2006)
3. Woo, J.H.: BIM (building information modeling) and pedagogical challenges. In: Proceedings of the 43rd ASC National Annual Conference (2006)
4. Laiserin, J.: To BIMfinity and Beyond! (AEC Insight Column), Building information modeling for today and tomorrow. http://www.cadalyst.com/aec/to-bimfinity-and-beyond-aec-insight-column-3686. Accessed 01 Sept 2017
5. McGraw-Hill: Interoperability in the Construction Industry, in SmartMarket Report. McGraw Hill Construction (2007)
6. Azhar, S.: Building Information Modeling (BIM): trends, benefits, risks, and challenges for the AEC industry. Leadersh. Manag. Eng. **11**(3), 241–252 (2011)
7. Eastman, C., Teicholz, P., Sacks, R., Liston, K.: BIM Handbook - A Guide to Building Information Modeling for Owners, Managers, Designers, Engineers, and Contractors, 2nd edn. Wiley, Hoboken (2011)
8. Buehler, M.: 10 ways aerospace can shape the future of construction. https://www.weforum.org/agenda/2016/11/future-of-construction-lessons-from-aerospace/. Accessed 15 Jan 2017
9. Azhar, S., Hein, M., Sketo, B.: Building information modeling (BIM): benefits, risks and challenges. In: The 44th Associated Schools of Construction National Conference, Auburn, AL (2011)
10. Barlish, K., Sullivan, K.: How to measure the benefits of BIM—a case study approach. Autom. Constr. **24**, 149–159 (2012)
11. Gallaher, M.P., O'Connor, A.C., Dettbarn, J., John, L., Gilday, L.T.: Cost analysis of inadequate interoperability in the U.S. capital facilities industry. The USA National Institute of Standards and Technology (NIST) (2004)
12. Eadie, R., Browne, M., Odeyinka, H., McKeown, C., McNiff, S.: BIM implementation throughout the UK construction project lifecycle: an analysis. Autom. Constr. **36**, 145–151 (2013)
13. Motawa, I., Almarshad, A.: A knowledge-based BIM system for building maintenance. Autom. Constr. **29**, 173–182 (2013)
14. Ghaffarianhoseini, A., et al.: Building information modelling (BIM) uptake: clear benefits, understanding its implementation, risks and challenges. Renew. Sustain. Energy Rev. **75**, 1046–1053 (2017)
15. Brucker, B.A., et al.: Building information modeling (BIM): a road map for implementation to support MILCON transformation and civil works projects within the U.S. Army Corps of Engineers. Engineer Research and Development Center, U.S. Army Corps of Engineers (2006)
16. Hosseini, M.R., et al.: BIM adoption within Australian Small and Medium-sized Enterprises (SMEs): an innovation diffusion model. Constr. Econ. Build. **16**(3), 71 (2016)
17. Commission, E.: User guide to the SME Definition. Publications Office of the European Union, Luxembourg (2015)
18. Arayici, Y., Khosrowshahi, F., Ponting, A.M., Mihindu, S.: Towards implementation of Building Information Modelling in the construction industry. In: Fifth International Conference on Construction in the 21st Century (CITC-V). Collaboration and Integration in Engineering, Management and Technology, 20–22 May 2009, Istanbul, Turkey (2009)

19. Succar, B.: Building information modelling framework: a research and delivery foundation for industry stakeholders. Autom. Constr. **18**(3), 357–375 (2009)
20. Gu, N., London, K.: Understanding and facilitating BIM adoption in the AEC industry. Autom. Constr. **19**(8), 988–999 (2010)
21. Jung, Y., Joo, M.: Building information modelling (BIM) framework for practical implementation. Autom. Constr. **20**(2), 126–133 (2011)
22. Khosrowshahi, F., Arayici, Y.: Roadmap for implementation of BIM in the UK construction industry. Eng. Constr. Architectural Manag. **19**(6), 610–635 (2012)
23. Takim, R., Harris, M., Nawawi, A.H.: Building information modeling (BIM): a new paradigm for quality of life within architectural, engineering and construction (AEC) industry. Proc. - Soc. Behav. Sci. **101**, 23–32 (2013)
24. Miettinen, R., Paavola, S.: Beyond the BIM utopia: approaches to the development and implementation of building information modeling. Autom. Constr. **43**, 84–91 (2014)
25. Morlhon, R., Pellerin, R., Bourgault, M.: Building information modeling implementation through maturity evaluation and critical success factors management. Proc. Technol. **16**, 1126–1134 (2014)
26. Smith, P.: BIM implementation – global strategies. Proc. Eng. **85**, 482–492 (2014)
27. Lindblad, H., Vass, S.: BIM implementation and organisational change: a case study of a large Swedish public client. Proc. Econ. Financ. **21**, 178–184 (2015)
28. Son, H., Lee, S., Kim, C.: What drives the adoption of building information modeling in design organizations? An empirical investigation of the antecedents affecting architects' behavioral intentions. Autom. Constr. **49**, 92–99 (2015)
29. Tulenheimo, R.: challenges of implementing new technologies in the world of BIM – case study from construction engineering industry in Finland. Proc. Econ. Financ. **21**, 469–477 (2015)
30. Bui, N., Merschbrock, C., Munkvold, B.E.: A review of building information modelling for construction in developing countries. Proc. Eng. **164**, 487–494 (2016)
31. Cao, D., Li, H., Wang, G., Huang, T.: Identifying and contextualising the motivations for BIM implementation in construction projects: an empirical study in China. Int. J. Project Manag. **35**, 658–669 (2017)
32. Hosseini, M.R., Namzadi, M.O., Rameezdeen, R., Banihashemi, S., Chileshe, N.: Barriers to BIM adoption: perceptions from Australian small and medium-sized enterprises (SMES). In: 40th AUBEA 2016 conference, Radical Innovation for Built Environment, pp. 271–280 (2016)

Environmental Factors on Concept Maps Design

Daniela Oliveira[1(✉)], Mickael Gardoni[1], and Kimiz Dalkir[2]

[1] École de Technologie Supérieure, Montreal, Canada
daniela.oliveira@mcgill.ca
[2] School of Information Studies, McGill University, Montreal, Canada

Abstract. Building Information Modeling (BIM) environments have a lot of potential to facilitate communication and support collective work, speeding construction times and increasing the overall quality of the project. A few ontologies creation efforts have been made by both academia and practitioners to foster the transmission of knowledge in BIM environments. This paper aims to add to the discussion by analyzing the notes of users of concept maps, knowledge structures similar to ontologies, and comparing them to BIM environment researchers'.

Keywords: BIM · Concept maps · Knowledge management
Knowledge transmission · Knowledge construction · Ontologies

1 Introduction

Building Information Modeling (BIM) environments are excellent candidates for the implementation of Knowledge Management (KM) techniques and tools. As Dalkir [8] points out, one of the problems KM can help solve in projects being object to BIM is the need for professionals in different disciplines to "speak the same language". It seems that while technical interoperability surrounding BIM has been addressed by the development of standards and long-term use of BIM tools [14], business interoperability is yet to be fully supported in order to expand collaboration [22]. The multi-disciplinary perspectives the same object can take in Architecture/Engineering/Construction (AEC) and the lack of tools that can support them seem to be in cause [20].

A bibliographic study of BIM literature has shown that in recent years ontologies have been considered as a means to foster collaboration in AEC environments exchanging BIM, but very few studies addressed different context or environmental elements in the interpretation process of ontologies [27]. This bibliographic investigation has justified Cerovsek's [5] perception that little attention was being paid to the semiotics of communication in AEC. In other words, the AEC field lacks studies on BIM projects and the different meanings and interpretations the same object or object characteristics may take.

Variance of meaning, or semiotics, is a natural element of human communication. As people have different backgrounds, beliefs and experience, it is natural that they accord different meanings to the same words and symbols. While semiotics account for

Published by Springer Nature Switzerland AG 2018.
P. Chiabert et al. (Eds.): PLM 2018, IFIP AICT 540, pp. 25–34, 2018.
https://doi.org/10.1007/978-3-030-01614-2_3

the cultural richness in society, in a performance-intensive environment, such as construction, it can be a source of misunderstandings, frustrations, and barriers to collective work.

2 Concept Maps and Ontologies

Concept maps are knowledge structures that codify objects and their relation to each other. Several perspectives are used to depict the various dimensions of a relationship between two objects. In educational settings, the process of creating a concept map helps students relate different concepts of the domain explored [9]. Once the concept map is ready, it serves as a tangible representation of the domain and helps the student recall the propositions of the domain [18]. In knowledge management, concept maps are used to produce "visual representations of complex knowledge domains that meet social scientists' standards for rigor and reliability, while being easily interpretable to practitioners" [38]. The collaborative design process of the concept map is itself a team-building activity and involves a lot of articulation and negotiation skills [12, 39]. Concept maps' capacity to promote the construction of shared meaning assured the tool the recognition as a feminist research method [3]. Concept maps are the first step for the creation of ontologies [2, 4, 28, 36]. Concept maps that conform to a specific format and are machine-readable are called Ontologies.

Ontologies have been developed and implemented in BIM projects to help increase knowledge flow and business interoperability. The Information Delivery Manuals (IDM), guiding BIM implementations, represent the effort to connect and describe the context [16]. They are intended to provide directives to represent what is the place of a process, what is its relevance, the actors around the information represented, the information itself and how it should be supported by applications [35]. However, as Eastman, one of the most prominent scholars studying BIM [37], argues, the use of IDM is only a first step towards answering the need for full interoperability in BIM tools [10].

3 Environmental Factors in KM and Education

In November 2017, I (Daniela) felt the urge to reflect on the influence and power imbalances surrounding the creation of concept maps. I have engaged myself in an exercise of critical reflection [7] on my own experiences facilitating concept maps creation in Knowledge management (KM) and education settings for the past five years. The production and treatment of the content followed Trochim's [30] method adapted to one single participant and low-volume data. Fifty-nine statements related to environmental factors around the creation of concept maps were produced. These statements were regrouped in fourteen categories, which were then named. Similarities between the labels of categories motivated a subsequent fusion and reorganization of categories, resulting in the eleven main elements that motivated this study.

Previous research had already suggested that contextual factors may be responsible for mixed findings in concept maps studies [1]. In the preliminary phase of this study, validation in the literature was sought for these elements emerging from practice. These elements may have considerable impact on concept maps and, as a consequence, in ontologies creation and use. They have been divided into four categories, explained as follows.

3.1 People Involved

Who Creates the Tool. Different people might produce different concept maps on the same subject [26].

In educational settings, concept maps may be created by the instructor or by the student [1], by a group of students having an instructor as a mediator and by a group of students working conjointly with an instructor. The number of participants representing knowledge influences the outcome of this representation [19].

In KM settings, concept maps may be designed by an information professional only, to express the results of document analysis, or in design sessions. Participants of design sessions tend to be admitted by invitation only [30]. The selection of participants usually takes into account their category [34] (external or internal client, subject matter expert, management level, for example); their potential to interact with other participants - power imbalances may be considered; their availability and their added value to the project. When conceiving how the concept map should be designed, the information professional considers what kind and level of endorsement would be most beneficial to the knowledge representation. The same participants may not take place in every step of the concept map production [21, 30].

The perception of the creators' authority in the field may represent a bias for the concept maps users, as would the creators' reputation and the support from senior management they are perceived to enjoy.

Importance of Participants' Knowledge and Scope. How concept maps users and facilitators see the importance of the knowledge of the participants involved in the design of the concept map is likely to vary. In educational settings, students are less credited of understanding of the knowledge domain than are instructors. Students' knowledge representation in concept maps is perceived as the expression of their knowledge, rather than a representation tailored to meet users' needs. This common perception has to be taken into account by the facilitator when choosing intervention techniques.

In situations where instructors have authored the concept map, the general perception is that a didactic reduction was made to adapt to novices' understanding, leaving important knowledge of the field unrepresented in the concept map.

In KM settings, the knowledge articulated either by participants or by the information professional alone is seen as the important knowledge in the field. The common perception is that a selection of the important concepts was made – and what was left out is not as important.

Who Uses the Tool. In educational settings, any student – being the concept map's author or not – may use concept maps produced by instructors or by students working with an instructor. Concept maps produced by one single student are usually only used by that single student.

The relationship between authors and users may create different user experiences. For instance, as mentioned, concept maps may perform the role of an individual's memory guide if they are both the sole author and user but will take the role of an exploration path if the author is the instructor and the user, a novice.

In KM settings, the number of users can largely outnumber the group of creators. Concept maps may be used by employees, clients, suppliers and government for regulation purposes, even if they have been authored by one single person. Concept maps authored by one single person may be used by a sole other person, for example, when expressing the reasoning used behind an algorithm or technical solution.

The target user population will certainly have its influence in the authoring process. Facilitators should take authors' view of the target population into account when planning for concept maps design sessions.

3.2 Trends

Purpose. In educational settings, concept maps may be used to portray a knowledge field to be explored, to serve as a guide to one's knowledge and to assess learning. The purpose of the concept map will certainly have an impact on how it is produced. A concept map created as a guide to the author's understanding and memory of the field will not be the same as one created to display the author's understanding of the field.

In KM settings, concept maps may be created to help specify the conceptual frameworks of programs [26, 31], to help attribute meaning to sets of data [15], to determine technological solutions requirements [11], or as an aid to navigate internal documents or content published on the organization's website [17], among other uses. When coupled with other tools, they may also be used to assess relevance of documents over time. The purpose for which the concept map was created suggests the point of evolution of the knowledge represented, or how much agreement exists in the field at that moment. In other words, the concept map portrays, in some way, the collective endorsement of the knowledge represented.

Evaluation Criteria. The purpose of the concept map may be attached to an evaluation strategy. Among other uses, evaluation strategies aim to assess the suitability of the concept map for the task it is intended to support or the coverage of its scope. Although there is still no acclaimed method for testing concept maps [33], it is reasonable to expect that evaluation criteria to be applied in a concept map influences the facilitator's choices of intervention techniques.

3.3 The Impact of Time

Number of Workshops over Time. Concept maps are usually produced in one session in educational settings, although they may be incremented over time. In KM settings, concept maps usually take one to five sessions to be considered final [30].

Momentum of Production. As the concept map portrays the author's vision of the knowledge field at a specific point in time, a concept map produced in the beginning of a course or a project will be drastically different from one produced by the end of a course or project. The momentum of production may affect participant's motivation and user's perception of reliability of the tool.

Time of Tool Consumption. Concept maps are used in educational settings while the user considers the knowledge important and the tool useful, which could mean for the duration of a course or an educational program. In KM settings, concept maps may be used long time after production, especially when they serve as guides for navigating documents or content [17].

3.4 Collaboration Issues

Facilitators and authors of concept maps will try to compensate for any perceived inadequacies regarding the preceding elements. For example, a facilitator conducting a concept design session in the beginning of a project for a concept map intended to hold a good level of maturity in concepts will stimulate participants to perform divergent thinking and will try to diversify interventions to achieve the desired level of maturity in concepts; a student might use shorter terms and clearer relationships when being evaluated through a concept map.

Variety. Focus groups, workshops, input from interviews [30] and document analysis [23], are some of the methods used to gather ideas for concept maps.

Collaboration. When concept maps are to be authored through collaboration, greater attention is given to staffing [21, 30]. That may include stimuli for different learning styles [32] and assuring representativeness of all participants in the end product.

Techniques for Animation. Different techniques might be used to assure accurate representativeness of the participants in the end product. The idea is to have participants exploring different points of view and relationships [24] and being able to name concepts, ideas [13] and, more rarely but also importantly, emotions [6].

Table 1 summarizes the design process differences and the different factors involved.

Table 1. Main aspects and factors related to concept maps use in KM and Education

Main aspect	Factor
People	Who creates the information; importance of participants' knowledge; who uses the information; individual endorsement
Trends	Purpose - why was the information codified; evaluation criteria - how is the information expected to be evaluated; collective endorsement
Time	Frequency of information generation; point in the process generating information; point in the process where information is consumed
Collaboration	Criteria for selection of people to be involved; how interactive was the creation process; how did people interact when generating the information

4 Ontologies Perspectives in AEC

Three very different perspectives in representing context were identified in the AEC. For Lee and Jeong [20], the people involved and the purpose of the information are the key elements to identify context in BIM projects. The authors describe a solution divided in a private and a public space. In the public space, the views of the objects depend on the qualification of the subject (e.g. an architect, a structural engineer and a mechanical engineer). For each object, the ontology would carry information describing the creator of the published data, the date of creation or modification, the qualifier of the relationships with other objects (e.g. a part of, a kind of) and "detailed description on reasons of creating or modifying the published data" [20].

The individual versus the shared space idea was originally explored by Cerovsek [5], who divides context description into various "standpoints". In the individual sphere, Resources, Process, Process result, BIM literacy and BIM tool would provide enough information for the evaluation of BIM support. In the shared space, the Reference Location, Time, Group, Teamwork, Business process, Information sharing, Application sharing and Communication channel would be the points helping evaluate BIM-enabled collaboration [5].

The framework conceived by Succar [29] identify fields, maturity and lenses/filters in a project. "Fields" relate to Technology, Process and Policy fields. "Maturity" aims to describe in much detail the point of the project where the object being described resides. "Lenses/Filters" present different views of the data. "Lenses" would present all the information that answer a specific criterion, while "Filters" would present all the information that does not answer the criterion.

Up to the submission of this paper, to our knowledge, no attempt to integrate these three perspectives was made. Although concern about contextual or environmental factors is present in AEC literature, the level of discussion seems to be considerably still too low to inform approaches in practice.

5 Discussion

Even though not much have been said about communication in BIM projects and its relation to ontology use [5, 27], some of the environmental factors identified in concept maps production and use were already identified in AEC literature. Environmental factors involved in the representation of knowledge in KM, Education and AEC are summarized in Table 2.

The identification of environmental factors of concept maps in AEC literature might indicate that research on the impact of these factors in ontology use would be welcomed in the AEC field. In practical terms, the correspondence suggests that there is a lot more to the process of knowledge building and consensus finding in BIM projects than the current ontology use supports. Therefore, BIM project managers and participants should be aware that BIM environments are not exempt from misconceptions and misunderstandings. Communication opportunities in a variety of channels should be encouraged to reduce conflicts having low positive impact in the construction process.

Table 2. Environmental factors of concept maps and their acknowledgement in AEC literature

Main aspect	Factor	KM/Education	In AEC
People	Who creates the information; importance of participants' knowledge; who uses the information; group; teamwork; individual endorsement	X	[5, 20]
Trends	Purpose - why was the information codified; evaluation criteria - how is the information expected to be evaluated; collective endorsement	X	
Time	Frequency of information generation; point in the process where information is generated; date of creation or modification; point in the process where information is consumed	X	[20, 29]
Collaboration	Criteria for selection of people to be involved; how interactive was the creation process; how did people interact when generating the information; information sharing; application sharing; communication channel	X	[5]

6 Conclusion

The creation of a concept map does not limit itself to the consignation of propositions into nodes and lines. A series of actions in design planning impact the actual design of the concept map and might influence how the concept map is perceived and put into use. If the same reasoning is applied to ontologies related to BIM, the information consigned in the ontology should not limit itself to the description of objects, but also the context in which those objects were created. Insight from the interaction between people and the knowledge representation in concept maps suggest that ontologies should also address the process of consensus building.

Similarities and differences between KM, Education and AEC in the description of context were identified. These preliminary findings suggest the usefulness of a larger and empirical research study on the context of objects represented in BIM tools.

Limitations. As this study originated in a single practitioner's experience, it might not represent an exhaustive list of environmental factors impacting knowledge representation in ontologies. Empirical, multi-participant, larger studies on environmental factors are encouraged. The results from the equivalence of factors in KM and Education and in AEC literature have to be considered taking into account the scarcity of literature in the AEC field. Exploration of the topic by AEC is also encouraged.

Acknowledgement. Daniela's work was supported by McGill University's Centre for Social and Cultural Data Science (CSCDS) grant number J1317026.

References

1. Adesope, O.O., Nesbit, J.C.: A systematic review of research on collaborative learning with concept maps. In: Handbook of Research on Collaborative Learning Using Concept Mapping, pp. 238–255. Information Science Reference, Hershey (2009)
2. Brilhante, V., Macedo, G., Macedo, S.: Heuristic transformation of well-constructed conceptual maps into owl preliminary domain ontologies. In: Workshop on Ontologies and their Applications, WONTO (2006)
3. Campbell, R., Salem, D.A.: Concept mapping as a feminist research method. Psychol. Women Q. **23**, 65–89 (1999). https://doi.org/10.1111/j.1471-6402.1999.tb00342.x
4. Castro, A.G., et al.: The use of concept maps during knowledge elicitation in ontology development processes – the nutrigenomics use case. BMC Bioinform. **7**, 267 (2006). https://doi.org/10.1186/1471-2105-7-267
5. Cerovsek, T.: A review and outlook for a “Building Information Model” (BIM): a multi-standpoint framework for technological development. Adv. Eng. Inform. **25**, 224–244 (2011). https://doi.org/10.1016/j.aei.2010.06.003
6. Ci, C., Choi, S.: How to manage a city’s image using the brand concept map and network analysis: a case of Seoul. Qual. Quant. **51**, 2441–2456 (2017). https://doi.org/10.1007/s11135-016-0402-6
7. Daley, A.: Reflections on reflexivity and critical reflection as critical research practices. Affillia **25**, 68–82 (2010). https://doi.org/10.1177/0886109909354981
8. Dalkir, K.: A Knowledge Management Approach for Digital Cultural Heritage Preservation, Istanbul (2017)
9. Dansereau, D.F.: Node-link mapping principles for visualizing knowledge and information. In: Tergan, S.-O., Keller, T. (eds.) Knowledge and Information Visualization. LNCS, vol. 3426, pp. 61–81. Springer, Heidelberg (2005). https://doi.org/10.1007/11510154_4
10. Eastman, C.M., Jeong, Y.-S., Sacks, R., Kaner, I.: Exchange model and exchange object concepts for implementation of national BIM standards. J. Comput. Civ. Eng. **24**, 25–34 (2010). https://doi.org/10.1061/(ASCE)0887-3801(2010)24:1(25)
11. Freeman, L.A.: The effects of concept maps on requirements elicitation and system models during information systems development. In: Cañas, A.J., Novak, J.D., González, F. (eds.) Concept Maps: Theory, Methodology, Technology. Proceedings of the First International Conference on Concept Mapping. Universidad Pública de Navarra, Pamplona, Spain, pp. 257–264 (2004)
12. Freeman, L.A., Jessup, L.M.: The power and benefits of concept mapping: measuring use, usefulness, ease of use, and satisfaction. Int. J. Sci. Educ. **26**, 151–169 (2004). https://doi.org/10.1080/0950069032000097361
13. González, H.L., Palencia, A.P., Umaña, L.A., Galindo, L., Villafrade, M.L.A.: Mediated learning experience and concept maps: a pedagogical tool for achieving meaningful learning in medical physiology students. Adv. Physiol. Educ. **32**, 312–316 (2008). https://doi.org/10.1152/advan.00021.2007
14. Howard, R., Björk, B.-C.: Building information modelling – experts’ views on standardisation and industry deployment. Adv. Eng. Inform. **22**, 271–280 (2008). https://doi.org/10.1016/j.aei.2007.03.001
15. Jackson, K.M., Trochim, W.M.K.: Concept mapping as an alternative approach for the analysis of open-ended survey responses. Organ. Res. Methods **5**, 307–336 (2002). https://doi.org/10.1177/109442802237114
16. Laakso, M., Kiviniemi, A.: The IFC standard - a review of history, development, and standardization. J. Inf. Technol. Constr. ITcon. **17**, 134–161 (2012)

17. Lambe, P.: Organising Knowledge: Taxonomies, Knowledge and Organisational Effectiveness. Chandos Publishing (Oxford) Ltd., Witney (2007)
18. Lambiotte, J.G., Dansereau, D.F., Cross, D.R., Reynolds, S.B.: Multirelational semantic maps. Educ. Psychol. Rev. **1**, 331–367 (1989). https://doi.org/10.1007/BF01320098
19. Larivière, V., Gingras, Y., Sugimoto, C.R., Tsou, A.: Team size matters: collaboration and scientific impact since 1900. J. Assoc. Inf. Sci. Technol. **66**, 1323–1332 (2015). https://doi.org/10.1002/asi.23266
20. Lee, J., Jeong, Y.: User-centric knowledge representations based on ontology for AEC design collaboration. Comput. Aided Des. **44**, 735–748 (2012). https://doi.org/10.1016/j.cad.2012.03.011
21. Linton, R.: Conceptualizing feminism: clarifying social science concepts. Eval. Program. Plann. **12**, 25–29 (1989). https://doi.org/10.1016/0149-7189(89)90018-9
22. Liu, Y., Van Nederveen, S., Hertogh, M.: Understanding effects of BIM on collaborative design and construction: an empirical study in China. Int. J. Proj. Manag. **35**, 686–698 (2017). https://doi.org/10.1016/j.ijproman.2016.06.007
23. Ridde, V.: "The problem of the worst-off is dealt with after all other issues": the equity and health policy implementation gap in Burkina Faso. Soc. Sci. Med. **66**, 1368–1378 (2008). https://doi.org/10.1016/j.socscimed.2007.10.026
24. Rogers, R.R.: Reflection in higher education: a concept analysis. Innov. High. Educ. **26**, 37–57 (2001). https://doi.org/10.1023/A:1010986404527
25. Rosas, S.R.: Multi-map comparison for group concept mapping: an approach for examining conceptual congruence through spatial correspondence. Qual. Quant. **51**, 2421–2439 (2017). https://doi.org/10.1007/s11135-016-0399-x
26. Rosas, S.R., Camphausen, L.C.: The use of concept mapping for scale development and validation in evaluation. Eval. Program. Plann. **30**, 125–135 (2007). https://doi.org/10.1016/j.evalprogplan.2007.01.003
27. Santos, R., Costa, A.A., Grilo, A.: Bibliometric analysis and review of Building Information Modelling literature published between 2005 and 2015. Autom. Constr. **80**, 118–136 (2017). https://doi.org/10.1016/j.autcon.2017.03.005
28. Starr, R.R., de Oliveira, J.M.P.: Concept maps as the first step in an ontology construction method. Inf. Syst. **38**, 771–783 (2013). https://doi.org/10.1016/j.is.2012.05.010
29. Succar, B.: Building information modelling framework: a research and delivery foundation for industry stakeholders. Autom. Constr. **18**, 357–375 (2009). https://doi.org/10.1016/j.autcon.2008.10.003
30. Trochim, W.M.: An introduction to concept mapping for planning and evaluation. Eval. Program. Plann. **12**, 1–16 (1989). https://doi.org/10.1016/0149-7189(89)90016-5
31. Trochim, W.M., Cook, J.A., Setze, R.J.: Using concept mapping to develop a conceptual framework of staff's views of a supported employment program for individuals with severe mental illness. J. Consult. Clin. Psychol. **62**, 766 (1994)
32. Vincent, A., Ross, D.: Personalize training: determine learning styles, personality types and multiple intelligences online. Learn. Organ. **8**, 36–43 (2001). https://doi.org/10.1108/09696470110366525
33. Weinerth, K., Koenig, V., Brunner, M., Martin, R.: Concept maps: a useful and usable tool for computer-based knowledge assessment? A literature review with a focus on usability. Comput. Educ. **78**, 201–209 (2014). https://doi.org/10.1016/j.compedu.2014.06.002
34. Windsor, L.C.: Using concept mapping in community-based participatory research: a mixed methods approach. J. Mix. Methods Res. **7**, 274–293 (2013). https://doi.org/10.1177/1558689813479175
35. Wix, J., Karlshoej, J.: Information delivery manual: guide to components and development methods. Build. Int. **5**, 10 (2010)

36. Yao, J., Gu, M.: Conceptology: using concept map for knowledge representation and ontology construction. J. Netw. **8**, 1708–1712 (2013)
37. Zhao, X.: A scientometric review of global BIM research: analysis and visualization. Autom. Constr. **80**, 37–47 (2017). https://doi.org/10.1016/j.autcon.2017.04.002
38. Petrucci, C.J., Quinlan, K.M.: Bridging the research-practice gap. J. Soc. Serv. Res. **34**, 25–42 (2007). https://doi.org/10.1300/J079v34n02_03
39. Stoyanova, N., Kommers, P.: Concept mapping as a medium of shared cognition in computer-supported collaborative problem solving. J. Interact. Learn. Res. **13**, 111 (2002)

A Conceptual Framework for Personalization of Indoor Comfort Parameters Based on Office Workers' Preferences

Saeed Mirzaeifar(✉), Pedram Daee, and Vishal Singh

Aalto University, Espoo, Finland
saeed.mirzaeifar@aalto.fi

Abstract. Prevention of building-related illnesses and improving indoor air quality has become an emerging research area not only because of the comfort of workers in an office or the quality of the perceived air, but also because it can provide financial benefits to both employees and employers through a potential reduction in prolonged sick leaves. Therefore, building facility managers attempt to achieve the most comfortable and healthy environment conditions for the office workers. However, the parameters associated with achieved comfort vary from person to person as workers` preferences, as well physiological characteristics, are heterogeneous. In the ideal case, the indoor health parameters should be personalized based on individuals` feedback. This paper presents a computational framework for personalization of environmental parameters based on limited office workers' feedback. We propose that by using current state of the art machine learning methods it is possible to learn the preference model of individuals, by employing both the limited feedback and the relevant literature on health-related symptoms. The framework is explained and discussed in a potential example scenario. Evaluation based on real data is left as a future work.

Keywords: Personalization · Building-related symptoms
Indoor health parameters · Building information modelling · Office building
Worker preference

1 Introduction

People in developed countries spend most of their time indoors [1, 2]. Therefore, the quality of indoor environment parameters such as temperature, humidity, lighting, noise level and even chemical contaminants can affect a person's health and productivity, especially during the worktime activity [3]. A few studies have pointed that the trending emphasis on transforming building technology primarily for energy savings may trigger inaccuracy and depreciation in Indoor Air Quality (IAQ) [4]. On the other hand, IAQ is defined in the terms of the reduction in building-related health problems, and increase in the occupants' satisfaction level of comfort [5]. Based on the World Health Organization report, a group of building health-related symptoms, which are mostly well-known such as nose, eye and throat irritation; sensation of dry mucous

Published by Springer Nature Switzerland AG 2018.
P. Chiabert et al. (Eds.): PLM 2018, IFIP AICT 540, pp. 35–45, 2018.
https://doi.org/10.1007/978-3-030-01614-2_4

membrane; headache and mental fatigue and etc. can be characterized as Building Related Symptoms (BRS) [3].

In parallel with the focus on indoor air quality, nowadays, modular and distributed office facilities are becoming popular, with the aim to eliminate the problems of megalopolises such as traffic congestion, accessibility, and to increase the energy savings [6]. Furthermore, modular offices can be located in different accessible points and even as home offices. The occupants are often given the ability to control the physical environmental parameters such as Heating Ventilation and Air-Conditioning (HVAC) and lighting in the modular offices [7]. However, it may also be desirable that the HVAC and other technical systems adjust themselves based on the occupant preferences as there is the individual difference in people susceptibility in feelings and perceived thermal comfort [8]. Hence, there is a need to train a system with appropriate user feedback data complemented with knowledge in literature, to identify user preferences for providing the most comfortable environmental condition as and when needed. In this respect, the research question can be formulated as: "How to learn and personalize the indoor health parameters based on the office workers' feedback?". The first step to resolve research question is to anticipate the situations when users feel uncomfortable during work time with the aid of feedback. In this respect, a review of the health-related symptoms and associated indoor parameters provides the proposed framework with the complementary knowledge. The second step is to employ suitable mathematical models for learning, based on the literature knowledge as well as the targeted data sources. The proposed mathematical model and the initial solution are presented in Section Three, with a high-level architecture for BIM integration with the aim to automate the process of data collection and analysis. In Section Four, a potential use case example before the conclusions, is introduced.

2 Comfort and Health-Related Parameters

The previous studies [9, 10] categorized the factors threatening the comfort or even health of human into three main groups:

- BRS: nonspecific symptoms with unknown cause.
- Comfort complaints: inconveniences about the environmental situation such as thermal, noise or malodor complaints.
- Building-related illnesses or building related diseases include health problems because of pollutants and contaminants coming from outdoor air and building materials.

This categorization aids to extract and classify the contributing indoor health problems parameters in office buildings, as shown in Fig. 1.

The first step in the personalization of parameters is to identify the factors that are associated with the user feedback. There are two types of questions in the questionnaire including IAQ factors and perceived health-related symptoms. Answer to IAQ factor questions provides clear knowledge about the user preferences and do not need additional processes for knowledge elicitation and formulation. An oversimplified scenario can be if the user feels too cold or dryness of the air, the temperature and

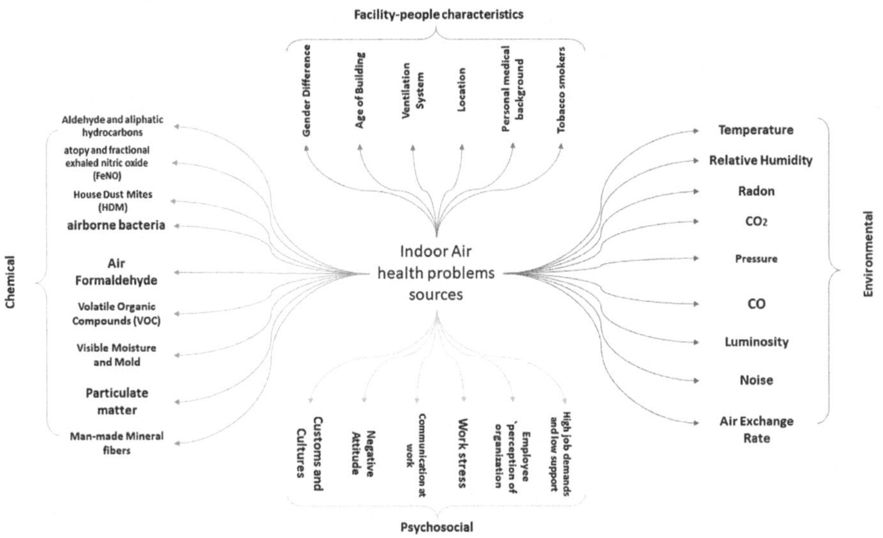

Fig. 1. Categorization of indoor health problem sources.

humidity should be regularized somehow until the uncomfortable feelings are resolved. On the contrary, the relation between building-related symptom and associated parameters needs more complicated processes to achieve the user preference knowledge. Next section explains how we aim to formulate this problem, and the initial solution is introduced. However, in this section, the association type between building-related symptoms and parameters measurable in research laboratories are discussed. These associations provide the basis to design the prediction model, building on the existing knowledge in the literature, as shown in Table 1.

Table 1. Health-related symptoms and associated (type) measurable parameters

Measurable parameter	Associated symptoms (positive+/negative−/not clear)	Reference(s)
Temperature	Nasal and skin symptoms(−) Fatigue(+) Sleepiness(+)	[11–13]
Humidity	Skin and nasal dryness(−) Eye irritation(−)	[12, 14, 15]
Lighting	Eyestrain Fatigue(−) Headache(+) Dizziness(−)	[16, 17]
CO2	Skin and eye irritation(+) Tiredness(+) Difficulty in concentration(−)	[13, 18]

(*continued*)

Table 1. (*continued*)

Measurable parameter	Associated symptoms (positive+/negative−/not clear)	Reference(s)
TVOC	Sensory irritation(+) Asthma symptoms(+)	[18–20]
NOx	Respiratory symptoms(+) Asthma(+)	[21, 22]
Radon	Lung cancer(+)	[23]
Noise level	Headache(+) Fatigue(+) Hypertension Aggression(+)	[24, 25]
Stress level	Anxiety(+) Fatigue(+) Eye irritation(+)	[26, 27]
Posture	Connective tissues of tendons Joint capsules and ligaments	[28, 29]

3 Personalization Framework

The goal of this conceptual framework is to predict a measure of comfort preference for each individual worker based on personalized feedback and literature knowledge on known health problems and related associations. There are two key points that make this problem challenging. First, the heterogeneous nature of preference makes the prediction problem ungeneralizable to all individuals. In other words, one worker's feedback cannot directly be employed to improve the prediction for another worker. This is an important challenge as it is only possible to collect limited feedback from each worker, compared to the impersonalized case where a huge number of feedback, from the sum of all workers, is available. Second, the knowledge available in the literature, i.e. health problems and associations such as those gathered in Table 1, is sparse and unorganized, and it would be difficult and cumbersome to formulate it in the prediction problem. In the following subsections, we formally introduce and review these challenges and available solutions from the machine learning point of view. We then propose how to employ the state of the art prediction models for the preference personalization and we explicate it with an example in Sect. 4.

3.1 Machine Learning Challenge

In many practical prediction applications, the input data with known target values, i.e., the training data, is significantly fewer than the number of attributes representing the data. In some cases, the number of data can be more than the attributes, but still, the training data may only cover some particular aspects of the search space, which would be equivalent to only having few effective training data. This can, in particular, happen in personalized systems where the feedback is limited or only few sets of configurations can be tried out. The limited effective training data poses constraints about how accurate the predictions can be [30]. Furthermore, many powerful machine learning methods, like deep neural networks, cannot be applied in this setup since they require huge amount of data. The dominant solution for these problems is to regularize the prediction model to constrain the search space and to avoid overfitting to training data.

A parallel fruitful direction to improve these types of prediction problems is to employ alternative available sources of information, other than training data, in the prediction. In many problems, prior information about the prediction task is available through experts or relevant literature. Prior elicitation is the process of extracting the available knowledge and employing them in the prediction task [31]. This is usually done by having a data scientist or statistician interviewing the field experts and then enforcing this knowledge on the parameters of the prediction model [31]. However, the classical prior elicitation methods are expensive and would require many iterations between the experts in the field and experts in the modeling. Recent works have proposed prior elicitation methods that remove the link between the data scientist and the field expert and directly put the expert in the prediction loop. This has become possible by defining intuitive ways for the experts to input their knowledge (priors) about the problem in a Bayesian prediction model. For example, [32] ask the experts to provide information about whether an attribute is relevant in a highly regularized prediction task or not, or to provide a value as their estimate of the regression coefficient. [33] ask about pairwise similarity feedback on different attributes, [34] about the direction of relevance (positive or negative), and [35] about the probability of an attribute being relevant. All these methods also investigate applications where there are only few training data sets available. We believe these approaches can also be employed in our personalized comfort prediction problem because different associations between attributes and the target variable (see Table 1) is known in our task.

In particular, [32] proposes a Bayesian sparse linear regression as the modeling solution to handle the limited training data problem. In their model, it is possible to intuitively add external knowledge about the relevance of attributes. We believe that this would be a proper fit for our personalized preference prediction problem. To use it, first, we need to gather the necessary data including the vector of attributes (here for example sensory measurements about the work environment and personal information like age and sex or any other related information) and the corresponding target values (for example personalized feedback about symptoms). Indeed, it is impossible to bother the user for a large number of feedbacks, and therefore, the number of data is always small. This is the ideal case for that method since in nature it assumes that the number of data is even less than the number of attributes.

This model is able to handle limited feedback challenge. However, we would still need to add the literature knowledge (Table 1) into the problem at hand. To do this, we can use the modeling solution in [34] (an extension of [32]) and consider the following types of literature knowledge:

- Knowledge about the relevance of the attribute for the considered prediction task.
- Knowledge about the direction of association (positive or negative) of the attributes to the target variable.

Given these two types of knowledge for the available attributes and the limited available data from individual feedback, [34] showed that it is possible to improve the accuracy of the prediction. Section 4 demonstrates how this approach can be used in an example scenario.

3.2 BIM Integration

The main aim of this study is to introduce a conceptual solution for personalization of the indoor health parameters based on the worker's preference. The building residents are considered as one of the building consituents in the context of facility management. Hence, the resident behavior can be modelled in BIM. Consequently, worker's preferences can be modeled and analyzed in building an information system for more efficient knowledge creation. In this respect, the required technical infrastructure should be provided for heterogeneous data collection and aggregation, data analysis and visualization, and knowledge creation. In addition to knowledge about the people preferences, the proposed framework is able to create the knowledge related to facility management utilizing the collected sensory data to make informed decisions about the health risks of the occupants. Through Internet of Things (IoT) communication, an infrastructure is developed where the sensor data and user feedback can be collected, and the generated knowledge can be applied for system behavior improvement [36]. BIM can play a vital role in automation and visualization of information for the built facility, and consequently, closing the information gap to provide comfort for building occupants, as shown in Fig. 2. From technical point of view, a service oriented architecture is developed, which each service oversees a module e.g. data aggregator and visualizer, in order to fulfil the technical requirements of the proposed framework. In data acquisition level, different streams of data are collected in related databases. In prototype level, the NoSQL database such as MongoDB[1] is preferred based on the volume and complexity of data. Data aggregator module will generate a timewise synchronized matrix out of data views in database. The machine learning service analyses the generated matrix which contains user feedback on collected psychological and environmental data to predict personalized model for each user. Trimble Connect[2] BIM engine is utilized to provide a knowledge base and data visualizer which can be used by the stakeholders to exploit of generated model and knowledge.

The proposed technical framework is able to aid facility managers in making decisions about building facilities based on the on knowledge created within the data analysis process e.g. the VOC data analysis can assist facility manager to identify mold growth in a building. In addition, the framework is able to provide the worker with a real-time warning about the inappropriate situation at work e.g. inconvenient posture of sitting.

[1] https://www.mongodb.com/.

[2] https://connect.trimble.com/.

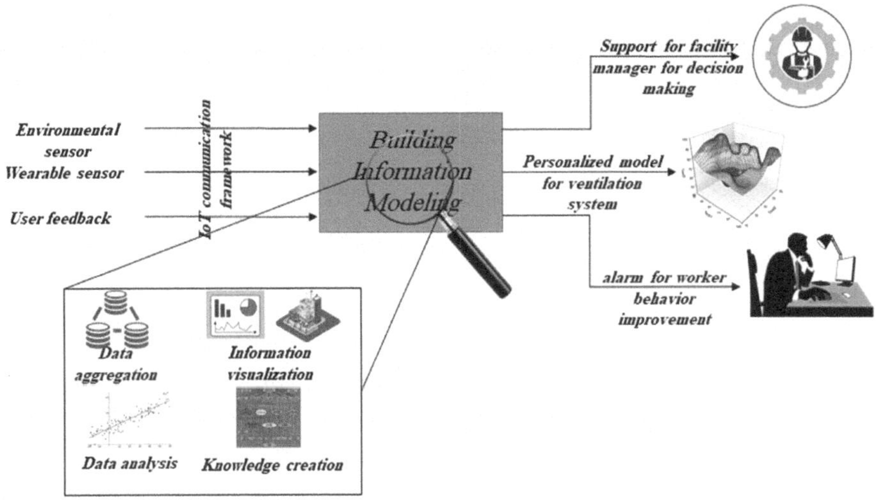

Fig. 2. The high level architecture of information flow

4 Use Case Scenario

In order to better understand and validate the proposed solution, a potential example scenario is provided in this section. This example describes how the algorithm works for personalization of all measurable parameters with respect to the worker feedback. Assume that we want to have a prediction system that would estimate the level of fatigue, i.e. subjective feeling of tiredness, for each individual worker in the building. The first step is to consider a list of attributes that may contribute to fatigue. These attributes can include both the sensory measurements about the environment (such as outdoor and office temperature, humidity, CO2 level, TVOC, NOx, Radon level and other measurable parameters listed in Table 1, and time and weather attributes such as time of the day, season, weather condition, and so on), and the personal level attributes (such as age, gender, health status, allergic disease, respiratory illnesses, smoking status). In the training phase, we ask about personal feedback of individual workers on their level of fatigue at different intervals. The feedback can be provided in a discretized preference scale such as Likert-type scale (1–5). Each feedback value along with the values of the corresponding attributes create one instance of the training data. Along with the gathered training data, we include the known associations between the attributes and the target variable (fatigue) in the Bayesian model of [34]. For example, we add the directional knowledge about stress level, CO2, lighting, and temperature to the model (e.g., it is known that CO2 has a positive association with fatigue). The model uses both the training data and the knowledge to learn the best prediction solution. After the training, the model can be used to estimate the level of fatigue of that worker at any time. This knowledge can be employed to find the most pleasant attribute ranges for that worker.

Figure 3 depicts this scenario where the worker provides feedback about his or her fatigue level in 3 intervals. These few data along with the association knowledge in the literature will feed the machine learning algorithm to learn the personalized fatigue prediction model.

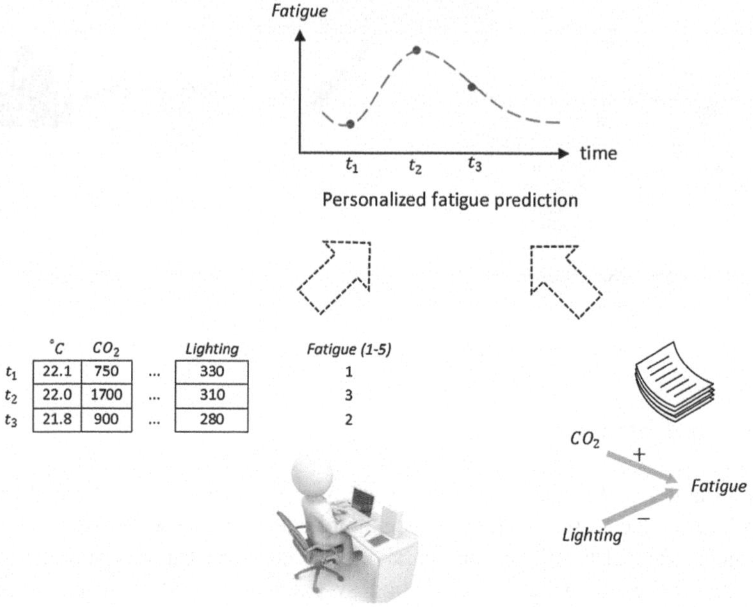

Fig. 3. Combining limited feedback from an individual worker with the available literature knowledge to achieve an accurate personalized prediction model.

5 Conclusion

Personalization in different domains is growing as people are looking for more customized solutions. Based on this preference, the expectations for the personalized indoor environment is not an exception either. In this respect, the purpose of this paper is to provide a technical framework to predict the measure of comfort preference for each individual worker based on personalized feedback and literature knowledge on known health problems and associations. The machine learning challenges are discussed in order to highlight the importance of the study. Subsequently, literature has been investigated to identify the prior knowledge about prediction models, and an example scenario is proposed to support the feasibility of the personalization model. A BIM-integrated technical solution is discussed for automating data aggregation and closing the information flow gap in built facilities.

Indoor health and well-being related parameters can affect employees' productivity during work time. So, it would be beneficial for employers to have healthier work environments to provide greater comfort for each individual worker, because different people may fall sick in different conditions based on their physiological attributes. Personalized indoor environmental conditions can potentially enhance productivity and reduce sick leaves. The objective of the proposed framework is to overcome the aforementioned challenges and the developed system according to this framework will be evaluated with real data in further studies.

References

1. Brasche, S., Bischof, W.: Daily time spent indoors in German homes–baseline data for the assessment of indoor exposure of German occupants. Int. J. Hyg. Environ. Health **208**(4), 247–253 (2005). https://doi.org/10.1016/j.ijheh.2005.03.003
2. Leech, J.A., Nelson, W.C., Burnett, R.T., Aaron, S., Raizenne, M.E.: It's about time: a comparison of Canadian and American time–activity patterns. J. Expo. Anal. & Environ. Epidemiol. **12**(6), 427 (2002). https://doi.org/10.1038/sj.jea.7500244
3. World Health Organization: Indoor air pollutants exposure and health effects report on a WHO meeting, Nordlingen, EURO Reports and Studies, 78 (1982)
4. Sterling, E., Sterling, T., McIntyre, D.: New health hazards in sealed buildings. Am. Inst. Archit. J. (United States) **72**(4) (1983)
5. Reijula, K., Sisäilmaongelmat, H.T.: Altistumisen arviointi ja potilaan tutkiminen [indoor air problems: Assessment of exposure and examination of the patient]. Finn. Med. J. **53**(36), 4215–4230 (1998)
6. Ghazanfari, E.: Applying product design and digital construction methodologies to conceptualize modular and distributed healthcare facilities. Master thesis, Aalto University, Finland (2016)
7. Gillespie I.: Modular Office (2002)
8. Jansz, J.: Theories and Knowledge About Sick Building Syndrome. In: Abdul-Wahab, S. (ed.) Sick Building Syndrome. Springer, Berlin (2011). https://doi.org/10.1007/978-3-642-17919-8_2
9. Hellgren, U.: Indoor air problems in Finnish hospitals-from the occupational health perspective (2012)
10. Norbäck, D.: An update on sick building syndrome. Curr. Opin. Allergy Clin. Immunol. **9** (1), 55–59 (2009). https://doi.org/10.1097/ACI.0b013e32831f8f08
11. Amin, N.D.M., Akasah, Z.A., Razzaly, W.: Architectural evaluation of thermal comfort: sick building syndrome symptoms in engineering education laboratories. Procedia - Soc. Behav. Sci. **204**, 19–28 (2015). https://doi.org/10.1016/j.sbspro.2015.08.105
12. Reinikainen, L.M., Jaakkola, J.: Significance of humidity and temperature on skin and upper airway symptoms. Indoor Air **13**(4), 344–352 (2003). https://doi.org/10.1111/j.1600-0668.2003.00155.x
13. Schiavon, S., Yang, B., Donner, Y., Chang, V., Nazaroff, W.W.: Thermal comfort, perceived air quality, and cognitive performance when personally controlled air movement is used by tropically acclimatized persons. Indoor Air **27**(3), 690–702 (2017). https://doi.org/10.1111/ina.12352
14. Shan, X., Zhou, J., Chang, V.W., Yang, E.: Comparing mixing and displacement ventilation in tutorial rooms: students' thermal comfort, sick building syndromes, and short-term performance. Build. Env. **102**, 128–137 (2016). https://doi.org/10.1016/j.buildenv.2016.03.025
15. Wolkoff, P., Nojgaard, J.K., Franck, C., Skov, P.: The modern office environment desiccates the eyes? Indoor Air **16**(4), 258–265 (2006). https://doi.org/10.1111/j.1600-0668.2006.00429.x

16. Godish, T.: Sick Buildings: Definition, Diagnosis and Mitigation. CRC Press, Boca Raton (1994)
17. Pitarma, R., Marques, G., Ferreira, B.R.: Monitoring indoor air quality for enhanced occupational health. J. Med. Syst. **41**(2), 23 (2017). https://doi.org/10.1007/s10916-016-0667-2
18. Lu, C., Lin, J., Chen, Y., Chen, Y.: Building-related symptoms among office employees associated with indoor carbon dioxide and total volatile organic compounds. Int. J. Environ. Res. Public Health **12**(6), 5833–5845 (2015). https://doi.org/10.3390/ijerph120605833
19. Dales, R., Raizenne, M.: Residential exposure to volatile organic compounds and asthma. J. Asthma **41**(3), 259–270 (2004). https://doi.org/10.1081/JAS-120026082
20. Venn, A.J., Cooper, M., Antoniak, M., Laughlin, C., Britton, J., Lewis, S.A.: Effects of volatile organic compounds, damp, and other env'l exposures in the home on wheezing illness in children. Thorax **58**(11), 955–960 (2003). https://doi.org/10.1136/thorax.58.11.955
21. Lim, F., Hashim, Z., Said, S.M., Than, L.T., Hashim, J.H., Norbäck, D.: Sick building syndrome (SBS) among office workers in a Malaysian university—Associations with atopy, fractional exhaled nitric oxide (FeNO) and the office environment. Sci. Total Environ. **536**, 353–361 (2015). https://doi.org/10.1016/j.scitotenv.2015.06.137
22. Mi, Y., Norback, D., Tao, J., Mi, Y., Ferm, M.: Current asthma and respiratory symptoms among pupils in Shanghai, China: influence of building ventilation, nitrogen dioxide, ozone, and formaldehyde in classrooms. Indoor Air **16**(6), 454–464 (2006). https://doi.org/10.1111/j.1600-0668.2006.00439.x
23. Joshi, S.M.: The sick building syndrome. Indian J. Occup. Environ. Med. **12**(2), 61 (2008). https://doi.org/10.4103/0019-5278.43262
24. Skov, P., Valbjorn, O.: The "sick" building syndrome in the office environment: the Danish town hall study. Env. Int. **13**(4–5), 339–349 (1987). https://doi.org/10.1016/0160-4120(87)90190-5
25. Teeuw, K.B., Vandenbroucke-Grauls, C.M., Verhoef, J.: Airborne gram-negative bacteria and endotoxin in sick building syndrome: a study in Dutch governmental office buildings. Arch. Intern. Med. **154**(20), 2339–2345 (1994). https://doi.org/10.1001/archinte.1994.00420200095010
26. Marmot, A.F., Eley, J., Stafford, M., Stansfeld, S.A., Warwick, E., Marmot, M.G.: Building health: an epidemiological study of "sick building syndrome" in the whitehall II study. Occup. Environ. Med. **63**(4), 283–289 (2006). https://doi.org/10.1136/oem.2005.022889
27. Nordström, K., Norbäck, D., Akselsson, R.: Influence of indoor air quality and personal factors on the sick building syndrome (SBS) in Swedish geriatric hospitals. Occup. Environ. Med. **52**(3), 170–176 (1995). https://doi.org/10.1136/oem.52.3.170
28. Grandjean, E., Hünting, W.: Ergonomics of posture-review of various problems of standing and sitting posture. Appl. Ergon. **8**(3), 135–140 (1977). https://doi.org/10.1016/0003-6870(77)90002-3
29. Leivseth, G., Drerup, B.: Spinal shrinkage during work in a sitting posture compared to work in a standing posture. Clin. Biomech. **12**(7–8), 409–418 (1997). https://doi.org/10.1016/S0268-0033(97)00046-6
30. Johnstone, I.M., Titterington D.M.: Statistical Challenges of High-Dimensional Data (2009). https://doi.org/10.1098/rsta.2009.0159
31. O'Hagan, A., et al.: Uncertain Judgements: Eliciting Experts' Probabilities. Wiley, Hoboken (2006)
32. Daee, P., Peltola, T., Soare, M., Kaski, S.: Knowledge elicitation via sequential probabilistic inference for high-dimensional prediction. Mach. Learn. **106**(9–10), 1599–1620 (2017). https://doi.org/10.1007/s10994-017-5651-7

33. Afrabandpey, H., Peltola, T., Kaski, S.: Interactive prior elicitation of feature similarities for small sample size prediction. In: Proceedings of 25th Conference on User Modeling, Adaptation and Personalization, pp. 265–269 (2017). https://doi.org/10.1145/3079628.3079698
34. Sundin, I., et al.: Improving drug sensitivity predictions in precision medicine through active expert knowledge elicitation (2017). arXiv Preprint arXiv:1705.03290
35. Daee, P., Peltola, T., Vehtari, A., Kaski, S.: User modelling for avoiding overfitting in interactive knowledge elicitation for prediction. In: Proceedings of the 23rd ACM International Conference on Intelligent User Interfaces, pp. 305–310 (2018). https://doi.org/10.1145/3172944.3172989
36. Mirzaeifar, S., Dave, B., Singh, V.: Development of systematic construction logistics using *'intelligent products'* (2017). https://doi.org/10.24928/2017/0295

Development of a Digital Platform Based on the Integration of Augmented Reality and BIM for the Management of Information in Construction Processes

Alice Schweigkofler[1(✉)], Gabriele Pasetti Monizza[1,2], Erdal Domi[2], Andrei Popescu[2], Julia Ratajczak[2,3], Carmen Marcher[1], Michael Riedl[1], and Dominik Matt[1,2]

[1] Fraunhofer Italia Research, Bolzano, Italy
alice.schweigkofler@fraunhofer.it
[2] Free University of Bozen-Bolzano, Bolzano, Italy
[3] Budimex S.A, Warsaw, Poland

Abstract. The construction industry is a project-based industry characterized by heterogeneity, extreme complexity and fragmented supply chain. Its complexity is increased by mutual relationships between different stakeholders involved in the creation, management and efficient exploitation of engineering data. Over the years, productivity and reliability in CI has been struggled by a difficulty in sharing information between construction project participants and in providing accurate information on site, which is a primary cause of poor performances.

Therefore, the adoption of enabling tools for managing product data and information flow as well as for better communication and collaboration appears crucial in the CI. This paper describes an approach to achieve significant improvements in managing of construction activities, thanks to the adoption of ICT technologies for the immediate information delivery. In particular, this research paper will describe the developing process of a digital platform that uses augmented reality combined with BIM to provide workers with relevant information in real-time, based on their current position on the construction site. This consists in a 3D model-based integration platform that can integrate and exploit BIM models, in order to provide context-aware "augmented" information in real-time at the right place.

The paper describes the main features of the developed tool and focuses on the actual topics of the study which are: (1) the location system using sensory information collected by mobile devices to give location awareness to the application; (2) the integration of 3D BIM model metadata in order to contextualize tasks and instructions and provide building components information.

Keywords: Augmented reality · BIM metadata · 3D model-based platform Industry 4.0 · Product development

---

G. P. Monizza—Presenting author.

Published by Springer Nature Switzerland AG 2018.
P. Chiabert et al. (Eds.): PLM 2018, IFIP AICT 540, pp. 46–55, 2018.
https://doi.org/10.1007/978-3-030-01614-2_5

1 Introduction

1.1 Construction Industry

The Construction Industry (CI) is an information-based industry, since a great amount of information need to be transferred and exchanged during the construction process. Its peculiarity regards the management of different challenges given by multiple parties participating towards the completion of a construction project. Construction processes are characterized by an extreme complexity, where various participants must collaborate, exchange information and often solve problems. Over the years, the CI has always been struggled by difficulties in sharing information between the involved participants. This fact represents a primary cause of poor performances. Different participants would spend a major effort on the individual work, rather than intelligently exchanging information with other parties [1]. Moreover, in major construction sites, information flow still depends on paper-based information management. Such aspect can easily result in misunderstanding between stakeholders [2]. Therefore, an efficient management of information flow is crucial to encourage a general improvement of construction processes.

1.2 ICT Technologies and Augmented Reality in the CI

In the most recent years, the adoption of ICT in the supply chain management has brought significant improvements in industries. The increasing digitization of information management in the Construction Industry is examined in [3] as an opportunity for new technologies to find valuable employment also in construction processes. The source states that while information is being more and more treated in a digital format, there is also the necessity of accessing and visualizing it in an intuitive manner. Several studies have therefore considered mobile applications integrating Augmented Reality technologies, as valid digital tools in the Construction Industry.

Augmented Reality (AR) is an emergent technology which allows the creation of a 3D virtual layer upon the reality, that enhances the normal experience of the user. Especially on the construction site, where a high level of flexibility is required due to rapidly changing conditions, there is urgent need of suitable information management support that can adapt as rapidly. Different studies argue that mobile applications integrating Augmented Reality technologies have the capabilities to satisfy such need, because they provide meaningful and updated information with respect to space and time [4]. Additionally, human perception is based primarily on three-dimensional objects. Therefore, a digital 3D representation supports a quick orientation in space and can be used to provide information in a context-based manner [5].

Building Information Modeling

Building information modeling (BIM) is a set of interacting policies, processes and technologies that generates a methodology to manage the essential building design and project data in digital format throughout the building's life cycle [6]. For more than ten years Building Information Modeling has been one of the most important innovation means to approach building design holistically, to enhance communication and collaboration among key stakeholders, to increase productivity, and to improve the overall quality of the final product (building) [7]. The integration of AR with BIM models can furthermore improve the assimilation of this innovative practices, making possible the exploitation of model-based software tools. Building models together with the encapsulated metadata, can conveniently be accessed and managed with an AR mobile application [8].

2 State of the Art

Many researches have focused on developing, analyzing and discussing different solutions for managing BIM data and information flow using digital enabling tools. Mobile computing has been the topic of different studies, as one promising technology which would extend the information management from offices to the actual site [9]. As described in the paper, managers would therefore be able to remotely collect information from the site. An example of another valid solution is [10], which aims to introduce the effectiveness of Google Glass as a technology for the information management on the construction site. One further study [11] analyses the inadequate management of resources in the CI, and discusses a framework for the implementation of the Virtual Reality technology with the purpose of data visualization. Such system would display real-time information in the virtual model, in order to avoid its manual monitoring.

As [12] writes, the real challenge lies in the provision of the position in time and discusses different indoor positioning techniques, their characteristics as well their accuracy, advantages and disadvantages. Only in recent years the focus has passed to indoor venues, and one technology identified for indoor location is Bluetooth. Positioning with BLE beacons has two major purposes, tracking and providing local-based services [12]. Indeed, BLE is a different and innovative solution for developing an indoor positioning system (IPS), by defining a real-time and environment-adaptive signal propagation model, based on the evolution of Received Signal Strengths Indicator over time.

Different studies have also considered mobile applications as useful instruments for the processing of BIM information. An effective theoretical input comes from [13], which discusses the possibility of integrating construction information coming from BIM software with Augmented Reality. As this study suggests, AR should include context awareness, in order to properly manage all BIM information.

It is also important to keep in mind the field of application, in order to provide enabling tools that properly addresses the construction site issues. It appears crucial to consider the dynamics in the construction site, where workers are in continuous movement and on different positions of interest. For example, [14] proposes a high-precision, image-based AR application for collecting information from the construction site, aiming at reducing the manual work. Generally, as [3] states, even if the idea of applying Mixed Reality in construction is not particularly new, a simple straightforward solution has not been yet available.

3 AR4Construction Research Project

Considering the discussion above, the final goal of the project AR4Construction has been identified in the development of an enabling tool for managing technical information in a dynamic and intelligent manner, in order to solve the issue of the rapid changes occurring on a construction site, that require immediate information delivery and ease of use. The main aim was to develop a mobile application for the digital transfer of BIM information on the construction site, though augmented reality and exploiting an indoor location system based on Bluetooth technology.

The application domain was defined to be a generic construction site. The application permit to visualize the whole, or only parts (e.g. windows), of the 3D BIM model in the "correct" place while walking through the construction site, and furthermore to extract relevant information in the construction phase (details or assigned tasks). The idea is to provide workers with a user-friendly digital tool which substitutes a consistent amount of paper-based material.

According to this, functional requirements are designed as follows:

- Users of the application are workers on the construction site;
- Explore the 3D BIM by walking in the real counterpart. The position of the worker in the building should always correspond to the position in the 3D model;
- Be able to filter the building components (e.g. walls, floors, windows), therefore to see only interesting components;
- Touch relevant components in order to access its information. This includes general information about the geometry and physical details but also specific notes attached to that component;
- Visualize tasks to be completed with respect to the worker position in the 3D model.

4 Development

Once the definition of the requirements and functionalities of the system has been completed, a conceptual scheme of the application structure was designed in order to support the implementation phase. The internal structure, considering the hardware and software components and the information flow of the AR4Construction platform was defined (Fig. 1). This section aims to describe the tools, the procedures, and various issues concerning the system's whole development phase.

4.1 Internal Structure

Among different hardware solutions available at the time of this research, the smartphone "Lenovo Phab 2 Pro", that integrates the platform "Tango", has been chosen as the mobile delivery device. With regard to the development environment, the application has been implemented in Unity, that allows the creation of system's required blocks and their interaction by means of C# scripts. The Unity game engine platform is essentially required for the 3D model management. The implementation's preliminary phase consisted of importing the necessary services and assets into Unity, such as the Tango API, the Firebase SDK, adopted for the creation of a remote database and its

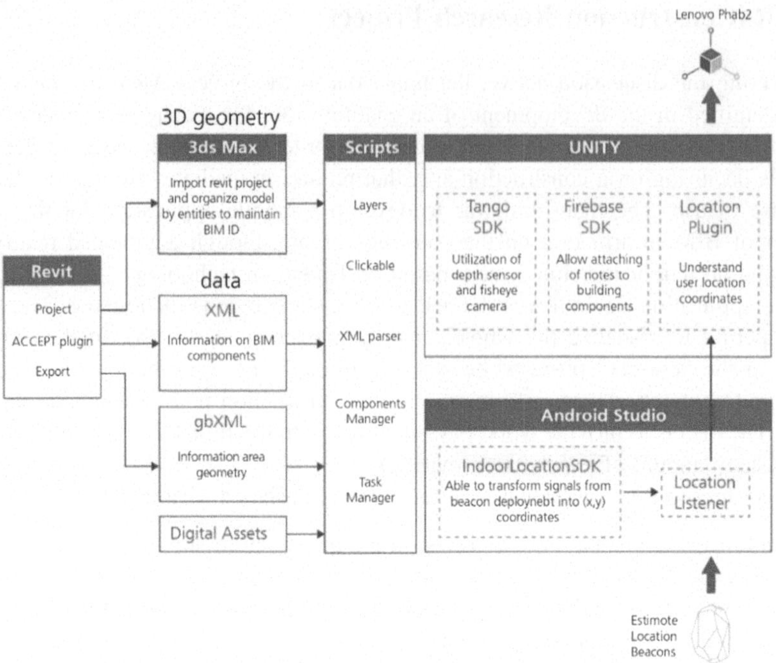

Fig. 1. Internal structure and information flow of the AR4Construction platform (Source: Fraunhofer Italia)

management through Unity, and a BIM model with associated XML metadata-file containing all building's relevant parameters. The development phase has been done using as a reference the BIM model of the Fraunhofer Italia offices, modeled by the authors. Thanks to this, each implementation step has been followed by a concrete testing phase inside the building.

The implementation advanced by developing a system to regulate all information incorporated in the model and metadata. For this purpose, the main work has been done in developing scripts that the authors called "Layers", "Cliccable", "XML parser", "Components manager" and "Task Manager". In such a way, data is available within the application for visualization and further processing. Furthermore, an Indoor Positioning System (IPS) has been structured exploiting the iBeacon technology, developing a script in Android studio, that the authors defined "Location Listener", that is able to transform signal from beacon deployment into coordinates.

An elementary Graphical User Interface (GUI) was consequently implemented in Unity in favor of convenient data handling. The GUI's features include a filter for the model's components, information retrieval by clicking the model's components and the possibility to insert component related notes. In the final phase, by means of the Firebase Storage Service, a cloud database has been created, in order to centralize all data that is relevant for multiple system's users.

In addition, the focus research topics of this paper are explained in the next section.

5 Research Focus

5.1 Indoor Positioning

Indoor Positioning System

Developing an AR application requires the understanding on the environment in order to offer contextualized information. The understanding required for the correct functioning of the developed application is related to the user positioning inside the building. To overcome potential complications deriving from the utilization of GPS systems, especially in complex environments, Indoor Positioning Systems (IPS) were here taken into consideration. There are many different approaches available to implementing IPS, and for this purpose the use of BLE (Bluetooth Low Energy) beacons has been chosen as the most suitable solution. Estimote Location Beacons were chosen as the hardware for the AR4Construction IPS.

Setting up Location Beacons

With the capabilities of the beacons in mind, a physical location was mapped. The most appropriate location for this purpose has been defined as the kitchen of the Fraunhofer Italia offices (Fig. 2). The area span is 4.5 by 9.1 m. Five beacons were placed at chest height, with a clear line of sight between each of them. An origin point was chosen, which serves as a point of reference for the beacons. After the positioning phase, a file with all relevant beacon information was uploaded to the Estimote Cloud.
This file serves to describe the relative placement of the beacons in terms of the origin point. Using this information, it is possible to calculate the position of a device found inside the frame of reference.

In order to gauge the setup accuracy, a testing phase followed. The smartphone (delivery device) was randomly placed in the mapped area and the position reported by the beacons has been compared with the actual real location. The measurements are shown below (Table 1).

During the testing phase, it was noted that for displacements less than 3 m, the software would not update the location. A large displacement in position triggers a recalculation. After the initial calculation, an error correcting phase occurs, until the estimated position converges to a fixed point.

5.2 Information Management

The 3D BIM Model Import Process

Fraunhofer Italia has provided the BIM model of the offices which correspond to the physical area mapped with the beacons. In order to import a BIM model in Unity, it must be in either .obj or .fbx format. Since the project file has been developed through the software Revit®, it must be transferred through 3DSMax® to be translated to FBX. The component names from this phase include an ID that links to the 3D elements. This model is then imported into Unity, where a camera displays it on the device screen. A camera in Unity is a device that captures and displays the view to the user. This camera has a three-dimensional position in the scene, which determines what is

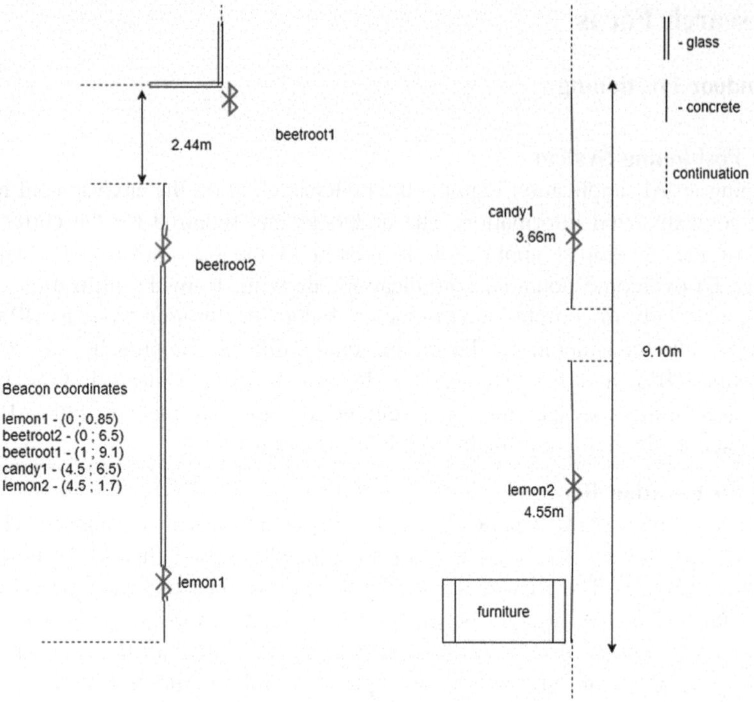

Fig. 2. Setup overview (Source: Fraunhofer Italia)

Table 1. Beacon accuracy measurements

Position #	Estimated location (X ; Y)	Actual location (X ; Y)
Position 1	(0.8 ; 3.8)	(1.5; 3.7)
Position 2	(1. 97 ; 6.6)	(0.3 ; 6 8)
Position 3	(3.03 ; 8.26)	(1.2 ; 8.2)
Position 4	(1.3 ; 9.4)	(1.2 ; 8.2)
Position 5	(4.1 ; 4.7)	(4.3 ; 4.7)
Position 6	(3.5 ; 8.6)	(4.3 ; 9.2)
Position 7	(2.2 ; 5.9)	(0.5 ; 7)
Position 8	(4.20 ; 0.27)	(3.8 ; 0.45)
Position 9	(0.24 ; 1.61)	(0.8 ; 2.2)
Position 10	(2.42 ; 4.57)	(2.17 ; 3.2)
Position 11	(1.9 ; 4.6)	(2.5 ; 8.3)
Position 12	(1.6 ; 4.9)	(2.7 ; 4.7)
Position 13	(1.5 ; 1.7)	(1.2 ; 1.6)
Position 14	(4.1 ; 3 4)	(0.9 ; 4.7)
Position 15	(1.3 ; 6.0)	(2.9 ; 6.6)

displayed or not. The whole system works around placing the virtual camera in the same position as the device camera. The "Location Listener" plugin reports the user initial location to the virtual camera so that it aligns itself and displays the 3D building components the user is looking at. By using the motion tracking capabilities of Tango, the device is able to track the user movement, so that the cameras always stay aligned.

Exporting BIM Data
The 3D model is not sufficient to provide the user with all the necessary information. Using a custom-made plugin for Revit®, the ACCEPT plugin[1], parameter information about every component is extracted in an XML format. This file contains the relevant information about the building component (e.g. height or width), related with an ID to the model-object. The script "Cliccable" allows each component of the model to be interacted with and permit, through a double click, to display this information.

```
selectedObject = hit.transform.gameObject; //the hit object
hitID = script.getComponentID(selectedObject); //get the id of
the selected component
component = script.getCompon(hitID); //retrieve the component
hitName = component.getGameObject().name;//BIM name
h = component.getHeight(); //geometry info
w = component.getWidth();
idField.GetComponent<Text>().text = compo-
nent.getID().ToString(); //update the GUI
nameField.GetComponent<Text>().text = hitName;
```

[Bridging 3D view with BIM information using the "Cliccable" script]

Through the export of a gbXML file from Revit®, it is also possible to capture information about areas of the project. An area is a subdivision of space within a building model. From this file it is possible to extract the bounding coordinates of all areas, therefore to be able to understand in which area the user is currently located. This allows the app to provide contextualized tasks that are linked to building components and specific locations on site. That means, the worker can quickly retrieve information about installation procedures, technical data, drawings, and quality checklists.

6 Results

The achieved result consists of a prototype application, which provides workers with relevant real-time information based both on the BIM model and on the user current position in the building. Users can perform the following actions (Table 2).

In this case, context-awareness, is achieved with respect to two dimensions: location and time. The Fig. 3. shows a demonstrative utilization of the application in the Fraunhofer offices, when they were still a construction site.

[1] Developed in the H2020 ACCEPT project, it is a BIM 4D plug-in to match BIM metadata data and MS-Project® scheduling and to import to the ACCEPT platform, in order to enable a more reliable construction scheduling and controlling.

Table 2. Functionalities of the AR4C application

Functionality	Description
Navigate 3D model	The worker navigates the 3D model in the application by walking in the real environment
Visualize element information	Allows the user to touch every element in the 3D model, and to extract information from that element
Read geometry information	The user can visualize a technical summary of a given component
Filter 3D Model	The user can enable and disable different levels of the 3D model
Consult task list	The user can consult a list of tasks currently available
Upload/Read note	Allows the worker to type/read a note related to a selected component and to upload/download it to/from the shared database by touching a button

Fig. 3. Using the AR4C prototype application.

7 Conclusions

In this research paper a platform for the integration of Augmented Reality and BIM was discussed. Usually, users adopt BIM for 2D and 3D visualization without exploiting full potentials of BIM approach and software. Moreover, Mixed Reality technologies have increasingly gained importance within the Construction Industry. The reason is given by their capability to manage different levels of reality perception. These can be combined with an efficient management of context-aware information and this combination could solve some of the most peculiar issues of the CI, namely communication and information flow management issues.

Considering these assumptions, it is clear that the implementation of innovative technologies as the AR4Construction platform, will be crucial in order to support the CI for the integral cooperation of all stakeholders in construction projects for the general increasing of productivity. Future developments might be to apply this application to a real construction site, in order to quantify its real potentiality. Furthermore, such system represents a stable starting point on top of which further functionalities can be built as extensions.

References

1. Dainty, A., Moore, D., Murray, M.: Communication in Construction, Theory and Practice. Taylor & Francis, New York (2006)
2. Tauscher, E., Mikulakova, E., Beucke, K., König, M.: Automated generation of construction schedules based on the IFC object model. In: International Workshop on Computing in Civil Engineering. ASCE, Austin, pp. 666–675 (2009). https://doi.org/10.1061/41052(346)66
3. Chi, H.-L., Kang, C.-C., Wang, X.: Research trends and opportunities of augmented reality applications in architecture, engineering, and construction. Autom. Constr. **33**, 116–122 (2013)
4. Izkara, J.L., Pérez, J., Basogain, X., Borro, D.: Mobile augmented reality, an advanced tool for the construction sector. In: CIB W078 24th International Conference on Information Technology for Construction, pp. 453–460 (2007)
5. Knoth, L., Mittlböck, M., Vockner, B.: Smart 3D building infrastructures: linking GIS with other domains. In: ISPRS Annals of the Photogrammetry, Remote Sensing and Spatial Information Sciences, 11th 3D Geoinfo Conference, Athens, Greece, vol. IV-2/W1 (2016)
6. Penttilä, H.: Describing the changes in architectural information technology to understand design complexity and free-form architectural expression. ITC Inf. Technol. Constr. **11**, 395–408 (2006)
7. Ratajczak, J., Malacarne, G., Krause, D., Matt, D.: The BIM approach and stakeholders integration in the AEC sector – benefits and obstacles in South Tyrolean context. In: Third International Workshop on Design in Civil and Environmental Engineering (2014)
8. Wang, X., Dunston, P.S., Skibniewski, M.: Mixed reality technology for construction equipment operator training. In: Proceedings, 21st International Symposium on Automation and Robotics in Construction, pp. 393–400 (2004)
9. Chen, Y., Kamara, J.M.: A framework for using mobile computing for information management on construction sites. Autom. Constr. **20**, 776–788 (2011)
10. Moon, S., Seo, J.: Integration of smart glass technology for information exchange at construction sites. In: Proceedings of the 32nd ISARC, Oulu, Finland, pp. 1–2 (2015). https://doi.org/10.22260/isarc2015/0018
11. Cheng, T., Teizer, J.: Real-time resource location data collection and visualization technology for construction safety and activity monitoring applications. Autom. Constr. **34**, 3–15 (2013)
12. Knoth, L.: Spatial information infrastructures for indoor environments. Master's thesis in Applied Geoinformatics, Interfaculty Department of Geoinformatics, Salzburg (2015)
13. Wang, X., Love, P.E.D., Kim, M.J., Park, C.-S., Sing, C.-P., Hou, L.: A conceptual framework for integrating building information modelling with augmented reality. Autom. Constr. **34**, 37–44 (2013)
14. Bae, H., Golparvar-Fard, M., White, J.: High-precision vision-based mobile augmented reality system for context-aware architectural, engineering, construction and facility management (AEC/FM) applications. Vis. Eng. **1**, 3–16 (2013). https://doi.org/10.1186/2213-7459-1-3

All-Automatic 3D BIM Modeling of Existing Buildings

D. Benarab[1,2(✉)], W. Derigent[1,2], D. Brie[1,2], V. Bombardier[1,2], and A. Thomas[1,2]

[1] Université de Lorraine, CRAN, UMR 7039, Campus Sciences, BP70239, 54506 Vandœuvre-lès-Nancy, France
{djamel-eddine.benarab, william.derigent, david.brie, vincent.bombardier, andre.thomas}@univ-lorraine.fr
[2] CNRS, CRAN, UMR 7039, Vandœuvre-lès-Nancy, France

Abstract. In order to ensure a reliable building life cycle management, it is essential to generate an accurate and up-to-date referential mock-up that will be used for renovation, extension and maintenance. Based on this statement, we carried out, in a previous work, a research study in the sake of reconstructing a 3D CAD model from a point cloud acquired using a Lidar. This point cloud is processed automatically to detect planes and contours and to generate the 3D CAD model. However, during the life cycle of the project, different actors from different fields intervene on the building, which creates several communication conflicts, and this means a loss of time, energy and money. In order to ensure a constructive collaboration and a simplified data exchange between the different contributors in the building, we continued our work to propose, in this paper, an automatic conversion of a point cloud to a 3D BIM file. This conversion induces the passage to the standard IFC format and the integration of a valuable knowledge in it. To do so, an automatic classification of contours into architectural elements is proposed. It consists in defining a hierarchical classification rule reproducing the human reasoning for classifying the architectural elements. Then, based on the classified set of polygons, an automatic generation of 3D IFC model is proposed.

Keywords: Point cloud · 3D reconstruction · Mock-up · CAD
Entity classification · IFC · BIM · PLM · Calibration

1 Introduction

Knowing that the maintenance phase represents the biggest part of the global building cost [1], it is essential to have an accurate and up-to-date referential model to approach this life cycle phase and ensure a sustainable monitoring during the whole life cycle of the building. For example, this accurate representation of the building could be used in (but not limited to) different rehabilitation phases.

Therefore, we first carried out a research study to define an automatic reconstruction process adapted to existing buildings. This one is able to generate a 3D CAD mock-up from a point cloud acquired using a Lidar 3D scanner. As will be detailed later, the reconstruction process automatically detects the planes of the building then

Published by Springer Nature Switzerland AG 2018.
P. Chiabert et al. (Eds.): PLM 2018, IFIP AICT 540, pp. 56–68, 2018.
https://doi.org/10.1007/978-3-030-01614-2_6

the polygonal contours in each plane. The exterior polygons are considered as facades and the interior polygons are considered as architectural elements: doors, windows and others. Afterwards, these polygons constitute our CAD model that can be saved, for example, into a DXF format file.

During the life cycle of the building, different actors from different fields intervene on the building such as constructors, carpenters, plumbers, etc. In order to ensure a constructive collaboration between these actors, the BIM (Building Information Modeling) has been proposed [2, 3]. This process allows an optimized collaborative work and a simplified data exchange between different actors coming from different backgrounds. This is possible thanks to the use of a common exchange format, namely, the standard IFC (Industry Foundation Classes) which is the most widely used standard currently.

For this reason, and in the sake of conceiving an all-automatic BIM modeling for the existing building, an automatic conversion of the point cloud to a standard IFC file is proposed in this paper. IFC allows to model building and construction elements (walls, windows, doors, etc.), their characteristics and relations between them. Indeed, unlike STEP and DXF formats, IFC is not limited to the sole geometry of an object but supports a richer semantic description, that we ought to use in our process by automatically generating a file composed of 3D building elements (walls, doors and windows). This requires completing our former reconstruction process with 2 additional steps:

1. The classification of the different interior polygons into building architectural elements (the exterior polygons are only known to be walls). These interior polygons can be classified into doors, windows and others;
2. The conversion of each detected building element into its corresponding IFC entity and the generation of the IFC file.

In this paper, we will start, in Sect. 2, by presenting the research works carried out in the field of 3D reconstruction and BIM file generation. In Sect. 3, we will illustrate a summary of our previous work of 3D reconstruction of existing buildings and introduce the first contribution, namely the polygon classification. In Sect. 4, the automatic generation of the IFC file based on the previously classified polygons is presented. After that, several real test cases are presented in Sect. 5, followed by a conclusion in Sect. 6.

2 Related Works

Recently, several researchers have focused on developing methods for the automation of existing buildings reconstruction and BIM model generation. In terms of 3D reconstruction of building elements, the focus has been on computational geometry algorithms to extract the 3D representation of building elements through segmentation, including surface normal approaches [4], plane sweeping [5] and region growing [1, 6].

Processing a point cloud in order to reconstruct a cured 3D model is a very difficult task. The main difficulties [2, 6–9] are the density distribution difference of the point all along the point cloud, the occlusion of the building parts which are not exposed to the Lidar, the reflection of laser beams and sometimes the complexity of the building itself. In the literature, different research works sought to overcome the difficulties of as-built 3D reconstruction model. We find, for instance, several semi-automatic reconstruction methods requiring limited user intervention as in [6, 9–11]. In [6] researchers proposed a method based on supervised learning in order to cope with the occlusion in interior reconstruction. In the same context of occlusion but in the exterior, researchers in [11] proposed to enhance the acquired data by a fusion of point clouds issued from laser scanning and photogrammetry. [9, 10] proposed to couple the point cloud with images in order to overcome reflection problems and enhance the exterior reconstruction. However, these methods remain insufficient and require a large number of parameters and their level of abstraction is often too high for the user.

In [12, 13] the researchers propose an automatic as-built 3D model reconstruction. These contributions have shown promising results, but they do not generate a parametric object-based model as we can find in BIM models but they generate a 3D CAD model that needs to be remodeled manually to create a BIM model.

In order to generate a BIM model, [2] proposed a semi- automatic system of the 3D reconstruction of existing buildings. Their goal is to develop a processing chain that automatically extracts the maximum amount of information from the point cloud of a building in order to integrate the result into a BIM model. To do this, they proposed to use RANSAC algorithm to segment the point cloud, the color intensity to detect the openings in each plane and the software FreeCAD to generate the IFC file.

Due to the limitations of the data collection processes as well as the complexity of as-built scenes, automated 3D modeling still presents many challenges and the majority of methods do not guarantee the accuracy of their results. Our aim, in this paper, is to propose an all-automatic and accurate 3D BIM reconstruction approach for existing buildings. For this, we start by reconstructing the 3D CAD model then we automatically generate an enriched BIM mock-up using the information parsed from the CAD model.

3 3D CAD Model Reconstruction

The 3D reconstruction process is detailed in Fig. 1. It is basically composed of 3 steps: point cloud segmentation, extraction of the different edges (or contours) of the building and ROI classification (regions of interest). Despite the classification step, the segmentation and extraction phases were already detailed in our previous works. Yet, to ensure a good understanding of the complete process, an overview of these two steps is briefly done in Sect. 3.1, knowing that further details can be found in [7]. The new step, i.e. the classification, is described Sect. 3.2.

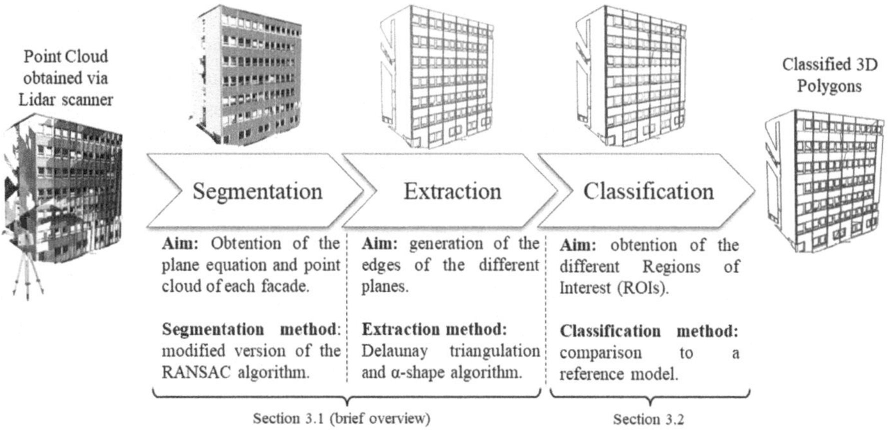

Fig. 1. The 3D reconstruction process

3.1 Segmentation and Contour Extraction

Point cloud segmentation consists in looking for the successive planes that maximize the number of consistent points (inliers). It is based on a modified version of the RANSAC algorithm, introduced by [14] in 1981. The initial algorithm is composed of three steps:

1. Proposition: In this step, the algorithm randomly chooses a sample composed of three points which implicitly define a plane equation.
2. Calculation of the cost function: The cost function consists in determining the number of inliers, which are the consistent points with the plane respecting an interval of tolerance. The other points are considered as outliers.
3. Model Ranking: Models are ranked according to the number of points that are consistent with each model. The model that maximizes the cost function is considered as the best.

These three steps can be iterated until the probability of finding a better model becomes low. A simplified (but time controlled) procedure consists of limiting the number of iterations to a fixed level. To further reduce the complexity and computation time of the algorithm, we can also consider the colorimetric data of the points cloud. Assuming the colorimetric homogeneity of the points belonging to the same geometric feature, the data point cloud is partitioned into homogeneous colorimetric clusters. Then the random sampling (step 1. of RANSAC) is selected from a single-color class. Further details can be found in [8].

The next step consists in detecting the contours of each set of co-planar consistent points. To do this, we applied the Delaunay triangulation then the α-shape algorithm. The Delaunay triangulation is an optimal triangulation that maximizes the smallest angle of all triangles with the tendency of avoiding acute angles. The α-shape is a generalization of the convex hull of a point set [15]. It is composed of a set of α-exposed segments. According to [16], a segment is said to be α-exposed if there exists an empty circle of radius α that circumcircles it. This results in a 2-D simplicial complex, which by definition is composed of vertices, edges and triangles (free and attached). A triangle edge is considered as a boundary (contour points), if it only belongs to a single triangle. The key design parameter is the radius α. Using a constant value α implicitly assumes a uniform point cloud density which is not the case in real applications for which multiple stations are used. Actually, the spatial sampling step varies with the azimuth and elevation angles of the laser beam and it is minimal (i.e. it has a maximal density) when the laser beam is orthogonal to the plane. The approach proposed in [7] approximates the density function of the point cloud. This allows to calculate the radius used in the α-shape algorithm.

Once we detect the exterior and the interior contours of each facade, the Hough line detection approach is used to detect segments, which are then gathered in a closed 3D polygonal model. This is detailed in Sect. 3.2.

3.2 Architectural Elements Classification

After the generation of the 3D geometric model of the building, a classification stage aims to provide a semantic description of the architectural elements existing inside the facade contours, in our case walls, doors and windows. For each plane, the exterior contour is considered as a wall, and interior contours are the remaining other architectural elements. For each interior polygonal contour, the identification as door or window is done by comparing the enclosing parallelepiped to the most common standard door and window geometrical models (which also are parallelepipeds).

Having defined these standard models, we measure the similarity by evaluating the quadratic distance between the enclosing parallelepiped and standard model vertices and choose the one having maximal similarity (minimal distance). The main geometrical features taken into account in order to classify entities are:

- **Shape**: Windows can take different shapes: square, rectangle, triangle, etc. However, doors are generally rectangular.
- **Dimensions**: Specific intervals are set to limit the acceptable dimensions for a window or a door. For instance, the standard model of a door is defined by a rectangle with a height between 1,7 m and 2,5 m and a length between 0,7 and 1.5 m. More than 1,5 m of length can be considered as a garage. On the other hand, the standard model of windows is more general.
- **Position**: Position makes it possible to differentiate between a window and a door. especially the Z coordinate which can define whether the entity touches the floor or no.

All these criteria allow us to calculate a set of similarity measures that are compared to empirical fixed thresholds and combined in a hierarchical classification rule which reproduces the simple human reasoning depicted in Fig. 2. This process allows to classify the polygons of a plane as: wall, window, door, unknown.

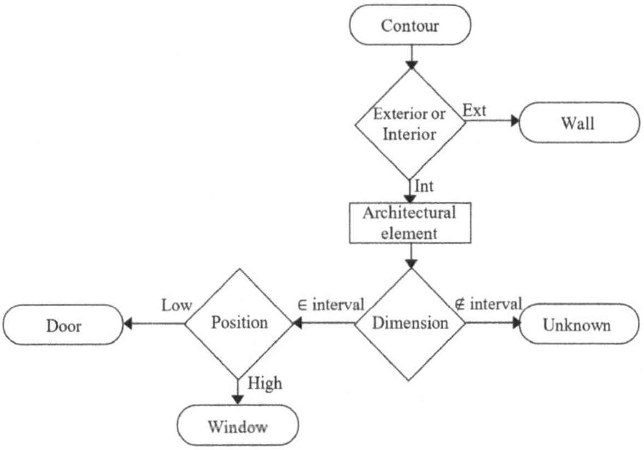

Fig. 2. A graph representation of the hierarchical classification rules

3.3 Computation of Additional Features

Once the 3D geometrical model (i.e. the set of labelled polygons) is available, several geometric, spatial and colorimetric characteristics can be computed from the point cloud and contours associated to each architecture element. From the different labelled door and window contours, we calculate the minimum surface enclosing and maximum surface enclosed parallelepipeds. For walls, the set of corresponding consistent points is used to evaluate the variance of the point clouds planarity error (granularity), and the thickness of wall in the B-rep model (see Fig. 3). In addition to this information, we export the mean plane, the minimum/maximum planes, the normal and the geometry of the plane. Moreover, some TLS generate point clouds where each point is associated with its colorimetric information. For each architectural element, the colorimetric description is description by averaging the colorimetric information over the set of consistent points.

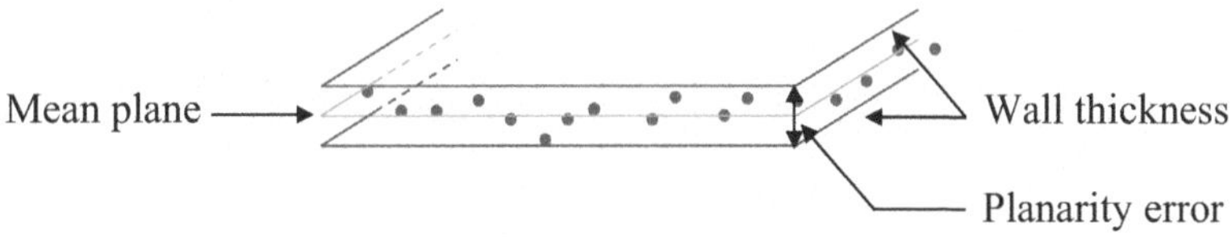

Fig. 3. Information extracted from the generated planes

4 IFC Model Generation

The previous step generates a set of classified polygons, that remains to be converted into an IFC file. The IFC standard, currently supported and maintained by the BUILDINGSMART consortium [17], is the most popular format in the construction industry. This standard, based on STEP [18] has the needed level of expression to model 3D shapes coupled with additional information. The IFC is a standard integrating common 3D objects with a clear semantic for the construction actors. Many building specialists import and export IFC file and many free IFC viewers are available on the market.

4.1 Modeling Types Supported by the IFC BIM Standard

Four modeling types are supported by the IFC standard: solid (B-Rep), surface, CSG, and tessellated models. To identify which modeling is the most appropriate for our purpose, several tests are realized using the files available on the Building Smart site, and different free IFC viewers. If all these different model types are authorized by the IFC standard, they are not all equally supported by BIM software tools (and especially by the free BIM viewers) available on the market. The choice of the modeling type to use has thus been guided by two constraints: *(1)* the chosen modeling must allow to represent surfaces issued from the contours detected by the previous steps and *(2)* must be compatible with a maximum number of BIM viewers, to ensure a good interoperability. As the set of classified polygons does not include the needed information to construct a building mesh, the tessellation modeling is not adapted to our use case. The remaining modeling modes has been tested on 12 different BIM viewers (11 among these are free). This list is based on our knowledge of the BIM offers and on listings available on the web[1]. Results presented in the table Table 1 show that the most interoperable modeling is the B-Rep one, compatible with all modelers and is thus the one chosen in our approach.

Table 1. Results of experimentations conducted on modeling types and BIM viewers.

	11 free BIM viewers											**Not free**
Modelling types	Lexocad	Tekla Bimsight	Solibri	BIM Vision 2.18	Autodesk Viewer	3D Repo	Simple BIM	Areddo 3.2	EveBIM V2	Bentley View V8.i	RDF Viewer	Solidworks
Surface	X	X	X	V	V	V	V	V	V	V	V	X
CSG	X	X	X	V	X	X	V	V	X	V	V	X
B-Rep	V	V	V	V	V	V	V	V	V	V	V	V

V: modelling type supported / X : modelling type not supported

[1] https://www.hexabim.com/blog/qui-a-teste-ces-15-viewers-ifc-gratuits.

The previous steps extract for each building element *E* (facade, window or door) its contour *C*, its normal vector *N* as well as a planarity value *P*, that corresponds to the maximum distance between the points belonging to the plane and the plane equation. As a result, the automatic IFC generation is decomposed into 2 sub-steps, *(1)* transform the wireframe structure into a B-Rep model, and *(2)* create the IFC objects needed to represent facades, windows and doors, as depicted in Fig. 4.

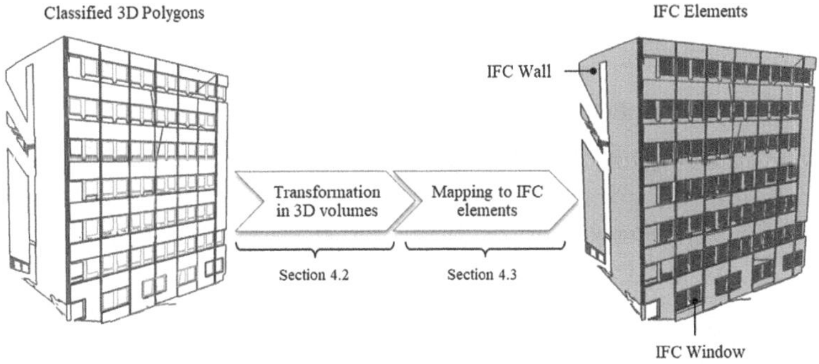

Fig. 4. IFC model generation

4.2 Generation of the B-Rep Model

In fact, the creation of an IFC element requires first the creation of the B-Rep elements needed to define its 3D shape. The complete process is described in Fig. 5. The final building model is not necessarily "closed", i.e. some surfaces could be missing. In fact, it is very difficult to do a complete scan of all the surfaces of a building because of diverse constraints related to accessibility and cost. As a result, building a single B-Rep for all the building is not achievable. We instead build a set of small B-Reps, one per facade, window or door, the whole set representing the final building model. This is completely in line with the IFC modeling philosophy.

Each building element *E* (facade, door and window) first undergoes a geometric process as illustrated in Fig. 5a. This algorithm is composed of two procedures:

1. Creation of duplicated and linking lines for the considered contour: the lines of the contour *C* are duplicated and moved along the normal vector *N* from a distance *P*. Then linking lines, joining vertices of both contours, are constructed. They are required to form a closed wireframe shape of the building element. Using *P* is a mean to add visual information to the final BIM model that could be used later by an engineer, in the case of a building external insulation for example. For instance, in our case, *P* is the planarity error calculated using the associated sub-point cloud.
2. Creation of the faces *F* and volume *V* of the final B-Rep model.

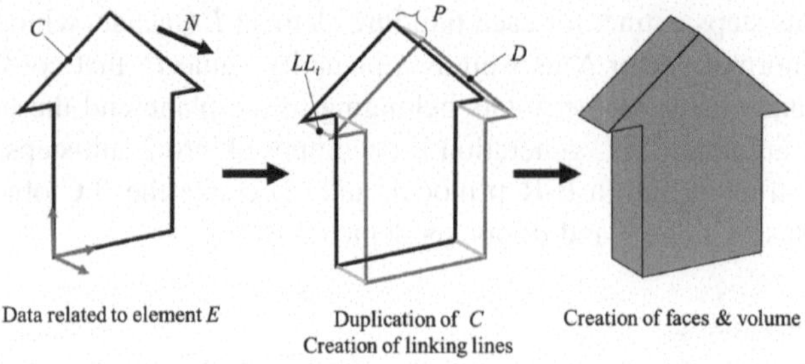

(a) Creation of the B-Rep Model of a building element *E*

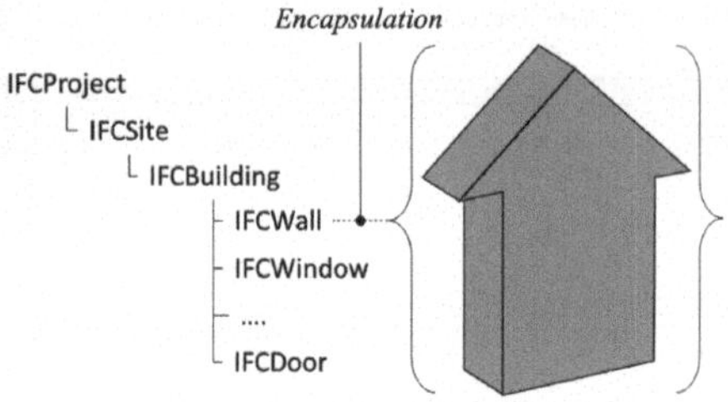

(b) Encapsulation of the B-Rep Model in an IFC structure

Fig. 5. Creation of the B-Rep model of a building element *E*

4.3 Mapping to IFC Elements

Once done, the second step is to associate the BRep model with an IFC element. In our case, four IFC elements are considered *IFCBuilding* that contains: *IFCWall* for facades, *IFCWindow* for windows and *IFCDoor* for doors. After the execution of the whole process, the final IFC file contains a list of all facades, doors and windows detected on the initial point cloud, and reconstructed as IFC elements as shown in Fig. 5b.

5 Two Real-Life Test Cases

A set of experiment has been conducted on different point clouds coming from different sites. In the following, 2 experiments are presented. The first one is a house (calles Liezey's house) and the second one is a small co-ownership accommodation (called La Bresse's co-ownership). Our objective is to generate automatically an accurate 3D BIM mock-up for the two buildings that will be used for thermal insulation purposes.

The point cloud acquisition is carried out using the TLS Leica C10. 3D CAD reconstruction (point cloud segmentation, contour extraction) is made using ModiBuilding software (developed by the University of Lorraine). The prototype of the conversion from CAD to IFC model is implemented with Matlab software. The tests are conducted on a 6 core Apple pro equipped with an NVIDIA graphical processor unit (GPU).

Figure 6a illustrates the complete experiment for the Liezey's house whereas Fig. 6b only shows the final IFC model obtained for La Bresse's co-ownership. In Table 2 we present an evaluation of the architectural elements classification process carried out on the two test buildings.

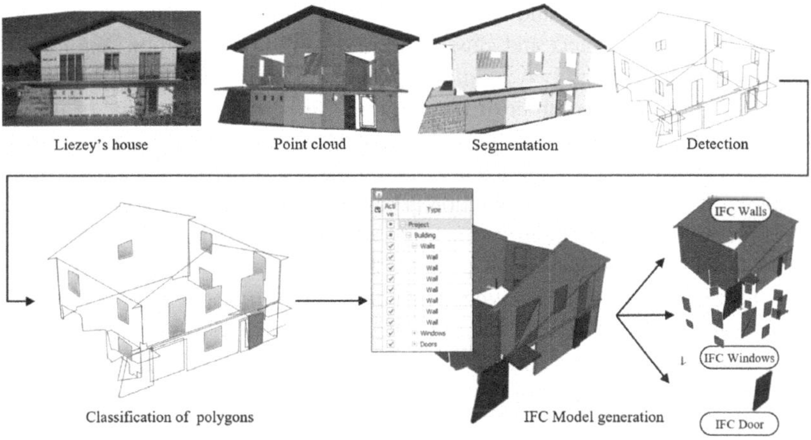

(a) Illustration of the complete process on Liezey's house

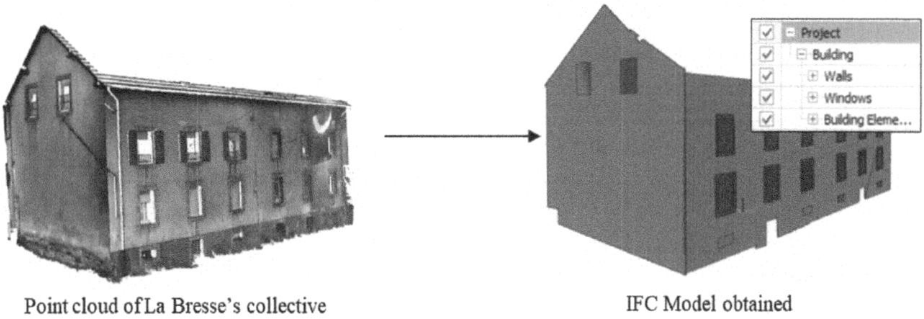

(b) IFC Model obtained from the point cloud of La Bresse's co-ownership

Fig. 6. Experiment realized on Liezey's house and La Bresse's co-ownership

Table 2. Evaluation of the architectural elements classification process

Object	Liezey	La Bresse
Number of windows	13	18
% of classified windows	100%	100%
Number of doors	2	2
% of classified doors	50%	0%

The windows in the two buildings were well classified because they fit the standard form and dimensions of windows. However, the door of the garage in Liezey's house could not be classified because it does not have the form of a standard door. In this case, an adaptation of the classification algorithm is needed. On the other hand, the two small doors in the big facade of La Bresse's co-ownership were classified as unknown because they do not respect the lowest tolerated dimensions of a regular door. In fact, only half of the two doors were scanned, and another occluded half is underground and accessible using stairs. In order to detect and classify these doors, the acquisition step need to be adapted and completed with two additional stations to scan the underground part.

The Table 3 presents an order of magnitude of the computation time of the reconstruction process for the two buildings. In the two cases, we didn't use the raw point cloud acquired with TLS, we applied a sampling method to lighten the point cloud and the computation time. Plane segmentation is based on the iterative algorithm RANSAC which is time consuming. Contour extraction took more time in La Bresse co-ownership because it is an old building which means a lot of planarity errors that creates false polygons to be analyzed and removed. The computation time needed for the architectural elements classification and the IFC model generation is within few seconds. Both IFC models were successfully opened using every BIM Viewers listed previously, except with SimpleBIM. The origin of this error has not been investigated yet.

Table 3. Computation time of 3D reconstruction process for the two buildings

Time computation	Liezey	La Bresse
Point cloud acquisition	9M points (1 day)	8M points (1 day)
Plane segmentation	50 mn	45 mn
Contour extraction	55 mn	58 mn
Classification	<1 s	<1 s

6 Conclusion

In this paper, a 3D BIM-oriented automatic modeling of existing buildings was presented. This process, starting from the building point cloud, is able to automatically generate 3D IFC models, fully compatible with available free BIM viewers. Our previous work has been completed by two other modules related to the classification of polygons and the IFC model generation. This improved process has been tested on numerous case studies, of which two were presented here. Experiments proved that the process is reliable but still time-consuming. However, because it is fully automatic, it may be launched in hidden time, during nights for example.

The process is for the moment limited to plane reconstruction, meaning that round shapes are discretized into numerous planes during the reconstruction process, which is not optimal. Nevertheless, this is not an important problem for applications related to building renovation of classic buildings, which is our main application target.

7 Acknowledgments

This research work has been carried out within the framework of the project ADEME ITE+(External Thermal Insulation). The authors want to thank the French Environment and Energy Management Agency (ADEME) for their financial support. A special acknowledgement goes to the University of Lorraine for the use of the Modibuilding Software.

References

1. Andrey, D., Mani, G.: Segmentation of building point cloud models including detailed architectural/structural features and MEP systems. Autom. Constr. **51**, 32–45 (2015). https://doi.org/10.1016/j.autcon.2014.12.015
2. Hélène, M.: From point cloud to building information model (BIM). 3D semi-automatic reconstruction of existing buildings. University of Strasbourg (2017)
3. Thomson, C., Boehm, J.: Automatic geometry generation from point clouds for BIM. Remote Sens. **7**(9), 11753–11775 (2015). https://doi.org/10.3390/rs70911753
4. Barnea, S., Filin, S.: Segmentation of terrestrial laser scanning data using geometry and image information. ISPRS J. Photogramm. Remote Sens. **76**, 33–48 (2013). https://doi.org/10.1016/j.isprsjprs.2012.05.001
5. Budroni, A., Boehm, J.: Automated 3D reconstruction of interiors from point clouds. Int. J. Archit. Comput. **8**, 55–73 (2010). https://doi.org/10.1260/1478-0771.8.1.55
6. Adan, A., Huber, D.: 3D reconstruction of interior wall surfaces under occlusion and clutter. In: Proceedings of the IEEE International Conference on 3D Imaging, Modeling, Processing, Visualization and Transmission (3DIMPVT), China, pp. 275–281 (2011). https://doi.org/10.1109/3dimpvt.2011.42
7. Brie, D., Bombardier, V., Baeteman, G., Bennis, A.: Local surface sampling step estimation for extracting boundaries of planar point clouds. ISPRS J. Photogramm. Remote Sens. **119**, 309–319 (2016). https://doi.org/10.1016/j.isprsjprs.2016.06.006
8. Benis, A.: Contribution to the 3D reconstruction of buildings using point cloud of terrestrial laser scanning. University of Lorraine (2015)
9. Frueh, C., Jain, S., Zakhor, A.: Data processing algorithms for generating textured 3D building facade meshes from laser scans and camera images. Int. J. Comput. Vis. **61**(2), 159–184 (2005). https://doi.org/10.1023/b:visi.0000043756.03810.dd
10. Pu, S., Vosselman, G.: Building facade reconstruction by fusing terrestrial laser points and images. ISPRS J. Photogram. Remote Sens. **64**, 2525–4542 (2009). https://doi.org/10.3390/s90604525
11. Böhm, J., Becker, S., Haala, N.: Model refinement by integrated processing of laser scanning and photogrammetry. In: Proceedings of the 3D Virtual Reconstruction and Visualization of Complex Architectures (3D-Arch) (2007)
12. Xiong, X., Adan, A., Akinci, B., Huber, D.: Automatic creation of semantically rich 3D building models from laser scanner data. Autom. Constr. **31**, 325–337 (2013). https://doi.org/10.1016/j.autcon.2012.10.006
13. Jung, J., et al.: Productive modeling for development of as-built BIM of existing indoor structures. Autom. Constr. **42**, 68–77 (2014). https://doi.org/10.1016/j.autcon.2014.02.021
14. Fischler, M.A., Bolles, R.C.: Random sample consensus: a paradigm for model fitting with applications to image analysis and automated cartography. Commun. ACM **24**, 381–395 (1981). https://doi.org/10.1145/358669.358692

15. Edelsbrunner, H., Kirkpatrick, D.G., Seidel, R.: On the shape of a set of points in the plane. IEEE Trans. Inf. Theory **29**, 551–559 (1983). https://doi.org/10.1109/TIT.1983.1056714
16. Edelsbrunner, H., Mucke, E.P.: Three-dimensional alpha shapes. ACM Trans. Graph. **13**(1), 43–72 (1994). https://doi.org/10.1145/174462.156635
17. ISO.: Industry Foundation Classes (IFC) for data sharing in the construction and facility management industries (2013)
18. Pratt, M.J.: ISO 10303, the STEP standard for product data exchange, and its PLM capabilities. Int. J. Prod. Lifecycle Manag. **1**(1), 86 (2005). https://doi.org/10.1504/IJPLM.2005.007347

Configuration Views from PLM to Building Lifecycle Management

Carla Di Biccari, Giovanna Mangialardi(✉), Mariangela Lazoi, and Angelo Corallo

Università del Salento, Campus Ecotekne, Lecce, Italy
{carla.dibiccari,giovanna.mangialardi, mariangela.lazoi,angelo.corallo}@unisalento.it

Abstract. This research is based on the envisaged necessity to improve Building Information Modeling (BIM) methodologies and technologies along the building or infrastructure life cycle leveraging lessons learned by Product Lifecycle Management (PLM) applications in aerospace and automotive industries. To this aim, the authors analyzed the concept of "configuration view", or better, "Product Structure configuration", of complex manufacturing and whether it has been already applied to process or information management of different lifecycle phases of the AEC industry. Starting from the representation of the configuration views in PLM, the final objective is to identify gaps in the current BIM technological process and to propose a customized Product Structure based on personalized configuration views in the Construction World to implementing the Building Lifecycle Management (BLM).

Keywords: BIM · PLM · BLM · Configuration view · Product Structure

1 Introduction

The social, environmental and economic benefits of digitalization are well recognized in the Construction industry and already implemented in Aerospace and Automotive industries. In both industries, the strategic vision based on information lifecycle management, provides significant efficiency benefits, time-saving, value creation, and they are a driver for country competitiveness.

Sometimes, the legislative framework could speed the technologies adoption, but the context is not always ready. For example, the Italian country struggles to follow innovation in the construction industry, even though nowadays it recognizes as fundamental. In detail, the "*Codice degli Appalti*" n. 50/2016, in article 23, paragraph 13, introduces the use of specific electronic methods and tools for complex works and the Ministerial Decree n. 560/2017 defines the methods and times of gradual mandatory introduction. The obligatoriness starts from the 1st January 2019 for works value of €100 million or more, and then gradually for minor amounts from the years after, until works for a value of less than € 1 million, for which the deadline starts from 1 January 2025. Although this Decree n. 560/2017 is known as the "BIM Decree", it never mentions the "BIM" term, but it focuses on electronic tools and methods in the building and infrastructure during the design, construction and management phases.

Published by Springer Nature Switzerland AG 2018.
P. Chiabert et al. (Eds.): PLM 2018, IFIP AICT 540, pp. 69–79, 2018.
https://doi.org/10.1007/978-3-030-01614-2_7

In general, in Architecture and Engineering Construction (AEC) Industry the process innovation through digitalization is usually associated with the BIM methodology/technologies, but the authors, in line with the Italian Decree, consider more focalized the adoption of the Building Lifecycle Management (BLM) [1–3] approach to cover the requirements of the asset management during their lifecycle.

On this basis, the present paper consists of the continuation of a previous authors research, named "BIM and PLM Associations in Current Literature" [4], in which the main result is that AEC industry innovation derives from PLM lessons learned. It emerges that it is necessary to extend the BIM technologies across the entire asset lifecycle, especially along the management and maintenance phases, like current PLM holistic applications for complex products, by reaching the BLM vision.

The functionalities already mature PLMs in the complex product manufacturing, should be customized to the specific context of the construction and infrastructure industry to effectively manipulate BIM complex models. Moreover, gaps discovered of learning from PLM "configuration views", better known as "Product Structure Configuration" since it is still missing a concrete comparison about configuration management in BIM against PLM. The BIM could be to the BLM what the PIM (Product Information Modeling) is to the PLM, and the Product Structure is the missing link [5] in the BIM approach to cover the full lifecycle, calling BLM the solution at the construction industry need for managing the whole lifecycle.

Starting from this assumption and considering the Product Structure as one of the most important features of BIM, the authors analysed the state of the art in this field in both industries, highlighting how the know-how of the manufacturing sector could be utilized in AEC industry.

Following the representation of the Configuration Views in PLM, the final objective is to identify gaps in the current BIM technological process and to propose a customized Product Structure through personalized Configuration views of the construction world to implementing the Building Lifecycle Management (BLM).

The next section of the paper describes the state of the art in the manufacturing complex product regarding Product Structure and PLM, with a focus on "Product Model", "Product Information Model" and "Product Structure" definition. In Section number 3, the Product Structure in AEC industry is analyzed. In section number 4 the authors try to integrate the Configuration Views in BLM approach. A final section of conclusion and further developments ends the paper.

2 Product Structure in PLM and Complex Products

2.1 Product Structure

A product is a materialized, artificially generated object or group of objects which form a functional unit. The materialization may contain mechanical parts, electrical components, electronic components, hydraulic components and other elements, even computer software and hardware components.

A product model contains relevant information including data, structures and algorithms, where algorithms are the links between user, data and structures [6].

The Product Structure (PS) is a concept well known for those familiar with PLM, typically the environment where complex products are developed, manufactured, used, maintained, disposed or re-introduced in the lifecycle through end-of-life treatments.

Even before PLM became a buzzword, the Product Structure represented one of the possible answers to the issue of product modeling and the needs of development of new products and maintain old ones.

The PS is defined in Krause et al. [6] as “the description of the product breakdown” and as the core of that particular branch of Product Models called “Structure-oriented Product Models” (is therefore a part of a more complete Product Model). The PS as a description of the product breakdown, is the kernel of structure-oriented Product Models. To represent the structure of products, several types of structures such as different bill-of-material structure types, classification structure, structures to describe versions and variants of a product can be used [6].

Saaksvuori and Immonen [7] defines the PS as “a model, which analyses the information on the product and how the information relates hierarchically to other pieces of information (…). It forms the heart of a PLM system, (since) parts, components, documents and assemblies are attached to the product and to each other through it”.

Stark [8] highlights the possible hierarchical characteristic of Product Structures mainly referring to the way of modeling relationships among parts, components, assemblies and the whole product. As the regards information the role of a Product Structures is defining the product requirements throughout its lifecycle and describing “the information that’s needed or is produced at each phase of the lifecycle”.

Different studies ([9–12]) agree on the hierarchical nature of Product Structures and on their role of describing relations among components, parts, assemblies and products.

Citing again, the study of Saaksvuori and Immonen [7], he specifically assigns five hierarchical levels to products structures, as the example of the ship Product Structure (Fig. 1).

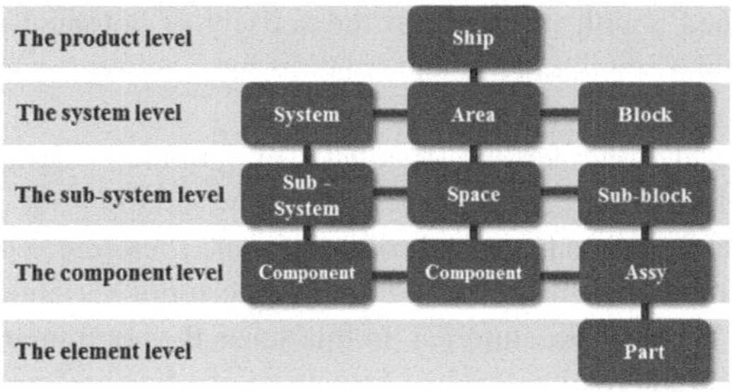

Fig. 1. The generic product structure (product model) of the ship [7]

Being an “information construct” [9], the contents that are usually attached to a Product Structure are: 3D models, attributes of products (data, part number material information, manufacturing processes, versions, engineering parameters etc. [12]) and generic classes of information (ingredients descriptions, assembly drawings, part drawings, NC programs, and user manual) [13]. References to the data from various application systems, which might own specific databases, are stored within a Product Structure. Information about order processing, its specific data and formats, access functions and the address within a computer network can be stored within structure-oriented Product Models [6]. It can represent how a particular division in a company needs to visualize the product (i.e. a particular view), for example, the design or the manufacturing point of view [14] or, the product development and engineering sales production and maintenance [7].

PS can be also a way of categorizing product information according to the product lifecycle phases of create, build (as built), support (as maintained) and dispose [9]. For complex product like airplanes, many views of the design phase can be defined at different point in time (as specified, as designed, as designed & as planned, and as prepared) [12].

Hence, the PS is a dynamic entity [14] and it evolves, furthermore, due maintenance activities [15] making the management of PS evolution over time "the most important technology requirement of PLM".

Many agree that the Bill of Material (BOM) is a particular Product Structure [6, 9], or better, a particular view of the Product Structure [14]. In fact, the Concept of Bill of Material is defined as "A comprehensive list of raw materials, components and assemblies required to build or manufacture a product. Hence it is a detail recipe of product which help to define, build and maintain a product. Since product goes through various lifecycle and interacts with various discipline or domain from Design to Manufacturing to Service to Finance, Bill of material also goes through similar lifecycle and various discipline or domain" [16].

Apart from efficiently showing the information organization depending on the needs of different company divisions or at different points in time, PS can be applied to various purpose: managing product variants [9], keep latest design information to prevent inconvenient design activities [12], cost efficient delivery of customized product variants [17], as base for DMU [18].

In Foufou et al. [19], "multiple Product Structure" are cited: "as-designed", "as-built", "as-maintained", with reference to the activity of "product definition" i.e. the description of product requirements and relationships between parts and assemblies within these multiple Product Structures.

In Saaksvuori and Immonen [7], Product Configuration refers to the process of customizing a product introducing physical property variations. It corresponds to the creation of a Product Structure from the Product Model. Therefore, a "configuration" is a specific Product Structure corresponding to a specific set of variations applied for customizing a generic Product Structure [7]. In this sense the configuration is a method of arrangement [13] and alternative Product Structures can be considered alternative configurations. PS can be called also system architecture, and, together with parts, components and relationships must contain the associated configuration documentation [11].

The configurations should cover the entire product lifecycle, assuming different denominations depending on the associated phase: "as-planned", "as-designed", "as-built", "as-maintained", "as-disposed of" [19]. The management and update through time of the configuration of a product is called Configuration Management (CM). CM is a formal discipline that aims at assuring the quality and long-term support of complex product through consistent identification and effective monitoring and control of all of this information [13] (Fig. 2).

Fig. 2. Lifecycle configuration views. Elaboration from [11]

The standard ISO 10007:2003, QMS - Guidelines for Configuration Management, describes the four related procedures and list the identification of the Product Structure as part of the first one, i.e. "Configuration identification". CM originated in the 50's in military and space contexts to ensure that the detailed specifications produced for these complex products where followed from design to manufacturing and even in the Maintenance Phase [14].

2.2 Product Structure, Product Model and Product Information Model

In this section, it is explored the relation among the terms "Product Model", "Product Information Model", "Product Structure" and "Configurations" in contexts that deal with complex products (military, automotive, aerospace) where it can happen that some are used interchangeably, due to their close meanings. In order to clarify these concepts, the definitions found in the literature are examined below.

The starting point of this analysis is the Product Model (PM), which is a container of information. The PM is an information model, i.e. "the representation of structure and semantics of information within a subject area, a formal description of types of ideas, facts and processes which together form a model of a portion of interest of the real world, and which provides an explicit set of interpretation rules" [20]. It is aimed at accumulating all relevant information of a product in digital (or computer interpretable) system/application independent form [6, 7, 21], including its behavior [22]. It describes the Product Structure and the configuration [11] for any lifecycle phase [6, 11]. The ISO 10303 (or Standard for the Exchange of Product model - STEP) defines the information modeling language EXPRESS to outline generic Product Models [19] and make them computer accessible [20]. STEP is supported by a series of Application Standards (AP), AP203 (focused on mechanical CAD) and AP214 (automotive industry) are the most widely applied. It is important to recall that the scope of AP203 revolves around Configuration Management, geometric shapes, Product Structure, and specifications. "It looks at the definition of product as an integration of the specification of its shape, its configurations, and the applicability of its possible multiple definitions to a particular configuration. It defines the exchange of product definitions with 3D shape representations together with the data, which defines and controls the configuration of those product definitions. In this AP, the configuration is about what parts compose a product and how they are composed together" [19].

Krause et al. [6] state the relationship between the Product Structure and the PM saying that the first is a type of Product Model (a structure oriented one), and adding that PMs can also be geometry oriented, feature oriented or knowledge oriented. When more types of PMs are clustered and connected, it is possible to indicate them as an "Integrated Product Model".

On the other hand, in Saaksvouri and Immonen [7], the PM is a general Product Structure "for a certain individual product", the author say that in many cases the Product Model is called "generic Product Structure". The Product Structure is what is created from the Product Model when a product is customized and therefore undergoes a number of variations, this process is the "Product Configuration" [7].

We can also find the term Product Information Model (PIM) both in the industrial language and in literature. For Saaksvouri and Immonen [7], PIM is more a "conceptual model of the product in which information on the product and the connections between various information elements and objects are analyzed at a general, generic level". Even if merely conceptual, the PIM should describe product-information relationships formally and carefully. An example of PIM is the one proposed by NIST [23], which includes geometry, structure and assembly. Van Renssen [22] adds the lifecycle concept to the PIM, in the sense that it can collect "facts about a product" and its operations under various conditions "including requirement specification, process and mechanical design (1,2,3D), cost estimation, procurement, fabrication, construction, commissioning, start-up operation, control, inspection, maintenance and demolition". One step of creating a PIM is defining its Product Structure.

3 Product Structure in AEC Industry

Van Nederveen et al. [24] recall that in the 80s and 90s what we now call BIM was referred as "Building Product Modeling" and "Product Modeling Of Buildings", showing the close relationship with the general product modeling applied in aerospace, automotive and mechanical engineering. The information models (IFC) expressed in EXPRESS computer readable language define the meaning of the data incorporated into the Product Model thus generating information.

In AEC industry the Product Structure is linked with the physic and functional breakdown of the building or the infrastructure project. The software tools commonly used are focused on the project structure organized in hierarchical levels without considering the evolution of the product during its life cycle. For example, in a top-down vision, the classes of the technological unit are the first level of a Work Breakdown Structure (WBS), Technological Unit are the second level, Technical Element classes as the third level. Further levels of decomposition, although not detailed in the individual items, may correspond, for example, to technical elements [25].

In UNI 11337-1:2017 regulation, the spatial decomposition of the asset informative structure is Building/Infrastructure, System, Sub-System and Component.

These examples of Product Structure do not correspond to the lifecycle information management of the building or infrastructure.

In general, the concept of configuration view in the AEC field is not as structured as in the manufacturing sector, and it is often missed in BIM software tool, which includes only an organized Product Structure at the design stage. For example, the functionality of checking/comparing the "as built" to the "as designed" configuration views of the Product Structure is missing.

Much work needs to be done in this direction in a BLM vision, even though Gielingh [21] had already stressed the importance of product information management, storage and control with computer systems integration, since 1990, using standards and organizing the "Product Structure & configuration management". Gielingh introduced "the General AEC Reference Model (GARM)", developed for AEC applications within the ISO/STEP standardization effort, to facilitate data-exchange between computer-applications for design, production and maintenance of the AEC products [26], in the full lifecycle of the building or infrastructure. In this sense, the GARM lists seven fundamental "stages" in the product lifecycle: "as required, as designed, as planned, as built, as used, as altered, as demolished", recognizable for the authors as the Configuration Views of the Product Structure.

In Eastman [27], he recovered and adapted the classification proposed by Gielingh, structuring the lifecycle according to its major transition points (Fig. 3). Eastman's lifecycle classification consists of six consequential phases and six resulting transitions connected by information flow, the integration and the automatization of linear processes. Furthermore, several others scholars ([28–31]) focused on "Building Product Models" as an integrated representation to be taken on for translating information.

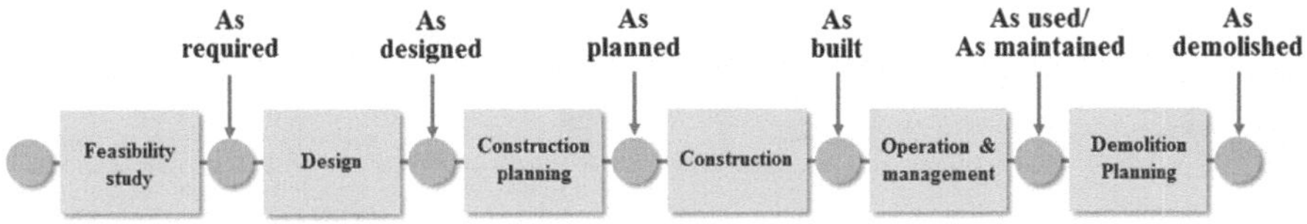

Fig. 3. One classification of the building lifecycle, addressing both phases and transitions. Elaboration from [27]

Another representation of the digital assets lifecycle evolution arrives from Ingram [32], which integrates data and model driven processes. This is organized in four group: "As Sold", including estimating, cost and change management; "As Designed", including design intent, design, specifications and geometry; "As Built", including integrated plan, 4D construction, work packages; "As Maintained", including as built/as maintained model, lifecycle visualization, smart work execution, IIoT and digital twin.

In AEC Industry, the use of the Configuration Management provides a means of tracking how the customer's expectations generated at the beginning of a project are turned at the completion of the project. In this field, different studies ([33, 34]) show how the CM approaches in complex engineering projects need further researches.

All these previous studies can become the foundation of an integrated Product Structure for the Building Lifecycle Management based on the lesson learned from holistic PLM platforms and relative configuration views, namely, Eastman's transitions.

4 Integrating Configuration View in BLM

Starting from the previous paragraphs, this research introduces the configuration views in the Building Lifecycle Management focusing on a Product Structure that enables the archiving of all the information, during the lifecycle in a circular vision, as reported in Boton et al. [5], in which the comparison between the PLM and BIM approaches are based on the standpoint of the Product Structure (PS).

Being Product Structure mostly arbitrary [9], the important thing is to make it consistent throughout the lifecycle in order to create a BLM Product Structure. To this end, it is proposed a Building/Infrastructure Product Structure in Fig. 4 that integrates the Product Structure of Saaksvuori and Immonen [7] and the information reported by Building SMART International [28] for domains. In detail, the System level coincides with the Domain Specific data schemas. The domain-specific data schemas contain final specializations of entities.

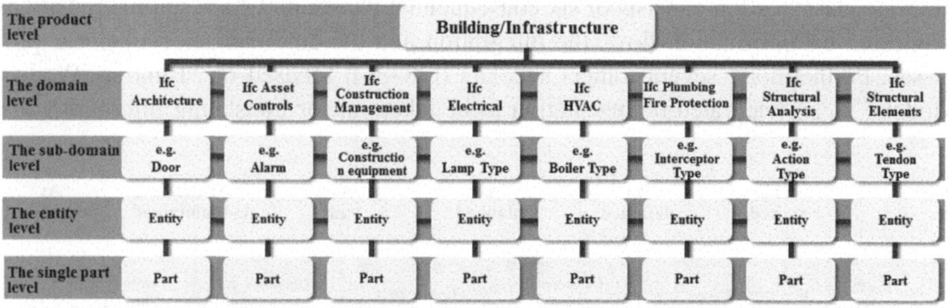

Fig. 4. Building/Infrastructure product structure. Elaboration from [7] and [35]

The Product Structure enables a dynamic Product Information Model that enriches the Product Model during its lifecycle. For the authors the "Configuration Views", of the PS, can manage Building/Infrastructure data, updating and archiving information over time (Fig. 5), in a suitable manner for each specific lifecycle phase.

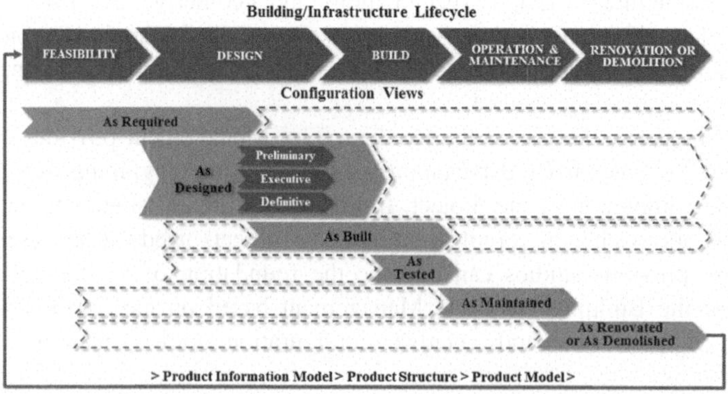

Fig. 5. Building/Infrastructure Lifecycle and corresponding Configuration Views.

Circularity consists in focusing on the digital twin in the common data environment BLM that includes document management, three-dimensional parametric modeling via BIM, etc., and it is enriched over the lifecycle of the Building/Infrastructure, including through the use of IoT, RFID or in situ sensors.

5 Conclusions and Further Developments

The purpose of this paper was to summarize the meaning of Product Structure and Product Model for both traditional complex industries and the construction industry to formulate research questions in a precise manner to guide further developments. In particular, this study is part of two doctoral research focused on the adoption of BIM methodology for the management of different contexts, namely Wastewater Treatment plants and Social Housing districts.

The use of different Product Structure lifecycle views, optimized according to the specific life-cycle phase of an infrastructure or building, is not widespread in current practice, despite the fact that some sources have been advocating them in literature for a long time [24, 26].

Given the large number of operations involving existing buildings and structures and their long lifecycle, BIM software tools and methodology should be more optimized for after construction phases. The Asset Information Management, organized through the Product Structure and the Configuration (Management) Views is the backbone of the Building/Infrastructure Lifecycle, because contains data regarding assets in a centralized environment, integrating as designed, as built and as maintained data. This vision enables the Building Lifecycle Management including Standards, like ISO 55000. The Configuration Management, in fact, aligns and synchronizes BOM data and lifecycle information.

The BLM approach, as a “single source” for all processes and metadata, is useful for owners that have to support a portfolio of buildings or civil infrastructure and needs to support both facility management and real estate management, including maintenance management and environmental sustainability.

Further research will be focused on modeling real-life example of construction lifecycle views and testing them in real contexts. In the light of these arguments, the following research will be gathering the requirements for as-maintained and as-used views for a wastewater treatment plant and social housing located in Puglia (i.e. an Italian region) from the related stakeholders and transforming them in functionalities of a BIM-integrated piece of software to be tested. Other further research will be on how to reconcile a view of the Product Structure and the link with the underlying standard IFC.

References

1. Bonandrini, S., Cruz, C., Nicolle, C.: Building lifecycle management. In: Proceedings of the International Conference on Product Lifecycle Management, vol. 1113, Lyon, France (2005)
2. Vanlande, R., Nicolle, C., Cruz, C.: IFC and building lifecycle management. Autom. Constr. **18**(1), 70–78 (2008). https://doi.org/10.1016/j.autcon.2008.05.001

3. Ustinovičius, L., Rasiulis, R., Nazarko, L., Vilutienė, T., Reizgevicius, M.: Innovative research projects in the field of building lifecycle management. Proc. Eng. **122**, 166–171 (2015)
4. Mangialardi, G., Di Biccari, C., Pascarelli, C., Lazoi, M., Corallo, A.: BIM and PLM associations in current literature. In: Ríos, J., Bernard, A., Bouras, A., Foufou, S. (eds.) PLM 2017. IAICT, vol. 517, pp. 345–357. Springer, Cham (2017). https://doi.org/10.1007/978-3-319-72905-3_31
5. Boton, C., Rivest, L., Forgues, D., Jupp, J.: Comparing PLM and BIM from the product structure standpoint. In: Harik, R., Rivest, L., Bernard, A., Eynard, B., Bouras, A. (eds.) PLM 2016. IAICT, vol. 492, pp. 443–453. Springer, Cham (2016). https://doi.org/10.1007/978-3-319-54660-5_40
6. Krause, F.L., Kimura, F., Kjellberg, T., Lu, S.Y., Alting, L., Elmaraghy, H.A., Week, M.: Product modelling. CIRP Ann.-Manuf. Technol. **2**(42), 695–706 (1993). https://doi.org/10.1016/s0007-8506(07)62532-3
7. Saaksvuori, A., Immonen, A.: Product Lifecycle Management. Springer, Heidelberg (2005). https://doi.org/10.1007/b138258
8. Stark, J.: Product Lifecycle Management (Volume 2), The Devil is in the Details. Springer, Geneva- Switzerland (2016). https://doi.org/10.1007/978-3-319-24436-5
9. Grieves, M.: Virtually Perfect, Cocoa Beach. Space Coast Press, LLC, Florida (2011). ISBN 978-0982138007
10. Shilovitsky, O.: PLM, product structure and multi-level BOM. Let's sort it out. 9 December 2016. http://beyondplm.com/2016/12/09/plm-multi-level-bom-vs-product-structure-lets-sort/ . Accessed 20 Feb 2018
11. United States of America - Department of Defense: MIL-HDBK-61A(SE). Military Handbook. Configuration Management Guidance (2001)
12. Mart, T., Cangelir, C.: Lessons learned for better management of master geometry. In: PLM 2013, IFIP AICT 409, Nantes, France (2013)
13. Stark, J.: Product Lifecycle Management, 21st Century Paradigm for Product Realisation, vol. 1. Springer, Geneva (2015). https://doi.org/10.1007/978-0-85729-546-0
14. Svensson, D., Malmqvist, J.: Strategiee for Product Structures Management in Manufacturing Firms. In: ASME Design Engineering Technical Conferences, Baltimore, Maryland, USA (2000). https://doi.org/10.1115/1.1471356
15. Hu, H., Lu, Y.-j., Hua-wu, L.: The product structure evolution model for maintenance based on finite automation. In: Advanced Materials Research, Vol. 472–475, pp. 3010–3016 (2012). https://doi.org/10.4028/www.scientific.net/AMR.472-475.3010
16. Tiwari, M.: January 2014. http://teamcenterplm.blogspot.it/2014/01/bill-of-material-concept.html
17. Womack, J., Dan, J.: Seeing the whole value stream, Lean Enterprise Institute (2011). ISBN 978-1-934109-32-8
18. Riascos, R., Levy, L., Stjepandić, J., Fröhlich, A.: Digital mock-up. In: Concurrent Engineering in the 21st Century, pp. 355–388. Springer, Cham (2015). https://doi.org/10.1007/978-3-319-13776-6_13
19. Foufou, S., Rachuri, S., Kemmerer, S.: NISTIR 7339. Analysis of Standards for Lifecycle Management of Systems for US Army — a preliminary investigation. National Institute of Standard and Technology (2006). https://doi.org/10.6028/nist.ir.7339
20. Sørensen, T.: On the implementation of product model interfaces in CIME. In: Computer Applications in Production and Engineering. IFIP TC5 International Conference on Computer Applications in Production and Engineering (CAPE 1997), Detroit, Michigan. USA (1997)

21. Gielingh, W.: Computer integrated construction. a major step forward. In: Proceedings of ARECDAO 12–14 April 1989, Barcelona (1989)
22. Van Renssen, A.: Semantic Information Modeling Methodology, Zoetemeer. Gellish.net, The Nederlands (2015). ISBN 978-1-329-65448-8
23. Le Duigou, J., Bernard, A.: Product lifecycle management model for design information management in mechanical field. In: Interdiscliplinary Design. Proceedings of the 21st CIRP Design Conference, Daejon, South Korea (2011). hal-00797992
24. van Nederveen, S., Beheshti, R., Gielingh, W.: Modelling concepts for BIM. In: Handbook of research on Building Information Modeling and Construction Informatics. Concepts and Technologies., Hershey-New York, Information Science Reference, pp. 1–15 (2009). https://doi.org/10.4018/978-1-60566-928-1.ch001
25. Ferrara, A., Eva, F.: BIM e project Management. Dario Flaccovio Editore, Palermo (2016). ISBN 978-88-579-0595-2
26. Gielingh, W.: General AEC reference model (GARM). ISO TC184/SC4 (1988)
27. Eastman, C.M.: Building product models: computer environments, supporting design and construction. CRC press a cura di (1999). ISBN-13: 978-0849302596
28. Eastman, C.M., Siabiris, A.: A generic building product model incorporating building type information. Autom. Constr. **3**(4), 283–304 (1995). https://doi.org/10.1016/0926-5805(94)00028-l
29. Eastman, C.M., Wang, F.L., You, S.J., Yang, D.: Deployment of an AEC industry sector product model. Comput.-Aided Des. **37**(12), 1214–1228 (2005). https://doi.org/10.1016/j.cad.2004.11.007
30. Tolman, F.P.: Product modeling standards for the building and construction industry: past, present and future. Autom. Constr. **8**(3), 227–235 (1999). https://doi.org/10.1016/s0926-5805(98)00073-9
31. Björk, B.-C.: Basic structure of a proposed building product model. Comput.-Aided Des. **21**(2), 71–78 (1989). https://doi.org/10.1016/0010-4485(89)90141-3
32. Ingram, K.: The digital evolution of the construction industry. In: COMIT Annual Conference (2017)
33. Hu, H.-T., Lin, C.-P., Lin, Y.-C.: Applications of configuration management in BIM Models management during the construction phase. In: icccbe2016 (2016). ISBN 978-4-9907371-2-2
34. Lindkvist, C., Stasis, A., Whyte, J.: Configuration management in complex engineering projects. In: Procedia CIRP 11 (2013)
35. B.S.I. Ltd.: 1996–2016. http://www.buildingsmart-tech.org/ifc/IFC4/Add2/html/

Model-Based Systems Engineering and Through-Life Information Management in Complex Construction

Yu Chen(✉) and Julie Jupp

School of Built Environment, University of Technology Sydney, Sydney, Australia
Yu.Chen@uts.edu.au

Abstract. With increasing maturity in model-based design and construction, a concomitant increase in the need for system-based methodologies and toolsets to support systems integration, requirements management, verification and validation and configuration management is evident if model-based information is to serve the operations of complex buildings and civil infrastructure projects. There is much to learn from best practices reported in complex discrete manufacturing. In particular, closed-loop product lifecycle management (PLM), systems engineering (SE) and model-based systems engineering (MBSE) are key to systems approaches to digital complex construction delivery and the reuse of model-based information for operations and maintenance (O&M). The paper reviews related research and investigates the role of the V-model in the development process, discussing its significance to structuring a through-life approach to information management. A discussion of Erasmus' PLM aligned V-model is presented, and missing links in current BIM-enabled environments are identified relative to requirements engineering, verification and validation, and configuration management. The paper closes with a discussion of the gaps in supporting model-based tool ecologies and lack of a central structuring infrastructure, as well as the deficiencies in current process and data standards. Closing with the identification of a future research agenda.

Keywords: Building Information Modelling
Through-life information management · Systems engineering
Model-based systems engineering

1 Introduction

Within the lifecycle of a building asset, different actor-groups are involved in generating and sharing data and information throughout the design, construction, and operations and maintenance (O&M) phases [1]. The fragmented nature of both the construction and facilities management (FM) industries leads to the inefficient exchange and low reuse of asset information [1, 2]. During the past decade more effective utilization of product and product-related information has improved in the development of new complex buildings and infrastructure [3]. Building Information Modelling (BIM) is widely regarded as a key enabler of this trend, and together with

P. Chiabert et al. (Eds.): PLM 2018, IFIP AICT 540, pp. 80–92, 2018.
https://doi.org/10.1007/978-3-030-01614-2_8

the increased use of sensors and the internet of things (IoT), the foundation of the fourth industrial revolution, or Industry 4.0 are being laid [3]. BIM is defined as "a new approach to design, construction, and FM, in which a digital representation of the asset process is used to facilitate the exchange and interoperability of information in digital format" [4]. The implementation of BIM in design and construction phases brings with it benefits regarding performance-based simulation and analysis, as well as greater cost and schedule control [5]. Yet these benefits are marginal in light of the potential gains to the O&M of a facility's assets [6]. The realization of a through-life approach to product data and information management faces a variety of persistent barriers. Issues relate to the highly fragmented nature of the construction supply chain, traditional procurement methods, and lack of process standardization [9]. These and other barriers related to technology infrastructures [10, 25] prohibit the integration and flow of model-based product information [7]. The knock-on effects of these barriers on the management of vast amounts of data and information generated are significant and prohibits an integrated systems approach to development processes [8].

To capitalize more fully on the potential of BIM to support the integrated flow of digital information and process activities, it is necessary to define a structuring concept linking BIM models, BIM uses, related information flows in the project together, with workflows that commence at requirements elicitation and analysis and include defined verification and validation (V&V) activities capable of supporting both functional product and information quality assurance together with linked with user profile information [9, 10]. Previous researchers have identified how the application of systems engineering (SE) activities in construction can structure the flow of data and information as well as process activities [11, 12]. SE is a multidiscipline approach that (i) supports the realization of complex systems integration, (ii) using requirements engineering methods increases the project team's ability to deliver high quality products, and (iii) services a variety of different business processes across the organization [13]. Key to SE is the emphasis on requirements traceability through-life to achieve the alignment of components, units, subsystems, and system [14]. However, whilst SE provides a robust set of methods and processes (e.g., information requirements management [3], configuration management [15, 16] and change management [17, 18]), gaps remain in how these methods translate to the complex nature of construction projects, where challenges persist in the implementation of BIM surrounding the way data is structured, verified, validated, reused and managed over the lifecycle of the asset [1, 3, 19, 20]. Recent initiatives to develop BIM Standards (e.g., PAS 1192 and ISO/DIS 19650) have sought to address such issues. However, an understanding of how SE methods and processes can be used to implement systems-based collaborative methodologies is currently lacking.

Against this backcloth, this paper presents a review and discussion of related literature surrounding BIM and through-life information management. The paper introduces the widely used V-model, popularized in the SE research in support of development processes in complex discrete manufacturing. The paper discusses BIM tool ecologies and standards in light of V-model objectives. Focusing on requirements management, verification and validation and configurations management activities, gaps are identified in construction practice. The paper ends with a discussion of the role of SE methods in support of in complex building and infrastructure projects.

2 Background

With the increasing uptake of model-based design and construction technologies during project delivery, opportunities for reusing information throughout the life of the asset have arisen. Accordingly, technologies supporting the required backbone infrastructure, data structuring, cloud provisioning services, and enterprise architectures have also emerged. Much effort has also been made to support interoperability, where data standards have sought to support data exchange across various AEC disciplines. Remaining challenges for the successful delivery of both the physical and digital asset surround the use of various data standards and immaturity in the use of BIM process standards that support the use of BIM in the delivery of 3D 'as-builts' and associated data for O&M. Whilst best practices in the specification of information requirements during project delivery to support BIM-enabled O&M/FM, the implementation requirements of through-life information management relative to key verification and validation processes, and configurations management remain relatively unknown. A significant issue remaining in the fragmented supply chains of construction and FM industries is the difficulty in determining "what data and context are required for each phase of the product lifecycle" [21].

Over the last three decades, the complex, discrete manufacturing industries have made significant progress in productivity increases and management efficiencies. This is in large part due to a more seamless integration of systems enabled by SE methods and the technology infrastructure that Product Lifecycle Management (PLM) platforms provide [9, 21, 22]. Similar improvements, however, have not been achieved in the construction and FM industries [9]. Given the increasingly cyber-physical nature of these industries in the last decade, SE and recent approaches to model based systems engineering (MBSE) have the potential to inform new approaches to BIM-enabled systems integration and through-life information management [9, 11, 14].

In the field of information processing, researchers investigating lifecycle approaches to BIM have explored the relevance of PLM. Whilst PLM is a business-oriented solution, at its core PLM is a software-enabled strategy streamlines the flow of information about the product and related processes throughout the product's lifecycle. As such, the right information, in the right context, at the right time can be made available [23]. By providing the backbone technology infrastructure to improve processes to conceptualize, design, develop and manage products, PLM implementations drive higher levels of productivity and product profitability [29]. Jupp [9] presents a typology for comparing PLM and BIM in a comprehensive literature review, undertaking comparative analysis between aerospace and construction. The study highlights that the similarities between PLM and BIM trajectories stem from a few common but key characteristics surrounding data requirements, object-oriented approaches to modelling and visualization, project level data sharing, and organization of teams around digital deliverables [9]. Jupp and Nepal [24] explore how BIM and PLM have impacted the professional practices in construction and manufacturing industries. They concluded that the level of BIM maturity across the construction industry is improving; increasing the possibility to reach a "common endpoint with manufacturing industries". Boton et al. [10, 25] present a comparison between the PLM and BIM approaches from the standpoint of the Product Structure (PS) and Bill of Material (BOM), highlighting significant differences in approaches to 3D modelling and systems decomposition, data structures and workflow automation [25].

Other notable research works include studies on the adoption of SE approaches in construction [1, 14, 26, 27]. Whyte [14] provides a comprehensive review of system integration research in the delivery and operation of infrastructure projects and suggests future directions for research on systems integration within the civil infrastructure. Whyte highlights the potential of combining "data-sets and model-based systems engineering, BIM and performance-based models" and using "new forms of data analytics to reveal new patterns" [14]. A chief concern raised by the translation of SE into a built environment context is the reliance on a single source of data and the potential for errors and significant failures in the absence of robust processes for information verification and validation throughout the project [14]. Hoeber and Alsem [1] present a way of working that utilizes open-standard BIM, SE ontologies, object libraries and an Information Delivery Manual to support information management throughout the life of infrastructures assets. Mata et al. [26] develop a 'Systems of Systems' model using SE concepts and Systems Modeling Language (SysML) to evaluate the sustainability performance of infrastructure projects. Notably, De Graaf et al. [27] assessed the level of SE applications in six construction projects of the Dutch Water Board based on the SE process model developed by the U.S. Department of Defense (DoD).

This growing body of literature signals the case for understanding SE methods and PLM functionalities relative to the unique context and requirements of designing, delivering and O&M of facility assets.

3 Model-Based Systems Engineering and the PLM V-Model

One of the most accepted definitions of SE is that proposed by INCOSE: "SE is an interdisciplinary approach and means to enable the realization of successful systems. It focuses on defining customer needs and required functionality early in the development cycle, documenting requirement, and then proceeding with design synthesis and system validation while considering the complete problem" [13]. Model-based systems engineering (MBSE), is an approach that is founded in SE, and is aimed at the use of models (instead of documents) to support system requirements, design, analysis, verification and validation of the system being developed [28]. The "V" model, one of the most widely used development process models in SE that takes a lifecycle approach, describing the through-life requirements management, and continuous verification and validation processes [13]. In typical V-model representations, traceability is ensured from both "horizontal" and "vertical" verification and validation linkages [29]. During system decomposition and definition, requirements, functions, and objects (R/F/O) are verified with higher-level R/F/O before then being validated against client expectations, which enable the "vertical" traceability [30]. The components of a system are then integrated and recomposed into the product. System components are therefore verified with corresponding R/F/O at each level with ongoing validation, which enable the "horizontal" traceability [30, 31]. In this way, V&V are not treated as separate phases but are integrated activities executed continuously throughout the MBSE process [30].

Erasmus et al. [32] have united the V-model development processes and PLM's backbone infrastructure to produce a framework that aligns objectives and capabilities to support model-based delivery processes. Figure 1 shows this alignment between PLM and a MBSE V-model. The model describes requirements [R], functions [F], logical solution elements [L], and physical elements [P]. Using a PLM platform, three information management capabilities can be harnessed to enabled MBSE, including the integration: (i) of product information across the entire lifecycle and the associated information, (ii) for improved collaboration between practitioners from different disciplines and business functions, and (iii) of people, data, processes and business systems to provide a product information methodology for the company and its extended enterprise [32].

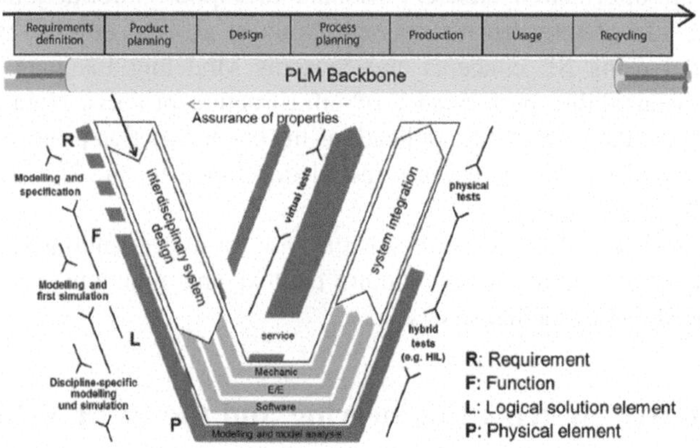

Fig. 1. PLM aligned V-model to enable model-based systems engineering [32]

In Erasmus' PLM V-Model, time and system maturity proceed from the left 'wing' (top-down) to the right 'wing' (bottom-up) [13]. Top-down processes reflect the definition and decomposition of the system into sub-systems and components; while the bottom-up approach enables the integration and verification from system components to the system level [31]. In MBSE approaches, the 'V' reflects the definition of model-based V&V plans during the top-down requirements developments process. In a BIM-enabled environment, the development of information management methodologies relies on similar approaches, for example as reflected in EIR definitions in PAS 1192.3-2014. However, Erasmus' combined PLM V-model highlights further deficiencies in the application of BIM, where as a model-based development process it should be supported by similar mechanisms that can facilitate the relationship between the various participants in the supply chain and their model-based deliverables, by enabling the exchange of the information that describes the product, its configuration, its intended use, and how it will be maintained.

4 New Complex Construction and Information Management

This section introduces a conceptual framework that attempts to describe the different approaches to model-based design, construction and operations. The framework illustrated in Fig. 2 provides a means of identifying and structuring the problem of implementing a through-life approach to information management in a construction context so as to highlight the gaps to model-based requirements management, verification and validation, and configuration management processes and infrastructures.

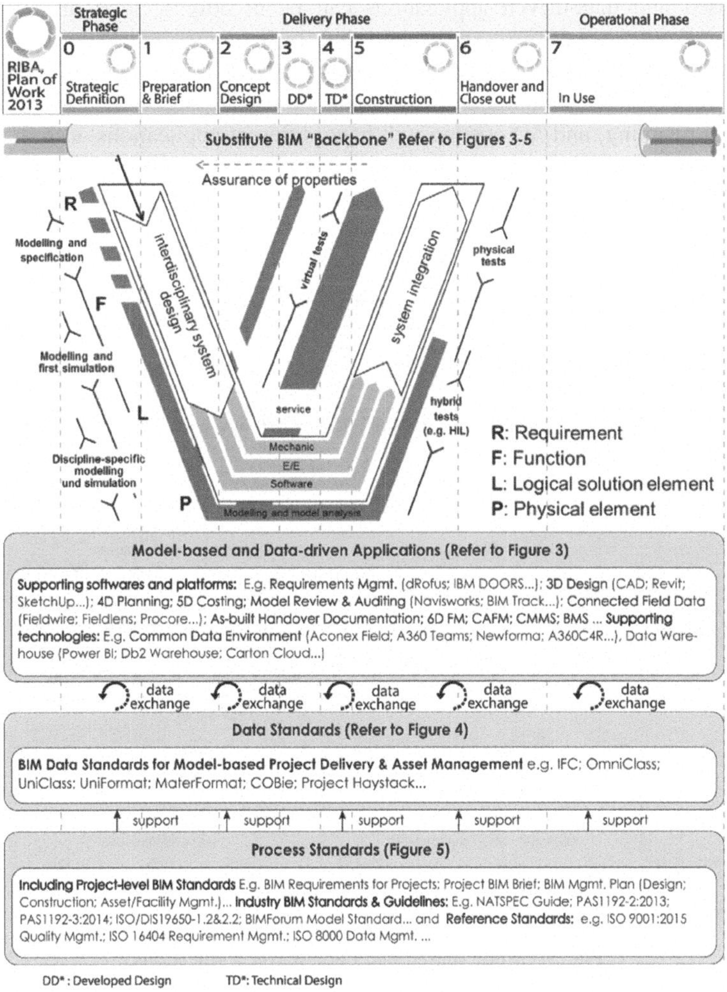

Fig. 2. Through-life information management in complex construction

The framework consists of five layers: (i) Construction Asset Lifecycle Phases according to RIBA [33], (ii) MBSE PLM aligned V-model, (iii) Model-based applications (iv) Data standards, and (v) Process standards. In this framework, the RIBA's project lifecycle stages are adopted [33]. There are eight phases in total: strategic definition, preparation and brief, concept design, development design (same as schematic design), technical design (also called detail design), construction, handover and close out, and in use. The following sub-sections discuss layers (iii) to (iv).

4.1 Model-Based and Data-Driven Applications

Model-based and data-driven applications can be broadly divided into two areas: supporting software/platforms and supporting technologies (as shown in Fig. 3). Typical software adopted in different phases were listed according to their corresponding function. Some applications span phases, e.g. requirements management; 3D design, 4D planning, and 5D costing will have different applications according to the minimum modelling requirements specified at each phase. Applications may also occur across multiple functions based on the multifunctional modules supported.

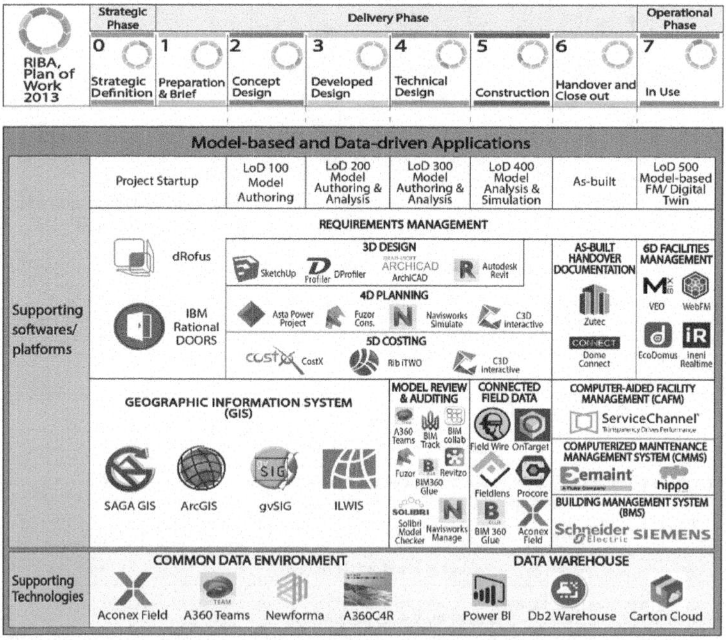

Fig. 3. Model-based and data-driven applications

The use of requirements management workflows and technologies are not widespread in the construction industry and appear to be somewhat more common in the civil engineering and infrastructure sectors. Within these sectors, the use of requirements management tools such as IBM Rational DOORS is increasing. In the health infrastructure sector, case studies documenting BIM applications also report limited use of planning and data management tools such as dRofus, which offer requirements management capabilities that utilize a space-based approach to requirements management [34]. However, interactions between multiple dependent requirements remain independent, and links to the model to automate traceability are seemingly uncommon according to our review of the few academic studies documenting its use. To support data integration, Common Data Environment (CDE) platforms and data warehouses are now essential to complex construction delivery. The CDE provides an environment to share geometric information as well as related information such as registers, schedules, contracts, reports and model information. The CDE therefore builds on the concept of a "federated" model by bringing everyone's information together in a virtual space. Cloud-based platforms such as Aconex, Trimble Connect, Autodesk BIM360, GroupBC, ProjectWise and a host of Autodesk Forge's applications including AEC Hub, provide different forms of CDE.

Due to the complexity of the tool ecologies utilized throughout complex construction project delivery phases, a variety of data and process standards have been developed and despite the growing maturity in collaborative modeling software and CDE, they remain bolt-on solutions to the systems integration problem that persist due to construction's fragmented supply chain and typical design and construct (D&C) delivery methods.

4.2 Supporting Data Standards

Data standards encompass a range of data exchange and data formats (as shown in Fig. 4). Data standards reviewed here are based on the classification systems proposed by Sabol [35]. Whilst standards are primarily applied during design and are directed towards supporting the onsite integration of asset equipment, recent data standards such as Project Haystack are designed for operations. One of the most commonly used data standard includes Industry Foundation Classes, or IFCs (ISO16739) were developed to support the data exchanges between different software. Uniclass is the main classification systems in the UK while the UniFormat and MasterFormat standards are well known and widely used in the North American construction context, the successor classification system, OmniClass (also known as ISO 12006-2) is also utilized worldwide [25]. COBie[1] was first proposed by the US Army Corp of Engineers in 2007 [36] and was adopted as a British Standard in 2014 [37]. More recent classification systems are aimed at the O&M phases are gaining traction in the industry. An example is the Project Haystack, which has developed an open set of tags for naming key building automation and energy components [38].

[1] Construction Operation Building Information Exchange.

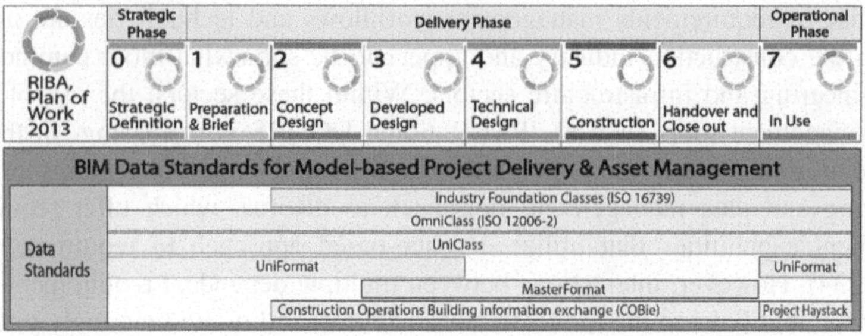

Fig. 4. Data Standards used in BIM-enabled complex construction

4.3 Supporting Process Standards

BIM process standards consist of the current developed project-level BIM standards informed by industry BIM standards and guidelines as well as its reference industry standards (as shown in Fig. 5). The project-level BIM standards include BIM requirements for projects, project BIM brief, and BIM execution plan (BEP), also known as a BIM management plan (BMP) for design, construction, and facility/asset management purposes. These three types of documentations are informed by relevant industry standards and guidelines. For example, in the UK, the British Standard Institute published the PAS[2] 1192-2: 2013 and later PAS 1192-3: 2014 focusing on information management process to support BIM Level 2 in the capital/delivery phase of projects, and operational phase [39, 40]. Both Standards introduce new concepts and system-level processes to BIM implementation. In the US there are Level of Development specifications while in Australia there are National BIM Guide and BEP template. Internationally, the ISO/DIS 19650-1.2 and 2.2 are aimed to support the information management during the life cycle of built assets when using BIM [41]. Industry BIM standards are supported or informed by several reference standards to support quality management (ISO 9001:2005), asset management (ISO 55000 series), data management (ISO 8000), requirement management (ISO 16404).

[2] Publicly Available Specification.

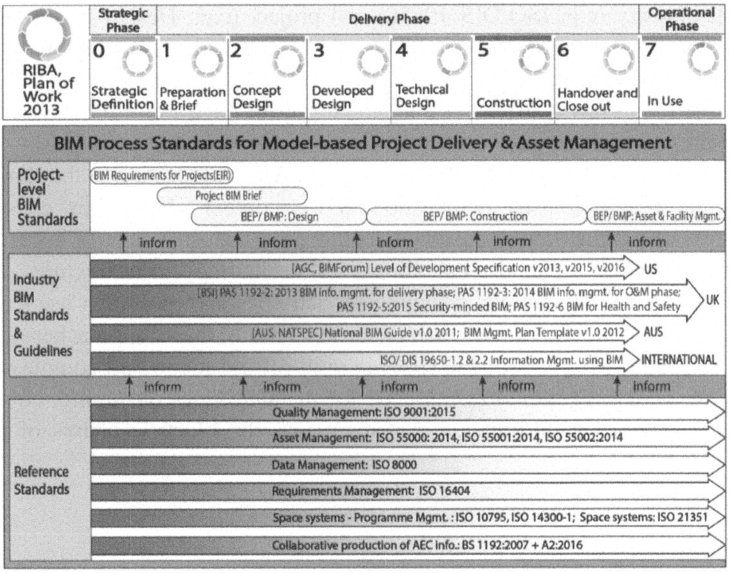

Fig. 5. Process Standards used in BIM-enabled complex construction

5 Conclusion and Ongoing Research

The development of BIM as an enterprise strategy that can integrate and streamline the flow of information about product and product-related processes through-life (supporting the right information, in the right context, at the right time) is a central motivator of this research project. This paper has therefore sought to investigate SE and MBSE and enumerate their relevance in support of a BIM-enabled approach, where through-life information management continues to prove to be challenging to AEC project teams [7]. The V-Model is a widely accepted approach to the development process in complex discrete manufacturing. By supporting requirements management, continuous V&V and configurations management of product and product-related information throughout development processes, this simple structuring of systems decomposition and integration demonstrates a relevant method and technology infrastructure that can benefit construction and FM industries. Erasmus' PLM V-Model [32] demonstrates how the backbone infrastructure and enterprise level approach of PLM is required to achieve model-based systems integration and its inherent relevance to V&V and configurations management throughout the development process. These capabilities, whilst developed in a complex discrete manufacturing context, have relevance in the model-based development and O&M of complex built assets; that is, where 3D deliverables are mandated by clients contractually.

Throughout the life of a built asset, different requirements come into and out of specification and management processes. To leverage the value of BIM in construction, system-based information management processes across all phase of the lifecycle must not only account for a variety of model-based applications and data standards, but also implement industry (e.g. ISO/DIS 19650) and project (e.g., Design BMP/BEP) standards without structured workflows. The need to include structured requirements management and V&V processes, supporting model-based data structures and backbone technology infrastructure is key to supporting through-life information management in complex construction.

The overall aim of this research is to develop new approaches to the through-life management of model-based information in the context of complex construction. Ongoing research is therefore focused on documenting industry practice in case studies that utilize SE/MBSE methods, including PLM technology infrastructures and supporting V&V and configurations management activities and toolsets. Case studies are targeting both complex discrete manufacturing where these approaches are more readily observable, but also notable cases in civil infrastructure and complex hospital projects. The goal is to minimize the need for manual, time-consuming, error prone, point-mapping between information systems across the lifecycle phases of complex built assets.

References

1. Hoeber, H., Alsem, D.: Life-cycle information management using open-standard BIM. Eng. Constr. Archit. Manag. **23**, 696–708 (2016). https://doi.org/10.1108/ECAM-01-2016-0023
2. Green, S.D., Newcombe, R., Fernie, S., Weller, S.: Learning across business sectors: Knowledge sharing between aerospace and construction. The University of Reading, Reading (2004)
3. Whyte, J.K., Hartmann, T.: How digitizing building information transforms the built environment. Build. Res. Inf. **45**, 591–595 (2017). https://doi.org/10.1080/09613218.2017.1324726
4. Eastman, C., Eastman, C.M., Teicholz, P., Sacks, R., Liston, K.: BIM Handbook: A Guide to Building Information Modeling for Owners, Managers, Designers, Engineers and Contractors. Wiley, Hoboken (2011)
5. Barlish, K., Sullivan, K.: How to measure the benefits of BIM — a case study approach. Autom. Constr. **24**, 149–159 (2012). https://doi.org/10.1016/j.autcon.2012.02.008
6. Love, P.E.D., Matthews, J., Simpson, I., Hill, A., Olatunji, O.A.: A benefits realization management building information modeling framework for asset owners. Autom. Constr. **37**, 1–10 (2014). https://doi.org/10.1016/j.autcon.2013.09.007
7. Jupp, J., Awad, R.: BIM-FM and information requirements management: missing links in the AEC and FM interface. In: Ríos, J., Bernard, A., Bouras, A., Foufou, S. (eds.) PLM 2017. IAICT, vol. 517, pp. 311–323. Springer, Cham (2017). https://doi.org/10.1007/978-3-319-72905-3_28
8. Anderson, A., Marsters, A., Dossick, C.S., Neff, G.: Construction to operations exchange: challenges of implementing COBie and BIM in a large owner organization, pp. 688–697 (2012)
9. Jupp, J.R.: Cross industry learning: a comparative study of product lifecycle management and building information modelling. Int. J. Prod. Lifecycle Manag. **9**, 258–284 (2016)
10. Boton, C., Rivest, L., Forgues, D., Jupp, J.: Comparing PLM and BIM from the product structure standpoint. In: Harik, R., Rivest, L., Bernard, A., Eynard, B., Bouras, A. (eds.) PLM 2016. IAICT, vol. 492, pp. 443–453. Springer, Cham (2016). https://doi.org/10.1007/978-3-319-54660-5_40

11. Blockley, D.I., Godfrey, P.: Doing it Differently: Systems for Rethinking Construction. Thomas Telford, London (2000)
12. Aslaksen, E.W., et al.: Guide for the application of systems engineering in large infrastructure projects. INCOSE Infrastructure Working Group San Diego (2012)
13. INCOSE: Systems Engineering Handbook. A Guide for System Life Cycle Processes and Activities, v.3. INCOSE, Seattle (2006)
14. Whyte, J.: The future of systems integration within civil infrastructure: a review and directions for research. INCOSE Int. Symp. Banner **26**, 1541–1555 (2016). https://doi.org/10.1002/j.2334-5837.2016.00244.x
15. Sage, A.P., Rouse, W.B.: Handbook of Systems Engineering and Management. Wiley, Hoboken (2009)
16. Lindkvist, C., Stasis, A., Whyte, J.: Configuration management in complex engineering projects. Procedia CIRP **11**, 173–176 (2013). https://doi.org/10.1016/j.procir.2013.07.046
17. Morris, P.W.: The Management of Projects. Thomas Telford, London (1997)
18. Whyte, J., Stasis, A., Lindkvist, C.: Managing change in the delivery of complex projects: configuration management, asset information and 'big data'. Int. J. Proj. Manag. **34**, 339–351 (2016). https://doi.org/10.1016/j.ijproman.2015.02.006
19. Xu, X., Ma, L., Ding, L.: A framework for BIM-enabled life-cycle information management of construction project. Int. J. Adv. Robot. Syst. **11**, 126 (2014). https://doi.org/10.5772/58445
20. Zadeh, P.A., Wang, G., Cavka, H.B., Staub-French, S., Pottinger, R.: Information quality assessment for facility management. Adv. Eng. Inform. **33**, 181–205 (2017). https://doi.org/10.1016/j.aei.2017.06.003
21. Hedberg, T., Feeney, A.B., Helu, M., Camelio, J.A.: Toward a lifecycle information framework and technology in manufacturing. J. Comput. Inf. Sci. Eng. **17**, 021010 (2017)
22. Lemberger, I.D., Erasmus, L.D.: Systems engineering management process maturity of South African manufacturing organisations. In: Portland International Conference on Management of Engineering & Technology (PICMET), pp. 2371–2380. IEEE (2014)
23. Ameri, F., Dutta, D.: Product lifecycle management: closing the knowledge loops. Comput. Aided Des. Appl. **2**, 577–590 (2005)
24. Jupp, J.R., Nepal, M.: BIM and PLM: comparing and learning from changes to professional practice across sectors. In: Fukuda, S., Bernard, A., Gurumoorthy, B., Bouras, A. (eds.) PLM 2014. IAICT, vol. 442, pp. 41–50. Springer, Heidelberg (2014). https://doi.org/10.1007/978-3-662-45937-9_5
25. Boton, C., Rivest, L., Forgues, D., Jupp, J.R.: Comparison of shipbuilding and construction industries from the product structure standpoint. Int. J. Prod. Lifecycle Manag. **11**, 191–220 (2018). https://doi.org/10.1504/IJPLM.2018.094714
26. Matar, M., Osman, H., Georgy, M., Abou-Zeid, A., El-Said, M.: A systems engineering approach for realizing sustainability in infrastructure projects. HBRC J. **13**, 190–201 (2017). https://doi.org/10.1016/j.hbrcj.2015.04.005
27. (Robin) de Graaf, R.S., (Rick) Vromen, R.M., (Hans) Boes, J.: Applying systems engineering in the civil engineering industry: an analysis of systems engineering projects of a Dutch water board. Civ. Eng. Environ. Syst. **34**, 144–161 (2017). https://doi.org/10.1080/10286608.2017.1362399
28. INCOSE T: Systems Engineering Vision 2020. INCOSE-TP-2004-004-02 (2007). http://www.ccose.org/media/upload/SEVision2020_20071003_v2_03.pdf

29. Eigner, M., Dickopf, T., Apostolov, H., Schaefer, P., Faißt, K.-G., Keßler, A.: System lifecycle management: initial approach for a sustainable product development process based on methods of model based systems engineering. In: Fukuda, S., Bernard, A., Gurumoorthy, B., Bouras, A. (eds.) PLM 2014. IAICT, vol. 442, pp. 287–300. Springer, Heidelberg (2014). https://doi.org/10.1007/978-3-662-45937-9_29
30. FHWA: Systems Engineering for Intelligent Transportation Systems (2007)
31. Locatelli, G., Mancini, M., Romano, E.: Systems engineering to improve the governance in complex project environments. Int. J. Proj. Manag. **32**, 1395–1410 (2014). https://doi.org/10.1016/j.ijproman.2013.10.007
32. Erasmus, J., Jacob, M., Erasmus, L.D.: The need for PLM in South Africa (2015)
33. RIBA Project stages. Imperial College London. http://www.imperial.ac.uk/admin-services/estates-projects/project-procedures/stages/. Accessed 5 Apr 2018
34. Product|dRofus. http://www.drofus.no/en/product.html. Accessed 27 Apr 2018
35. Sabol, L.: Challenges in cost estimating with Building Information Modeling. IFMA World Workplace, pp. 1–16 (2008)
36. East, W.E., Brodt, W.: BIM for construction handover. J. Build. Inf. Model. **2007**, 28–35 (2007)
37. Pärn, E.A., Edwards, D.J., Sing, M.C.P.: The building information modelling trajectory in facilities management: a review. Autom. Constr. **75**, 45–55 (2017). https://doi.org/10.1016/j.autcon.2016.12.003
38. Home – Project Haystack. https://project-haystack.org/. Accessed 17 Mar 2018
39. BSI. PAS 1192-3:2014 Specification for information management for the operational phase of assets using building information modelling. The British Standards Institution (2014)
40. BSI. PAS 1192-2:2013 Specification for information management for the capital/delivery phase of construction projects using building information modelling. The British Standards Institution (2013)
41. ISO: ISO/DIS 19650 Organization of information about construction works - Information management using building information modelling, Draft (2018)

InBookModE: An Interactive Book and Model Environment to Link BIM and AEC Education

Vishal Singh(✉)

Aalto University, Espoo 02150, Finland
vishal.singh@aalto.fi

Abstract. Building Information Modeling (BIM) tools have become a knowledge resource in the Architecture Engineering and Construction (AEC) sector. While effective BIM use requires knowledge and skills with the tools, BIM tools can also become a good source of learning about the core domain area e.g. architecture, engineering, etc. However, effective teaching and learning of BIM and core domain knowledge is challenging, especially when BIM tools are becoming specialized and complex. So how do we train and skill people both in the use and potential of technology, as well as in their core domain knowledge? To address this challenge, we propose a learning platform, InBookModE (Interactive Book and Model Environment), that integrates acquisition of BIM knowledge with domain knowledge. The main objectives of the proposed approach are to (1) Implement and test the efficacy of an interactive learning platform that integrates the BIM tools with the information encoded in textbooks (2) Combine the interactivity and usability of ebooks with BIM applications to enhance wider adoption and learning, and (3) Create the basis for a long-term goal of a digital repository of interactive BIM case studies. This paper introduces the key ideas and concepts behind the InBookModE, with a brief discussion on the current status of the project and the findings so far.

1 Introduction

Building Information Modeling (BIM) provides digital tools and approaches to effectively create and manage built facilities across the lifecycle (Eastman et al. 2008), which can have potentially huge economic, environmental and societal impact. This belief in the potential capabilities and impacts of BIM has resulted in global attention towards BIM across the Architecture Engineering and Construction (AEC) industry, academia and the policy makers (Bew and Underwood 2010). For example, a McGraw-Hill Research (Bernstein et al. 2012) reports that within five years, between 2007 and 2012, BIM adoption in the US grew from 17% to 70%. Given this growing interest in BIM and its potential wide-ranging scope, the number of BIM-based products and services have increased manifold. As a result, more and more expert knowledge is being encoded into the BIM software for targeted purposes such as performance analysis, code checking, etc., which are making the BIM tools increasingly complex. The increasing emphasis on BIM in AEC, combined with the increasing complexity of BIM tools, is creating the following unintended effects and challenges that need to be addressed:

Published by Springer Nature Switzerland AG 2018.
P. Chiabert et al. (Eds.): PLM 2018, IFIP AICT 540, pp. 93–103, 2018.
https://doi.org/10.1007/978-3-030-01614-2_9

1. There is an extreme shortage of multi-skilled AEC professionals with a combination of domain expertise (core disciplinary and traditional knowledge) and BIM and ICT expertise (to augment their competence)
2. The increasing complexity of BIM tools means there is greater cognitive and learning load on individuals to simultaneously gain domain expertise as well as the expertise in using BIM technologies efficiently
3. There is an increasing need and pressure in the tertiary institutes to rethink AEC curriculum and pedagogy to balance and seamlessly integrate BIM and technology education with core disciplinary education

Besides these challenges, there are new opportunities for improvements in AEC education and learning through cross-disciplinary knowledge transfer from other fields. The emergence of learning technologies, and self-learning and distributed learning platforms such as MOOCS (massive open online courses) have created further opportunity and need to rethink teaching and learning (Eckerdal et al. 2014).

Therefore, this paper presents the details and preliminary results from an ongoing research project aimed at addressing these gaps and opportunities at the interface of BIM and AEC education. The key research questions are: (Q1) How can BIM education be seamlessly integrated with the education and learning about AEC? (Q2) How can the contents and tools required for BIM education be integrated with the traditional contents and tools used in AEC education, for example, textbooks? And, (Q3) How can we leverage the advancements in learning technologies to address the problems stated in Q1 and Q2? (Q4) What will be the intended and unintended cognitive effects and impacts of *InBookModE* for learning, skills development and technology integration in AEC? And, (Q5) What new educational methods and techniques will emerge as a result of the *InBookModE*? These fundamental research enquiries will lead to new knowledge and theories in the context of BIM and AEC education.

2 Background

The potential impact of BIM on the AEC sector is globally recognized, which has fuelled rapid growth and interest across the industry, academia and the policy makers. For example, government agencies across countries such as Australia, US and the UK have recently taken steps towards national BIM guidelines, regulations and policy interventions to facilitate BIM integration and adoption across the AEC sector (e.g. Fussel et al. 2009, AIA 2007, Bew and Underwood 2010). The UK government has even mandated that all public sector, centrally procured, construction projects will be delivered using BIM by 2016. Similarly, the Finnish government's real estate organization, termed Organization-S here, has already mandated the submission of BIM model for all its new projects since 2007. Despite such mandates, there is growing concern on the alarming shortage of multi-skilled AEC professionals with a combination of domain expertise and BIM expertise (CIOB 2013). This shortage of BIM skilled AEC professionals is significant because it poses serious threats to achieving the targeted levels of BIM adoption and usage, which in turn can jeopardize the desired levels of productivity and performance improvements in AEC sector that can be achieved using BIM tools and approaches. For example, in the case of Organization-S, despite the mandated use of BIM since 2007, the organization has failed to use BIM to the intended effect due to shortage of AEC professionals that could deliver quality BIM models, as well as those who could use and integrate the delivered models in their activities (Holmström et al. 2014). Consequently, BIM education and training, skills development and integration are seen as critical bottlenecks that need immediate attention for the advancement and productivity improvements in the AEC sector. In the AEC literature and academic research, BIM education and training is beginning to emerge as a significant research topic (Sacks and Barak 2010). Yalcinkaya and Singh's (2015) analysis shows "BIM education and curriculum development" as one of the most popular theme within BIM research with significant jump between 2012–2014. Academic research so far has been focused on BIM curriculum development, multi-disciplinary classroom environments, and project-based learning, but considerably little has been reported towards the development of BIM-related learning technologies.

On the other hand, the research and development in learning technologies in recent years has shown significant advancements in the areas of rich interactive learning tools, and self-learning and distributed learning platforms such as MOOCS (Brusilovsky et al. 2014, Korhonen et al. 2013). These developments provide opportunities for cross-disciplinary knowledge transfer. This has opened up new opportunities for transforming BIM and AEC education, and there are potentially significant theoretical and practical contributions that are yet to be made.

2.1 Notable Trends in Learning and Teaching

The learning and teaching approaches, especially at the level of tertiary education is seeing significant changes brought about by technology mediation, increasing awareness and recognition of modern pedagogical methods and approaches in engineering education, and changes in educational policies and expectations. Some of the notable trends relevant to this study include:

- Emphasis on *blended learning,* which combines online digital media with traditional classroom methods. There is expectation that while the face to face sessions and contact teaching continue with the physical presence of both the teacher and the students, there would be complementary elements of the courses that allow some of the control in the hands of the students, including when they learn, where they learn, in what order do they learn the content, and at what pace? Thus, there is a clear trend to combine face-to-face classroom practices with computer-mediated activities regarding content and delivery. In BIM-related courses where students also need hands-on computer-based sessions such a combination is natural. However, the combination and integration between lecture sessions in AEC courses and BIM exercises and assignments are still not seamlessly streamlined, and there is opportunity for better blended learning experience.
- *Online and open learning:* With the explosion of online learning material and learning sources, and with increasing acceptance of distance learning and open learning approaches, there is greater demand and expectation on quality online and open learning opportunities. Regular students as well as open learning students

might be enrolled in the same courses, and hence, several courses are expected to have well developed delivery methods to support online learning.

- *Flipped-classroom:* Together with blended learning and online learning, flipped classroom is intended to facilitate learner driven teaching practice. Students explore the topics and learning material of their interest, and the student picked contents become the focus of classroom discussions. Consequently, one of the roles of the teachers and instructors is to curate quality content for the students to explore and choose from for classroom discussions. This creates opportunity as well as the need to have online databases and libraries of interactive content, which can foster content search, filtering, self-driven exploration, and follow-up activities.
- *Case-based and Project-based learning:* In various traditional disciplines, best practices have evolved over years of experience. For example, design-based courses such as in architecture, software design, and engineering design are mostly planned around project-based learning, whereas courses in management departments are often planned around case-reviews and case-based learning. Consequently, with the growing emergence of multi-disciplinary courses case-based and project-based learning are becoming increasingly central to teaching and education. Since BIM and Product Lifecycle Management (PLM) courses are multidisciplinary at the interface of engineering, design and management, case-based and project-based learning is in particularly relevant to these courses.
- *Virtual learning environments (VLEs)* in engineering education: VLEs have been proven to be more engaging and attractive to students. With increasing maturity of Virtual Reality (VR) and Augmented Reality (AR) kits, the role and scope of VLEs is expected to grow exponentially in coming years. So far one of the biggest drawbacks of VLEs have been its development cost and skills. On the other hand, VR and AR applications based on BIM could provide students clear view of the learning content, more complete and detailed visual information, and also an ability to study all the architectural details, structures, constructions and joints within the augmented environment. With greater availability of BIM and PLM models and libraries, the basis for VLE content development is available.

2.2 Challenges in Planning and Delivering BIM Courses

The expectation and need from BIM educators and teachers to be able to respond to the emerging trends, together with the breadth of topics to cover in typical BIM courses, poses several challenges for academics offering such courses. Several factors need to be considered in developing BIM courses and the learning material, such as

- *Connecting the dots* between the different AEC theories and topics and methods and the practical tools that need to be introduced in the courses. Collectively, the amount and breadth of content to cover has increased. Besides the traditional and fundamental engineering content that needs to be covered, additional content related to tools and their applications needs to be covered.
- *Managing workload for students:* Not only do the instructors and teachers need to consider their own workload, there is growing recognition that students' workload in courses should allow them time and space to reflect on their learning. This means

better selection of material and content which facilitates comprehension, and allows learning in more comfortable and informal settings.

- *Developing and updating content which is rapidly changing:* Several aspects of relatively new topics such as BIM and PLM tend to change frequently. New tools, applications, and research-based findings need to be introduced into the courses as they emerge, and hence, the teaching material and content should be easy to update.
- *Increasingly provide more content via interactive and digital media:* Digital natives differ in how they learn and how they consume data. With various aspects of everyday life shifting to digital media, interactive learning is becoming a norm, and teaching material and delivery needs to take advantage of this change.
- *Facilitating social processes and interaction:* As is emphasized in modern pedagogical approaches, situated learning and interaction among learners is desirable. Several authors have noted that social interactions facilitate and reinforce learning (e.g. Singh et al. 2013). In particular, for courses such as BIM and PLM, several soft skills are desirable which can only be developed in how the content and course is delivered, rather than the content itself. Thus, online and digital learning environments also need to support such interaction, especially when it may limit some of the modes of interaction that are available in collocated settings. Furthermore, tertiary education increasingly involves diverse set of students, including those attending courses from remote locations. Thus, it is important to ensure mechanisms that allow these diverse set of students to interact as well.

2.3 Unique Opportunities for BIM and PLM Based Learning Platforms

BIM and PLM tools and applications offer unique features and characteristics that are particularly conducive to integrate them in learning platforms. For example,

- BIM and PLM tools can be viewed as knowledge resources (Jupp and Singh 2014) where a lot of domain knowledge is encoded in form of object libraries and attributes, standards and regulations, relationships and constraints between objects, performance analysis and code- checking rules, etc. BIM tools and applications are increasingly viewed as collaboration tools allowing exchange of ideas, representations and comments, and at the same time facilitating documentation of the generated knowledge (Singh et al. 2011). The concepts and models created by one set of designers may also be available to the next set of designers and team members in form of custom libraries and templates within organizations and project teams (Gu et al. 2014). With a range of BIM applications and tools available to support 'nD' simulations and modeling, BIM can also be viewed as a decision support system, providing knowledge support to the project team members. All this documentation, makes BIM models and platforms particularly useful as learning resources.
- As shown in Fig. 1, there are different ways and levels of detail in using BIM as a source of learning. At the basic level access to details of BIM objects and object attributes can allow learning about building and construction objects, materials, etc. For example, a window BIM object can be used to explain how a window is detailed, what kind of material is used, what are the attributes to consider, etc.

Similarly, case projects and buildings are often used to explain design and engineering principles. Such case projects allow limited context and content, but focused learning objectives. For instance, the design of a specific building (e.g. FallingWater) could be used to explain its designer's (e.g. Frank Lyod Wright) design philosophy or a design principle specifically applied or demonstrable in the chosen case. Thus, a single BIM model of a specific case can be used for targeted learning objectives. In contrast, access to all the resources available in a BIM software could allow much wider content and learning possibility. For instance, a structure engineering BIM software would typically have a large repository of structural elements and components that follow one or more standard, rules and constraints defining relationships between different objects and object attributes, etc.

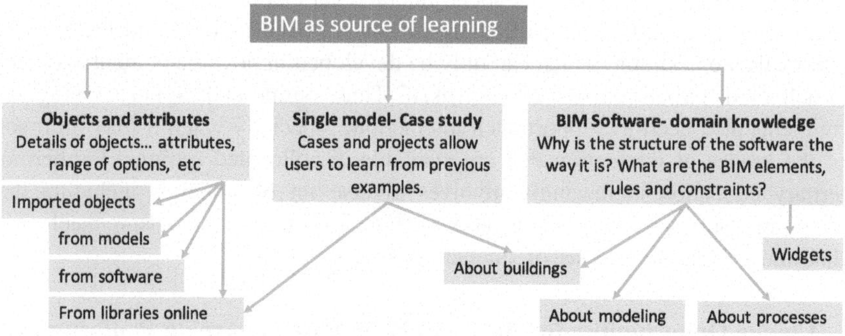

Fig. 1. Opportunities with BIM as a source of learning

- However, all the information and knowledge encoded in the BIM objects, or models, or software are not particularly structured in a way that is directly conducive to learning. Typically, descriptive text is required to explain the content. Thus, BIM related content needs to be integrated with textbooks or reports explaining that content. While BIM objects and models can be integrated in a separate learning platform, access to all the content within BIM software would require interoperable interfaces with the BIM software or embedding the learning platform within a BIM software. Since there are numerous BIM software, each with their own proprietary solutions, implementing a learning system that can be embedded within different BIM software applications is challenging. Therefore, the InBookModE research currently focusses on developing a learning platform that can use BIM objects and BIM models as learning resources. Future work would aim at developing widgets and plug-ins allowing the InBookModE platform to be used within BIM software.
- There is a trend towards both vertical and horizontal integration of BIM education in AEC curricula (Suwal and Singh 2016). Vertical integration refers to the level of education such as undergraduate or postgraduate level. Horizontal integration refers to multidisciplinarity and breadth of education such as architecture, engineering, mechanical-electrical-plumbing (MEP) education, etc.

- Suwal and Singh (2016) found that online BIM learning platforms are highly rated by students as a positive learning experience. They also found that the integration of easy-to-use online BIM learning platforms where students can learn at their own pace, and practice their skills, results in improved engagement and learning.

3 Development and Implementation

The InBookModE development and implementation is currently underway. A working prototype has been developed with basic functionalities, but full-scale user testing to validate and test the research questions and hypotheses is still to be done. Preliminary details and some findings from the implementation so far are presented here.

3.1 What Has Been Implemented so Far?

A working prototype of InBookModE with separate authoring and reader interface and login has been implemented. The system is based on integration between open BIM-Server to access open standard BIM data, Unity engine for interactive game interface, and web-technologies. Figure 2 shows the system architecture. Figures 3 and 4 show snapshots from the current implementation, each supported with a brief description.

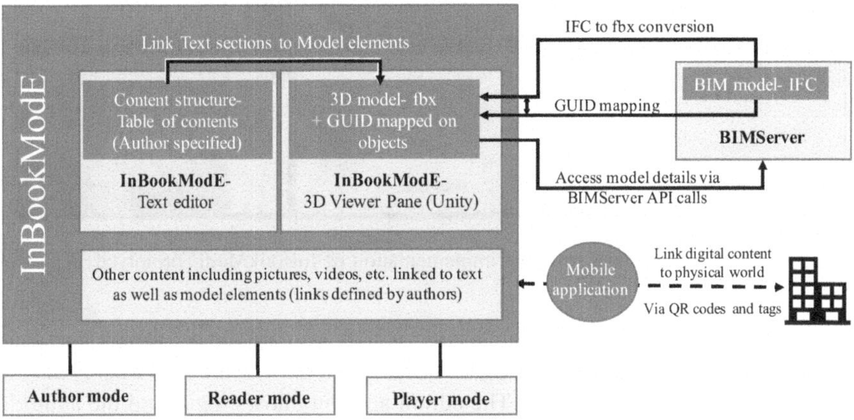

Fig. 2. System architecture for InBookModE

The 'user' in Fig. 3 refers to students, who can login (Fig. 4a) into the InBook-ModE library, access the books and the interactive 3D models associated with the books. A bookstore has been implemented where all books chosen by the students are maintained in their bookshelf (Fig. 4b).

The 'admin' refers to the teachers and content providers who have access to the back end. These actors have the ability to create book content, including uploading and connecting BIM models relevant to the book contents, link the model data with the book data. The admin users can also maintain user accounts, and check usage patterns.

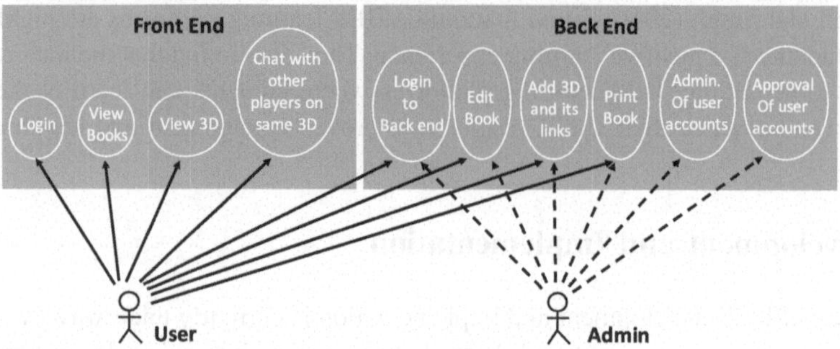

Fig. 3. Use case diagram

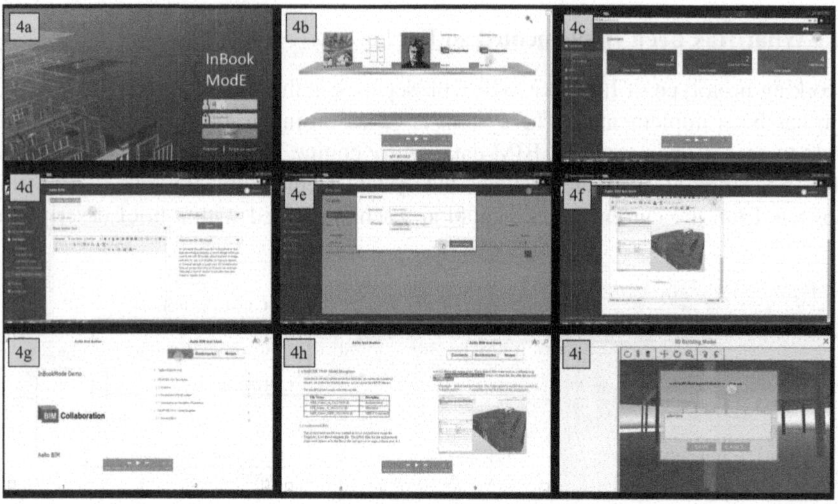

Fig. 4. Snapshots from the implementation of InBookModE prototype

The admin or the teacher can see details such as who are the active and non-active users, what are activity logs, how long do users spend on which book, what is the total number of books, etc. (Figure 4c). The admin account allows login into the authoring mode, whereby the teachers can create new content (Figs. 4d–f). The interface allows content developers to organize their book and preview as it progresses. Help tips such as how to add 3D content etc. are also provided.

InBookModE has a book interface (Fig. 4g) with standard book elements such as table of contents, bookmarks, ability of tagging and taking notes, etc. InBookModE platform also allows embedding and linking processed BIM models into the book interface (Fig. 4h). The BIM model is processed to make it lighter, while the GUIDs of the model elements are retained. Using these GUIDs it is possible to fetch relevant data from BIMServer, while allowing interactive navigation of the model. The authors can also link the model elements with parts of the book text. The model elements can be linked directly to book sections, or paragraphs, or sentences and words, etc. The 3D model can be navigated within the frame or can be viewed on a pop-up window.

To enhance interactive experience, including social and situated learning, a multi-user learning session has been implemented (4i). More than one user, including students and teachers can interact with the same content, and interact with chats. The typed text can be tagged to different model elements and saved for later reference and use. The left side of the interface allows showing model tree structure based on IFC or other classification of the model data.

3.2 Testing and Validation

While a full-fledged testing with students has not been achieved yet, the research team was able to test the usability and functionality of the initial working prototype, especially during development of sample content. This was done to explore different implementation features and how usable these functionalities were. The images above are based on such sample testing. Currently, two case projects are being detailed with respect to BIM models as well as reports relating to those models. Some of the insights from the implementation and sample content development so far include:

- Even though the number of available BIM models is increasing rapidly, in most BIM models the meta-data is either not well documented, or is not directly suitable for direct training and education. Nonetheless, even without adequate and relevant meta-data the models can be useful for interaction and visualization.
- Following on the previous point, it is important to prune BIM models to be linked into the InBookModE such that only the relevant and filtered data is accessed. Otherwise it leads to performance issues as large models can slow down the interactions. In some cases, it is perhaps desirable to develop well-documented BIM models specifically for the purpose of education and training.
- Mapping and structuring the book content with the used BIM content offers various possibilities, which vary with the types of books and specific cases to be written. This means, it is desirable to develop default templates to support authors and reduce the complexity of the mapping and linking activities.

4 Conclusion

This paper reports the development of a BIM-based learning platform, InBookModE, which allows interactive links between digital books and associated BIM models. Thus, it is possible for students to bi-directionally navigate between models and textbooks, or even between related models, textbooks and other linked or embedded sources from the InBookModE interface. Preliminary functionalities and sample content has been developed to test the technical feasibility and integration of the different requirements. A full-scale testing with students to validate whether the learning platform enhances and augments learning experience and comprehension is part of the future work.

References

AIA: Integrated project delivery: A Guide (2007). http://www.aia.org/contractdocs/AIAS077630

Bernstein, H.M. (ed.): The Business Value of BIM in North America: Multi-year Trend Analysis and User Ratings (2007–2012), SmartMarket Report. McGraw-Hill Res. Findings, Belford (2012)

Bew, M., Underwood, J.: Delivering BIM to the UK Market. In: Underwood, J., Isikdag, U. (Eds.) Handbook of Research on BIM and Construction Informatics: Concepts and Technologies, pp. 30–64 (2010)

Brusilovsky, P., Edwards, S., Kumar, A., Malmi, L. (co-chairs), et al.: Increasing Adoption of Smart Learning Content for Computer Science Education, ITiCSE Working group report (2014)

CIOB: A report exploring skills in the UK Construction Industry, The Chartered Institute of Building, April 2013

Eastman, C., Teicholz, P., Sacks, R., Liston, K.: BIM Handbook: A Guide to BIM for Owners, Managers, Designers, Engineers and Contractors. Wiley, NewYork (2008)

Eckerdal, A., Kinnunen, P., Thota, N., Nylén, A., Sheard, J., Malmi, L.: Teaching and learning with MOOCs: computing academics' perspectives and engagement. In: Proceedings of the Conference on Innovation and Technology in Computer Science Education (ITiCSE 2014). ACM, NY, pp. 9–14 (2014)

Fussel, T., Beazley, S., et al.: National guidelines for digital modelling. Brisbane, QLD (2009)

Gu, N., Singh, V., London, K.: BIM Ecosystem: The Coevolution of Products, Processes, and People. In: Kensek, K., Noble, D. (Eds.) Building Information Modeling: BIM in Current and Future Practice, pp. 197–211 (2014)

Holmström, J., Singh, V., Främling, K.: BIM as Infrastructure in a Finnish HVAC Actor Network: Enabling Adoption, Reuse, and Recombination over a Building Life Cycle and between Projects. J. Manag. Eng. https://doi.org/10.1061/(asce)me.1943-5479.0000305, A4014006 (2014)

Jupp, J., Singh, V.: Similar concepts, distinct solutions, common problems: learning from PLM and BIM deployment. In: International Conference on Product Lifecycle Management, Yokohama, Japan (2014)

Korhonen, A., Naps, T., Boisvert, C., et al.: Requirements and design strategies for open source interactive computer science eBooks. In: ITiCSE Working Group Reports Conference on Innovation and Technology in Computer Science Education-WGR 2013, pp. 53–72. ACM, NY (2013)

Sacks, R., Barak, R.: Teaching building information modeling as an integral part of freshman year civil engineering education. J. Prof. Iss. Eng. Edu. Prac. **136**(1), 30–38 (2010)

Singh, V., Dong, A., Gero, J.S.: Social learning in design teams: The importance of direct and indirect communications. Art. Int. Eng. Des. Anal. Manuf. **27**, 167–182 (2013)

Singh, V., Gu, N., Taylor, C., London, K., Brankovich, L.: Collaboration Platform: Final Report. CRC for Consortium Innovation, Australia (2009). http://eprints.qut.edu.au/27997/1/27997.pdf

Singh, V.: BIM and systemic ICT innovation in AEC: perceived needs and actor's degrees of freedom, Construction Innovation: Information, Process, Management, **14**(3) (2014)

Singh, V., Gu, N., Wang, X.: A theoretical framework for BIM-based multi-disciplinary collaboration platform. Autom. Constr. **20**, 134–144 (2011)

Suwal, S., Singh, V.: Assessing students' sentiments towards the use of a Building Information Modelling (BIM) learning platform in a construction project management course. European Journal of Engineering Education (2016). https://doi.org/10.1080/03043797.2017.1287667

Yalcinkaya, M., Singh, V.: Patterns and trends in Building Information Modeling (BIM) research: A Latent Semantic Analysis. Autom. Constr. **59**, 68–80 (2015)

PLM and BIM Approach to Support Information Management in Nuclear Decommissioning: A Synthesis

Vincent Cheutet[1], Aicha Sekhari[2(✉)], and Nathalie Corbeaux[3]

[1] University Lyon, INSA Lyon, DISP Laboratory, EA4570 Villeurbanne, France
vincent.cheutet@insa-lyon.fr
[2] University Lyon, Université Lumière Lyon 2, DISP Laboratory, EA4570 Bron, France
aicha.sekhari@univ-lyon2.fr
[3] EDF-DP2D, Lyon, France
nathalie.corbeaux@edf.fr

Abstract. Nuclear decommissioning is a huge disaster and cumbersome mechanism to handle, after critical analysis and rigorous review it is found that PLM and BIM approaches seem interesting in this field to support the business needs in terms of collaboration, information exchange and traceability all over the decommissioning process. This paper analyses the scientific and industrial literature to extract the requirements for the deployment of a mixed BIM-PLM approach in the nuclear decommissioning context.

Keywords: Information management · PLM · BIM
Nuclear decommissioning

1 Introduction

At this time, the first generation of Nuclear Power Plants (NPPs) is gradually being taken out of service and decommissioned. Around 300 nuclear facilities will be stopped around the world in the next 20 years and more than 10 decommissioning operations are on-going in France. A decommissioning process is long, complex and requires the determination and the description of the decommissioning scenario of the installation, which means the description of all the operations which are run from the final shutdown of the NPP units.

Amount of data are needed to establish a physical and radiological inventory of the totality of the NPP [1]. The main challenge is to ensure the access to the right information at the right time to the right person, in order to provide a consistent basis to the decision support framework. Such information must be well storage, managed and controlled, meaning that the user has to be aware of the level of maturity and uncertainty attached to such information to complete our mastery of nuclear-based energy all along its lifecycle. In order to efficiently support, manage and control such activities, **information management is so of prior interest**.

Published by Springer Nature Switzerland AG 2018.
P. Chiabert et al. (Eds.): PLM 2018, IFIP AICT 540, pp. 104–114, 2018.
https://doi.org/10.1007/978-3-030-01614-2_10

Nevertheless, the intrinsic characteristics of Nuclear Facilities Decommissioning (NFD) process make this information management very complex and requires new approaches. In this research work, the authors aim to precisely characterize the NFD process in order to specify the key characteristics that a dedicated information system should gather in order to successfully support the activity. Based on this analysis, the authors compare some promising approaches in information management and information systems by proposing a digital roadmap for NFD information management.

The paper is structured as follows. Section 2 characterizes the NFD process and the information generated and required to support this process. Section 3 defines the objectives two promising approaches with these key characteristics: PLM (Product Lifecycle Management) and BIM (Building Information Management). Section 4 synthesizes the comparison between these two concepts. Section 5 analyses their appropriation in the context of NFD and opens new research perspectives.

2 Information Management for Nuclear Decommissioning

2.1 NFD Process Characteristics

IAEA (International Atomic Energy Agency) proposes this definition for decommissioning process: “The administrative and technical actions taken to allow the removal of some or all of the regulatory controls from a facility” [2]. It implies that decommissioning does not restrain to the dismantling activities and covers all operations from the preparation to the final site clean-up (Fig. 1). In particular, it begins before the end of nuclear operations.

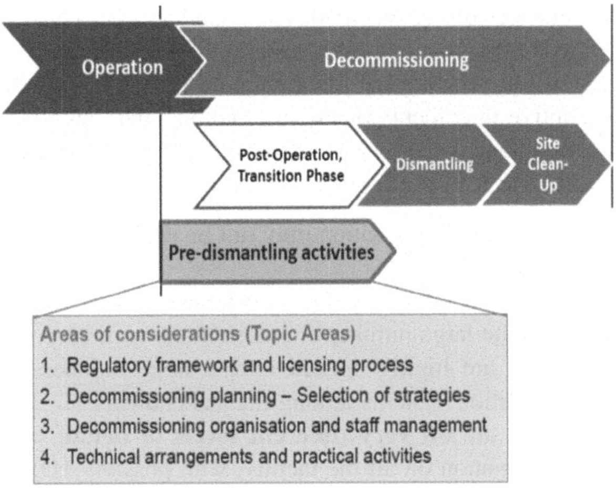

Fig. 1. IAEA definition of nuclear facility decommissioning [3]

A nuclear facility can be seen as a complex system with a very long lifetime. The ones that are currently decommissioned in France were put into service in the 1960s.

Even if the first decommissioning activities have finished in the recent years, there is still very few experience and feedback on these activities that can be shared among the nuclear community. Moreover, even if it exists some classification of nuclear facilities, their very long operation time and the diversity of needs at their design period imply that there is very few standardisation between nuclear facilities: each of them can be seen as a unique complex system with its particular history. It makes the reusability of information and knowledge more complex for the community. As a consequence, NFD can be considered as **project-based**, with a perspective of standardisation.

Decommissioning process is also a long-time activity. In France, for PWR (Pressurized Water Reactor), it may last at least 22 years. This process is highly guided by regulations, for instance in France by ASN (Autorité de Sûreté Nucléaire) that validates the dismantling scenario proposed the decommissioner, authorizes the operations and ensures the information and knowledge capitalization.

A large number of stakeholders are implied in the NFD process, from the NF designer that provides any information (digitalized or not) on the facility, the operators (with a special attention on all maintenance operations realised during the operating phase), the regulation authorities (ASN, ANDRA - Agence Nationale pour la gestion des Déchets RAdioactifs - in France), the decommissioner that is responsible of the dismantling scenario design and operation and all the subcontractors that may take part in some activities overall the process.

2.2 Information Characteristics

With the characteristics listed in the previous section, one can imagine the complexity that occurs in information management for NFD process. In the NFD process, data and information are focusing on three essential elements: **the nuclear facility, nuclear wastes and the decommissioning scenario**. The main focus is so on a specific instance of elements that is central to the NFD. Some examples of data and information required by the regulations in the process are: requirements (project, regulatory, functional, technical …), descriptive documents of the installations, data on hardware, operating history, physical and radioactive inventory, costs, etc. Among others, one can list these specificities that will have a strong impact on data and information management:

- A large number of data and information **may not be digital**, due to the long lifetime of facilities,
- Data and information are **strongly heterogeneous**, due to few standardization between facilities, to the large number of stakeholders with very specific expertise,
- Data and information are **highly spread** over a large number of dedicated and heterogeneous information systems among the stakeholders,
- Data and information are **on very different levels of detail**, with data on very specific parts or information on all the facility, with possibly 1D, 2D or 3D digital mock-up.
- The **quality** of data and information is **untrusty**, with problems of redundancy, inconsistency, uncertainties, inaccessibility and unsuitability for end users that occurs.

Finally, due to the lack of experience and feedback, information management is non-mature at that time and so a strong effort is required to define and share these specifications. With all these constraints and specificities, it is not complicated to understand why there is few research works that have tackled this problem of information management in the context of NFD. Among the literature, one can cite [1, 4 and 5] that have proposed an integrated information systems for NFD but which implantations are still limited, or [6] that focuses on information management for dismantling planning.

In the current research works, the authors analyses the EIS (Enterprise Information Systems) families that have been developed with a different objective [7] to find if an adaptation is possible. Among the listed EIS (Enterprise Resource Planning (ERP), Supply Chain Management (SCM), Manufacturing Execution Systems (MES), Customer Relationship Management (CRM), Product Lifecycle Management (PLM) and Business Intelligence (BI)) with addition of BIM and Enterprise Asset Management [28], two are promising according to their nature: PLM and BIM. In fact they are both by nature project-based, centred on a specific instance of elements and they aim at enhancing the collaboration among a large number of heterogeneous stakeholders. This finding is enhanced by the strategic choices of the Digital Transformation program of our industrial partner (EDF).

3 PLM-BIM Definitions and Objectives

PLM can be mostly understood as the information backbone of the organization attached to the all lifecycle of a product. The Product Lifecycle Management (PLM) concept holds to integrate all the information produced throughout all phases of a product's life cycle to everyone in an organization at every managerial and technical level, along with key suppliers and customers [8]. The lifecycle model consists of three phases during which information must be tracked and knowledge capitalized: The Beginning-of-Life (BOL), the Middle-of-Life (MOL) and finally, the End-of-Life (EOL). PLM tools are based on technologies such as the Cloud and SOA architecture, and integrate functionalities to enhance collaboration, workflow engine to automate processes, approaches to manage product variants and versions, PLM is supposed to fill the gap between enterprise business processes and product development processes. In other terms, PLM works as glue which adhere all the processes that have something to do with product and connects all functional silos to make them horizontally integrated [9].

BIM is defined as the method of generation execution and monitoring of the "building data" during its life process. Moreover, BIM is also known as a combination of process and technology to improve efficiency and effectiveness of delivering a project from inception to operation and maintenance [10]. In construction projects, BIM has been used by architecture, engineering and construction or facilities management (AEC/FM) to implement collaborative management of construction projects between all stakeholders. The term generally refers both the model(s) representing the physical characteristics of the project and to all the information contained in and attached to the component of theses model [11]. As a clear and practical example, while a door represented in a 2D CAD drawing is just a collection of lines, in BIM it is an intelligent object containing information on its size, cost, manufacturer, schedule and more. According to [12], BIM should be used as a building model repository. A building model repository is a database system whose schema is based on a published object based format. It is different from existing project data management (PDM) systems and web-based project management systems in that the PDM systems are file based, and carry CAD and analysis package project files. Building Model repositories are object based, allowing query, transfer, updating and management of individual project objects from potentially heterogeneous set of application.

While BIM has existed for some time, advances in information and communication technologies (ICTs) have strongly encouraged the adoption of the concept. Recently, BIM has attracted the market demand from engineering, designing, building and warehousing domains. It creates and manages huge landscape of opportunities by associating with like-minded and in-lined areas and processes. In [10], they state that BIM is a process that brings all data or information on project design together in one parametric model giving benefits to construction projects in terms of time, cost and quality and helps design team to solve the design clashes early in pre-construction stage. As a summary, BIM consists of at least three dimensions: process, technology and people. The findings from the literature revealed some barriers and challenges in BIM implementations. In an NBS report [13], 67% of BIM users and 64% of non-BIM users confirmed cost was a major barrier to BIM uptake. The same sources revealed that the lack of knowledge about different BIM software packages is a major barrier to their adoption. Up-to-now, very few works focus on BIM implementation for end-of-life activities and one can cite [27] that elicits the essential functionalities for a BIM-based deconstruction tool in the context of classical facilities.

The focus on entire aspect of BIM exemplifies its close proximity to PLM. The evolution of BIM, and its analogy with PLM provides a platform to expand current knowledge of these ideas, introduce new fields of research, and develop innovative scientific information domains. The following paragraph deals with a comparative study between PLM and BIM.

4 PLM-BIM Comparative Study

When looking to PLM and BIM, many sharing concepts come in play. They take into consideration the entire vision of effectively managing and connecting all information related to the Process, People, Data and integration of this information to other business systems across the entire lifecycle of the products companies manufacture or construction industry. PLM and BIM are not just technology, but an approach in which processes are as important as data. Similarities between the two approaches are creation, integration and reuse of project information, the concept of 'digital mock-up' and project management practices. PLM and BIM both have same common objective, i.e. to increase collaboration, productivity, optimization, and to deliver better value to the client. Inter-relations between BIM and PLM have already been addressed in previous works. But the subject is still very interesting and it is not always easy to clarify what is the role and advantages of each of them and how they can accept each other.

There are only a few documented efforts on PLM and BIM integration benefit. One of the main gaps identified in the literature relates to the lack of research surrounding the role of PLM in the BIM methodology [15]. Few works that consider the research on the implementing of PLM systems in the AEC companies.

These previous research work has shown that it is possible to improve BIM with the features and the best practices from Product Lifecycle Management (PLM) approach [26]. Authors of [16] identified the BIM management requirements that reflect core PLM functions, including data organization, version management, release management and role/responsibility identification. Authors of [15] analysed the consequences of incomplete BIM implementation. The study identified three types of problems: process-based issues, technology based issues and policy-based issues. The results are that PLM can actually be an opportunity to expand existing applications of BIM. However the study also suggests that the transverse application of a BIM-PLM solution that is based on discrete manufacturing processes might lead to other types of problems due to the complexity of interfaces observed in construction projects [26].

To summarize, BIM and PLM share a number of similarities relative to their approach to data sharing, project management, organization of teams around deliverables and timelines, and object-based visualization activities [14].

At the same time, the literature count a number of key differences between BIM and PLM concepts and their practical deployment. These differences can be seen to stem from the different structures, backgrounds and traditions of their respective industries. BIM has amazing features to manage the different process of the building from design to construction but lacks the monitoring and management mechanism, and this the main point where both PLM and BIM are discriminated. PLM offers the strong management capabilities for the lifecycle of the any constructed project. Using the BIM we can know the state of building at present time whereas with PLM it is possible to know what were the modifications made at such moment and thus to know what was the condition of building at some point in the past. Besides, there is lack of BIM standards for model integration and is being managed by multidisciplinary teams. Integrating multidisciplinary information in a single BIM model requires multiuser access to the BIM model. At the moment, since there are no standard protocols available, each firm adopts its own standards. This could create inconsistencies in the model, which if not properly detected, could lead to inaccurate and inconsistent BIM model. The exclusion of PLM's activities in the deployment of the BIM methodology can lead to failures in presenting the merits of BIM to tasks and lessen its importance to customers:

On one hand, we have BIM, a unique data model that allows the collaboration of the different actors and focuses mainly on the visualization functions, the calculations of the properties, and the verification of the interactions between the different elements of the digital model. But which does not deal with document management or the control of reports and versions of documents. On the other hand, we have the PLM which allows the management of the lifecycle of the construction project and formalizes the processes of modification, validation, exchange.

As a conclusion, it can be claimed that BIM is a subset of PLM and major part of any organization is based on the accurate management and the monitoring of the assets. As addressed by the national BIM standard project committee that BIM is a digital representation of physical and functional characteristics of a facility, besides it is a shared knowledge resource for information about a facility forming a reliable basis for decisions during its lifecycle; defined as existing from earliest conception to demolition. PLM is an integrated, information-driven approach to all aspects of a product's life from its design inception through its manufacture, deployment and maintenance, culminating in its removal from service and final disposal. Table 1 proposes a synthetic comparison of PLM and BIM approach.

Table 1. Comparisons between BIM and PLM

	PLM	BIM
Information management	-Data retrieved from various models are managed and **stored in vault** **-Data exchange standards** have often been criticized for their inability to capture well-defined business processes, work flow patterns/systems, and underlying business rules -Capabilities of PLM system have been enhanced to capture, manage and preserve the created information for the **entire product portfolio** of a company	-It does not distinguish between requirements, functional and physical documents -The information maintained and produced in the BIM approach includes both the geometric and non-geometric data -Limited to **single project or product**
Approach	-Product-driven PLM paradigm **-REX -** The focus is instead on the overall business process -With PLM, companies think of the standard processes, standard data and standard systems that they, and the numerous suppliers, customers, and partners, can use to save an enormous amount of time and money -PLM implementation team work closely with the cross-functional business teams	-Technology led BIM paradigm -BIM is an interdependent network of processes, technologies and policies, which constitutes a 'methodology to manage building design and project data in digital format throughout the **building's lifecycle'** **-Rules and requirements** have not yet been developed nor established within current BIM approaches -BIM emphasizes open communication and information exchange, collaborative decision making, early participation and contribution of knowledge and expertise by downstream stakeholders (contractors and suppliers), and greater levels of risk sharing
Domain	-PLM in the manufacturing sectors is more established In the construction sector, BIM is still considered a recent concept and should therefore benefit from the lessons of PLM implementation	-Construction industry is still in the early phases of BIM adoption In the construction sector, BIM is still considered a recent concept and should therefore benefit from the lessons of PLM implementation

5 PLM-BIM in Nuclear Facilities and Perspectives

With this perspective, we can analyse how these two approaches have been deployed in nuclear facilities context. PLM and BIM are considered as important collaborative approach in delivering a safe, secure and cost effective nuclear as well as other emerging domains or example, construction, manufacturing and architectural platform [17].

A large literature exists on the deployment of PLM and/or BIM to support the BOL (Beginning of Life) or MOL (Middle of Life) phases of NPPs [18–20]. One can cite for instance [18] that address the digitized concept of the nuclear industries by deploying PLM and BIM merely focusing on the UK's nuclear sector. In their discussion, they all claim that both PLM and BIM play the remarkable rôle in the manufacturing and constructing the innovative NPP and industries.

Some authors are enlarging the scope of BIM and/or PLM to tackle the entire NPP lifecycle [21–24]. As an example, authors of [24] examine that one of the critical challenges while keeping the foundation of NPP from set-up to decommission phase is the proper and accurate management of the resources in the short span of time. Besides, most of the societal needs are inter-related to the efficient utilization of the power plants due to various hurdles and expenses to tackle, so PLM is the dire need of the overall nuclear facility environment.

Nevertheless, none of these works are properly tackling the specificities of NFD and only consider this process as part of EOL (End-of-Life) phase of NPP lifecycle. In our understanding of these concepts, applying them specifically to this process can improve the overall performance and safety.

In this research works, we extensively synthesize the leading role of both BIM and PLM on the basis of their significant contribution in the NFD process. After deep analysis and critical examination of the literature, a list of functionalities that are required for NFD can be drawn (Fig. 2), with PLM specific ones, BIM specific ones, BIM-PLM common ones and NFD specific one that does not exist at that moment neither in BIM nor PLM.

In perspective, if BIM and PLM are definitively interesting approach to support NFD process, some questions remain open, among them: what is the "Product" in this approach? A model mixing the plant, the wastes and the dismantling scenarios in the product concept is being experimented in [25], with configuration management as key characteristics to handle the diversity of products and lifecycle.

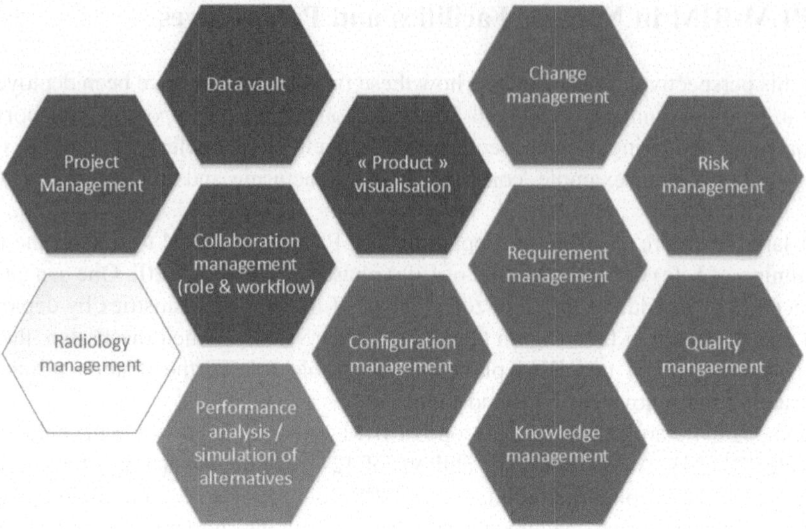

Fig. 2. BIM-PLM functionalities elicited for NFD: in green PLM-specific functionalities, in red BIM-specific ones, in blue BIM-PLM common ones and in white NFD-specific one. (Color figure online)

References

1. Chou, I.H., Fan, C.F.: Developing integrated decommissioning information management system (IDIMS) of nuclear facilities. J. Nucl. Sci. Technol. **43**(5), 596–604 (2006). https://doi.org/10.1080/18811248.2006.9711138
2. IAEA: Standard format and content for safety related decommissioning documents. International Atomic Energy Agency, Safety Reports Series No. 45 (2005)
3. Michal, V.: IAEA perspectives on preparation for decommissioning. In: International Symposium on Preparation for Decommissioning – PREDEC 2016, Lyon, France (2016)
4. Leclair, A.N., Lemire, D.S.: 26–Information management for nuclear decommissioning projects. In: Laraia, M. (Ed.) Woodhead Publishing Series in Energy, Nuclear Decommissioning, pp. 777–798. Woodhead Publishing (2012)
5. Iguchi, Y., Kanehira, Y., Tachibana, M., Johnsen, T.: Development of Decommissioning Engineering Support System (DEXUS) of the Fugen Nuclear Power Station. J. Nucl. Sci. Technol. **41**(3), 367–375 (2004). https://doi.org/10.1080/18811248.2004.9715497
6. Yanagihara, S., Sukegawa, T., Shiraishi, K.: Development of computer systems for planning and management of reactor decommissioning. J. Nucl. Sci. Technol. **38**(3), 193–202 (2001). https://doi.org/10.1080/18811248.2001.9715021
7. Romero, D., Vernadat, F.: Enterprise information systems state of the art: past, present and future trends. Comput. Ind. **79**, 3–13 (2016). https://doi.org/10.1016/j.compind.2016.03.001
8. Sudarsan, R., Fenves, S.J., Sriram, R.D., Wang, F.: A product information modeling framework for product lifecycle management. Comput. Aided Des. **37**(13), 1399–1411 (2005). https://doi.org/10.1016/j.cad.2005.02.010
9. Ameri, F., Dutta, D.: Product lifecycle management needs, concepts and components. Product Lifecycle Management Development Consortium (2004)

10. Latiffi, A.A., Mohd, S., Rakiman, U.S.: Potential Improvement of Building Information Modeling (BIM) implementation in Malaysian construction projects. In: Bouras, A., Eynard, B., Foufou, S., Thoben, K.-D. (eds.) PLM 2015. IAICT, vol. 467, pp. 149–158. Springer, Cham (2016). https://doi.org/10.1007/978-3-319-33111-9_14
11. Haron, A.T., Marshall-Ponting, A.J., Aouad, G.: Building information modelling in integrated practice. In: 2nd Construction Industry Research Achievement International Conference. Kuala Lumpur, Malaysia (2009)
12. Eastman, C.M., Eastman, C., Teicholz, P., Sacks, R.: BIM Handbook: a guide to building information modeling for owners, managers, designers, engineers and contractors. Wiley, Hoboken (2011)
13. NBS: NBS National BIM Report 2014 (2014). https://www.thenbs.com/knowledge/nbs-national-bim-report-2014
14. Jupp, J.R., Nepal, M.: BIM and PLM: comparing and learning from changes to professional practice across sectors. In: Fukuda, S., Bernard, A., Gurumoorthy, B., Bouras, A. (eds.) PLM 2014. IAICT, vol. 442, pp. 41–50. Springer, Heidelberg (2014). https://doi.org/10.1007/978-3-662-45937-9_5
15. Jupp, J.R.: Incomplete BIM implementation: exploring challenges and the role of product lifecycle management functions. In: Bernard, A., Rivest, L., Dutta, D. (eds.) PLM 2013. IAICT, vol. 409, pp. 630–640. Springer, Heidelberg (2013). https://doi.org/10.1007/978-3-642-41501-2_62
16. London, K., Singh, V., Taylor, C., Gu, N., Brankovic, L.: Building information modelling project decision support framework. In: Proceedings of the Twenty-Fourth Annual Conference Association of Researchers in Construction Management (ARCOM) (2008)
17. Aram, S., Eastman, C.: Integration of PLM solutions and BIM systems for the AEC industry. In: Proceedings of 30th International Symposium of Automation and Robotics in Construction and Mining, Montréal, pp. 1046–1055 (2013)
18. Walker, A.: Big benefits for nuclear sector by going digital Building Information Modelling (BIM) and Project Lifecycle Management are transforming the nuclear industry for lifecycle value and assurance (2016). http://www.infrastructure-intelligence.com/article/apr-2016/big-benefits-nuclear-sector-going-digital
19. Yalcinkaya, M., Singh, V.: Building Information Modeling (BIM) for facilities management – literature review and future needs. In: Fukuda, S., Bernard, A., Gurumoorthy, B., Bouras, A. (eds.) PLM 2014. IAICT, vol. 442, pp. 1–10. Springer, Heidelberg (2014). https://doi.org/10.1007/978-3-662-45937-9_1
20. Tommila, T., Alanen, J.: Conceptual model for safety requirements specification and management in nuclear power plants. VTT-VTT Technol. **238**, 120 (2015)
21. Cronin, B.: BIM in Nuclear Decommissioning (2015). https://thebimhub.com/2015/04/06/bim-in-nuclear-decommissioning/#.WqvfG2rOW71
22. Pottelberg, P., Tremblay, R.: The Turnover Process at Chalk River Laboratories from Operations to Decommissioning. In: PREDEC 2016 Conference, Lyon (France) (2016)
23. Calais, T., Rauber, J.C.: Control and maintenance of the Superphenix knowledge and its specific sodium skills through an innovative partnership between EDF and AREVA, PREDEC. In: 2016 Conference, Lyon (France) (2016)
24. IAEA-TECDOC-1305: Safe and Effective Nuclear Power Plant Life Cycle Management towards Decommissioning, pp. 1–36 (2002)
25. Cheutet, V., Sekhari, A., Corbeaux, N.: A PLM approach to support nuclear decommissioning process. In: DEM 2018 - Dismantling Challenges: Industrial Reality, Prospects and Feedback Experience, Avignon (France) (2018)

26. Boton, C., Rivest, L., Forgues, D., Jupp, J.: Comparing PLM and BIM from the product structure standpoint. In: Harik, R., Rivest, L., Bernard, A., Eynard, B., Bouras, A. (eds.) PLM 2016. IAICT, vol. 492, pp. 443–453. Springer, Cham (2016). https://doi.org/10.1007/978-3-319-54660-5_40
27. Akinade, O.O., et al.: BIM-based deconstruction tool: towards essential functionalities. Int. J. Sustain. Built Environ. **6**(1), 260–271 (2017). https://doi.org/10.1016/j.ijsbe.2017.01.002
28. Kraft, D., Francisco, W.: Establishing a governance framework to provide leadership to a new enterprise asset management program. In: Asset Management Conference (AM 2016), (2016). https://doi.org/10.1049/cp.2016.1403

Collaborative Environments and New Product Development

A Discussion on Current Issues for Semantic Interoperability in an Integrated Product Development Process

Athon Francisco Curi Staben de Moura Leite[1], Anderson Luis Szejka[1(✉)], Osiris Canciglieri Junior[1], and Rafael Christiano Annunziato[2]

[1] Industrial and Systems Engineering Graduate Program, Pontifical Catholic University of Parana, Curitiba, Brazil
{athon.leite, anderson.szejka, osiris.canciglieri}@pucpr.br

[2] NHS Electronic Systems, Curitiba, Brazil
rafael@nhs.com.br

Abstract. Through past decade, the complexity of integrated product development process has been significantly increased, due to highly elaborated customer's needs, market requirements and their multi-disciplinary nature. In this context, the meaning and formal structure of such information must be well managed since initial stages of product development, in order to avoid semantic heterogeneity and subsequent mistakes in interpretation. The aim of this paper is to understand the current issues related to this scenario, through the study of later works and research regarding Semantic Interoperability through ontologies in multiple domains, applicable in the field of Product Development and Manufacturing. Search material points out that a significant issue regards the input of information, since most of current models merely translate information from different sources, instead of understanding its nature and stablish a common standard to extract and structure it. Research has suggested that Knowledge Extraction models may be a viable path to filter and refine the quality of the input information, as means to improve the accuracy and effectiveness of new knowledge. This research structured its findings in a model that explores the issues of semantic interoperability through reference ontologies, to bring light to new research themes, validated through further research.

Keywords: Semantic interoperability · Multiple domains
Product development and manufacturing · Formal models · Reference ontology

1 Introduction

In order to fulfill customer's needs, a wide range of knowledge from multiple domains is used during Product's Lifecycle Management. The complexity of client's requirements generates a remarkable quantity of information, which can be misinterpreted across different development stages and compromise the quality of final product, increasing its development and manufacturing cost. These impacts are caused mainly

Published by Springer Nature Switzerland AG 2018.
P. Chiabert et al. (Eds.): PLM 2018, IFIP AICT 540, pp. 117–125, 2018.
https://doi.org/10.1007/978-3-030-01614-2_11

by the heterogeneity within and across different domains of knowledge in a semantic manner.

Currently, researchers are addressing the problem of semantic heterogeneity through the concept of ontology-driven semantic interoperability. This concept is based on the communication of different systems by using ontologies as means to develop a formal and shareable taxonomy that standardizes, verifies and infers information by a set of rules and axioms, improving its interpretation, traceability and integration [1]. Semantic Interoperability addresses the meaning of information exchanged in virtual environments, assuring that the same intent is captured across different systems [13]. In the context of an Integrated Product Development Process (IPDP), there are issues that challenges the quality of information flow and imposes barriers to a semantically interoperable system across multiple domains for product development and manufacturing [2, 3].

One of the most difficult challenges carried through IPDP is related to the different notations in which knowledge is represented across different development phases and domains. The necessary information is mostly structured in distinct taxonomies and extensions that are not, in most cases, designed to interoperation and further integrated applications [4].

This paper aims to analyze the current issues regarding semantic interoperability within a requirement notation perspective. Information will be gathered through the review of later works, which will be later discussed and analyzed, considering the current issues on the implementation of semantically interoperable systems in the field of integrated product development and manufacturing.

2 Problem Statement

The different requirements from multiple domains of knowledge might result in several *a posteriori* negative effects in a semantically interoperable system for product development and manufacturing. The information from each IPDP phase comes from different domains, e.g. CAD/CAM systems, CRM software, etc., having a unique notation to represent its knowledge, which requires translation [5]. This process involves restructuring information into a standard pattern for further interoperable applications, implying in issues during the requirement's analysis, such as: inconsistencies, incoherence, lack of uniqueness and unfeasible, untraceable, unverifiable information [6, 7].

In another aspect, the multiple perspectives of Product Development require a range of specialists to solve it, from different fields of study and backgrounds, using a varied set of informational tools [8]. The different experiences result in a lack of standardization during the solving process by human decisions, which may lead into misunderstanding and perpetuation of wrong assumptions for further applications [8]. In this matter, research consider increase the level of automation of the decision-making process, in order to reduce misinterpretation [9–11].

In a system's perspective, ontology-driven semantic interoperability offers a way of systems communicate by sharing knowledge from various sources [9, 14]. The use of ontologies throughout the product design and manufacture may offer a differential in terms of standards and requirement's traceability, as long as the quality of knowledge gathering and structuring process is maintained through all development phases. By formalising this knowledge, the correct meaning of exchanged information might assure fewer mistakes and consequently reduce costs during PDP [12, 14].

Currently, semantic interoperation issues are addressed by authors, such as [12–14], which focus on requirement's engineering (in a broader sense) in its semantically interoperable system models. The idea of such system focused on product development and manufacturing is still a theme for debate and analysis, since there are still technical and conceptual barriers that need to be overcome to a provide a seamless information interoperation [15].

3 Related Works

The related works of this research were structured as a qualitative literature review, based on the nature of issues in a semantically interoperable system focused on product development and manufacturing, as follows: (i) cross-domain issues, (ii) cross-IPDP phases' issues and (iii) cross-requirement representation issues.

3.1 Cross-Domain Issues

The complexity of new products demands participation of specialists from multiple domains, providing a holistic view that ensures the best solution to fulfill customers' needs [16]. Although this approach provides a better product, it ends up generating a set of heterogeneous information that represents the interests and background from different groups of stakeholders, which may not have the same meaning. This heterogeneity in information may result in divergence and misinterpretation of the correct meaning of information, due to lack of formalism and standards, affecting negatively in further product life-cycle management, by increasing costs, re-work and the overall lead time of PDP [12, 17].

One of the reasons for divergence and misinterpretation resides in the expertise of specialist being restricted to their respective domains, as pointed by [18]. In addition, requirements coming from clients and software, across multiple domains, have their own structure, which results in a semantic problem that challenges the success of development process [18]. In another aspect, there is no current system capable of translate all requirements from all stakeholders in product features. This results in the necessity to manage the heterogeneous knowledge from multiple domains in different systems and product life-cycle phases, which intensifies the cross-domain issues.

Literature points to the use of different models to standardize the structure of information in different domains, such as UML (Unified Modelling Language), Model-Driven Engineering (MDE), Domain Specific Language (DSL), and others [2, 9, 19]. Although those models present an intent to formalize and represent knowledge from domains in a standard way, those approaches do not present the dynamic nature of requirements and knowledge from different product development phases [20].

Currently, a few models consider the consistency of requirements and performance in a dynamic environment. In [21], the authors explore a design framework for cyber-physical systems, based on design rationale, linking unique design parameters and requirements from various sources. In [22], authors explore the domain of Manufacturing and the acquisition of requirements from different domains of knowledge. Both [21] and [22] have combined different models to achieve verifiable and validated information with dynamic requirements, but still, there is the need for specialists' decisions during the translation of requirements process. That approach implies in semantic issues, as there are subjective factors and a range of different methods related to each domain, resulting in different inputs among different specialists.

3.2 Cross-IPDP Phases' Issues

The Integrated Product Development Process refers to a multi-disciplinary and communicative product development approach, which relates to the concept of Transdisciplinary Engineering applied to traditional PDP [23, 24]. There are several models and standards focused on the process, defining each of its phases, methods of verification and related tools, as pointed by [25]. However, each model is different and cannot, in an explicit way, represent all life-cycle situations in the necessary level of abstraction [26]. Although they can represent different life-cycle phases, there are particularities that make each of them more suitable for different and specific phases [25, 27].

In theory, each model is a closed loop and do follow a sequential flow of information while performing its activities. In a practical manner, though, most of the information do not follow a linear path and there is constant change in information in previous phases due to new findings in later activities [24, 25, 27, 28]. This end up causing inconsistencies that may increase the cost and time of development, as well as reworks and other negative impacts [28].

The communication, a basis for every integrated model, relies heavily on the semantic interpretation of each agent [24]. Across different phases, the different set of information may cause misinterpretation due to variable meanings for a term, e.g. 'orange' as a color and 'orange' as a fruit. This occurs due to the different knowledge background of developers and their experience [24, 25, 20]. Corroborating that affirmation, [20] states that the knowledge required for a phase of development may have different implications in later activities and can be as well changed due to the dynamic nature of product development.

Current literature, as demonstrated in [12], proposes a formalization through semantic annotations for interoperable applications, from different views in Product Life-Cycle Management. There were no annotations, however, that represented dynamic requirements. In [13], the author proposed a solution based on a model-driven ontology, which was limited to two domains and presented no evidence of further expansion and integration for more domains.

3.3 Cross-Requirement Representation Issues

Requirements are a component of every system, coming from various sources and in varied representations. In the context of product development and manufacturing, requirements may be classified as Functional (Parts Design, Functionality, etc.) and Non-Functional (International Standards, Quality objectives, Regulations, etc.) [18, 29]. Those requirements represent knowledge from different stakeholders' needs, and must be assured as complete, coherent and unique, to offer a trustworthy representation of reality [29, 30].

The requirements represent the main inputs in an ontology-driven semantic interoperability system [14]. As entries to such system, all of this knowledge must be 'semantically whole', as means to avoid further interoperation issues, by means of formal structures and well defined statements [14, 18]. In most cases, though, the process of abstraction of poorly defined statements end up generating divergent interpretation, which might have negative impacts related to uniqueness, comprehensiveness and, most important, traceability [14].

In [31], authors point that a correct, consistent and traceable information prevents further inconsistencies across product life-cycle. In the same research, though, authors do not provide a model to ensure requirements' traceability and no model, whatsoever on ways of optimizing the knowledge gathering and structuring process. [32] presented an interoperation model in multiple domains to ensure traceability through validation and verification methods. However, this model was limited only to early phases of a system.

Current literature, as found in [14], points out to standardized ways collected information and ensure traceable information through verification and validation. Despite that, the requirement gathering standard still relies in specialists' expertise and may require further research to develop a methodology extensible to other domains.

4 Discussion

One of the reasons for semantic issues occurrence in product development, as pointed out by literature, relates to the representation of requirements of a product by developers. Specialists tend to focus on a single phase of development, domain and requirement notation, e.g. the detailed design of mechanical components in a specific CAD software file. To enhance comprehension on the pointed-out issues, a model is proposed in Fig. 1. Three perspectives compose the three dimensions of the problem, detailed as follows:

- **Domain Perspective:** The Domain perspective reflects the multiple knowledge sources necessary to develop new products and its particularities;
- **Integrated Product Development Process Perspective:** The IPDP perspective reflects the whole process of development for a new product and/or customization. Each phase may spam through different domains of knowledge and requirement notations;
- **Requirements' Notation Perspective**: This perspective reflects the taxonomy and modeling of the represented knowledge from different requirement sources (Design, client's specifications, among others). The Requirement Notation has significant impacts on a programming level (XML models, RDF schema, for instance) and conceptual structure (representation of product's features) across different IPDP phases and domains.

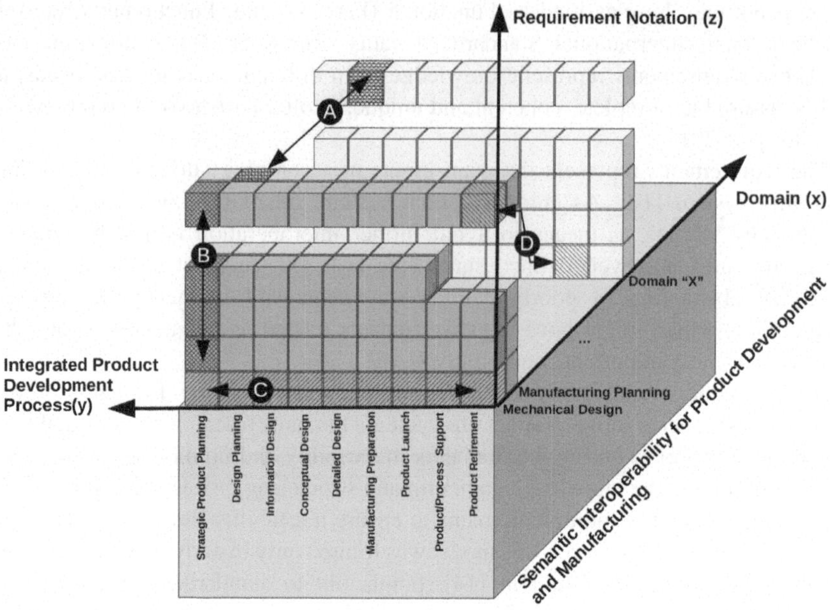

Fig. 1. Model of current issues in semantic interoperability for an integrated product development process

Each axis of the model contains one or more semantic interoperability issues related to product development and manufacturing. Each block represents a "piece" of structured knowledge. Across the 'Domain' dimension (x axis), the variety of knowledge of different domains implies in heterogeneous information that may cause semantic inconsistency along the process (Detail A of Fig. 1). Within a domain and a product development phase, there is a wide range of notations (z axis) to structure and represent knowledge, e.g. the product taxonomy and format of different CAD software files, presenting semantic interoperation issues on a conceptual level (Detail B of Fig. 1). Along the product development, the communication of different phases might present divergent information, resulting in issues related to information transfer, uniqueness, and traceability, among others (Detail C of Fig. 1). Last, but not least, there are the issues related to knowledge structures communicating without any similarity, which imply in lack of verifiable, trustworthy, unique, complete, coherent and traceable information (Detail D of Fig. 1).

As depicted, each perspective (depicted in three axis) have a related issue, showing that each dimension of the model might be responsible for misinterpretations in their way. Despite the role of each of these perspectives, a complex system must consider all three operating simultaneously, to better represent a real development process. In this aspect, the fourth issue represent the relation of these perspectives, which must be considered in equal importance as the other issues.

An important observation is that this model considers as source of information the needs of consumers and developers, translated into computational language and represented as "blocks" of structured knowledge. The dynamic nature of such requirements characterizes the complexity of managing and sharing such information without losing the original meaning.

The proposed model is a representation of the current issues on Semantic Interoperability for Product Development and Manufacturing, by a Requirement Notation perspective. Such model can provide a holistic view to the problems presented on selected research and act as a starting point for further research on the area. Further applications on semantic interoperability might be benefited from the model, as it provides a clear view on the current issues that might be addressed through new computational systems and methodologies.

As an inference on the model, the current issues for semantic interoperability in integrated product development process occur, in general, due to systems that heavily rely on the expertise of specialists and developers. As different specialists create singular solutions, it is necessary to develop a standardized way of collecting and structuring knowledge from products' requirements. Thus, such formal approach should benefit from a deeper study on the information flows and relations between domains.

Issues related to the requirements′ notation, as pointed out by literature, are still not well defined and do not present a formal and effective method for solution. The input of information has significant impacts on the final product and should be cautiously gathered. In this sense, a knowledge extraction model for semantic interoperability would benefit the final quality and completeness of information.

5 Conclusion

This paper presented a research that led to a model for current issues on semantic interoperability within an integrated product development process context. The model offers a fresh view on several issues related to semantically interoperable system through a requirement notation perspective, offering new questions for further research.

Current literature points out several challenging issues that need to be addressed to provide seamless information interoperation. Authors are already developing solutions, but there are still points to be observed in further research. In future applications, the notation aspect of requirements may be a differential aspect which will improve products, customers' satisfaction and reduce costs.

The high level of abstraction and needs for specialists may be a challenge to overcome in further models. By an input perspective for product life-cycle, a model to improve and increase automation in decision-making processes related to knowledge gathering and structuring is still necessary.

An aspect of this research, noted throughout its development is that further literature review by a systematic approach is necessary, to validate and define the state-of-the-art on related topics of study, covering all recent and relevant literature.

In order to expand this research further works are suggested, such as a systematic literature review on semantic interoperability through requirements′ notation perspective in PLM, development of a knowledge extraction model for semantic interoperability in IPDP and an integration of knowledge extraction models and a semantic reconciliation process.

References

1. Chungoora, N., Canciglieri, O., Young, R.I.M.: Towards expressive ontology-based approaches to manufacturing knowledge representation and sharing. Int. J. Comput. Integr. Manuf. **23**, 1059–1070 (2010)
2. Canciglieri Jr., O., Young, R.I.M.: Information sharing in multiviewpoint injection moulding design and manufacturing. Int. J. Prod. Res. **41**(7), 1565–1586 (2003)
3. Anjum, N., et al.: Verification of knowledge shared across design and manufacture using a foundation ontology. Int. J. Prod. Res. **51**, 6534–6552 (2013)
4. Chen, D., Doumeingts, G., Vernadat, F.: Architectures for enterprise integration and interoperability: past, present and future. Comput. Ind. **59**, 647–659 (2008)
5. Chungoora, N., Young, R.I.M.: Semantic reconciliation across design and manufacturing knowledge models: a logic-based approach. Appl. Ontol. **6**, 295–315 (2011)
6. Szejka, A. L., Canciglieri Jr., O., Loures, E.R., Panetto, H., Aubry, A.: Requirements interoperability method to support integrated product development. In: 45th Computers and Industrial Engineering, vol. 147, pp. 1–8 (2015)
7. Imran, M., Young, R.I.M.: The application of common logic based formal ontologies to assembly knowledge sharing. J. Intell. Manuf. **26**, 139–158 (2013)
8. Song, W., Ming, X., Wang, P.: Collaborative product innovation network: status review, framework, and technology solutions. Concurr. Eng. **21**, 55–64 (2013)
9. Schmidt, D.C.: Model-Driven Engineering. IEEE Comput. **39**(2), 25–31 (2006)
10. Strasunskas, D., Hakkarainen, S.E.: Domain model-driven software engineering: a method for discovery of dependency links. Inf. Softw. Technol. **54**(11), 1239–1249 (2012)
11. Barbieri, G., Fantuzzi, C., Borsari, R.: A model-based design methodology for the development of mechatronic systems. Mechatronics (2014)
12. Liao, Y., Lezoche, M., Panetto, H., Boudjlida, N., Loures, E.R.: Semantic annotation for knowledge explicitation in a product lifecycle management context: a survey. Comput. Ind. **71**, 24–34 (2015)
13. Chungoora, N., Young, R.I., Gunendran, G., Palmer, C., Usman, Z., Anjum, N.A., CuttingDecelle, A.F., Harding, J.A., Case, K.: A model-driven ontology approach for manufacturing system interoperability and knowledge sharing. Comput. Ind. **64**(4), 392–401 (2013)
14. Szejka, A.L., Júnior, O.C., Loures, E.R., Panetto, H., Aubry, A.: Proposal of a Model-Driven Ontology for Product Development Process Interoperability and Information Sharing. In: Harik, R., Rivest, L., Bernard, A., Eynard, B., Bouras, A. (eds.) PLM 2016. IAICT, vol. 492, pp. 158–168. Springer, Cham (2016). https://doi.org/10.1007/978-3-319-54660-5_15
15. Chungoora, N., Young, R.I.M.: The configuration of design and manufacture knowledge models from a heavyweight ontological foundation. Int. J. Prod. Res. **49**, 4701–4725 (2011)
16. Pereira, J.A., Canciglieri Jr., O., Lazzaretti, A.E., Souza, P.M.: Application of inte grated product development model oriented to R&D projects of the Brazilian electricity sector. Adv. Mater. Res. **945–949**, 401–409 (2014)
17. Stechert, C., Franke, H.J.: Managing requirements as the core of multi-disciplinary product development. CIRP J. Manufact. Sci. Technol. **1**(3), 153–158 (2009)
18. Szejka, A.L., Aubry, A., Panetto, H., Junior, O.C., Loures, E.R.: Towards a Conceptual Framework for Requirements Interoperability in Complex Systems Engineering. In: Meersman, R., et al. (eds.) OTM 2014. LNCS, vol. 8842, pp. 229–240. Springer, Heidelberg (2014). https://doi.org/10.1007/978-3-662-45550-0_24

19. Haveman, S.P., Bonnema, G.M.: Requirements for high level models supporting design space exploration in model-based systems engineering. Proc. Comput. Sci. **16**, 293–302 (2013)
20. Nattermann, R., Reiner, A.: Approach for a data-management-system and a proceeding model for the development of adaptronic systems. In: International Mechanical Engineering Congress and Exposition (ASME), pp. 1–10, Vancouver (2010)
21. Moneva, H., Hamberg, R. Punter, T.: A design framework for model-based development of complex systems. In: 32nd IEEE Real-Time Systems Symposium and 2nd Analytical Virtual Integration of Cyber-Physical Systems Workshop, pp. 1–8, Vienna, (2011)
22. Chungoora, N., et al.: A model-driven ontology approach for manufacturing system interoperability and knowledge sharing. Comput. Ind. **64**, 392–401 (2013)
23. Rozenfeld, H., Forcellini, F.A., Amaral, D.C., Toledo, J.C., Silva, S.L., Alliprandini, D.H., Scalice, R.K.: Gestão de Desenvolvimento de Produtos: Uma Referência Para a Melhoria do Processo. Saraiva, São Paulo (2006)
24. Stechert, C., Franke, H.J.: Managing requirements as the core of multi-disciplinary product development. CIRP J. Manuf. Sci. Technol. **1**(3), 153–158 (2009)
25. Pereira, J.A., Canciglieri Jr., O.: Product development model oriented for the R&D projects of the Brazilian electricity sector. Appl. Mech. Mater. **518**, 366–373 (2014)
26. de Moura Leite, A.F.C.S.M., Canciglieri, M.B., Szejka, A.L.: Canciglieri Jr., O.: The reference view for semantic interoperability in Integrated Product Development Process: The conceptual structure for injecting thin walled plastic products. J. Ind. Inf. Integr. **7**, 13–23 (2017)
27. Young, R.I.M., Gunendran, A.G., Cutting-Decelle, A.F., Gruninger, M.: Manufacturing knowledge sharing in PLM: a progression towards the use of heavy weight ontologies. Int. J. Product. Res. **45**(7), 1505–1519 (2007)
28. Kim, K.-Y., Manley, D.G., Yang, H.: Ontology-based assembly design and information sharing for collaborative product development. Comput. Des. **38**, 1233–1250 (2006)
29. Ramesh, B., Jarke, M.: Toward reference models for requirements traceability. IEEE Trans. Softw. Eng. **27**, 58–93 (2001)
30. Spanoudakis, G., Zisman, A., Pérez-Miñana, E., Krause, P.: Rule-based generation of requirements traceability relations. J. Syst. Softw. **72**(2), 105–127 (2004)
31. Pohl, K.: The three Dimensions of Requirements Engineering: a framework and its applications. Inform. Syst. **19**(3), 243–258 (1994)
32. Cleland-Huang, J., Chang, C.K., Sethi, G., Javvaji, K., Haijian, H., Jinchun, X.: Automating speculative queries through event-based requirements traceability. In: Proceedings of IEEE Joint International Conference on Requirements Engineering, pp. 289–296 (2002)

Current Issues in Multiple Domain Semantic Reconciliation for Ontology-Driven Interoperability in Product Design and Manufacture

Matheus Beltrame Canciglieri[1], Anderson Luis Szejka[1(✉)], Osiris Canciglieri Junior[1], and Lucy Yoshida[2]

[1] Industrial and Systems Engineering Graduate Program, Pontifical Catholic University of Parana, Curitiba, Brazil
{matheus.canciglieri,anderson.szejka, osiris.canciglieri}@pucpr.br
[2] NHS Electronic Systems, Curitiba, Brazil
lucy@nhs.com.br

Abstract. The competitive environment in which the manufacturing industries are inserted ensures that to achieve competitiveness the businesses must react quickly to change and understand the balance of possible options when making complex decisions. For a high quality, timely decision across a range of complex factors, it is necessary high-quality information and knowledge available at the time of the decision making. However, each business sector requires its own view on the enterprises information it needs. This represents a problem as current software solution provide local support but do not provide trans-disciplinary interoperability that is critical to long term competitiveness. The exploration of semantic technologies has the potential to solve this problem using formalizations to share the knowledge across multi-domain environments, these systems can provide more comprehensive solutions than the approaches employed to date. The aim of this paper is to study the current issues regarding the application of ontology-driven interoperability for Product Development and Manufacture. This objective will be achieved through a literature review on Semantic Interoperability, Semantic Rules and Multiple Domains and a Discussion on the current issues of each topic. This research showed that the knowledge enrichment introduced by knowledge translation models aids the creation of an interoperable environment between the product design and its manufacture.

Keywords: Semantic interoperability · Semantic rules · Multiple domains
Product design and manufacture

1 Introduction

In recent years the trend of product design is towards the formation of business collaborative alliances between enterprises and as consequence the manufacturing companies have been focusing on a more knowledge intensive product development

Published by Springer Nature Switzerland AG 2018.
P. Chiabert et al. (Eds.): PLM 2018, IFIP AICT 540, pp. 126–135, 2018.
https://doi.org/10.1007/978-3-030-01614-2_12

process with the aim of reduce the overall product design time and increase its activities efficiency. To achieve this aim, the enterprises relay more heavily in emerging computer network technologies, such as, the Semantic Web [1–3].

The Semantic Web is a web of relations among entities, therefore its role is to operate as a virtual model base in a way where the product design collaborators can have ubiquitous access to the product model, through a client interface, while understanding the semantic and context of the information.

Interoperability, a systemization of knowledge, is one of the key aspects of the semantic web and is reached through ontological integration with the aim to create a common ontology for all the information sources in a scenario of information exchange [4–7].

An ontology is an explicit, formal specification of terms in a domain and the relations between these terms. [8], that is, an ontology is a data structure of a knowledge domains concepts and how they relate with each other, in a machine-readable format [9, 27].

The knowledge from each node within the product development and manufacture may be formalized which will result in multiple viewpoints associated to the representation of artifacts and different depictions of similar concepts [10, 27].

To [11], these multiple representations of an artifact or a concept is known as semantic heterogeneity, which is an obstacle to semantic interoperability to solve this problem the process of semantic reconciliation is used. This process is traditionally made by hand by the database administrator or a designer due to its complexity. However, with the introduction of the semantic web this process shifts towards a more automated environment.

Therefore, the aim of this paper is to is to study the current issues regarding the application of ontology-driven interoperability for Product Development and Manufacture in order to provide sustenance to a proposal of an ontology-driven semantic reconciliation model that aims to use ontology mapping techniques to aid the product design and manufacture processes knowledge share.

2 Problem Statement

Globalization, collaboration and cooperation have contributed to the emergence of a knowledge sharing culture in open and large environments [12, 13, 27]. However, communication between project teams is often hindered by the lack of clarity in the terms used. This represents that the context in which the information is exchanged affects the overall meaning and interpretation of the shared implicit and explicit knowledge. Therefore, two problems may appear: (I) the same term is being applied to different concepts (semantic problem) and (II) different terms are being applied to the same concept (syntax problem) [14]. These problems are known as semantic heterogeneity.

One approach to solve these problems, is the creation of an ontology in which a specific domain's concepts and terms are defined and can be understood through the different teams across that domain. Nevertheless, this presents a different issue: *How can the knowledge be shared effectively through multiple domain systems without the problems caused by semantic heterogeneity?*

The use of different ontology throughout the product design and manufacture may hinder the creation of an interoperable environment as the different domains have different concepts and the exchange of this information through the product development without the proper processing may result in loss of product quality, greater development time and costs.

3 Current Issues

The current issues were researched and structured according to the main topics related to the research objective: (i) Semantic Interoperability; (ii) Semantic Reconciliation; (iii) Semantic Rules.

3.1 Semantic Interoperability

Even though the product development process presents a holistic approach to provide the necessary information to the different phases of the product design and manufacturing, it has been identified misinterpretations and mistakes during the latter stages of the product development [15]. These mistakes become more significant when the activities of the design and manufacture cost 85% of the products final cost [16]. Consequently, the information sharing across the different stages of product development and manufacture must be done efficiently to ensure that the product developed has the desired quality with cost and time optimization.

This is a semantic interoperability problem for which the meaning associated to the captured information must be shared across different domains inside a system without any loss of meaning and intent during the exchange process [17]. The most common method to ensure that there is no loss of meaning in the information exchange process has been the definition of common information models [18, 19]. In this context, the construction of ontologies is a viable solution on the formalization of these common information models and on the sharing of the formal information throughout the stages of the product development process, which, consequently, provides increased knowledge in the domains of application [19, 20].

An Ontology is defined as "a lexicon of specialized terminology along with some specification of the meaning of terms on the lexicon" [21], where the lexicon is the vocabulary of a knowledge domain. Therefore, an important differentiation can be made between ontologies by their degree of expressiveness. In this differentiation, simple ontologies, which formalizes only a taxonomy of concepts and basic relations between them are referred as lightweight ontologies. When a lightweight ontology is enriched through the insertion of axioms in the form of constraints, they are classified as a heavyweight ontology. Nevertheless, the use of ontologies is restricted to the purpose of its application, that is, the knowledge structure formalized in an ontology has little reusability outside the scope of its application [17].

Despite the semantic formalism created using ontologies, a limitation appears when the need to work in multiple knowledge domains is presented, as the semantic formalism of the ontology cannot ensure the sharing of the information and its meaning through different domains. However, this problem is moderated with the development of ontology mapping methodologies, which can create relationships between terms in different ontologies of different domains [16].

3.2 Semantic Reconciliation

The increase in the perception that to make better decision, it is essential to have usable ou actionable information, which can be defined as knowledge, in an integrated environment between diverse resources. Therefore, the importance of resolving semantic heterogeneity has gained attention in various domains [17, 22].

The emerging semantic web, which is a specific form of formal logic that can be used efficiently in a virtual environment, has used descriptive logic based ontologies as one of its primary applications. These ontologies can take advantage of better expressive constructs, however, when used in a multiple domain environment they suffer from limitations to share the knowledge efficiently between them [16, 17, 22].

For example, consider two different classification systems, a simple query is finding all the data corresponding to a term in both information sources, however, this query can only be efficiently answered if both of the systems have their semantics well understood. If these systems are conceptualized in two different ontologies the comparation of terms is a challenge due to the great variation of the detail level and logic between these ontologies [17, 22].

To solve this limitation a shared ontology approach can be adopted. This approach enables terminological reasoning over the definition of classes in the descriptive logic ontologies by considering the axioms, set of relations and set of class definitions defined in the shared ontology [23, 26].

Even with the considerable effort that has been input to address the obstacles of semantic interoperability brought by semantic mismatches, there are still several challenges to improve the semantic reconciliation techniques [25, 26]. Nowadays, the most popular techniques are the ontology mapping/matching.

Initial work on these techniques focused mainly on the overall nomenclature of the ontologies, which lead to various conflicts in a multiple domain environment or even in similar domain ontologies that uses different taxonomies [25]. However ontology mapping techniques have been a key direction to solve semantic heterogeneity issues using the reconciliation of the semantics of the ontology based models. Even though, several perspectives of the ontology mapping methods have been proposed, there is a consensus over the types of methods that can be applied to do a ontology mapping/matching. Figure 1 presents these methods [2, 10].

Ontology mapping methods can be classified as one of 4 categories or as hybrids of these. The ontology mapping categories are, as shown in Fig. 1: (i) techniques that merge two ontologies to construct a new ontology from the individual ontologies (Detail A); (ii) methods that through a transformation function, transforms a given ontology into another based on the rules specified (Detail C); (iii) techniques that establish binary relations between the vocabularies of two ontologies (Detail B) and (iv) methods that enable specific portions of two ontologies to be reconciled with the use of semantic mappings made through an articulation ontology (Detail D) [2, 10, 17].

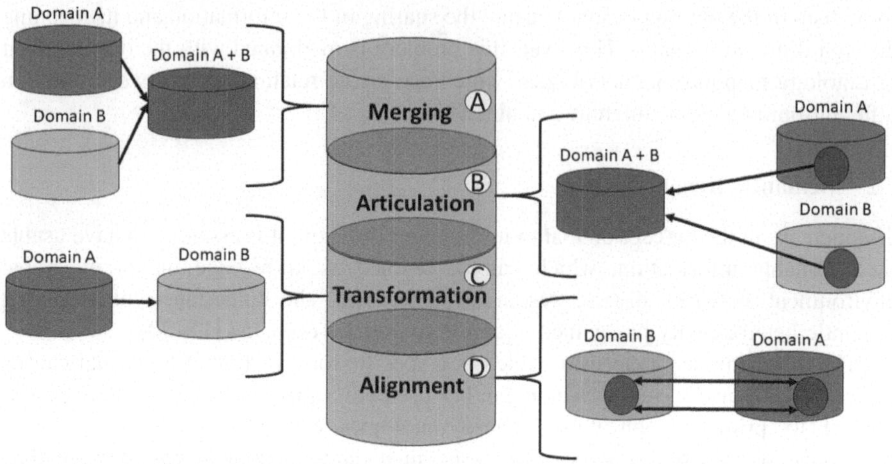

Fig. 1. Ontology mapping/matching techniques categorization. Adapted from [10].

Even though ontology mapping/matching has been key to solve semantic heterogeneity problems, there is presently of methods that rely on lexical similarity matching, which is not optimal from a semantic interoperability viewpoint. This is because in a multiple domain environment similar terms are used across different groups to refer to diverse concepts. Ergo, it is only through the semantics associated to these terms that existing differences can be identified, highlighting the need to capture semantics in the first place [10].

On the other hand, ontological formalisms lite the Web Ontology Language (OWL) support built-ins for ontology mapping, however, these built-ins have limitations when mapping the semantic content of manufacturing ontologies and their associated knowledge bases [10, 17, 26].

Moreover, there are requirements to aid the construction of mapping/matching techniques which can be formally interpreted and are focused at indentifying potential solutions for semantic mismatches. Therefore, enabling the reconciliation process at several levels, including the instance level, of ontology based models. These requirements aid the reconciliation process to have better accuracy, automation and reduces the time that takes to resolve cross-model correspondences [17, 25].

3.3 Semantic Rules

The web ontology language (OWL) relies only on description logic, however both description logic and rules are required for a semantic web application because they can overcome expressiveness limitations through extensions of different knowledge domains. Nevertheless, each paradigm supports specific reasoning services and for them to work efficiently there is a need to a close integration between the description logic and semantic rules [3].

The semantic web rule language (SWRL) extends the description logic of the OWL with the ability to write rules and permitting the addition of horn logic rules to the

OWL descriptions. This characteristic allows the construction of more complex relations and can be used to define more precisely the concepts in the ontology. The SWRL rules are an implication between an antecedent and a consequent that can be read as when the conditions specified in the antecedent are true then the conditions on the consequent must also be true [3, 4, 24].

Although the SWRL is supported by the Protégé ontology editor and by several rule inference engines such as Pellet, it has been around fore more than 10 years making it very unlikely that it will become a W3C standard, therefore difficult to reach out to the industrial world [24].

An alternative to the SWRL is the SPARQL Inference Notation (SPIN), which has become an industrial standard and uses representations of the SPARQL inqueries to construct rules and constraints in semantic web models. SPIN combines concepts from object oriented languages, query languages and rule based systems to describe objects behaviors in the semantic web, that is, it links class definitions with queries in order to capture constraints and rules that will formalize the expected behavior of those classes.

Since SPIN is represented in RDF, the rules and constraints can be shared with the class definitions they are associated with. This attachment of rules to the classes they refer to aids in the maintenance of the database.

The SPIN vocabulary defines several properties that can be used to attach SPARQL queries to the classes and the reasoning engines will construct inferred RDF triples from the currently asserted information in the model. These queries are interpreted in the context of the classes to which they refer to [24].

The use of SPIN to create the constraints and relationships of the concepts described in a semantic web model allows it to have an object oriented view in which the SPARQL queries play similar role to the functions and methods. The Inheritance is treated in the sense that any rule defined for super classes will also be applied to the subclasses. This means SPIN rules can only further restrict what has been defined in the upper classes of the model [24].

4 Discussion

This research works towards finding evidence that demonstrates the current issues regarding semantic interoperability, semantic reconciliation and semantic rules in a multiple domain environment. These issues provide sustenance to the proposal of an ontology-driven semantic reconciliation model that aims to use ontology mapping techniques to aid the product design and manufacture processes knowledge share, therefore, ensuring higher quality products and cost reduction of the product design steps and its manufacture. Additionally, the model aims uses semantic rules to better simulate the behaviour of the concepts thus optimizing the reconciliation and translation process of the model.

The mapping of the current issues revealed the limitations of a ontology driven interoperability system when it is used in a multiple domain environment, and, also, how the sharing of ambiguous information in such an environment can reduce the competitiveness of an enterprise as it will raise the costs and diminish its products quality.

In order to ensure a semantic interoperability environment across multiple domains, ontology mapping/matching techniques are necessary as through them it is possible to create a multiple domain ontology that contains all the relevant information to the domains and has translation mechanisms which will translate the concepts within this ontology to all other domains. However, these techniques are made mostly by hand which makes them expensive and time demanding. This makes their use in industrial applications limited.

The semantic rules aid in the creation of a semantic interoperable environment as they create more complex class expressions and enable the simulation more accurate of the concepts behaviour and, therefore, infer the behaviour of similar concepts integrating the different knowledge domains. Yet there are limitations to their use as there is not a method to conceive these rules outside the determination of an expert, which makes their creation an expensive and long process. The main language to the development of semantic rules, SWRL, has some limitations that are being solved through SPARQL based rule languages as SPIN.

During the product development and manufacture the departments envolved must manage their resources and at the same time need to communicate, cooperate efficiently with the other teams in the process. Therefore the issues presented in this research represent the biggest problems that interfere with the application of an efficiently

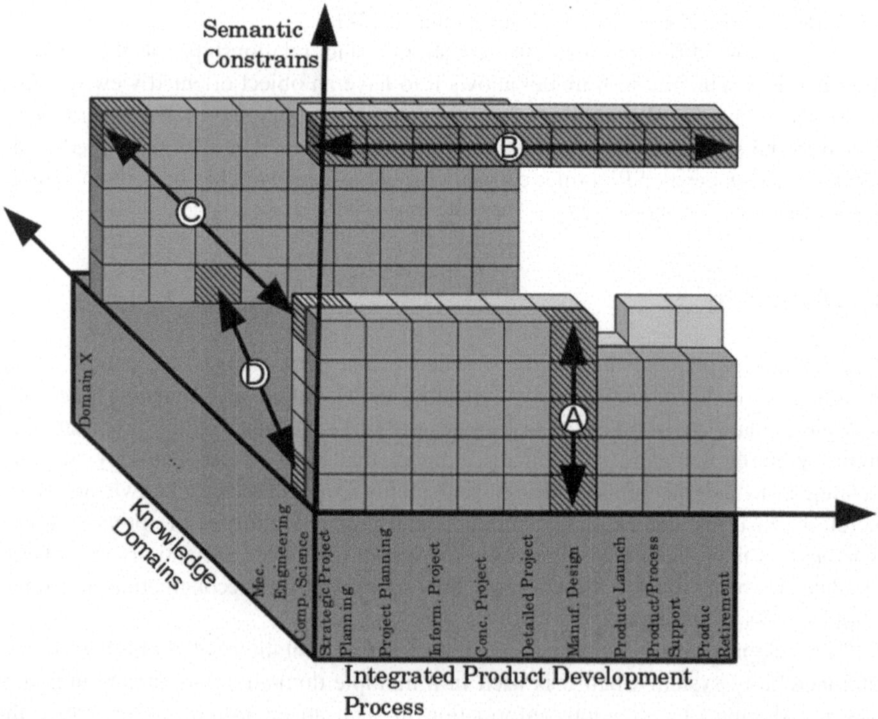

Fig. 2. Diagram of interoperable limitations regarding product deign and manufacture, multiple domains and semantic constrains.

multiple domain communication and cooperation system that creates a true knowledge share environment which reduces the product's development and manufacture time, cost and ensures its quality.

Thus, the essential requirements for effective and efficient collaboration among enterprises are agility and interoperability.

Through the analysis of multiple domains and their semantic constrains throughout the product development process, a model can be developed which represents the points where the semantic constrains and rules may hinder the development of an interoperable environment as can be seen in the Fig. 2.

Detail A represents the possibility of ambiguous constraints present in a same domain and same product design stage. Detail B shows the possibility of having heterogeneous constraints in a same domain but in different stages of the product development process. Detail C characterises the heterogeneity between constraints in the same development stage, however, between different knowledge domains. Finally, Detail D represents the heterogeneity between constrains in different stages of the product design and in different domains.

5 Conclusion

This paper presented a research that lead to the development of a model which shows some of the critical issues that hinder the development of a true ontology-driven interoperable environment between product design and manufacture. These areas are essential to ensure a competitive position for an enterprise in the global competitive environment it is inserted.

The standardized and formalised knowledge that is captured by an ontology driven system allows it to be retrieved, shared and reused in different stages of the product development and manufacture and, also, through the process of relating concepts made in the ontology design the information can be captured in its entirety as well as extended as the need arrises. This integration improves the collaboration in a multiple domain environment and across network based designs as it conveys several characteristics, that are often ambiguous, in a non-ambiguous manner. These knowledge structures can, also, be used to create optimization models.

The high degree of expressiveness of a ontology-driven structure enables the establishment of resolvable and meaningful mappings across knowledge models which help support the consistency of the ontology matching while also avoiding the drawbacks of subjectivity in the mapping transaction that are a consequence of extensive human intervention.

In order to continue this research several subjects are proposed for future works: Research semantic rules development methods for ontology mapping/matching; Map product development and manufacture structures and important concepts for the development of reference ontologies which can be then specialized to specific projects; Research and define a Semantic Reconciliation Method for Multi-Domain Environments.

References

1. Engineous. In: Engineous International Symposium Workshop, Novi, Mi, October 10–12 (2005)
2. Kim, K.-Y., Chin, S., Kwon, O., Ellis, R.D.: Ontology-based modeling and integration of morphological characteristics of assembly joints for network-based collaborative assembly design. Artif. Intell. Eng. Des. Anal. Manuf. **23**, 71–88 (2009)
3. Zhao, W., Liu, J.K.: OWL/SWRL representation methodology for express-driven product information model part I. Implementation methodology. Comput. Ind. **59**, 580–589 (2008)
4. Biletskiy, Y., Vorochek, O., Medovoy, A.: Building ontologies for interoperability among learning objects and learners. In: Orchard, B., Yang, C., Ali, M. (eds.) IEA/AIE 2004. LNCS (LNAI), vol. 3029, pp. 977–986. Springer, Heidelberg (2004). https://doi.org/10.1007/978-3-540-24677-0_100
5. Mizoguchi, R.: Tutorial on ontological engineering part 1: introduction to ontological engineering. New Gener. Comput. **21**(4), 365–384 (2003)
6. Mizoguchi, R.: Tutorial on ontological engineering part 2: ontology development tools and languages. New Gener. Comput. **22**(2), 61–96 (2004)
7. Mizoguchi, R.: Tutorial on ontological: engineering part 3 advanced course of ontological engineering. New Gener. Comput. **22**(2), 198–220 (2004)
8. Gruber, T.R.: A translation approach to portable ontology specification. Knowl. Acquis. **5** (2), 199–220 (1993)
9. Fensel, D.: Ontologies: A Silver Bullet For Knowledge Management And Electronic Commerce, 2nd edn. Springer, Heidelberg (2004). https://doi.org/10.1007/978-3-662-09083-1
10. Chungoora, N., Young, R.I.M.: Semantic reconciliation across design and manufacturing knowledge models: a logic-based approach. Appl. Ontol. **6**(4), 295–315 (2011)
11. Gal, A., Anaby-Tavor, A., Trombetta, A., Montesi, D.: A framework for modeling and evaluating automatic semantic reconciliation. Int. J. Very Large Databases **14**(1), 50–67 (2005)
12. Beau, S., Taouil, F.-T., Hassanaly, P.: Elaborate knowledge between necessity and opportunity. In: Proceedings of the Third International Conference of Information Systems and Economic Intelligence (SIIE), Sousse, Tunisia, pp. 317–330 (2010)
13. van Sinderen, M.: Challenges and solutions in enterprise computing. Enterp. Inf. Syst. **2**(4), 341–346 (2008)
14. Harding, J.A., Shahbaz, M.: Manufacturing system engineering ontology for semantic interoperability across extended project teams. Int. J. Prod. Res. **42**(24), 5099–5118 (2004)
15. Penciuc, D., Durupt, A., Belkadi, F., Eynard, B., Rowson, H.: Towards a PLM interoperability for a collaborative design support system. Procedia CIRP **25**, 369–376 (2014)
16. Rozenfeld, H., et al.: Gestão De Desenvolvimento De Produtos: Uma Referência Para A Melhoria Do Processo Product Development Management: A Reference To Improve The Process. Saraiva, São Paulo (2006)
17. Chungoora, N., Young, R.I.M.: A framework to support semantic interoperability in product design and manufacture. Ph.d. Thesis, Loughborough University, Loughborough (2010)
18. Junior, O.C., Young, R.I.M.: Information mapping across injection moulding design and manufacture domains. Int. J. Prod. Res. **41**(7), 4437–4462 (2010)
19. Yang, A., et al.: A multi-agent system to facilitate component-based process modeling and design. Comput. Chem. Eng. **32**(10), 2290–2305 (2008)

20. Gomez-Perez, A., Corcho, O., Lopez, M.F.: Ontological Engineering: With Examples from the Areas Of Knowledge Management, E-Commerce and the Semantic Web, p. 404. Springer, London (2004). https://doi.org/10.1007/b97353
21. ISO 18629, Industrial Automation Systems and Integration – Process Specification Language (2005)
22. Durbha, S.S., King, R.L., Shah, V.P., Younan, N.H.: A framework for semantic reconciliation of disparate earthobservation thematic data. Comput. Geosci. **35**, 761–773 (2009)
23. Stuckenschmidt, H., Harmelen, F.V.: Information Sharing on the Semantic Web, p. 276. Springer, Heidelberg (2005). https://doi.org/10.1007/b138282
24. Bassiliades, N.: Swrl2spin: a tool for transforming SWRL rule bases in owl ontologies to object-oriented spin rules, pp. 1–14. Arxiv (2018)
25. Kumar, S.K., Harding, J.A.: Ontology mapping using description logic and bridging axioms. Comput. Ind. **64**(1), 19–28 (2013)
26. Song, S., Zhang, X., Qin, G.: Multi-domain ontology mapping based on semantics. Cluster Comput. **20**(4), 3379–3391 (2017)
27. Nagy, M., Vargas-Vera, M.: Multiagent ontology mapping framework for the semantic web. IEEE Trans. Syst. Man Cybern. Part A Syst. Hum. **41**(4), 693 (2011)

A Consumer Centric VMI Methodology for a Collaborative Supply Chain Model – An Answer to Demand Volatility

Abhro Choudhury[1,2(✉)], Nicolas Maranzana[1], Frederic Segonds[1], and Sandrine Gautier[2]

[1] Arts et Métiers, LCPI, ParisTech, 151 Boulevard de l'Hôpital, 75013 Paris, France
abhro.choudhury@ensam.eu

[2] Procter & Gamble, 163 Quai Aulagnier, 92600 Asnières-sur-Seine, France

Abstract. The increase in the market competitiveness and demand volatility is urging organizations to be more responsive to the customer needs. An out of stock scenario is a huge loss in the consumer products sector as it is a loss of revenue and a loss of brand loyalty which cannot be afforded. This raises the need for a consumer centric collaborative supply chain model. A Vendor Managed Inventory (VMI) practice is a collaborative inventory replenishment technique engaging the suppliers and the retailers. This paper proposes a next generation VMI methodology which is based on a cloud environment which can integrate the customer demand in the entire value chain. This would eventually result in higher customer service levels and inventory on-shelf availability. This proposed methodology has been implemented as a case study with one of the major clients, various parameters such as customer satisfaction and demand fluctuations were studied and compared with the present scenario. The methodology proposed here will benefit both sides of the supply chain (suppliers and retailers) by improving the visibility ultimately resulting in an improved collaborative supply chain model. This paper also intends to highlight the importance of collaboration of all role players in the entire end to end chain.

Keywords: Collaborative supply chain · Vendor managed inventory Cloud · Demand forecast

1 Introduction

In today's complex business structure, managing order-delivery processes has been a major issue in supply chain management. With the advancement in information technology, a supply chain has progressed a lot through information sharing. Despite the advancement and enablement of having higher visibility in the entire supply chain, there a lot of areas which are still left unattended and thus having a scope of improvement.

Vendor Managed Inventory (VMI) is one of the most widely discussed alternative for order replenishments for improving multi-firm supply chain efficiency. It is a replenishment strategy where the traditional ordering process is eliminated, and the

P. Chiabert et al. (Eds.): PLM 2018, IFIP AICT 540, pp. 136–146, 2018.
https://doi.org/10.1007/978-3-030-01614-2_13

supplier has the right and responsibility to make stock replenishment decisions based on regular automatic inventory and/or sales data from buyer (ECR handbook) [1]. It was popularized by Procter & Gamble and Wal-Mart in 1980s and since then the use of VMI has grown in various industries. VMI is a way to cut costs and keep inventory levels low in the entire supply chain and evidences has shown the it has significantly improved the supply chain performance [2]. VMI partnership is a collaborative method where the suppliers are authorized to manage the inventory and make inventory replenishment decisions for the buyer. The integration of operations between suppliers and buyers is done through information sharing using technologies such as Electronic Data Exchange (EDI) or other internet-based protocols which is on a real-time basis. One of the major benefits of the supplier controlling the stocks is that using this information the whole chain can be more organized. This enables to do have better production planning, delivery schedules and eventually managed order volumes and having a control over the inventory levels. The reason why VMI is getting popular among industries is reduced inventory costs for the supplier and the buyer, improved customer service levels and higher vehicle fill rates [3]. More accurate sales forecasting and improved inventory distribution helps in achieving the better efficiency. VMI also play a substantial role in diminishing the bull whip effect as there is elimination of decision making and elimination of time delays in information flows. The research question which is studied in this work is what the future of Vendor Managed Inventory would be and how can this next version of VMI would help an enterprise to improve and synchronize the entire end to end supply chain. The article has been divided in sections and we start with a detailed state of the art analysis in Sect. 2, the proposed methodology in Sect. 3, followed by a case study implementation in Sect. 4 and then in Sect. 5, the conclusion and future work.

2 State of the Art

An in-depth review of the existing literature has been done to understand the difference in functionality of a VMI based supply chain over a traditional one and eventually to identify the gaps in the system.

2.1 Overview of a Traditional Supply Chain

A supply chain is a system consisting of material suppliers, production facilities, distribution centers and customers who are all linked together via the downstream feed-forward flow of materials (deliveries) and the upstream feedback flow of information (orders), as shown in Fig. 1 [4]. In a traditional supply chain, each player is responsible for his own inventory control and production or distribution ordering activities. One fundamental characteristic and problem that all players in a traditional supply chain face is the decision making of the quantity to be ordered to the suppliers, to enable a supply chain which can satisfy the customers' demands which leads to inventory control issues.

According to Axsater [5] the purpose of an inventory control system is to transform incomplete information about the market place into coordinated plans for production

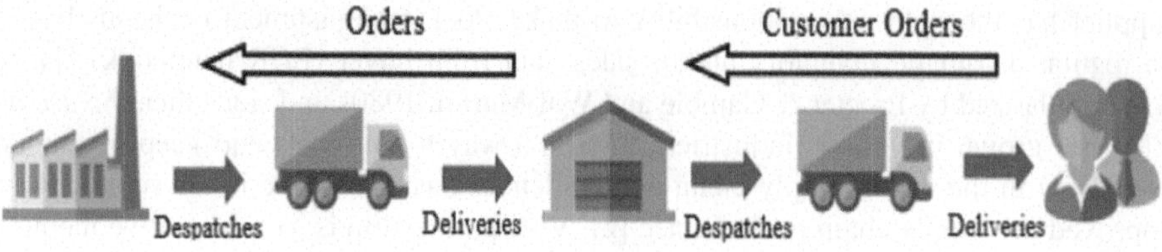

Fig. 1. Overview of a traditional supply chain

and replenishment of raw materials. Normally users tackle the inventory control problem by inspecting data relating to demands, inventory levels and orders in the pipeline and either, in a structured, mathematical way (for example, by using a decision support system and a designed replenishment rule), or in a less formal way (by using their own experience and judgement), place orders up the supply chain. In the real world, the ordering process is frequently biased according to who is perceived as the most important customer. The traditional supply chain is characterized by each player in the supply chain basing his production orders or delivery orders solely on his sales to his customer, on his inventory levels. Each player in the supply chain only has information about what their immediate customers want and not on what the end customer wants. This does not allow suppliers to gain any insight into what their customers are ordering to cover their own inventory-based customer service level and cost requirements and what the customers are ordering to satisfy immediate customer demand [6]. This lack of visibility of real demand can and does cause several problems in a supply chain if it is not properly designed and even then, fluctuations cannot be eliminated.

2.2 Overview of VMI Supply Chain

In reacting to this scenario, many companies have been compelled to improve their supply chain operations by sharing demand and inventory information with their suppliers and customers. VMI is a supply chain strategy where the vendor or supplier is given the responsibility of managing the customer's stock.

VMI has become more popular in the grocery sector in the last 15 years due to the success of retailers such as Wal-Mart [7, 8]. Additionally, it is only relatively recently that the necessary information and communication technology has become economically available to enable the strategy. A research work has implemented VMI in a supply chain using data available from a popular ERP system and a spreadsheet-based decision support system [9]. Moreover, VMI is not a new strategy; it was eloquently discussed in a presentation of a conceptual framework for designing a production control system [10].

VMI comes in many different forms. Familiar names are quick response (QR) [11], synchronized consumer response (SCR), continuous replenishment (CR), efficient consumer response (ECR) [12], forecasting and replenishment (CPFR) [13] depending on sector application, ownership issues and scope of implementation. However, they are all specific as applications of VMI, as summarized conceptually in Fig. 2.

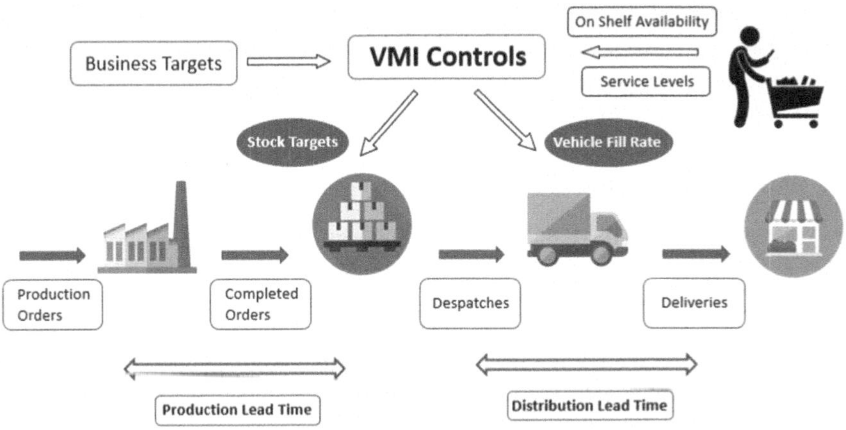

Fig. 2. Overview of a VMI supply chain

2.3 Information Sharing and Integration

The implementation of VMI requires both the sharing of information and the coordination and integration of processes between buyers and suppliers. In general, buyers share demand and inventory status information with their suppliers (information sharing) so that suppliers can take over the inventory control and purchasing function from the buyers (process integration).

A stream of research has quantitatively studied the value of information sharing in supply chains, especially the causes and consequences of the bullwhip effect. The bullwhip effect is the phenomenon whereby the size of inventory overages and shortages increases the further a firm is from final consumer demand in a supply chain. Much of this literature has shown that the bullwhip effect can be minimized through information sharing in the supply chain [14, 15]. The result of a decrease in the bullwhip effect is an improvement in supply chain performance (e.g., the lowering of inventory levels and the reduction in cycle times) [16]. Another work presented an analytical model for coordinating inventory and transportation decisions in VMI systems and found that the vendor's actual inventory requirement is partly determined by the parameters of the shipment-release policy in use [17]. This result holds because vendors have the autonomy to retain orders until an agreeable dispatch time is reached, with the expectation that an economical consolidated dispatch quantity will accumulate before an order is dispatched.

It was predicted that information technologies would allow for closer integration of adjacent firms in the supply chain through the development of electronic linkages (e.g., electronic data interchange). The ability to smooth supply and demand, and thus reduce the possibility of inventory overages or shortages, has been suggested as a key benefit of systems like VMI, Just in Time, quick response, and efficient consumer response that integrate the operations of supply chain members [18]. However, several studies have found that supply chain integration does not necessarily result in benefits for both suppliers and buyers. A buyer's inventory costs may be reduced only because costs are transferred to the supplier [19, 20]. A cloud-based service-oriented Demand Driven Supply Network could eventually increase business interoperability thus giving a global visibility of the entire cycle [21]. In the next section, we would discuss the future of VMI systems which we name it as VMI 2.0 – Smart Replenishment.

2.4 VMI Model Functionality

The working of the VMI Model is being explained by using the working model of Procter & Gamble and its service provider Datalliance [22] which has a SaaS working model thus forming a link between P&G and its VMI Client. It is a cyclic process which starts by Datalliance sending an inquiry based on the demand forecasts to P&G and then an order is created by the analysts. This order is transmitted to the client for addition of prices and eventually it returns to P&G thus completing the entire cycle of the information flow (Fig. 3).

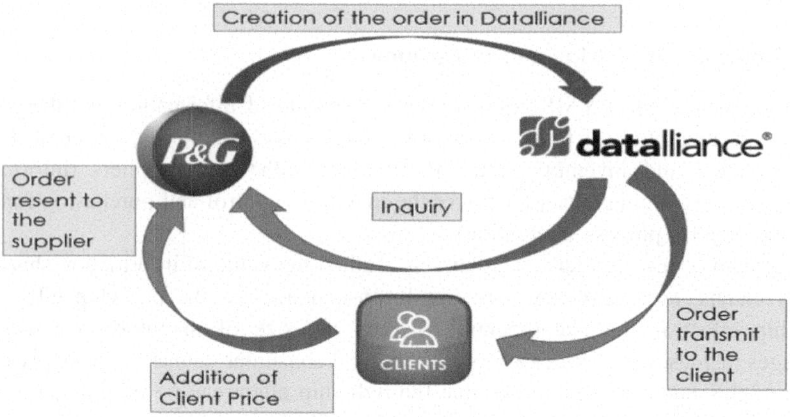

Fig. 3. Information flow and interaction between P&G, Datalliance and Client

2.5 Synthesis

The sections above discuss about the existing methods and the critical analysis shows there are quite a few gaps. The research gaps have been well mentioned out in the recent extensive literature study [23]. Therefore, we have focussed on every individual player of the supply chain and have attempted in reducing the existing gaps by our proposed methodology discussed in Sect. 3. The work also focuses on the importance of having an entire end to end view to the methodology eventually leading in a more synchronised Supply Chain.

3 Proposal of a Methodology

This article proposes VMI 2.0 – Smart Replenishment which is the next step in the domain of vendor managed inventory and thus would be trying to close the gaps in the existing process. We have defined the major segments which is the customers/shoppers, customer interface, distribution and manufacturing. We have touched each of the four segments aiming to have an end to end synchronized supply chain. The first step is store order forecasting which is basically having a better forecast at a store level thus being more precise demand forecasts. It calls for a very good collaboration with the client as it is based on the data sharing at the actual buying level. The second step is the product segmentation which allows us to concentrate on the product which are more profitable and have market penetration for the future. Then it is followed by smart ordering which is the even distribution of the promotional and shelf orders to avoid peaks. The fourth stage enables us to know the economic order quantity balancing to transportation and inventory costs. The last being the live availability check which is a real time check on the products at the production level thus ultimately having better vehicle fill rates as we would order only the products which are available (Fig. 4).

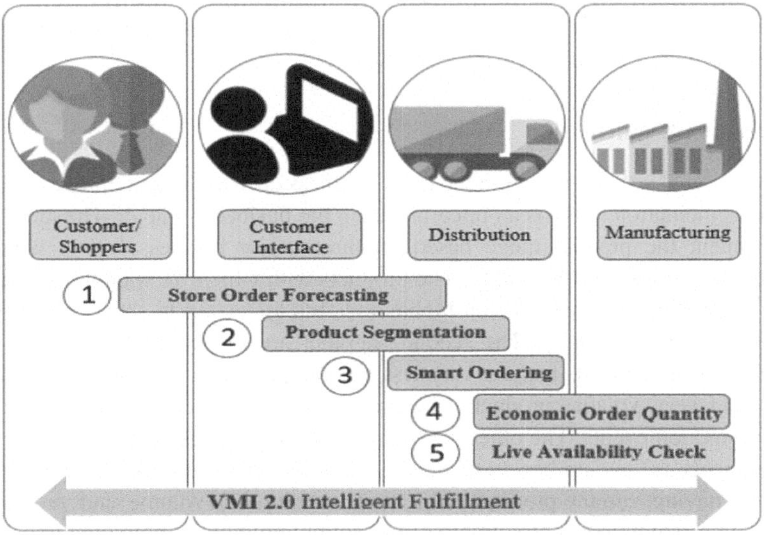

Fig. 4. Proposal of a VMI 2.0 – smart replenishment

The coming sub sections in the paper deals with all the methodology phases which were deployed and tested at P&G and the results were analyzed.

4 Case Study - Implementation

The proposed methodology has been explained in further details in this section and mode of implementation and the expected outcomes. The realized results have been discussed later.

4.1 Store Order Forecasting

The idea here is to leverage store order forecasting data thus allowing us to have a more precise demand forecasts eventually enabling to be proactive rather than reactive. The key role player is the collaboration which and then finally using the real-time data at store level to optimize the replenishment of the Promotional only products. And for the shelf products which are played in promotion to have no impact on the on-shelf availability. The parameters like which time of the year, type of promotion, a promotion done recently or not, location of the store etc. were considered to predict the sales. We took two years history to create predict the sales but till now we have not achieved in do exact prediction for all type which clearly means there are other parameters which are affecting the sales. One of them is the climate/weather which we think is impacting the results. This is still under development for higher precision but at this present stage we can estimate, and this is heling the sales team to push for more volumes and thus helping in business intelligence.

4.2 Product Segmentation

Categorization is very important in the retail business decision making process and thus product segmentation today is an integral part in the business strategy. The idea behind is to segment the product range based on three major business factors which are Volume, Profitability and Volatility. The products with which we want to penetrate the market which may or may not be profitable now, but the idea is to create a perturbation in the market as a strategy. The second segment are the products which has high volumes as well as profits and are very less volatile products. The third being high on volume and very volatile products, these are mainly products which perform only during promotion events. The objective would be to do most of the business in the first three segments as they are beneficial for the company and for the consumers. Then we would be having certain products which are medium in volume and profitability. Finally, the products which are low in volume and very less profitable which is not at all of interest to the company thus business of such products to be discontinued. We can very well say that the percentage volume covered by the Strategic, Priority and Agile segments is around eighty and thus saying the focus should be in these segments and we should not have the best customer service levels and should have no out of stock scenarios.

4.3 Smart Ordering

This forms the next step of the proposed methodology which would be making smart orders and would allow us to be more intelligent in creating the orders thus optimizing the whole delivery logistics. Sales promotion in certainly the most essential element in the consumer goods sector [23] and thus from a supply chain point of view we have very often to deliver promotional orders which could be products only in promotions as well as shelf products which are played in promotion to have an influence in the sales.

The existing process is to deliver the total promotional quantity at once (by completing full trucks) and then the rest demand of the shelf products would be delivered differently. To summarize, the delivery is partitioned in promotional orders and shelf orders. This eventually results in peaks in inventory and we deliver more shelf orders which is not necessarily needed at that moment because we need to deliver complete trucks which becomes a constraint. The methodology proposed would divide the promotional quantity evenly in the number of deliveries which is done in a week (based of the data analysis), and the rest of the truck is completed with the shelf orders (Fig. 5). The real need of shelf products at the DC is 63 palettes and but since we must complete the 4th truck we fill it with more shelf stock, this increases the stock of the DC. The proposed solution was to distribute evenly the promotion in 3 deliveries (average delivery frequency per week) and filling the trucks with the shelf products. We see that we deliver the actual need of the DC and reducing the number of trucks per week.

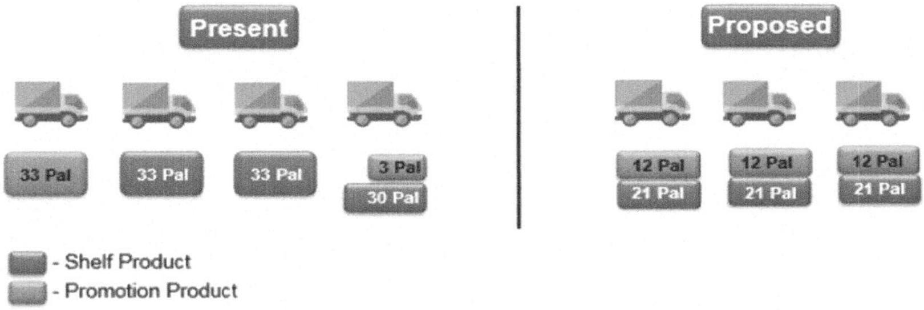

Fig. 5. Smart ordering of shelf and promotional products

This would avoid from having promotional order peaks since the quantity is evenly distributed and we would be far more accurate for the shelf order needs. The outcome would be no peaks in deliveries, reduction in inventory and reduction in the number of trucks making the system more sustainable. The realized results were increase in service by 0.5% as the frequency of the shelf products were more regular thus reducing the out of stock scenarios. This had an impact on the work experience as we are more regular and resulting in increase in productivity and was appreciated by the customer.

4.4 Economic Order Quantity

A synchronized Supply Chain will source, produce and ship daily what the consumers require and the flow this need seamlessly through the network. For more than a century, the act of determining order quantity (or lot sizing) for a firm's requirements has been a primary consideration. As early as 1913 Harris developed a simple model for determining order quantity based on basic economic considerations (including holding and ordering costs) that was called an Economic Order Quantity (EOQ) model [24]. In this paper, we emphasize on another factor which is Days Between Next Shipment. (DBNS) which is basically how frequently we ship tout item to a customer distribution center. This value in a state of utopia should be equal to one which means we ship everyday but considering today's logistics capabilities we cannot achieve this. The cost of shipping an item reduces if we have higher days between next shipment, basically meaning that we would be shipping a huge quantity in one go but this will eventually increase the inventory holding cost which is a linearly increasing graph. Thus, the ideal situation is to find balance between the both which would be the minimum of the total cost curve as shown in Fig. 6. (a DBNS of 7 days). The possible ordering measurements were palettes, layers and cases. The preparation of layers and cases were costly as they involved human intervention which would increase the price.

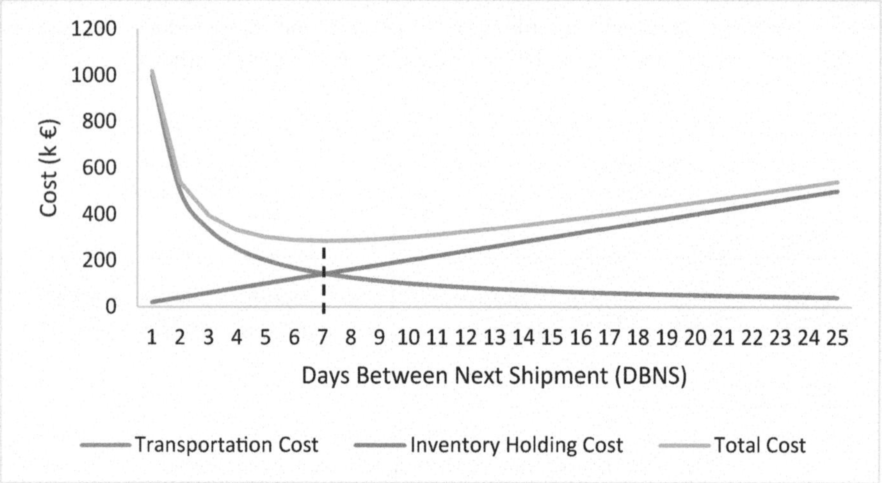

Fig. 6. Estimation of the economic order quantity (EOQ)

The implementation of EOQ based on the DBNS resulted in cost saving both for P&G and the client's distribution centers too. A decrease from palette to layer would not always mean an increase in cost when we take the inventory keeping cost in mind. This analysis was done keeping the product segmentation in mind thus giving us a clearer picture of the frequencies of deliveries.

4.5 Live Availability Check

This plays a very important role in our proposed methodology of the future of VMI systems which helps the user to have an idea about the availability of the product in real time. Not knowing about the availability of the product in the plant had huge impacts on the vehicle fill rates (VFR). We would have ordered certain products which might not be available and thus while the order is being loaded in the truck we would miss out certain quantities leading to the truck being partially filled and impacting VFR. This new functionality would not allow any unavailable product to be put on order and alert the user about certain products which might be at risk of being unavailable at real-time which resulted in increased VFR. This functionality was successfully tested for two distribution centers and we have seen an improvement of 0.5% in VFR and it eventually goes on to an increase of 0.5% in customer service. This now would be implemented in remaining all distribution centers.

5 Conclusion and Future Work

The proposed methodology answers the research question defined in the Sect. 1, VMI 2.0 touches each part of the entire supply chain starting from consumers to the manufacturing unit and thus resulting in a more End to End Synchronized Supply Chain. The methodology was implemented, and the results were analyzed, we had an improvement in the on-shelf availability of the products and the customer service levels. One major change in the ordering mindset is using the shelf products as a filler quantity in the truck which has a positive impact in the entire supply chain. The major KPIs of supply chain were also studied and this methodology resulted in reduction in inventory, increase in on shelf availability of the product and reduction in lost sales. The realized increase in service by 1% and an increasing in On Shelf Availability of the product by 1% which is surely in line with the objectives and is planned to be implemented all over They are less than the expected results as these KPIs are dependent on numerous other factors thus showing there is some scope of improvement. The live availability check however poses potential risk at masking the real demand of the products at the store level. There might be demand but since we have production issues and it is at risk the system would not order it thus masking the real demand. This opens an area of future work. End to end synchronization cannot be achieved without client involvement as the pattern of their deliveries to different stores is also the part of the entire chain. Thus, the integration of their shipment into our supply chain would be an area to work on to reduce the bull whip effect.

References

1. ECR Handbook, Best Practices in implementing VMI (2016)
2. Emigh, J.: Vendor-managed inventory. Computerworld **33**(34), 52–55 (1991)
3. Waller, M., Johnson, M.E., Davis, T.: Vendor-managed inventory in the retail supply chain. J. Bus. Logist. **20**(1), 183–203 (1999)
4. Stevens, G.: Integrating the supply chain. Int. J. Phys. Distrib. Logist. Manage. **19**(8), 3–8 (1989)
5. Axsäter, S.: Control theory concepts in production and inventory control. Int. J. Syst. Sci. **16**(2), 161–169 (1985)
6. Kaipia, R., Holmström, J., Tanskanen, K.: VMI: what are you losing if you let your customer place orders. Working Paper, Department of Industrial Management, Helsinki University of Technology, Finland (2000)

7. Andel, T.: Manage inventory, own information. Transp. Distrib. **37**(5), 54–58 (1996)
8. Stalk, G., Evans, P., Shulman, L.E.: Competingon capabilities: the new rules of corporate strategy. Harvard Bus. Rev. **70**(2), 57–70 (1992)
9. Disney, S.M., Towill, D.R.: The effect of VMI on the Bullwhip effect. In: International Conference on Production Research, Prague, Czech Republic, July 30–August 2 (2001)
10. Magee, J.F.: Production Planning and Inventory Control, pp. 80–83. McGraw-Hill Book Company, New York (1958)
11. Lee, H.L., Padmanabhan, P., Whang, S.: Information distortion in a supply chain: the Bullwhip Effect. Manage. Sci. **43**, 543–558 (1997)
12. Cachon, G., Fisher, M.: Campbell Soup's continuous replenishment program: evaluation and enhanced inventory decision rules. Prod. Oper. Manage. **6**(3), 266–276 (1997)
13. Holmstrom, J., Framling, K., Kaipia, R., Saranen, J.: Collaborative planning forecasting and replenishment: new solutions needed for mass collaboration. Working Paper, Department of Industrial Management, Helsinki University of Technology, Finland (2000)
14. Chen, F., Drezner, Z., Ryan, J.K., Simchi-Levi, D.: Quantifying the bullwhip effect in a simple supply chain: the impact of forecasting, lead times, and information. Manage. Sci. **46**(3), 436–443 (2000)
15. Lee, H.L., So, K.C., Tang, C.: The value of information sharing in a two-level supply chain. Manage. Sci. **46**(5), 626–643 (2000)
16. Xu, K., Dong, Y., Evers, P.T.: Towards better coordination of the supply chain. Transp. Res. Part E Logist. Transp. Rev. **37**, 35–54 (2001)
17. Cetinkaya, S., Lee, C.Y.: Stock replenishment and shipment scheduling for vendor-managed inventory systems. Manage. Sci. **46**(2), 217–232 (2000)
18. Dong, Y., Xu, K.: A supply chain model of vendor managed inventory. Transp. Res. Part E Logist. Transp. Rev. **38**(2), 75–95 (2002)
19. Romero, B.P.: The other side of JIT in supply management. Prod. Inventory Manage. J. **32**(4), 1–4 (1991)
20. Harris, F.W.: How many parts to make at once. Factory Mag. Manage. **10**(135–136), 152 (1913)
21. Gnimpieba Zanfack, D.R., Nait-Sidi-Moh, A., Durand, D., Fortin, J.: Publish and subscribe pattern for designing demand driven supply networks. In: Bouras, A., Eynard, B., Foufou, S., Thoben, K.-D. (eds.) PLM 2015. IAICT, vol. 467, pp. 45–55. Springer, Cham (2016). https://doi.org/10.1007/978-3-319-33111-9_5
22. Datalliance. https://www.datalliance.com/
23. Salem, R.W., Elomri, A.: Vendor managed inventory: from theory to practical implementation – a literature review. Int. J. Supply Chain Manage. **6**(1), 68–93 (2017)
24. Neslin, S.A.: Sales promotion. In: Weitz, B., Wensley, R. (eds.) Handbook of Marketing. Sage Publications, Thousand Oaks (2002)

Goal-Oriented Approach to Enable New Business Models for SME Using Smart Products

Jan Hicking(✉), Violett Zeller, and Günther Schuh

Institute for Industrial Management, FIR at the RWTH Aachen University, Aachen, Germany
{Jan.Hicking,Violett.Zeller, Gunther.Schuh}@fir.rwth-aachen.de

Abstract. The manufacturing industry has to exploit trends like "Industrie 4.0" and digitization not only to design production more efficiently, but also to create and develop new and innovative business models [1, p. 2]. New business models ensure that even SMEs are able to open up new markets and canvass new customers [2, p. 82ff.]. This means that in order to stay competitive, SMEs must transform their existing business models [3, p. 2ff.]. The creation of new business models require smart products [4, p. 1, 5, p. 235, 6, p. 13, 7, p. 2, 8, p. 322, 9, p. 7]. The required data base for new business models cannot be provided by SMEs alone, whereas smart products are able to provide a foundation, given the creation of smart data and smart services they enable [5, p. 235]. These services then expand functions and functionality of smart products and define new business models [10, 6f.]. However, the development of smart products by small and medium-sized enterprises is still lined with obstacles [11, p. 640]. Regarding the product development process the inclusion of smart products means that new and SME-unknown domains diffuse during the process [12, p. 2]. Although there are many models regarding this process there appears to be a substantial lack of taking into account the competencies enabled by the implementation of digital technologies. Hence, several SME-supporting approaches fail to address the two major challenges these enterprises are faced with [13, p. 8]. This paper generally describes valid objectives containing relevant stakeholders and their allocation to the phases of the product life cycle. Within each objective the potential benefit for customers and producers is analyzed. The model given in this paper helps SMEs in defining the initiation of a product development project more precisely and hence also eases project scoping and targeting for the smartification of an already existing product.

Keywords: Smart product development · Smartification

1 Introduction

Since the industrial revolution product development processes have constantly been making progress. While early products of mechanical engineering comprised basically on mechanical, physical parts, today's products are far more digital. With the VDI 2221

Published by Springer Nature Switzerland AG 2018.
P. Chiabert et al. (Eds.): PLM 2018, IFIP AICT 540, pp. 147–158, 2018.
https://doi.org/10.1007/978-3-030-01614-2_14

and the basic works of Pahl u. Beitz 1977 a generic problem-solving approach was disseminated to support challenges of mechanical engineers in any type of form. The product development process was dominated by one single domain, the mechanics. Hereinafter new domains diffused in the development process to face disruptions during automation and other aspects [14, p. 24f., 15], for example the diffusion of informatics and electronics in mechanics created the field of mechatronics. This evolution of including more and more unknown requirements lead to several new product development process models: V-Model [15], Simultaneous Engineering [16], Mechatronics design model [17], Three-cycle Model [18], Model-based systems engineering [19], W-Model [20], Multi-Domain Matrix (MDM) [21] and more. All these models try to unite all named domains to reduce time and costs of development, while new, relevant aspects driven by trends like digitization and "Industrie 4.0" aren't faced properly. These trends carry new requirements like product intelligence, connectivity and smarter product services [10, p. 6f., 12, p. 2] (Fig. 1).

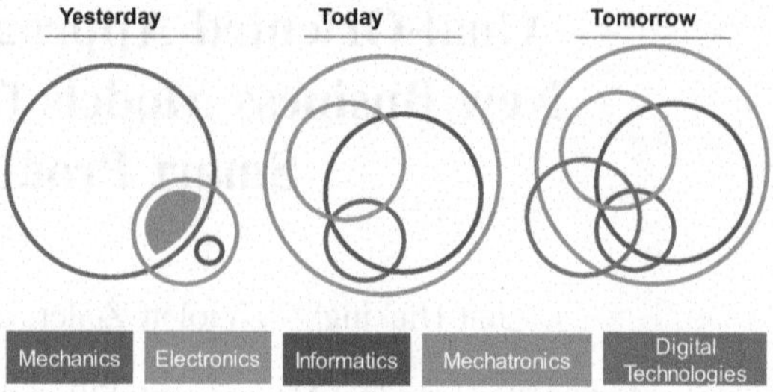

Fig. 1. Domain diffuse in the product development

The question for SMEs at this point in time has to be which kind of influence this evolution has on existing products. Even today, customers gravitate towards the product that has the highest scope of performance in comparison with other products of similar or identical price [12, p. 2f.]. As mentioned before, existing products must change in order to serve customer needs in the future and stay competitive, which means that SMEs have to transform their product-centered business models into new user-centered business models [10, p. 8f.]. Therefore, SMEs must develop smart products which act as the needed data collector for the creation of new business models [10, p. 6f.]. Because smart products can collect, analyze and processes data, they are the basis for smart data [10, p. 6ff.], which in turn is the basis for smart service, which ultimately enhances smart products [5, p. 235ff.]. Thus, smart products enable new business models [4, p. 1, 5, p. 235, 6, p. 18, 8, p. 322, 9, p. 7] (Fig. 2).

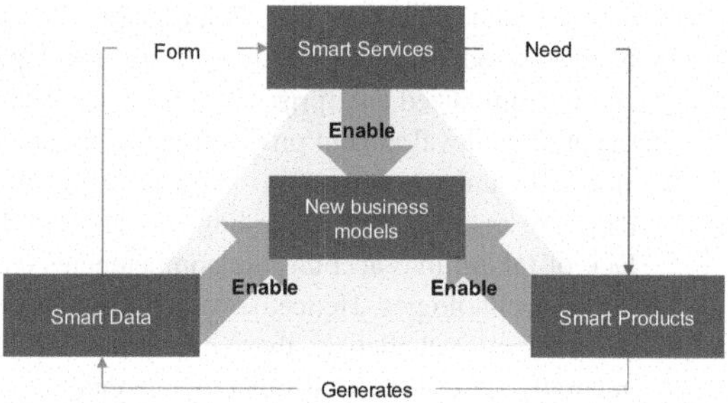

Fig. 2. Influence of smart products on new business models

As already stated, certain developments in creating business models and the need for smart products bring two enormous challenges along.

The first challenge describes the development task we can define as "smartification". Many of the aforementioned development models fail to provide transformability from product to smart product. The second and most significant challenge for SMEs are ambiguous requirements due to missing target-oriented deriving methodologies.

This paper takes the first step towards dealing with these challenges by defining the term smart product properly and generally describing valid targets containing relevant stakeholders and an allocation to the phase in a product's life cycle. Taking into account a proper definition and valid targets for smart product, SMEs are able to plan a smartification project more precisely.

In the following chapter a definition of smart products is attempted in order to provide a general understanding of this type of product. Taking into account the frequency and the described content of the definitions, a universal definition is derived. Based on experiences of the German research project "Mittelstand 4.0-Kompetenzzenztrum Dortmund" and a literary research, generally valid targets for smart products will be presented while describing the potential benefits for SMEs and their customers.

2 Definition: Smart Products in the Manufacturing Industry

In this chapter a definition of smart products is presented. The literary analysis has shown that there exists a great amount of varying definitions of smart products. First it is shown why "smart" is the right description for those products, which are able to offer more than just a single defined function. Second it is shown what "smart products" actually means and what such a product has to be capable of (Table 1).

Table 1. Different designations of "smart" products

Source/designation	Smart, connected product	Smart product	Intelligent product	Intelligent technical system	Cyber-physical product	Cyber-physical system	Digitalized product	Digitized product	Product service system	Digital product
[22]	X									
[23–30]			X							
[5, 31–35]		X								
36]				X						
[37, 38]						X				
[39, 40]					X					
[3, 41, 42]										X
[1, 43, 44]							X			
[45]									X	
[45–50]								X		

Following the definition of Porter and Heppelmann, smart products have physical, smart and connected components. "The result is a virtuous cycle of value improvement." [22, p. 5]. Abramovici describes smart products as cyber-physical products which are capable of condition monitoring and communication with several IT-System and are extended by product-related services [40, p. 2]. Taking Schuh's definition, we can state that smart products are based on digitized products like cyber-physical products and are extended with intelligent components [1, p. 22]. The table shows that there are many different interpretations of "smart" products. Combining these interpretations with the author's definitions we can conclude that the designation "smart" is a synonym for intelligent or smart, connected. The designations "cyber-physical", "digitalized" and "digitized" are descriptions for "digitized" products. Digitized products are one of the primary stages of smart products [1, 22, 40]. Based on the definitions and designations of Schuh, Porter and Heppelmann and Abramovici, we can define smart products: smart products are based on digitized (or cyber-physical) products, they consist of physical, intelligent and connected components and are capable of a digital upgrading through internet-based services (Fig. 3).

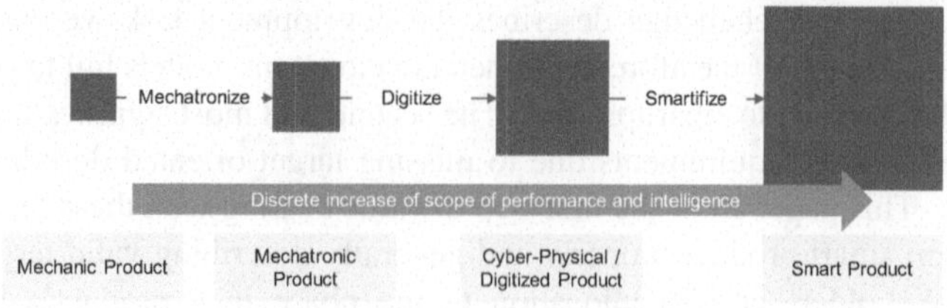

Fig. 3. Definition of smart products

3 Goal-Oriented Development of Smart Products

This chapter presents several targets of smart products. In order to structure the targets we will use a matrix which shows, in horizontal direction, the life cycle phases of a product, segmented into "development", "production", "usage", and "recycling" [51, 52, p. 41, 53, p. 2]. The phase "development" contains all relevant steps in the product development process, starting with product planning via requirements management through to construction and testing [53, p. 2]. The phase "production" includes all relevant steps of production and delivery. The phase "usage" contains all interaction between customer and producer in usage, from general usage of the customer via maintenance support through to after-sales support. The phase "recycling" describes all relevant steps from disposal to decomposition of the product. In addition, the matrix's vertical direction shows the strategic success factors, which includes: productivity, costs, time, quality, flexibility [54, p. 397ff.]. By analyzing the experiences of the research project "Mittelstand 4.0-Kompetenzzentrum Dortmund" and the literary research, relevant targets are assigned to product life cycle phases and to strategic success factors. The relevance of each target was validated within the interviews with project partners in the research project. The target description follows a consistent structure: each target contains its name, (1) usage potential for producers, (2) usage potential for customers and the according life cycle phase.

Following the literary analysis, we can conclude that new business models enabled by the usage of smart products are very important. When using smart products the first target is to support the transformation from a product-centered towards a user-centered business model [3, p. 142, 55, p. 32f., 56, p. 9, 57, p. 1359, 58, p. 25ff.]. Pursuing this goal means that a company is able to increase its productivity, for example a company offers the smart product as a service in the future, which means that customers pay for a service in a different manner than before. Thus, the company achieves a constant cash flow. The new business model requires a smart product which allows the offering of products as a service. Therefore, pursuing the target "**Enable new business models**" addresses a development task in correspondence with the product's life cycle phase.

1. Realize constant cash flow by offering product functions as a service
2. Only used product functions and frequency of usage is factored in

The second target describes the way field data is used to analyze the product usage and how this can be used to optimize product adjustments [56, p. 9, 59, p. 244, 60, p. 145, 61, p. 101], which enables a constant improvement of the product even while it is used by the customer in the field. This is realized by analyzing condition data. If the producer adjusts the product parameters based on the analysis, the user will be able to observe a performance increase. The productivity of the product and by this, the productivity of producer and customer is increased. Taking into account that this target "**Increase product performance**" requires for the product to be in the field we can state that it has to be assigned to the life cycle phase "usage".

1. Increase product value and effectiveness; Increase customer satisfaction
2. Creates more individualized products which fit customer requirements better; Higher product availability

The third target "**Increase product efficiency**" describes how field data is used to increase the efficiency of products which leads to e.g. less downtimes [59, p. 244, 62, p. 14]. Similar to target two, this target is assigned to the phase "usage", as the product is used by customers in the field, too. The difference is that this target addresses relevant quality aspects of the product. Possible product adjustments lead to less downtimes and thus a more efficient product. Like target 2 an immediate added value for customers is achieved.

1. Increase product value and effectiveness; Increase customer satisfaction
2. Product is tailored to customer requirements; Less malfunctions reduces process costs

The fourth target "**Optimize product development**" describes how field data is used to support the product development process [1, p. 22, 4, 60, p. 145, 63, p. 325]. Real customer data, which describes how customers use a product is fundamental in order to develop products fitting customers more individually than before. Getting field data of a product means being able to learn about customer behavior and built up customer knowledge. This knowledge enables the creation of individualized products with lower costs.

1. Enable a learning product development; Customer experience (Customer knowledge)
2. Creates more individualized products which fit customer requirements better; Individualized customer product functions

The fifth target "**Increase flexibility**" describes the way smart products dissolve inflexible production systems [27, p. 6, 35, p. 11, 54, p. 401, 61, p. 101]. Flexibility in production systems allows producing a broader product range in less time with less costs.

1. Enhance competitiveness; Increase customer satisfaction
2. More flexibility in production systems due to a smart product

The sixth target "**Increase product's range of function**" describes how updates enable new product functions even while the product is in the field [1, p. 22, 46, 50, p. 1, 56, p. 9, 62, p. 13, 64]. In the past, a product's functions were limited even after the product left its producer. Smart products are able to offer more functions even when they are already in the field. Based on field data, producers are allowed to release new functions which increase the productivity of a product. Assigning this target to a product's life cycle phase, a division has to be made. One the one hand, this means that new product functions are assigned to the life cycle phase "development" for producers, for costumers on the other hand the product is assigned to the phase "usage".

1. Increase customer satisfaction; Offer customers individual functions which extend the product life cycle
2. New functions allow for the product to be used in different ways than before

The seventh target "**Optimize after sales**" describes how field data is used to predict product downtimes and failing components [65, p. 32]. Companies are able to plan the production of components for after-sale activities more precisely, as information about failing components predicts component lifetimes. For customers, this means that downtimes of the used product e.g. a machine tool can be prevented.

1. Production of failing components can be planned earlier, which leads to lower costs
2. Downtimes are prevented, costs regarding process interruptions are reduced

The eighth target "**Optimize internal service processes**" describes how field data is used to monitor the product and predict downtimes [56, p. 9]. By preemptively realizing a product failure will occur, producers are able to calculate resources for maintenance activities more precisely. Internal service processes are optimized by analyzing and incorporating field data of products. For customers, this means that downtimes of the used product e.g. a machinery tool, can be prevented.

1. Early knowledge of product failure leads to better planning of maintenance measurements and resources
2. Downtimes are prevented, costs regarding process interruptions are reduced

The ninth target "**Service flexibility**" describes how field data is used to create entirely new product-related services [57, p. 1359, 61, p. 101, 65, p. 31]. With smart products companies are able to learn more about customer behaviors, which must be analyzed during the development process to identify new customer demands. Based on these demands a company is able to develop and create entirely new services which address each customer individually.

1. Service portfolio can be developed more precisely due to knowledge of customer demands
2. More individual services are provided

The tenth target "**Efficient recycling**" describes how information about a product's base materials and new components, which were added during maintenance measures, is saved to support the recycling process [9, p. 6].

1. Transparency of all product ingredients even after delivery
2. Tracking of spare part changes in the product is not necessary anymore

Besides interviews with SME two use cases are taken into account. First a smartification of an evacuation chair which is used in safety concepts in official buildings. Second a smartification of punching machine which is used in clothing industry. Scope of both projects was to realize the target "**Optimize internal service processes**" by monitoring the conditions of both products.

Regarding the assignment of each target to the phases of the product life cycle and the critical success factors we can observe that they can be divided into two groups. The first shows which targets have in common that they are using field data to create customer experience. The usage of field data influences cost and time aspects in the development and production of a product. Constantly learning about customer's means that products or services can be created which are tailored to customer requirements more efficiently than before. Unsuccessful product developments are minimized. Reducing costs through better planning of internal resources as well as saving time are key factors for SME's success. Building a broader understanding of customer needs, new business models can be developed and employed. Creating a product service system which covers all needs of the customer increases productivity. The second group of targets addresses an

Fig. 4. Smartification of an evacuation chair

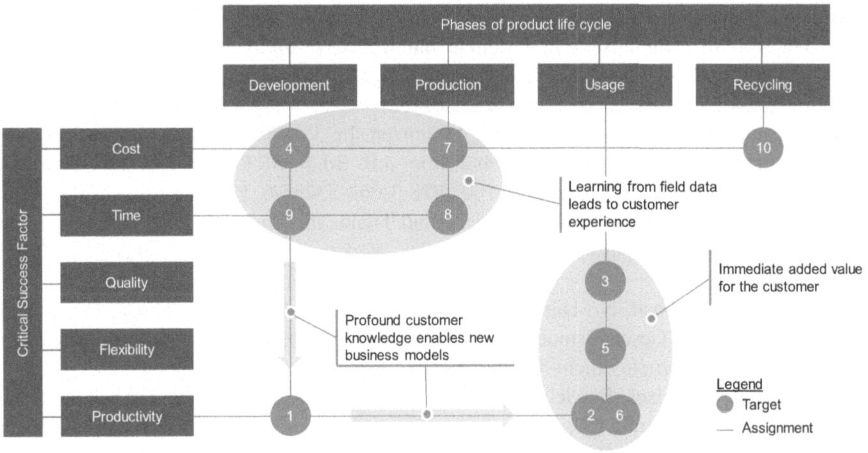

Fig. 5. Assigning targets for smart products

immediate increase of product value. New functions, which are updated while the product is in the field as well as new services which support the customer more individually are bound to lead to a higher customer satisfaction, higher flexibility and productivity (Fig. 4).

Employing one or more of these targets while developing smart products, SMEs develop more goal-oriented and efficiently than before (Fig. 5).

4 Conclusion and Further Research

This paper presented both a definition of smart products as well as several targets for smart products, as well as a number of reasons why SMEs should incorporate and develop them. Based on experiences of the German research project "Mittelstand 4.0-Kompetenzzentrum Dortmund" and a literary research the targets are validated. Since SMEs are able to integrate these targets into their development processes it is important to expand this approach. A goal-oriented product development can be achieved when the targets are used to derive the relevant requirements for smart products.

Acknowledgement. This article arose during the work of the authors, within the context of the research project "Mittelstand 4.0-Kompetenzzentrum Dortmund" (project number: 01MF15001C) funded by the Federal Ministry for Economic Affairs and Energy in Germany. The authors want to thank all donors, supporter and critics.

References

1. Schuh, G.: Industrie 4.0 in der Produktentwicklung, Aachen, 14 March 2017
2. Kagermann, H.: IT-Driven Business Models: Global Case Studies in Transformation. Wiley, Hoboken (2011)
3. Gassmann, O., Frankenberger, K., Csik, M.: Geschäftsmodelle entwickeln: 55 innovative Konzepte mit dem St. Galler Business Model Navigator, 2nd edn. Hanser, München (2017). https://doi.org/10.3139/9783446452848
4. Michel, S.: Mit Digitalisierung Produkte und Prozesse optimieren. Digitale Produktentwicklung. http://www.maschinenmarkt.vogel.de/mit-digitalisierung-produkte-und-prozesse-optimieren-a-545414/. Accessed 04 June 2017
5. Kagermann, H.: Chancen von Industrie 4.0 nutzen. In: Vogel-Heuser, B., Bauernhansl, T., ten Hompel, M. (eds.) Handbuch Industrie 4.0 Bd.4. SRT, pp. 235–246. Springer, Heidelberg (2017). https://doi.org/10.1007/978-3-662-53254-6_12
6. Bellersheim, V.: Digitale Geschäftsmodelle und Trends im Maschinenbau. Vortrag auf dem Jahrestreffen des Europäischen Verbandes der Werkzeugmaschinenhersteller (CECIMO), November 2016
7. Röglinger, M., Urbach, N.: Digitale Geschäftsmodelle im Internet der Dinge. Diskussionspapier, Bayreuth, Geschäftsmodelle in der digitalen Welt, August 2016. https://fim-rc.de/Paperbibliothek/Veroeffentlicht/589/wi-589.pdf
8. Wildbihler, M., Stelzer, B., Schiebel, E., Brecht, L.: Internet der dinge. In: Schallmo, D., Rusnjak, A., Anzengruber, J., Werani, T., Jünger, M. (eds.) Digitale Transformation von Geschäftsmodellen. SBMI, pp. 311–331. Springer, Wiesbaden (2017). https://doi.org/10.1007/978-3-658-12388-8_12

9. Barbian, M., et al.: Digitale Chancen und Bedrohungen - Geschäftsmodelle für Industrie 4.0, Statusreport, o.O., May 2016
10. Lauenroth, K., Schreiber, F., Schreiber, F.: Maschinen- und Anlagenbau im digitalen Zeitalter: Requirements Engineering als systematische Gestaltungskompetenz für die Fertigungsindustrie Industrie 4.0, 1st ed. s.l.: Beuth Verlag GmbH (2016)
11. Issa, A., Lucke, D., Bauernhansl, T.: Mobilizing SMEs towards Industrie 4.0-enabled smart products. In: Tseng, M.M., Tsai, H.-Y., Wang, Y. (eds.) Manufacturing Systems 4.0 – Proceedings of the 50th CIRP Conference on Manufacturing Systems, vol. 63, pp. 670–674. Elsevier, o.O.: (2017). https://doi.org/10.1016/j.procir.2017.03.346
12. Brauckmann, O.: Smart Production: Wertschöpfung durch Geschäftsmodelle. Springer Vieweg, Berlin (2015). https://doi.org/10.1007/978-3-662-45302-5
13. Gonzales, A.A., Becker, K., Cheng, C.-H., Döricht, V., Duchon, M.: Digitale Transformation: Wie Informations- und Kommunikationstechnologie etablierte Branchen grundlegend verändern. fortiss GmbH, München (2016)
14. Kühnl, C.: Software gibt den Takt vor. Mechatronic & Fertigung **2010**, 20–21 (2010)
15. Design methodology for mechatronic systems 2206 (2004)
16. Bullinger, H.-J., Warschat, J., Bading, A. (eds.): Forschungs- und Entwicklungsmanagement: Simultaneous Engineering, Projektmanagement, Produktplanung, Rapid Product Development. Teubner, Stuttgart (1997). https://doi.org/10.1007/978-3-663-05946-2
17. Hollauer, C., Becerril, L., Kattner, N., Weidmann, D., Chucholowski, N., Lindemann, U.: Adaptable mechatronic engineering design processes: process reference model and methodology. In: Chakrabarti, A., Chakrabarti, D. (eds.) ICoRD 2017. SIST, vol. 65, pp. 597–607. Springer, Singapore (2017). https://doi.org/10.1007/978-981-10-3518-0_52
18. Gausemeier, J., Ebbesmeyer, P., Kallmeyer, F.: Produktinnovation: Strategische Planung und Entwicklung der Produkte von morgen. Hanser, München [u.a.] (2001)
19. Beier, G., Rothenburg, U., Woll, R., Stark, R.: Modellbasiertes systems engineering: Durchgängige Entwicklung mit erlebbaren Prototypen. In: Digital Engineering, pp. 14–17 (2012). https://www.digital-engineering-magazin.de/sites/default/files/magazine-pdf/de_2012_03_inhalt_farm.pdf
20. Nattermann, R., Anderl, R.: Approach for a data-management-system and a proceeding-model for the development of adaptronic systems. In: Design and Manufacturing, Parts A and B, Vancouver, British Columbia, Canada, vol. 32, pp. 379–387 (2010). https://doi.org/10.1115/imece2010-37828
21. Ponn, J., Lindemann, U.: Konzeptentwicklung und Gestaltung technischer Produkte: Systematisch von Anforderungen zu Konzepten und Gestaltlösungen, 2nd edn. Springer, Heidelberg (2011). https://doi.org/10.1007/978-3-642-20580-4
22. Porter, M.E., Heppelmann, J.E.: How smart, connected products are transforming competition: spotlight on managing the internet of things. Harvard Bus. Rev. **65**, 64–88 (2014)
23. Anderl, R., Picard, A., Albrecht, K.: Smart engineering for smart products. In: Abramovici, M., Stark, R. (eds.) Smart Product Engineering. Lecture Notes in Production Engineering, pp. 1–10. Springer, Heidelberg (2013). https://doi.org/10.1007/978-3-642-30817-8_1
24. Hermann, M., Pentek, T., Otto, B.: Design principles for Industrie 4.0 scenarios: a literature review (2015). https://doi.org/10.13140/rg.2.2.29269.22248
25. Weyrich, M.: Industrie 4.0 und intelligente Produkte: Wie Automatisierungs- und Softwaresysteme der nächsten Generation die Produktentwicklung und Produktion verändern, München, 17 June 2015
26. Anderl, R.: Industrie 4.0 - Advanced Engineering of Smart Products and Smart Production (2014). https://doi.org/10.13140/2.1.1039.4406

27. Schlick, J., Stephan, P., Loskyll, M., Lappe, D.: Industrie 4.0 in der praktischen Anwendung. In: Vogel-Heuser, B., Bauernhansl, T., Hompel, M. (eds.) Handbuch Industrie 4.0 Bd.2. SRT, pp. 3–29. Springer, Heidelberg (2017). https://doi.org/10.1007/978-3-662-53248-5_46
28. Vogel-Heuser, B., Bauernhansl, T., Ten Hompel, M. (eds.): Handbuch Industrie 4.0: Bd 2: Automatisierung, 2nd ed. Springer Vieweg, Berlin (2017). https://doi.org/10.1007/978-3-662-53248-5
29. McFarlane, D., Giannikas, V., Wong, A.C.Y., Harrison, M.: Intelligent products in the supply chain - 10 years on. In: Borangiu, T., Thomas, A., Trentesaux, D. (eds.) Service Orientation in Holonic and Multi Agent Manufacturing and Robotics. Studies in Computational Intelligence, vol. 472, pp. 103–117. Springer, Heidelberg (2013). https://doi.org/10.1007/978-3-642-35852-4_7
30. Kiritsis, D.: Closed-loop PLM for intelligent products in the era of the Internet of things. Comput.-Aided Des. **43**(5), 479–501 (2011). https://doi.org/10.1016/j.cad.2010.03.002
31. Vogel-Heuser, B.: Preparing for the 4.0 Future: Industry strategies in anticipation of 4.0. Munich [u.a.], 21 August 2015
32. Janzen, S., Maass, W.: Smart Product Descprition Object (SPDO). In: Eschenbach, C., Gruninger, M. (eds.) Frontiers in Artificial Intelligence and Applications, Formal Ontology in Information Systems: Proceedings of the Fifth International Conference (FOIS 2008), vol. 183, pp. 25–30. IOS Press, Amsterdam (2008)
33. Meier, H., Uhlmann, E. (eds.): Integrierte Industrielle Sach- und Dienstleistungen: Vermarktung. Entwicklung und Erbringung hybrider Leistungsbündel. Springer, Heidelberg (2012). https://doi.org/10.1007/978-3-642-25269-3
34. Seidenschwang, P.: Smart Products Engineering. White Paper, Eschborn (2013)
35. Scheibe, H.-G.: Smart Products: Neue Spielregeln für die Industrie. In: ROI Dialog, ROI Management Consulting AG, Ed., pp. 10–11 (2016)
36. it's OWL, So intelligent können Produkte sein, Paderborn (2015)
37. Krause, T., et al.: IT-Plattformen für das Internet der Dinge (IoT): Basis Intelligenter Produkte und Services. Fraunhofer Verlag, Stuttgart (2017)
38. Sapatnekar, S. (ed.): Proceedings of the 47th Design Automation Conference on - DAC 2010. ACM Press, New York (2010)
39. Sendler, U. (ed.): Industrie 4.0 Grenzenlos. Springer Vieweg, Heidelberg (2016). https://doi.org/10.1007/978-3-662-48278-0
40. Abramovici, M.: Smart products. In: Laperrière, L., Reinhart, G. (eds.) CIRP Encyclopedia of Production Engineering, the International Academy for Produ, pp. 1–5. Springer, Heidelberg (2014). https://doi.org/10.1007/978-3-642-35950-7_16785-1
41. Samulat, P.: Die Digitalisierung der Welt: Wie das Industrielle Internet der Dinge aus Produkten Services macht. Springer Fachmedien Wiesbaden, Wiesbaden (2017). https://doi.org/10.1007/978-3-658-15511-7
42. Westkämper, E., Spath, D., Constantinescu, C., Lentes, J. (eds.): Digitale Produktion. Springer, Heidelberg (2013). https://doi.org/10.1007/978-3-642-20259-9
43. Janata, S.: Leitfaden Digitalisierung: Strategien, Technologien und Ökosysteme, Kassel (2016)
44. Kreutzer, R., Land, K.-H.: Digitaler Darwinismus: Der stille Angriff auf Ihr Geschäftsmodell und Ihre Marke; das Think!Book, 2nd edn. Springer Gabler, Wiesbaden (2016). https://doi.org/10.1007/3-211-27349-2_42
45. Herterich, M.M., Mikusz, M.: Looking for a few good concepts and theories for digitized artifacts and digital innovation in a material world. In: 37th International Conference on Information Systems (ICIS 2016): Dublin, Ireland, 11–14 December 2016, Association for Information Systems (AIS), Ed., Curran Associates Inc, Red Hook, pp. 750–771 (2017)

46. Yoo, Y., Henfridsson, O., Lyytinen, K.: Research commentary —the new organizing logic of digital innovation: an agenda for information systems research. Inf. Syst. Res. **21**(4), 724–735 (2010). https://doi.org/10.1287/isre.1100.0322
47. Yoo, Y.: The tables have turned: how can the information systems field contribute to technology and innovation management research? JAIS **14**(5), 227–236 (2013)
48. Yoo, Y., Boland, R.J., Lyytinen, K., Majchrzak, A.: Organizing for innovation in the digitized world. Organ. Sci. **23**(5), 1398–1408 (2012). https://doi.org/10.1287/orsc.1120.0771
49. Yoo, Y.: Computing in everyday life: a call for research on experiential computing. MIS Q. **34**(2), 213–231 (2010). https://doi.org/10.2307/20721425
50. Novales, A., Mocker, M., Simonovich, D.: IT-enriched "Digitized" Products: Building Blocks and Challenges. Paper, AMICS, San Diego, USA (2016). Accessed 17 Dec 2017
51. Hill, T.: Production/Operations Management. PHI Prentice-Hall International, Englewood Cliffs (1983)
52. Feldhusen, J., Gebhardt, B.: Product Lifecycle Management für die Praxis: Ein Leitfaden zur modularen Einführung. Umsetzung und Anwendung. Springer-Verlag, Heidelberg (2008). https://doi.org/10.1007/978-3-540-34009-6
53. Eigner, M., Stelzer, R.: Product Lifecycle Management: Ein Leitfaden für Product Development und Life Cycle Management, 2nd edn. Springer, Dordrecht (2013). https://doi.org/10.1007/b93672
54. Schuh, G. (ed.): Produktionsplanung und -steuerung: Grundlagen. Gestaltung Und Konzepte. Springer, Dordrecht (2006). https://doi.org/10.1007/3-540-33855-1
55. Kagermann, H., et al.: Smart Service Welt: Umsetzungsempfehlungen für das Zukunftsprojekt Internetbasierte Dienste für die Wirtschaft, Berlin, March 2014
56. Herterich, M.M., Eck, A., Uebernickel, F.: Exploring how digitized products enable industrial service innovation – an affordance perspective. In: 24. European Conference on Information Systems (ECIS), İstanbul, Turkey, 2016 4, Istanbul (Türkei), Research Papers 156 (2016). http://aisel.aisnet.org/ecis2016_rp/156. Accessed 17 Dec 2017
57. Santos, K., Loures, E., Piechnicki, F., Canciglieri, O.: Opportunities assessment of product development process in Industry 4.0. Procedia Manufact. **11**, 1358–1365 (2017). https://doi.org/10.1016/j.promfg.2017.07.265
58. Schallmo, D., Rusnjak, A.: Roadmap zur digitalen transformation von geschäftsmodellen. In: Schallmo, D., Rusnjak, A., Anzengruber, J., Werani, T., Jünger, M. (eds.) Digitale Transformation von Geschäftsmodellen. SBMI, pp. 1–31. Springer, Wiesbaden (2017). https://doi.org/10.1007/978-3-658-12388-8_1
59. Cronin, M.J.: Smart Products, Smarter Services: Strategies for Embedded Control. Cambridge University Press, Cambridge (2010)
60. Schaupp, E., Abele, E., Metternich, J.: Potentials of digitalization in tool management. Procedia CIRP **63**, 144–149 (2017). https://doi.org/10.1016/j.procir.2017.03.172
61. Demont, A., Paulus-Rohmer, D.: Industrie 4.0-geschäftsmodelle systematisch entwickeln. In: Schallmo, D., Rusnjak, A., Anzengruber, J., Werani, T., Jünger, M. (eds.) Digitale Transformation von Geschäftsmodellen. SBMI, pp. 97–125. Springer, Wiesbaden (2017). https://doi.org/10.1007/978-3-658-12388-8_4
62. Meyer, G.G., Främling, K., Holmström, J.: Intelligent products: a survey. Comput. Ind. **60** (3), 137–148 (2009). https://doi.org/10.1016/j.compind.2008.12.005
63. Herterich, M.M., Uebernickel, F., Brenner, W.: The impact of cyber-physical systems on industrial services in manufacturing. Procedia CIRP **30**, 323–328 (2015). https://doi.org/10.1016/j.procir.2015.02.110

64. Porter, M.E., Heppelmann, J.E.: How smart, connected products are transforming companies. Harvard Bus. Rev. **96–112**(114), 2015 (2015)
65. Schuh, G., Kreutzer, R.: Utility potentials of cyber-physical systems′ field data. In: Akay, H. U., Bendsoe, M.P., Brezzi, F., Castellano, M.D. (eds.) IJERD - International Journal of Engineering Research and Development, 14, vol. 1, pp. 24–35. IJERD, o.O. (2018)

Sustainability of Cascading Product Lifecycles

The Need for Adaptive Management to End-of-Life Supply Chains

Matthias Kalverkamp[1(✉)], Alexandra Pehlken[1], Thorsten Wuest[2], and Steven B. Young[3]

[1] Cascade Use Research Group, Carl von Ossietzky University of Oldenburg, 26111 Oldenburg, Germany
{matthias.kalverkamp,alexandra.pehlken}@uol.de

[2] Industrial and Management Systems Engineering, West Virginia University, Morgantown, WV 26506, USA
thwuest@mail.wvu.edu

[3] School of Environment, Enterprise and Development, University of Waterloo, Waterloo, ON, Canada
sb.young@uwaterloo.ca

Abstract. Product lifecycles can contain several waste management steps after the production of a product. At each step, 'end-of-life' supply chains can separate, each emerging supply chain representing an intended lifecycle or an unintended, though not necessarily inferior lifecycle in terms of sustainability. This variety demonstrates the complexity arising at the end-of-life and indicates that not necessarily a single actor coordinates these supply chains. The cascade use methodology targets this complexity by identifying sustainable supply chains, possibly managed by alternative actors. This study applies the methodology to a novel case of vehicle reuse and conversion discussing its sustainability and implications for decision makers. The authors argue for more adaptive management approaches to address sustainability in product lifecycles more holistically.

Keywords: Cascade use · Recycling · Reuse · Remanufacturing
Product lifecycle management · Closed-loop supply chains
Open-loop supply chains

1 Introduction

The circular economy is popular in industry, policy, as well as research, and as such widely supported [1–3]. The concept of a circular economy reinforces triple bottom line objectives: (i) conserving environmental and (ii) economic resources (such as materials, energy, labor and capital value) that are incorporated into products as well as (iii) contributing to the social dimension of sustainability [3].

The waste management hierarchy (WMH) considers different strategies for resource conservation in a descending order of its environmental friendliness from prevention of (primary) production to recovery and disposal of products and materials. For products

Published by Springer Nature Switzerland AG 2018.
P. Chiabert et al. (Eds.): PLM 2018, IFIP AICT 540, pp. 159–168, 2018.
https://doi.org/10.1007/978-3-030-01614-2_15

(after production), the subsequent steps of reuse and recycling aim to preserve resources in the form of products (reuse) or materials (recycling). The second to the last step, recovery, aims at recovering energy from materials. After energy recovery, disposal remains as the final, generally undesirable treatment option [4].

Reuse and recycling transactions are fundamental for a functional circular economy and they regularly form some sort of cascade utilization. Product lifecycles can contain several of the WMH steps after the production of a product, namely reuse, recycling and recover. Reuse contains various circular strategies that relate to different degrees of additional treatment and resource inputs, i.e. direct reuse (without further treatment), repair, refurbish or remanufacturing [5]. At each of these steps, 'waste' supply chains of end-of-life and end-of-use products could separate (end-of-life and end-of-use are hereafter subsumed as end-of-life for simplicity; for a more detailed discussion of end-of-life perspectives, the interested reader may refer to Kalverkamp *et al.* [6]). While some products (or components) remain at the reuse level, others move towards recycling or recovery. However, in reality, the corresponding supply chains may separate at each level of the WMH. Furthermore, each supply chain may represent an intended lifecycle or an unintended, though not necessarily inferior, lifecycle in terms of sustainability. This variety demonstrates the complexity at the end-of-life of products and components. It further indicates the importance of reuse and recycling as critical steps of the WMH where products potentially enter some sort of cycle not necessarily managed by one actor or a defined group of actors.

The objective of this paper is to demonstrate how the 'cascade use' perspective on product lifecycles relates to different types of supply chains by considering the complexity and market dynamics at products' end-of-life. The predominant consideration of either single businesses and their ('closed-loop') supply chains or product-service-systems sets boundaries that may neglect this complexity [7] and thereby undermine the sustainability potential of alternative supply chains, usually considered as 'forward' supply chains. This paper focuses on how the cascade use methodology can support alternative perspectives on the management of sustainable supply chains. Therefore, we outline the 'cascade use methodology' (Sect. 3) and apply the methodology to a case that visualizes the dynamics of global used car markets and corresponding supply chains (Sect. 4). The discussion highlights the potential for supply chain management to contribute to sustainability and derives practical implications for management and policy (Sect. 5). An outlook on future research concludes this paper (Sect. 6).

2 Product Lifecycles and Closed-Loop Supply Chains

The product lifecycle approach is fundamental in the development and management of sustainable products, such as in product design (e.g., design for repair) or corresponding business models [8]. In the context of reuse and recycling in product lifecycles, products return to the manufacturer or they reach third parties (e.g., remanufacturers or material recyclers). In this context, reverse supply chains support the management of product returns with different tools to establish circularity in product lifecycles, popularized under the term 'closed-loop supply chains' (CLSC). CLSCs are supposed to recover value from product returns and are usually dominated by a central actor who intends to control the entire product lifecycle [9]. Nevertheless, third-party organizations take advantage of materials dedicated to waste management or that 'leak' from CLSCs and thereby also close product lifecycles [10].

The term 'product lifecycle' is used differently throughout literature [11]. Two lifecycle perspectives are predominantly considered, namely a marketing [12] and a technical/engineering [13] one. The marketing perspective identifies up to five stages: introduction, growth, maturity, saturation and decline [12]. When considering different product classes, forms and models, the complexity of this perspective increases substantially [12]. The more technical perspective usually considers three phases, beginning-of-life; middle-of-life; and end-of-life [14]. Prominent domains using this technical view are life cycle assessment, business process management and product lifecycle management. The latter uses data and information technology to enable product lifecycles [13, 14]. These two perspectives are relevant when considering the real-world complexity of market-oriented manufacturing in the context of sustainability [11]. For increasing sustainability, it is especially relevant to consider the end-of-life 'and beyond' from both lifecycle perspectives.

In addition to the outlined lifecycle perspectives, there is a process-related perspective in marketing that comprises all market transactions from the (primary) seller to the final consumer, also referred to as 'transvections'. These transvections reflect the technical processes 'from extraction to consumption' eventually merging in the concept of supply chain management [15]. This illustrates linkages and interdependencies of the two different lifecycle perspectives in common business practice.

Illustrations in literature model the product lifecycle differently with a variable number of process steps or different allocations of reverse flows, although often with the focus on reverse supply chains that connect with actors of the forward supply chain to enable CLSC's [16, 17]. This leads to an implicit or explicit focus on central actors that manage these supply chains hence the product lifecycles. Consequently, an implicit assumption made by most stakeholders and many researchers is that products need to be returned to the original producer; this, however, limits the field of vision and underestimates end-of-life complexity and possibilities.

3 The Cascade Use Methodology

The authors refer to those lifecycles that split-up at the reuse level eventually flowing into yet again different 'steams', i.e. supply chains, at the recycling level as 'cascading utilization'. The cascade use methodology aims to integrate the broad variety of end-of-life options into the management of product lifecycles. The cascade use methodology acknowledges the complexity at the end-of-life, and shows how products and eventually materials cascade through reuse and recycling to recovery (ideally avoiding landfill). The idea of cascade use derives from the biomass domain where it describes the different processes that renewable resources happen to pass before treated as an energy source (e.g. from wood through boards and recycled fibers to fibers as fuel for energy production) [18]. In addition to the biomass domain, the term 'cascade' is used in contexts of lifecycle management and reuse. Related to quantitative approaches in CLSCs, Guide and van Wassenhove [19] use the term 'cascade reuse opportunities';

they further state research gaps regarding a 'life-cycle approach' that considers all the different types of product returns. Therefore, there is no general definition for the term 'cascade'.

However, the cascade from the biomass domain serves as a blueprint that is combined with the WMH steps 'reuse', 'recycle' and 'recovery'. Figure 1 shows the cascade use methodology and depicts clearly the increasing complexity and variety of end-of-life options at the levels reuse, recycle and recovery. The downwards inclination conceals that products and materials can remain at each cascade level through iterations of reuse (e.g. remanufacturing) or recycling (up-/down-cycling). In addition, this cascade does not consider landfill, because landfill does not contribute to circularity [4].

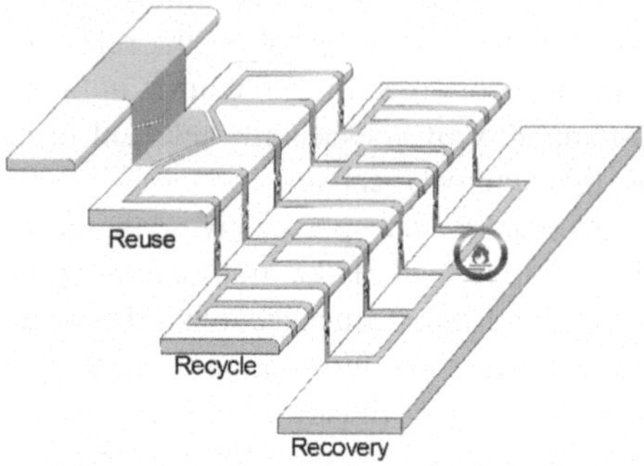

Fig. 1. Cascade use methodology [6]

Thinking in cascades influences the product lifecycle from the start, for example, through design principles facilitating cascade levels. This applies similarly to components replaced during the product lifetime. However, even products that were designed for lifecycle iterations or that are part of a circular business model do not always reach the corresponding CLSC. In such cases, third parties may take advantage of these flows and perform activities mimicking the CLSC. Therefore, various supply chains can co-exist at the reuse level and, similarly, at the recycling level of the cascade.

The visualization of different cascades fosters alternative end-of-life solutions, in supporting decision makers to identify economic and environmental potential in the different 'streams' of the cascade. It integrates market realities of trade with used products and of changing end-of-life options. The realities at the end-of-life are neither a perfect circular flow towards known stakeholders nor are they as one-directional as critics of classic forward supply chains may claim. Hence, the narrow perspective on a predefined lifecycle potentially supported through CLSC management limits the view on opportunities for alternative and maybe even more sustainable subsequent lifecycles. The cascade use methodology acknowledges these different supply chains and recognizes that one supply chain owner can hardly manage all potential end-of-life scenarios.

4 Results

Challenges regarding used-product collection in general, further complicated by dynamics on real-world markets, foster the previously described complexity. The cascade use methodology, applied and discussed below, addresses this gap regarding new and alternative actors in the management of product lifecycles with a real-world case. The methodology further underlines that the management of product lifecycles must consider additional supply chains than those corresponding to the originally planned product lifecycle. The cascade use methodology has been demonstrated and applied before using two original cases [6]; those cases focused on product components (vehicle parts). This paper applies the methodology to a novel case focusing on the product (vehicles) through a similar empirical, case-based approach. However, a distinct emphasis is placed on the supply chain perspective. The product perspective motivated the case selection reasonably complementing the preceding methodology applications. The presented case addresses vehicle reuse across different markets with details on the quantities of end-of-life products that reach the reuse level and split into different supply chains. The case contextualizes the discussion on CLSCs at the reuse level and provides details on notable deviations from predicted supply chains due to market dynamics.

4.1 From Japan to Chile: Notable Used-Vehicle Export Supply Chains

Despite some differences and somewhat slowing sales, new car sales in developed countries of the European Union, North America and Japan result in numerous used vehicles that enter reuse at local or export markets or directly to material recycling. Between 2009 and 2013, the U.S. exported on average 762,000 cars per year mainly to lower-income countries [20]. In 2014 the US and Canada reached a combined export value of used cars of USD 1.4 billion [21]. The EU officially exports approximately 1.2 million used cars per year. However, the real number of exported used cars is not known and can be safely assumed to be significantly higher considering that the number of cars classified as 'unknown whereabouts' reached 4.75 million vehicles in 2014. Some of these vehicles reach unofficial recycling channels, others are simply exported legally but not monitored [22]. Japan exports approximately one million passenger cars per year [23] especially to Asian, Oceanic and African countries—but also to South America [24]. Figure 2 shows the top–ten export destinations of used vehicles from Japan in 2015. Noteworthy are two destinations in this list that are strict right-hand traffic countries that, as best determined, do not allow right-hand-drive vehicles on their roads. Japan is a left-hand traffic country hence exports used right-hand-drive vehicles.

These streams of used vehicles at the reuse level of the cascade usually appear in classic forward supply chains through the transfer of ownership. Even if vehicles were previously managed in a CLSC facilitated by leasing or renting business models, these CLSCs eventually become forward supply chains for reuse. Either way, for the case of Chile, the transfer of ownership after a first use in Japan results in a transfer into a different region with different rules and legal obligations. Furthermore, the repair and recycling infrastructure may be different in the importing region.

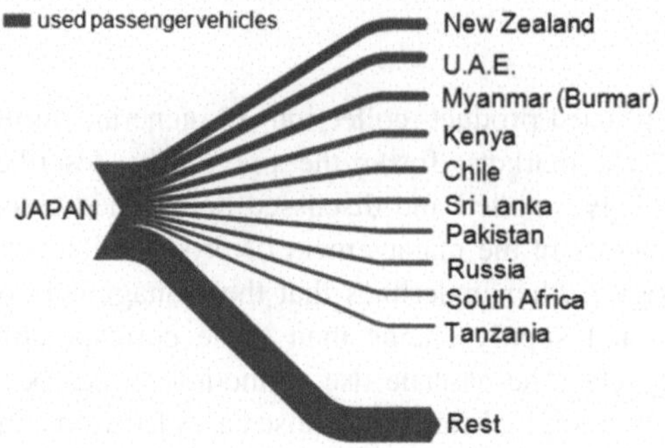

Fig. 2. Top 10 export destinations of used passenger cars from Japan (strict left-hand-drive countries marked red; own representation, data source: http://jevic.com) (Color figure online)

4.2 'Cambio Volante': Market Dynamics Spur Remarkable Reuse Activities

The authors followed the export supply chain of Japanese used vehicles to a remarkable reuse activity in Chile in the port of the city of Iquique, which is part of the free trade zone ZOFRI (Zona Franca de Iquique). Tax exemptions and a demand for low-cost transportation in the surrounding region of Tarapacá and neighboring countries like Peru and Bolivia, as well as Paraguay, provide demand for used-vehicles. Although used-vehicles from Japan are relatively young (generally ~6–7 years; some only 4 years according to local source) and in relatively good condition, they need to be converted to left-hand-drive to be used in these countries. Thus, in the vicinity of the port of Iquique, mechanics convert vehicles in so-called 'cambio volante' (steering wheel 'changeover') workshops. Although this case may raise concerns about the safety of converted vehicles, it is notable that Japanese exporters provide conversion kits and even full conversion services that are conducted in Japan before export (see for example, www.japan-partner.com/LHD-conversion.php; www.globalauto.co.jp/reason_e.html), which indicate some formal acceptance of the conversion process. Nevertheless, the conversion workshops suffer from shortages with regard to parts that must be replaced, such as the steering rack. Other parts, like the ventilation ducts and the A/C unit, can be refitted with limitations. In general, all these parts are readily available as new spare parts (for left-hand-drive vehicles) provided within Japanese-sourced conversion kits. However, either the workshops cannot afford the retail prices of OEMs or such parts are not exported to Chile. In few cases, some OEMs install convertible components such as steering racks that can be 'flipped' hence used both in left-hand-drive and right-hand-drive vehicles. Such solutions substantially facilitate the conversion process. Workshops further intend to source alternative parts such as copies though often the identification of suppliers is difficult and the transport and import costs can raise to a prohibitive level. Used parts are an alternative to new parts (whether original or copies) though it can be difficult to acquire such in the required qualities or quantities. Therefore, the workshops constantly search for parts that cannot be 'flipped' such as steering racks. However, they manually rework and modify parts that need to be converted (e.g., the dashboard and retrofitting of A/C components), which establishes reasoned objections against conversion. Figure 3 depicts the case and its supply chains using the cascade use methodology.

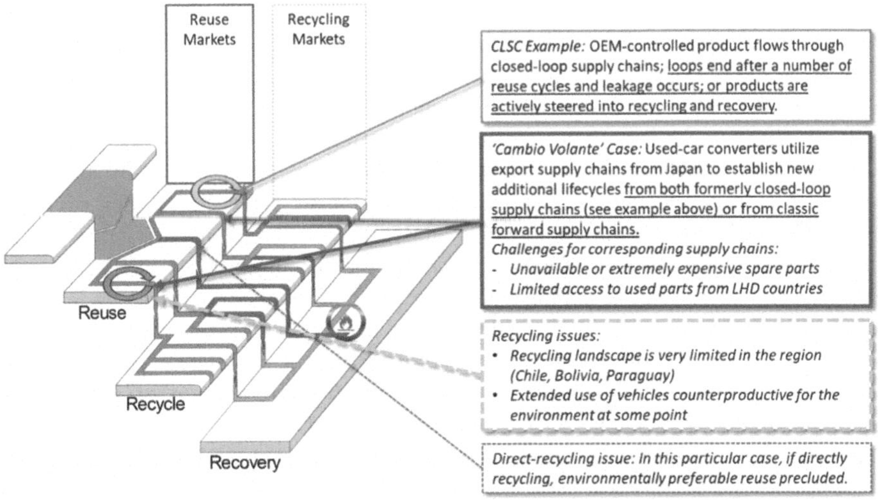

Fig. 3. Lifecycle and supply chain cascade for used-vehicle exports from Japan to Chile (the direct recycling route in red is not discuss in detail; adopted from Kalverkamp *et al.* [6]) (Color figure online)

5 Discussion

The exemplary case of vehicle conversion in Chile represents one of the many different supply chains that emerge from vehicle end-of-life in Japan. Similar forward supply chains may reach other countries too. Exports of used vehicles in developed countries before their optimal end-of-life makes vehicle reuse through these supply chains reasonable from an environmental perspective. In addition to the benefits in these supply chains due to trade gains and for customers due to affordable individual mobility, the (re-)manufacturing-like process of 'cambio volante' increases the demand for skilled labor, which addresses the societal dimension of sustainability. However, this particular cascading product lifecycle has limitations, such as stresses on the recycling infrastructure in the importing country, which may increase environmental impacts (compared to the home country) once the converted vehicle is reaching its ultimate end-of-life (in the import country). Furthermore, the export supply chain of used vehicles lacks an accompanying supply chain for spare parts or the parts provided raise the conversion costs to a prohibitive level. This may lead to a 'do-it-yourself' approach when converting vehicles and raises reasoned objections against such conversion. The case showed that some solutions exist, such as the design-stage solution of making steering racks that can be used both ways (left-hand-drive/right-hand-drive). Although it is more likely that OEMs designed these steering racks to improve their purchasing power and to reduce costs, it also facilitates the conversion of vehicles. However, further components and parts must be changed during the conversion process and their supply is limited as well.

From this case, the cascade use methodology highlights a hidden 'stream' in the automobile lifecycle and thereby indicates where additional product lifecycles emerge. The case makes evident that the complexity at the end-of-life involves many different actors in addition to OEMs and that 'open-loop' supply chains can complement CLSC to provide sustainable outcomes in supply chains.

From the perspective of the cascade use methodology, the Chilean case is an example where OEMs and other actors can contribute to sustainability by amending their product lifecycle and corresponding supply chain perspectives. For example, OEMs could provide certain components and parts to conversion workshops, potentially through special licenses. OEM arguments emphasizing product safety and risks due to the conversion can be anticipated, however, the conversion services by Japanese exporters indicate that some design thinking and a standardized conversion process is possible. Furthermore, the involvement of third-parties in activities such as remanufacturing is similarly criticized by OEMs despite the contribution of independent remanufacturers for sustainable outcomes of remanufacturing systems [25]. Such arguments seem to fall short in cases of contraventions that harm OEM customers, such as the recent and infamous emission scandal. Hence, this idea might not be popular with OEMs though should be discussed when sustainability is truly valued.

Other potential suppliers such as vehicle dismantlers and parts dealers, could be more prominent actors in 'spare part supply chains for vehicle conversion'. These actors have the knowledge and access to used products. However, parts dealers from North America and Europe, being right-hand-drive regions, would be particularly relevant here, though trade is limited due to various barriers (such as taxes and regulations). Innovative solutions that improve the complex global reuse supply chains could support a safer conversion process. Recycling infrastructures have to accompany these developments in order to cover subsequent levels of cascading lifecycles.

Policy could utilize this knowledge and discuss tax exemptions for selected reuse-products or even develop strategies to attract refurbishing or remanufacturing businesses. Combined with an enforced extended producer responsibility for importers of new and used products (like the recycling legislation recently introduced by the Chilean government; http://leydereciclaje.mma.gob.cl) resulting in economic activities could contribute to all three dimensions of sustainability.

Neither CLSC nor product lifecycle management address unintended or unwanted supply chains emerging from the end-of-life. Those supply chains often develop due to dynamics on markets. The used product of one market can serve the needs at another market. The cascade use methodology sheds light on supply chains that complement CLSC in a sustainable manner without the management of a central actor. Therefore, the rather centralized control of CLSCs may require managerial approaches that complement existing supply chain strategies as a supporter of product lifecycle management. In addition, economic and environmental considerations may sometimes require governmental involvement to steer the streams of the cascade.

6 Conclusion and Outlook

The cascade use methodology aims to shed light on circular economy opportunities in addition to and beyond the CLSC. It broadens the perspective on market dynamics occurring at the end-of-life and affecting product lifecycles. The study recognized that less control over end-of-life decisions might not be the preferred choice for OEMs. However, if the variety of end-of-life waste streams were considered as an opportunity for lifecycle management, environmental and economic benefits could arise that also complement the originally designed lifecycle.

Complexity at the end-of-life and limitations in the current management of product lifecycles and in corresponding PLM solutions affect sustainability. The cascade use methodology suggests identifying the current cascades of a product to locate those cascade streams where a company can support reuse and recycling in a sustainable manner: Although concerned by less control over the value and supply chain, a motivation could be to regain certain influence over end-of-life decisions. However, the study only examined one case. Further cases are necessary to better assess the potential of 'open-loop supply chains' and to motivate practitioners and researchers to investigate the 'unseen or unwanted' supply chains. In addition, developing criteria for decisions on open- vs. closed-loop supply chains and investigating how management could benefit from open-loop supply chains provides fruitful ground for research.

Acknowledgements. MK and AP were financially supported by the German Federal Ministry of Education and Research (Grant No: 01LN1310A).

References

1. EC: Circular Economy Strategy. http://ec.europa.eu/environment/circular-economy/index_en.htm. Accessed 31 May 2016
2. NPC: Circular economy promotion law of the People's Republic of China: adopted at the 4th session of the standing committee of the 11th national people's congress of the People's Republic of China. Standing Committee of the National People's Congress (NPC), China, August 2008
3. Ellen MacArthur Foundation: Towards the Circular Economy: An economic and business rationale for an accelerated transition. https://www.ellenmacarthurfoundation.org/publications/. Accessed 13 July 2016
4. European Commission: Closing the loop - An EU action plan for the Circular Economy. COM (2015). 614 final. http://eur-lex.europa.eu/legal-content/EN/TXT/?uri=CELEX:52015DC0614. Accessed 05 July 2016
5. Thierry, M., Salomon, M., van Nunen, J., van Wassenhove, L.: Strategic issues in product recovery management. Calif. Manag. Rev. **37**(2), 114–135 (1995). https://doi.org/10.2307/41165792
6. Kalverkamp, M., Pehlken, A., Wuest, T.: Cascade use and the management of product lifecycles. Sustainability **9**(9), 1540 (2017). https://doi.org/10.3390/su9091540
7. Tukker, A.: Product services for a resource-efficient and circular economy – a review. J. Clean. Prod. **97**, 76–91 (2015). https://doi.org/10.1016/j.jclepro.2013.11.049

8. Moreno, M., de Los Rios, C., Rowe, Z., Charnley, F.: A conceptual framework for circular design. Sustainability **8**(9), 937 (2016). https://doi.org/10.3390/su8090937
9. Guide, V.D.R., van Wassenhove, L.N.: The evolution of closed-loop supply chain research. Oper. Res. **57**(1), 10–18 (2009). https://doi.org/10.1287/opre.1080.0628
10. Majumder, P., Groenevelt, H.: Competition in remanufacturing. Prod. Oper. Manag. **10**(2), 125–141 (2001). https://doi.org/10.1111/j.1937-5956.2001.tb00074.x
11. Borsato, M.: Bridging the gap between product lifecycle management and sustainability in manufacturing through ontology building. Comput. Ind. **65**(2), 258–269 (2014). https://doi.org/10.1016/j.compind.2013.11.003
12. Tibben-Lembke, R.S.: Life after death: reverse logistics and the product life cycle. Int. J. Phys. Distrib. Log. Manag. **32**(3), 223–244 (2002). https://doi.org/10.1108/09600030210426548
13. Terzi, S., Bouras, A., Dutta, D., Garetti, M., Kiritsis, D.: Product lifecycle management - from its history to its new role. IJPLM **4**(4), 360 (2010). https://doi.org/10.1504/IJPLM.2010.036489
14. Jun, H.-B., Kiritsis, D., Xirouchakis, P.: Research issues on closed-loop PLM. Comput. Ind. **58**(8–9), 855–868 (2007). https://doi.org/10.1016/j.compind.2007.04.001
15. Svensson, G.: The theoretical foundation of supply chain management. Int. J. Phys. Distrib. Log. Manag. **32**(9), 734–754 (2002). https://doi.org/10.1108/09600030210452422
16. Ziout, A., Azab, A., Atwan, M.: A holistic approach for decision on selection of end-of-life products recovery options. J. Clean. Prod. **65**, 497–516 (2014). https://doi.org/10.1016/j.jclepro.2013.10.001
17. Hu, G., Bidanda, B.: Modeling sustainable product lifecycle decision support systems. Int. J. Prod. Econ. **122**(1), 366–375 (2009). https://doi.org/10.1016/j.ijpe.2009.06.011
18. Haberl, H., Geissler, S.: Cascade utilization of biomass: strategies for a more efficient use of a scarce resource. Ecol. Eng. **16**, 111–121 (2000). https://doi.org/10.1016/S0925-8574(00)00059-8
19. Guide, V.D.R., Wassenhove, L.N.: Closed-loop supply chains: an introduction to the feature issue (part 1). Prod. Oper. Manag. **15**(3), 345–350 (2006). https://doi.org/10.1111/j.1937-5956.2006.tb00249.x
20. Coffin, D.: Used vehicles are an important component of U.S. passenger-vehicle exports. USITC Executive Briefings on Trade, USITC, January 2015
21. Coffin, D., Horowitz, J., Nesmith, D., Semanik, M.: Examining Barriers to Trade in Used Vehicles. Working Paper ID-044, USITC - Office of Industries, August 2016. https://www.usitc.gov/publications/332/used_vehicle_wp_id-44_final_web_0.pdf. Accessed 13 September 2017
22. Sander, K., Wagner, L., Sanden, J., Wilts, H.: Development of proposals, including legal instruments, to improve the data situation on the whereabouts of end-of-life vehicles. Umweltbundesamt, Dessau-Roßlau (2017)
23. Kumar, S., Yamaoka, T.: System dynamics study of the Japanese automotive industry closed loop supply chain. J. Manufact. Technol. Manag. **18**(2), 115–138 (2007). https://doi.org/10.1108/17410380710722854
24. Zaun, T., Singer, J.: How Japan's second-hand cars make their way to third world: Sophisticated market handles big used-vehicle surplus; way station in Dubai. Wall Street J. (2004). https://www.wsj.com/articles/SB107352145936011400
25. Kalverkamp, M., Raabe, T.: Automotive remanufacturing in the circular economy in Europe: marketing system challenges. J. Macromarketing **38**(1), 112–130 (2017). https://doi.org/10.1177/0276146717739066

How Food Companies Manage Their Innovation Process: A Multinational Food Company Point of View

Claudia Pinna(✉), Monica Rossi, and Sergio Terzi

Department of Management, Economics and Industrial Engineering, Politecnico di Milano, Piazza Leonardo da Vinci, 20133 Milan, Italy
{claudia.pinna,monica.rossi,sergio.terzi}@polimi.it

Abstract. This current research, as a natural consequence of previous findings, focuses on the first phase of the New Food Development (NFD) process. Being this phase the most creative and innovative, it comes naturally to think it is also the most chaotic, very difficult to standardize and to control. At the same time, this phase is considered one of the most important of the overall process, because it adds the most value to the product that is going to be created. Starting from these considerations, the aim of this paper is to enrich the previous study by understanding how food companies could enhance their competitiveness by leveraging on their front-end process, with a special focus on the use of structured approaches for creativity and innovation and on the PLM solution. An important multinational food company has been used as a case study to investigate the above research objectives and to provide a preliminary conceptual framework to model the impact of structured front-end process on the overall NFD success. This study allowed to identify how the FFE food process is structured, the main CSFs and KPIs, as well as which methods and IT tools are used to support the analyzed process. Concerning the latest, a deeper analysis has been done focusing on the PLM solution, understanding how its functionalities are used to support the different FFE process sub-activities. Finally, this work confirms the results identified in the previous study, affirming the lack of adoption that the PLM solution plays in the FFE phase.

Keywords: Food sector · Innovation process · New Food Development
New product development · NPD

1 Introduction

Over the last years, the food industry has become increasingly relevant since it represents excellence in the worldwide economy [1]. However, despite the growing importance of this sector, food firms still face many challenges in managing their products and competing in the market. This research starts from the results of previous works, focused on the new product development process - called New Food Development process (NFD) for the food context, being recognized as an added value process for food companies [2, 3]. NFD generates value for the product that they have to introduce to the market, contributing consequently to greater success. This is

Published by Springer Nature Switzerland AG 2018.
P. Chiabert et al. (Eds.): PLM 2018, IFIP AICT 540, pp. 169–180, 2018.
https://doi.org/10.1007/978-3-030-01614-2_16

necessary since in a highly competitive market food companies must develop new products valued by consumers. While previous studies from the authors [3–7] discuss how multinational food firms could increase their competitiveness in the market and improve their performance by leveraging on the use of the Product Lifecycle Management (PLM) solution to support the NFD process, this current research, as a natural consequence of previous findings, focuses on the first phase of the same process, called 'upfront' or 'Fuzzy Front-End' (FFE). Important considerations have emerged from the results of such study. In particular, being the FFE phase the most creative and innovative of the process taken into consideration, it is also the most chaotic, very difficult to standardize and to control. At the same time, this phase is considered one of the most important of the overall process because it adds the most value to the product that is going to be created. The aim of this paper is to understand how food companies could enhance their competitiveness by leveraging on their FFE process - considering the use of structured approaches for creativity and innovation and on the possible tools, with a particular focus on the PLM solution. Therefore, the study focuses on: (i) how the process is structured, (ii) the main tools and methods as well as (iii) the main Critical Success Factors (CSF) and KPIs. This study is part of a wider research project - started in January 2018 and still ongoing - that has the main objective to understand the role of methods and tools on FFE food performances, with a specific focus on the role of the PLM solution. The work was carried out independently, in collaboration with an Italian company which has been used as case study. The company is a historic Italian firm operating in the bakery sector and part of a group that is the owner of several brands. It deals also with production on behalf of third parties and private labels. This collaboration allows to investigate the research objectives and to validate the preliminary conceptual framework and questionnaire developed. The paper starts, in Sect. 2, with a state of the art about methodologies and tools used to support the fuzzy front end process in the food industry. Following, Sect. 3, describes a preliminary empirical research, which defines the research methodology, as well as the meaning and scope of the difference from each part of the questionnaire. In Sect. 4, results of the case study have been presented and developed with the aim to validate the questionnaire. In this section, particular attention has been given to the PLM solution. Finally, Sect. 5 concludes the paper, presenting some thoughts about future research.

2 State of the Art: Methodologies and Tools for FFE

The literature review has been conducted with the aim to investigate if there are some scientific studies concerning the use of methodologies and/or tools supporting the FFE process phase. The FFE is the first phase of the NPD process. It begins when an opportunity is first considered worthy of further ideation, exploration, and assessment and it ends when a firm decides to invest in the idea, commit significant resources to its development and launch the project [8–10]. Thus, the FFE could be defined as the period between when an opportunity is first considered and when an idea is judged ready for development. The FFE phase, contrary to the development phase, is intrinsically non-routine, dynamic and uncertain. The idea-development and subsequent idea-selection stages typically involve ad hoc decisions and ill-defined process [11].

This phase can be further divided in order to better manage it. Griffin (1997), for example, divides the predevelopment phase by the 'concept generation stage', this latter begins when the idea for the product first surfaces, and also by the 'project evaluation stage', which starts when the product strategy and target market have been approved and the project has been given a 'go' to develop specifications [12].

According to Monteiro et al. (2010), FFE is an essential phase leading to the success of innovation [13], this is the reason why various software tools have been proposed to support FFE activities. The aforementioned authors conducted a systematic literature review analyzing 1090 articles published between 1997 and 2009. The results obtained show that the use of software tools supporting the FFE process can generate many benefits, among which to: speed up the FFE, reduce costs, increase collaboration, improve decision quality and knowledge management, reduce risks, and enhance overall creativity [13]. Therefore, companies may support their FFE using different tools, methods, and techniques [14]. Thus, the use of tools, methods, and techniques that support the FFE of innovation seems to have a positive influence on innovation performance. Starting from these considerations, the main aim of the next sections is to understand with a practical study which tools and methodologies are used to support the FFE phase by food companies.

3 Preliminary Empirical Research

3.1 Theoretical Framework and Research Questions

To achieve the research aim, a methodology based on 6 different activities have been proposed. These activities are focused on the identification of:

1. the main activities characterizing the FFE food process,
2. the main information characterizing each phase of the FFE food process,
3. the methods used to support the FFE food process,
4. the tools used to support the FFE food process,
5. the actors involved in the FFE food process,
6. the main KPIs and CSFs used to measure the FFE food process.

To develop these actions, a questionnaire was developed. Figure 1 shows the theoretical framework and the logic sequence used to develop the different sections of the questionnaire.

3.2 Methodology – Research Strategy

In this work, Case Study [15] has been utilized as a research strategy.

Questionnaires were used as a research tool. In January 2018, it was tested and validated through a Pilot Case with the help of an important Italian food company. Company actors who mostly interface with this solution were chosen (R&D and IT managers). The pilot case questionnaire has been first submitted to the R&D and IT managers by email and a face to face interview have been developed. A standard protocol was followed and identified to be valid for each case study. Up to now, the

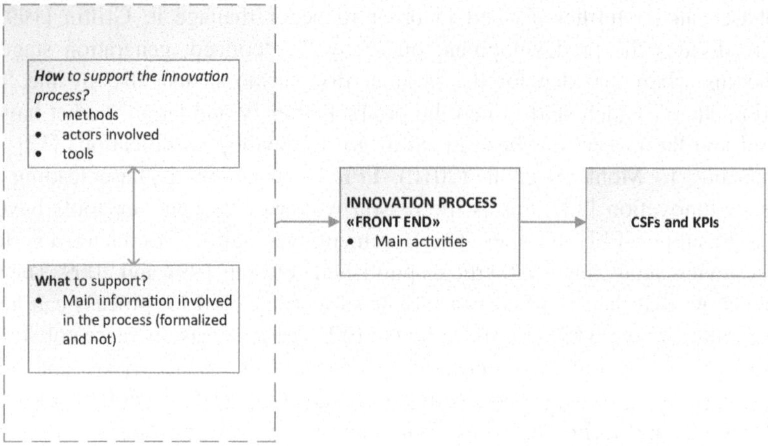

Fig. 1. Research framework

paper is structured following the main section of the protocol. Results of this pilot case are presented in the following section.

4 A First Empirical Research

4.1 Company Overview

The company interviewed is a historic Italian company of bakery products. It mostly produces traditional Italian bakery products such as panettone, pandoro, colomba, and croissants. The group is also the owner of several brands. They also deal with production on behalf of third parties and private label. Accordingly, their products could be essentially divided into three categories, that are: recurring products (those products that are typically sold during the Catholic holidays), pre-recurring products (really tasted products offered before festivities by supermarkets) and dairy products (snacks are their main daily consumption products and specifically the naturally leavened croissants).

Company CSFs and KPIs

The first section of the questionnaire is dedicated to the company overview. This phase allows understanding the company, and specifically, the sector its belonging to, as well as the strategic objectives (CSFs) and the indicators used to measure their achievements (KPIs). Usually, CSFs are used to define key areas of activity and to identify the strategic indicators of the company [8].

In the case of analysis, two main CSFs have been identified: (i) *Company growth through geographical expansion* and (ii) *product quality*.

Concerning the indicators used to measure the company performances, two main KPIs are mostly used (i) *financial measures*, defined as an estimation of the achievement of certain turnover targets linked to the new products, both for the Italian and the international market and (ii) *volume measures* defined as quantity, number of pieces produced or kilos. At this point, authors decided to focus on one specific category of product and of innovation (incremental innovation), in order to limit the boundaries of this research and obtain more precise results. From that point until the end, the analysis focuses on the daily product category and specifically on the healthy segment products.

4.2 Company New Food Development Process: Phases, Activities, CSFs and KPIs

The second section of the questionnaire allows to better understand how the NFD process is carried out. Starting from results of a previous research [3–5, 7, 16], the main phases and activities characterizing the NFD process, reported in Table 1, have been validated. Furthermore, CSFs and KPIs have been identified, with a specific focus on the research boundaries. Results from this section of the questionnaire are shown in the following table:

Table 1. Company NFD phases, activities, CSFs and KPIs.

Phases	Activities	CSFs	KPIs
FFE or Pre-development	Concept generation	- Concept and product adequacy with respect to consumers expectations	- Consumer satisfaction test compared to some predefined indicators
	Feasibility analysis		- Turnover derived from product innovation
	Planning		- Contribution derived from product innovation
Recipe development	Recipe definition	- The ability of the new products to generate incremental volumes and turnover	- Number of successful ideas
	Recipe test and feasibility		- On time launches
	Product internal feasibility		- Compliance with product target cost
Prototyping and test	Product external feasibility	- Time	- Compliance with project objectives
	Prototyping		
Industrialization	Industrial tests		
	Quality tests		
Production, Launch and Commercialization	Bulk production		
	Timing		

As shown from the table, the main strategical objectives of the company (concerning the NFD process) are customers' expectations, revenue and time.

4.3 Company Fuzzy Front End Phase (Pre-development)

The aim of this questionnaire section is to identify the main phases, activities, and sub-activities characterizing the company FFE phase. Furthermore, the main CSFs and KPIs have been identified for most FFE sub-activities.

Company FFE process is characterized by three main activities (concept generation, feasibility analysis, and planning) which in turn are characterized by some sub-activities. Specifically, those sub-activities describe how each activity is carried out.

Analyzing Tables 1 and 2, some common objectives could be identified, particularly linked to the customer's expectations. However, the FFE food phase puts more emphasis on the sensory aspect and the quality of the product (intended as the use of a low number of natural ingredients).

Table 2. Company FFE phases, activities, CSFs and KPIs

Activities	Sub-activities	Company actors	CSFs	KPIs
Concept generation	- Analyze markets - Consumers usage and attitudes (U&A) - Survey customers - Generate product ideas	- Marketing - Trade marketing - R&D	- Correspondence between product and consumer expectation (mostly related to the presentation and sensory features)	- testing with consumers - generation of a number of ideas that succeed the concept test phase - correspondence between generated ideas and company general objectives
Feasibility analysis	- Technical, legal and regulatory feasibility	- Marketing - R&D - Finance - Sales - Operations - Quality - Legal	- the possibility of a product with certain sensory characteristics, with an extremely limited number of ingredients and without adding ingredients that prolong the shelf-life - trade-off good product (few ingredients and natural) and economic competitiveness	- respect of the maximum target cost - compliance with current regulations - feasibility in "itself" (i.e. Is it possible to produce a biscuit without additives?)

(*continued*)

Table 2. (*continued*)

Activities	Sub-activities	Company actors	CSFs	KPIs
Planning	- Prioritize and approve ideas - Define programs - Create product/project/marketing briefs	- Marketing - R&D - Finance - Sales - Operations - Quality		- Project time - Project cost

In this phase of the NFD process, many company actors are involved. The multidisciplinary skills of the team are crucial in this preliminary phase in order to generate a product that has to: be aligned with the customer needs (marketing, trade marketing, sales), respect the regulatory compliances (legal), feasible both economically and technically (finance, operations, R&D), respect certain quality levels (quality).

4.4 Information, Tools and Methods Supporting Company FFE Activities

In this section, the main information characterizing the company FFE activities as well as the main methods and tools supporting these activities are identified and shown in Table 3.

Table 3. Information, Tools and Methods supporting company FFE activities

Sub-activities	Information	Source	Methods	IT Tools	Methods and tools users
Analyze markets	- category size - consumption per capita - average price - number of competitors - market ability to innovate	- data banks (i.e. nielsen, iri) - data on innovation (i.e. mintel, innova)	- open innovation	No	- R&D - Marketing
Consumers usage and attitudes (U&A)	- consumers information	- research institutes	- statistical methods - data collection	No	- Marketing
Survey customers	- shelf space for a certain category - average price - % product sold at a discount	- clients (distribution chains)	No	No	- Trade marketing

(*continued*)

Table 3. (*continued*)

Sub-activities	Information	Source	Methods	IT Tools	Methods and tools users
Generate product ideas	- new ingredients - new technologies - new packaging	- supplier	- open innovation - TRIZ - Design thinking - workshop with suppliers	- open innovation portals - PLM (mostly as a repository)	- R&D - Marketing
Feasibility analysis	- possibility to realize the product, in an economically valid and sustainable way and according to the law	- technical specifications - target destination country laws and regulations - details of the income statement, company financial data	- there is no developed method, it is specific to each company	- PLM	- R&D - Marketing - Finance - Sales
Prioritize and approve ideas	- economic considerations - strategic considerations (advantages to enter a new market, new segment, etc.)	- company internal evaluations	- Open innovation	No	- Marketing - Finance
Define programs	- available resources detection - functions involved - time allocable for resources - available budget	- company business functions	- project management	- PLM	- R&D - Marketing
Create marketing briefs	- target cost - target of time - target of product - timing - resources	- all the previous phases (formalized summary previous info)	No	- PLM	- R&D - Marketing

Table 3 highlights which are the main information used to develop each sub-activity of the FFE food process and also the main source used to find that information. Tools and methods supporting each sub-activity have been also identified. In general, the main methods used are open innovation, statistical methods, data collection,

TRIZZ, design thinking, the involvement of suppliers (that are considered the main source of innovation) and methods belonging to the project management subject. At the same time, some tools supporting those sub-activities have been identified, and specifically PLM and open innovations portals.

How the PLM Solution Support the FFE Food Phase

Focusing on the use of the PLM solution, functionalities have been identified supporting some the company FFE sub-activities. The sub-activities identified supported by the PLM functionalities are:

- *Generate product ideas*: PLM is used mostly as a repository. In this phase information coming from previous products already developed by the company, from market analysis focused on the customers' needs as well as from other product life cycle phases are collected and used to support the creation of new ideas; specifically, the main PLM functionalities supporting the information needed by this activity are: *product portfolio and program management* and *specifications management*.
- *Feasibility analysis*: the PLM functionality called *regulatory compliance* is used to support the regulatory feasibility. This functionality supports tools enabling companies to identify what regulations, policies and obligations are applicable to them. It allows companies to proactively ensure compliance throughout the product life cycle and fully integrate product quality and food safety into the process of developing and managing products;
- *Define programs*: the PLM functionality called *project management* is used to support the definition of programs. It supports the project, collecting data and results along all the phases of the project in order to drive the company decisions. This functionality supports the management workflow by automating process workflows, as well as the related ability to create, archive, trace and search documents. Change management workflows direct information (which could be new or changed) to the right people in order to be reviewed and approved, allowing to find mistakes, ensure accuracy and consistency;
- *Create marketing briefs:* in this phase, all the information and decision taken along the FFE process phase are formalized in order to generate a common brief that has to be used to support the next product development phases. In this sense, the PLM help to keep the information available, constantly updated and also achievable. This allows facilitating the brief creation, ensuring data availability and reliability. The *project management* functionality is used to support this activity.

5 Conclusions and Further Research

As previously mentioned, this study is part of a wider research project that has the main objective to understand the role of methods and tools on FFE food performances, with a specific focus on the role of the PLM solution. This paper shows the results of a case study analysis, developed with the aid of an Italian company operating in the bakery sector. This study allowed to identify how the FFE food process is structured (activities and sub-activities), the main CSFs and KPIs, as well as which methods and tools are used to support the analyzed process. Concerning the IT tools (open innovation portals and PLM functionalities), a deeper analysis was done for the PLM solution, understanding how its functionalities are used to support the different FFE process sub-activities. This work confirms the previous work results, affirming the lack of adoption that the PLM solution plays in the FFE phase. Specifically, in the previous work [7], Authors stated the interest to understand why PLM functionalities are not implemented in this phase. They also made some hypotheses, that are the following: (i) a lack of understanding of real benefits PLM systems applications might have on those phases, (ii) PLM functionalities might miss to specifically support those phases or simply (iii) implementation of software solutions in such phases are not easy to apply and be sustained on a daily work basis. Analyzing the interview, some considerations have emerged confirming all of these hypotheses. Starting from that, this work defines the main activities and sub-activities characterizing the FFE process. Moreover, special attention has been given to the company strategical objectives. The main company objectives are company growth through geographical expansion and quality. Focusing on the NFD process, the main objectives identified are customers' expectations, revenue and time. Moving to the specific FFE phase, some commonalities have been found concerning the CSFs, and in detail about the customer's expectations aspect. However, the FFE food phase puts more emphasis on the sensory and quality of the product. Moreover, the main methods used for FFE food have been identified. At the same time, some IT tools supporting those sub-activities have been identified. Particular attention has been given to the PLM functionalities supporting the FFE sub-activities. This choice derived from the fact that, even if the majority of the sub-activities are not supported by any tool, among those supported all use the PLM solution. Therefore, this consideration pushed to further investigate the way the PLM solution support the analyzed process. In this concern, PLM functionalities for FFE sub-activities have been identified. In order to understand how to measure the achievement of the CSFs, many KPIs have been identified. The interview confirmed what found in the literature review, concerning the relation between the use of tools and technologies in the FFE process and the related performances. In fact, according to Ester Val-Jauregi and Daniel Justel (2007), the use of tools, methods and techniques that support the FFE of innovation seems to have a positive influence on innovation performance [14]. This statement could be considered true also for the specific food sector. Another important result of this research is related to the company actors involved in the FFE food phase. In fact, the multidisciplinary aspect is considered very important in this context because allow developing a concept aligned with different needs and requirements.

Despite the interviewed company is considered as a big company, it still operates in a very traditional way. From the analysis of the interview, it emerged that they are willing to have a new supporting tool but they are not still ready to introduce it. In fact, this transformation involves first of all the workers that have to deal with it. In order to support this change, some training sessions have to be done in the company allowing the introduction of the mindset needed to support this important company evolution.

Despite the relevance of the research topic, some research limitations have been identified, concerning specifically the fact that only one case study has been developed in this study. The methodology adopted needs further analysis to generalize the results: a quantitative approach with a higher number of food firms adopting methods and tools to support the FFE food phase is necessary. Moreover, this research is explorative in nature, representing the first step toward a complete understanding of the phenomenon analyzed. A quantitative methodology could be developed assess more in detail the impact of the use of methods and tools on FFE food performances.

References

1. Lehmann, R.J., Reiche, R., Schiefer, G.: Future internet and the agri-food sector: state-of-the-art in literature and research. Comput. Electron. Agric. **89**, 158–174 (2012)
2. Rossi, M., Terzi, S.: CLIMB: maturity assessment model for design and engineering processes. Int. J. Prod. Lifecycle Manag. **10**(1), 20 (2017)
3. Pinna, C., Plo, L., Robin, V., Girard, P., Terzi, S.: An approach to improve implementation of PLM solution in food industry – case study of Poult Group. Int. J. Prod. Lifecycle Manag. **10**(2), 151–170 (2017)
4. Pinna, C., Avolio, E., Bandinelli, R., Terzi, S., Rinaldi, R.: Product development KPIs : a case study analysis in Food and Fashion companies. In: XXII Summer School "Francesco Turco" – Industrial Systems Engineering Product (2017)
5. d'Avolio, E., Pinna, C., Bandinelli, R., Terzi, S., Rinaldi, R.: Analysing product development process and PLM features in the food and fashion industries. In: Ríos, J., Bernard, A., Bouras, A., Foufou, S. (eds.) PLM 2017. IAICT, vol. 517, pp. 509–521. Springer, Cham (2017). https://doi.org/10.1007/978-3-319-72905-3_45
6. Pinna, C., Taisch, M., Terzi, S.: PLM in the food industry: an explorative empirical research in the italian market. In: Harik, R., Rivest, L., Bernard, A., Eynard, B., Bouras, A. (eds.) PLM 2016. IAICT, vol. 492, pp. 238–247. Springer, Cham (2016). https://doi.org/10.1007/978-3-319-54660-5_22
7. Pinna, C., Galati, F., Rossi, M., Saidy, C., Harik, R., Terzi, S.: Effect of product lifecycle management on new product development performances: evidence from the food industry. Comput. Ind. **100**, 184–195 (2018)
8. Smith, P.G., Reinertsen, D.G.: Shortening the product development cycle. Res. Manag. **35**(3), 44–49 (1992)
9. Cooper, R.G.: Winning at New Products: Accelerating from Idea to Launch, 2nd edn. Addison-Wesley, Reading (1993)
10. Khurana, A., Rosenthal, S.R.: Towards holistic 'front ends' in new product development. J. Prod. Innov. Manag. **15**(1), 57–74 (1998)
11. Montoya-Weiss, M.M., O'Driscoll, T.M.: From experience: applying performance support technology in the fuzzy front end. J. Prod. Innov. Manag. **17**(2), 143–161 (2000)
12. Griffin, A.: The effect of project and process characteristics on product development cycle time. J. Mark. Res. **34**(1), 24–35 (1997)
13. Monteiro, C., Arcoverde, D.F., da Silva, F.Q.B., Ferreira, H.S.: Software support for the fuzzy front end stage of the innovation process: a systematic literature review. In: 2010 IEEE International Conference on Management Innovation and Technology, pp. 426–431 (2010)

14. Val-jauregi, E., Justel, D.: Use of tools, methods and techniques during the fuzzy front end of innovation: their impact on innovation performance – a survey based exploratory study of companies in the basque country. Innovation, 1–12 (2007)
15. Yin, R.K.: Case study research. Des. Methods **26**(1), 93–96 (2003)
16. Pinna, C., Taisch, M., Terzi, S.: PLM in the food industry: an explorative empirical research in the italian market. In: Harik, R., Rivest, L., Bernard, A., Eynard, B., Bouras, A. (eds.) PLM 2016. IAICT, vol. 492, pp. 238–247. Springer, Cham (2016). https://doi.org/10.1007/978-3-319-54660-5_22

Product Lifecycle Management Strategy for the Definition and Design Process of Face Implants Oriented to Specific Patients

Cristian C. Ardila-Mejia(✉), Clara Isabel López-Gualdrón, and Javier Mauricio Martínez-Gómez

Universidad Industrial de Santander, Santander, Colombia
cristianc.am9310@gmail.com,
{clalogu, javimar}@uis.edu.co

Abstract. The main purpose of this research was oriented to generate a structured model from an organizational vision to the definition and development of precise osteosynthesis prosthesis. Implants were adapted to the Colombian population anthropometry allowing fracture reductions and craniofacial defects corrections based on technologies for specific patients. This research was developed taking into account the first three PLM stages: Imagination, definition, and realization. Procedures, stages, roles, and activities that take part in the design and pre-surgical planning were identified for the patient-specific implants PSI, carried out through a study case. It was established as a definition model for design and fabrication process of patient-specific implants (PSI). It was possible that technology included in a collaborative workflow wherein the roles which intervene in the design process and the pre-surgical planning were related. The ability to design implants for specific patients and surgical guides was obtained different pathology situations including face trauma. According to the PLM strategy for designing custom implant, it would be possible to build innovation capabilities. With those, an organization could generate a collaborative workflow integrating stages, roles, activities, applying technology and local human resource. Further work related to the subject is necessary to enhance the process by iteration and improve the clinical cases management.

Keywords: Collaborative workflow · Digital manufacturing
Patient-specific device · PLM model · Virtual surgical planning

1 Introduction

Development of new medical devices influences strongly in the surgical quality, that increases a better anatomical situation, real quantity of bone, and reconstruction demands. Therefore, functional restoration is achieved through those devices [1]. From those is obtained a surer, shorter and time predictable surgery [2].

Nowadays, plastic surgery is the health specialty with more influence in the reconstructive field for patients with osseous craniofacial defects [3, 4]. Surgeons have found complex defects that have been corrected through medical devices such as

Published by Springer Nature Switzerland AG 2018.
P. Chiabert et al. (Eds.): PLM 2018, IFIP AICT 540, pp. 181–190, 2018.
https://doi.org/10.1007/978-3-030-01614-2_17

surgical guides and patient-specific implants (PSI). These devices, also known as patient-specific devices (PSD), are designed according to the patient osseous structure and allowing restoration of anatomical appearance looking for aesthetic and functional properties [3]. However, virtual technology and digital manufacturing make possible application, which is necessary to medical procedures, such as diagnosis, pre-surgical planning, and surgery, becoming less complex by reducing uncertainty [5].

The main four steps in PSI development are: First, making a digital reconstruction model. Second, design process and device simulation. Third, evaluate the accuracy of the PSI compared with the biological surface. Fourth, piece evaluation [2]. The development of those steps in the process of PSI device involve tools such as reverse engineering (RE), computer-aided design - manufacturing- engineering (CAx), 3D modeling, and rapid prototyping (RP) techniques [6, 7].

Although the importance of the virtual technologies to guarantee PSI development, there would be uncertainty in the development process of this product related to its application on surgery. Implant design process is complex. To achieve medical requirement it demands lots of time and effort. That is why a specialized staff is mandatory, as well a complete evaluation of skull condition, soft tissue bundle, greater accuracy, and time during trauma treatment [1, 2]. The use of specialized software allows reducing the vagueness in precision and accuracy [5]. This implies that a multidisciplinary team must articulate different profiles in the organized structured way inside a collaborative workflow, defining roles and activities atPSI development.

PLM strategy has been implemented successfully in the automotive and aerospace industry [7]. They have defined an integrative vision of PLM strategy, that led to optimizing development time and resources, reducing mistakes on design and manufacture stages, increasing productivity and change controlling [8]. Product Lifecycle Management (PLM) has been set to control RE procedures, to take geometric or organic models as input. RE is been applying in the design process due to its feature to bring human models and the instance of using CAx tools to modify components [8, 9]. PLM strategy involves product data management PDM software, an information technology resource that enables a company to structure a collaborative workflow in safety database. It is useful to planning resources and creating a communication path among different stages, like design, manufacture, sales, support, and elimination. Its value resides in control procedures and selects the accurate tools to intervene through lifecycle product [9, 10]. Quality control and traceability of the process are crucial for medical device, topics which could be covered by PLM implemented strategy [11, 12]. This research defines the application of a PLM strategy looking for improving the development process of medical devices in a public university hospital from a developing country. The main contribution of this paper is related to the proposal of a visual model for PLM strategy in a non-traditional field such as Health. This paper was structured into four parts: first, materials and methods. Second, a PLM strategies structure proposed. Third, a case report is presented. Fourth, the conclusion of PLM implementation related to study case.

2 Materials and Methods

This research was developed in the following way: The first stage was to understand the current situation. This stage was divided in two: first, an exploratory study was conducted to defining procedures for PSI development in a Public University Hospital. Field observation was executed in the subject of context through collecting data about people, artifacts, and procedures, with non-structured interviews. Data were organized according to the timeline for patient attention, specifically on maxillofacial surgery field. Second, a non-structured literature review was conducted, related with PSI for skull and face recovery cases, in order to identify software tools for imaging, virtual reconstruction, modeling and 3D printing of custom medical devices. The second stage was to propose a process line with in the public university hospital for developing a PSI, by implementing a PLM strategy to make decision process and pre-surgical planning. In order to meet this objective, current sequential flow from user perspective was first identified. Then, process areas were established according to fundamental activities from diagnosis, to design, and manufacture. Then, it was analyzed how the proposed PLM strategy could be according with a process to obtaining a PSI. Once workflow and software tools were defined, PLM strategies through project data management (PDM) were applied.

Finally, in the third stage, according to previous evaluation, a new workflow was proposed according to PLM strategies, in order to get a design process for craniofacial implants. For verification purposes, the new workflow was applied to one study case. The evaluation scope was to confirming the design solutions proposed. The accuracy of PSI was verified by physician concept. With that in mind, activities for implant development in the case study were integrated through a PDM.

3 PLM Strategy Structuration Results

A strategy based on product lifecycle was proposed to define craniofacial implants design from current workflow patient service, which showed opportunities to improve the service. Implementation of a visual model allows for controlling productivity associated with equipment, according to each stage involved in the development of the product. This model provides transparency from a Top-down approach [13].

To establish a PLM strategy visual framework, main stages were specified. From academic scope, covered lifecycle just include the initial three: imagination, definition, and realization. Then, process areas involved in main stages were identified: requirements, design, manufacturing, testing, and knowledge management. Each one has a workflow that connects among others, through every activity performed by a specific role. Thought decomposition graphics in every activity, a role is understanding, as well as its skills, tools, and input or output items [13].

3.1 Current Process Description

Through observation techniques and non-structured interviews, the process related to surgical treatment was drawn. A business process model BMP was made to get a graphic flow that showed activities in the timeline when a patient asks for health attention. It is established that in complex craniofacial trauma cases, use of PSI implants is applied where standard implants performance would be no adequate, although in many cases the surgeon had no other choices. Figure 1 shows an opportunity to include design area in pre-surgical planning procedure. That would enhance endogenous advance of PED under a service procedure based on PLM strategy that facilitates collaboration among multidisciplinary roles.

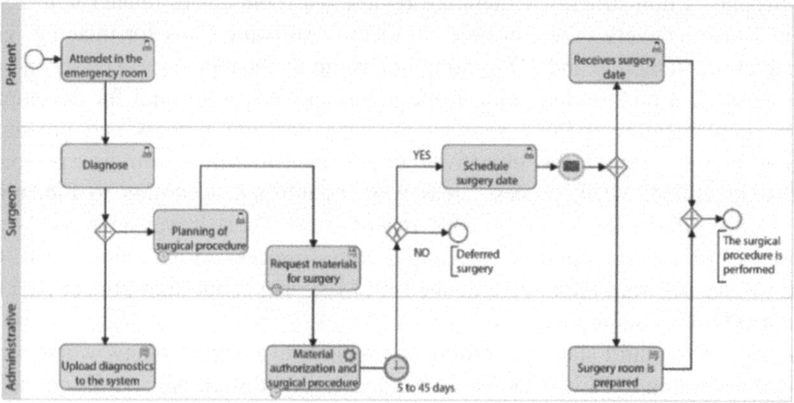

Fig. 1. Workflow in the Hospital. Sequential process observed by authors.

3.2 Building a Visual Model. Stage/Areas Description

Activities involved in the process of obtaining a PSI implant must match by correspondence. Related works in literature are focused on digital workflow in reconstructive implants [14], and how to share complex and heavy data from imaging [15, 16]. A few works presented exchange problems between roles in health [17], specifically how people must conduct a PLM implementation according to organization objectives would be a lack [18]. That gap was identified in the literature review, and next, it was proposed a PLM strategy in order to adapt it to a public university hospital.

The process areas framed in the initial three stages of the PLM approach suggested by Stark were adopted, which correspond to the stages of imagination, definition, and realization [19] as shown in Fig. 2. That also corresponds with the research scope, in order to reduce complexity on technical data management [20].

First, imagination stage. Diagnosis and analysis area has to get information about the patient situation. In this process area, a specialist identifies a defect. Specialist generates a list of requirements that a specific device must accomplish for the patient. Second, definition stage. Three process areas interact as following: first, 3D reconstruction process area, the one in charge to translate Digital Imaging and Communications in Medicine DICOM images [21] from tomography to a 3D biomodel by means of RE technologies [22]. Second, the design area, where the PSI should be virtually made following specifications is previously given by the specialist [23]. Third,

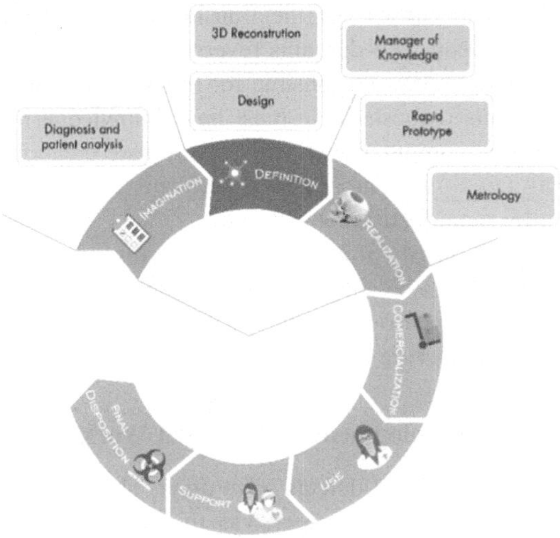

Fig. 2. The initial stage of Lifecycle and Process areas involved, proposed by authors.

knowledge management, where practices related to acquiring information for current and future products are established. Third, realization stage. Rapid prototyping processes are established, rather a biomodel, a PSI, or a surgical guide would be needed, according to any case. Validation must perform by testing quality, or metrology process area, where the evaluation, measurement, and verification of product quality are carried out. Knowledge management area acts again, to creating information manuals for the production process and user manuals for PED. See Fig. 2.

3.3 Roles and Technology Integration

Once the process area was established, roles that are involved in PSI development procedures were identified with his respective technological tools. These roles were integrated by a public access PDM. Selection from PLM services are complex and deepens of organization resources [13]. Due economic limitation, a public PDM service was selected, the GrabCAD workbench from Stratasys [24]. That tool allows interaction among different roles, being possible to visualize change estates on 3D files. Although a role could be performed at least by one person, roles definition corresponds to:

- *Surgeon specialist:* Who generates requirements from the patient about a product and asks the designer for a service according to needs. He is an expert on the surgical correction that requires repair or replaces a craniofacial bone structure.
- *Requirements analyst*: Who directs requirements process area. That role coordinates to obtaining requirements from the indirect user (the surgeon) to define product functionality. Analyst deployed activities in PDM, looking for controlling requirement to accomplishing or updating in every process areas.

- *Reverse Engineer:* Who carries out the translation from DICOM to 3D reconstruction. A trained person who domains reverse engineering techniques.
- *Designer:* The designer role is responsible for the design process according to the needs and requirements requested. He must have knowledge regarding creativity, innovation and design, computational skills in software creation PSI products.
- *Rapid Prototyping Operator:* The one who performs 3D printing according to the indications given by manufacture requirements.
- *Knowledge manager*: Consists of identifying, collecting, managing and storing the knowledge, so that this can be shared, reviewed, and modified in a safety way.
- *Metrology Engineer*: Who carries out the inspections and product verifications. He finally evaluates manufacturing costs from other areas.

3.4 Medical Prosthesis Development. A Proposed Workflow

Three study cases with craniofacial defects were done. The cases need to be attended by a physician specialist. The main target was to know the common activities to develop each case. Then, a collaborative workflow was performed where roles that intervene in a PSD design interact constantly along the whole procedure. Next, study cases related to PSD (pre-surgical planning, surgical guides, and PSI) was shown. In Fig. 3, a workflow for PSI development was suggested. Procedures were according to activities and steps in a public hospital, which was taken as reference. Those activities flow through different professionals, whom could accept or reject inputs and outputs form each activity, taking into account custom conditions for each device. Proposed workflow is described as follows:

First, the surgeon specialist SS identifies the defect that should be treated. Specialist generates a diagnosis and requests a service based on the cost analysis and justification about advantages. In this stage, procedure requested is assessed by requirements analyst, is appropriate or not for the patient. The PS probably requests the service in an iterative way until all changes suggested over the first proposal were defined, including overall schedule and a probable price.

Once the proposal is accepted, reverse engineer intervenes, getting TAC images from Hospital, traducing DICOM to a virtual 3D shape, and correcting mesh. Next, designer structures all ideas to be developed using 3D imaging as input. When the designer has already done a concept, PS intervenes again in establishing if concept accomplishes expectations or must be modified. Once SS concedes his approval, detailing design, materialization and refinement are carried out. At this point, idea evolves to the product, and designer recommends specifications for each device. It is verified whether rapid prototyping could be done or it must be configured from concept refinement again. With a final design, metrology engineer ME could evaluate the performance virtually or physically by testing. If ME approves, knowledge manager could create a product manual for the application, bringing a compact product to SS.

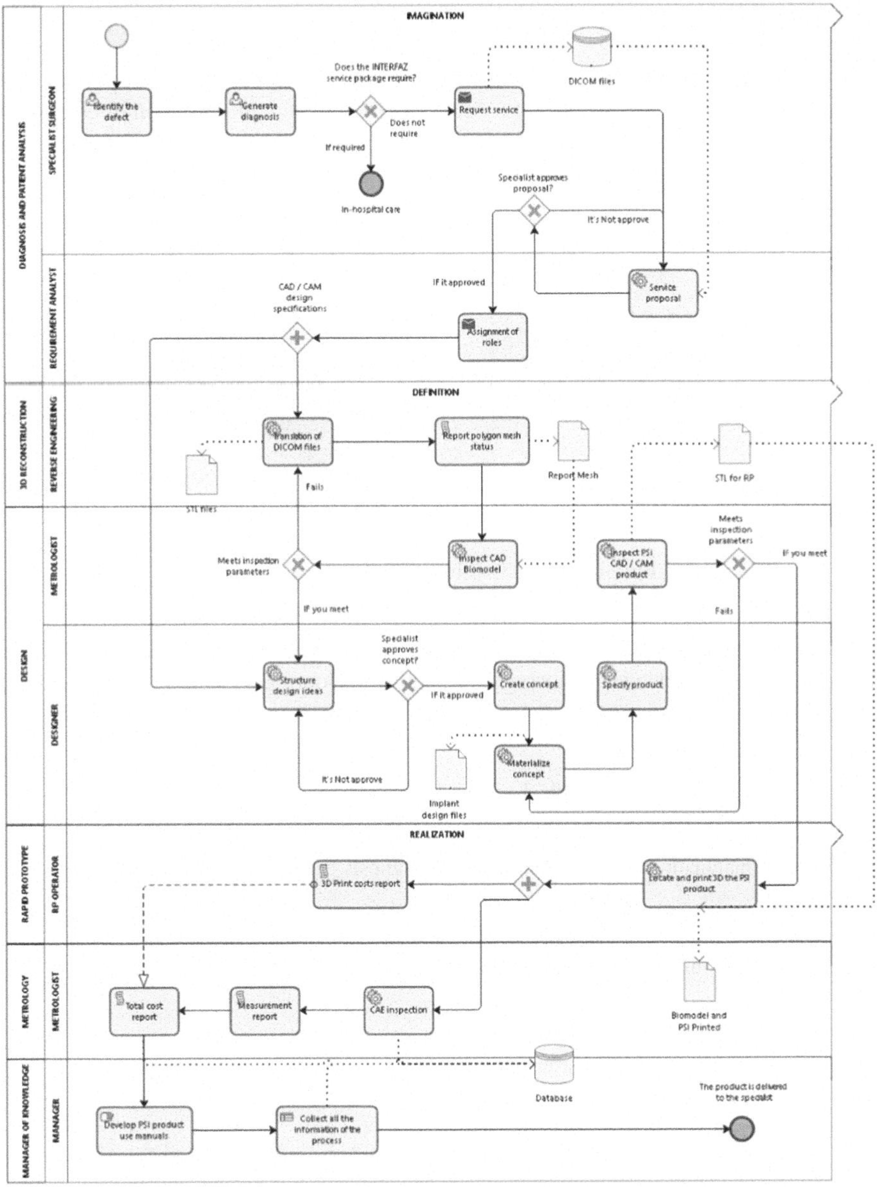

Fig. 3. Systematic Workflow proposed by authors.

4 Study Case

The collaborative workflow was proposed and implemented for a study case. The patient was diagnosed with sequels Le-fort 1 of cleft palate with retrusion of congenital type maxilla, see Fig. 4. The surgeon specialist requests the design of a cutting guide for osteosynthesis, and the pre-surgical planning to improve the patient's bite.

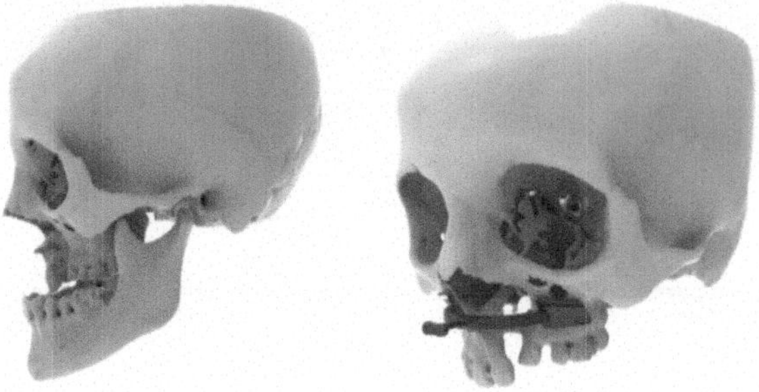

Fig. 4. Study case. Image drawn by authors.

Roles communication and technology integration were taken into account. Table 1 shows time spent in each stage according to activity. Comparing with other works [25], time reduction must be a goal for future developments.

Table 1. Time for each activity

Stage	Activities	Time (h)
Imagination	Defect identification/Diagnosis generation	8
	Requesting service	0.5
	Requirements management	3
Definition	Roles assignation	1.5
	Reverse engineering	8
	Mesh correction	8
	Ideas structuration	5
	Concept creation	14
	Concept evaluation	1
	Concept materialization	4
	Product specification	1
	Measure verification	0.5
Realization	Rapid prototyping	5.7
	Knowledge management	2
	Information manuals generation	2

Finally, a prototype was brought to surgery to check, according to surgeon specialist observation, if it fits osseous geometry or not. That cutting guide was not used along the surgical procedure. It was sterilized and its contact was less than 10 s. Integration of RE, CAx, and RP technologies was established, founding guidelines and procedures to development. Co-creation among key roles and technological tools were also defined. Technology inclusion was possible within a collaborative workflow where roles are constantly interacting. The capability to generate PED must be obtained by experience by attending different situations of pathology treatment.

5 Conclusions

Based on the PLM strategy for the design of the patient-specific implant it is possible to build capabilities to generate a collaborative workflow integrating stages, roles, activities and a workflow with technology and local human resource. PLM strategy improves the development of the case in an organized manner allowing to knowledge management. However, it is necessary to implement cost validation and control scheduling in activities, in order to measure biomodel results, starting with academic validation. Developing PDM software could be recommended to improve roles interaction and interface, easing exchange formats requested for each case. Develop the four remaining stages of the PLM strategy(commercialization, use, support, and disposal) will imply further research and effort, to develop stages which were not taken into account on this paper reducing complexity and because that would be beyond research scope.

References

1. Hassfeld, S., Mühling, J.: Computer assisted oral and maxillofacial surgery - a review and an assessment of technology. Int. J. Oral Maxillofac. Surg. **30**(1), 2–13 (2001)
2. Zhang, J., et al.: Customized titanium mesh for repairing cranial defects: a method with comprehensive evaluation. J. Craniofac. Surg. **26**(8), e758–e761 (2015)
3. García, A., Morey, M.Á., Ramos, M., Janeiro, S., Molina, I., Iriarte, J.I.: Reconstrucción de la articulación temporomandibular postraumática con prótesis a medida. Planificación quirúrgica virtual. Rev. Esp. Cir. Oral y Maxilofac. **33**(2), 53–60 (2011)
4. González de Santiago, M., Chaurand, L., Sandoval, B.: Cranial reconstruction with a custom-made implant. Rev. Esp. Cir. Oral Maxilofac. **3333**(1), 40–44 (2011)
5. Rengier, F., et al.: 3D printing based on imaging data: review of medical applications. Int. J. Comput. Assist. Radiol. Surg. **5**(4), 335–341 (2010)
6. Goh, B.T., Teoh, K.H.: Orbital implant placement using a computer-aided design and manufacturing (CAD/CAM) stereolithographic surgical template protocol. Int. J. Oral Maxillofac. Surg. **44**(5), 642–648 (2015)
7. Grieves, M.W., Tanniru, M.: PLM, process, practice and provenance: knowledge provenance in support of business practices in product lifecycle management. Int. J. Prod. Lifecycle Manag. **3**(1), 37 (2008)
8. Saaksvuori, A., Immonen, A.: Product Lifecycle Management, 3rd edn., Helsinki, Finland (2008)

9. Segonds, F., Maranzana, N., Veron, P., Aoussat, A.: Collaborative reverse engineering design experiment using PLM solutions. Int. J. Eng. Educ. **27**(5), 1037–1045 (2012)
10. Martínez, J., Sauza, J., Ricci, F., Chiabert, P.: Validation process model for product lifecycle management. Int. J. Prod. Lifecycle Manag. **7**(2/3), 230 (2014)
11. Scott, F., Mcdonnell, W., Burkett, M.: Designing medical devices to improve patient outcomes (2011)
12. Lantada, A.D., Morgado, P.L.: Introduction to modern product development. In: Lantada, A. (ed.) Handbook on Advanced Design and Manufacturing Technologies for Biomedical Devices, pp. 1–17. Springer, Boston (2013). https://doi.org/10.1007/978-1-4614-6789-2_1
13. Martínez, J.M.: Visualization model for product lifecycle management: processes, activities, roles and items involved in product lifecycle. Politecnico di Torino (2013)
14. Unkovskiy, A., Spintzyk, S., Brom, J., Huettig, F., Keutel, C.: Direct 3D printing of silicone facial prostheses: a preliminary experience in digital workflow. J. Prosthet. Dent., 1–6 (2018)
15. Pham, C.C., et al.: How to share complex data and knowledge: application in bio-imaging. IFAC-PapersOnLine **49**(12), 1098–1103 (2016)
16. Allanic, M., Hervé, P.-Y., Durupt, A., Joliot, M., Boutinaud, P., Eynard, B.: PLM as a strategy for the management of heterogeneous information in bio-medical imaging field. Int. J. Inf. Technol. Manag. **16**(1), 5–30 (2015)
17. Ngo, T., Bernard, A., Belkadi, F.: Interest of PLM for data sharing in the patient treatment process requiring prosthesis implantation. In: 15e Colloque National AIP-Priméca, no. 73, pp. 1–6 (2017)
18. Schuh, G., Rozenfeld, H., Assmus, D., Zancul, E.: Process oriented framework to support PLM implementation. Comput. Ind. **59**(2–3), 210–218 (2008)
19. Stark, J.: Product Lifecycle Management, vol. 2, 3rd edn. Springer, Geneva (2016)
20. Labbi, O., Ouzizi, L., Douimi, M., Aoura, Y.: A model to design a product and its extended supply chain integrating PLM (Product Lifecycle Management) solution. Int. J. Sci. Eng. Res. **7**(10), 1190–1205 (2016)
21. Kucklick, T.R.: The Medical Device R&D Handbook, vol. 21. CRC Press, Boca Raton (2005)
22. Jardini, A.L., et al.: Cranial reconstruction: 3D biomodel and custom-built implant created using additive manufacturing. J. Cranio-Maxillofac. Surg. **42**(8), 1877–1884 (2014)
23. Aitchison, G.A., Hukins, D.W.L., Parry, J.J., Shepherd, D.E.T., Trotman, S.G.: A review of the design process for implantable orthopedic medical devices. Open Biomed. Eng. J. **3**(1), 21–27 (2009)
24. Wu, D., Terpenny, J., Schaefer, D.: Digital design and manufacturing on the cloud: a review of software and services. Artif. Intell. Eng. Des. Anal. Manuf. **31**(1), 104–118 (2017)
25. Numajiri, T., Nakamura, H., Sowa, Y., Nishino, K.: Low-cost design and manufacturing of surgical guides for mandibular reconstruction using a Fibula. Plast. Reconstr. Surg. Glob. Open **4**(7), e805 (2016)

PLM for Digital Factories and Cyber Physical Systems

Implementation of "Digital Twin" Concept for Modern Project-Based Engineering Education

S. Nikolaev(✉), M. Gusev, D. Padalitsa, E. Mozhenkov, S. Mishin, and I. Uzhinsky

Skolkovo Institute of Science and Technology, Moscow, Russia
s.nikolaev@skoltech.ru

Abstract. The main focus of this work is simulation-driven product development methodology for MSc students' education. The educational process is built around real product development process; small Unmanned Aerial Vehicle is used as a case-study. The bunch of simulation and optimization tools (NX CAD, Simcenter 3D, LMS System Synthesis, LMS Amesim, ANSYS, STAR-CCM) is used in the educational process for creating so-called "digital twin" of a real product and to achieve the continuity and transparency of the development process. Product Lifecycle Management (PLM) system is used to manage requirements, changes and integrate all simulation results. The global trend in engineering education is in the transition from the training of narrowly specialized engineers for high-tech industries. In the new reality, the industry needs specialists with broad knowledge and system thinking, which are able to solve problems that require cross-disciplinary expertise. These specialists should be able to use the most advanced methods and tools of numerical simulation, optimization, product lifecycle management, configuration management, advanced manufacturing techniques. The aim is to enhance the classical methodology for systems engineering with a digital environment in order to develop an MSc level courses teaching latest practices for innovative product design based on real case problems. A modeling of the system to be developed enables the comprehensive analysis and its quantitative assessment. Such approach demonstrates both a thorough investigation of a problem and quantitative estimation of the system's efficiency.

Keywords: Simulation-driven product development
Learning-by-doing · Project-based education

P. Chiabert et al. (Eds.): PLM 2018, IFIP AICT 540, pp. 193–203, 2018.
https://doi.org/10.1007/978-3-030-01614-2_18

1 Motivation

1.1 The Problems of Traditional Engineering Education

Classic engineering education approach implies courses devoted to some particular discipline. Usually, the course consists of the theoretical part, practical and/or laboratory parts. Theoretical part includes different means of physical processes mathematical description and some empirical experience, while seminars/labs aim to provide students with practical skills during test examples solution. In most cases, test examples are easy, easily verifiable and more or less abstract. This approach results in graduates with deep and narrow knowledge in particular field of engineering science. Traditional engineering education gives graduate all required knowledge for developing some type of engineering systems (mechanical, hydraulic, aerodynamics, electronics, etc.) in particular industry (aerospace, automotive, heavy machinery, etc.). These "traditional" engineers mainly are supposed to work inside the group of specialists with similar background, don't getting outside particular field of knowledge very often. This approach works very well for the products with lightly coupled subsystems.

1.2 The Global Trend to Digitalization

In the 21st century, more and more products are becoming not just complicated, but complex, which means that more subsystems are becoming interconnected with each other. That leads to the fact that development using big, highly specialized departments is replaced by the principle of working in small mobile interdisciplinary groups. This trend implies increasing demand in cross-disciplinary educated employees, especially for advanced, MSc level. Nowadays, many Universities try to adjust their education programs in order to satisfy industry needs [1]. One more defining trend is enterprises digitalization [2], which changes the product development and its lifecycle management (see Fig. 1).

Product Lifecycle Management (PLM), as defined by CIMdata, is a business strategy that supports the development of products including the information needed to support them throughout their lifecycle. Digitalization affects PLM strategy of enterprises since now the software tools become the main instrument of companies PLM transformation and product development. Companies always tried to manage the lifecycle of their products; but, in most cases, they have done it using manual methods. Manual PLM cannot deal with today's complex products and multi-disciplinary requirements. Moving engineering education into new ways of approaching and supporting product development and the complete lifecycle is essential to help companies exploit innovation that leads to continued business success [3].

Digitalization requires that physical product development has to be accompanied by its "digital twin" development in order to increase the data traceability and perform optimization with a minimum number of physical tests. This process is based on multi-scale, multi-domain physical simulation and so-called virtual testing. This could not be done by any single software tool. Modern PLM

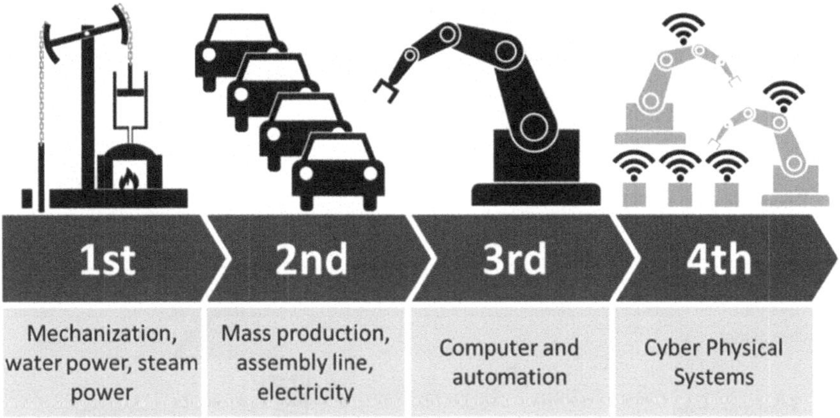

Fig. 1. Digitalization, a massive trend in Industry 4.0 [2]

systems include product data management (PDM), mechanical CAD (MCAD), electrical CAD (ECAD), computer-aided engineering tools, simulation and analysis tools (SA and CAE), digital manufacturing, computer-aided manufacturing (CAM and NC), reporting and analytics, portfolio planning, requirements management, and many others [4]. Therefore, the practical skills in a bunch of software are in great demand in modern industry companies, which make their steps to digitalization.

2 Project-Based Engineering Courses Description

2.1 Systems-Driven Product Development for Engineering Education

Summing up, modern engineering courses should be based on the practical project-based activity, highly focused on real product "digital twin" development and testing. So-called systems driven product development (SDPD) is the state-of-the-art simulation-based methodology which allows to unite different phases of complex systems development and reuse created models for designing new products in the future [5]. In that approach, the whole process of system development is maintained under a single project, where all created models are interconnected and, hence, affect each other [6]. As a result, analysts can inspect influence of high-level models on specific system assemblies and architects can change high-level templates with a further automatic update of all affected submodels. Knowledge expansion from engineering area to related fields (Change Management, Configuration Management, Systems Engineering, Business processes, etc.) within PLM system is essential too as shown at [7]. The principle of the described approach is schematically presented in Fig. 2. The proposed approach should cover both branches of this diagram, with focusing on systems from a particular industry. Since the education process should be project-based the particular product is the basis of the courses. The small Unmanned Aerial Vehicle (UAV) was chosen as an object for the course, described in this paper.

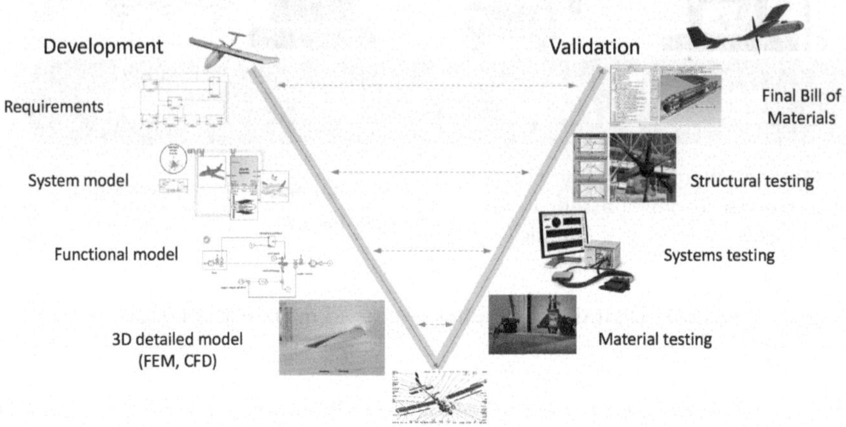

Fig. 2. V-diagram and systems-driven product development stages

The proposed approach is realized by the authors in two interconnected MSc level courses. The first-course "Advanced PLM I: Digital Design and Optimization" is dedicated to model-based systems engineering, design, and simulation, whereas the second-course "Advanced PLM II: Testing and Model Validation" is devoted to the UAV manufacturing and testing.

2.2 Course Description

The experimental course series was held for 2nd year MSc students from "Advanced and Digital Engineering Techniques" program. They were 6 students with a different background in aerospace, mechanical engineering, electrical engineering, applied physics. The duration of each course is 2 months, overall duration is 4 months. There are 3 classes per week, each 3 h long. 25% of the class time was dedicated to the lectures aiming to introduce different PLM principle and tools. All the lectures included some case studies from real life. Some of the classes have been held by external lecturers from industry. The rest time (75%) was devoted to practical work with software tools. It's worth noting that despite students didn't have an experience of using needed software minimum time was spent on tutorials (no more than 2 h) for every software tool. The courses finish with a final presentation, during which the project defence takes place and individual contribution of each student is evaluated.

2.3 Small Tube-Launched UAV Case Study

The task was to develop special UAV, which is able to be launched from the tube for fast take-off (Fig. 3). Such type of UAV has unusual structure caused by deployable wings, stabilizer, and propeller. Students had to design it from system level to detailed design level, produce the prototype and perform all required tests to verify the UAV "digital twin". Multidisciplinary optimization techniques were used to obtain the optimal parameters of the UAV subsystems. The 3D-printing technology for UAV prototyping was chosen to maximize production automation.

The course was divided into several stages:

- Model-based systems engineering, system architecture development;
- Functional simulation using multi-domain models;
- 3D-detailed design and Computer-Aided Engineering;
- Optimization;
- Manufacturing and testing for models' verification.

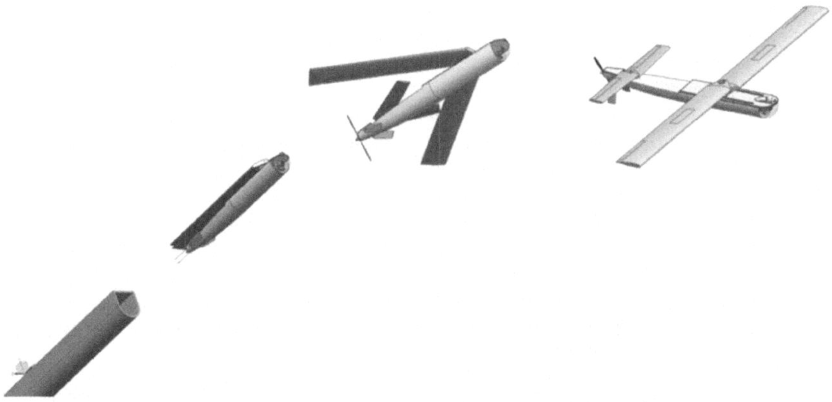

Fig. 3. Tube-launched UAV concept

2.4 Model-Based Systems Engineering and 1D-simulation of UAV

Just basic requirements were given to the students at the beginning of the course, therefore they had to analyze and work it out themselves. The base architecture is built by the students, using LMS System Synthesis software, and systems engineering principles. Also, the requirements were created using Teamcenter PLM system. When the architecture is completed, it is possible to create different sets of simulation architectures, where unique parameters and physical configuration of the system are defined for each simulation. Then, the UAV architecture was divided into major subsystems which have been modeled by different students' groups (Fig. 4).

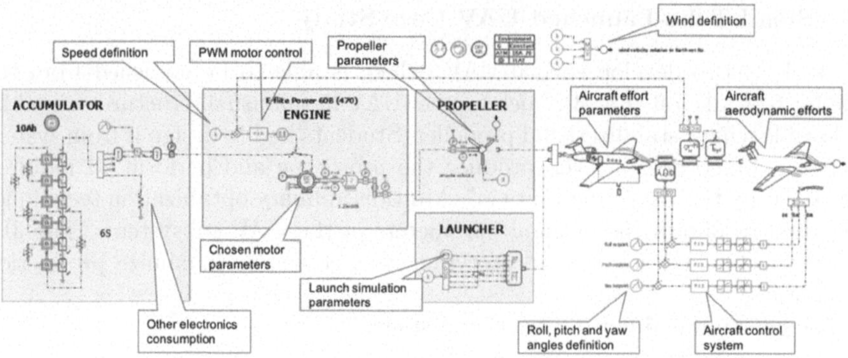

Fig. 4. UAV functional model and its main subsystems

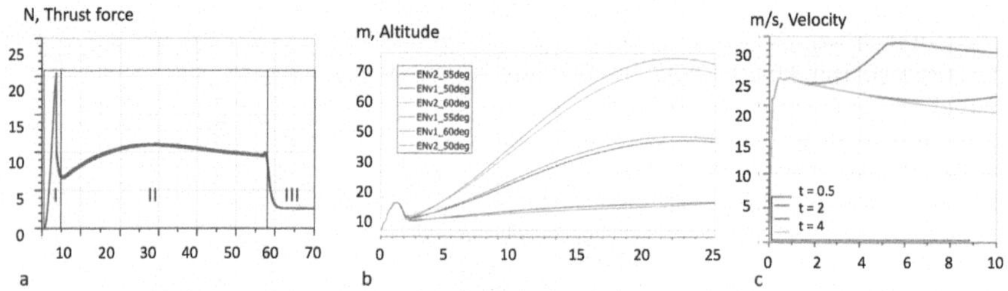

Fig. 5. UAV absolute altitude position during different stages of motor launch (a), influence of launch angle on altitude position (b) and comparison of different engine launch strategies by absolute UAV velocity (c)

These subsystems are power supply system, propulsion system, the launch system, structure and flight dynamics system. Each group created a set of models for the particular subsystem in LMS Amesim software. LMS Amesim software uses the bond-graph method to deal with multiphysical systems modeling. The advantage of such a software is an easy way to assemble the models of big multi-domain systems using libraries of verified components. During working on each subsystem model, students collaborate between groups in order to find appropriate parameters and link the subsystems together satisfying the conditions for the energy, heat and mass balance. Some results of systems design and analysis are presented in Fig. 5 (stage I - take-off; II - climbing; III - cruise flight).

After the area of the stable solution was found the global optimization was performed using differential evolution method in Optimus software and optimal parameters have been found for each subsystem. The conceptual design of UAV arrangement was made during this stage too. In considered case, the students made a decision to choose canard scheme.

2.5 3D Simulation and Design of UAV

Computational Fluid Dynamics (CFD) analysis using ANSYS Fluent/CFX and STAR-CCM+ for Lift and Drag calculation and polar curves plotting was performed (see Fig. 6) Particular attention was paid to CFD results verification. This was done by comparing results, obtained by different solvers (ANSYS CFX, ANSYS Fluent, CTAR-CCM) and different turbulence models. The maximum difference in Lift coefficient was less than 5%, whereas for Drag coefficient it was 12%. The ability to estimate the correctness of numerical simulation results is essential for engineers, therefore significant efforts were spent to this during the course.

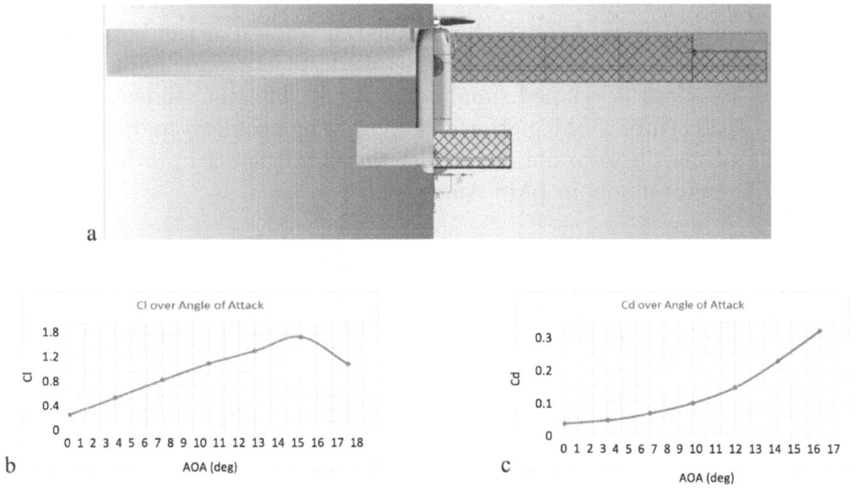

Fig. 6. CFD analysis of UAV (a), Polar curves for Lift (b) and Drag (c) coefficients over angle of attack

The wing structural analysis was performed using Finite Element Analysis. Siemens Simcenter 3D was used to calculate the stresses due to aerodynamic forces considering different load cases (take-off, climbing, cruise). The optimization of the wing structure was performed using a surrogate-based algorithm (Fig. 7). The wing consists of plastic body and composite spar. The connection between the spar and plastic wing root is the weakest place, where maximum stresses occur. The main task for the students was to reduce the stresses with constraints on wing mass using the parametric model of the wing and external optimization solver. The wing structure was obtained as a result.

In addition, nonlinear dynamic drop analysis in Abaqus software was performed for hard landing simulation and coupled Thermal-Flow simulation in Comsol software was made for UAV motor cooling estimation. Comprehensive 3D design and analysis allowed to obtain the detailed UAV model validated by virtual tests and reduced a time needed for prototype manufacturing.

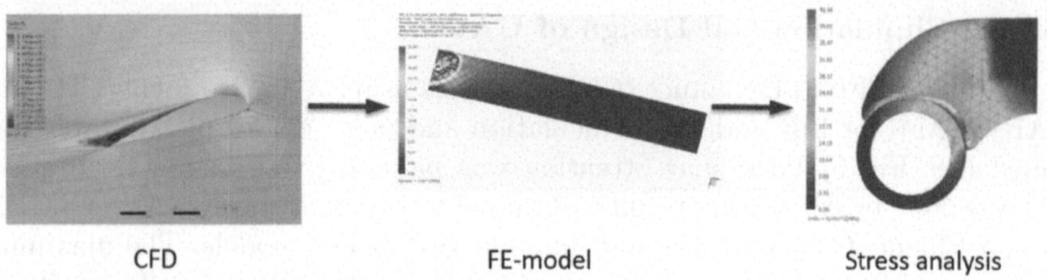

Fig. 7. Combination of finite-element analysis and Computational Fluid Dynamics for structural analysis and optimization

After 1D and 3D-simulations have been performed, the structural and subsystems parameters were defined, the detailed 3D design of the UAV structure was implemented in NX software. The detailed structure including electronic components has been developed simultaneously by different students and managed using Teamcenter PLM platform (Fig. 8). The geometry parameters such as moments of inertia were obtained from the CAD model in order to update the flight dynamics model in LMS Amesim.

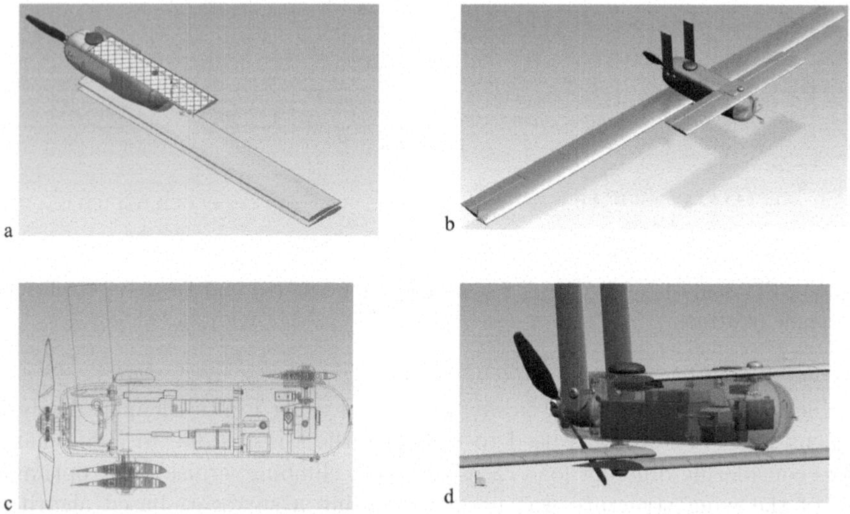

Fig. 8. CAD models of the UAV in folded (a) and deployed (b) state, side view (c) and components view (d)

2.6 Testing and Prototyping

The UAV testing including static material tests for material selection, Hardware-in-the-Loop testing of UAV control system and destructive static tests of the wings was performed. The main purpose of the tests was to verify and validate UAV "digital twin". First of all, static tests were held for material properties evaluation (see Fig. 9). The tests have shown that PLA plastic is the optimal choice among compared materials. The properties, obtained from static tests (Young module and Poisson ratio) were used to update the UAV FE-models. The structure then was manufactured using Fused Deposition Modeling 3D-printers.

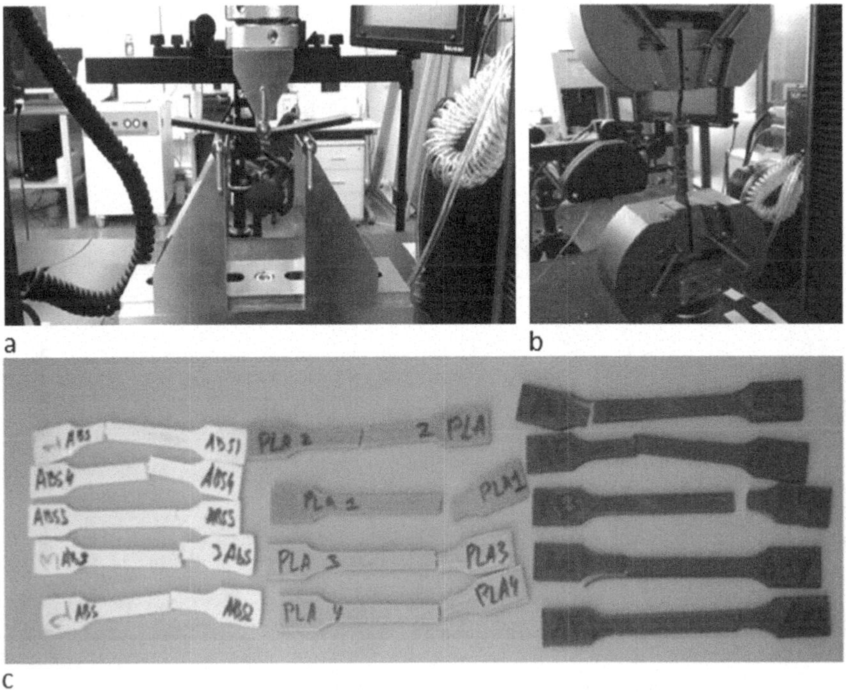

Fig. 9. Material testing and evaluation: 3-points bending (a), tensile test (b), specimen after testing (c)

In order to validate the 1D-model of the UAV including control system model the Hardware-in-the-Loop (HiL) approach was used. HiL testing involves putting the UAV 1D-model on the real-time board and co-simulation between real prototype (using LabView) and digital prototype (using LMS Amesim) under the same conditions (Fig. 10). The parameters to be verified included propeller rotary speed, engine temperature, control servos feedback current and thrust force. The HiL testing allowed students to verify the models, built in LMS Amesim and obtain the functional model, capable to predict dynamic behavior under transient conditions.

Finally, The UAV prototype was assembled and launched for test flights with wings, fixed in deployed position (Fig. 11).

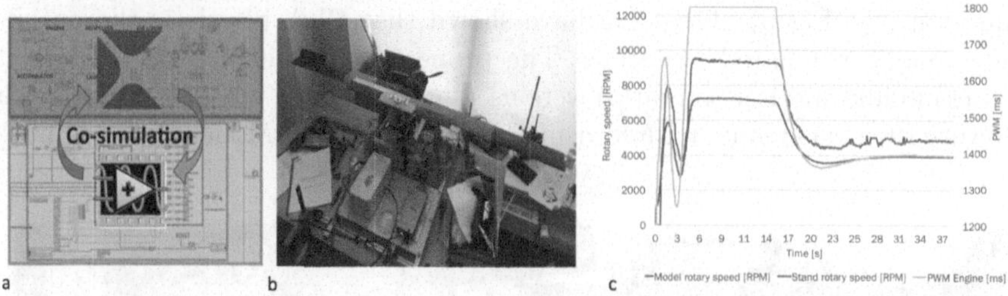

Fig. 10. Hardware-in-the-Loop scheme (a), HiL test-bench (b), HiL test-model comparison results (c)

Fig. 11. UAV prototype and students team

3 Conclusions

3.1 Results of the Experimental Course

Small students team managed to design, prototype and test complex system on a very tight schedule. They got familiar with PLM/CAD/CAE tools and learned to work in a team. The feedback from the students is totally positive and resulted in increasing the number of course attendees to 22, this year. Very important knowledge obtained during the course is a hands-on experience of end-to-end design of the real product. All the students successfully graduated from University and will bring their SDPD experience to the industrial enterprises. Several aerospace companies representatives visited the project defence and appreciated the course results. There is a lack of time as a shortcoming of the course, so some important testing procedures (vibration and modal testing, autopilot testing, tube launch test) weren't done. Therefore, future course series will be elongated to 6 months and will consist of three courses devoted to Design, Prototyping and Testing.

3.2 Future Work

To make the transition from "digital prototype" to real "digital twin" the described educational process should include working with Internet of Things (IoT) platform, collecting data and updating the model in real-time. The IoT platforms such as GE Predix or Siemens Mindsphere should be used for this purpose.

References

1. Onar, S.C., et al.: The changing role of engineering education in industry 4.0 era. In: Onar, S.C., et al. (eds.) Industry 4.0: Managing The Digital Transformation. Springer, Cham, pp. 137–151 (2018)
2. Roser, C.: "Faster, Better, Cheaper" in the History of Manufacturing: From the Stone Age to Lean Manufacturing and Beyond, 1st edn. Productivity Press, USA (2016)
3. CIMdata white paper: are Students 'Real-World' Ready? https://www.cimdata.com/en/news/item/8127-cimdata-publishes-are-students-real-world-ready. Accessed 10 May 2018
4. Siemens PLM white paper: Systems-Driven Cross-Industry Product Development. https://www.plm.automation.siemens.com/en/products/teamcenter/systems-engineering-software/. Accessed 10 May 2018
5. Pavasson, J., et al.: Challenges and opportunities within simulation-driven functional product development and operation. Procedia CIRP **22**, 169–174 (2014)
6. Lindstrom, J., et al.: Functional product development: what information should be shared during the development process? Int. J. Prod. Dev. **16**(2), 95–111 (2012)
7. Motyl, B., et al.: How will change the future engineers' skills in the Industry 4.0 framework? A questionnaire survey. Procedia Manufact. **11**, 1501–1509 (2017)

Digital Twin Requirements in the Context of Industry 4.0

Luiz Fernando C. S. Durão[1], Sebastian Haag[2], Reiner Anderl[2], Klaus Schützer[1], and Eduardo Zancul[1](✉)

[1] University of São Paulo, São Paulo, Brazil
{luiz.durao, ezancul}@usp.br, schuetzer@scpm.unimep.br
[2] Technische Universität Darmstadt, Darmstadt, Germany
{haag, anderl}@dik.tu-darmstadt.de

Abstract. Digital Twin (DT) is being considered a significant enabler for Industry 4.0 initiatives. Within Industry 4.0, the amount of digital product information generated and collected over the entire lifecycle has been growing. Current information and communication technologies, including data storage, data processing, and wireless data transmission, may be leveraged to digitally mirror the lifecycle of a corresponding physical product with increasing level of detail. A DT creates a link between physical products and their virtual models with more comprehensive data and accumulation of knowledge. Therefore, a DT may be applied to enhance simulation, traceability and to support the offering of value-added services along the lifecycle. However, the definition of a DT and its requirements are not yet fully established. The characteristics a DT model should possess to be widely used in manufacturing remains an open question in the literature. The concept is still broad and dependent on the lifecycle stage and industry sector of application. Therefore, the objective of this paper is to propose an initial synthesis of DT requirements based on a literature review and industry interviews. The literature review focuses on the content analysis of papers published from 2010 to 2018 and indexed in the ISI Web of Science database. The interviews were conducted with industry representatives in Brazil. The results show that DT requirements are related to real-time data, integration, and fidelity. Besides, it shows that industry requirements are close to literature and the actual implementation of DT is the future of research in this field.

Keywords: Digital Twin · Industry 4.0 · Product lifecycle management

1 Introduction

Industrial revolutions alter product manufacturing processes as well as how consumers interact with production, allowing sophistication of the demand for different consumer goods [1]. Before the first Industrial Revolution, the products were manufactured in a handmade way, according to the individual demands of each consumer and taking the time of the artisan to be manufactured. From the first Industrial Revolution, production processes began to be mechanized (first revolution), to be treated as massive processes (second revolution), and to be automatized (third revolution), standardizing the products in exchange for an increase in the efficiency of the production line [2]. The fourth

Published by Springer Nature Switzerland AG 2018.
P. Chiabert et al. (Eds.): PLM 2018, IFIP AICT 540, pp. 204–214, 2018.
https://doi.org/10.1007/978-3-030-01614-2_19

Industrial Revolution - or Industry 4.0 - comes with the proposal to unite the advantages of large-scale production with the individualization. Hence, virtual product models, which are frequently referred to as Digital Twins, are used as fuel to shortening time to market and to create further benefits along the entire lifecycle [3].

The convergence between physical and virtual spaces has gained wide attention recently [4]. Digital Twin (DT) is defined as a very realistic model of the current state of the process and their own behavior in interaction with their environment in the real world [5]. It is used not only for representation purposes but also for predicting the product behavior [3]. Besides, Digital Twin's ability to link enormous amounts of data to fast simulation makes it possible to perform real-time optimization of products and production processes [6].

However, the definition of a DT and its requirements are not yet fully established and lack of conceptual basis [3]. The characteristics a DT model should possess to be widely used in industry remains an open question in the literature.

Therefore, this paper aims to narrow this research gap by proposing an initial synthesis of Digital Twin requirements. The paper seeks to answer the following research question (RQ1): what are main requirements for developing a Digital Twin? Besides, it aims to investigate (RQ2): what industry understands as Digital Twin?

A systematic literature review, merging bibliometrics and content analysis [7], was applied to identify the main requirements listed in literature for Digital Twins. The literature review focused on a content analysis of articles published from 2010 to 2018 in the ISI Web of Science database. After literature review, a set of interviews with industry representatives were conducted in Brazil.

The paper is structured in five sections. After the introduction of the research topic in Sect. 1, Sect. 2 provides the research approach developed in the paper. In Sect. 3, the requirements brought by literature to the Digital Twin concept are presented. Section 4 presents industry requirements for Digital Twin. Finally, the conclusion and an outlook on further research needs are discussed in Sect. 5.

2 Methodology

To acquire a broad knowledge about Digital Twins, this research firstly took into consideration the possible ways a literature review can be developed [8]. The research design combines quantitative and qualitative strategies. It merges bibliometrics and content analysis, to study a research topic, as they are complementary methods [7]. Mainly, this kind of methodology is used not only to probe the existing literature and to identify relevant patterns, words, and authors of the particular field of research, but also to investigate the evolution of the publications stratified by journals [9].

Decisions on which research method to apply are mainly taken based on the results from the databases, particularly the sample size to be reviewed [7]. The bibliometric approach is particularly useful for large sample sizes since it focuses on metrics based on the number of publications and the metadata. Content analysis, on the other hand, focuses on in-depth review of the sample but allows analytical flexibility [9, 10].

The second part of the research methodology consisted of industry interviews target at discovering the implications of Digital Twin in real cases and the requirements given by manufacturing companies to the concept deployment.

2.1 Sampling

For this paper, an initial sample was elaborated using the ISI Web of Science, aiming to cross-check their results and enhance some documents to be studied. The article search was performed in January and February 2018. The following search string was used, and no restrictions were considered: "Digital Twin" and ("Industry 4.0" or "Requirement*"), and "Digital Twin". This first search resulted in 52 entries in ISI Web of Science.

The first exclusion criteria were based on the abstracts and title reading. All these papers had their abstracts read for identifying those that did not fit within the scope of the study, excluding them from the final list, resulting in 20 papers. It was not possible to have access to the full paper of one article, resulting in 19 articles. All the papers from the final list were read to identify the Digital Twin requirements contained in the papers to be used in the content analysis.

All the 52 papers had been published from 2010 to 2017, in 47 different journals and conferences, and 85% of the papers had their publication concentrated in the last three years. Among the conferences and journals, the "IFAC papersonline", the "IEE access", and the "Manufacturing Systems 4.0" have the most papers in the subject (3), and there are 198 authors and the authors that have the most articles possess two publications.

2.2 Industry Selection and Questions

Interviews with six industry representatives from Brazil and Germany have shown that there is growing interest in Digital Twin technologies. However, there are many reservations regarding feasibility, and application. These issues will be discussed in more detail in Sect. 4 to derive the industry-specific requirements for Digital Twin. The companies answered five different questions regarding Digital Twin:

1. Have you heard about Digital Twin concept?
2. What do you understand by Digital Twin?
3. Do you use Digital Twins in your processes?
4. What are, in your point of view, the main requirements for the implementation of Digital Twins in your processes?
5. What is your future plan concerning the use of Digital Twin?

Interviews were conducted by telephone with 7 representatives from 6 different companies: two automotive OEM, three manufacturing technology providers, and one ERP software provider.

After answering the questions, the requirements showed in literature were compared with the requirements and concerns defined by the industry.

3 Literature Requirements

In this section, it is presented a discussion of three different topics, Industry 4.0 (3.1), and Digital Twin (3.2). At the end of this section, as a result of the literature review, Table 1 is presented summarizing the requirements brought by literature to the Digital Twin concept.

3.1 Industry 4.0

Industry 4.0 is a new approach to the manufacturing chain that aims to integrate manufacturing systems creating a self-controlled and intelligent environment. A controlled environment can promote information about the lifecycle and close the product information loop [11].

Connected environments, promoted by Industry 4.0, consider the production of more individualized products without interrupting the production line, since consumer orders are directly connected to production planning via the network [2, 12].

Factories are rapidly becoming adaptable while remaining economically productive. This situation allows the decentralization of production - through autonomous tasks based on Cyber Physical Production Systems [13–15]. Intelligent factories will be connected in a collaborative network sharing information relevant to a database and thus creating a dynamic environment with the use of technologies such as Artificial Intelligence, Internet of Things among others [2].

The implementation of intelligent factories is possible considering the evolution of manufacturing and information technologies, being able to receive different information from different sources and produce items that are more complex in a reduced time and in different locations. This change in production technologies requires a new representation of manufacturing processes and product models. This representation would be reached by a Digital Twin.

3.2 Digital Twin

Digital Twin is a multi-physical, multi-scale, and probabilistic simulation model of a complex product. It uses updated sensors and physical models to mirror physical life in the digital world and vice versa [16, 17]. Technologies for mapping Digital Twins are being developed for approximately 20 years [17].

However, it was the digital manufacturing and the Cyber Physical Production Systems (CPPS) that allowed the enrichment of the Digital Twin models through production and operation data [3]. More specifically, the development of sensing technologies and information technologies allowed the integration of digital models with the real-time information of the physical product [3].

Information such as sensor readings, alarms, assembly, disassembly, shipping event, and other information related to the entire product lifecycle needed to be exchanged between products and systems [18]. The role of the PLM system is collecting and managing data of product definitions, processes, resources and decisions across the whole product lifecycle supporting changes and enabling traceability of these changes through a Product Model [19].

Table 1. Literature requirements for Digital Twin

Requirement	[21]	[17]	[22]	[23]	[24]	[25]	[26]	[5]	[3]	[16]	[4]	[27]	[28]	[29]	[30]	[6]	Total
Real-time data			1			1	1						1		1	1	**7**
Integration			1	1		1								1	1	1	**6**
Fidelity				1	1		1		1		1		1				**6**
Interaction	1									1	1						3
Communication	1										1						2
Convergence										1	1						2
Automatically updated		1															1
Autonomy								1									1
Connectivity								1									1
Data acquisition													1				1
Data capture														1			1
Data quality							1										1
Data security												1					1
Data warehousing													1				1
Efficiency					1												1
Expansibility									1								1
Globally available in real-time		1															1
Independently expanded		1															1
Interoperability									1								1
Modularity								1									1
Process planning														1			1
Real-time location												1					1
Scalability									1								1
Scalable	1																1
Stable data acquisition												1					1
Stable operation												1					1

The product model that supports the data interfacing (and then systems interoperability) should describe, with the same semantic, various data. In low trust level, the product model is used to manage the product information separately in different databases [20]. Therefore, managing the interaction between the physical and digital world starts from the product model. The DT must manage the interaction of the product model and the physical world and its requirements must reflect that.

The different understandings of the term Digital Twin can be observed in cases in the industry. Some manufacturers focus on building a link between the virtual product and the physical product, increasing manufacturing flexibility. Other manufacturers are looking to use Digital Twin to improve product design; and others are using DT to map the product throughout its life cycle improving quality in manufacturing [3]. The challenge lies in the fact that there are few possibilities for the synchronization between the physical world and the digital world making it difficult to close the information loop.

To be considered a Digital Twin, the model must have some specific characteristics such as: scalability (ability to analyze different scales of information); interoperability (ability to convert, match and establish equivalence between representation models); expansibility (ability to integrate models); and fidelity (ability to conform to the physical model) [3].

Considering the comprehensive study of the "Digital Twin" definitions shown previously, the numbers of requirements to describe "Digital Twin" are numerous. The different characteristics are summarized in Table 1, which demonstrates the relations between the parameters (lines) and the citation (columns) and total citation (final column Total).

The data from Table 1 enables us to state that the most frequent requirements of Digital Twins are real-time data, integration, and fidelity. These are crucial requirements for connecting the Product Model and the real conditions of the product.

As revealed by Table 1, real-time data was mentioned by 6 among the researched sample of 19 articles being the most cited parameter for Digital Twin requirements. For instance, in [6], real-time data is used for the optimization of products and production processes. The importance of this requirement is also shown by [22], that concludes that, real-time data is important for knowing the status of the product. In [25], real-time data requirements focus on the management and optimization of processes through monitoring and data analytics.

Data integration is the second most cited parameters for Digital Twin requirements. Integration is the most important value creation in the Digital Twin world [28]. A real-world object is represented by different subgraphs of nodes and edges. The integration of the different nodes is essential for creating valuable data [22]. In [23], integration is shown as the way to create the visual abstract that represents the anatomy of Digital Twin.

Fidelity, the third most cited parameter, is essential to mirror physical entities [4]. A high fidelity simulation model has several potential uses in organizations. It allows an operator to train on virtual machine, provide a basis for increasing the self-awareness of the machine [26]. The abstract representation of the Digital Twin allows the description of different operations in the real world. It is the fidelity of the model that provides the closeness to the physical product [3].

With the literature requirements defined, it is possible to collect industry requirements.

4 Industry Requirements

In this section it is presented the main results from interviews conducted at industry partners aiming at understanding:

(a) The current use of digital twin concept;
(b) The vision of the industry about this topic; and
(c) The requirements imposed by industry for the development of digital twins.

From the six companies that were interviewed, all were familiar with the Digital Twin concept and claimed to use this model on processes. The interviewed companies demonstrated to understand this component as a digital representation of the physical world and a physical representation of the digital world. It is seen as composed by two different visions a real one, and a utopic one. The utopic is described as the intersection between the digital and the physical. The real one is described as the use of DT as a simulation model for the physical world, without instant connection of data.

One company claimed to use DT model in large scale, simulating the manufacturing lines before the actual implementation of the factory. The system of this company is then alimented with real data. Other companies claimed to use DT concept as part of their business model, selling solutions that englobe DT.

For the future, the companies intend to implement integration platforms that collect physical data to create an abstraction model which mirrors the physical world with high fidelity allowing real-time control of the manufacturing lines. Each company has a different strategy to achieve that, such as startups acquisitions and in-house development of technology.

Therefore, it is possible to conclude that however industry is well familiar with Digital Twin concept and many of them claimed to already use DT, most of them only use DT as simulation model. The main obstacles to the implementation of DT are a robust integration of data to allow a representation with high fidelity and real-time control of the line. The requirements demanded by industry are the same ones required in literature.

5 Conclusions and Future Work

This paper set out to answer the RQs: (RQ1) what are main criteria for developing a Digital Twin? Besides, it aims to investigate (RQ2) what industry understands as Digital Twin?

For answering the RQ1, this paper provides a rich description and analysis of the Digital Twin requirements in literature. This article contributes to the literature by surveying DT requirements. A total of 19 articles were analyzed, coming from the ISI Web of Science databases.

An analysis of the most frequent related topics on Digital Twin reveals that real-time data, integration, and fidelity are the DT requirements mostly dealt with and valued by the literature.

For the industry, DT is seen as a combination of an academic vision of coexistence of digital and physical world and a real vision of simulation models to improve and implement physical manufacturing lines. All interviewed companies claimed to understand the Digital Twin concept, however the current state of the practice is anchored on simulation models. They understand the difficulties to integrate digital and physical world and described their future strategy as more concerned about actual implementation of real-time control, not only simulation.

Besides, using the same data to draw an evolution of the topics in recent years - Table 2 - it is possible to see that, more recently, topics related to the system independence and implementation are becoming more cited in the literature in the last year. Approaching DT by a combination of implementation and reliability requirements

Table 2. Parameters evolutions in recent years

Factors	2015	2016	2017	Total
Real-time data		1	6	7
Integration		1	5	6
Fidelity			5	5
Interaction			3	3
Communication			2	2
Convergence			2	2
Scalability			1	1
Modularity	1			1
Data acquisition			1	1
Data security			1	1
Data capture			1	1
Data warehousing			1	1
Data quality			1	1
Efficiency			1	1
Interoperability			1	1
Expansibility			1	1
Process planning			1	1
Stable operation			1	1
Real-time location			1	1
Stable data acquisition			1	1
Scalable			1	1
Connectivity	1			1
Autonomy	1			1
Independently expanded			1	1
Automatically updated			1	1
Globally available in real-time			1	1

appears to be an academic challenging issue for the upcoming research agenda, showing that the actual implementation is gaining more attention than the DT design requirements.

This research has limitation due to the methodological choices, particularly related to the sample analyzed. The database choices, the search strings applied and topic analyzed have possible bias; hence, important articles can be missed in the process. Moreover, interviews were limited in number and to only one country.

The future of the research into the field is still open. Just recently, new parameters have been discussed as part of DT requirements. Especially the ones related to the actual implementation of DT models in manufacturing industries. Based on current DT requirements definition, future research in the field could explore additional DT requirements related to the actual implementation of DT models in manufacturing industries. Therefore, future work may focus on real DT case simulations – such as in labs and learning factories –, and pilot implementations.

Acknowledgments. The authors thank the Coordination for the Improvement of Higher Education Personnel (Capes), the Brazilian National Council for Scientific and Technological Development (CNPq), and the German Research Foundation (DFG) for supporting related projects. The authors also thank the companies involved for providing real case applications.

References

1. Hobsbawn, E.: The Age of Revolution (1961)
2. Kagermann, H., Wahlster, W., Helbig, J.: Recommendations for implementing the strategic initiative INDUSTRIE 4.0. Final report of the Industrie 4.0 Working Group 82 (2013)
3. Schleich, B., Anwer, N., Mathieu, L., Wartzack, S.: Shaping the digital twin for design and production engineering. CIRP Ann. Manufact. Technol. **66**, 141–144 (2017). https://doi.org/10.1016/j.cirp.2017.04.040
4. Tao, F., Zhang, M.: Digital twin shop-floor: a new shop-floor paradigm towards smart manufacturing. IEEE Access **5**, 20418–20427 (2017). https://doi.org/10.1109/ACCESS.2017.2756069
5. Rosen, R., Von Wichert, G., Lo, G., Bettenhausen, K.D.: About the importance of autonomy and digital twins for the future of manufacturing. IFAC-PapersOnLine **28**, 567–572 (2015). https://doi.org/10.1016/j.ifacol.2015.06.141
6. Zhang, H., Liu, Q., Chen, X., et al.: A digital twin-based approach for designing and decoupling of hollow glass production line. IEEE Access 1 (2017). https://doi.org/10.1109/access.2017.2766453
7. Carvalho, M.M., Fleury, A., Lopes, A.P.: An overview of the literature on technology roadmapping (TRM): contributions and trends. Technol. Forecast Soc. Change **80**, 1418–1437 (2013)
8. Boote, D.N., Beile, P.: Scholars before researchers: on the centrality of the dissertation literature review in research preparation. Educ. Res. **34**, 3–15 (2005). https://doi.org/10.3102/0013189X034006003
9. Durão, L.F.C.S., Grotti, M.V.F., Maceta, P.R.M., et al.: A review of the soft side in project management: concept, trends and challenges. GEPROS Gestão da Produção Operações e Sist **12**, 157–176 (2017). https://doi.org/10.15675/gepros.v12i2.1644

10. Duriau, V., Reger, R., Pfarrer, M.D.: A content analysis of the content analysis literature in organization studies research themes, data sources, and methodological refinements. Organ. Res. Methods **10**, 5–34 (2007)
11. Anderl, R.: Industrie 4.0 - advanced engineering of smart products and smart production. In: 19° Seminário Internacional de Alta Tecnologia, Piracicaba (2014)
12. Piccard, A., Anderl, R.: Integrated component data model for smart production planning. In: 19° Seminário Internacional de Alta Tecnologia, Piracicaba (2014)
13. Brettel, M., Friederichsen, N., Keller, M., Rosenberg, M.: How virtualization, decentralization and network building change the manufacturing landscape: an Industry 4.0 perspective. Int. J. Mech. Aerosp. Ind. Mechatron. Eng. **8**, 37–44 (2014)
14. Lee, J., Bagheri, B., Kao, H.: A cyber-physical systems architecture for Industry 4.0-based manufacturing systems. Manufact. Lett. **3**, 18–23 (2015). https://doi.org/10.1016/j.mfglet.2014.12.001
15. Monostori, L.: Cyber-physical production systems: roots, expectations and R&D challenges. Procedia CIRP **17**, 9–13 (2014)
16. Tao, F., Cheng, J., Qi, Q., et al.: Digital twin-driven product design, manufacturing and service with big data. Int. J. Adv. Manufact. Technol. (2017). https://doi.org/10.1007/s00170-017-0233-1
17. Brenner, B., Hummel, V.: Digital twin as enabler for an innovative digital shopfloor management system in the ESB logistics learning factory at Reutlingen - University. Procedia Manufact. **9**, 198–205 (2017). https://doi.org/10.1016/j.promfg.2017.04.039
18. Kubler, S., Robert, J., Hefnawy, A., et al.: Open IoT ecosystem for sporting event management. IEEE Access **5**, 7064–7079 (2017). https://doi.org/10.1109/ACCESS.2017.2692247
19. Wiesner, S., Freitag, M., Westphal, I., Thoben, K.D.: Interactions between service and product lifecycle management. Procedia CIRP **30**, 36–41 (2015). https://doi.org/10.1016/j.procir.2015.02.018
20. Belkadi, F., Bernard, A.: Trust-based patterns for the management of inter-enterprises collaborations in context of extended enterprise. IFAC-PapersOnLine **28**, 1186–1191 (2015). https://doi.org/10.1016/j.ifacol.2015.06.245
21. Alam, K.M., El Saddik, A.: C2PS: a digital twin architecture reference model for the cloud-based cyber-physical systems. IEEE Access **5**, 2050–2062 (2017). https://doi.org/10.1109/ACCESS.2017.2657006
22. Canedo, A.: Industrial IoT lifecycle via digital twins. In: Proceedings of the Eleventh IEEE/ACM/IFIP International Conference on Hardware/Software Codesign System Synthesis - CODES 2016, vol. 1 (2016). https://doi.org/10.1145/2968456.2974007
23. DebRoy, T., Zhang, W., Turner, J., Babu, S.S.: Building digital twins of 3D printing machines. Scr. Mater. **135**, 119–124 (2017). https://doi.org/10.1016/j.scriptamat.2016.12.005
24. Knapp, G.L., Mukherjee, T., Zuback, J.S., et al.: Building blocks for a digital twin of additive manufacturing. Acta Mater. **135**, 390–399 (2017). https://doi.org/10.1016/j.actamat.2017.06.039
25. Konstantinov, S., Ahmad, M., Ananthanarayan, K., Harrison, R.: The cyber-physical E-machine manufacturing system: virtual engineering for complete lifecycle support. Procedia CIRP **63**, 119–124 (2017). https://doi.org/10.1016/j.procir.2017.02.035
26. Rodič, B.: Industry 4.0 and the new simulation modelling paradigm. Organizacija **50**, 193–207 (2017). https://doi.org/10.1515/orga-2017-0017
27. Uhlemann, T.H.J., Lehmann, C., Steinhilper, R.: The digital twin: realizing the cyber-physical production system for industry 4.0. Procedia CIRP **61**, 335–340 (2017). https://doi.org/10.1016/j.procir.2016.11.152

28. Uhlemann, T.H.J., Schock, C., Lehmann, C., et al.: The digital twin: demonstrating the potential of real time data acquisition in production systems. Procedia Manufact. **9**, 113–120 (2017). https://doi.org/10.1016/j.promfg.2017.04.043
29. Vachálek, J., Bartalský, L., Rovný, O., et al.: The digital twin of an industrial production line within the Industry 4. 0 concept. In: 21st International Conference on Process Control, pp. 258–262 (2017)
30. West, T.D., Blackburn, M.: Is digital thread/digital twin affordable? a systemic assessment of the cost of DoD's latest Manhattan project. Procedia Comput. Sci. **114**, 47–56 (2017). https://doi.org/10.1016/j.procs.2017.09.003

Is Openness Really Free? A Critical Analysis of Switching Costs for Industrial Internet Platforms

Karan Menon[1(✉)], Hannu Kärkkäinen[1], Thorsten Wuest[2], and Timo Seppälä[3]

[1] Tampere University of Technology, Tampere, Finland
{karan.menon,hannu.karkkainen}@tut.fi

[2] West Virginia University, Morgantown, USA
thwuest@mail.wvu.edu

[3] ETLA, The Research Institute of the Finnish Economy, Helsinki, Finland
timo.seppala@etla.fi

Abstract. The core idea of Industrial Internet, Industry 4.0, Smart Manufacturing and Cyber Physical Systems (CPS) is to utilize Internet of Things (IoT) based technologies and applications for the purpose of enhanced operations productivity. These IoT technologies and applications help companies to integrate their business as well as their engineering, manufacturing and service processes making their operations more robust, efficient and sustainable (green) with supreme quality. Switching cost and openness of the industrial internet (II) platform has many short and long-term impacts on the end-users' business. Hence the openness is often considered to be free or synonymous to open source. The purpose of this paper is to understand and analyze the impact of II-platform's increased openness and its dimensions on switching costs framework. For empirics and to test the developed framework we conducted a training and a workshop, where 11 manufacturing and service industry representatives describe the main types of switching costs that would be impacted because of increased openness of II-platforms. As a managerial implication this new switching cost framework seem to provide a tool to evaluate the specific preferences and potential positive and negative impacts of II openness on their respective businesses.

Keywords: Industry 4.0 · Industrial internet · Smart Manufacturing Platforms · Openness · Switching costs · Lock-in · IIoT · IoT

1 Introduction

Industrial Internet or Industry 4.0 utilizes internet of things (IoT) based technologies to combine business and engineering processes improving the production efficiency, robustness as well as producing high quality products at lower costs [1,2]. Various Industrial internet or industry 4.0 platforms allow the manufacturing companies to manage data and information efficiently in order to implement

P. Chiabert et al. (Eds.): PLM 2018, IFIP AICT 540, pp. 215–226, 2018.
https://doi.org/10.1007/978-3-030-01614-2_20

IoT related technologies to enhance their business and create value for the customers [3–5].

Platforms and platform economy has been of increasing academic and industrial interest, both in general as well as in the specific context of industrial internet. Some common topics in platform research include, platform business models [6,7], platform related network effects [6,8], platform openness [9,10], interoperability, lock-in [11], to name few. In the manufacturing companies' context, platform related openness is considered very important for technology implementation and creating business value [4,12–14]. This requirement from the industrial end-users also enforces platform providers to make critical decisions on platform openness [5,12,15].

Industrial internet platform openness has many benefits for manufacturing companies such as, enhanced interoperability with different machines because of open standards, diverse and high end applications made by core as well as third party developers. Literature primarily discusses about the downsides or risks of platform openness from the platform supplier or provider perspective and not from the platform end-user perspective [12,16]. In our previous work we have discussed the downsides of industrial internet platform openness for platform end-users [4]. Lock-in, which is understood to be one of the long-term downside of openness, can be a result of multiple factors including increased switching costs. However relatively little is known about the impact of switching costs in a B2B context. Furthermore the impact of increased openness on switching costs is also not studied well. Hence, in this paper we apply a multi-dimensional switching cost concept together with the multi-dimensional openness concept to evaluate the impact of increased openness for manufacturing companies that use industrial internet platforms.

We have derived the following research questions to address the identified research gap related to platform openness and related switching costs especially in the context of industrial internet platforms' end-users:

RQ1 *What types of switching costs would be perceived impacted by increased openness of industrial internet platforms?*

RQ2 *How would increased openness of industrial internet platforms impact the identified perceived switching costs?*

The remainder of the paper is divided into theoretical background, research methodology and design, results and findings, discussion and conclusions.

2 Theoretical Background

2.1 Industrial Internet Platforms and Related Trends

Today, innovation and value creation is happening more and more digitally and online. This stands true across all industries, from marketing to manufacturing. The increasing pace of this development can be credited to some extent to the available infrastructure, on which digital offerings and applications are built upon. This development is commonly referred to as platform economy [17]. In this paper we follow the platform definition by [18], that defined industry platforms as "products, services, or technologies developed by one or more firms, that serve as foundations upon which a larger number of firms can build further complementary innovations and potentially generate network effects." In essence, platforms provide a structure to utilize connectivity (through the internet), analytics (computational resources) and data.

Platforms can be designed narrowly for a specific purpose or industry. However, in this paper, we focus on platforms that can be utilized on an eco-system level across different industries and/or purposes. These platforms have in common that they allow a variating degree of customization and openness towards, e.g., third party developers. Platforms in an industrial setting are often used in unison with paradigms like Industrial Internet, Industry 4.0, Internet of Things (IoT), Cyber-Physical Systems (CPS) and Smart Manufacturing. [19] argue that Industrial Internet Platforms are one of the key enabling technologies for Smart Manufacturing Systems. Industrial Internet Platforms can be used to access, store, aggregate and analyze data from a variety of sources in a manufacturing environment (e.g., machine tools, sensors, ERP or MES systems) as well as provide access to data to dedicated applications and services throughout the smart factory and beyond. One major aspect of high relevance to industrial end-users is the openness of a platform (see following chapter) and the impact on the (direct and indirect) switching costs associated with it.

2.2 Industrial Internet Platform Openness

From the literature, we can see that platforms are not just open or closed, they belong on a continuum between open and close [4,14,20–22]. Manufacturing companies need to select the right industrial internet platform in order to attain optimal openness between their customers, suppliers, sub-contractors and partners. Eisenmann et al. 2009 [23] defined that a platform is "open", as long as, (1) no restrictions are placed on participation in its development, commercialization or use; or (2) any restrictions, for example, requirements to conform with technical standards or pay licensing fees, are reasonable and non-discriminatory, that is, they are applied to all the potential platform participants [23]. This is applicable to all the actors participating in the use and propagation of the platform. These platform actors are divided into three categories; (1) Demand-side user (end-users of the platform) (2) Supply-side users (application developers in the platform) (3) Platform providers and sponsors (platform companies) [4,13,15,18].

Platform openness is divided into three broader dimensions keeping the above mentioned platform actors in mind and then further divided into sub-dimensions, which results into a multi-dimensional framework for platform openness [4,22]. The impact of industrial internet platform openness on platform providers' strategy and platform end-users' strategy has been discussed in our previous work using the same openness framework mentioned above [4,22].

2.3 Platform Openness and Switching Costs

Some of the major effects of platform openness decisions are related to the interoperability (of platform users), network effects, as well as transaction costs and switching costs [15,18,22,24]. Choosing an optimal level of platform openness is crucial for companies that design and maintain the platforms (e.g. [12,23,25]), as well as companies that use those platforms [13]. In determining the level and type of openness, switching costs are one approach that can be utilized to understand especially the longer-term impacts of openness [11,13].

Blut et al. [26] define switching costs as "the customer's perception of the magnitude of additional costs required to conclude the current relationship, and secure an alternative supplier." However, they state that relatively little is known about the relevance of switching costs, yet, particularly in industrial and B2B markets. Furthermore, switching costs should be seen in B2B-context as a multifaceted construct [26]. Thus, part of the novelty of this study is derived from the use of multi-dimensional switching cost concept, and reflecting the importance of platform openness from the perspective of individual switching cost components in the relatively little studied industrial B2B context, as well as the little studied perspective of industrial internet platform use, and the platform user perceptions on the impact of openness to switching costs. We present the multi-dimensional openness (see [4] for details) versus the multi-dimensional switching costs (see [26] for details) evaluation framework in Table 1.

On the supplier side, significant part of management practices and tactics are often aimed at increasing switching costs, for instance through introducing loyalty schemes or offering unique customer solutions. It is rather commonly experienced that increased openness is generally something positive when viewed from the perspective of platform users: from the perspective of platform users and related switching costs, platform openness can e.g. allow the end users to reduce the switching cost to an alternative platform, thus allowing the end users to avoid a lock-in to the used platform ([27]).

One challenge with the proper understanding of the role of switching costs, as well as the impact of openness to switching costs is related to the nature of switching costs developing and often increasing in the course of time (see e.g. [26]). It has also been demonstrated that users have a tendency to fail to anticipate the impact of future switching costs, while having a preference of minimizing immediate costs, and thus, this leading to lock-in. Furthermore, due to common difficulty of anticipating future switching costs, as well as the many-dimensionality of both openness and switching cost concepts, it may be difficult for a platform user to identify the multitude and the importance of different impacts of openness to switching costs, especially in the long run.

Table 1. Platform openness [4] and switching cost framework [26]

			Switching Costs							
			Procedural				Financial		Relational	
			Uncertainty costs	Search costs	Training costs	Setup costs	Sunk costs	Lost performance costs	Brand relationship and psychological costs	Personal relationship and psychological costs
Openness Dimensions	End-user related openness	Access to information								
		Cost of access								
		Control in terms of rules to use the platform								
	Application developer related openness	Core developers								
		Extension or 3rd party developers								
		Data aggregators								
	Provider or sponsor related openness	Proprietary model								
		Licensing model								
		Joint venture model								
		Shared model								

3 Research Methodology and Design

The empirical material for this paper stems from a qualitative questionnaire, training and workshop of eleven manufacturing and service companies. The material and data were collected in February, 2018. The logic of the data collection resembles that of a multiple case study. [28] Table 2 describes the industry focus and the role of the respondent in the company.

Table 2. Information on companies

Company	Industry	Role of the respondent
Company A	Manufacturing	Production director
Company B	Manufacturing	Production manager
Company C	Manufacturing	Production manager
Company D	Manufacturing	Vice President Sourcing
Company E	Manufacturing	Production manager
Company F	Manufacturing	Supply chain project manager
Company G	Manufacturing	Supervisor
Company H	Manufacturing	Program manager
Company I	Industrial service	Business operations senior manager
Company J	Media company	-

We collected data following methods; (1) a qualitative questionnaire was sent to the eleven participants three working days before the training and workshop. This is because we wanted to understand: (a) the level of general knowledge of the participants about the platform economy and its characteristics and (b) what are the platforms of industrial internet the participating companies are applying for their operations and services, and (2) an in-depth qualitative training and workshop was executed of the platform economy. All participants who participated the questionnaire, training and workshop work as senior operations manager positions of participating companies. Furthermore, separate discussions about the platform economy and its characteristics were conducted with the participants during the training and the workshop. In this paper we will present results only from the workshop, i.e. point (2), which focuses on the switching cost framework.

The qualitative training and workshop were conducted in a structured way: first, the participants received a three-hour introduction to the topic of platform economy and its characteristics; second, the participants received and 30 min introduction to the switching cost analysis model and to its characteristics; third, the participants executed the switching cost analysis from the openness perspective as an individual task. The analysis took 60 min and iterative discussions were allowed to take place during the analysis between the two instructors and the participants. The data collected in training and workshops were supplemented and elaborated through the feedback collected after the training and workshop by the organizers.

During the workshop, the participants were introduced to the switching cost and openness framework, presented in Table 1. They were asked to evaluate the switching costs that would be impacted if individual sub-dimensions of openness were significantly more opened up either by their own platform or a new platform. Once they finished pointing out the switching costs, they were asked to give a +H to the switching costs that would have a maximum impact on their business and give a reason next to every +H that they mark.

4 Results and Findings

In this section, we report the results of our initial workshop focusing on switching costs in conjuncture with our Industrial Internet Platform Openness Framework. The results are based on the data provided by ten participants with variating backgrounds regarding their companies and II platforms used. In this section, the results are strictly reported and not interpreted. An interpretation of the results and a detailed discussion with regard to the initial research question, including possible limitations of the study, is presented in the following section.

We merged the answers that the individual participants provided within the framework table depicted in Table 1 in a combined table (Table 3). This allowed us to see general patterns that emerged across the different participants feedback.

However, before describing emerging patterns, we will present ***general results***. It is noticeable that each participant, all of them working with different platforms in their daily life, have identified multiple areas where openness relates to switching cost.

The two individual cross sections with the overall highest response count are at the intersection of the openness sub-dimension 'Access to information' and procedural switching costs category 'Setup Costs' with 10 total responses as well as 'Access to information' and 'Training Costs' with 9 total responses. The same ranking occurs when only counting individual 'high impact' responses, with a score of 5 for 'Access to information'/ 'Setup Costs' and 4 for 'Access to information'/ 'Training Costs'.

After merging the individual answers of the participants in one template, several ***patterns within the answers emerged***. One very prominent pattern is that the *openness dimension* 'End-User related openness' received the most attention with a combined total of 80 selected boxes across the participants. The second openness dimension 'Application Developer related openness' is a close second in total number of 68 selected boxes. The third and final openness dimension, 'Provider or Sponsor related openness' lags behind with only 32 reported correlations. In this sense, it is also noteworthy that while all 10 participants have a minimum of 6 (dimension 1) and 3 (dimension 2) ticked boxes while a total of four participants reported no impact for dimension 3.

Looking closer at the *openness sub-dimension level*, there is a clear preference visible with the first openness sub-dimension 'Access to information' receiving

Table 3. Results from the workshop

			Switching Costs								
			Procedural				Financial		Relational		Total
			Uncertainty costs	Search costs	Training costs	Setup costs	Sunk costs	Lost performance costs	Brand relationship and psychological costs	Personal relationship and psychological costs	
Openness Dimensions	End-user related openness	Access to information	4	5	9 (four +H)	10 (five +H)	3	6	3	2	42
		Cost of access	1 (one +H)	5	3	4 (one +H)	2	1			16
		Control in terms of rules to use the platform	2	2	8 (two +H)	2	2	1 (one +H)	3 (one +H)	2	22
	Application developer related openness	Core developers		4 (one +H)	5 (one +H)	5 (one +H)	4	2 (one +H)	4	2	26
		Extension or 3rd party developers	3	2 (one +H)	5	5 (one +H)		4	5	3	27
		Data aggregators	2	4 (one +H)	2 (one +H)	2 (one +H)			2	3	15
	Provider or sponsor related openness	Proprietary model	1	1	1	2	1	1	1		8
		Licensing model	1	3	1	1 (one +H)	2	1	4 (one +H)	1	14
		Joint venture model		1	2		1		1	1	6
		Shared model		1	1		1			1 (one +H)	4

Ranked 1 in High Impact on business responses
Ranked 2 in High Impact on business responses
Ranked 1 in responses to openness dimensions
Ranked 2 in responses to openness dimensions
Ranked 3 in responses to openness dimensions
No responses

a total of 42 responses with openness sub-dimensions five - 'Extension or 3rd party developers, and four - 'Core developers' accumulate 27 and 26 responses respectively. The highest score of any individual sub-dimension within openness dimension 3 is achieved by 'Licensing Model' with 14 responses, making up almost half of the total responses for this dimension.

It has to be noted that there are *two intersections of between openness* dimension and switching costs category standing out. Openness dimension one 'End-User related openness' and 'Procedural Switching Costs' have the most 'high impact' +H responses with a count of 13. Followed by the intersection of openness dimension two 'Application Developer related openness' with the same switching cost category scoring a total of 8 'high impact' responses.

Another interesting pattern that emerging from the accumulated data is that the openness sub-dimension 'Cost of access' has no reported correlation with 'Relational Switching Cost'. Similarly, the participants reported no correlation of the openness sub-dimension 'Data aggregators' with 'Financial Switching Costs'.

The participants were asked to provide ***reasoning for their top-three 'high impact' cross-sections*** of openness related switching cost. We clustered and condensed the individual reasons to provide an overview of the reported impacts. Switching the platform to more open would mostly affect the set-up cost as well as training costs of the company. Typically, these terms set-up cost and training cost denote money and time used as an investment to benefit the company (for more information about the training costs see [29]). In our study the respondents considered that set-up cost and training cost would be quite high or high for their companies. They also considered that companies sometimes have difficulties in obtaining financial resources for such cost, especially training. Additionally, the openness of the platform would lead to even higher set-up cost and training cost.

Hence, the respondents considered that set-up cost and training cost also add value for the company (it is not always a bad thing one of the respondents said) and will lead to higher licensing revenues from the platform. They also identified new opportunities for larger indirect network effects by implementing shared revenue business models. Adding developers to the platform would lead to even larger indirect network effects (more developers make the platform better another respondent said). Furthermore, a more open platform, from the end user perspective, allow companies to get much more innovations out of it such as new data, new knowledge and new patents. However, sometimes openness might lead to higher search cost, lost performance, lost competence and for more varied systems architecture.

5 Discussion and Conclusions

It can be seen from Table 3 that the overall procedural costs get impacted by increased openness of end-user related openness and application developer related openness dimensions. Procedural costs are associated with the costs that involve time and effort in searching, adopting and using a new platform as well as the uncertainty associated with the new platform. On increasing openness for end-user related dimension certain procedural costs (for example setup and training costs) increase to an extent that they have a significant impact on the platform end-user's business. This happens because the end-user manufacturing company incurs costs with respect to setting up either new servers, databases or systems related to the new platform. There is also an additional training cost associated with the features of the new platform. Similarly, increased openness for application developer related dimension also has a substantial impact on procedural costs. New applications can mean concentrated effort and investment on infrastructure as well as training the personnel on how to efficiently use these applications. Hence, it is important to understand that increased access to data, better control over the use of the platform and increase in the number of applications can increase the switching costs significantly in long term.

One of the various findings of this study was that increased openness for access to information was commonly perceived to increase the switching costs related to training and setup costs. This means access to more data and information, which can result into investments in infrastructure as well as training the personnel. None of the respondents consider increased openness towards cost of access, i.e. cost of the platform usage reduces, will impact the relational switching costs. This means that for industrial manufacturing companies it is the access to data and information that is more vital when compared to the cost of access to the platform. Another interesting finding of the study was that if the openness towards 3rd party developers would increase then some of the perceived procedural costs will have a significant impact. The is because it is the 3rd party developers or application developers, in general, that create business opportunities for the platform end-users by developing novel applications. Hence, if the openness increases for 3rd party developers then more applications will be developed on the platform motivating the end-user to stay on the platform for a long time and therefore, increasing the switching costs.

There are several limitations that need to be mentioned regarding the nature of this study and the conclusions drawn. One limitation is the size and setup of the group surveyed. While all participants have some form of experience with industrial internet platforms, they are all from different companies and serve in different roles. This might result in a bias in the answers provided. Another limitations might be inherited in the framework itself. Given the time limit of 60 min for the whole exercise, the participants might spend more time on the top part of the matrix and rush through the later parts. This might have an effect on the number of responses for the different parts (higher for earlier parts, lower for later parts). The complexity of the framework itself and the explanation given to the participants can also be perceived as a possible limitation that should be taken into consideration when interpreting the results.

It is imperative that the managers while making an industrial internet platform selection take into consideration, not only, the benefits of openness but also the long term risks or downsides. Openness versus the switching costs framework gives an indication towards long term lock-in. It was observed in our workshop that the managers were interested to learn new kinds of costs related to switching that their company would incur if the selection is made purely based on the positives of increased openness. It is important that the managers in collaboration with different users of the platform in the company make the decision related to the impacts of openness on their business.

As part of the future studies, it would be interesting to interview multiple people from the same company, involved in platform strategy as well as platform usage related senior roles. After understanding the role of switching costs towards lock-in, it would be beneficial to understand the role of different factors, such as, network effects, transaction costs, interoperability and others.

Overall, openness in industrial internet platform brings many benefits in short and long term but understanding the long term risks such as lock-in related switching costs gives us an understanding that openness is not always "free" as it is perceived occasionally.

Acknowledgement. This work was part of funding received by Wihuri Foundation (Grant Number: 00170247) & Välkky Project-Project Number-720118 We would like to thank our Master of Science researcher Pilar Aldama Marin for her contribution towards the study.

References

1. Wang, S., Wan, J., Li, D., Zhang, C.: Implementing smart factory of industrie 4.0: an outlook. Int. J. Distrib. Sens. Netw. **12**(1), 3159805 (2016)
2. Jeschke, S., Brecher, C., Meisen, T., Özdemir, D., Eschert, T.: Industrial internet of things and cyber manufacturing systems. In: Jeschke, S., Brecher, C., Song, H., Rawat, D.B. (eds.) Industrial Internet of Things. SSWT, pp. 3–19. Springer, Cham (2017). https://doi.org/10.1007/978-3-319-42559-7_1
3. Ehret, M., Wirtz, J.: Unlocking value from machines: business models and the industrial internet of things. J. Mark. Manag. **33**(1–2), 111–130 (2017)
4. Menon, K., Kärkkäinen, H., Wuest, T.: Role of openness in industrial internet platform providers' strategy. In: Ríos, J., Bernard, A., Bouras, A., Foufou, S. (eds.) PLM 2017. IAICT, vol. 517, pp. 92–105. Springer, Cham (2017). https://doi.org/10.1007/978-3-319-72905-3_9
5. Kotiranta, A., Seppälä, T., Tahvanainen, A.J., Hemminki, M., Mattila, J., Sadeoja, S., Tähtinen, T.: Roadmap for Renwal. A Shared Platform in the Food Industry. The Research Institute of the Finnish Economy, October 2017
6. Rochet, J.C., Tirole, J.: Two-sided markets: a progress report. RAND J. Econ. **37**, 645–667 (2006)
7. Hagiu, A., Wright, J.: Multi-sided platforms. Int. J. Ind. Organ. **43**, 162–174 (2015)
8. Parker, G.G., Van Alstyne, M.W.: Two-sided network effects: a theory of information product design. Manag. Sci. **51**(10), 1494–1504 (2005)
9. Gawer, A.: Platforms Markets and Innovation. Edward Elgar, Cheltenham, UK (2009)
10. Ghazawneh, A., Henfridsson, O.: Balancing platform control and external contribution in third-party development: the boundary resources model. Inf. Syst. J. **23**(2), 173–192 (2013)

11. Opara-Martins, J., Sahandi, R., Tian, F.: Critical analysis of vendor lock-in and its impact on cloud computing migration: a business perspective. J. Cloud Comput. **5**(1), 4 (2016)
12. Parker, G., Van Alstyne, M.: Innovation, openness, and platform control. Manag. Sci. 2973–3468 (2017)
13. Eisenmann, T.R.: Managing proprietary and shared platforms. Calif. Manag. Rev. **50**(4), 31–53 (2008)
14. Benlian, A., Hilkert, D., Hess, T.: How open is this platform? The meaning and measurement of platform openness from the complementors' perspective. J. Inf. Technol. **30**(3), 209–228 (2015)
15. Parker, G.G., Van Alstyne, M.W., Choudary, S.P.: Platform Revolution: How Networked Markets Are Transformin the Economy - And How to Make Them Work for You (2016)
16. McIntyre, D.P., Srinivasan, A.: Networks, platforms, and strategy: emerging views and next steps. Strateg. Manag. J. **38**, 141–160 (2017)
17. Zysman, J., Kenney, M.: The rise of the platform economy - issues in science and technology. Issues Sci. Technol. **32**(3), 61–70 (2016)
18. Gawer, A., Cusumano, M.A.: Industry platforms and ecosystem innovation. J. Prod. Innov. Manag. **31**(3), 417–433 (2014)
19. Mittal, S., Khan, M.A., Romero, D., Wuest, T.: Smart manufacturing: characteristics, technologies and enabling factors. In: Proceedings of the Institution of Mechanical Engineers, Part B: Journal of Engineering Manufacture, p. 095440541773654, october 2017
20. Stefi, A., Berger, M., Hess, T.: What influences platform provider's degree of openness? – measuring and analyzing the degree of platform openness. In: Lassenius, C., Smolander, K. (eds.) ICSOB 2014. LNBIP, vol. 182, pp. 258–272. Springer, Cham (2014). https://doi.org/10.1007/978-3-319-08738-2_18
21. Hilkert, D., Benlian, A., Sarstedt, M., Hess, T.: Perceived software platform openness: the scale and its impact on developer satisfaction. In: ICIS, pp. 1–20 (2011)
22. Menon, K., Kärkkäinen, H., Gupta, J.P.: Role of industrial internet platforms in the management of product lifecycle related information and knowledge. In: Harik, R., Rivest, L., Bernard, A., Eynard, B., Bouras, A. (eds.) PLM 2016. IAICT, vol. 492, pp. 549–558. Springer, Cham (2016). https://doi.org/10.1007/978-3-319-54660-5_49
23. Eisenmann, T.R., Parker, G., Van Alstyne, M.: Opening platforms: how, when and why? Platforms Mark. Innov., 131–162 (2009)
24. Henten, A.H., Windekilde, I.M.: Transaction costs and the sharing economy. info **18**(1), 1–15 (2016)
25. Gawer, A., Cusumano, M.: Platform Leadership: How Intel, Microsoft, and Cisco Drive Industry Innovation, p. 305 (2002)
26. Blut, M., Evanschitzky, H., Backhaus, C., Rudd, J., Marck, M.: Securing business-to-business relationships: the impact of switching costs. Ind. Mark. Manag. **52**, 82–90 (2016)
27. Matzler, K., Strobl, A., Thurner, N., Füller, J.: Switching experience, customer satisfaction, and switching costs in the ICT industry. J. Serv. Manag. **26**(1), 117–136 (2015)
28. Eisenhardt, K.M.: Building theories from case study research. Acad. Manag. Rev. **14**(4), 532–550 (1989)
29. Swanson, R.A., Cullen, J.G., Sawzin, S.A., Sisson, G.R.: Cost Effectiveness: A Model for Assessing the Training Investment (1978)

A Case Study in Learning Factories for Real-Time Reconfiguration of Assembly Systems Through Computational Design and Cyber-Physical Systems

G. Pasetti Monizza[1,2](✉), R. A. Rojas[1], E. Rauch[1], M. A. Ruiz Garcia[3], and D. T. Matt[1,2]

[1] Free University of Bolzano, Bolzano, Italy
gabriele.pasettimonizza@fraunhofer.it
[2] Fraunhofer Italia Research, Bolzano, Italy
[3] Sapienza University of Rome, Rome, Italy

Abstract. Digitalization in manufacturing, also known as Industry 4.0, and Cyber Physical Systems (CPS) may turn ordinary manufacturing systems, usually designed for mass-production, into highly flexible and reconfigurable manufacturing system for mass customization purposes. The huge potential of the digital information management and real-time data management introduced by Industry 4.0 will be a key enabler for further developments in mass customization manufacturing. Increasing customization capabilities means increasing product variability and producing small quantities in a highly flexible way; this impacts the production process and the business process as well. Such reconfigurable CPS promise improvements of the production processes efficiency. In order to disseminate this production strategy to students and industry, the authors created a simple case study in order to introduce these aspects in a learning factory environment. This paper presents a pilot case study implemented in the Smart-Mini Factory laboratory at the Free University of Bolzano for educational and research purposes. The pilot case study aims at introducing a digital information management since the early first steps of the business process, combining Computational Design techniques and CPS. The authors discuss a simple pilot case that will be used mainly for dissemination purposes towards people not addicted to CPS and digital environments such as students and SME's entrepreneurs. In the upcoming academic year, the demonstrator will be tested for the first time in the course Production Systems and Industrial Logistics with engineering students. In addition, the use of the demonstrator in industry seminars on mass customization and computational design is planned.

Keywords: Learning factory · Mass customization · Computational design Visual recognition

P. Chiabert et al. (Eds.): PLM 2018, IFIP AICT 540, pp. 227–237, 2018.
https://doi.org/10.1007/978-3-030-01614-2_21

1 Introduction

The increasing request for individuality of customers intensifies the trend towards mass customization. The producer, which is able to produce a product to low prices and with customer specific characteristics as quickly as possible, has the highest competitive advantage on the market. Therefore, mass customization is also an issue in engineering education and consequently also in the context of education in learning factories. In the sense of Industry 4.0, it would be an extensive goal if the production system could adapt to the requirements of the individual product in real time and therefore automatically adjust its production and assembly processes. Learning Factories should try to communicate these ambitious goals to students or seminar participants from industry by means of practical demonstrators.

This paper describes a case study at the Smart-Mini Factory (a learning factory lab) of the Free University of Bozen-Bolzano, which implemented such a demonstrator. In the case study, the assembly system is adapted to an individual product in real time by using Computational Design and CPS. The paper is structured as follows: after a short introduction, the state of the art in mass customization, reconfigurable production systems, Computational Design and the integration of CPS is shown. Subsequently, the concept of the case study or the demonstrator is explained and its implementation is described.

2 State of the Art

2.1 State of the Art in Reconfigurable Production Systems and Mass Customization

The concept of mass customization was first expounded formally in the book "Future Perfect" by Davis in 1989 [1]. It means the production of products, which have been customized for the customer, at production costs similar to those of mass-produced products [2]. Mass customization allows customers to select attributes from a set of predefined features in order to design their individualized product, by which they can fulfil their specific needs and take pride in having created a unique result [3, 4]. Mass customization brings radical changes to methods used to operate traditional manufacturing enterprises [5–10]. Manufacturing systems in a mass customization environment should be able to produce small quantities in a highly flexible way and to be rapidly reconfigurable [4, 11].

In the past, several concepts for manufacturing system design have been discussed in scientific literature: from flexible manufacturing systems (FMS) [12] to reconfigurable manufacturing systems (RMS) [5] as well as the concept of changeable and agile manufacturing systems [13]. Such manufacturing systems fit the needed requirements for mass customization manufacturing better than a traditional one.

The latest trend in mass customization is digitalization in manufacturing, also known under the term Industry 4.0 or CPS. The large potential of Industry 4.0 will be a key enabler for further developments in mass customization manufacturing [14]. Intelligent, cognitive and self-optimizing manufacturing systems can learn and there-by perform self-determined changes in production systems [15]. To reach such a next level of changeability it is necessary to equip manufacturing systems with cognitive capabilities in order to take autonomous decisions in even more complex production processes with a high product variety [16].

2.2 State of the Art in Computational Design

Computational Design is a term widely adopted to describe all the disciplines and the approaches that lead the design and the engineering processes applying computer aided methods and tools, such as: Parametric Design, Algorithmic Design, Generative Design, etc. Nowadays is mostly applied in constructions and building industry, but may be effectively applied to all Engineer-to-Order (EtO) industries, according to Wortmann classification [17].

The definition provided by Jabi in 2013 [18] summarizes a complex debate in the scientific community since the 1940s' writings of architect Luigi Moretti [19] and the mathematical origins of parametric modelling. Lots of authors argue that everyone from Architecture, Design and Art disciplines always adopted parametric models to generate their ideas, such as Burry [20]. This complex framework generates difficulties in providing a clear definition about Parametric Design technique. After 70 years, the debate still goes on.

According to Woodbury [21], Parametric Design may be considered a huge family that includes all techniques leading geometry changes through parameters changes. Generative Design is based on algorithmic and parametric modelling and is a fast technique to explore design possibilities or design optimizations. Mostly, it applies nature's evolutionary approach to design [22, 23].

Schumacher in his Parametricist Manifesto [24] points out stylistic application of Parametric and Generative Design techniques. Unfortunately, Schumacher neglects the difference between tool use and tool making as defined by Aranda and Lasch et al. [25, 26]. Beyond stylistic application, Scheurer [27] and Arnold Walz (designtoproduction) are supporting architects, planning experts and manufacturers in order to reach new standards of efficiency, safety and quality in complex and highly customized projects. They handle geometry optimization, computation of quantities, production planning and machine data to facilitate the installation process on construction sites. The authors successfully tested the application of Computational Design techniques in EtO environment pushing mass customization capabilities, for further details, they kindly invite readers to refer to previous publications [28].

2.3 State of the Art in Integration of CPS

Contrary to what common sense could say, heterogeneity of components in modern industrial systems may be a favourable condition due to several facts [29], as spanning industrial activities through different norms or application-specific requirements. Moreover, CPS are intrinsically heterogeneous systems due to the natural difference between its constitutive layers, i.e., physical, platform and software [30]. In this context, integration may be understood as the necessary steps that permits a body of disparate systems to be treated as a whole [31]. Because the authors are only interested in integration of software layers, their specific concern is that of interoperability, i.e. the ability of a software layer to use and share information and/or functionalities of another software layer by adhering to common standards [32]. Interoperability may be technical, syntactic and sematic [33].

At this point, integration of Cyber-Physical Production System (CPPS) becomes familiar with a long history of effort to integrate disparate digital platforms that begins in office environments and the term Enterprise Service Bus (ESB) appears to describe the software and hardware infra-structure capable of enabling seamless interoperability between systems [34]. In industrial environments, term Manufacturing Service Bus (MSB) was coined as an equivalent to ESB [35].

The integration of the IT landscape of the factory floor with enterprise level IT systems have been approached by several authors and technical reports. In [36] the concept of Service Oriented Architecture (SOA) is widely explained from the perspective of manufacturing systems and an architecture for MSB is presented. The European Innovation Project SOCRADES [37] presents a MSB system based on web services. The European In-novation project IMC-AESOP [38] (Architecture for Service-oriented Process, Monitoring and Control) proposes an integration approach for CPPS based on cloud technologies. Authors in [39] describe the integration of the shop floor with the ESB and other business activities of the Business Domain.

Those approaches rely heavily on web-services and XML-based technologies, which are dominant in office/enterprise systems and ISA-95 standard [40]. Unlike the precedent works, in this paper the authors prefer to focus in communication technologies that are more suitable for CPS, focusing in efficiency and speed of the data transfer. For this reason, they decided to rely in the communication system available in ROS (Robot Operative System) [41] to assure the integration of the nodes per-forming the assembly process. This approach behaves the challenge of adapting the software layer of every CPS to be compatible with ROS, that was primarily developed for Linux platforms. In fact, address the challenge of developing the necessary software tools to integrate the required systems via network with ROS. Further, the authors still rely in XML-based technologies to integrate the assembly system with the frontend dedicated to the customer.

3 Concept of the Case Study

3.1 Computational Design for Reconfigurable Product Engineering

During their previous research activities [28], the authors analyzed a relationship between the adoption of CPS and the digitalization of design and engineering processes though a pilot case study. This research activities tested the efficiency and the effectiveness of Parametric and Generative Design techniques within a real production system, highlighting huge benefits which can be achieved without huge investments on the production system itself. The lack of controlling strategies and information management based on CPS has been identified as the main limit.

Following these promising results and according to the planned activities within the Smart-Mini-Factory laboratory, the authors developed a specific algorithm that aims at simulating a high reconfigurable product within different x-to-order environments. The algorithm should offer a prototype mock-up of an information management platform based on Parametric and Generative design techniques.

In order to fulfil the objectives previously identified, the algorithm has been developed according to a free customization, defining these specific design intents:

- the reconfiguration of the product must be performed both at features level and at geometrical level in an assembly space that could change time-by-time;
- the reconfiguration of the product must be performed real-time and the algorithm should transmit assembly information and trigger the production process any time by a real-time connection within the intelligent and hybrid assembly system of the Smart-Mini-Factory Laboratory;
- any scripting skill should not be required during the reconfiguration of the product, in order to make the algorithm accessible to any figure who could lead the process (e.g. final customer, selling agent, product developer, etc.).

According to the first design intent, the authors identified the TETRIS© game as the best example of performing a high-reconfigurable product design task. Number of pieces are limited to four, but, differently to the game, the user can select which piece he would use and freely change the order during the design task. Furthermore, the algorithm does not limit the alignment of the pieces (in the game limited to the bottom line) but let the user free of placing the pieces within the assembly space.

The reconfiguration of the product can be performed real-time thanks to the capability by the user of controlling all the parameters that lead the assembly. User can transmit assembly information and trigger the production process anytime, though a XML-RPC communication protocol.

The algorithm is structured though four main steps:

- assembly space (domain), pieces and geometric transformation definitions (see Fig. 1);

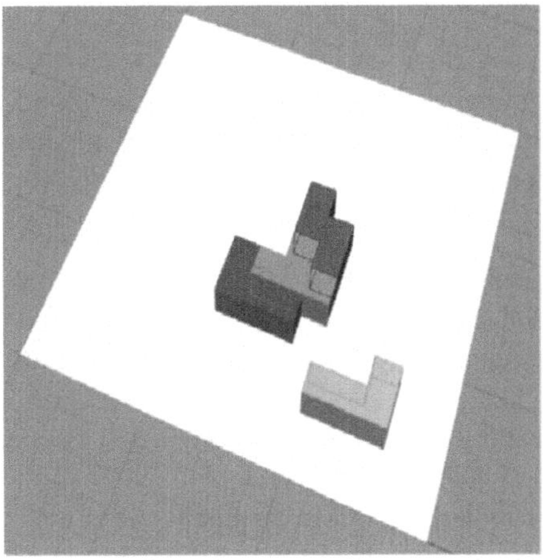

Fig. 1. Assembly space (domain)

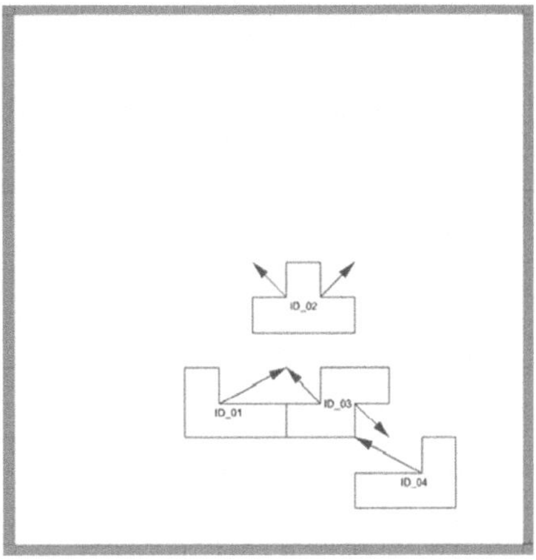

Fig. 2. Convexity analysis

- geometry analysis;
- assembly information and communication protocol definitions;
- GUI definition.

In a first step the algorithm defines the assembly domain, which has been defined as a 2D plane for convenience. The algorithm can apply parametric transformations on the main definition of the pieces: rotations of 90 degrees steps and translations according to the grid definition.

During a second step, the algorithm performs a geometry analysis in order to detect the following issues that may compromise a correct assembly:

- collision detection;
- assembly order (or priority).

The assembly order (or priority) has to be defined depending on the assembly process that has to be leaded. Whether the assembly is performed in a horizontal plane, any priority definition should not be performed. Whether the assembly is performed in a vertical plane, the algorithm must define the correct assembly order, identifying priorities of the pieces that have to be placed on bottom, under the condition that the assembly robot usually operates from the top according to a convexity analysis (see Fig. 2).

During a third step, the algorithm collects the assembly information that has to be transmitted to the assembly robot. The assembly information has been identified as follow:

- piece ID;
- assembly position (though coordinates) within the assembly domain;
- rotation on the main definition of the piece (in degrees or rad).

This information is transmitted to the assembly robot though a XML-RPC call.

In the last step the algorithm defines a GUI for controlling the algorithm and all the parameters leading pieces and geometric transformation definitions. The interface is shortly described in the description the next section.

3.2 Components of the Assembly System

Following the agent paradigm, the assembly system's design addresses each component of the manufacturing station as an autonomous entity capable of making its own decisions and autonomously retrieve any necessary resource of the network. The components are:

- An adept Cobra i400 robots, a four-axis manipulator with a SCARA base and one additional wrist joint. Its controller is a SmartController CX with Ethernet capability. It runs the V+real-time operating systems is capable of execute concurrently up to 24 processes.
- The Adept FlexiBowl is a rotary feeder for loose parts with less than 80 g. It can be actuated using a specific protocol based on UDP/IP over Ethernet.
- A Basler scout Giga-Ethernet camera. It handles the image acquisition and automatically sends it using the GiGe protocols, which is based over UDP/IP.
- A gateway server.

By then self, the FlexiBowl system and the Basler camera do not cope with the requirements of a CPS, so they cannot be integrated into the CPPS. This problem is overridden using the concepts of administration shield [42]. In practice, the FlexiBowl is connected to an Arduino YUN to its Ethernet port and the Balser camera is connected to a desktop computer running Linux with 3 Gb or RAM and an Intel i7 processor to reach the requirements of processing characteristics of computer vision system. Both systems as CPS will be called Smart Feeder and Smart Vision System respectively. Finally, the authors underline that the Adept Cobra i400 robot is already a CPS thanks to its Adept V+multitasking real-time operating systems and its hardware. Moreover, this robot will be the central entity of the CPPS that will receive the product assembly order and retrieve the required resource of the system to autonomously complete the order.

4 Implementation in the Smart-Mini Factory

4.1 User Interface Applied for Reconfigurable Product Engineering

The GUI is structured in two main sections (see Fig. 3):

- control windows;
- preview window.

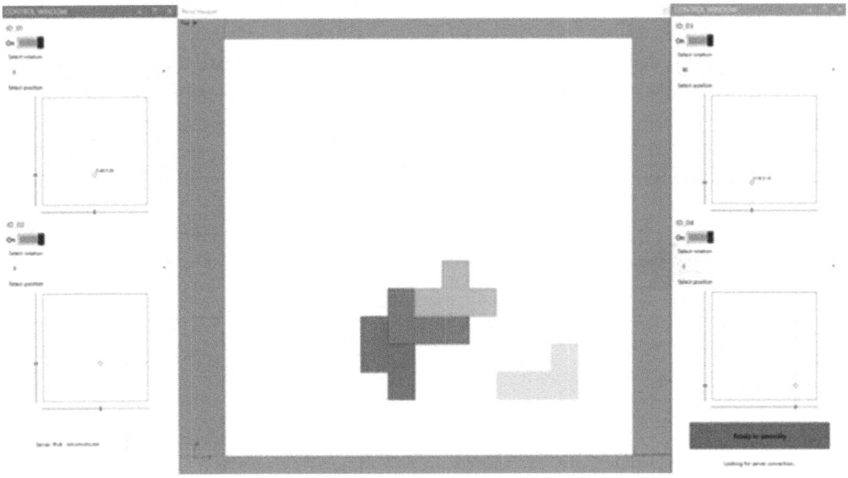

Fig. 3. The programmed GUI

The control windows are located at the side of the screen and they are the main interface for the user. The user can check parameters and assembly results though the preview window that is located in the middle of the screen. Changing parameters in control windows, starts algorithm's geometry analysis step that is performed in the background and controls the activation of the "Ready to assembly" button. This button communicates to the user whether collision occurs and invites him to check the geometry. As soon as any issue is not detected, the user can transmit assembly information through the "Ready to assembly" button that let the algorithm open the communication channel with the listeners terminal and transmit the information to the assembly robot.

The algorithm and the GUI have been installed and adapted for a Touch Table available in the laboratory (Fig. 5). This system provides a simple and attractive interaction with the GUI thanks to its multi-touch feature, highlighting algorithm capabilities to be used in different scenarios according to the second and the third design intents. Though the Touch Table, students, visitors, professionals and researchers as well, could appreciate the capabilities of an information management platform based on Parametric and Generative design techniques and having a better understanding of benefits provided by CPS aiming at enhancing mass customization capabilities of production system within the "Industry 4.0" vision.

4.2 Network Specifications, CPS Coordination and Orchestration

There are mainly two different kind of data exchanged in industrial systems: (i) configuration data, that is related to remote management of systems and operation support and (ii) process data that is related to the state of process. Each category of data as its own requirements regarding network latency, jitter and reliability. To cope those requirement, the authors selected Publish and Subscribe for process data and Services for configuration data. Due to the pervasiveness of Ethernet compatibility in the available devices the authors chosen as the back-bone of the network of the CPPS a VLAN on switched Ethernet inside the Campus Area Network (CAN) of the Free University of Bolzano. The ROS-compatible Publish and Subscribe and services system and the XML-RPC messaging define two separate networks as in Fig. 4.

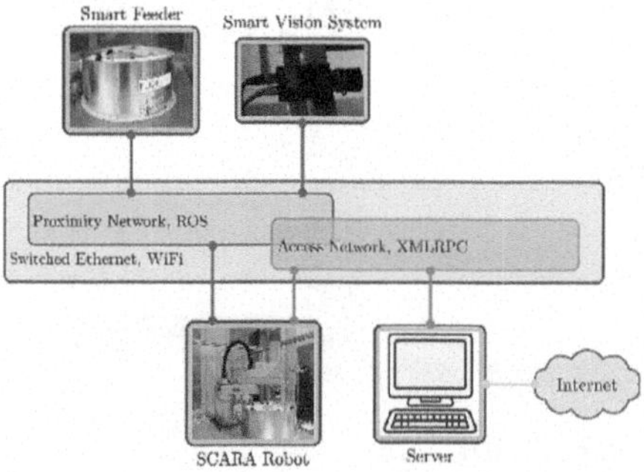

Fig. 4. Subdivision of the system network

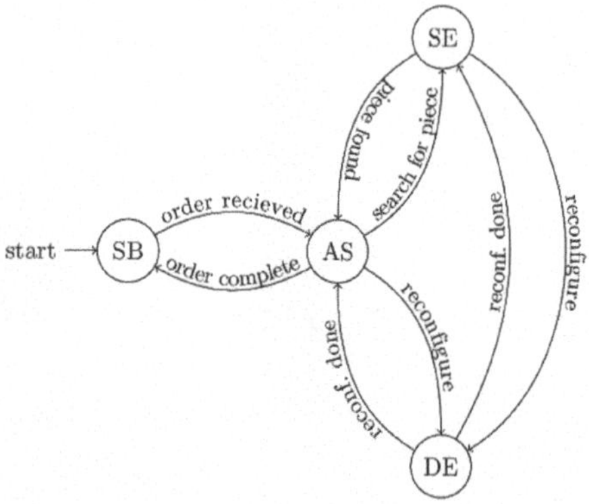

Fig. 5. States of the assembly process

At a high level the authors differentiate their systems in 4 states as represented in Fig. 5, namely AS assembling, DE disassembling, SE searching and SB stand-by. The pro-cess begins in the SB state, where the robot is waiting for the external call from the

Customer Relationship Management (CRM) product customization web-based front-end. Once the order is sent to the robot the system pass to the AS state, where the algorithm runs the pick and place operation for the assembly of the product. When a piece is required the system pass to the state SE, where the camera and the feeder will be used to search the required piece. Once the required piece is found, the system pass to the AS state. If the reconfiguration order is received the system pass, only if necessary to the state DE, where the necessary pieces are dissembled in order to reconfigure the product.

As stated before, all the assembly algorithm is placed inside the SCARA robot which is able to retrieve the state of the other CPS through Publish and Subscribe mechanism and to command them using services.

The image processing technique was based in the optimized Canny Algorithm presented in [43]. After a noise removal and contour detection, lines where extracted using the Hough transform [44]. Once the proper lines are filtered, the shapes were classified by noting that edges of the shapes under study are proportional to either one, two or three times the length of the underlying square. Such property allows us to verify the geometry of all shapes and also to discriminate between T and S shapes. The easiest approach to discriminate between Right-L and Left-L shapes, consist in the computation of the (signed) angle between the longest orthogonal segments of the L.

5 Conclusions

This paper discusses a case study for a simple reconfigurable CPPS used as a showcase and a demonstrator at the Smart-Mini Factory (a learning factory lab) of the Free University of Bozen-Bolzano. The case study has been completed applying both Computational Design techniques and connectivity of CPS. The connectivity layer has been developed over an Ethernet hardware assuring seamless integration of the Touch Table and the assembly system as well all its components. The authors would like to encourage other initiatives in order to explore capabilities of a wider digitalization along the whole value-chain system towards real-time reconfigurable CPPS.

Since the laboratory has been newly founded, the presented case study and the demonstrator have not yet been tested in teaching. In the upcoming academic year, the demonstrator will be tested for the first time in the course Production Systems and Industrial Logistics with engineering students. In addition, the use of the demonstrator in industry seminars on mass customization and computational design is planned.

References

1. Davis, S.M.: From “future perfect”: mass customizing. Plan. Rev. **17**(2), 16–21 (1989). https://doi.org/10.1108/eb054249
2. Kaplan, A.M., Haenlein, M.: Toward a parsimonious definition of traditional and electronic mass customization. J. Prod. Innov. Manag. **23**(2), 168–182 (2006). https://doi.org/10.1111/j.1540-5885.2006.00190

3. Schreier, M.: The value increment of mass-customized products: an empirical assessment. J. Consum. Behav. **5**(4), 317–327 (2006). https://doi.org/10.1002/cb.183
4. Qiao, G., Lu, R.F., McLean, C.: Flexible manufacturing systems for mass customisation manufacturing. Int. J. Mass Cust. **1**(2–3), 374–393 (2006). https://doi.org/10.1504/IJMASSC.2006.008631
5. Koren, Y.: Reconfigurable manufacturing and beyond (Keynote Paper). In: Proceedings of CIRP 3rd International Conference on Reconfigurable Manufacturing, Ann Arbor, Michigan, USA (2005)
6. Terkaj, W., Tolio, T., Valente, A.: A review on manufacturing flexibility. In: Tolio, T. (ed.) Design of Flexible Production Systems, pp. 41–61. Springer, Heidelberg (2009). https://doi.org/10.1007/978-3-540-85414-2_3
7. Mourtzis, D., Doukas, M., Psarommatis, F.: Design and operation of manufacturing networks for mass customisation. CIRP Ann. Manuf. Technol. **62**(1), 467–470 (2013). https://doi.org/10.1016/j.cirp.2013.03.126
8. Bednar, S., Modrak, V.: Mass customization and its impact on assembly process' complexity. Int. J. Qual. Res. **8**(3), 417–430 (2014)
9. Matt, D.T., Rauch, E., Dallasega, P.: Trends towards distributed manufacturing systems and modern forms for their design. Procedia CIRP **33**, 185–190 (2015). https://doi.org/10.1016/j.procir.2015.06.034
10. Smirnov, Y.: Manufacturing planning under uncertainty and incomplete information. In: American Association for Artificial Intelligence Spring Symposium (1999)
11. Thirumalai, S., Sinha, K.K.: Customization of the online purchase process in electronic retailing and customer satisfaction: an online field study. J. Oper. Manag. **29**(5), 477–487 (2011). https://doi.org/10.1016/j.jom.2010.11.009
12. Wiendahl, H.P., et al.: Changeable manufacturing-classification, design and operation. CIRP Ann. Manuf. Technol. **56**(2), 783–809 (2007). https://doi.org/10.1016/j.cirp.2007.10.003
13. ElMaraghy, H.A., Wiendahl, H.P.: Changeability–an introduction. In: ElMaraghy, H. (ed.) Changeable and Reconfigurable Manufacturing Systems, pp. 3–24. Springer, London (2009). https://doi.org/10.1007/978-1-84882-067-8_1
14. Kull, H.: Intelligent manufacturing technologies. In: Kull, H. (ed.) Mass Customization, pp. 9–20. Apress, Berkeley (2015). https://doi.org/10.1007/978-1-4842-1007-9
15. Schmitt, R., et al.: Self-optimising production systems. In: Brecher, C. (ed.) Integrative Production Technology for High-Wage Countries, pp. 697–986. Springer, Heidelberg (2012). https://doi.org/10.1007/978-3-642-21067-9
16. Brettel, M., Fischer, F.G., Bendig, D., Weber, A.R., Wolff, B.: Enablers for self-optimizing production systems in the context of industrie 4.0. Procedia CIRP **41**, 93–98 (2016). https://doi.org/10.1016/j.procir.2015.12.065
17. Wortmann, J.C.: A classification scheme for master production schedule. In: Wilson, B., Berg, C.C., French, D. (eds.) Efficiency of Manufacturing Systems, pp. 101–109. Plenum Press, New York (1983). https://doi.org/10.1007/978-1-4684-4475-9_10
18. Jabi, W.: Parametric Design for Architecture. Laurence King, London (2013). ISBN 1780673140
19. Bucci, F., Mulazzani, M.: Luigi Moretti: Works and Writings. Princeton Architectural Press, Hudson (2002). ISBN 1568983069
20. Burry, M.: Scripting Cultures. Wiley, Chichester (2011). ISBN 0470746416
21. Woodbury, R.: Elements of Parametric Design. Routledge, Abingdon (2010). ISBN 0415779871
22. Soddu, C.: Generative design futuring past. In: GA2015 – XVIII Generative Art Conference (2015). http://www.generativeart.com/ga2015_WEB/FuturingPast_Soddu.pdf
23. Maeda, J.: Design by Numbers. The MIT Press, Cambridge (2001). ISBN 0262632446

24. Schumacher, P.: Parametricism as style - parametricist manifesto. In: Dark Side Club1, 11th Architecture Biennale, Venice 2008 (2008). http://www.patrikschumacher.com/Texts/Parametricism%20as%20Style.html
25. Aranda, B., Lasch, C.: Pamphlet Architecture 27: Tooling. Princeton Architectural Press, New York (2005). ISBN 1568985479
26. Aish, R.: From intuition to precision. In: Proceedings of 23rd eCAADe Conference, pp. 62–63. Lisbon: Technical University of Lisbon (2005). https://cumincad.architexturez.net/system/files/pdf/2005_010.content_0.pdf
27. Scheurer, F.: Materialising complexity. In: Theories of the Digital in Architecture, p. 287. Routledge, New York (2014). ISBN 0415469244
28. Pasetti Monizza, G., Rauch, E., Matt, D.T.: Parametric and generative design techniques for mass-customization in building industry: a case study for glued-laminated timber. Procedia CIRP **60**, 392–397 (2017). https://doi.org/10.1016/j.procir.2017.01.051
29. Lin, S.W., Miller, B.: Industrial internet: towards interoperability and composability. Technical report, Industrial Internet Consortium (2016)
30. Sztipanovits, J., et al.: Toward a science of cyber–physical system integration. Proc. IEEE **100**(1), 29–44 (2012). https://doi.org/10.1109/jproc.2011.2161529
31. Bellman, K.L., Landauer, C.: Towards an integration science. J. Math. Anal. Appl. **249**(1), 3–31 (2000). https://doi.org/10.1006/jmaa.2000.6949
32. Vernadat, F.B.: Interoperable enterprise systems: principles, concepts, and methods. Annu. Rev. Control **31**(1), 137–145 (2007). https://doi.org/10.1016/j.arcontrol.2007.03.004
33. Rojas, R.A., Rauch, E., Vidoni, R., Matt, D.T.: Enabling connectivity of cyber physical production systems: a conceptual framework. In: Faim 2017 Conference Proceedings (2017). https://doi.org/10.1016/j.promfg.2017.07.184
34. Chappell, D.: Enterprise Service Bus. O'Reilly, Sebastopol (2004)
35. Monostori, L., et al.: Cyber-physical systems in manufacturing. CIRP Ann. Manuf. Technol. **65**(2), 621–641 (2016). https://doi.org/10.1016/j.cirp.2016.06.005
36. MESA. Soa in manufacturing guidebook. Technical report, MESA International, IBM Corporation and Capgemini (2008)
37. de Souza, L.M.S., Spiess, P., Guinard, D., Köhler, M., Karnouskos, S., Savio, D.: SOCRADES: a web service based shop floor integration infrastructure. In: Floerkemeier, C., Langheinrich, M., Fleisch, E., Mattern, F., Sarma, Sanjay E. (eds.) IOT 2008. LNCS, vol. 4952, pp. 50–67. Springer, Heidelberg (2008). https://doi.org/10.1007/978-3-540-78731-0_4
38. Colombo, A.W., et al. (eds.): Industrial Cloud-Based Cyber-Physical Systems. Springer, Cham (2014). https://doi.org/10.1007/978-3-319-05624-1
39. Minguez, J., Ruthardt, F., Riffelmacher, P., Scheibler, T., Mitschang, B.: Service-based integration in event-driven manufacturing environments. In: Chiu, D.K.W., et al. (eds.) WISE 2010. LNCS, vol. 6724, pp. 295–308. Springer, Heidelberg (2011). https://doi.org/10.1007/978-3-642-24396-7_23
40. ANSI/ISA-95.00.01-2010 (IEC 62264-1 Mod) Enterprise-Control System Integration - Part 1: Models and Terminology
41. O'Kane, J.M.: A Gentle Introduction to ROS. Jason M. O'Kane, Coleraine (2014)
42. Adolphs, P., Bedenbender, H., Ehlich, M., Epple, U.: Reference architecture model industrie 4.0 (rami 4.0). Technical report, VDI/VDE, ZVEI (2015)
43. Deriche, R.: Using Canny's criteria to derive a recursively implemented optimal edge detector. Int. J. Comput. Vis. **1**(2), 167–187 (1987). https://doi.org/10.1007/BF00123164
44. Matas, J., Galambos, C., Kittler, J.V., Robust detection of lines using the progressive probabilistic Hough transform. CVIU **78**(1), 119–137 (2000). https://doi.org/10.1109/cvpr.1999.786993

How Digital Twins Enable the Next Level of PLM – A Guide for the Concept and the Implementation in the Internet of Everything Era

Christian Voell(✉), Prodip Chatterjee(✉), Andreas Rauch(✉), and Julius Golovatchev(✉)

Detecon International GmbH, Sternengasse 14–16, 50676 Cologne, Germany
{Christian.voell, prodip.chatterjee, andreas.rauch, julius.golovatchev}@detecon.com

Abstract. The idea of a digital twin as a virtual representation of a product is not new. However, the modern IoE (Internet of Everything) technology is able to cover a new dimension in terms of monitoring and controlling an operating state of a products or process. The potential is high to reach a new maturity level in all PLM processes. Unfortunately, it is a very complex topic and has a high impact on internal and external processes. The technical challenges are spread in different domains. The business value is hard to see. Therefore the risks are also high and a well-grounded strategy is necessary. This includes an organic growth with customer benefit and a consistent change management in the company.

Besides a successful implementations of digital twins this guide provides a pragmatic approach to get access to the digital twin technology. It covers the range from the conceptual understanding of a digital twin to a successful implementation with a prototype.

Keywords: Digital twin · Internet of Everything (IOE) · PLM
Prototyping · Traceability and performance

1 Introduction

The idea of a digital twin (DT) develops within PLM experts. It is a virtual representation of a product. A CAD model provides the geometry. A PLM tool provides functional and architectural information. But what is special about a DT? It brings realtime information to a model. This is why the application of digital twins gains momentum with technical progress in Internet of Everything (IoE).

IoE provides a solution to bring PLM to a next level. Producers are able to observe their product in the field. They are able to get insights to the use of the product [1]. A direct feedback loop from the customer to the producer will be established. Producers can make adjustments to the product while it is in use by the customer. Major changes and decisions for the product become obvious. The DT has the potential to significantly change methods and tools in every phase of the PLM [2]. Now the

Published by Springer Nature Switzerland AG 2018.
P. Chiabert et al. (Eds.): PLM 2018, IFIP AICT 540, pp. 238–249, 2018.
https://doi.org/10.1007/978-3-030-01614-2_22

question is why does not every company have a digital twin or at least is working to implement one?

It is easy to get the idea of a virtual representation, but it is hard to understand the whole idea. It is even harder to convince people of the idea. Of course there has to be a use case with a business value and the technology is far from the level of plug and play. In the following paper we want to discuss these hypothesis and give a proven way to make a DT in a company feasible.

2 Conceptual Foundation

2.1 The Digital Twin in Our View

Within five years, there will be over 21 billion connected machines, cars, buildings and other forms of smart devices in the world [3] all developed to collect, analyze and share all kinds of data. In total, by 2020, our accumulated digital universe of data will grow to around 44 trillion gigabytes [4]. This development is accompanied by the increasing sophistication of data processing technologies. Just think of recent advancements in AI, high performance- or quantum computing. One of the most recent examples being Google's AI algorithm beating a professional player at the Chinese board game Go, which is considered the world's most complex board game. As a result, the world is currently at the dawn of a technology-driven revolution which is fueled by a combination of the explosion in data production and data processing technologies. The combined effect of those two forces is changing the way we operate every "object" and manifests itself in the form of DTs.

So what are DTs? And why are companies so excited about them? A DT is a virtual dynamic model which includes everything that is known about an object. In other words, DTs are exact replica of their physical counterparts that change with the current environment in real time to help companies (and people for that matter) monitor, test, treat and maintain any number of systems [5]. They are continuously getting richer with data by integrating real-time location data, temperature data, energy consumption and other relevant data.

At a conceptual level, research of the Fraunhofer Institute for Intelligent Analysis and Information Systems [6] identified a couple of key features of DTs.

Comprehensiveness: DTs can include multiple features of physical things in order to anticipate broad use cases. These features may be spatial, material, structural and design attributes or include aspects of their close environment such as usage, weather or schedules. Still, the level of granularity with which a physical object is represented by its twin can range based on the requirements of its use: from a mere identification to a representation at an atomic level. Note that DTs can be virtual aggregated views of data and information located at various sources.

Linkage: DTs can be linked to other DTs in various ways. Relationships between DTs may be described as "part of", "requires", "communicates with" etc. A linked data representation of a DT facilitates the linking between two twins through the use of a unique identifier.

Interoperability: Interoperability is an important prerequisite of linkage. It means that DTs can reason and make decisions with each other rather than operating in isolation. Why is this interesting? Think of humans having DTs. To understand how the body works and improve its health, your DT must model more than the physical parts of the body. It must model how your entire body works together. This model includes not just organs, bones and other parts but also describes processes like blood flow, metabolism and the interactions among organs. Leg pain may be caused not by a leg problem but rather by a pinched nerve in the spine. A standalone model of a leg won't help you diagnose that problem. And if you only gave medication for the leg pain, without finding a treatment for the root problem, you condition would not improve.

Instantiation: It is important to differentiate between an instantiated an uninstantiated abstract DT. An abstract twin may be compared to "abstract class" in object-oriented programming. They cover features that all DTs have in common, but is in itself not a fully functional DT. An instantiated DT is fully functional. Its instance defines specific features not shared with other DTs.

Evolution and Traceability: DTs evolve over time as a physical object evolves, but keeps track of its evolution. In order to allow for independent maintenance and version-control, the properties from different domains related to the physical object should be represented in mutually distinct submodules of the overall DT.

Importantly, DTs are more than just a 3D model of a physical thing. They are also not just a mere user interface that enables remote control over a physical thing or a digital view on a thing/subject which focuses on only a particular aspect.

2.2 Current Players with a Successful Implementation of a DT

DTs are emerging everywhere across every industry, in business and in consumer markets. DT industrial use cases typically target maintenance and equipment health, predictive maintenance as well as operations and performance optimization [7]. DTs are already adding tremendous benefits in terms of efficiency gains and innovation. For example, GE is embracing the concept of the "digital twin"—a data model of a specific physical asset—in a bid to eliminate unplanned downtime of aircraft engines and other systems [8].

GE factory twins integrate operational analytics at the edge to ensure the efficient operation of the factory's entire assets, e.g. predicting failures, and find ways to optimize against a multiplicity of KPIs, e.g., balancing revenue against remaining life [9].

In a similar vein, Lufthansa Technik is working towards digitally modelling every single customer aircraft throughout the entire lifecycle as part of a digital aircraft twin. That way they can perform predictive maintenance effectively across their entire fleet [10].

Moreover, Siemens has built a fully automated auto factory which not only produces physical cars but also their DTs including all relevant data. These twins are continuously fed with real-time data once the car has left the factory halls reducing time to market from 30 to 16 months [11].

Dassault 3DEXPERIENCE creates a DT of a city which attempts to capture the complex spatial and temporal implications of life and work to support planners as they seek to imagine, develop and experience sustainable urban solutions [12].

3 Research Method

The key goals of this research is to understand how customers across industry verticals see the state of DT for themselves, how relevant they see the approach on their business and what are the barriers they have to implement DT solutions into their operations. We analyzed and integrated approaches how to ease the transition to DTs by generating a practical guide towards it. This paper will give practitioners a profound understanding of the underlying architecture of DTs and provides practical ways to organically integrate DT models that create undisputed business and customer value. The research was in cooperation with companies of Deutsche Telekom Group, industrial clients of Detecon across verticals (e.g. automotive), business consultants of Detecon Consulting (Member of Deutsche Telekom Group) and further subject experts. We conducted a series of interviews and surveys, combined with practical learnings that derived from DT projects undertaken by Detecon for clients. This way of validation offered the chance to hypothetically check the developed approach with experiences from client projects.

4 The Benefit of DTs in General

The reason why DTs are becoming more and more widespread is mainly because of two factors: their ability to integrate large amounts of static, real-time, structured and unstructured data and to combine this data with advanced data processing methods such as AI, machine learning or high-performance computing [7].

Let us consider analytics. Importantly, the business value which is created by means of DTs depends on the analytics proficiency with which it is used. Because DTs have become a single source of truth for all information related to an asset, they can be used for descriptive analytics. Informing operators about what happened based on trending information on historical or current events represents the lowest or basic business value, which can be created by employing DTs. At the next higher level, DTs are used for diagnostic analytics. Diagnostic analytics helps operators understand the reasons for a current situation by leveraging past data to understand why something has taken place. Even higher business value is created, if DTs are used for predictive analytics. Using current and historical facts to predict the future or unknown events can help operators of machines to perform maintenance before a part breaks down. The highest business value is generated by means of prescriptive analytics. In this case DTs examines a set of possible actions to recommend actions and support decision-making based on diagnostic and predictive analyses of complex data. More specifically, DTs can not only anticipate and predict problems they also issue proactive measures accordingly. This is done by combining real-time data of its precise state with similarity learning techniques accessing the knowledge of thousands of other similar DTs and running thousands of simulations to optimize individual outcomes, and provide mitigation. Additionally, the DT may provide operators with a forecast on the impact of implementing the suggested options along with an estimation of its confidence for that impact to actually realize itself, allowing the operator to make the optimal decision.

In general, the application of analytics moves from descriptive to prescriptive. Thus the nature of how to apply data and analytics changes from merely collecting information and doing basic trending to instead focusing on how to leverage data and analytics for true optimization. We see a shift in leveraging data to protect physical assets from financial downside (equipment failure leading to unavailability and expensive repairs) to enabling an upside (purposefully timed maintenance that balances operational risk and reward). As the analytics provide more valuable insights on the operational risks and opportunities, they need to be connected to both the people who make operational decisions and to the advanced controls that can adapt and maneuver the machines towards the desired outcomes.

Finally, our experience in client projects shows the DT is used to create demonstrable business value along several axes:

- Individual: The DT is applied to individual assets, tracking history and performance over the asset's lifetime.
- Adaptable: The DT infrastructure and models are adaptable. For example, they can transfer to another part or asset class, or adapt to new scenarios or new factors.
- Continuous: The DT models are continuously updated as the physical asset is operated. At any moment the DT represents a faithful representation of the current state of the asset; the output of the model changes with every fuel burn hour.
- Scalable: Benefit is derived when hundreds or thousands of like assets have a DT. A DT tracking a single asset learns from similar assets.

5 Challenges to Face for an Implementation

5.1 Understanding and Communicating the Digital Twin

If the intend to implement a digital twin is there, then it is absolutely necessary to understand the concept behind it. However, not only a visionary or missionary must understand the concept, but also the rest of the company.

Based on our experience the problem starts with the understanding. As seen in Sects. 2.1 and 2.2 there are several views and implementation on the topic. A general definition of a digital twin is hard to find because it is always customized. After a common understanding the management needs to be confident about the idea. They always ask for a business value behind it. So our recommendation is to identify a real business value in the company.

The investments may vary between the different use cases. Especially if the reference is a big project. Then it will be hard to state the value because the management is afraid of the investment. Indeed some use cases can be implemented with a lower investment. As a practitioner, we recommend to develop a prototype which is covered in detail in Sect. 6. It will also help to capture all technical challenges which will be covered in Sect. 5.3. If the used technology is clear for the use case then it will be much easier to calculate the cost. Consequently it is easier to calculate the business case behind it.

The prototype also helps to communicate the potential of the DT. People must experience the digital twin live. The enthusiasm rises as the idea matures in the head of the management or other employees. They start thinking on different use cases beside the intended one without saying anything else.

Once the idea is in everybody's head, the structured preparation remains. The following questions get relevant:

- Which use cases are relevant?
- Which ones will be prioritized and implemented?
- Which are the major steps?
- What efforts are necessary to achieve the desired benefit?
- What timetable is achievable?
- Is the organization in a position to implement the project?

Although the potential seams endless, the implementation requires consistent action. There will be a transition phase where the expenses are made, but the benefit cannot yet be generated. Especially here, it is important to communicate the value of the idea.

5.2 Use Case, Business Value and Business Model – How to Get Started

During our research, we found out that many clients face challenges in getting the right orientation in the endless use cases and opportunities that digital twins provide [5]. Developing a short, mid- and long-term strategy that is holistic and consistent at the same time is not easy. Related to this, allocating the right level of internal and external resources (monetary and personnel) is even harder. The most important takeaways according to our analysis is to take the customer experience/impact at the center of any digital twin strategy, use case or activity. We have seen the negative side effects of an approach that is technology focused ("What can I do with the digital twin?") and then looks for a suitable use case. The more effective way is to have a systematic and relentless focus on where the company can massively enhance customer experience. We have developed a four-step process that aims to help setting up a functional framework for clients who are in the early stages of their digital twin maturity (Fig. 1).

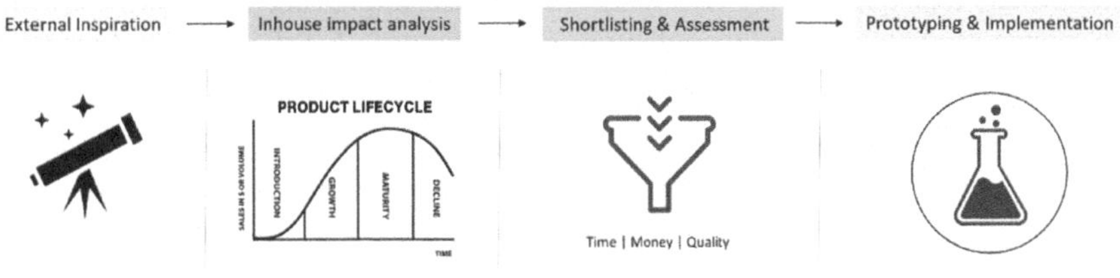

Fig. 1. Four-step process for identifying, selecting and implementing digital twins

Step 1 | External Inspiration: Due to its relative nascent stage, digital twins are still very new to the majority of clients (especially in the manufacturing sector). Given the vast array of potential use cases and the strong level of abstraction, it is difficult to get a tangible idea on use cases. Therefore, it is strongly recommend conducting a detailed understanding of use cases and activities that other clients from other verticals are working on by meeting and engaging with them. On top of that, these conversations with other clients have to be supplemented with dialogues from technology suppliers and innovative startups in order to get a holistic picture. Receiving external inspiration is potentially very helpful to get tangible input, that fosters ideation and though process about relevant use cases for the clients own company. It is recommended to get external help and advice from agencies/consultancies, who proved to have a strong network and access in the field of digital twins across clients, vendors and start-ups.

Step 2 | Inhouse impact analysis: As a next step, the focus has to come into the internal potentials of applying digital twins. Digital twins are able to have impact across the entire product lifecycle, starting from early stage prototyping until shipping of final products incl. aftersales. We recommend to conduct the inhouse analysis according to the phases of product lifecycles in order to distinguish between those and have clear focus. A very helpful exercise is, to jointly work out the Top 5 most important challenges that exist today in each of the phases and also working out a few use cases that would potentially add significant impact on customer delight. It is extremely important to have a relentless customer focus at this stage. In this step, it should be aimed to develop relevant use cases in each phase of the product lifecycle.

Step 3 | Shortlisting & Assessment: Post creating a longlist in each of the phases, it is now crucial to conduct a rigorous and systematic assessment of each these ideas with subject matter experts (advisors, vendors, internal employees, customers) in order to filter out which topics are worth working on first. The assessment has to conducted in these four areas:

- Technical: How complex would a digital twin be for the use case?
- Customer: How much would customers directly or indirectly benefit?
- Commercial: What costs occur for prototyping and scaling?
- Strategic: Is this use case going to exist and be relevant in 5+ years?

In order to assess how customers would benefit from the use case, it is helpful to assess the impact in three dimensions: time (e.g. does it make a process faster), money (cut costs with predictive maintenance or drive revenue by monetizing data or complete digital twins) and quality (e.g. reducing error rates, improving engineering quality). Most clients especially in the manufacturing sector care a lot about these dimensions. The use case must have significant impact on one or more of these areas.

Step 4 | Prototyping & Implementation: After the detailed assessment has been conducted, clients now should move on to build functional prototypes that are piloted in the field and post that implement the final solution at scale [13]. At this stage, it is very important to deeply consider the interdependencies of any solution for the entire product lifecycle, internal operations and processes. Especially for clients who have so far a nascent level of development in the area of digital twins, building prototypes that are not deeply integrated into IT-Systems and don't require large scale platforms are a vital way to understand if the solution is promising, how internal employees and external customers perceive it. Piloting the prototype for a few months is providing valuable feedback and prevents a company to make large-scale investments into solutions that are not suitable.

5.3 Technical Challenges that Come with the Architecture

The value chain plays an important role to get an overview about it, mainly because DT architecture has a lot in common or rather is identical with an Internet of Things (IoT) architecture (Fig. 2):

Fig. 2. Architecture of a digital twin

The architecture consists of physical devices, an optional device management system, a connectivity solution, a platform, and the actual application. The physical devices capture the data from the real twin. It transports the information to the platform or it will be stored temporarily in the device management. The device management has the task to control all devices. This is sometimes necessary when the devices are from different suppliers or the device itself is complex. It can also be implemented in the device. That is why it is not mentioned consistently in literature. Usually a cellular network establishes the connectivity between the device and the platform. The platform itself is the managing part of the architecture on the software side. At the end we have the actual application for the end user. While the general architecture is always the same, the characteristic of the whole system is always different. It highly depends on the technology for connectivity, platform and especially the application.

The DT has in contrast to the IoT platform a context information through dependencies and interactions. Its information is not limited to the object depicted, but also includes its environment. Furthermore, a DT differs in its application. It has always a relation to its product life cycle. The level of detail depends on the phase.

Based on the high potential that we have seen in prior chapters one question arises: Why does not every company have a digital twin or starts to develop one? Some challenges still remain even with great progress in technology. Here is an extract of the most important technical challenges. They not always apply in a specific use case, but it might happen:

Device

On the one hand the processor has to be small to attach it easily on a device. On the other hand energy consumption has to be low so that it last long for long time periods like several month or even years. The scope needs to be defined with the right kind of measurements. Only those who are important to model the functionalities of the product. One step further, it is also possible to collect data from other digital twins or IoT infrastructure. The DT then needs a connection to those infrastructures and we are not there yet, but as soon as the amount of digital twins increases this option becomes more feasible.

Device Management

At first it is a managing device so it needs to be connected to the digital twin devices. It controls the information flow and possible signals for actuators. The device management also controls the batteries of the devices. This has a significant impact on the architecture of the digital twin depending on the architecture of physical twin and how the energy will be provided. At this point we have to decide where the processing takes place. Does it happen at the local device, in the device management or completely on the platform? An additional device management increases the complexity, but it can make live easier.

Connectivity

The connectivity is crucial because if no data is transferred there is no digital twin. The connectivity has to be managed within the devices and among the devices. The indoor reception has to be guaranteed. In the case of an edge application the connectivity with low signal needs to be established. Sometimes the connection has to be around the world. This is especially important if the connection is established with cellular networks. Furthermore the connection needs to consist of a secure connection with high security standard. Almost every information is critical because it is related to sensitive product data.

Platform

A powerful cloud platform is the first point that comes into mind when you think about a digital twin platform. Indeed, it is a very important part. There are many cloud providers on the market. Every provider has its own specialty. At this point the actual use case of the digital twin plays a significant role. Does the digital twin concentrate on controlling and monitoring or are realtime observations and actuation necessary? The option to get access or guarantee access for other digital twins is an important point. Even though it might not be important nowadays but it has a huge effect when more companies establish digital twins.

A different point is the information access within the twin. Mastering the data about components and modules require a detailed concept. The correct interpretations are only valid if specification about the physical twin and its components is available. This information must be either stored in the platform with the challenge to keep them up to date or the data is available through the access of the device or device management. Then the platform needs to have an interface for that. This question becomes even more important if information exchange of digital twins will be considered.

Application

Challenges that occur with the application mostly occur on the relevant systems and tools. The information is available for everyone on the platform, but every user gets access through the PLM system. This might be a central software with interfaces to more specific software like CAD. An alternative is the access through the specific software itself which is harder to implement. The easy way is to introduce system only for digital twin application.

No matter which way the system needs to manage big data volumes because the amount of data will explode sooner or later. Furthermore, the software needs to be capable of AI implementation and other advanced analytics methods. This is the intelligence of the digital twin where the raw data will be transformed to actual information.

6 Prototyping

It is recommended for clients who are early stage in their digital twin maturity and who don't have large internal teams of Hardware- & Software developers to have an organic way to implement use cases. The outlined four-step process outlined in Sect. 5.2. is aimed to shortlist high-impact use cases and prototype them. The motivation of prototyping and piloting those prototypes is to get early stage feedback from real users and customers and the usefulness and modifications necessary for a full scale solution. It is a lean way to experiment before scaling up. Implementing digital twin solutions require very often far reaching and disruptive resources across hardware, software, connectivity and analytics – resulting into significant change management required for the internal teams of a client and external customers. Before deciding to go "all in" and invest into solutions that run in real operations, it is crucial to build prototypes that are mature enough that they can be piloted internally [7]. Also, for digital twins to be used across the organization, we see an organic implementation as more successful especially with internal acceptance compared to a tradition top-down approach of implementation [14]. There are four success factors for the prototyping stage:

Target Picture: Clearly define what a prototype must be able to achieve so that it can be piloted in a way where users can provide valuable feedback. Also it should be layed out how a end-product/solution shall be designed.

"Silo-Prototyping": The prototype shall ideally not be integrated to the existing IT-Infrastructure and processes of a client, hence it shall operate in complete autarky. IT integration is very often a complex process and in many cases prototypes can be build in a way that engineers can still test and provide relevant feedback to it.

Off-the-Shelve/Frugal Prototyping: As outlined in Sect. 5.3. the technical architecture compromises Device, Device Management, Connectivity, Platform and Application. For the prototyping stage, it is recommended to use very simple forms in each of these dimensions for the prototype in order to keep prototyping costs in balance and operative quickly. As an example, using Arduino & IoT Kits for the device part, 4G or Wifi for connectivity and Public Cloud Infrastructure for the Platform part might be good enough for the prototyping stage.

Development: The developers needed for building digital twin prototypes are crucial for the development and pilot phase. Experienced teams are important due to the complexity and interdepencies of digital twins. It is therefore recommended to work alongside technology partners/innovation centers who have experienced developers and outsource the prototyping phase to certain extend [15]. Combining internal and external teams is helpful to achieve an early stage knowledge transfer, also contributing to the change management process required while implementing digital twins in an organization.

Each prototype shall be piloted for a few months inside the organization, allowing internal and external users to provide qualitative and quantitative feedback [14]. This helps to design and develop the strategy of large scale implementation. This section has to be planned in detail with domain experts (advisors, vendors, system integrators etc.).

7 Outlook

Digital twins are undoubtedly at a very early stage of their evolution, with many uncertainties existing in the marketspace and ecosystem. However, the value add to manufacturers and customers are undisputed across many areas of the product lifecycle. Digital twins are here to stay – and they will in the future become a standard, similar like Computer Aided Design (CAD) models are ubiquitous today. The pace of innovation and variety of IoT sensors will make digital twins much more heterogeneous and the multi-fold architecture adds complexities alongside. Over the next five years, we see digital twins being adopted by more and more manufacturers with the twins they design become more sophisticated. Penetration rate will grow and change the PLM landscape significantly. Key barriers of adoption today, such as missing standardization, interoperability and vendor lock-ins will disappear slowly. It is not decided yet who will drive the change – large-scale enterprises (top-down approach) or midsize companies (bottom-up approach). Customers who are in the very early stage of digital twin adoption should now start designing a comprehensive short-/mid- and long-term strategy that is holistic, customer centric and organic. Implementing digital twins at scale is comparable with a full switch to an Enterprise Resource Planning (ERP) system – it is complex, will take a lot of resources and needs significant change management. With the technology becoming more mature over time, we see the internal change management as one of the most important and most underestimated success factors in this transition. Different teams across the organization have to work together and support during the implementation phase. This cannot be dictated by a traditional top-down management approach, but more through an organic and inclusive method based on experimenting, prototyping, piloting and then scaling digital twins in those areas with most significant customer value.

References

1. Glaessgen, E.H., Spargel, D.S.: The digital twin paradigm for future NASA and U.S. air force vehicles. In: 53rd Structures, Structural Dynamics, and Materials Conference, Honolulu, Hawaii, 23–26 April 2012
2. Tao, F., Cheng, J., Qi, Q., et al.: Digital twin-driven product design, manufacturing and service with big data. Int. J. Adv. Manuf. Technol. **94**, 3563–3576 (2018). https://doi.org/10.1007/s00170-017-0233-1

3. Gartner Says 8.4 Billion Connected "Things" Will Be in Use in 2017, Up 31 Percent From 2016 (2017). https://www.gartner.com/newsroom/id/3598917
4. Marr, B.: Big Data: 20 Mind-Boggling Facts Everyone Must Read. Forbes (2015). https://www.forbes.com/sites/bernardmarr/2015/09/30/big-data-20-mind-boggling-facts-everyone-must-read/#376956da17b1
5. Grieves, M.: Origins of the Digital Twin Concept, pp. 226–242. Springer, Montreal (2016). https://doi.org/10.13140/RG.2.2.26367.61609. enterprises
6. Auer, S., Lange-Bever C.: Digital Twin, Concept, State and Reference Model. Working Paper (2017)
7. Lukowski, G., Rauch, A., Rosendahl, T.: The virtual representation of the world is emerging. In: Krüssel, P. (eds.) Future Telco. Springer, Cham (2018). https://doi.org/10.1007/978-3-319-77724-5_14
8. Warwick, G.: GE Advances Analytical Maintenance With Digital Twins. Aviation Week (2015). http://aviationweek.com/optimizing-engines-through-lifecycle/ge-advances-analytical-maintenance-digital-twins
9. Darling, D.: Meet your digital twin, they will change your business. Australian Financial Review (2018). http://www.afr.com/technology/meet-your-digital-twin-they-will-change-your-business-20180422-h0z3t2
10. Presseportal: Lufthansa Technik präsentiert "AVIATAR" (2017). https://www.presseportal.de/pm/55257/3620492
11. DesignNews: PLM and Digitalization Will Redefine Engineering and Manufacturing (2015). https://www.designnews.com/alternative-energy/plm-and-digitalization-will-redefine-engineering-and-manufacturing/93473115047495
12. Moore, C.: The Virtual Singapore project aims to digitize an entire city. Digital Trends (2017). https://www.digitaltrends.com/home/virtual-singapore-project-mapping-out-entire-city-in-3d/
13. Budde, O., Golovatchev, J.: Produkte des intelligenten Markts. In: Aichele, C., Doleski, O.D. (eds.) Smart Market, pp. 593–620. Springer, Wiesbaden (2014). https://doi.org/10.1007/978-3-658-02778-0_22
14. Golovatchev, J., Schepurek, S.: Early prototyping in the digital industry: a management framework. In: Bouras, A., Eynard, B., Foufou, S., Thoben, K.-D. (eds.) PLM 2015. IAICT, vol. 467, pp. 335–343. Springer, Cham (2016). https://doi.org/10.1007/978-3-319-33111-9_31
15. Golovatchev, J., Felsmann, M.: Modulare und durchgängige Produktmodelle als Erfolgsfaktor zur Bedienung einer Omni-Channel-Architektur – PLM 4.0. In: Doleski, O.D. (ed.) Herausforderung Utility 4.0, pp. 199–210. Springer, Wiesbaden (2017). https://doi.org/10.1007/978-3-658-15737-1_11

Uzbekistan Towards Industry 4.0. Defining the Gaps Between Current Manufacturing Systems and Industry 4.0

Ikrom Kambarov[1(✉)], Gianluca D'Antonio[2(✉)], Khurshid Aliev[2(✉)], Paolo Chiabert[2(✉)], and Jamshid Inoyatkhodjaev[1(✉)]

[1] Turin Polytechnic University in Tashkent, Kichik Halqa Yuli 17, 100095 Tashkent, Uzbekistan
{ikrom.kambarov, j.inoyatkhodjaev}@polito.uz

[2] Politecnico di Torino, corso Duca degli Abruzzi 24, 10129 Turin, Italy
{gianluca.dantonio, khurshid.aliev, paolo.chiabert}@polito.it

Abstract. With the advancements in industry technology and applications, many concepts have emerged in manufacturing. Since the term Industry 4.0 was published to highlight a new industrial revolution, many manufacturing organizations and companies in Europe, North and South America are researching on this topic. Even the Industry 4.0 concept is included on government duty, sponsored by national initiatives and research funding. However, developing country like Uzbekistan, with high industrial potential are experiencing a different position and the technology roadmap of accomplishing Industry 4.0 is not clear yet. In the last 20 years, Uzbekistan managed to join the group of lower-middle income countries; the ultimate development goal of the country in the next stage is to reach the development benchmark comparable to the higher-middle income group by 2030. Therefore, this paper aims to depict the current state of manufacturing systems in Uzbekistan and identify the gaps with the Industry 4.0 requirements. The findings of this paper can serve for researches from emerging countries as technological roadmap towards Industry 4.0 paradigm and can assist industrial people in understanding and achieving the requirements of Industry 4.0.

Keywords: Industry 4.0 · Manufacturing systems · Developing countries

1 Introduction

In the past three decades, there are significant development took place information technology in general. In order to compete and offer more value to the customers, developed countries started to apply advance technologies on production level. In USA and some other countries, such initiatives are termed as fourth industrial revolution, Internet of Things, or next generation systems. Whereas in Germany, it is driven by German government and referred as Industry 4.0 [1].

Industry 4.0 will change supply chains, business models and business processes significantly. However, researchers hold different opinions of the specific requirements

Published by Springer Nature Switzerland AG 2018.
P. Chiabert et al. (Eds.): PLM 2018, IFIP AICT 540, pp. 250–260, 2018.
https://doi.org/10.1007/978-3-030-01614-2_23

of Industry 4.0 and its accomplishment, acting on their various industrial technology applications [11].

Industry has had an important role in the economic development of Uzbekistan. Since its independence in 1991, attraction of advanced technologies, foreign investments and modern management paradigms have been set as a priority policy of the government. In the last years, the industrial sector has shifted its focus from capital-intensive basic industries towards developing manufacturing sectors that produce goods of higher technological level and contribute more to the growth of productive employment, leading to an increased share of industry in GDP of the country.

According to investigations of the Center of Economic Research [2], the ultimate development goal for the Uzbekistan is to join the group of upper middle-income countries by 2030. With this end in view, it is important to maintain stable economic growth rates at 7–8% per annum over the next years and a structural transformation of the economy in a number of directions is required. A sector worth of development efforts is manufacturing: its share in the country GDP was 9% in 2012 and has to increase up to 22% by 2030 to achieve the aforementioned target (Figs. 1 and 2).

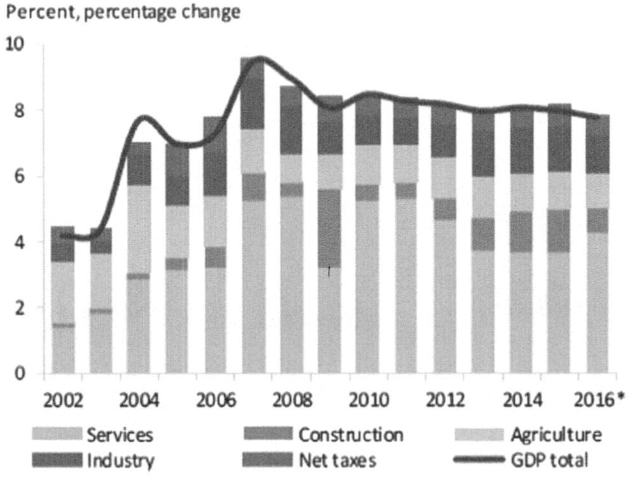

Fig. 1. Structural Changes in the Uzbek Economy over the Last Years, GDP structure [2].

The digitalization technologies that are promoting the Industry 4.0 paradigm can boost the manufacturing development also in developing countries like Uzbekistan, thus leading to a sort of re-industrialization resulting in increased product quality and technological content, improved process performance and higher work quality.

Therefore, Industry 4.0 may play an important role for economy development and support Uzbekistan in achieving the desired target. However, despite the wide thematic coverage and the depth of elaboration of various aspects of Industry 4.0 in the research of European and American scientists, the Smart Manufacturing paradigm is not fully formed in Uzbek manufacturing systems yet. Some of the technology advances representing the basis for Industry 4.0 are already used in manufacturing systems of the

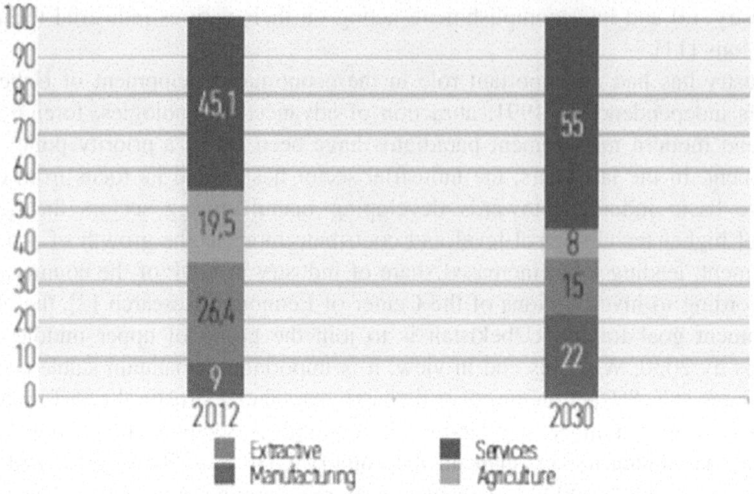

Fig. 2. Uzbekistan GDP composition by sector in 2012 (left) and target for 2030 (right) [2].

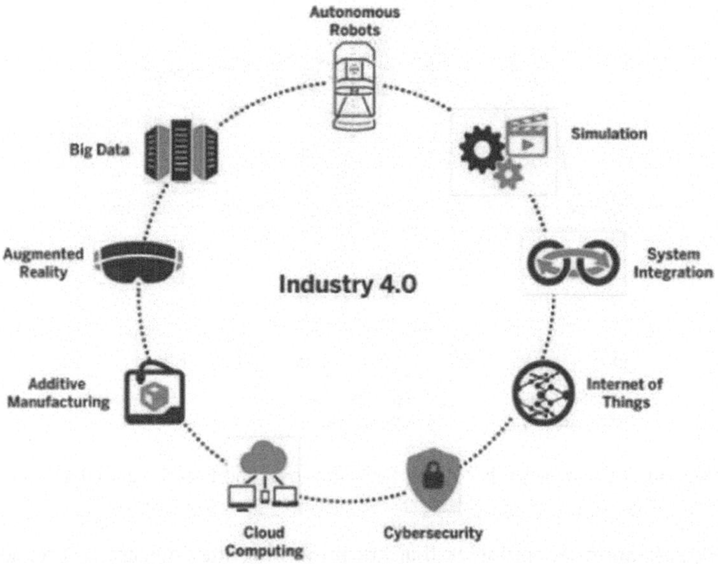

Fig. 3. The nine technologies enabling the Industry 4.0 paradigm [6].

country. Nonetheless, a systematic approach for Industry 4.0 has not been developed and additional research is necessary to support a comprehensive adoption of this paradigm adapted to the Uzbek cultural background. In particular, the definition of requirements for implementation, the development methods and models for implementing smart production are necessary.

Therefore, the goal of this study is to define the gaps between Uzbek manufacturing systems and Industry 4.0 requirements with particular concern for automobile industry. The remainder of this paper is organized as follows. In Sect. 2, the vision of Industry 4.0 concept and its requirements are shortly reviewed; further, the advanced technologies of the Smart manufacturing are presented. In Sect. 3, the current state of Uzbekistan automotive manufacturing technologies are defined, and the gaps with respect to Industry 4.0 requirements are presented. In Sect. 4, some proposal will be given to transform towards Industry 4.0. Last, in Sect. 5 some conclusive remarks are presented.

2 The Industry 4.0 Paradigm

According to [1] Industry 4.0 is considered as future of manufacturing enabled by application of advanced ICT tools at production level to bring new values and services for customers and organizations. This new paradigm also brings flexibility and quality to fulfill demands. The digitalization and virtualization are tools to bring end-to-end services throughout a product life cycle and in a cost effective way for customers.

A formal definition of industry 4.0 is defined in [3] as follows: "Industry 4.0 will involve the technical integration of CPS into manufacturing and logistics and the use of the Internet of Things and Services in industrial processes".

Many researchers in Europe believe that industry is at the beginning of a new revolution, considered as fourth industrial revolution. The concept of Industry 4.0 is based on the German government initiative that was adopted as part of the "The new High-Tech Strategy Innovations for Germany" [4]. This new paradigm holds the promise of increased flexibility in manufacturing, mass customization, increased speed, better quality and improved productivity [5].

To capture these benefits, industries will need to adopt a number of new and innovative technological advances, which are considered as building blocks of the Industry 4.0 [6].

These technologies can be grouped as follows, according to their effect on the production systems.

Increased Production Flexibility. The development of autonomous robots capable of quick configuration and human cooperation [7], and the development of additive manufacturing technologies enable to produce a huge variety of products in the same manufacturing process [8]. This capability is boosted by integrating the manufacturing operations, both from the internal point of view (e.g. logistics) and the external perspective (e.g. suppliers). These abilities make the company able to rapidly adopt the customer-supplier specifications, properly adapt the process and profitably produce even small batches.

Shortened Time-to-Market. With the implementation of advanced technologies of Industry 4.0, the production pace can be also improved. 3-D simulation, augmented and virtual reality of the manufacturing process [9], tools for virtual product development and automation systems for production can reduce the time necessary for designing and manufacturing a product, this being able to quicker satisfy the demand of new products.

Increased Product Quality. Integrating product development through manufacturing chain with the help of Internet of Things (IoT) will lead to improve product quality [10]. This also directs decentralization of manufacturing process, enabling real-time decision-making. Embedded systems give the opportunity to implement total quality control practices, rather than using sampling to detect errors. Within the Industry 4.0 framework, products are provided with an embedded system (e.g. a RFID tag) since their early manufacturing stage of to collect data concerning its evolution over the production facility. This type of small, but critical, application of IoT in manufacturing results in reduced downtime, increased quality, reduced waste and less overall costs. This kind of products is known as Smart products [10].

Increased Productivity. Process productivity can be increased through various effects of Industry 4.0 advanced technologies. For example, by using cloud-based software in manufacturing facilities data sharing across sites and company boundaries will increase. As a result, by advantage of cloud technologies and big data, performance of the manufacturing process can be improved, enabling more data-driven service for production systems [11].

Cybersecurity. One of the last technology advancements of Industry 4.0 is Cybersecurity. With increasing data generation across manufacturing systems, increasing connectivity, sharing data with partners in the value network will increase importance of the cybersecurity to protect critical industrial systems and lines from cyber-attacks [12].

3 Industry 4.0 and the Uzbek Automotive Manufacturing System

The Uzbek manufacturing environment is populated by companies in the fields of automotive, machinery, chemical industry and transportation services. However, according to the results of the Center of Economic Research [2], automotive is the most developed field and, thus, the driver of the country manufacturing.

The adoption of advanced technologies in Uzbek manufacturing has begun in the past years: additive manufacturing systems and autonomous robots have been implemented, as well as ICT solutions for simulation and systems integration have been adopted. Nevertheless, the deployment of such tools is still in its early stage and a well-established structure is necessary for further improvements. In the following, the current level of Industry 4.0 technology adoption is described and assessed through a scale ranging from 5 (high) to 1 (low). The evaluation of the Uzbek manufacturing systems led to design the graph in Fig. 4. A score equal to 5 has been assigned to technologies already implemented and highly experienced. Grade 4, is for technologies already implemented in industrial environments requiring further experience and training. Grade 3 is assigned to technologies investigated in research activities but not yet implemented in manufacturing systems. The score equal to 2 is assigned to technologies into an early stage of deployment: few research activities and/or prototypal installations have been done. Last, grade 1 denoted technologies in their infancy that are totally new for the country background high level of research.

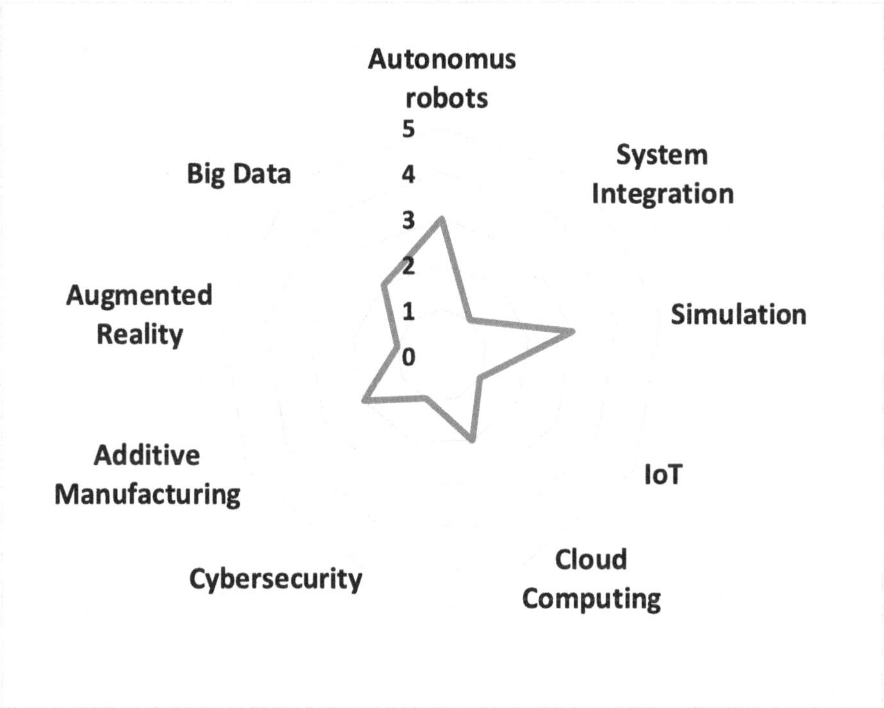

Fig. 4. Adoption level of technological advances into Uzbek automobile industry [14, 15, 17].

Autonomous Robots. Manufacturers in Uzbekistan started to widely deploy robotic, flexible systems to tackle complex assignments. For example, in the vehicle assembly plant in Asaka [14] line-tracking robots have been already introduced in the assembly line. These robots are interconnected with the main production line and are in charge of picking and placing engines in the desired assembly position. A system of high-end sensors and control units has been installed to enable close and safe collaboration with both human operators and the surrounding production system.

As another example, the GM-Powertrain system consists of flexible production lines and automated machining systems for cylinder block, cylinder head and crankshaft manufacturing assisted by computers.

Big Data Analytics. Over the last 20 years' experience of automobile industry, data collection and analytics methods and technologies are increased. There are various methods and techniques for long-term strategic design decisions focusing on sites or the entire production process. Each supplier is using analytical tools and methodologies for improving product quality, equipment service level and energy saving. Even special department are organized for such specific analytics. For example, the most reasonable database for the current production control is the master data. Master data is used to execute the production process and quality control of the process. All changes of products characteristics, processes or resources in the manufacturing systems ultimately lead to changes in production master data.

Simulation. The effort in adopting ICT solutions has been mainly devoted to product design (CAD) and process design (CAM) tools. However, the spread of this technology should arise: simulation tools should be used to evaluate the performance of the manufacturing process in different operating scenarios and to identify the best strategy to react to possible issues, thus adapting on-the-fly the process and the supporting services (e.g. supply of components, logistics, maintenance). Nonetheless, the mere adoption of such tools is not sufficient for improving process performance: training programs must be developed to exploit as much as possible the advantages of such technologies.

Additive Manufacturing. The technology of 3-D printing has been adopted for a few years, mainly for rapid prototyping and to produce individual components only by research intuitions. In addition, this technology is also deployed in cooperation with reverse engineering technology of the small sized plastic vehicles part localization process. At this point academic site Tashkent Turin Polytechnic University [15] has great effort. Currently in the country, printing technology is more spread rather UV lasers and extrusion technologies.

Cloud Computing. A few companies are already using cloud-based software for some analytics applications, but analytics are more related to financial services than production. For example, the Cloud Computing SAP HANA technology began to be implemented into production process of GM-Powertrain. This experience mostly relies on logistics design and some analytical purposes.

In addition, Audit Company Deloitte in Uzbekistan implements SAP S/4HANA Finance for auditing some vehicle manufacturing companies like GM-Uzbekistan or GM-Powertrain.

Furthermore, digital marketing framework is implemented in other sectors like textile engineering, banking systems, electric power industry of the country.

Internet of Things. The application of Internet of Things (IoT) in industrial environments is supposed to be one of the strongest enabling technologies of Industry 4.0. However, in order to implement IoT applications, efforts for ICT infrastructures must be spent.

In the last few years, the Uzbekistan government has strongly invested to develop ICT infrastructures to support IoT applications. Recent applications include, for example, monitoring of traffic congestion (based on Yandex, Google, and other maps services) as well as taxi booking or sharing. In a short time, these solutions changed the way to exploit mobility services in large cities such as Tashkent. Despite this diffusion in broad application, IoT is not yet applied in industrial environments: further efforts for educating technicians and operators to design, develop, implement and use this technology is necessary.

System Integration. Companies, suppliers and customers are still rarely linked over production process. In some cases, even the departments within the enterprise such as engineering, production, service, planning are not fully integrated along the value chain, through integrated IT systems. To overcome these problems, producers as well as suppliers must work to adapt new infrastructure within their production facilities and strengthen approaches to increase IT-related skills.

Cybersecurity. Since Uzbekistan is at first steps towards Industry 4.0, Cybersecurity is at infancy level. However, cybersecurity starting from 2018 is under governmental duty and it will be involved all resources for further developments. International forum on 2 February 2018 on Digitalization in Almaty (Kazakhstan) [16] can serve as first stage towards Cybersecurity of the Central Asian countries, including Uzbekistan.

Augmented Reality. In Uzbekistan, Augmented reality (AR) is still in the early stages as in other developed countries. For example, in tourism industry authors of [17] developed android based mobile AR smartphone application which can act as a guide book for tourists of Uzbekistan. Conversely, the implementation of AR in industrial manufacturing in Uzbekistan would take some time since before AR we have to adapt our educational system to new technologies. Luckily, it will not take as long time as for developed countries since now information spreading very fast.

Table 1 represents the comparison between Uzbekistan today's factories and Industry 4.0 factories based on Technology and Production System.

Table 1. Comparison of Uzbekistan today's factories and an Industry 4.0 factory.

	Today's Factories in Uzbekistan	Industry 4.0 Factory
Technology	Precise Smart Sensors and Fault detection, Condition based monitoring and Diagnostics (quality and throughput)	Self-aware, self-predictable, self-compared, predictive health monitoring, remaining useful life monitoring
Production system	Based on Lean principles, GMS systems	Self-configured, decentralized, integrated, self-organized, cloud-based

4 A Roadmap for Industry 4.0 in Uzbekistan Manufacturing

Uzbekistan created a car industry from the ground up. Today, this industry produces more than 120,000 cars and their engines [20]. The production of new vehicle models that meet international standards concerning environmental impact, quality and safety is one of the main priorities of the Uzbekistan's automotive car manufacturers. In order to increase the country export potential, create value chain along production facilities, increase manufacturing speed and productivity, and develop flexible manufacturing systems, the following measures must be further adopted in the next future.

Workforce Qualification. To deal with the technologies shown in Fig. 3, high skilled workforce is necessary: besides competences on manufacturing, skills concerning process modelling, programming, simulation, and data analysis are required. Further, creativity for problem-solving and decision making will be increasingly necessary. According to an investigation promoted by the European Parliament, high skilled workforce is considered one of the core challenge of the future of manufacturing [19].

Therefore, to undertake the journey towards Industry 4.0, car manufacturers in Uzbekistan need to work on employee qualification. Industries need to define short, medium and long term strategies to address training of the already available employees, and manage vocational trainings.

Education and Research Activities. Institutions, research centers and manufacturing organizations must cooperate to adapt university programs and train workforce capable to work into an Industry 4.0 environment. Academic curricula must be updated to focus the attention on up-to-date information technologies and novel models for company management.

Research is an essential condition for realizing the potential of the advanced technologies. In Sect. 3, the adoption level of the Industry 4.0 enabling technologies has been discussed; however, for further development deeper analyses and research activities are required on each direction. Such efforts must also include frameworks and methodologies for technology adoption and deployment.

Adoption of Cloud Based Software. Uzbek enterprises poorly adopted automation and IT tools, which allow to improve process planning and control, as well as to enhance the performance of each step of the manufacturing process. They do not make use of complex simulation tools or planning models, like elaborated above. In many cases, none of the employees of enterprises has experiences with such tools and therefore the possible advantages are often ignored.

As introduced in Sect. 3, the SAP cloud software is mainly implemented for financial analysis. Nonetheless, to increase monitoring and control capabilities, further cloud tools must be adopted and mutually integrated for production control, supply chain control and other manufacturing related functions. This will lead to integrating the value chain across all the production process. However, to successfully use such tools, employees must be properly trained and educated. Therefore, SAP tool can be possible solution for production integration process.

Adoption of New Manufacturing Infrastructures. Innovative business models are willing to be introduced in Uzbek manufacturing systems. To achieve this result, integrated value chains must be realized between the departments of a company and, then, across suppliers and customers. This transformation requires high IT, data managing and analytics skills for decision-making.

Investments and National Initiatives. Since the term Industry 4.0 was published, funding investments are the main critical challenge of this paradigm. To adopt and manage advanced technologies companies must dedicate great efforts, and need to be supported by institutions to meet the strategic national guidelines.

For this reason, on 2017, June 1st the President of Uzbekistan signed a resolution entitled "On measures on further improving management and accelerated development of the automotive industry for 2017–2021". This program includes a list of investment projects, which will be implemented in the automobile industry [20].

5 Conclusions

The present work focused on development and adoption of Industry 4.0 paradigm in Uzbekistan automobile system and introduces the common vision of future manufacturing. The main concepts of the future manufacturing have been identified and current state of the Uzbekistan automobile manufacturing technologies in terms of Industry 4.0 requirements has been defined.

Some gaps between the current state of the automobile manufacturing sector and the requirements of future manufacturing environments have been highlighted and some lines to be adopted have been proposed. The research showed that manufacturing industries must invest in research and development activities as well as on staff qualification into the Industry 4.0 paradigm.

References

1. Khan, A., Turowski, K.: A survey of current challenges in Manufacturing Industry and Preparation for Industry 4.0. In: Abraham, A., Kovalev, S., Tarassov, V., Snášel, V. (eds.) Proceedings of the First International Scientific Conference "Intelligent Information Technologies for Industry" (IITI'16). AISC, vol. 450, pp. 15–26. Springer, Cham (2016). https://doi.org/10.1007/978-3-319-33609-1_2
2. Center for Economic Research: Uzbekistan towards 2030. A new social protection model for a changing economy and society (2014). http://www.cer.uz/upload/iblock/6fd/bunxjnse%20pwvc%20en%209.pdf. Accessed 9 Mar 2018
3. Kagermann, H., Helbig, J., Hellinger, A., Wahlster, W.: Recommendations for implementing the strategic initiative industrie 4.0: securing the future of german manufacturing industry. Final report of the industrie 4.0 working group (2013)
4. The German Federal Ministry of Education and Research: The new high-tech strategy innovations for Germany (2014). https://www.bmbf.de/pub/HTS_Broschuere_eng.pdf
5. Burke, R., Mussomeli, A., Laaper, S.: The Smart Factory. Responsive, Adaptive, Connected Manufacturing. Deloitte University Press, London (2017)
6. Gerbert, P., et al.: Industry 4.0: the future of productivity and growth in manufacturing industries. BCG Group (2015). https://www.bcg.com/it-it/publications/2015/engineered_products_project_business_industry_4_future_productivity_growth_manufacturing_industries.aspx
7. Thoben, K.D., Wiesner, S., Wuest, T.: "Industrie 4.0" and Smart Manufacturing–a review of research issues and application examples. Int. J. Autom. Technol. **11**(1), 4–16 (2017)
8. Ford, S., Despeisse, M.: Additive manufacturing and sustainability: an exploratory study of the advantages and challenges. J. Clean. Prod. **137**, 1573–1587 (2016)
9. Mourtsiz, D., Doukas, M., Berdinaki, D.: Simulation in manufacturing: review and challenges. Procedia CIRP **25**, 213–229 (2014)
10. Onder, O., Gupta, S.: Quality management in product recovery using Internet of Things: an optimization approach. Comput. Ind. **65**(3), 491–504 (2014)
11. Qin, J., Liu, Y., Grosvenor, R.: A categorical framework of manufacturing for Industry 4.0 and beyond. Procedia CIRP **52**, 173–178 (2016)
12. Zong, R., Klotz, E., Newman, S.: Intelligent manufacturing in the context of Industry 4.0: a review. Engineering **3**(5), 616–630 (2017)

13. Hutchins, M.J., Bhinge, R., Micali, M.K., Robinson, S.L., Sutherland, J.W., Dornfeld, D.: Framework for identifying cybersecurity risk in manufacturing. Procedia Manuf. **1**, 47–63 (2015)
14. http://uzavtosanoat.uz/en/JSC-GM-UZBEKISTAN.html
15. https://polito.uz/index.php?lang=en
16. http://kazakh-tv.kz/2015en/view/news_kazakhstan/page_190699_
17. https://www.morebooks.shop/store/us/book/mobile-ar-application-for-tourism-industry-of-uzbekistan/isbn/978-3-330-51698-4
18. https://www.azernews.az/region/125414.html
19. Davies, R.: Industry 4.0 Digitalization for productivity and growth (2015)
20. https://www.uzdaily.com/articles-id-39812.htm

Towards Cloud Based Collaborative Design – Analysis in Digital PLM Environment

Siddharth Sharma[1,2](✉), Frédéric Segonds[1], Nicolas Maranzana[1], Damien Chasset[2], and Vincent Frerebeau[2]

[1] Arts et Métiers, ParisTech, LCPI, 151 Boulevard de l'Hôpital, 75013 Paris, France
Siddharth.sharma@ensam.eu

[2] Dassault Systèmes, 10 Rue Marcel Dassault, 78140 Vélizy Villacoublay, France

Abstract. This paper proposes a cloud-based PLM methodology to carry out collaborative design by implementing industrial scenario representing realistic collaboration among all the stake holders. In a world of advancing information technology and more than ever demand in the requirement of spatially inter connected collaborative work space, cloud based generic design process methodology seems to be a viable option. However, it has been noticed that there has been little effort directed towards Cloud Based Design (CBD). It is a widely accepted fact that nearly 80% of the manufacturing cost of a product is determined by its design process and hence targeting the very same process of PLM is the prime focus in this paper. With an increase in the complexity of products along with the squeezed budget across all industries, there has been a growing demand to have cross company collaboration. To deal with such a complex requirement of communication and coordination between all the players in the design process, this paper links the field of collaborative design and cloud computing to propose paradigm-based solution to cater generic design process. This paper showcases the main advantages when CBD data and legacy CAD data are used to create a unified digital model to achieve a true cross company collaboration by the means of Cloud Based Collaborative Design (CBCD) methodology.

Keywords: Cloud · Collaborative design · PLM · Interactive design
Legacy users

1 Introduction

The globalization is gripping the world much more quickly and this has induced new models of industries where fierce competition, addition of disruptive technologies, and inter connected collaborative workspace are becoming a reality. Not so long ago, Cloud Computing was limited to only some specific industries, but now cloud computing has emerged as one of the major enablers for the product development industries by transforming the traditional design and development process by aligning product innovation with business strategy and has created big collaborating network of geographically dispersed industries. As 80% of the manufacturing cost comes from the

P. Chiabert et al. (Eds.): PLM 2018, IFIP AICT 540, pp. 261–270, 2018.
https://doi.org/10.1007/978-3-030-01614-2_24

design process of a product [1], it is evident that coupling cloud computing with design process was a viable option. Based on the same reasons, many researchers have pursued Cloud Based Design (CBD) and even merged it with another similar concept called Cloud Based Manufacturing (CBM). There is no indication of the existence of ideal CBD systems which represent a model where collaboration happening between legacy systems and the new CBD users, thus making it impossible to have a cross company collaboration between Small and Medium-sized Enterprises (SMEs) and big enterprises. This paper will focus on Cloud based Collaborative Design (CBCD) and explore its main constituents, merits over other systems. This paper first starts with literature review about importance of cloud, evolution of design. This is followed by CBCD methodology and case study to test it. The paper ends up with results, discussion, conclusion and future work about CBCD systems.

2 Literature Review

The literature review focusses on the main constituents of CBCD system that is cloud, design and collaboration and communication to explore their importance in the methodology and how they impact the design process holistically.

2.1 Cloud - Highlights

As per the hype cycle proposed by Gartner in 2017 [2], different portions of cloud computing fall in the 5 categories, right from "Innovation trigger" to the phase "Plateau of productivity" where Software as a Service (SaaS) falls in the latter category, thus showing a great opportunity to be explored as also visible in the hype cycle proposed by Gartner [3]. From the perspective of design, cloud allows to access, review and modify design easily from geographically diverse locations, allows data continuity and fluidity based on cloud-based PLM methodology, secured exchange of knowledge management and data exchanges and real time collaboration for true concurrent design engineering. In the same context, SaaS which has embarked upon a journey of revolutionizing the sector of CBDM (Cloud Based Design and Manufacturing) has been able to provide customers licensing combined with maintenance and monitoring, management of IT infrastructure related to cloud and a network of multitenant data centers to ensure maximum performances and protection from emerging security threats. In the recent times, cloud computing paradigms have received a lot of excitement from the world but despite having such reputation (IT buzzword); many industries have not explored its full potential which offers a space of research to be done.

2.2 Design – from Past to Future

In this section, the past is referred as traditional design process, present is the conventional computer aided design tools/systems and the future is CBD. As per the literature survey, many descriptive models of design process have been proposed over the years and among them, the famous ones were proposed by Pahl and Beitz that consists of 4 main design phases: planning & clarifying the tasks, conceptual design, embodiment design and detailed design [4] in a linear chain. Most of the approaches of design process developed afterwards in form of extension or modification are found to be related to the fundamental approach of Pahl and Beitz [5]. But when it comes to concurrent engineering there is a scope of improvement in the process and hence, this paper proposes a generic design process with steps and sub steps, which works for a cross company collaboration involving legacy and CBD users.

The IT advancements over the period introduced CAD systems which can be hosted on cloud, allows multi-tenancy, SaaS based pay per use model among many other benefits of Cloud based Design thus providing a unique experience of distributed and collaborative design [6] and is now being experienced across all the industries who have completely migrated all their data. However, there are ample of industries who carry out design work in file based legacy CAD systems (Dassault Systemes CATIA V5, PTC Creo™etc. [7]) and hesitate to migrate into the cloud platform because of difficulty in migration in terms of cost, time and technical difficulties among many other reasons. Thus, a big population of legacy system users miss out from the advantages a CBCD system has to offer. Therefore, to have a cross company collaboration among all the industries, it is necessary to connect legacy systems users to the cloud-based software while maintaining their data in file based legacy format.

In general, design process has been claimed by many is composed of three sets of group functions such as the first group that involves designers taking technical decisions followed by the second group that considers design process as workflow with task dependencies and product information exchange comprises of actors associated with operation and project management and finally the third group that evaluate the meaning of collaborative designs as people accessing product data and sharing the design information comes from the group of CAD and CAE functional areas [8]. An effective collaboration among them is important to have fluidity in the design process. Even with the addition of CAD system, the problem of communication persisted because engineers are still communicating with each other via emails and sharing data via multiple resources like pen-drives for bigger files and small files via email. It further gets complicated by the CAD/CAM/CAE systems which are standalone system and are required to be installed individually on premise [9]. All these different applications hosted by different providers require maintenance and operational cost which turns out to be higher as compared to the CBD systems when compared the holistically [9]. The major thing which is found to be missing in CBD process is the lack of common platform where all the activities of working and sharing can be carried out including architecture of product, BOM management etc. to have an effective and efficient communication and collaboration. Additionally, many collaborations can be carried out in web-based apps instead of native applications (requires installation on system) and this has been leveraged in the proposed methodology where certain activities have been moved to web based applications from the native applications. To achieve a unified digital model comprising of legacy users and cloud users, it becomes clear that new forms of apps need to be developed to move more activities into the web, whose functionalities can be accessible from mobile devices. One of the example of current process of design activity includes problems like CBD and legacy users can't merge the data or legacy users can't simulate data in a CBD software and the future where a unified model is used by all the companies involved in design process can be seen in the Fig. 1. Therefore, hence this paper aims to target this aspect by envisaging Cloud Based Collaborative Design (CBCD) to investigate how cross company collaboration can be carried out where design process uses a unified digital model concept in a design process and discusses the learning outcomes of this new methodology to support collaboration between large enterprises and SMEs by bringing CBD and legacy users together.

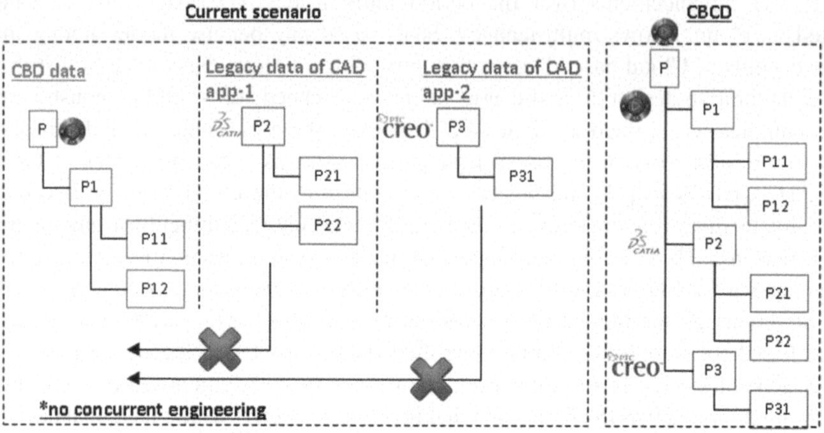

Fig. 1. Product architecture in current scenario vs CBCD [7]

3 Cloud Based Collaborative Design (CBCD)

CBCD is evolved from the best practices of CBD systems along with an addition of legacy system users in the process as discussed in the following sections

3.1 CBD Systems

Many definitions of CBD have been proposed in the past and one of such widely circulated in many papers "Cloud-Based Design (CBD) refers to a networked design model that leverages cloud computing, service-oriented architecture (SOA), Web 2.0 (e.g., social network sites), and semantic web technologies to support cloud-based engineering design services in distributed and collaborative environments" [10]. There is very less literature available which specifically study the characteristics and key constituents of CBD system except few like Andreadis, et al. [11], who in their work analyzed the contribution of collaborative design in the era of cloud computing but it doesn't follow design process for analysis and rather consider one-stage process to focus more on CBDM in totality. In most of the case CBD becomes a sub-part of CBDM where only certain aspects like early design stages or only data created in CBD are considered and thus loses their importance during adoption. It can be said that CBD has not been explored a lot even though design process is responsible for majority of the cost incurred in product development.

3.2 Conceptual CBCD Process Methodology

In CBCD environment, multiple stakeholders can be involved to do design and development activities like project manager, design engineer etc. of both Original Equipment Manufacturer (OEM) and suppliers. Taking in into account, all the problems identified in the literature review, CBCD design methodology for a cross company collaboration is envisaged as shown in Fig. 2. It consists of 4 stages where at each stage, sub steps involved are as shown in the series of images.

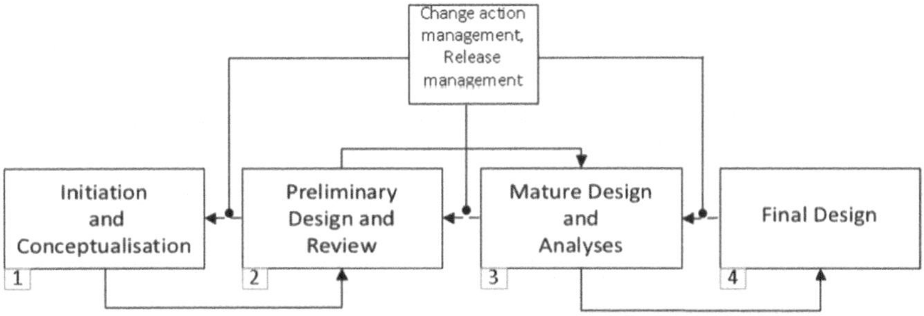

Fig. 2. Proposed CBCD methodology

The process starts with Initiation and conceptualization (Fig. 3) where project manager uses the historical data, CR (customer requirement), market analysis, RFQ etc. to create a project scope, roles required, estimated time and cost. This is followed by creation of collaborative space for cross company collaboration, assignment of tasks, roles. At this point component designer role is offered to legacy user to connect with the collaborative process on cloud. The first mockup in form of sketch or adding annotation to an existed similar product in cloud is added to start conceptualization. At the end of this stage, a mockup (digital or file based) and comments are shared to start the preliminary design and review phase. The process has been simplified by taking some activities which were possible only on system installed software/native applications to the web-based applications which can be accessible by mobile devices as represented by yellow boxes. Cloud user can use native applications (represented by purple boxes) for simple mockups if necessary. Legacy users will enter the process during the first sharing of the task and the collaborative space on cloud at the authority of the administrator.

The second phase (Fig. 4) starts with the mockup and parallel involvement of cloud and legacy users in creation of product definition and creation/addition of legacy CAD parts/assembly in the cloud to create a first UPS (Unified Product Structure). This is the beginning of unified digital model to achieve an end to end digital thread. This stage starts with identification of an already existing engineering items in the cloud which can either be modified or reused. At the time when CBD users are creating or reusing the part, legacy users can do the same thing in a parallel session and add their part to the cloud. Activities like product definition, unified 3D model have been moved to web based applications to reduce the activities which were more time consuming on native

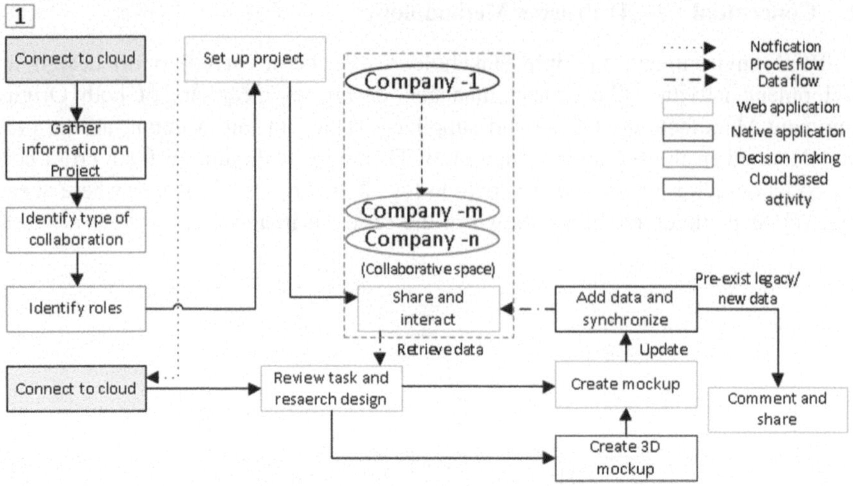

Fig. 3. Phase 1: initiation and conceptualization

applications. This is the stage where first review of the structure and drawing happens. As all thing stored in the cloud, with the help of web-based application, only part in contention of modification will be opened in the native applications thus reducing the load on the native application. Engineering connection between the CBD and legacy CAD parts remains intact during the process after the creation of UPS.

The third phase (Fig. 5) starts either with the entry of other legacy products/CAD product into the cloud or direct usage of UPS created in the second stage. This is the phase when again both legacy and cloud users can see the structure in the platform but holds authorization to change the part only in the software in which the part was created to reduce the complexity. Any modifications or creation of part, assembly and drawings can be carried out as per the comments coming from the previous stage. Once the assembly is finalized for the core view or an individual review, further roles can be added to carry out analyses like structural simulation etc. on the UPS.

The analyses files are saved back in the cloud so to allow for a review in web-based applications. Again, the main aim of this process is to simplify the reviewing task by allowing to be carried out in the web-based applications (3D and 2D annotations review) other than on the installed applications which requires more time and cost. Items here can have their maturity change if required. All the "in working" parts that are cleared in the review can be released. This stage ends with the submission of UPS with all the analyses files shared in the cloud and accessible easily through the web applications.

The fourth stage (Fig. 6) starts with the assessment of the reviewer's comments to check the product architecture again before releasing the assembly. All tasks are later closed and the project manager who initiated the task can send an approval for the product to be sent for further usage like marketing or manufacturing.

At any stage a separate change action management or release management action plan can be initiated.

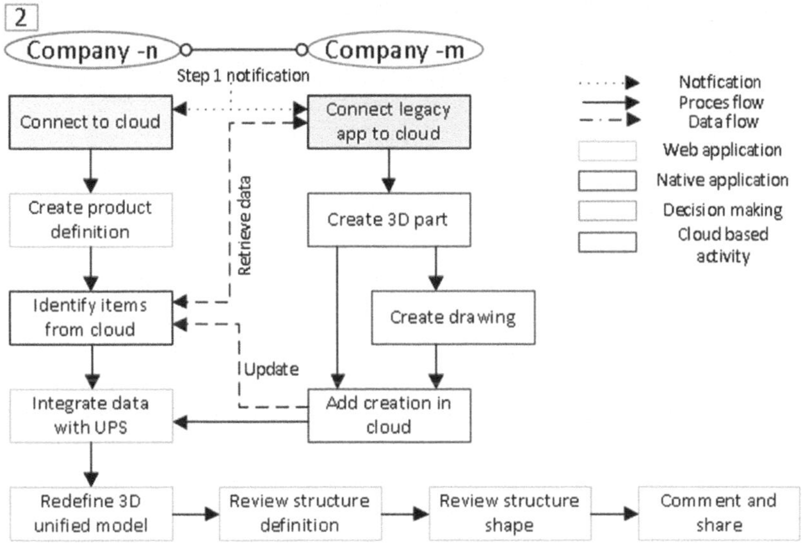

Fig. 4. Phase 2: preliminary design and review

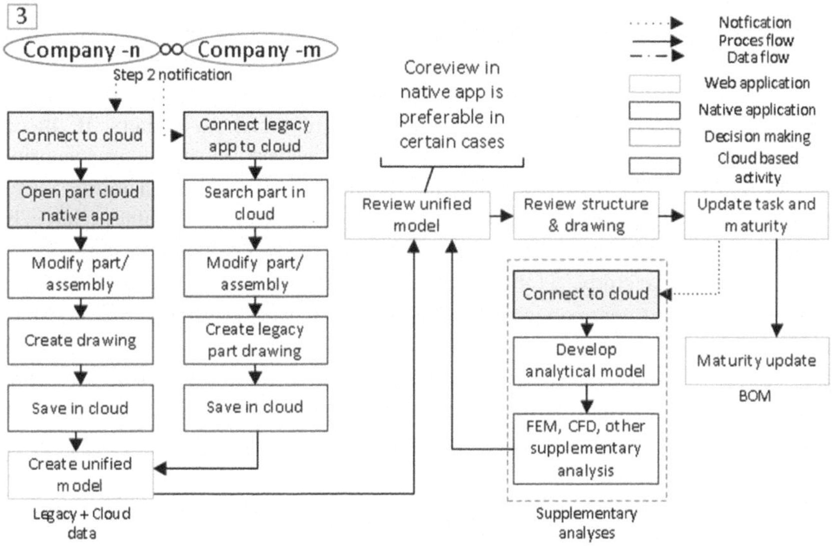

Fig. 5. Phase 3: mature design and analysis

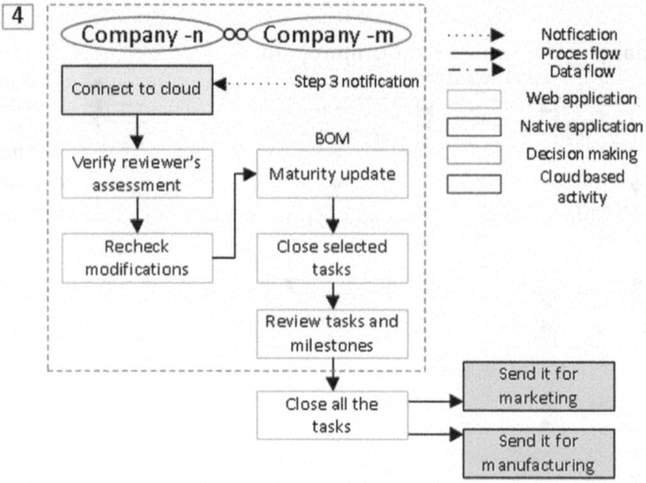

Fig. 6. Phase 4: final design

3.3 CBCD Case Study

As to understand the value of CBCD system proposed in form of its methodology, a case study (Fig. 7) was formulated where one type of users used legacy systems and others used cloud based system. For Cloud based system, Dassault Systemes's 3D experience platform was chose as a test bed and for legacy system, CATIA V5 was chosen as a test bed. Two software can be replaced by others if there is network/connection exist between legacy and CBD system. In the given scenario, an interaction between OEM and supplier has been studied and its feasibility was test based on the user experience during the design process and advantages have been identified.

In the current case study, a OEM is chosen which has access to cloud platform and all its services. Department concerned in the case study is a design department. There is a supplier which is responsible for providing certain CAD designs to be used by OEM as per request to form a new assembly of wheel as a unified digital model (aim of CBCD) comprising of both legacy data and CBD data. Supplier is equipped with a legacy system like CATIA V5 and can be given access to cloud only by the OEM as per the project requirement.

The acquisition of data was carried out by using "3DSearch", "3DSwym" web applications whereas the legacy user was able to access the same thing via "CATIA V5" when it was connected to the cloud. Communication was carried out by "3DMessaging" apps which was done via mobile phone. During co review, PMO (OEM project manager) and DEO (OEM design engineer) carried out in real time co-review in "3DEXPERIENCE CATIA" in the stage 3 and rest of the co review was carried out in web-based application "3DReview" accessible from mobile devices. The product architect was designed and visualized in the web application "Product Structure Editor". All stakeholders were added in the "3DSpace" connected to the cloud. Exploration of the existing component and comparing it with the existing engineering

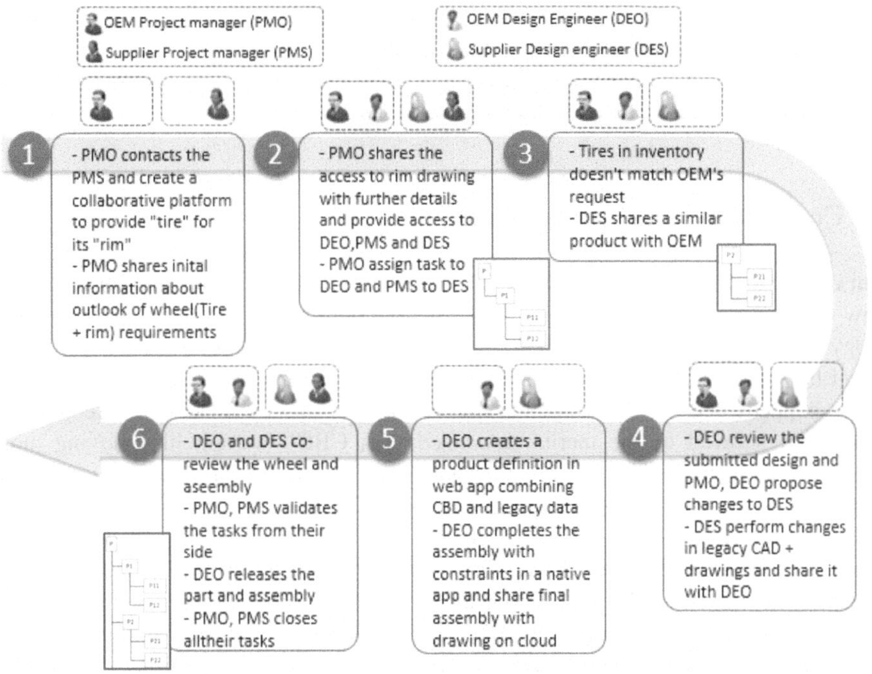

Fig. 7. Cross company collaboration process flow

item was carried out using “Product Explorer” and “Compare “web applications. Once the part was uploaded in the cloud, a new UPS was created in the web application Product Structure editor and near actual assembly was created in 3D Compose web for which later engineering connections were created in the CBD native application.

4 Results

When CBCD methodology was carried out, following observations were made:

- Single unified digital model comprising of multi CAD structure was found to bring fluidity in the design process
- File based legacy CAD data became engineering items in the CBCD which can be accessed, used and indexed again thus extending their life
- Tenancy offers legacy users to experience the advantages of the cloud platform without migrating their data
- Visualization of CBD data in CATIA VS is still not available in legacy system
- Transfer of certain functionalities were found to be interoperable like publications, materials and catalogues
- Product architecture, changing maturity, 3D and 2D review, collaborative tasks, cloud search, engineering items comparison, metrics reader, community, mail, product exploration, route tasks, cloud news via web applications really speed up

the design process because of non-requirements of doing things in native applications and their accessibility on mobile devices

- Locking mechanism with multi users was found to be robust as it took less than a minute for update across all the CBD and legacy systems.

5 Conclusion and Future Work

Our research started with the identification of issues related to Cloud Based Design and how it has not been explored fully. Our research presented a generic CBCD methodology involving all kind of design activities in cross company collaboration fashion via cloud by representing a complex scenario of big and small industries where collaboration happens between CBD system users and legacy users. Successful execution of case study showed us the merits associated with CBCD system like moving more activities on web based applications, challenges like issues with visualization and authoring of hybrid models and the importance of creating a truly hybrid digital data collaboration by involving different types of CAD data such that all collaborators can use just one data model even though the parts are authorized in their respective CAD origins. The future works involves testing the CBCD methodology with the other famous CAD systems available in market with the existing cloud test platform in order to understand the collaboration scenario, challenges of hybrid model usage, advantages of unified digital model to achieve start to end digital thread based on UPS.

References

1. Clark, K.B.: Product Development Performance: Strategy, Organization, and Management in the World Auto Industry. Harvard Business Press, Brighton (1991)
2. Kasey, P.: Top Trends in the Gartner Hype Cycle for Emerging Technologies, Gartner (2017)
3. Smith, D.M., Anderson, Ed.: Hype Cycle for Cloud Computing, Gartner (2017)
4. Pahl, G., Beitz, W.: Engineering Design, vol. 984. Design Council, London
5. Hicks, B., Culley, S., McMahon, C.A.: The barriers to improving information management in engineering organizations. In: Proceedings of International Conference on Engineering Design, ICED 2007 (2007)
6. Barham, P., et al.: Xen and the art of virtualization. ACM SIGOPS Oper. Syst. Rev. **37**(5), 164–177 (2003)
7. Datakit: Datakit value to CAM, CMM & control vendors (2018). www.datakit.com
8. Lu, S.C.-Y., Cai, J., Burkett, W., Udwadia, F.: A methodology for collaborative design process and conflict analysis. CIRP Ann. **49**(1), 69–73 (2000)
9. Red, E., French, D., Jensen, G., Walker, S.S., Madsen, P.: Emerging design methods and tools in collaborative product development. J. Comput. Inf. Sci. Eng. **13**(3), 031001 (2013)
10. Wu, D., Rosen, D.W., Schaefer, D.: Cloud-based design and manufacturing: status and promise. In: Schaefer, D. (ed.) Cloud-Based Design and Manufacturing (CBDM), pp. 1–24. Springer, Heidelberg (2014). https://doi.org/10.1007/978-3-319-07398-9_1
11. Andreadis, G., Fourtounis, G., Bouzakis, K.-D.: Collaborative design in the era of cloud computing. Adv. Eng. Softw. **81**(11), 66–72

Ontologies and Data Models

A Preliminary Methodological Approach to Models for Manufacturing (MfM)

Fernando Mas[1(✉)], Jesus Racero[2], Manuel Oliva[1], and Domingo Morales-Palma[2]

[1] Airbus, Seville, Spain
{fernando.mas,manuel.oliva}@airbus.com
[2] Universidad de Sevilla, Seville, Spain
{jracero,dmpalma}@us.es

Abstract. To enhance multidisciplinary design and simulation of complex systems, MBSE (Model Based Systems Engineering) is a methodology where computer aided graphical modeling authoring tools are used to specify functions and behaviors of the systems. Simulation tools bring about a system behavioral abstraction required for the design of complex products. MBSE enables more robust systems engineering, because it results in models and their associated behavioral abstraction [1].

A research approach for modelling manufacturing systems in the aerospace industry, and in particular for FAL (Final Assembly Line), has been proposed by the authors in several research papers during the last years [2, 3]. Functional and data models have been published and deployed using data structures available from commercial PLM systems [4].

Recently a new approach for modelling manufacturing systems has been coined as an extension of the previous research to introduce MBSE in manufacturing. A new architecture based on 3-Layers Model (3LM) has been defined: a Data layer, an Ontology layer and a Service layer. Ontology layer is the core of the 3LM. The Ontology layer defines: Scope model, Data model, Behavior model and Semantic model, to further instance information from databases. Scope model is mandatory because manufacturing is a large and wide part of the artifact lifecycle and Data model can cover different several uses across it.

This paper presents a preliminary methodology for Models for Manufacturing (MfM) trends and issues that can be addressed in order to support the generation and management of manufacturing ontologies.

Keywords: Models for Manufacturing (MfM) · industrial DMU (iDMU)
Ontologies · 3-Layers Model (3LM)
Model-Based Systems Engineering (MBSE)

1 Introduction

The motivation for this preliminary approach to an MfM methodology is to provide MPT (Method, Processes and associated Tools) to help the engineers to perform the Industrial Design and manufacturing of an aerospace product. The MfM methodology

Published by Springer Nature Switzerland AG 2018.
P. Chiabert et al. (Eds.): PLM 2018, IFIP AICT 540, pp. 273–283, 2018.
https://doi.org/10.1007/978-3-030-01614-2_25

aims to provide a set of processes, methods and associated tools to support the discipline of manufacturing in a model-based context.

Currently, in the aerospace industry, the 3D definition of the product using PLM, CAx tools and MBSE models in a huge improvement in the Functional Design processes. Therefore, in the manufacturing side of the lifecycle, despite the use of ERP, PLM, MES CAx tools and bespoke tools that has been improved along the last years modelling is still undergoing.

The novelty of this work relays on the development of a reference framework, the 3LM, based on the definition of a manufacturing ontology and enabling simulation, behaviors and analytical capabilities, capitalizing the Company knowledge. Currently the research is doing in parallel with the development of architecture, prototypes tools and manufacturing use cases. Still it is in preliminary phase.

Following to the rest of the document, Sect. 2 contains more detailed review of the problem to solve. Section 3 is devoted to present a non-exhaustive literature review about MBSE research close-to-industrial research. Section 4 contains the methodology under development, supported by a 3LM, referred to as Data, Ontology and Service layers. Section 5 discloses the discussion and conclusions from this work and to present the topics for further research.

2 Review of MBSE Research Initiatives for Manufacturing

Model-Based Systems Engineering is a methodology that has gained a foothold over the past 10–15 years and continues to be refined and improved today. One of the main goals of MBSE is to substitute the classic 3D centric approach and document-oriented information in favor of a simulated model-oriented definition that has several benefits [5, 6]:

- The model is the core of the development (requisites, design, and manufacturing).
- Ability to manage complexity and to capture knowledge.
- Analysis and trade-off and early detection of issues.
- Keep consistency between requisites along the lifecycle.
- Allow flexibility when changes appear.

Bergenthal [12] defines MBE (Model Based Engineering) in the Model Based Engineering final report for US NDIA (National Defense Industrial Association): "an approach to engineering that uses models as an integral part of the technical baseline that includes the requirements, analysis, design, implementation, and verification of a capability, system, and product throughout the lifecycle", extending MBE to the whole lifecycle.

Frechette [8] defines a Model-based Enterprise: "an organization that applies modeling and simulation technologies to integrate and manage its technical and business processes to define, execute, control, and manage all enterprise processes", insisting in the extension of MBSE to the whole lifecycle.

MBSE has been worldwide accepted by the aerospace and automotive industry during the last few years [7], with hundreds of development and deployment in the Functional Design processes and with special emphasis in the area of systems design.

Several researches, developments, deployments and projects has been conducted using MBSE, but only recently the interest is turning to manufacturing. Industrial Design of the product, manufacturing and assembly, balancing lines, configuration and change management, and many others tasks performed during the serial production phase of the lifecycle are taken the attention of the researchers.

Friedenthal et al. [5] proposed a 2010 status and a 2020 vision on MBSE. Some topics selected for the 2020 vision are applied to manufacturing:

- Extends to domains beyond engineering to support complex areas.
- Enable the engineer to focus on abstract modeling of the user domain.
- Modeling standards supporting high fidelity simulation and real representations.
- Extensive reuse of model libraries, taxonomies, and design patterns.
- Standards supporting integration and management across a distributed repository.

The iDMU, as proposed in [14] can be designed under the paradigm of MBSE, and the most relevant potential opportunities are integration of knowledge, reusability, and traceability, reduced costs, higher quality, and decreased time-to-market in addition with the automation of manufacturing document generation.

Kulvatunyou et al. [9] presents several ontologies for industrial problems that have been a topic of research for several years, most of the projects in the EU Horizon 2020 program have adopted ontology as a component and similarly, in the US NIST (National Institute of Standards and Technology), manufacturing projects also have ontology as a component. In fact, reinforces the concept of commonality between the ontologies, long term interoperability between the different engineering, manufacturing, and supply chain disciplines.

NIST organized a workshop to explore the idea of a framework for curating ontologies, an IOF (Industrial Ontologies Foundry) [10]. The goal for the workshop was to identify industry needs, to develop consensus and to identify the issues that need to be addressed to move forward. Workshop participants reported the main reason in seeing an industrial ontology foundry is interoperability, information linking, and formalization of requirements through information constraints, incorporation of business process aspects, and quality and traceability.

Several authors [15–18] are researching on the development and deployment of MBSE methodologies and tools in manufacturing. Aspects like process planning, human resources, robotics, IoT (Internet of Things) are recently research topics.

Ontologies are in the core of MBSE methodology. According Uschold and Gruninger [19], ontology is the term used to refer to the shared understanding of some domain of interest which embodies some sort of world view with respect to the given domain.

Ontology model development is today a worldwide research topic and ontology Engineering refers to the set of activities that concern the ontology development process and the ontology lifecycle, the methods and methodologies for building ontologies, and the tool suites and languages that support them [20].

3 Problem to Solve

The objective of the presented research work is to propose a MBSE methodology able to be applied along the Industrial Design, Serial Manufacturing and In-Service Support phases of an aerospace artifact lifecycle. Figure 1 shows the typical lifecycle of a commercial aircraft [13]. Despite the Functional Design is a huge human and financial effort, only takes around 10 years with some isolate upgrading efforts along the lifecycle. Production and in-service support takes a long period, around 40 years, covering both Functional and Services Design, manufacturing, assembly, and management of the supply chain, MRO (Maintenance, Repair and Overhaul) and product services activities.

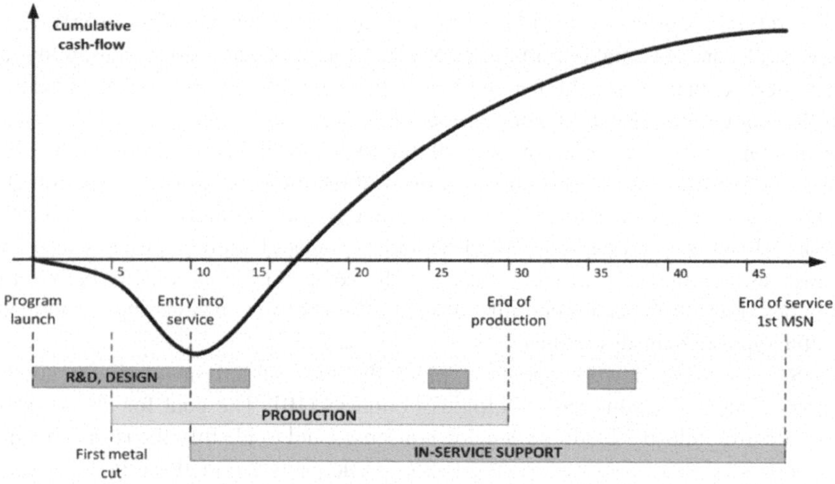

Fig. 1. Typical commercial aircraft program lifecycle [13].

As an example, considering the aerospace lifecycle phases [11], there are four main software systems used to generate, manage and exploit the aircraft related data or information: Computer Aided applications (CAx), Product Lifecycle Management (PLM), Enterprise Resource Planning (ERP) and Manufacturing Execution System (MES) and several bespoke and legacy tools.

Aerospace artifact data are dispersed through a number of databases belonging to different software systems (e.g. PLM, ERP, MES, bespoke and legacy systems), which are operated along the lifecycle. Every software system considered has a full vertical approach: Database, Data model and Service. Databases are usually provided by a vendor (Oracle, MySQL, and others). Data model, the core of the system is defined and developed by the provider with little or none user influence. Service is the mathematical, simulations, behaviors or business functions to apply. Even though each system ensures the consistency of its data, the approach fails to ensure a data model consistency along the aerospace artifact whole lifecycle.

Manufacturing is a large and wide part of the lifecycle and covers several different stages with similar models. Nowadays many different software applications are running with interfaces between them without a full common model. Data continuity is devoted to interfaces between the applications, simulation is done partially and consistency with the Company processes is done via customization, legacy software add-ons or Excel sheets.

The proposed solution is the 3LM framework and the MfM methodology and associated tools. It supports splitting functions and data, and creating ontology to define, manage and maintain the Company knowledge.

4 Models for Manufacturing (MfM) Methodology

4.1 3-Layers Model (3LM)

Model-Based for Manufacturing methodology proposed is based on a 3-Layers Model shown in Fig. 2. The 3LM ensures the independence between layers, maintaining both Data Layer and Ontology Layer isolated. The result is independence on the definition of the Ontology, the knowledge of the Company, against Data layer and Services layer. In fact, the 3LM decouples the traditional vertical system developed by the software vendors giving to the users the independence to migrate software services inside the Service Layer easily.

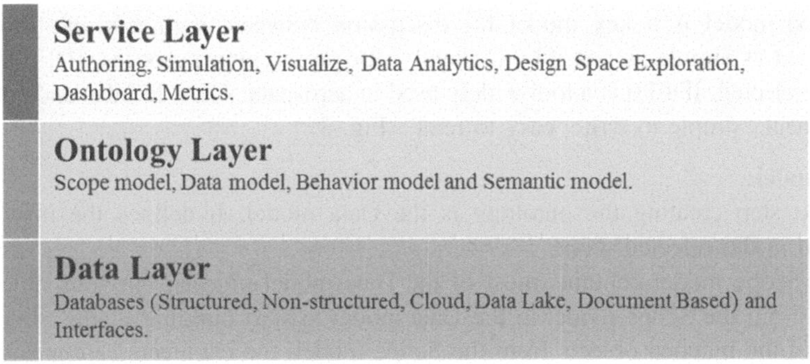

Fig. 2. 3-Layers Model (3LM) framework.

The lower layer, Data layer, collect all the databases and interfaces: legacy databases from the legacy software, databases from the commercial software applications, clouds and data lakes databases and many others. Included in the Data layer are those databases to hold the information instanced using Ontology layer.

The medium layer, the Ontology layer, is the core of the model. It holds all the Company processes and scope, data and semantic models, and the associated simulation or behavior requirements.

The upper layer, Service layer, holds the software services. The behaviors of the different services are defined in the Ontology layer as part of the ontology definition. Service layer holds software as authoring and simulation tools, visualizers, data analytics and dashboard and space design exploration tools. Services are exploited using information stored in the Data layer, instanced through the Ontology layer.

4.2 Ontology

The Ontology layer is the core in the 3LM framework and is where the knowledge of the Company is created, stored, managed and used. Ontology Layer includes Scope model, Data model, Behaviour model and Semantics model. Ontology layer is defined in an agnostic way; it is not linked to any model language or software tools. A survey of the current existing ontology software tools shows that a big amount of tools existing on the market and a significant set of them are frequently used [22]. The MfM methodology states a few declarations:

- Define an agnostic methodology. Do not have preferred tools or languages.
- Promote the use of simple modelling tools; simple to write models and extremely easy to share, read, understand and discuss by skilled engineers on the model topic.
- Establish and assure procedures for creation, enrichment and reuse ontologies.
- Establish a procedure to manage lifecycle, configuration and effectivity from different parts and objects in the ontologies. Promote the use of a PLM tool to fulfill this requirement.

Scope Model

The first step creating the ontology is the Scope model. It defines the limits where the model works and contains all main Data model objects, and the definition of the simulation behaviors.

Scope model is a key model for discussion between engineers and should be maintained as simple as possible. Currently, for prototyping purposes, IDEF0 [23] is the tool selected. IDEF0 is a tool widely used in aerospace since decades and cover the requirement "simple to write, easy to read" (Fig. 3).

Data Model

The next step creating the ontology is the Data model. It defines the information managed in the selected scope.

The Scope model contains most of the Data model objects, thus this objects are mapped from the Scope model to the Data model to start building it (Fig. 4).

Using the mapped objects from the Scope model, the engineers can enrich, reuse and complete the Data model. Currently, for prototyping purposes, CMAP [24] is the tool selected. CMAP is a tool widely used to define Data model and cover the requirements "simple to write, easy to read" (Fig. 5).

To support and to manage the objects lifecycle, configuration and effectivity, MfM methodology promotes the use of a PLM system. A PLM system can hold and manage easily ontology objects and let the engineers manage, upgrade, reuse and enrich the objects. An initial prototype, based in a FOSS PLM, is building by the authors.

Behavior Model

The Behavior model defines the simulation or other software defined in the Scope model needed to check the full system. It is still on development and currently it is not included in the MfM methodology.

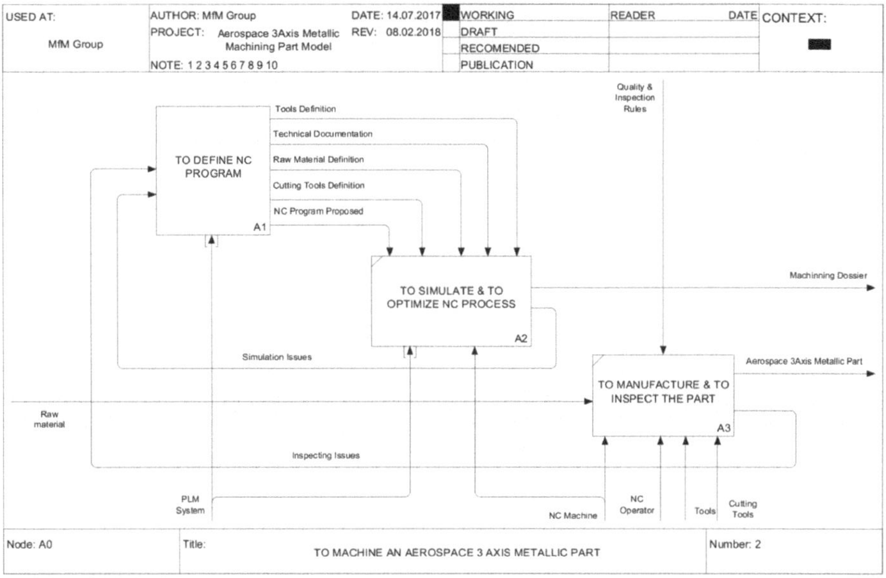

Fig. 3. Example of a Scope model modelled in IDEF0 for NC milling 3 Axis metallic parts.

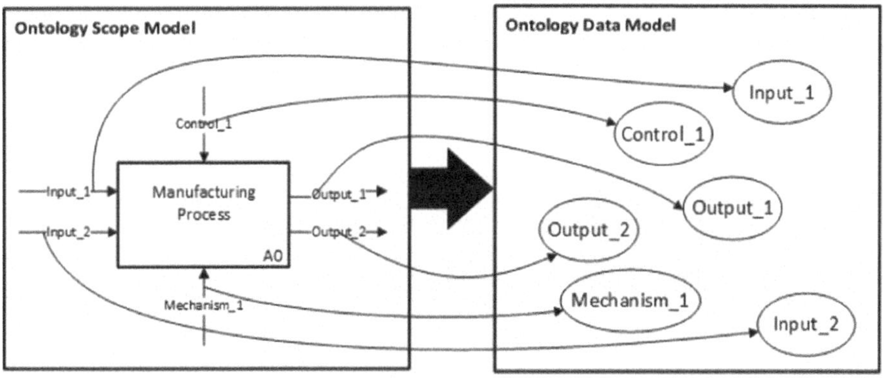

Fig. 4. Mapping objects between Scope model and Data model.

Semantic Model

The Data model in the ontology should be instance with real data in the prototypes and to run real use cases. Information coming from the databases (commercial applications, bespoke and legacy systems) is defined in different ways, different languages or different formats (i.e. Date in American or European format). Semantic model lets also to maintain connection between models among the lifecycle given digital continuity to the ontologies.

Figure 6 shows a simple example about the application of Semantics in the 3LM. A basic concept in product design, the fillet radius between two planes, is part of a product data model. Corner radius, a useful concept in manufacturing, is part of a

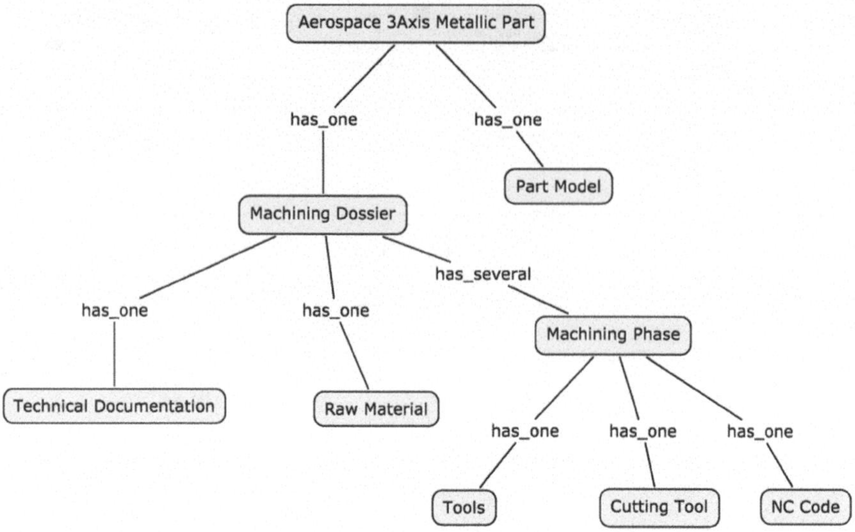

Fig. 5. Example of a Data model modelled in CMAP for NC milling 3 Axis metallic parts.

manufacturing data model and finally a concept like Rc, is part of a procurement data model. All three concepts have the same meaning: radius: the Semantic model translates and unifies the different definitions, and let the ontology make data instance using radius as a unique concept.

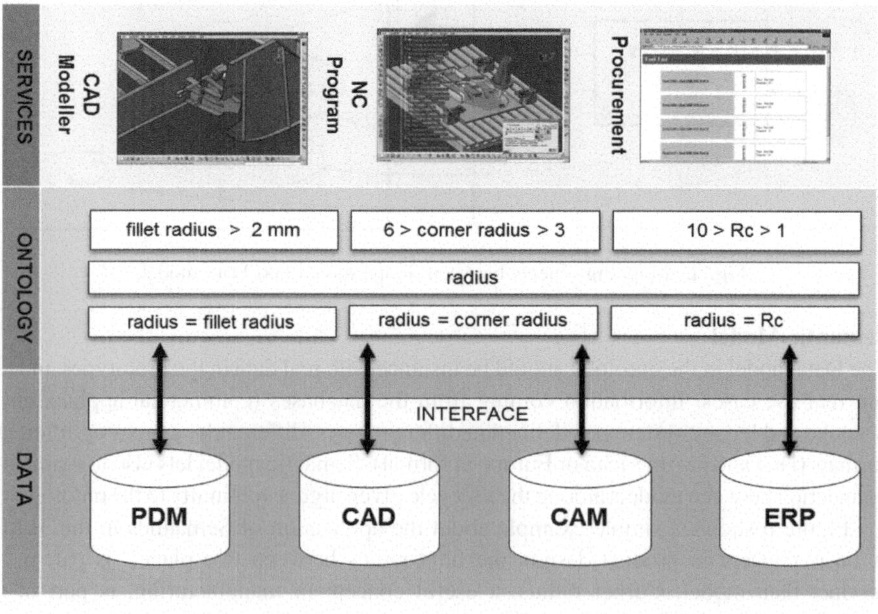

Fig. 6. Semantics. Same object with different names in data models.

5 Discussion and Further Work

A preliminary approach for a methodology to apply Models for Manufacturing has been proposed and described. A 3LM framework is included on the methodology to assure the full applicability. The methodology is an agnostic methodology, independent of languages or modelling tools.

The feasibility of the applicability of the MBSE methodology to manufacturing has been done using a basic example: a preliminary study applied to Incremental Sheet Forming technology has been developed [21], modelled following the methodology and proposed tools [22].

MfM methodology has been successfully applied to build a prototype in a different use case: an approach to gender analysis in Airbus R&T organization [25].

The research team is working in the improvements of the MfM methodology, the development of the associated tools and the modelling of real manufacturing use cases. The team is working using AGILE for research and development, building prototypes as fast as possible to test and get feedback. As result, research and develop are running in three lines at the same time: MfM methodology, associated tools and prototypes, and use cases. The further MfM methodology tasks planned are:

- Improve the definition of relationships between Scope model and Data model.
- Improve the lifecycle management between Scope model and Data model.
- Define methods to include behavior and simulation from the Scope model definition and from the Data model definition to complete the ontology.
- Research on "MBSE Design in Context" or "Collaborative MBSE" using MfM during the conceptual phase of the product lifecycle [14].
- Research on building a virtual manufacturing environment to simulate MfM prototypes and use cases.

Acknowledgement. The authors would like to thank Ignacio Eguia, Jose Carlos Molina, Andres Padillo, and other Sevilla University colleagues, Julio Ortegon, and other Cadiz University colleagues, Rebeca Arista, Tamara Borreguero, and other AIRBUS colleagues for their support and contribution during the development of this work.

References

1. Holland, O.T.: Model-based systems engineering. In: Loper, M.L. (ed.) Modeling and Simulation in the Systems Engineering Life Cycle. SFMA, pp. 299–306. Springer, London (2015). https://doi.org/10.1007/978-1-4471-5634-5_23
2. Mas, F., Rios, J., Menendez, J.L., Gomez, A.: A process-oriented approach to modeling the conceptual design of aircraft assembly lines. Int. J. Adv. Manuf. Technol. **67**(1–4), 771–784 (2013). https://doi.org/10.1007/s00170-012-4521-5
3. Mas, F., Oliva, M., Rios, J., Gomez, A., Olmos, V., et al.: PLM based approach to the industrialization of aeronautical assemblies. Procedia Eng. **132**, 1045–1052 (2015). https://doi.org/10.1016/j.proeng.2015.12.594

4. Gómez, A., Rios, J., Mas, F., Vizan, A.: Method and software application to assist in the conceptual design of aircraft final assembly lines. J. Manuf. Syst. **40**, 37–53 (2016). https://doi.org/10.1016/j.jmsy.2016.04.002
5. Friedenthal, S., Griego, R., Sampson, M.: INCOSE model based systems engineering (MBSE) initiative. In: INCOSE International Symposium (2007)
6. Dickerson, C.E., Mavris, D.: A brief history of models and model based systems engineering and the case for relational orientation. IEEE Syst. J. **7**(4), 581–592 (2013)
7. D'Ambrosio, J., Soremekun, G.: Systems engineering challenges and MBSE opportunities for automotive system design. In: 2017, IEEE International Conference on Systems and Cybernetics, Banff, AB, pp. 2075–2080 (2017)
8. Frechette, S.: Model based enterprise for manufacturing. In: 2011, 44th CIRP International Conference on Manufacturing Systems, Madison, WI, United States (2011)
9. Ivezic, N., Kulvatunyou, B., Brandl, D., Cho, H., Yan, L., et al.: Drilling down on Smart Manufacturing – enabling composable apps. Manuf. Lett. **08**, 10 (2016)
10. Ivezic, N., Kulvatunyou, B., Lu, Y., Lee, Y., Lee, J., et al.: OAGi/NIST Workshop on Open Cloud Architecture for Smart Manufacturing. Report number: NISTIR 8124
11. Ríos, J., Hernández, J.C., Oliva, M., Mas, F.: Product avatar as digital counterpart of a physical individual product: literature review and implications in an aircraft. In: 22nd International Conference on Concurrent Engineering, vol. 2, pp. 657–666. IOS Press. https://doi.org/10.3233/978-1-61499-544-9-657
12. Bergenthal, J.: Final Report Model Based Engineering (MBE) Subcommittee. NDIA Systems Engineering Division, M&S Committee (2011). https://www.ndia.org/-/media/sites/ndia/meetings-and-events/3187-sullivan/divisions/systems-engineering/modeling-and-simulation/reports/model-based-engineering.ashx. Accessed Mar 2018
13. European Commission: Aeronautics and Air Transport: Beyond Vision 2020 (Towards 2050). Official Publications of the European Communities, 2010, Luxembourg. http://bookshop.europa.eu. Accessed Mar 2018
14. Mas, F., Menendez, J.L., Oliva, M., Rios, J., Gomez, A., et al.: iDMU as the Collaborative Engineering engine: research experiences in Airbus. In: International Conference on Engineering, Technology and Innovation (ICE), Bergamo, pp. 1–7 (2014). https://doi.org/10.1109/ICE.2014.6871594
15. Fiorini, S.R., Bermejo-Alonso, J., Gonçalves, P., de Freitas, E.P., Alarcos, A.O., et al.: A suite of ontologies for robotics and automation [industrial activities]. IEEE Robot. Autom. Mag. **24**(1), 8–11 (2017)
16. Mayer, S., Hodges, J., Dan, Yu., Kritzler, M., Michahelles, F.: An open semantic framework for the industrial Internet of Things. IEEE Intell. Syst. **32**(1), 96–101 (2017)
17. Perini, S., Arena, D., Kiritsis, D., Taisch, M.: An ontology-based model for training evaluation and skill classification in an Industry 4.0 environment. In: Lödding, H., Riedel, R., Thoben, K.-D., von Cieminski, G., Kiritsis, D. (eds.) APMS 2017. IAICT, vol. 513, pp. 314–321. Springer, Cham (2017). https://doi.org/10.1007/978-3-319-66923-6_37
18. Lundgren, M., Hedlind, M., Kjellberg, T.: Model driven manufacturing process design and managing quality. Procedia CIRP **50**(1), 299–304 (2016)
19. Uschold, M., Gruninger, M.: Ontologies: principles, methods and applications. Knowl. Eng. Rev. **11**(2), 93–136 (1996)
20. Kiritsis, D.: Closed-loop PLM for intelligent products in the era of the Internet of Things. Comput. Aided Des. **43**(5), 479–501 (2011)
21. Morales-Palma, D., Mas, F., Racero, J., Vallellano, C.: A preliminary study of Models for Manufacturing (MfM) applied to Incremental Sheet Forming. In: Chiabert, P., Bouras, A., Noël, F., Ríos, J. (eds.) PLM 2018. IFIP AICT, vol. 540, pp. 284–293. Springer, Cham (2018)

22. Slimani, T.: Ontology development: a comparing study on tools, languages and formalisms. Indian J. Sci. Technol. **8**(24) (2015)
23. NIST: Integration Definition for Function Modeling (IDEF0). Computer Systems Laboratory of the National Institute of Standards and Technology, December 1993. http://www.idef.com/wp-content/uploads/2016/02/idef0.pdf. Accessed Mar 2018
24. Cañas, A.J., et al.: Concept maps: integrating knowledge and information visualization. In: Tergan, S.-O., Keller, T. (eds.) Knowledge and Information Visualization. LNCS, vol. 3426, pp. 205–219. Springer, Heidelberg (2005). https://doi.org/10.1007/11510154_11
25. Arista, R., Mas, F.: A preliminary model-based approach for Gender analysis of Airbus Research Organization. In: IEEE International Conference on Engineering, Technology and Innovation (ICE/ITMC), Stuttgart, pp. 1-6 (2018). https://doi.org/10.1109/ICE.2018.8436319

A Preliminary Study of Models for Manufacturing (MfM) Applied to Incremental Sheet Forming

Domingo Morales-Palma[1(✉)], Fernando Mas[2], Jesús Racero[1], and Carpóforo Vallellano[1]

[1] Universidad de Sevilla, Seville, Spain
{dmpalma, jrm, carpofor}@us.es
[2] Airbus, Seville, Spain
fernando.mas@airbus.com

Abstract. Models for Manufacturing is a new approach proposed by the authors to apply Model-based Systems Engineering concepts to Manufacturing. The methodology under development is supported by a 3-layer framework (referred to as Data Base and Interfaces, Ontology and Software Tools layers) and simple and easy-to-use software tools. This work presents a preliminary implementation of Models for Manufacturing to SPIF, an innovative incremental sheet forming that makes use of CNC technology and usually requires a numerical study to validate the manufacturing process. The work introduces the proposed methodology and presents the model in development with special emphasis on the Ontology layer.

Keywords: Models for Manufacturing (MfM)
Model-based Systems Engineering (MBSE) · Ontologies
Manufacturing process modelling · Single-Point Incremental Forming (SPIF)

1 Introduction

Model-based Systems Engineering (MBSE) is a methodology that uses computer aided graphical modelling authoring tools to design and simulate complex systems and specify their functions and behaviours. MBSE has emerged as a viable method for multidisciplinary collaboration of stakeholders, communication of ideas and increase of productivity and quality [1]. MBSE results in models and their associated behavioural abstraction that enable more robust systems engineering [2]. MBSE has conducted several works in the aerospace and automotive industry during the last few years [3], with hundreds of developments focused in Functional Design processes. However, only recently the interest is turning to manufacturing and related tasks performed during the production phase, such as Industrial Design of the product, assembly, balancing lines or configuration and change management, among others.

Modelling of manufacturing systems in the aerospace industry has been investigated by some of the authors in recent years [4–6]. Recently, Models for Manufacturing (MfM) has been proposed by the authors as a new approach to apply MBSE

Published by Springer Nature Switzerland AG 2018.
P. Chiabert et al. (Eds.): PLM 2018, IFIP AICT 540, pp. 284–293, 2018.
https://doi.org/10.1007/978-3-030-01614-2_26

concepts to Manufacturing. The novelty of the proposed MfM methodology consists of the development of a reference 3-layer framework based on the definition of a manufacturing ontology and enabling simulation, behaviours and analytical capabilities. The three layers of the framework are referred to as Data Base and Interfaces, Ontology and Software Tools layers. This work focuses on the development of the Ontology layer whereas aspects related to system architecture and methodological approach of MfM are further discussed in [7]. The MfM methodology is still in the preliminary phase.

The MfM methodology is planned to be applied to different manufacturing technologies of interest to the authors' research, such as assembly processes of aeronautical components, CNC machining and metal sheet forming processes. This work presents a preliminary implementation of MfM to an incremental sheet forming process: Single-Point Incremental Forming (SPIF). This novel technology is a flexible and economical manufacturing process with a great potential for the manufacture of small and medium-sized batches of parts with a high degree of customization [8]. SPIF combines several simulation technologies that makes it very attractive to its implementation by MfM, such as CAD/CAM modelling, CNC machine control and analysis of elasto-plastic material behaviour by FEM (Finite Element Method). Furthermore, the research work on SPIF by some of the authors has also motivated the choice of this manufacturing process [9–13]. Next sections briefly introduce the proposed MfM methodology, describe the most relevant aspects of manufacturing by SPIF, present the current state of the SPIF model and discuss the results obtained.

2 Methodology

The proposed MfM methodology is supported by a 3-layer framework referred to as Data Base and Interfaces, Ontology and Software Tools layers. The MfM methodology is carried out through the following steps:

1. Create the system scope to define the limits of the model.
2. Define the ontology (Ontology layer).
3. Define behaviour (Software Tools layer).
4. Instance the data bases through the interfaces using the defined ontology (Data Base and Interfaces layer).

The system scope is needed because manufacturing is a large and wide part of the lifecycle and models can cover several topics. The scope clearly establishes the main concepts of the model related to manufacturing activities or functions, materials, equipment, tools, design, modelling, simulation, analysis, etc. It must be approved by all stakeholders before defining the next steps of the system ontology.

The Ontology layer is the core of the 3-layer model and is supported by models that are easy to read, understand, reuse and enrich. It provides the tools and methods necessary to collect knowledge of the manufacturing system. It is defined by the system scope applicable to the model, the data model and semantics itself, and the simulation requirements or behaviours.

The Software Tools layer allows analysing different models and instantiating real cases from models. Its implementation depends on the type of manufacturing model and related simulations. Previously, the system scope has already defined the functionalities that should be implemented in this layer and even the tools to be used.

The Database and Interfaces layer is being implemented by PLM solutions to manage all the information related to the models and their use. The proposed methodology aims the use of simple tools that allow to easily write an ontology to discuss with skilled people in a collaborative way.

3 Single-Point Incremental Forming (SPIF)

Incremental forming is an innovative sheet forming process that makes use of computers and CNC technology to plastically deform a raw material through the progressive and local pressure of a small-size forming tool. This technology has been used for the last few years to obtain a variety of industrial parts due to its benefits compared with conventional manufacturing processes, such as non-dedicated equipment requirements, dieless process, flexibility, low costs and improvement of material formability, among others. Many variations of incremental forming have been explored, but by far the most widely used is the single-point incremental forming (SPIF) configuration [8].

Figure 1 presents the basic components of the SPIF process: the blank sheet, the forming tool, and tools for clamping and holding the sheet in its position (blank holder and backing plate). The backing plate opening defines the maximum working area of the forming tool. The tool trajectory is generated by a CNC machine. The tool action is performed on the front surface of the sheet and there is no backup die supporting the back surface.

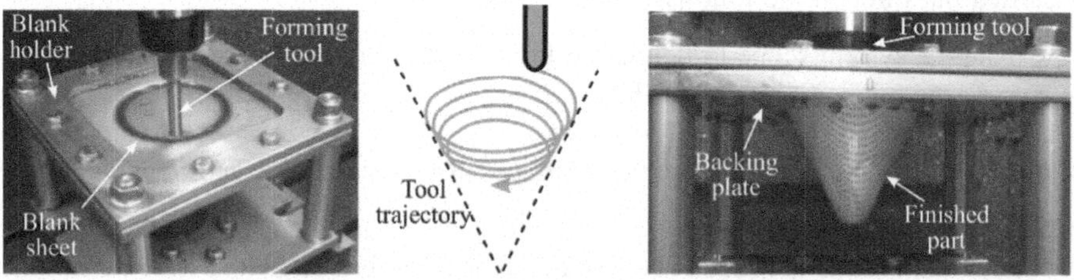

Fig. 1. Basic components to produce a cone by SPIF: (a) recently started process; (b) schema of the tool trajectory; and (c) finished sheet part.

SPIF is mainly applied in the automotive and aeronautical sectors, either to obtain functional parts or prototypes, as well as for biomedical prosthesis [9]. Figure 2 shows some CAD models and manufactured parts by SPIF carried out for experiments that demonstrate the viability of the process [10]. Part design as well as tools definition and programming of CNC code are carried out frequently by conventional machining-based CAD/CAM systems. Often the SPIF process is decomposed in several forming stages to homogenize deformation. Thus, the design of the forming strategy is a fundamental factor to take into account to produce successful parts using SPIF.

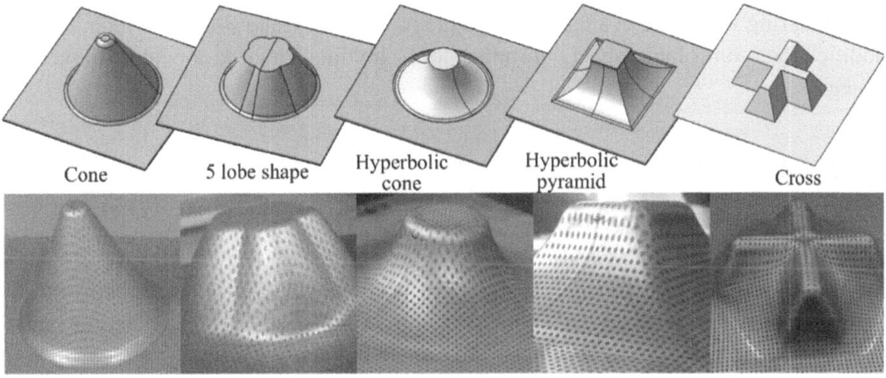

Fig. 2. CAD models and sheet parts manufactured by SPIF.

The design evaluation of the SPIF process is carried out through simulations of both tool movements and material deformation [11]. The former are accomplished by analysing tool trajectories and collisions in the CAD/CAM system. The latter simulations are achieved through numerical studies by finite element analysis (FEA) systems. Figure 3(a) illustrates a numerical simulation of a SPIF process to produce a circular hole-flanged part [12]. Typical objectives of these studies include the calculation of forces and geometrical deviations after elastic spring-back, and the evaluation of sheet failure, among others.

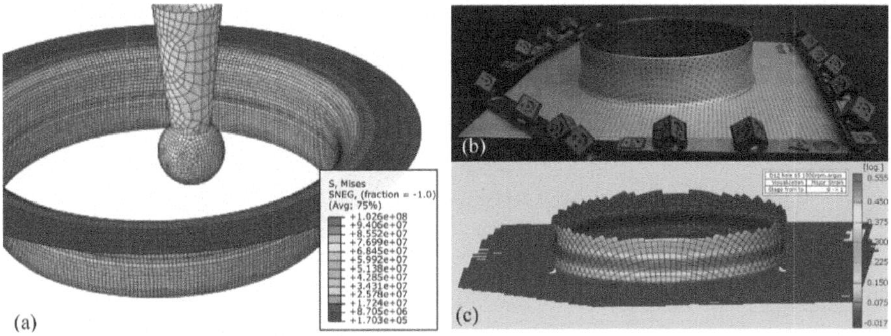

Fig. 3. Analysis of a hole-flanged sheet part manufactured by SPIF: (a) numerical study by FEA; (b) setup for capturing digital images of a manufactured specimen; and (c) analysis of strains by DIC techniques.

Sheet parts manufactured by SPIF are inspected according to the quality and inspection rules of the manufacturing organization. Figure 3(b–c) presents a dimensional inspection of the hole-flanged part using digital image correlation (DIC) techniques [13]. The technique used in this example consisted of marking the sheet with a circle pattern before the forming operation and measuring the strains of resulting ellipses by the DIC software. For pieces rejected by the quality control, manufacturing issues are evaluated to find the most appropriate solution which includes modifications on blank sheet, forming tool, holding devices or tool movement strategies.

4 Results

4.1 Scope Model

The Scope model for the SPIF process is developed with IDEF0 [14] diagrams. IDEF0 assists the modeller in identifying what functions are performed (represented as boxes, see Fig. 4) and what is needed to perform those functions (labelled arrows) in four categories: inputs, outputs, controls and mechanisms. The main function is *Produce Part by SPIF* that transforms the input *Raw Material* into the output *Finished and Tested Part*, according to controls *Part Model* and *Quality and Inspection Rules*, and carried out with mechanisms *NC Machine*, *Forming Tool* and *Tools*. Another relevant mechanism is *PLM System* that represents software tools used to generate the NC program and analyse the SPIF process. Since the blank sheet, the forming tool and tools are customized to produce each sheet part, their definitions are also modelled as an output *SPIF Setup Definition* of the main function.

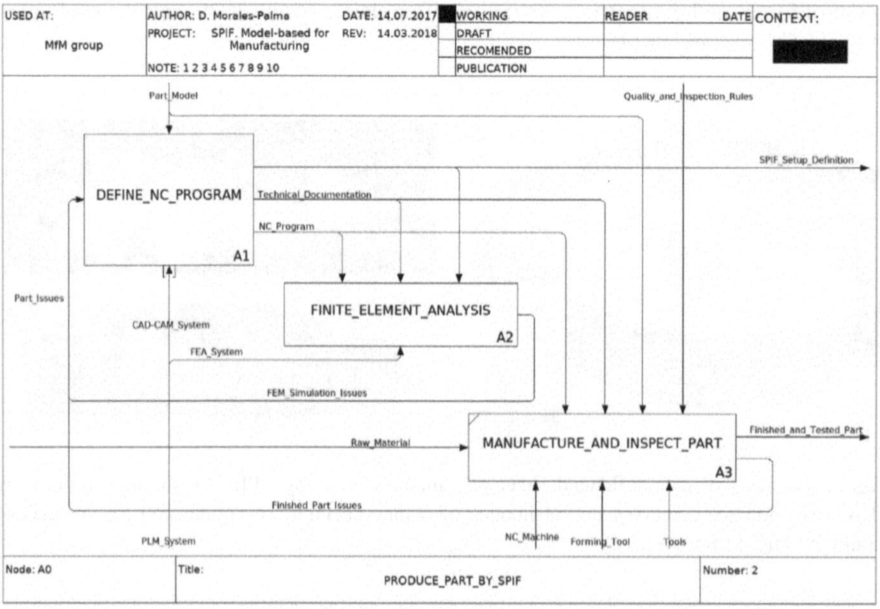

Fig. 4. Scope definition for SPIF with IDEF0 diagrams: *Produce a part by SPIF* (level A0).

The current Scope model contains many IDEF0 diagrams but only two are shown in this document. Figure 4 displays the decomposition of the main function into three subfunctions that operate simultaneously with each other, while the interface arrows constraining when and how operations are triggered and controlled. For example, *Part Model* is a control element used to *Define NC Program* and *Manufacture and Inspect Part* (for inspection) but not to develop *Finite Element Analysis* (FEA). *Part Issues* represents all the possible problems predicted by FEA (*FEM Simulation Issues*) or found when inspecting the part (*Finished Part Issues*). *NC Program* and *Technical Documentation* are generated from *Define NC Program* which are required to control FEA, manufacturing and inspection of the part.

Figure 5 represents a lower level IDEF0 diagram to detail function *Define NC Program*. As can be seen, *Part Model* is used to *Define Blank and Tools*, *Define Forming Tool* and *Define Forming Strategies* using a *CAD/CAM System* (note that this mechanism is "tunnelled" in Fig. 4 as represented as a snippet of the arrow in brackets, which means that is a mechanism element for all subfunctions). The function *Define Forming Strategies* generates a *SPIF CNC Model* that contains decisions about number of stages and geometry of manufactured parts between stages, as described in a lower level IDEF0 diagram. The *SPIF CNC Model* is used to *Simulate and Generate NC* with the CAD/CAM system. Figure 5 also shows that if *NC Program Issues* occurs, they must be resolved by modifying the definition of forming tool or forming strategies.

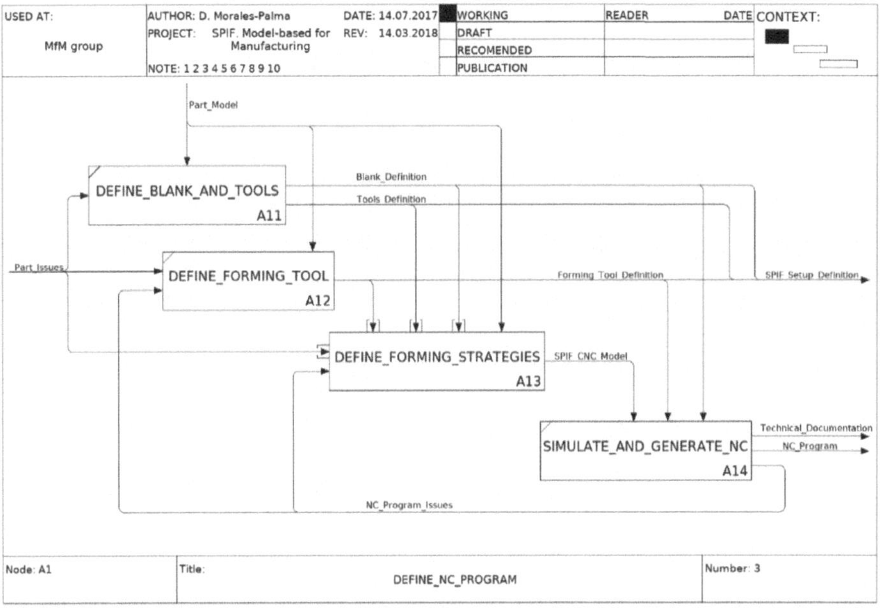

Fig. 5. Scope definition for SPIF with IDEF0 diagrams: *Define NC Program* (level A1).

From the Scope model, IDEF0 "inputs" and "outputs" are used as main classes of the ontology whereas "functions" and "mechanisms" will be used to implement the

Software Tools layer. However, a "control" element can be either an ontology class, as is *Part Model* (see Figs. 4 or 5), or an object for the Software Tools layer, as is *Quality and Inspection Rules* (see Fig. 4). In the current system prototype, a tag has been added to IDEF0 element names to allow the system to recognize the ontology classes from those that are not. This tag has been removed from this document for clarity. Nevertheless, this solution is provisional and will be replaced by a more functional one in future developments.

Once the Scope model is finished and approved by the work team, the IDFEØ model can be uploaded to the system (in IDL format) and converted to an OWL document containing the main classes of the ontology. This document can be downloaded and opened with IHMC CMapTools software to define the Data Model as a concept map.

4.2 Data Model

A concept map or conceptual diagram is a graphical tool for structuring and representing knowledge. In the proposed methodology, the modeller organizes the concepts or main classes (represented as boxes, see Fig. 6) in a hierarchical structure, creates relationships between concepts (as labelled arrows) and enriches the concept map by adding new concepts and attributes.

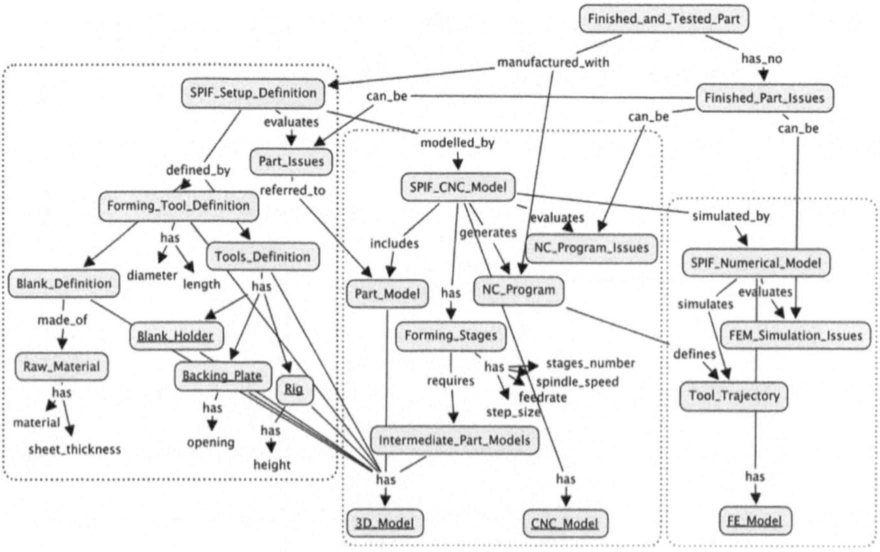

Fig. 6. Ontology definition for SPIF with concept maps.

Figure 6 depicts the concept map for the SPIF process. The focus question is: "How is a sheet part produced by SPIF?" The most general concepts are at the top of the diagram and can be described as follows: the *Finished and Tested Part* is *manufactured with* the *SPIF Setup Definition* and the *NC Program* and, given that the part has been already tested, it *has no Finished Part Issues*; the *SPIF Setup Definition* is *modelled by* a *SPIF CNC Model* in order to *generate* the *NC Program*; and the *Finished Part Issues can be* of different type: *Part Issues*, *NC Program Issues* or *FEM Simulation Issues*.

The concept map elements in Fig. 6 have been arranged inside dotted boxes to highlight three fields of knowledge of the proposed ontology. The former represents the definition of physical components of the *SPIF Setup Definition*: blank, forming tool, etc. The second group depicts the *SPIF CNC Model* to be developed in a CAD/CAM system to design the SPIF process and generate the *NC Program*. The latter represents the *SPIF Numerical Model* to simulate the *Tool Trajectory* and analyse the SPIF process in a FEA system to overcome any *FEM Simulation Issue*.

In the proposed methodology, a secondary class of the Data model is a class added to the concept map that was not included in the Scope model. Some secondary classes have been added to the concept map for SPIF to illustrate this concept, represented as boxes with underlined name in Fig. 6. For example, *Blank Holder*, *Backing Plate* and *Rig* were included as "children" of *Tools Definition*, see the lower left corner of Fig. 6. Actually, whether these classes are primary or secondary depends on the degree of detail of the Scope model. Indeed, the above secondary classes would be primary if the IDEF0 element *Tools Definition* of the Scope model would be decomposed into *Blank Holder*, *Backing Plate* and *Rig* in a similar way that *SPIF Setup Definition* (see Fig. 5) was decomposed into *Blank Definition*, *Tools Definition* and *Forming Tool Definition* in order to be related with different IDEF0 functions.

A valuable feature of the proposed methodology is the reuse of other ontologies, already existing or to be developed. The relationship between classes of the proposed ontology for SPIF and classes of other ontologies is implemented through secondary classes in the concept map. For instance, the following secondary classes in Fig. 6 aim to fulfil this purpose: *3D Model* and *CNC Model* represent the CAD and CAM models of CAD/CAM systems, respectively, and *FE Model* is used by FEA systems. The related ontologies as well as the data type of class attributes (integer, string, etc.) are set at a later stage of the proposed methodology. Class attributes are represented as simple labels at the end of arrows in Fig. 6.

5 Conclusions

A new methodology based on a 3-layer architecture has been proposed for modelling manufacturing systems. In this work the methodology has been applied to an innovative incremental sheet forming (SPIF) and the development of both system scope and ontology has been presented.

It can be concluded that designing the system scope model among all project participants is an efficient method to establish the starting point for development of both Ontology and Software Tools layers. Furthermore, the combination of more than one modelling technique allows to define a more robust ontology from different perspectives. In this work, IDEF0 diagrams and concept maps have been used to define a successful ontology for SPIF. Nevertheless, the proposed methodology is not limited to these two schemes of knowledge representation and could be replaced by others more suitable in future developments.

The current project is still under development and further work is required to evaluate the success of the proposed methodology. Future work includes the implementation of the Software Tools layer, the instantiation of real cases from the ontology model and the investigation of alternatives to computer modelling tools.

Acknowledgement. The authors would like to thank Ignacio Eguía, Jose Carlos Molina, Andrés Padillo and other Sevilla University colleagues, Julio Ortegón and other Cádiz University colleagues, Rebeca Arista, Tamara Borreguero and other AIRBUS colleagues, for their support and contribution during the development of this work.

References

1. Ramos, A.L., Ferreira, J.V., Barceló, J.: Model-based systems engineering: an emerging approach for modern systems. IEEE Trans. Syst. Man Cybern. Part C (Appl. Rev.) **42**(1), 101–111 (2012). https://doi.org/10.1109/TSMCC.2011.2106495
2. Holland, O.T.: Model-based systems engineering. In: Loper, M.L. (ed.) Modeling and Simulation in the Systems Engineering Life Cycle. SFMA, pp. 299–306. Springer, London (2015). https://doi.org/10.1007/978-1-4471-5634-5_23
3. D'Ambrosio, J., Soremekun, G.: Systems engineering challenges and MBSE opportunities for automotive system design. In: 2017 IEEE International Conference on Systems and Cybernetics (SMC), Banff, AB, Canada, p. 2075 (2017). https://doi.org/10.1109/smc.2017.8122925
4. Gómez, A., Ríos, J., Mas, F., Vizán, A.: Method and software application to assist in the conceptual design of aircraft final assembly lines. J. Manuf. Syst. **40**, 37–53 (2016). https://doi.org/10.1016/j.jmsy.2016.04.002
5. Mas, F., Rios, J., Menendez, J.L., Gomez, A.: A process-oriented approach to modeling the conceptual design of aircraft assembly lines. Int. J. Adv. Manuf. Technol. **67**(1–4), 771–784 (2013). https://doi.org/10.1007/s00170-012-4521-5
6. Mas, F., Oliva, M., Ríos, J., Gómez, A., Olmos, V., García, J.A.: PLM based approach to the industrialization of aeronautical assemblies. Procedia Eng. **132**, 1045–1052 (2015). https://doi.org/10.1016/j.proeng.2015.12.594
7. Mas, F., Racero, J., Oliva, O., Morales-Palma, D.: A preliminary methodological approach to Models for Manufacturing (MfM). In: Chiabert, P., Bouras, A., Noël, F., Ríos, J. (eds.) PLM 2018. IFIP AICT, vol. 540, pp. 273–283. Springer, Cham (2018). https://doi.org/10.1007/978-3-030-01614-2_25
8. Behera, A.K., Sousa, R.A., Ingarao, G., Oleksik, V.: Single point incremental forming: an assessment of the progress and technology trends from 2005 to 2015. J. Manuf. Process. **27**, 37–62 (2017). https://doi.org/10.1016/j.jmapro.2017.03.014
9. Centeno, G., Morales-Palma, D., Gonzalez-Perez-Somarriba, B., Bagudanch, I., Egea-Guerrero, J.J., Gonzalez-Perez, L.M., García-Romeu, M.L., Vallellano, C.: A functional methodology on the manufacturing of customized polymeric cranial prostheses from CAT using SPIF. Rapid Prototyp. J. **23**(4), 771–780 (2017). https://doi.org/10.1108/RPJ-02-2016-0031
10. Morales-Palma, D., Martínez-Donaire, A.J., Centeno, G., Vallellano, C.: Teaching experience for the virtualization of machine tools and simulation of manufacturing operations. Mater. Sci. Forum **853**, 79–84 (2016). https://doi.org/10.4028/www.scientific.net/MSF.853.79

11. Centeno, G., Martínez-Donaire, A.J., Bagudanch, I., Morales-Palma, D., Garcia-Romeu, M. L., Vallellano, C.: Revisiting formability and failure of AISI304 sheets in SPIF: experimental approach and numerical validation. Metals **7**, 531 (2017). https://doi.org/10.3390/met7120531
12. Morales-Palma, D., Borrego, M., Martínez-Donaire, A.J., Centeno, G., Vallellano, C.: Preliminary investigation on homogenization of the thickness distribution in hole-flanging by SPIF. Procedia Manuf. **13**, 124–131 (2017). https://doi.org/10.1016/j.promfg.2017.09.101
13. Borrego, M., Morales-Palma, D., Martínez-Donaire, A.J., Centeno, G., Vallellano, C.: Experimental study of hole-flanging by single-stage incremental sheet forming. J. Mater. Process. Technol. **237**, 320–330 (2016). https://doi.org/10.1016/j.jmatprotec.2016.06.026
14. NIST: Integration Definition for Function Modeling (IDEF0). Computer Systems Laboratory of the National Institute of Standards and Technology, December 1993. http://www.idef.com/wp-content/uploads/2016/02/idef0.pdf. Accessed March 2018

Application of Optimization in the Early Stages of Product Development, Using a Small UAV Case Study

M. P. Gusev(✉), S. M. Nikolaev, I. K. Uzhinsky, D. I. Padalitsa, and E. R. Mozhenkov

Skolkovo Institute of Science and Technology, Moscow, Russia
m.gusev@skoltech.ru
https://www.skoltech.ru/en/

Abstract. Innovative product development involves a lot of tools, methods, and approaches to create a better product faster and satisfying customer's need. Two wide spread approaches are Product Lifecycle Management (PLM) and Model-Based Systems Engineering (MBSE). However, there are not many software tools, combining methodologies PLM MBSE; one can mention LMS System Synthesis software, now is actively developing. It is used to create system models which include functional models able to describe system behavior in multiphysics domain. Therefore, when the system model of a product is multidisciplinary it's not obvious what the parameters values describe the optimal state of the system. For these reasons, it is vital to apply multidisciplinary optimization techniques with the specific tools to calculate appropriate parameters of the developed system in the early stages of product development. This research is devoted to different optimization tools application, such as pSeven and Optimus Noesis, to the numerical models constituting digital twin for a small Unmanned Aerial Vehicle (UAV). The results of this research, specifically formulation of the optimization problems, detailed numerical models and the calculations results, are presented in this paper. The main idea is that optimization should be applied not as additional tool for separate numerical models, but one has to apply it as a powerful means along with PLM and MBSE tools in order to ensure that the product will meet all requirements and reduce time-to-market.

Keywords: Optimization · Product Lifecycle Management
Model-based systems engineering · Small UAV · Digital twin

1 Introduction

Innovative product development requires a lot of software tools which allows to create a different representation of a developed product. All this software creates a lot of data which is needed to manage and Product Lifecycle Management

Published by Springer Nature Switzerland AG 2018.
P. Chiabert et al. (Eds.): PLM 2018, IFIP AICT 540, pp. 294–303, 2018.
https://doi.org/10.1007/978-3-030-01614-2_27

(PLM) platform performs this function. In order to realize product to a market in a faster and proper way: PLM approach [1] combines with Model Based System Engineering (MBSE) methodology [2,3]. In this case, 1D numerical models which describe product behavior are developed in early stages of a product development, which allows to check all the requirements for the product. Also, 3D Computer-Aided Design (CAD) and Computer-Aided Engineering (CAE) models represent different level of the system, such as the geometric design, and various analytical perspectives such as performance and reliability. In order to meet all requirements in a faster and easy way, it is proposed to implement optimization approach to all numerical models and to different stages of a product development.

All stages of a product development can be represented by V-diagram [4], shown in Fig. 1.

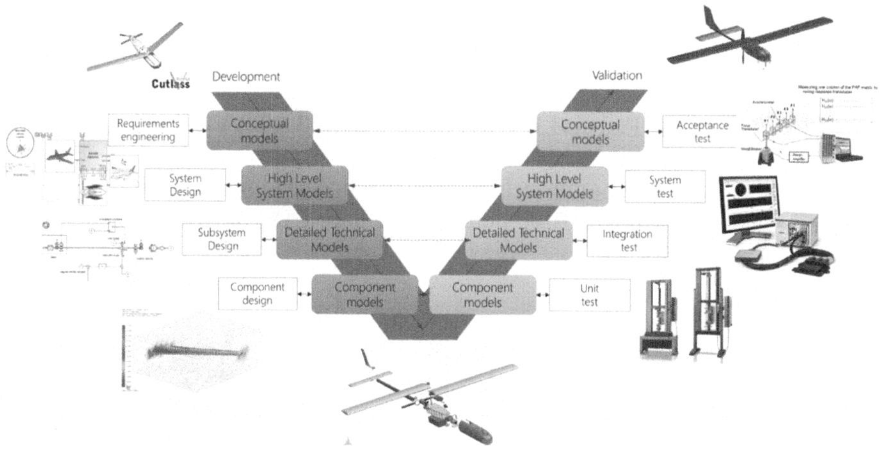

Fig. 1. V-diagram in product development

According to V-diagram, the product development starts from the requirements, conceptual design and system design. Researchers develop a lot of frameworks based on the System Model Language (SysML) on the level of system design [2,5,6]. These frameworks include different structures and seems to be not appropriate to all variety of real product cases. The one model based system modelling tool is LMS System Synthesis for now is actively developing [7]. System Synthesis is an architecture-driven approach for model-based systems engineering which allows engineers to reduce model design effort thanks to traceability and reusability of simulation models for different types of analyses such as requirements analysis or "what if" analysis. Models created in System Synthesis tool is linked with subsystems or functional model which may be created in LMS Amesim software or another tool. The architecture of a product is determined on the level of system design and after the choosing of architecture, it is proposed to apply optimization to narrow the limits of various parameters of the system. The example of a such approach will be presented in next sections of this paper.

After the stages of system and functional level design, the component design of a product is performed. On the stage of component design the parametric or topology optimization of specific part of a product is usually applying. For example, for aircraft a lot of research is devoted to structural optimization [8–10], because the aircraft has high degree of reliability and at the same time should have a minimum weight. For all other products, it is important to apply optimization approach in order to reduce the number of testing and decrease time to market.

This paper aims to present optimization approach on different levels of product development based on the Unmanned Aerial Vehicle (UAV) development case study. UAV was developed according to V-diagram and optimization was performed to the numerical models of a UAV on system model to determine the angle of launch, on the functional level to determine the launch system parameters and on the component level to obtain structural parameters of a wing. The presentation of the material in the paper follows the sequence indicated above.

2 Case Study: Tube-Deployable Small UAV

Applying of optimization approach to the system level and structural design is considered on the example of tube-deployable small UAV, presented in the Fig. 2.

Fig. 2. Concept of launch system and tube deployable small UAV

UAV has wings, which are may folded and unfolded. In initial state, when UAV is inside the tube the wings are folded. The pressure inside tube creates the force which acts to UAV. The force accelerates the UAV and it flies out of the tube (Fig. 2 left). Tube has a given angle of a slope. Then the wings open for a certain time and the plane gains altitude.

The UAV consists of four subsystems: engine, accumulator, launch subsystem and flight dynamics. The system model (Fig. 3) for UAV was developed in LMS System Synthesis software to describe how each subsystem works.

System model also includes four subsystems: Accumulator, Engine, Launch and Flight Dynamics. Accumulator generates required power, the engine transforms electric energy into mechanical energy, mechanical energy of a motor transforms to the ability of flight in flight dynamics subsystem, and Launch subsystem produces the mechanical energy required to fly out UAV from the tube. There are links between subsystems, which transmit energy in different forms. For UAV case study each subsystem was built in LMS Amesim software (Fig. 4).

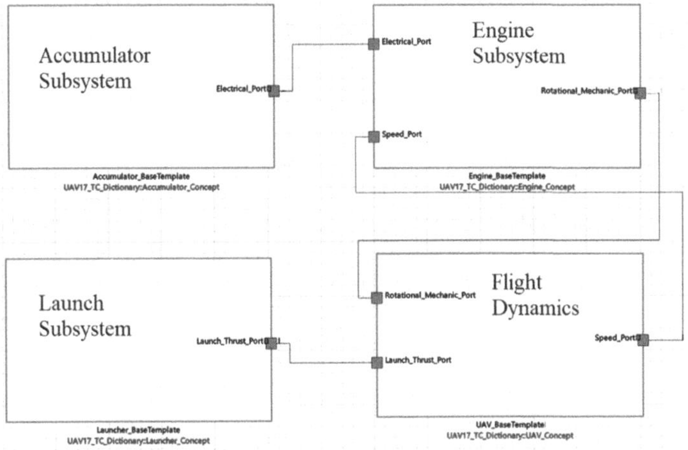

Fig. 3. System model for a small UAV in LMS System Synthesis software

3 Architecture Choice

Different simulations were performed based on the system model. Simulation performed in System Synthesis solves the problem of architecture choice. Simulation allows to choose appropriate Engine Subsystem for UAV case study. Based on the simulation, the problem of appropriate angle of a launch system (Fig. 2) was solved. It is obvious, that the incorrect angle of a launch system can lead to the improper take off of the aircraft.

The altitude dependency over time for two architectures with different Engine subsystems is presented in Fig. 5. Two different engines are modeled, which are on the market. The difference between two engines lies in the coefficients, such as armature winding resistance and armature winding inductance.

The altitude climbing is better for Engine 1, and the 60° is a better angle for all architectures as seen from the Fig. 5. Therefore, for further research architecture with Engine 2 was chosen. The next step is applying optimization to clarify the exact value of an angle to achieve maximum altitude.

4 Optimization of a Launch Angle

After choosing the rational variant of architecture by analyzing Fig. 5, it is required to calculate and set the optimal angle of launch in order to achieve

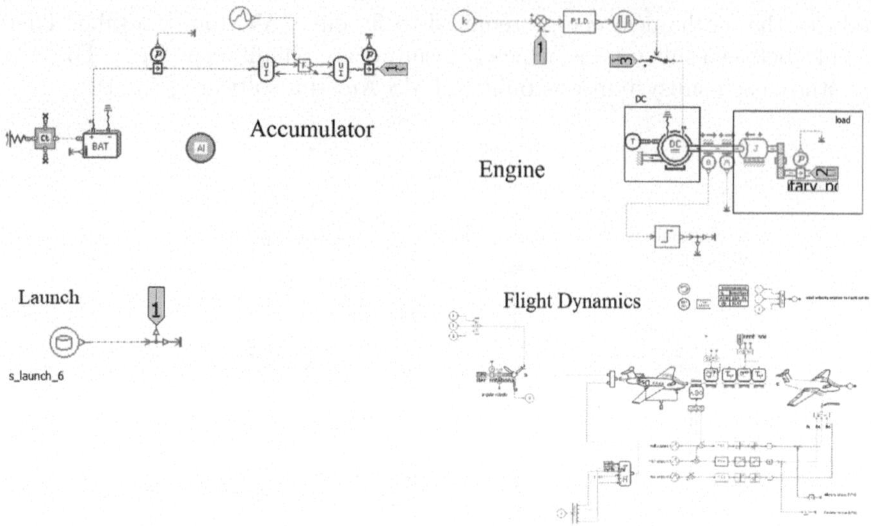

Fig. 4. Subsystems of a system model for a small UAV in LMS Amesim software

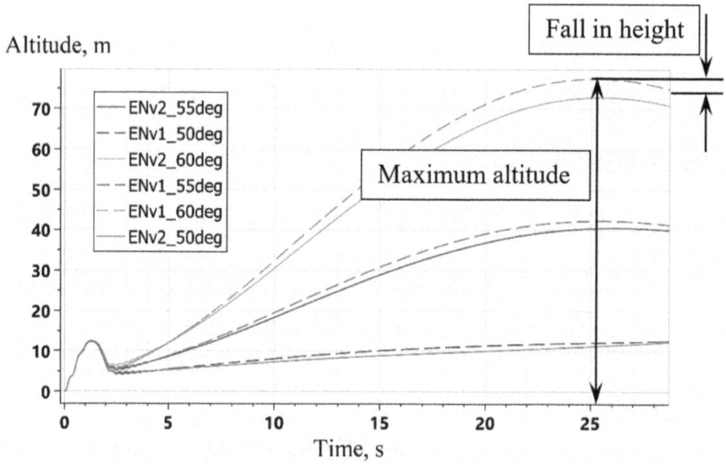

Fig. 5. Altitude dependency for two different engines and angles of launch

maximum altitude and minimize fall in height after the point of maximum altitude, Fig. 5. Therefore, the statement of optimization problem can express as follows: to find launch angle which maximizes maximum altitude and minimize fall in height.

This problem was solved in Noesis Optimus software. The outline of optimization is presented on Fig. 6.

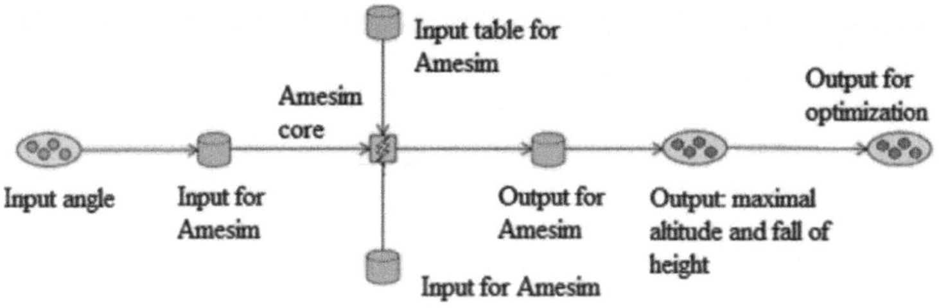

Fig. 6. Outline of optimization for search optimal angle

Blocks in outline are Input angle: the only angle, which varies from 40 to 80°; Amesim block, which has its own input and output blocks and the output block.

The results of optimization are presented below on Fig. 7.

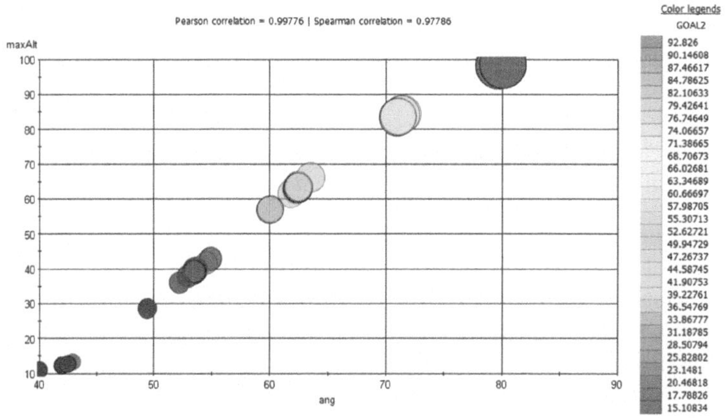

Fig. 7. Results of angle optimization (Color figure online)

Figure 7 shows the dependency of the maximal altitude over angle. The size and color of a bubble represent fall of height after the maximal altitude. Increasing the maximum height leads to an increase in the fall (Goal2 in Fig. 7). Thus, when the problem has two or more objectives, the researcher chooses a more appropriate variant. In this case, the optimal solution is 62° of the angle which leads to 63.3 m maximum altitude and 46.5 m of fall in height. It should be noted, that to avoid falling, it is necessary to work out the elevator.

This was the example of applying optimization on the system level and launch angle was determined as one of the important parameters in order to achieve better altitude gaining. Another example of applying optimization on the system level is parameters determination for the pneumatic tube.

5 Optimization of Parameters for a Launch System

The problem is to find better parameters for pneumatic tube (Fig. 2), which capable to provide flying out UAV and achieve for UAV a flight speed no less than 30 m/s. 30 m/s is speed when UAV has appropriate lifting force.

A mathematical model for pneumatic tube was developed in LMS Amesim software to solve the indicated problem. The outline of a model is presented in Fig. 8.

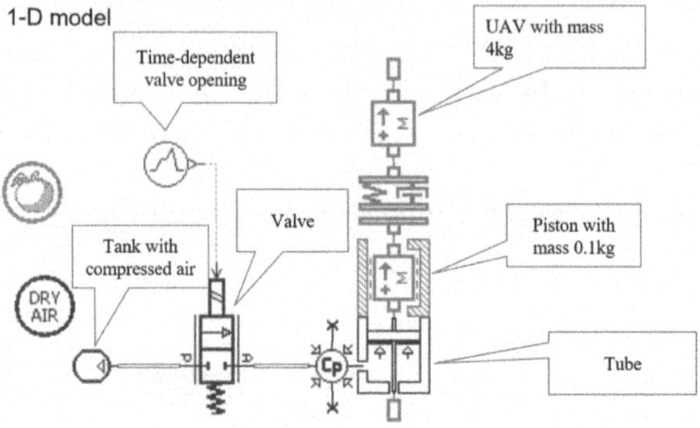

Fig. 8. 1-D model of a pneumatic launch system

Seven parameters need to be determined for presented model. Table 1 represents the list of these parameters and the limits of their variation.

Internal optimization tool of LMS Amesim software was chosen to solve the problem and Generic algorithm was the method of optimization. Optimal solution for this problem is on the Table 1 and some graphical results are presented in Fig. 9. They are length and pressure over iteration.

It should be noted that such a large number of iteration in the optimum search (Fig. 9) is caused by a large number of parameters, and by the choice of the

Table 1. Bounds for initial parameters and results of the optimization of a launch system.

Parameters	Lower boundary	Upper boundary	Optimal value
Length of tube	0.7 m	2 m	1.9 m
Tank volume	2 L	10 L	9.9 L
Tank pressure	2 bars	10 bars	8.1 bars
Interior tube diameter	20 mm	100 mm	48.1 mm
Valve opening time	0.02 s	0.1 s	0.093 s
Valve interior diameter	15 mm	45 mm	41.4 mm
Pipes interior diameter	10 mm	50 mm	43.9 mm

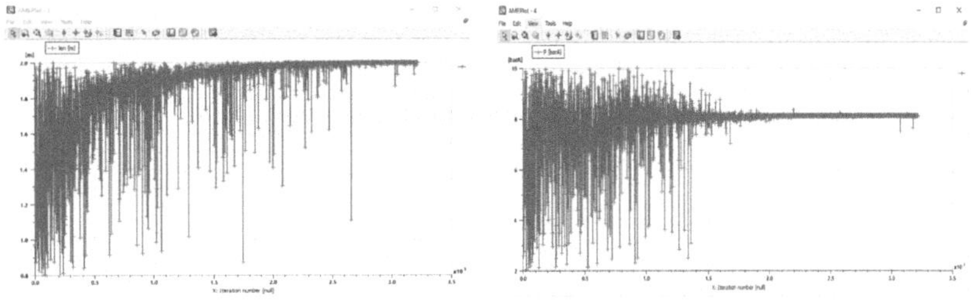

Fig. 9. Length of tube and pressure over iteration, during the optimization process

genetic algorithm as an optimization method. Another appropriate optimization algorithms in LMS Amesim led to local minima, but a global one was required. This was the reason for choosing a long-term processing genetic algorithm.

Example above illustrates optimization on the functional level with help of specific optimization tool. It is not so crucial what tool to use for optimization but it is very important to use the optimization approach for all significant numerical models of a system to accelerate the process of product design. The next section will be devoted to structural optimization of a wing.

6 Structural Optimization of UAV Wing

It should be noted, that for UAV case study the first prototype was produced from PLA plastic. Therefore, the parts were designed directly for 3D printing. The internal volume of the wing was filled with the honey structure as seen from Fig. 10.

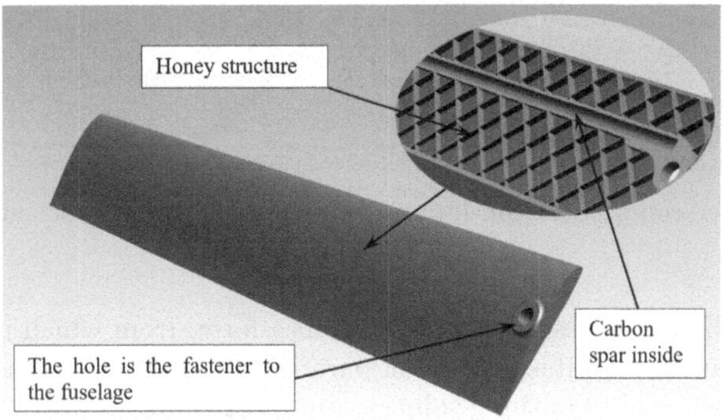

Fig. 10. Structure of a wing for small UAV

In the wing, force structure is carbon spar. The plastic around the spar is the place where the spar is located. In this task, the mass of plastic around the spar was optimized. Figure 11 represents force structure of a wing.

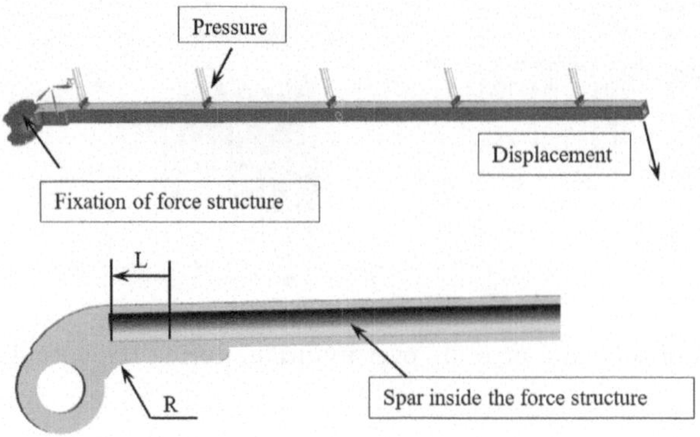

Fig. 11. Force structure inside the wing

The input parameters for optimization are L and R (Fig. 11). L is the distance of increase the spar towards hole. R is fillet radius. There are two objectives in optimization: minimum of a displacement for the tip of force structure and minimum of a stress. The problem was solved in pSeven 6.12 software. Figure 12 presents the results of optimization.

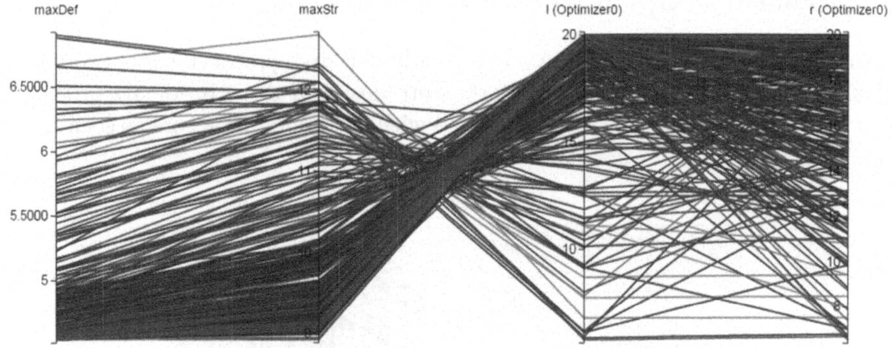

Fig. 12. Parallel coordinates for input parameters L, R and for output maxDef, maxStress

Figure 12 shows results of optimization in a form, from which it can be seen the solution: maximal values of input parameters lead to minimal objectives. The values which lead to optimal solution are L = 20 mm, and R = 20 mm. Under these conditions the face of the composite spar approaches the center of the hole and minimum displacement and stress occur.

7 Summary and Outlook

The central objective of the research was to demonstrate an integration of optimization approach with PLM and MBSE methodologies by means of applying optimization to small UAV case study. Meaning integration is followed: data in the form of numerical models is taken from PLM platform, then the important parameters are chosen and optimization is performed. Along with that, the requirements are checked and the optimization helps to meet these requirements in a faster way. Despite this tube deployable small UAV is not an industrial case and not all aspects of modeling and design of the UAV is presented in this paper, but optimization approach is supposed to be expanded towards the development of any innovative product. This approach implies optimization on the system, functional and structural numerical models over the process of product development and implementation of the optimization decreases the time of product development. The essence of the optimization approach technique is the appropriate choice of parameters and numerical models to optimize on each level of product development. Therefore, the combination of PLM, MBSE and Optimization approach creates strong methodology in which models are the core of product development, the optimization precise the models and the PLM allows to manage data efficiently.

References

1. Danesi, F., et al.: P4LM: a methodology for product lifecycle management. Comput. Ind. **59**(2–3), 304–317 (2008). https://doi.org/10.1016/j.compind.2007.06.013
2. Vosgien, T., Nguyen Van, T., Jankovic, M., Eynard, B., Bocquet, J.-C.: Towards model-based system engineering for simulation-based design in product data management systems. In: Rivest, L., Bouras, A., Louhichi, B. (eds.) PLM 2012. IAICT, vol. 388, pp. 612–622. Springer, Heidelberg (2012). https://doi.org/10.1007/978-3-642-35758-9_55
3. Fisher, A., et al.: 3.1. 1 model lifecycle management for MBSE. In: INCOSE International Symposium, vol. 24. No. 1 (2014). https://doi.org/10.1002/j.2334-5837.2014.tb03145.x
4. Tahera, K., Eckert, C., Earl, C.: Highlighting the importance of testing in the product development process (2015)
5. Peak, R.S., et al.: 9.3. 2 Simulation-based design using SysML part 1: a parametrics primer. In: INCOSE International Symposium, vol. 17. No. 1 (2007)
6. https://www.plm.automation.siemens.com/en/products/lms/imagine-lab/system-synthesis/
7. Rihtaršic, J., Žavbi, R., Duhovnik, J.: Sophy-tool for structural synthesis of conceptual technical systems. In: The 11th International Design Conference on DS 60: Proceedings of DESIGN 2010, Dubrovnik, Croatia (2010)
8. Chase, N., et al.: Structural optimization of composite aircraft. In: 12th AIAA Aviation Technology, Integration, and Operations (ATIO) Conference and 14th AIAA/ISSMO Multidisciplinary Analysis and Optimization Conference (2012)
9. Chedrik, V., Tuktarov, S.: Structural design of aircraft wing based on topology and global-local optimization. In: 11th World Congress on Structural and Multidisciplinary Optimization.-Sydney, Australia (2015)
10. Kachel, S.: Optimization of wing parameters to achieve minimum weight at defined aerodynamic loads. J. Theor. Appl. Mech. **51**, 159–170 (2013). May 2018

Modeling Manufacturing Resources: An Ontological Approach

Emilio M. Sanfilippo[1(✉)], Sergio Benavent[4], Stefano Borgo[2], Nicola Guarino[2], Nicolas Troquard[3], Fernando Romero[4], Pedro Rosado[4], Lorenzo Solano[5], Farouk Belkadi[1], and Alain Bernard[1]

[1] ECN, Laboratory of Digital Sciences of Nantes, UMR CNRS 6004, Nantes, France
emilio.sanfilippo@ls2n.fr
[2] Laboratory for Applied Ontology ISTC-CNR, Trento, Italy
[3] Free University of Bozen-Bolzano, Bolzano, Italy
[4] Universitat Jaume I, Castellón, Spain
[5] Universitat Politècnica de València, Valencia, Spain

Abstract. Resource management is at the core of different manufacturing tasks, which need to be seamlessly integrated to optimize production in manufacturing environments. The development of knowledge-based systems led to the use of ontologies to systematically organize data. Unfortunately, ontologies for resource knowledge representation lack maturity and often rely on context-dependent modeling choices. As a result, the notion of manufacturing resource is treated in disparate, non-homogeneous ways at the expenses of communication and application systems interoperability. The purpose of the paper is to lay down a conceptual framework on manufacturing resources based on ontology engineering principles. By the end of the paper we will see how different approaches can be harmonized with the proposed approach.

Keywords: Manufacturing resource · Ontology · Process planning

1 Introduction

Management of manufacturing resources is of primary concern for manufacturing enterprises. Resources have indeed to be managed for various purposes like process or resource planning, resource scheduling, and work improvement study, just to mention a few tasks. As a consequence, enterprises require models to handle resource information in a uniform and transparent manner to smooth data exchange across the actors involved in the manufacturing chain.

Various data modeling standards, conceptual models, and ontologies have been proposed over the years for this goal. In particular, the use of the latter is increasing in application domains that require heterogeneous data to be consistently organized and exchanged while preserving their original meaning. Examples are Product Lifecycle Management (PLM) systems [1], but also emerging paradigms like Cyber Physical

Published by Springer Nature Switzerland AG 2018.
P. Chiabert et al. (Eds.): PLM 2018, IFIP AICT 540, pp. 304–313, 2018.
https://doi.org/10.1007/978-3-030-01614-2_28

Production Systems (CPPS) [2], Smart-Sensitive-Sustainable (S3) Manufacturing [3], and Cloud Manufacturing [4].

Several information models addressing such domains have been developed, each one with its own specific view and application context. Consequently, various and not well-aligned modeling frameworks co-exist, a fact that complicates the efficient interoperation of organizations and information systems [5]. This situation has stimulated the creation of the international effort called *Industrial Ontologies Foundry* (IOF)[1] aimed at the design of a library of open-source ontologies to facilitate the interaction between applications and communities. 'Resource' is one of the key notions being analyzed within the IOF, which calls for a conceptual clarification despite the plethora of models proposed over the years.

The aim of this work is to contribute to this clarification with the ultimate purpose of supporting the development of an ontology for manufacturing resources based on principled modeling choices. Instead of presenting a computational ontology, we provide here a reference conceptual framework that can be used to both harmonizing existing models and develop domain ontologies tuned on specific requirements.

As a modelling notation, we shall rely on OntoUML to convey *graphically* the core meanings of the notions at stake. OntoUML is a UML extension for ontology-driven conceptual modeling [6] that has been successfully employed in a number of industrial projects in several different domains[2]. Thanks to its formal semantics, OntoUML diagrams can be straightforwardly translated (with some loss of expressivity) in a computational language like the Web Ontology Language[3] (OWL).

The paper is structured as follows. In Sect. 2 we give an overview of the state of the art on resource modeling. In Sect. 3 we analyze the notion of manufacturing resource and propose a conceptual analysis based on ontological theories like [6, 7]. Section 4 shows how the analysis can be extended to integrate resource classifications based on multiple criteria. Section 5 concludes the paper by addressing the advantages and limits of our work.

2 Manufacturing Resource Modeling: A Conceptual Overview

The interpretation of what can be considered as manufacturing resource changes considerably across the literature. According to the standard MANDATE [8], a resource is "any device, tool and means, except raw material and final product components, at the disposal of the enterprise to produce goods and services". The standard hence distinguishes what is transformed during a manufacturing activity (e.g., raw materials) from its final outcomes (products), and the physical means (machines, etc.) that bring about the transformation. From the definition, only the latter – humans

[1] http://www.industrialontologies.org.

[2] http://www.menthor.net/ontouml.html.

[3] https://www.w3.org/TR/owl2-overview/.

included – are manufacturing resources. Differently, other proposals identify incoming material and/or transformed entities as resources as well [9, 10].[4]

Several approaches rely explicitly on the relationship with (manufacturing) processes to characterize the notion of resource (e.g., [12–14]), while others complement this approach with the modeling of capabilities [14, 15]. According to ISO 15704 [16], for example, a resource is "an enterprise entity that provides some or all of the capabilities required by the execution of an enterprise activity and/or business process." Hence, the idea is that a resource can be employed for manufacturing because of its capabilities or – more generally – a*ttributes* [17] that are relevant to execute the desired processes. This idea leads us to think of resources in tight connection with application contexts, since one and the same resource can be ascribed with different attributes in relation to the process where it is employed.

The diversity concerning the conceptualization of manufacturing resources has a radical impact on how data is organized; it can also hamper data exchange if not properly handled. For example, by relying on MANDATE, reference to capabilities and processes is not required, differently from the case in which data is structured on the basis of ISO 15704. Additionally, if one takes seriously the *contextual nature* of resources, it should be possible for the same entity to be and not to be a resource across different contexts, as suggested in [12, 18]. Current approaches have not treated contextual knowledge in a systematic manner. This easily leads to undesired interpretations, since persons, materials or tools, among others, are classified as resources independently of the contexts where they may happen to be in.

In the next section we dig into the analysis of manufacturing resources. By the end of the paper, we show how the proposed framework can deal with the diversity of views found in the literature.

3 Foundational Aspects of Manufacturing Resources

In order to represent manufacturing resources in a manner that is coherent with both ontological and engineering knowledge, we first need to introduce some general notions, which are then specified to the manufacturing domain.

Following existing standards [19] and ontologies [10, 20], we hold a basic distinction between (*physical) objects* and *processes*, e.g., drillers and drilling operations. The former are primarily extended in space, whereas the latter unfold through time. *Participation* is the most general link between objects and processes. Objects, but also processes, are characterized by qualities (*attributes* in the terms of [17]) like weights, which are said to *inhere* in objects (processes). Some objects are made of material, while others lack material constitution. Among the latter, *information objects* stand for the immaterial content of technical documents, e.g., Computer-Aided Design (CAD) models encoded on a physical support. For instance, when two computer files are copies of the same CAD model, in our framework this means that they share the

[4] Recall that several standards, e.g., ISO 10303 AP-238, ISO 14649 (STEP-NC), ISO 13399, and ASME B5.59-2, deal with (CNC) manufacturing resources (see [11]).

same information object. Accordingly, an information object can be encoded in multiple supports, for instance, different computer files.

With these basic notions, we now dig into the OntoUML diagram showed in Fig. 1.[5] The idea is to consider a manufacturing resource as an entity that is related to a manufacturing process plan because it is relevant for some goal specified in the plan. We shall see throughout the section how this is represented in the model.

For our purposes, we understand agents as (physical) objects with sensors, actuators, and the capability of acting on the environment by adopting plans to reach some goals. Goals are intentional states inhering in agents and referring to desired states of the world. We assume that agents have at least one goal,[6] whereas plans are ways (strategies) to achieve goals. For example, if an agent has the goal of creating a table, this goal is satisfied in all states of the world where a physical table, bearing the qualities desired by the agent, exists. To achieve one of such states, a suitable plan must be realized.

Manufacturing plans (*MfgPlan*) are information objects (like workflows) that specify the sequence of actions to be performed to realize a goal. We assume that manufacturing goals are goals such that a manufacturing plan exists for them. So we assume a relation *has-plan* between manufacturing goals and manufacturing plans such that for a manufacturing goal there is at least a plan, and vice versa.

The class *MfgPlanRealization*, subsumed by *Process*, refers to the actual manufacturing processes that realize manufacturing plans. A plan may not be always realized; this is why the multiplicities of the relation *realizes* from *MfgPlanRealization* to *MfgPlan* is *0..** on the side of the former class.

For the purposes of this paper, an important part of a manufacturing plan is the description of the various resources to be used to realize the plan. We introduce therefore the class *MfgResourceDescription,* whose instances are proper parts of a *MfgPlan.* For each *MfgPlan*, at least one *MfgResourceDescription* must exist. Like manufacturing plans, manufacturing resource descriptions are information objects

We are now in the position to define a manufacturing resource as something that *satisfies* a *MfgResourceDescription* that is part of a *MfgPlan*. A resource is *relevant-for* a specific plan if and only if it satisfies a resource description that is part of that plan (the *relevant-for* relation appearing in Fig. 1 is therefore a *derived relation*). The notion of *satisfaction* of a description has been discussed in [21], and will be taken here as a primitive. In general, a given entity may satisfy or not a resource description depending on its qualities. Within manufacturing resources, we distinguish between physical objects and amounts of matter, since these are the most general classes of entities to which one commonly refers (see Sect. 2).

An instance of *MfgResource* has to satisfy at least one instance *MfgResourceDescription.* On the contrary, a *MfgResourceDescription* may have no resources that satisfy it. Note that a resource may be *relevant-for* a certain plan even if

[5] Classes with names prefixed by *Mfg* or *MR* are specific to manufacturing. *Mfg* stands for manufacturing, *MR* for manufacturing resource. Classes in green are taken from [21].

[6] The *has-goal* relation between *MfgAgent* and *MfgGoal* is of the same type of relation holding between qualities and, e.g., physical objects or processes. For simplicity, these latter relations are not showed in Fig. 1.

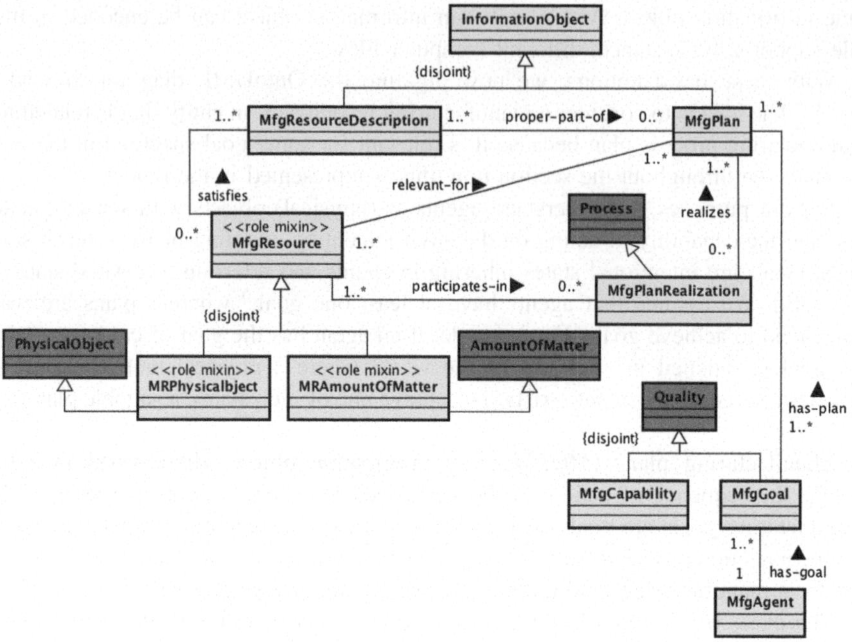

Fig. 1. Core elements for the conceptual representation of manufacturing resources

it does not *participate* in its realization. For instance, we typically require that all the resources that are relevant for a certain plan must exist (and be *available*, see below) before a realization process starts. On the contrary, entities of different kinds (such as air or dust particles) may actually participate in a process without being considered as resources. In conclusion, we can see resources as entities such that, in virtue of their qualities, are considered as *relevant* for a manufacturing plan and may therefore play the role in manufacturing processes by participating to certain activities.

As a final comment, let us highlight the *role* nature of resources that emerges from the analysis of the state of the art.[7] In ontology engineering, roles are properties which are always *contingent,* being satisfied only within certain contexts [6, 7, 21]. Generalizing, the idea is that talking of manufacturing resources means referring to entities that are primarily classified by *non-role* classes and that may play certain roles when employed for manufacturing. This is why in Fig. 1 *MRPhysicalObject* and MR*AmountOfMatter*, referring to object and amount of material resources, are subsumed by both *MfgResource* (role class) and *PhysicalObject* and *AmountOfMatter*, respectively, the latter two being non-role classes. With this approach, based on [6, 7], the conceptual model provides the flexibility to isolate manufacturing resources in their contexts. It is important to stress that the attribution of a (manufacturing) resource role

[7] By looking at Fig. 1, *MfgResource, MRPhysicalObject* and MRAmountOfMatter are marked with the stereotypes *role mixin* to make explicit their role nature. A *role mixin* class has instances of different types [6], e.g., persons, products, etc.

is strictly dependent on a process plan. By looking at Fig. 1, the relation *relevant-for* between *MfgResource* and *MfgPlan* means that a manufacturing resource role is necessary to achieve some goal specified in the plan.

4 High-Level Classification of Manufacturing Resources

We now distinguish between different manufacturing resource roles according to both ontological and engineering criteria. In particular, the classification is based on three orthogonal principles: (i) agentivity, (ii) mode of deployment, and (iii) control. The classification is not meant to be exhaustive; it rather provides a high-level taxonomy that can be extended to cover specific scenarios. For simplicity, we refer only to physical resources, whereas their corresponding descriptions can be easily introduced.

First, we distinguish between *agentive* and *non-agentive* resources, depending on whether the entity ascribed with the resource role is an agent or not. A standard milling machine is an example of non-agentive resource; a milling machine embedded with a cyber-physical architecture may be an example of agentive resource.[8]

Second, in line with the engineering literature, we want to make sense of the distinction between (i) resources that 'passively' undergo manufacturing processes, e.g., planks of wood, (ii) resources that 'actively' act on the former, e.g., milling machines, and (iii) resources that result from manufacturing processes, e.g., products. Taking inspiration from IDEF0[9] and previous works [10, 14], these correspond in our approach to *input*, *mechanism*, and *output manufacturing resources*, respectively. Differently from the agent *vs* non-agent dichotomy, the latter notions are not disjoint, since one object can act on itself, i.e., it can be input, mechanism, and output in the same process like a robot changing its configuration.

Third, we distinguish between *allocated*, *dedicated*, and *available* manufacturing resources, which refer to temporary states. Allocated resources are assigned and employed in manufacturing processes (plan realizations). Dedicated resources are assigned to processes, which may not however employ them. The fact that a resource is dedicated to an individual process p implies that it cannot be assigned to another process occurring at the same time of p. Available resources are present (in a factory), although they are neither allocated nor dedicated. An example is a screwdriver available at the shop floor meaning that any agent in the shop floor could use it if necessary.

Since the classification criteria are orthogonal, they can be (consistently) combined. Figure 2 shows the extension of the class *MfgResource* with the classes presented above,[10] whereas Table 1 suggests some examples at the intersection between the agentivity and mode of deployment criteria.

The classification presented in Fig. 2 can be used as high-level taxonomy to integrate multiple classifications. For instance, following [13], mechanism resources may be further specialized into *primary* and *auxiliary* resources to emphasize the

---

[8] It is assumed that only objects can be agentive in our ontology; amounts of matter cannot.

[9] http://www.idef.com/.

[10] The relationships *input-of*, *output-of*, and *mechanism-of* specialize *participates*.

Table 1. Intersection between agentivity and mode of deployment

	Agentive resource	Non-agentive resource
Input resource	Drilling robot	Plank of wood
Mechanism resource	Employee	Cutting tool
Output resource	Drilling robot equipped with drill bit	Table

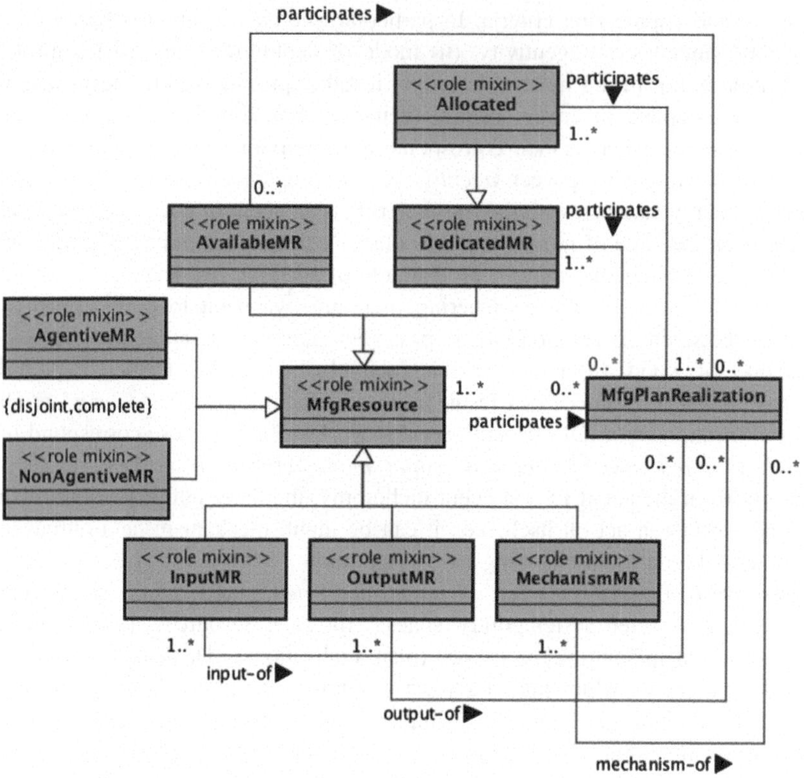

Fig. 2. High-level taxonomy of manufacturing resources

distinction between resources "that are in charge of executing operations", and resources "that are defined in relation to primary resources that employ them", respectively. In Industry 4.0 contexts [2], the classification of resources with a cyber-physical architecture plays a fundamental role, and different classes of cyber-physical systems (CPS) can be distinguished because the characteristics that must be shown for each level of abstraction may be different [22]. Also, for specific application domains, the taxonomy may be extended to cover, e.g., machining or additive manufacturing resources, among others.

5 Discussion and Conclusions

The conceptualization of manufacturing resources presented in the paper provides a general framework for their representation in application ontologies and data models for manufacturing. As said, our purpose was not the proposal of an ontology for computational applications. Rather, we presented a conceptual analysis with the purpose of making clear the properties that manufacturing resources have to satisfy independently from specific application requirements. The proposed framework gives a high-level perspective on manufacturing resources, and needs therefore to be extended to cover specific domain knowledge. The generality of the proposal makes it suitable to harmonize various views under the same umbrella, which has therefore the potentiality of acting as integration schema across multiple sources. Consider, e.g., the notion of resource in MANDATE [8] that, as we saw in Sect. 2, is restricted to what we call mechanisms, differently from the approaches in [10, 12] which cover products (outcomes) and raw materials (inputs), too. At the current state, these models are not interoperable, whereas their alignment to our ontology can enable their smooth interaction. From this perspective, the ontology can be used to compare various approaches and to assess their (conceptual) similarities and differences.

Additionally, differently from the state of the art, the proposed framework allows one to consider explicitly the *contextual dimension* of manufacturing resource classes, an approach that is coherent with both ontological and engineering knowledge. Consider, e.g., the specific milling machine *mch_id21*. From an ontological perspective, *mch_id21* is an artifact, i.e., an object intentionally designed and created to satisfy customers' needs. For manufacturing purposes, we want to say that *mch_id21* can be a mechanism resource *if* employed to perform certain processes. This means that *mch_id21* is an artifact for its very nature, whereas it is considered as a mechanism resource only with respect to certain manufacturing contexts. Hence, if *mch_id21* is never considered as relevant with respect to a manufacturing goal, it is never a resource, while it remains a machine with specific qualities and capabilities. The same reasoning applies to human resources, among others.

The proposed approach has interesting consequences from a modeling perspective. First, objects (and amounts of matter) can assume different resource roles within and across manufacturing processes and organizations. For example, one and the same machining tool can be the outcome resource of process p_1 and the mechanism resource of process p_2 occurring after p_1. Also, as previously seen, nothing prevents the same object to participate consistently as input, mechanism, and output resource in the same process. Second, by using our approach, one can revise models like, for instance, that in [17], where classes like *Person*, *Tool*, and *Material* are subsumed by *Resource*, to make them ontologically more tenable and, in turn, more reusable. Indeed, once we take *Resource* as a role, the taxonomical link between these classes cannot hold, since it would lead to the undesired classification of instances of the former classes as being always instances of *Resource*. Differently, our ontology allows referring to, e.g., tools independently from the resource role they may have in manufacturing processes, hence to classify them as resources only when needed.

Further work on our proposal is necessary to consolidate the approach with respect to both ontological modeling principles and engineering application scenarios. For example, a deeper analysis of resources' capabilities is necessary to establish a stronger link with processes. Also, even though our OntoUML model can be straightforwardly translated into computational languages like OWL, further work is required to a more expressive ontology in formal languages like first-order or common logics; these would allow exploring the semantic of the employed terms in a broader manner to check coherence with respect to the engineering domain.

References

1. El Kadiri, S., Kiritsis, D.: Ontologies in the context of product lifecycle management: state of the art literature review. Int. J. Prod. Res. **53**(18), 5657–5668 (2015). https://doi.org/10.1080/00207543.2015.1052155
2. Monostori, L., et al.: Cyber-physical systems in manufacturing. CIRP Ann. **65**(2), 621–641 (2016). https://doi.org/10.1016/j.cirp.2016.06.005
3. Weichhart, G., Molina, A., Chen, D., Whitman, L.E., Vernadat, F.: Challenges and current developments for sensing, smart and sustainable enterprise systems. Comput. Ind. **79**, 34–46 (2016). https://doi.org/10.1016/j.compind.2015.07.002
4. Lu, Y., Morris, K.C., Frechette, S.: Current standards landscape for smart manufacturing systems. Natl. Inst. Stand. Technol. NISTIR **8107**, 22–28 (2016). https://doi.org/10.6028/NIST.IR.8107
5. Chungoora, N., et al.: A model-driven ontology approach for manufacturing system interoperability and knowledge sharing. Comput. Ind. **64**(4), 392–401 (2013). https://doi.org/10.1016/j.compind.2013.01.003
6. Guizzardi, G.: Ontological foundations for structural conceptual models. Twente University (2005)
7. Guarino, N., Welty, C.A.: An overview of OntoClean. In: Staab, S., Studer, R. (eds.) Handbook on Ontologies, pp. 201–220. Springer, Heidelberg (2009). https://doi.org/10.1007/978-3-540-92673-3_9
8. Industrial Automation Systems and Integration – Industrial Manufacturing Management Data – General Overview: Part 1 (2004). ISO TC184/SC4, ISO IS 15531-1
9. Browning, T.R., Fricke, E., Negele, H.: Key concepts in modeling product development processes. Syst. Eng. **9**(2), 104–128 (2006). https://doi.org/10.1002/sys.20047
10. Solano, L., Romero, F., Rosado, P.: An ontology for integrated machining and inspection process planning focusing on resource capabilities. Int. J. Comput. Integr. Manuf. **29**, 1–15 (2016). https://doi.org/10.1080/0951192X.2014.1003149
11. Vichare, P., Nassehi, A., Newman, S.: A unified manufacturing resource model for representation of computerized numerically controlled machine tools. Proc. Inst. Mech. Eng. Part B: J. Eng. Manuf. **223**, 463–483 (2009). https://doi.org/10.1243/09544054JEM1363
12. Labrousse, M., Bernard, A.: FBS-PPRE, an enterprise knowledge lifecycle model. In: Bernard, A., Tichkiewitch, S. (eds.) Methods and Tools for Effective Knowledge Life-Cycle-Management, pp. 285–305. Springer, Heidelberg (2008). https://doi.org/10.1007/978-3-540-78431-9_16
13. Bonfatti, F., Monari, P.D., Paganelli, P.: Resource-free and resource-dependent aspects of process modelling: a rule-based conceptual approach. Int. J. Comput. Integr. Manuf. **11**(1), 60–76 (1998). https://doi.org/10.1080/095119298130985

14. Solano, L., Rosado, P., Romero, F.: Knowledge representation for product and processes development planning in collaborative environments. Int. J. Comput. Integr. Manuf. **27**, 787–801 (2014). https://doi.org/10.1080/0951192X.2013.834480
15. Newman, S.T., Nassehi, A.: Machine tool capability profile for intelligent process planning. CIRP Ann. Manuf. Technol. **58**, 421–424 (2009). https://doi.org/10.1016/j.cirp.2009.03.031
16. ISO 15704. Industrial automation systems – requirements for enterprise-reference architectures and methodologies (2000)
17. Inden, U., Mehandjiev, N., Mönch, L., Vrba, P.: Towards an ontology for small series production. In: Mařík, V., Lastra, J.L.M., Skobelev, P. (eds.) HoloMAS 2013. LNCS (LNAI), vol. 8062, pp. 128–139. Springer, Heidelberg (2013). https://doi.org/10.1007/978-3-642-40090-2_12
18. Fadel, F.G., Fox, M.S., Gruninger, M.: A generic enterprise resource ontology. In: 3rd IEEE Workshop on Enabling Technologies, Morgantown, 17–19 April 1994. https://doi.org/10.1109/enabl.1994.330496
19. ISO 18629-1. Industrial automation systems and integration – process specification language – part 1: overview and basic principles (2004)
20. Borgo, S., Masolo, C.: Foundational choices in DOLCE. In: Staab, S., Studer, R. (eds.) Handbook on Ontologies, pp. 361–381. Springer, Heidelberg (2009). https://doi.org/10.1007/978-3-540-92673-3_16
21. Masolo, C., et al.: Social roles and their descriptions. In: KR, pp. 267–277 (2004)
22. Röpke, H., Hell, K., Zawisza, J., Lüder, A., Schmidt, N.: Identification of "Industrie 4.0" component hierarchy layers. In: 2016 IEEE 21st International Conference on Emerging Technologies and Factory Automation (ETFA), pp. 1–8 (2016). https://doi.org/10.1109/etfa.2016.7733752

Multi-aspect Ontology for Semantic Interoperability in PLM: Analysis of Possible Notations

Alexander Smirnov[1] and Nikolay Shilov[2(✉)]

[1] ITMO University, St. Petersburg, Russia
smir@iias.spb.su
[2] SPIIRAS, St. Petersburg, Russia
nick@iias.spb.su

Abstract. Product lifecycle management covers a number of stages that deal with different tasks and apply different methods but require intensive information exchange to be efficient. Information support of these stages has to address this problem. However, successful implementation of information support systems requires solving the problem of interoperability of heterogeneous information related to different PLM stages. The paper investigates the problem of developing a single ontology for PLM support taking into account differences between terminologies (multi-aspect ontology) used at various stages of the PLM cycle. Different options of designing ontologies covering multiple domains have been considered. Three of them: (i) ontology localization/multilingual ontologies (ii) granular ontologies, and (iii) ontologies with temporal logics are considered in details and analysed. The analysis is based on the case study of PLM support at the automation equipment producer Festo AG & Co KG.

Keywords: Information management · Interoperability · Multi-aspect Ontology

1 Introduction

Product lifecycle management covers a number of stages that deal with different tasks and apply different methods but require intensive information exchange to be efficient. Information support of these stages has to address this problem. However, successful implementation of information support systems requires solving the problem of interoperability of heterogeneous information related to different PLM stages.

The paper develops the earlier presented work [1, 2] based on a long-time collaboration with automation equipment producer Festo AG & Co KG. This is a worldwide provider of automation technology for factory and process automation with a wide assortments of products (more than 40 000 products of approximately 700 types, with various configuration possibilities) ranging from simple products to complex systems (Fig. 1).

During a number of years of collaboration, an eco-system of software tools aimed at support of various PLM stages within the company has been developed as shown in Fig. 2. Below, the elements of the figure are described in detail.

Published by Springer Nature Switzerland AG 2018.
P. Chiabert et al. (Eds.): PLM 2018, IFIP AICT 540, pp. 314–323, 2018.
https://doi.org/10.1007/978-3-030-01614-2_29

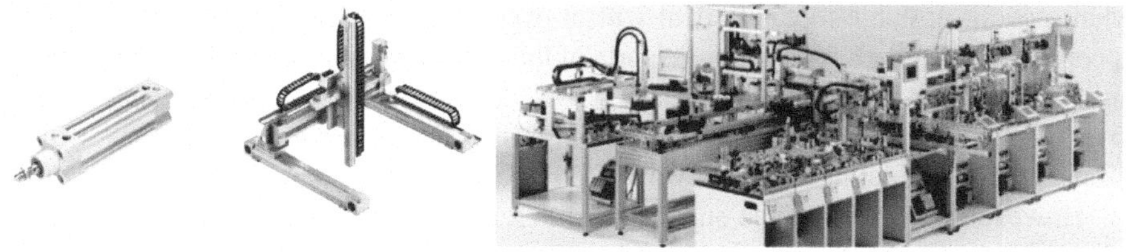

Fig. 1. Assortment range: from simple products to complex systems.

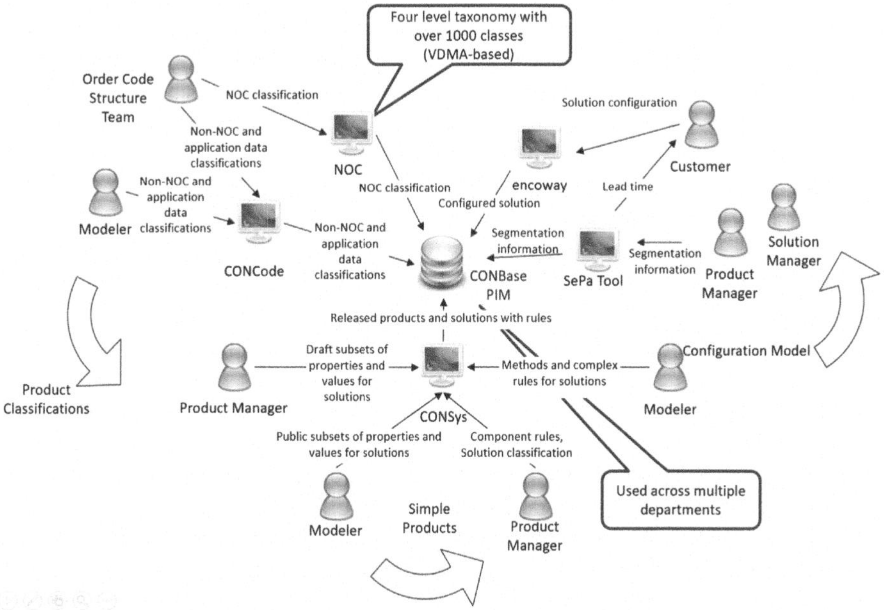

Fig. 2. Information and knowledge management systems developed by the moment.

One of the first projects of the considered company related to this problem was launched in 2010 [3]. It was aimed at modification of work and information flows related to configuration of product combinations. The business process reorganization started with setting up a product ontology in a semi-automatic way originally aimed at product codification (order code scheme) by the NOC tool [3]. The resulting ontology (described in detail in [4]) consisted of more than 1000 classes organized into a four level taxonomy, based on the VDMA (Verband Deutscher Maschinen- und Anlagenbau/Mechanical Engineering Industry Association) classification [5].

The same taxonomy was used in the company's PDM (Product Data Management) and ERP (Enterprise Resource Planning) systems. The ontology structure enabled separation of various types of entities (e.g., physical products and software services) what made it possible to easily deal with it even though it was rather large. Different specialists could work with different parts of the ontology without the need to overview and manage the whole ontology at once (CONBase Product Information Management). Overall, application of the common ontologies in this particular project has proved itself as a convenient and reliable way of product and system knowledge organisation.

However, extension of the support of different PLM stages has caused appearance of extensions of the central ontology aimed at particular processes (e.g., CONCode to support products, which have descriptions incompatible with the ontology). Complex product modelling and design system (CONSys tool) together with product segmentation policy definition tool (SePa) also introduced additional information to be managed. E.g., application data (an auxiliary component used for introduction of some additional characteristics and requirements to the product, for example, operating temperatures, certification, electrical connection, etc.) had to be added for marketing purposes and combined with other features through defined rules. Development of the product configuration tool (CONFig) was aimed at testing the possibility to configure systems based on the rules stored in the CONBase. The tool supported the configuration process in terms used within the company.

Although some significant results have been achieved in the area of complex product and system information management and configuration, still a lot has to be done to support the whole lifecycle of this type of products. One of the key tasks is to provide a coherent way of integration of different extensions into the common ontology.

Having a number of ontologies is not an efficient way due to the necessity to continuously translate information and knowledge between them. However, plain integration is not possible either. For example, the customers are used to operate different terminology, which does not correspond one-to-one to that used within the company. Besides, customers from different industries also operate different terms.

The paper is aimed at investigating the problem of developing a common ontology for PLM supporting differences between terminologies (multi-aspect ontology) used at various stages of the PLM. Different options of designing ontologies covering multiple domains have been considered. Three of them: (i) ontology localization/multilingual ontologies, (ii) granular ontologies, and (iii) ontologies with temporal logics are considered in details and analysed.

2 Related Work

Ontologies are a mean to represent knowledge about a problem domain in a machine-readable way. They enable obtaining, exchanging and processing information and knowledge based on their semantics rather than just syntax. Ontology is a formal conceptualisation of a particular domain of interest shared among heterogeneous applications [6, 7]. Usually, it consists of concepts existing in the problem domain, relationships between them and axioms. Ontologies are a well-proven tool to solve the interoperability problem, but the problem of applying ontologies to PLM is due to different terminologies used at PLM stages even within one company [8, 9]. E.g., in [10] a model-driven interoperability framework is presented as a technical support of co-evolution strategy of products and manufacturing systems. The authors address connecting possible product modules managed in the PLM tool to all possible production capabilities managed on the Manufacturing Process Management tool through establishing "connector framework" to match different ontologies.

The whole scale of the problem was identified in [11] and presented in Fig. 3.

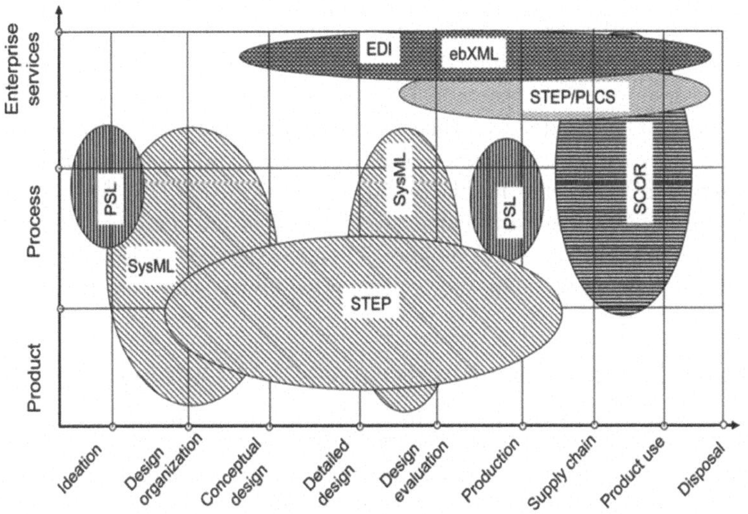

Fig. 3. Usage of different standards at various PLM stages [11].

In [12] a solution is proposed based on semantically annotated multi-faceted ontology for product family modelling to automatically suggest semantically-related annotations based on the design and manufacturing repository on the example of laptop computers. A fragment of the solution is shown in Fig. 4.

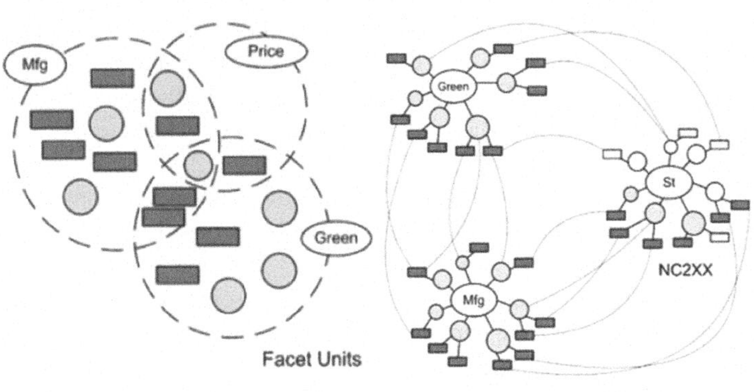

Fig. 4. Building a multi-faceted ontology for PLM (adapted from [12]).

Thus, ontology matching is one of the techniques to solve the problem. However, automatic ontology matching is not very reliable and manual ontology matching requires significant time and efforts. There are efforts aimed at enriching ontologies with additional information (e.g., extension of DAML+OIL for description of configuration problems [13], introducing semantic annotations [14], etc.), however, they still cannot solve the problem of integrating heterogeneous information and knowledge described in different terminology. For example, it is common understanding that domain specific models (e.g., configuration models) can be derived by inheriting or subclassing the ontologies within the general model. Thus, SWRL is a rule-based language for description of constraints is based on OWL and the resulting ontology is an extension of OWL ontology. Then, actual configuration system is implemented using JESS what requires mapping of OWL-based configuration knowledge and SWRL-based constraints into Jess facts and Jess, respectively [15].

As it can be seen there are many efforts aimed at integration of heterogeneous knowledge into a single complex ontology. After an extensive study of the domain, we have identified three main and most promising possibilities, which are discussed below.

3 Possible Notations for Multi-aspect PLM Ontology

In this section we consider three different notations that can be used for implementation of the multi-aspect PLM ontology. The aspects are assumed as different PLM stages, however, in some cases the aspects can be more narrow and assume PLM processes.

3.1 Multilingual Ontology

Multilingual ontologies are aimed at solving terminological issues arising from usage of different languages. Among the terminological issues the following can be selected [16]:

1. Existence of an exact equivalent. This is the easiest case when two terms have completely the same meaning. In real life (when talking of regular languages such as English or German) this is a rear situation, however in a company most of terminology would be the case. For example, "product" would mean the same both during the design stage and the production stage, or in the considered company, "feature" during the design stage means the same as "characteristic" during the production stage.
2. Existence of several context-dependent equivalents. This case assumes that one can choose the right translation (the right equivalent) based on the situation. An example could be the term "modular product" that can stand for both product consisting of several modules or product with some variable characteristics. Treating such ambiguity for a person could be relatively simple but for a machine it can cause significant difficulties.
3. Existence of a conceptualization mismatch. This is an important issue for regular languages, standing for a lack of semantic equivalent for a given term. In case of

PLM this is a much less common issue since the lack of a certain term at a PLM stage usually means that it is just not used (not needed) at this stage.

Usually, such ontologies are built as an ontology with language specific fragments with relationships between terms and it might be a straightforward enough solution for multi-aspect domains. This really helps to overcome the terminological issues, as well as to solve the problem of heterogeneity of information and knowledge between different lifecycle stages.

However, a multilingual ontology is formulated in a single formalism and collecting together for example, configuration knowledge with procurement knowledge would not be possible without losing some semantics. As a result this approach could not solve the problem formulated. On the other hand, multilingual support could be really useful for global companies that have employees speaking different languages, which is actual for the company considered but out of the scope of the presented here research.

3.2 Granular Ontology for PLM

Granular ontologies are based on the integration of ontology-based knowledge representation with the concept of granular computing. Granular computing is based around the notion of granule that links together similar regarding to a chosen criteria objects or entities ("drawn together by indistinguishability, similarity, proximity or functionality" [17]). The granules can also be linked together into bigger granules forming multiple levels of granularity.

From the knowledge representation point of view, a granule can be considered as a chunk of knowledge made about a certain object, set of objects or sub-domain [18]. When speaking about PLM, higher-level granules can combine knowledge related to a certain PLM stage, and lower-level granules can be related to particular PLM processes (Fig. 5). A level is a collection of granules of similar nature. The hierarchy of granules then would form a hierarchy of PLM processes.

Granular ontologies seem to be a suitable solution to support various PLM stages: they enable splitting the domain in smaller areas with consistent terminology and formalisms. The possibility to form a hierarchy (generalisation) is also beneficial due to the possibility to define generic concepts and relationships at higher levels.

However, PLM stages usually overlap in terms of used information and knowledge (Fig. 6). This means that there exist multiple processes that assume collaboration and usage of the same information and knowledge. Pure granular ontologies cannot solve the problem of terms having different meaning at different PLM stages or different company departments. There are multiple efforts in the area of rough granular computing [19–21], however, they are not directly related to ontology design. As a result, additional research in this area is required. Another possibility is to extend a granular ontology with a concept that would enable certain "roughness" of it, and the following section proposes such a possibility.

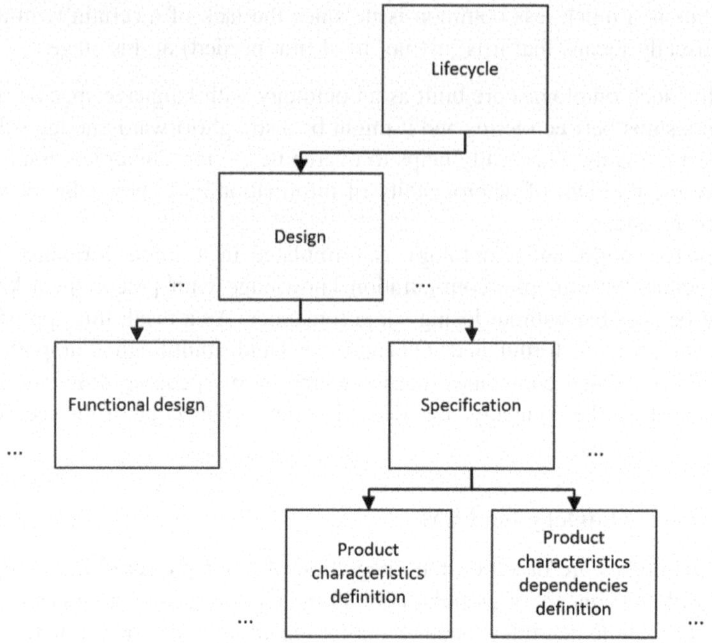

Fig. 5. Example of PLM ontology granules from whole lifecycle down to particular processes.

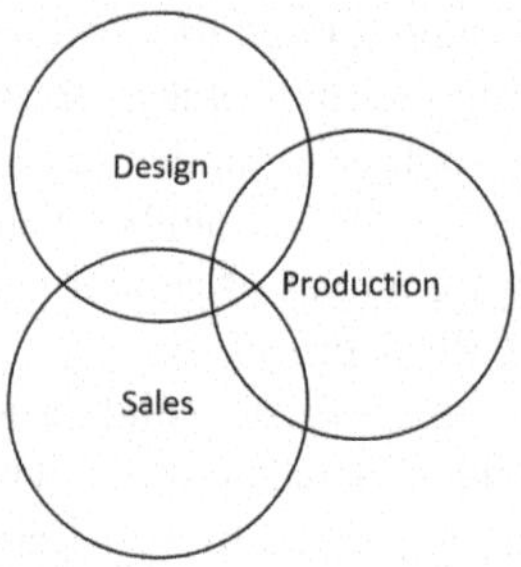

Fig. 6. Example of overlapping PLM stages.

3.3 Temporal Logics-Based Ontology for PLM

The authors of [22] propose to address the problem of terms having different meaning at different PLM stages or different company departments through usage of temporal logics. The idea of using temporal logics in describing PLM originates from the fact that most of product related information and knowledge is used in the product lifecycle only during some stages.

PLM is basically always associated with time. The most often met PLM schemes are "time arrow" (when the PLM stages follow one after another) and "time wheel" (when the time arrow of PLM stages is connected into one or several circles). Time is also considered as one of the key resources in PLM, when, for example one speaks of decreasing lead time or increasing the product usage period.

The approach presented in [22] is based on the fuzzy extension of temporal logics to enable links and overlapping between different stages of the lifecycle. The metaphor used in the approach is based on the idea of representing lifecycle stages as time intervals with fuzzy duration.

The ontology (ONT_{LC}) is described by the following formula:

$$ONT_{LC} = <C_{LC}, R_{LC}, O_{LC}, T_{LC}> \text{, where}$$

C_{LC} is the set of concepts related to lifecycle (all the concepts of the ontology used at all stages of the lifecycle),
R_{LC} is the set of relations between the concepts (including structural relationships between products and their characteristics),
O_{LC} is the set of operations over concepts and/or relations,
T_{LC} is the set of temporal characteristics for lifecycle.

Since the ontology is aimed at separation of concepts between lifecycle stages, the lifecycle systemic kernel is represented as the following triple:

$$ONT_S = <S, R_S, O_S> \text{, where}$$

S is the set of lifecycle stages,
R_S is the set of relations between the stages,
O_S is the set of operations used on the stages.

As it was mentioned the lifecycle stages are considered as time intervals $s = [t, t^+]$, with starting and ending time points t and t^+ respectively. However, in order to indicate the overlapping of stages, the intervals are considered to be fuzzy.

Though the usage of granular ontology with temporal logic as a notation for multi-aspect PLM representation looks complex, it can solve the heterogeneity problem arising from different mental models at different product lifecycle stages. Besides, the "complexity" of this approach makes it possible to include different representations related to different processes of the lifecycle preserving the expressiveness of the representations and languages used unlike multilingual ontologies. As a result, it was concluded define that in the considered case the semantic interoperability support in PLM based on a multi-aspect ontology should be implemented via the notation of granular ontology with temporal logic.

4 Conclusion and Future Work

The paper represents an analysis of the possible notations for building a multi-aspect ontology supporting semantic interoperability in PLM.

Building a multi-aspect segmented ontology basically consisting of a number of ontologies (sub-ontologies) can be based on using unchanged source ontologies and the overall structure of such an ontology would be simple and easy to process. However, this would lead to the necessity of continuous translation of information and knowledge between different representations and standards, which is not an easy task. The dynamic structure of the terminology would make this issue even more complex for solving. As a result, this solution was not accepted.

Multilingual ontologies can solve the problem of heterogeneity of information and knowledge but lack the possibility to support multiple problem-specific formalisms. This solution was not accepted wither but it was noted that multilingual support could be useful for global companies like the considered one, which has employees speaking different languages.

It was identified that in the considered case the semantic interoperability support in PLM should be based on granular multi-aspect ontology extended with temporal logics elements. The pilot efforts related to building smaller ontologies with the purpose of methodology validation proved its viability and potential efficiency. The future research is aimed at building a larger-scale ontology including real company data.

Acknowledgements. The paper is due to collaboration between SPIIRAS and Festo AG & Co KG, State Research # 0073-2018-0002, projects funded by grants ## 18-07-01201, 18-07-01272 of the Russian Foundation for Basic Research. The work has been partially financially supported by Government of Russian Federation, Grant 074-U01.

References

1. Smirnov, A., Kashevnik, A., Teslya, N., et al.: Knowledge management for complex product development framework and implementation. IFIP Adv. Inf. Commun. Technol. **409**, 110–119 (2013)
2. Smirnov, A., Shilov, N., Oroszi, A., Sinko, M., Krebs, T.: Changing information management in product-service system PLM: customer-oriented strategy. In: Ríos, J., Bernard, A., Bouras, A., Foufou, S. (eds.) PLM 2017. IAICT, vol. 517, pp. 701–709. Springer, Cham (2017). https://doi.org/10.1007/978-3-319-72905-3_62
3. Oroszi, A., Jung, T., Smirnov, A., et al.: Ontology-driven codification for discrete and modular products. Int. J. Prod. Dev. **8**, 162–177 (2009). https://doi.org/10.1504/IJPD.2009.024186
4. Smirnov, A., Shilov, N.: Ontology matching in collaborative recommendation system for PLM. Int. J. Prod. Lifecycle Manag. **6**, 322–338 (2013). https://doi.org/10.1504/IJPLM.2013.063210
5. VDMA. German Engineering Federation (2018)
6. Gruber, T.R.: A translation approach to portable ontology specifications. Knowl. Acquis. **5**, 199–220 (1993). https://doi.org/10.1006/knac.1993.1008
7. Staab, S., Studer, R.: Handbook on Ontologies. Springer, Heidelberg (2009). https://doi.org/10.1007/978-3-540-92673-3
8. Asmae, A., Souhail, S., El Moukhtar, Z., Hussein, B.: Using ontologies for the integration of information systems dedicated to product (CFAO, PLM…) and those of systems monitoring (ERP, MES..). In: 2017 International Colloquium on Logistics and Supply Chain Management (LOGISTIQUA), pp. 59–64. IEEE (2017)

9. Palmer, C., Urwin, E.N., Young, R.I.M., Marilungo, E.: A reference ontology approach to support global product-service production. Int. J. Prod. Lifecycle Manag. **10**, 86 (2017). https://doi.org/10.1504/IJPLM.2017.083003
10. Lafleur, M., Terkaj, W., Belkadi, F., Urgo, M., Bernard, A., Colledani, M.: An onto-based interoperability framework for the connection of PLM and production capability tools. In: Harik, R., Rivest, L., Bernard, A., Eynard, B., Bouras, A. (eds.) PLM 2016. IAICT, vol. 492, pp. 134–145. Springer, Cham (2016). https://doi.org/10.1007/978-3-319-54660-5_13
11. Rachuri, S., Subrahmanian, E., Bouras, A., et al.: Information sharing and exchange in the context of product lifecycle management: role of standards. Comput. Des. **40**, 789–800 (2008). https://doi.org/10.1016/j.cad.2007.06.012
12. Lim, S.C.J., Liu, Y., Lee, W.B.: A methodology for building a semantically annotated multi-faceted ontology for product family modelling. Adv. Eng. Inform. **25**, 147–161 (2011). https://doi.org/10.1016/j.aei.2010.07.005
13. Felfernig, A., Friedrich, G., Jannach, D., et al.: Configuration knowledge representations for semantic web applications. Artif. Intell. Eng. Des. Anal. Manuf. **17**, 31–50 (2003). https://doi.org/10.1017/S0890060403171041
14. Liao, Y., Lezoche, M., Panetto, H., Boudjlida, N.: Semantic annotations for semantic interoperability in a product lifecycle management context. Int. J. Prod. Res. **54**, 5534–5553 (2016). https://doi.org/10.1080/00207543.2016.1165875
15. Yang, D., Miao, R., Wu, H., Zhou, Y.: Product configuration knowledge modeling using ontology web language. Expert Syst. Appl. **36**, 4399–4411 (2009). https://doi.org/10.1016/j.eswa.2008.05.026
16. Espinoza, M., Montiel-Ponsoda, E., Gómez-Pérez, A.: Ontology localization. In: Proceedings of the Fifth International Conference on Knowledge Capture - K-CAP 2009, pp. 33–40. ACM Press, New York (2009)
17. Zadeh, L.A.: Is there a need for fuzzy logic? Inf. Sci. (Ny) **178**, 2751–2779 (2008). https://doi.org/10.1016/j.ins.2008.02.012
18. Calegari, S., Ciucci, D.: Granular computing applied to ontologies. Int. J. Approx. Reason. **51**, 391–409 (2010). https://doi.org/10.1016/j.ijar.2009.11.006
19. Jankowski, A., Skowron, A.: Toward rough-granular computing. In: An, A., Stefanowski, J., Ramanna, S., Butz, C.J., Pedrycz, W., Wang, G. (eds.) RSFDGrC 2007. LNCS (LNAI), vol. 4482, pp. 1–12. Springer, Heidelberg (2007). https://doi.org/10.1007/978-3-540-72530-5_1
20. Inuiguchi, M., Hirano, S., Tsumoto, S.: Rough Set Theory and Granular Computing. Springer, Heidelberg (2003). https://doi.org/10.1007/978-3-540-36473-3
21. Polkowski, L., Skowron, A.: Rough mereological calculi of granules: a rough set approach to computation. Comput. Intell. **17**, 472–492 (2001). https://doi.org/10.1111/0824-7935.00159
22. Tarassov, V., Fedotova, A., Stark, R., Karabekov, B.: Granular meta-ontology and extended Allen's logic: some theoretical background and application to intelligent product lifecycle management systems Valery. In: Schwab, I., van Moergestel, L., Gonçalves, G. (eds.) INTELLI 2015: The Fourth International Conference on Intelligent Systems and Applications, St. Julians, Malta, pp. 86–93 (2015)

Education in the Field of Industry 4.0

PLM for Education. The Next Generation of Engineers

Andrés Padillo(✉), Jesús Racero, Jose Carlos Molina, and Ignacio Eguía

Universidad de Sevilla, Seville, Spain
Andrespadillo88@gmail.com, {jrm,jmolinal2,ies}@us.es

Abstract. Industry of the Future (IoF) or Industry 4.0 is bringing a new model of industry wherein it is necessary to acquire new skills by the new generation of engineering students.

The following paper pursues as a main objective the design and implementation of a new subject for students of Engineering at the University of Sevilla (Spain). In this subject, fundamentals aspect of PLM business models and engineering relationship are collected, and students are equipped of necessary knowledges and skills to customize PLM tools according to business requirements. As a practical application, students must undertake a real case based on a collaborative engineering study between design and manufacturing areas.

To achieve this goal, software architecture is described and provided to students for the management, configuration and industrialization of the data product, as well as the assignment of the tasks necessary to successfully achieve the different milestones involved in the project. This work describes the tools used to implement a practical application: ARAS INNOVATOR as PLM software, a LEGO product as DMU (Digital Mock-Up) and Redmine for project management.

Keywords: PLM tools · Education · Collaborative engineering Industry 4.0

1 Introduction

The globalisation of markets and rapid changes experienced by the industry through digital transformation are bringing significant changes in how to design and manufacture products, where the collaborative engineering plays an essential role.

The use of PLM tools to manage lifecycle is essential to achieve success and more and more of European companies increasing use of them. As a result demand has heightened significantly over the last several years. However, lack of professional skilled specialized in this area in order to respond companies requirements is limited.

In Spain, nowadays the use of PLM is based on different roles associated to several CAx PLM tools. However, does not exist a role or a specific profile such a PLM engineer to interact with the different tools each other and customize them according to business models requirements.

Published by Springer Nature Switzerland AG 2018.
P. Chiabert et al. (Eds.): PLM 2018, IFIP AICT 540, pp. 327–337, 2018.
https://doi.org/10.1007/978-3-030-01614-2_30

Actually, many of PLM courses are focus on the design of products and processes, using the standard configuration provided by software default. However, it is very difficult to find any company whose needs can fit the software.

The new generation of PLM systems allows a great customization and parameterization, enabling its adaptation to any business process and company. This competence has not been exploited, although it more is demanded every day.

Based on this problematic, arise an initiative to include in engineering studies subjects related to PLM Systems where collected fundamental requirements that should fulfill a PLM engineer to design and customize the systems according to business requirements.

The following paper describes the design, deployment and results achieved of introduction and customization PLM skills into aeronautical education engineering. The desired aim are cover knowledge:

- Concepts and fundamentals of the PLM systems and its interaction with engineering
- PLM Tools & customization
- A use case based on acquired skills
- Evaluation methods

This paper is organized as follows. Section 2 introduces others experience into PLM training into higher education, it focus on skill and curriculum. Section 3 describes competence or skills, design of contents, hardware architecture and evaluation method. Section 4 shows the deployment experience and the results. Finally, the paper presents the conclusions obtained.

2 Pedagogical Renewal. PLM & Industry 4.0

PLM systems are solutions that seek to manage the product life cycle and allow the companies connect all information improving the operational efficiencies as well as working faster (recovery and exchange of electronic information, reuse of data, automated capabilities, and data security).

PLM is not only a software. When a PLM System is described, must support business solutions in collaborative creation, management and product and process definition. In Industries PLM is commonly used for:

- Centralize and organize product data
- Design & management product development projects
- Integrate design process & industrialization

PLM systems aim to connect and cover the entire cycle of a product (From conception to market debut). A set tools that provide a platform through a collaborative environment to optimize flow and information Exchange between different actors involved in lifecycle.

To achieve this purpose, these tools have the ability to customize and model their data, which allows companies to adapt them according to the different requirements of the business [7].

Currently, this is a gap to cover nowadays between industry and PLM systems. The lack of consultants and training engineers in this area makes it difficult a correct implementation and execution of PLM systems in a company.

From different educational institutions as well as PLM software companies are beginning to promote the use of CAX-PLM tools through subjects and training courses focusing on using tools to became a professional PLM engineer.

With that aim, in 2016 the project named 'Accelerating the adoption of Industry of the Future (IoF) supporting technologies by Spanish universities'; was launched. It is an educational project, with a focus on manufacturing related competences and partially funded by La Fondation Dassault Systèmes [10].

Current educational cases dealing with CAX-PLM technologies in some spanish universities:

- University Jaume I of Castellón. The educational model is based on projects or module assignments that integrate several courses. This case comprises a training module on the methodological use of CAX applications, integrating the product design and development process with a PLM application to support the collaborative teamwork [11, 12].
- University of Cádiz. The I4.0 support technologies dealing with CAD/CAM/CAE and PDM/PLM systems are within the scope of the Manufacturing Processes Engineering Area [10].
- Polytechnic University of Madrid – Industrial Engineering School. Currently, in the Degree and Master studies, only different CAX applications are used in different courses.

Therefore, there is no an integrating solution, based also on the use of a PLM system and the customization, that allows students developing a multidisciplinary collaborative project.

The aim of the project called ProVerStand ("Produktentwicklung über Verteilte Standorte" – "Product Development Involving Distributed Locations") is to provide universities and similar institutions access to state of the art PLM systems, such as PDMS, CAE and CAD [4]. The Project defines a PLM scenario from preparatory level to master level (Fig. 1).

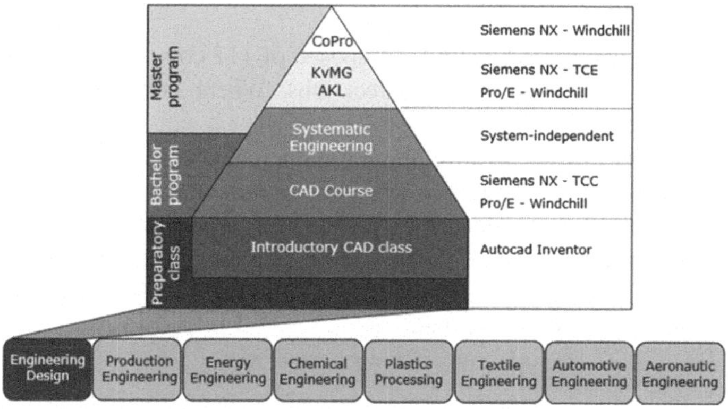

Fig. 1. PLM education scenario [4]

Research Institute of Aoyama Gakuin University in Japan has developed effective educational curriculum. The goal of this lesson is an understanding of effective PLM when a new product is developed using e-Learning as the educational tool [6]. The training focus on the business processes in PLM, designs the curriculum of the PLM education by e-Learning.

The content is structure in 5 subjects where it develop the following concepts: Product Design (EBOM), production design (Layout & systems production) production management (MRP, Material Requirements Planning) and process design.

The faculty at Purdue University has been working together to reform existing PLM-related courses. The new curriculum provides three courses at junior years to build a student's basic PLM knowledge and skill sets and two senior level electives course based on project-based learning environment to help the students synthesize what they have learned during the past academic years [3].

The importance of include trends of industry 4.0 in the engineering training, is reflected in different courses in several European universities: the polytechnic university of Torino [2] developing courses around the framework Small Factory Project. The courses focus on training the students in ERP and PLM tools.

The HSR (university of applied science of Rapperswil) [13] covers trends of industry 4.0 & digitalization based on a scenario around the product using very common technologies (Lego, Arduino, etc.) and IT tools (PLM, CAD, ERP, etc.)

Finally, it is note that in the literature review a training destined to customize PLM system based on customer requirements was not found.

This gap is taken advantage for design and implement a new subject with a first approach to cover these requirements.

3 Design and Development of a PLM Subject

The incipient demand on PLM & Industries 4.0 has seduced students and therefore engineering schools to include PLM training in their curricula. All this is encouraged because the A400M program will further strengthen the importance of Andalusia (in the south of Spain) as one of the country's main aerospace-production regions. The all-new A400M military aircraft made its first flight from Andalusia's Seville San Pablo Airport after its assembly at the EADS CASA factory, the third largest Airbus production plant in the world.

The Andalusian aerospace cluster is composed of 117 companies (engineering and consulting 18.8%), generating 14.463 direct jobs. Where 26% are highly qualified employees (Engineers).

This environment has led to develop an optional subject in the aeronautical engineering master degree at the University of Sevilla. In order to provide students of cross-cutting skills to plan, design, manage & certification procedures, infrastructures and systems that support the aerospace industry with activities related to industry 4.0. As well as specific skills related to use and customization of PLM tools focus on development of business in professional field.

As a prerequisite, the student must be graduated in an engineering field and is highly recommended possess knowledges of data modeling and production management.

With a total of 125 h distributed as face-to-face classes and cooperative homework, the subject is divided into two blocks:

- Theoretical classes: teaching class 25 h (face to face) and 50 h analysis and study (non-presential)
- Computing practices: teaching class 15 h (Face to face) and 35 h (non presential)

The structure of the subject is divided in four large modules. Each module in turn, is structured into theoretical and applied sub-modules. The first one, is composed by an introductory part and general concepts associated with the relevant module and the second one by a practical part. In such a way that the student progressively acquires the skills necessary for each of them.

Module 1: Product Lifecycle Management in Aerospace Industry.

Theoretical part: Introduction and basic concepts about product lifecycle. Differences between sequential engineering and concurrent engineering and first approach concept of collaborative engineering across PLM systems. Definition of PLM system and their relationship with the Industy 4.0.

Practical part: Analyze and develop with a project management tool a collaborative framework collecting the following aspects:

- Project management
- Teamwork management
- System virtualization concept, software and PLM architecture

Module 2: PLM System in Aerospace Industry

Theoretical part: Introduction and concepts about PLM Systems in aerospace industry. Programs and projects management in aerospace industry. Main activities:

- Planning, managing and controlling
- Organizational structure OBS and Work Breakdown Structure Work.
- Requeriments management & product specification.

Practical part: Design and modeling an aerospace program with several projects associated with a PLM tool where it is collected the following aspects:

- Analysis of requirements associated with the project
- OBS (Organizational Breakdown Structure) the structure of the project
- Analysis and modeling users permissions in the tool
- Creation of identities
- Modify permissions and users
- Update items and relationships
- Allocation and configuration of roles in the teamwork

Module 3: Product Data Management

Theoretical part: Introduction and concepts of industrial digital mock-up (iDMU, [9]): 3D virtual prototypes and information contain. Product data management: concept of BOM, EBOM, MBOM. Configuration management, versions and variants & Product lifecycle management.

Practical part: Design and modeling a product lifecycle with a PLM tool where it is collected the following aspects:

- Set the product lifecycle & models
- Products and models creation
- Definition states and permission associated with states
- Creation of bill of material BOM
- Creation new attributes

Module 4: Process Data Management in PLM Environment

Theoretical part: Introduction and concepts about virtual product and collaborative design. Definition of a process management data and process plan. The concept of PPR (Product, Process, Resource) structure and data explode in the manufacturing area (Work instructions and Maintain Resource Operation).

Practical part: Design, modeling and adapt a process plan in a PLM tool where it is collected the following aspects:

- Setting up the environment to include the concept of PPR in a tool
- Design data model and implementation of a classical PPR structure and relationships between Product, Process and Resource)

4 Case Study. Configuration & Customization a PLM Tool

4.1 Architecture Software

For the implementation and development of practices, it is necessary to set up an infrastructure allowing the student to interact with the different tools in a collaborative framework through two main systems: a production system that allows students to work in a collaborative environment for the implementation project and a development system, through a virtual machine in each student machine for developing and testing solutions. Previous implementation in the productive system (Fig. 2).

Fig. 2. Architecture software

4.2 Software and Material Support

The Information systems, material and complementary information used in practice are described below:

- **ARAS INNOVATOR** is a software, which offers integration services for PLM and PDM solutions on a single platform.

The structure is divided in 3 mains modules:

- PLM to manage processes throughout the life cycle
- PDM to manage CAD data: product, part and documentation
- PLATFORM to adapt, extend and build applications
- **Redmine** is a free and open source, web-based project management and issue tracking tool. It allows users to manage multiple projects and associated subprojects. It features per project wikis and forums, time tracking, and flexible, role-based access control. It includes a calendar and Gantt charts to aid visual representation of projects and their deadlines. Redmine integrates with various version control systems and includes a repository browser and diff viewer [5].
- **A Lego helicopter model 6745-H**, composed by 247 pieces, to define the assembly process (6745 Model Propeller, [1]). The implementation must be defined in the Aras Innovator tool under the Schema control of the production model defined as well as Lego designer software tool (Lego Designer, [8]), a free software available for mac and windows to design through the pc any Lego assembly.

4.3 Rubric Evaluation

A rubric is typically an evaluation tool or set of guidelines used to promote the consistent application of learning expectations, learning objectives, or learning standards in the classroom, or to measure their attainment against a consistent set of criteria. In instructional settings, rubrics clearly define academic expectations for students and help to ensure consistency in the evaluation of academic work from student to student, assignment to assignment, or course to course.

The rubric applied has 9 points. From 1 to 6 evaluate the PLM skills achieve in the subject. The 7th and 8th point is an optional section to increase marks and the last point evaluates project management skills.

The practical part is developed in groups. The groups consist of a minimum of 3 students and a maximum of 4. Each group defines a project manager who manages and monitors tasks for a satisfactory conclusion.

1st point collected the sections related to the OBS structure and will be assessed the following aspects

- User definition: the student must define different roles.
- Teamwork definition: the student must define different groups that share common functions.
- Permission definition: The student must define permissions according to the role, lifecycle and data type associated.

2nd point collected the sections related to the program & project management and will be assessed the following aspects

- Program definition. The student must define at least one program and define life-cycle (state, transition) and the users and permissions involved.
- Project definition. The student must define a project based on a template that should be extended with tasks and activities. The project must be associated with a model as well as a life cycle and access permissions.

3rd point includes paragraphs related to the customization of a PLM tool

- Parts and Products definition: the student must define new attributes to the structure of a Part, identify the types of parts and design forms & new attributes.
- Definition of the life cycle: the student must design a cycle of life for each item type as well as the permissions and allocation of transitions.

4th point includes the concept of EBOM (As Design concept)

- Definition of the EBOM where the student must design the product structure with a LEGO model and implementation into PLM System.
- Definition the Vault File concept applying import and export data associated to parts.

5th point. It is used to define the Manufacturing model (as planned and as prepare structure), design of the manufacturing structure (MBOM)

- Definition and design manufacturing parts, implementing the idmu data model into PLM system.
- Definition of the MBOM structure for 6745 Lego propeller model. The student must incorporate new structures in the PLM tool (processes and resources) as well as define their lifecycle, forms and relationships between elements (structure PPR).

6th point. Documentation of the technical evaluation report: the student must upload documentation associated with the project that reflects the following aspects:

- Introduction and objectives
- Scope
- Analysis and requirements capture
- Design
- Implementation
- Tests
- Conclusions
- Extensions

7th point an alternative option for students. It evaluates the automatic software programming included into PLM System. For example, develop import and export data in batch modes.

- Definition data model. Description of the level of implementation of the description of the procedures.

8th point: included aspect related to extensions where the student puts to the test the skills acquired going a step and beyond.

- Design and implementation Work Instruction.
- Engineering change order. Definition business process to change management.
- Effectivities

9th point collected aspects of project management. To know the activities done by students in the subject.

- Work distribution. Hours to develop task.
- Task type distribution. Balanced work distribution by rubric point.
- Analysis learning curves. Evaluation of group members.

4.4 Results

In the literature review, the experience is focusing on describing content and skills acquired by the students.

This experience starts in 16/17 academic year. The following table describes the level of achievement in percentage (by work team) of competencies acquired by students (Fig. 3).

Work Team	1	2	3	4	5	6	7	8
1	1,0	1,00	1,00	1,00	1,00	1,00	1,00	0,50
2	1,0	1,00	1,00	1,00	0,89	1,00	0,50	0,00
3	1,0	1,00	1,00	1,00	1,00	1,00	1,00	0,75
4	1,0	1,00	1,00	1,00	0,56	1,00	0,00	0,25
5	1,0	0,67	0,71	0,67	0,89	1,00	0,00	0,25
6	1,0	1,00	1,00	1,00	0,89	1,00	0,00	0,25
7	1,0	1,00	1,00	1,00	1,00	1,00	0,00	0,25
8	1,0	1,00	1,00	1,00	0,89	1,00	0,00	0,00
Average	1,0	0,96	0,96	0,96	0,89	1,00	0,31	0,28

Fig. 3. Comparative table (**expressed as a percentage)**

The results reflect that all Works teams have acquired 75% of competences defined. Likewise, these competencies have been achieved completing over 80% of activities.

On the other hand, software development skills that involves using customization PLM Tools and not included in theoretical lessons and practices, have not been achieved. One of the possible causes is the dedication time at developing competences and skills. The average dedicated by the Works teams was 156 h; 45 h theoretical-practical and 116 for developing out of classes.

A disaggregate analysis, student by student, shows that the workload is balanced. The difference between the hardworker is around 11% while the deviation respect from the average stands is about 8%. The work division has been balanced (deviation less than 15%).

5 Conclusions

This paper has described the development and results of the implementation of a subject oriented towards the acquisition of skills in the customization of PLM systems. A very demanded area nowadays by companies and not included in the current aeronautical engineering curricula.

During the design and the planning stages of the subject, several doubts emerged about the reception from the students as an optional subject with unknown content.

However, the result reflected in the information systems of the University of Sevilla through satisfactions surveys, shows that not only the subject has well accepted by the students but also the number of students has doubled respect from the last course and assessed positively in the study plans.

Finally, another important factor to consider and perhaps the most important from the point of view as educator have been the result reflected in the workload required to the student outside school hours. It can be observed the similarity between the estimated and actual hours in the study plan and how the most of students have achieved the aims and competences successfully.

References

1. Propeller Model Instructions. LEGO. https://www.lego.com/en-/us/service/building-instructions/search?initialsearch=6745#?text=6745. Accessed 17 Mar 2018
2. Bedolla, J., D'Antonio, G., Chiabert, P.: A novel approach for teaching IT tools within learning factories. Procedia Manuf. **9**, 175–181 (2017). ISSN 2351-9789
3. Chang, Y., Miller, C.L.: PLM curriculum development: using an industry-sponsored project to teach manufacturing simulation in a multidisciplinary environment. J. Manuf. Syst. **24**(3), 171–177 (2005). (C. Dept. of Computer Graphics Technology, Purdue University, West Lafayette, Indiana, USA)
4. Feldhusen, J., Löwer, M., Brezing, A., Neis, J.: DS 62: Proceedings of E and PDE 2010, the 12th International Conference on Engineering and Product Design Education - When Design Education and Design Research Meet
5. Kanai, K., Anderson, M.: Redmine as a web-based collaboration tool in engineering design courses. In: 120th ASEE Annual Conference & Exposition (2013)
6. Kakehi, M., Yamada, T., Watanabe, I.: PLM education in production design and engineering by e-Learning. Int. J. Prod. Econ. **122**(1), 479–484 (2009). https://doi.org/10.1016/j.ijpe.2009.06.028
7. Javvadi, L.: Product life cycle management an introduction (2011)
8. Lego Designer Software. https://www.lego.com/en-us/ldd. Accessed 17 Mar 2018
9. Mas, F., Menendez, L., Servan, J., Gomez, A., Rios, J.: Aerospace industrial digital mock-up exploitation to generate assembly shopfloor documentation (2012)

10. Ríos, J., et al.: Accelerating the adoption of industry 4.0 supporting technologies in manufacturing engineering courses. Mater. Sci. Forum **903**, 100–111 (2017)
11. Vila, C., Abellán, J.V., Estruch, A.M., Bruscas, G.M.: Project-based collaborative engineering design and manufacturing learning with PLM tools. In: Luo, Y. (ed.) CDVE 2009. LNCS, vol. 5738, pp. 367–371. Springer, Heidelberg (2009). https://doi.org/10.1007/978-3-642-04265-2_55
12. Vila, C., et al.: Collaborative product development experience in a senior integrated manufacturing course. Int. J. Eng. Educ. **25**, 886–899 (2009)
13. Fradl, B., Sohrweide, A., Nyffenegger, F.: PLM in education – the escape from boredom. In: Ríos, J., Bernard, A., Bouras, A., Foufou, S. (eds.) PLM 2017. IAICT, vol. 517, pp. 297–307. Springer, Cham (2017). https://doi.org/10.1007/978-3-319-72905-3_27

Development of Product Engineering Skills with PLM Applications Through Collaborative Educational Projects

Carlos Vila(✉), Rafael Torres, Santiago C. Gutiérrez, and Amparo Meseguer

Universitat Politècnica de València, Camino de Vera s/n, 46022 Valencia, Spain
carvipas@upv.es

Abstract. In the industrial discipline of product design and manufacturing, training and learning methods for last academic course engineering students is difficult and complex since they have to integrate technical knowledge with computer-aided applications (CAx) and new skills in collaborative work. With the trends of Industry 4.0, companies request new talents and improved competences from the very first time. The fact that Product Lifecycle Management (PLM) platforms with a huge variety of tools support structured collaborative practices drives us to use them as a gear to integrate all the engineering and put it into practice for engineering content creation. In this contribution we present an innovative academic project for the last academic course students integrating several subjects in order to develop an industrial project working in a PLM platform. The platform allows us to control not only the data but also the scheduled activities of a project while the participants use different engineering applications in each phase of the project. Traditionally, engineering education deals with the learning of CAD, CAE and CAM tools separately, giving a partial learning experience and vision to the students. This communication presents a structured integrated vision of this learning project and the achieved results.

Keywords: Project based learning · Collaborative engineering
Design for manufacturing · Industry 4.0 skills · PLM implementation

1 Introduction

Manufacturing companies are in continuous product lifecycle improvement. From the perspective of manufacturing, emerging technologies such additive manufacturing, hydroforming and composites molding, can help in obtaining more quality parts and products. However, previous activities to manufacturing, particularly design and development, are difficult to improve since they need not only the latest information and communication technologies but also cultural changes.

Since early nineties new work philosophies such as Concurrent Engineering (CE), Collaborative Engineering (CoE), or Integrated Product, Processes and Resources Development (IPPRD) have been topics of interest. Conversely, many corporations find very complicated to implement this cooperative way of working and, at the same time, updated groupware.

P. Chiabert et al. (Eds.): PLM 2018, IFIP AICT 540, pp. 338–347, 2018.
https://doi.org/10.1007/978-3-030-01614-2_31

This major change of implementing virtual and collaborative environments represents not only a great investment but also a great effort in terms of time and team training. From this perspective, there is a claim from the industry that engineering formation must incorporate these new skills [1].

In this contribution, we will present the current situation for the companies and the implementation of some 4.0 Industry enablers and the collaborative engineering pilot project for academia that we are developing.

This communication has the following structure: Sect. 2 provides a review of computer support for collaborative practices, Sect. 3 explain the proposed method, Sect. 4 the experimental procedure, Sect. 5 the results discussion and Sect. 6 shows the conclusions and future work.

2 Issues in Computer Support for Collaborative Work

Engineers from design and manufacturing disciplines, and Academic Researchers, view Collaborative Engineering as a key issue for reducing working time of product lifecycle stages and achieving product quality and reliability. The accomplishment of Collaborative Engineering within any organization is based on the premise of how prepared are the different working team actors for collaboration among the different working teams involved in the different product life cycle stages [2].

In that way, we must give to the working teams the tools for an effective communication and collaboration to ease the sharing of data and information related to product design, manufacturing process planning and product industrialization. It is important to highlight that Computer Support for Collaborative Work (CSCW) discipline includes many perspectives to achieve the integration of tools, methodologies and people.

There are different definitions of CSCW, depending on the nature of the application. CSCW is primarily concerned to people and computers. It is an environment where computers provide support to a group of people to accomplish a common goal or task. More concisely, CSCW is a “set of software, hardware, language components and procedures that support a group of people in a decision related meeting”.

The type of CSCW environment is, basically, determined by time and place dimensions. The different types of interactions based on these two dimensions can be the combination of different scenarios. On one hand, working sessions at the same time (synchronous) or at different time (asynchronous). On the other hand, working meetings in the same place (face to face) or in geographically dispersed locations (distributed).

From the CSCW perspective, there are four main areas for training engineers in collaborative skills: *Organizational*, *Sociological*, *Psychological* and *Technological* [3]. Organizational training deals with how to structure data, information and knowledge, how to control the access and how to use and to distribute it, as well as project management. Sociological training is focused on how to manage groups and the way they work in new environments. Psychological training tries to empower the behavior of individual people not only in real but in virtual teams. Finally, technological training can be the easiest one since it is about empower the use of computer applications.

If we structure and balance the learning process, team collaboration can be potentially enhance and the productivity and effectiveness of the engineering group will be a real fact according to concurrent engineering principles. In order to support collaboration we can use methodologies and tools but they should come with metrics and incentives system.

With this structured vision, we can address the main issues to handle and the skills to improve for engineers working in collaborative environments (Fig. 1).

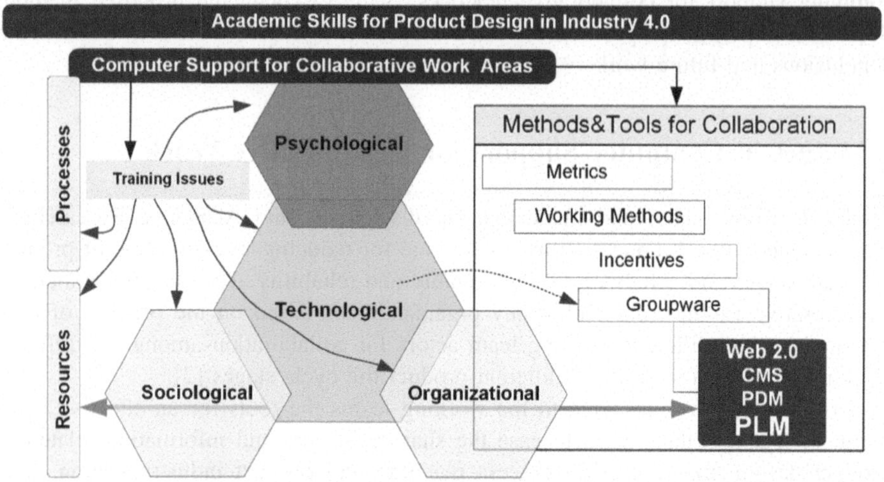

Fig. 1. CSCW issues, methods and tools.

Computer tools for collaboration are defined as Groupware and a PLM system can be qualified as the most complete one, due to many of its capabilities. For example, the emergence and widespread use of web 2.0 offers an incredible potential for information sharing among geographically distributed people in different locations that work at different timetable [4]. However, they do not provide support for structured collaboration and information sharing including data management access control and project schedule.

Therefore, it is important in this context to focus the characteristics of a groupware if we are planning to implement and train engineering teams in collaborative development processes.

2.1 Groupware Features

An important point about Groupware is to detect the different functionalities that it can have. Moreover, we need to understand how the software will support procedures, methods and applications for the activities of the working groups. For instance, a functionality or feature for the early stage activities is how it can manage the brainstorming during the initial process to generate ideas, structure them and evaluate them.

Another desired feature could be how the software manage collaborative part/product designs and if it facilitates revisions over the web. According to this reasoning, basic features that we should look for are:

- ***Interaction*** facilities for synchronous or asynchronous meetings.
- ***Coordination*** of performed tasks among team members.
- ***Distribution*** of data when needed through web platforms.
- ***Visualization*** and access to data according to roles and workflows.
- ***Data hiding,*** separating public and private data.
- ***Sharing of data***, engineering drawings, applications, and so on among participants.

These features are crucial for Collaborative Engineering but, although they are aligned with industry 4.0 principles, this technology does not guarantee a successful implementation of collaborative environments [5]. These features together provide a complete architecture to support engineering activities and decision-making process. It is what we will call Product Lifecycle Management (PLM) system. However, it is needed a formation in the tools and in methods that support this new way of working within environments full of data and information.

2.2 Team Formation for Collaborative Engineering

Engineering working teams or multidisciplinary teams that work under the umbrella of industry 4.0 will have to use these groupware applications. The problem is that, up to now, engineering students have not had an integrated formation putting together all the technical knowledge and information and communication technology [6]. The main reasons why academic organizations does not have incorporated this way of formation is complex but we summarize them as follows:

- Regular Academic are based on isolated subjects.
- Vertical integration and planning is sometimes difficult although it is supposed that some subjects are required prior to others.
- Horizontal integration is complicated since academic staff does not want to be integrated in a global academic project.
- It requires a great effort to put together some multiple points of view, perspectives and expertise in a common project with a practical objective.
- It requires extra work to define the academic project and the metrics.
- Finally, to communicate and train in all the skills and best practices to the students and, at the same time, summarize all the features of the collaboration.

The efficient use of PLM tools goes beyond simply purchasing the platform and its applications. Particularly, these platforms, demands a deep knowledge on how to use it effectively to support team members' interactions while working with advanced authoring applications [7]. Therefore, it is a key issue to define a correct implementation and customized training scenario [8].

The nonexistence of an integrated perspective in the engineering curriculum overlooks the necessity of teaching valuable skills in the areas of: *project and work-group management in cross-functional distributed teams, identification and resolution of design and manufacturing problems, efficient collaboration and workflow management.*

The academia is working to overcome these curriculum limitations and some works claim for more initiatives to broaden vision of the professional activities in engineering [9], however, this ongoing process still requires many issues to be improved.

3 Methodology

3.1 PLM Performances Approach

In order to draw a rational curriculum, we have done a deep analysis of this new way of working with PLM platforms. For the experimental procedure, we have grouped performances of these platforms and, then, we have tried to use most of the performances in the regular academic engineering course. For this work, and based on previous works [10], several main categories have been defined and, within each one of them, we have identified functionalities or applications that should be included for engineering tasks (Table 1).

Table 1. PLM tool grouped performances and functionalities

Category	Description and functionalities
Personal data	Professional data for inside and outside of the organization and meeting tools. *Contact list/manager, group calendar*
Social	Communication tools and exchanging of data, information and ideas. There are many of them free, the problem is to synchronise them with the process. *e-mail- news group - web conferencing - instant messaging/chat, audio conferencing, whiteboard*
Application	Applications related with modelling, assembly simulation, virtual manufacturing and many other needed for the product design and development CAD/CAE/CAM. *Modelling, simulation, machining*
Data management	Applications related with CAx data and other electronic documents. *File sharing-management, version control, search system, ole based access control, access control/security*
Decision support	Applications for interaction between the members of the team, synchronous or asynchronous, and decision-making. *Discussion forum/group, voting system, survey and feedback*
Project management	Collaborative process need tools for planning and resources assignment. Theses apps must enable the project time scheduling and tasks coordination. *Project planning, workflow, tasks reminder, new events e-mail notification*
Miscellaneous	Includes different applications that could be used during the collaboration. All of them are based on web 2.0 similar to social networks. *Reporting, time card system, integration with other system, personalised profile*

The table briefly shows the set of functionalities included within each of the main categories. Such functionalities list has helped to characterize a PLM platform and match a particular application for developing skills in concurrent engineering environments. According to the project objectives and planning, the initial formation can be customized and limited just to the needed tools or applications among all of the selected PLM platform.

3.2 Collaborative Training for Enhance Product Design Skills in Industry 4.0

PLM systems provide a technological framework, where the interactions among participants can be scheduled and documented, but collaboration processes must be defined and documented to recreate real processes and to train engineers, and those aspects are still very limited. Project-Based Learning (PBL) can be seen as a way to recreate a limited and simple product design and engineering context, where students must collaborate to achieve the objectives of an engineering project and where Computer Aided Applications (CAx) and PLM applications are the technological enablers.

For the academic project, we have planned a two-semester design project that integrates several subjects (Fig. 2).

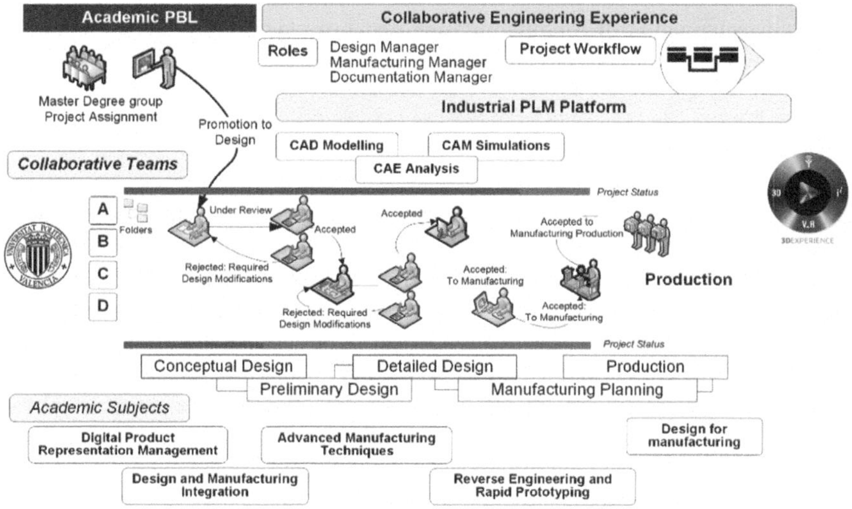

Fig. 2. CSCW project based learning with PLM platform.

The academic subjects are mainly related with design and manufacturing skills and all of them belong to the specialization within the last year of a two-years Master Degree. Therefore, we have designed a project that, in some tasks, needs the technical knowledge and the tools or authoring applications for creating components.

The project has been structured in six main phases with simple tasks, milestones, deliverables and gates for going through the next phase.

After agreeing the structure of the project, it has been implemented in the PLM platform using the project management functionality (Fig. 3).

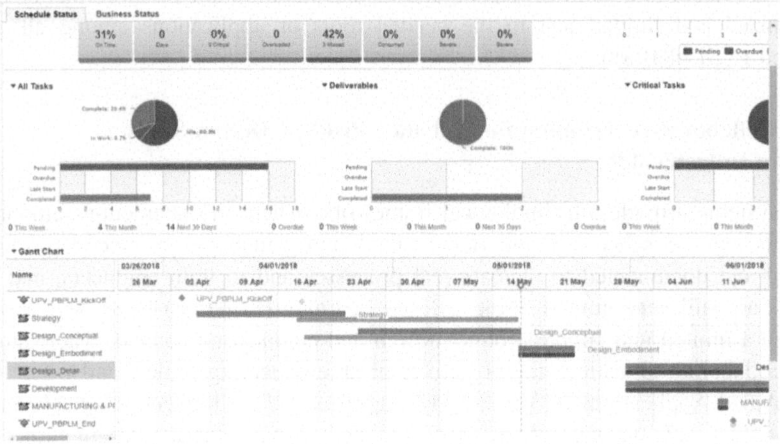

Fig. 3. Project structure used for the academic learning.

The characterization of a product design and manufacturing project template has helped to review the project progressions of each academic team.

4 Experimental Procedure

The pilot project started at the beginning of the academic year with the objective of reproducing a real case with a PLM industrial tool. Although individual courses are focused on teaching fundamentals in design, CAD design and manufacturing, we created a learning environment of how to work in design and manufacturing engineering environments with CAD/CAE/CAM and PLM systems in a collaborative way.

The key element has been not only to design and to deploy several experiences with a CAx-PLM software framework but also to explore how to face commercial tools integrating technical knowledge from the academia perspective. It has included also the analysis of how to manage the learning process of advanced applications among all the previously proposed categories and functionalities. For this academic project, we have used the 3DEXPERIENCE platform from Dassault Systemes.

The software framework provides a wide range of apps for unstructured collaboration, structured collaboration, information intelligence, and engineering content creation and management. The students started the learning process by practicing through activities such as 3D modeling, 3D tolerance analysis, 2D drawings creation, component analysis and simulation, and material removal processes definition and simulation, which they will carry out collaboratively. In order to handle this advanced educational scenario, an action has been launched to create and share learning experiences promoting collaborative engineering education.

5 Results and Discussion

Once the environment was arranged, the kickoff of the projects has been launched and all the collected information is being processed to enrich the academic training oriented to future engineers and new experiences. The project includes three parallel projects that collaborate and compete at the same time.

Although new platforms are based on the web with social interfaces, there are some new issues in these platforms. For example, how to integrate social apps with complex tools. Therefore, the first step was to create the learning interface and the training exercises repository. Abilities of viewing 3D parts is really important at least in engineering (Fig. 4).

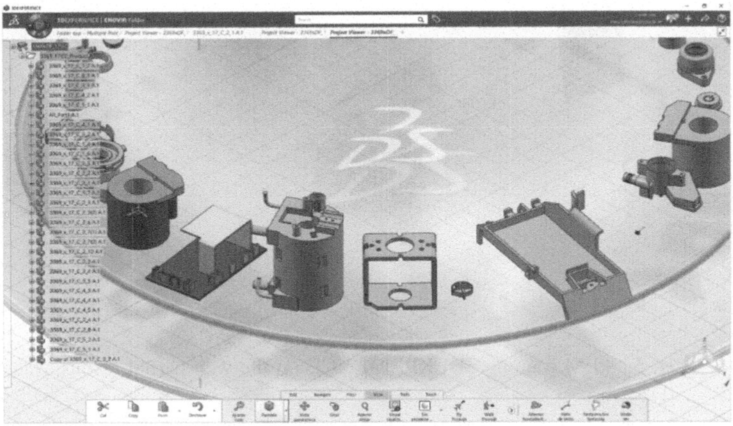

Fig. 4. PLM training workspace in 3DEXPERIENCE platform.

Then, we had to manage the parallel learning of PLM platform, particular CAx tools and social applications with regular technical content while achieving partial project milestones.

If we focus on the barriers, we have found that the first barrier to overcome is to commit with the project planning and the sequence of tasks. Students are used to work directly on the CAD tool without preparing the work. The learning curve of the apps at this level is not easy and the problem is to transmit the knowledge in short academic sessions. Another barrier is the complexity of the platform due to its completeness, it has many courseware materials for self-learning, but they last too many hours that is good for specific but goes against a fist approach to the lifecycle general vision.

We could say that the main barrier has been not the technical but the cultural change that the student has to achieve using the platform that allows showing what other colleagues are doing in real time, which has not been usual until now.

It is important to highlight that the execution had to overcome the difficulties in learning a new tool with many applications. Under the lecturer supervision, students have reviewed, designed and simulated the manufacturing process.

Regarding to the evaluation of the skills, we can say that although it is difficult to get students to work in parallel on the web but once they are familiar with the new way of working results arise spontaneously. Because the platform is web based, instructor can review what they are doing online and has a general vision of all the engineering projects (Fig. 5). The evaluation of the acquired skills is done reviewing the quality of the results obtained from a dedicated application.

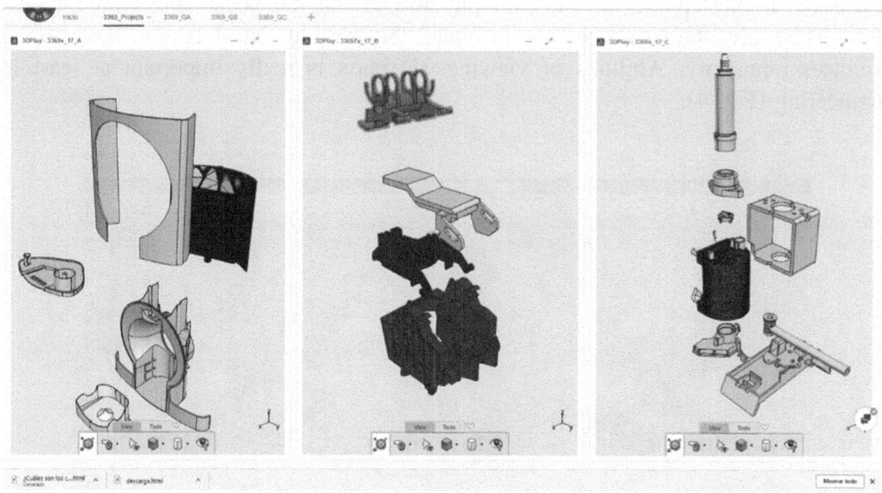

Fig. 5. PLM training 3DEXPERIENCE on the web partial results.

Concerning to the factual evaluation and measurement of the results these platforms record all the activities. Therefore, you cannot only review the quality of the project but also the participation of each member and content creation, which can be reflected in the final individual mark including skills evolution.

Another advantage is that all the CAx apps are integrated and there is a possibility of revision including from the tablets or smart phones similar to social networks. For the pilot we have used an example of designing a product doing reverse engineering. It is divided in projects for each subassembly and team and they share parts and restrictions through the platform. Therefore in this case study is complicated to compare since they are parts of a hole product and the only thing in this case we could compare was the different tasks and the fulfillment of times.

6 Conclusions and Future Work

Lessons learned from project based learning experiences have allowed us to identify different collaborative engineering skills problems that can be translated to company engineer's training. Firstly, the architecture, structure and templates of each learning project are different but there is a baseline that can be shared in each learning project. Secondly, the students output and feedback on from each project will help to correct the learning issues, since we have to control the learning if we want to succeed in this tools training.

Current practices have showed the need to define templates and collaboration procedures to make an appropriate and efficient use of the features and to accelerate the students' learning curve. This aspect is critical, especially where the available functionalities are extremely large and students are unable to identify which capabilities use and for what.

Concerning future works, we have to be able to define real projects in collaboration with industry. An initial step could be to define digital twin labs not only inside the university but also with other one to test the real distributed collaboration.

Acknowledgements. The authors would like to thanks to La Fondation Dassault Systèmes for its funding support and to Universitat Politècnica de València for its support to the project "*Competences Development in Collaborative Engineering through Project Based Learning of Industrial Design and Development with PLM tools*".

References

1. Burchardt, C.: Establishing product-lifecycle management education at university in industry context. In: IEEE International Conference on Engineering, Technology and Innovation (2015). https://doi.org/10.1109/ice.2015.7438666
2. Lu, S.C.Y., Elmaraghy, W., Schuh, G., Wilhelm, R.: A scientific foundation of collaborative engineering. CIRP Ann. Manuf. Technol. **56**(2), 605–634 (2007)
3. Monplaisir, L., Singh, N.: Collaborative Engineering for Product Design and Development. American Scientific Publishers (2002). https://doi.org/10.1016/j.cirp.2007.10.010
4. Grieves, M.: Product Lifecycle Management: Driving the Next Generation of Lean Thinking. McGraw-Hill Education, New York (2005)
5. Hermann, M., Pentek, T., Otto, B.: Design principles for industrie 4.0 scenarios: a literature review (2016)
6. Gogan, L.M., Popescu, A.-D., Duran, V.: Misunderstandings between cross-cultural members within collaborative engineering teams. Procedia Soc. Behav. Sci. **109**, 370–374 (2014). https://doi.org/10.1016/j.sbspro.2013.12.474
7. Vila, C., Abellán, J.V., Estruch, A.M., Bruscas, G.M.: Project-based collaborative engineering design and manufacturing learning with PLM tools. In: Luo, Y. (ed.) CDVE 2009. LNCS, vol. 5738, pp. 367–371. Springer, Heidelberg (2009). https://doi.org/10.1007/978-3-642-04265-2_55
8. Vila, C., Abellán-Nebot, J.V., Estruch, A.M., Siller, H.R.: Collaborative product development experience in a senior Integrated manufacturing course. Int. J. Eng. Educ. **25**(5), 886–899 (2009)
9. Rajala, S.A.: Beyond 2020: preparing engineers for the future. Proc. IEEE **100**(Spl. Content), 1376–1383 (2012). https://doi.org/10.1109/jproc.2012.2190169
10. Albiñana, J.C., Vila, C.: A framework for concurrent material and process selection during conceptual product design stages. Mater. Des. **41**, 433–446 (2012). https://doi.org/10.1080/00207543.2015.1110632

Closing the Lifecycle Loop with Installed Base Products

Martin Imboden(✉), Bernhard Fradl, and Felix Nyffenegger

HSR, Rapperswil, Switzerland
imbodenmartin@hotmail.com,
{bernhard.fradl, felix.nyffenegger}@hsr.ch

Abstract. Industry trends indicate that in the future, more systems will be rented then sold. The customer rents production capacity and demands a guaranteed high operational readiness, which is hard to achieve with conventional maintenance. Downtimes can never be completely ruled out. In order to solve this problem and guarantee high operational reliability, the predictive maintenance approach is widely discussed: By means of indicators, measured by sensors, a potential problem can be identified before it actually occurs. The application of this concept to new products gets a lot of attention in many areas. However, industrial products such as machines or plants are long living objects. It seems interesting to extend these new technologies and eventually new services business models to the installed base, too.

This paper explores and demonstrates, what it takes to upgrade an operating product in its mid-of-life stage to a smart, connected products with predictive maintenance capabilities. The showcase consists of a jointed-arm industrial robot with six axes. The robot's motions will be retraced in order to determine the state and position of the robot and finally predict, what the robot is about to do. To achieve this, the robot was made IoT-capable by attachment of sensors which communicate directly to a cloud database. Finally, a trained machine learning model allows predication on the robots' behavior. On the way to the final result, many little lessons about sensing, protocols, the right place to process or tag data in the IoT stack had to learnt and will be shared in this publication.

Keywords: Closed-loop PLM · Predictive maintenance · Machine learning IoT · Installed base

1 Introduction

Within the framework of the "Lifecycle Lab", a virtual world is being set up at HSR (university of applied science of Rapperswil) in order to discuss various concepts in the field of digitization (Industry 4.0, Industry 2025) and Closed Loop Product Lifecycle Management [1]. This is illustrated by the example of two virtual companies called "Sortic" and "DropKick". **Sortic** manufactures automation solutions, which are sold in accordance with the "machine as a service" business model. The customer does not buy the machine itself, but only "sorting capacity". This includes 98% operational readiness, defined response times and services for upgrades and retrofitting of the system.

Published by Springer Nature Switzerland AG 2018.
P. Chiabert et al. (Eds.): PLM 2018, IFIP AICT 540, pp. 348–357, 2018.
https://doi.org/10.1007/978-3-030-01614-2_32

The functional model of the machine was developed as a pick and place machine based on Lego and Arduino (electricity and software).

DropKick is a user of the Sortic system and uses it to complete its business model. The company is a delivery service startup that is strongly digitized. The interaction between the two companies is the basis for explaining and researching a digital ecosystem and closed-loop PLM. The ideas around the closed loop lifecycle will be put into practice on a real machine, since simulated systems only show the real world to a limited extent. This "installed base" is an example of a system in operation. It consists of a machine with a jointed-arm industrial robot that should be retrofitted or upgraded so that it becomes IoT-capable. This means the machine needs to be outfitted with sensors, which communicate (in this case via Bluetooth) with a microcomputer, who then communicates with a database in the cloud. Using machine learning and cloud computing correlations and trends can be identified. Based on this, predictions on the robot's motions are made [2].

Background of this project is Industry 4.0, which means to interlink Industrial production with modern information and communication technology. Intelligent and digitally networked systems are the technical basis for this. With their help, a largely self-organized production is possible. This means that people, machines, plants, logistics and even products communicate directly with each other. Interconnection should make it possible to optimize the entire supply chain in all phases of the product lifecycle and not just one single production step in a single phase [3].

Industry 4.0 consists of four basic principles that support companies in identifying and implementing industry 4.0 scenarios [4].

- **Interconnection:** machines, devices, sensors and people can connect and communicate with each other via the internet of things or the normal internet (internet of people).
- **Transparency of information:** In order to create a virtual image of the real world, information systems of digital factory models are extended with sensor data.
- **Technical assistance:** People are physically supported in exhausting, unpleasant or dangerous tasks. Assistance systems also help people with aggregated, visualized and understandable information so that they can make informed decisions and solve problems more quickly.
- **Decentralized decisions:** Industry 4.0 systems are capable of making autonomous decisions and thus carrying out tasks independently. In exceptional cases, tasks are transferred to a higher authority, for example in accidents.

2 Related Work

In this paper, machine learning is used to monitor how a system behaves and when and how something changes, i.e. applying predictive maintenance.

Orhan, Aktürk and Celik found out that vibration monitoring and analysis in rotating machines produces information about the internal structure of the machines. With this knowledge, maintenance activities can be planned and scheduled [5].

Pedregal, García and Schmid developed with RCM2 a predictive maintenance system for railway turnouts. By combining the maintenance techniques Reliability Centered Maintenance (RCM1) and Remote Condition Monitoring (RCM2), they have created a system that detects errors at an early stage and thus massively improves system safety and reliability of the turnouts [6].

Gilabert and Arnaiz dealt with Predictive Maintenance for non-critical machines such as elevators and machine tools. The elevators were modeled with neural networks and the machine tools were monitored with vibration systems. The final system consists of a sensor-processing unit and a remote maintenance module system [7].

Based on this previous work, this study aims to develop a simple applicable and vendor neutral solution to upgrade installed base products.

3 Methods and Theories

3.1 Machine Learning

Machine Learning can be described as a computer system that improves itself with experience and as a method that converts data into software. Machine Learning is a sub-area of predictive analytics, the art of estimating or calculating the future from historical data. It consists of a collection of methods used to create software models that are trained by large amounts of data and are then able to recognize certain patterns or trends or even make predictions.

What drives the development of Machine Learning? An infinite amount of data is available through digitized historical data or real-time data from embedded systems. Data storage space is globally available for a low cost and there is a number of mechanisms to capture the endless stream of data from portable devices and public clouds. Computing power is virtually endless trough cloud computing services which are available everywhere trough a large number of cloud and hosting partners. The successful use of the economic power of predictive analytics in many business use cases clearly indicates the rise of predictive analytics.

Examples of predictive analytics and Machine Learning can be seen in the behavior of spam filters, which is triggered by the content, title and origin of messages. Another example is pattern recognition, which is used in speech or face recognition. Also, there are ads in web search engines which are tailored for users based on their search history [8, 10].

3.2 Data Science

Data Science addresses the following five fundamental questions. Each of these questions is answered with different algorithms i.e. Machine Learning methods. One can imagine the algorithm as a recipe and the input data as ingredients. The algorithm specifies how the data is to be combined and mixed in order to get a response.

Is that A or B? Simple classification algorithms are used for questions with two possible answers, multiclass classifications for questions with more than two possible answers.

Is this strange? Detection of patterns and anomalies are used to identify unexpected or unusual events or behaviors. This indicates where to look for problems.

How much? How many? Regression algorithms make numerical predictions and therefor help answer questions regarding numbers.

How is this organized? The structure of a dataset needs to be understood. Clustering separates data into natural clusters, simplifying interpretation. Understanding how data is organized makes it easier to understand and predict behavior and events.

What should I do next? A group of algorithms called „in-depth learning" answers this question. These algorithms learn from results and choose the next action (reward driven).

In-depth learning is generally well suited for automated systems that require many small decisions without human guidance. Algorithms for in-depth learning collect data during operation and learn through systematic try and error [9].

3.3 Predictive Maintenance

By comparing a sufficient amount of real-time data with previous data, errors can be detected in their origin. Cross comparisons can be used to find correlations and thus not directly related disturbances. Predictive maintenance can eliminate faults long before damage occurs [10].

To put it bluntly, one wants to find out when something breaks before it breaks, so that a reaction can be planned and implemented at an early stage. This principle applies to large machines, hand-held devices, software and even to humans.

The general approach is to gather suitable data. This data must be prepared, and incorrect or flawed data must be removed to enable Machine Learning. The prepared data then needs to be tagged for recognition while training a machine learning model. After tests and possible alteration, the model is able to do predictions when it is fed with new and unknown data (Fig. 1).

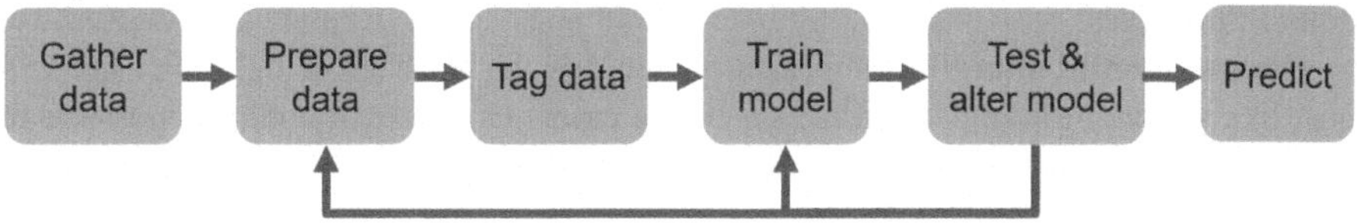

Fig. 1. General approach in predictive maintenance

3.4 The IoT Stack

"IoT Stack" refers to the overall structure of an IoT application with all layers. In simple terms, an "IoT Stack" consists of three layers. At the bottom is the first layer, consisting of a device that generates data, e.g. a sensor. The second layer includes the communication between the device and the cloud, like a gateway. The third and last layer is located in the cloud and consists of a cloud storage and software, which turns the stream of data into insights and uses.

4 Use Case to Showcase IoT on an Installed Base Product

4.1 The Sample Product

The existing system, also referred to as "installed base", consists of a handling robot of the type M20iA from Fanuc. The System has various interfaces such as ProfiBus, TCP/IP and digital as well as analog inputs and outputs. In this work, the Fanuc robot is considered a black box, which does not communicate. The measurement setup, which is attached to the robot, must work independent.

4.2 Use Cases

Detect Motion Patterns. If the robot performs a motion program, the attached sensors send acceleration data via Bluetooth to a microcomputer, which in turn sends combined data packets to a cloud storage. In the cloud, the data will be prepared and built into datasets. Those datasets will then be fed to a machine learning model to identify the active motion.

Predict Load-Dependent Drift. Like before, acceleration data will be gathered end sent to a cloud storage, built into datasets and then fed to a machine learning model. Additionally, the information on which motion is active and with which load weight is given. Based on that, the machine learning model then predicts a drift in motion or acceleration of the loaded robot.

4.3 Measurable Parameters for Both Use Cases

Acceleration data in three axis directions will be measured. Based on that, conclusions on the values and directions of acceleration during a motion can be drawn. Also, the alignment of the sensors and therefor the alignment of the robot can be calculated on the "direction" of the earth's gravitation.

Gyrometer data describes the rotational acceleration which will be measured around three axes.

Environmental data like temperature, humidity, air pressure or light intensity will most likely have little impact on the given use cases. However, it could be possible to draw conclusions about the season, the daytime and whether someone was near the machine or not.

5 Communication Concept

5.1 Key Considerations

In the case of the used jointed-arm industrial robot, several questions needed to be answered.

How Many Sensors? Nearly any number of sensors can be linked to a single microcomputer. The question is how many should actually be used. A single sensor is not enough because not all of the joints can be observed. With three sensors, a motion can theoretically be recorded precisely enough depending on various factors. Furthermore, it would probably be possible to reconstruct the position and alignment of the robot axes with three correctly placed sensors.

Where to Put the Sensors? The positioning of the sensors on the robot arm has an influence on the quality of the measurement. Possible positions for sensors could be directly on the wrist of the robot or at the end of axis 5, a sensor on the elbow or directly after axis 3, and also on axis 2 or on the upper arm of the robot.

How to Communicate? There are several ways to transfer measurement data from the sensors to a cloud database. Data can be sent directly from the sensors to the database via a smartphone or microcomputer. It would also be imaginable to collect the measurement data with a microcomputer and then send it to the cloud via the robot controller, or to send it from the sensors directly to the robot controller and then on from there on.

Sampling Frequency? In order to be able to retrace a motion, a sufficiently high sampling frequency is required, which can be determined experimentally. However, a higher sampling frequency also means higher data throughput.

5.2 Components

Sensors: The TI SimpleLink SensorTags CC2650STK are used as sensors. In addition to environmental sensors for temperature and humidity, these include acceleration sensors and gyroscopes.
It would be possible to use other sensors, but the TI sensor tags include the most relevant sensors to cover the desired values for this work.

Apart from that and a reasonable price, the TI sensor tags have a preconfigured Bluetooth interface, which makes further work easier.

Gateway: For grouping and forwarding the sensor data a Raspberry Pi 3 microcomputer is used which runs with the operating system Raspbian Jesse. Again, other microcomputers would be possible. However, the operation of the Raspberry is generally known and very simple, which is why it is preferred. If only a single sensor tag is used, it can also be connected to a smartphone.

Software: For data handling, Node-Red is to be used, which with its simple, graphical programming is very easy to use. Self-written functions can also be implemented with little effort.

Database: The data is stored on the Microsoft Azure environment. Several different database types are available, for the use case SQLite was chosen, again for simplicity reasons.

5.3 Communication Along the IoT Stack

Three sensor tags are used to trace the motions of the robot. With three sensor tags, acceleration and rotation can be monitored at three different positions. Those positions are at the wrist, elbow and shoulder of the robot (axes 2, 3 and 5, as seen on the picture below) (Fig. 2).

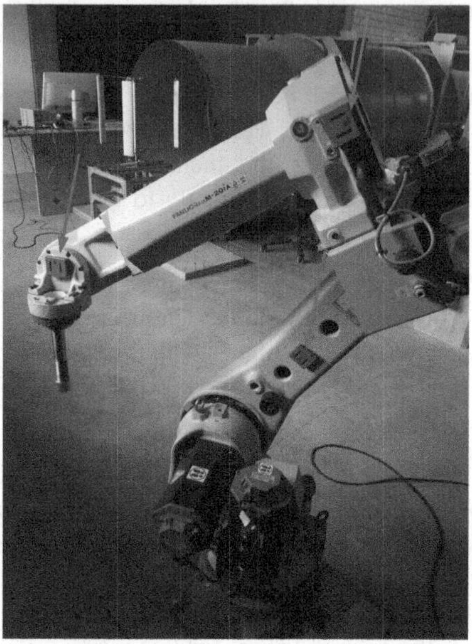

Fig. 2. Installed base with mounted SensorTags

The datasets travel from the sensor tags via Bluetooth to a Raspberry Pi3, representing the local factory system. There, the datasets get accumulated and slightly reshaped before they are sent to a virtual computer in the IoT Gateway in the cloud via a web socket. In this setup a NodeRed instance serves as IoT Gateway. On the virtual computer, the datasets get their final form, which is compatible to the logic of the database. Also, identifying information is added here to make machine learning possible.

From there on the datasets get forwarded to a cosmosDB database on Microsoft Azure cloud services. A prescript is necessary to ensure an automated connection to the database and a graphical user interface shows the user the current sensor values (Fig. 3).

xpos1p	ypos1p	zpos1p	xpos1n	ypos1n	zpos1n	xpos2p	ypos2p	zpos2p	xpos2n	ypos2n	zpos2n	xpos3p	ypos3p	zpos3p	xpos3n	ypos3n	zpos3n
108	1	1	0	1	0	44	6	0	0	0	0	0	1	0	0	0	0

Fig. 3. Example dataset used for training the machine learning model

From the database the prepared datasets get imported into Microsoft Azure Machine Learning Studio using simple sql-query language. The datasets are used to train a Machine Learning Model, which is then able to make (inaccurate) predictions. Tests of that model show if it works or if further improvements are necessary.

With a tested and approved Machine Learning Model, predictions can be made. For that a web service must first be set up, which then forwards the prediction of the Machine Learning Model back to the user. Again, node-red is used to show the user graphically what is happening and what the results of the prediction are (Fig. 4).

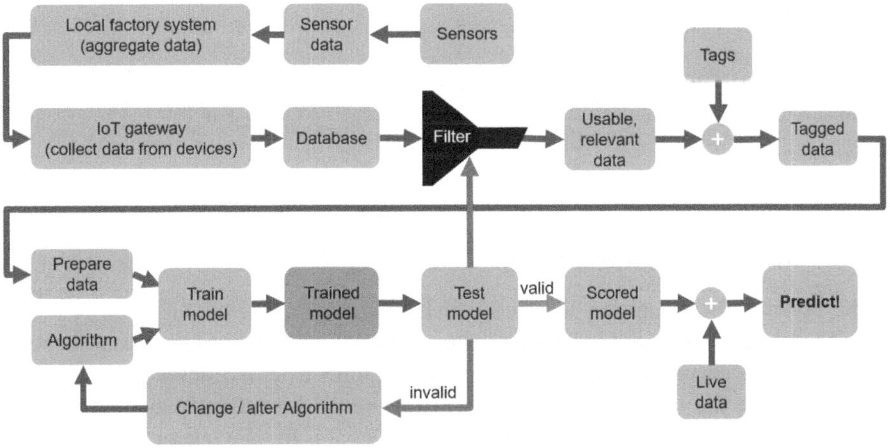

Fig. 4. Communication along the IoT-stack

6 Implementing Machine Learning

6.1 Providing Learning Data

Machine Learning requires that prepared data is available, so-called learning data. Based on this data, a model is trained. The trained model then contains rules and instructions with which it can assign incoming data to the corresponding patterns and thus make predictions.

Depending on the kind of prediction that is to be made, different approaches on recording learning data are possible

In this case for example, there was no use to feed acceleration curves to the machine learning model as it "learns" row by row and thus will completely loose the time-information of the data. That's why the time-information needs to be extracted beforehand. A simple one-line dataset is needed that contains all the important data points. The data had to be prepared so that it was simple enough, yet accurate enough for the learning. Eventually, we ended up using a rather simple approach: From the sample shown in Fig. 5, the values which were greater than one g or smaller than minus one g per sensor and axis were counted. Such that a complete motion can be represented a one single sample.

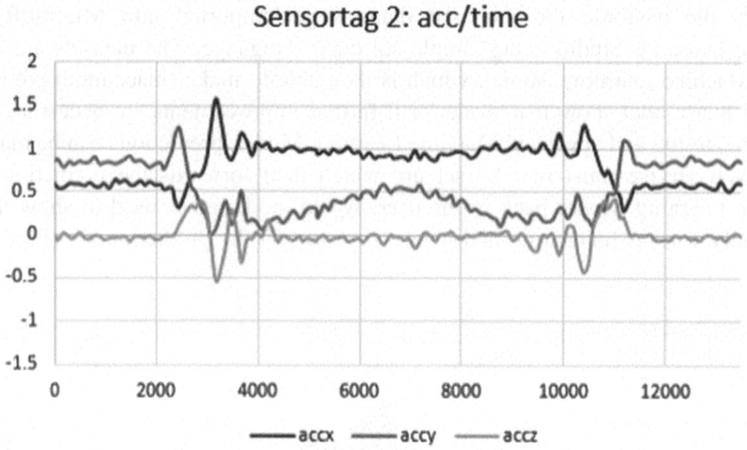

Fig. 5. Data sample

6.2 Choosing a Learning Strategy

In the given work a question is asked which has several possible answers. A robust learning strategy is required. Although there are selection guidelines and cheat sheets, it is not trivial to choose a learning strategy and requires extensive tests.

In our case the task will be managed using multi-class classification, since they produced the most promising results. The ultimate goal is to train one or more Machine Learning Models so that they can identify robot motions and positions when fed with life data. To train a model one feeds it with prepared and tagged data and an algorithm. This algorithm contains the logic. Which algorithm to use can be determined via the type of the problem or experimentally.

7 Conclusion and Outlook

It is possible to upgrade existing installed base products to make them IoT capable with simple technologies and tools. However, on the way to the presented solution a lot of unexpected barriers had to be conquered. E.g. unexpected updates of cloud providers can change the complete communication pathway.

Machine learning needs a lot of data. In the frame of this work only a limited number of samples was recorded, which led to unsatisfying predictions. Much more samples are needed to get reliable predictions.

The aim of this study was to use standard tools and algorithms. Machine Learning means an infinitely large collection of tools. It is extremely difficult to understand how these tools interpret data.

Furthermore, the preprocessing of data has an immense influence on the quality of the predictions. It would be thinkable to try out the mathematical programming language "R" to prepare datasets or even to write learning-algorithms. This would probably increase transparency of data processing a lot.

In this work acceleration sensors where the main source of data, it would be conceivable to use other sensors or even other sensor principles.

References

1. Fradl, B., Sohrweide, A., Nyffenegger, F.: PLM in education – the escape from boredom. In: Ríos, J., Bernard, A., Bouras, A., Foufou, S. (eds.) PLM 2017. IAICT, vol. 517, pp. 297–307. Springer, Cham (2017). https://doi.org/10.1007/978-3-319-72905-3_27
2. Nyffenegger, F.: Aufgabenstellung_BA_2017_imboden. HSR, Rapperswil (2017)
3. Plattform Industrie 4.0. http://www.plattform-i40.de/I40/Navigation/DE/Industrie40/WasIndustrie40/was-ist-industrie-40.html;jsessionid=D7ED4118DED525F176F382A8F939369D. Accessed 18 May 2017
4. Hermann, M., Pentek, T., Otto, B.: Design principles for industrie 4.0 scenarios. In: 2016 49th Hawaii International Conference on System Sciences (HICSS), Hawaii (2016)
5. Orhan, S., Aktürk, N., Çelik, V.: Vibration monitoring for defect diagnosis of rolling element bearings as a predictive maintenance tool: comprehensive case studies. NDT E Int. **39**(4), 293–298 (2005)
6. Pedregal, D.J., García, F.P., Schmid, F.: RCM2 predictive maintenance of railway systems based on unobserved components models. Reliab. Eng. Syst. Saf. **88**(1), 103–110 (2004)
7. Gilabert, E., Arnaiz, A.: Intelligent automation systems for predictive maintenance: a case study. Robot. Comput.-Integr. Manuf. **22**(5–6), 543–549 (2006)
8. Barnes, J.: Azure Machine Learning - Microsoft Azure Essentials. Microsoft Press, Redmond (2015)
9. Microsoft: Data science for beginners. https://docs.microsoft.com/de-de/azure/machine-learning/machine-learning-data-science-for-beginners-the-5-questions-data-science-answers. Accessed 15 March 2017
10. Diamond, S., Marfatia, A.: Predictive Maintenance for Dummies. Wiley, Hoboken (2013)

A Reference Model for PLM in the Area of Digitization

Felix Nyffenegger[1(✉)], Roman Hänggi[1], and Adrian Reisch[2]

[1] University of Applied Sciences HSR, Rapperswil, Switzerland
{felix.nyffenegger, roman.haenggi}@hsr.ch
[2] Ernst & Young GmbH, Berlin, Germany
adrian.reisch@de.ey.com

Abstract. With the uprising discussion around digitization, the value of product data has reached a new level. Product Lifecycle Management aims to play a core role in enabling the digital transformation in industry. The focus of PLM has traditionally been on the management of processes and data to define product types while many concepts of digitization rest upon individual product instances. In the context of current PLM implementations, this new perspective is not yet widely understood. A model that explains the interaction of product type and its instances along the business processes is missing. This essay suggests a PLM reference model that separates the lifecycles of product types and product instance. Four phases in a closed loop process explain the interaction between type and instance and how they are connected to the business processes of a company. The model results from a series of workshops with industrial experts and was applied in several industrial projects.

Keywords: Product lifecycle management · Reference model
Closed loop PLM · Digitization

1 Introduction

During the past two decades the importance and value of product lifecycle management (PLM) has been continuously rising. Many companies today consider PLM as a core strategic topic. During this period, the scope of PLM and its impact on business processes has been growing. Today it is understood as a business activity to efficiently manage products and its digital representation along the complete lifecycle [1]. Typically, PLM emphasizes multiple processes inside and outside of a company.

Along with the expansion of PLM, its complexity has been growing a lot. To understand the impact of PLM in a company we need to understand many aspects such as interdisciplinary design processes, change management, sales configuration, global supply chain management, the role of variants in product structures, installed base and service subjects, and many more [2, 3]. In other words, establishing value adding and sustain-able PLM concepts involves collaboration between experts from various disciplines inside and outside a company. Each of them has its own technical language and its own specific models to explain his domain. However, cross-functional

Published by Springer Nature Switzerland AG 2018.
P. Chiabert et al. (Eds.): PLM 2018, IFIP AICT 540, pp. 358–366, 2018.
https://doi.org/10.1007/978-3-030-01614-2_33

discussions turn out to be difficult, since a common language is missing. Even the term "product" is often discussed controversially.

The presented reference model intends to add a new perspective to explain the role of product lifecycle management on both sides: the product type and the product instances. We aim to give experts from different domains such as designers, supply-chain planners, service suppliers, IT-specialists, or PLM vendors a common and understandable framework to discuss PLM topics. In terms of education it helps to give PLM a novel, holistic structure. Eventually, it might contribute to shape the profile of PLM in the area of digitization and hopefully foster the discussion in research.

2 Related Research

Current reference models for product lifecycles can be divided in models suggested by researches, vendors of PLM solutions, and models from reference architectures suggested by standards. Also, they can be classified into linear approaches (birth to death) or circular approaches.

Eigner, one of the PLM pioneers in Europe, describes PLM as a holistic approach to enable information access and decision support throughout the complete lifecycle of a product [4]. He points out, that PLM must sup-port collaboration in business processes (e.g. design, sourcing and production) along the supply chain. In his reference model, the lifecycle stages of a product are: requirements, product-planning, development, process-planning, production, operation, and recycling. Many authors [1, 5] and system vendors describe similar linear models of the product lifecycle in order to address capabilities, concepts, or concerns in the implementation of PLM systems.

Kiritsis et al. suggest an easy-to-use model defined by three main phases [6]: Beginning-of-life (BOL) including design and manufacturing, Middle-of-life (MOL) including distribution use and support in terms of repair and maintenance, and End-of-life (EOL) where products are retired. He intro-duces the term "closed loop lifecycle" and points out the lack of information flow between EOL and BOL. Later in [7] he proposes an ontology that is able to map all phases into one sematic model that supports both, the evolvement of the design of a product type as well as optimization in the MOL phase.

Porter and Heppelmann address a shift of paradigm in PLM in the area of smart, connected products [8] focusing on a business perspective. They show the immense power of closed loop information systems to gain competitive advantage. Additionally, they call attention to the necessary in-vestment in connected product capabilities in order to achieve long-term success of such an approach. From this perspective, the scope of PLM includes the "IoT technology stack" and the integration of filed product data into business systems.

Silventoinen et al. [2] describe a holistic PLM model emphasizing different aspects that need to be addressed: strategy, culture and people, processes, product structures, and IT architecture. PLM in their view is a holistic business concept that requires balanced actions in all these aspects.

Terzi et al. summed up the history of PLM and set a reference for many PLM publications in research [3]. The authors, knowing the research community very well, agree on three major phases suggested by Kiritsis et al. and define three fundamental elements of PLM: processes, methodologies, and ICT (information and communication technology). They point out that every phase can gain substantial value from information provided by the other two phases, but the information loops need to be closed. The authors assign PLM a central role to close these loops with all its elements.

The community of industry 4.0 in Germany describes a reference model for the lifecycle of a product called RAMI 4.0 [9]. The model has three dimensions: layers (from asset to business), hierarchical levels (from product to work-center to connected world), and the lifecycle value stream. In the third dimension, the lifecycle value stream is separated into two subsequent sections: the lifecycle of the type (as designed) and the lifecycle of the instances (as produced).

However, none of the models mentioned above separates the lifecycle of a product type and the lifecycles of its instances. Although the phases of operation and recycling clearly belong to the product instances and every instance has a different life. Especially for digitized or connected products, it is interesting to include the aspects of these individual lives into the PLM thinking. Production by its nature forms the transition from type to in-stance and therefore plays a key role in this thinking pattern. Closing the loop from EOL to BOL in that sense then must be the opposite to production.

Complementary to the literature mentioned above, that strongly influenced the presented work, we would like to share the following thoughts.

3 Description of the Reference Model

3.1 Overview

The general reference model, illustrated in Fig. 1, can be divided into two main areas. The lower area shows the scope of the product types, while the upper area represents the scope of the product instances. The separation of type and instance is a fundamental concept in the presented model and probably the most relevant difference to traditional models.

The product type is the concept of a product. It is the offering presented on the market. The description of a product type includes everything that is needed to promote, sell, build, operate, servitize [10, 11], and recycle product instances. Examples of information describing a type are product requirements, master data for production such as drawings, BOMs, operation plans, and manufacturing methods, or recycling instructions. Also, configuration knowledge for the sales process or instructions and tools to fulfill a service are typical items that describe a product type.

The product instance, on the other hand, represents a single physical or logical object that was produced based on a certain type. The instance is what we buy and consume as customers or users. The design of a type might include many variants while each instance represents an individual configuration of that product type. Even due to environmental conditions and the spectrum in tolerances every instance is as slightly different. Instances are individuals. Instance-related information documents the history of that instance and includes: “as built”, and “as maintained” BOMs, serial numbers,

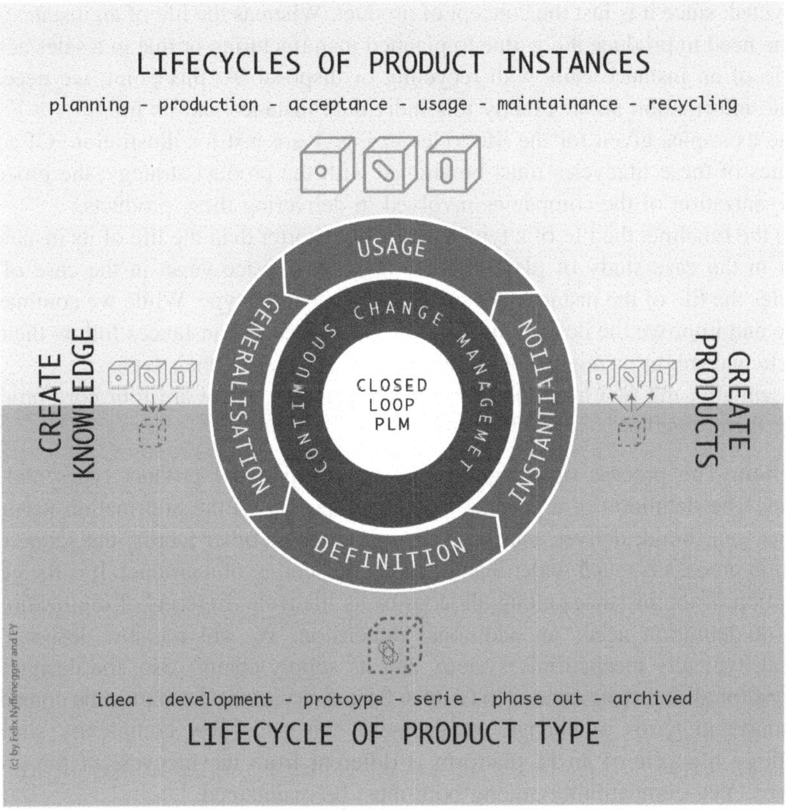

Fig. 1. The essence of product type and product instance and the 4 processes of interaction between them

test certificates, information about its customer, and ultimately sensor data measured by the product, its component, or its environment.

Ever since ERP world separates master data from transaction data. Similarly, we can separate type and instance, but not just in terms of data. In the perspective of closed loop lifecycle management, the complete life of a product type and all its instances must be in focus. This includes master data, transaction data, the physical products and all their components, data produced by the product instances during their life – often referred to as the "digital twin" [12] – but also the knowledge we gain from observing the product instances and the people around them.

3.2 Two Lifecycles for Type and Instance and How They Interact

Looking more closely on the concept of type and instance leads to the conclusions that type and instance must have different lifecycles. Unlike traditional models that describe the lifecycle of a product from idea to re-cycling, the life of the type starts with a market opportunity or idea and ends with the phase-out of this type. A type will never be recycled, since it is just the concept of product. Whereas the life of an instance starts with the need to produce it e.g. due to planned manufacturing or due to a sales activity. The life of an instance ends with recycling or disposal. At this point, we need very accurate information about exactly this individual instance and its life.

The examples given for the lifecycles in Fig. 1 are just for illustration. Of course, the states of these lifecycles must be aligned with the product strategy, the processes, and organization of the companies involved in delivering these products.

On the timeline, the life of a type can be a lot shorter than the life of its instance, as shown in the case study of plant engineering below. Vice versa in the case of consumables the life of the instance is usually shorter than its type. While we continuously change and improve the definition of our product types, the instances follow their own lifecycle and might or might not be affected by changes of their types.

Essentially, the two lifecycles are not independent. There are four core processes linking them together.

Definition. The process of designing and maintaining the product types and their services. The definition of a product type encompasses all the information needed, to promote, sell, build, deliver, and serve its instances. In other words, the scope of the definition process is much wider than just the engineering of a product. It is the generic description of the instances along all steps of its lifecycle. In terms of digitization, the scope of definition needs an additional dimension. We are not just designing the physical, typically mechatronic system, and its supply chain. Also, the design of IT solutions for all future instances (IoT Hubs, Cloud services, etc.…) must be considered. Particularly in terms of change management, this adds new complexity since the technology lifecycle of an IT platform is different from the lifecycle of the product instances. Yet, compatibility among both must be maintained.

Instantiation. The process of creating a product instance, based on the current state of its type. While creation of course comprises some way of manufacturing the product, the complete procedure from sales to delivery must be considered in this context. The instantiation process not only includes the creation of a physical product, but also its digital representation, the "digital twin". From the perspective of digitization and industry 4.0 new approaches (such as smart factories) help us to efficiently acquire accurate information about the "birth" of a product instance. Therefore, the more traditional aspects of PLM and integrated product data currently experience a renaissance.

Usage. The process of using, servicing, and maintaining a product in-stance. During this process, the product instances can collect data about its behavior and the conditions or events around it. In this phase, the aspects of digitization seem to have one of the strongest leverage potentials. With the help of IoT or similar concepts product instances are able to continuously communicate to centralized data hubs and provide the instances with generalized knowledge (e.g. for predictive maintenance or decision support based on artificial intelligence). This offers potential for new services or even new business models.

Generalization. The process of learning from the product instances and the data they collected. One key concept in this process is the aggregation of information acquired from many instances. This knowledge can be applied for both sides. It can improve the quality of service on existing instances and might lead to a better understanding of the market needs. Eventually, it leads to an improved design of the next generation product type or to the development of new services for the existing products. Again, in terms of digitization new technologies such as big data, machine learning, etc. are available to execute the generalization on a new level.

These four core processes are of a very generic nature but help to characterize the processes along the lifecycles of product type and instances on a holistic level. In reality, these processes are described by a variety of sequential and parallel business processes. Every organization looks different, however Fig. 2 pictures a common understanding of this process landscape. In the area of digitization, new aspects need to be considered along these processes as briefly discussed in the sections above.

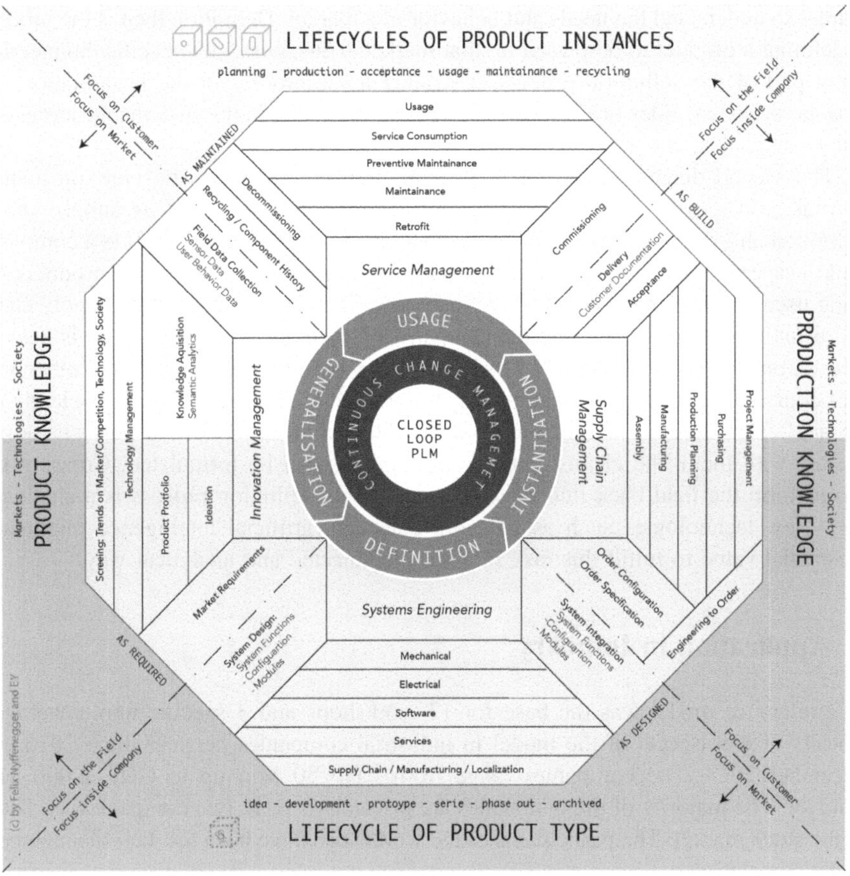

Fig. 2. Business processes along the reference model

3.3 The Boundaries of Company, Field, Customer, and Market

There is another interesting aspect to the four processes. As illustrated in Fig. 2, they form two diagonals across the complete picture. These diagonals help to understand the focus of the different processes.

The diagonal from top left to bottom right characterizes a boundary between the focus on customers and the focus on markets. Instantiation and usage are usually processes with one specific customer in focus. Particularly, the instantiation process is about breaking down the product type to the need of one specific customer. To achieve this in an efficient way, various concepts such as "assemble to order" strategies and configurators have become state of the art. On the other side, generalization and definition aim to understand and serve the need of a complete market. As mentioned above, generalization is about generating knowledge from many instances and other sources to understand the needs and behavior of a market. Definition then is the process of defining a product to be placed on that market. Thus, customer specific engineering is not part of the definition process, it's rather a sub-process of the instantiation. To separate these two sides of engineering or design is crucial in the sustainable success of many companies.

The second diagonal from top right to bottom left separates the view on mainly internal processes from what happens outside of a company and its supply chain. Definition and instantiation are processes that are typically managed inside a company, while usage and data acquisition for generalization take place where the products are being used. Even if manufacturing is outsourced, the management of the supply chain will usually be controlled inside the company that delivers the instance and is heavily focused on matching the internal processes. Innovation management on the other side is of course organized inside a company, but the focus of these processes is clearly on the field. The more we learn from product instances in the field and how customers interact with them, the clearer market requirements can be formulated. Crossing the barrier form the field back into the company and its definition process is a challenge [13]. New technologies such as IoT, big data, and artificial intelligence might add substantial value to fulfill this task in a more connected and analytical way.

4 Application in Industry

This reference model was the base for 13 workshops and 3 specific implementation projects of the aspects of the model in industrial companies between June 2016 and December 2018. The companies range from CHF 50 Mio up to CHF 2'000 Mio turnover. The majority of the companies are privately owned, two companies are listed on the stock market. The participants of the workshops have been the Top Management of the companies.

The findings on these projects can be summarized as follows:

- In particular, the model has proven to be helpful to explain the value of PLM and integrated information flows on C-level. This is a major accomplishment in light of the difficulties aligning all different aspects and complexity that digitalization brings to the industrial companies.

- The model seems to be capable to represent and align the views of the different organizational functions (product management, design disciplines, manufacturing, sales or service management).
- The complexity of the model and the generic terms for definition and instantiation is rather high. Often in workshops, definition and instantiation were replaced by "design phase" and "the factory". While this clearly is a simplification of the original intention, it still helps the understanding.
- Interesting discussions resulted with several engineer-to-order (ETO) companies. It is agreed that the design effort of ETO is part of the instantiation.
- Since design effort only scales on the definition side more focus must be spent on the definition of ETO products. This finding resulted in the "ETO-corner" shown in Fig. 2.
- During usage phase, change management of the instances does matter for services, but also affects the generalization of knowledge, particularly on long living product instances.
- Digitization of products (smart, connected products and new digital services) heavily relay on the provided quality of definition and instantiation data. PLM initiatives are no longer pushed by engineering departments but rather pulled by service or even new business model initiatives.

This model has been proven as the base for many digitalization strategies:

- The understanding of the importance of the definition phase as the base for the implementation of digital services in the usage phase is widely shared and owned by Top Management. This focus resulted often directly in an increase of budgets for this phase to drive the digital transformation.
- The generalization phase has today an increasing importance through the focus on learning from collected data. This requires a structured process based on this model.

5 Conclusion and Outlook

The presented reference model results from the learnings of long term experience in PLM implementations and a series of projects to create smart, connected products, that focus on the usage phase. Digitization requires a holistic understanding on product data, how it is created, and how physical product instances are connected to the digital world. In that sense, the presented reference model was helpful to start the discussion and add "PLM thinking", particular in the ideation phase of new product concepts or business models in a wide range of applications.

Feedback form industry as well as two mapping case studies that are currently in work indicate that the phases of definition, instantiation, and usage are well understood and can be easily mapped to the process landscape of a company. The generalization phase is discussed controversially and offers potential for further research. Generalization of data from many product instances starts to be a common strategy to develop new service products (e.g. predictive maintenance) or even new business models. Yet, only few understand generalization as a tool to better understand the behavior of a product, its users, and its environment in the market.

In academic education, the authors use the reference model to give courses a structure. It acts as a leitmotiv to put the various topics of PLM into context.

References

1. Stark, J.: Product lifecycle management. In: Product Lifecycle Management: 21st Century Paradigm for Product Realisation, pp. 1–16. Springer, Heidelberg (2011). https://doi.org/10.1007/978-0-85729-546-0_1
2. Silventoinen, A., Pels, H.J., Kärkkäinen, H., Lampela, H.: Towards future PLM maturity assessment dimensions. In: Proceedings of 8th International Conference on Product Lifecycle Management, pp. 480–492 (2011)
3. Terzi, S., Bouras, A., Dutta, D., Garetti, M., Kiritsis, D.: Product lifecycle management – from its history to its new role. Int. J. Prod. Lifecycle Manag. **4**(4), 360 (2010)
4. Eigner, M., Stelzer, R.: Produktdaten-management und product lifecycle management. In: Product Lifecycle Management - Ein Leitfaden für Product Development und Life Cycle Management, pp. 27–45. Springer, Heidelberg (2008). https://doi.org/10.1007/b93672_3
5. Saaksvuori, A., Immonen, A.: Product Lifecycle Management. Springer, Heidelberg (2008). https://doi.org/10.1007/978-3-540-78172-1
6. Kiritsis, D., Bufardi, A., Xirouchakis, P.: Research issues on product lifecycle management and information tracking using smart embedded systems. Adv. Eng. Inform. **17**(3–4), 189–202 (2003)
7. Kiritsis, D.: Closed-loop PLM for intelligent products in the era of the Internet of things. Comput. Des. **43**(5), 479–501 (2011)
8. Porter, M.E., Heppelmann, J.E.: How smart, connected products are transforming competition. In: Harvard Business Review, November 2014
9. VID/VDE. Reference Architecture Model Industrie 4.0 (RAMI4.0). Igarss 2014, no. 1, p. 28 (2015)
10. Vandermerwe, S., Rada, J.: Servitization of business: adding value by adding services. Eur. Manag. J. **6**(4), 314–324 (1988). https://doi.org/10.1016/0263-2373(88)90033-3
11. Baines, T., Lightfoot, H.: Made to Serve. How Manufacturers Can Compete Through Servitization and Product-Service Systems, vol. 1 (2013)
12. Parrott, A., Lane, W.: Industry 4.0 and the digital twin. Deloitte University Press, pp. 1–17 (2017)
13. Rossi, M., Cattaneo, L., Le Duigou, J., Fugier-Garrel, S., Terzi, S., Eynard, B.: Lean product development and the role of PLM. In: Harik, R., Rivest, L., Bernard, A., Eynard, B., Bouras, A. (eds.) PLM 2016. IAICT, vol. 492, pp. 183–192. Springer, Cham (2016). https://doi.org/10.1007/978-3-319-54660-5_17

Design for IoT Business Modeling Workshop: A Case Study of Collaborative University–Industry Education Program

Satoshi Goto[1,2,3(✉)], Osamu Yoshie[1,2], and Shigeru Fujimura[1,2]

[1] Graduate School of Information, Production and Systems (IPS), Waseda University, Tokyo, Japan
satoshi-goto@fuji.waseda.jp, {yoshie, fujimura}@waseda.jp
[2] Waseda University IPS Kitakyushu Consortium, Kitakyushu, Japan
[3] PTC Japan Co., Ltd., Tokyo, Japan

Abstract. On January 11, 2017, Waseda University launched a university–industry collaboration program with a local government body in Kitakyushu City, Japan and 20 local businesses in the area. Officially called the "Waseda University IPS Kitakyushu Consortium (IPSKC)," the program aims to change the direction of local society and to develop innovative business and technology solutions in the era of Industry 4.0. In addition, it seeks to contribute to future global business development with neighboring Asian countries. As a first step, one of the program's key initiatives was to offer consortium members an Internet of Things (IoT) business modeling workshop as part of the University's industrial IoT/business engineering education program. This paper discusses an approach to facilitate workstream as a case study. We present the key results of the workshop; and discuss the future outlook of IoT and PLM education program.

Keywords: Internet of Things · Business engineering
University–industry collaboration · Industry 4.0 · Engineering education
Workshop facilitation · Design thinking

1 Introduction

The Graduate School of Information, Production and Systems (IPS) at Waseda University focuses on academic studies related to the integration of manufacturing industry and information communication technology. The IPS campus is located in the middle of Kitakyushu City, the birthplace of Japan's modern industries (Fig. 1). Kitakyushu City is an industrial success story that managed to overcome environmental pollution that plagued the city in the 1960s [1]. However, the global business trend is changing to a new frontier of Industry 4.0. Therefore, it is also necessary to consider the impact of a new innovative business on the regional economy around Kitakyushu area (Fig. 2).

In that context, Waseda University's IPS graduate school launched its new university–industry collaboration initiative, called the Waseda University IPS Kitakyushu Consortium (IPSKC), which involves partnering with the local government of Kitakyushu City and 20 local companies. As the area is a hub to the East Asia, IPSKC is

Published by Springer Nature Switzerland AG 2018.
P. Chiabert et al. (Eds.): PLM 2018, IFIP AICT 540, pp. 367–376, 2018.
https://doi.org/10.1007/978-3-030-01614-2_34

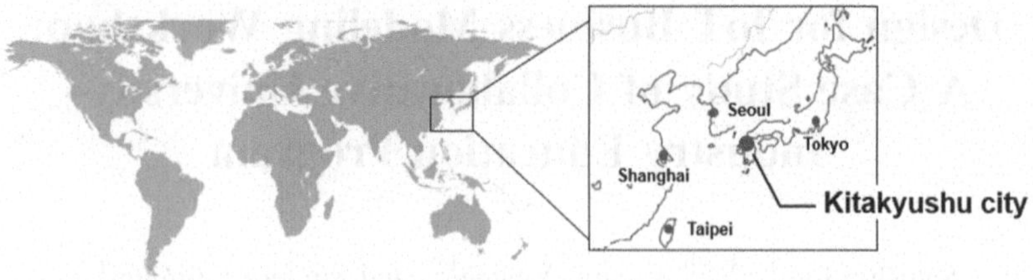

Fig. 1. The location of Kitakyushu City, Fukuoka prefecture, Japan

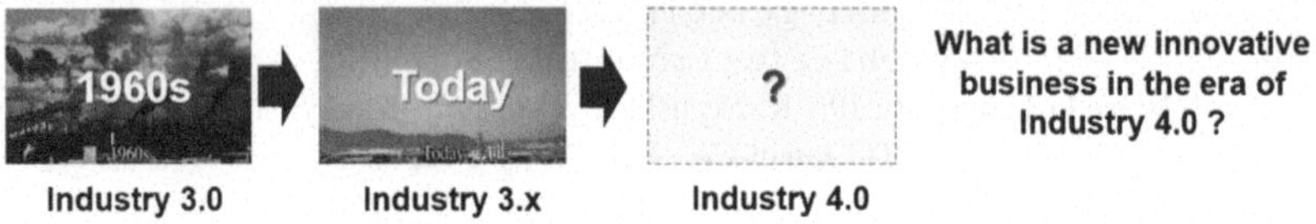

Fig. 2. New innovative business direction on Industry 4.0 for Kitakyushu area

also expected to contribute to future global business development for neighboring Asian countries. One of the key initiatives of the IPSKC in 2017 was to develop and deliver a first version of the university–industry collaborative workshop on the Internet of Things (IoT) as it relates to the business engineering education program.

This paper is a case study of the first IPSKC workshop. It begins with some background information on the key objectives of the IPSKC and on our previous studies on industrial IoT business workshop design. The paper focuses on the IPSKC IoT business modeling workshop that was held in spring of 2017. The workshop invited consortium members and IPS graduate students to participate. The intensive two-day workshop generated new insight and ideas about IoT-based business models. Finally, the key findings on the workshop along with a summary of its significance are presented.

2 Mission of IPSKC Program

The IPSKC [2] aims to be a model university–industry consortium in which the university collaborates with multiple IPSKC member companies rather than individual companies. It seeks to move beyond the conventional collaborative or commissioned research defined by contractual relationships to a dynamic ecosystem in which consortium activities spontaneously propagate between collaborative R&D projects.

IPSKC members can serve as visiting faculty members of Waseda University IPS school in charge of the university–industry collaboration program. In 2017, it appointed four IPSKC members as lecturers. They taught the following industrial management courses: Leadership for Small Organization, Experiment on Industrial Internet of Things, Corporate Innovation, and New Industry Strategy. These types of academic activities, available to both IPSKC members and IPS students, are a way of imparting practical business skills to students by IPSKC professional members (Fig. 3).

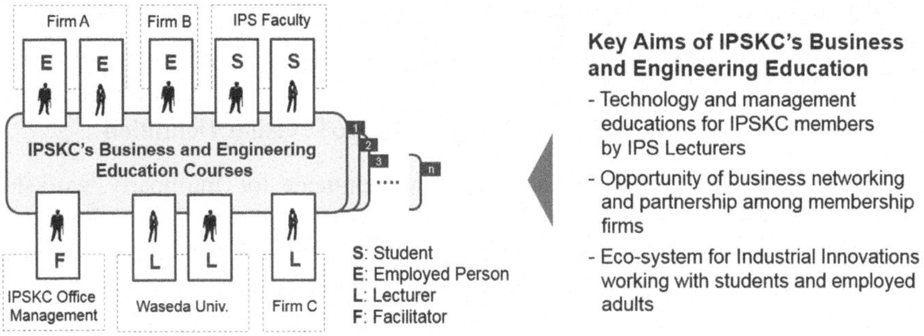

Fig. 3. Concept of IPSKC's collaborative educational program

The program is also a means for companies to recruit IPS students and to provide IPS students with employment opportunities. It aims to have a positive impact on employment matching between students and companies. Furthermore, information shared through the IPSKC may be disseminated worldwide, thus establishing Kitakyushu City as the innovative center of smart manufacturing.

3 Study Questions and Preliminary Activities

3.1 Study Questions

When the IPSKC program was launched, we considered that only conducting conventional class room lectures does not promote innovation among students. The students should get a hands-on experience of Industry 4.0.

For example, many universities have been providing students a conventional sensor and PC board as an IoT starter kit [3, 4]. However, this kit is used on a generic beginner scale and complex tools should be provided. This does not enable the participants to learn innovative business modeling.

With regards to business innovations, business schools have been already deployed and contributed for business strategy and management programs for adult employees and entrepreneurs. However, those are not always specific hands-on experience of IoT technology and solutions.

In terms of active learning type of group discussion, design thinking methodology is well-known in Japan as well as other counties [5]; customer value chain analysis, value graph, and paper prototyping are highly intriguing for the participants as they have a high potential to induce innovative thinking. However, it is hardly seen that references of design thinking workshops are included Industry 4.0 discussion themes.

Therefore, we have decided to test the following three preliminary studies that are combined with some state-of-the-art academic workshop practices. It can originally define a new workshop method on IoT-related business engineering for IPSKC members:

- Preliminary Study 1 - Design Thinking for IoT Vision Definition
- Preliminary Study 2 - Hands-on Technology Experience and Field Trip

- Preliminary Study 3 - New Business Modeling by Small and Medium sized Enterprises (SMEs) Employees.

3.2 Preliminary Study 1 - Design Thinking for IoT Vision Definition

In January 2015, we started methodology development for multiparty workshop facilitation on IoT vision definition. This methodology adopted the design thinking methodology, which was developed by d.School of Stanford University (https://dschool.stanford.edu/), so that it efficiently builds a mutual new idea of IoT vision. Since 2013, design thinking was widely adopted in the university–industry collaboration programs in Japan.

However, fewer reports on design thinking have been identified in the IoT-related academic education field in Japan than in other countries in which design thinking has been adopted widely. Therefore, the first step was to propose a pragmatic IoT visioneering workshop framework as a preliminary study in Japan. In preliminary study 1, the framework evaluated 26 types of various IoT use cases defined by PTC Inc., which was systematized along entire product lifecycle management process [6]. The IoT use cases assisted in efficiently examining IoT business solutions. To discuss the 26 use cases efficiently, the authors proposed five progress steps as a IoT workshop facilitation (Table 1). When we had an opportunity to deploy this facilitation method to a Japanese manufacturing company at the time, they could define some new visions of the IoT business model in a very short time (within just two hours). It was able to get high evaluation from participants. However, owing to the short durations of the workshops, the participants suffered from pressure and stress.

Table 1. Five Steps for group facilitation at a visioneering session [7]

Step	Group discussion topic
1	***Identify Stakeholder***—utilizing Customer Value Chain Analysis (CVCA)
2	***Select Top 6 IoT Use Cases***—aligning with corporate value drivers
3	***Narrow-down the Use Cases***—selecting 3 out of 6 for to be more specific
4	***Craft IoT Value Roadmap***—positioning the use cases on the value maturity
5	***Set Metrics (KPIs)***—qualifying business goals

In terms of such IoT discussion, understanding the technology was important as along with business management discussion. However, such a technology was not provided during the trial workshop sessions. As a result, the participants pointed out to the authors that the definition of IoT business model was undefined without the experience of IoT's technical knowledges. In addition, this workshop was designed and implemented for large sized global companies.

Therefore, it could not recognize a real value of university–industry collaboration program for SMEs.

3.3 Preliminary Study 2 - Hands-on Technology and Field Trip

On September 2016, we recruited some IPS student volunteers to participate in a 3-day workshop [8], which included a hands-on IoT technology session using Thing-Worx, a leading commercial IoT technology platform powered by PTC Inc. (http://www.ptc.com/).

In addition, the day 3 included a field trip event around the industrial areas of Kitakyushu City, where many IPSKC member companies are located. In other words, we incorporated a business tour to discover new business model opportunities as much as possible during the workshop days (Fig. 4). This allowed the participants to develop the ability of insights on IoT technology and solution development that the participants could not imagine in classroom lectures.

Fig. 4. The target local town for fieldwork activity as the workshop day 3

Workshop participants were active IPS students and university officials. It was a great opportunity for them to understand the reality of the local society situation in which the IPSKC member are located.

However, since a lot more topics were covered in this workshop than those in the previous design thinking workshop, this workshop lasted for three days. This amount of time would discourage most working people from attending.

3.4 Preliminary Study 3 - New Business Modeling by SMEs Employees

Through the results of previous preliminary studies 1 and 2, we identified that the combination of engineering and business education was valuable for the participants; the field trip was also a great activity to develop new insights for the business model for the participants. Therefore, we worked further as the third preliminary study to develop a workshop facilitation method on IoT business model design in March 2017. This was enhanced version of the past preliminary study 1 and 2.

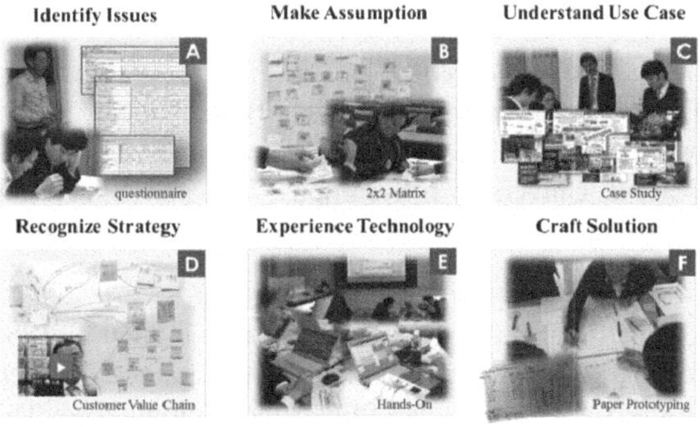

Fig. 5. Configured six sessions: A to F [9]

During the study, one of the IPSKC member companies (a local SME) was significantly interested in our workshop idea and tentative six sessions: Step A to F (Fig. 5). The CEO proposed that he wanted to implement the workshop as a part of their employee education. This CEO feared about the existing business model becoming obsolete in the future. He raised expectations on the manner in which they could efficiently define ideas of new business models in a short time.

The result was quite positive according to the participants and their CEO. Particularly, while adopting customer value chain analysis (CVCA) [10], the participants could think of a new business model and its value chain, which they had never considered before. Because the workshop was conducted in a single day, it was highly satisfactory for adult workers.

However, this did not serve the original purpose of IPSKC as IPS students did not participate in this workshop.

4 Case Study of IoT Business Modeling Workshop for IPSKC Members

4.1 Workshop Opportunity to IPSKC Members

During the inception of the consortium in 2017, we reported to the board members on the outcomes of those three preliminary studies and proposed to deploy an industrial IoT business modeling workshop for selected IPSKC members. The proposed workshop agenda was an enhanced version adopting improvements and outcomes through the preliminary empirical studies. It was reinforced as more pragmatic session contents for the SMEs. The consortium board members have approved our proposal and implemented an IoT business modeling workshop.

4.2 Workshop Agenda

The following shows the workshop activities the authors recently executed with the IPSKC members.

Date, Time, and Venue

The workshop was held on June 8 and June 9, 2017; for the total duration over these two days was 13 h (Table 2). The venue was a student lecture room in a building in Waseda University IPS campus. The participants gathered from individually owned companies and IPS graduate student communities.

Involved Members

The participants of the workshop were invited by IPSKC members. Twelve employees from IPSKC membership companies gathered; three graduate students from IPS of Waseda University also joined these employees. These 15 participants were divided into three groups during the two days. To efficiently conduct the workshop sessions, one professional workshop facilitator was assigned, who was a board member of IPSKC. One external IoT specialist supported them during the hands-on session of IoT application development (Fig. 6).

Table 2. The agenda and timetable of the trial workshop

Step	Session agenda	Interval	Clock time
Day 1 (8-Jun-2017)			
1	Warming up, self-introduction	15	10:00–10:15
2	Review of pre-questionnaire by participants	30	10:15–10:45
3	Understand of existing IoT user cases	45	10:45–11:30
Group lunch		60	11:30–12:30
4	Discuss about business objective adapting IoT apps.	45	12:30–13:15
5	Lecture of IoT global case study	30	13:15–13:45
Break time		15	13:45–14:00
6	Hands-on of commercial IoT technology platform	120	14:00–16:00
Break time		15	16:00–16:15
7	Define customer value chain for IoT value propositions	60	16:15–17:15
8	Paper prototyping of IoT solution candidates	30	17:15–17:45
9	Group presentation	15	17:45–18:00
Day 2 (9-Jun-2017)			
10	Reflection of day 1	30	10:00–10:30
11	Identify target market and customers	45	10:30–11:15
12	Define delivery model and resource planning	45	11:15–12:00
Group lunch		60	12:00–13:00
13	Discuss about revenue stream and cost structure	45	13:00–13:45
Break Time		15	13:45–14:00
14	Re-design of business model	30	14:00–14:30
15	Final group presentation	30	14:30–15:00

Fig. 6. The IPSKC members involved during the two-day workshop

Adopted Technology

During the workshop sessions, ThingWorx was used as the IoT development platform, which was developed by PTC Inc. Figure 7 shows the user interface and system architecture that was used by the participants in the hands-on technology session.

Session Agenda and Timetable

The workshop was configured for 15 sessions for two days. It was designed as an intensive program so that the participants could learn many IoT business and technology methodologies in a short time. The first day focused on understanding IoT

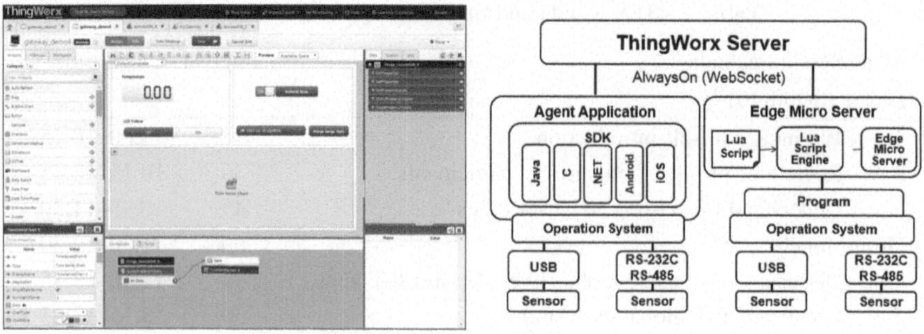

Fig. 7. User interface (left) and system architecture (right) of commercial IoT technology platform: an example of ThingWorx by PTC Inc.

solution development based on business strategy and experience of technology. The second day had a specific agenda of defining IoT-related business modeling via the business model canvas method [11]. This workshop aimed to comprehensively capture the participants' potential abilities through a group effort.

4.3 Fieldwork at the Student Cafeteria: Developing an IoT Solution for a Future School Meal Management System

One of key functions of the workshop was that we had been developing the process through which significant fieldwork should be provided to participants. Although field trips around the city and visits to companies allowed the participants to gain many insights, they were too time-consuming. We needed to create a realistic program that was not time-consuming.

Therefore, we conducted an activity in the student cafeteria located at IPS campus while the participants were having lunch. The participants were requested to observe the product and service lifecycle management and operations, such as carrying in foodstuffs, cooking, setting up meals, delivery provisions, payment, in service for eat-in space, disposal, dish-washing, which were similar to those observed in an industrial manufacturing site.

Then, the participants were presented with the question "Please imagine what the student cafeteria will be in 2030?" They had to envision the business model that utilizes IoT solution for a future school meal management as a group work. The group members discussed the problems of the current school cafeteria concerning food processing and production system.

5 Discussions

The purpose of the study was to determine whether participants were able to design an IoT-based business model built for the Industry 4.0 era during the workshop. To achieve this, we used a questionnaire that the participants had to answer at the end of the workshop.

We received feedback from 12 among the 15 participants. The results of the questionnaire are summarized below:

Question 1: Please evaluate your overall satisfaction of the workshop.

Results: 58% of participants reported being "strongly satisfied," and 42% reported being "satisfied." No participant reported being "not satisfied."

It appears that the majority of the participants comprehensively understood the value of the workshop agenda and contents.

Question 2: What methodology did you to consider to be the most effective in generating new ideas?

As stated in Fig. 8, the trial workshop was an opportunity for many participants to learn about market-proven design thinking methodologies, such as CVCA, business model canvas, and value graph.

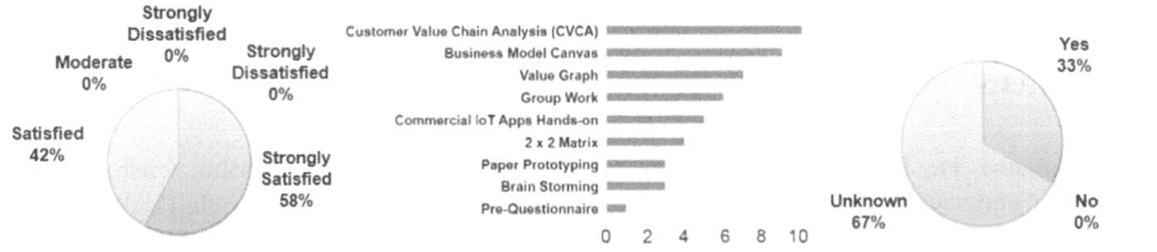

Result of Question 1 Result of Question 2 Result of Question 3

Fig. 8. Evaluation results of workshop by participants

Question 3: Did you discover a new IoT business model during the workshop?

Among the participants, 33% reported that they were able to formulate a new IoT business model using the methodologies provided and within the workshop timeframe. No participant reported not defining a new business model at all. However, 67% reported "It was unknown," meaning that it was unclear to them whether they did manage to come up with a new innovative business model during the workshop. We will need to thoroughly investigate the "it was unknown" response.

6 Conclusion and Future Work

The two-day IoT business modeling workshop was designed to provide IPSKC participants. This was an opportunity to engage in industrial IoT business modeling using technologies and business strategies introduced in the workshop. The following outcomes were identified:

- The basic method of design thinking was adopted to gather many of insights. This contributed to efficiently produce an innovative business hypothesis.
- The user experience of state-of-the-art commercial IoT application software supported the participants to make the innovative business hypothesis.

- There was a possibility to create new business models while working with multi-party groups involving adult employees as well as students.
- To create a new business model, the agenda of workshop was needed to enhance more of the current workshop agenda and contents.

The short-term intensive business workshop conducted over two days enabled a sense of achievement among the participants.

Future work includes a several days intensive education program offered to IPSKC members in summer 2018, which would be an expansion of the IoT business modeling workshop and a plan to convert the modeling program to a university credited course combined with PLM education category.

Acknowledgments. This work was supported by The Japan Society for the Promotion of Science (JSPS) Grant-in-Aid for Scientific Research (C) No. 15K00495.

References

1. Shiroyama, H., Kajiki, S.: Case study of eco-town project in Kitakyushu: tension among incumbents and the transition from industrial city to green city. In: Loorbach, D., Wittmayer, J.M., Shiroyama, H., Fujino, J., Mizuguchi, S. (eds.) Governance of Urban Sustainability Transitions. TPUST, pp. 113–132. Springer, Tokyo (2016). https://doi.org/10.1007/978-4-431-55426-4_7
2. Waseda University IPS Kitakyushu Consortium. https://www.waseda.jp/fsci/ipsrc/about/#anc_9. Accessed 11 Mar 2018. (in Japanese)
3. Cai, K., Tie, F., Huang, H., Lin, H., Chen, H.: Innovative experiment platform design and teaching application of the Internet of Things. Int. J. Online Eng. (iJOE) **11**(6), 28–32 (2015)
4. He, J., Lo, D.C.T., Xie, Y.: Integrating Internet of Things (IoT) into STEM undergraduate education: case study of a modern technology infused courseware for embedded system course. In: Frontiers in Education Conference (FIE). IEEE (2016)
5. Koh, J.H.L., Chai, C.S., Wong, B., Hong, H.-Y.: Design Thinking for Education. Springer, Singapore (2015). https://doi.org/10.1007/978-981-287-444-3
6. PTC Inc.: IoT Value Roadmap. https://www.ptc.com/en/products/iot/use-cases. Accessed 11 Mar 2018
7. Goto, S., Trolio, E., Yoshie, O., Tamaki, K.: Multi-party interactive visioneering workshop for smart connected products in global manufacturing industry considering PLM. In: Harik, R., Rivest, L., Bernard, A., Eynard, B., Bouras, A. (eds.) PLM 2016. IAICT, vol. 492, pp. 501–511. Springer, Cham (2016). https://doi.org/10.1007/978-3-319-54660-5_45
8. Goto, S., Yoshie, O., Fujimura, S., Tamaki, K.: Preliminary study on workshop facilitation for IoT innovation as industry-university collaboration PLM program for small and medium sized enterprises. In: Ríos, J., Bernard, A., Bouras, A., Foufou, S. (eds.) PLM 2017. IAICT, vol. 517, pp. 285–296. Springer, Cham (2017). https://doi.org/10.1007/978-3-319-72905-3_26
9. Goto, S., Yoshie, O., Fujimura, S.: Industrial IoT business workshop on smart connected application development for Operational Technology (OT) system integrator. In: The IEEE International Conference on Industrial Engineering and Engineering Management (2017)
10. Donaldson, K., Ishii, K., Sheppard, S.: Customer value chain analysis. Res. Eng. Des. **16**(4), 174–183 (2006)
11. Osterwalder, A., Pigneur, Y.: Business Model Generation: A Handbook for Visionaries, Game Changers, and Challengers. Wiley, Hoboken (2010)

Ontology-Based Platform for Sharing Knowledge on Industry 4.0

Giulia Bruno(✉) and Dario Antonelli

Politecnico di Torino, Corso Duca degli Abruzzi 24, 10129 Turin, Italy
{giulia.bruno,dario.antonelli}@polito.it

Abstract. Industry is currently undergoing a digital transformation for strengthening its competitiveness through the convergence between industrial automation and data exchange technologies. This trend exploits a multiplicity of technologies from Cyber Physical Systems and intelligent robotics to PLM and big data management, in order to transform the manufacturing systems in a network of smart and autonomous agents. Even if most of the technologies are already available nowadays, the key obstacle lies in the lack of experience in operating with such technologies. To develop the required skills, different strategies for learning should be adopted. The paper describes the first outcomes of TIPHYS (http://www.tiphys.eu/), an EU funded project for the development of 'social network based doctoral education on Industry 4.0'. The project organizes the learning material as small didactic elements that are accessed through an ontology-based platform. PLM concepts are applied to allow learners to customize their learning path, to provide them with a dynamic repository, whose content evolves and is enriched by the collaborative contribution of students themselves. The ontology structure is described with the help of selected examples.

Keywords: Industry 4.0 · PLM · Ontology · Collaborative learning

1 Introduction

The term Industry 4.0 refers to the so-called "fourth Industrial Revolution". The purpose of Industry 4.0 is to create a smart factory characterized by a strong digitalization of processes and based on Cyber Physical Systems (CPS). The basic concept is to exploit mature ICT technologies by implementing them in the manufacturing sector in order to develop an interconnected production system.

Industry 4.0 is characterized by the integration along three dimensions: vertical integration together with networked manufacturing systems, horizontal integration through value networks, and end-to-end digital integration of engineering across the value chain of a product's life-cycle. CPS platforms are where the specific requirements for horizontal and vertical integration of CPS, applications, and services arise in business processes [1].

The technologies specific to this fourth industrial revolution defined as "enabling" are nine [2]: horizontal and vertical system integration, industrial IoT, cybersecurity,

Published by Springer Nature Switzerland AG 2018.
P. Chiabert et al. (Eds.): PLM 2018, IFIP AICT 540, pp. 377–385, 2018.
https://doi.org/10.1007/978-3-030-01614-2_35

cloud, big data analytics, simulation, augmented reality, autonomous and collaborative robots, additive manufacturing.

It is apparent that there is a common set of concepts that pervades the different and apparently unrelated technologies. The need of explicating the underlying concepts that justify the clustering of all the technologies is pointed out by [3].

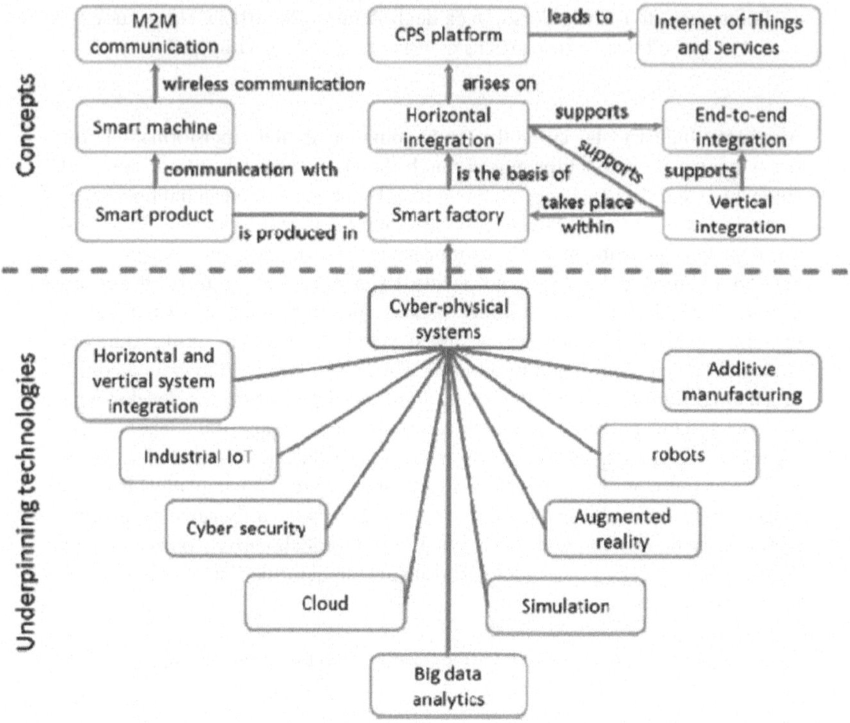

Fig. 1. The relationship among Industry 4.0 enabling technologies and the related core concepts (from [3]).

A study carried out among a large group of companies both adopting and non-adopting I4.0 technologies revealed a spread lack of knowledge on the subject [4]. It emerged that the non-adopters were not familiar with the issues of the fourth industrial Revolution that appeared as an evolution too far in the future.

An alarming feature common to adopters and non-adopters companies lay in their mentality that attributed scarce importance to the formation of the management on the issues of digital and smart factory.

The justification of present work is exactly the set up of a learning platform for the dissemination and the collaborative learning of Industry 4.0 concepts. The idea has given life to the EU project TIPHYS [5], whose preliminary results are presented here.

TIPHYS aims at developing a platform that allows students to customize their learning path through a modular approach. It relies on building blocks defined through a design approach based on Constructive Alignment.

The adopted approach relies on defining and populating two ontologies: one of the learning process and the other on the concepts that constitute the core principles of I4.0. Defined the concepts and the relationships among them, it is possible to design a learning path that lead to the desired outcome in terms of knowledge of a specific enabling technology.

In the paper the TIPHYS project outcomes and its methods are shortly described in Sect. 2. In Sect. 3 the problem of learning I4.0 is described with the help of a storyboard. In Sect. 4, the ontologies are described and in Sect. 5 they are implemented for a chosen case study. Finally, Sect. 6 draws conclusions and states future works.

2 The TIPHYS Project

The objectives of the TIPHYS project is to build an Open Networked Platform for the learning of Industry 4.0 themes dedicated to university students and to industrial technicians by adopting modern learning strategies. Such strategies are Social Network-Based Education (SNE) and Constructive Alignment (CA). In the view of educational paradigms, the concept of SNE could be a model that integrates features of the education 3.0 paradigm [6]. In SNE, students and teachers are participants that form a network, in which the network structure, communication, learning process and behavior exhibit features of a social network.

Constructive Alignment (hence CA) has emerged from the work of John Biggs as outstanding principle for devising effective and efficient pedagogical activities in higher education. CA builds upon two main concepts: the constructivist understanding of the learning process and the practical need for aligned and outcome-based curricula designing [7].

Therefore, SNE is focused on teamworking, building of interaction networks among students and teachers of different Universities and Countries. CA gives the necessary common framework for sharing educational objectives among different institutions and different teaching methodologies.

The ICT technologies supporting the project are the MOOC (Massive Open Online Courses) platforms and the virtual reality. MOOC allow offering a networked multinational learning content without the need of physical movement of students and teachers among the Universities. Virtual reality allows enriched interaction between the students when laboratory activities are needed for gaining specific skills. This is particularly important as the object of the present action is education in the field of Factory Automation.

The objectives of the project are to build an Open Networked Platform for the learning of Industry 4.0 themes. The project doesn't just create an open platform but a set of models to standardize the learning and physical processes as a "virtual copy" of the learning activities. The models are structured in a modular approach in order to promote the integration in the existing mechanisms as well as for future necessary adaptations.

The students will be able to co-create their learning track and the learning contents and dynamic student teams will be created for every specific learning requirement. Teams will interact using a Social Network application, without the necessity for physical presence.

3 Motivation

Learning to exploit I4.0 enabling technologies is a challenging task as they have a consistent number of connections with several disciplines and it is not known what exactly are the knowledge needed to implement the technology, to maintain the technology or simply to use it in a factory.

In the storyboard a fictitious manufacturing technician, with an electronic background, needs to setup a Cyber Physical System where a number of sensors mounted on a CNC are connected together and feed a simulator of the machine state for predictive maintenance purposes. As happens in I4.0, when ICT techniques are applied to factory machines, two completely different knowledge sets are involved. In this case the technician knows how to connect sensors to the factory network and how to extract relevant information to redirect to the LAN where the simulator receives inputs. On the contrary she doesn't know how to program CNC to slow down or stop the machine when a possible failure mode is detected or predicted.

Figure 2 shows the storyboard of this situation. Without a learning platform, the learner has to find the materials on her own, and they cannot be in the right order. For example, she firstly finds a lesson on CNC with programming examples, but they are hard to understand without a previous knowledge of cutting processes and related parameters. Thus, she understands she has to find a lesson more general of cutting processes, and then finally come back to the details of the programming language (G-code).

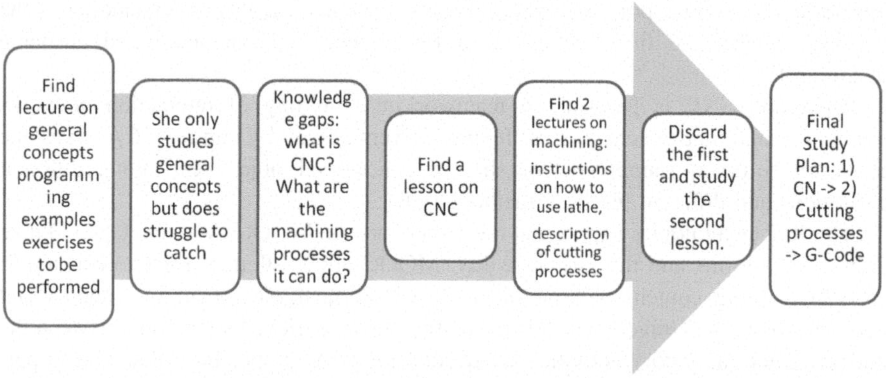

Fig. 2. Storyboard of a wrong learning path, due to the incorrect order of lessons found.

By exploiting the TIPHYS learning platform, the precedence constrains among lessons are known, thus the learning path will be firstly studying the cutting processes, then the CNC and finally the G-code, as reported in Fig. 3.

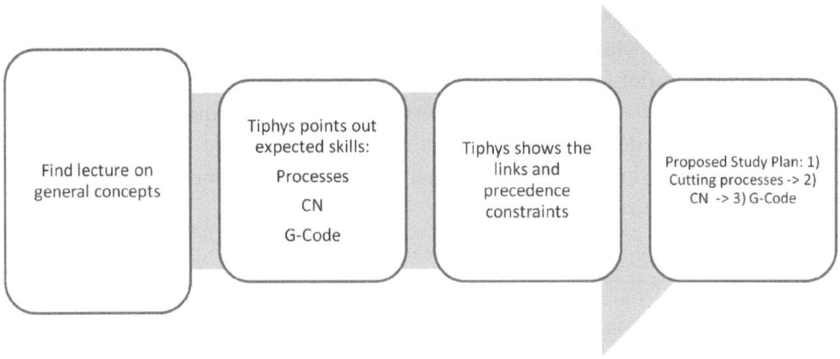

Fig. 3. Storyboard of a correct learning path, due to the exploitation of the TIPHYS learning platform.

4 Ontology for Learning Industry 4.0

Ontologies plays a fundamental role in knowledge management because they formally specify the key concepts, properties, relationships, and axioms of a given domain [8]. They are used to structure and represent knowledge in a variety of industrial domains [9, 10]. According to Imran and Young [11] the process of defining an ontology starts from the identification of the set of relevant concepts, then proceeds with the organization of concepts in a formal model representing the ontology structure, and finally performs the implementation of the model in ontology web language (OWL). This procedure was followed to define the two ontologies necessary for our purpose: one for Industry 4.0 and another for the learning process. They are described in the following subsections. Both of them are created by using the Protégé ontology editor (http://protege.stanford.edu).

4.1 Industry 4.0 Ontology

The Industry 4.0 ontology contains all the concepts related to Industry 4.0, and the relationships among them. We take as reference the concepts and technologies represented in Fig. 1 and created the corresponding ontology in OWL.

Smart factory is a core concept component of Industry 4.0 [3]. It is the place where vertical integration together with networked manufacturing systems takes place. In a smart factory, products and machines communicate with each other, cooperatively driving production. Horizontal integration refers to the integration of multiple smart factories through value networks. Smart product is another critical concept component. Smart products can refer to objects, devices, and machines that are equipped with sensors, controlled by software and connected to the Internet.

Industry 4.0 will give rise to novel CPS platforms geared toward supporting collaborative industrial business processes and the associated business networks. Technologies of nine aspects related to CPS involved in the process of turning the current industrial production to Industry 4.0 have been identified [3]. The application of CPS bring both cybersecurity issues and the generation of industrial big data, which requires cloud technology and data analytics for storage and analysis. The virtual world of CPS consists of a great variety of models of the production facilities, for which simulation can play an important role. Augment reality technology is required for operators to interact with CPS, while additive manufacturing and robots are essential parts of the CPS-based manufacturing systems of Industry 4.0. All these concepts are organized in the Industry 4.0, as shown Fig. 4.

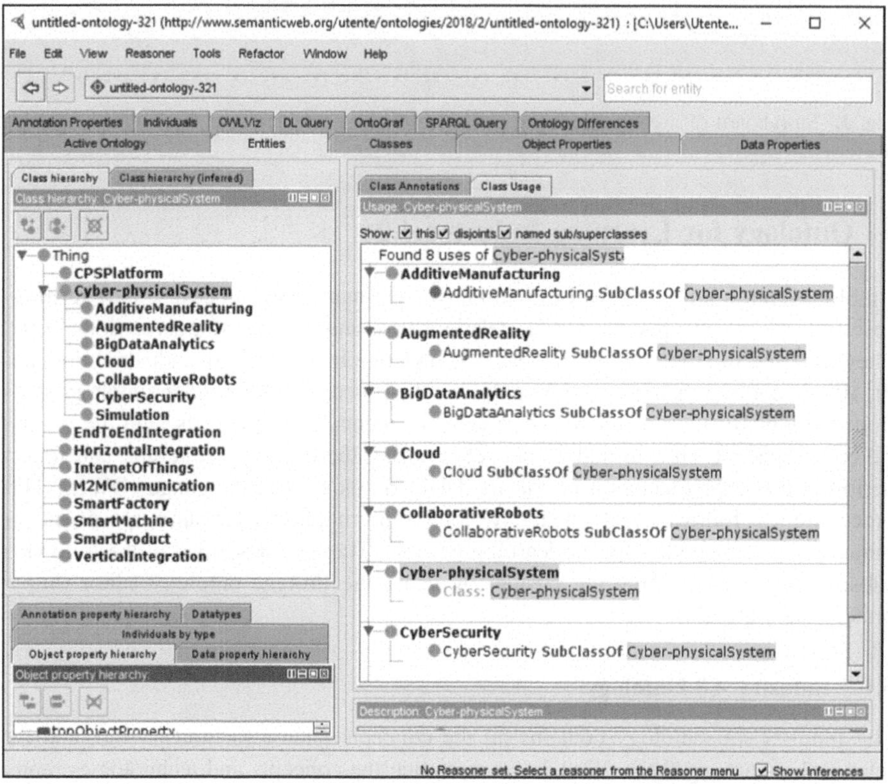

Fig. 4. Implementation in Protégé of the Industry 4.0 ontology.

4.2 Learning Ontology

The learning ontology, accordingly to the constructive alignment philosophy (i.e., the CONALI ontology) was previously defined in [7]. The main concepts of this ontology are the intended learning outcomes (ILO), the teaching activities (TA), the assessment tasks (AT), and the educational goal verbs (EGV). An ILO is connected with the corresponding TAs, ATs and ECGs. Also TAs and ATs are connected to the involved EGV. We adopted this ontology by adding a relationship to represent the constraints between ILOs, i.e., which ILOs are preparatory to reach another ILO. The implementation of the learning ontology is shown in Fig. 5.

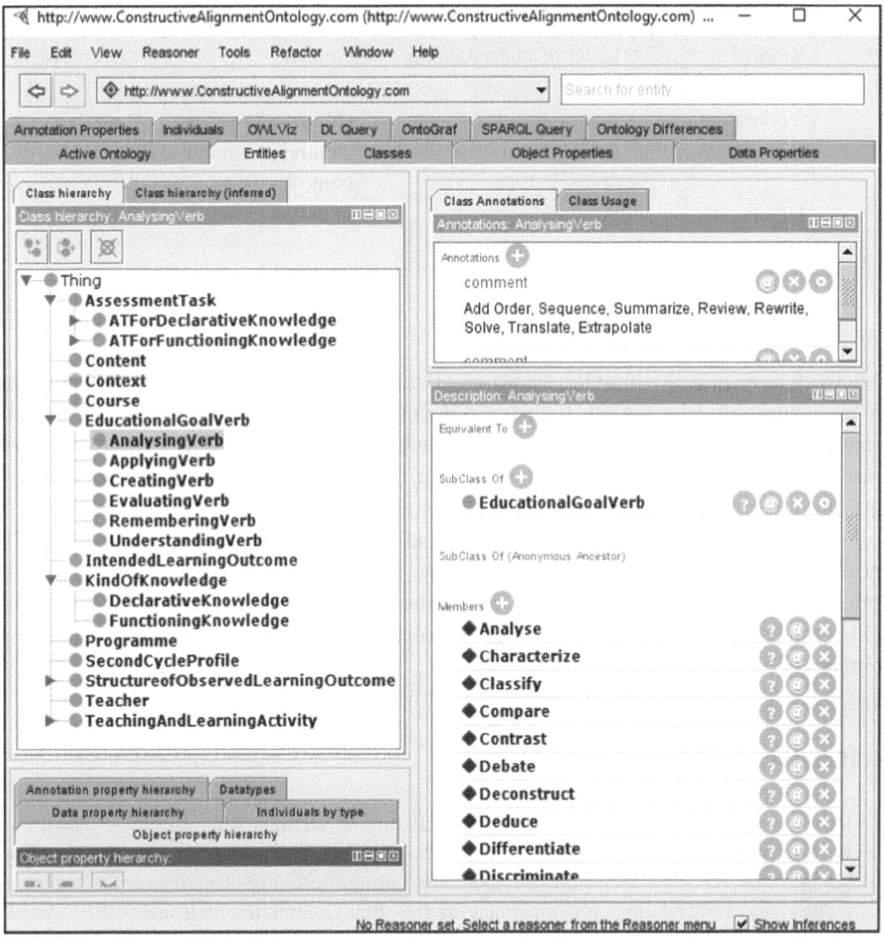

Fig. 5. Implementation in Protégé of the learning ontology.

5 Ontology Population and Usage

Both the ontologies have to be populated in order to be used. The Industry 4.0 ontology is populated with the concepts that specify the ones described in Sect. 4.1. For each concept, one or more learning outcome with the corresponding teaching activities and assessment tasks is added in the Learning ontology described in Sect. 4.2. Furthermore, the precedence constraints among ILOs are lso inserted.

By making reference to the example described in Sect. 3, Table 1 represents the ILOs available in the Learning ontology. In this case the precedence is limited to the ILOs associated to the same topic, but it is possible to have precedences also between different topics of Industry 4.0.

Table 1. Example of ILOs stored in the learning ontology.

# ILO	Kind of knowledge	Level of understanding (Verb)	Content	Precedent
1	Declarative	Assess	Cutting processes	–
2	Declarative	Select	Computer numerical control	1
3	Functional	Program	G-code	2

6 Conclusion

This work aims at describing the set up of a learning platform for the dissemination and the collaborative learning of Industry 4.0 concepts, the main objective of the EU funded TIPHYS project. The adopted approach relies on defining and populating two ontologies: one of the learning process and the other on the concepts that constitute the core principles of I4.0. Defined the concepts and the relationships among them, it is possible to design a learning path that lead to the desired outcome in terms of knowledge of a specific enabling technology. Future works will focus on the development of a networked platform, based on the two ontologies developed, where students will be able to communicate and co-create their learning track and the learning contents.

References

1. Industrie 4.0 Working Group: Securing the Future of German Manufacturing Industry—Recommendations for Implementing the Strategic Initiative, acatech, Munich, Germany (2013). https://www.acatech.de/Publikation/securing-the-future-of-german-manufacturing-industry-recommendations-for-implementing-the-strategic-initiative-industrie-4-0/. Accessed 28 Aug 2016
2. Rüßmann, M., et al.: Industry 4.0: The Future of Productivity and Growth in Manufacturing Industries. The Boston Consulting Group, Boston.https://www.bcg.com/publications/2015/engineered_products_project_business_industry_4_future_productivity_growth_manufacturing_industries.aspx. Accessed 28 Aug 2016
3. Liu, Y., Xu, X.: Industry 4.0 and Cloud Manufacturing: A Comparative Analysis. University of Auckland, New Zealand (2017)
4. Federmeccanica: I risultati dell'indagine Industria 4.0 condotta da Federmeccanica (2016)
5. Tiphys: Social Network Based Doctoral Education on Industry 4.0. Erasmus Plus KA2 Strategic Partnership, Project No: 2017-1-SE01-KA203-034524
6. Putnik, G.D., Putnik, Z.: A semiotic framework for manufacturing systems integration–Part I: generative integration model. Int. J. Comput. Integr. Manuf. **23**(8–9), 691–709 (2010)
7. Maffei, A., Daghini, L., Archenti, A., Lohseb, N.: CONALI ontology. A framework for design and evaluation of constructively aligned courses in higher education: putting in focus the educational goal verbs. In: 26th CIRP Design Conference (2006)

8. Bruno, G., Antonelli, D., Korf, R., Lentes, J., Zimmermann, N.: Exploitation of a semantic platform to store and reuse PLM knowledge. In: Grabot, B., Vallespir, B., Gomes, S., Bouras, A., Kiritsis, D. (eds.) APMS 2014. IAICT, vol. 438, pp. 59–66. Springer, Heidelberg (2014). https://doi.org/10.1007/978-3-662-44739-0_8
9. Bruno, G., Antonelli, D., Villa, A.: A reference ontology to support product lifecycle management. Procedia CIRP **34**, 41–46 (2015)
10. Bruno, G., Villa, A.: An ontology-based model for SME network contracts. In: Herrero, P., Panetto, H., Meersman, R., Dillon, T. (eds.) OTM 2012. LNCS, vol. 7567, pp. 85–92. Springer, Heidelberg (2012). https://doi.org/10.1007/978-3-642-33618-8_16
11. Imran, M., Young, B.: The application of common logic based formal ontologies to assembly knowledge sharing. J. Intell. Manuf. **26**(1), 139–158 (2013)

Product-Service Systems and Smart Products

A Methodological Approach for the Identification of Context-Specific Reconfiguration Options in the PLM-Context

Philipp Savarino(✉), Michael Abramovici, and Jens Christian Göbel

Chair of Information Technology in Mechanical Engineering (ITM), Ruhr-University Bochum, Bochum, Germany
philipp.savarino@itm.rub.de

Abstract. Current changes of traditional products towards intelligent, connected smart products require a fundamental adaption and enhancement of traditional Product Lifecycle Management approaches. In our previous activities we showed that lifecycle management approaches lack suitable methods and IT tools for smart products especially during their use phase. In particular the reconfiguration in the use phase has been addressed, as the characteristic properties of smart products enable a tremendous potential. As an approach virtual product twins were introduced in our previous activities in order to manage both virtual product models as well as product usage data across all engineering domains including environmental data. This contribution describes the core enabler, such as the reconfiguration lifecycle and virtual product twins for the reconfiguration of smart products during their use phase including the necessity of designing the architecture of reconfiguration options. The scope is the introduction of a methodological approach, which allows the identification of context-specific reconfiguration options.

Keywords: Reconfiguration · Smart products · Product Lifecycle Management
Virtual twin

1 Introduction

Innovations in Information and Communication Technology (ICT) have led to drastic changes of traditional products towards intelligent smart products. Smart products are defined as intelligent products with the ability to communicate and interact with other smart products and their environment by using internet-based services [1]. Among others, characteristic properties of smart products are their high degree of personalization and automation, autonomic behavior in decision making and their vast number of multidisciplinary components. In the scope of this contribution their capability to react in real-time and their tremendous potential for dynamic reconfiguration especially during their use case is of particular interest. Here, suitable methodological approaches and IT-tools, e.g. for the lifecycle-spanning management of both virtual product instance models as well as product usage data, are scarcely covered by common Product Lifecycle Management (PLM) approaches [2].

Published by Springer Nature Switzerland AG 2018.
P. Chiabert et al. (Eds.): PLM 2018, IFIP AICT 540, pp. 389–399, 2018.
https://doi.org/10.1007/978-3-030-01614-2_36

In general it can be distinguished between two types of reconfiguration: type-specific reconfigurations such as common software updates and context-specific reconfigurations like smart services generated individually for each product instance. The paper at hand addresses the context-specific reconfiguration, where every product instance, based on a permanent, individual management across all engineering domains, is confronted with the question, which reconfiguration option can be individually offered. Approaching this challenge, the normative standard ISO 10007 introduced a configuration management model including the definition of configuration units (CU). These configuration units can be considered as entities within an instance configuration that provide a specific end use function. The norm introduced a change management approach, which shares characteristics with a reconfiguration process that are not limited to any lifecycle phase [3]. However, it rather addresses type-specific than context-specific reconfigurations, as it requires otherwise knowledge of all product instance configuration units along the entire lifecycle.

This idea was approached by the idea of virtual product twins, which was originally introduced by the NASA's technology roadmap "Modeling, Simulation, Information Technology& Processing". The virtual twin was defined as an integrated multiphysics, multiscale simulation of a vehicle or system that uses the best available physical models and sensor updates to mirror the life of its corresponding twin [4]. This approach however focused mainly the simulation of the physical twin in order to predict its behavior, instead of using the product instance knowledge for compatibility checks in order to solve reconfiguration option issues, for example.

The IEEE 828 standard for configuration management in systems and software engineering introduced a description of the configuration management process, including the configuration identification process, which is a necessary element for the offering of compatible reconfiguration options. The identification is focusing primarily physical and functional characteristics and a semantic-based description though and excludes to tackle the question on how configuration units can be systemized to allow the description of a product instance's context [5].

An approach for a model-based, consistent management of control unit configurations by using function blocks is defined by the IEC 61499 standard. It focuses rather on the architecture of distributed agile manufacturing systems and thus does not consider the whole lifecycle of a smart product [6]. This standard has been enhanced in several research activities, however by mainly considering the automation of production by solving reconfiguration issues of electronic and software components [7, 8].

None of these research activities identified the potential of smart product reconfiguration in the use phase while considering the virtual twin concept as a basis for the reconfiguration process. Additionally, the necessary design of the reconfiguration options architectures has not been in the scope of research activities so far, which is why these issues will be addressed in the following sections.

2 Enabling the Reconfiguration Lifecycle of Smart Products

This chapter describes the core enabler for the reconfiguration of smart products during their use phase. It consists of the reconfiguration lifecycle and virtual product twins, which are both integral components of smart products. Apart from that, the methodological approach for the design of reconfiguration options architectures is introduced in order to be able to offer context-specific reconfiguration options.

2.1 The Reconfiguration Lifecycle of Smart Products

The characteristics of smart products, as mentioned in Sect. 1, lead to a highly expanding set of capabilities regarding the reconfiguration compared to traditional products. Here, the reconfiguration of smart products during the use phase is of particular interest. It enables for example a vast amount of personalization potential, due to the continuous awareness of its own configuration and environment. This continuous reconfigurability during the use phase can be regarded as a reconfiguration lifecycle as shown in Fig. 1.

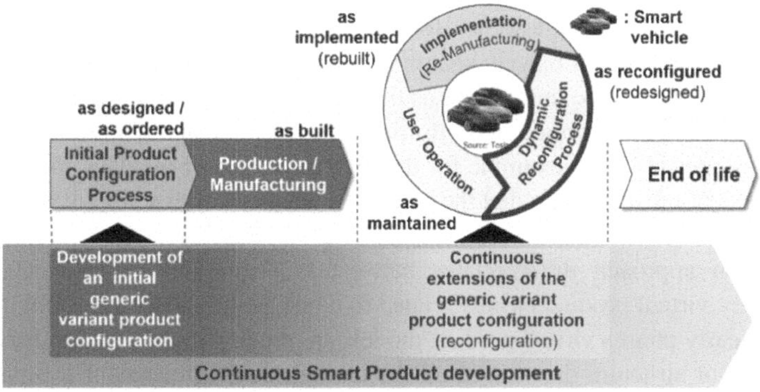

Fig. 1. The reconfiguration lifecycle of a smart product [9].

The process of configuration starts at the beginning of a smart product's lifecycle. The development of an initial generic variant product configuration in a company's product portfolio establishes the possibility to choose a specific instance configuration, e.g. based on a customer's order (as designed/as ordered). The configuration process is characterized by rules that define the relationship between elements, which can be described as configuration units [3]. Due to variation in the production/manufacturing process, for example related to deviation of production resources, the smart product is built (as built). Parallel to the smart product's lifecycle, the generic variant product configurations available for possible reconfiguration differ, as some variants may have left the product portfolio e.g. for external reasons, such as changes in legislation. This diverse set of reconfigurations is now available in the smart product's use phase. They can be offered during maintenance processes (as maintained) or used to offer a new set of IT-driven functions to the product, e.g. by offering higher degree of personalization for the customer (as reconfigured). Subsequently, the new configuration has to be implemented (as implemented) and reopens a new use/operation phase of the smart product until it reaches its end of life.

2.2 Virtual Product Twins

As in the previous chapter introduced, the reconfiguration of smart products during the use phase enables possibilities like a higher degree of personalization. Therefore, a higher attention to the management of both virtual product models from previous lifecycle stages as well as the present models need to be at hand in order to determine the given configuration. Apart from that, especially environmental information can enable reconfiguration offers that can be described as context-specific. A context in this particular angle can be understood as the circumstances that form the setting for an event [10]. For example, a context-specific reconfiguration offer can be described as a triggered event, which is happening based on the smart product's current situation. The possibility to describe a smart product's current state or the surrounding environment is given by product use data. Thus, a holistic approach to describe both virtual product models as well as product use data along the entire lifecycle is shown in Fig. 2 by considering virtual product twins. In the past, various approaches with different terms addressed similar research questions, for example product avatars where the product-instance is the centre of a lifecycle-spanning management concept [11]. In general, the virtual product twin can be considered as the notion, where data from each stage of the product lifecycle is transformed into information which is made seamlessly available to subsequent stages [12]. An example for the transformation of the data into information can be the use of the data to predict the product's behavior after setting it in its semantic context.

The given approach differentiates between a virtual and a physical lifecycle, because every virtual product twin is related to a physical instance mirroring a physical twin. In the early phases virtual product models are created in the virtual lifecycle, such as CAD data or structure data based on the configuration process for example. In the following phases, for example manufacturing data, maintenance reports or material data provide information about the current state of the product instance. In the early phases of the physical lifecycle e.g. measurement data can be collected from early prototypes. Subsequently, machine, condition or service data provide knowledge about either the current product instance's own state as well as its environment. As previously described, the data gathered and transformed into information and is then made seamlessly available to subsequent phases. Thus, the amount of information along the entire lifecycle is increasing from every phase as well as from every reconfiguration. This leads to a higher set of context-specific deployment possibilities of the virtual twin especially during the use phase [13].

2.3 Design Methodology for Reconfiguration Options in the Scope of Context-Specific Smart Product Reconfiguration

In order to offer reconfiguration options that can be considered as context-specifically adequate, the architecture of reconfiguration options need to be addressed. Especially

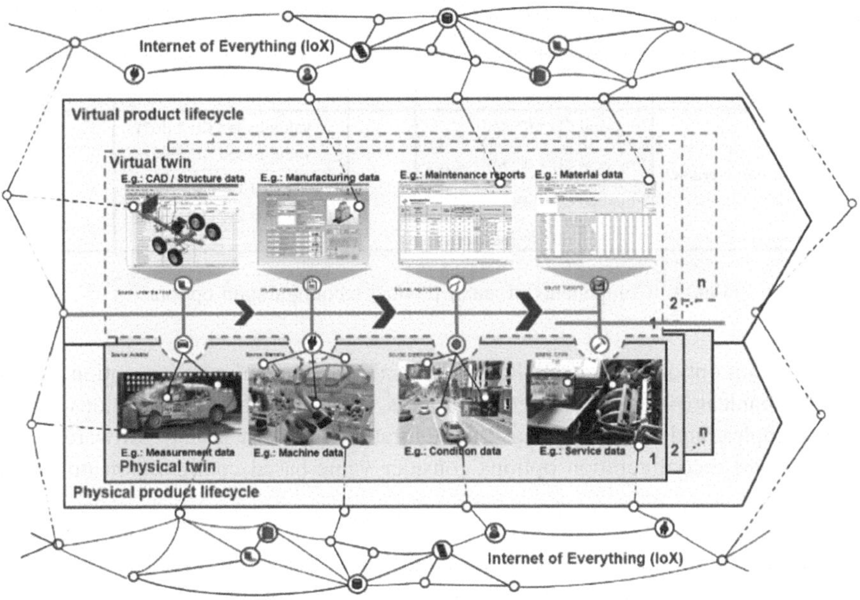

Fig. 2. Virtual product twins as a holistic approach for the consideration of virtual product models and product use data along the entire lifecycle [13].

for the reason that some reconfiguration options can have a high amount of overlapping configuration units with other reconfiguration options, a systematic approach will be introduced that indicates all necessary components for smart product reconfiguration options. In general, there are two types of configuration units (CU) that can be differentiated: physical configuration units and value-based configuration units. Physical CUs are referring to models describing physical parts such as CAD-data or manufacturing data. The relationship between these physical configuration units is described by considering metadata, which defines the relationship in form of hierarchical levels. Thus, for instance, an assembly between two parts can be described by using metadata that define the structural interdependence between them. Value-based CUs are addressing the context-specific attributes of smart product reconfiguration options. They define a certain value or value-interval of a sensor, for example. In order to successfully offer a reconfiguration option, these values has to be satisfied by the corresponding values of the product's instance sensor. Both physical and value-based CUs can be embedded in a three-layered architecture (Fig. 3):

- Class list of characteristics group
- Class list of characteristics
- Characteristics

The class list of characteristics group is defining the nature of a reconfiguration option. This classification is nevertheless challenging, as the tremendous amount of interdisciplinary parts in products increase. Therefore, a continuum between mechanical-based and smart reconfiguration options allow a rough classification of a

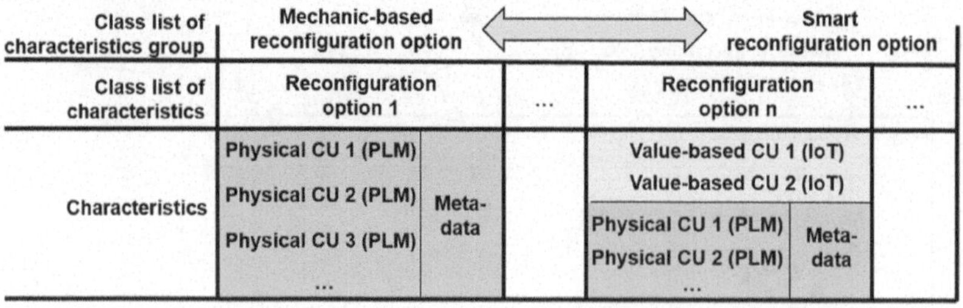

Fig. 3. Components of smart product reconfiguration options.

reconfiguration options nature. While mechanical-based reconfiguration option address solely mechanical (physical) configuration units, smart reconfiguration options include highly complex and interdisciplinary configuration units, including software. Additionally, smart reconfiguration options consider value-based configuration options as well.

The class list of characteristics describes the reconfiguration option itself. Those are more specifically described by their characteristics located in the third layer, which are simultaneously responsible for the classification of the reconfiguration options nature.

3 Approach for the Identification of Context-Specific Reconfiguration Options in the PLM-Context

In this chapter the architecture and the components for the identification of context-specific reconfiguration options for smart products are outlined. While the first part describes a three-layered structure, the second part identifies the necessary components and their interdependencies.

3.1 Architecture of the Methodological Approach

A structural systematization of the required components for the identification of context-specific reconfiguration options in the PLM-context shows is shown in Fig. 4. It consists of three layers each bearing a different character of information considering the given input and output in the form of value-based and physical configuration units (cf. Sect. 2.3). Additionally, each layer is differentiating between a physical and a virtual lifecycle, where the physical lifecycle can be regarded as the source of the value-based configuration units (e.g. the value of sensors) and the virtual lifecycle as the source of the physical configuration units (e.g. CAD-data).

The generic layer contains rules that define the relationship between them. This refers for example to configuration units that hold an incompatibility in certain assemblies. The total amount of configuration units as well as its values in the generic layer are discrete as the reconfiguration options are fully defined by the reconfiguration provider. Concrete, all reconfiguration options with its physical and value-based configuration units are determined and are the basis for further consideration for context-specific reconfiguration offers for each product instance.

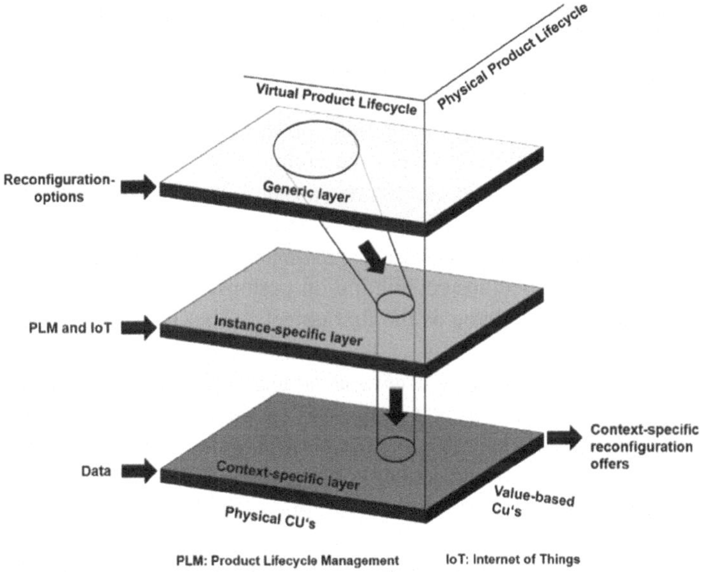

Fig. 4. Structural systematization of the context-specific reconfiguration components in the PLM-context.

Part of the instance specific layer are the data of the Product Lifecycle Management (PLM) as well as the Internet of Things (IoT). It contains all product relevant data such as structure, behavior or product usage that can be part of a product instance data for example. Therefore, as it combines all product relevant data from the virtual and the physical lifecycle, it can be considered as the virtual product twin layer. In order to identify compatible context-specific reconfiguration options, generic reconfiguration options have to be matched with the instance-specific data. Considering the compatibility mainly physical and value-based configuration units including structural information between them have to be checked. Therefore, only a small part of the whole instance-specific layer is relevant for the successful identification of context-specifically matching reconfiguration options.

On the context-specific layer product instance data is constantly updated in order to check the compatibility of the generic reconfiguration options with the product instance models and data. Therefore, the concrete product structure data with its physical configuration units as well as the product usage data in form of value-based configuration units. However, these physical and value-based configuration units are similar to those predetermined by the generic reconfiguration units and congruent to those from the instance-specific layer. Consequently, after a successful compatibility check, a reconfiguration option that is matching to the product instance's context can be identified and offered.

3.2 Components of the Methodological Approach

Necessary components for the offering of reconfiguration options by considering a two-staged methodological approach are shown in Fig. 5. The approach bases on the generic layer with all possible reconfiguration options that can be offered by a provider. The reconfiguration options derive from the architectural framework as presented in Sect. 2.3. Here, the characteristics of each reconfiguration options, namely the physical and value-based configuration units, are of particular interest for the methodological approach. The physical configuration units provide the input for the first stage for the identification of context-specific reconfiguration options. Therefore, the physical configuration units can be considered as the first objective that has to be successfully met by the physical configuration units of the product instance as part of the product reconfigurator. The aim is to find a general compatibility of the product instance's physical configuration units and its assembly. For example, if there is a necessity for specific configuration units in order to offer a reconfiguration option like an autonomous parking service for a smart vehicle, such as ultrasonic sensors or wheels, those are predefined by the generic reconfiguration options and checked for presence in the product instance. Thus, also the physical configuration units of the product instance have to be considered for this compatibility checks. These physical configuration units are part of the product instance's virtual twin, concrete the part concerning the virtual product lifecycle such as product models related to physical units like CAD data from an engine part. For the first compatibility check are mainly virtual product models relevant, which describe the configuration unit (e.g. CAD-data) including metadata like structural information. Of particular interest are only those configuration units, which are part of the reconfiguration option architectures and contain the physical configuration units of a product instance within its assembly unit. These data can be retrieved from PLM-systems and analyzed in a product reconfigurator tool, e.g. by exporting the configuration unit describing data including its metadata on a predefined temporary basis. Such a product reconfigurator tool is capable of matching determined sets of rules between the physical configuration units in the generic reconfiguration units and those present by the structure models of a product instance.

If the general compatibility between generic reconfiguration option's physical configuration units and those of the product instance have been proven successful, these reconfiguration options are taken into further consideration for context-specific offerings. However, as soon as physical configuration units are replaced at either the formal description of the reconfiguration offers or the product instance, for example due to a product portfolio change (generic) or a maintenance processes (instance), this first stage of compatibility checks have to be repeated. The second stage of the identification of context-specific reconfiguration options is particularly describing the current product instance's condition and its environment. In general, a product's condition and its environment can be determined by analyzing sensor data, for example. Thus, the value-based configuration units of the generic reconfiguration options are the basis for this stage. Concrete, every value-based configuration unit, such as the necessary value interval of a supersonic sensor for a reconfiguration option like an autonomous parking service, is defined in the generic reconfiguration options and is considered as a reference during the compatibility checks with the value-based configuration units

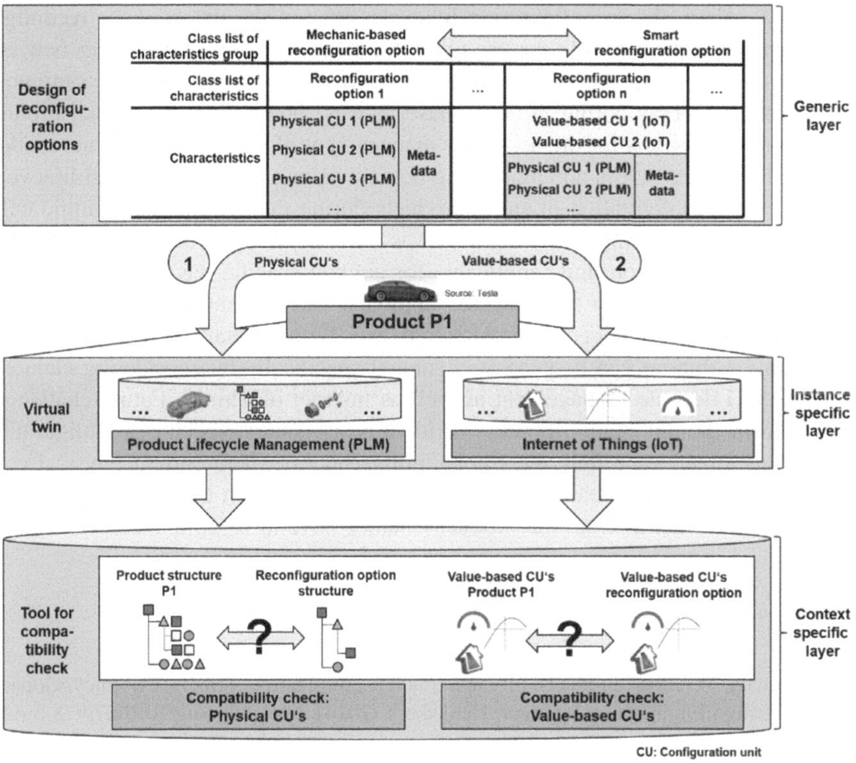

Fig. 5. Approach to identify context-specific reconfiguration options for smart products.

(condition and environmental data) of the product instance. The actual condition and environmental data of a product instance can be provided by managing a smart products physical lifecycle data with the help of an internet of things (IoT) platform. However, these data need to be provided for the compatibility check on a constant basis. The shorter the query cycles can be implemented, the better the context of the product on basis of the value-based configuration units can be determined. Consequently, the values of the value-based configuration units have to be matched with those described in the generic reconfiguration options. If the values of value-based configuration units match with those of the reconfiguration options, context-specific reconfiguration offers can be realized.

4 Summary and Future Challenges

Smart products enable a huge potential for reconfiguration scenarios during their use phase. One main driver are their multidisciplinary properties, which reflect their vast amount of multidisciplinary components. This contribution pointed out the main enabler for the reconfiguration of smart products during their use phase, concrete the reconfiguration lifecycle, virtual product twins and the design of reconfiguration option architectures. Here, the reconfiguration lifecycle stressed the potential for reconfiguration of smart products during the use phase by describing the dependencies between the initial configuration process at the product creation process and the continuous reconfiguration process during the use phase. It was shown, how the virtual product twin can serve as a basis for the necessary management of both virtual product models and product use data across all engineering domains along the entire product lifecycle, to support the reconfiguration of smart products during their use phase. Additionally, the architecture of reconfiguration options was introduced, by stressing the characteristics of the configuration units applicable for context-specific reconfiguration offers. Deriving from this point, a three-layered approach was presented with all necessary inputs and outputs. Finally, this architecture was further detailed by showing how reconfiguration options can be generated context-specifically by considering elements from Product Lifecycle Management as well as Internet of Things. Future challenges will remain in the automation process of identifying context-specific reconfiguration options. This affects especially the compatibility checks, where current physical configuration units and value-based configuration units both from the generic reconfiguration options as well as from the product instance have to be combined.

References

1. Abramovici, M.: Smart Products. In: Lapierriére, L., Reinhart, G. (eds.) CIRP Encypclopedia of Production Engineering. Springer, Heidelberg (2014). https://doi.org/10.1007/978-3-642-35950-7
2. Lutters, E., van Houten, F.J.A.M., Bernard, A., Mermoz, E., Schutte, C.S.L.: Tools and techniques for product design. CIRP Ann. Manuf. Technol. **63**(2), 607–630 (2014)
3. DIN ISO 10007: Qualitätsmanagement. Leitfaden für Konfigurationsmanagement (2003)
4. NASA Technology Roadmap, Modeling, Simulation, Information Technology & Processing Roadmap Technology Area 11 (2010)
5. IEEE standard for configuration management in systems and software engineering, Institute of Electrical and Electronics Engineers, New York (2012)
6. DIN EN 61499: International Electrotechnical Commission 61499-1: Function Block - Part 1 Architecture (2013)
7. Zoitl, A., Sunder, C., Terzic, I.: Dynamic reconfiguration of distributed control applications with reconfiguration services based on IEC 61499. In: IEEE Workshop on Distributed Intelligent Systems: Collective Intelligence and Its Applications, DIS 2006, 15–16 June 2006, Prague, pp. 109–114. IEEE, Piscataway (2006)
8. Olsen, S., Wang, J., Ramirez-Serrano, A., Brennan, R.W.: Contingencies-based reconfiguration of distributed factory automation. Robot. Comput. Integr. Manuf. **21**(4–5), 379–390 (2005)
9. Abramovici, M., Göbel, J.C., Savarino, P.: Reconfiguration of smart products during their use phase based on virtual product twins. CIRP Ann. – Manuf. Technol. **66**(1), 165–168 (2017)
10. Oxford Dictionaries: Definition of context. https://en.oxforddictionaries.com/definition/context Accessed 5 Sept 2017
11. Hribernik, K.A., Rabe, L., Thoben, K.D., Schumacher, J.: The product avatar as a product-instance-centric information management concept. IJPLM **1**(4), 367 (2006)

12. Rosen, R., von Wichert, G., Lo, G., Bettenhausen, K.D.: About the importance of autonomy and digital twins for the future of manufacturing. IFAC-PapersOnLine **48**(3), 567–572 (2015)
13. Abramovici, M., Göbel, J.C., Savarino, P., Gebus, P.: Towards smart product lifecycle management with an integrated reconfiguration management. In: Ríos, J., Bernard, A., Bouras, A., Foufou, S. (eds.) PLM 2017. IAICT, vol. 517, pp. 489–498. Springer, Cham (2017). https://doi.org/10.1007/978-3-319-72905-3_43

What Affect Manufacturers Approaching Servitization: A Case Study in HVAC Industry

Claudio Sassanelli[1(✉)], Giuditta Pezzotta[2], Fabiana Pirola[2], and Sergio Terzi[1]

[1] Department of Management, Economics and Industrial Engineering, Politecnico di Milano, Via R. Lambruschini 4/b, 20156 Milan, Italy
{claudio.sassanelli,sergio.terzi}@polimi.it

[2] Department of Management, Information and Production Engineering, University of Bergamo, Viale Marconi, 5, 24044 Dalmine, BG, Italy
{giuditta.pezzotta,fabiana.pirola}@unibg.it

Abstract. Product Service System (PSS) development involves both manufacturing and service workers, carrying them great potential to pursue industrial competitiveness, customer satisfaction and sustainable improvement. The belief is that the development level of PSS design is slowly evolving through a path strongly driven by the evolution of the technology and the progressive involvement of the industry in its application. However, on one side some companies still need to understand the relevance of the development process related to their service offer, on the other best practices able to improve the PSS development processes performances more systematically are needed. The paper proposes a case study, first providing a mapping of the service offer of Company A, an Italian company in the humidifiers industry. Then, it investigates, through a content analysis, what could affect companies both positively or negatively to switch their approach from a product-centric to a service integrated one. This transition would enable them in the future to develop more advanced PSSs, opening new market opportunities and being more capable of satisfying customer needs.

Keywords: Product Service System (PSS) · Product service system development · Servitization · Case study · Humidifiers industry

1 Introduction

The manufacturing world, increasingly absorbed by Service Economy [1, 2], has today to cope with the need of navigating the "servitization" phenomenon [3]. To do this, companies are compelled to change their traditional business model, based on the development and sale of pure product, in a Product-Service System (PSS) based one, where new services are added and bundled to physical products [4]. However, due to the high complexity of this process, this transition is slow and gradual [5, 6] and composed of several sequential and parallel steps [7]. Indeed, it requires companies not only to raise their awareness and capacity of consistently designing combined products and services but also to plan other changes inside and outside themselves, as the type of

Published by Springer Nature Switzerland AG 2018.
P. Chiabert et al. (Eds.): PLM 2018, IFIP AICT 540, pp. 400–409, 2018.
https://doi.org/10.1007/978-3-030-01614-2_37

relationship with customers, the cash flows dynamics and the business costs and risks [8]. Indeed, in order to adequately act on these different dimensions, new PSS customized business models are needed, enabling manufacturers to go through this gradual "service infusion" [8–10], [11] and to fulfil customer-focused value creation, long-lasting productions [12] and sustainable consumption patterns [13].

Thus, this paper aims at understanding what could affect companies along with their transition from a product-centric approach to a service integrated one. To do this, a case study has been conducted starting with a mapping of the service offer of the company involved. With this objective, the paper is organized as follow. Section 2 introduces the concept of PSS, unveiling the issues and hurdles occurring during the companies switch from being a product manufacturer to become a product-service integrated provider and proposing the theoretical framework to conduct this research. Then, Sect. 3 reports a detailed description of the adopted methodology. Formerly the used criteria in the case study approach are reported, then an introduction of the assessed company is given. Section 4 explains the results of the study, showing the outputs of the coding analysis, and Sect. 5 is dedicated to their discussion. Finally, Sect. 6 concludes the paper, triangulating results with theory and providing further researches and limitations.

2 The Servitization Issues for Manufacturers

Companies are beginning to consciously realizing the importance of the servitization phenomenon [5], but they still have to prepare themselves in effectively designing integrated PSSs, complex systems made of product and service components and supported by suitable infrastructures and networks. [14] gave the first formal definition of PSS in 1999. Goedkoop et al. gave the first formal definition of PSS in 1999. Along the time, different definitions confirmed that PSSs are made to pursue industrial competitiveness, customer satisfaction and sustainable development [15]: as stated by [16], PSS represents a new business model [17] enabling firms to generate new sources of added value and competitiveness, empowering the relationship with customers through customized, innovative and long-lasting integrated solutions. There is, however, an open issue on how to detect the real customer demand and how to convert it from an intangible to a tangible dimension [16] to exploit the service offer potential. [7] explained the dynamic of this slow process by three sequential hurdles to be overcome in making such a transition. First, firms might not believe in the economic potential of the service component for their product. Second, although a firm might realize the service market potential, it may decide that providing services is beyond the scope of their competencies. Finally, a firm might realize the service market potential, decide to enter that market but fail in deploying a successful service strategy. Indeed, transitioning from product manufacturer into service provider constitutes a significant managerial challenge. Services require organizational principles, structures and processes new to the product manufacturer: the need of new capabilities, metrics and incentives highlights the shift on the business model changes from transaction to relationship-based. Developing this new set of capabilities necessarily diverts financial and managerial resources from manufacturing and new product development, the traditional sources of competitive advantage for the organization. Related to this, [7] revealed some hurdles for manufacturers to move into services, specifically the evaluation of the Installed Base (IB) service potential and the extent to which a firm should enter the service market. Just as product and market attributes determine the profitability potential from the IB, they believe that organizational attributes dictate the extent to which a firm should move along the product-service continuum. In this regard, [18] identified and structured five main tactics for PSS implementation: contracts, marketing, network, product and service design, and sustainability. Each of these tactics has been declined in several particular aspects per each PSS business model category (product, use or result oriented). However, the relationship between PSS business models and these five tactics deserves further investigation, since internal and external organizational conditions can influence it. Indeed, due to the high complexity, if managed wrongly, these possible heterogeneous factors occurring during the servitization path can often lead manufacturers to fail, making them fall in the service paradox [10, 19]. Furthermore, [20] defined three possible service growth trajectories in system suppliers, based on how much manufacturers infuse higher levels of services in their offerings: (1) availability provider, those who promise to achieve availability offering service activities during the system lifecycle in an use-oriented, customized, relational and output-based way; (2) performance provider, similar to project-based sales and requiring a major offer differentiation; and (3) 'industrializer', standardizing previously customized solutions to enable repeatability and scalability. They also assumed that firms need to keep balanced business expansion and standardization activities but also to manage the co-existence of different system supplier roles. Summing up the contributions from literature about such a complicated transition, in Table 1 are reported the elements identified by the authors as relevant to understand how to enter the servitization effectively, supporting to detect and keep into consideration what can foster and hinder such pursuit. These elements, constituting a theoretical framework, have been used to build the protocol to analyze Company A: both the internal and external factors, faced during their approaching to servitization, were detected to exploit their offer under a service perspective.

Table 1. Theoretical framework: elements to effectively assess servitization

	Context	Elements to be investigated to pursue servitization
1	Customer	The type of customers and their needs [16]
2	(AS-IS) offer provided	The type of offer provided by the company: what is provided to satisfy the customer needs so far and how (through which kind of revenue stream) [7, 20]
3	(TO BE) Product/Installed Base potential service offer	The potential service offer that can be implemented based on the products provided, to satisfy the unfulfilled customer needs [7, 20]
4	Knowledge and cultural aspects	The internal and external processes needing to be improved to foster a cultural servitization shift in the company [18, 20]

3 The Case Study: The Methodology and the Company

In this chapter, formerly a detailed description of the used methodology is reported. Then, the company assessed in the case study is introduced, and its current service offer is mapped. Then, the framework defined in Table 1 were used to build the protocol to conduct the case study and to obtain the results reported in Sect. 4.

In order to investigate the transition leading the integration of services into the product offering, an explanatory case study has been conducted: it included semi-structured interviews to gather data and content analysis to achieve multifaceted information [21, 22] through a hierarchic approach. A list of topics to be investigated in the interview protocol were the starting point in coding analysis to detect variables, categories and labels [23]. The first step has been the definition of the unit of analysis on the basis of the primary aim of the research: the choice fell on Company A Climate Business Unit (BU). The case study approach used is indeed a holistic single-case design approach [21]. Through content analysis, first the main categories were identified, condensed, abstracted and labelled with codes, then patterns were traced: eight main categories were founded and linked together. Even though three interviews were conducted in the different BU of the same company, this paper describes only the Climate BU case, representing a particular context in Company A since it is the only division in the company providing a complete final solution to customers.

Case selection is a complex matter [24]: Company A, an Italian company founded in the early Seventies, has been chosen. The strategy of focusing on technology, quality and innovation – regarding both process and product – allows Company A to achieve a significant role in the world market of Refrigeration, Air Conditioning and Air Humidification and to become a specialist in the development of control systems. The company has two main divisions: HVAC (Heating, Ventilation, Air-Conditioning) and REF (Refrigeration), involving different Original Equipment Manufacturers (OEMs), Dealers and Projects. One of the main issues of the company is represented by a weak value proposition in the service context lacking a structured service design and development process, intended for both its direct customers and the final users of the proposed solutions. Indeed, Company A service offer is limited to commissioning, installation assistance to OEMs, corrective maintenance (mainly towards OEMs), training to OEMs and branches and spare parts provision. The main issue for Company A is due to their focus on the development of the physical product against the need and will of developing new PSSs, creating a bundle of existing products and add new services.

4 Results

The preliminary result from the interview is an AS-IS analysis of Company A and of its offer in terms of products, services and PSS/solutions,, with a particular focus on the HVAC Business Unit (BU): this part is useful to realize if it already develops PSSs according to the models proposed by [16]. The division deals with different technologies for humidifiers and control systems, being able to deliver products for different types of applications: industrial environments, process industries, clean rooms, conservation and wellness. In this division different typologies of customers are involved: wholesalers (32%), contractors/installers (22%), affiliate/importers (19%), system integrators (9%), distributors (8%) and others actors (10%) placed in the value chain between OEMs and the final users. Regarding services, while for Air Conditioning and Refrigerator products, generally, the OEMs provide services to the final user since Company A produces only a part of the final product (air condition and refrigeration control system). On the other hand, for Humidifiers, maintenance, installation and commissioning are either mainly provided by the installers or outsourced to three assistance centers in Italy (which are not exclusive for Company A business). Indeed, the service revenue in this division is only the 2% of the total (mainly coming from commissioning) while spare parts count for the 35% of the total division profit. In particular, on the humidifiers market, the company provides only two services to its customers. As illustrated in Fig. 1, the proposed PSS offer in this division corresponds to product-oriented PSS, more specifically either advice and consultancy or product related services. More precisely, the first is given by Company A's HVAC BU Project and Dealers to installers regarding advice and consultancy to give them the useful information to correctly install their different products in the several contexts they are called to be used. The other service is instead delivered by installers to final users and consists in the practical installation of the solution in the plant of the customer. Furthermore, it is very rare to have the direct selling of the product to the final user: in this case, indeed, Company A's HVAC BU OEM provides the products to OEMs which are then in charge of the selling to the final users. Starting by this assessment, the next step of the analysis deals with evaluating which are the elements that could affect, positively or negatively, Company A in moving towards servitization: the interview allowed the authors to detect which are considered by the interviewee the enabling capabilities of developing service integrated solutions and of enhancing PSS offering in a systematic way.

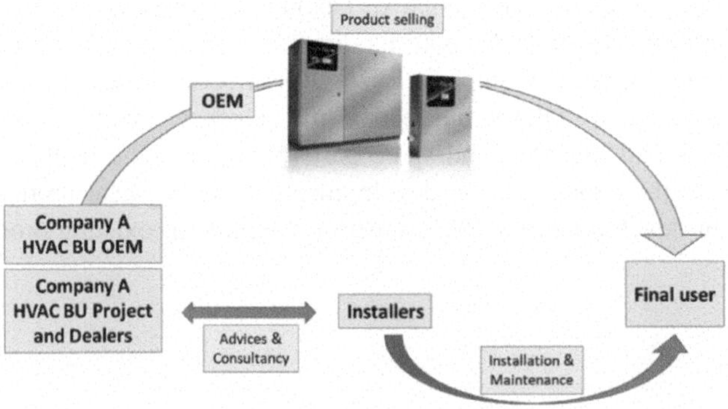

Fig. 1. Company A - HVAC BU (for humidifiers) AS-IS product oriented PSS model

The conducted content analysis brought to several results: coding allowed to detect some hidden concepts (Table 2) and to identify positive and negative patterns and relations among them (Fig. 2). The analysis started from the four main contexts of the theoretical framework of Table 1, which have been reported in the first column of Table 2 to be linked to the different coding dimensions detected.

Table 2. Coding results: categories and codes

Framework context	Coding main category	Code	Sub-category
1. Customer 2. Offer provided	Actors	pssp	PSS provider
		oem	OEM
		intc	Intermediate customer
		finu	Final customer (user)
	Relationship	rel	
	Customer heterogeneity	het	
	Willingness to develop integrated services	will	
3. Potential service offer 4. Knowledge and cultural aspects	Market constraints	know	Brand awareness & industry know-how
		dmdet	Customer (decision maker) detection
		oaint	Other industry actors interests
	Tool	chan	Channel
		plat	Platform
	External practices	extp	
	Company constraints	flex	Flexibility
		usfr	User-friendliness
		servc	Service competencies
		busap	Business approach

Table 2 and Fig. 2 show coding results: the humidifiers context is characterized by an extensive heterogeneity of customers, which brought the actors to establish several types of strategic relationships. Indeed, product and market attributes, which determine the profitability potential from the IB [7], enabled Company A to act as an availability provider [20]. Also, the company demonstrates a good willingness to develop enhanced integrated services to be included in its offer. However, positive and negative elements were detected, the company's organizational attributes, affecting its attempt to act in that direction [7]. In this specific case, to enhance its organizational setting, on one hand, the company identified some examples among its competitors and other industries, to be used as best practices, and also some tools, mainly communication channels and development platform, which could allow it to better understand the customer needs and to satisfy them more suitably [25, 26]. On the other hand, it knows that different hurdles, either at the company or market/industry level, impede them to move in a direct way to the so-called performance provider trajectory [20]. Internally they need more flexibility, user-friendliness, service competencies and more B2C oriented approach; externally they must, first of all, detect the real customer they look at (with

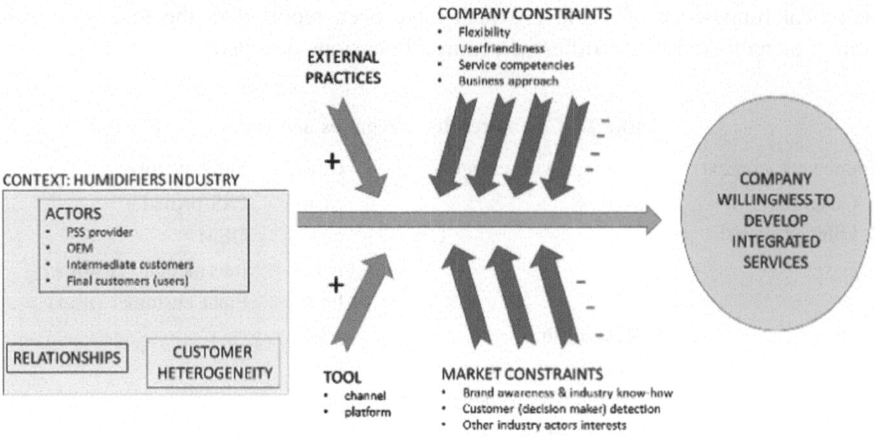

Fig. 2. Patterns: relation among the main coded categories

their characteristics and the amount of the relative business), coping with improving the brand awareness & know-how of customers about the industry complexity and also facing competitors and other actors (mainly intermediate customers as installers) interests. In this situation, the creation and introduction of new services thought exclusively for the final users and able to directly reach them, could be useful. For example, to exploit the spare parts business, Company A could install on the product a control system able to suggest in advance the need of a spare part and to send the order directly to them. This would simplify the ordering process, avoid the product failure and then increase the customer satisfaction. Since in this market the final customer is not the decision maker, but the installers select the system to be installed for each application, the company currently works to strengthen the relationship with these actors. In addition to this, since a large amount of different applications characterizes this BU, the company needs a higher level of flexibility in its solutions. However, a "plug and play" solution able to adapt to the different applications is still missing. It would support the company to have a better understanding of the customer needs and a market segmentation based on it: how many types of users could be interested in buying such solutions, which are the communication means and channels needed to reach the different users, how to understand what is the real value for each of them and what they need to know about the product before the purchasing. The "plug and play solution" would support Company A to move towards the 'industrializer' trajectory [20], balancing business expansion and standardization activities to enable repeatability and scalability.

5 Discussion

The pattern traced in the results of this paper through the coding analysis furtherly raises some open issues already reported in the literature. After having ascertained that Company A is at the beginning of its route in the product-service continuum, the case study confirmed that the first steps to be fulfilled are consistent with what reported by [7], i.e. the consolidation of the product-related service offering and the entrance to the IB service market. Given that the product and the market attributes determine the profitability potential from the IB [7], the main issue for the company resulted to be the evaluation of the potential market and the understanding of which channel should be used to penetrate it. To this purpose Company A is willing to implement an analysis of how users approach the humidification market and of what they try to search on the web when they want to solve their problems. Through a consistent assessment of data, that could be the used keywords on research engines by customers and the feedback coming from the users, the potential market could be detected and characterized and thus their needs better defined and satisfied. These hurdles contribute to make also Company A route in the product-service continuum relatively relaxed and careful [7]. This happens because even though organizations consider services an important component of the consumer satisfaction indicators, firms often realize that providing services is beyond the scope of their competencies and their business approach. The interviewee stated indeed that, also due to the company traditional B2B setting, they do not own the required competencies to develop services internally even if they strongly desire it. PSS design and development is, in fact, a process that requires a considerable effort in terms of several backgrounds, like technical specialization, business organization, data and knowledge management. New organizational principles, structures and processes are required. Company A in this specific case is thinking to remedy to this establishing some new partnerships that could improve the offered service level: however, this could not be enough. To improve the delivery of services, the creation of a single organizational unit, identifying the profit opportunity within the service arena, and the setting up of the structures and processes to exploit it would be required. This is what the analyzed company desires to implement, not hiding in the meanwhile the internal and external constraints it is already coping with. [27] explained how a company acting in the same humidification industry, Danfoss A/S, created a dedicated business unit to offer services and move up the supply chain from its position of the component supplier, creating a stronger and more direct relationship with its customers. The importance of the business model from transaction to relationship-based is strategic.

6 Conclusions and Further Researches

This paper proposed a theoretical framework to understand what can affect companies during their transition from a product-centric approach to a service integrated one. To do this, first the offer of a company has been mapped according to the eight PSS archetypes. Related to this, the open issue reported by [16] is confirmed: even if the importance of services is progressively growing, also in this case, the company has several difficulties in identifying the real customer demand and convert it from an intangible to a tangible dimension. The content analysis supported in uncovering the solution to this problem: the use of new tools, i.e. the exploitation of the extensive amount of data available on the new communication channels to come up with a consistent segmentation of the market, and the adoption of a platform for integrated service design. About the methodology, a theoretical framework, based on the analysis of the literature, was built. The case study presented in this paper was conducted to conduct the framework verification and triangulate the hints coming from the literature with practical findings, confirming that an effective service orientation assessment of a company needs to start from a focus on the type of customers, of the offer and of the revenue stream generated (composing part of the theoretical framework proposed in Table 1). Moreover, the content analysis suggested that different elements deserve attention along the servitization path: the product and the industry characteristics, the customer heterogeneity and the relationships along the value chain can affect the potential from the IB. Instead, market (e.g. brand awareness & industry know-how, customer detection, industry actors interests) and company (e.g. flexibility, user-friendliness, service competencies, business approach) constraints, together with external practices and supporting tools (channel, platform), can affect companies capacity to internally modify their organization and pursue a more service-oriented trajectory.

Finally, some limitations can be highlighted for this research. The paper presents only one of the BU of the company of enhancing a servitization strategy. Further researches will be conducted: first, also the other two interviews already performed in the company about claim management and product monitoring platform could be included in the coding analysis, getting a comparison among different contexts. Then, on the basis of the next results, the unit of analysis could be enlarged to other companies and industries to obtain complete information about the service infusion phenomenon and to understand how much the context could affect its evolution. Moreover, while this work is only limited to map a company service offering according to the PSS archetypes, a structured approach can be defined and proposed to enable the assessment of the company service orientation to move along the product-service continuum, starting from the framework proposed and the results obtained with this case.

Acknowledgements. This work was funded by the European Commission through Diversity Project, GA 636692, under the H2020 program.

References

1. Fuchs, V.R.: The service economy. National Bureau of Economic Research (1968)
2. Santamaría, L., Nieto, M.J., Miles, I.: Service innovation in manufacturing firms: Evidence from Spain. Technovation **32**(2), 144–155 (2012)
3. Vandermerwe, S., Rada, J.: Servitization of business: adding value by adding services. Eur. Manag. J. **6**(4), 314–324 (1988)
4. Baines, T.S., et al.: State-of-the-art in product-service systems. Proc. Inst. Mech. Eng. Part B J. Eng. Manuf. **221**(10), 1543–1552 (2007)
5. Jacob, F., Ulaga, W.: The transition from product to service in business markets: an agenda for academic inquiry. Ind. Mark. Manag. **37**(3), 247–253 (2008)
6. Ulaga, W., Reinartz, W.J.: Hybrid offerings: how manufacturing firms combine goods and services successfully. J. Mark. **75**(November), 5–23 (2011)
7. Oliva, R., Kallenberg, R.: Managing the transition from products to services. Int. J. Serv. Ind. Manag. **14**(2), 160–172 (2003). https://doi.org/10.1108/09564230310474138

8. Kowalkowski, C., Kindström, D., Alejandro, T.B., Brege, S., Biggemann, S.: Service infusion as agile incrementalism in action. J. Bus. Res. **65**(6), 765–772 (2012)
9. Ostrom, A.L., et al.: moving forward and making a difference: research priorities for the science of service. J. Serv. Res. **13**(1), 4–36 (2010)
10. Brax, S.: A manufacturer becoming service provider – challenges and a paradox. Manag. Serv. Qual. An Int. J. **15**(2), 142–155 (2005)
11. Barquet, A.P.B., de Oliveira, M.G., Amigo, C.R., Cunha, V.P., Rozenfeld, H.: Employing the business model concept to support the adoption of product-service systems (PSS). Ind. Mark. Manag. **42**(5), 693–704 (2013)
12. Porter, M.E., Heppelmann, J.E.: How smart, connected products are transforming competition. Harv. Bus. Rev. **2015**, November 2015
13. Ayres, R.U.: Peer reviewed: toward a zero-emissions economy. Environ. Sci. Technol. **32**, 366A–367A (1998)
14. Goedkoop, M.J., Van Halen, C.J.G., te Riele, H.R.M., Rommens, P.J.M.: Product service systems, ecological and economic basics. Report for Dutch Ministries of Environment (VROM) and Economic Affairs (EZ), vol. 36, no. 1, pp. 1–122 (1999)
15. Tukker, A., Tischner, U.: Product-services as a research field: past, present and future. Reflections from a decade of research. J. Clean. Prod. **14**(17), 1552–1556 (2006)
16. Tukker, A.: Eight types of product-service system: eight ways to sustainability? Experiences from suspronet. Bus. Strateg. Environ. **13**(4), 246–260 (2004)
17. Zaring, O., et al.: Creating eco-efficient producer services, Gothenburg (2001). http://www.score-network.org/files/828_18.pdf
18. Reim, W., Parida, V., Örtqvist, D.: Product–Service Systems (PSS) business models and tactics – a systematic literature review. J. Clean. Prod. **97**, 61–75 (2014)
19. Gebauer, H., Fleisch, E., Friedli, T.: Overcoming the service paradox in manufacturing companies. Eur. Manag. J. **23**(1), 14–26 (2005)
20. Kowalkowski, C., Windahl, C., Kindström, D., Gebauer, H.: What service transition? Rethinking established assumptions about manufacturers' service-led growth strategies. Ind. Mark. Manag. **45**(1), 59–69 (2015)
21. Yin, R.K.: Case Study Research Design and Methods, 4th edn., vol. 5 (2009)
22. Eisenhardt, K.M.: Building theories from case study research. Acad. Manag. Rev. **14**(4), 532–550 (1989)
23. Berg, B.L.: Qualitative Research Methods for the Social Sciences, 7th edn. Allyn & Bacon, Boston (2001)
24. Henn, M., Weinstein, M., Foard, N.: A Short Introduction to Social Research, p. 296. Social Research, New York, (2006)
25. Sassanelli, C., Terzi, S., Pezzotta, G., Rossi, M.: How lean thinking affects product service systems development process. In: XX Summer School Francesco Turco 2015 - Operational Excellence Experiences, pp. 97–104 (2015)
26. Sassanelli, C., Pezzotta, G., Rossi, M., Terzi, S., Cavalieri, S., Boucher, X.: Towards a lean product service systems (PSS) design: state of the art, opportunities and challenges. In: Procedia CIRP, vol. 30, pp. 191–196 (2015)
27. Tan, A.R., Matzen, D., McAloone, T.C., Evans, S.: Strategies for designing and developing services for manufacturing firms. CIRP J. Manuf. Sci. Technol. **3**(2), 90–97 (2010)

Improvement of the Containerized Logistics Performance Using the Unitary Traceability of Smart Logistics Units

S. Wattanakul[1(✉)], S. Henry[2], L. Bentaha[1], N. Reeveerakul[3], and Y. Ouzrout[1]

[1] DISP Laboratory, University of Lyon, University Lyon 2, Lyon, France
siraprapa.wattanakul@univ-lyon2.fr
[2] DISP Laboratory, University of Lyon, University Lyon 1, Lyon, France
[3] College of Arts, Media and Technology, Chiang Mai University, Chiang Mai, Thailand

Abstract. Based on the emergence of the Internet of Things, smart logistic units (container, pallet, cardboard) offers a new opportunity to improve the responsiveness to disturbances of the supply chain and to develop robust scheduling approach based on the knowledge extracted from the historical data of traceability on the smart logistic units. The limitations of the current traceability solutions are related in particular to the insufficient level of detail, the late availability of data and the scattering of data in databases of different actors in the supply chain who are reluctant to exchange them. Then, the unitary traceability based on the Internet of Things with a real-time tracking of multiple parameters of each object (position, temperature, vibration, humidity, etc.) is a solution which makes it possible to improve reactivity in real time when facing disturbances and to extract knowledge from historical data. Therefore, this paper proposes a conceptual framework based on seven activities that exploit smart container traceability data for real-time analysis and decision to monitor risks of disruptions and to mitigate the impact of disruptions.

Keywords: Supply chain performance · Smart container · Unitary traceability Disruption management · Reactivity

1 Introduction

Maritime shipping is the most significant mode of transport for international trading. Ships carry more than 80% of global trading volume. It reached 10.3 billion tons in 2016. This amount values above 70% of total international trading values. Specifically, containerized transportation is the fastest growth, more than triple times in 20 years, from about 45 million TEUs (20-foot equivalent units) in 1996 to 140 million TEUs in 2017 [1]. A large number of containers are handled by container ships and ports. In each year since 2012, more than 600 million TEUs flows in and out ports around the world [2].

The containerized shipment is expected to operate under the just-in-time (JIT) production and the "Punctuality/Delivery in time" is a most critical factor [3]. For example, the case of container transhipment(s), the shipment has a limited time to

Published by Springer Nature Switzerland AG 2018.
P. Chiabert et al. (Eds.): PLM 2018, IFIP AICT 540, pp. 410–419, 2018.
https://doi.org/10.1007/978-3-030-01614-2_38

transfer to the next scheduled vehicle. In a very competitive field where the service offered must be the most efficient (cost-time-sustainability), logistics operations are also planned in the JIT with very short of buffer time to minimize the costs on each operation. Thus, an unexpected disruption can influence the initial planning with very quickly consequences on the date of delivery. A single plan of the robust route (cost, time, sustainability) estimated under normal conditions is no longer the best solution. In an uncertain context consisting of disruptions, an additional solution which is invulnerable to disruptions and improves the operation performance such as the delivery time, the condition of product quality and cost becomes a supplementary approach.

To be more specific, as illustrated in Fig. 1, an optimization of the operation planning is generally captured from the real world situation. Based on the historical data, some significant attributes of norm cases which represent the majority of situations are selected to construct the expert model. To support a decision, the expert model predicts and plans a robust solution. However, the expert model and the real world situation are different in some extent. While executing the plan, the operation may face a disruption and the performance declines from the expectation.

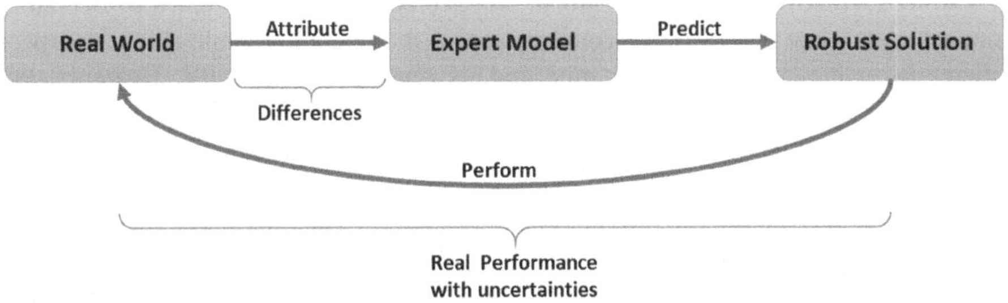

Fig. 1. The uncertainty of operation

There are two approaches to improve the operation performance. First, to adjust the expert model by collecting feedback from the recent experienced operation to adjust the model [4]. This approach improves accuracy to the prediction. Still, not every scenario, in reality, can be included into the expert model. The operation takes risks on the uncertainty of operation performance. Another approach is to be proactive and reactive to disruptions in order to prevent and/or mitigate their impact. During the proactive period, the disruption is not yet critical to the performance. The operation monitors risk factors and raises awareness to prevent or to prepare for the incoming situation. In the other case of reactive approach, a disruption occurred and the operation performance is decreasing. The reactive approach analyses situation and suggests a method to minimize the impact [5, 6].

The emergence of the Internet of Things and in particular with smart logistics unit (container, pallet, cardboard) offers a new opportunity through a more precise and real-time monitoring of the logistics operation. These real-time sensing units allow visibility to explore the real operation and knowledge of disruptions. Later, the model of disruptions can further apply to their prediction, their detection and the assessment of their impact.

The remainder of this paper is organized as follows: performance of the logistics chain and the performance measurement is discussed in Sect. 2. The uncertainty in the supply chain with its impact is presented in Sect. 3. Framework to integrate container traceability data to minimize the impact of disruption is described in Sect. 4. Finally, Sect. 5 summarizes our contributions and announces perspectives of this work.

2 Performance of the Logistics Chain

Generally, the logistics ***operation performance*** is measured in the view of process owner to identify the vulnerability in the chain. For the logistics chain, each function performance is measured by the operation cost, time and resource consumption [7]. A process modelling tool such as the SCOR model is used to point out the inefficient functions. The bottleneck functions or high-cost operations is then improved using these efficiency factors [8].

In the viewpoint of customer expectation, the ***service performance*** is rarely measured and clarified. Besides, the customer satisfaction to the container transport results in low to average in a survey of global shipper 2017 [17]. On each trip, operators concern costs, time and resource consumption of the operation while shippers expect differently in the package arrival time and its quality condition [9]. However, the current traceability system has a limitation in data accessibility of the package throughout the logistics chain. In consequence, the measurement of service performance is limited.

Current global traceability standard offered by GS1, each traceable unit is tracked and traced under the Electronic Product Code Information Services (EPCIS) as shown in Fig. 2. Each chain partner captures events of the tracing units (date-time, location, event-type e.g. departure, arrival, transfer). Data of the operation are scattered in partners' storages and the data sharing is in reluctance. Especially the data that can imply the performance [3, 10]. Towards two major objectives of the transportation, a shipment should arrive safely and on-time, the existing traceability system limits the evaluation of the service performance regarding these objectives as follows:

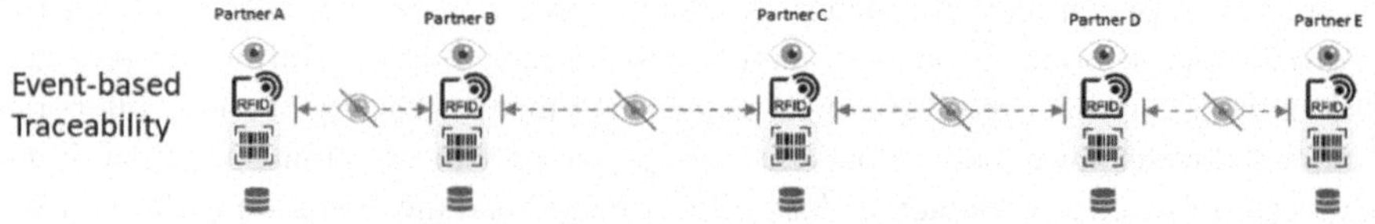

Fig. 2. The current traceability system (EPCIS)

2.1 Limitation in the Product Quality Assurance

The EPCIS tracks and traces the logistics units such as vehicle, container, pallet and carton. The traceability records the trajectory flow and events of each tracking items. The parameters related to the goods quality are not included. The environment or condition of the transportation storage is not maintained [11]. However, environment parameters such as temperature and humidity are essential to products which are sensitive to the time and condition such as perishable products. In extra to the GS1 traceability standard, the monitoring and controlling of storage condition should be cautious [12–14].

Furthermore, in case of the product lost or damage in the supply chain with several partners, it is difficult to investigate the root cause due to the unavailability of supply chain information and the communication of the whole logistics is limited [14, 15].

2.2 Limitation in the On-Time Shipment Assurance

Disruptions can initiate a delay to the shipment. Handling disruptions requires visibility of the operation through the logistics chain in real time. Then, the pattern of the normal operations and the operations with disruption can be distinguished. Risks and impact of disruptions should also be monitored in real time. Further, the decision time for disruption response is shortened and the disruption impact such as delay time can also be minimized. However, as mentioned, the supply chain visibility is currently limited by scattered traceability data storage.

Traceability data of the logistics operation seems to be a critical resource to evaluate the service performance in terms of the product quality surveillance and the delivery punctuation. Delay time is a significant factor that degrades the goods quality and the customer satisfaction [17].

3 Uncertainty in Logistics

3.1 Disruptions

Planning the logistics operation, the carrier considers routes and scheduling based on several factors in order to secure the plan and to minimize the operating costs. Factors such as the transportation network, route, vehicle, facility equipment and service operators are estimated on the consumption demand [18]. However, during the operation execution, disruptions can threaten the plan such as port congestion, accident, weather, tide condition, operator's mistake or even the consequence effect of the previous event. For example, the US West Coast labour dispute in February 2015 for a month affected the liner network globally for a year. From that time on the dispute, the liner delay had increased every five months and reached the highest average of delay at 38.3% in February 2016 [19]. Furthermore, the logistics operation time can be affected by more than one event. Currently, it is hard to distinguish and quantify the delay of February 2016 effected by the labour disputation, by the seasonal event of Chinese New Year or by any other disruptions.

3.2 Impact of Disruptions

Disruptions can directly impact customer expectations in terms of shipment delay, reduced product value, damaged or lost. Moreover, the negative impact also effects indirectly to the operation performance of partners. Not only the shipment carrier loses reliability from shippers. Nearly 90% of shipment stakeholder throughout the chain believes that a disruption is relevant to the loss of their reputation and their clients. Even the delay occurred previously in the chain by the other actors or any disruption, delays in delivery are frequently considered as a responsibility of the company that customer is dealing [20].

4 A Conceptual Framework for Real-Time Management

According to the previous study proposed in [21], the technology of Smart Container [22, 23] offers the capturing of container status parameters through the operation seamlessly in real-time as shown in Fig. 3. The operation of each container is recorded to the historical database. The situation awareness of containers enables the logistic chain analysis in all decision level (operational, tactical, strategical). This research aims to extend the ability of the smart container by improving the service performance of the container logistics operation in disruptions.

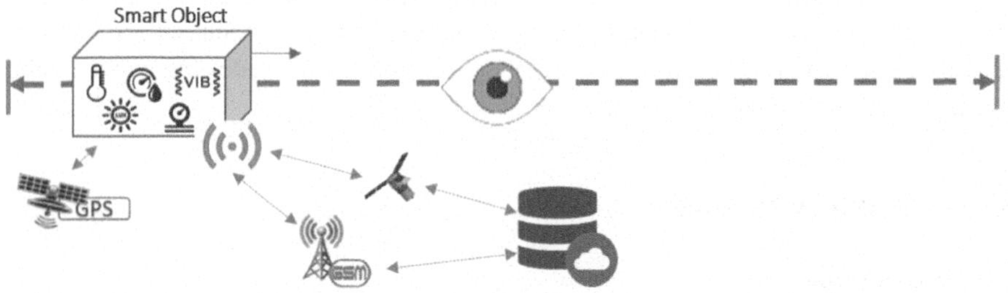

Fig. 3. The traceability system using the smart container

4.1 Smart Container for Extended Real-Time Traceability

The traceability data of the smart container is capable to measure the service performance in the product quality assurance and the on-time shipment assurance. The parameters of temperature, humidity, vibration and door opening status enables the monitoring of the product quality by means of proper storage condition and storage safety. The parameter of GPS location can interpret the trajectory of the container and the time spent on each logistics leg. Then, the detection of anomaly determines the container movement pattern and the location of incident is specified. Furthermore, the surrounding environment such as weather and traffic can be observed and comprehended to the operation situation. The prediction of on-time shipment service can be proactive.

4.2 Performance Improvement Based on the Smart Container

With the capability of the smart container, two strategies are proposed to improve service performance of the logistics operation.

The 1st strategy – Finding the "robust" Route

In order to identify the route for a container or a shipment from the route network offered by liners, each shipper or forwarder has a different preference. Based on an individual preference of shippers or forwarders, the "robust" route can be considered based on the criteria of the efficiency of the operation performance (cost, time, sustainability) and the robustness of the service performance (delay, goods quality):

- *Cost* – the logistics cost is a part of product capital cost. Minimizing the cost of shipment delivery benefits value to the business.
- *Time* – the supply chain concerns the planning of warehouse, production and time to market so the arrival time of material, parts or product affects to the plan and value of the product. The Estimated Time of Arrival (ETA) of shipment is included in the supply chain planning.
- *Sustainability* – logistics consume high volume of fuels and emits pollution. This raises the chance of higher cost in the future. Minimizing the emission on logistics trips becomes a highlight of shippers and carriers' interest [24].
- *Robustness in delay* –This criterion is to identify the route configuration with minimized chance and impact of the delay.
- *Robustness in goods quality* – a hazard treatment or the improper condition of the container storage can damage goods and its value. This criterion identifies the route that has least chance of the product quality lost from logistics.

These criteria are conflicted on one another. For example, choosing the cheapest route carrier, it may consume a long time of travelling with high emission rate and in the high risk of delay and product damage. Moreover, each shipper can have different interests and different acceptable range and weight balance on each. The shipment route selection then should be in multi-criteria to identify the route that is the most robust to the shipper preference. However, the information of the ETA and Sustainability criteria are based on the normal situation. It may not be true in real operation so shippers still have to take a risk on these criteria.

The 2nd strategy – Being Proactive and Reactive to disturbances

In order to enhance the risk of the first strategy on the route planning, this strategy aims to improve the service performance of the operation when a disruption occurs, the traceability data raises situation awareness of each container as follows:

1. *Being proactive by predicting and detecting disruptions* – as the traceability data is captured in real-time. When a disruption occurred, the behaviour of data is changed differently from the normal operation pattern. The situation of the disruption is detected and becomes aware. The incoming shipments then predict the possibility of the disruption impact based on the container status, the disruption situation and the historical data.
2. *Being reactive by diagnosis root causes of the disruption* – based on the historical data of the containerized logistics with the extended situation information, the root cause should be identified to support the reactivity decision.
3. *Being reactive by predicting the impact of disruption* – in order to make a decision on the reactivity planning precisely, each container considers its delay time caused by the disruption.

4. *Being reactive by making the operation decision in a short time* – a decision is made to choose a reactivity that minimizes the disruption impact.

Conducting these two strategies can be performed under the following conceptual framework for the containerized logistics.

4.3 Conceptual Framework for the Containerized Logistics

Regarding the proposed strategies, this study proposes a conceptual framework intend to maximize the performance of the containerized operation and also raising the satisfactory of shippers. The framework is as shown in Fig. 4. There are seven major activities to handle though the lifecycle of containerized logistics operation including normal operation and under a disruption such as port congestion. Each container continuously monitors, analyses its own status and adjust its operation in a near real time.

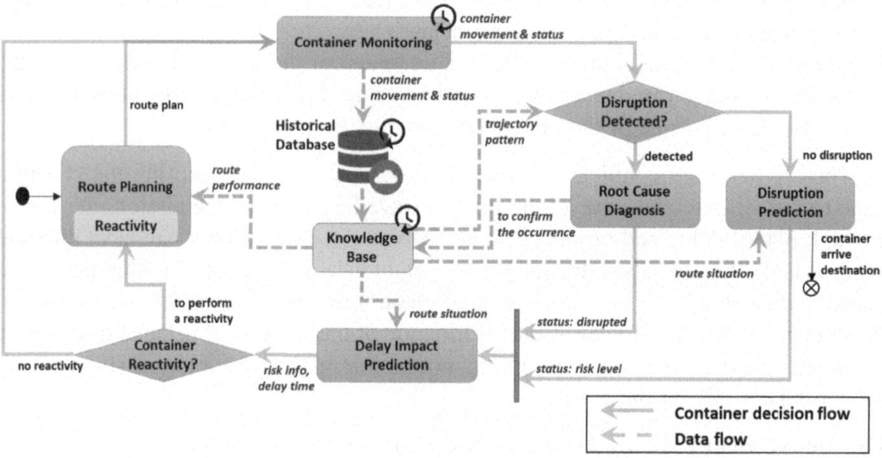

Fig. 4. Conceptual framework for the containerized logistics

Once the container starts the logistics process as defined in its route plan ("*Route Planning*" by a tool of robust route planner e.g. Navigate). Each smart container seamlessly captures data parameters such as GPS location, temperature, humidity, vibrating rate and door opening in real time through the travel trip by the "*Container Monitoring*". These real-time container data are used to support the analysis of decision functions along the container decision flow. Also, all these raw data are stored in the central cloud as a historical database. The "*Knowledge Base*" uses the historical data to classify the trajectory patterns of smart containers by an artificial intelligent approach e.g. Bayesian Network. The recent movement of containers can then be compared with the classified pattern to distinguish the container in the normal operation from the operation with occurred disruption.

Based on the classified trajectory patterns and the others abnormal traceability data such as the fluctuation of vibration, the change of temperature or humidity level, the container operation can detect the disruption.

- In case of normal operation - the container proactively predicts the risk of encountering a disruption by considering *its own situation* and *the route situation* provided by the knowledge base. '*the container own situation*' means to recent captured parameters e.g. position, trajectory, timestamp, etc. and '*the route situation*' is clustered from the recent trajectory of containers on the same route to identify traffic and disruption status of the travelling route.
- In another case of confronting a disruption – e.g. accident or long waiting time. The root cause should be diagnosed to identify significant features that characterize the disruption. This may improve the classification of trajectory patterns to detect and predict the disruption in the future.

After that, based on the clustering of route situation and the historical of disrupted trajectory pattern, the total delay along the remaining travel trip is predicted for the container. Each container considers its predicted situation and expects to achieve as its robust plan, otherwise, it should execute a reactivity to adjust the operation process. Containers are able to communicate and making a deal on the reactivity e.g. operation sequencing. The process adjustment decision should fulfil the goal of containers robust plan while the operation productivity rate is not reduced. Repeatedly, smart containers are monitored and adapted until it reached the destination. The overall delay time of containers is expected to be reduced and the position of incidents can also be identified by this approach.

This conceptual framework intends to enhance the service performance from the customer view of the containerized logistics service as a major. However, the Knowledge Base contains information of the logistics network which can offers a support on decisions to the other viewpoints in logistics such as liners, shippers, freight forwarder and port operator.

5 Conclusions

In the maritime container industry, the customer satisfaction is in positive impressed. By chance of an uncertainty, disruptions can impact logistics in both the product quality and on-time delivery. This study focuses on improving the performance of the containerized logistics service. A conceptual framework for planning, monitoring and controlling the container shipment under the shipper's expectation is proposed based on two major strategies. First, shippers select a robust route based on their preference (route efficiency and service robustness). Second, each container is proactively monitored for disruptions and when facing a disruption, the reactive control persists the container flow in shipper's expectation. These activities are limited by the visibility of the logistics chain operation to monitor and analyse the operation situation, and also to make decisions on disturbance mitigation in a near real-time.

The emerging of smart container technology offers traceability data that improve visualization of the logistics operation. The availability of traceability data in container storage condition and its movement can extend the awareness to the logistics situation. Data are recorded in the central knowledge base. With seamless data visibility and quality, the improvement of logistics chain performance can be conducted using the proposed strategies.

The central knowledge base provides the classified trajectory patterns to support decisions in a near real time. Along the travelling, each smart container proactively perceives the situation of itself by using data provided by the knowledge base to predict the chance of confronting to disruption and the possible delay time. A reactivity may be required to adjust the operation process in order to improve the performance.

In the near future, the proposed framework will be simulated using AnyLogic to proof the concept. Elements such as the knowledge base, prediction models of disruption and delay impact will be developed.

Acknowledgement. This work is supported under the Erasmus Mundus's SMARTLINK (South-east-west Mobility for Advanced Research, Learning, Innovation, Network and Knowledge).

References

1. UNCTAD: The United Nations Conference on Trade and Development: The Review of Maritime Transport 2017 (UNCTAD/RMT/2017). United Nations Publication, New York and Geneva (2017). http://unctad.org/en/PublicationsLibrary/rmt2017_en.pdf
2. The World Bank: Statistics of Container Port Traffic (TEU: 20 foot equivalent units) (2017). https://data.worldbank.org/indicator/IS.SHP.GOOD.TU
3. SEALS Consortium: Final Report: Statistical coverage and economic analysis of the logistics sector in the EU (SEALS) prepared for the European Commission, DG Energy and Transport. Technical report. ProgTrans AG (2008)
4. Kridel, D., Dolk, D., Castillo, D.: Adaptive modeling for real time analytics: the case of "Big Data" in mobile advertising. In: 48th Hawaii International Conference on System Sciences (HICSS), pp. 887–896. IEEE, Hawaii (2015). https://doi.org/10.1109/hicss.2015.111
5. Elluru, S., Gupta, H., Kaur, H., Singh, S.P.: Proactive and reactive models for disaster resilient supply chain. Ann. Oper. Res. 1–26 (2017). https://doi.org/10.1007/s10479-017-2681-2
6. Chung, S.H., Tse, Y.K., Choi, T.M.: Managing disruption risk in express logistics via proactive planning. Ind. Manag. Data Syst. **115**(8), 81–1509 (2015). https://doi.org/10.1108/IMDS-04-2015-0155
7. Verdouw, C.N., Wolfert, J., Beulens, A.J.M., Rialland, A.: Virtualization of food supply chains with the internet of things. J. Food Eng. **176**, 128–136 (2016). https://doi.org/10.1016/j.jfoodeng.2015.11.009
8. Aboulaid, H., et al.: Process re-engineering and success of integration projects of information technologies case study: process modeling of a cross docking platform of a car manufacturer. In: 3rd Logistics Operations Management, pp. 1–6. IEEE (2016). https://doi.org/10.1109/gol.2016.7731697
9. Balci, G., Cetin, I.B., Tanyeri, M.: Differentiation of container shipping services in Turkey. Transp. Policy **61**, 26–35 (2018). https://doi.org/10.1016/j.tranpol.2017.10.004

10. Fisseler, D., Kemény, Z., Reiners, R.: Monitoring and control framework for business processes in ubiquitous environments. In: Ubiquitous Intelligence & Computing, Advanced and Trusted Computing, Scalable Computing and Communications, Cloud and Big Data Computing, Internet of People, and Smart World Congress, pp. 863–868. IEEE (2016). https://doi.org/10.1109/uic-atc-scalcom-cbdcom-iop-smartworld.2016.0136
11. GS1 AISBL: EPC Information Services (EPCIS) Standard, Release 1.2 (2016). https://www.gs1.org/epcis
12. Wang, J., Yue, H.: Food safety pre-warning system based on data mining for a sustainable food supply chain. Food Control **73**, 223–229 (2017). https://doi.org/10.1016/j.foodcont.2016.09.048
13. Xiao, X., Wang, X., Zhang, X., Chen, E., Li, J.: Effect of the quality property of table grapes in cold chain logistics-integrated WSN and AOW. Appl. Sci. **5**(4), 747–760 (2015). https://doi.org/10.3390/app5040747
14. Kim, W.R., Aung, M.M., Chang, Y.S., Makatsoris, C.: Freshness Gauge based cold storage management: a method for adjusting temperature and humidity levels for food quality. Food Control **47**, 510–519 (2015). https://doi.org/10.1016/j.foodcont.2014.07.051
15. Guo, X., Wei, D.: Under the environment of supply chain logistics outsourcing decision and risk research. In: International Conference on Logistics Engineering, Management and Computer Science, pp. 168–171. Atlantis Press (2014). https://doi.org/10.2991/lemcs-14.2014.39
16. Yuen, K.F., Thai, V.: Barriers to supply chain integration in the maritime logistics industry. Marit. Econ. Logist. **19**(3), 551–572 (2017). https://doi.org/10.1057/mel.2016.10
17. Drewry and ESC: Satisfaction survey in container transport: customers rate service quality of ocean carriers "poor to average". Drewry Supply Chain Advisors and European Shippers' Council, London and Brussels (2017). https://www.drewry.co.uk/news/news/satisfaction-survey-in-container-transport-customers-rate-service-quality-of-ocean-carriers-poor-to-average
18. Meng, Q., Wang, S., Andersson, H., Thun, K.: Containership routing and scheduling in liner shipping: overview and future research directions. Transp. Sci. **48**(2), 265–280 (2013). https://doi.org/10.1287/trsc.2013.0461
19. Drewry: Service reliability falls to 12-month low (2016). https://www.drewry.co.uk/news/news/service-reliability-falls-to-12-month-low
20. Angel, M., Salazar, F.: Proposal for the implementation of a wireless sensor network system for container transportation. In: Proceedings of the Industrial and Systems Engineering Research Conference, pp. 2074–2083. IISE (2013)
21. Wattanakul, S., Henry, S., Bentaha, M.L., Reeveerakul, N., Ouzrout, Y.: Improving risk management by using smart containers for real-time traceability. In: 9th International Conference on Logistics and Transport: Supply Chain 4.0 Challenges and Prospects, pp. 222–230. ICLT (2017). http://www.iclogisticstransport.org/uploads/files/ICLT2017 Full Papers.pdf
22. Traxens: Traxens Technology (2017). https://www.traxens.com/en/technology
23. Mersk: Smart containers listen and talk (2016). https://www.maersk.com/stories/smart-containers-listen-and-talk
24. Bask, A., Rajahonka, M., Laari, S., Solakivi, T., Töyli, J., Ojala, L.: Environmental sustainability in shipper-LSP relationships. J. Clean. Prod. **172**, 2986–2998 (2018). https://doi.org/10.1016/j.jclepro.2017.11.112

Innovating Performing Arts Management Through a Product Lifecycle Management Approach

Corallo Angelo, Lazoi Mariangela, Marra Manuela(✉), and Quarta Lorenzo

Dipartimento di Ingegneria dell'Innovazione, University of Salento, Campus Ecotekne, via Monteroni, 73100 Lecce, Italy
manuela.marra@unisalento.it

Abstract. Cultural and Creative industry is a wide sector with different specializations and application areas. It refers to the creation and distribution of services or products of a cultural or artistic nature such as gaming, visual arts, movie, performing arts, music and theatre.

IT systems supporting this sector are not widely used and there is a lack of tools supporting the activities management and data and information retrieval, sharing and systematization. With a focus on Performing Arts, existing tools do not help to manage completely three critical areas: Tour Management, Stage Configuration Management and Social Network Analysis.

With particular attention to configuration management, that refers to how change the structure of artists and instrumentations on the stage in different performances, the study aims to analyze the context of Cultural and Creative Industries, studying the concept of Product (Live Event), its lifecycle and relative critical areas. A new integrated Data Model is proposed to help managers in cultural and creative events organization and management and extending the view of complex products on this industry result prospective. Data model entities and attributes will be discussed for evaluating an extension of current PLM systems also in this field.

Keywords: PLM · Product lifecycle · Performing arts
Cultural and creative industries

1 Introduction

Cultural and Creative Industries (CCIs) are industries whose principal purpose is production or reproduction, promotion, distribution or commercialization of goods, services and activities of a cultural, artistic or heritage-related nature" [1]. In recent years, CCIs have been characterized by great income (US$2,250 billion of global revenues in 2013) [1] and are the target of many public and private initiatives (regional and European) to drive economic growth and create jobs.

Despite their importance and potential value, there are few definitions about what Industries are part of the Cultural and Creative domain. One of these has been provided by UNESCO and includes the following eleven sectors: Advertising, Architecture,

Published by Springer Nature Switzerland AG 2018.
P. Chiabert et al. (Eds.): PLM 2018, IFIP AICT 540, pp. 420–431, 2018.
https://doi.org/10.1007/978-3-030-01614-2_39

Books, Gaming, Music, Movie, Newspaper and Magazines, Performing Arts, Radio, TV and Visual Arts [1].

The sales of physical products, for years the main source of income for artists and CCIs organizations, have dramatically decreased due to a different way to consume a product by customers. On the other hand, digital sales are growing steadily, but they do not compensate the loss resulting from the decrease in physical sales.

In this scenario, events can represent a great source of income and a perfect means of advertising a cultural and creative product.

Starting from this observation, the need to organize increasingly attractive and efficient events emerges in order to attract as more paying spectators as possible and media attention.

The cultural and creative products like festivals, concerts, events, tours, exhibitions, theater performances, etc. have their own life cycle that could be managed in a more efficient way by borrowing technologies and approaches used in the management of complex products (Product Lifecycle Management, Business Process Management, Social Network Analysis, Virtual Reality and simulation, etc.). The concept of new product risk is more complex in an arts context. Firstly, many of the risk factors that apply to commercial products apply also to performing arts products - perhaps even more so. Colbert [2] argues that three factors make performing arts products particularly risky - the impossibility of testing the new product, planned limited life cycle of the product and inability to stock the product - and that these elements "prove that cultural enterprises are high-risk ventures that have no equivalent in other sectors of the economy". It could be argued, however, that these are in fact similar to the challenges faced by those involved in developing new services.

Furthermore, in the organization of a Cultural and Creative Event, it is important to consider the definition of Project that citing the PMI (Project Management Institute) is "a temporary endeavour undertaken to create a unique product or service" [3]. It is possible to say that a Cultural and Creative Event is no more than a Project with a specific Scope: the cultural and creative one. Both have a Life Cycle and the running of performance is just the latest of several steps that usually involve a lot of people and stakeholders with heterogeneous skills and different roles and several risks to consider and deal with.

Based on these premises and on the preliminary studies carried out for the start of the MYA (Manage Your Arts) research project, which involves University and companies operating in the performing arts industry, the paper aims to propose phases and areas of the entire Lifecycle of an event and suggests a new and integrated Data Model. This one will be the basis for defining a set of technological solutions enabling the improvement of cultural and creative events organizational processes.

In the next sections of the paper, the studies related to the topic of interest, the research methods used and the reached results are described. A section of conclusions ends the paper.

2 Background

PLM stands for Product Lifecycle Management and its value is increasing particularly in the manufacturing and high-tech sectors [4]. Today, PLM is recognized as a necessity for organizations that want to become more innovative and meet the challenges of the competitive environment. Being an innovative business not only means creating innovative products, but also improving the processes by which those products are manufactured and supported throughout their life cycle [5]. At the highest level, the objective of PLM is to increase product revenues, reduce product-related costs, maximize the value of the product portfolio, and maximize the value of current and future products for both customers and shareholders [6].

PLM can be defined as a strategic business approach that supports all phases of a product's life cycle, from concept to disposal, providing a unique and timed source of product information. By integrating people with processes and technologies and ensuring consistency of information, traceability and long-term archiving, PLM enables organizations to collaborate within the extended enterprise [7, 8]. The objective of the PLM is to track and manage all activities, data and information flows during the product development process and then during maintenance and support phase [9].

PLM methodologies and tools have continued to grow in traditional sectors such as automotive [10], aerospace and defence industries [11, 12]. They have recently begun to emerge in non-traditional markets such as life sciences, energy [13], architecture [14] and shipbuilding.

Further studies analyze the application of PLM in non-conventional sectors such as fashion [15], luxury [16] and food industry [17, 18]. In this field starting from the analysis of the specific new product development (NPD), authors try to deepen the application of PLM in the industry, evaluating also technology suppliers' offer.

D'Avolio et al. study [15] describes the main characteristics of PLM implementation in the fashion industry. Starting from an overview of fashion NPD, they studied in depth PLM adoption through a descriptive exploratory research, based on interviews and information, available on websites and industry-specific magazines thanks the growth of PLM projects within the fashion industry and the increasing number of industry-specific tools. They presented how through PLM, fashion companies are able to manage standardized processes, based on timely and correct decisions. PLM technologies support several core tasks, such as material and colour management, merchandise planning, product sourcing and visual merchandising, but also manufacturing and retailing. The advantages of its adoption are shorter product development process, a greater control of information, a reduction in inventory, non-value-added tasks and time to market.

Vezzetti et al. [16] analysed PLM in luxury fashion scenario adopting a user centred approach. They formalized the key luxury NPD processes, in terms actors involved, information/data received and produced, tools/methodologies involved for each process, and possible constraints. This task was preparatory to the collection of the real functional requirements of a Collaborative Product Development and Management solution identifiable with a PLM solution.

Pinna et al. [17, 18] analysed the level of knowledge of PLM systems in the food sector from the literature and the markets points of view, observing how it is still low even if many vendors of PLM solutions offer dedicated and customized solutions for the food industry. The researchers aimed to understand how the use of PLM systems could enhance the performances related to the different phases of the NPD in food industry studying in depth the related processes. They complete the analysis interviewing some of the main Italian and foreign food companies about actors participating to the process, the kind of performances considered important for the food NPD, the forces (internal and external) that lead to the decision to develop a new product and how long lasts the process (from concept to the launch stages). Their final goal was to understand how the PLM functionalities can affect the performance of the various activities of the NPD process taking into account four strategical interest of the PLM solution deployment: the sharing of information, the optimization of its processes, the deploying a structured NPD methodology, and the analysis and the anticipation of the risks linked to the product/process data.

Although studies carried out in different sectors cannot make direct contributions to the identification of life-cycle stages due to the specificity of the cultural product, many insights and suggestions can be made by comparing the methods and approaches adopted in these sectors.

There are still no cases of applications of PLM approaches in the context of CCIs. It is a world that has recently become made up of professionals and the need to innovate, improve and standardize processes is beginning to emerge.

Some authors examined the application of NPD models to performing arts [19, 20] or in general, to the arts industry, that is nourished and sustained by innovation and creativity. They assumed a marketing perspective, focusing more on initial phase of concept definition. The nature of artistic products appears ill-suited to traditional NPD model witch assume the new development from idea generation to launch as a response to consumer need. Crealey [19] pointed out that arts organizations do not formally consider the management of a product's lifecycle, although it is a critical stage in the NPD process. The life cycle of a performing arts product can encompass the initial season, repeat performances in later years, re-staging, school performances and tours. Life-cycle management can lead to sustainability in the arts, since repositioning one product offering for different audience segments will save money and time.

Others instead have compared managerial works in performing arts, although dealing with the fine arts and concerned with creativity, audience appreciation and good art, to similar task of managers in industry and project management activities [21]. Lindgren and Packendorff [22] analyzed theatres as project-based organisations, considering project management as a part of a general trend towards the 'manageri-alisation' of the performing arts.

Finally, Holmes and Ali-Knight [23] discussed about the importance of lifecycle of events mainly in the tourism field where also others scholars have done different research (e.g. [24]). They suggests extending the TALC (Tourism Area Life Cycle) model to the events and festivals context, considering events and festivals as products.

Although the model created in tourism literature links the development cycle of tourism destinations to that of products in the product life cycle model, they did not explicitly mention PLM but just suggested seven event trajectories offering event managers the means for managing their events' future plans.

3 Research Design

The paper aims to address the research questions: *What are the lifecycle phases of an event and the main process areas impacted by a lifecycle approach? How can be events elements systematized in a Data Model useful to guide technological developments?*. These research questions are emerged during a workshop in which engineers and technicians involving on research activities in the manufacturing field discussed PLM impacts and extension.

To answer the research questions firstly, six semi-structured interviews were carried outwith different profiles involved in the management of performing arts: musician, band, event organizer, sound manager, theatres manager and cultural association.

The collected evidences were organized in a framework and proposed for implementation in a research project based on a public call in Apulia Region in the South of Italy. The project is named MYA (*Manage Your Arts*) and has as partners University of Salento, Bass Culture, Cantieri Teatrali Koreja, Officine Cantelmo and Cool Club. The industrial partners cover the field of music booking agency, and production and organization of concerts, ballets, theatrical performances, conventions and congress. Apulia Region is the only Region in Italy with a productive District related to Creative and Cultural Industry and to recognize a significant role of new technologies and methods for this industry among the regional strategic areas of innovation. Therefore, it is the right context to implement the proposed idea.

To enforce the preliminary view originated by the interviews, and as preliminary phase for the starting of the project, five focus groups were launched to create a common background, defines best practices and to identify area, elements and phases of cultural events lifecycle. Four focus groups were specific to share information about the activities of each companies and a last one, was realized to discuss the observed practice and define common elements.

In the following figure, the main steps of the research method are summarized (Fig. 1).

For the analysis of the collected data, an interactive approach has been used to analyse and integrate the contributions of the different interviews and focus groups. During the interviews and focus groups, notes have been taken by two researchers per time. Notes have been useful to remember about the meaning of terms and create a structured set of information. After, each interviews and focus groups, the notes have been read and coded in order to highlighting the main concepts to be also further exploited in the later interviews and then, in focus groups, until the last one. The highlighted concepts describe the different activities and related characteristics for a live performance implementation with several levels of details. Concepts have been organized in categories representing the different lifecycle phases of an event. In the last focus group the followed approach, the emerged concepts and how they are

Data Collection Method	Interviewees Characteristics	Gathered Information
Semi-structured interviews ***N.6***	Different Profiles involving in Performing Arts: *musician, band, event organizer, sound manager, theatres manager and cultural association*	▪ Issues to be managed for events organizations; ▪ Problems; ▪ Involved Roles; ▪ Used Documents; ▪ Needs.
Focus Group ***N.5***	*Booking Activity Managers* *Concert and Tour Organizers* *Theatre producers and managers* *Congress Organizers*	• Activities; • Phases for cultural events; • Actors involved and Responsabilities; • Software used; • Success Factors of an event
	Booking Agency Managers, Concert Organizers, Theatre producers and managers, Congress Organizers	• Comparison and Discussion of the results of the previous Focus Groups in order to share experience and identify best-practices

Fig. 1. Research method steps

integrated in categories were presented; feedbacks have been collected to re-arrange specific points and validate the overall picture. The result is, therefore, a chain of concepts explored and interrelated with the different actors involved and systematized in specific categories.

4 Results

The results section is organized in three parts: the description of event lifecycle phases and relevant process areas and the proposal of a data model for further developments.

4.1 Event Lifecycle Phases

Through the analysis of the information collected and the comparison and validation done in the last focus group, five phases of a lifecycle of an event emerges (Fig. 2):

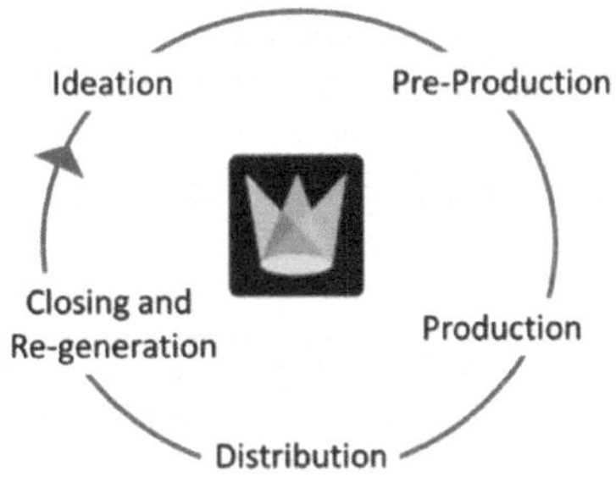

Fig. 2. Event lifecycle phases

1. Ideation: it is the phase in which the need of a new event arises. In this phase, the type of event (e.g. concert, ballet), the place (e.g. a city, a Region or a square, a theatre), the typology of performance (e.g. rock music, hip hop music, drama, comedy), and the period (e.g. month, season) are defined.
2. Pre-production: all the critical decisions are taken, risks are evaluated and emerging problems are solved. Booking of artists, definition of date and place, evaluation of budget and available instrumentation, search of sponsors, the definition of the ticket costs are managed by a team of different professionals.
3. Production: it is full of activities to be executed to prepare the live performance. Negotiation with the artists and with the proposers are faced, the technical rider is received/generated. The location is evaluated and the different permissions are asked (e.g. use of public land authorization, serving food/alcohol to the public authorization, security and disability access prevision, copyright collecting agency permission). Service for audio and video are also defined. Timing of the event is also important to be analysed and established. Booking activities of the same event in different places are also carried out.
4. Execution and Distribution: it implies the activation of a tour and the live performance in the different established location. The technical rider is managed.
5. Closing and re-generation: when the tour is finished or the event is not more replicated (even in the case of once) or are not planned replication, the realized event is closed. Parts of the same event can be used to lead the conceptualization of new ones.

Monitoring of performance and activities is relevant in all the lifecycle phases, even if it is not currently completed done by all the actors and in all the phases. The use of indicators can be of time, costs and spectators reaction. It is also important to keep track of all the evaluation done in order to support decisions for future projects.

4.2 Relevant Process Area

Managing the whole lifecycle of a Cultural and Creative Event is a very hard job and, often, it requires several people with different competencies to be completed successfully. As emerged from data collection, three Process Areas, that could be better managed with digital tools, have been identified: 1. Tour Management; 2. Configuration Management; and 3. Social Network Analysis.

In reference to the lifecycle phases, in the following figure there are reported the relations between processes areas and phases (Fig. 3).

PROCESS AREAS	Impact on Event Lifecycle				
	Ideation	Pre-Production	Production	Distribution	Closing and Re-Generation
Tour Management		●	●	●	●
Configuration Management		●	●	●	●
Social Network Analysis	●			●	●

Fig. 3. Processes areas and phases

4.2.1 Tour Management Process Area

The organization of a Tour is an activity that regards existing shows, probably tested with a pilot or a preview. It is possible to state that Ideation phase of the single event is not part of a Tour Management Area, although organizing a tour requires a certain amount of creativity, but more related to the advertising than to the contents.

An Event is unique but, usually, it is only one small part of a more complex set of shows called Tour. Thinking to the tour of a musician or to the one of a cirque, they both move from a location to another performing the same show each time. Tours can last a day or months and they can include events in one single or in more locations.

Although each event has its own characteristics, is important to manage some aspects of the whole Tour because it requires a great use of resources to move materials, manage accommodation, and comply with administrative obligations and so on.

The process to organize and manage a Tour is the Tour Management. In this process area, booking agents, artists, artist managers, tour managers and personal managers are mainly involved. It is becoming an increasingly important aspect in cultural and creative field, because always often the tour is one of the first sources of income.

4.2.2 Configuration Management Process Area

A Configuration refers to how the structure of artists and instrumentations changes on the stage, in different performances. Configuration Management is related to the close connection that exists between a stage and the way to act a performance on that stage. It depends not on the performance itself but more on the physical space that the crew can use to make it. Different stages require different ways to make a performance and different configurations of the stage itself.

Moreover, the performance itself can change each time though the stage is the same. This is the case of Cirque du Soleil, the most famous cirque in the world. While a lot of Events are part of roadshows, a part of them is performed in the fixed locations (Montreal, Las Vegas, New York, and so on) the company has got. Each event is made up by several exhibitions, which differ for instrument used and number of people involved. Therefore, it is extremely important to plan the configuration of all of them and switch from one to another in the quickest possible way.

The Technical or "Contract" Riders are the documents that contain all the technical information useful for the preparation of the stage and can be useful in all the configuration management activities.

4.2.3 Social Network Analysis Process Area

Social Network Analysis is a topic extremely important in the cultural and creative industries context, because usually a good marketing or promotion campaign on Social Networks can lead to an increase of products and tickets sold.

Social Networks are one of the most important sources of data and primary point of contact with the audience. Social Network analysis refers to the usage of data, taken from Social Networks, to evaluate a performance but also to create it. Thanks to the

Social Networks, today is possible to understand users' preferences and receive, immediately, feedbacks about a performance done. These data could be used, for example, to improve the later performances and so they could affect ideation phase of a following event.

Furthermore, understand what are the most central members in a network is extremely important, because their role is essential to spread an information or influence the behavior of the other members of the network. Today, central members of a network are called *influencer* and their role is officially recognized on many social networks such as Twitter or Instagram.

Promoting an event on social networks, observing feedbacks both pre-event, during the event and post-event can release, therefore, important information for managing the event lifecycle.

4.3 A Data Model to Manage Cultural and Creative Product Lifecycle Information

In the following section will be proposed a data model to support the Lifecycle Management of a Cultural and Creative Event. The Data Model proposed will be a valid starting point from which developing future software. It describes not only all the Data entities that a manager needs to take care while organizing an Event or a Tour, but it will be analyzed also the set of all the relationships existing among them.

Six different groups of Classes have been identified. They represent the type of entities needed to manage the Cultural and Creative Event Lifecycle. *People Group* includes all the human resources involved in the Event both required to organize, manage and execute the Event, but also who will pay. *Document Group* includes all the information required to accomplish bureaucratic tasks and to keep track of technical requirements. *Logistic Group* includes all the aspects related to accommodation and transport, both for human and material resources. Also, the stage on which the performance will be executed is part of this cluster. *Performance Group* is the most important class because it represents the final product that prompts the end users to pay and the entity to which all the other ones are connected. *Sales Group* includes not only the tickets payed from final user but also all the income related to merchandise and advertising. Finally, the *Social Network Group* includes all the information and data extracted from web and social channels that can be used to evaluate the Event and to create new products.

The proposed data model (Fig. 4) is highly comprehensive and covers all the business cases analysed but can be further extended and specified in terms of entities and relationships, also depending on the needed implementation granularity.

The most important class, represents the Event object. It will be named as **EventProduct** and its attribute list includes (Fig. 5):

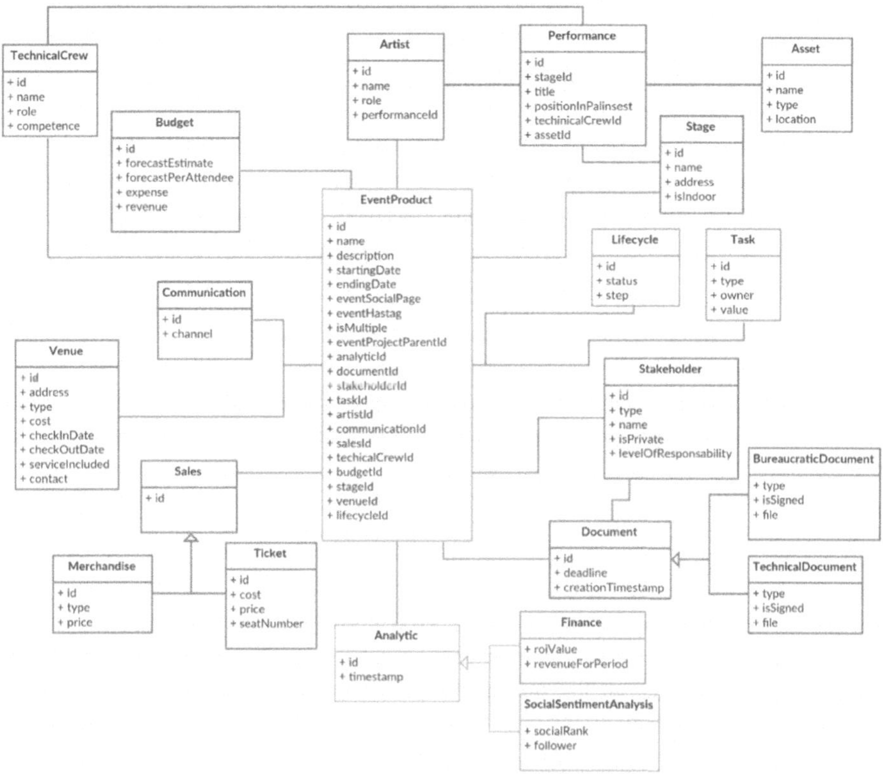

Fig. 4. Data model class diagram

id: entity key
name: the event project name
description: the event project description
startingDate: the event starting date
endingDate: the event ending date
eventSocialPage: the social network page of the event
eventHashtag: the event tag
isMultiple: the attribute defines whether the event is single or repeated.
eventProjectParentId: the any pre-existing event to which the present one relates
analyticId: relation to Analytic entity
documentId: relation to Document entity
stakeholderId: relation to Stakeholder entity
taskId: relation to Task entity
artistId: relation to Artist entity
communicationId: relation to Communication entity
salesId: relation to Sales entity
technicalCrewId: relation to TechicalCrew entity
budgetId: relation to Budget entity
stageId: relation to Stage entity
venueId: relation to Venue entity
lifecycleId: relation to Lifecycle entity

Fig. 5. EventProduct object entities

5 Conclusion

Compared to the studies in the literature concerning the application of PLM in unconventional sectors (food, fashion, luxury) where PLM applications in companies exist and scholars tried to assess how PLM is adopted, its limits and challenges, in the area of CCIs, the concept of PLM is not yet widespread. This study proposes a first approach focusing on performing arts among the different areas of the CCIs.

Event can be managed as a complex product with different parts, actors, responsabilities and risks involved and different tools to be used. Although the PLM is not considered, the issue of event lifecycle has already been addressed by few scholars [19, 23], who focused on the application of NPD models and assuming a marketing or managerial perspective.

The needs of improve and innovate activities and lifecycle of events are emerged in different discussion with actors involved in the organization and execution of live performance.

The proposed lifecycle phases, processes areas and data model are the preliminary results of a structured study that will be carried out with a deep participation of the involved actors using a living lab methodology in order to reflect the real needs of the wide set of actors involved in an event.

As emerged by the paper results thus, a PLM thinking for events could support the CCIs for different processes. Benefits can be related to the information and asset management but also about the management of a whole event. Further studies will analyse in deep the benefits of the proposed approach in order to provide an appropriate evaluation based on the analysis of real cases.

Future research will deepen the lifecycle phases correlating for each phase also the information about actors involved, documents created/shared and software used. A methodology for proposing a more structured approach in event management will be defined and customized for specific targets of actors. A software solution will be developed in order to integrate and support the highlighted process areas and to establish a lifecycle management view.

References

1. EY: Italia Creativa (2016)
2. Colbert, F.: Marketing Culture and the Arts, Montreal: Chair in Arts Management, 2nd edn. (2001)
3. Project Management Institute: A Guide to the Project Management Body of Knowledge (PMBOK® Guide), 5th edn. 589 p. Project Management Institute (2013)
4. Saaksvuori, A., Immonen, A.: Product Lifecycle Management, 2nd edn. Springer, Heidelberg (2005). https://doi.org/10.1007/b138258
5. CIMdata: Product Lifecycle Management - Empowering the Future of Business (2002)
6. Stark, J.: Product Lifecycle Management (Volume 3): The Executive Summary. Springer, Cham (2018). https://doi.org/10.1007/978-3-319-72236-8
7. Corallo, A., Maria Elena, L., Mariangela, L., Lettera, S., Marra, M., Verardi, S.: Defining product lifecycle management: a journey across features, definitions, and concepts. ISRN Ind. Eng. **2013** (2013). https://doi.org/10.1155/2013/170812

8. Grieves, M.: Product Lifecycle Management: Driving the Next Generation of Lean Thinking. McGraw-Hill, New York (2006)
9. Stark, J.: Product Lifecycle Management. 21st Century Paradigm for Product Realisation, 2nd edn. Springer, London (2011). https://doi.org/10.1007/978-0-85729-546-0
10. Tang, D., Qian, X.: Product lifecycle management for automotive development focusing on supplier integration. Comput. Ind. **59**(2–3), 288–295 (2008). https://doi.org/10.1016/j.compind.2007.07.002
11. Alemanni, M., Grimaldi, A., Tornincasa, S., Vezzetti, E.: Key performance indicators for PLM benefits evaluation: the alcatel alenia space case study. Comput. Ind. **59**(8), 833–841 (2008). https://doi.org/10.1016/j.compind.2008.06.003
12. Cantamessa, M., Montagna, F., Neirotti, P.: Understanding the organizational impact of PLM systems: evidence from an aerospace company. Int. J. Oper. Prod. Manag. **32**(2), 191–215 (2012). https://doi.org/10.1108/01443571211208623
13. Corallo, A., Lazoi, M., Margarito, A., Pinna, D.: Developing a PLM framework: a case study application in an energy company. In: Bernard, A., Rivest, L., Dutta, D. (eds.) PLM 2013. IAICT, vol. 409, pp. 149–158. Springer, Heidelberg (2013). https://doi.org/10.1007/978-3-642-41501-2_16
14. Aram, S., Eastman, C.: Integration of PLM solutions and BIM systems for the AEC industry. In: Proceedings of the 30th ISARC International Symposium of Automation and Robotics in Construction and Mining, Montréal, Canada (2013)
15. D'Avolio, E., Bandinelli, R., Rinaldi, R.: Improving new product development in the fashion industry through product lifecycle management: a descriptive analysis. Int. J. Fash. Des. Technol. Educ. **8**(2), 108–121 (2015). https://doi.org/10.1080/17543266.2015.1005697
16. Vezzetti, E., Alemanni, M., Morelli, B.: New product development (NPD) of 'family business' dealing in the luxury industry: evaluating maturity stage for implementing a PLM solution. Int. J. Fash. Des. Technol. Educ. **10**(2), 219–229 (2017). https://doi.org/10.1080/17543266.2016.1250286
17. Pinna, C., Taisch, M., Terzi, S.: PLM in the food industry: an explorative empirical research in the Italian market. In: Harik, R., Rivest, L., Bernard, A., Eynard, B., Bouras, A. (eds.) PLM 2016. IAICT, vol. 492, pp. 238–247. Springer, Cham (2016). https://doi.org/10.1007/978-3-319-54660-5_22
18. Pinna, C., Plo, L., Rossi, M., Robin, V., Terzi, S.: Impact of PLM system in the new food development process performances: an empirical research. In: Ríos, J., Bernard, A., Bouras, A., Foufou, S. (eds.) PLM 2017. IAICT, vol. 517, pp. 532–543. Springer, Cham (2017). https://doi.org/10.1007/978-3-319-72905-3_47
19. Crealey, M.: Applying new product development models to the performing arts: strategies for managing risk. Int. J. Arts Manag. **5**(3), 24–33 (2003)
20. Bennett, R., Kottasz, R.: Lead user influence on new product development decisions of UK theatre companies: an empirical study. Int. J. Arts Manag. **3**(2), 28–39 (2001). http://www.jstor.org/stable/41064721
21. Shone, A., Parry, B.: Successful Event Management, A Practical Handbook, 3rd edn. Cengage Learning EMEA, Andover (2010)
22. Lindgren, M., Packendorff, J.: Performing arts and the art of performing – on co-construction of project work and professional identities in theatres. Int. J. Project Manag. **25**(4), 354–364 (2007). https://doi.org/10.1016/j.ijproman.2007.01.005
23. Holmes, K., Ali-Knight, J.: The event and festival life cycle – developing a new model for a new context. Int. J. Contemp. Hosp. Manag. **29**(3), 986–1004 (2017). https://doi.org/10.1108/ijchm-10-2015-0581
24. Getz, D., Page, S.J.: Progress and prospects for event tourism research. Tour. Manag. **52**, 593–631 (2016). https://doi.org/10.1016/j.tourman.2015.03.007

The Benefits and Impact of Digital Twins in Product Development Phase of PLM

Ilkka Donoghue[1(✉)], Lea Hannola[1], Jorma Papinniemi[1], and Aki Mikkola[2]

[1] Industrial Engineering and Management, Lappeenranta University of Technology, PL 20, 53851 Lappeenranta, Finland
{ilkka.donoghue, lea.hannola, jorma.papinniemi}@lut.fi
[2] Mechanical Engineering, Lappeenranta University of Technology, PL 20, 53851 Lappeenranta, Finland
aki.mikkola@lut.fi

Abstract. The concept of the Digital Twins offers opportunities for business-to-business (B2B) manufacturing companies to co-create and maintain Product-Service-Systems. This facilitates closer relationship with customers over the lifespan of the delivered solution. However, the definition of the Digital Twin is not yet established in the companies that took part in this research that forms the basis to understand the relationship between the Digital Twins and Product-Service-Systems.

The objective of this paper is to define the concepts of Digital Twin and real-time simulation, and increase understanding of the benefits and impacts that B2B companies face when applying real-time simulation, and understand where the transformation should start in Product Lifecycle Management. The case companies that participated in this research are mobile work machine manufactures, but the findings are applicable to other B2B manufacturing companies which have complex solution deliveries that are managed over the lifecycle.

Results of this study show that B2B manufacturing companies are using real-time simulation to create digital twins of their real-world solutions. The companies participating in the research project create functioning digital twins but managing them is tedious and not integrated to the Product Lifecycle Management operations. First, only applying this to product development is not enough, but the management must cover the entire lifecycle of the product from Beginning (BOL), Middle (MOL) and End-of-Lifecycle (EOL). Second, the need to rethink the approach to product development and management is a key for success. Otherwise, the result is a virtual representation of the real world that is impossible to maintain at industrial level.

Keywords: Digital twin · Real-time simulation
Product Lifecycle Management · PLM · Product-service system
Digital Mock-Up

Published by Springer Nature Switzerland AG 2018.
P. Chiabert et al. (Eds.): PLM 2018, IFIP AICT 540, pp. 432–441, 2018.
https://doi.org/10.1007/978-3-030-01614-2_40

1 Introduction

The focus of this paper is to increase understanding how digital twins, especially built on real-time simulation, impact and create benefits already in the product development phase. This paper increases understanding for B2B companies when applying real-time simulation based digital twins, and to understand how the transformation should start in Product Lifecycle Management (PLM). The integration of the Digital Twin and PLM is becoming important to B2B companies. To understand the benefits and limitations to the products, services, and ways of working, requires understanding of the different elements defining the digital twin. However, agreement what a digital twin is depends on the audience. In simplicity, it can just be the meta data that describes the product or as a complex real-time IoT-based simulation model. The Digital Mock-Up (DMU) is closely related concept to the digital twin and they have similarities. Typically, the DMU is a 3D definition of the product over its lifecycle. However, here the digital twin is connected to the physical world representation (via IoT) and is able to integrate machine learning to improve its operations and its real-world counterpart over the lifecycle. In addition, it can simulate, in real-time the multibody dynamics of the real-world counterpart throughout the lifecycle. For product development, this means that the digital twin is developed as a real-world counterpart and integrated to it once it is delivered. This paper tries to understand, through two case companies, the relationship between the digital twin and real-time simulation in the product development and management phase of PLM.

Figure 1(A) presents the current way digital tools are used in the existing organisations. Typically, real-time simulation is a practice that is managed in product development or is used for training purposes instead of being a transparent value-add process to benefit the users or customers. Currently, this slows feedback from users and the overall development process. In addition, actual errors or shortcomings can occur in new products. Figure 1(B) disrupts the existing working ways in the case companies by bringing the users part of the product development process instigating a co-creation environment which is built on the real-time simulation in a real-time co-creation environment. This approach could shorten the development times and increase user and customer satisfaction creating a positive customer experience (Mikkola et al. 2014).

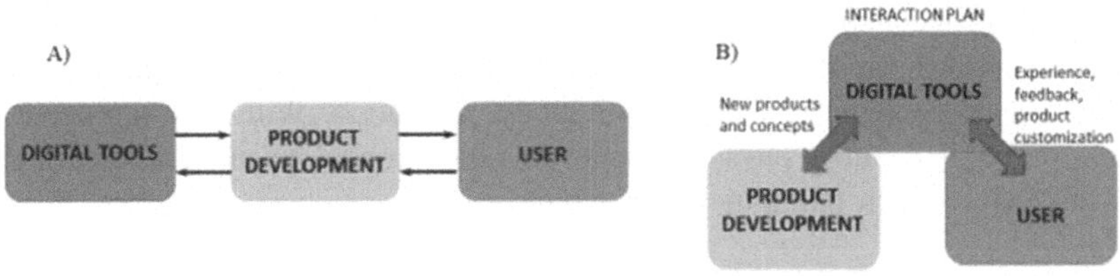

Fig. 1. Real-time simulation can offer ways co-develop product and services with customers creating disruption in the traditional product development operations (Mikkola et al. 2014)

The relevance of digital twins is growing in manufacturing companies and the opportunities to create new business models based on services is increasing. The current understanding is that there are multiple elements that influence the digital twin. Research has been published on the key elements, but they have not been integrated into a concept where the different elements are organized in a framework to use in manufacturing business. The underlining question is the relationship of real-time simulation and digital twins in creating value and minimizing disruption for manufacturing companies over the lifecycle.

2 Related Research

The research on the key elements that constituent the digital twin in PLM have be reviewed in the following. The objective is to understand the relationship, if exist, of these different elements for the research carried out with the case companies.

2.1 Digital Twin

The Digital Twin is not a new concept and it can be seen part of the Product Lifecycle Management (PLM) vision (Grieves 2006). The Digital Twin can be defined according to Bilello (2017, pp. 9) as "*Digital surrogate (i.e., the Digital Twin) is a physics-based description of the system resulting from the generation, management, and application of data, models, and information from authoritative sources across the system's lifecycle*". The Digital Twin is at the core of digitalization and is based on the use of digital technologies. However, the usability and maintenance of the virtual product over the lifecycle has not been efficient with traditional metadata and structure-based definitions of products. The Digital Twin must consist of the virtual product and the virtual process definition, and most importantly it requires end-to-end connectivity and physics-based simulation. When this alignment is achieved, the Digital Twin can create new business models that provide new revenue, value propositions and business opportunities to companies (Bilello 2017).

A complete Digital Twin representation consists of four elements that are (1) real space, (2) virtual space, (3) the data link from real space to virtual space, (4) and information link from virtual space to real space and virtual sub-spaces (refers to one or more digital representation of the product). A physical product operates in real space whereas a virtual machine (i.e. simulation model) is created in virtual space. A virtual machine can be constructed using a multibody simulation. With this approach, it is possible to build detailed physics-based simulation model to analyse dynamics of complex products such like a mobile machine.

2.2 Product Lifecycle Management

There is a variety of related concepts and definitions in the literature on Product Lifecycle Management (PLM), depending on the focus of the authors. According to Stark (2018), PLM is the business activity of managing, in the most effective way, a company's products all the way across their lifecycles; from the very first idea for a product all the way through until it is retired and disposed of. From the executive's point of view, PLM is the management system for the company's products.

In context, Product Lifecycle Management is an integrative information-driven approach comprised of people, processes/practices, and technology to all aspects of a product's life and its environment, from its design through manufacture, deployment and maintenance. Product Data Management (PDM) is a systematic, directed set of tools by which to manage and develop an industrially manufactured product. Information systems of PDM and with wider frame-oriented PLM systems are based on data model, enable accessing, updating, manipulating and reasoning about product information that is being produced in a fragmented and distributed environment (Grieves 2006; Saaksvuori and Immonen 2008). The required capabilities on PLM systems are for example product data and structure management and data exchange of Computer-Aided Design (CAD) models (Siller et al. 2008).

Product knowledge management throughout the lifecycle of the product and the related services has attracted increasing consideration in research and (mainly manufacturing) company practices in recent years. New digital tools and solutions, e.g. Internet of Things, Virtual Reality, Digital twins and simulation, for managing product related data and information across lifecycles, enable new kind of smart services and product-service systems.

2.3 Product-Service-Systems

The term Product-Service-Systems (PSS) has been gaining attention from research and industry in recent years, which takes the "Servitization" approach of manufacturing companies of switching from a physical product-based business to a service-oriented strategy (Cedeño et al. 2018). Tukker and Tischner (2006) define PSS as *"a specific type of value proposition that a business network offers to or co-produces with its clients, and it consists of a mix of tangible products and intangible services designed and combined so that they jointly are capable of fulfilling final customer needs"*. According to Tukker and Tischner, the PSS concept focuses on the following two pillars:

1. Taking the final functionality that the user wants as a starting point of business development (instead of the product fulfilling this functionality).
2. Expanding the system that provides this functionality with a 'greenfield' mindset (instead of taking existing structures, routines and the position of the own company therein for granted).

Xin et al. (2017) have made a systematic literature review of empirical PSS studies between 2006 and 2016, and they found that PSS practices are widely applied across different research and geographical areas. In addition, the PSS studies indicate that the evolution of PSS is still in its early development stage (Xin et al. 2017).

2.4 Multibody Real-Time Simulation

Multibody real-time simulation techniques have enabled the precise description of complex mechanical systems such as mobile and industrial machinery and the subsequent solution of the relevant equations of motion in real time. This capability has been available for more than three decades. Currently, real-time simulation models based on multibody dynamics can account for a large number of rigid (Garcia de Jalon and Bayo 1994) and flexible bodies (Garcia de Jalon and Bayo 1994), and contact models (Garcia de Jalon and Bayo 1994). These multibody-based approaches can be combined with models of actuators enabling the description of multi-physical systems as the one shown in Fig. 2.

Fig. 2. An excavator model operating on deformable ground

3 Research Process

The research process applied design science research approach (Hevner et al. 2004; Hevner 2007) and data collection was made through semi-structured interviews. These methods were selected based on the goal to understand what is the current state of the case companies and provide insights on how to bring value to the case companies. The case companies that participated in this research are mobile work machine manufactures. To maintain anonymity, the companies are referred to company Ox-cart and Have-Blue. Ox-cart provides intelligent mobile material handling solutions and services and Have-Blue provides vehicles, service and solutions to the mining and construction industry.

The research was divided into two phases; (1) the first to understand the as-is status of product development and management in the companies, and (2) impacts and benefits in the transformation towards the future state when digital twins and real-time simulation is applied into practice. The research focus was on the application of real-time simulation. The research method was divided into the following phases:

1. Review into related research to understand previously published concepts that impact the research area. A superficial review of social media was also done.
2. Interview the case companies' product development and product management representatives to understand the as-is state and opportunities and impacts when applying digital twins.
3. Identify possible business benefits and impact on current product development and management.

4 Benefits and Impacts of the Digital Twin

The results can be divided into benefits that improve the way of working and the impact that a digital twin has on the product development and PLM. The adoption of real-time simulation, that forms the digital twin, requires a change in the way companies execute product development and PLM in future. Based on the work carried out with companies, the digital twin is a feasible option when it is full physics based real-time simulation. However, the maturity level of the two companies are different. Company Ox-cart has piloted digital twins based on real-time simulation in product development but are still evaluating the business case for full implementation across the company's operations. However, the first area of implementation is product development. On the other hand, Company Have-Blue have implemented and are using real-time simulation-based digital twins in certain product lines. This implementation has focused on product development and management, but it has also been piloted in other areas for example sales and manufacturing. Common benefits are closer customer relationship and dialogue that enables faster product development. This need for transparent communication with customers is not often present in product development. The main goals for the case companies from real-time simulation based digital twins are:

- Improved R&D and Product Management Processes improving efficiency and cost.
- Better understanding of customer needs with co-creation during development.
- New Product-Service-System (PSS) possibilities due to integration of operations data and connected digital twins (virtual-PSS).

Both case companies' product and service portfolios are diverse and the customer segments that they support are heterogeneous. Each product and service line have different needs and maturity levels. The Have-Blue portfolios consist of, for example, software, automation, equipment and process solutions that from product-service-systems. The companies use traditional simulation in the product development processes and have also invested in real-time simulation solutions. A key issue for real-time simulation is the need for specialised expertise, and the effort to manage complex models. The opinion is that benefits can be achieved if the productization of real-time simulation software is improved and the code development is replaced with ready user interfaces. Building a re-useable library of simulation products, modules and services across or in product platforms is key for adoption in these companies. As an example, a re-usable module is a control logic used in the drive system or the boom.

Table 1 positions the different simulation dimensions that exist and identifies the simulation areas where value could be brought to product development and management in the companies. The goal of Table 1 was to create insight what is the as-is and vison for real-time simulation driven digital twins. In Table 1, the columns represent the different simulation domains that were identified in the case companies. The *Simulation Column* covers traditional simulation methods used by most companies. These include, for example, CFD of FEM simulations. The *Realtime Simulation Column* covers the full physics real-time simulation which is an accurate physics-based representation of the mobile work machines, e.g., excavator. The 3rd column *Collaborative Realtime Simulation* uses real-time simulation, but in a virtual environment that enables the simultaneous use of multiple real-time simulation models where the environment is a real-time simulation, for example, mine, airport or harbour, and are cloud based. The *Faster than Realtime Column* represents real-time simulations where the simulations can be carried out faster than the real-world occurrence.

Table 1. Digital twin domains and simulation approaches. Green areas are under development and blue areas are concepts of interest to the case companies

Digital Twin	Simulation	Realtime Simulation	Collaborative Realtime Simulation (1	Faster than Realtime Simulation
Virtual Reality model	Used	Limited use	Not in use	Used
Human in the VR loop	Used	Limited use	Not in use	Concept
Hardware in the loop	Used	Limited use	Not in use	Concept
Augmented reality	Used	Not in use	Not in use	Concept
ANI in the loop	N/A	Concept	Vision	Vision
AGI in the loop	N/A	Vision	Vision	Vision
ASI in the loop	N/A	Vision	Vision	Vision
N/A = Not Applicable				

The rows represent the different simulation approaches. The 1st row *Virtual Reality* represents the model where human interaction is not present. The 2nd row *Human in the VR loop* is controlled and operated by a human. The 3rd line *Hardware in the VR loop* is when the digital twin has a real-world element connected to it or vice versa. The 4th line *Data in-the-loop* is when the simulations are run based on real-time data collected from Product-Service-System. The 5th line *Augmented Reality* is when the digital information is shown in the real world in real-time. Line 6 and Line 7 represent Artificial Narrow (ANI) and General (AGI) Intelligence where the simulation model can make different levels of decisions independently with or without operational data. Line 8 is when Artificial Super Intelligence is in the loop. AGI and ASI are visions only. The vision is to apply Narrow AI to the connected system, but the basics must be in place first. ANI with degrees of autonomy has interesting possibilities in connected digital twin and PSS.

The case companies use different simulation and IT tools to create the digital twin. However, the simulation solutions are used interpedently in product development and PLM. The case companies use real-time simulation, but it is not fully integrated to the Enterprise Architecture (EA) and is difficult to maintain meaning few true digital twins based on real-time simulation exist.

The implementation of digital twins impacts the architecture of the case companies because it changes how the companies manage product development processes and involve external and internal stakeholders. The real-time simulation maturity level in the architecture areas were:

- Specialist exist in organisations (Organisation Architecture and Role Descriptions).
- Realtime simulation and digital twin not integrated to process (Process Architecture).
- Realtime simulation models built from scratch (Information Architecture).
- Realtime simulation not integrated to Information System (IS architecture).

However, if implemented as part of the enterprise architecture, real-time simulation and therefore digital twins will improve the product development and management processes reducing cost through faster feedback and earlier involvement of the customer in the development phase. The case companies' objectives were to understand how real-time simulation can bring value and to create a business case for the digital twin. The interviews uncovered benefits and pains in product development and PLM that real-time simulation can improve. These most important areas, based on the interviews with the companies were:

- Time-to-Market can be reduced with real-time simulation.
- Improved marketing & sales of new PSS capabilities and features to customer.
- Collecting end-user and customer feedback and needs.
- Building concepts and prototypes to get customer insight faster at lower cost.
- Release time between prototypes after testing feedback can be reduced.
- Replacing time consuming and costly product testing with real-time simulation-based.
- Threshold to start new product development does not need significant drop in sales (especially company Ox-cart).
- Deeper view how services are used and integrated in customer PSS.

In both companies, product development time must be reduced in the future and getting it first-time right is critical for success, as is cost. In Ox-Cart, the key elements for equipment success is operator visibility, driving and loading experience. These areas can be developed faster with real-time simulation with the near real-world operator experience. Realtime simulation was used to collect operator feedback on improvements e.g. maintenance procedures and accessibility. For Have-Blue, the integration of the digital twin to products can create an augmented real-time simulation to test and verify improvements to the product. This data was used to understand the traditional asset-based service's needs. The time and cost to build new real-world prototypes is a risk that impacts internal and supplier resources. Using a configurable real-time simulation models, in the early stage of development for prototyping, enabled customer feedback and improved requirement collection in early stages of development. The suppliers develop and deliver more than half of the assemblies in the products and many of these assemblies are developed at the same time as the end-product. If a digital twin is used, the possibility to test, e.g. control software, would ensure quicker development cycles and identify supplier errors early in the development phase. Real-time simulation, if is used for testing and certification, would reduce physical prototypes.

5 Discussion and Conclusions

Digital Twins are not only tools for product development to gain better customer commitment to new concepts. The real opportunities lie in creating digital products and services that integrate the real and digital worlds together and form a connected solution (Fig. 3). If a real-time simulation based digital twin is implemented, this digital representation can change the way companies view their products and services in the future. The virtual product becomes the asset that opens new business opportunities, for example, connected information-based services. This enables the creation of Product-Service-Systems (PSS) that can be used to simulate the PSS different lifecycle phases.

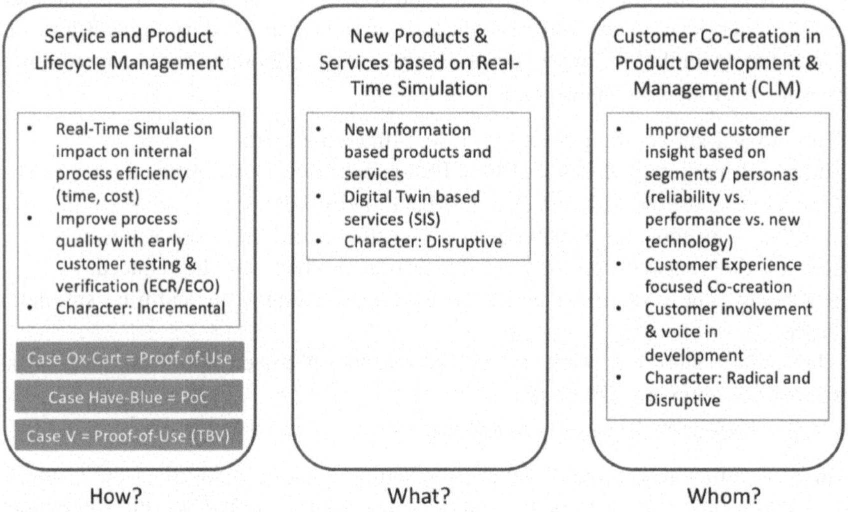

Fig. 3. Digital twin high-level benefits achievable through application of real-time simulation when connected to real-world counterpart

The digital twin concept impacts the case company core from R&D to install base management. The value comes from the lifecycle management of PSS where the connected product can provide information to the digital twin. This information can verify the real-time simulation accuracy but can form the basis to continuously test new development and operational scenarios. Therefore, real-time simulation based digital twins can create a digital-PSS with predictive services in the form of product efficiency services, customer process support, and process delegation services.

For real-time simulation to have an impact on the way an organisation operates, the digital twin and the enabling real-time simulation software must be an integrated part of the operating model. Realtime simulation is the essential element of the digital twin concept that builds new capabilities. Therefore, real-time simulation can redefine business processes and impact how information is managed, and IT architecture defined. For successful digital twin implementation, based on real-time simulation, a company must evaluate its; simulation maturity and capabilities, product-service-system maturity and capabilities, and customer lifecycle management maturity. Future research should concentrate on the benefits that the digital twin can create over the complete lifecycle of the product and how machine learning can create new services and for customers and the companies offering them.

References

Mikkola, A., Hannola, L., Handroos, H., Rantanen, H., Ullako, K.: LUT Research Platform on Sustainable Product Processes Through Community-Based Real-Time Simulation. Lappeenranta University of Technology, Lappeenranta (2014)

Bilello, P.A.: The Digital Twin has Landed, CIM Data (2017)

Grieves, M.: Product Lifecycle Management: Driving the Next Generation of Lean Thinking. McGraw-Hill, New York (2006)

Saaksvuori, A., Immonen, A.: Product Lifecycle Management. Springer, Berlin (2008). https://doi.org/10.1007/978-3-540-78172-1

Siller, H., Estruch, A., Vila, C., Abellan, J., Romero, F.: Modeling workflow activities for collaborative process planning with product lifecycle management tools. J. Intell. Manuf. **19**(6), 689–700 (2008)

Stark, J.: Product Lifecycle Management (Volume 3): The Executive Summary. Springer, Cham (2018). https://doi.org/10.1007/978-3-319-72236-8

Cedeño, J.M.V., Papinniemi, J., Hannola, L., Donoghue, I.: Developing smart services by internet of things in manufacturing business. LogForum **14**(1), 59–71 (2018). https://doi.org/10.17270/J.LOG.2018.268

Tukker, A., Tischner, U.: Product-services as a research field: past, present and future. J. Clean. Prod. **14**(2006), 1552–1556 (2006)

Xin, Y., Ojanen, V., Huiskonen, J.: Empirical studies on product-service systems – a systematic literature review. Procedia CIRP **64**, 399–404 (2017)

Garcia de Jalon, J., Bayo, E.: Kinematic and Dynamic Simulation of Multibody Systems: The Real Time Challenge. Springer, New York (1994). https://doi.org/10.1007/978-1-4612-2600-0

Hevner, A.: A three cycle view of design science research. Scand. J. Inf. Syst. **19**(2), 87–92 (2007)

Hevner, A., March, S., Park, J., Ram, S.: Design science research in information systems. Manag. Inf. Syst. Q. **28**(1), 75–105 (2004)

Donoghue, I, Hannola, L., Papinniemi, J.: Product lifecycle management framework for business transformation. In: 24th International Conference on Production Research (2017)

Does End of Life Matter in Smart Cities?

Ahmed Hefnawy[1(✉)], Abdelaziz Bouras[2], and Chantal Cherifi[1]

[1] DISP Lab, Université Lumière Lyon 2, Lyon, France
{ahmed.hefnawy, chantal.cherifi}@univ-lyon2.fr
[2] DCSE, College of Engineering, Qatar University, Doha, Qatar
abdelaziz.bouras@qu.edu.qa

Abstract. In the smart city ecosystem, smart systems go through different phases of development from conception and design, through deployment and operation till end of service and retirement. Normally, city operators pay less attention to End of Life activities, compared to other phases of lifecycle. however, in the End of Life, the decommission of certain smart system shall be subject to applicable laws and regulations, like data privacy and cyber security. In addition, the outage of such smart system should be strategically aligned with the vision of the smart city. In this paper, we present the scenario of FIFA World Cup™ 2022, where Qatar has committed to donate part of its sports infrastructure to other countries. We particularly focus on the lifecycle of an IoT-enabled smart parking use-case in Lusail City.

Keywords: Smart city · IoT · Lifecycle management · End of Life Ecosystem

1 Introduction

Smart city ecosystems, like other kinds of systems, consist of elements, functions and interconnections, but elements are intelligent and adaptive [1]. In addition, smart city ecosystems include humans, whether users, policy makers, regulators, vendors; and have business models and processes. It is also subject to applicable legal and regulatory frameworks. As many stakeholders adopt smart solutions in the city environment, the level of complexity increases from smart devices, to smart systems, to a compound system of interrelated/interdependent systems. The lifecycle aspect of smart city systems is very important, like other engineered systems, and even more important in the case of complex SoS [9, 10].

Smart city system development, operation and maintenance are very complex tasks and involve numerous stakeholders from different disciplines and domains. In most cases, these systems are at different phases of design, deployment and operation, i.e. at different phases of lifecycle. Moreover, in such an innovative and responsive ecosystem, due to very rapid technological changes and altered consumer requirements, smart city systems can have multiple versions, variants and upgrades. Hence, lifecycle management concepts are very important to better manage smart city development as a complete ecosystem across different phases of lifecycle [5, 6].

Published by Springer Nature Switzerland AG 2018.
P. Chiabert et al. (Eds.): PLM 2018, IFIP AICT 540, pp. 442–452, 2018.
https://doi.org/10.1007/978-3-030-01614-2_41

Qatar is the host of FIFA World Cup™ 2022. The Supreme Committee of Delivery and Legacy (SCDL) is responsible for the delivery of the required infrastructure to provide world-class services and create lasting legacy for Qatar. Qatar has committed, as per the bid file to FIFA, to donate parts of infrastructure and systems to future mega-event hosts. In this paper we propose the application of lifecycle management to manage different phases of a smart parking system, with a special focus at the End of Life (EoL). The remainder of this paper consists of four sections. Section 2 presents the background of smart city lifecycle management and importance of its applications. Section 3 includes the lifecycle-based modeling of smart city ecosystem. Section 4 demonstrates the lifecycle approach in a smart parking use-case. Section 5 includes conclusion of this paper.

2 Background

Lifecycle management is more than a technology solution; it is a strategic approach that enables more efficiency, higher quality, cost effectiveness, rapid innovation and better collaboration between stakeholders. As lifecycle management has enabled large enterprises to better manage their portfolio of products and services; similarly, lifecycle management can enable city administrators to better manage public services and supporting infrastructure. Hence, lifecycle management is important to manage business processes and data associated with heterogeneous connected objects in the smart city context [3].

For a smart city, lifecycle management is particularly important due to the following reasons [7, 8]:

- Diversity of application domains, heterogeneity of data sources, big number of stakeholders and interdependency between different smart systems.
- In a complex smart city ecosystem, boundaries between sectors are blurring; different stakeholders are required to work together to design, deploy and maintain smart services.
- Being customer-focused, smart city service systems should be responsive to user requirements and customizable to public as well as personal requirements.
- Being technology-intensive makes "time to market" very critical factor for the smart city ecosystem that should be also agile and adaptable to technology and business disruptions.
- As a complex ecosystem, smart city is subject to multiple jurisdictions across different domains, and has to validate and prove compliance to all relevant regulatory obligations at all stages.

In the same time, absence of a clear lifecycle management vision can result in the following:

- Vertical "siloed" model of smart city with inefficient system design and disjointed operation process.

- Actors and partners – at different lifecycle phases – use different platforms and different ways of handling data, which consequently result in difficult collaboration, inefficient and delayed exchange of data/information.
- In a "siloed" ecosystem, data is scattered, difficult to trace and less reliable. Moreover, there is lack of efficient change notification process between interdependent/interrelated smart systems; and, engineering change processes are difficult to implement and track.
- Regulatory failure at different phases of lifecycle that may incur expensive fines, rework and write-offs.
- Delay in "time to market" which has severe business impact, in such an innovative and dynamic ecosystem, if a competitive smart solution gets to market first.

The vision of applying lifecycle management in the smart city context is to address the aforementioned issues to better integrate all smart city systems. To achieve such a holistic vision of complete smart city ecosystem, interrelated/interdependent systems can exchange system data that include Bill of Material (BOM), versions, variants, stats and other lifecycle related data. Through lifecycle management systems, stakeholders can connect to a single platform to collaborate across lifecycle phases. They can access and share information, monitor and manage activities throughout lifecycle, and produce accurate reports.

3 Smart City Lifecycle-Based Modeling

Lifecycle-based modeling is essential to support the evolutionary path of smart city development, where smart city service systems can be consistently designed, built and operated in phases and in a modular way. Lifecycle-based modeling encourages innovators and entrepreneurs to develop endless number of new smart services and applications over the top of existing smart infrastructure and wealth of information. In addition, lifecycle management joins up many previously separate and independent processes, disciplines, functions and applications. It also maximizes reuse of smart city knowledge between different domains at different phases. In short, lifecycle management offers managers visibility about what is really happening with smart city systems and with their development, modification and retirement projects.

Hefnawy, Bouras and Cherifi [4–6] proposed a lifecycle-based model, as illustrated in Fig. 1, that combines the following three viewpoints: First, a layered architectural framework to deliver a common basis for the description of smart city systems. Second, domain representation to reflect different application domains, such as energy supply, traffic and public health. Third, lifecycle (time) viewpoint to represent the development of smart city systems and mentions roles of all involved stakeholders across time.

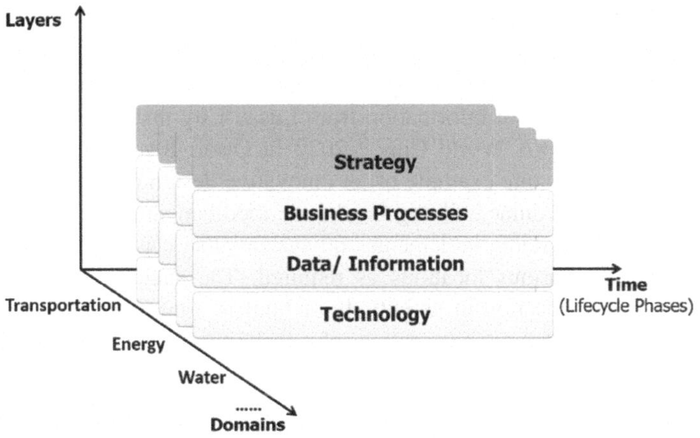

Fig. 1. Three-dimensional smart city modeling approach

Combining the three mentioned viewpoints provides a holistic view of smart city as a comprehensive ecosystem to better integrate people, processes, data and systems; and assure strategic alignment, and information consistency, traceability, and long-term archiving. Considering the big number of stakeholders involved in public service delivery, lifecycle management enables interoperability between different stakeholders at different levels of the multi-layered architecture. In line with the European Interoperability Framework (EIF), presented in Fig. 2, lifecycle management addresses interoperability requirements:

> "...enabling disparate and diverse organizations to interact towards mutually beneficial and agreed common goals, involving the sharing of information and knowledge between the organizations, through the business processes they support, by means of the exchange of data between their respective ICT systems" [14].

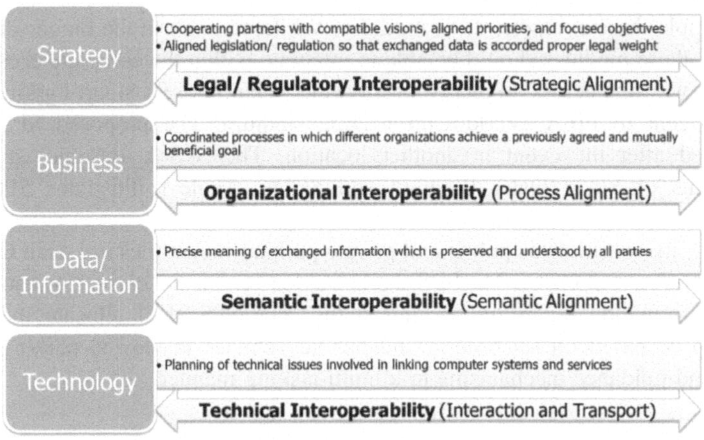

Fig. 2. Interoperability against layers and time

4 Smart Parking Use-Case

To better understand the proposed approach, the following use-case is a high-level example that is based on real information from Lusail City that will host the opening and final matches of FIFA World Cup™ 2022 in Qatar. Ras Abu Aboud stadium, shown in Fig. 3. [12], is one example of an innovative design concept using modular building blocks. The modular building blocks are modified shipping containers, each containing fundamental stadium elements and systems that can be quickly assembled and disassembled at various locations as required. The stadium is intended to be reassembled in a new location in its entirety or built into numerous small sports and cultural venues. This commitment entails physical infrastructure and smart system handover, as well as knowledge transfer.

Fig. 3. Ras Abu Aboud stadium

In this use-case, we aim to build a scenario of a smart parking service system that is integral part of a complete smart city ecosystem to serve FIFA World Cup™ 2022. The smart parking system is promised to be decommissioned and donated to other countries after the event. The reassembly of stadiums and supporting infrastructure and systems can be in entirety or in parts. For this purpose, it is required to design, build, operate and dissemble these components in modules. While, to achieve the bigger vision of a smart city, these modules should be able to integrate within the complete ecosystem in a seamless way and across all phases of lifecycle. We propose a Smart Parking System (SPS) adjacent to FIFA World Cup™ 2022 stadium. The proposed SPS will be reassembled after the event in another location. The SPS is designed as per the requirements of Smart Qatar Program and SCDL. Table 1 illustrates SPS design considerations across SPS lifecycle.

Lusail City consolidates public and private parking inventories in Lusail Command and Control Centre (LCCC). The SPS shall be able to exchange correct system data and relevant information regarding parking status. The SPS shall allocate the optimal parking space based on set criteria and handle vehicles inside the parking through tracking and guidance mechanisms in a multi-tasking manner.

Table 1. Smart parking system considerations

- **Strategic Alignment:** Design in modular way (BoL); Reassembly after event in a new location (EoL);
- **Compliance:** All personal data should be retired (EoL) in compliance to Personal Data Protection Law;
- **KPIs:** Parking Cruising Time and Vehicle Mile Travel (MoL);
- **Processes:** Approval, Modification, Notification, between SCDL Construction (BoL, EoL), Smart Parking Sites' Operators (MoL, EoL), Technology Vendor (MoL, EoL);
- **Data Exchange:** Static and Dynamic Data in DATEX II format, between Smart Parking Sites' Operators;
- **Knowledge Preservation:** from BoL, MoL, and EoL to be transferred to the new location operator;
- **Technology:** The Open Group Standards as an Open IoT Standards and Platforms: Aras Innovator as lifecycle management system.

- **Operating Environment**
  The SPS is proposed to operate as part of an integrated parking system, within Lusail smart city environment. Marina district (in Lusail City) has total of 2,200 public parking spaces in 4 identical underground parking sites, 3 basement level each. Currently, only one site is operational by Qatari Diar VINCI Park (QDVP[1]). QDVP contract includes management, operation, maintenance and repairs. Operators of the remaining 3 sites have not been yet selected. The presentation of QDVP operation in Lusail in Fig. 4 below [11].
- **System Description**
  As described in Fig. 5, the SPS is operating within a smart city environment. All smart city systems are interacting with Lusail Command and Control Centre (LCCC). The SPS will interact through external interfaces with Database System, Web Portal System, and LCCC.
- **Integration of SPS within the Smart City Ecosystem**
  To ensure integration of the SPS within the smart parking system of Lusail City, which is part of the complete smart city ecosystem, we ensure interoperability at different architectural levels and between different platforms, as illustrated in Fig. 6 and explained in the following sub-sections.

[1] QDVP is a joint venture owned 51% by Qatari Diar Real Estate Investment Company (a subsidiary of the Qatar sovereign fund, Qatar Investment Authority) and 49% by Indigo.

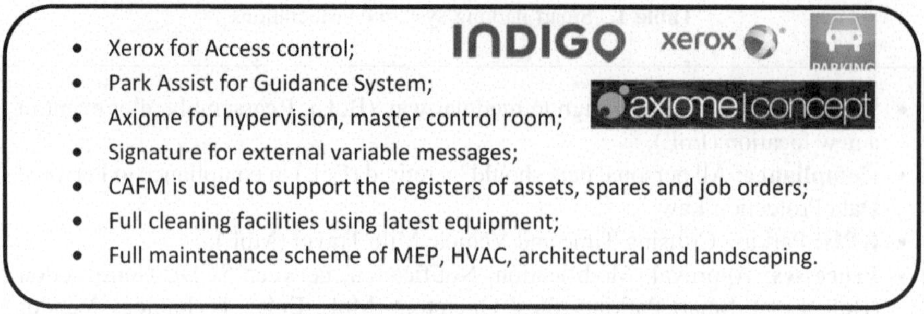

Fig. 4. Presentation of QDVP operation

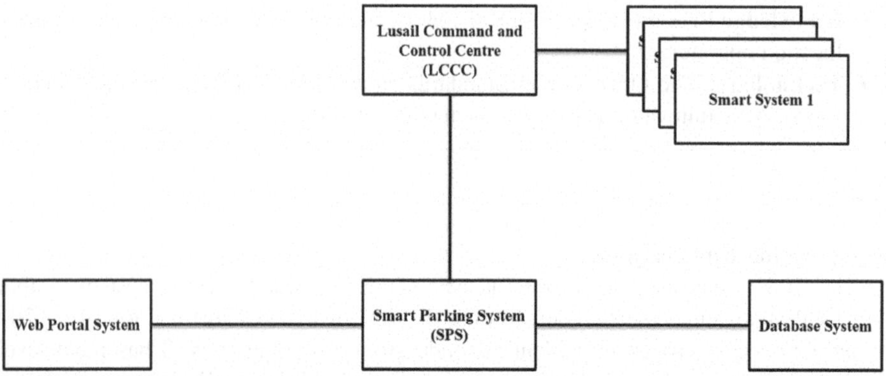

Fig. 5. SPS overall description

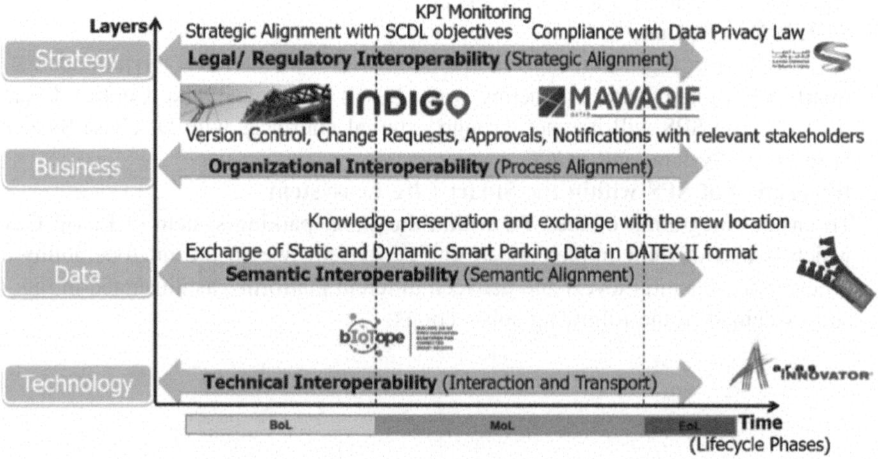

Fig. 6. Multi-level interoperability of SPS

– Strategic Alignment
The SPS is aligned to Smart Qatar [13] strategic objectives and SCDL requirements for FIFA World Cup™ 2022. The following are the strategic objectives that the SPS contributes to:

- Giving back 96 h per year per person of time lost in traffic;
- Reducing CO_2 emissions equivalent to 29,000 homes annually;
- Attracting 600,000 visitors to sports events.

The proposed SPS, as part of the bigger city parking system, contributes towards the achievement of the above strategic objectives. This contribution shall be continuously measured across lifecycle, through KPI monitoring. In addition, legal and regulatory compliance shall be verified and recorded at all phases. Legal and regulatory compliance includes adherence to Qatar's Transportation Master Plan, Open Data Policy and Personal Data Protection Law. SPS shall open up its parking related data during MoL. All personal data that will be used by SPS shall be ensured retired before the decommission of the system at the EoL.

– Business Processes
The use of lifecycle management system integrates all relevant stakeholders, according to their roles/access rights, in approval, modification, and notification processes. Figure 7 compiles relevant stakeholders who are involved in business processes. Lifecycle management ensures continuity of processes amongst stakeholders at different phases of lifecycle.

Fig. 7. SPS relevant stakeholders

– Information/Data: Semantic Interoperability
To realize the full promise of a complete smart city ecosystem, SPS integrates in a bigger smart mobility system that is together with other smart systems form Lusail smart city. For this purpose, we use DATEX II standards to exchange information between different parking site operators, LCCC, and traffic management centers. We use static parking publications for parking infrastructure, facilities and geo-referencing, which is low frequency in nature. While, we use dynamic parking publications for high

frequency data about occupancy, status of facilities and temporary changes of static data. DATEX II provides a very extensive parking model (data catalogue). For the purpose of this use-case, we have selected limited number of classes and attributes. We have used DATEX II conversion tool, presented in Fig. 8. [2], to select relevant parts of the UML model and to create a Sub-Schema.

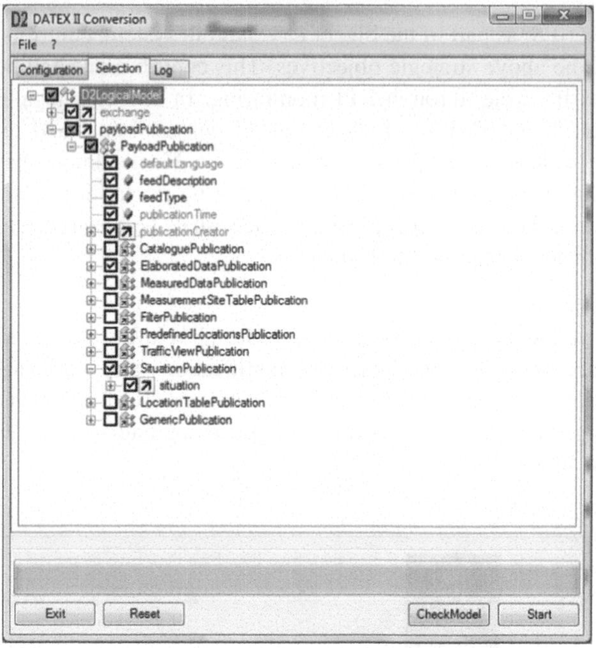

Fig. 8. DATEX conversion tool

– Technology

In this use-case, we use The Open Group Standards for IoT. To enable peer-to-peer publication and discovery of parking-related information, several O-MI edge nodes have been implemented in an aggregated form. The implementation of the O-MI nodes is in accordance to the XSD schema released by DATEX II conversion tool for the selected classes. Figure 9 illustrates the Object Tree structure in O-MI node, as pushed by Java agent.

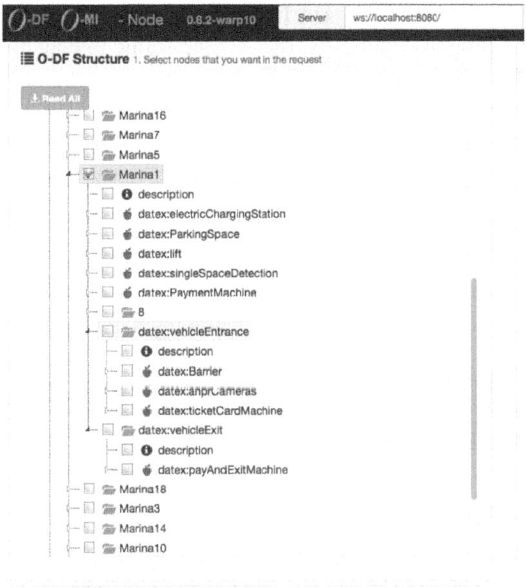

Fig. 9. SPS O-MI node implementation

5 Conclusions

This paper examines the proposed lifecycle-based approach in a smart parking system. The lifecycle-based approach is proved very relevant to this use-case for many reasons: need to manage End of Life Activities, and in general the whole lifecycle; need to integrate with other smart parking operators and with other smart city services; time-to-Market is very critical in a time constrained event like FIFA World Cup™ 2022.

We start by designing the SPS itself and ensure it fulfils all business and customer requirements. The SPS is designed to report a correct information regarding the current parking status online, and allocate the optimal parking space based on set criteria and handle vehicles inside the parking through tracking and guidance mechanisms in a multi-tasking manner. The SPS detects the vehicles as they enter the facility, providing a real time visual aid to direct the vehicles to a specific space.

The SPS is designed in a modular way to ensure integration within Lusail City parking system and within the bigger smart city ecosystem. For this purpose, we align the SPS with the operating environment on 4 levels: strategy; business processes, information/data, and technology. KPIs of the SPS performance shall be continuously monitored across lifecycle. In addition, regulatory compliance shall be verified and recorded at all phases. Legal and regulatory compliance includes Qatar's Transportation Master Plan, Open Data Policy and Personal Data Protection Law. The use of lifecycle management system integrates all relevant stakeholders, according to their roles/access rights, in approval, modification, and notification processes. For semantic interoperability purposes, we use DATEX II standards to exchange information between different parking site operators, LCCC, and traffic management centers. While, we use The Open Group Standards for IoT technology.

References

1. Anthopoulos, L., Janssen, M., Weerakkody, V.: A Unified Smart City Model (USCM) for smart city conceptualization and benchmarking. Int. J. Electron. Gov. Res. **12**(2), 77–93 (2016). https://doi.org/10.4018/IJEGR.2016040105
2. DATEX II Browser (2017). http://datexbrowser.tamtamresearch.com/#/package/D2LogicalModel
3. Främling, K., Kubler, S., Buda, A.: Universal messaging standards for the IoT from a lifecycle management perspective. IEEE Internet Things J. **1**(4), 319–327 (2014). https://doi.org/10.1109/JIOT.2014.2332005
4. Hefnawy, A., Bouras, A., Cherifi, C.: Lifecycle based modeling of smart city ecosystem. In: Springer Proceedings of the 14th International Conference on Information & Knowledge Engineering, Las Vegas, 27–30 July 2015 (2015)
5. Hefnawy, A., Bouras, A., Cherifi, C.: IoT for smart city services: lifecycle approach. In: ICC 2016, Proceedings of the International Conference on Internet of things and Cloud Computing, Article No. 55, Cambridge, 22–23 March 2016 (2016). https://doi.org/10.1145/2896387.2896440
6. Hefnawy, A., Bouras, A., Cherifi, C.: Relevance of lifecycle management to smart city development. Int. J. Prod. Dev. (2018, accepted)
7. Hefnawy, A., et al.: Combined use of lifecycle management and IoT in smart cities. In: IEEE Xpress Proceedings of 11th International Conference on Software, Knowledge, Information Management & Applications, Colombo, Sri Lanka, 06–08 December (2017)
8. Hefnawy, A., et al.: Lifecycle management in the smart city context: smart parking use-case. In: Harik, R., Rivest, L., Bernard, A., Eynard, B., Bouras, A. (eds.) PLM 2016. IAICT, vol. 492, pp. 631–641. Springer, Cham (2016). https://doi.org/10.1007/978-3-319-54660-5_56
9. Kubler, S., Robert, J., Hefnawy, A., Främling, K., Cherifi, C., Bouras, A.: IoT-based smart parking system for sporting event management. In: Proceedings of the 13th Annual International Conference on Mobile and Ubiquitous Systems: Computing, Networking and Services, Hiroshima, Japan, 28 November–1 December 2016 (2016)
10. Kubler, S., Robert, J., Hefnawy, A., Främling, K., Cherifi, C., Bouras, A.: Open IoT ecosystem for sporting event management. IEEE Access. **5**(1), 7064–7079 (2017). https://doi.org/10.1109/ACCESS.2017.2692247
11. QDVP: Qatari Diar VINCI Park (2017). http://www.mawaqifqatar.com/about. Accessed 17 Dec 2017
12. SCDL: Supreme Committee for Delivery and Legacy (2017). https://www.sc.qa/en. Accessed 17 Dec 2017
13. Smart Qatar. https://tasmu.gov.qa/en. Accessed 3 Dec 2017
14. SmartCities: Creating Municipal ICT Architectures: A Reference Guide from Smart Cities (2015). http://www.smartcities.info/ict-architecture. Accessed 13 Oct 2016

Lean Organization for Industry 4.0

How to Manage People Underutilization in an Industry 4.0 Environment?

Gianluca D'Antonio(✉) and Paolo Chiabert

Politecnico di Torino, Corso Duca degli Abruzzi 24, 10129 Turin, Italy
{gianluca.dantonio,paolo.chiabert}@polito.it

Abstract. For long time, Lean manufacturing has been often mis-defined as "doing more with less" and relied on Taiichi Ohno's taxonomy made of seven classes of wastes. More recently, the definition of Lean Manufacturing has been mostly centered on the continuous improvement approach and an eighth class of waste has been defined: skills, or non-utilized talent. This kind of waste occurs when organizations introduce a huge separation between the management and the process operators, thus obstructing the continuous improvement routines. The spread of the Industry 4.0 paradigm, based on a massive ICT deployment, may lead to two possible risks. First, decisions may be taken based only on the data acquired on the process, without involving the people performing a task who are most capable and experienced to develop appropriate solutions. This would lead to enlarge the gap between management and operators and, in turn, the waste of skills. On the other side, appropriate skills are necessary to manage the Industry 4.0 tools. The latest literature advances in these two fields are discussed in the present paper.

1 Introduction

Today enterprises are required to face challenging scenarios: on the one hand, companies have to deal with competitors spread all over the world and working in a variety of different conditions. On the other hand, customers' expectations increase at a high pace: high quality products must be available at a low price, delivered in short times and provided with a high innovative content.

In order to profitably fulfill such expectations, different initiatives can be undertaken. Among them, the adoption of Lean Manufacturing practices is one of the most powerful approaches. This term has been introduced in 1990 [1] to denote the working philosophy developed in the Toyota Production System and then adopted by many Japanese companies. The power of this approach consists in the scientific, systematic approach for distinguishing the product features that match the value desired by the customer (or even increase the perceived value) from the low added-value characteristics. This analysis, in turn, can be reflected on the manufacturing processes, to focus efforts on the operations that really increase product value or are strictly necessary for its management, enabling to discard useless tasks, and deploy continuous improvement routines for performance increase.

P. Chiabert et al. (Eds.): PLM 2018, IFIP AICT 540, pp. 455–464, 2018.
https://doi.org/10.1007/978-3-030-01614-2_42

For this reason, the Lean approach is often synthesized as "doing more with less". Nonetheless, such synthesis may be misleading, as it does not include one of the foci of the Lean approach: the successful implementation of such practices is strictly committed to the active role of the human, who is the main source of intelligence and creativity in any manufacturing environment; thus, his role cannot be discarded in the continuous improvement journey.

The digitalization technologies are further enriching this framework, driven by the diffusion of the Industry 4.0 paradigm: this term has been introduced during the Hannover Fair in 2011; although a well-established and shared definition is still lacking, scientists and practitioners agree in stating that Industry 4.0 relies on the application of Internet of Things within industrial environment. The diffusion of technologies for non-invasive, easy-to-use monitoring systems (e.g. wireless sensors), the increased storage capacity available at low price, the enhanced available computing power led to the availability of intelligent systems for data acquisition, data analysis, decision making and information dispatching that are permeating manufacturing environments at a high-pace.

Such systems may boost the performance of a manufacturing environment, provided that an enterprise is able to extract value from the collected information. The role of human is crucial for this purpose: high-level professional functions and skills are necessary to take technical, organizational and strategical decisions in agreement with the Lean principles, supported by the information systems powered by the Industry 4.0 technologies. Nonetheless, a recent survey realized by Frey and Osborne [2] showed that automation and digitalization will result in deleting more than 700 occupation profiles in the USA and that 47% of total USA employment is at risk. A similar analysis performed in Europe [3] shows that 40% to 60% of workers may be displaced because of technological changes.

Therefore, the following research questions are dealt in the present paper: (i) How can information systems support human operators in taking the right decision at the right time? (ii) Which competences are necessary for an operator to profitably work into an Industry 4.0 environment? To answer such questions, a literature analysis has been performed.

The reminder of this paper is organized as follows: the background concerning the role of human according to the Lean approach is presented; in particular the issue of people underutilization is discussed. The research methodology is presented in Sect. 3. Sections 4 and 5 are devoted to answering the two research questions. Finally, conclusive remarks are provided in Sect. 6.

2 Background

Womack and Jones [1] use the term 'waste' to denote any activity that absorbs resources without creating value. In the late 1980 s, Ohno [4] proposed a classification of the wastes that may affect any manufacturing process; he defined the following 7 classes: transportation, inventory, unnecessary movements, waiting, overproduction, inappropriate processing and defects. Later, an eight waste has been added to this taxonomy, which is still quite under-investigated in literature: underutilized people [5].

Cattaneo et al. [6] recently made an effort to systematize knowledge on the connections between the Lean approach and the Industry 4.0 technologies through a systematic literature review. Over a basis of 42 documents (including both journal and conference papers), they found that about one third take into account human resources management, a strategic approach aimed to employ and develop qualified employees to achieve company's objectives [7]. The development of human resources plays a crucial role for the performance of any organization and may be split into three main functional areas: personal development (competencies), team development (collaboration) and organizational development (structure and processes) [8].

According to the Lean perspective, the waste of underutilized people can be considered from different points of view: for example, an uneven work distribution results in involving more people than necessary for a given task and, in turn, in wasting workforce. Nonetheless, considering people as simple workforce is a limited perspective: humans are the main source of creativity within any working environment. Therefore, people underutilization may also result from mis-using skills: this occurs when employees are not provided with the right information to correctly perform the assigned tasks and support the improvement process or, conversely, when they are lacking the skills necessary for a proper interpretation of the events that are taking place.

In a recent work, Ras et al. [9] identify four challenges for shop floor workers to perform well in modern manufacturing environments:

1. The workforce needs to understand the underlying processes and their dependencies, to develop the know-how needed for collecting and utilizing data, and leverage digitization in the intelligent production of smart products with flexible lot sizes.
2. Intelligent assistance systems need to be standardized, developed, and deployed in order to real-time guide operators, train workforce, and assess performance from observation.
3. Job profiles have to be updated as tasks needed in the Industry 4.0 context are more interdisciplinary and combine, for example, elements of mechatronics with design, data analytics, and business administration. Development and appraisal procedures for the existing workforce must be built, and a map for the new needed skills to be developed is to be drawn.
4. Socio-technical approaches are necessary to allow grounded participatory design of an interdisciplinary workplace, and re-organize lifelong learning in ways that positively impact on the work life balance.

Therefore, accordingly with our research questions, operators need to be properly guided by intelligent systems supporting observation and decision making. Some approaches available in literature concerning this issue are presented in Sect. 4. Further, operators need mental routines as well as interdisciplinary and social skills to profitably operate in complex environments cooperating with the rest of the company. A review of the existing models defining the necessary competences is presented in Sect. 5.

3 Methodology

To perform a literature review capable to answer our research questions, the two main databases of scientific papers have been consulted: Scopus and Web of Science (WoS). The search strings have been defined to find papers containing at least one of the keywords "Industr* 4.0" or "Smart manufactur*" and one of the keywords "skill*", "competenc*" and "knowledge". The wildcard "*" has been used to select papers containing nouns in both the singular and the plural forms and to include in the search also papers containing the German term Industrie 4.0.

The results provided by Scopus and WoS provided 419 and 222 papers, respectively. Some papers were available on both the two databases; thus, a cleaning operation has been made resulting in a sample made of 516 original papers. The first result of this search is the increasing impact over time of the investigated topic. Only 17 papers have been published before 2013; then, the number tends to roughly double every year: 25 papers in 2014; 64 papers in 2015; 142 papers in 2016; 229 papers in 2017. The sample of papers published in 2018 is already sized 36 (the research has been made on the February, 20th).

However, many of these papers do not tackle issues tied to the role of human in industrial environment. As an example, papers concerning information systems for knowledge management in smart factories may appear in the results, although is not related with the research questions at stake. Therefore, a sub-sample of papers has been defined: for each paper, we read title, keywords and abstract, and discarded the publications not significant for our scopes. After this selection, the sample has been restricted to 70 papers which have been read carefully.

4 Intelligent Systems to Support Human Operators

According to the Final Report of the Industrie 4.0 Working Group [10], the work of employees will be supported by smart assistance systems with multimodal, user-friendly interfaces. In this field, Longo et al. [11] propose a human-centered approach (HCA) aiming to align and enhance the capabilities and the competencies of operators with the new smart factory context. In particular, they define the paradigm of "augmented operator". The term "augmented" is used because the Industry 4.0 technologies enable the operator to enhance his ability to perceive and act within the physical world by providing a virtual reality (VR) environment where different levels of contents superimpose each other. Moreover, augmented reality (AR) applications enable to add digital resources to a current view of the physical world. Therefore, the augmented operator may own an increased knowledge of the working environment deriving from operational tasks and traditional procedures as well as from a variety of value added contents that are suited to increase his abilities to perceive and act within the working environment. An example of AR-based assistance system is provided by Kerpen et al. [12], who developed a solution for weaving machine operators in textile production. When an operator needs support to fix a broken weft, he can focus the insertion device with the camera of the developed tool. A software application detects the position where the weft yarn is broken and provides the operator with a case-specific, AR-based support. For this solution, smartphones, tablets, or smart glasses can be used as runtime platforms.

A further effort has been made by Krugh and Mears [13]: they extended the 5C architecture describing CPS [14] to humans, obtaining a paradigm for the Cyber Human System (CHS). They interestingly found that the most difficult activities in the cyber world are naturally performed by humans because of the inherent intelligence that can be naturally leveraged for self-adaptive, corrective, and preventative actions. Conversely, the easiest activities for the CPS are more complicated for humans: while instrumenting a machine with sensors for data collection is quite simple, issues concerning human privacy, ethical data usage and storage, or acceptance by workers must be considered in the CHS.

However, although many concepts for smart assistance systems can be developed, the implementation into a manufacturing environment is not trivial. Arndt et al. [15] attempted to fill this gap by defining a methodology based on five steps, with particular focus on assembly production systems: (1) Analysis of the actual condition and challenges for the process at stake; (2) Definition of the requirements for the system, for handling personal data, and for supply process information; (3) Creation of a concept for documenting and processing data, as well as for presenting process information; (4) Implementation of the concept; (5) Validation and eventual optimization.

Nonetheless, besides the changes in the workplace, manufacturers also have to deal with the changes in workforce that are already taking place. Demographic changes are reshaping work design. It is estimated that by 2050 around 20% of the world population will be aged 60 years or older [16]. Several changes take place in the human body as age increases, and some of them are significant for the working environment, e.g. sensory, senso-motoric and cognitive capabilities. Further, the degrade of capabilities occurs individually at different speeds; therefore, the inter-individual differences increase as a population gets aged and companies need to address such changes in order to remain competitive [17]. To tackle the issue of aging workforce, Peruzzini and Pellicciari [18] developed a human-centered system capable to take into account the individual workability for a woodworking NC machine. Before the intervention, the process exhibited a high impact of human errors and downtimes to manually adjust the machine, as well as a high number of manual operations. The assistance system is made by hardware components to improve process ergonomics and to monitor the state of the machine and the surrounding environment. When an unexpected behavior occurs, the system intelligence browses the past cases to find a similar event and propose a solution to the operator; in case the issue is totally new, the system manager defines a solution that is added to the database of rules. Further, the system is able to recognize the user and automatically adapts according to the user needs: for example, the graphical interface may change in case of vision or memory problems, or the task sequence can be adapted to support an operator with limited motion abilities. user is recognized and the system automatically.

A further role of assistance systems is to support workers in training to deal with increasingly complex environments. For example, before the operators are allowed to perform assembly operations in a manufacturing line, they perform a training program to learn and practice their duties. Hardware prototypes are commonly used; nonetheless, they are costly and space-consuming. Further, a limited set of product variants can be tested and devices are available only at late development stages. Virtual training can play a significant role in overcoming such limitations. Gorecky et al. [19] developed an advanced training system for assembly in automotive industry based on affordable solutions like Microsoft Kinect and Nintendo Wii capable to access relevant data from the company information systems (e.g. Product Lifecycle Management) and automatically compile a training scenario. The system showed a high user-acceptation and exhibits a high potential for integration into diverse industries with complex products and processes, such as aerospace or train industries.

5 Competence Models for Industry 4.0

This section aims to discuss the importance of competencies for workers operating into an Industry 4.0 environment. The increased level of automation generally leads to a reduced number of workers in the shop-floor environment. As an example, Pfeiffer [20] reports a plant for car body production with a high automation level. Each operator is responsible for around 8 robots for material handling and welding, and usually intervenes 20 to 30 times per shift to adjust the system in order to prevent possible issues. To do this, workers need formal qualification: operators in this plant have at least a three-years vocational training. This example shows that one of the Industry 4.0 effects is the shift of human jobs towards non-routine tasks. Further, the higher is the technological level, the higher is the need of highly-skilled and well-trained people to make systems resilient and fix the failures that inevitably take place.

As pointed out by Ras et al. [9], the workforce operating in such scenario needs to integrate theoretical and practical knowledge. Technical competences and expertise is necessary to observe systems, extract implicit knowledge and use it for decision making. Nonetheless, technical skills are not sufficient to profitably operate in such a complex scenario: many additional competences are required, such as creativity, social intelligence, innovation competence and complex problem solving. In particular, they define three main categories of skills that are necessary to deal with a manufacturing environment: (i) STEM: Science, Technology, Engineering and Mathematics; (ii) MES: Mechanics, Electronics, Software and Manufacturing Technique; (iii) soft skills.

Also, the roles of the so-called "white" and "blue" collars are undergoing a transformation. The former class is now made of the designers of Industry 4.0 products and processes, while the latter group is shifting towards the Operator 4.0 defined by Romero et al. [21]. They envisage a human cyber-physical system where operators' abilities are improved through the interaction with machines, which can be classified in the following two categories. Physical interactions take place through exoscheletons supporting correct movements and ergonomics, wearable systems to collect and access information, collaborative robots to execute complex tasks. Cognitive interactions occur through augmented and virtual reality, intelligent personal assistants, social networks and big data analytics.

Thus, given the increased technological level that characterizes an Industry 4.0 environment, the role of human is still crucial: employees have to contribute in organizational learning, and innovate processes. Further, the rate of change is accelerating with greater force and frequency, and firms have to be very sensitive to new needs of customers and new type of competitors. Shamim et al. [22] argue that, to remain competitive, companies have to foster a climate of innovation and learning.

As a result, scientists proposed different competence models for the employees of an Industry 4.0 environment.

Pinzone et al. [23] performed an exploratory study aimed to depict the skills that a company must own for a successful exploitation of Industry 4.0 technologies. The study resulted in a set of both hard and soft skills classified according to the following five functional, key areas:

1. Operations management, including the definition of a roadmap to adopt Industry 4.0 technologies, active technology skills to use and program collaborative robots, additive manufacturing, augmented and virtual reality, monitoring systems, ICT tools, and soft skills such as human resources management;
2. Supply chain management, including the abilities to design and build digital supply networks, to analyze Big Data for predicting market behavior, to develop IT strategies for supply chain management;
3. Product-service innovation management, including capabilities to analyze innovative materials and processes, to design smart products and to design the service model;
4. Data science management, including capabilities to design Big Data architectures and software platforms, to develop tools for Big Data analytics, to use cloud platforms for computing and storage, to design info-graphics for intuitive representations;
5. IT-OT integration management, based on the development of a strategic roadmap for integrating information technologies (IT) with operations technologies of industrial automation (OT). This requires the capability to implement IT architectures and networks, the selection of appropriate communication protocols, and the design of strategies for cybersecurity.

Conversely, the classification performed by Pinol et al. [24] is based on the type of skills that needs to be owned by an Industry 4.0 employee:

1. Technological skills: abilities to work with IoT, collaborative robots, additive manufacturing systems, simulation tools and big data analytics;
2. Skills techniques: languages, business management planning, expertise in coasching;
3. Soft skills: adaptation to changes, flexibility and autonomy, effectiveness and leadership, teamworking and networking.

Hecklau et al. [8] provide a more detailed mode by aggregating the necessary competencies in four categories:

1. Technical competencies, including state of the art knowledge and skills on process understanding, media, coding, IT security;
2. Methodological competencies, including creativity, entrepreneurship, problem and conflict solving, decision making, research orientation, analytical and research skills;

3. Social competencies, including languages, communication, networking, team working, cooperation, leadership and intercultural skills
4. Personal competencies, including flexibility, motivation, ability to work under pressure, compliance, sustainable mindset.

The taxonomy provided by Fantini et al. [25] takes into account two possible roles for human operators in manufacturing environment. The first type is named Human-in-the-Loop (HitL) and encompasses activities such as overseeing and adjusting machines, directly commanding the system, being a source of data (for identification, early detection, reporting, etc.), as well as introducing deviations or disturbances due to errors, oversights, voluntary of involuntary deviations from the standards. This scenario corresponds to the levels 1 and 2 defined in the ISA95 standard. The second integration type is named Human-in-the-Mesh (HitM) and involves activities related to the interactions with the CPS network and applications – including the supported interaction with other human roles – corresponding to the levels 3 and 4 in the ISA95 standard. Their analysis results in a skills classification based on three categories: Human resource management and organization; Production management and methods; Technology. However, these three categories contain different skills according to the scenario to be dealt.

For the HitL scenario, competences in the area of human resource include flexibility, teamworking, confidence with feedback mechanisms, technological competences, ability to perform process and quality analyses. Conversely, Humans-in-the-Mesh need responsibility and authority, decision-making skills, complex systems modeling and simulation, capability to align objectives and incentives with the desired performances and to transfer knowledge.

The skills in production methods required for HitL include routine training, monitoring of human tasks and generation of alerts in case of possible errors or unexpected events, development of condition-based instructions to support diagnosis and reporting and to guide interventions. HitM need confidence with incremental models, multi-objective (multi-stakeholder) decision making, caption of decision-making patterns by experts.

Finally, technological skills for HitL comprise the deployment of mobile devices, the deployment of (wearable) sensors for inspection, testing and monitoring, multi-modal interaction (voice, image, gesture recognition, sound lights, etc.), asset tracking to detect tools and spare parts. HitM are required to support the deployment of mobile devices, the intuitive representation of alternatives and trade-offs, and the decision support enhanced by experts' decision- making patterns.

6 Conclusions

The present paper aimed to present the major literature trends concerning the role of humans within Industry 4.0 environments. The discussion in the previous sections shows that the developers of IT systems are beginning to take into account the needs of individual workers: customized interfaces can be realized to compensate with workers shortcomings (e.g. sights issues or concentration lacks) and to provide personalized information. On the other side, workers need to extend the range of their knowledge: technical competences are necessary but no more sufficient, and need to be complemented with social and soft skills. A general competence model, however, is not sufficient to deal with the complexity of Industry 4.0: different models for different job profiles have to be designed. In this field, a first interesting step has been made by Fantini et al. [25].

Acknowledgements. The results presented in this paper has been developed within the research program DISLOMAN - *Dynamic Integrated ShopfLoor Operation MANagement for Industry 4.0*, funded by Regione Piemonte (Italy).

References

1. Womack, J.P., Jones, D.T., Roos, D.: The Machine that Changed the World. Free Press, New York (1990)
2. Frey, C.B., Osborne, M.A.: The future of employment: how susceptible are jobs to computerisation? Technol. Forecast. Soc. Chang. **114**, 254–280 (2017). https://doi.org/10.1016/j.techfore.2016.08.019
3. Bowles, J.: The computerisation of European jobs (2015). http://bruegel.org/2014/07/the-computerisation-of-european-jobs/
4. Ohno, T.: Toyota Production System - Beyond Large Scale Production. Productivity Press, New York (1988)
5. Abdul Wahab, A.N., Mukhtara, M., Sulaiman, R.: A conceptual model of lean manufacturing dimensions. Procedia Technol. **11**, 1292–1298 (2013). https://doi.org/10.1016/j.protcy.2013.12.327
6. Cattaneo, L., Rossi, M., Negri, E., Powell, D., Terzi, S.: Lean thinking in the digital era. In: Ríos, J., Bernard, A., Bouras, A., Foufou, S. (eds.) PLM 2017. IAICT, vol. 517, pp. 371–381. Springer, Cham (2017). https://doi.org/10.1007/978-3-319-72905-3_33
7. Armstrong, M., Taylor, S.: Armstrong's Handbook of Human Resource Management Practice, 13th edn. Kogan Page, London (2014)
8. Hecklau, F., Galeitzkea, M., Flachsa, S., Kohlb, H.: Holistic approach for human resource management in Industry 4.0. Procedia CIRP **54**, 1–6 (2016)
9. Ras, E., Wild, F., Stahl, C., Baudet, A.: Bridging the skills gap of workers in Industry 4.0 by Human performance augmentation tools - challenges and roadmap. In: Proceedings of the 10th International Conference on Pervasive Technologies Related to Assistive Environments (PETRA 2017), pp. 428–432 (2017)
10. BDI (The Federation of German Industries), Roland Berger: The digital transformation of industry. How important is it? Who are the winners? What must be done now? (2013). https://www.rolandberger.com/publications/publication_pdf/roland_berger_digital_transformation_of_industry_20150315.pdf
11. Longo, F., Nicoletti, L., Padovano, A.: Smart operators in industry 4.0: a human-centered approach to enhance operators' capabilities and competencies within the new smart factory context. Comput. Ind. Eng. **113**, 144–159 (2017). https://doi.org/10.1016/j.cie.2017.09.016
12. Kerpen, D., Löhrer, M., Saggiomo, M., Kemper, M., Lemm, J., Gloy, Y.-S.: Effects of cyber-physical production systems on human factors in a weaving mill: implementation of digital working environments based on augmented reality. In: Proceedings of the 2016 IEEE International Conference on Industrial Technology (ICIT), pp. 2094–2098 (2016). https://doi.org/10.1109/icit.2016.7475092

13. Krugh, M., Mears, L.: A complementary Cyber-Human Systems framework for Industry 4.0 Cyber-Physical Systems. Manuf. Lett. (2018, in press). https://doi.org/10.1016/j.mfglet.2018.01.003
14. Lee, J., Bagheri, B., Kao, H.-A.: A cyber-physical systems architecture for Industry 4.0-based manufacturing systems. Manuf. Lett. **3**, 18–23 (2015). https://doi.org/10.1016/j.mfglet.2014.12.001
15. Arndt, A., Auth, C., Anderl, R.: Guideline for the implementation of human-oriented assistance systems in smart factories. In: Trzcielinski, S. (ed.) Advances in Ergonomics of Manufacturing: Managing the Enterprise of the Future. AISC, vol. 606, pp. 85–96. Springer, Cham (2018). https://doi.org/10.1007/978-3-319-60474-9_8
16. Fornalczyk, A., Stompor-Swiderska, J., Slazyk-Sobol, M.: Age management within organizations-employees' perceptions of the phenomenon - research report. J. Intercult. Manag. **7**(3), 39–51 (2015). https://doi.org/10.1515/joim-2015-0020
17. Schinner, M., Calero Valdez, A., Noll, E., Schaar, A.K., Letmathe, P., Ziefle, M.: 'Industrie 4.0' and an aging workforce – a discussion from a psychological and a managerial perspective. In: Zhou, J., Salvendy, G. (eds.) ITAP 2017. LNCS, vol. 10298, pp. 537–556. Springer, Cham (2017). https://doi.org/10.1007/978-3-319-58536-9_43
18. Peruzzini, M., Pellicciari, M.: A framework to design a human-centred adaptive manufacturing system for aging workers. Adv. Eng. Inform. **33**, 330–349 (2017). https://doi.org/10.1016/j.aei.2017.02.003
19. Gorecky, D., Khamis, M., Mura, K.: Introduction and establishment of virtual training in the factory of the future. Int. J. Comput. Integr. Manuf. **30**(1), 182–190 (2017). https://doi.org/10.1080/0951192X.2015.1067918
20. Pfeiffer, S.: Robots, Industry 4.0 and humans, or why assembly work is more than routine work. Societies **6**(2), paper no. 16. https://doi.org/10.3390/soc6020016
21. Romero, D., et al.: Towards an Operator 4.0 typology: a human-centric perspective on the fourth industrial revolution technologies. In: Proceedings of the International Conference on Computers & Industrial Engineering (CIE46) (2016)
22. Shamim, S., Cang, S., Yu1, H., Li, Y.: Management approaches for Industry 4.0 - a human resource management perspective. In: Proceedings of the 2016 IEEE Congress on Evolutionary Computation (CEC), pp. 5309–5316 (2016). https://doi.org/10.1109/cec.2016.7748365
23. Pinzone, M., Fantini, P., Perini, S., Garavaglia, S., Taisch, M., Miragliotta, G.: Jobs and skills in Industry 4.0: an exploratory research. In: Lödding, H., Riedel, R., Thoben, K.-D., von Cieminski, G., Kiritsis, D. (eds.) APMS 2017. IAICT, vol. 513, pp. 282–288. Springer, Cham (2017). https://doi.org/10.1007/978-3-319-66923-6_33
24. Piñol, T.C., Artigas Porta, S., Rodríguez Arévalo, M.C., Minguella-Canela, J.: Study of the training needs of industrial companies in the Barcelona area and proposal of training courses and methodologies to enhance further competitiveness. Procedia Manuf. **13**, 1426–1431 (2017). https://doi.org/10.1016/j.promfg.2017.09.159
25. Fantini, P., et al.: Exploring the integration of the human as a flexibility factor in CPS enabled manufacturing environments: methodology and results. In: Proceedings of the 42nd Annual Conference of the IEEE Industrial Electronics Society (IECON 2016), pp. 5711–5716 (2016). https://doi.org/10.1109/iecon.2016.7793579

Possibilities of Maintenance Service Process Analyses and Improvement Through Six Sigma, Lean and Industry 4.0 Implementation

Katarzyna Antosz and Dorota Stadnicka(✉)

Faculty of Mechanical Engineering and Aeronautics,
Rzeszow University of Technology, Rzeszow, Poland
{katarzyna.antosz,dorota.stadnicka}@prz.edu.pl

Abstract. The paper deals with problems concerning a maintenance process realized by maintenance service companies. In the paper the concept of wastes identification in such companies is presented. Then, a case study company is analysed. The company designs, manufactures, implements and performs maintenance processes of installations used in products control, sorting and packing in clients' factories. The analysed problems concern data collection as well as their analysis in order to improve the maintenance company efficiency. The authors propose to implement the Six Sigma methodology to collect and analyse data, elements of the Lean concept to identify wastes and Industry 4.0 concept in order to improve the maintenance service processes.

Keywords: Maintenance · Six Sigma · Lean concept · Industry 4.0
Efficiency improvement

1 Introduction

Maintenance processes play a significant role in maintaining the efficiency of technical equipment. Maintenance processes can be realized by different participants: by a user of equipment (1), by a manufacturer (2), by a company which delivered the service of an equipment installation (3), by an external company on the principle of outsourcing (4), in a mixed way (5). A maintenance process depends on many factors such as: selection of the right maintenance strategy [1], ensuring a certain technical infrastructure for a maintenance process [2], selection of the qualified employees [3] and, the most important, gathering the right data for a decision making in the maintenance process planning [4]. In order to manage a maintenance process correctly, it is essential to identify factors critical to quality (CTQ) from the point of views of clients as well as a company which delivers a maintenance service. Then, it is necessary to identify these factors which have real influence on CTQs. To do it Six Sigma methodology can be applied [5]. On the basis of the knowledge coming from the analyses performed in Six Sigma project, the maintenance information systems can be developed to be used in a decision making process. In the work [6] maintenance information systems were highlighted as one of the six important research areas in maintenance processes. Additionally, the work [7] shows how the collected data can be converted into

Published by Springer Nature Switzerland AG 2018.
P. Chiabert et al. (Eds.): PLM 2018, IFIP AICT 540, pp. 465–475, 2018.
https://doi.org/10.1007/978-3-030-01614-2_43

information, and then into knowledge in maintenance processes. A decision making system in maintenance can be supported by different methods and tools. The systems such as: CMMS (Computerized Maintenance Management Systems) [7, 8] or ERP (Enterprise Recourse Planning) [9] allow to store the data from a maintenance process, and then use them in analyses in many different ways. Different decision scenarios can be analyzed [10]. The works [11, 12] present the use of fuzzy logic in the analyses of the data gathered from a maintenance process, and then the prioritization of the maintenance activities. Additionally, the work [13] shows the use of a genetic algorithm in optimizing an aircraft maintenance plan. It is advantageous for companies to use such solutions in maintenance processes. Considering the fact that software might be expensive, analyses might be too complex and time consuming, the mentioned solutions are not very popular in small and medium enterprises (SME). However, in the light of Industry 4.0 concept it is predictable that more and more data which can be used for maintenance planning will be available [14]. Therefore, a cyber-physical system (CPS) can be proposed to support a maintenance process. A holistic approach for the quality oriented maintenance planning presented in the work [15] and an approach which uses historical data presented in the work [16] can be taken into consideration in CPS development.

Another important issue is connected to the wastes which may exist in a maintenance process. In order to identify wastes and then to eliminate them Lean concept can implemented [17]. Therefore, in this paper, the authors propose a methodology which uses Six Sigma and Lean concepts for a problem definition and identification of important factors influencing a decision making in a maintenance service process (MSP). It also combines a lot of data and analyses together, as well as the concept of Industry 4.0 to propose a direction for CPS development. The proposed methodology was developed for a case study company and it is currently implemented in this company.

In Sect. 2, the research problem and work methodology are presented. Section 3 describes a business organization in the case study company. Section 4 presents description of the MSP. In Sect. 5 the adopted the Six Sigma methodology is presented. Section 6 describes a company problem. Section 7 specifies the data which are collected. Section 8 presents the proposed statistical tests to be conducted to verify the research hypotheses. Section 9 indicates proposals for improvements and it presents a concept of MSP monitoring with the support of CPS. The last section concludes the work and identified limitations as well as the future research.

2 The Research Problem and Work Methodology

The research problem the authors deal with is that a simple methodology which can be applied in an SME maintenance service company and leads to the key factors identification and maintenance process improvement is not presented in the literature.

In order to develop such a methodology, the authors first analysed the business organization in the case study company and the activities undertaken in an MSP, then they adopted the Six Sigma methodology and Lean concept to the case study.

3 The Business Organization in the Case Study Company

The case study company designs, manufactures, implements and performs maintenance processes of the installations used in products control, sorting and packing in clients' factories. In order to create an installation, the company uses different kinds of elements: (1) elements which are manufactured in the company, (2) elements which are bought as standard elements (e.g. engines) and (3) elements which are delivered to order by other companies (e.g. industrial robots).

When an installation is started, the case study company takes responsibility for the maintenance process of the installation, if included in the contract. If not, the company takes responsibility only for hidden defects during the warranty period. In this work, only the cases in which a maintenance process is included in the contract are discussed.

The strategy of maintenance activities is presented in Fig. 1. A supplier of the elements delivered on order, which are composed into an installation, takes responsibility for a maintenance process of these elements (e.g. industrial robots). An installation supplier, i.e. the case study company, takes responsibility for the rest of the installation elements as well as for a trouble-free operation of the entire installation. Additionally, a user of the installation should plan internal maintenance processes to the necessary extent, of which the frequency depends on the installation utilization.

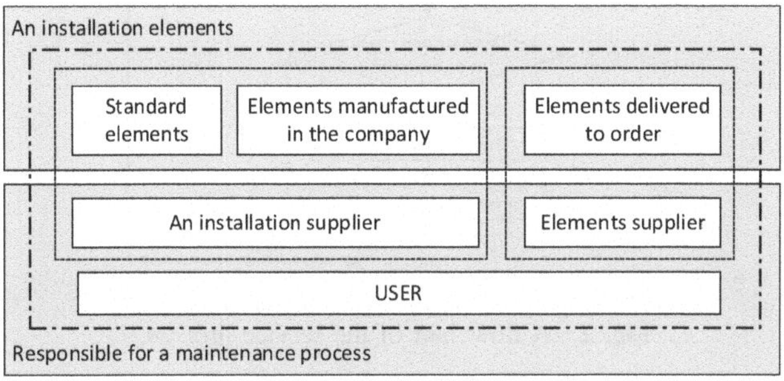

Fig. 1. A maintenance strategy.

In order to avoid failures, a preventive maintenance process is recommended. This kind of maintenance activities is undertaken by an installation supplier and elements suppliers in accordance with the provisions of the contracts, as well as by a client (user). Unfortunately, clients very often do not plan and do not undertake any preventive maintenance activities what causes the installation failures and increases the costs of the maintenance process undertaken by an installation supplier and elements suppliers. Therefore, in order to find the possibilities to decrease the costs of a maintenance process, this problem will be discussed in this work.

4 Description of a Maintenance Service Process

The MSP analysis is started from the identification of the steps of the process (Fig. 2). The process begins when a problem is reported or a company orders a preventive MSP. Then, a report is registered and a preliminary diagnosis or analysis of the activities that should be undertaken in a preventive MSP is performed. At this point, the kind of activities that should be done on the installation have to be pre-decided.

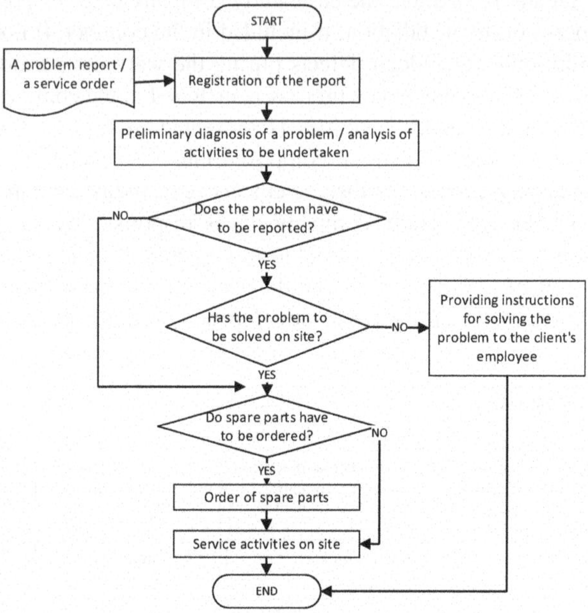

Fig. 2. A flowchart of the service process.

There are situations, related to problems reporting, when a problem can be solved remotely. It means that an employee can solve the problem based on the instructions of a supplier's maintenance employee, given by phone. Then, the MSP is finished. If a problem cannot be solved remotely, a maintenance employee or employees have to go to the installation place to perform a diagnosis and undertake maintenance service activities on site. Spare parts are sometimes needed. If this is the case, spare parts are ordered. Sometimes they have to be manufactured by the supplier. It takes time. When the spare parts are available, the MSP on site begins. One or more service employees (depending on the needed skills) have to go to the client's to undertake any necessary activities. If both an elements supplier and an installation supplier have to undertake service activities connected to the same reported problem, a client wants them to do it at the same time, because the running process must be stopped for the time of repair. Many factors have a potential influence on an MSP on each step of the process.

5 The Six Sigma Methodology with Additional Indicators

The authors proposed a project to be realized in the case study company. It involves the Six Sigma methodology and Lean tools in order to identify problems and factors which have an influence on the MSP outputs. The methodology consists of 5 steps based on DMAIC: Define, Measure, Analyse, Improve, Control, and it is presented in Table 1.

Table 1. Steps of the analysis

Step	Description	Results
Define	Identification of important outputs	Identified *Y*s
	Identification of inputs which can have a potential influence on the outputs	Identified *X*s
Measure analysis	Data collection	*Y*s and *X*s
	Analysis of *Y*s distributions	Normality test results
	Selection of statistical tests (for continuous data and attribute data)	Chosen tests
	Performing statistical tests	Test results
	Calculation of additional indicators	Values of indicators
	Qualitative analysis – identification of high costs and long lead time causes with the use of the quality and Lean tools (VSM)	Problems causes
Improve	Proposals for MSP improvements based on Industry 4.0 concept	Improvements
Control	Process monitoring based on Industry 4.0 concept	Stable processes

In order to evaluate the effectiveness of machines, devices and the MSP, the following performance indicators will be calculated: *MTBF* (Mean Time Between Failures), *MTTR* (Mean Time To Repair), *OA* (Operational Availability) calculated with the use of Eq. (1) and *MLD* (Mean Logistic Delay).

$$OA = \frac{MTTM}{MTTM + MMT + MLD} \tag{1}$$

where: *MMT* – Mean Maintenance Time, *MTTM* – Mean Time To Maintenance.

In order to perform the presented analyses, the company needs to gather a lot of different data. Then, detailed analyses of the values of the presented indicators have to be performed to show the problems as well as the directions of improvements in a MSP.

Additionally, for the assessment of the quality and flexibility of an MSP, the following analysis, among other, are planned to be performed: (1) the analysis of the frequency of emergence of particular types and (potential) causes of failures; (2) the analysis of the frequency of emergence of individual ways to eliminate failures; (3) the analysis of the number and specialization of the employees involved in a maintenance process; (4) the analysis of the type and costs of the spare parts used; (5) the analysis of the waiting time for the spare parts. Then, the Lean tool, such as Value Stream

Mapping (VSM), will be used to analyse the details of a single MSP and to identify additional problems which can cause, for example, delays or which can increase the maintenance service costs, as done in the work [18]. The detailed VSM methodology will not be presented in this work. In order to recognise the causes of the identified problems, the Ishikawa diagram can be applied. The results of the analysis will be taken into consideration in proposing improvements.

The project is established to be realized in the period of six months. The initial steps of the project are presented in this paper as well as the whole methodology developed to realize the project.

6 Define: Description of the Problem and SIPOC Development

The case study company is struggling with the problem of failures. These failures cause high costs of maintenance activities. Additionally, the lead time of failures elimination is long what, in consequence, causes customer's dissatisfaction. Therefore, the following problem has been defined.

Identification of the factors influencing the number of failures, maintenance service costs and lead time of a maintenance service process (MSP), and determination of activities which should be undertaken to minimize the costs and lead time.

In order to analyse the problem, first SIPOC was developed and it is presented in Fig. 3. There are several suppliers for a maintenance process such as: a client who provides the installation to be maintained; elements suppliers who perform a maintenance process of the chosen installation elements; and spare parts suppliers.

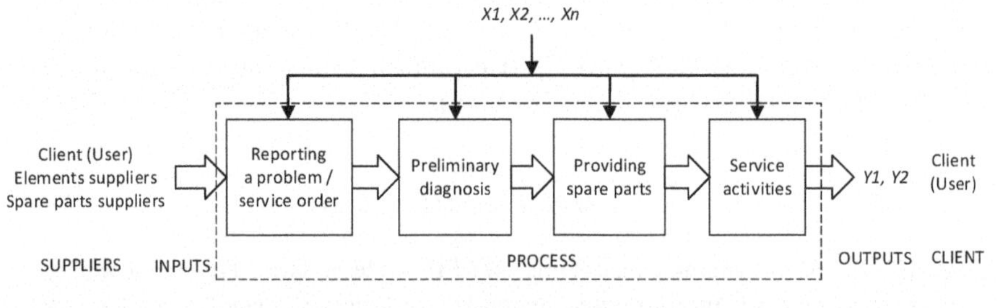

Fig. 3. The factors influencing the service process.

The input is the installation which will be the object of a maintenance process. The process consists of the following steps: registration of a report (a problem/a service order), a preliminary diagnosis, spare parts provision and service activities. From the client's point of view, the lead time (*Y1* [days]) of a service process is crucial. From the supplier's point of view, the cost (*Y2* [Euro]) of an MSP is also important. Therefore, these factors will be treated as the outputs of the process (CTQs). A customer is a user of the installation. The process can be influenced by different factors (*X1*, *X2*, ..., *Xn*). In order to identify these factors, first an MSP has to be carefully analysed.

7 Measure: Data Collection

Among the factors which can have a potential influence on the steps of a service process, these presented in Table 2 were identified. These data are currently being collected in the case study company and they will be used in further analyses. There are two kinds of data: attribute data and continuous data. The attribute data are coded as presented in Table 2. The outputs of the process might depend on some or on all of the inputs. However, in order to discover which inputs have a real influence on the outputs, further statistical analyses are indispensable.

Table 2. Factors having potential influence on the service process

Group of factors	Kind of factor	Symbol	Kind of data
Factors depending on a client	Kind of agreement with a client	*X16*	S, NS
	Kind of installation	*X3*	S, W, P, L, O
	Time since the installation of the work stand	*X17*	[days]
	Duration of the client's employees' training	*X23*	[hrs.]
	Time since the last preventive actions	*X21*	[days]
	Time since the last failure	*X22*	[days]
	Time since the installation of the oldest robot	*X18*	[days]
	Manufacturer of the robot	*X19*	M1, M2
	Number of collaborating equipment elements	*X20*	[pcs]
	People responsible for preventive actions	*X24*	S, C
	Day of the week when a problem was reported	*X32*	M, T,...
Reporting a problem/service order	Client	*X1*	C1, C2,...
	Industry	*X2*	I1, I2,...
	Way of reporting	*X15*	M, P
	Kind of an order	*X26*	P, F
	Comment of a client	*X27*	Descript. data
Preliminary diagnosis	Type of failure	*X4*	M, A, E, O
	Causes of failure	*X5*	C1, C2,...
	Distance to the client's site	*X11*	[km]
	Timeliness of preventive maintenance activities	*X25*	Y, N
Providing spare parts	Type of spare parts	*X8*	T1, T2,...
	Cost of spare parts	*X29*	[Euro]
	Waiting time for spare parts	*X31*	[days]
	Availability of spare parts	*X30*	A, NA
Service activities	Way of failure elimination	*X6*	W1, W2,...
	Additional actions	*X7*	T, D, R
	Way of the order realization	*X12*	C, S, SS
	Elements supplier	*X13*	SS1, SS2,...
	Number of employees engaged in the process	*X9*	[persons]
	Time for repairs	*X14*	[h]
	Specializations of employees	*X10*	S1, S2,...

8 Analyse: Proposed Statistical Tests

When the data are complete, first of all, statistical tests will be performed to identify the factors which have an influence on *Y1* and *Y2*. Therefore, the hypotheses were developed, taking into account the identified CTQs. Table 3 shows statistical tests which can be used in the presented hypotheses verification. In case of GLM application for H1 hypothesis testing, all *X*s can be tested in one GLM test, what is possible if *Y*1 distribution is normal. In case when *Y*1 distribution is not normal the Kruskal-Wallis test can be applied and each *X* has to be tested separately.

Table 3. Hypotheses to be tested and proposed statistical tests

	Hypotheses	Input	Output	Statistical test
H1	There is a significant difference in the lead time when *X*s take different attributes	*X1–X7, X10, X12, X13, X15, X16, X19, X24–X26, X30, X32*	*Y1* [days]	GLM or Kruskal-Wallis test
H2	There is a significant difference in the costs of an MSP when *X*s take different attributes	*X1–X7, X10, X12, X13, X15, X16, X19, X24–X26, X30, X32*	*Y2* [Euro]	GLM or Kruskal-Wallis test
H3	There is a significant difference in the lead time when *X*s take different values	*X9, X11, X14, X17, X18, X20–X23, X29, X31*	*Y1* [days]	Regression analysis
H4	There is a significant difference in the costs of an MSP when *X*s take different values	*X9, X11, X14, X17, X18, X20–X23, X29, X31*	*Y2* [Euro]	Regression analysis
H5	There is a significant difference in the types of failures (*X*4), failures causes (*X*5) and in additional actions (*X*7) in different kinds of installations	*X3*	*X4, X5, X7*	Chi^2
H6	There is a significant difference in the ways of an order realization within a different distance from the clients' site	*X11* (data have to be transformed into attribute data)	*X12*	Chi^2
H7	There is a significant difference in the number of employees engaged in different kinds of the installations maintenance process	*X3*	*X9*	Anova one way or Kruskal-Wallis test

The same situation occurs for hypothesis H2. For H3 and H4 regression analyses can be performed. For the next hypotheses, H5 and H6, we propose to use Chi^2 tests, however in case of H6, first the data (*X11*) have to be transformed into attribute data. In order to test H7 hypothesis, we recommend to use Anova one way or Kruskal-Wallis test depending on the distribution of *X9*.

On the basis of the results of the presented analysis, significant factors which have an influence on the outputs will be identified.

9 Improve and Control

The results of the above analyses will show the strengths and weaknesses of the MSP realized in the case study company. Additionally, the results will show the directions and ways of the MSP improvements. In order to improve the MSP on-line monitoring of the chosen installations' parameters such as: a number of working hours of the chosen elements of the equipment (1), vibration of the chosen elements of the equipment (2), work temperature of the chosen elements of the equipment (3), power consumption of the chosen elements of the equipment (4) and environmental working conditions (5) can be performed. Then, a decision making process that uses artificial intelligence, neutral networks or fuzzy logic, which on the basis of the data will suggest preventive maintenance activities on the grounds that a failure can appear, can be implemented [11, 12]. Other improvements can be proposed on the basis of the results of the analysis.

In order to control the MSP, the data concerning the process realization should be collected. Until now, the data concerning a certain client's order were registered partly in a database and partly on paper forms. The authors propose to implement a Cyber Physical System (CPS) with mobile devices which will allow to input the data concerning a maintenance process on site, where the installation functions, without a necessity of filling paper documents. This way, all the necessary data will be available just after the MSP completion and they will be the inputs for a decision making process supported by the developed algorithms.

10 Conclusions and Future Research

This paper presents a Six Sigma project which is currently run in a maintenance service company. The finished stages of the project concerned the problem definition, recognition of the current situation (flowchart of the service process), SIPOC development, identification of the factors which can have a potential influence on the maintenance process lead time (*Y1*), the costs of the maintenance service (*Y2*) and selection of statistical tests which can be used in further analysis to test the developed hypotheses. This allowed to understand the problem and plan further steps of the Six Sigma project.

The paper shows that the efficiency of an MSP depends on a number of factors. The realization of the process can be supported by different methods and tools. In order to support the MSP, more or less complex solutions can be applied in the same company. The main problem is data collection and integration, and then adequate responding to the performed analyses results. The presented approach shows the way of integrating the Six Sigma methodology, Lean philosophy and Industry 4.0 concept in order to increase the quality, efficiency and flexibility of an MSP.

The proposed methodology presents types of data and the way of data collecting as well as the possibilities of their statistical and qualitative analyses. the implementation of this methodology may allow companies to identify the possibilities of improvements, especially in the reduction of costs and lead time of an MSP.

The proposed methodology has its limitations which are connected to the fact that the methodology was developed on the basis of one company, and it has not been fully applied in practice yet. Therefore, in the future publications, the authors will present analyses which will be performed on the basis of the data which are currently being collected.

References

1. Swanson, L.: Linking maintenance strategies to performance. Int. J. Prod. Econ. **70**(3), 237–244 (2001)
2. Iung, B., Levrat, E., Crespo-Marquez, A., Erbe, H.: Conceptual framework for e-Maintenance: illustration by e-Maintenance technologies and platforms. Annu. Rev. Control **33**(2), 220–229 (2009)
3. Tretten, F.P., Normark, C.J.: Human factors issues in aircraft maintenance activities: a holistic approach. In: Human Factors and Ergonomics Society Annual Meeting: A Holistic Approach, Proceedings of the Human Factors and Ergonomics Society Europe Chapter 2014 Annual Conference, 08–10 October 2014 (2014)
4. Duffuaa, S.O., Raouf, A.: Intelligent maintenance. In: Planning and Control of Maintenance Systems, pp. 271–280. Springer, Cham (2015). https://doi.org/10.1007/978-3-319-19803-3_13
5. Zasadzien, M.: Application of the Six Sigma method for improving maintenance processes – case study. In: Proceedings of the 6th International Conference on Operations Research and Enterprise Systems, ICORES 2017, pp. 314–320 (2017)
6. Garg, A., Deshmukh, S.G.: Maintenance management: literature review and directions. J. Qual. Maint. Eng. **12**(3), 205–238 (2006)
7. Candell, O., Karin, R., Söderholm, P.: eMaintenance-Information logistics for maintenance support. Robot. Comput.-Integr. Manuf. **25**, 937–944 (2009)
8. Claverley, J.D., Leach, R.K.: A review of the existing performance verification infrastructure for micro-CMMs. Precis. Eng. **39**, 1–15 (2015)
9. Klos, S., Patalas-Maliszewska, J.: The impact of ERP on maintenance management. Manag. Prod. Eng. Rev. **4**(3), 15–25 (2013)
10. Loska, A.: Scenario modeling exploitation decision-making process in technical network systems. Eksploatacja i Niezawodnosc – Maint. Reliab. **19**(2), 268–278 (2017). https://doi.org/10.17531/ein.2017.2.15
11. Ratnayake, R., Antosz, K.: Risk-based maintenance assessment in the manufacturing industry: minimisation of suboptimal prioritisation. Manag. Prod. Eng. Rev. **8**(1), 38–45 (2017)
12. Antosz, K., Stadnicka, D.: An intelligent system supporting a maintenance process of specialised medical equipment. In: Burduk, A., Mazurkiewicz, D. (eds.) ISPEM 2017. AISC, vol. 637, pp. 23–32. Springer, Cham (2018). https://doi.org/10.1007/978-3-319-64465-3_3
13. Yang, Z., Yang, G.: Optimization of aircraft maintenance plan based on genetic algorithm. Phys. Proc. **33**, 580–586 (2012)
14. Erol, S., Jäger, A., Hold, P., Ott, K., Sihn, W.: Tangible Industry 4.0: a scenario-based approach to learning for the future of production. Proc. CIRP **54**, 13–18 (2014)

15. Glawara, R., Kemeny, Z., Nemetha, T., Matyas, K., Monostoric, L., Sihna, W.: A holistic approach for quality oriented maintenance planning supported by data mining methods. Proc. CIRP **57**, 259–264 (2016)
16. Pogačnik, B., Duhovnik, J., Tavčar, J.: Aircraft fault forecasting at maintenance service on the basis of historic data and aircraft parameters. Eksploatacja i Niezawodnosc – Maint. Reliab. **19**(4), 624–633 (2017). https://doi.org/10.17531/ein.2017.4.17
17. Gupta, S., Gupta, P., Parida, A.: Modeling lean maintenance metric using incidence matrix approach. Int. J. Syst. Assur. Eng. Manag. **8**(4), 799–816 (2017)
18. Stadnicka, D., Ratnayake, R.M.C.: Minimization of service disturbance: VSM based case study in telecommunication industry. In: 8th IFAC Conference on Manufacturing Modelling, Management and Control, MIM, Troyes, 28–30 June (2016). IFAC PAPERSONLINE **49** (12), 255–260

Towards a Smart Manufacturing Toolkit for SMEs

Sameer Mittal[1], David Romero[2], and Thorsten Wuest[1(✉)]

[1] Industrial and Management Systems Engineering, Benjamin M. Statler College of Engineering and Mineral Resources, West Virginia University, Morgantown, WV, USA
samittal@mix.wvu.edu, thwuest@mail.wvu.edu
[2] Tecnológico de Monterrey, Mexico City, Mexico
david.romero.diaz@gmail.com

Abstract. Technology, human and financial capitals will always be a significant constraint for manufacturing Small and Medium-sized Enterprises (SMEs). Keeping that in mind, this paper introduces a modular Smart Manufacturing (SM) Toolkit for SMEs as a set of technologies, methods, tools, and practices that can help manufacturing enterprises to increase their SM capabilities. The modular SM toolkit is composed of seven individual specialized toolboxes, which cover both technical and business management aspects of a successful digital transformation in a manufacturing SME. In addition, the various SME functions that can be supported with each individual toolbox are presented as well. The paper concludes with two short demonstration case studies as a means of an early validation mechanism for the SM toolkit in refinement.

Keywords: Digitalization · SMEs · Industry 4.0 · Smart Manufacturing Intelligent manufacturing · Toolboxes · Toolkit

1 Introduction

The goal of a *Smart Manufacturing (SM)* initiative is to optimize a production system with the help of a set of digital practices, technologies and other enabling factors that support the operations of a manufacturing enterprise [1, 2]. The discretion of practices, technologies and enabling factors that may be deployed by a manufacturing enterprise will depend on the degree of *digitalization* of its industrial sector (i.e., push-adoption) and/or self-conviction in pursuit of a new (digital) competitive advantage (i.e., pull-adoption). In this sense, it is important to emphasize that developing an *SM system* represents both a technological and managerial challenge [3]. Therefore, shifting towards an *SM practice* should be both profitable and sustainable for a manufacturing enterprise. Although, the scientific literature has suggested a number of assessments, frameworks, maturity models and roadmaps for supporting the *digital transformation* of manufacturing enterprises towards the development of *SM capabilities,* the body of knowledge is lacking methods, tools and support systems for Small and Medium-sized Enterprises (SMEs).

Published by Springer Nature Switzerland AG 2018.
P. Chiabert et al. (Eds.): PLM 2018, IFIP AICT 540, pp. 476–487, 2018.
https://doi.org/10.1007/978-3-030-01614-2_44

According to Esmaelian et al. [4]: *"Manufacturing is continuously evolving from concept development to methods and tools available for the production of goods for use or sale. Traditionally, manufacturing refers to an industrial production process through which raw materials are transformed into finished products to be sold in the market. However, these days manufacturing is considered to be an integrated concept at all levels from machines to production systems to an entire business level operation".*

The evolution in the definition of "manufacturing" [4] has led to the establishment of new requirements for the development of *manufacturing toolkits* as a set of methods, tools, and practices. Different manufacturing initiatives, such as *lean manufacturing* [5] and *digital manufacturing* [6] have developed their own toolkits over the years that may help manufacturing enterprises in their shift towards more efficient production operations. These toolkits include a diverse range of items from cutting-edge CAx technologies, working tools, managerial principles, training methods, organizational practices, etc. However, when it comes to the recent *SM initiative* [1, 2], there is a void, or at least a very limited number, of toolkits aimed at supporting manufacturing enterprises (i.e., SMEs), in adopting the new 'smart' ways of production operations. Therefore, there is a need for systematizing the currently available SM methods, tools and practices in a modular toolkit providing a step-by-step and building-block approach for SMEs to develop SM capabilities in their own individual manufacturing systems.

This paper discusses the importance of SM toolkits for SMEs in the context of the Fourth Industrial Revolution or Industry 4.0. Section 2 focuses on available toolkits in the scientific body of knowledge. Section 3 proposes a *modular SM toolkit* that aims to help SMEs to develop SM capabilities. Following, two case studies validating the proposed toolkit are discussed in Sect. 4. Section 5 presents conclusions and further research work.

2 Literature Review

Toolkits may be considered as the set of organized working methods, physical and software tools, and managerial practices [7]. Every toolkit has its own objective. When it comes to manufacturing, there are a few toolkits available that may be considered as precursors for the development of an SM toolkit.

[5] categorized different *lean tools* and *methods* under five families to develop a modular toolkit: (a) JIT (pull-system, takt-time and Kanban systems), (b) TPM (OEE, SMED and 5S), (c) Automation (poka-yoke, andon and full work systems), (d) VSM (current state map, future state map and flow diagrams), and (e) Kaizen (brainstorming, continuous flow, five whys, Pareto-chart and Gantt-chart). The selection of the best *lean toolkits* for manufacturing SMEs has also been discussed in the literature [8], emphasizing the toolkits specific SME characteristics.

A target toolset, or toolkit, for *digital manufacturing* has been suggested by [6], considering five families: (a) manufacturing design and production simulation tools - focus on value addition and waste reduction - e.g.: manufacturing planning, layout planning, process simulation and lean manufacturing, (b) production automation tools, e.g.: CNC machining, remote monitoring, PLC programming, machine vision, RFID and barcode technology, (c) robotic tools - which can be an alternative for human labour with a positive effect on production rate and quality, e.g.: office programming, material handling, welding and trimming, (d) additive manufacturing tools - for cost-reduction - e.g.: pre-moulding, prototyping and 3D-printing, and (e) digital scanning and measuring (metrology) - for economical design and process innovation, e.g.: 3D-laser scanning, reverse engineering and quality assurance.

[9] mentioned the following tools, or toolkit, for *e-manufacturing:* (a) predictive intelligence (e.g.: agents, algorithms, software), (b) scalable platform, (c) information compatibility between devices and business, (d) data-to-information-to-knowledge transformation tools, (e) synchronization systems for dynamic decision-making (e.g., CRM, SCM, B2B e-commerce systems), (f) tether-free communication systems, (g) employee education and training, and (h) flexible enterprise culture.

Similarly, a toolset or toolkit for *small-scale intelligent manufacturing systems* has been proposed by [3], where three broad categories were defined: (a) ICT as the use of information and communication technology for production management, e.g.: agent technology, cloud computing, mobile technology and remote monitoring, (b) artificial intelligence (AI) techniques in manufacturing as well as technologies like CAD, CNC machines, robots and virtual reality, and (c) others technologies like rapid prototyping, 3D measurements & inspection, reverse engineering and reconfigurable machine tools.

An *Industry 4.0 toolbox* has been proposed by [10], for both product and process levels, including six distinct toolboxes each. At the product level: (a) sensor and actuator integration, (b) communication/connectivity, (c) functionality of data storage and information exchange, (d) monitoring, (e) product related IT services, and (f) business models. Similarly, at the process level: (a) data processing, (b) Machine-to-Machine (M2M) communication, (c) company-wide networking with production, (d) ICT-infrastructure, (e) man-machine interfaces (HMIs), and (f) efficiency with small batches.

ICT has been considered as a fundamental technology in the aforementioned toolkits [3, 5, 6, 8], but an *operationalization perspective* has been only offered by the Industry 4.0 toolbox [10]. The need of ICT, data and other application technologies such as CAD, CAM and recently 3D-printing, are the other vital factors that can be observed. Business models, charts, brainstorming, employee education, training, and skills enhancement programs are other organizational practices that were contemplated. Therefore, the available scientific literature presents several (general) toolboxes from both a technical and a managerial perspective. However, based on the literature review conducted in SCOPUS and Web of Science databases, there are a limited number of SM toolkits. Although there is an Industry 4.0 toolkit [10] available, this covers only the technical perspective (i.e., product and process families) and neglects the managerial view (i.e., employees' skills enhancement and business model aspects).

Due to the imminent pressure by OEMs to *digitalize* their whole value chains, SMEs need more than ever support in their *digital transformation.* A possible way to effectively support SMEs is by providing them with a *modular SM toolkit,* which can help them to follow a step-by-step and building-block approach for the needed actions to adopt SM technologies and business practices, and deliver both short-term and long-term results to themselves and their value chains. The short-term benefits/results should motivate SMEs to lower the entry barrier and start their *digitalization journey* towards new SM capabilities, whereas the long-term benefits should bring new competitive advantages to the manufacturing enterprise.

3 Towards a Smart Manufacturing Toolkit for SMEs

[6] proposed a *Digital Manufacturing (DM) toolkit* for SMEs. *DM* allows SMEs to virtually prototype and test multiple products and process designs; thus reducing design risks and ultimately costs. Whereas, *SM* will allow/enable SMEs to connect all their manufacturing resources with each other and with their products in order to optimize their operations. Therefore, there is a need to provide a specific *SM toolkit* for manufacturing SMEs, which is currently not available in literature.

Table 1 presents a set of toolboxes that integrate and conform the proposed *modular SM toolkit for SMEs*. The proposed *SM toolkit* has been developed with the help of a literature review, discussions with experts from academia based in India, Mexico, and the United States, and further refined with the help of SME managers. As a result, some of the toolboxes, which were already partially available in the literature, were refined. Others, not available yet, were developed as part of this research work. Table 1 presents a list of toolboxes and their corresponding features, various technologies, methods, tools and practices that are considered under the proposed *SM toolkit* and the enterprise functions that the toolboxes serve (see also Tables 2, 3, 4, 5, 6, 7, 8 and 9).

A *modular SM toolkit for SMEs* must be a stepwise and building-block instrument, always considering a continuous improvement process and various maturity levels towards developing new SM capabilities. The proposed levels are: (a) *novice,* when a manufacturing SME is not aware of the benefits of adopting SM technologies, (b) *beginner,* when an SME is informed about the benefits of adopting SM technologies and has taken the first step towards the adoption of one or more SM technologies, (c) *learner,* when an SME has already started its 'digitalization journey' towards SM practices, (d) *intermediate,* when an SME has spent sufficient time, effort and resources in practicing the SM paradigm and has develop new SM capabilities, and (e) *expert,* when an SME has realized new competitive advantages through its SM capabilities.

Tables 2, 3, 4, 5, 6, 7, 8 and 9 present seven toolboxes as key components of the *modular SM toolkit for SMEs* composed by various technologies, methods, tools, and practices (from Table 1), which act as enablers for the progress of a manufacturing SME through the different maturity levels to achieve new, value-adding SM capabilities. Some toolboxes may require inputs from other toolboxes for their functioning. Therefore, in Tables' column three, those inputs of other toolboxes are specified.

Toolbox 1 - Fabrication/Manufacturing Tools (FMTs): This toolbox involves production processes where humans are directly involved in the operation of different machinery tools. It might even be considered as the traditional form of manufacturing. This research work assumes the presence of manufacturing machine tools such as lathe, mill, etc. at the SME. Table 2 shows the evolution of manufacturing systems based on the inputs (enablers) required to move forward to the next SM maturity level [11, 12] when developing SM manufacturing/fabrication capabilities. [11] and [12] consider the following inputs as enablers to develop new SM capabilities in a manufacturing/

Table 1. SM toolkit: features, examples and corresponding SME functions

Toolboxes	Features	Examples	SME Functions
Manufacturing/ Fabrication Tools	• Used for manufacturing. • Human involved	• Lathe, Casting, Carpentry, Mill, Welding, etc.	• Manufacturing/Production
Design and Simulation Tools [3] [6]	• Deployed during design phase & simulating production	• Process Simulation, CAD, G-codes, 3D-printing, etc.	• Product Design • Process Planning • Operation(s) Times Estimation • Manufacturing/Production
Robotics and Automation Tools [6]	• Tools that can perform repetitive work. • Automated and modular	• Material Handling, Conveyor Belts, AS/RS, etc. • Scanners/Printers, etc.	• Part/Product/Transportation/ Storage • Quality Control and Inspection • Reverse Engineering • Manufacturing/Production
Sensors and Connectivity Tools [3] [9]	• Convert outputs to readable formats. • Support communication.	• Microcontrollers, Boards, Sensors, Actuators, Wi-Fi, M2M, Digital Readouts, Mobile Apps, etc.	• Quality Control • Repair and Maintenance • IT • Dispatching • Safety
Cloud/Storage Tools	• Provide space for data storage. • Stored data is shareable by host.	• Google Drive, Microsoft OneDrive, MS Azure etc. • External Hard-/ Optical-Drives, etc.	• IT • Supply Chain Management • Storing Investments, Expenses, Sales, Payrolls, Tax and Compliance, etc.
Data Analytics Tools	• Support data analytics.	• Data Analytics, AI, Optimization, Statistics, Machine Vision, etc.	• Decision Making • Purchasing & Sales • Evaluation Methods/Products/ Process/Employees • Production Planning • Statistical Quality Control • Data Management • Product Development
Business Management Tools/Principles [3] [8]	• Support development of business models, awareness and organizational culture.	• Collaboration, • Attending workshops, • Reading reports, Lean Practices, etc.	• Employee Relations • Employee Development • Realizing organizational short-term and long-term goals • Change Management Strategies • Strategic Planning • Deploying Standards

fabrication system (see Table 2). The novice level requires working dextrously with raw materials that require only hand-tools for their transformation into products, whereas at the beginner level, power-tools such pneumatic and/or electric energy machines are now needed to work more efficiently with (new) raw materials. At the learner level, numerical control machines take the stage at the shopfloor for enabling larger production volumes (of parts/products), and for the later introduction of the first manufacturing information systems (e.g. CAD in Toolbox 2) & MES) at the intermediate level. As both learner and intermediate stage need to mention the number of parts and products, the data analytics (see Toolbox 6) may be used as well. Finally, at the expert level, an SME starts to be concerned with the sustainability of its production resources, once it has managed to effectively achieving its production objectives.

Table 2. Fabrication/manufacturing toolbox (FMTs) and maturity levels

Inputs required	Levels	Toolbox
Raw materials	Novice	FMTs
Energy	Beginner	FMTs
Parts	Learner	FMTs, DATs
Orders	Intermediate	FMTs, DATs, DSTs
Sustainable resources	Expert	FMTs

Toolbox 2 - Design and Simulation Tools (DSTs): This toolbox considers the use of simulations of how actual production process should work. It involves the digital imitation of the manufacturing process environment. DST might be used during the design and ramp-up phase of a production line (see Table 3). The design and simulation process begins with paper-based designs, next level is when a design environment and model are present, a more sophisticated level involves software that can actually simulate how a product/part will behave in real-world, subsequently prototypes deploying 3D-printing (see Toolbox 3) may be produced using the design in the next level, and finally an interface is available for both producers and customers to actually interact with the product/part.

Table 3. Design and simulation toolbox (DSTs) and maturity levels

Inputs required	Levels	Toolbox
Paper-based design	Novice	CSTs
Environment & model (Design environment)	Beginner	DSTs
Simulation software	Learner	DSTs
3D Prototypes	Intermediate	RATs
Interface (Configurators)	Expert	SCTs

Toolbox 3 - Robotics and Automation Tools (RATs): This toolbox will support the elimination of strenuous and repetitive work by means of automation. Robots and other automation tools will be able to perform repetitive tasks more efficiently as compared to humans. Robots and other automation solutions will need to be installed as part of the manufacturing systems. RATs are the first step towards production automation. Since RATs need a separate investment, SMEs may consider purchasing them on the basis of their critical operations. Therefore, they can be classified in different levels that may require new hardware acquisitions during the SM maturity journey (see Table 4). The novice level of this toolbox requires manually-operated machines, whereas the beginner level involves non-programmable machines, which can be controlled by changing their basic parameters like speed, direction, etc. Moreover, at the learner level, programmable machines are introduced, while at the intermediate level, collaborative robots mimic human-motions and learn with experience. Finally, at expert level, the collaborative robots operate by deploying AI. Different families of RATs based on their functions have also been considered (see Table 5).

Table 4. Robotics and automation tools (RATs) and maturity levels

Inputs required	Levels	Toolbox
Manually-operated machines	Novice	RATs
Non-programmable machines	Beginner	RATs
Programmable machines	Learner	RATs
Collaborative robot (mimic human)	Intermediate	RATs
Collaborative robot (based on AI)	Expert	RATs

Table 5. Robotics and automation tools families and functions (RATs)

Family	Function
Quality & Inspection	They are used for maintaining quality in the manufacturing systems
Pick-n-Place	They are used for inter- and intra-departmental transportation

Toolbox 4 - Sensors and Connectivity Tools (SCTs): This toolbox includes sensors that can convert manufacturing processes outputs into readable formats. Their installation in machine tools helps to measure the required data for a better production management. Thus, helping in networking and sharing the data/information needed for a smart production planning and control [13]. The first level of this toolbox requires a source in the form of a physical body like raw materials (see FMT) or tools (see RBT), the second level requires sensors that can sit on the source, in the third level, the sensors will be able to convert the signals in readable formats, at the fourth level, the data can be stored, and finally at the expert level the user is able to operate with the help of an interface (see Table 6).

Table 6. Sensors and connectivity toolbox (SCTs) and maturity levels

Inputs required	Levels	Toolbox
Source	Novice	FMTs, RBTs
Sensors	Beginner	SCTs
Signals and converters	Learner	SCTs
Storage	Intermediate	CSTs
Interface	Expert	SCTs

Toolbox 5 - Cloud/Storage Tools (CSTs): This toolbox enables to store and share data. Nowadays, there is an abundance of online/cloud platforms that provide various facilities for data storage and sharing. For SMEs, the CST toolbox (see Table 7) begins with registering data by manually entering it in paper-based logbooks or spreadsheets to store data, in the second level, data storage is made in built-in hard drives (HDs), whereas in the third level, data store is made in shared HDs (i.e., flash drives, intranet, etc.), finally as data increases, massive data storage may be required based on *cloud* and/or *fog* solutions corresponding to the fourth and fifth maturity levels respectively. The difference between these two levels is minor as both fog and cloud have similar resources and services. But fog is able to reduce network congestion and latency [14].

Table 7. Cloud/storage toolbox (CSTs) and maturity levels

Inputs required	Levels	Toolbox
Registers, Logbooks, Spreadsheets	Novice	CSTs
Built-in HDs	Beginner	CSTs
Shared HDs	Learner	CSTs
Cloud	Intermediate	CSTs
Fog	Expert	CSTs

Toolbox 6 - Data Analytics Tools (DATs): This toolbox contains methods for data analytics. It includes a large family of statistical methods, optimization techniques, heuristics, etc. There are five main levels of data analytics [15]. During the first level, data collection is done by the input sources mentioned in Table 7; in the beginner level, data is cleaned; in the learner level, the meaningful data from various sources is combined; at the next level, data is reduced with the help of various rules; and finally data is transformed or normalized to avoid, e.g., redundancies (Table 8).

Table 8. Data analytics toolbox and maturity levels (DATs) [15]

Inputs required (Processes)	Levels	Toolbox
Data collection	Novice	CSTs
Data cleaning	Beginner	DATs
Data integration	Learner	DATs
Data reduction	Intermediate	DATs
Data transformation	Expert	DATs

Toolbox 7 - Business Management Tools (BMTs): This toolbox involves a lot more than technology. For example, it deals with practices that manufacturing SMEs need to develop and follow as part of a new SM culture. This toolkit considers managerial oriented aspects towards an SM culture such as employees' skills enhancement, lean culture, employee/employer shared mind-sets, positive organizational culture, keeping the organization updated about the latest trends in SM with the help of workshops, seminars and reading grey papers. Since this toolbox motivates the SME at all levels towards an SM culture and practice, therefore, this toolbox is one of the most essential and might be considered as a foundation for successfully developing SM capabilities. This toolbox considers also the five maturity levels defined for each of the business principles included, since the adoption of new business practices comes together with the adoption of the other technology-based SM toolboxes and vice versa. Selected BMT tools have been described in Table 9.

Table 9. Business management toolbox (BMTs) [Adapted from 16]

Principle/Practices	Description
Lean thinking	Eliminating all forms of waste in a production process
Organizational culture	System where employees share the same set of beliefs and values
Employee involvement	Activity where employees (not involved in R&D) can share their ideas, knowledge and play a role in organisation's decisions
Customer involvement	Products are designed based on customer voice/feedbacks
Collaboration	Products are designed considering supplier feedback.

As observed from Tables 2, 3, 4, 5, 6, 7, 8 and 9, a combination of different tools from several toolboxes might be required before the stepwise deployment of a particular toolbox. Implementing IoT technology requires sensors and actuators to be installed, Wi-Fi connectivity, data storage, and data analysis. Therefore, it will need to integrate SCTs, CSTs and DATs toolboxes.

4 Demonstration Case Studies

In addition to introducing the toolboxes as a means of integrating the proposed modular SM toolkit, it is important to identify the issues faced by SMEs during their adoption as well as how the proposed toolboxes may be deployed. As a result, this paper presents two short cases studies, where we present a stepwise deployment of the SM toolkit.

Digital Read Outs in Lathes and Mills: Two seasoned analogue lathe and mill machines had been lacking the needed accuracy on the shop floor. Job accuracy was mainly dependent on the skill and the experience of their individual operators. Considering budget constraints, the SME owner installed digital readouts (DROs). The DROs deployment made possible to ensure that the actual displacement with reference point is shown on the screen and the operator was no longer expected to set the zero for DROs repeatedly. The DROs may be considered as a part of the SCTs toolbox. Since a screen was attached to the lathe and mill itself (see Fig. 1), therefore, the wireless connectivity was not required in this case. Table 10 presents the various levels for installing the DROs in lathe and mill machine tools and shows how the toolbox helped the lathe and mill to shift from a "novice" to a "learner" – in the SCT toolbox levels.

Fig. 1. Smart Lathe (left) and Smart Mill (right) after DROs installation

Table 10. SCTs toolbox for DRO installation in Lathe and Mill machine tools

Inputs required	Levels went through	Toolboxes required
Lathe/Mill	Novice	FMTs
DRO Sensors	Beginner	SCTs
Signals, Converters	Learner	SCTs

Visual Inspection in Garment Industry: The SME was facing problems with manual inspections. The defects identification in the garment varied based on the subjective judgement of the worker the hour of the day. As a result, to improve the consistency in identifying defects and quality problems, an installation of a fabric inspection machine was suggested. For this improvement project, the RATs toolbox would be used and it will help the SME to make the cloth inspection more consistent. The fabric inspection machine will have a light box installed under the platform for inspecting the garment, also allowing the worker to adjust the speed of roll. Since the visual inspection machine will be operated by a human, therefore, it can be considered that the inspection process in the Garment industry shifted from a "novice" to a "beginner" (see Table 11). Additionally, if a digital fabric inspection machine is installed the fibre defects can be detected with the help of the sensors [17].

Table 11. RATs toolbox for visual inspection installation in garment industry

Inputs required	Levels went through	Toolboxes required
Manually-operated machines	Novice	RATs
Non-programmable machines	Beginner	RATs

5 Conclusions and Further Research

This paper presents a *modular SM toolkit for SMEs* consisting of *seven individual toolboxes.* Six toolboxes are technical in nature (fabrication/manufacturing; design and simulation; robotics and automation; sensors and connectivity; cloud/storage; data analytics), while one is managerial-oriented (business management). Moreover, the robotics toolbox has been accompanied with a robotics tools' families and functions sub-toolbox.

The technically oriented toolboxes have been complemented by selected business management tools via the seventh business management toolbox (see Table 9). The reason for this seventh toolbox is that to deploy successfully the SM toolkit, a change in the SMEs mind-set is required as well as a change in their organizational culture and other management aspects. Therefore, the proposed *SM toolkit* includes both technical and business management toolboxes. The stepwise and building-block approach of the *SM toolkit* is matched with SME specific requirements for its easy adoption by SMEs.

Although, the application of selected *toolboxes* (i.e. [3, 5, 6, 8, 10]) has been demonstrated in an industrial setting, their full evaluation is a long-term commitment. Hence, the full validation of the proposed *modular SM toolkit for SMEs* is part of our planned future work. Our future work will additionally include the deployment of all presented SM toolboxes in more SMEs and the development of a corresponding SM maturity model for SMEs (SM^3E) creating a comprehensive support system for SMEs.

References

1. Kusiak, A.: Smart manufacturing. Int. J. Prod. Res. **56**(1–2), 508–517 (2018)
2. Mittal, S., Khan, M.A., Romero, D., Wuest, T.: Smart manufacturing: characteristics, technologies and enabling factors. Part B: J. Eng. Manuf. (2017). https://doi.org/10.1177/0954405417736547
3. Huang, T.: Development of small-scale intelligent manufacturing systems (SIMS): a case study at Stella Polaris AS. Master thesis. Arctic University of Norway (2017)
4. Esmaeilian, B., Sara, B., Ben, W.: The evolution and future of manufacturing: a review. J. Manuf. Syst. **39**, 79–100 (2016)
5. Belekoukias, I., Garza-Reyes, J.A., Kumar, V.: The impact of lean methods and tools on the operational performance of manufacturing organisations. Int. J. Prod. Res. **52**(18), 5346–5366 (2014)
6. Kaartinen, H., Pieskä, S., Vähäsöyrinki, J.: Digital manufacturing toolbox for supporting the manufacturing SMEs. In: 7th IEEE International Conference on Cognitive Infocommunications, pp. 71–76 (2016)
7. Odedairo, B.O., Bell, D.: Framework for introducing and implementing value methods: a novel toolkit for small & medium scale industries in developing nations. Int. J. Basic Appl. Sci. **9**(10), 130–146 (2010)
8. Alaskari, O., Ahmad, M.M., Pinedo-Cuenca, R.: Development of a methodology to assist manufacturing SMEs in the selection of appropriate lean tools. Int. J. Lean Six Sigma **7**(1), 62–84 (2016)
9. Lee, J.: e-Manufacturing: fundamental, tools, and transformation. Robot. Comput.-Integr. Manuf. **19**(6), 501–507 (2003)
10. Anderl, R., et al.: Guideline Industrie 4.0: guiding principles for the implementation of Industrie 4.0 in small and medium sized businesses. In: VDMA Forum Industrie, vol. 4 (2015)
11. Cusumano, M.A.: Shifting economies: from craft production to flexible systems and software factories. Res. Policy **21**(5), 453–480 (1992)
12. Bi, Z., Da Xu, L., Wang, C.: Internet of things for enterprise systems of modern manufacturing. IEEE Trans. Industr. Inf. **10**(2), 1537–1546 (2014)

13. Nelles, J., Kuz, S., Mertens, A., Schlick, C.M.: Human-centered design of assistance systems for production planning and control: the role of the human in Industry 4.0. In: IEEE International Conference on Industrial Technology, ICIT, pp. 2099–2104 (2016)
14. Osanaiye, O., et al.: From cloud to fog computing: a review and a conceptual live VM migration framework. IEEE Access **5**, 8284–8300 (2017)
15. Han, J., Pei, J., Kamber, M.: Data Mining: Concepts and Techniques. Elsevier, Amsterdam (2011)
16. Vrande, V., De Jong, J., Vanhaverbeke, W., De Rochemont, M.: Open innovation in SMEs: trends, motives and management challenges. Technovation **29**(6–7), 423–437 (2009)
17. Li, Y., Ai, J., Sun, C.: Online fabric defect inspection using smart visual sensors. Sensors **13** (4), 4659–4673 (2013)

Optimization of Multi-part 3D Printing Build Strategies for Lean Product and Process Development

Nicola Garzaniti(✉), Alessandro Golkar, and Clément Fortin

Skolkovo Institute of Science and Technology, Space Center, Nobel Street 3, 464, Skolkovo, Moscow 143026, Russia
nicola.garzaniti@skoltech.ru

Abstract. In recent years, the engineering community realized the potential of additive manufacturing (AM) technology to be a game changer in product development and manufacturing. The capability of AM to build tailored products within short lead-time can make it a key contributor to Industry 4.0 in a lean manufacturing perspective.

This paper aims to assess how additive manufacturing can enable the implementation of lean product and process development practices, within a Product Lifecycle Management (PLM) perspective. We propose the use and the implementation of Design of Experiments (DoE) in a PLM tool to evaluate how part orientation, nesting and support strategy affects the total costs and time for product development and manufacturing. Then, we use the results of DoE analysis to optimize the multi-part 3D printing build strategies, to reduce waste of raw material and increase the overall quality of the final component.

Finally, we foresee the integration of this work in a wider multidisciplinary approach to comprehensively evaluate the use the of AM in the design of systems as early as at the conceptual design phase.

In this paper we present one of the case studies experimentally tested and validated.

Keywords: Additive manufacturing · Lean manufacturing
Cost-effectiveness analysis · PLM

1 Introduction

Over the last decade, manufacturing companies are facing significant challenges concerning the disruptive concept of Industry 4.0 [1]. It refers to a wide range of ideas, which cover several aspects related to product development and manufacturing [2].

In this context, Additive Manufacturing (AM) technologies drew significant interest from both academia and industry [3]. The engineering community realized the potential of AM to be a game changer in product development [4–6]. The capability of AM to build tailored products within short lead-time can make it a key contributor to Industry 4.0 in a lean manufacturing perspective [7].

The lean philosophy aims at minimizing waste within a manufacturing process. Originally, it was focused on eliminating rework, unnecessary processing steps, waiting

Published by Springer Nature Switzerland AG 2018.
P. Chiabert et al. (Eds.): PLM 2018, IFIP AICT 540, pp. 488–497, 2018.
https://doi.org/10.1007/978-3-030-01614-2_45

time, excess inventory and overproduction. Nowadays, it covers all the aspects of product development starting from the early stage of product life cycle, such as conceptual design, over to the manufacturing and distribution [8].

To enable the implementation of lean practices in product development and manufacturing, we focus on AM technology and analyze how to implement lean practices in the manufacturing process. Currently, market offers several PLM solutions to support 3D printing (i.e. solid and surface modeling, geometry meshing, STL slicing, G-code generation or its equivalent); however, most of them do not provide comprehensive information aimed to optimize multipart build strategies within a given volume.

Therefore, a lack of fundamental design guidelines of lean manufacturing practices suitable for AM can be observed. These guidelines, once well-defined can be implemented in a PLM optimization module that could be used early in the product lifecycle at the product development and the manufacturing stages. They could thus lean the product and process development for AM.

This paper investigates this concern by addressing two research questions:

1. Which design variables affect mostly the cost-effectiveness of AM processes?
2. How can we define a set of optimal levels of these parameters to enhance the cost-effectiveness of the process?

We limit our scope to *Powder Bed Fusion (PBF)* [9] for metals, which is the AM technologies that has been identified as the most industrially relevant at the time of writing of this paper.

The remainder of the paper is structured as follows. Section 2 illustrates the proposed approach. Section 3 discusses the results. Section 4 draws conclusions from the research and identifies avenues of future work.

2 Approach

We propose the use and the implementation of Design of Experiments (DoE) in a multidisciplinary PLM tool to identify lean practices in additive manufacturing (AM). The DoE method [10] consists of a set of statistical techniques, that provide a systematic way to sample the design space and to study the effects of the input variables on the output parameters.

Considering the overall steps to move from virtual CAD description to physical artifact development (Fig. 1), the approach we prose focuses on data preparation. It analyzes how the design variables involved in the building processes affect time and cost. The output of DoE is useful for identifying an optimal set-up [11] to reduce waste, particularly time and cost, in building parts using AM.

The first step consists in identifying the parameters we want to investigate, called *factors*, and defining appropriate design variable ranges, called *levels*. In the second step we select the most appropriate DoE techniques. Then, we delineate the *Matrix of Experiments*, where each row corresponds to one *observation*. Finally, we evaluate cost and time for each combination of variables stated in the matrix.

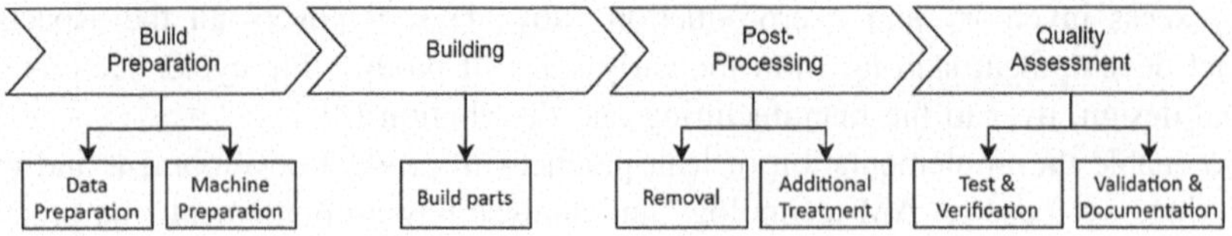

Fig. 1. AM overall workflow [12]

In data preparation phase, engineers have to select the nesting, part orientation and to define the support strategy. Therefore, we identified five factors which can influence cost and time needed to build parts using AM. In Table 1 we list them while providing a brief description.

Table 1. Factors

Factors	Description
Nesting	Process of laying out parts on the building plate to maximize the chamber filling and minimize the raw material waste
Z-height	Height along z direction of the component we want to build using AM
Solid supports volume	Volume of supports that have to provide a robust attachment to the build plane
Solid supports surface area	Area of supports that have to provide a robust attachment to the build plane
Wafer supports surface area	Area of a non-solid supports which are used to dissipate the heat

The definition of those factors has been mainly driven by the scan strategy associated to the generic PBF process. In this technology, each feature is built layer by layer, starting from the contour subsequently filled with a raster scan. Therefore, considering all the layers, contours become surfaces and filled areas become volumes. Literature provides many other parameters, which could be considered [13]. Nevertheless, most of them have a higher influence on the mechanical properties rather than cost [14], therefore, as a first approximation, they have not been considered in this discussion. However, they could be included into future improvements of this approach.

For each factor, a proper number of levels needs to be defined. The level of granularity must be sufficient to characterize the problem, without unacceptably penalizing computational cost.

Concerning nesting, we consider the parts' bounding box, therefore, we define l levels corresponding to the maximum number of components we can allocate to fill the chamber. Concerning the height along the z-direction, we define l levels included between the minimum size of parts' bounding box, corresponding to one of its side, and the maximum one, that corresponds to the internal diagonal. Therefore, depending on the orientation selected, it may happen that z-height is greater than the nominal bounding box dimensions.

With regards to the support strategy, we decided to define the levels as a percentage of the volume or area of the components in question. A minimum value of 5% to a maximum of 30% has been considered.

In the second step, we need to select the DoE techniques and delineate the Matrix of Experiments. The full factorial design is the best choice if it is computationally feasible. If a complete investigation is too expensive, the use of the one or two-factor technique can be considered.

Subsequently, we evaluate cost and time for each experiment stated in the matrix. To perform this task, we used the AM evaluation tool developed by the authors [12]. It consists of a manufacturing cost model, based on actual process flows foreseen for powder-based process. As input, the user has to provide information about the part to manufacture. As output, the tool presents a detailed cost and time breakdown structure. The model is based on two general equations, one for the recurring cost (RC) and one for non-recurring cost (NRC). The total cost is the sum of each of them.

$$\begin{cases} RC_i = \sum_j \left(hr_{i_j} \cdot t_{i_j}\right) & \textit{if phase} \neq \textit{building part} \\ RC_i = rm_c \cdot m_p + e_c \cdot e_p \cdot t_i & \textit{if phase} = \textit{building part} \end{cases} \tag{1}$$

Where:

RC_i - Recurring cost concerned with *ith* manufacturing phase (€)
hr_{i_j} - Hourly rate of the jth task concerned with *ith* manufacturing phase (€/h)
t_{i_j} - Time concerned with *jth* task of the *ith* manufacturing phase (h)
rm_c - Raw material cost (€/kg)
m_p - Total mass of the building job (parts and waste material) (kg)
e_c - Energy consumption (kW/h)
t_i - Time concerned with *ith* manufacturing phase (h)
e_p - Energy price (€/kW).

$$NRC_i = \frac{CapEx}{d_t \cdot u_t} \cdot t_i + \frac{OpEx}{u_t} \cdot t_i + NRC_{pv_i} \tag{2}$$

NRC_i - Non- recurring cost concerned with ith manufacturing phase (€)
$CapEx$ - Capital Expenditure (€)
$OpEx$ - Operating Expenditure (€/y)
d_t - Depreciation time (y)
u_t - Machine usage (h/y)
t_i - Time concerned with ith manufacturing phase (h)
NRC_{pv_i} - NRC, concerned with ith manufacturing phase, amortised on a specific part type, therefore affected by production volume (e.g. data preparation) (€).

Then, we used the results to calculate the main effect of a factor. It is the effect of a factor on the output averaged across the levels of other factors.

The output of DoE analysis exhibits the relationship between the different variables. It offers information useful to identify factors that mostly affect the costs and time of building parts using AM. The results are therefore used to optimize the AM process to reduce waste in a lean perspective.

3 Results

In this paragraph, our approach applied to a concrete case study is presented. We considered the hydraulic manifold of an aircraft. Its function is to regulate fluid flow between pumps and actuators in a hydraulic system. It lets the operator control how much fluid flows between components of the system, therefore controlling the behavior of actuators. This component has been identified as one of the most suitable to be manufactured using AM.

We adopt a simulation driven design approach [15] (i.e. to use PLM methods and tools to support design decisions) to move from a preliminary design to a topology optimized design [16]. Figure 2 shows the overall workflow foreseen to achieve the design which benefits most from the great geometry freedom enabled by additive techniques. We start selecting the component to be optimized: a hydraulic manifold made of Ti-6Al-4V (Fig. 2(1), green element). Then we define the design domain, the overall loads, and the preliminary properties and constraints of the part (Fig. 2(2), purple areas). Subsequently, we run the optimization code (Fig. 2(3)) and finalize the design (Fig. 2(4)).

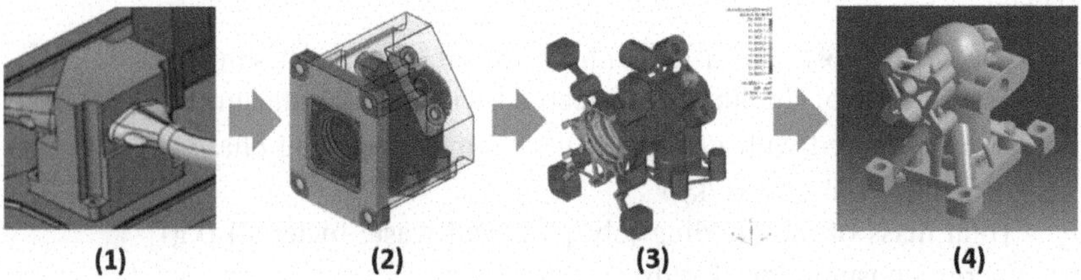

Fig. 2. Workflow to move from a preliminary to a topology optimized design (Color figure online)

In Table 2 we summarize the geometrical characteristics of the manifold selected (size of bounding box, effective volume and area) needed for the subsequent analysis.

Table 2. Hydraulic manifold geometrical characteristics

Item	Value	Metric
Length	75	mm
Width	75	mm
Height	85	mm
Volume	76178	mm^3
Surface area	43000	mm^2

In order to set up properly the DoE, the definition of the machine model, thus the build volume is required. A SLM 3D printer for metal, with a build volume of 250 × 250 × 315 mm, has been considered.

The second step is to define an appropriate number of levels, then select a proper DoE technique and delineate the matrix of experiments.

Considering the component size and the machine characteristics, we decided to define six level for each factor. We set a nesting value from one up to six. Concerning the height along the z-direction, we set equispaced value from 75 mm to 136 mm. As regards the support strategy, we define equispaced levels in the range from 5% to 30% of part's volume or area (Table 3).

Table 3. Factors and levels

Factor	Levels					
Nesting	1	2	3	4	5	6
Z-height (mm)	75	87.2	99.4	111.6	123.8	136
Solid s. volume	5%	10%	15%	20%	25%	30%
Solid s. surface area	5%	10%	15%	20%	25%	30%
Wafer s. surface area	5%	10%	15%	20%	25%	30%

If we want to perform a full factorial design, 7776 observations are needed. This investigation is complete but too expensive.

$$l^n = 7776\, observations \tag{3}$$

Where:

- n is the number of factors
- l is the number of levels.

Considering the use of one-factor method, we have to perform 26 observations.

$$1 + n(l - 1) = 26\, observations \tag{4}$$

Therefore, we decided to use the one-factor method and built the corresponding matrix. Subsequently, we evaluated cost. In Table 4 the matrix of experiments and related cost and time is exhibited.

We use the data in Table 4 to calculate the effect of factors. The analysis highlighted that nesting and z-height have a higher impact on cost and time than other factors. The first one has a coefficient of variation, also known as relative standard deviation, of 0.55 and the second of 0.09, the others lower than 0.01.

The results of DoE analysis offer preliminary information aimed at selecting a set of optimal parameters to reduce waste in manufacturing parts using AM.

The cost-effectiveness of the process is greatly influenced by the volumetric packing density of the part within the build chamber. Therefore, it is highly recommended to define a part orientation that most efficiently enables other parts (similar or different in geometry) to fit around it. In some circumstances, parts may also be clustered into groups and supported from one another.

Table 4. Matrix of experiments, cost and time

Exp No.	Nesting	z-height (mm)	Solid s volume	Solid s S area	Wafer s S area	Cost €	Time h
1	1	75	5%	1	5%	2815	25
2	2	75	5%	5%	5%	1553	16
3	3	75	5%	5%	5%	1133	13
4	4	75	5%	5%	5%	922	12
5	5	75	5%	5%	5%	796	11
6	6	75	5%	5%	5%	712	10
7	6	87.2	5%	5%	5%	757	10
8	6	99.4	5%	5%	5%	803	10
9	6	111.6	5%	5%	5%	848	11
10	6	123.8	5%	5%	5%	893	11
11	6	136	5%	5%	5%	939	11
12	6	75	10%	5%	5%	719	10
13	6	75	15%	5%	5%	726	10
14	6	75	20%	5%	5%	733	11
15	6	75	25%	5%	5%	740	11
16	6	75	30%	5%	5%	747	11
17	6	75	5%	10%	5%	713	10
18	6	75	5%	15%	5%	714	10
19	6	75	5%	20%	5%	714	10
20	6	75	5%	25%	5%	715	10
21	6	75	5%	30%	5%	716	10
22	6	75	5%	5%	10%	713	10
23	6	75	5%	5%	15%	715	10
24	6	75	5%	5%	20%	716	10
25	6	75	5%	5%	25%	718	10

The cost and time are directly proportional to the maximum height of components along the z-direction. The expenses grow with the increase of height due to the increment of the number of layers. It is therefore preferable to minimize the size along the z-axis.

Orientation of components in the chamber also has significant effect on the build-up quality, because parts' properties change according to layer direction. It influences the surface finish (roughness), the part strength in a specific direction, the geometric accuracy and the part stability in the building process. Therefore, all those issues should also be taken into account within the data preparation practice.

As in most engineering problems, criteria to minimize cost and time while ensuring appropriate quality of the product can conflict. So, the objective is to identify and select the best compromise solution for the scenario being considered.

All the results presented here were obtained by the implementation of DoE analysis in a PLM tool, tailored for AM process. It performs the analysis and it provides the data summarized in Table 4 and Fig. 3 as output.

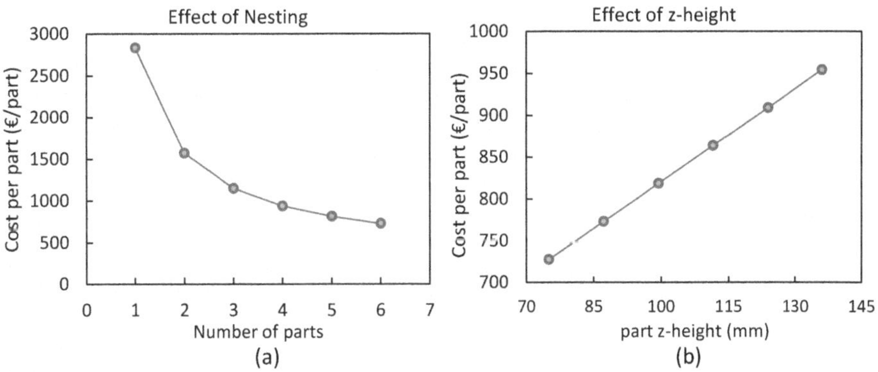

Fig. 3. Effect of nesting (a) and height along z on cost (b)

Furthermore, considering the two factors with the highest effect, the tool evaluates cost (or time) for different combination of those factors, while increasing number of levels. The infeasible solutions (i.e. max building chamber's dimensions exceeded) are automatically excluded from the analysis.

This is useful to identify the solution that minimize cost and time, constrained to the production volume foreseen/required. Figure 4 shows that in case of one-off component it is possible to minimize z-height (blue dots), meanwhile increasing the production volume it is not possible to reduce under a given threshold (green marks).

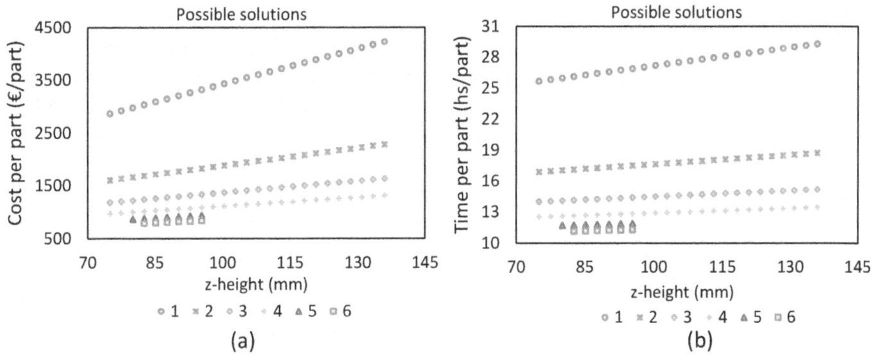

Fig. 4. Optimization (a) cost – (b) time (Color figure online)

The research work presented here has been experimentally tested and validated on different builds, including multiple geometries and different quantities. In this paper we presented one of the case studies analyzed.

The tests have been performed in the Additive Manufacturing Laboratory of a European aerospace company. The laboratory also provided the facilities and tools to manufacture the components involved in the analysis.

The estimations and the experimental data are in very good agreement: we have a level of uncertainty lower than 5% for the manufacturing cost and time. This proves the validity of the proposed guidelines that can be implemented in a PLM system.

4 Conclusions

Deployment of AM technologies represents a highly effective way to enable the implementation of lean philosophy within Industry 4.0. The main objective of this paper was to propose a methodology to identify lean practices in additive manufacturing and implement it in a PLM tool. Here we briefly summarize main findings of the research highlighting potential and limitation of our approach.

We introduced the use of DoE to identify the design variables which most affect the cost-effectiveness of AM process. Then we used the results to define a set of optimal parameters to reduce waste in manufacturing using AM.

The research investigates the relationship between orientation, support strategy, nesting and cost/time, and provides a systematic approach to perform quantitative analysis of the cost-benefit for AM process. Furthermore, we present some preliminary results to be used for optimization of design variables to reduce raw material waste and shorten lead time.

The analysis highlighted that z-height and nesting have a higher impact on cost and time than other variables. Therefore, we can identify and select the best compromise solution for the scenario being considered, in order to minimize cost and time while ensuring appropriate quality.

The work presented here has to be considered in a wider perspective and it opens the potential for several other topics to be investigated. It shall be integrated in a multidisciplinary PLM tool aimed to comprehensively evaluate the use the of AM in the design of systems already. This wider approach would provide information on how to support the prototyping and manufacturing technique decision-making process.

Several research works have been dedicated to the different AM core topics making this technology to be key contributor to the Industry 4.0. However, we also need improvements in systems engineering practices and PLM approaches to make it more competitive on the global market. This work intended to contribute to this future and this vision shaping a strategy to enable the deployment of lean practices within AM technologies.

Acknowledgments. The authors would like to thank Mr. Jonathan Meyer form Airbus for his valuable contribution, and for giving access to the data used to test and validate the tool.

References

1. Schumacher, A., Erol, S., Sihn, W.: A maturity model for assessing Industry 4.0 readiness and maturity of manufacturing enterprises. Proc. CIRP **52**, 161–166 (2016). https://doi.org/10.1016/j.procir.2016.07.040
2. Lasi, H., Fettke, P., Kemper, H.G., Feld, T., Hoffmann, M.: Industry 4.0. Bus. Inf. Syst. Eng. **6**, 239–242 (2014). https://doi.org/10.1007/s12599-014-0334-4
3. Gao, W., et al.: The status, challenges, and future of additive manufacturing in engineering. Comput.-Aided Des. **69**, 65–89 (2015). https://doi.org/10.1016/j.cad.2015.04.001
4. I. Wohlers Associates, Wohlers report 2017: 3D printing and additive manufacturing state of the industry : annual worldwide progress report (2017). https://wohlersassociates.com/2017contents.htm
5. Yang, S., Zhao, Y.F.: Additive manufacturing-enabled design theory and methodology: a critical review. Int. J. Adv. Manuf. Technol. **80**, 327–342 (2015). https://doi.org/10.1007/s00170-015-6994-5
6. Priarone, P.C., Ingarao, G.: Towards criteria for sustainable process selection: on the modelling of pure subtractive versus additive/subtractive integrated manufacturing approaches. J. Clean. Prod. **144**, 57–68 (2017). https://doi.org/10.1016/j.jclepro.2016.12.165
7. Santos, C., Mehrsai, A., Barros, A.C., Araújo, M., Ares, E.: Towards Industry 4.0: an overview of European strategic roadmaps. Proc. Manuf. **13**, 972–979 (2017). https://doi.org/10.1016/j.promfg.2017.09.093
8. Mrugalska, B., Wyrwicka, M.K.: Towards lean production in Industry 4.0. Proc. Eng. **182**, 466–473 (2017). https://doi.org/10.1016/j.proeng.2017.03.135
9. ASTM F42.91, F2792-12a: Standard Terminology for Additive Manufacturing Technologies, pp. 1–3. ASTM International, West Consh (2012). https://doi.org/10.1520/f2792-12a
10. Uy, M., Telford, J.K.: Optimization by design of experiment techniques. In: 2009 IEEE Aerospace Conference, pp. 1–10. IEEE (2009). https://doi.org/10.1109/aero.2009.4839625
11. Montgomery, D.C.: Design and Analysis of Experiments. Wiley, Hoboken (2013)
12. Garzaniti, N.: Influences of additive manufacturing in concurrent engineering process for aerospace applications. Thesis, Department of Mechanical and Aerospace Engineering, Politecnico di Torino (2017)
13. Sun, S., Brandt, M., Easton, M.: Powder bed fusion processes. In: Laser Additive Manufacturing, pp. 55–77. Elsevier (2017). https://doi.org/10.1016/b978-0-08-100433-3.00002-6
14. Calignano, F., Cattano, G., Manfredi, D.: Manufacturing of thin wall structures in AlSi10Mg alloy by laser powder bed fusion through process parameters. J. Mater. Process. Technol. **255**, 773–783 (2018). https://doi.org/10.1016/j.jmatprotec.2018.01.029
15. Sellgren, U.: Simulation-driven design - motives, means, and opportunities. KTH (1999)
16. Sigmund, O., Maute, K.: Topology optimization approaches. Struct. Multidisc. Optim. **48**, 1031–1055 (2013). https://doi.org/10.1007/s00158-013-0978-6

Perceived Risks and Benefits of Advanced Pay-Per-Use Type of Business Models Based on Industry 4.0 Enabled Technologies in Manufacturing Companies

Mikko Uuskoski(✉), Karan Menon, Hannu Kärkkäinen, and Kari Koskinen

Tampere University of Technology, Tampere, Finland
{mikko.uuskoski, karan.menon, hannu.karkkainen, kari.t.koskinen}@tut.fi

Abstract. There is a growing interest in the pay-per-outcome business models in manufacturing industries because of novel technologies provided by Industry 4.0 implementations. These business models for the software companies cannot be directly applied for manufacturing companies because of the scalability issues as well as complexity issues. The purpose of this paper is to identify perceived benefits and risks of Industry 4.0 enabled pay-per-outcome models for manufacturing companies (machine builders). We conducted qualitative interviews of machine building companies. We identified and selected companies that have been experimenting with novel Industry 4.0 enabled pay-per-outcome business models. We were able to create understanding the perceived benefits and risks of these advanced industry 4.0 enabled PPU/PPO type business models for machine builders. Since there is a limited amount of practical implications especially in case of investment heavy machine builders thus there is little understanding about related benefits and risks of implementing these novel Industry 4.0 enabled pay-per-outcome business models. This study can facilitate decision making of managers about implementing these novel business models by taking into account the expected benefits as well as bottlenecks encountered.

Keywords: Industry 4.0 · Industrial internet of things · Business models
Pay per use · Pay per outcome

1 Introduction

Services in product-oriented companies have grown to be one of the most active areas in research in the service research domain (e.g. [1]). There is a growing interest in novel types of business models in manufacturing industries because of the novel opportunities provided by technologies related to Industry 4.0 implementations. Pay-per-use (PPU) and pay-per-outcome (PPO) are some of the business models which have recently grown strongly in interest by researchers and practitioners alike. Some of the well-known examples of such business models are, for example, Rolls Royce's "power by hour" business model [2], as well as Michelin's usage-based pay-per-kilometer or

P. Chiabert et al. (Eds.): PLM 2018, IFIP AICT 540, pp. 498–507, 2018.
https://doi.org/10.1007/978-3-030-01614-2_46

performance-based (pay-per-reduction in fuel consumption) models [3]. In machine building, these models would mean that instead of customers investing in and owning the production line machines and related software, they pay at least partly from the use or related valuable outcomes.

There is a multitude of research on PPU and PPO business models when it comes to the software companies [4, 5]. However, these business models for the software companies cannot be directly applied for manufacturing companies because of the scalability issues (selling software as a service can be much more easily offered and scaled up as a service than heavy investment products), as well as issues related to the complexity of machines (e.g. related to automation, electricity and mechanical hardware).

The purpose of this paper is to study PPU and PPO business models from the perspective of little studied SME-sized manufacturing companies (machine builders), instead of the huge companies, such as Rolls Royce and Michelin, and instead of the widely studied software companies' business models. Moreover, we presume, on the basis of our wide review of related literature, that there are no complete or 100% pay-per-outcome business models like in the software companies, that would allow us to compare or validate the research findings from software companies. Furthermore, we focus on Industry 4.0-enabled PPU and PPO models, which is still relatively little understood in academic literature. We aim to identify perceived benefits and risks of especially Industry 4.0 enabled pay-per-outcome models for manufacturing companies. Our main research question is: "What are the perceived benefits and risks of Industry 4.0 enabled PPU and PPO business models for machine building companies?

To study the above research question, we conducted qualitative interviews of machine building companies in the SME or close to SME category. In order to gain as useful information about the plans and implementations of these models, we identified and selected especially manufacturing companies that have been already experimenting with novel Industry 4.0 - enabled business models, such as PPU and PPO models. We thus expect the companies to give us in-depth insights on the PPU and PPO business model related benefits as well as risks because of their experience and use of Industry 4.0 based technologies. Most of the companies that are planning or experimenting with these novel business models are yet in the very early phases of the implementation of these novel Industry 4.0 enabled pay-per-outcome business models. The remainder of the paper is divided into theoretical background, research methodology and design, results and findings, discussion and conclusions.

2 Theoretical Background

2.1 Industry 4.0 Technologies

Industry 4.0/Industrial Internet can be defined as industrial systems that integrate computational and physical capabilities of machines in order to provide advanced real time or near real time analytics and interact with humans [6–9]. The application or use of Industry 4.0/Industrial Internet in the real world is possible due to the integration of several enabling or key technologies.

These enabling technologies can be divided into three core elements in the form of a technology stack as shown in Fig. 1; physical product/asset, connectivity and product/asset cloud. The first one, physical product/asset, is divided into two subcategories, Software and Hardware which contain technologies such as sensors and actuators, and embedded operating systems respectively. Connectivity category refers to protocols and technologies that enable the product communication with the cloud or other products creating the network [10] and connecting the physical with the digital world. It has been divided into three subcategories: Internet protocols (e.g. IPv4 and IPv6), Middleware and Communication technologies and protocols such as RFID, NFC among others. Finally, the Product/Asset Cloud category refers mainly to software applications running in remote servers, data analytics, platforms, etc. It has been split into two subcategories: Analytics and a generic one named. Others conformed by technologies for storage, database, etc.

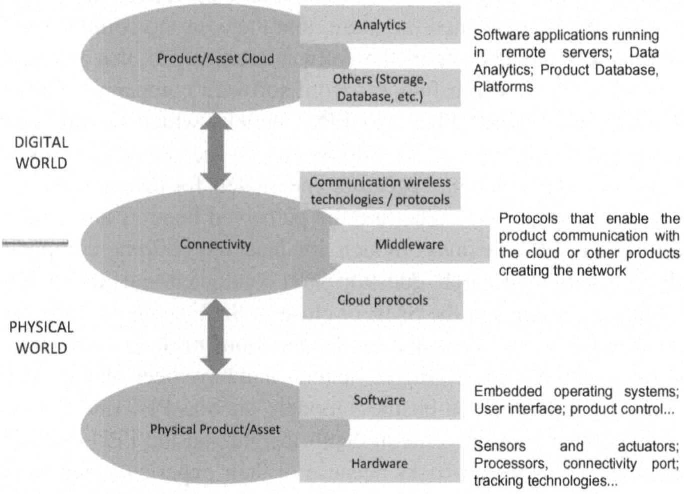

Fig. 1. Industrial internet technology stack. Adapted from [10]

2.2 Industry 4.0 Enabled Advanced Business Models

As far as the Industrial Internet/Industry 4.0 technologies are concerned the impact is not only restricted to production-technical change but also towards extensive organizational changes and benefits [11, 12]. These organizational benefits result into influencing the business model of the manufacturing company. Hence, the only way to make the most of the emergence of industry 4.0 based technologies to adapt new business models (such as pay-per-use, pay-per-outcome) or to innovate the existing business models [10, 11, 13]. Literature has discussed about these business models by using tools like the business model canvas for some industries specifically but also very broadly covering the manufacturing sector [12–14].

Industrial Internet/industry 4.0 technologies bring in the advantages related to real time or near real time connectivity of machines over the cloud that can result into advanced analytics of the condition of the machine as well as the process optimization related issues. This kind of technological advancement can give rise to new business models such as the pay per use [11] and pay per outcome [15] type of advanced business models. The primary idea behind these novel advanced business models is to move the risk from the customer end to the manufacturer's end and as a result building on earnings and profit for the manufacturer.

In case of machine builders or production line manufacturers, their business is dependent on the investment heavy product, that would be a machine or a production line [16]. In order to implement Industry 4.0 enabled novel business models such as the pay-per-use for example, it is important for the machine builder to strategize the implementation of the new business model in a hybrid manner, where the equipment can be rented or leased and the added Industry 4.0 enabled services can be sold to the customer based on the customer's use [11].

2.3 Benefits and Risks of Ind. 4.0 Enabled Advanced Business Models

Industry 4.0 technologies in themselves bring a lot of benefits and risks to production and manufacturing related processes as well as to the business models of the companies that use these advanced technologies. Literature has documented these Industry 4.0 technologies' related benefits and risks very well [10, 17, 18]. But there is a scarcity of research related to the implications of these advanced business models (PPU/PPO) that are enabled by industry 4.0. In general, there is research which discusses the technology related enablers or hindrances that industry 4.0 technologies can have on the implementation of advanced business models [11, 12].

Implications, benefits and risks, of these advanced business models (PPU/PPO) enabled by industry 4.0 technologies will benefit manufacturing companies both small and large companies. Benefits and risks of advanced business models need to be evaluated from internal, market (customer and competition) and shareholder's perspective in order to get a full picture of the potential impacts of these business models.

3 Research Methodology and Design

The aim of this research is to understand the benefits and risks of advanced business models, such as PPU and PPO enabled by Industry 4.0 technologies. To study this, we conducted qualitative interviews of three machine building companies in the SME or close to SME category. In order to gain as useful information about the plans and implementations of these models, we identified and selected especially manufacturing companies that have been already experimenting with novel industry 4.0 - enabled business models, such as PPU and PPO models. We thus expect the companies to give us in-depth insights on the PPU and PPO business model related benefits as well as risks because of their experience and use of Industry 4.0 based technologies. Following companies were selected because they have used Industry 4.0 based technologies to implement PPU business model to a certain extent. They are all machine builders who specialize in manufacturing systems and production lines.

The details of the companies after anonymizing explicit information is as follows:

Company A
The turnover level for company A is 100–150 million € and the range of number of employees is 200–500. Company supplies machines and systems for sheet metal related operations. Their manufacturing facilities are in Europe, North America and Asia. Their sales and service network is present in over 80 countries.

Company B
The turnover level for company B is 50–100 million € and the range of number of employees is 200–500. The main customer segments are engineering and machine building industries, aircraft and aerospace industries, manufacturers of construction and mining machinery, parts manufacturing and assembly.

Company C
The turnover level for company C is 100–150 million € and the range of number of employees is 200–500. Company's operations are divided into the Machines and Services business areas. Machines business product portfolio covers a wide and technologically advanced range of building material processing Services business provides machine maintenance services, machine upgrades and modernizations, spare parts and the tools.

The main themes of the questionnaire that was used to collect the qualitative data is as follows: Implementation of Industry 4.0 and the significance of Industry 4.0 in their business.

1. Types of PPU/PPO models that the companies have implemented or plan to implement.
2. Benefits and Risks of Industry 4.0 enabled advanced business models such as PPU/PPO type business models.

We had roughly 60 to 80 min of discussion with the experts who are responsible for implementing Industry 4.0 based technologies and related strategy and business model development.

4 Results and Findings

In this section, we present results and findings from the three interviewed companies. First, we present the results related to the significance of Industry 4.0 based technologies in implementing the advanced business models such as PPU/PPO. Finally, we present our findings on perceived benefits and risks of these advanced business models in Tables 1 and 2.

The three companies share their views on the significance of Industry 4.0 based technologies in the advanced business models such as the PPU/PPO in the following manner: company A: The data from the machines is stored into the cloud., which is then converted into useful information using advanced analytics using Industry 4.0 based technologies, and sold to the customer using the PPU model. Company B: Industry 4.0 technologies are vital for two purposes, one for digitalization of

Table 1. Benefits of PPU business model

	Company A	Company B	Company C
Internal	There is a benefit and motivation that PPU BM brings in terms of combining Data, AI and own know-how in new ways	PPU BM helps in getting new deals faster than the competing companies	-The benefit of this kind of PPU BM when compared to the traditional BM is that it will enable continuous turnover and eventually build on the profits
Market related	-The benefit of the PPU BM is that it reinforces the position of the company as a technology leader and eventually makes it stronger -The benefit of PPU BM is that it can help the company compete with competitors who sell the equipment at a lower price. They can do this by putting more intelligence in the machines by PPU BM based services	-The benefit of the PPU BM is that it allows faster deals to happen with the customers and eventually it gives a competitive edge to the company -The PPU BM also makes sure that the customers get the advanced services quickly or rather immediately -Customer sees the benefit for the PPU BM if the company sells functionalities like, automated ordering (automatic order management)-it can save person months for the customer	-The benefit of PPU BM is that it will allow them to move to Outcome based models quickly -The added benefit of PPU BM is that it will allow the company to keep the advanced software and services updated all the time at the customer end
Shareholder related	Major shareholder is forcing them towards the PPU kind of new BMs because they see the benefits towards growth in these BMs i.e. it improves the profit margin for the shareholders	–	-The benefit of this kind of a PPU model is that it will allow continuous turnover and eventually build on the profits
Others	–	–	–

Table 2. Risks of PPU Business Model

	Company A	Company B	Company C
Internal	-PPU business model must have defined certain service quality level and if the delivery doesn't meet promised level customer requires compensation -Internal sales need to educate the customers about the advantages of PPU BM or the risk is customers do not believe in advantages of PPU business model	-PPU BM is a risk if it does not contribute to the overall sales in a significant manner	Internal Mind-set in the sales organization, because they still prefer turnover from hardware sales as the most important factor instead of PPU sales
Market related	-The new service/software system which could be under PPU business model is not good enough to show correct data and information at this point and hence the risk is the customer might not pay for it	-Forcing the PPU model on the customer can create a risk of losing the deal or the customer. (Implication is) Sales process should be synchronized with the customer mind-set -Customer gets sceptical about the hardware if the PPU BM only sells machine/hardware related simple added services and that is a risk	-Customer finds that PPU billing is difficult hence they have to agree for a new smart type of contract -The risk for a PPU BM related to services is that it is intangible and customers might not realize the benefits like they would in case of a tangible product
Shareholder related	–	–	Business model requires patience from the shareholders because the outcomes/results are not immediate
Others	–	-If the advanced leasing contract will be implemented, who will be responsible for a needed capital? -There will be more layers between machine builder and customer, which can leave space to new actors, who will take bargaining power	The competition will implement PPU Business Models offering faster

manufacturing processes and second to create PPU based services for example automatic order management type PPU services. And company C: For the more advanced business model like the pay per outcome or outcome as a service, it will be very important to have the Industry 4.0 based technologies to increase the integration from machine level to ERP level.

In Table 1, above we present the results and finding based on benefits of PPU business model for the interviewed companies. The logic used to distribute the perceived benefits as well as risks was to distribute them in internal, market related, shareholder related and others.

Table 2 presents findings related to the perceived risks that the respondents pointed out towards the Industry 4.0 enabled advanced business models, such as the PPU/PPO type business models. Based on these results and findings we discuss the major conclusions as well as managerial implications in the next section.

5 Discussion and Conclusions

We aimed to answer to the main research question "What are perceived benefits and risks of Industry 4.0 enabled pay per outcome business models for machine building companies?" This study will provide academic novelty by creating new understanding about the possibilities and limitations of Industry 4.0 - enabled advanced business models in SME-sized machine builders operating in production line machine building and in investment heavy businesses, the models being hybrid models between traditional and PPU/PPO models. Existing empirical qualitative studies have not identified benefits and risks of Industry 4.0 enabled pay-per-outcome business models in the above types of machine building companies.

From the perspective of identified advanced business models (PPU/PPO), the Industry4.0 - enabled technologies played a pivotal role in all the studied manufacturing companies. This was true from two different perspectives: both them being able to support the digitalization of manufacturing-related processes, such as monitoring and controlling the manufacturing process in new ways, and the order management process, and them enabling the creation of new PPU-based services, such as remote monitoring and automatic order management.

First, we found that the studied companies had the PPU component in their business model repertoire (two had already implemented it, and one said that they would soon implement it). In addition, all of them were currently thinking of including also the PPO type of advanced business model in the near future, the planning being already very far. More concretely, two companies were found to already have a relatively concrete plan towards outcome based (PPO) business models, and the third one was planning to go there, as well, if the capital will be provided to the customers of the advanced leasing model by a third party. Furthermore, at least one of the companies was able to already define their outcome in the above PPO model as delivery reliability.

Concerning the perceived benefits, we were able to recognize internal, market-related as well as shareholder- related benefits. All companies saw that PPU business model components were beneficial for them from the strategic perspective to e.g. allow new sources for growth, while earnings from mere hardware and traditional services was seen to be getting more and more difficult, and for other ways of gaining competitive advantage. In overall, we found that PPU and PPO type of business models were genuinely interesting for the studied machine building companies because of the strategic and the other mentioned benefits. In more detail, even if there were some similarities in perceived benefits, when going more into detail, it seemed that the expressed perceived benefits were relatively unique to the companies, and it seemed to be the core business, their unique features in machine building, and the related markets that fundamentally impacted the perceived benefits.

Concerning the perceived risks, all companies saw that there were also clear and important risks related to the customer understanding and the acceptance of the advanced PPU models.

Some of the risks were expressed to be of a "show-stopper" type: these included, internally, for instance that the mindset of sales towards the advanced PPU/PPO models had to be strongly changed before more fully implementing the new models (i.e. those related to the current selling of tangible goods instead of selling of use or outcome). Furthermore, one of the companies considered that the capital related to the purchase of the hardware/machines required essentially a third party in the planned advanced leasing model because of the large required machine investments, or else the PPU model would not be implemented. As one important further risk towards the implementation was the need of shareholders to change their traditional view towards their profit expectations, because the returns of PPU/PPO models would take more time to develop compared to the traditional investment-oriented model.

This study can facilitate decision making of managers about implementing these advanced business models by taking into account the expected benefits as well as risks and potential bottlenecks encountered. As for further managerial implications, in order to establish novel types of PPU/PPO business models enabled by Industry 4.0, managers should make sure that there is clear product strategy also for the pay-per-use-type of products and services. They should also be able to make customers to understand and be guaranteed for what they would be getting by the novel business models. For instance, detailed long term break-even calculations should be carried out for customers, while they should also be quite concrete and realistic. Furthermore, it should be made sure that especially the first launched products making use of new PPO/PPU business models will be clearly defined and are clearly selected so that they can be shown to be valuable to the customers.

Considering the limitations of this study and future research, the possibilities of actual PPO models should be further studied in various types of especially SME-sized manufacturing companies, while our studied companies had not yet implemented such models, and while there are very few earlier academic studies that have studied PPO models in such contexts. Second, we would like to extend our study to include respondents from several company viewpoints to include e.g. CEO and managing director levels, as well as persons responsible for automation technology and IT. Furthermore, since the transition to such advanced business models is not an easy one in manufacturing companies, it would be important to research how the overall transition to implementing such business models can be done, what kinds of novel competences and capabilities are needed for implementing PPU/PPO models in the case of

SME machine builders, and what different types of concrete options a machine builder could have concerning the designing of hybrid PPU/PPO business models.

References

1. Ostrom, A.L., et al.: Moving forward and making a difference: research priorities for the science of service. J. Serv. Res. **13**(1), 4–36 (2010)
2. Gebauer, H., Saul, C.J., Haldimann, M., Gustafsson, A.: Organizational capabilities for pay-per-use services in product-oriented companies. Int. J. Prod. Econ. **192**, 157–168 (2016)
3. Gebauer, H., Joncourt, S., Saul, C.: Services in product-oriented companies: past, present, and future [Servicios en empresas orientadas a productos: Pasado, presente y future]. Univ. Bus. Rev. **2016**(49), 32–53 (2016)
4. Vaquero, L.M., Rodero-Merino, L., Caceres, J., Lindner, M.: A break in the clouds. ACM SIGCOMM Comput. Commun. Rev. **39**(1), 50 (2008)
5. Fishburn, P.C., Odlyzko, A.M.: Competitive pricing of information goods: subscription pricing versus pay-per-use. Econ. Theory **13**(2), 447–470 (1999)
6. Hermann, M., Pentek, T., Otto, B.: Design principles for industrie 4.0 scenarios. In: 2016 49th Hawaii International Conference on System Sciences (HICSS), pp. 3928–3937 (2016)
7. Lee, I., Lee, K.: The internet of things (IoT): applications, investments, and challenges for enterprises. Bus. Horiz. **58**(4), 431–440 (2015)
8. Evans, P.C., Annunziata, M.: Industrial internet: pushing the boundaries of minds and machines. General Electric (2012)
9. Iansiti, M., Lakhani, K.R.: Digital ubiquity. How connections, sensors, and data are revolutionizing business. Harv. Bus. Rev. **92**(11), 90–99 (2014)
10. Heppelmann, J., Porter, M.E., Heppelmann, J.E.: How smart, connected products are transforming competition. Harv. Bus. Rev. **92**(11), 64–88 (2014)
11. Gebauer, H., Saul, C.J., Haldimann, M., Gustafsson, A.: Organizational capabilities for pay-per-use services in product-oriented companies. Int. J. Prod. Econ. (2015)
12. Arnold, C., Kiel, D., Voigt, K.-I.: How the industrial internet of things changes business models in different manufacturing industries. Int. J. Innov. Manag. **20**(8), 1640015 (2016)
13. Laudien, S.M., Daxböck, B.: The influence of the industrial internet of things on business model design: a qualitative-empirical analysis. Int. J. Innov. Manag. **20**(8), 1640014 (2016)
14. Ehret, M., Wirtz, J.: Unlocking value from machines: business models and the industrial internet of things. J. Mark. Manag. **33**(1–2), 111–130 (2017)
15. Gierej, S.: Techniques for designing value propositions applicable to the concept of outcome-economy. Eng. Manag. Prod. Serv. **9**(1), 56 (2017)
16. Copani, G., Marvulli, S., Tosatti, L.M.: An innovative pattern to design new business models in the machine tool industry. In: Azevedo, A. (ed.) BASYS 2008. ITIFIP, vol. 266, pp. 317–324. Springer, Boston, MA (2008). https://doi.org/10.1007/978-0-387-09492-2_34
17. Kagermann, H.: Change through digitization—value creation in the age of industry 4.0. In: Albach, H., Meffert, H., Pinkwart, A., Reichwald, R. (eds.) Management of Permanent Change, pp. 23–45. Springer, Wiesbaden (2015). https://doi.org/10.1007/978-3-658-05014-6_2
18. Menon, K., Kärkkäinen, H., Lasrado, L.: Towards a maturity modeling approach for the implementation of industrial internet. In: PACIS 2016 Proceedings (2016)

A Customizable Lean Design Methodology for Maritime

Brendan P. Sullivan(✉), Monica Rossi, and Sergio Terzi

Department of Management, Economics and Industrial Engineering - Politecnico di Milano, via Lambruschini 4/B, 20156 Milan, Italy
{brendan.sullivan,monica.rossi, sergio.terzi}@polimi.it

Abstract. Lean focuses on the reduction of wastes, optimization of processes and consideration of the production of highly customized systems. Over the past decade the maritime industry has been working to apply unique solutions capable of improving their design and development performances by focusing heavily on production time and quality, however work and progress has been limited due to the competitive nature of the market [1–4]. Despite efforts, design methodologies applied in the industry have remained rather unchanged, regardless of demand for the incorporation of new technologies and materials. Literature and multiple case studies were utilized to develop a design methodology, that aims to transform the design process into a lean process that is measurable and capable of addressing multiple areas of improvement. Through a holistic lean transformation methodology developed through this work, sociotechnical variables were incorporated to allow for maritime vessel designers to customize the method to overcome unique deficiencies. The paper describes the approach and work being undertaken as well as outlines the Lean Design Methodology for Maritime.

Keywords: Vessel design · Maritime design · Shipbuilding · Lean design
Lean transformation · LTF

1 Introduction

Technological innovation and economic growth are closely related, and the ability to conquer them will facilitate the continued growth and development of European industries. Globally, the maritime industry continues to be a hugely important part of the economy due to the delivery of valuable raw material, components and finished products [5, 6]. The maritime industry is the backbone of global trade there are critical areas that must be advanced to leverage technological and social capabilities [7].

Surrounded by 136,000 km of coastline, a blue economy of 5.4 million jobs and almost €500 billion a year of gross added value, Europe has traditionally been a world leader in the maritime activities. Like other industries it has become increasingly important for companies to improve their processes to maintain competitiveness, prosperity, and survival. European maritime industry faces constant competition, as ports represent strategic poles of distribution for traffic to/from emerging countries.

Published by Springer Nature Switzerland AG 2018.
P. Chiabert et al. (Eds.): PLM 2018, IFIP AICT 540, pp. 508–519, 2018.
https://doi.org/10.1007/978-3-030-01614-2_47

The maritime industry has been working to apply unique solutions capable of improving their development performances [4]. To remain competitive, Europe needs to identify and develop new value-added solutions, products and services that can accommodate the changing demands. Focusing on industrial repositioning, by incorporating new technologies and materials that are unfamiliar to many of the engineering and design practices in the industry today (i.e. tools, methods, techniques).

This paper introduces a customizable lean design methodology that was developed alongside industry partners to reduce design time, and wastes encountered in the design of maritime vessels. To achieve this, a case study methodology was used to contribute to state of the art based on 3 industrial cases active in the design/development and manufacturing of maritime vessels in Europe.

2 State of Art and Practice

We investigated how design in the maritime industry was managed and how lean has been previously applied. Literature was in accordance to the research approach evaluated to provide a review of design principles, approaches, and tools, suitable for the maritime industry and capable of resolving deficiencies identified.

2.1 Lean Design and Development

The original definition of lean thinking aims at "Creating more value, defined from the customer's perspective, while consuming fewer resources" [8]. Lean design is an aspect and consideration of product development that facilitates, impacts and allows for the realization of products. When appropriately considered in early-stage design decisions, the incorporation of lean tools and processes has proven capable to improve system lifecycle value and system performance, while reducing waste. Systems are being designed to operate with longer lifecycles in rapidly changing environments, there is a shift from traditional mission centric optimization strategies to complex systems that are robust, and value optimized, requiring improved methods of delivering value. The creation of value in lean product and process development consists of enabling the whole enterprise to generate everything the customer is willing to pay to establish operations that produce and deliver quality products [10].

Lean in the Maritime Industry. The publication of lean in shipbuilding is limited due to the novelty and the restriction of the concept, particularly related to the approaches being employed. However, process efficiency, delay rectification and cost control are all principal areas where work has been undertaken and measured improvement has been demonstrated [2, 11, 12]. According to [1] elements of lean can be found throughout the industry however there are few organizations that utilize lean principles in an organized manner.

The maritime industry has been working to advance vessel development approaches by focusing heavily on production time and quality [1–4]. A key difference between automotive companies that have adopted skills/approaches and methods from the Toyota and the maritime industry is that in general vessel design and development prohibits the utilization of assembly lines since vessels are designed and developed in limited or single cases. Features that characterize the shipbuilding industry focus primarily on the design and development of complex one-of-a-kind products [13, 14]. Lean vessel design and development is a very specialized, field of lean and is seen as "one of the extensions beyond Lean Construction" [15].

2.2 Maritime Design Process

Vessel design is a complex, iterative and multifaceted process, influenced by a number of factors (both internal and external) [16]. Depending on the vision or requirements set forth by the customer, designers are required to develop cost efficient vessels capable of performing specific tasks, while maintaining strict adherence to both international and national rules or regulations. However, finding the best balance within these restrictions is a challenge for the designer, system integrator, and the ship yard.

The vessel design type has a strong influence on the design choices and the design process that will be undertaken from conception to final customer delivery, due to both customer expectations and legal rules/regulations. One of the most common vessel design processes is the spiral design process. The vessel design spiral is a conceptual model of a process for maritime vessel design [17]. The establishment of requirements is the first step of this process and is a fundamental starting point before entering the concept design phase, leading to preliminary power estimations, a propulsion system, hull shape, and preliminary cost estimations. Within each phase of the process, solutions become specific and options are set, culminating in a design ready for authorization. Incremental development and improvement have been developed and applied to maritime. One approach is PDCA (plan–do–check–act or plan–do–check–adjust) which is a four-step method used for the control and continual improvement of processes and products, another variation is OPDCA, which incorporates observation.

3 Research Approach

The research covered in this paper utilized a case study method which was selected due to its ability to facilitate a close examination of the lean design process in the maritime industry. Through a multiple-case design, it was possible to acquire and analyze data during a real-time project from various perspectives.

In addition, product design state of art was applied to develop a comprehensive methodological foundation that included elements of lean systems engineering, and lean design. The literature reviewed was identified and evaluated based on relevancy to lean design, lean product and process development and product development (Fig. 1).

In each case, interviews and on-site visits were undertaken to understand how the companies design maritime vessels. Through the identification of existing practices as well as the incorporation of best practices identified through literature, a lean design methodology was constructed based on the unique needs and expectations of the maritime cases. From there, a comprehensive list of steps and sub-procedures are introduced into design process to improve efficiency and reduce waste within the cases.

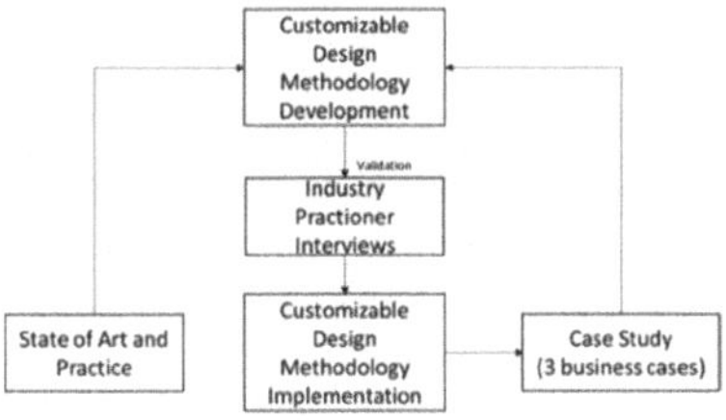

Fig. 1. Research approach

4 Empirical Research

The authors performed an empirical research study in Europe with multiple cases from March 2017 to February 2018. The cases were studied based on three areas: (a) context understanding and data gathering, (b) identify design challenges, and measures for analysis, and (c) strategy setting where business needs were elicited.

The design process, wastes and lean tools were evaluated in 3 different cases in Europe, who are all active in the design and development of maritime vessels. This allowed for different design processes, tool and issues related to the design process to be evaluated at multiple levels. In each case there was an opportunity to interview employees with similar experience, and the design process was able to be observed.

4.1 Classification Structures

Development of maritime vessels is a considerable challenge for engineering and design professions, with different challenges expected depending on the levels of complexity inherent to the vessels. The industry tends to be dominated by the experience and expertise of engineering, and customization is understood in several areas of the industry as a promising approach to compete in the fragmented market. By using flexible processes and organizational structures, customization enables companies to provide variety and individualized solutions. The cases were classified in Fig. 2 according to businesses classification (1) business size [18], (1a) operating structure, and vessel classification (2) Sea-Related Sector [19], and (2a) vessel type [20, 21].

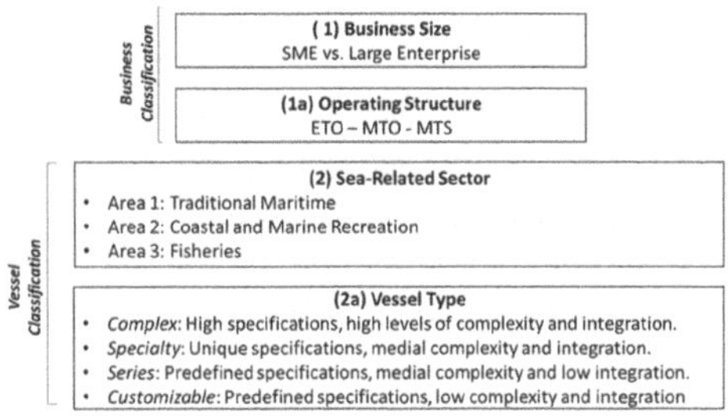

Fig. 2. Classification of case study

4.2 Interview

Interviews were conducted using a reference questionnaire, comprised of 33 questions identified through literature and best practices. At each case, the technical director (or delegate) was interviewed, lasting roughly 3 h. Information about the company and its products and markets was also collected, in addition using open resources (web site, databases, etc.). In all cases, secondary interviews were conducted to clarify design and industrial positioning, this semi-structured interview lasted 1 h.

4.3 Interview Analysis

Data was categorized to determine the design process maturity in each of the 3 cases and the average used as an initial benchmark [22]:

1. **Organization** (*blue textbox*) how people are involved in daily activities: *Work Organization*), coordination of people and activities, roles of engineers and designers (*Roles and Coordination*), skills/expertise of practitioners (*Skills and Competences*).
2. **Process** *(Yellow textbox)* how NPD is performed, based on four areas: design rules and methodologies (*Methods*), control mechanisms and improvement of the process (*Process Management*), how decisions are taken every day (*Decision Making Factors*) and competitors and customers (*Activities and Value*).
3. **Knowledge Management** *(light blue textbox)* how companies create, share, represent and re-use tacit and explicit knowledge: *Formalization* (how knowledge is formalized and shared) and *Computerization* (how IT tools and platforms are used for supporting knowledge storing, sharing and reusing along the NPD process).

Based on the maturity level established by the CLIMB assessment method, efficacy of the practice was determined [22, 23] (Fig. 3).

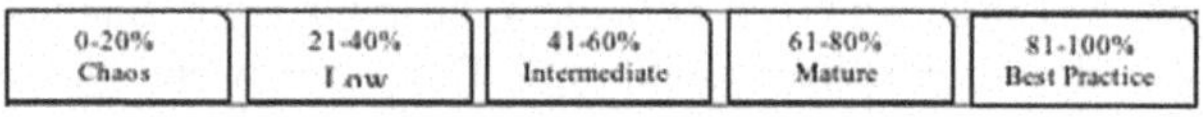

Fig. 3. CLIMB maturity levels [22]

For each of the process maturity levels being evaluated the questions were scored using a Likert scale (5 points scale; 1, 3, 5, 7, 9), so the respondent could choose if their company's practice level. The lowest levels scored with 1 correspond to a poor practice, while the highest-level cane be scored 9 which corresponds to a best practice. The score for each area was calculated using an additive scale (summing the single scores of the questions describing the area) then normalized in % [23]. The following formula according to the CLIMB method was utilized to score each generic area (A_i):

$$a_i = \frac{\sum_1^{m_i} q_{ij}}{8 * m_i}$$

Where:

a_i is the score corresponding to i-th area, expressed in %

$i = 1...8$, is the indicator for the areas

q_{ij} is the score of the answer to the question j, belonging to the i-th area

$j = 1...m_i$, is the indicator for the questions, depending on the area the number of questions changes

m_i, is the number of questions of the i-th area

$8*m_i$ is the maximum score the area can assume in the case the respondent declares.

The level of maturity achieved in each area of analysis is represented in the radar chart (Fig. 4) to show a picture of the level of implementation in each area of the analysis (Table 2) and displays the positioning of the company related to the corresponding CLIMB maturity level (%). The highest levels of maturity were found in Case 2, and in Organization, as seen in Table 2, the absolute average maturity score was 64.08%.

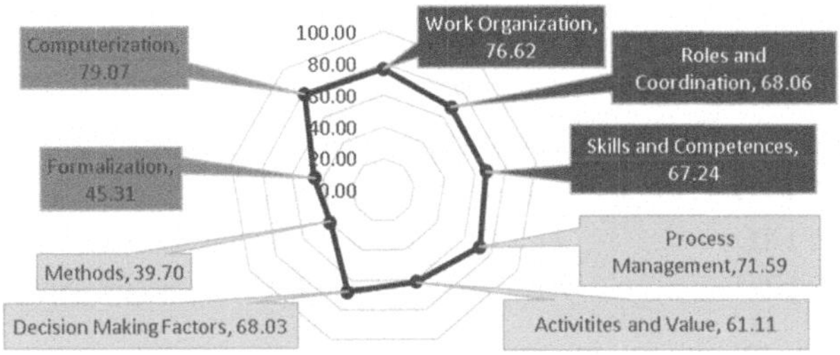

Fig. 4. Average interview management process radar chart (Color Figure Online)

4.4 Waste Analysis

The waste analysis served as a tool applied for methodological development and as a component within the greater lean objectives. This analysis required designers/ engineers categorically associate a series of information to translate waste in the design process focusing on: cause, effect, severity, probability, detectability, detection way and avoidability. Examples of waste are: too many meetings organized inside company, time spent for bad definition of priorities and inability to reuse previous knowledge.

Each of the 10 wastes (Table 3) were measured within each case to identify non-value-added process and then compared to the average waste within traditional SMEs (production, automotive, services) [24]. In respect to the wastes based on vessel classification commonalities as well as differences can be identified. As seen in Fig. 5 there is a difference between the two classes, with the only common waste being W1 Change Priorities (which is high, however follows the case study average) and W10 Over Engineered Products (which has a low value and is the case average).

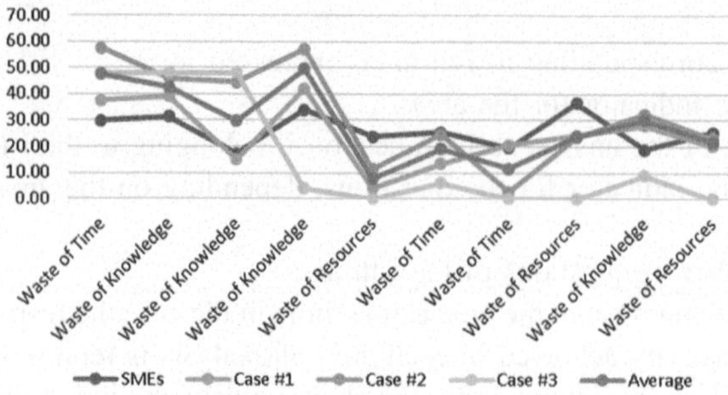

Fig. 5. Waste analysis within each case

Based on the classification of each case, all were found to be SMEs (ETOs) operating within the same sea-related sector, though a variation in the vessel type was noted as shown in Table 1.

Table 1. Case study classification and characteristics

Case	Business classification	Vessel classification	
Case #1	SME; ETO	Area 1: Traditional Maritime Sector	Series Vessel
Case #2	SME; ETO	Area 1: Traditional Maritime Sector	Series Vessel
Case #3	SME; ETO	Area 1: Traditional Maritime Sector	Specialty Vessel

Table 2. Case study maturity level according to CLIMB

Case	Organizational ML	Process ML	Knowledge Mgmt. ML
Case #1	(Mature) 67.8%	(Intermediate) 58.9%	(Intermediate) 55.7%
Case #2	(Mature) 74.3%	(Mature) 65.3%	(Mature) 75.7%
Case #3	(Mature) 69.8%	(Intermediate) 56.1%	(Intermediate) 55.2%
Average	(Mature) 70.6%	(Intermediate) 60.1%	(Mature) 62.2%

While the business classification and sea-related sectors for the Business Cases were the same the vessel classification amongst the three cases were different, there was a distinction related to the vessel classification, however the limited sample size requires further work to be conclusive. Recognizing the single case that was classified under this criterion there remains a level of bias that will require additional cases (wastes) to be measured before a definitive interpretation can be made at that level.

Table 3. Waste analysis process areas

	Area	Description
W1	Change priorities	Time making changes, reviews, modifications and reworks
W2	Reworks - incomplete data	Projects (of parts of projects) must be re-done due to incorrect, incomplete, unreliable data, information, specifications, test, etc.
W3	Non-necessary product functionalities	Functionalities and features that are not necessary or required.
W4	Knowledge retrieval	Difficulty to retrieve and access previous knowledge.
W5	Project leftovers	Projects are realized that never reach the market.
W6	Manual data transcoding	The information and data related to the product and project need to be inserted and coded manually.
W7	Missing authorization	Projects are delayed due to authorizations challenges.
W8	Defect products are designed	Defective products are introduced; requiring modifications.
W9	No knowledge reuse	Projects, developed in the past, are redone due to previous knowledge not being retrieved.
W10	Over-engineered projects	Over-engineering; cost increase without adding value to the product.

5 Customizable Lean Design for Maritime

To achieve a lean transformation in maritime design it is necessary for three aspects to be considered:: process, people, and technology, which are all interrelated and interdependent, collectively affecting an organization's ability to achieve goals and objectives [25]. As shown above, the traditional design process has areas of low maturity that can be strengthened through the inclusion of lean and can only be rectified through a lean transformation. The methodology employs a holistic approach since each phase of the development process must to be considered. The cases used in this research stressed a need for improvements that could reduce costs and times in the design and development process through a comprehensive, long-term, improvement methodology. The Customizable Lean Design Methodology was developed to address the lean management of design processes through the reduction of wastes in the industry through a sequential structure of decision-making.

Based on the outputs of the use case interview and waste analysis high-level and functional requirements were used to ensure the methodology addressed necessary objectives. High-level requirements mandate the considerations and behaviors that are to be addressed in the Customizable Lean Design Methodology for Maritime Industry. While functional requirements were established to mandate how the Customizable Lean Methodology addressed these established behaviors.

5.1 Maritime Lean Transformation

Like product development which deals with information and processes, involving a multitude of choices and iterations that are used for problem solving and decision-making activities. The maritime industry is confronted with the management of iterations and complex development, and through the development of unique solutions the customizable lean design methodology aims at improving development performances. To facilitate the optimization of this initiative, an evaluation of diffused strategies was undertaken to develop a Lean Transformation Framework (LTF), that seeks to maximize value while minimizing waste and resources in a sustainable and environmentally conscious manner. LTF was introduced by the Lean Institute by John Shook to combat delays and complications being faced in implementation of lean [26].

5.2 Practices and Approaches for Maritime Lean Transformation

Within this study, the authors identified more than 24 best practices proposed in literature to establish a multidimensional lean transformation. Practices and approaches were identified based on the objectives of the LTF to confirm suitability to deliver skills and improvements based on business and industrial objectives.

The methods and practices focus on the outputs they can facilitate based on high-level requirements set by the 3 cases. The outputs adopted correspond to the five areas of improvement related to the LTF and ultimately are comprised of several different yet interrelated elements that facilitated the establishment of multifunctional teams, the use of modularization and standardization for parts and components, and the use of design for x. Through this process, an easy-to-implement methodology was developed that allows businesses to adapt the methodology to satisfy their specific needs. The methods, practices and approaches focus on the outputs they facilitate. The outputs adopted, correspond to the outputs generated from the case interviews and waste analysis to visualize how methods and practices relate to LTF principles.

5.3 Customizable Lean Design Methodology for the Maritime Industry

The Customizable Lean Design Methodology targets SMEs in the maritime vessel design and engineering sector, that are seeking to improve or implement lean into their organization to reduce time for development and waste within the process. The methodology offers a customizable set of tasks and steps that can be easily modified to facilitate the successful implementation of lean in various maritime design process (Fig. 6).

The methodology was built based on organizational objectives and case study commitments to deliver and increase stakeholder value. Through a series of questions, rather than explicit steps, the LTF methodology for maritime focuses on obtaining support within the organization to promote a path for continuous improvement in the design process by addressing [26], [27].

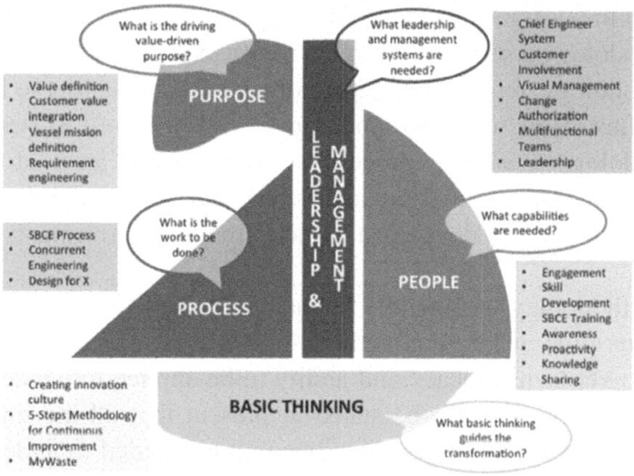

Fig. 6. Customizable lean transformation methodology for maritime

- **Purpose**: What is the value for the stakeholder?
- **Process**: How the industry/organization can better deliver value?
- **People**: What skills, attributes, or characteristics are needed/required to engage in these processes to best deliver value to the stakeholder?
- **Leadership and Management**: What is the management system and leader behaviors utilized to achieve goals and objectives?
- **Basic thinking**: What considerations and values/goals can guide the transformation?

The methodology is committed to deliver and increase stakeholder value through the 5 concurrently lean aspects, presented above. To customize the methodology, consideration of each aspect must take place to explain the main objectives of the case and the most appropriate means to reduce design time and facilitate the total lean transformation. Collectively this supports the definition and design of new vessels in an innovative, efficient, eco-friendly and cost-effective manner.

6 Discussion, Conclusion and Future Work

This paper aimed to introduce a lean transformation methodology that is customizable and easily implementable in the maritime industry. The methods and processes introduced support the adoption and implementation of lean in the design of maritime vessels as well as techniques that can be relevant to specific vessel types. Based on design processes and waste analysis best practices were positioned, to allow for unique wastes throughout the industry to be targeted. The is expected to give designers a complete view of the design process and abridge the duration of implementation.

This methodology seeks to extend the advantages of lean to a new area of the industry to improve the Value Added of SME offerings. Designed to be easily customizable, the methodology provides a solution for organizational lean transformation that respects people and integrates knowledge sharing, feedback and continual improvement into the design process. Following the development of the customizable lean design methodology a series of interviews with experts in the field were utilized to confirm the methodology, relating to context, objectives, and ability to be implemented. Post-interview adjustments to the methodology were then used to strengthen the customizable methodology regarding 'process' so that multiple areas of knowledge generation could be leveraged through simulation and knowledge-based engineering approaches. KPIs will be later developed to measure the improvements provided by the methodology.

While the methodology is generally applicable to the design process of vessels in the Traditional Maritime Sector, the methodology will require broader application and implementation to verify its efficacy and ability to be applied to the design of different vessel types. Particularly, it can't be stated at present that all the findings related to vessel types are conclusive. Additional studies will be needed to understand if the use of the methodology and best practices are context dependent. Currently, validation and implementation (process improvement measurements) of the methodology are underway and additional cases are being identified to extend the data evaluation process.

Acknowledgments. The content of this paper is based on the LINCOLN project (EU H2020 727982) that is currently under development (www.lincolnproject.eu). We wish to express our deep gratitude to all LINCOLN partners.

References

1. Liker, J., Lamb, T.: Lean shipbuilding. In: Ship Production Symposium, Ypsilanti, MI, June 2001
2. Koenig, P.C., Narita, H., Baba, K.: Lean production in the japanese shipbuilding industry? J. Sh. Prod. **18**(3), 167–174 (2002)
3. Radovic, I., Macclaren, B.J.: Lean six sigma in shipbuilding. In: European Shipbuilding and Repair Conference on 2 November 2004, London (2004)
4. Milanovic, V.: Application of set-based concurrent engineering to shipbuilding projects, Norwegian University of Science and Technology, (2016)
5. European Commission: Report on the Blue Growth Strategy: Towards more sustainable growth and jobs in the blue economy, SWD/2017/128 Final, pp. 1–62 (2017)
6. Corbett, J.J., Winebrake, J.: The impacts of globalisation on international maritime transport activity, In: Global Forum on Transport and Environment in a Globalising World (2008)
7. Ki-moon, B.: Maritime Transport Is 'Backbone of Global Trade and the Global Economy', Says Secretary-General in Message for International Day (2016)
8. Womack, J.P., Jones, D.T.: Lean Thinking: Banish Waste and Create Wealth In Your Corporation. Simon & Schuster, New York (1996)
9. Womack, J.P., Jones, D.T.: The Machine that Changed the World. Rawson Associates, New York (1990)
10. Rossi, M., Morgan, J., Shook, J.: Lean product and process development. In: The Routledge Companion to Lean Management (2017)
11. Storch, R.L., Lim, S.: Improving flow to achieve lean manufacturing in shipbuilding improving how to achieve lean manufacturing in shipbuilding. Prod. Plannning Control **7287**(November), 127–137 (1999)

12. Lang, S., et al.: Shipbuilding and lean manufacturing - a case study, Soc. Nav. Archit. Mar. Eng., no. 201 (2001)
13. Longva, K.K.: Warehouse Management in a Lean Shipbuilding Perspective - An Exploratory Case Study of Ulstein Verft, Høgskolen Molde (2009)
14. Salem, O., Solomon, J., Genaidy, A., Minkarah, I.: Lean construction: from theory to implementation. J. Manag. Eng. **22**(4), 168–175 (2006)
15. Dugnas, K., Uthaug, I.: Can Lean Philosophy Strengthen and Develop Cluster Advantages? - An Exploratory Research towards Lean Shipbuilding (2007)
16. Vossen, C., Kleppe, R., Randi, S.: Ship design and system integration, September 2013
17. Mistree, F., Smith, W.F., Bras, B.A., Allen, J.K., Muster, D.: Decision-based design: a contemporary paradigm for ship design, Soc. Nav. Archit. Mar. Eng. Annu. Meet. (1990)
18. E. European Commission: What is an SME, Internal Market, Industry, Entrepreneurship and SME (2018). http://ec.europa.eu/growth/smes/business-friendly-environment/sme-definition_en
19. P. R. Corporation.: The role of maritime clusters to enhance the strength and development of maritime sectors (2008)
20. Kolić, D.: Lean manufacturing methodology for shipyards. Brodogradnja **63**, 18–29 (2012)
21. Gaspar, H.M., Ross, A.M., Rhodes, D.H., Erikstad, S.O.: Handling complexity aspects in conceptual ship design. In: International Maritime Design Conference, pp. 1–14, June 2012
22. Rossi, M., Terzi, S., Taisch, M.: Engineering and design best practices in new product development: an empirical research. Procedia CIRP **21**, 2 (2014)
23. Rossi, M., Terzi, S.: CLIMB: maturity assessment model for design and engineering processes. Int. J. Prod. Lifecycle Manag. **10**(1), 20–43 (2017)
24. Rossi, M., Kerga, E.T., Taisch, M., Terzi, S.: Proposal of a method to systematically identify wastes in new product development process. In: 2011 17th International Conference on Concurrent Enterprising, ICE, pp. 1–9 (2011)
25. Morgan, J., Liker, J.K.: No The Toyota Product Development System: Integrating People, Process, and Technology (2006)
26. Shook, J.: The Lean Transformation Framework. The Lean Enterprise Institute (2018)
27. Rossi, M., Taisch, M., Terzi, S.: Lean product development: a five-steps methodology for continuous improvement. In: 2012 18th International Conference on Engineering Technolory and Innovtion ICE 2012 - Conference Proceedings (2012)

Knowledge Management and Information Sharing

Investigating the Evolving Knowledge Structures in New Technology Development

J. A. Gopsill[1(✉)], P. Shakespeare[2], C. M. Snider[3], L. Newnes[2], and B. J. Hicks[3]

[1] University of Bath, Bath, UK
J.A.Gopsill@bath.ac.uk
[2] National Composites Centre, Bristol, UK
[3] University of Bristol, Bristol, UK

Abstract. The development of new technology has been identified as one of the key enablers to support business and economic growth in developed countries. For example, the United Kingdom (UK) has invested £968 Million into the creation of Catapult centres to provide 'pull through' of low Technology Readiness Level (TRL) research and science. While these Catapults have been instrumental in developing new technologies, the uptake of new technology within industry remains a considerable challenge.

One of the reasons for this is that of skills and competencies, and in particular, defining the new skills and competencies necessary to effectively apply and operate the new technology within the context of the business. Addressing this issue is non-trivial because the skills and competencies cannot be defined a priori and will evolve with the maturity of the technology. Therefore, there is a need to create methods that enable the elicitation and definition of skills and competencies that co-evolve with new technology development, and what are referred to herein as knowledge structures.

To meet this challenge, this paper reports the results from a dynamic co-word network analysis of the technical documentation from New Technology Development (NTD) programmes at the National Composites Centre (NCC). Through this analysis, emerging knowledge structures can be identified and monitored, and be used to inform industry on the skills & competencies required for a technology.

Keywords: Knowledge management · Competency mapping
Knowledge structures · Graph theory · Dynamic network analysis
Co-word analysis

1 Introduction

New Technology Development (NTD) has been identified as one of the key enablers to support business and economic growth in developed countries. This is one of the reasons that many developing countries are investing in specialist centres to support the growth of NTD. One example of this is in the United Kingdom (UK), where the government has invested £968 Million into the creation of Catapult centres to provide 'pull through' of low Technology Readiness Level (TRL) research and science [1].

Published by Springer Nature Switzerland AG 2018.
P. Chiabert et al. (Eds.): PLM 2018, IFIP AICT 540, pp. 523–533, 2018.
https://doi.org/10.1007/978-3-030-01614-2_48

These centres provide state-of-the-art facilities to further research and innovation, and provide a nexus for blue-skies University research to be developed into commercially viable technologies. Although the provision of state-of-the-art facilities is paramount to NTD, the uptake of NTDs within industry remains a considerable challenge. A critical barrier to this uptake is not in the access and/or cost of new equipment but in the development of the skills, competencies, and knowledge structures around NTD.

Given the largely digital nature of modern-day NTD, there now lies an opportunity to investigate how knowledge structures evolve through the dynamic co-word analysis of technological terms within NTD reports. Understanding the evolution of these knowledge structures could support the adoption of NTD through enhanced identification of the skills & competencies pertaining to an NTD and the development of best practice in ensuring the appropriate knowledge structures around NTD's are built.

To investigate this potential, this paper reports the initial findings from a dynamic co-word network analysis of a set of reports generated from NTD projects at the UK's National Composites Centre (NCC). The centre is a specialist facility aimed at developing low TRL research into high TRL commercially viable technologies.

The paper first provides an overview of dynamic co-word network analysis with a discussion of the types of insight and information that can be generated (Sect. 2). This is followed by a discussion of the context in which the reports have been generated and statistics of the resulting dataset (Sect. 3). Section 4 then discusses how dynamic co-word network analysis has been applied to the dataset and the results that will be produced. This continues into Section Five, which presents the results and discusses the insights it has brought to understanding the evolving knowledge structure around NTD. The paper then concludes by highlighting the key findings, limitations and future work.

2 Dynamic Co-word Network Analysis

Dynamic co-word analysis is the investigation of the semantic structure of a corpus of textual data through the co-occurrence of terms over time. By analysing the co-occurrence of terms, a network of connected terms (a.k.a. nodes) is generated, which enables the application of algorithms developed in graph theory to uncover underlying structures within the network and examine the nature of the connections behind the terms. For example, centrality measures are often used to identify the most important and influential terms within the network structure. In addition, clustering algorithms, such as Louvain community partitioning [2, 3], seek to identify groups of highly connected nodes within a network. In the context of co-word analysis, the clustering of terms is often referred to as the identification of topics.

The dynamism of the network comes from the continual addition of new documents. As new documents are added to the corpus, the connected nature of the terms is updated, and leads to a change in the structure of the network. The analysis of these temporal networks can reveal patterns in how knowledge around NTD evolves and matures. It is the hypothesis of this paper that NTD's that have been widely adopted will contain particular patterns in the development of the associated knowledge structure. Identifying these patterns would then enable the development of new processes and best practice to encourage the development of appropriate knowledge structures in future NTDs.

Dynamic co-word analysis has been particularly successful in identifying research topics within scientific communities [4–6]. Whilst [7] has demonstrated the potential of the technique to support engineering project management through the monitoring of topics being discussed and potential requirements/scope creep. It is this ability of identifying and monitoring the evolution of these topics in real-time that is the current state-of-the-art within research [6].

Also, it is not only the quantitative metrics afforded by this analytical technique but the ability to aggregate and visualise a large corpus of information into a more manageable form for users to interpret and make decisions on that makes dynamic co-word network analysis an attractive proposition. Example visualisation techniques include: re-arranged matrices in relation to the clustering of the terms [8]; force-based network diagrams to reveal the connected nature of the terms [6]; and, quadrant diagrams that show the movement of clusters of terms (i.e. topics) and how their influence evolves over time [9].

It is for these reasons that dynamic co-word analysis has been selected as the technique to elicit and characterise the Knowledge Structures of NTD.

3 Context and Dataset

The National Composites Centre (NCC) is a world-leading research & development centre for UK composites. Established in 2009 as a result of the UK Composite strategy, it is now part of the UK government's CATAPULT programme to develop world- leading centres designed to transform the UK's capability for NTD and help drive future economic growth. The NCC currently provides R&D support for over 40 companies.

This analysis looks at the research projects performed over a four-year period with projects typically lasting between 6–12 months. Each research project results in a set of reports detailing methods, tools and key findings pertinent to NTD. Due to the sensitivity of some of their projects, the analysis has been performed on a sub-set of documents generated from publicly funded projects. This represents approx. 20% of the total projects by the NCC. Table 1 provides a detailed breakdown on the number of final project reports produced year-on-year from publicly funded projects.

Table 1. Dataset statistics

Year	No. of documents	Sum no. of words	Mean words	Max. words	Min. words
2012	5	31.9×10^3	6.4×10^3	9.4×10^3	3.6×10^3
2013	6	56.2×10^3	9.4×10^3	17.8×10^3	2.8×10^3
2014	7	83.8×10^3	12.0×10^3	20.4×10^3	999
2015	8	68.1×10^3	8.5×10^3	19.0×10^3	4.0×10^3
Combined	26	240.0×10^3	9.2×10^3	20.4×10^3	999

4 Dynamic Co-word Analysis of Technical Reports

In order to apply co-word analysis to full-text engineering reports, this paper applies a four-step process.

Step 1. Keyword extraction
Step 2. Co-word network generation
Step 3. Topic identification
Step 4. Dynamic analysis through Quadrant Charts.

Compared to previous research where co-word analysis has been applied to keywords within academic reports and/or short texts such as e-mails, instant messaging or tweets, the application of co-word analysis on full-text documents necessitates a greater amount of pre-processing [4, 6, 9]. In particular, it is necessary to include keyword identification and extraction to identify and define topics pertaining to NTD. Following this, Step 2 covers the generation of the co-word network. The co-word network is formed of nodes that represent the key terms identified in Step 1, and edges and associated weightings representing the number of times terms co-occur.

With the terms connected to one another within a network, clustering techniques can then be applied to generate the topics relating to NTD (Step 3). These clusters are then further post-processed in Step 4 to analyse how the topics connectedness and density evolve over time. These metrics are then plotted over time using quadrant charts where insights into the knowledge structures of NTD can be drawn. Each step is now discussed in detail.

4.1 Keyword Extraction

All documents were archived in portable document format (PDF) and required parsing to extract the text in UTF-8 format. The majority of the documents were purely digital whilst a few had been scanned and required Optical Character Recognition (OCR) to parse the text. Regular expressions were used to extract the year in which the report was created and generate the list of n-grams contained within the report. The n-grams are further post-processed where any n-grams containing terms from the Natural Language Toolkit (NLTK) [10] stopwords list for the English Language as well as stopwords list for commonly used technical terms within the organisation were removed. This left 1.2×10^3 terms whose frequencies and number of documents they featured in are shown in Fig. 1.

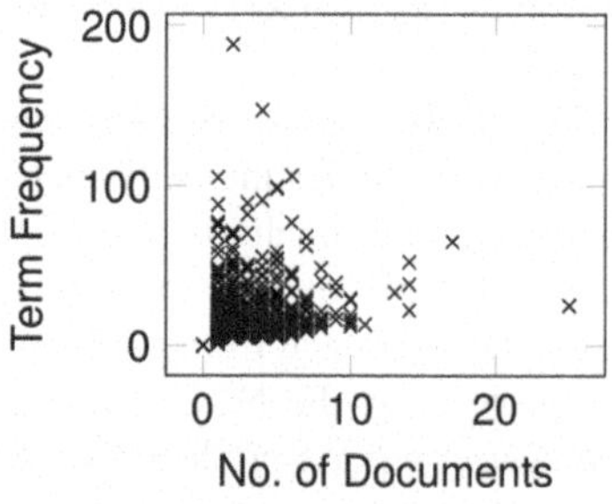

Fig. 1. Keyword statistics

4.2 Co-word Network Generation

With the final set of terms being identified, the document set is parsed further to identify the co-occurrence of terms within the documents. First, a network is generated containing nodes that represent each of the terms. The process iterates through each document and identifies the number of terms that exist within the document. Edges are then made between two nodes (terms) if they exist within the same document. The edges are weighted based on the number of documents that the two terms co-occur. This is further normalised to adjust for the effects of the range of occurrences for the different terms as shown in Eq. 1. Where $n_{i,j}$ is the normalised edge weighting and is determined by the number of times the two terms have co-occurred $(w_{i,j})$ divided by the minimum occurrence f_i or f_j for terms i and j respectively.

$$n_{i,j} = \frac{w_{i,j}}{\min(f_i, f_j)} \tag{1}$$

4.3 Topic Identification

As the measurements of co-occurrence are transactional and continuous, and there exists a degree of error in relating terms to one another given the length of the reports (i.e. a report may be discussing two studies where terms would be related in Step 2 but do not actually feature in the same context), Louvain community clustering algorithm has been selected as the method for identifying topics in the network.

The objective of the Louvain community algorithm is to generate a set of topic for the network that returns the highest modularity value. Modularity (Q) is an assessment of the quality of the network clustering and is defined as [11]:

$$Q = \frac{1}{2m} \sum\nolimits_{ij} \left[A_{ij} - \frac{k_i k_j}{2m} \right] \delta(c_i, c_j) \tag{2}$$

Where $m = 1/2 \sum_{i,j} A_{ij}$ is the number of co-occurrences within the network. δ is the Kronecker delta function and is 1 if a co-occurrence exists between two models and 0 otherwise. $k_i k_j / 2m$ is the probability that a co-occurrence may exist between two terms, where k_i is the number of terms that have co-occurrences with term i and k_j is the number of terms that have co-occurrences with term j. And, A_{ij} is the normalised weighted co-occurrence between the two terms.

In order to obtain the highest modularity, the algorithm iterates between two modes. The first assigns each term to its own topic. This is then followed by the algorithm sequentially moving one term to a different topic and calculating the change in modularity. From this, the maximum modularity change can be identified.

The second mode merges the terms together to form a topic of terms and combines the co-occurrences of the terms to form single value for the co-occurrence that links the topic to the rest of the network. In addition, the edge weightings within the topic are combined to identify the strength of the internal connection within the topic. The aim is to achieve a clustering whereby each topic is highly connected internally and weakly connected to one another.

Thus, it can be considered a form of hierarchical clustering and the algorithm iterates until the modularity can no longer be increased by further aggregation of the terms. This paper uses the community API implementation of the Louvain community partitioning algorithm within the NetworkX python package [3].

4.4 Quadrant Charts

With the topics defined, one can now investigate the features of these topics and how they change over time. To achieve this, Quadrant Charts can be used. Quadrant Charts use normalised axes with lines drawn along the mid-axes to form four equal quadrants. A and third measure can be represented by altering the size of the markers on the chart (Fig. 2).

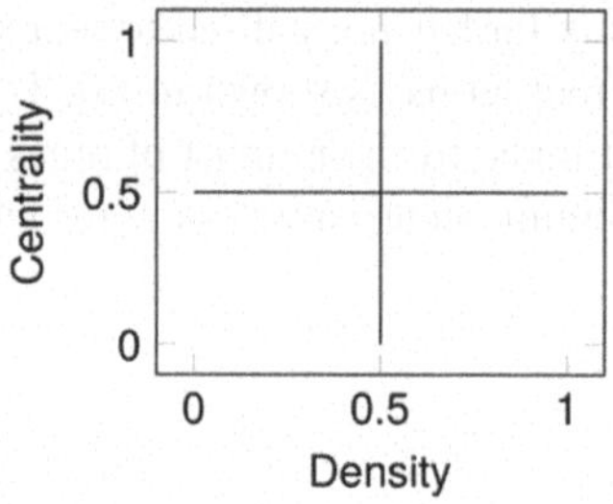

Fig. 2. Quadrant chart example

Quadrant charts have been widely used in business to support decision makers [12] and new market identification, and in network analysis to investigate potential correlations in network characteristics [6]. A particular affordance of quadrant charts is to provide a fixed space to monitor and observe the evolution and movement of partitions within a network. For example, [9] analysis of topics within an engineering project highlighted the chart's potential to provide 'actionable' information with respect to how topics are emerging, declining and/or becoming core to the projects activities. This enabled the project managers to compare their hypotheses on project activities with the actual topics being discussed in the project.

In this case, the metrics used are the cluster density and eigenvector centrality. Cluster density (D_c) is the number of edges connecting the terms within a cluster (m) divided by the possible number of edges connecting all the terms within the network ($n(n-1)/2$). Thus, 1 shows that all terms are connected with one another within the cluster and is considered a measure of how well-defined a topic is.

$$D_c = \frac{2m}{n(n-1)} \tag{3}$$

Eigenvector centrality is used to measure the influence of a cluster within the network. Relative scores are assigned to all clusters in the network based on the idea that edges to high-scoring clusters contribute more to the score of the cluster in question than equal edges to low-scoring clusters. A high eigenvector score means that a node is connected to many nodes who themselves have high scores. Equation 4 is the

Eigenvector equation where **A** is the weighted co-occurrence matrix, $\boldsymbol{x}$ are the nodes and λ are the eigenvectors.

$$\mathbf{A}\boldsymbol{x} = \lambda\boldsymbol{x} \tag{4}$$

In addition, as this analysis is monitoring the development of topics over time, one can also measure the similarity of the topics from one year to the next. To do this, the terms within each topic of the previous year is compared to the terms within the topic of the current year. A ratio of the number of terms that occurs in both topics can then be generated and a full pair-wise comparison leads to a matrix of ratios for the topics. This pair-wise comparison can then indicate where the majority of the terms from the previous topics have moved to and is used to show how topics have merged and developed across the years. Table 2 provides an example of comparing the evolution of topics from 2012 to 2013. The values in bold highlight the topics that are most similar based on the occurrence of terms.

Table 2. Pair-wise comparison of topics between years to identify mergence and growth of NTD topics

		2012 Topics					Notes
		1	2	3	4	5	
2013 topics	a	0.00	0.04	0.03	0.03	0.17	New topic
	b	**0.87**	**0.52**	0.00	0.06	**0.67**	Mergence of 1, 2 and 5
	c	0.07	0.07	**0.84**	0.30	0.04	Expansion of 3
	d	0.13	0.19	0.10	**0.56**	0.05	Expansion of 4
	e	0.13	0.19	0.03	0.05	0.08	New topic
Sum		1.00	1.01	1.00	1.00	1.01	

It can be seen that there is significant movement of terms between the topics generated in the years. Topics *a* and *e* appear to be new topics with little relation to the previous years, whilst *b* is a mergence of topics *1*, *2* and *5* from 2012. Topics *c* & *d* show expansion of topics *3* & *4*. It is these dynamic behaviours that are of interest for determining the maturity of NTD. Table 3 provides further insight into the mergence of topics *1*, *2* and *5* from 2012 to form topic *b* of 2013 as well as evidence to show the effectiveness of method to group terms. One such example of this is the term u-shape male tool, u-shape male and u-shape cut, which are all related terms to a technique used in carbon composite manufacture.

Table 3. Terms within topics

2013-a	2012-1	2012-2	2012-5
u-shape male tool	**u-shape male tool**	**Ceramic block material**	End effector
Ceramic block material	First ply	Bond line	Link arms
Woven preforms	**Woven preforms**	Carbon fibre	System integration
in-plane shear	**in-plane shear**	Mechanical performance	**Flexible membrane**
Tool surface	**Male tool**	Mechanical properties	**Core automation**
Male tool	**u-shape cut**	**Ceramic block**	**Ply cutting**
u-shape cut	**Fibre misalignment**	High temperature	Wide range
u-shape male	**ud tape**	Tests conducted	Surface area
Woven fabric	**Woven material**	Surface finish	Laser system
Fibre misalignment	**Single ply**	Block material	Robot arm
Flexible membrane	**u-shape male**	Residual stresses	Robot cell
ud tape	**Woven fabric**	Paste adhesive	Kuka robot
Core automation	4ply stack	Material surface	Initial concept
Woven material	Fibre direction	Relatively low	Press schemes
Single ply	Ambient temperature	Bonded together	Robotic pick
Ceramic block	Red line	Material suppliers	Dry fabric
Ply cutting	Elevated temperatures	Epoxy filler	Scoring matrix
...	...	...	...

5 Results

Table 4 reveals the development of topics over the four-year period. As one would expect, more terms are being added to the knowledge structure as more research and studies are being performed. In addition, there is an increase in the number of edges connecting the terms within the evolving network. Reviewing the network density (Table 4), it reveals that there is little change over the areas and is very low. This indicates that there is a high-level of structure relating these terms to one another.

Table 4. Dynamic network statistics

Year	No. of terms	No. of edges	Network density	No. of clusters	Modularity score
≤ 2012	239	1.1×10^3	20×10^{-3}	7	0.644
≤ 2013	557	3.0×10^3	10×10^{-3}	15	0.660
≤ 2014	847	6.1×10^3	10×10^{-3}	16	0.638
≤ 2015	1009	8.1×10^3	10×10^{-3}	19	0.614

Further evidence of this is provided by the number of topics being generated by the analysis and the high modularity score of 0.6. Scores of >0.3 are considered typical of highly-structured networks [13].

Continuing from the descriptive statistics, Fig. 3 shows the topics plotted on the quadrant chart of density against centrality and the node size relating to the number of terms within the topic. New topics are generated each year and the bracketed values indicate similarity with a topic in the previous year. In 2012 (Fig. 3a), it can be seen that all the topics are of density 1 highlighting that all the terms are connected with all the other terms within the topic. Given this is the starting point of the analysis, this would seem a logical finding as it is most likely that these topics will represent individual reports with little transfer of knowledge between them.

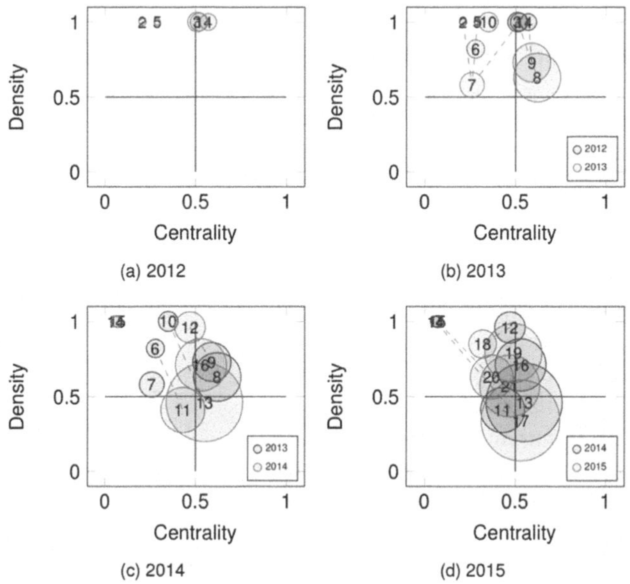

Fig. 3. Quadrant chart of evolving technology knowledge structures

Moving to 2013 (Fig. 3b) and the addition of further reports, the results show an increase in size of the topics and a decline in the density of the topics. It is interesting to note that topic 7 is a combination of 1, 2 & 5 from 2012 demonstrating there has been some work on relating these topics. The decrease in density shows that these topics have yet to be fully combined and the low centrality highlights that this topic has little influence on the rest of the NTD. In addition, a further separation of the topics based on the centrality begins to occur. The topics 8 & 9 are indicative of core NTD's as they have grown in size and have built-up from previous work (3 & 4, respectively) whilst maintaining a high-density and centrality with other topics within the network. Topics 6 & 10 represent new topics that are being introduced into NTD.

In 2014 (Fig. 3c), it can be seen that there is the addition of new topics into NTD (14 & 15). It also appears that topics 12, 16, 11, & 13 represent existing topics as they are linked to one previous topic respectively and show continued growth through the addition of more terms. It is also interesting to see an alignment of the topics along the mid-line of centrality indicating that neither has more influence than the other. This may be a key feature of topics surrounding NTD.

This trend continues in 2015 (Fig. 3d) where the topics maintain an equal influence with one another. In addition, previous topics 14 & 15 have now been integrated into the main group of topics by their mergence with topics 17 & 20, respectively. At this stage of NTD, it is the density and size that are key differentiating factors. It could be that these indicate the topics that represent the NTD with the other topics representing key features of the NTD.

6 Discussion and Future Work

The results from the dynamic co-word analysis of NTD reports has highlighted the complex dynamics surrounding the generation of topics and their relations to one another. The high-level of dynamism observed shows there is potential for patterns to be identified that would relate to best practice structuring of knowledge around NTD.

However, to reach this stage, further work is required on capturing the secondary data in terms of identifying NTDs that have been easily adopted by industry. This is currently ongoing work at the NCC. With this, patterns within the co-word analysis can then be correlated to easy adoption of NTD.

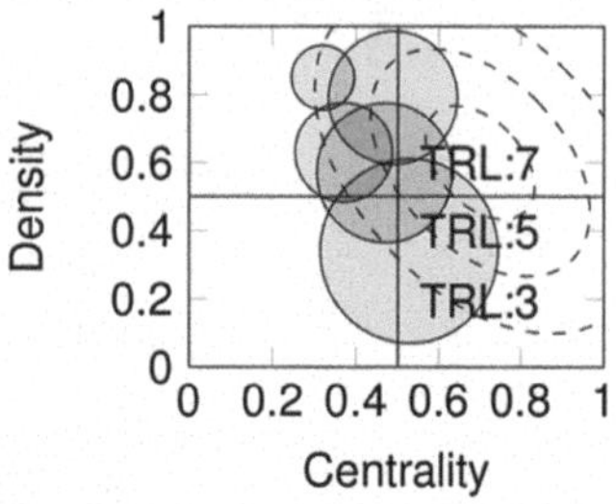

Fig. 4. Setting TRL regions based on density & centrality

In addition, it is a further hypothesised that Technology Readiness Levels (TRLs) could be mapped to these quadrant charts, which would then enable project managers to identify the readiness of their R&D (Fig. 4). The authors are actively working on this through questionnaires with experts at the NCC to qualify the TRL of different topics. The aim is to then correlate these results with the metrics from the co-word analysis.

The last aspect that is being expanded upon is in the contents of the network itself. Examples include in mapping topics to individuals, projects, companies and equipment in order to gain a better understanding of how the distribution of skills and competencies within an organisation may help or hinder the adoption of NTD.

7 Conclusion

New Technology Development (NTD) has been identified as one of the key enablers to support business and economic growth in developed countries. Facilities have now been created to ensure developed countries maintain their advantage of being at the forefront of NTD. Although these facilities provide state-of-the-art tools and equipment, challenges exist in the development of the skills and competencies, and the body of knowledge concerning NTDs.

This paper has presented results from a dynamic co-word analysis of NTD reports within the NCC and has demonstrated the viability of this technique to provide insights into the evolution and growth of the knowledge structure surrounding NTD. The evolution of the topics concerning a matured NTD have equal influence on one another with the topic density and size being the differentiating factor on the role within NTD.

Acknowledgements. The work reported in this paper has been funded by the Engineering and Physical Sciences Research Council (EPSRC). Grant references EP/K014196/2, EP/R513556/1 & EP/R013179/1.

References

1. Catapult. https://catapult.org.uk. Accessed 20 Feb 2018
2. Blondel, V.D., et al.: Fast unfolding of communities in large networks. J. Stat. Mech: Theory Exp. **2008**(10), P10008 (2008)
3. Hagberg, A.A., et al.: Exploring network structure, dynamics, and function using NetworkX. In: Proceedings of the 7th Python in Science Conference (SciPy2008). Pasadena, CA USA, August 2008, pp. 11–15 (2008)
4. Ding, Y., et al.: Bibliometric cartography of information retrieval research by using co-word analysis. Inf. Process. Manag. **37**, 6 (2001)
5. Coulter, N., et al.: Software engineering as seen through its research literature: a study in co-word analysis. JASIST **49**(13), 1206–1223 (1998)
6. Liu, Y., et al.: CHI 1994-2013: mapping two decades of intellectual progress through co-word analysis. In: Proceedings of the 32nd Annual ACM Conference on Human Factors in Computing Systems, pp. 3553–3562. ACM (2014)
7. Gopsill, J., et al.: The evolution of terminology within a large distributed engineering project. In: ICED (2015)
8. Gopsill, J.A., et al.: Automatic generation of design structure matrices through the evolution of product models. Artif. Intell. Eng. Des. Anal. Manuf. **30**(4), 424–445 (2016). https://doi.org/10.1017/s0890060416000391
9. Jones, S., et al.: Subject lines as sensors: co-word analysis of e-mail to support the management of collaborative engineering work. In: ICED (2015)
10. Loper, E., et al.: NLTK: the natural language toolkit. In: Proceedings of the ACL-02 Workshop on ETMTNLP, Philadelphia, Pennsylvania, pp. 63–70. Association for Computational Linguistics (2002). https://doi.org/10.3115/1118108.1118117
11. Newman, M.E.: Analysis of weighted networks. PRE **70**(5), 056131 (2004)
12. Vargo, J., et al.: Crisis strategic planning for SMEs: finding the silver lining. IJoPM **49**(18), 5619–5635 (2011). https://doi.org/10.1080/00207543.2011.563902
13. Newman, M.E.J.: Modularity and community structure in networks. Proc. Nat. Acad. Sci. **103**(23), 8577–8582 (2006)

Multicriteria Evaluation Method in PLM Environment: A Pilot Study

Kevin Audoux[1(✉)], Floriane Laverne[1], Gianluca D'Antonio[1], Frédéric Segonds[2], Olivier Kerbrat[3], Paolo Chiabert[2], and Ameziane Aoussat[1]

[1] LCPI/Arts et Métiers Paristech, 151 Boulevard de l'Hopital, 75015 Paris, France
kevin.audoux@ensam.eu

[2] Politecnico di Torino, C.so Duca degli Abruzzi 24, 10129 Turin, Italy

[3] Univ Rennes, ENS Rennes, CNRS, Gem - UMR 6183, 35000 Rennes, France

Abstract. During the whole design process, evaluation stages are required and should consider more and more criteria but some of them are not mastered by designers. They also need support tools or methods to ease the product evaluation during the design process and avoid the subjectivity of this task, to limit the choice's risks and to allow the repeatability of the whole process. This article presents through an experiment the necessity of evaluation tools by comparing assisted and not-assisted evaluation of 9 products.

Keywords: Evaluation method · Innovation · Sustainable development

1 Introduction

To win the innovation race firms must set up innovation management evaluation during their design process to control the evolution of their products. This race reduces the time allowed for product development. This modification of the design requirements promotes the use of evaluation method during the design process. Each evaluation phase needs its own performance indicators and method to fit with the product's progress. As a performance criterion, the innovative characteristic of the product must be evaluated to validate the economic and functional viability.

However, the performance of the product depends on design and politic goals. More and more criteria of performance are added to suit the consumers' evolution and the policy evolution as the sustainable development.

Sustainable development is "development that meets the needs of the present without compromising the ability of future generations to meet their own needs" [1]. It is composed of three aspects: social, as the human being, environment, as the respect of the nature and economy as the industrial development. This approach is currently growing and is described as the next world problem is global warming as presented in the Climate change conference in 2015 [2]. Environmental impact reduction is supported by Policy [3] and is also promoted by consumers as a selection criteria [4]. By considering the sustainability impact of their product, firms can increase their

Published by Springer Nature Switzerland AG 2018.
P. Chiabert et al. (Eds.): PLM 2018, IFIP AICT 540, pp. 534–542, 2018.
https://doi.org/10.1007/978-3-030-01614-2_49

profitability and improve the life cycle of their products by optimising the end of life of their product or reduce the consumption of the product manufacturing.

Innovation and sustainability are therefore promising opportunities for designing new products. The requirements relative to its themes must be integrated as soon as possible into the design process that means during the early design stages, to provide the market with innovative and sustainable products.

The motivation of this work is to expose the difficulty of multiple performances evaluation during the design process. The state of the art positioned the design methodologies in PLM approach and described the limits of evaluation tools for multiple performance assessment. An experiment is proposed to highlight the benefit of tools during the design process.

2 State of the Art

Our study is focused on the evaluation stage of innovation and sustainability during the design process. The state of the art first aims to position the Product Lifecycle Management into the design process. In a second time, the integration of innovation and sustainability in the design process are investigated. In the third part of the state of the art, a description of evaluation tool typology is proposed.

2.1 Early PLM and Design Methodologies

Design methodologies are widely used in our community. For engineering design practices in industry, engineers and managers are concerned with the results of design by following specific design process more rigorously to ensure that the final design result meets the objectives of the product design and development projects [5]. PLM is an approach to support this complexity, including the design methodology and the complete product life cycle [6, 7]. As PLM addresses the entire lifecycle of the product, it has a cross-functional nature and deals closely with the way a company runs [8]. With the development of Product Data Management (PDM), PLM and associated workflows, software firms have proposed solutions to the everyday problems of engineering design departments (versioning of documents, naming etc.). PLM aims to cover all the stages of product development, by integrating the processes and people taking part in the project [9]. Thus, PLM is an approach in which processes are just as important as data, or even more so. Thus, when dealing with PLM implementation, the design process is naturally the starting backbone to define processes and associated workflows. Hence, if one wants to provide a successful PLM environment, it is mandatory to structure the methodologies that will be supported. Design process is also the backbone of an innovation process and early design stages, starting from the research of concepts to the delivery of a preliminary layout, are the key stages of the innovative design [10] as presented in Fig. 1. If we focus on the early design stages, current «PLM methodological backbones» are not evaluated by designers or end-users. This paper presents the benefit these kinds of tools could provide.

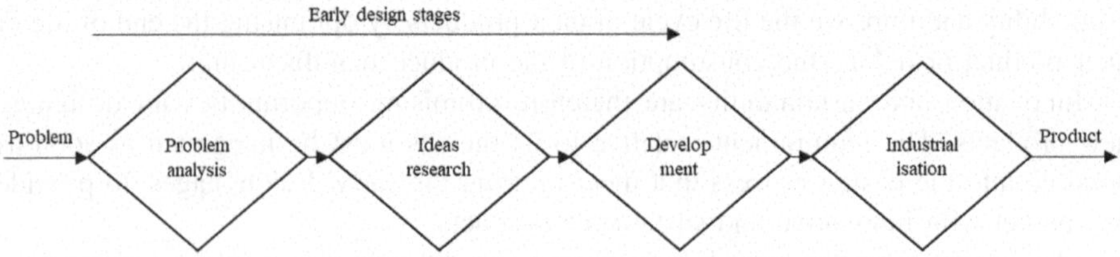

Fig. 1. Design process and position of the early design stages

2.2 Innovation and Sustainability in the Design Process

The innovative aspect of a product is created during early design stages [11]. Two kinds of innovations are differentiated: incremental innovation which ameliorate a product and breakthrough innovation which corresponds to new products for new needs [12]. Saunders identifies characteristics of innovative products based on the study of popular products [13]. This study permits to identify innovation criteria for product development. The innovative aspect of a product can be managed by two approaches:

- An innovative design process: The whole process is modified and managed to increase the innovative characteristic of the product.
- An innovative evaluation of the project: each intermediate representation of the product is evaluated to control the innovative characteristic of the product.
- Throughout the rest of the article, we proposed to study only the second approach, suitable for every type of design process.

As opposed to innovation, sustainability is not specific to early design stages. It can be evaluated during the whole process. The complexity of methods follows the evolution of the product during all design stages. First, method permits to identify the product scenario of use based on the environmental impact criteria [14], then select and improve the ideas [15, 16] also improve the product concept or architecture [17, 18] and then optimise the life cycle of the whole defined product [19].

Innovation and sustainability aspects of the product have to be evaluated and monitored during the design process. The different kinds of evaluation tool are described in the following part.

2.3 Typology of Evaluation Tools in Design Process

2.3.1 Design Evaluation

Each successive stages of the design process is the alternation of generation and evaluation of intermediate representation of the product [20]. It means that firstly designers must answer the specific problems of the product design and then select with the appropriate criteria the best intermediate representations.

According to Blessing [21], criteria "are used to be able to focus the investigation of the existing situation; to assess the contribution of the findings of such investigations to the research goal; to focus the development of support on the most relevant factors;

to plan the appropriate evaluation; to focus the realization of the support on this evaluation; and to assess the evaluation results."

Two types are defined:

- Successful criteria: they represent the benefit generated by the placing on the market of the product
- Measurable success criteria: they represent the possible success of the product, innovative and sustainable indicators are used here for measuring the performance of the product.

2.3.2 Typology of Evaluation Tools

To quantify these measurable success criteria, a specific evaluation method is needed. Literature distinguishes two types of evaluation:

- Expert evaluation based on the knowledge of experts in the domain. This type of method is well used for innovation projects and relies on evaluation grids [22].
- Tools evaluation based on the quantification of product criteria. This kind of method needs tangible measurement and is used to determine environmental impact of intermediate representation with survey [15] or, matrix [23]. It is based on the measurement of objective criteria.

Evaluations are crucial during the design process and even more during the early design stage where the greater part of the engaged cost is defined. Innovation and sustainable require experts. To reduce the resource dedicated to the evaluation stage and to draw on objective indicators, tools are the best compromise.

3 Evaluation Needs During Design Process

In this section, an experiment made to investigate the impact of evaluation tools for designers is proposed. Twelve M.Sc. students attending courses on sustainable manufacturing have been involved: subjective and objective evaluation sessions are performed to understand whether the use of tools during evaluations is a benefit for designers or not. Secondly, a method for tool evaluation is proposed and tested.

3.1 Protocol

First, a set of products to be evaluated has been identified: nine heterogeneous products designed with particular concerns for the purpose of sustainability or innovation, or manufactured with innovative technologies (such as additive manufacturing) have been selected. The whole list of products is provided in Table 1.

Table 1. Product description

Product	Description	Categories
1	Single-blade electric razor used like classic one	Innovation
2	Optimised leg prosthesis for runners	Innovation
3	Electric car	Sustainability
4	Desk made with carton	Sustainability
5	Glasses manufactured by additive manufacturing	Innovation
6	Neckless manufactured by additive manufacturing	Innovation
7	Bicycle saddle/lock	Innovation
8	Edible water bubble	Sustainability
9	Plate made with leaf	Sustainability

The experiment is composed of two main steps and lasted 1h30 as described in Fig. 2.

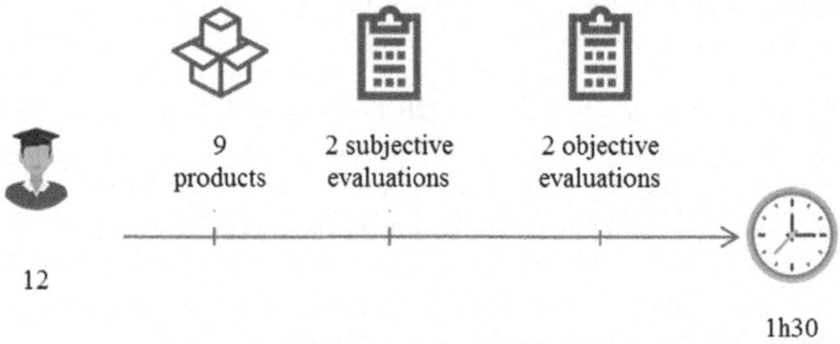

Fig. 2. Planning for experiment

In the first stage, each participant has to assess the sustainability and the innovation levels for each product without any support tool. Participants have to access a Google form and provide a subjective answer to the question "how much is the innovative aspect?" through a Likert scale (1–5): 1 is for bad and 5 is for good.

After this evaluation, the same set of products is evaluated by using two appropriate tools for sustainability [15] and innovation [13]. These tools were adapted in a Google form.

Then, the results have been collected and compared to identify whether differenced among the two evaluations can be found.

3.2 Results

This pilot study needs the use of non-parametric methods due to the sample size. For each product, we analyse the distribution and the difference between the two kinds of evaluation by using the following method:

Table 2. Kolmogorov-Smirnov results

	Tools	Product	1	2	3	4	5	6	7	8	9
sustainability	with	mean	1,61	2,75	3,33	3,33	2,58	2,81	2,17	3,75	3,89
		standard deviation	0,45	0,81	0,90	0,42	0,62	0,40	1,04	0,42	0,64
		coefficient of variation	28,0%	29,5%	27,0%	12,6%	24,0%	14,2%	47,9%	11,2%	16,5%
		signification	0,70	0,97	0,96	1,00	0,92	0,91	0,98	1,00	0,99
	without	mean	2,58	3,00	4,18	3,58	3,07	2,57	3,08	4,73	4,75
		standard deviation	1,24	0,60	0,81	1,16	1,00	1,28	0,96	0,59	0,58
		coefficient of variation	48,1%	20,0%	19,4%	32,4%	32,6%	49,8%	31,2%	12,5%	12,2%
		signification	0,69	0,14	0,21	0,32	0,33	0,62	0,46	0,00	0,00
innovation	with	mean	1,48	2,11	2,11	2,02	1,11	1,03	1,70	2,05	2,02
		standard deviation	0,50	0,48	0,61	0,83	0,61	0,53	0,47	0,68	0,65
		coefficient of variation	33,8%	22,7%	28,9%	41,1%	55,0%	51,5%	27,6%	33,2%	32,2%
		signification	0,83	0,55	0,94	0,76	0,97	0,94	0,37	0,98	0,70
	without	mean	2,75	4,25	3,88	3,50	2,29	2,36	4,08	4,73	3,56
		standard deviation	1,29	1,06	0,86	1,45	0,99	1,01	0,76	0,46	1,26
		coefficient of variation	46,9%	24,9%	22,2%	41,4%	43,2%	42,8%	18,6%	9,7%	35,4%
		signification	0,41	0,12	0,20	0,22	0,32	0,57	0,48	0,04	0,65

– Kolmogorov-Smirnov method is used for non-parametric sample. It compared each sample with a normal distribution. The results of each product are shown on Table 2. This method provide four criteria:

- the mean value of the evaluation
- the standard deviation
- the coefficient of deviation
- the signification that describe if the normal distribution is validated.

– Wilcoxon method permits to identify if the evolution between two samples of data are correlated. The results are shown on Table 3.

Table 3. Wilcoxon test

	Signification								
Product	1	2	3	4	5	6	7	8	9
Sustainability	0.31	0.498	0.465	1	0.686	0.269	0.416	0.109	0.109
Innovation	0.023	0.002	0.003	0.018	0.021	0.013	0.003	0.003	0.007

Most of the results on Table 2 show that the hypothesis of a normal distribution is never rejected when the tool is used (signification value higher than 0.05) for both sustainability and innovation. When the tool is not used, the hypothesis of normal distribution is not accepted in three cases only (see the results highlighted in orange). In 14 out of the 15 remaining evaluation pairs, exhibit a reduced sustainability or innovation average score: therefore, if the participants are not guided during the evaluation process, they tend to overestimate products' performances. Further, in 12 out of 15 cases the overall standard deviation is smaller, although a clear pattern for the coefficient of variation (given by the ratio between the standard deviation and the mean value) cannot be identified: so, the overall evaluation range is reduced but, since also the average values are usually lower, the relative dispersion may increase.

For the case study, final products are evaluated, the use of tools permit to standardize and homogenize this step.

The results of Table 3 show the results of Wilcoxon test. It compared two linked-samples and test whether their evolutions are constant. If the signification is under 0.05, the hypothesis is invalidated. For innovation evaluation, the hypothesis is rejected that means that participants change significantly their point of view between the two evaluations. This result is in accordance with the Table 2, the range is clearly different with and without tools. This test shows that innovation is clearly a subjective characteristic and it is difficult to evaluate without tools.

3.3 Analysis and Conclusion of the Experiment

This experiment shows that it is difficult to evaluate products regarding to different subjects. The Table 2 shows how much participants overestimate the performance of product. Moreover, it permits to identify that tools reduce the deviations. The Table 3 permits to understand how evolve the evaluation between the two steps. For sustainability aspect, the participants overestimate the performances but in average follow the same distribution with or without tools. For innovative aspect, the subjectivity of this characteristic can explain why the participants change drastically their evaluation.

This experiment was made with final products which are easier than during the design process. The less the product is developed the better the benefit of evaluation tool is.

These results show the need of assistance for evaluation stages. The next part of this article aims to validate a method of classification for evaluation method.

One limit of this experiment could be the reduce number of participants.

4 Conclusion

This article proves through the experiment the necessity of evaluation tool during design by the comparison of two evaluations: an evaluation subjective and an evaluation with tools. This experiment was performed by engineering students and highlighted that tangible constraint as the sustainability is more valuable than subjective characteristic as innovation. Evaluation tools permit for both types of feature to reduce the uncertainty. Assistance makes repeatable and reliable evaluation stages.

The choice of evaluation tool depends of different condition link to the design process or designers' knowledge or product goals, and makes the selection more and more difficult. The second experiment is a validation of an evaluation method of tools. This method is using unlabelled criteria to fit with each disciplinary found in the design process. Engineering students had to make their own evaluation of scientific papers by following the proposed method.

References

1. Brundtland, G.H.: Rapport Brundtland. Ministère Aff. Étrangères Dév. Int. L'Odyssée Dév. Durable (1987)
2. The Paris Agreement - main page. http://unfccc.int/paris_agreement/items/9485.php. Accessed 25 Jan 2018
3. Rosiek, J.: The impact of the eu climate policy on green jobs creation. Econ. Manag. **18**(4), 697–714 (2013)
4. Young, W., Hwang, K., McDonald, S., Oates, C.J.: Sustainable consumption: green consumer behaviour when purchasing products. Sustain. Dev. **18**, 20–31 (2009)
5. Tomiyama, T., Gu, P., Jin, Y., Lutters, D., Kind, C., Kimura, F.: Design methodologies: industrial and educational applications. CIRP Ann. - Manuf. Technol. **58**(2), 543–565 (2009)
6. Bergsjö, D.H.: Management of Mechatronic Product Data in PLM Systems. Chalmers University of Technology, Sweden (2007)
7. Sellgren, U., Törngren, M., Malvius, D., Biehl, M.: PLM for mechatronics integration (2018)
8. Garetti, M., Terzi, S., Bertacci, N., Brianza, M.: Organisational change and knowledge management in PLM implementation. Int. J. Prod. Lifecycle Manag. **1**(1), 43–51 (2005)
9. Schuh, G., Rozenfeld, H., Assmus, D., Zancul, E.: Process oriented framework to support PLM implementation. Comput. Ind. **59**(2–3), 210–218 (2008)
10. Laverne, F., Segonds, F., D'Antonio, G., Le Coq, M.: Enriching design with X through tailored additive manufacturing knowledge: a methodological proposal. Int. J. Interact. Des. Manuf. **11**(2), 279–288 (2017)
11. Perrin, J.: Concevoir l'innovation industrielle: méthodologie de conception de l'innovation. In: CNRS (2001)
12. Encaoua, D., Foray, D., Hatchuel, A., Mairesse, J.: Les enjeux économiques de l'innovation, the economics of innovation: trends and issues. Rev. Déconomie Polit. **114**(2), 133–168 (2004)
13. Saunders, M.N., Seepersad, C.C., Hölttä-Otto, K.: The characteristics of innovative, mechanical products. J. Mech. Des. **133**(2), 1–9 (2011)
14. Cluzel, F., Yannou, B., Millet, D., Leroy, Y.: Eco-ideation and eco-selection of R&D projects portfolio in complex systems industries. J. Clean. Prod. **112**, 4329–4343 (2016)
15. Bocken, N.M.P., Allwood, J.M., Willey, A.R., King, J.M.H.: Development of an eco-ideation tool to identify stepwise greenhouse gas emissions reduction options for consumer goods. J. Clean. Prod. **19**(12), 1279–1287 (2011)
16. O'Hare, J.A.: Eco-innovation tools for the early stages: an industry-based investigation of tool customisation and introduction. University of Bath (2010)
17. Hassan, M.F., Saman, M.Z.M., Sharif, S., Omar, B.: An integrated MA-AHP approach for selecting the highest sustainability index of a new product. Procedia - Soc. Behav. Sci. **57**, 236–242 (2012)
18. Halog, A., Schultmann, F., Rentz, O.: Using quality function deployment for technique selection for optimum environmental performance improvement. J. Clean. Prod. **9**(5), 387–394 (2001)
19. Contreras, A.M., Rosa, E., Pérez, M., Van Langenhove, H., Dewulf, J.: Comparative life cycle assessment of four alternatives for using by-products of cane sugar production. J. Clean. Prod. **17**(8), 772–779 (2009)
20. Howard, T.J., Culley, S.J., Dekoninck, E.: Describing the creative design process by the integration of engineering design and cognitive psychology literature. Des. Stud. **29**(2), 160–180 (2008)

21. Blessing, L.T.M., Chakrabarti, A.: DRM, A Design Research Methodology. Springer, London (2009). https://doi.org/10.1007/978-1-84882-587-1
22. Yannou, B., Zimmer, B., Farel, R., Jankovic, M., Cardinal, S.L.: Proofs of utility, innovation, profitability and concept for innovation selection. In: ICED, Seoul Korea (2013)
23. Binz, M., Reichle, H.: Evaluation method to determine the success potential and the degree of innovation of technical product ideas and products. In: 35 Proceedings of ICED 05 15th International Conference on Engineering Design, Melbourne, Australia, 15–18 August 2005 (2005)

How the ALIENNOR Platform Supports the Identification of Eco-Ideation Stimulation Mechanisms During an Eco-Ideation Phase

Cong Cuong Pham[1(✉)], Flore Vallet[2,3], Benjamin Tyl[4], Olivier Pialot[5], and Benoit Eynard[1]

[1] Sorbonne Universités, Université de Technologie de Compiègne, CNRS, UMR 7337 Roberval, Centre de Recherche Royallieu - CS 60 319, 60 203 Compiègne Cedex, France
phamcong@utc.fr
[2] CentraleSupélec, Laboratoire Genie Industriel, Université Paris-Saclay, Paris, France
[3] IRT SystemX, Paris-Saclay, Paris, France
[4] APESA, Saintes, France
[5] Laboratoire QUARTZ, Supmeca, Saint-Ouen, France

Abstract. Creativity stage or ideation phase is one of the most important step of innovation process where ideas with high potential of environmental and social impact reduction are generated. Therefore, many eco-ideation tools (stimuli, mechanisms, etc.) have been proposed. These tools are mainly at micro level (providing technical solutions) or at macro-level (providing a systemic view). The research project ALIENNOR (http://www.agence-nationale-recherche.fr/Project-ANR-15-CE10-0001) aims at providing a set of Eco-Ideation Stimulation Mechanisms (ESMs) at meso-level compromising both systemic vision and technical solutions. This paper presents how ALIENNOR platform (a part of ALIENNOR project) supports the identification of appropriate ESMs used in eco-ideation phase.

1 Introduction

By integrating both of environmental and social factors, eco-innovation could be defined as *"inventions, designs and new solutions for fulfilling human's and nature's needs in ecologically effective ways"* [1]. Eco-ideation is an important phase that takes place upstream the eco-innovation process [2] since in which, ideas with great potential for reducing environmental impact are proposed [3]. Problem finding - the starting point of any eco-ideation process plays a crucial role and often requires some techniques or supported tools to foster the generations of useful ideas such as ideation stimuli (heuristics), mechanisms, wheels or diagrams. Proposed methods are mainly technical solutions (at micro levels) or systemic approaches (at macro levels). They can be simple tools (simple to implement and to use) that don't require specific knowledge such as Eco-design Strategy wheel [4], BEC synergy diagram [5] or complex approaches such as TRIZ-based tools [6–9].

Published by Springer Nature Switzerland AG 2018.
P. Chiabert et al. (Eds.): PLM 2018, IFIP AICT 540, pp. 543–553, 2018.
https://doi.org/10.1007/978-3-030-01614-2_50

The ALIENNOR project aims to develop a method supporting companies in their innovation process at three levels: (a) the idea generation; (b) eco-innovation evaluation; and c) idea generation and concept evaluation coordination.

In the idea generation phase, a set of seven stimulation mechanisms (Eco-ideation Stimulation Mechanisms – ESMs) has been proposed to support eco-ideation sessions (see Table 1). However, only two or three (at most) ESMs should be used during the eco-ideation phase of a particular eco-innovation case. With seven pre-defined mechanisms and a base of pre-selected eco-innovation cases, three methods can be used to identify the most appropriate ESMs:

Table 1. Seven Eco-ideation Stimulation Mechanisms used in eco-ideation sessions [13].

No	ESM	Raises questions about
1	Innovate with stakeholders	Stakeholder network, through the value creation for the users, the environment, society, and all other relevant actors value creation for all stakeholders
2	Innovate through biomimicry	The similarities between man-made industrials practices and natural strategies of development at several system levels (organ, organism, ecosystem)
3	Innovate through sustainable mode of consumption	The unsustainable use of products/services and how the system can fit the system to end users and territorial specificities (skills, resources, etc.)
4	Innovate through Product Service Systems	The optimization the functionality of the materials and energy consumed by the system (use intensity, dematerialization) and of dissociating the product property and the consumption
5	Innovate through territorial resources	The integration of territorial capitals in design strategy: natural capitals, industrial ecosystems, social capitals and anthropic
6	Innovate through circularity	The different ways to design a product in closed loop (of material, energy, information). It also questions the question of recycle, repair, upgradability
7	Innovate through new technologies	The possibility to integrate new technologies, new process and organization, new material, in the design of the system

(a) Identification of relevant ESMs through an analysis of the environmental problems from the design brief;
(b) Identification of relevant ESMs through a systematic reformulation of the design brief according to each ESM and
(c) Identification of the ESMs through inspiring case studies.

Each method requires a group of participants coming from various disciplines (scientists in eco-innovation, designers or students). This paper presents "*how ALIENNOR platform is used to support participants to identify the most relevant ESMs used in eco-ideation phase?*" according to each method listed above. The rest of the article is structured as follows: In Sect. 2, we review some existing eco-ideation ICT (Information and Communication Technology) based tools, in Sect. 3 we present main functions of the ALIENNOR platform and three usage scenarios corresponding to three methods, we describe in detail in Sect. 4 how the platform is used in the third method with a real example of eco-innovation cases. The paper ends at Sect. 5 with some conclusions and perspectives.

2 Related Work of Ideation-Tools and Ideation-Mechanisms Identification Approaches

In this section, we review some existing ideation-tools and eco-innovation platforms that have been used to promote the eco-innovation design/process. We present also three approaches used in the ALIENNOR project to identify appropriate ideation-mechanisms.

2.1 Existing Ideation-Tools and Eco-Innovation Platforms

Many ideation-tools have been proposed such as Eco-design Strategy wheel [4], BEC synergy diagram [5] or TRIZ-based tools [9, 10]. These tools are mainly stimulus, mechanisms, a diagram or a wheel that help to foster the generations of useful ideas for the eco-innovation process. However, for a particular eco-innovation case, only a few stimuli, mechanisms are used and we have found a lack of interest from the community in developing ICT (Information and Communication Technologies) solutions such as web-based platform, desktop software, etc. that facilitate the identification of the appropriate ESMs to be used. Only a few works that has been proposed. Two among them are *Information/inspiration* [11] and *IDEATRIZ Innovation software* [12] but they aims to facilitate the whole eco-innovation process instead of eco-ideation phase.

Information/inspiration proposed by Bhamra and Lofthouse [11] is a sustainable design web-based tool combining sustainable design information with a selection of inspirational ideas. As stated by authors, a web-based format was chosen since it *"allows content presented in a highly visual and interactive way, supports the opportunity for the user to access content on demand, provides a good opportunity for the eco-design information to be kept up to date"*. Two types of data are included: *"Information"* and *"Inspiration"*. The former aims to be as appropriate as possible to the type of work that industrial designers become involved in: strategies, recycling, use, materials, packaging, etc. The later contains case studies grouped according to the product type: 'electrical products', 'white goods', 'packaging', etc. *"The aim of 'Inspiration' is to encourage, inspire and educate designers, by providing them with product examples of eco-design work, to help them build up their tacit eco-design knowledge, and/or support idea generation at the beginning of an eco-design project"* [11]. By selecting a particular product, users can see detail information about it such as description, image, functions, eco-design strategies, etc. The platform was developed a long time ago, the web interface is too simple and not really intuitive. It lacks also filter functions or navigation tools to move between eco-design cases.

IDEATRIZ Innovation software is a desktop software, based on IDEATRIZ methodology proposed by Carvalho et al. [12] that aims at generating ideas that are both new and valuable to company's customer. The software allows users to create new product and provides them a list of heuristics (from IDEATRIZ methodology) to freely generate ideas without have to worry about storing them in the eco-ideation phase. The main limitation of IDEATRIZ Innovation software is that it doesn't allow a collaboration work among different users.

The next sub-section presents three methods used to identify relevant ESMs for ideation phase, proposed in the context of ALIENNOR project[1].

2.2 Three Methods to Identify Relevant ESMs

The Table 1 describes in detail seven Eco-Ideation Stimulation Mechanisms (ESMs) proposed in the ALIENNOR project. These mechanisms are used mainly in the very first phase of the eco-innovation process to generate ideas with high environmental and social impacts. However, for a particular eco-innovation cases, only two or three (at most) should be used. Three methods have been proposed to facilitate the selection of appropriate ESMs to be used.

- **Method 1: Identification of relevant ESMs through an analysis of eco-innovation problems**. In this approach, the participants identify environmental problems from the design brief and connect them to the most appropriate ESMs using Problem-ESM relationships sheet (Fig. 1).

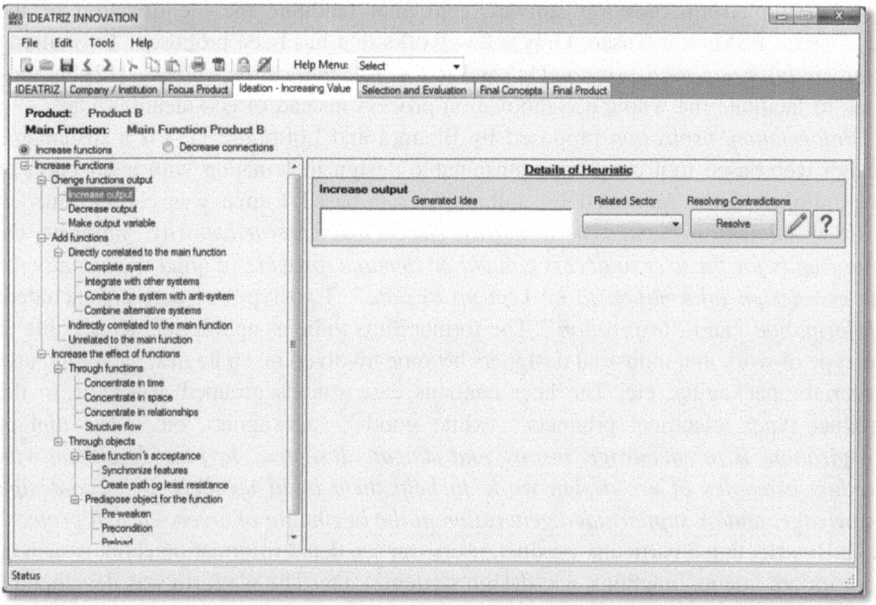

Fig. 1. IDEATRIZ Innovation software – Ideation tab [12].

- **Method 2: Identification of relevant ESMs through a systematic reformulation of the design brief according to each ESM**. Each participant reformulates the design brief according to each ESM. All reformulations are then grouped and summarized to deduce which ESMs are the most relevant for the case study.
- **Method 3: Identification of relevant ESMs through inspiring case studies**. Participants choose from a predefined base of cases the ones that they evaluate as the most associated to the current case study (same category, same environmental issues, etc.). Selected cases are then grouped and clustered into different categories according to types of issues faced by the current case study. Relevant ESMs are then identified from these clusters.

In the next section, we present how the ALIENNOR platform can be used to support these three methods.

3 ALIENNOR Platform

Three methods presented in Sect. 2 require the participants from different disciplines: eco-innovation scientists, designers, students, etc. A web-based platform enables geographically distributed participants to work remotely together instead of going to face-to-face work sessions. It also allows to capture and summarize discussion sessions' results in a more efficient way.

3.1 Platform's Functions Summary

The main advantages of the ALIENNOR platform (Fig. 2) can be summarized as follows:

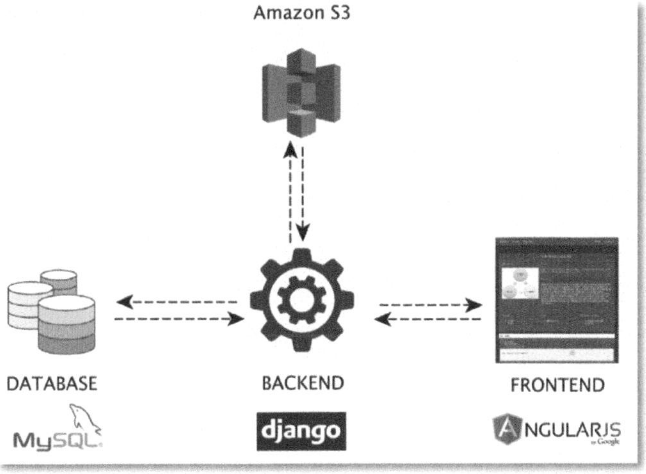

Fig. 2. Overview of web-based ALIENNOR platform's architecture. Eco-innovation cases are stored in a MySQL database while the Amazon S3 service is used to stock cases' images.

- **Provides a rich base of 120 eco-innovation cases** classified in two groups: tagged and non-tagged. The first group contains cases that are already linked to two or three ESMs and will be used as inspiring cases in the method 3 (see above). Cases in the second group have not been tagged yet, that means they are not linked to any ESM and the main purpose of all three above methods is to identify what ESMs are relevant for these cases.
- **Provides a detailed presentation of each ESM** among seven ESMs (Table 1) with description, explanation of each step to follow, etc. User can consult the content of each ESM directly on the platform or through the attached.pdf document.
- **Provides navigation tools** between eco-innovation cases and seven mechanisms that allow users to easily consult all cases associated to a particular ESM. Some **filters** have been implemented to refine eco-innovation cases based on categories or associated mechanisms. All **links between eco-innovation cases and mechanisms are also represented visually** through a graphical representation. These functions help users more understand eco-innovation cases and facilitate them in querying particular cases (Fig. 3).

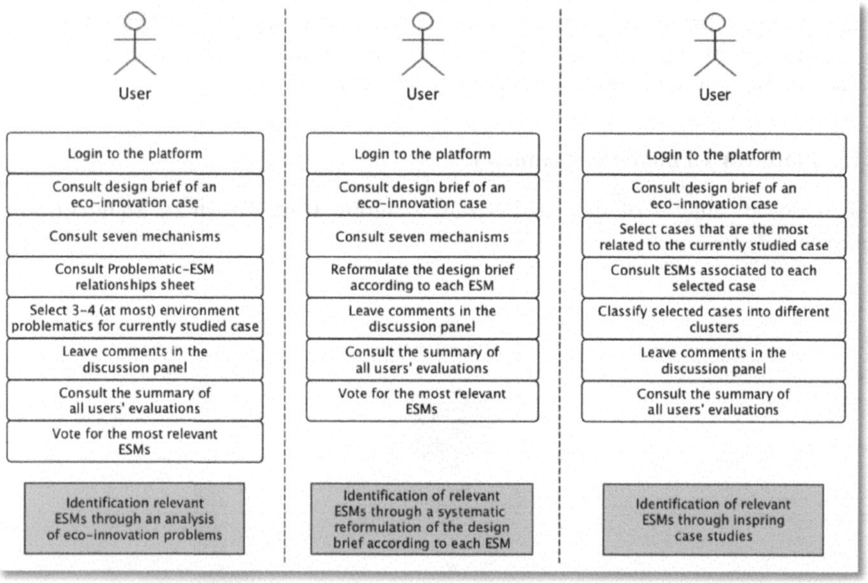

Fig. 3. Three scenarios of ALIENNOR platform corresponding to three ESMs identification methods.

3.2 Scenarios

With eco-innovation cases and mechanisms implemented, the ALIENNOR platform allows the creation and animation of a community between scientists, small and medium companies, and students the helps to promote the eco-innovation product design. Besides, it can also be used (as mentioned above) to facilitate the identification of relevant ESMs used in eco-ideation phase. Three scenarios have been identified according to three methods (presented in Sect. 2):

- **Scenario 1**: After logged in to the platform, users consult the design brief of a particular eco-innovation case through its detail page. This page contains different fields such as title, promise, visualization (product's photo, company's logo etc.) and description with information about environmental factors, economic values, etc. Users then consult seven mechanisms and the Problematic-ESM relationships sheet to select from 3 to 4 at most environment problematics related to the currently studied case. They can leave any comment in the discussion panel to discuss more about their decisions or view evaluations of other users. Platform's admin can decide which ESMs are the most relevant based on users' evaluations or users can vote for them directly on the detail page of eco-innovation case.
- **Scenario 2**: Like in the scenario 1, after logged in, consult the design brief of a particular eco-innovation case and seven ESMs, users have to reformulate the design brief according to each ESM through a dedicated page. They can also leave their comments for each reformulation in the discussion panel and view the evaluations' summary of all other users. The most relevant ESMs are selected by platform's admin based on the voting results of all users.
- **Scenario 3**: After logged in and consult the design brief of a particular eco-innovations, users use implemented filters and navigation functions to navigate through all eco-innovations cases existing in the database and select a set of cases that are the most related to the currently studied case. Users can see what ESMs are associated to each selected eco-innovation case in its detail page. They then classify the set of cases into different clusters according to types of issues faced by the studied case. They can leave comments in the discussion panel to explain the why a case is classified into a cluster but not the others. The most relevant ESM are then selected by the platform's admin according to the clusters established by all users.

We are going to illustrate in the next section the third scenario: *"Identification of relevant ESMs through inspiring cases studies"* with real examples of eco-innovation cases.

4 Identification of the ESM Through Inspiring Case Studies on ALIENNOR Platform

With 120 implemented eco-innovation cases and 7 mechanisms, the ALIENNOR platform is notably helpful in the third approach. It facilitates the selection of inspiring cases by providing users a structured and intuitive representation of all eco-innovation cases with appropriate navigation, visualization functions.

In order to identify ESMs adapted to a non-tagged case, after logged in, users consult the design brief included in its detail page (see Fig. 4). In the next step, users select from the database a set of tagged cases (inspiring cases) that are the most related to the currently studied non-tagged case. To facilitate this selection, the platform provides users with an overview page of all tagged-cases represented in grid. In this

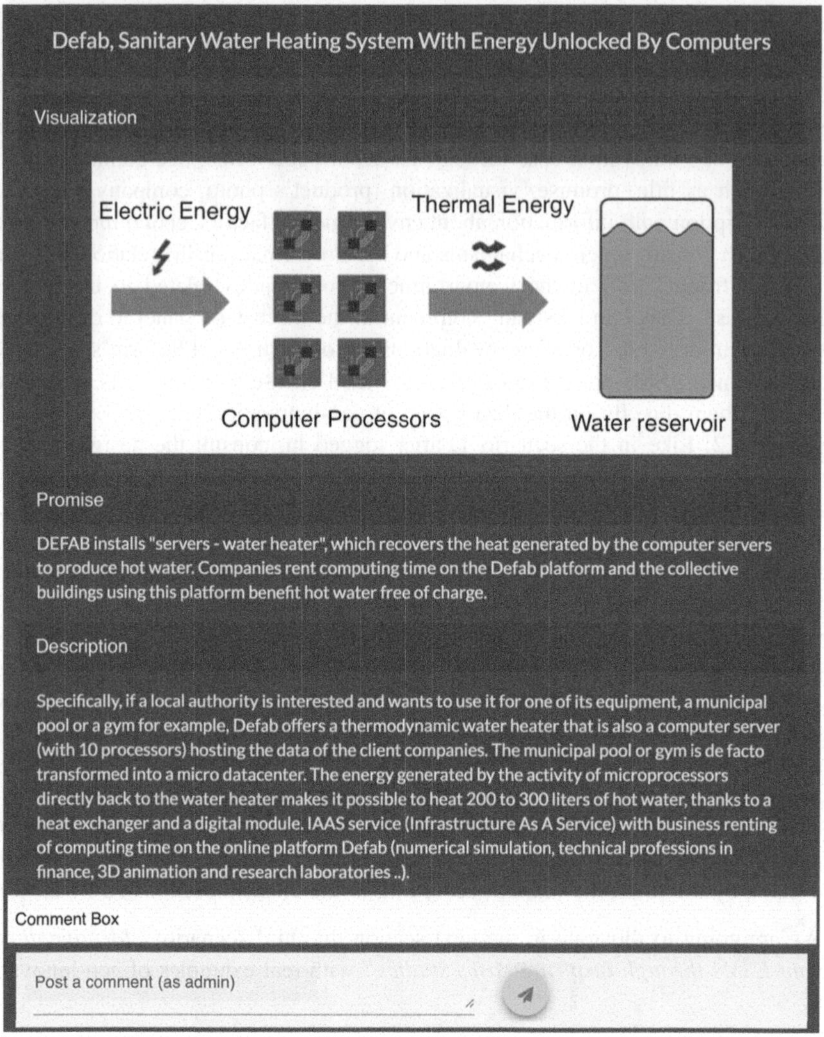

Fig. 4. Detail page of a particular eco-innovation case. Different fields are included: Visualization, Promise, Description. Users can leave their comments at the discussion panel.

grid, each cell contains case's title and a product's image or a logo of the company that the product belongs to. Users can refine tagged cases by associated mechanisms or categories. Tagged cases selected as inspiring cases are marked with a blue tick (see Fig. 5).

In the same time, users can consult all cases associated to a particular mechanism through the visualization panel. In the Fig. 6, orange circles represent cases that are linked to the mechanism *'Innovate by territorial resources'* as the best matching mechanism while green circles represent cases that are linked to the mechanism as the second most relevant mechanism.

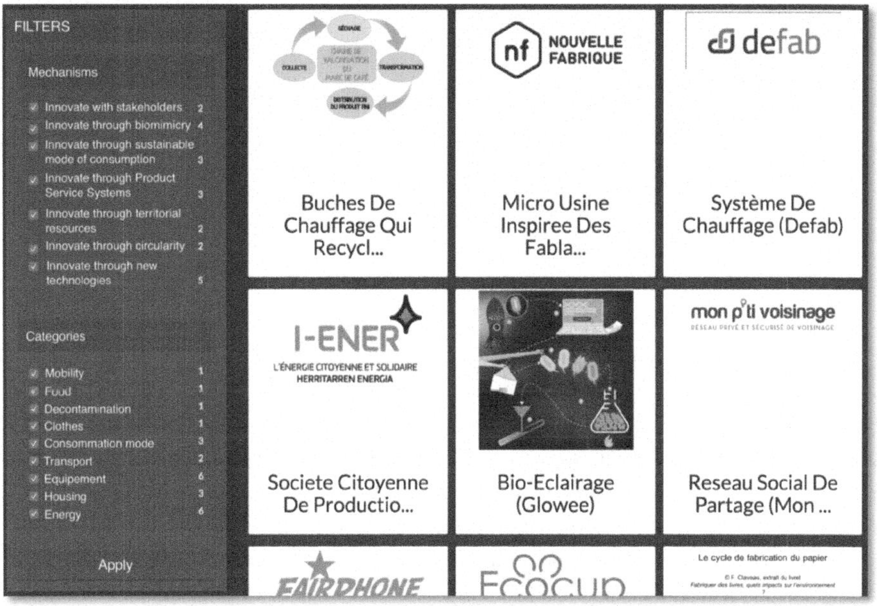

Fig. 5. Tagged cases are represented in grid and can be refined by mechanism or category. Users click on each cell to see detail page of corresponding eco-innovation case. Selected inspiring cases are marked with blue tick.

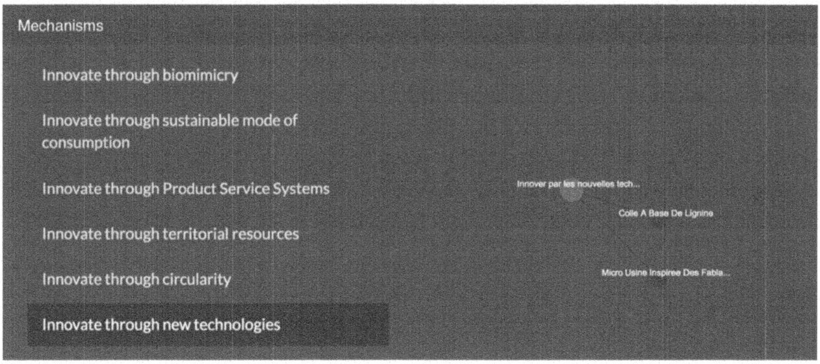

Fig. 6. Graphical representation of all tagged cases associated to the selected mechanism.

Platform's admin groups and classifies inspiring cases selected by all users into different clusters. Users then vote for the most relevant ESMs according to these clusters classification. Voting results are represented at the end of the detail page as we can see in Fig. 7.

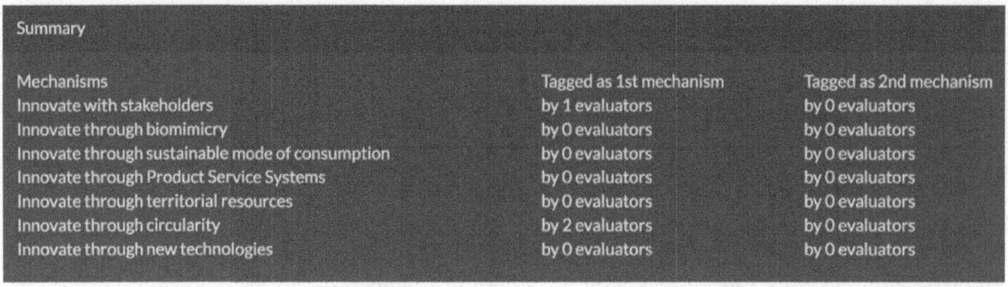
Summary

Mechanisms	Tagged as 1st mechanism	Tagged as 2nd mechanism
Innovate with stakeholders	by 1 evaluators	by 0 evaluators
Innovate through biomimicry	by 0 evaluators	by 0 evaluators
Innovate through sustainable mode of consumption	by 0 evaluators	by 0 evaluators
Innovate through Product Service Systems	by 0 evaluators	by 0 evaluators
Innovate through territorial resources	by 0 evaluators	by 0 evaluators
Innovate through circularity	by 2 evaluators	by 0 evaluators
Innovate through new technologies	by 0 evaluators	by 0 evaluators

Fig. 7. Summary of voting results for the most relevant ESMs.

5 Conclusions and Perspectives

Eco-ideation phase is crucial for any eco-innovation process. Seven ESMs have been proposed in the ALIENNOR project to facilitate the generation of useful ideas in this important phase. This paper presents ALIENNOR platform as a supportive tool for the identification of relevant mechanisms used in the eco-ideation phase.

The ALIENNOR platform provides necessary tools to support users in three different ESMs identification methods: *Identification of relevant ESMs through an analysis of the environmental problems from the design brief*; *Identification of relevant ESMs through a systematic reformulation of the design brief according to each ESM* and *Identification of the ESMs through inspiring case studies*. The main advantage of the platform is it provides an intuitive and user-friendly interface, implemented navigation, visualization and filters tools that help users to understanding quickly integrated eco-innovation cases and mechanisms. It enables also the collaboration of users coming from different disciplines in geographically distributed locations.

As perspective, some additional tools will be implemented such as the "**community module**" (to improve the collaboration among users). Besides, currently implemented visualizations need further testing to be enhanced.

Acknowledgement. The authors wish to thank the French National Research Agency (ANR) for its funding of the ALIENNOR project (project reference: ANR-15-CE10-0001).

References

1. Hofstra, N., Huisingh, D.: Eco-innovations characterized: a taxonomic classification of relationships between humans and nature. J. Clean. Prod. **66**, 459–468 (2014)
2. Tyl, B., Vallet, F., Pialot, O., Millet, D., Le Duigou, J., Graves, G.: The ESM approach: 8 mechanisms to efficiently support eco-ideation. In: Proceedings International Design Conference (2016)
3. Bocken, N.M.P., Allwood, J.M., Willey, A.R., King, J.M.H.: Development of an eco-ideation tool to identify stepwise greenhouse gas emissions reduction options for consumer goods. J. Clean. Prod. **19**, 1279–1287 (2011)
4. Brezet, H.: Ecodesign, a promising approach to sustainable production and consumption. U. N. Environ. Program UNEP (1997)

5. O'Hare, J., Dekoninck, E., Liang, H., Turnbull, A.: An empirical study of how innovation and the environment are considered in current engineering design practise. In: Takata, S., Umeda, Y. (eds.) Advances in Life Cycle Engineering for Sustainable Manufacturing Businesses, pp. 213–218. Springer, London (2007). https://doi.org/10.1007/978-1-84628-935-4_37
6. Kobayashi, H.: A systematic approach to eco-innovative product design based on life cycle planning. Adv. Eng. Inform. **20**, 113–125 (2006)
7. Mann, D., Jones, E.: Sustainable services & systems (3s) through systematic innovation methods. J. Sustain. Prod. Des. **2**, 131–139 (2002)
8. Yang, C.J., Chen, J.L.: Accelerating preliminary eco-innovation design for products that integrates case-based reasoning and TRIZ method. J. Clean. Prod. **19**, 998–1006 (2011)
9. Tyl, B.: Contribution of creativity in the eco-innovation process - proposition of an EcoASIT tool to foster the eco-ideation of sustainable systems, Theses, Université Sciences et Technologies - Bordeaux I (2011). https://tel.archives-ouvertes.fr/tel-00662434
10. Turner, S.: ASIT—a problem solving strategy for education and eco-friendly sustainable design. Int. J. Technol. Des. Educ. **19**, 221–235 (2009)
11. Bhamra, T.A., Lofthouse, V.A.: Information/inspiration: a web based sustainable design tool. In: DS 31 Proceedings of ICED 03 14th International Conference Engineering Design Stockholm (2003)
12. de Carvalho, M.A., Grillo, J.G.B., Tessari, R.K.: Methodology and software for new product ideation. Procedia Eng. **131**, 352–358 (2015)
13. Tyl, B., Pialot, O., Vallet, F., Millet, D.: Éco-innover à l'aide de méso Mécanismes de Stimulation d'Éco-idéation (MSE), Ref TIP695WEB - Éco-Concept. Innov. Responsab. (2017)

Preserving Design Intent in Feature-Based Parametric CAD Data Exchange

Jullius Cho(✉) and Detlef Gerhard

Vienna University of Technology, Vienna, Austria
{jullius.cho,detlef.gerhard}@tuwien.ac.at

Abstract. The proliferation of 3D technology on many different platforms has made CAD data exchange vital to industrial engineering innovation. The need to share and integrate CAD data, information, and knowledge amongst systems involved in product development has become an important requirement. This requirement is largely determined by a proper communication of design intent, which is usually expressed implicitly within CAD models or tacitly as experiential knowledge from domain experts. However, solutions for CAD data exchange are mostly restricted to the exchange of pure static shape information, restricting their applicability in many downstream processes. This paper suggests methods and strategies for preserving design intent in CAD data exchange. A test case is undertaken to demonstrate the idea and as evidenced in the results, the method proposed helps in capturing and preserving design intent.

Keywords: Engineering knowledge · Design intent · Data exchange
Geometric parameters

1 Introduction

With current trends of automation as well as the proliferation of 3D technology on many different platforms, the need to integrate and share CAD data, information and knowledge among systems involved in product development becomes an important requirement. Over time, computer-aided geometric design systems have evolved from modeling 3D solid models containing geometric and dimensioning information to models, which are embodiments of rich engineering data [1]. This data can be analyzed to deduce information and knowledge that is valuable across the entire life cycle of a product. This knowledge includes the degree of flexibility and the ease of alteration of a CAD model which strongly depend on the modeling methodology [2]. Further, the principles of geometric and solid modeling, feature-based parametric and variational modelling form the foundation of computer-aided design. In general, these support the creation, exchange, visualization, animation, interrogation, and annotation of digital models of physical objects [3, 4]. For greater productivity, easier maintenance, scalability, tractability, and efficiency, CAD model reusability is inevitable and therefore, a dire industrial need. This need is largely determined by a proper communication of design intent [5, 6], which is usually expressed implicitly within CAD models [7] or tacitly as experiential knowledge from domain experts. However, the inherent lack of consideration of design intent and associated parameters, constraints, rules etc. in

Published by Springer Nature Switzerland AG 2018.
P. Chiabert et al. (Eds.): PLM 2018, IFIP AICT 540, pp. 554–565, 2018.
https://doi.org/10.1007/978-3-030-01614-2_51

existing (standard) CAD data exchange systems greatly restricts their applicability in many downstream processes. There is therefore, a need to propagate design intent present in CAD models and in the minds of domain experts to a structured and reusable format.

This paper focuses on the preservation of design intent in feature-based CAD data exchange. Using automatic knowledge acquisition techniques coupled with a structured elicitation of experiential knowledge from experts [8, 9], design intent is captured in geometric parameters, constraints, rules. These are controlled by an inference mechanism based on functional requirements and experiential knowledge. This preservation mechanism is an integral part of a broader framework for the modeling of a high-level neutral representation of engineering knowledge for reuse in feature-based parametric modeling systems described in [8, 9]. A test case is presented to demonstrate the idea and as evidenced in the results, the methods proposed are effective for preserving design intent in CAD data translation and transformation.

2 Background

To set up the scene for this paper, we begin with a brief overview of a scenario where design intent is actively mined and used. One of our industrial partners produces high quality hinges and drawer pull-out systems for kitchens cabinet drawers and shutters. The company works very closely with carpenters, suppliers, and solution providers who are mostly software vendors. This symbiotic association is to provide each associate with the required data, information, and knowledge to be morphed into resources, products, and services to satisfy their individual and collective needs. One pertinent objective of the company is to provide these associates with the right engineering data at the right time to fulfill specific requirements. This multifaceted data therefore, has to be consistent, accommodating updates across all systems that use this data, and across all associates involved. The data requirements are generally broad, including data for visualization, product configuration, analysis, process planning, etc. Because these associates inevitably use different CAD, analysis, visualization and other downstream authoring tools, the data provided has to be translated and/or transformed to meet their needs. To maintain a single source of data, the data has to be presented in a generic way, independent of any underlying authoring system [3]. For the data to be complete and useful, it should be multifaceted, encompassing the static geometry as well as the parameters, rules, constraints and inference mechanism for data manipulation. This inference mechanism is what is referred to as the design intent as it enforces the intention(s) of the designer. With CAD systems and technologies abound, how can the design intent be preserved when translating and transforming CAD data?

The main approach for automatically extracting data in CAD models is explained in [8]. The approach uses applications programming interfaces (APIs) to interrogate CAD systems to gain access to CAD model data. In addition, the knowledge acquisition and formalization assistant (KAFA) enables the elicitation of experiential knowledge for integration into a "generic" XML CAD representation named XmlCad. While the APIs of CAD systems offer access to the internals of their systems, there still exist some problems. In their work "Data exchange of parametric CAD models using ISO 10303-

108" [10], Kim, Pratt, Iyer, and Sriram, outline the main problems observed in developing translators, which read and write information through the APIs of CAD systems. These include semantic differences, implicitly created information, design rationale, granularity of processing, numerical accuracy, and other implementation issues.

STEP has been established in the CAD/CAM environment for several years as a stable, neutral interface for data exchange including information of the entire life cycle of a product model [11–13]. STEP's biggest limitation however, is that, implementers do not implement the handling of features, constraints, or construction history, which are important in a commercial CAD system. After a data exchange, there is largely only information of the model that is presented with the description of B-Rep and contains no more engineering design intentions in the receiving CAD system [10, 13]. The editable representation (Erep) project proposed by Hoffmann and Juan [3] defines a neutral file format that specifies modeling features, constraints, and assembly models thereby providing a means of transmitting the indent of a design. The company Proficiency provides interoperability software for CAD/CAM/CAE systems based on The Universal Product Representation (UPR). The UPR was proposed by [14], exchanges parametric information to support the union of data types supported by commercial CAD systems. Another important aspect related to the transfer of design intent is that oftentimes the lack of tools for the visualization and analysis of relationships between features in CAD models presents an important barrier for understanding design intent [6]. Based on the researches described in [9] and [8], we describe the design intent preservation process by first of all, examining the basic structure of a CAD model.

3 CAD Structure

Parametric or variational modeling systems enable the designer to enforce design intent in a geometric model, which can be either a drawing, part or an assembly. Our approach to design intent preservation in CAD data exchange involves CAD parameters, constraints, and rules of logic, which define and shape solid models. To communicate our approach effectively, a brief discourse on the static CAD structure to be made dynamic is necessary. This includes assembly and/or part representation including topological and geometrical data. For the discussion in this paper however, it suffices to describe a simplified structure of a CAD model, paving the way to describing the preservation of the design intent.

A CAD model is either an assembly, part or drawing. In this write-up however, we will not talk about drawings and will assume that CAD models are assemblies. Using a top-bottom approach describing the level of granularity, a basic CAD model comprises an assembly, parts, features, and entities. The assembly is an amalgam of parts bound together by set of constraints. Parts consists of basic features such as sketches, fillets, chamfers, holes, etc. which in turn are built from basic entities. The basic entities include a point, a line segment, an arc, a parabola, an ellipse, and a spline, etc. The mathematical definitions (see Tables 1 and 2) and management of these units to preserve the shape and function of a modeled physical object constitutes design intent. In addition to the description, the composition of each component from its basic low-level entities to high-level representations are structured according to Fig. 1. Each entity has a unique identification and is classified according to its type, relating it to other entities. Furthermore, each entity has a geometric description as well as a clear definition of the parameters and relationships that rule coexistence in an assembly. This decomposition is used extensively in the MultiCAD API as shown in Figs. 2 and 3.

Table 1. Cartesian and parametric representation of basic CAD topological objects

Topological object	Cartesian representation	Parametric representation
Arc	$(x-h)^2+(y-k)^2=r^2$	$x=h+r*cos(t)$ $y=k+r*sin(t)$
Circle	$(x-h)^2+(y-k)^2=r^2$	$x=h+r*cos(t)$ $y=k+r*sin(t)$
Ellipse	$\frac{(x-h)^2}{a^2}+\frac{(y-k)}{b^2}=1$	$x=h+a*cos(t)$ $y=k+b*sin(t)$
Line segment	$\frac{x-x_0}{a}=\frac{y-y_0}{b}=\frac{z-z_0}{c}$	$x=a+\mu*r_x$ $y=b+\mu*r_y$ $z=c+\mu*r_z$
Parabola	$(x-h)^2=4p(y-k)$	$x=2at$ $y=-at^2$
	$(y-k)^2=4p(x-h)$	$x=h+at^2$ $y=k+2at$

3.1 Basic CAD Topological Objects

Feature-based design is based on functional elements or features having particular significance in the design [3]. This view can be extended to include basic entities, which can be used to drive the defined features. Table 1 shows possible mathematical representations of some basic CAD entities that are the main enablers of design intent. These basic topological objects can be represented mathematically either in Cartesian (rectangular) or parametric forms. These definitions lend themselves particularly useful for the definition of parameters, which can be changed in an authoring system to model the shape, relationships, and other properties of these entities. For example, a circle in a particular plane can be manipulated when the center point *(h, k)* and radius *(r)* are known. Also, an ellipse can be manipulated if the center *(h, k)* as well as the lengths of the major *(a)* and minor *(b)* axes are known.

3.2 Basic CAD Features

CAD features form the basis for feature-based modeling. As mentioned in Sect. 3.1, CAD features can be viewed as functional elements having particular significance in a design. For example, the basic CAD features shown in Table 2 correspond to functional elements, which from the feature-based modeling view can be represented conveniently by entities and parameters.

Table 2. Basic CAD features

Features	Composition
Extrusion	Sketch entities, extrusion distance
Hole	Circle, radius, depth
Chamfer	Radius, angle
Fillet	Radius, angle
Revolution	Axis, sketch
Face	Edge, vertex
Edge	Line segment
Body	Face, edge
Vertex	Point, line segment
Sketch	Arc, ellipse, parabola, line segment, point, spline

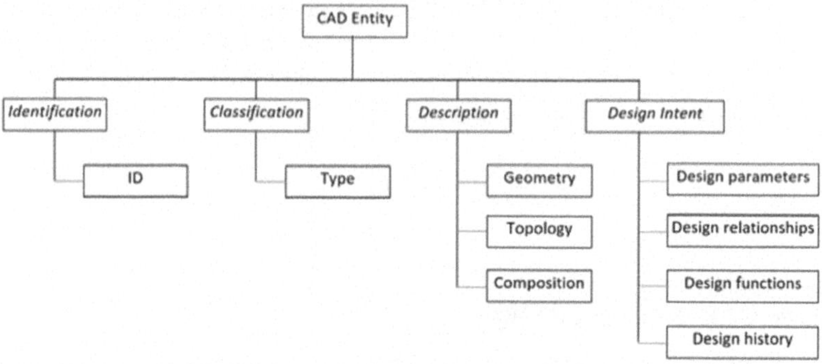

Fig. 1. CAD entity decomposition

3.3 CAD Constraints

Constraints are associations and restrictions applied CAD entities and features to define shape and functionality. Conceptually, constraints mate or align surfaces, curves and points, until the relative position of the part, with respect to the partial assembly, has been completely specified [3]. There are two general types of constraints: geometric constraints control the relationships of objects with respect to each other and dimensional constraints control the distance, length, angle, and radius values of objects. A list of some major constraints is shown in Table 3.

4 Design Intent Formalization for Feature-Based Parametric CAD Data Exchange

One of the initial stages of product development is requirement gathering. These requirements may be the result of business, mechanical, or manufacturing considerations. Integrating these requirements in specific tools to manage the behavior of a

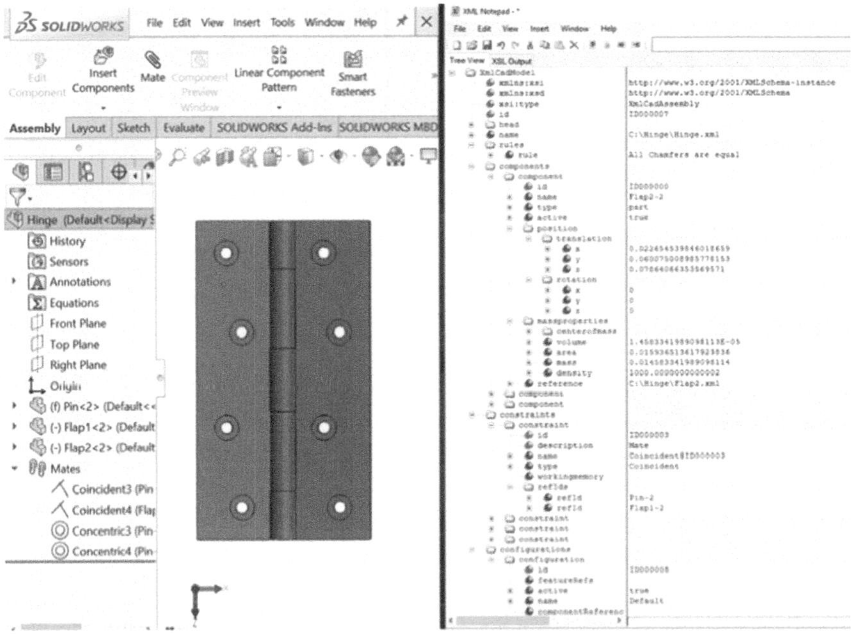

Fig. 2. Simple door hinge with two flaps and a pin in SolidWorks and partial view in XmlCad (XmlCad is a proprietary Software to represent and manipulate/edit CAD models represented in XML Format. The software is still under development)

model in a particular context is the challenge of capturing the designer's intent. Data translation and transformation entails conveying both the static representation of models in as well as the knowledge required to edit these models in the destination systems. Generally, design intent is a term used to describe how a model should be created and how it should behave when it is changed [5–7, 15, 16]. The essence of preserving the design intent in CAD data exchange is that there be a dynamic model available in the receiving system. This provides the user of the receiving CAD system with the possibility to modify the shape and other properties using the information (parameters, geometrical constraints, and features) exchanged during the transfer. This would enhance an imported model from a so-called "dumb model" to a so-called intelligent model" or "smart model" [11].

One approach is to provide the missing information held by current static models. This information can be divided into geometric definition, parameters, constraints, rules, and an inference mechanism. For this information on the designer's intentions to be effectively shared and used across systems, its representation should be independent of any system. Moreover, any changes made should seamlessly propagate to all systems that interface the data and data-manipulation instruction systems. Our approach to preserving design intent in CAD data exchange is to provide the missing information held by current static models. Using the MultiCAD API Manager proposed in [8] and the KAFA proposed in [17], engineering knowledge can be extracted from existing CAD models and experiential knowledge elicited from domain experts respectively.

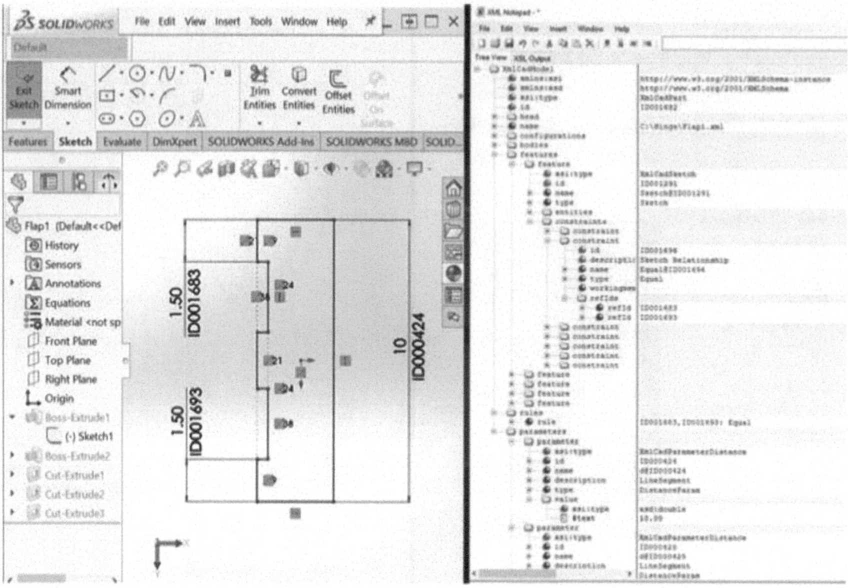

Fig. 3. Base sketch of a hinge flap in SolidWorks showing parameters and constraints of plus partial view in XmlCad

Table 3. Geometric and dimensional constraints

Constraints	Representation
Coincident	A coincident constraint between endpoints of lines/circles/arcs and other segments
Collinear	A collinear constraint between line segments
Concentric	A concentric circle or arc constraint
Equal	An equal-length curve constraint on lines and circles/arcs
Fix	A fixed-geometry constraint for line/circles/arcs
Horizontal	A horizontal constraint on line segments
Parallel	A parallel constraint between two line segments
Perpendicular	A perpendicular constraint between two lines or a line and circle/arc segment
Tangent	A tangent constraint between lines and circle/arcs or between two circles/arcs
Vertical	A vertical constraint on line segments

This information is then structured into an editable representation [8, 9] which can be interfaced by various authoring systems. This representation is both in XML and Json formats. It is best to describe the approach of preserving design intent in CAD data exchange by means of a succinct example. Before we expound on an example, let us first describe the main enablers of design intent: these include parameters (and variables), constraints, rules, and an inference mechanism.

4.1 Design Intent in Parameters, Variables, Constraints and Design Rules

In this paper, the concepts of parameters and variables will be kept simple. A parameter is assumed to be a constant in an equation describing a model while a variable is the way in which an attribute or quantity is represented. In CAD systems, parameter define the scope of variational entities such as the length of a line or the magnitude of an angle or a Boolean condition of a particular process or activity. Parameters and constraints can be used to determine the size, shape, and other properties of the different modeling elements [3]. Constraints are associations and restrictions applied to geometric entities to achieve a desired shape and/or function [18]. Constraints control the relationships of objects with respect to each other or control the distance or length and angle values of entities and features. Constraint based systems allow the position and size of geometric elements or entities to be specified using variables, allowing the designer to create a model which is easily modifiable during the design process. These constraints could be either at the assembly or at geometric levels. Some of the basic constraints include concentricity, tangentiality, parallelism, perpendicularity, etc.

Design rules can be either assignment operations assigning values to attributes, or a sequence of expressions comprising conditions and consequent actions if the conditions are evaluated to be true or false. [17] proposed the Knowledge Acquisition and Formalization Assistant (KAFA) which can be effectively used by experts to define explicit rules describing the functional relationships of entities and features in a CAD model. Rules are expressions of the form:

$$if < conditions > then < actions > \quad (1)$$

where conditions are expressions involving attributes and the logical connective *and* [19].

When variables representing parameters are given specific values depending on the designer's requirements, the inference mechanism reacts to the changes, executing instructions that manage the propagated effects of this change. In general, when rules are examined by the inference engine, actions are executed if the information supplied by the user satisfies or does not satisfy the conditions in the rules [20]. The inference mechanism involves assigning values to attributes, evaluating conditions, and checking to see if all of the conditions in a rule are satisfied or not. Two methods of inference are often in use - forward and backward chaining. Forward chaining is a top-down method which takes facts as they become available and attempts to draw conclusions leading to actions being executed while backward chaining is the reverse [19].

4.2 Example

Returning to the example, we show how a basic line segment (see Table 1) can by interrogated and all associated geometry, parameters, constraints, and rules safeguarded for reconstruction and manipulation in another CAD system or another appropriate authoring system. Let us assume the parametric equation of a line segment in three dimensions consists of a known point $p = (a, b, c)$, a direction vector $\vec{r} = (r_x, r_y, r_z)$

and a parameter μ which determines how long the line should be from the fixed point p in the direction $\vec{r}$. This equation can be written as follows:

$$\begin{pmatrix} x \\ y \\ z \end{pmatrix} = \begin{pmatrix} a \\ b \\ c \end{pmatrix} + \mu \begin{pmatrix} r_x \\ r_y \\ r_z \end{pmatrix} \tag{2}$$

where $x = a + \mu * r_x$, $y = b + \mu * r_y$ and $z = c + \mu * r_z$. For the sake of this discussion, it is assumed that the direction vector $\vec{r} = (r_x, r_y, r_z)$ is a unit direction vector. This means that it has a magnitude of one (1): $\left(|\overrightarrow{r}| = \sqrt{r_x^2 + r_y^2 + r_z^2} = 1\right)$. In this case, μ is a variable representing the length parameter that defines the length of the line starting from the fixed point $p = (a, b, c)$ and stretching in the direction of $\vec{r} = (r_x, r_y, r_z)$. In an appropriate authoring system, it should be possible to identify the length *parameter* (μ) through a unique identification. It should also be possible to define a *rule* which will assign a user defined length to the parameter, for example, $\mu = 10$. With this assignment, the length of the line will be increased or decreased to 10 units. *Constraints* attached to the line such as perpendicularity, parallelism, tangentiality etc. will be enforced, and associated constraints propagated accordingly to other entities and features by the *inference mechanism.* All these attributes can be mathematically defined using vector analysis. This procedure can be applied to other geometric entities such as an arc, ellipse, spline or to features such as the extrude length. Because each CAD or authoring system and downstream application does handle parameter allocation, rules, and constraints differently, it makes sense to manage the static geometry, parameters, constraints, rules, and inference mechanism differently from each other. There should however, be a system in place to trace and relate these to each other. Our approach is a persistent naming convention based on a prefix relating to the entity, the @ sign and a Globally Unique Identifier (Guid). For example, the Line Segment above will have an identification such as **d@ID419** that is unique in the whole representation. This unique identifier associated to the length parameter is used to trace this particular line in the database.

5 Test Case

To exemplify the aspects of design intent preservation described above, we provide a simple test case. A simple hinge consisting of three parts – two flaps and a pin holding the flaps together but providing coordinated movement so that a shutter attached could be moved as desired (see the left image in Fig. 2). While the three components have independent geometries, they are bound together by constraints, which enforce the coordinated movement. Figure 2 shows the hinge assembly in SolidWorks including components and constraints. The right side of Fig. 2 shows a partial view of the generic xml representation generated with the MultiCAD API Manager. The constraints are defined with a name, a type, a unique identification, and a description.

Figure 3 provides more detail by showing the parameter and constraints of one hinge flap. The image to the left shows the base sketch of the flap with three lengths annotated (ID001683, ID001693, and ID000424), two of which are equal and collinear (ID001683 and ID001693). The image to the right is a partial view of the XML representation of a hinge flap showing amongst other things features, parameters, and constraints.

6 Results, Discussions and Conclusion

Although design intent is a well-established required aspect in the context of CAD and downstream application systems, it remains a complex concept with different experts approaching it in different ways [5, 7, 10, 13, 15, 21]. Generally, the anticipated reaction of a CAD model to changes is commonly understood as design intent [5–7, 19]. The authoring tools as well as strategies employed do influence design intent communication. Recognizing the fact that tools and strategies do influence design intent communication, we are developing a set of optimized tools to cater for the various aspects of design intent preservation. With the MultiCAD API Manager, the KAFA and the neutral representation, we successfully extract and formalize CAD geometry, parameters, and constraints from existing CAD models. We further enrich this knowledge with experiential knowledge from experts thereby hoarding information that makes it possible for geometry to be editable in the target authoring system.

Different CAD systems represent and store different objects in different ways. However, the mathematics behind these objects are generally translatable. Using the principle of rewrites introduced in the UPR [14], it is possible to translate the data from the general representation to suit the requirements of particular CAD systems. Our editable representation takes two form – XML and Json – the two main data representation and transportation formats. With these, most authoring systems can parse and get the required data and information for further use.

Parametric or variational modeling systems have been developed to enable the designer to "capture design intent" in the geometric model of a part or assembly. Preserving the designer's intent during CAD translation or transformation is a challenge. This paper presented a test case, which shows how design intent propagated by the bearers geometric parameters, constraints, rules and an inference mechanism can be preserved during CAD exchange. The goal of the preservation is to enable the transmission of design intent information during a model transfer so that the model can be edited in the receiving system as though it had originally been created there.

In combination with the researches presented in [8, 9], the next stage in this project is to provide a complete software solution to manage engineering knowledge for reuse in different authoring applications.

References

1. Bordegoni, M., Rizzi, C. (eds.): Innovation in Product Design. Springer, London (2011). https://doi.org/10.1007/978-0-85729-775-4
2. Camba, J., Contero, M., Johnson, M., Company, P.: Extended 3D annotations as a new mechanism to explicitly communicate geometric design intent and increase CAD model reusability. Comput.-Aided Des. **57**, 61–73 (2014)
3. Hoffmann, C.M., Juan, R.: Erep An Editable High-Level Representation for Geometric Design and Analysis (1992)
4. Xu, X.: Integrating Advanced Computer-Aided Design, Manufacturing, and Numerical Control: Principles and Implementations. Information Science Reference, Hershey (2009)
5. Camba, J., Contero, M., Otey, J.: Explicit communication of geometric design intent in CAD: evaluating annotated models in the context of reusability. In: ASME 2014 International Design Engineering Technical Conferences and Computers and Information in Engineering Conference, p. V007T07A014 (2014)
6. Otey, J., Company, P., Contero, M., Camba, J.D.: Revisiting the design intent concept in the context of mechanical CAD education. Comput.-Aided Des. Appl. **15**(1), 47–60 (2018)
7. Li, M., Langbein, F.C., Martin, R.R.: Detecting design intent in approximate CAD models using symmetry. Comput.-Aided Des. **42**(3), 183–201 (2010)
8. Cho, J., Vosgien, T., Gerhard, D.: Engineering knowledge extraction for semantic interoperability between CAD, KBE and PLM systems. In: Ríos, J., Bernard, A., Bouras, A., Foufou, S. (eds.) PLM 2017. IAICT, vol. 517, pp. 568–579. Springer, Cham (2017). https://doi.org/10.1007/978-3-319-72905-3_50
9. Cho, J., Vosgien, T., Prante, T., Gerhard, D.: KBE-PLM integration schema for engineering knowledge re-use and design automation. In: Harik, R., Rivest, L., Bernard, A., Eynard, B., Bouras, A. (eds.) PLM 2016. IAICT, vol. 492, pp. 43–55. Springer, Cham (2016). https://doi.org/10.1007/978-3-319-54660-5_5
10. Kim, J., Pratt, M.J., Iyer, R., Sriram, R.: Data exchange of parametric CAD models using ISO 10303-108. NIST intergovernmental report. National Institute of Standards and Technology, Gaithersburg (2007)
11. Bondar, S., Shammaa, A., Stjepandic, J., Tashiro, K.: Advances in parameterized CAD feature translation. In: ISPE CE, pp. 615–624 (2015)
12. Maier, F., Stumptner, M.: Enhancements and ontological use of ISO-10303 (STEP) to support the exchange of parameterised product data models, pp. 433–440 (2007)
13. Pratt, M.J.: Extension of the standard ISO 10303 (STEP) for the exchange of parametric and variational CAD models. In: The Globalization of Manufacturing in the Digital Communications Era of the 21st Century: Innovation, Agility and the Virtual Enterprise, vol. 4. Springer, Heidelberg (1998)
14. Rappoport, A.: An architecture for universal CAD data exchange. In: Proceedings of the Eighth ACM Symposium on Solid Modeling and Applications, pp. 266–269 (2003)
15. Ault, H.K.: Using geometric constraints to capture design intent. J. Geom. Graph. **3**(1), 39–45 (1999)
16. Contero, M., Jeffrey, O., Pedro, C., Jorge, D.C.: A Review of the Design Intent Concept in the Context of CAD Model Quality Metrics, p. 10, July 2014
17. Gerhard, D., Lutz, C.: IT-based configuration and dimensioning of customer specific products – towards a framework for implementing knowledge based design assistant systems. In: DS 68-6 Proceedings of the 18th International Conference on Engineering Design, ICED 2011, Impacting Society through Engineering Design, vol. 6, Design Information and Knowledge, Lyngby/Copenhagen, Denmark, 15–19 August 2011 (2011)

18. Shah, J.J.: Designing with parametric CAD: classification and comparison of construction techniques. In: Kimura, F. (ed.) Geometric Modelling. ITIFIP, vol. 75, pp. 53–68. Springer, Boston, MA (2001). https://doi.org/10.1007/978-0-387-35490-3_4
19. Griffin, N.L., Lewis, F.D.: A rule-based inference engine which is optimal and VLSI implementable. In: IEEE International Workshop on Tools for Artificial Intelligence, Architectures, Languages and Algorithms, pp. 246–251 (1989)
20. Orsvärn, K., Axling, T.: The Tacton view of configuration tasks and engines. In: Workshop on Configuration, Sixteenth National Conference on Artificial Intelligence (AAAI 1999), pp. 127–130 (1999)
21. Piegl, L.A.: Knowledge-guided NURBS: principles and architecture. Comput.-Aided Des. Appl. **3**(6), 719–729 (2006)

Design of Self-assessment Tools to Measure Industry 4.0 Readiness. A Methodological Approach for Craftsmanship SMEs

R. Brozzi[1(✉)], R. D. D'Amico[1], G. Pasetti Monizza[1,2], C. Marcher[1], M. Riedl[1], and D. Matt[1,2]

[1] Fraunhofer Italia Research, Bolzano, Italy
riccardo.brozzi@fraunhofer.it
[2] Free University of Bolzano, Bolzano, Italy

Abstract. The ongoing transition to digitalization will inevitably require companies to shift their manufacturing processes towards the Industry 4.0 paradigm, to remain competitive on the market. An increasing number of companies worldwide are initiating integrated 4.0 solutions, catching up with this revolution in the very concept of production processes and the dynamics among producers, suppliers and end-users. SMEs will be particularly challenged to integrate IT and automation to gain market segments in an increasingly globalised playing-field. SMEs will either seize it by identifying opportunities and risks or succumb it. Against the background that there is no such a thing as a one-size-fits-all solution on the way to Industry 4.0, the self-assessment of firm-specific starting circumstances is an essential step prior to any digital implementation. However, the analysis of a diverse pool of existing online self-assessment tools demonstrated main application fields in the context of large companies. This paper will present a methodology developed to design self-assessment tools for Industry 4.0 readiness level, in the framework of two publicly funded EU projects, targeting small-scale craftsmanship companies in the manufacturing and construction sector. The results indicate the importance to scale existing tools to the specific framework conditions of SMEs as well as valuable approaches and concrete recommendations to consider during the conceptual and design phase.

Keywords: Industry 4.0 · Self-assessment tool · Craftsmanship SMEs

1 Introduction

Industry 4.0 will lead to significant changes in the way of conceiving production along the entire value chain ultimately requiring companies to adapt existing business strategies and models [1–3]. In general, a change towards better networking and more flexible working is projected, concerning both the work processes as well as the role of employees in the company [3, 4]. Through the introduction of Cyber-Physical Systems (CPS), which will be accompanied by Industry 4.0 (I4.0), employees and machines will, in future, work hand in hand on complex tasks. The emergence of such trends will

P. Chiabert et al. (Eds.): PLM 2018, IFIP AICT 540, pp. 566–578, 2018.
https://doi.org/10.1007/978-3-030-01614-2_52

require companies to tackle various challenges such as rethinking their production processes and dynamics along the entire supply chains, increasing their digitalization level as well as redefining the organization of tasks between humans and machines [5, 6]. Small- and medium-sized enterprises (SMEs) will be particularly challenged to adapt their current business strategies to I4.0, involving higher levels of industrial automation and information technologies. In fact, while several large companies have already anticipated the potential and risks of digitization and initiated innovation processes, on the other hand, SMEs are facing difficulties to adopt I4.0 solutions [7, 8]. SME specific challenges concern limited knowledge of I4.0 potential [9, 10], proper qualification of employees [11–13], lack of a comprehensive strategy [14], limited IT competences and technological knowledge [5, 7]. Hence especially in the starting phase, small companies need tailored external support to initiate innovation processes aimed at implementing I4.0 solutions [15]. To the extent that the focus of several companies in the near future will be oriented to I4.0, the assessment of their current willingness and ability to implement I4.0 solutions is compelling [16]. With respect to such an evidence, an increasing number of scholars claim a great need for a systematic approach to introduce I4.0 in enterprises respectively for a tool indicating the maturity level [17].

In the literature, several tools on this topic have been found, generally distinguishing between surveys such as self-assessment tools assessing the readiness [16, 18, 19] and maturity level [20–24] of firms toward radical technological and organisational changes. Schumacher et al. [23] consider differences in the development stage as a reason justifying the adequacy of either readiness or maturity assessment tools, for firms at initial and advanced stages of strategic planning respectively. However, further research and tools addressing this topic have been mainly tailored to the characteristics and needs of large companies. Against the background that differentiated approaches to foster innovation in large and small companies exist [25, 26], this paper will explore the research question whether existing self-assessment tools match appropriately the requirements of SMEs and can hence accurately assess their readiness toward I4.0. The identification of the current development stage of SMEs toward I4.0 is essential to promptly recognize market opportunities, derive adequate business and production strategies. Notably, Schumacher et al. [23] identified the need and developed new methods and tools to guide manufacturing companies aligning business strategies and operations. This paper, while affirming the validity of existing tools, attempted to scale the content and structure to the context and needs of SMEs. Furthermore, the approach employed to design a self-assessment tool tailored to the characteristics of small and medium craftsmanship enterprises will be presented. This entails, for instance, SMEs specific considerations which influenced the way in which questions were phrased, results displayed and communicated.

The paper is organised as follows. Following this introduction, the next section will provide a clear definition of the methods employed to derive a self-assessment tool tailored to the specific needs of small and medium craftsmanship companies. The results will firstly summarize the structure of the main existing self-assessment tools considered in the literature. Further analyses sampled the most recurring dimensions used across the selected self-assessment tools, providing a matching with current challenges SMEs should consider to this respect. Existing self-assessment tools were portrayed against number of dimensions and items to provide an overview of their respective complexity and enable their categorization. Finally, considering specific requirements of local craftsmanship companies, the resulting tailored self-assessment tool will be introduced and discussed with respect to previous scientific literature on the topic and useful recommendations for an effective design and presentation of results.

The proposed research provides local trade associations and regional business development agencies evidences on the design of tools assessing the industry 4.0-readiness particularly in case of small and medium craftsmanship companies. The further development and application of such tools can result in an improved understanding of SME's development goals in industry 4.0, as well as define measures for supporting technology and knowledge transfer at regional level through the collaboration of trade association, companies and research institutes. The approach and findings presented in this study will also feed the scientific debate on this topic of growing research interest for universities, applied research institutes and business consulting agencies.

2 Methodology

The methodology employed to scale existing self-assessment tools to the needs of small-scale craftsmanship companies has been structured in three stages. In the first stage, a comprehensive literature review both in German and English language was conducted to identify existing self-assessment tools evaluating the readiness- and maturity-levels of firms toward industry 4.0 and digitalisation. In the second stage, metrics to classify the collected self-assessment tools were defined in terms of number of dimensions and item considered to derive a measure of their overall level of complexity (Fig. 1). Dimensions were considered expression of the overall degree of detail, i.e. higher number of dimensions accounts for a lower detail of the tool. This relation proved reasonable since a high amount of dimensions results in tools dealing with the assessment of several different areas of the company, without a detailed analysis of individual areas. Conversely, a lower amount of dimensions results in tools specifically assessing certain areas of the company, with a relatively high level of detail. Collected self-assessment tools were portrayed according to defined metrics. Number of items, instead, stand for the general complexity of the tool. In the literature items are also named as "maturity items" [23] referring to fields of analysis (e.g. Data security) within a specific dimension (e.g. Production). Tools with a high number of items, indeed, are time consuming. Considering the challenges facing SMEs identified in the literature review, in the third stage, a list of potential dimensions and items was created out of which the authors designed a self-assessment tool for industry 4.0 specifically tailored to the needs of craftsmen. Figure 1 shows the two-axis diagram, where the horizontal axis identifies the dimensions, while the vertical one identifies the items. The area of the diagram can be split in 4 parts: (i) *specific*, few dimensions and high number of items. Tools in this area are designed for a specific kind of recipients, high degree of detail identified by the number of dimensions and deep analysis identified by the number of items. (ii) *Comprehensive*, high number of items and dimensions. Tools in this area are addressed to a general and wide comprehension of the recipients thanks to the high number of items spread in all dimensions. (iii) *General*, few items and high number of dimensions. Tools in this area have a generic approach, covering several dimensions with few items, a fast and generic tool. (iv) *Selective*, few dimensions and few items.

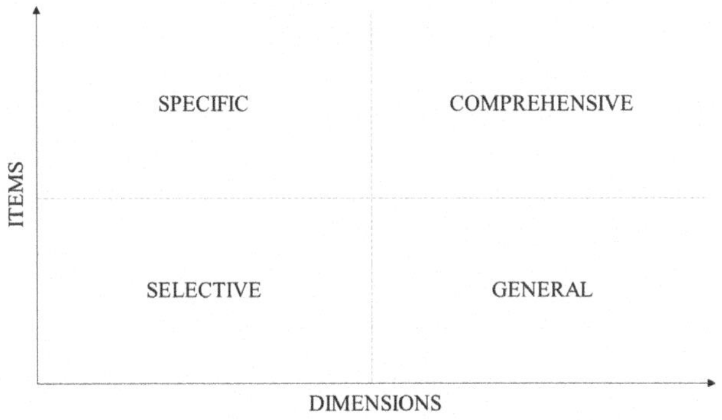

Fig. 1. Metrics analysis of the complexity of self-assessments

3 Results

3.1 Literature Review

The primary focus of the literature review targeted industry 4.0 tools assessing the readiness of companies toward digitalisation and I4.0. The literature review was conducted both for I4.0 readiness as well as for digital maturity models. Schumacher et al. [23] notably clarified the difference between readiness and maturity in the matter that *"readiness assessment takes place before engaging in the maturing process whereas maturity assessment aims for capturing the as-it-is state whilst the maturing process"*. Although such models have different characteristics and degrees of complexity [27], certain structures such as dimensions and items are recurrent. Dimensions can be considered process areas [27] namely aspects within the company to be assessed such as IT-Security, production processes and organisation. Items are detailed parts of each dimension to be assessed individually with respect to digitalisation. The latter case refers, for instance, to items such as implemented technologies, innovation management with respect to dimension such as organisation. After the exclusion of works that did not portray a necessary degree of detail of the number of dimensions and items, a total amount of 7 tools remained. These are characterized by a large variation with respect to both the number of dimensions and items (Table 1).

The existing maturity and readiness assessment tools range from 3 to 9 and from 7 to 62 in terms of dimensions and items respectively. Out of the 10 tools collected, 6 of them specifically targeted the assessment of the maturity of companies. The collected tools show a high degree of applicability across different sectors while scarce differentiation exists for SMEs and craftsmanship companies. Although not designed as maturity or readiness assessment tool, the "Checklist for process digitalisation" specifically targets craftsmen companies and comprises 9 dimensions and 63 items mainly composed of open text questions [28]. The mode of visualisation of results is not provided in detail. A similar example, also not specifically addressing industry 4.0 readiness level, is represented by the "Need-Analysis for Digital Craftsman" consisting of a questionnaire intended to provide craftsman businesses with information about the degree of digitisation in their company and potential for further development [28]. A study conducted by Telekom and techconsult, developed a digitalisation index considering the following dimensions: IT-Security, business model, customer relations, productivity [29]. This tool foresees the possibility to indicate whether the user belongs to a craftsmen company and access to survey to SMEs is not excluded. For such reasons, the Digitalisation index presents a suitable structure for the assessment of craftsmanship companies with respect to digitalisation.

Table 1. Existing self-assessment tools.

Self-assessment	Developer	Structure and design
IMPULS – Industrie 4.0 Readiness	VDMA, RWTH Aachen, IW Consult	6 dimensions, including 18 items
Industry 4.0 – Digital Operations Self-assessment	PricewaterhouseCoopers	6 dimensions, including 33 items
Benchmarking Readiness I4.0	Fraunhofer ISI	3 dimensions, including 9 items
I4.0 Reifegradmodell	FH-Oberösterreich	3 dimensions, including 13 items
I4.0 Maturity Model	Fraunhofer Austria; Vienna University of Technology	9 dimensions, including 62 items
The Digital Maturity Model 4.0	Forrester Research	4 dimensions, including 28 items
The Digital Maturity Check	EY	7 dimensions, including 14 items
Achieving Digital Maturity	Deloitte	5 dimensions, including 35 items
Digitalisation Index	Telekom-techconsult	4 dimensions, including 56 items
Digital Maturity Assessment Test	Ericsson	7 dimensions, including 7 items

An emerging limit of such a tool is the scarce focus on industry 4.0, particularly compared to another valid conceptual tool for SMEs maturity assessment, namely the I4.0 Maturity Model [23]. Against this background, Table 2 provides an overview of specific challenges SMEs and related craftsmanship companies face with respect to frequently used dimensions of selected assessment tools. In fact, craftsmanship companies are potential profiteers of the digitalization [29] while facing analogous challenges of SMEs toward I4.0 and having at disposal few appropriate tools measuring their readiness and maturity levels. Besides relatively low number of employees and revenue level, making the majority of craftsman business belonging to SMEs, other aspects which need to be considered while developing self-assessment tools, characterize the craftsmanship sector, such as the predominant local structure of operations, limited technological production endowments and inseparable ownership and management structure [30] i.e. the owner acts simultaneously as operator of the company.

Table 2. Self-assessment dimensions and related challenges to consider for SMEs

Dimension	SMEs challenges	Source
Products and services	Need to consider technology intelligence in product engineering process	[31]
Customer relation	Challenges along the entire supply chain	[6, 32]
Organisation/Knowledge Management/Innovation approach	Scarce adoption of knowledge management practices	[33]
Strategy/Leadership/Roadmap	lack of a strategy, roadmap, business model to I4.0	[14, 34, 35]
Production	lack of knowledge regarding the possibility and potential of using the current technology	[36]
IT-Security/Infrastructure	Improving existing IT infrastructure proved costly for SMEs	[37]
Employees	Proper qualification of employees required. Limited IT competence and knowledge	[5, 7, 38, 39]
Ecosystem/Digital business enablement	Expected frequent recourse to external expertise	[14]
Legal and regulatory issue	Emerging legal challenges and risks not yet fully tackled. Legal uncertainty	[14, 40]

Further analysis detected specific elements not fully considering SMEs as potential users of selected assessment tools. The well-designed tool developed by PriceWaterhouseCoopers to assess industry 4.0-readiness, for instance, does not permit to differentiate between small, medium and large enterprises, setting as the lowest annual revenue option a general value smaller than 100 Mio. Business processes may also differ substantially between SMEs and large companies, portraying questions about the use of application software such as ERP, MES, and CRM as inadequate [5] which are often mentioned in different tools. Lower emphasis should be devoted to leadership assessment considering the relatively simple structures recurring in craftsmanship companies.

On the base of the challenges and the insights discussed during expert interviews with representatives of the local craftsmen association, the following requirements for the design of the tool were also collected:

- Use of language avoiding too technical terms/concepts to enable users with limited knowledge of Industry 4.0 to complete the survey. Structure of the tool should be simple and limited compilation time required.

- Focus should regard current level of digitalisation under different perspectives (to assess readiness for digital transformation) and expected level in the future.
- Besides deriving digital level of companies, indication on application fields and typology of support required by research institutions and trade association should be assessed.

3.2 Analysis of the Self-assessment Tools Structures

On the base of the metrics defined in the methodology, the different assessment tools were portrayed in a chart against the individual number of dimensions and items used, as illustrated in Fig. 2. Most of the assessment tools considered occupy the bottom right area i.e. tools offering a general overview across different process areas.

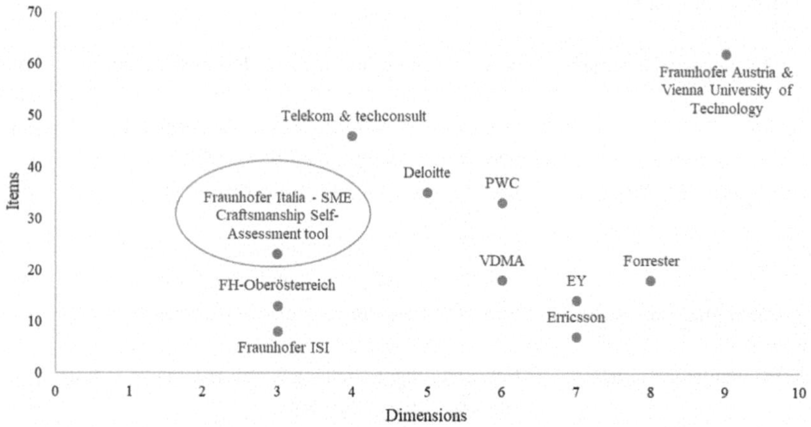

Fig. 2. Scatterplot items against dimensions in selected self-assessment tools.

The I4.0 Maturity Model developed by Fraunhofer Austria and the Vienna University of Technology positions itself on the upper right namely exhibiting a relatively high number of both items and dimensions. The structure and level of detail of this tool correspond to the comprehensiveness that tools encompassed within this area should exhibit. Remaining tools considered covered the bottom right area, expression of tools designed specifically on selected process areas with a relatively low level of detail of items foreseen. The characteristics of our tool developed for assessing SME Craftsmanship companies aimed at exhibiting a selective orientation. This is justified by the requirements previously identified for SME craftsmanship companies and particularly the need of simple structures enabling high participation of users in the compilation. Compared to the existing tools in this area, the analysis suggested sufficient room to deepen the assessment including additional items in the evaluation, without altering the selective orientation of the tool. In this regard, the tool acquires a relatively higher degree of accuracy, without assuming the complex structure that specific tool may entail.

3.3 Definition of the Self-assessment for Craftsmen Companies

After having collected and defined categories in terms of characteristics of the individual self-assessment tools, together with the consideration of SMEs specific challenges in approaching digital transformation projects, the authors designed the structure of a self-assessment tool targeting SME craftsmanship companies (Table 3).

Table 3. Structure of SME craftsmanship self-assessment tool

Dimension	Item	Assessment
Production and operations	Use of digital devices in the company	•
	Purpose to use the internet	•
	Quality of internet connection	•
	Data security	•
	Distribution and typology of sales channels	•
	Flexibility in producing products/offering services	•
	Degree of digitalization of work processes	•
	Perceived importance of new technologies	•
	Use of software to analyse and collect data	•
	Importance and utilization of collected data	•
	Use of technologies related to I4.0	•
Digitalisation	Perception of the trend digitalisation	•
	Level of knowledge regarding I4.0	•
	Perceived importance of I4.0 for the company	•
	Expected impact of I4.0 (company organisation)	•
	Expected impact of I4.0 (competition, market demand)	•
	Perceived advantages of I4.0	
	Perceived challenges of I4.0	
	Capabilities and qualifications of employees	•
	Allocated resources for digitalization (EUR)	
Ecosystem	Collaboration with other institutions on I4.0 projects	•
	Perceived assistance provided by supporting institutions	
	Application field in which support to SMEs is required	

• Values considered to calculate average score determining the profile and attitude of users

The number of dimensions was limited to 3 (*Production and operations, Digitalisation, Ecosystem*) with a total of 23 items. The evaluation of each item was based on a Likert-scale ranging from 1 to 5 similarly to other tools. Items not included in the calculation were those considering the advantages and disadvantages of I4.0, the allocated resources for digitalisation, as well as the degree of collaboration with other institutions. Likewise, the item to assess the perception of support by institutions were excluded from the average calculation. While some tools considered a standard Likert-scale [23], others required a double compilation in terms of "Relevance for the firm" and "Realization in the firm" [29], the present self-assessment tool considered the approach proposed by PriceWaterhouseCooper in which user should state their perception in terms of the "current state" of the company and the "target state" the company aims to achieve in 5 years [18]. In the SME Craftsmanship Self-Assessment tool, the reference time-frames in which users should evaluate their digital level are named "current" and "expected" level of digitalisation. The scale for each item was distributed along 5 levels, the descriptions of the lowest and the highest ranks were described with individual examples depending on the item topic Table 4.

Table 4. Example of individual Likert-scale definition

Item: To what extent are digital devices used in your company?
Level 1: *The company uses mainly PCs, laptops, printers and fax machines. New technologies are not being used.*
Level 5: *In addition to traditional devices such as PCs, laptops and printers, tablets, mobile phones (such as smartphones) and servers are used. The first 3D printers, barcode scanners or smart glasses are also available.*

The evaluation process considers separately the scores resulting from the average of values assigned as perception of the current state and those referring to the expected state to achieve in the future (Fig. 3).

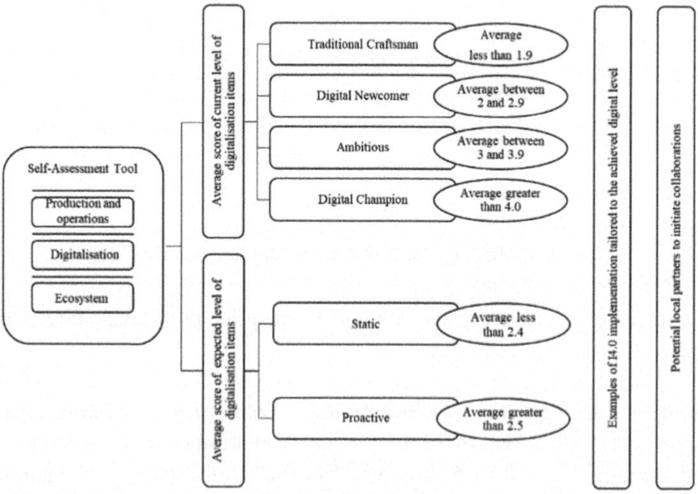

Fig. 3. Graphical representation self-assessment evaluation process

The "current" average values serve to determine one of four levels of predetermined profiles of craftsman namely the *Traditional Craftsman*, the *Digital Newcomer*, *Ambitious* and the *Digital Champion*. The individual profile achieved according to the average score, is shown immediately after completion of the assessment and offers guidance and recommendations for digital actions from same or similar sector of the respondent. The "expected" average score serves to portray the attitude of responding craftsmen and thus measures the willingness to initiate projects of I4.0 applications in the company. The two resulting attitudes, depending on the average expected score achieved, can vary from *Static* to *Proactive*. Description of the resulting profile and attitude achieved are presented, together with examples of I4.0 implementation in companies operating in the same sector of the responding user and potential partners at local level supporting the company in creating a network to initiate concrete collaborations. In addition to the proposed scheme, the tool provides users with the possibility to display definitions (in form of a brief dictionary statement) for several technologies and I4.0 concepts. The visualization will consist of graphs, generated from the average values corresponding to the three dimensions, differentiating for the current and future digital level of the company.

4 Discussion and Conclusions

4.1 Results Summary

The present research is aimed at presenting the approach used to design a self-assessment tool to measure industry 4.0 readiness of SMEs and particularly those of craftsmanship nature. The analysis demonstrated the need to develop self-assessment tools specifically targeting SMEs, since existing tools may not have an adequate focus on the several challenges such entities face. However, the authors also acknowledge an increasing interest to scale existing tools to the requirements of SMEs, particularly from craftsmanship trade unions, national development agencies and research centres. While considering adaptation of the content (mainly scaled on the structure and level of operations), tools addressing SMEs should also foresee consideration of structure and design. To confer a relatively simple structure to the tool, as also requirements outlined, the selection of dimensions and items - with respect to Fig. 1 - permitted to position the SME Craftsmanship Self-Assessment encompassing selective and specific features, avoiding a rather general and too detailed structure. General structures may not persuade users from SMEs about their utility, while time-consuming tools may not be fully considered. Furthermore, the use of simple wording in describing dimensions and items, possibility to visualise the definition of certain topics or technology, aided guidance on metrics proposed to measure readiness are considered means facilitating access of SMEs to the self-assessment tool. Furthermore, practical examples related to the achieved level of readiness including the description of real case technological implementation for a potential advancement are supposed to provide SMEs both an overview of their digital level, as well as insights on future steps to consider. Such examples were designed to be displayed according to the sector of the user, to stimulate interest and motivation.

4.2 Future Work

The presented findings result from the activities carried out in the framework of two publicly funded projects from the European Regional Development Fund, namely I4.0 Roadmap (B53D07000290008) and CRAFTech (B56G17000000008). The latter project recently released a free online survey encompassing the dimensions and items, described in the proposed SME Craftmanship Self-Assessment. The analysis of results derived from the assessment completed by representatives of local companies represents a reasonable follow up of the present research. It will aim at presenting the digital readiness level of local craftsman companies as well as potential application fields and typology of support required to support SMEs along the digital transformation. On the base of the feedback from respondents on the structure and contents of selected dimensions and items, further research will attempt determining the level of compliance of the SME Craftmanship Self-Assessment tool and related design features (such as concrete examples, glossary function, etc.) to the specific requirements of SMEs. In this regard, further methods and concepts need to be developed, to derive useful information from users contributing to the continuous improvement of such tools for SMEs. Furthermore, future works should encompass the analysis of additional aspects indicating internal and external readiness level, such as the willingness to share information and awareness of data security protocols.

References

1. MacDougall, W.: Industrie 4.0 - Smart Manufacturing for the Future. Trade & Invest, Berlin (2014)
2. Peßl, E., Ortner, W., Schweiger, J.: Industrie 4.0 - Informationstechnologie verschmilzt mit Produktion. Prod. Manag. **19**(1), 59–62 (2014)
3. Spath, D., Ganschar, O., Gerlach, S., Hämmerle, M., Krause, T., Schlund, S.: Produktionsarbeit der Zukunft - Industrie 4.0. Fraunhofer IAO (Institut für Arbeitwirtschaft und Organisation), Stuttgard (2013)
4. Rauch, E., Dallasega, P., Matt, D.: Critical factors for introducing lean product development to small and medium sized enterprises in Italy. Elsevier. Procedia CIRP **60**, 362–367 (2017)
5. Gabriel, M., Pessl, E.: Industry 4.0 and suitability impacts. Critical discussion of suitability aspects with a special focus on future of work and ecological consequences. Ann. Faculty Eng. Hunedoara – Int. J. Eng. **14**(2), 131–136 (2016)
6. Matt, D., Rauch, E.: Chancen zur Bewältigung des Fachkräftemangels in KMU durch Urbane Produktion von morgen. In: Kersten, W., Koller, H., Lödding, H. (eds.) Industrie 4.0 Wie intelligente Vernetzung und kognitive Systeme unsere Arbeit verändern, Berlin, pp. 155–176 (2014)
7. Dassisti, M., et al.: Industry 4.0 paradigm: the viewpoint of the small and medium enterprises. In: 7th International Conference on Information Society and Technology, Kopaonik, Serbia, pp. 50–54 (2017)
8. Schmeiss, J., Dopfer, M.: Die digitale Geschäftsmodell-Transformation - Chancen, Risiken und Strategien für den deutschen Mittelstand. In: Mittelstand-Digital. Wissenschaft trifft Praxis. Digitale Geschäftsmodelle: Erfolgsfaktoren und Praxisbeispiele, pp. 7–13. Bad Honnef: Begleitforschung Mittelstand-Digital WIK (2017)

9. Wischmann, S., Wangler, L., Botthof, A.: Industrie 4.0: Volks- und betriebswirtschaftliche Faktoren für den Standort Deutschland (2015)
10. Sommer, L.: Industrial revolution - Industry 4.0: are German manufacturing SMEs the first victims of this revolution? J. Industr. Eng. Manag. **8**(5), 12–32 (2015)
11. Universität Bremen: Industrie 4.0 - Auswirkungen auf Aus- und Weiterbildung in der M+E Industrie. Die bayerischen Metall- und Elektro-Arbeitgeber (2016)
12. PricewaterhouseCoopers: Industry 4.0: Building the Digital Enterprise (2016)
13. McKinsey&Company: Industry 4.0 how to navigate Digitization of the manufacturing sector. McKinsey Digital (2015)
14. Schröder, C.: The Challenges of Industry 4.0 for Small and Medium-Sized Enterprises (2016)
15. Kochan, D., Miksche, R.: Advanced manufacturing and Industrie 4.0 for SME. Newtech. In: 5th International Conference on Advanced Manufacturing Engineering and Technologies (2017)
16. Lichtblau, K., et al.: Industrie 4.0 – Readiness. Stiftung für den Maschinenbau, den Anlagenbau und die Informationstechnik (VDMA), Aachen, Köln (2015)
17. Pessl, E., Sorko, S., Mayer, B.: Roadmap Industry 4.0 - implementation guideline for enterprises. Int. J. Sci. Technol. Soc. **5**(6), 193–202 (2017)
18. PricewaterhouseCoopers: Industry 4.0 - Digital Operations Self-assessment (2016)
19. Fraunhofer ISI: Internet-based self-assessment instrument Industrie 4.0 for Baden-Württemberg. Fraunhofer-Gesellschaft (2015). https://www.isi.fraunhofer.de/. Accessed 10 Mar 2018
20. Kane, G.C., Palmer, D., Phillips, A.N., Kiron, D., Buckley, N.: Achieving digital maturity. Adapting your company to a changing world. MISSloan Manag. Rev. Deloitte Univ. Press (2017)
21. Ernst & Young: Digital Maturity Check. https://digitalmaturitycheck.ey.com/. Accessed 10 Mar 2018
22. Forrester Research: The Digital Maturity Model 4.0 (2016)
23. Schumacher, A., Erol, S., Sihn, W.: A maturity model for assessing Industry 4.0 readiness and maturity of manufacturing enterprises. Procedia CIRP **52**, 161–166 (2016)
24. Schuh, G., Anderl, R., Gausemeier, J., ten Hompel, M., Wahlster, W.: Industrie 4.0 Maturity Index. Managing the Digital Transformation. Herbert Utz Verlag, Munich (2017)
25. Rammer, C., Frietsch, R.: Global Champions und Hidden Champions: Internationale Konzerne und KMU im Innovationswettbewerb. Fraunhofer ISI, Karlsruhe (2015)
26. Spithoven, A., Vanhaverbeke, W., Roijakkers, N.: Open innovation practices in SMEs and large enterprises. Small Bus. Econ. **41**(3), 537–562 (2013)
27. De Carolis, A., Macchi, M., Kulvatunyou, B., Brundage, M.P., Terzi, S.: Maturity models and tools for enabling smart manufacturing systems: comparison and reflections for future developments. In: Ríos, J., Bernard, A., Bouras, A., Foufou, S. (eds.) PLM 2017. IAICT, vol. 517, pp. 23–35. Springer, Cham (2017). https://doi.org/10.1007/978-3-319-72905-3_3
28. Handwerkskammer Koblenz-Kompetenzzentrum Digitales Handwerk Schaufenster West, 10 May 2017. https://handwerkdigital.de/. Accessed 8 Mar 2018
29. Deutsche Telekom: Der digitale Status Quo im Handwerk (2016)
30. Cr@ftsman Project: Report on the situation of craftsmanship in Europe (2011)
31. Placzek, M., Eberling, C., Gausemeier, J.: Conception of a knowledge management system for technologies. In: International Association for Management Technology (IAMOT 2015) (2015)
32. Pfohl, H.-C., Yashi, B., Kurnaz, T.: The impact of Industry 4.0 on the supply chain. In: Hamburg International Conference on Logistics (2015)

33. Cerchione, R., Esposito, E.: Using knowledge management systems: a taxonomy os SME strategies. Int. J. Inf. Manag. **37**(1B), 1551–1562 (2017)
34. Rudtsch, V., Gausemeier, J., Gesing, J., Mittag, T., Peter, S.: Pattern-based business model development for cyber-physical production systems. Procedia CIRP **25**, 313–319 (2014)
35. Kagermann, H., Wahlster, W.: Recommendations for implementing the strategic initiative Industrie 4.0. acatech - National Academy of Science and Engineering (2013)
36. Andulkar, M., Le, D.T., Berger, U.: A multi-case study on Industry 4.0 for SME's in Brandenburg, Germany. In: Proceedings of the 51st Hawaii International Conference on System Sciences, Hawaii (2018)
37. Deloitte: Challenges and solutions for the digital transformation and use of exponential technologies, Zurich (2015)
38. Bauer, W., Schlund, S., Marrenbach, D., Ganshar, O.: Industrie 4.0 - Volkswirtschaftliches Potenzial für Deutschland, Bundesverband Informationswirtschaft Telekommunikation und neue Medien e. V. (2014)
39. Grass, K., Weber, E.: EU 4.0 - the debate on digitalisation and the labour market in Europe. Institute for Employment Research of the Federal Employment Agency (2016)
40. Plöger, I., Sahl, J.C., Willems, H., Bräutigam, P., Hinerasky, C., Klindt, T.: Industrie 4.0 – legal challenges of digitalisation. An input for the public debate. Bundesverband der Deutschen Industrie e. V., Berlin (2015)

The Methodological Challenges Related to Assess the Outcomes of Knowledge Management Initiatives: The Case of Communities of Practice

Patrick Mbassegue[1] and Mickaël Gardoni[2(✉)]

[1] Ecole Polytechnique, 2900 Bd Edouard Montpetit, Montreal H3T1J4, Canada
patrick.mbassegue@polymtl.ca
[2] Ecole de Technologie Supérieure,
1100 Notre-Dame, Montreal H3C1K3, Canada
mickael.gardoni@etsmtl.ca

Abstract. In any organizational project where the use of limited resources represents a challenge, it's necessary to assess the outcomes generated. The methodological approach on how to assess outcomes reveals many questions, namely: What is the best way to do so? What dimensions to assess? From what criteria? How to estimate them? In the case of communities of practice (CoP), these questions become accurate. Indeed, in the case of Communities of Practice, the participants represent the cornerstone of the project because there are the ones who generate knowledge. So to assess outcomes generated by CoP within an organization, it's necessary to identify an adapted methodological frame which will allow to take into account the critical aspects of the CoP and the user perspective. Our proposal aims to present a hybrid path (qualitative-quantitative) in order to minimize the limits and uplift advantages related to both approaches. The addition of these two approaches must generate a more stronger one and a better reliability of concept. For that purpose, the structure of the article concerns the following aspects: the context of knowledge management initiatives and particularly communities of practice; notions of assessment and outcomes; the current methodologies used to assess the outcomes of the CoP as well as their limits; the criteria to be respected for the choice as a strong methodology; the choice of a new approach (qualitative-quantitative) and its future application in the CoP.

Keywords: Communities of practice · Mixed methodology · Assessment

1 The Context of Knowledge Management (KM), Communities of Practice (CoP) and Product Lifecycle Management (PLM)

1.1 The Link Between Knowledge Management (KM) and PLM

PLM and KM are two frameworks that are improving organizational performance. PLM is about managing and optimizing every step of product development across the

Published by Springer Nature Switzerland AG 2018.
P. Chiabert et al. (Eds.): PLM 2018, IFIP AICT 540, pp. 579–589, 2018.
https://doi.org/10.1007/978-3-030-01614-2_53

entire lifecycle. In this sense, PLM can generate effective solutions that contribute to value creation. In addition, all these activities and solutions are based on knowledge management. For example, knowing how to manage knowledge make PLM enabled activities and solutions efficient. So, by establishing KM practices that promote organizational performance, PLM activities are also being improved.

Several authors establish the need to associate PLM and KM [1–3]. For McMahon et al. [4], KM is an enabler of PLM and vice versa because the activities of codification, dissemination, sharing, re-use and creation of knowledge underlie all PLM activities. As well as the lessons learned from PLM activities enrich the stock of knowledge available in the organization [5]. On this basis, we believe that KM and PLM are efficient by integrating the activities of the two frameworks (Fig. 1).

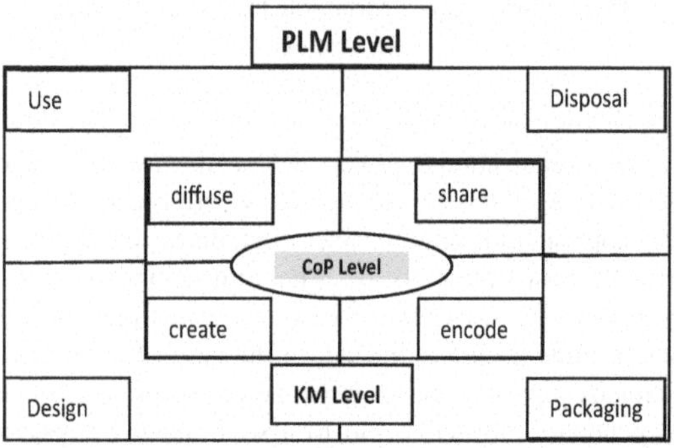

Fig. 1. Illustration of the KM-PLM integration

Incidentally, to establish how to capitalize on this integrated framework, the CoP is one of the knowledge management initiatives that can support continuous PLM improvement. But for that, it is necessary to identify the challenges and issues related to the benefits that can be generated by CoPs. But to do this many methodological challenges arise.

1.2 Knowledge Management (KM) and Communities of Practice (CoP): Benefits and Perspective

Knowledge management refers to activities of production, dissemination, sharing and acquisition of knowledge. In a context where organizations (public, private, community, professional) are submitted to deliver better performance, knowledge management activities lead to better results [6, 7]. In the same way as new technologies (equipment) or intangible resources (patents, software, applications), knowledge management improves organizational efficiency by improving productivity and processes that contribute to produce better services with quality, speed and effective decrease in the consumption of resources [8]. Knowledge management concerns different types of projects, namely COP, interactive data base, best practices [9].

CoP is viewed as a group where participants and experts share their knowledge on an ongoing basis. For Zboralski et al. [10], CoP represent a group of people who interact with each other in, both inside and outside of the organization. They are both sharing the same interest. CoP is one of the most effective project in knowledge management initiatives [11]. It is a framework in which employees as participants are both beneficiaries and producers of knowledge. Different mechanisms and conditions are at stake to ensure the implementation of the CoPs [10, 12]. But the essential element remains the participant. CoP requires different types of resources (human, financial, logistics, informational), so it's important for any given organizations to answer the crucial question of return on investment, namely benefits and impacts generated [13, 14]. To answer to the concern of those who carry out this type of initiative in different organizational contexts (large or medium-sized enterprises, manufacturing companies, research centers, professional groups, etc.), great attention must be paid to evaluate the benefits. The benefits can be viewed as impacts for the participants of a CoP, because they are the one who generated value added. For Mitchell et al. [15] these benefits are on three levels, namely individuals, organizational practice and productivity (Table 1).

Table 1. Benefits of communities of practice [15]

Benefits on organizational practice	Benefits on organisational productivity	Benefits for individuals
1- Generate knowledge and encourage skills development 2- Use knowledge management to drive strategy 3- Disseminate valuable information and transfer best practice 4- Iniate new lines of business including new products and services	1- Facilitate rapid responses to customer needs and problems 2- Decrease the learning curve for new employees 3- Help companies recruit and certain talent	1- Enable employees to manage change 2- Provide access to new knowledge 3- Forster trust and a sense of common purpose 4- Add value to professional lives

1.3 The Need to Evaluate the Benefits of a CoP Through Impacts Assessment

Impacts correspond to the changes of a state in a given situation. Two different moments are identified, namely before and after the implementation of the CoP. The gap between these two situations symbolizes the impact. An impact is a specific outcome that is linked to what has been implemented. The impact can therefore be of different types, including social, cultural, financial, technological, behavioral, learning, etc. Moreover, it can be identified at different levels: personal, collective, organizational, administrative, operational, departmental. In addition, as the core of the CoP is the participants and they play a critical role, the impacts to be determined are those that the participants experienced.

To identify such impacts, emphasis should be placed on the assessment function which is different from the one of the measure. Assessment consists of a systematic collection and analysis of information of a phenomenon or system. With an assessment method, it's possible to establish logical links of cause and effect and to determine the changes and modifications obtained by employees involved in a CoP. In this sense assessment allows a construction of meaning of a transformation dynamic to reach different goals. It's also a basis to identify outcome, to ensure the relevance of the organizational response. It's about providing information to understand progress and the degree of success. In this sense, assessment is a process that concerns different components [10, 15].

Thus, different types of assessment are available, namely: formative, summative, process and results. All these forms are for specific purpose. Nevertheless, they can all be realized on the same organizational system thus allow to have a richer understanding of the system to be evaluated. The choice of the type of assessment is made according to various criteria among others: the objectives, the priorities, the goals, the ways in which the results will be used. The nature of questions also differs according to the type of assessment. Finally, in terms of method, there are mainly 3 main stages: (1) stage 1 = before (at the beginning of the process); (2) stage 2 = during the process; (3) stage 3 = after (at the end of the process). These 3-step can be accompanied by a quasi-experimental approach with a control group or without one. In both ways, it's important to compare the two periods, namely before and after. With the presence of a control group, one can distinguish between an exposed and an unexposed reference group, so one can ensure that the result obtained is directly related to the actions and practices implemented. On the other hand, mobilizing a control group is often difficult to apply and expensive.

In addition, there are two types of methods, qualitative and quantitative research [16–19]. With qualitative evaluation the emphasis is on non-numerical data. The focus is to understand a phenomenon. Thus, the focus is on why, and how the event materializes. It allows first to establish the presence of an impact and in the second time to give a rich picture. It is difficult to use a large sample since the emphasis is on better explanation (richness of explanation). There is therefore a limit to the generalization of the results. The qualitative approach helps to understand behaviors. The analysis based there is to compare. The quantitative evaluation is based on numerical data. Thus, the focus is on the what questions. The need of statistical indicators is necessary to establish links and to give robustness to result. The generalization can be made. Consequently, to assess impacts of communities of practice raises many questions that will be discussed in the following paragraph and based on literature review. It is therefore necessary to establish the methodological bases to be able to determine the impacts in a robust way, by assuming validity, and reliability of the components of the evaluation model. For this, it is important to identify the methodological frameworks found in the literature on CoP assessment.

2 Review of Literature for Methodological Approach to Assess CoP

2.1 What Dimensions Are at Stake to Assess CoP$? A Problematic Review

The assessment function is a proven approach in many descriptions to establish the impacts, particularly in education, management, engineering [10]. But one of the issues lies in the methodology to be retained. It appears that the situation of the CoP is specific for a variety of reasons, including: knowledge belongs to individuals, evaluation is a process, impacts are assumed to evolve over time. It is therefore important to integrate the temporal dimension, the diversity of the forms of evaluation induces to identify the appropriate methodology [20, 21]. For the moment, valuation models focus on financial, operational, functional or strategic impacts: these represent structural dimensions of the organization. However, the point of view of the users-participants is essential, because in the initiatives of the communities of practice, their role is critical since they are the ones who possess the knowledge [22–24]. Therefore, the viability of the CoP rests with them, and also the results pursued by the organization implementing this type of project.

Given these observations, this proposal aims to develop an impact assessment framework from the point of view of the participants by using an approach based on the transformation of inputs into outputs. However, knowledge management, and particularly CoPs require the development of a dedicated assessment framework that favors the perspective of users or participants. In addition, since it is recognized that assessment is a process, impacts are assumed to evolve over time [14]. It is therefore important to integrate the temporal dimension, the diversity of the forms of assessment induces to identify the appropriate methodology. Indeed, the approach advocated to establish the impacts is linked to the robustness of the results, especially in the case of the COPs, because it represents an organizational system filled with humans. Therefore, interactions established by the participants contribute to the formalization of the impacts. Should we favor a qualitative or quantitative approach? Should the profile of the participants be taken into account? Should the duration of participation or the clear statement of objectives be taken into account beforehand?

2.2 Dimensions Related to Methodological Approach

From the literature, it has been possible to establish the limits and advantages of current methodological frameworks that have been used in the case of various studies and research on communities of practice. To highlight what is known about the methodological approaches used in the literature review, six specific dimensions were selected. These six dimensions make it possible to adequately describe a methodological approach. We distinguish for this purpose: (1) The inductive or deductive approach; (2) The type of context chosen (specific or generic); (3) The method of data collection; (4) The unit of analysis; (5) The existence of a theoretical model a priori; (6) The type of research. These six dimensions are summarized in Table 2. The analysis of the various parameters makes it possible to identify a certain number of advantages and limits. Benefits are new ways of doing things. Thus, among the aspects that seem important, let us underline, among others: (1) the type of research; (2) the theoretical framework; (3) methods of data collection.

Indeed, the distinction of the type of research makes it possible to be able to carry out a variety of research: this allows to enrich the understanding that one can have of this object of study. And therefore a richer understanding, ("rich picture") will also help develop more robust intervention tools. Being able to carry out as much qualitative as quantitative studies brings a lot of latitude in the design of the research. In addition, identifying the research contexts, specifying the sectors, the types of organization, appears also important, insofar as specifically in the field of knowledge management, the contextual dimensions are critical. Finally, the identification of the various means of data collection related to the methodological frameworks analyzed shows that it is necessary to rely on a variety of instruments to obtain specific data. And it is from these diverse data that we can produce fine and rich analyzes. In short, these three dimensions noted in relation to the methodologies analyzed deserve to be taken into account in the development of our research design.

Table 2. Dimensions related to methodological process to assess CoP

Dimensions	Result and references
Inductive or deductive approach	Inductive = 20% of cases studies [16, 25]
	Deductive = 80% of cases studies [26, 27]
Context	Organization specified = 30% of cases studies [22, 25]
	Sector specified = 60% of cases studies [23, 28]
Method of data collection	Questionnaire specified = 50% of cases studies [7, 25]
	Interview specified = 40% of case studies [25, 28]
	Internal documentations specified = 40% of cases studies [15, 29]
	Observations in situ specified = 30% of case studies [16, 28]
Unit of analysis	Individual level = 5% of case studies [25]
	Group level = 35% of case studies [28]
	Organizational level = 75% of case studies [26, 30]
Identification of a theoretical model	Identified = 80% of case studies [22]
	Not Identified = 20% of case studies [16]
Type of research	Qualitative = 50% of case studies [16]
	Quantitative = 50% of case studies [29, 31]

Nevertheless, a number of limitations deserve to be emphasized. First, the emphasis is on the level of analysis. Preponderance is at the organizational level. The individual level seems less taken into account, but knowledge belongs to individuals. This would be a gap to be filled. Second, the methodologies analyzed do not capture all the organizational ramifications that are specific in a community of practice. These ramifications ensure that many organizational aspects are inevitably affected and transformed, including: input-output processes, technologies, human resources, production volumes, performance, interaction dynamics, productivity and management of team's work. Given that many authors [26, 31] emphasize and recognize that knowledge management projects target and touch different aspects of the organization, it would therefore be appropriate to link these different affected aspects as inputs, outputs and processes. The analysis of the limitations that affect the methodological frameworks used in research related to communities of practice assessment shows that there are various critical aspects that are not taken into account. Therefore, in the context of this work, it is necessary to propose methodological avenues that will make it possible to fill these gaps.

3 Result for a Proposal of a New Approach to Assess CoP

3.1 Basis and Presentation of a New Methodological Approach

Based on literature review, qualitative and quantitative assessments are present. Qualitative assessments rely on induction and rich descriptions that take into account the individual experience [20, 32]. It is undeniable that given the contextual dynamics of a CoP characterized by a system of collective action and interactions between the participants, all this leads to the recognition of a certain complexity. This complexity requires an interest in the changes that users experienced, the behaviors and the knowledge they acquired. Identifying and understanding the changes that are taking place among CoP participants is needed. Not only will we be able to identify the impacts, but also explain the reasons behind them. Thus, to arrive at the description of the point of view of the users-participants in the CoP, a qualitative approach is to be considered [20].

This dual qualitative-quantitative position leads us to consider a hybrid methodological approach [19, 32]. This position is relevant given the specification of the evaluation function and the specific context of the CoPs. In addition, the classification of qualitative studies on one side and quantitative studies on the other do not conventionally permit the combination of the two approaches. However, the hybrid approach that we propose is a viable methodology. The hybrid approach therefore makes it possible to combine qualitative and quantitative data. Thus, the hybrid methodological framework elaborated is divided into 4 stages:

1. Stage 1 = identification of critical variables from the literature review.
2. Stage 2 = testing of critical variables with users. This action aims to better understand and characterize the object of research. This anchoring is necessary in view of the complexity and peculiarities of any evaluation process and the knowledge management dynamics within a CoP.
3. Stage 3 = validation of the built model: this requires checking the validity of construct or conceptual and internal validity and reliability. Reliability refers to the degree of accuracy with which an instrument measures the concept, in this case the benefits of a CoP. Construct or conceptual validity ensures that the instrument, in this case the conceptual model is well constructed and that it offers an adequate measure of the theoretical model mobilized. The occurrence of input-output model

can also be associated with the validity of content that aims to determine whether the measuring instrument and its components represent the concept.
4. Stage 4 = the application of the model in specific organizational situations. The case study is the preferred approach in this phase. Since the focus is on impacts, a more qualitative approach is preferred. Indeed, the case study makes it possible to clearly define the situation and the context to analyze. We can therefore have a rich understanding of how participants get their benefits.

The hybrid method approach established a structured CoP evaluation model with six components: income, inputs, throughput, output, outcomes, maturity and auditing initial conditions. This systemic model makes it possible to establish a logical link between the various components. Thus, it is possible from the perspective of users to determine the outcomes and impacts they have achieved based on their participation in the COP.

3.2 Results and Benefits of the Mixed Methodology

This methodological approach is necessary to meet the dual objective of the study, mainly the validation of the model on the one hand and the identification of impacts due to participation in a CoP. This reduces the weaknesses inherent in each of the initial approaches (qualitative and quantitative). There are several advantages inherent to the strength of the hybrid approach: complementarity, explanation and exploration [19, 32]. Complementarity allows for analysis at different levels regarding the impact of CoPs on participants. The qualitative approach enriches this understanding by focusing on users' experiences. The explanation is richer because the qualitative data provide deeper insights. The observation of the presence of phenomena is not only established by a quantitative basis, but it is also explained by aspects and strategies of appropriation. Exploration is necessary because the benefits and impacts are based primarily on ownership and changing individual practices. Exploration allows to discover the variety of individual situations that illustrates the materialization of the fallout.

In the proposal of an evaluation model, two important criteria for ensuring its robustness and relevance are reliability and fidelity. Both criteria require a statistically significant sample that favors a quantitative approach. The use of statistical tests is necessary. Adherence to the acceptance or rejection criteria is the main criterion, notably by calculating, Cronbach's alpha, coefficient of variation, KMO factor, kurtosis and skewness factors and so on. The quantitative approach thus favored makes it possible to base the model built on a statistically reliable basis since the respondents to the validation questionnaire are in agreement with their knowledge, their interests, their expectations, their practices, in short what they are looking for in an impact assessment model. In addition, a specific important advantage of the hybrid or mixed method is also the process of data collection and processing [19, 32]. Thus, it is to begin first with a quantitative study (testing or conceptualization or theoretical validation) followed by a qualitative study (exploration of cases). It is also possible to start with a qualitative study to discover the parameters constituting the phenomenon under study and then continue with a quantitative study for recurrences and generalization from a random sample that meets the rules of statistical generalization. The proposed hybrid approach identifies different methodological benefits, including: (a) The use of numeric and non-numerical data; (b) The diversity of data; (c) The triangulation of data. The use of statistical tests to validate the model ensures that the components retained in the conceptual model are relevant and can be applied in different contexts.

Finally, the specific situation of the CoP requires consideration of the concepts of change and stakeholder; which is needed, because in a CoP, the participants play a critical role. Therefore it's important to compare the situation of participants before they participate in knowledge sharing activities and after doing so. This type of evaluation also requires taking into account the time frame: this is easily achievable with a case study. The proposed hybrid methodological approach thus brings benefits both at the conceptual level (model development framework) and empirically (validation and field testing). Which ultimately results in informative, robust and pragmatic results.

4 Conclusion and Future Work

The application of the methodological approach is the next step, that of collecting data to obtain factual results. One of the stakes in this strategy of research refers to the type of sample to be compiled both for the quantitative and the qualitative part.

For the quantitative approach, a survey will be conducted among participants in communities of practice regardless of their organizational context. The aim is for them to express themselves on the conceptual model from their experience, practices, expectations and targets they seek by participating in a CoP. From their answers, we will be able to validate the conceptual model.

For the qualitative part, the sample to be selected corresponds to a convenience sample in so far as the east and the data collection are in a specific organization. These are accessibility and practical reasons that will make it possible to identify the case studies in which the conceptual model will have to be tested.

The idea is to extend the application of the conceptual model to different cases in different contexts and by different types of users taking into account also different levels of maturity. This multiplication of application will make it possible to arrive at the theoretical saturation necessary, thus, allowing to reach a double validation as much on the conceptual level as practical. The next steps are aimed at achieving these results.

References

1. Folkard, B., Keraron, Y., Mantoulan, D., Dubois, R.: The need for improved integration between PLM and KM: a PLM services provider point of view. In: Rivest, L., Bouras, A., Louhichi, B. (eds.) PLM 2012. IAICT, vol. 388, pp. 85–98. Springer, Heidelberg (2012). https://doi.org/10.1007/978-3-642-35758-9_8
2. Bernell-Garcia, P., Fan, I.-S.: Practitioner requirements for integrated knowledged based engineering in PLM. Int. J. Prod. Lifecycle Manag. **3**(1), 3–20 (2008). https://doi.org/10.1504/IJPLM.2008.019968

3. Beylier, C., Pourroy, F., Villeneuve, F., Mille, A.: A collaboration centered approach to manage engineering knowledge; a case study of an engineering SME. J. Eng. Des. **20**(6), 523–542 (2003). https://doi.org/10.1080/09544820801898482
4. McMahon, C., Lowe, A., Culley, S.: Knowledge management in engineering design: personalization and codification. J. Eng. Des. **15**(4), 307–325 (2003). https://doi.org/10.1080/0954482041000l697154
5. Trotta, M.G.: PLM: sustainability and knowledge management as keys in a complex system of product development. J. Ind. Eng. Manag. **3**(2), 309–322 (2010). https://doi.org/10.3926/jiem.2010
6. Carrillo, J.E., Gaimon, C.: Improving manufacturing performance through process change and knowledge creation. Manag. Sci. **46**, 265–288 (2000). https://doi.org/10.1287/mnsc.46.2.265.925
7. Marqués, D.P., Simon, F.J.G.: The effect of knowledge management practices on firm performance. J. Knowl. Manag. **10**(3), 143–156 (2006). https://doi.org/10.1108/13673270610670911
8. Lesser, E.L., Storck, J.: Communities Of practice and organizational performance. IBM Syst. J. **40**, 831–841 (2001)
9. Siddique, C.M.: Knowledge management initiatives in the United Arab Emirates: a baseline study. J. Knowl. Manag. **16**(5), 702–723 (2012). https://doi.org/10.1108/13673271211262763
10. Zboralski, K., Gemunden, G.H.: Encyclopedia of Communities of Practice in Information and Knowledge Management. IDEA GROUP Reference, London (2006). https://doi.org/10.1108/09504120710775246
11. Heisig, P.: Harmonisation of knowledge management. comparing 160 knowledge management frameworks around the globe. J. Knowl. Manag. **13**(4), 4–31 (2009). https://doi.org/10.1108/13673270910971798
12. Wenger, E., McDermott, R., Snyder, Y.M.: Cultivating Communities of Practice: A Guide to Managing Knowledge. Harvard Business School Press, Boston (2002)
13. Fontaine, M.A., Millen, D.R.: Understanding the value of communities: a look at both sides of the cost/benefit equation. Knowl. Manag. Rev. **5**(3), 24–27 (2002). 10.11/1985500
14. Chetty, L., Mearns, M.: Using communities of practice towards the next level of knowledge management maturity. SA J. Inf. Manag. **14**(1), 503–509 (2002). https://doi.org/10.4102/sajim.v14i.503
15. Mitchell, J., Wood, S.: Benefits of Communities of Practice. John Mitchell & Associates, Toronto (2001). www.jma.com.au/pages/communities-of-practice/c-of-p-benefits.pdf?
16. Harlow, H.: The effect of tacit knowledge on firm performance. J. Knowl. Manag. **12**(1), 148–163 (2008). https://doi.org/10.1108/13673270810852458
17. Zaim, H., Tatoglu, E., Zaim, S.: Performance of knowledge management practices: a causal analysis. J. Knowl. Manag. **11**(6), 54–67 (2007). https://doi.org/10.1108/13673270710832163
18. Pillania, R.K.: Information technology strategy for knowledge management in India automotive components SMEs. Knowl. Process. Manag. **15**(3), 203–210 (2008). https://doi.org/10.1002/kpm.311
19. Teddie, C., Tashakkori, A.: Foundations of Mixed Methods Research. Integrating Quantitative Approaches in The Social and Behavioral Sciences. Sage, Thousand Oaks (2009)
20. Creswell, J.W.: Research Design: Qualitative and Quantitative Approaches. Sage, Thousand Oaks (1994)
21. Molina-Azorin, J.: The use and added value of mixed methods in management research. Electron. J. Mix. Methods Res. **5**(1), 7–24 (2010). https://doi.org/10.1177/1558689810384490

22. Verburg, R.M., Andriessen, J.H.E.: The assessment of communities of practice. Knowl. Process Manag. **13**(1), 13–25 (2006). https://doi.org/10.1002/kpm.241
23. Yanklin, S., Igel, B.: Communities of practice purposefully designed for improving business performance. Knowl. Process Manag. **19**(4), 189–202 (2012). https://doi.org/10.1002/kpm.1398
24. McDermott, R.: Measuring the impacts of communities. How to draw meaning from measures of communities of practice. Knowl. Manag. Rev. **5**(2), 26–29 (2002). www.melcrum.com/e-library/
25. Lee, P.-S., Tseng, S.-M.: The effects of knowledge management capability and dynamic capability on organizational performance. J. Enterp. Inf. Manag. **27**(2), 158–179 (2014). https://doi.org/10.1108/JEIM-05-2012-0025
26. Yang, J.-T.: The impact of knowledge sharing on organizational learning and effectiveness. J. Knowl. Manag. **11**(2), 83–90 (2007). https://doi.org/10.1108/13673270710738933
27. Zack, M., McKeen, J., Singh, S.: Knowledge management and organizational performance. J. Knowl. Manag. **13**(6), 392–409 (2009). https://doi.org/10.1108/13673270710738933
28. Goldoni, V., Oliveira, M.: Knowledge management metrics in software development companies in Brazil. J. Knowl. Manag. **14**(2), 301–313 (2010). https://doi.org/10.1108/13673271011032427
29. McKellar, K., Pitzul, K., Yi, Y., Cole, D.: Evaluating communities of practice and knowledge networks: a systematic scoping review of evaluation frameworks. EcoHealth **11**, 383–399 (2014). https://doi.org/10.1007/s10393-014-0958-3
30. Perrin, A.: The practices of knowledge managers in lafarge. J. Knowl. Manag. **16**(2), 204–214 (2012). https://doi.org/10.1108/13673211218825
31. Yahya, S., Goh, W.K.: Managing human resources towards achieving knowledge management. J. Knowl. Manag. **6**(5), 457–468 (2000). https://doi.org/10.1108/13673270210450414
32. Tashakkori, A., Teddie, C.: Mixed Methodology: Combining Qualitative and Quantitative Approaches. Sage, Thousand Oaks (1998)

PLM Infrastructure and Implementation

Developing Key Performance Indicators for Shipbuilding PLM

Sehyun Myung(✉)

Youngsan University, Yangsan, Korea
msh@ysu.ac.kr

Abstract. This paper describes how to develop key performance indicators (KPI) for shipbuilding PLM. The decision maker can evaluate product development performance and risk by analyzing key performance indicators (KPI). Establishment of KPIs in the shipbuilding industry involves analyzing existing performance indicators and benchmarking other industry's performance indicators. In this paper, the KPIs are classified into three categories: project management viewpoint, business unit viewpoint, and enterprise management viewpoint.

Keywords: Shipbuilding · PLM · Performance management
Key performance indicators · Big data analysis

1 Introduction

Product Lifecycle Management ("PLM", henceforth) is started from CAD and CAD data management, and evolved to enterprise IT system which includes project management, requirement management, portfolio management, quality management, R&D strategy management, technical asset management, performance management and so on. PLM has been adopted gradually by industry from aerospace to shipbuilding, automotive, electronics and heavy industry. PLM can be a key innovation tool to be a great company, and PLM system regarded as one of major ICT solutions with ERP and SCM for the enterprise company. This paper describes how to develop KPI for shipbuilding PLM. The decision maker can evaluate product development performance and risk by analyzing KPI.

The performance indicator (PI) is an index that measures the extent to which an organization achieves its goals. In business informatics, KPIs represent current business conditions and are used to predict what will happen in the future. Real-time monitoring of KPI is called business activity monitoring. In addition, KPI provide layer-by-layer visibility and enable quick decision support. The KPI building and management process is conducted in the order of information provision, cause analysis, decision making and direction, and change management.

Establishment of KPI in shipbuilding industry involves analysis of existing KPI and benchmarking of KPI of other industries. The derived KPI can be used for product development performance evaluation and risk assessment services using Big Data

Published by Springer Nature Switzerland AG 2018.
P. Chiabert et al. (Eds.): PLM 2018, IFIP AICT 540, pp. 593–599, 2018.
https://doi.org/10.1007/978-3-030-01614-2_54

analysis methodology. In this paper, the KPIs are classified into three categories: project management viewpoint, business unit viewpoint, and enterprise management viewpoint.

2 Related Research

The start of KPI application is 'management by objectives' advocated by Peter Drucker. Peter Drucker insisted that in order for an enterprise company to achieve performance, each task should focus on the enterprise-wide goals. The goal here is to be concrete, measurable, achievable, realistic and time-sensitive [1].

Studies on KPIs have been conducted in various ways. Issa et al. [2] described environmental performance indicators (EPI) related to products for environmentally friendly design in manufacturing, and derived 261 EPIs from 500 indicators.

Rodrigues et al. [3] categorized the product development process into seven stages: product strategy planning, informational design, conceptual design, detailed design, production preparation, production launch, product accomplishment and monitoring, and derived 787 KPIs in product development.

Alemanni et al. [4] studied KPI for the benefits of introducing PLM systems to the aviation industry and derived 54 KPIs for quality, time, cost, infrastructure, and communication.

Myung [5] described Samsung Electronics' implementation of enterprise PLM and referred to performance management using KPI as a module of PLM system.

Folan et al. [6] described that performance management evolved from the recommendation of performance management to the establishment of performance management framework, the establishment of performance management system, and the management of performance between organizations.

3 Development of KPIs

3.1 Collect and Analyze Performance Indicators

Hundreds of PIs are already in use in the shipbuilding industry. The PI is the kind of artifact that changes from time to time. Depending on the business environment, the calculation formula and the upper/lower thresholds are different.

This research investigates and evaluates PIs of shipbuilding design PLM and non-shipbuilding PLM and derives KPIs that can be applied to the shipbuilding field.

PI includes name, definition and purpose, process to which KPI belongs, performance measurement/registration cycle, calculation method, calculation formula, evaluation unit, threshold and target value, quantitative evaluation/qualification evaluation, application department and others.

Figure 1 shows the general PI derivation process. After the goal setting, the PI is determined after the investigation, and then the threshold value and the target value of the PI are determined, and the result is analyzed.

Fig. 1. Performance indicator definition process

Figure 2 shows the KPI derivation method for shipbuilding PLM. After investigating the KPIs in the shipbuilding and non-shipbuilding industry, KPIs are derived from the viewpoints of 3 categories in the shipbuilding PLM. The calculation formula is determined and the KPI contents are checked through the module for visualization.

54 KPIs of three companies in the shipbuilding industry were collected, including 18 KPIs from company A, 28 KPIS from company B, and 8 KPIS from company C. The major categories of shipbuilding KPIs can be classified into design, procurement, and manufacturing by category, and they can be classified into strategic KPI, intrinsic KPI, and cost KPI by characteristic.

In the non-shipbuilding industry, 220 KPIs, 46 KPIs in the electronics industry and 38 KPIs in the construction/plant industry were collected and analyzed.

Performance management based on KPI in mass production industry is centered on EQCD (efficiency, quality, cost, delivery) during development and centered on PQCD (productivity, quality, cost, delivery) during production.

At the time of development, performance management is carried out focusing on development efficiency, quality, material cost, and delivery. In production, performance management is carried out focusing on productivity, quality, cost, and delivery.

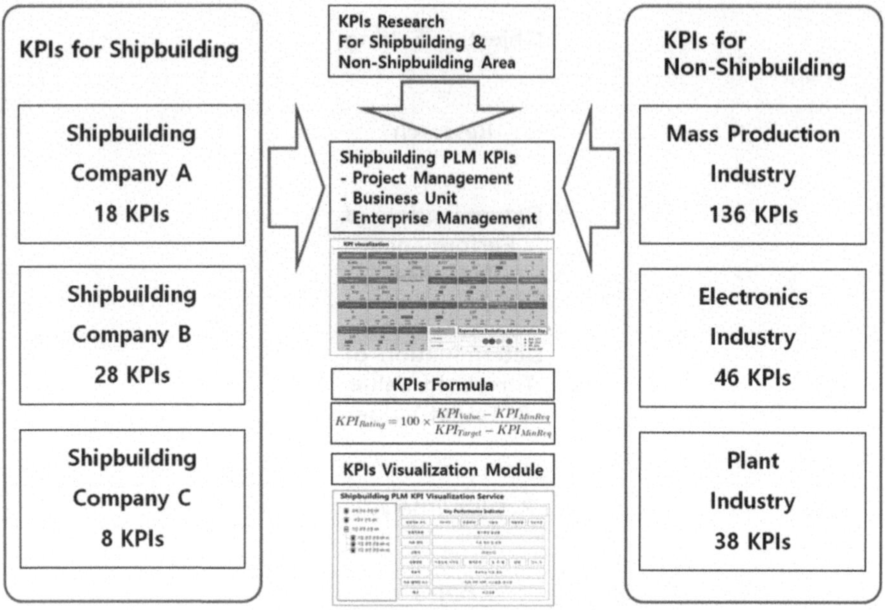

Fig. 2. KPI development process of shipbuilding PLM

However, if we look closely, efficiency, delivery, and quality can all be converted into cost. The KPI of the mass-production industry is different from the shipbuilding industry, which is an order-taking business. In the shipbuilding industry, which is a contractor, performance management is carried out on the total volume of a vessel that are constructed without taking into consideration the material cost considering the cost per production unit.

3.2 Developing KPIs

In this research, KPIs in the shipbuilding industry and KPIs in the non-shipbuilding industry were analyzed and then KPIs were established for the shipbuilding PLM sector. Also, the KPI is classified into three categories. The project management viewpoint is applied to each vessel line, and the business unit viewpoint is divided into business units such as merchant ships or special ships, and the enterprise viewpoint is handled at the whole company level. Therefore, enterprise KPIs are large scale, enterprise wide and financial.

In this research, 5 kinds of KPIs from the viewpoint of enterprise management, 10 kinds of KPIs from the viewpoint of business unit, and five kinds of KPIs from the viewpoint of project management were derived.

The 5 KPIs from the perspective of enterprise management are cost reduction achievement rate, estimating accuracy rate, order margin ration, securing advanced technology/strengthening internal capacity, and reducing material costs.

The 10 KPIs from the business unit point of view are the number of unique technologies, new CAD application rate, on-site feedback rate, design man-hour reduction achievement, accomplishment project performance, major equipment contracts, steel material achievement rate, design man-hour efficiency, steel scrap rate, internal information delay issue.

The 5 KPIs from the viewpoint of project management are the incidence rate of drawing change by the design cause in the production field, the compliance rate of the design process, the approval drawing acceptance rate, the ship owner/classification approval comment status, and the preceding outfitting ratio.

Figure 3 shows the example of KPI description. It contains KPI code, name, definition, managing team, sector, formula, method of calculation, period, unit, target, data source and remarks.

KPI Code	PM-002	Managing Team	Development Team	Sector	Development
KPI Name	Compliance Rate of the Design Process				
KPI Definition	Percentage of Drawings created in Planned Schedule				
Formula	Actual Number of Drawings / Planned Number of Drawings				
Method of Calculation	Automatic	Period	Monthly	Unit	%
Target	100%				
Data Source	PLM Project Management Module				
Remarks	N/A				

Fig. 3. Example of KPI description

Figure 4 shows the Shipbuilding PLM platform with big data analysis. Based on this platform, shipbuilding PLM system will be completed in connection with shipyard PLM service.

Through the KPI derived from this research, the risk assessment service is provided, the execution evaluation of the development work using the shipbuilding PLM is performed, and the decision making of the executives and the managers through the risk assessment is made possible.

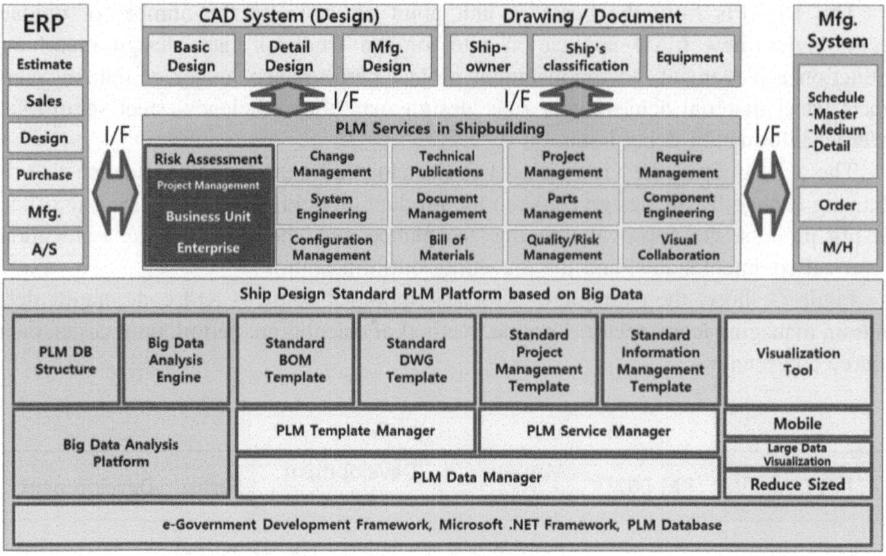

Fig. 4. Shipbuilding PLM platform with big data analysis

4 Conclusion and Further Research

In this paper, the methodology for establishing KPIs in the shipbuilding PLM is described.

In the future, product development performance and risk assessment will be linked to information systems that support monitoring, evaluation, and risk prediction of product development using KPIs of 3 viewpoints and design big data accumulated in PLM.

Acknowledgement. This work was supported by National IT Industry Promotion Agency (NIPA) grant funded by the Korea government (MSICT) (S1106-16-1025: Development of ship design standard PLM platform based on Big Data) and Y'sU (Youngsan university).

References

1. Drucker, P.F.: The Practice of Management, pp. 181–204. Hankyung, Seoul (2006)
2. Issa, I.I., Pigosso, D.C.A., McAloone, T.C., Rozenfeld, H.: Leading product-related environmental performance indicators: a selection guide and database. J. Clean. Prod. **108** (Part A), 321–330 (2015). https://doi.org/10.1016/j.jclepro.2015.06.088
3. Rodrigues, V.P., Pigosso, D.C.A., McAloone, T.C.: Process-related key performance indicators for measuring sustainability performance of ecodesign implementation into product development. J. Clean. Prod. **139**, 416–428 (2016). https://doi.org/10.1016/j.jclepro.2016.08.046

4. Alemanni, M., Alessia, G., Tornincasa, S., Vezzetti, E.: Key performance indicators for PLM benefits evaluation: the Alcatel Alenia Space case study. Comput. Ind. **59**(8), 833–841 (2008). https://doi.org/10.1016/j.compind.2008.06.003
5. Myung, S., 2008, Implementation process of enterprise PLM system, *Proceedings of International Conference on Product Lifecycle Management 2008*
6. Folan, P., Browne, J.: A review of performance measurement: towards performance management. Comput. Ind. **56**(7), 663–680 (2005). https://doi.org/10.1016/j.compind.2005.03.001

Engineering Project Health Monitoring: Application of Automatic, Real-Time Analytics to PDM Systems

Chris Snider[1(✉)], James Gopsill[2], David Jones[1], and Ben Hicks[1]

[1] University of Bristol, Bristol, UK
chris.snider@bristol.ac.uk
[2] Universtiy of Bath, Bath, UK

Abstract. Modern engineering work, both project-based and operations, is replete with complexity and variety making the effective development of detailed understanding of work underway difficult, which in turn impacts on management and assurance of performance.

Leveraging the digital nature of modern engineering work, recent research has demonstrated the capability and opportunity for implementation of broad-spectrum data analytics for development of detailed management information. Of key benefit is that these analytics may be both real-time and automatic.

This paper contextualises such analytics with respect to PDM through exploration of the potential for driving the analytics directly from data typically captured within PDM systems. Through review of twenty-five analytics generated from engineering-based digital assets, this paper examines the subset that may be applied to PDM-driven analysis on systems as-is, examines the coverage of such analytics from the perspective of the potential managerial information and understanding that could be inferred, and explores the potential for maximizing the set of analytics driven from PDM systems through capture of a minimal set of supplementary data. This paper presents the opportunity for integration of detailed analytics of engineering work into PDM systems and the extension of their capability to support project management and team performance.

Keywords: Data analysis · Engineering management · Analytics

1 Introduction

The continued increase of technological capability in engineering brings with it many challenges. Accompanied by globalisation [1], high complexity [2], and large operational scales [3], modern engineering projects require significant effort for effective management and control. Where 70 years ago engineering typically occurred through the efforts of tens to hundreds of personnel working concurrently and often co-located, engineering now routinely involves the concerted efforts of tens of thousands, developing millions of parts in hundreds of countries [4].

Published by Springer Nature Switzerland AG 2018.
P. Chiabert et al. (Eds.): PLM 2018, IFIP AICT 540, pp. 600–610, 2018.
https://doi.org/10.1007/978-3-030-01614-2_55

Driven by this change, challenges in engineering industry have manifested both in the control and management of the vast amounts of information now produced, and in the effective management of complex engineering project and operations. This has led to the development of sophisticated, through-life computational data management such as embodied in Product Lifecycle Management (PLM) and Product Data Management (PDM) systems, which have shown rapid uptake and high utilization across engineering industry.

While these systems provide game-changing capability for data management, storage, and retrieval, there remains significant opportunity for greatly extended utilization of the data held for analysis and support of effective management and enhancement of work performance. Recent work has shown great potential in development of broad-spectrum and low-level analytics of digital files for direct interpretation of higher-level work performance [5–7], beyond commonly applied techniques supporting process and workflow management. Of key benefit here is the potential for automatic and near-real-time analysis directly extracted from data held within PDM systems.

This paper presents an exploration of the potential for such analytics for the purposes of engineering management and support of high work performance. Through meta-analysis of 25 different analytic approaches targeted at automatic analysis of digital files (DFs - reports, communications and models) it identifies capability for analytics directly applied to PDM systems as-is, presents coverage of underlying understanding that may be developed, and identifies extensions to PDM systems for maximization of analytic capability.

2 Performance of Engineering Work

In interpretation of performance of work, two highly inter-related perspectives are frequently adopted. The first focuses on metrics of performance and direct measurement. Typically utilizing the classic "iron triangle" of time, cost, and quality, but extending to metrics such as stakeholder and user interpretation of work outputs [8] that attempt to provide quantifications of process and output that are resultant of work performance. In each, the values measured must be contextualized against the desired or expected for the case. The second perspective is concerned with *critical success factors* (CSFs) [9] and embodies descriptions of those characteristics of a work situation that will influence eventual performance dependent on their state. Examples include the cohesion of teams [10], definition of specification, and availability of information [11]. In application, CSFs (see Table 1) are characterized in the individual case, and then interpreted by management to support decision-making and intervention with a goal of eventual performance enhancement.

Table 1. Critical Success Factors (CSFs) in engineering management

Ref.	Critical success factor categories
[12]	Corporate environment, sponsorship/ownership, relationship management, project management, scope, requirements, funding, scheduling, development process, personnel, staffing, technology, external dependencies, planning

CSFs highlight a wealth of complex and inter-related factors which create significant complication in the effective management of engineering work. Managerial decision-making must identify the factors that are of influence upon performance, the means of their measurement, and the nature of consequent action and intervention that will support enhancement. This difficulty is exacerbated in practice by the distinct nature of each situation in that the key performance-influencing factors of one case may or may not be relevant to another case, in turn impacting their correlation with consequent work performance and appropriate methods of measurement.

Recent work has shown the viability of application of a condition-monitoring approach to work monitoring in engineering [5, 6], in which broad-spectrum and low-level data analysis is applied to work activity and used to infer higher work characteristics. This approach gives significant proven scope to detail work activity automatically and in real-time through algorithmic monitoring and analysis, thus providing managerial workers with detailed description of the situation under their responsibility and supporting their decision-making processes. This capability is in addition to managerial toolsets such as EVM, PMBOK, and Prince2.

As a digital repository of engineering data PDM systems provide high compatibility with this approach, where the digital files held within form the dataset on which analysis could be driven and from which understanding of the specific situation may be built. From effective application of analytics to PDM data, there is therefore potential to provide direct analysis and interpretation of specific engineering situations to decision-makers, thus increasing managerial capability while reducing investigative effort.

3 Data Analysis in PDM

Of vital importance in engineering workflow, PDM systems provide data storage, management, and structure that enable version control, information access, and process modelling for data management, amongst other capabilities [13]. While varying in sophistication from simple file structures to complex databases the value of PDM system capability is widely recognized, with successful implementation shown to give such benefits as increased flexibility and reliability of products, shorter time-to-market, and reduced development costs [14].

Due to variation in company structures, product, product purpose, and PDM system, utility of the data and data formats captured within PDM systems are often ad-hoc, specific to the engineering software in use, and oriented to the design itself [15]. Data captured within PDM systems typically consists of the file itself and accompanying meta-data, itself comprising a combination of manually and automatically categorized fields describing the file itself or the product it represents [16].

Dependent on the data held within the system, analytics employed within PDM systems are also of an ad-hoc nature, with focus on workflow, data and information characterization, and analysis of product, process, and programme structures [13, 16]. While these analytic methods support managerial practice through description of system/process characteristics, particularly in control and specification of process, this work contends that the data held within PDM systems provides a rich source from which interpretation of work performance characteristics may be derived directly.

Further, as explored within this paper, scope exists for many analytics to be applied in an automatic and real-time manner, with all data inputs extracted directly from files without manual categorization or description of meta-data. As such, scope exists to provide analyses general to all work situations, extend capability within PDM systems, and address the significant complexities in understanding of performance within varying engineering contexts described in Sect. 2.

4 PDM Data for Analysis of Engineering Work Performance

As the direct outputs of the activities of engineers working within an engineering context, the digital files (DFs) created, modified, and captured within PDM systems are a result of the multiplicity of internal and external influences upon the engineering situation in which the engineers work. Dependent on the characteristics of the engineering situation the type and properties of the DFs and the nature of their creation/modification will vary. Accordingly, through study of the characteristics of DFs there exists scope to understand the ongoing activity within the engineering situation and as such to infer information about the characteristics of the situation itself; information that supports managerial understanding of project performance. For example, characteristics of communicative activity are dependent on team cohesion and conflict [10], which in turn are related to project success [17]. This relation between characteristics of the engineering situation, activity, and the DFs created forms the basis for the analytics studied.

4.1 Types of Analysis and Outputs of Analysis

Given this relationship between data, activity, and performance, analysis techniques may either directly describe current engineering activity, or may infer the state of CSFs (see Sect. 2). In the former, the onus rests on the manager to interpret activity patterns observed and infer performance, while in the latter the manager must compare resultant descriptions of the state of the engineering situation against expectation.

In this work, analyses are classified according to these distinctions, with all categorized as providing a description of ongoing activity or according to the CSFs to which they relate. The CSFs used for categorization are given in [6], and for brevity here separated into four primary categories, with a total of 10 sub-categories:

Person; (team/individual) - CSFs relating to the characteristics of the persons directly involved in the ongoing work.

Design - CSFs relating to characteristics of the output of the engineering work.

Process – CSFs relating to characteristics of the processes by which the ongoing engineering work proceeds.

Context; (management/information/stakeholders/resource/environment/personnel)– CSFs relating to the broader context of the company and ongoing engineering work, according to the listed categories above.

4.2 Data Types

Current PDM systems capture a variety of data-types, often bespoke to the specific company or work, with focus on those representative of the product and process (i.e. CAD files, reports). DFs in this work are classified as one of three types, the former two being commonly captured in PDM, and the third not commonly captured:

Representation: including all virtual representations and models of the object of the work, including CAD models, virtual prototypes, analysis models (e,g. FEA).

Report/Documentation: Including all textual or numerical documentation that addresses the output, process, or project, including technical and managerial reports, presentations, excel spreadsheets, databases, etc.

Communication: including all digital communications sent between workers, including email, social network, and instant messaging.

All files are analyzed through focus on their properties at one of two levels:

Physical attributes: the characteristics of a file as an entity within the digital system, typically meta-data - including, for example, size, creator, creation/modification date, filetype, etc. This data is common in PDM systems.

Content attributes: the content of the file including, for example, textual data within communication, numerical data within spreadsheets, coordinate data within CAD models. This data is common in PDM systems, but less commonly used in analysis.

4.3 Data Analytics Studied

This work compares 25 analytics developed as part of a 5-year project into analytics of engineer work. Each interprets either activity or CSFs from low-level digital files produced in engineering work. For brevity in this format these are detailed in summary only in Table 2, with further detail available from the authors on request. These analytics are not considered exhaustively representative but include all identified in the 5-year project, and thereby describe the breadth of those identifiable within the project scope. All are (a) automatic in their application to data, and (b) provide near-real-time outputs allowing quick understanding and action from decision makers. Stemming from engineering work many analytics are applicable across context, where data-type available is the enabler. Utility of analytic is dependent on the context and should be assessed on a case-by-case basis dependent on priority and apparent issues. Further detail is available from the authors on all analytics and their validation.

To identify the elements of work performance to which the output of each analytic relates, all were classified by the CSF categories and if their output provided a description of underlying activity. This is shown in Table 3.

Through this meta-analysis a summation of the inferencing power of each analytic technique is produced, with a particular focus on the capabilities of analyses applied to different data-types against the types of CSF to which they relate. In so doing this work clarifies the manner in which such analyses may support understanding of work performance. Following categorization, the capabilities of analytics with respect to the data inputs required and the CSFs to which they relate can be summarized, thereby allowing contextualization to data held within PDM systems (see Table 4).

Table 2. Analytics of low-level digital files explored

	Summary of analytic	Data input
1	Assessment of the type and distribution of engineering work	All digital assets
2	Assessment of the type and distribution of project work	All digital assets
3	Assessment of the status (level of development of a design)	CAD files
4	Tracking and typing topics in communication by diffusion characteristics	Email
5	Tracking the evolution of clusters of topics in communications	Email
6	Tracking the relative levels of attention of actors to a topic	Email
7	Monitoring associations and interconnections between work areas	Email, reports, presentations
8	Elicitation of the product architecture/structure from project communication and documentation	Email, reports, presentations
9	Typing and tracking of communications by management purpose	Email/social media
10	Typing of communications by subject	Email/social media
11	Monitoring patterns of exchange within the communication networks of projects	Email/social media
12	Monitoring the composition of community by contribution to the communications network	Email/social media
13	Assessment of the sentiment, affect and tone of project members	Email/social media
14	Assessment of the sentiment, affect and tone of members with regard to a project topic	Email/social media
15	Assessment of the spread and diffusion of topics within the project team	Email/social media
16	Assessment of conformance of content to standard operating procedures	Models, reports, CAD files, code
17	Eliciting potential project dependencies through co-occurrence of modifications to types of digital file	Models, reports, CAD files, code
18	Evaluate the level of reuse of content from previous projects	Models, reports, CAD files, code
19	Predicting the time to complete a task through the rate of modification of a typed file	Models, reports, CAD files, code
20	Predicting the time to complete activity or stage through the occurrence of typed events	Models, reports, CAD files, code
21	Assessing the similarity of projects through comparison of the content of project briefs	Project documentation
22	Assessing the similarity of projects through comparison of the sequences of workflow in past projects	Project documentation
23	Assessing the normality of a project's workflow through comparison with past projects	Project documentation
24	Assessing the complexity level of a project through comparison of workflow with previously categorised projects	Project documentation
25	Elicitation of the development of knowledge and competencies within a team or organisation	Technical reports

Table 3. Coverage of analytics against CSFs and activity. Headers indicate CSF categories - Act: Activity, Ind: Individual, Des: Design, Pro: Process, Man: Management, Info: Information, Env: Environment, Per: Personnel, Sta: Stakeholder, Res: Resource. M - metadata only; B – both metadata and content attributes must be studied.

Analytic			Person		Des	Pro	Context					
	Data	Act	Ind	Team		Pro	Man	Info	Env	Per	Sta	Res
1	**M**	*										
2	**M**	*				*						*
3	**M**	*			*	*						
4	**M**	*				*		*				
5	**B**	*		*	*	*				*		
6	**B**	*										
7	**M**	*				*						
8	**B**				*			*				
9	**B**	*				*	*	*				*
10	**B**	*			*	*						
11	**M**	*	*	*			*			*		
12	**M**	*	*	*						*		
13	**B**		*	*						*		
14	**B**	*	*	*						*		
15	**B**	*	*	*				*		*		
16	**B**				*	*						
17	**M**				*	*						
18	**B**	*			*	*	*	*				
19	**M**	*			*	*						
20	**M**	*			*	*						
21	**B**				*	*		*				
22	**M**					*						
23	**M**					*						
24	**M**					*						
25	**B**	*	*	*				*		*		*

5 Discussion and Conclusion

From Table 3, a summation can be drawn of the possibility for extension to analytic capability within PDM systems, based on automatic and near-real-time analysis of DFs held within (see Table 4). From Table 4, several observations can be made about the capability of analytics based on low-level data held within PDMs to support interpretation of work performance.

Table 4. Analytic capability of extension to PDM systems.

Analysis extension	No. of analytics	Analytic capability
Current PDM	N/A	Largely bespoke, dependent on meta-data; process and workflow focus
Extend analysis on PDM as-is	10	**Analytics: 6, 7, 9, 10, 15, 16, 17, 18, 19, 20.** Significant extension across design and process category CSFs
Extend to directly include data-type content in analysis	14	**Analytics: as above + 5, 8, 12, 13.** Extension evaluates above + information re-use, conformance, and personnel competency
Extend to capture communications data-types, meta-data analysis only	13	**Analytics: As row 2 + 3, 4, 21.** Extension evaluates as row 2 + information sharing, team structure, work focus, and detection of work events
Extend to capture communications data-types, meta-data and content analysis	25	**Analytics: All.** Extension evaluates all above, + many aspects of person-based CSFs

There is high capability to monitor work performance via automatic and real-time analytics of DFs, including those held within PDM systems. Much benefit may be derived from addition of meta-data only analytics applied to existing data, while further benefit can be derived from inclusion of content analysis. The integration of such presents a significant area for future work in PDM system development. This has impact on integration into PDM systems in that the system must be able to fully open all DFs that it contains and parse content for analysis.

All 25 analytics provide description of activity, and as such demonstrate the potential for PDM data to provide automatic, detailed, and real-time monitoring capability. The breadth of description of analytic outputs is particularly exciting, describing many and varied aspects of engineer activity.

Data held within current PDM systems allows analysis of process-based and design-based CSFs, but with little capability to evaluate CSFs related to person and context categories. Extension to communication data enhances evaluation of person categories, but not context. As each of these areas is of vital importance to high performance this suggests a weakness in analysis as applied to PDM systems – it will not capture performance entirely.

Extension of PDM systems to capture and analyse communications sent as part of engineering work has great potential to inform of performance in person-based CSFs and extend the analytic capability of PDM systems generally. These specifically include areas of performance in which PDM systems are unable to inform.

Many analytics inform multiple CSFs, thereby providing a means through which limited implementation may provide broader information and understanding.

5.1 Benefits and Challenges in Implementation of Analytics

In context of management of engineering work through implementation of such analytics, several benefits and opportunities exist. First, this work demonstrates (1) opportunity for extension of analyses based on current PDM data, (2) opportunities for extension of PDM analytic capability through content-analysis, and (3) opportunity for extension via communication data capture and analysis. Each of these creates opportunity to address key challenges in engineering management. The applicability to PDM systems is highly significant, in that their near-ubiquitous implementation and data-neutrality of analytics build on infrastructure already in existence. Second, the broad categories of CSF against which analytics inform show the usefulness of such an approach in generating broad understanding. This is particularly true where single analytics relate to multiple CSFs, and through the emergent effect of simultaneous analysis of many aspects of engineering work. Third, the autonomy of each analytic provides significant capability, in that the investigative effort of managers may be reduced while simultaneously increasing their understanding of work performance. Fourth, analytics may be applied directly to data currently held within PDM systems, initially to basic meta-data created as part of the DF creation and modification process, and later through expansion of PDM capabilities to analysis of DF content directly.

There remain, however, several challenges to full implementation. First, as with the methods of implementation and data capture of PDM systems themselves, analytics applied must be selected and validated on a case-by-case basis. While general applicability to simple data-types exists, the uniqueness in data-types across engineering industry introduces significant complication. Further, as high performance may manifest in different ways for each unique work situation, the interpretation of performance from any analytic must be contextualized to the specific situation by managers before actions may be taken. Next, while usefulness of such analytics has been demonstrated, capability given current PDM data is limited primarily to CSFs concerning the Design and Process, hence away from the Persons involved in work and the situation Context. This presents both a difficulty and an opportunity; for full analysis of work performance PDM data capture must be expanded, and that capture and analysis of ongoing communications provides an avenue by which this may be best achieved. Finally, application of such analytics face technical challenges in their implementation that must be overcome. These include such well-documented issues as the formation of dictionaries for linguistic analysis (as required by email and report content analysis), issues associated with data privacy and security in autonomous analysis (i.e. for email), consistency in input data structure and standardisation across industry and analytic implementations, and complexity and demonstration of validity of big-data approaches.

5.2 Conclusion

Application of analytics such as those studied have broad capability to support and enhance the capabilities of PDM systems, particularly in that many have direct applicability to the data PDM systems currently capture. This work has shown the opportunity for immediate and detailed analysis of performance utilizing only existing PDM data, and the potential for extension of capability using content analysis and the additional capture of communications sent as part of engineering work. These analytics have strength in autonomy and speed, with potential for near real-time provision of information that has previously been unavailable to managerial decision makers.

References

1. Cataldo, M., Nambiar, S.: The impact of geographic distribution and the nature of technical coupling on the quality of global software development projects. J. Softw. Evol. Process **24**, 153–168 (2012)
2. Earl, C., Eckert, C., Clarkson, J.: Design change and complexity. In: 2nd Workshop on Complexity in Design and Engineering (2005)
3. Floricel, S., Miller, R.: Strategizing for anticipated risks and turbulence in large-scale engineering projects. Int. J. Proj. Manag. **19**(8), 445–455 (2001)
4. Watson, J.: Keynote address at the University of Bath (2012)
5. Snider, C., Škec, S., Gopsill, J.A., Hicks, B.J.: The characterisation of engineering activity through email communication and content dynamics, for support of engineering project management. Des. Sci. **3** (2017)
6. Snider, C., Gopsill, J.A., Jones, S., Shi, L., Hicks, B.: Understanding engineering projects: an integrated vehicle health management approach to engineering project monitoring. In: Proceedings of the International Conference on Engineering Design, ICED 2015, vol. 3, no. DS 80–03 (2015)
7. Snider, C., Emanuel, L., Gopsill, J.A., Joel-Edgar, S., Hicks, B.J.: Identifying the influences on performance of engineering design and development projects. In: International Conference on Engineering Design, ICED 2017 (2017)
8. Toor, S.-R., Ogunlana, S.O.: Beyond the 'iron triangle': stakeholder perception of key performance indicators (KPIs) for large-scale public sector development projects. Int. J. Proj. Manag. **28**(3), 228–236 (2010)
9. Baccarini, D., Collins, A.: Critical success factors for projects. In: Surfing the Waves: Management Challenges; Management Solutions (2003)
10. Hill, A., Song, S., Dong, A., Agogino, A.M.: Identifying shared understanding in design using document analysis. In: Proceedings of the 13th International Conference on Design Theory and Methodology (2001)
11. Hansen, M.T.: Knowledge networks: explaining effective knowledge sharing in multiunit companies. Organ. Sci. **13**(3), 232–248 (2002)
12. Schmidt, R., Lyytinen, K., Keil, M., Cule, P.: Identifying software project risks: an international Delphi study. J. Manag. Inf. Syst. **17**(4), 5–36 (2001)

13. Mesihovic, S., Malmqvist, J., Pikosz, P.: Product data management system-based support for engineering project management. J. Eng. Des. **15**(4), 389–403 (2004)
14. Sackett, P.J., Bryan, M.G.: Framework for the development of a product data management strategy. Int. J. Oper. Prod. Manag. **18**(2), 168–179 (1998)
15. Palos, S., Kiviniemi, A., Kuusisto, J.: Future perspectives on product data management in building information modeling. Constr. Innov. **14**(1), 52–68 (2014)
16. Li, J., Tao, F., Cheng, Y., Zhao, L.: Big data in product lifecycle management. Int. J. Adv. Manuf. Technol. **81**, 667–684 (2015)
17. Patrashkova-Volzdoska, R., McComb, S., Green, S., Compton, W.: Examining a curvilinear relationship between communication frequency and team performance in cross-functional project teams. IEEE Trans. Eng. Manag. **50**(3), 262–269 (2003)

Robot Interaction Through Smart Contract for Blockchain-Based Coalition Formation

Alexander Smirnov and Nikolay Teslya(✉)

SPIIRAS, 14th Line 39, 199178 St. Petersburg, Russia
{smir, teslya}@iias.spb.su

Abstract. Nowadays robots are able to perform decisions independent from the operator. Also, they are able to form a various kind of unions, such as swarms, schools, or coalitions to perform joint task solving. The most powerful and flexible type of union is coalitions. Due to each robot acts like an independent agent it is important to provide trusted interaction between them. It is quite hard to do this with existing methods based only on the knowledge representation using ontologies and reasoning techniques. The paper proposes to use smart contracts in blockchain to enrich the knowledge-based system by functions, specific for blockchain such as immutable transaction log, consensus between all participants as well as possibility to automate control on task resolving. The paper describes the new environment framework based on integration of cyberphysical system and blockchain, and interaction model between all framework elements using BPMN 2.0 notation. Smart contracts presented in the paper provide functions for tasks distribution between robots, resource allocation, and monitoring the task execution and reward distribution.

Keywords: Coalition · Robot · CPS · Blockchain · Smart contract

1 Introduction

Nowadays robots are able to make independent decisions in unknown situations to perform planned actions considering current context. It becomes available by equipping robots with a large number of various sensors to check the physical environment parameters, actuators to make actions in it, microcontrollers that provide high computation power as well as computational algorithms that allow making decisions based on information received from embedded sensors of the robot or external information sources.

Also, robots can perform the joint work to solve a common problem under current conditions. There are a large number of various solutions dedicated to the joint work performed by a group of robots. Among them, such models of joint work can be distinguished, like swarms, schooling and collective (coalition) work. The first two models are based on imitating wildlife swarms or schools, such as fish schools or insect swarms. Robots in such models use simple behavior patterns that allow them to make decisions based on a limited amount of information provided by nearest neighbors.

Published by Springer Nature Switzerland AG 2018.
P. Chiabert et al. (Eds.): PLM 2018, IFIP AICT 540, pp. 611–620, 2018.
https://doi.org/10.1007/978-3-030-01614-2_56

In a coalition model, each robot is viewed as a separate entity also known as agent, which allows the use of approaches developed for multi-agent systems [1, 2]. Robots can form a coalition when they are faced a problem and plan joint actions to solve it. Each robot in the coalition operates independently from the others, but within the scope of the developed plan and taking into consideration the current context. This approach provides possibility to make maximum use of the capabilities of individual robots to achieve a common goal. However, robot coalition formation with the distribution of tasks among all coalition members is very difficult NP-complete task. To date, many solutions have been proposed that provide an approximate solution to the coalition forming task [2–6]. Another important task in the robots coalition formation is the organization of an information interaction environment between them, which allows information exchanging about the current situation and the distribution of tasks among the participants in the coalition.

Tasks distribution and assignment among the coalition participants requires specific functions to be implemented in the interaction environment of cyberphysical system (CPS) formed by physical environment, robots and software [7]. The interaction based only on the knowledge representation using ontologies and reasoning techniques to distribute tasks among coalition participants can not provide a full picture of how the tasks were distributed [8]. Coalition members can get an approximate idea of this, only by making full reasoning among the knowledge of other members. This behavior is more typical for swarm interaction models and reduces overall efficiency of the coalition.

To enrich existing interaction methods, it is proposed to use a central or distributed ledger, in which results or coalition participants' work are displayed. Such ledger allows to reduce the number of calculations on the coalition formation stage and to distribute tasks taking into account the capabilities and characteristics of all the participants in the coalition. At the same time, each participant at any time will have a view of task distribution as well as when it is expected to receive the result from other participants and what resources are involved in solving the overall problem. The overall view makes it possible to reconfigure the coalition on the fly by adding new or replacing participants which will know what they should do from the very beginning.

The paper presents a usage of blockchain to enrich existing robots coalition formation approach based on context management methodology and publish/subscribe-based semantic interoperability mechanism. During the coalition creation, robots are negotiating to spread own knowledge about the task being solved, their current state and parameters of the environment. The negotiation process is carried out in a common information space also known as smart space, and the result of negotiations is the coalition in which the common complex problem is divided to tasks distributed among the coalition members. The separate tasks are bond to the robots, as well as the required resources, and the remuneration for solving the problem. Assignment and binding of tasks, resources and remuneration is proposed to be carried out using a smart contract that is based on the blockchain technology.

The rest of the paper is structured as follows. Section 2 provides description of related works in field of blockchain usage for robots and Internet of Thing components interaction. Section 3 provides a framework structure for robot negotiation during the coalition formation based on the cyberphysical smart space concept and blockchain, and model of the framework's components interaction using the BPMN 2.0 notation. Section 4 describes types of smart contracts used for negotiation and code examples for each type of contract.

2 Related Work

This section is aimed to provide examples of blockchain usage for organizing interaction between coalition participants in various models

The paper [8] considers the use of blockchain technology to create a logically centralized system for managing the distribution of tasks among coalition members. The blockchain technology itself is considered as a mechanism for recording and tracking transactions between participants performing control over the distribution of tasks. At the same time, it is possible to create a virtual ledger that contains all distributions of the assets available among the coalition participants.

The paper [9] provides an example of the E-Business model for decentralized autonomous corporations based on IoT and blockchain. The blockchain network is used here to create smart contracts and perform payment transactions using Bitcoin and system's own currency - IoTcoin. The presented approach provides the following advantages that can also be used in robot coalitions: internal resources of the system are presented in the form of payment system tokens; distributed ledger for transactions, built-in mechanism of digital signature; and protection of transactions by linking blocks with a hash function of a given complexity. Interaction between elements is carried out by transactions passing through four phases: preparing a transaction, negotiating, signing a contract, and fulfilling the terms of the contract.

A similar method is considered in relation to a Smart Home scenario in [10]. Also, there is an unchanged transaction ledger as an advantage of integrating IoT and Blockchain technologies. The proposed framework provides the following transaction processing functions: transaction storage, access to the transactions history and real-time monitoring. Also, due to the adaptation of the hierarchical structure of the proposed framework (which includes three levels: the smart home, overlay network, and cloud storage), optimization of resource consumption is achieved, and scalability of the network is increased. The functions of the block are focused on the level of interaction of elements in the overlay network.

It is also noted that the combination of the peer-to-peer network and the cryptographic algorithms that are underlying the blockchain technology allow for a negotiation process and consensus building without the presence of any controlling authorities. The distributed nature of the blockchain can be used in swarm robotics to store global knowledge about swarm actions [11]. At the same time, due to blockchain, the security of the transmitted data is ensured (garbage data can affect the achievement of a common goal), distributed decision making (creating a distributed voting system for the solution and use of the multi-signature), separation of robots behavior (switching between behavior patterns depending on the robot's role in the swarm), the emergence of new business models using the swarm. In addition, the availability of a distributed transaction ledger allows new robots to join the swarm and gain all the knowledge they have gained prior to the moment of inclusion by downloading and analyzing the transaction history.

3 Robot Interaction Framework

3.1 Framework Description

Robot interaction for coalition creation and functioning is based on the cyberphysical framework. The proposed framework implements publish/subscribe mechanism to provide real-time information sharing between robots. The conceptual scheme of the framework for the robots interaction is presented on Fig. 1. The framework is based on the smart space concept that implements publish/subscribe interaction mechanism using the "blackboard" interaction model. It allows to organize interaction of robots in the physical and cyber (virtual) spaces that includes solo and joint actions of robots with various physical objects into the operation environment, information exchange about the current state of robots, objects, and environment for planning further joint actions during the coalition formation.

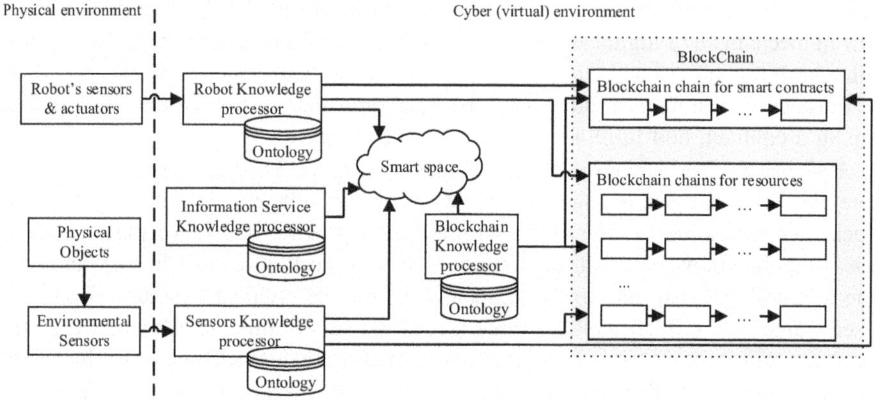

Fig. 1. Framework for robot coalition interaction

Large number of different robots and sensors, from different manufacturers and with different software, connected using different data transfer network raises a problem of the great heterogeneity of provided information and function as well as distribution of coalition participants that should be taken into account during their interaction. To provide interoperability between all coalition participants, the information exchange between them is implemented based on the ontologies usage. Such approach allows to expand the context by providing additional information about the semantic meaning of individual context parameters of shared information, for example, robot characteristics or object measurements. Each member of the CPS is presented by a knowledge processor (KP). KP implements functions of processing information from CPS member, as well as interaction (sharing and requesting the information) with other KPs using ontologies. For this purpose the common ontology can be developed for the whole system, or ontologies of individual components can be used, and information exchange between them is carried out using ontology matching methods [12, 13] including usage of background knowledge for matching process [14]. The concept of cyberphysical smart space in this case allows providing all CPS members a common information space through which they can distribute information. All the members have equal access rights to read and write information in cyberphysical space.

CPS itself cannot be viewed as trusted environment due to the lack of mechanisms to check authorship and correctness of the information shared through the cyber environment. To provide trustiness, information exchange that requires long-term immutable storage and the impossibility of unauthorized access to stored information it is proposed to use blockchain technology. These properties of the blockchain are required to solve several tasks at once, namely: monitoring the implementation of the basic norms of coalition interaction and agreements recorded in the smart contracts, as well as control over the expenditure of resources, including the basic resources of the system, specific to the problem area of the problem being solved. Several independent chains are created in the blockchain to store the distribution state of each of the available resources (Fig. 1). A separate chain of blocks is used to share smart contracts that store the basic norms of behavior in the coalition and agreements formed based on the norms for the distribution of tasks among the coalition members.

3.2 Interaction Model

The interaction between all components of framework for coalition interaction is presented on Fig. 2 using BPMN 2.0 notation. Robots interact with each other through the cyberphysical smart space and through the blockchain by using of KP located on the robots' control block. KP provides the functions of processing data from physical components of robots, as well as sharing information through the cyber space. In addition, KP implements functions for robots interaction with each other during the coalition formation and accessing to the blockchain to obtain information about the available resources required to solve the bond subtask as well as to obtain the required amount of resource according to the corresponding smart contract.

Physical and cyber resources are also presented in the framework by corresponding KPs—Sensors KP for control the physical resources and information service KP to control the information resources. They perform control on resources state and timely informing all participants of cyberphysical system about changes in resources state and their characteristics as well as storing large data sets from sensors and robots in the cyber space (Fig. 2). Resource characteristics changes are displayed in the smart space, while a changes of available amount of resources are displayed in the corresponding blockchain chain, which allows tracking its consumption and arrival. In order to ensure trust when changing the amount of resource, access to the blockchain is provided for all KPs directly using the private-public key pair from blockchain platform.

Cyber space is connected to the blockchain through blockchain KP. This KP provides consistency between information in cyber space and blockchain. It can be necessary for automatic control over the performance of smart contract conditions based on information located in smart space.

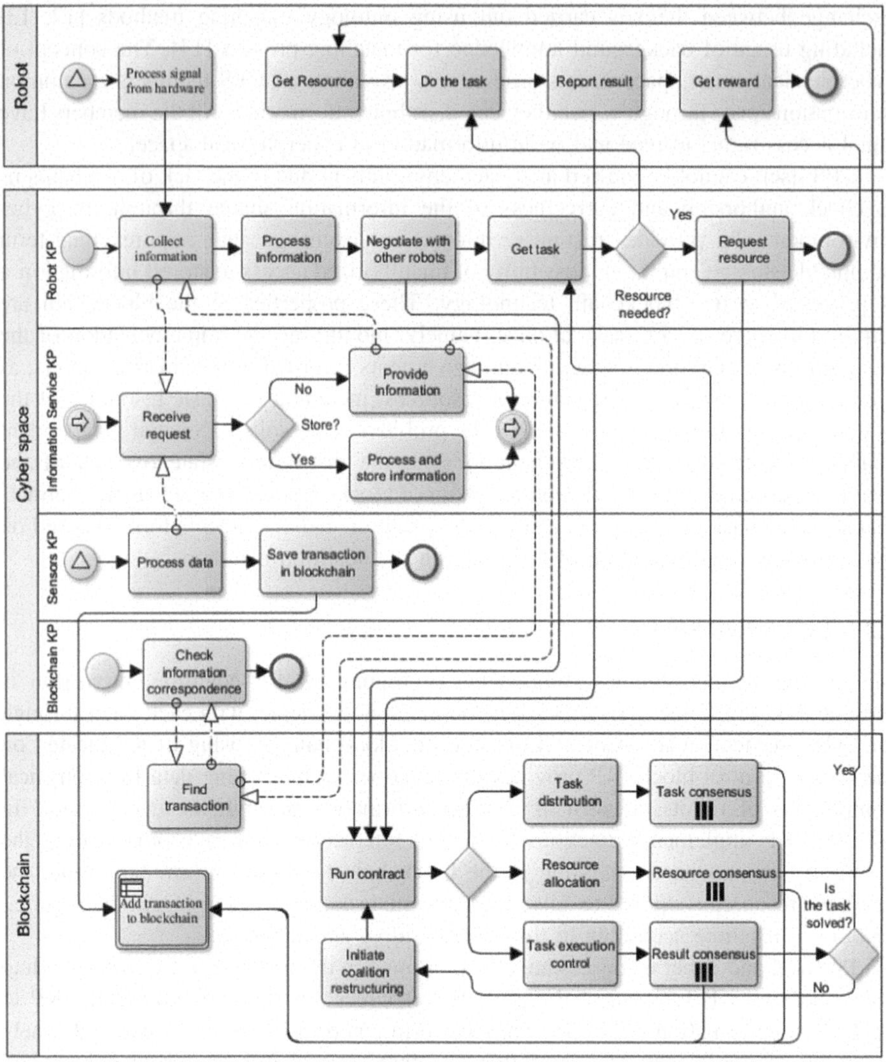

Fig. 2. Robot interaction model

When robot processes collected information required for the task it negotiates with other robots to make an agreement which task have to be solved by it. Conditions of the agreement are fixed into a smart contract that is placed in the blockchain's separate contract-oriented chain. To fox the task distribution new blocks are added to the blockchain that bind robots and subtasks. If robot needs some resource, it should provide request to the blockchain and allocation will be stored into the new transaction. In the subtask was successfully resolved the robot receives a bonus, which is to increase the competence parameter associated with the task being solved or some amount of internal currency. In case of non-fulfillment of the contract, the robot gets a lowering of the relevant competence, and the other participants receive an automatic notification about faults to adjust the plans for performing their tasks.

4 Smart Contract Examples for Robots Negotiation

Automation of robots interaction for the coalition formation and joint work is carried out through smart contracts. They describe the basic interactions of robots among themselves and during resources consumption. There are three types of contracts in the system, according to the functions provided:

- Contract for the tasks distribution between robots;
- Contract for resource allocation;
- Contract for monitoring the task execution.

A description of each of the contract types is presented below taking into account the platform used for blockchain creation. It is proposed to use the Hyperledger Fabric platform to build the blockchain environment for robots' interaction [15]. This choice can be explained in the way that the Fabric provides extensive architecture capabilities for configuring the platform for various tasks, as well as the ability to organize private blockchains. The platform provides a key-value storage for recording transactions, the ability to replace the mechanism for achieving consensus (by default, the Byzantine Fault Tolerance (BFT) mechanism is implemented using the BFT-SMaRt software module [16]), as well as the creation of contracts using the programming languages Go and Java, and contracts are executed in containers based on Docker. The declared speed of the platform satisfies the needs for interaction between robots due to the possibility of processing 3500 transactions per second [15].

4.1 Contract for the Tasks Distribution Between Robots

The distribution of tasks between robots is based on an analysis of the robot's correspondence to the requirements of the task to solve it, as well as the robot's requirements for rewarding for the task solution. It is believed that the dividing of a complex task into sub-tasks is predetermined and known at the time of the coalition formation. Correspondence of the robot to a certain subtask is determined by analyzing its equipment and comparing the onboard equipment to the one that is required to solve the subtask. At the same time robots, spending their energy and work resource can demand a reward in the form of an internal currency of the system, which can later be used to repair or charge by the owner of the robot. The contract presented here describes the search for robots to solve subtasks and binds the subtask to the robot, which can and is ready to perform it.

```
var robot, robot2 Robot    // Robots of the system
var task Task             // Task to be solved
func findRobot(stub shim.ChaincodeStubInterface, args
[]string) (string, error) {
  robot, robot2, task = args[0], args[1], args[2]
  if robot.properties == task.requirements{
    if robot.work_cost < robot2.work_cost {
    // bind task to robot, calculate end time and write
to the ledger
      stub.PutState(task.id, robot.id)
      stub.PutState(task.time, calc_end_time(robot))
    }
  }else return error
}
```

4.2 Contract for Resource Allocation

The resources used by robots are represented in the blockchain as tokens. Each resource has its own token, and the total number of tokens for the resource cannot exceed the maximum amount of the resource in the system (for example, for plant fertilizer in case of agriculture task or drugs in case of medicine task this quantity can be limited by the storage capacity of the warehouse), and the token itself is indivisible, corresponding to the minimum available unit of resource.

To account for the distribution of resources in the blockchain, a separate chain is created, which is realized in Hyperledger Fabric through channels. Each channel is accessible only to those participants who have an appropriate smart contract, which makes it possible to isolate the channels from each other.

```
func allocateResource(stub shim.ChaincodeStubInterface,
args []string) (string, error) {
  robot, amount = args[0], args[1]
  if getState(resource) > amount { // allocate resource
      stub.PutState(robot.id, amount)
      stub.PutState(resource, getState(resource)-amount)
  } else return error
}
```

4.3 Contract for Monitoring the Task Execution

The task execution process is also tracked through a smart contract. This approach allows real-time notification of other coalition participants about the fact of the solving ending and automatically verifies the correctness and reliability of the subtask solution by interested coalition participants, for whom the result is important. If they agree with the results, the robot who solved the subtask is paid a reward and the performance of the entire task is progressing further according to the plan. If the robot has not coped with the solution, the contract condition is not met and, accordingly, the robot is not paid a reward, and the robot itself is replaced by another having the required competencies. At the same time, the plan for solving the common task must be recalculated taking into account the change in the composition of the coalition.

```
func setResolved(stub shim.ChaincodeStubInterface, args
[]string) (string, error) {
  robot, task, state = args[0], args[1], args[2]
  if state == "Resolved" {
      stub.delState(robot.id, task.id)
      stub.setState(task.id, "resolved")
  }
} else return crror
```

5 Conclusion

The use of blockchain technology and smart contracts has been proposed to provide immutable distributed storage of transactions about robot actions and resource allocation available for all coalition participants. This kind of storage is important on the negotiation stage when the coalition is formed to bind separated tasks with concrete coalition participants as well as on the execution stage to check the tasks execution process. Integration of blockchain and cyberphysical smart space had allowed to reduce the number of calculations on the coalition formation stage and to distribute tasks taking into account the capabilities and characteristics of all the participants in the coalition.

Interaction model has been developed for the proposed framework components. It allowed to detect main interaction between components and formalize types of contracts needed for robots negotiation and joint task solving. These types are: tasks distribution between robots; resource allocation; and monitoring of the task execution. For each type of contract the examples had been proposed taking into account the Hyperledger Fabric blockchain platform specific. This platform has been selected for the proposed framework because it provides extensive architecture capabilities for configuring the platform for various tasks, as well as the ability to organize private blockchains and high performance in transaction processing.

As a result of the smart space and blockchain integration each robot is provided a possibility to have a view of task distribution at any time as well as have a view of what is expected time to receive the result from other participants and what resources are involved in solving the overall problem. The overall view makes it possible to reconfigure the coalition on the fly by adding new or replacing participants which will know what they should do from the very beginning.

Acknowledgments. The presented research was supported by the projects funded through grants # 17-29-07073, 17-07-00247 and 17-07-00327 of the Russian Foundation for Basic Research, and State Research # 0073-2018-0002.

References

1. Kaliaev, A.: Multiagent approach for building distributed adaptive computing system. Procedia Comput. Sci. **18**, 2193–2202 (2013). https://doi.org/10.1016/j.procs.2013.05.390
2. Guerrero, J., Oliver, G., Valero, O.: Multi-robot coalitions formation with deadlines: complexity analysis and solutions. PLoS One **12**, 1–26 (2017). https://doi.org/10.1371/journal.pone.0170659
3. Ayari, E., Hadouaj, S., Ghedira, K.: A dynamic decentralised coalition formation approach for task allocation under tasks priority constraints. In: 2017 18th International Conference on Advanced Robotics (ICAR), pp. 250–255. IEEE (2017). https://doi.org/10.1109/icar.2017.8023526
4. Mouradian, C., Sahoo, J., Glitho, R.H., Morrow, M.J., Polakos, P.A.: A coalition formation algorithm for multi-robot task allocation in large-scale natural disasters. In: 2017 13th International Wireless Communications and Mobile Computing Conference (IWCMC), pp. 1909–1914. IEEE (2017). https://doi.org/10.1109/iwcmc.2017.7986575
5. Dukeman, A., Adams, J.A.: Hybrid mission planning with coalition formation. Auton. Agents Multi-agent Syst. **31**, 1424–1466 (2017). https://doi.org/10.1007/s10458-017-9367-7
6. Agarwal, M., Agrawal, N., Sharma, S., Vig, L., Kumar, N.: Parallel multi-objective multi-robot coalition formation. Expert Syst. Appl. **42**, 7797–7811 (2015). https://doi.org/10.1016/j.eswa.2015.05.032
7. Guerrero, J., Oliver, G.: Multi-robot coalition formation in real-time scenarios. Rob. Auton. Syst. **60**, 1295–1307 (2012). https://doi.org/10.1016/j.robot.2012.06.004
8. Verma, D., Desai, N., Preece, A., Taylor, I.: A block chain based architecture for asset management in coalition operations. In: Pham, T., Kolodny, M.A. (eds.) Proceeding of SPIE 10190, Ground/Air Multisensor Interoperability, Integration, and Networking for Persistent ISR VIII, p. 101900Y (2017). https://doi.org/10.1117/12.2264911
9. Zhang, Y., Wen, J.: The IoT electric business model: using blockchain technology for the internet of things. Peer-to-Peer Netw. Appl. **10**, 983–994 (2017). https://doi.org/10.1007/s12083-016-0456-1
10. Dorri, A., Kanhere, S.S., Jurdak, R.: Towards an optimized blockchain for IoT. In: Proceedings of the Second International Conference on Internet-of-Things Design and Implementation - IoTDI 2017, pp. 173–178 (2017). https://doi.org/10.1145/3054977.3055003
11. Ferrer, E.C.: The blockchain: a new framework for robotic swarm systems (2016). arxiv:1608.00695
12. Smirnov, A., Kashevnik, A., Shilov, N., Balandin, S., Oliver, I., Boldyrev, S.: On-the-fly ontology matching in smart spaces: a multi-model approach. In: Balandin, S., Dunaytsev, R., Koucheryavy, Y. (eds.) NEW2AN/ruSMART - 2010. LNCS, vol. 6294, pp. 72–83. Springer, Heidelberg (2010). https://doi.org/10.1007/978-3-642-14891-0_7
13. Euzenat, J., Shvaiko, P.: Ontology Matching. Springer, Heidelberg (2013). https://doi.org/10.1007/978-3-642-38721-0
14. Smirnov, A., Teslya, N., Savosin, S., Shilov, N.: Ontology matching for socio-cyberphysical systems: an approach based on background knowledge. In: Galinina, O., Andreev, S., Balandin, S., Koucheryavy, Y. (eds.) NEW2AN/ruSMART/NsCC - 2017. LNCS, vol. 10531, pp. 29–39. Springer, Cham (2017). https://doi.org/10.1007/978-3-319-67380-6_3
15. Androulaki, E., et al.: Hyperledger Fabric: A Distributed Operating System for Permissioned Blockchains, p. 15 (2018). arxiv:1801.10228
16. Bessani, A., Sousa, J., Vukolić, M.: A byzantine fault-tolerant ordering service for the hyperledger fabric blockchain platform. In: Proceedings of the 1st Workshop on Scalable and Resilient Infrastructures for Distributed Ledgers - SERIAL 2017, pp. 1–10. ACM Press (2017). https://doi.org/10.1145/3152824.3152830

Knowledge Capture and Reuse Through Expert's Activity Monitoring in Engineering Design

Harvey Rowson[1,3](✉), Matthieu Bricogne[1], Lionel Roucoules[2], Alexandre Durupt[1], and Benoit Eynard[1]

[1] Université de Technologie de Compiègne, Compiègne, France
harvey.rowson@utc.fr
[2] Ecole Nationale Supérieure d'Arts et Métiers, Aix-en-Provence, France
[3] DeltaCAD, Lacroix Saint-Ouen, France

Abstract. This paper deals with artificial intelligence driven product engineering support. Many software systems are available to support the product lifecycle, especially during product design, such as CAD, PDM, CAE, SDM, etc. Most product development process is performed using these systems, which through their rich user interfaces allow skilled professionals to express their expertise and knowledge using the tools and functions the software is willing to provide them. At the end of the day, the result of their work is a model, built through a user interface, and stored in a repository. The goal of our research is to reverse engineer the user's knowledge by analysing his/her actions with the software system, based on the assumption that the process will itself be meta-knowledge driven and that we will focus on engineering software which provide semantically rich user interfaces. The aim of this paper is to investigate the idea of building reusable expert knowledge from actions on engineering software user interfaces. It first outlines existing works from different fields and identifies remaining issues. It then suggest an approach to address these issues and put together an operational system.

Keywords: Artificial intelligence · Knowledge based engineering
Engineering design · GUI monitoring · Computer vision

1 Introduction and Objective

(Rocca 2012) observe that product engineering could be improved in order to reduce time spent on sometimes repetitive and other times trivial tasks. This would allow designers to focus their attention and time on higher value-added undertakings. They analyse the subject from a Knowledge Based Engineering (KBE) point of view and explores how different paradigms, including Information Technology (IT), Artificial Intelligence (AI) and Computer Aided Design (CAD), can lead to miscellaneous approaches to KBE. One conclusion is that an important improvement would be "lowering the accessibility level", suggesting improving the ability for non-programmers to be able to define the KBE application, in particular by closing the gap between so called KBE languages and natural languages (Rocca 2012).

Published by Springer Nature Switzerland AG 2018.
P. Chiabert et al. (Eds.): PLM 2018, IFIP AICT 540, pp. 621–630, 2018.
https://doi.org/10.1007/978-3-030-01614-2_57

More generally, (Intharah et al. 2017) state that much time is wasted using software non-creatively, on repetitive and tedious tasks. They introduce an approach based on Computer Vision (CV) and Graphical User Interface (GUI) analysis stated as "learning-by-demonstration in a GUI world". They perform extensive experimentations with these concepts. Although this clearly could help addressing some of the issues observed by (Rocca 2012) a few years earlier, they nevertheless identify a number of shortcomings. These range from misclassification issues of user actions to unawareness of the system's (and software's) state. (Dominic et al. 2016) elaborate an AI based approach to capture, store and reuse knowledge within bridge structure calculation, which is demonstrated through usage of Bayesian networks to optimise parametric design. These works all strive at enhancing the user's efficiency while using software systems, by bringing some assistance in some form, known as KBE in the engineering community.

Our research tackles the problem from a complementary angle, combining many of the previously mentioned approaches, by suggesting the use of what we will call an Engineering Personal Assistant (EPA). An EPA is a software agent designed to help engineers use their dedicated software to perform their product designs. The focus of the EPA is twofold, first it ambitions to capture knowledge by monitoring the usage of the engineering software (it thus learns by example), and second it aspires to reuse this knowledge to help guide the user in future usages (it thus helps by pertinent suggestion). We believe that many by-product applications are possible for both of these aspects, as the captured knowledge could be used in many ways, and the advisory agent could rely on multiple knowledge sources. The EPA concept has some similarities with other forms of assistance to software usage, such as the Microsoft Clippy assistant[1]. This was integrated in office 1997 and abandoned around 2004, it was used mostly as a contextual user friendly online help system. Virtual assistants[2] are other examples, such as Amazon Alexa, Apple Siri, Microsoft Cortana or Google Assistant. These focus mainly on providing a voice control interface to regular actions (dial contact, create calendar event, perform Web search, …).

Our proposal, which is in an early state, aspires to achieve a robust approach, at least conceptually for now, by building upon CV, AI and KBE technologies in a predefined context, which is that of product engineering and design. Regarding the knowledge capture aspect, CV is used to monitor and log the system state and actions. KBE structures and principles, and the focus on product engineering methods and tools, are transverse to the whole approach, providing an overarching domain specific background allowing the necessary paradigmatic foundations. This paper therefore summarises related works from the two main fields which we plan to build upon and then proposes an operational process to enable the vision we have developed, which we plan to implement in a forthcoming demonstrator which is in progress.

---

[1] See https://en.wikipedia.org/wiki/Office_Assistant for additional information.

[2] See https://en.wikipedia.org/wiki/Virtual_assistant_(artificial_intelligence) for details.

2 State of the Art of Related Works

2.1 The Field of Knowledge Based Engineering (KBE)

When investigating the state of the art of works targeting a software solution to optimize product engineering activities, KBE is a recurring approach. (Danjou et al. 2008) timestamps the birth of KBE to be around 1980 and present an approach focused on encapsulating knowledge in customized features in order to achieve capitalization and reuse in a CAD based environment, which now underlies many knowledge-based systems embedded in engineering tools, as discussed further.

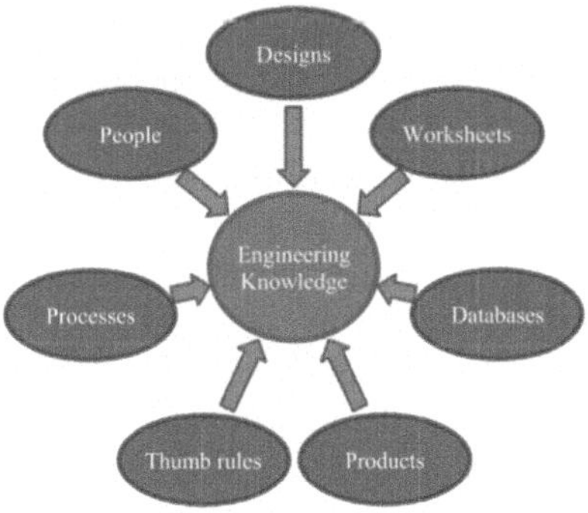

Fig. 1. Different elements of knowledge according to (Reddy et al. 2015)

(Reddy et al. 2015) present a survey of KBE approaches which illustrates the strong activity of this field and the diversity of approaches and results one can observe. They identify KBE as being a paradigmatic evolution over parametric design, with the advantage, amongst others, to be better suited for rapid development of customisable product families. Technologically, they identify KBE to be supported by information technologies, artificial intelligence and knowledge management. The popularity of KBE is rooted in the competitive advantage it brings for efficiently developing new products including customisation and component reusability. With Fig. 1, they clarify the concept of knowledge engineering and propose a diagram illustrating how it relates to its environment.

According to their analysis, 80% of design activities can be considered to be recurrent, and KBE can have great impact on these activities. An important step identified for KBE implementation is that of knowledge capturing and formalisation, and they list a number of methods and technics targeting this activity, such as MOKA, KOMPRESSA, DEKLARE or DEE (Reddy et al. 2015) whisle noticing that these produce knowledge bases which are not readily usable, as they require some tooling technology to support them. On the other hand, they also observe that engineering tool providers also implement internal knowledge-based systems[3]. They however state that this produces somewhat limited knowledge basis, as they tend to be specific to the system rather than the field, and also the knowledge is not easily extractable and reusable in different environments. They finally conclude that one of the strongest drawbacks of current KBE approaches, regardless of the two previously mentioned paths, is the difficulty to collect and formalise the knowledge in a robust manner, and believe better usage of Wiki like methods could bring solutions to this.

[3] Some examples of this approach could be Unigraphics NX Knowledge Fusion or Dassault Systemes CATIA Knowledgeware.

(Quintana-Amate et al. 2015) take a focused look at the knowledge sourcing issue. They first account for the successful usage of KBE systems in many industries, with more in-depth analysis of an Aeronautic example, and some of the issues encountered. One of these is the recurring difficulties raised by the need to fuel the KBE system with the required knowledge in the required formalism (often parameterized rules and constraints). They propose an extensive review of methods targeting this upstream phase of most KBE projects, and conclude that this area requires more work in order to solve the many remaining issues and to improve the overall process. They follow with a review of different related approaches in order to suggest finally a set of technologies which are identified as being of higher potential to address the knowledge generation phase. They suggest that artificial intelligence approaches should be pushed to handle this capitalization phase in order to significantly reduce the need of manual structuration and input of information to generate the required knowledge. They conclude with the concept of "learning by doing", which should be promoted in order to use artificial intelligence in a partially automated knowledge acquisition process.

Focusing on civil engineering, and more specifically bridge structure optimization, (Dominic et al. 2016) use modern artificial intelligence results, in the form of Bayesian networks, to establish a model and a method which is able to learn optimization strategies through analysis of existing studies within a bridge management system. They use a training set to perform machine learning processes which result in a fitting of the Bayesian network they designed. Although they do not demonstrate the approach's ability to support advisory actions, they believe this is possible for example by using machine learning technics to bridge the remaining gaps in the different modules of their knowledge management system. In (Dekhtiar et al. 2018), a review on the use of deep learning in CAD and PLM is also proposed.

Section 3 analysis these elements in regards of the EPA objectives and outlines the main aspects which our proposal (in Sect. 4) should focus on in order to fulfil its objectives, in particular automating the capitalisation phases and building a transparent while pervasive solution.

After this look into the field of product engineering, we will now turn towards the field of software testing in which a wealth of highly valuable input can be taken from. As illustrated in the following section, one approach to software testing is the technic consisting in capturing and replaying action sequences on the software through its GUI (in a similar way a human tester would do it).

2.2 The Field of Software Testing and Automation

Software editors, since the advent of GUIs, have faced the daunting task of testing and validating their products. Batch and script-based testing of command file applications have long driven the field of software testing, but these approaches fall short when it comes to software which is not only driven by such command files, and which results are not only so-called output files. The process for testing this type of software, without GUI, is basically to create a test case suite, with a set of input command files and a set of corresponding expected output files. These are then run to check that new versions of the software produce acceptable results as compared to the reference output files.

Although this does present some challenges of its own (especially when the notion of acceptable is fuzzy), it certainly misses the point of testing the GUI layers. (Alégroth and Feldt 2017) seek new solutions to this problem, and start by establishing a clean taxonomy of the existing approaches they have collected from existing tools and existing academic works, focusing on validating the GUI layers of software systems. They identify three distinctive steps in the history of the art of software testing. They go on to classify following three categories: pixel coordinate approaches, event interception methods and computer vision paradigms.

Table 1. Methods from (Qureshi and Nadeem 2013)

		Evaluation Parameters		
		Input representation of GUI under Test	*Intermediate representation*	*Coverage Criteria*
1.	R. Shehady *et. al* (1997)	Input, Output, Variables,States	VFSM Model, FSM Model which is used by Wp Method	All-paths, All-transitions
2.	A.M.Memon *et. al.* (99, 00, 01)	Source file of GUI	Hierarchical Model Scenario (Initial State, Goal State, Operators, Objects)	All-transitions
3.	S. R. Dalal *et. al.* (1999)	Req. & constraints of GUI	Data Model (Specification of inputs for AETGSpec)	Pairwise-interaction event-interaction
4.	L. White and H. Almezen (2000)	Identification of CIS	Reduced FSM (Trace all distinct paths)	All-paths, event-interaction
5.	Belli (2001)	Identification of CIS & FCIS	FSM Model (Trace all valid & invalid paths)	All-paths, event-interaction All-IPs, All-FIPs
6.	Kai-Yuan Cai *et.*	Identification of	Mealy machine/ FSM Model(Convert	All-path,

(Qureshi and Nadeem 2013) propose an extensive analysis of approaches falling into the second generation identified by (Alégroth and Feldt 2017). The interesting point of this is that it illustrates the maturity of this field in contrast to the third generation which is still emerging at the time. Their work breaks down the second generation into 12 families of methods, synthesized in a table classifying them following a number of interesting criteria, namely: Input representation of GUI under test, Intermediate representation, Coverage criteria, Automation, Tool Support, Case study, Fault model, Fault injection. This is illustrated in the Table 1.

(Börjesson and Feldt 2012) state the importance of focusing on the GUI layer of the system under test (the third generation of approaches reported by (Alégroth and Feldt 2017)). They first proceed to outline and analyse the weaknesses associated to event capturing and replay, as done within second generation approaches and summarized above. They then detail existing methods relying on Visual GUI Testing approaches, and provide further analysis of two tools, one which is a commercial software system and the second is the open source software application. They demonstrate the usage of these systems on some experimental cases and conclude to some of the limitations and difficulties mentioned above. They also point out some interesting distinctions between the fields of software testing and software automation, as they point out that the first have a focus on exhaustivity and coverage whereas the second have a focus on understanding and intelligence.

(Moreira and Lopes de Matos 2014) provide some important complementary ideas resulting from their work within the European "FCOMP-01-0124-FEDER-020554" project. Their approach strives to integrate and leverage the fact that GUIs often are built and designed relying on partly shared and standard design patterns and schemes (linked, amongst others, to ergonomic and implementation considerations). They propose a specific model, named DSL PARADIGM, which is able to model these similarities and shared features, and they demonstrate its usage on a number of test cases.

These elements are further analysed in Sect. 3 in the light of the EPA's objectives in order to identify the main aspects our approach (described in Sect. 4) should focus on, particularly targeting a specific type of software and activity, leveraging use interface richness and accepting extensive customisation.

The existing works summarised here within these two areas, although non-exhaustive, show that many scaffolding principles of our approach (detailed in Sect. 4) are already quite developed and should be built upon to elaborate the conceptual and technical elements of our solution. Overall, the field is wealthy and attracts high interest from the international product engineering and software engineering communities, with no sign of slowing down, and with new paradigms regularly emerging and yielding new hopes (for example around the current artificial intelligence trend). It also shows a number of areas where things could be improved if the idea is to promulgate higher robustness and efficiency of product engineering activities, as presented in the below section.

3 Towards a New Kind of Software to Enhance User Support and Efficiency

This section analysis the above state of art at the light of our research objectives, which, as stated in introduction, is to propose an EPA whose purpose is to support efficient knowledge capitalisation and reuse within product engineering activities. More precisely, it aims at capturing the expert's knowledge by monitoring the expert's interactions with the engineering software she/he is using, in a somewhat similar way a human could learn from observing someone else perform a task. However, here we limit the span to an activity consisting in using a software system and we only consider the explicit interactions between the user and system. We expect this capitalisation phase to rely on computer vision (CV) to capture the on-screen actions, and to use some form of advanced processing to transform these actions into reusable knowledge. The EPA then aims at reusing this knowledge through proposals to the user while she/he is interacting with his software. This supposes an identification of the ongoing interaction as being related to a capitalised interaction (again, likely relying on CV and advanced processing). It also implies being able to fit the capitalised interactions to any existing variations, and only then suggesting some support to the user. This can be for example in the form of automating the end of a multi-step but recurrent interaction.

The objective therefore leads us to identify a number of specificities relative to the current state of art in the identified fields we summarised in Sect. 2.

In particular, relative to the field of software testing, it can first be observed that the EPA focuses on a specific type of software, which supports a specific type of activity, respectively engineering support software and product engineering activities. The assumption is that specialising the concepts to this more specific field will reduce complexity and help achieve robust results in capturing interactions. Second, an interesting characteristic of the targeted software (CAD, CAE and PLM systems) is that they display rich user interfaces. This means they have a large variety of widgets (buttons, lists, checkboxes, fields, toolbars, menus, …) and a structure which is viewed as a facilitator in making sense out of the actions. They are hence coined as being semantically rich user interfaces. Third, the method integrates the idea of customisation, meaning that initial work is accepted to adapt the solution to any specificity identified in the target environment which seems of help to achieve the goal. This opens the path to parametrising and fine tuning the approach as to account for variabilities which could otherwise tend to hinder robustness. In particular, this aspect allows to establish a meta-knowledge base (which can include any information deemed useful for the purpose, including in particular static data, dynamic data, algorithms and workflows) which we can use to guide our overall process, more of which will be said in Sect. 4.1

Relative to the field of KBE, one can observe first that a valuable aspect here is the automating of the capitalisation phase through automatic observation and learning. This is seen as complementary to widespread knowledge capitalisation methods mentioned above in Sect. 2.1. Second, the EPA, as its name implies, is a software agent which should be as transparent as possible to the user, who should barely know of its existence except from benefitting from its suggestions and proposed automations. The EPA should seamlessly blend into the user's environment (operating system and engineering software) and will not replace any other system and will not bring any constraints (only possibilities). Third, the solution should not be hard linked to any specific software, and in particular, it should not require changes to the existing software, unlike for example KBE solutions which could be integrated into the CAD systems (Workbenches in CATIA for example). Fourth, the two aspects of the EPA, namely knowledge capturing and knowledge reuse, could be leveraged independently, assuming that the captures knowledge could be of interest for many applications and the advisory engine could maybe be powered by knowledge from other sources than its own capturing.

The research proposal, which is currently in early state and is planned to be developed during upcoming works, is presented in the following as we understand it currently. It consists mainly in building the EPA system as characterised above, starting by outlining its main architectural dimensions and its major operational principles. Different methods are planned for the validation of its conceptual and operational capability. A first goal is to use the EPA to monitor usage videos (such as Catia tutorials found on youtube) and extract and capitalise knowledge from these. A second will be to reuse the acquired knowledge in order to replay the tutorials progressively different settings, for example by first changing technical aspects (screen resolution, colour depth, …) and going towards higher level changes (initial model state, adaptable parameters, …).

4 How to Help Engineers Use Product Engineering Software

The envisioned approach is hence based on the elements introduced above with the main idea being to bridge the gap between existing concepts and the target goals. This section brings further details around these and provides an overall overview of the conceptual framework that is planned to be experimented in future works, as for now it is more of a scaffolding than a framework. To ease understanding, the solution is presented as if modules were independent, processes were sequential and things are monomorphic (viewed along one perspective), more of which will be said at the end of this section. We will first look at the capitalisation process, which will bring us also to the concept of meta-knowledge. We will then move onto the reuse phase, and elaborate on potential by-products the system can open to.

4.1 Capitalisation Through Monitoring and Meta-Knowledge

A central aspect of the solution is that of monitoring the user's interactions. Monitoring in this context is the activity of capturing and tracing the interactions the user has with the software she/he is using (Satama 2006). Examples of such interactions could be when the user activates a button, enters values into fields, activates a toolbar, selects a menu, … (Sadeghi et al. 2016) present a model of such a process, where they relate the development of a product part with the sequence of actions on a CAD software and the related impact within the product model. With this first step in mind, the next step is to look at how this can be performed. As presented in Sect. 2, work has already been done on capturing user actions on graphical user interfaces, and many results have been achieved within these works, whether to bring automation or to support software testing activities. As the EPA is non-intrusive, any approach that involves instrumenting of the target software will be discarded. Therefore, screen content analysis will be the preferred path, using mainly computer vision technology applied to identifying GUI widgets on the screen, and the changes of state of these to help identifying actions without needing to hook (Memon et al. 2003) the operating system's event stack.

To simplify matters, and with no apparent drawback in the frame of our work, it is planned to help this process by providing it with as rich and extensive as necessary data beforehand. (Satama 2006) explore this via the idea of domain specific models to ease testing. This will be part of the aforementioned meta-knowledge base which will be elaborated as required and with accepted overhead work. In particular, this will include information about the possible graphical representations of the interaction widgets (buttons, toolbars, …) and the nature of the actions these widgets generate. This includes contextual variations and the means to identify them as such. For example, the fact that a same widget could perform different actions depending on how it's embedded in the GUI hierarchy. This should be achievable by combining the computer vision technics presented, such as those overviewed in (Leo et al. 2017), and possibly pushing further towards machine learning algorithms in order to benefit from multi representation of each widget, and the purposely created widget base which will be designed specifically for the targeted scenarios.

4.2 Reusing Through Contextual Similarity Identification During Operations

The primary usage of this knowledge base within the EPA paradigm is its reuse to help the user perform tasks where the capitalised knowledge can help automate sequences of tasks the user is encountering. The first step to make this possible (assuming the knowledge base exists that is) is to identify in the current flow of actions an opportunity for reuse. This means analysing the ongoing interactions, with the same technologies and methods as during the capitalisation phase, and identifying in real time a resemblance between the script under elaboration and schemes in the knowledge base. Obviously, the difficulty is predicting the extrapolation of the script, as the script is under construction while the scheme is completed, and the goal is to estimate the chances of any given ongoing script to result into an existing scheme. If a match is identified, and an existing scheme is deemed pertinent regarding the current interactions, the EPA can suggest help to the user. It should present the proposed scheme, and the potentially required customisations. The EPA can then finalise the interaction sequence for him in an automatic manner using again computer vision technologies to identify related widgets and activate them as in (Chang et al. 2010).

It should be noted here, that the usage process is in fact possible regardless of the capitalisation process, providing that the EPA has access to the knowledge in the required formalism, which for testing purposes could be hand produced. This is an interesting feature as it allows working on the subject in a breadth first method rather than a depth first, the latter been subject to deadlock should the capitalisation process reveal unexpected shortcomings. Symmetrically, the capitalisation process can hold value even if the reuse process falls short. Indeed, analysing the usage logs, scripts and schemes could be used in many ways, for example to help promote and enhance best practices or standards across users and teams. Both the capitalisation and reuse aspects can also be imagined coupled with existing KBE systems, either as tools to generate the knowledge, or as agents to use it on the fly, providing that interoperability concerns are accounted for in the knowledge structures and operational principles.

5 Conclusions

This paper has presented a global vision of the Engineering Personal Assistant (EPA) as a Knowledge Based Engineering (KBE) inspired approach hoping to help product engineering and design activities by bringing partial automation of software usage. However, it takes a complementary approach to the current ones, by focusing on automatic capture and learning of the knowledge from monitoring of the user's interactions on the software. State of the art artificial intelligence technologies are the foundational enablers of the process, particularly computer vision linked to machine learning and template matching, and text processing of the logs to extract and build knowledge. Lots of work is planned in putting all this together and elaborating the central informational structures. Current work is focused on formalising the concepts (and models) while experimenting the envisaged technologies, with already some issues identified with the computer vision aspects for example (which seem more sensitive to video encoding and artefacts than expected), but workarounds seem possible.

References

Alégroth, E., Feldt, R.: On the long-term use of visual gui testing in industrial practice: a case study. Empir. Softw. Eng. (2017). https://doi.org/10.1007/s10664-016-9497-6

Börjesson, E., Feldt, R.: Automated system testing using visual GUI testing tools: a comparative study in industry. In: Proceedings of IEEE 5th International Conference Software Testing, Verification Validation, ICST 2012, pp. 350–359 (2012). https://doi.org/10.1109/icst.2012.115

Chang, T.H., Yeh, T., Miller, R.C.: GUI testing using computer vision. In: Proceedings of 28th International Conference Human Factors Computing Systems, pp. 1535–1544 (2010). http://doi.acm.org/10.1145/1753326.1753555

Danjou, S., Lupa, N., Koehler, P.: Approach for automated product modeling using knowledge-based design features (2008)

Dekhtiar, J., Durupt, A., Bricogne, M., Eynard, B., Rowson, H., Kiritsis, D.: Deep learning for big data applications in CAD and PLM – research review, opportunities and case study. Comput. Ind. **100**, 227–243 (2018). https://doi.org/10.1016/j.compind.2018.04.005

Dominic, S., Bügler, M., Borrmann, A.: Knowledge based bridge engineering - artificial intelligence meets building information modeling (2016)

Intharah, T., Turmukhambetov, D., Brostow, G.J.: Help, it looks confusing. In: Proceedings of the 22nd International Conference on Intelligent User Interfaces - IUI 2017, pp. 233–243. ACM Press, New York (2017)

Leo, M., Medioni, G., Trivedi, M., Kanade, T., Farinella, G.M.: Computer vision for assistive technologies. Comput. Vis. Image Underst. **154**, 1–15 (2017). https://doi.org/10.1016/j.cviu.2016.09.001

Memon, A., Banerjee, I., Nagarajan, A.: GUI ripping: reverse engineering of graphical user interfaces for testing (2003)

Moreira, R., Lopes de Matos, M.: Pattern-Based GUI Testing. PQDT - Glob 180 (2014)

Quintana-Amate, S., Bermell-Garcia, P., Tiwari, A.: Transforming expertise into knowledge-based engineering tools: a survey of knowledge sourcing in the context of engineering design. Knowl.-Based Syst. **84**, 89–97 (2015). https://doi.org/10.1016/j.knosys.2015.04.002

Qureshi, I.A., Nadeem, A.: GUI testing techniques: a survey. Int. J. Future Comput. Commun. 142–146 (2013). https://doi.org/10.7763/ijfcc.2013.v2.139

Reddy, E.J., Sridhar, C.N.V., Rangadu, V.P.: Knowledge based engineering: notion, approaches and future trends. Am. J. Intell. Syst. **5**, 1–17 (2015). https://doi.org/10.5923/j.ajis.20150501.01

La, R.G.: Knowledge based engineering: between AI and CAD. Review of a language based technology to support engineering design. Adv. Eng. Inform. **26**, 159–179 (2012). https://doi.org/10.1016/j.aei.2012.02.002

Sadeghi, S., Dargon, T., Rivest, L., Pernot, J.-P.: Capturing and analysing how designers use CAD software (2016)

Satama, M.: Event capturing tool for model-based GUI test automation (2006)

Machine Vision Systems for Industrial Quality Control Inspections

Ricardo Luhm Silva, Marcelo Rudek, Anderson Luis Szejka(✉), and Osiris Canciglieri Junior

Industrial and Systems Engineering Graduate Program, Pontifical Catholic University of Parana, Curitiba, Brazil
{marcelo.rudek, anderson.szejka, osiris.canciglieri}@pucpr.br

Abstract. In this paper we introduce Machine Vision System (MVS) for industrial quality control inspections presenting new perspectives with the recent developments of Artificial Intelligence (AI). A brief literature review is provided which indicates a substantial growth of machine vision new studies and an improved workflow is proposed to include these findings. Besides already existing machine vision solutions there is space to increase detection in quality control inspection and reduce current implementation constraints and technical limitations. The paper shows MVS new development and evinces that a deeper understanding of AI, MVS limitations is needed to provide a clearer path for future studies.

Keywords: Machine vision · Industrial inspection · Machine learning Artificial intelligence

1 Introduction

Visual inspection is an important process in an industry to recognize defective parts, to assure quality conformity of a product and fulfill customer demands [1, 2]. In assembly and manufacturing activities, product and process inspection are usually performed by human inspectors, but due fatigue, small parts, small details, hazardous inspection conditions and process complexity this task may not achieve the desired quality or be almost impossible to detect some types product non-conformities. In this cases a machine vision solution is recommended [1, 3, 4].

Machine Vision System (MVS) consist in applying computer vision to industrial solutions [8]. MVS can be used to perform visual inspection and fulfill industrial and factory performance, consequently improving product quality outcomes. To meet industrial expectations, MVS has been used to reduce product quality problems through improved inspections. Inspection system must be adapted to a scenario which have a wide variety of product features and high production speed assembly lines with complex environment variables from the MVS perspective [5, 6].

The purpose of this article is to provide an overview of MVS concepts and theirs current status for industrial inspection, identifying the main Artificial Intelligence (AI) concepts and application to quality in the automotive industry.

Published by Springer Nature Switzerland AG 2018.
P. Chiabert et al. (Eds.): PLM 2018, IFIP AICT 540, pp. 631–641, 2018.
https://doi.org/10.1007/978-3-030-01614-2_58

2 Theoretical Foundation

2.1 Machine Vision with Artificial Intelligence Techniques Machine Vision System Concepts and Applied Technologies

MVS systems have become imperative in many modern manufacturing facilities as forms of automatic quality inspection. These systems are integrated with manufacturing process where all products must pass through. Most systems consist of a camera (or cameras), PC and usually a controlled lighting environment within an enclosure [7].

2.2 Machine Vision with Artificial Intelligence Techniques

Machine learning and deep learning are data-driven artificial intelligence techniques, which may be applied to MVS. Both techniques uses neural network architecture concepts. which transforms raw data into representative information for decision making. Machine learning can be applied to feature extraction and classification where each step is constructed separately, and it may be highly dependent of an expert knowledge. In the other hand deep learning is applied in both feature extraction and classification steps as an unified neural network solution with requires minimum human interference. Figure 1 shows a comparison between machine learning and deep learning [8].

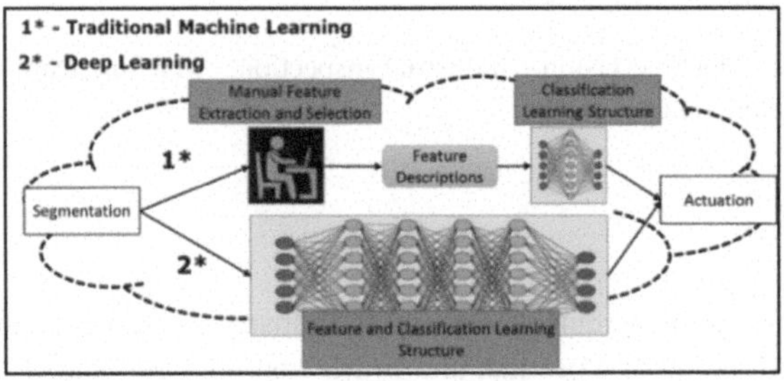

Fig. 1. Comparison between machine learning and deep learning. Adapted from [8].

One major drawback of MVS system without artificial intelligence techniques is that it cannot learn with all the processed images. Every image detail or new fault detection that may occur after the MVS initial setup may not be detected, which can lead to an incorrect information output while MVS with learning features has the potential to learn with new images incomes.

Golbani and Asadpour [4] proposed a block diagram for a typical vision system operation when artificial intelligence techniques were still being developed for MVS, as shown in Fig. 2. A new diagram was built containing the original block together with new AI techniques identified in recent literature. In this new framework is important to emphasize the need of an image knowledge database, which contains object features and quality criteria definitions, which may be used to assist and improve the current learning methods [1, 8].

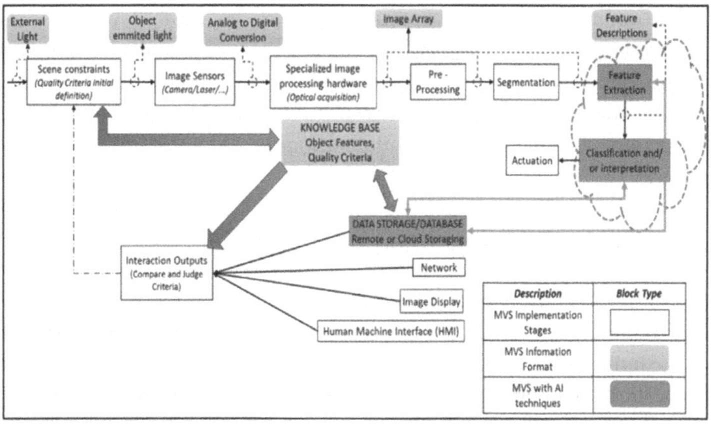

Fig. 2. A block diagram for a typical vision system operation and applicable AI techniques. Adapted from [1, 4, 8].

2.3 1-D and 2-D MVS Industrial Applications

One (1-D) and two dimensional (2-D) MVS have a wide range of applications such as measurement, surface and depth inspection, thermal inspection and robot vision. Each kind of application has its own characteristic equipment with different image gathering source, such as photoelectric sensor, lasers, cameras and so on. Some MVS source types and applications are shown in Fig. 3.

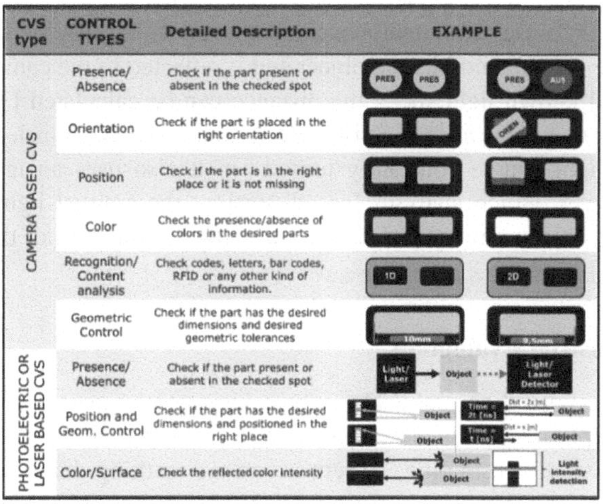

Fig. 3. Conventional MVS types and detection modes. Adapted from [1, 9].

Camera based MVS for industrial applications are commonly used to verify presence or absence of components, verify if the components are in their correct position and orientation, verify if components has the desired colors, analyze and recognize image content such as code bars and inspect size and measure of parts and assembly components [4].

Photoelectric and laser-based MVS inspections can also be used to presence or absence of components, check component positioning and verify desired colors, mainly to measure parts.

2.4 3-D MVS Industrial Applications

Optical non-contact 3-D measurement technique has been used to measure an image of an object and extract its geometrical information. It can be divided in passive and active 3-D sensing systems, where passive works with natural lighting from the scene without controlling the light that goes to the inspected object. While active sensing systems uses an external light, such as laser or a known projected light, by measuring speed of light, laser coherence or applying triangulation techniques [10].

Structured light is an active 3-D sensing system, which illuminates the object with predefined patterns and analyses how these patterns are deformed by the object when observed from a different angle of the projection. Some systems adopt non-visible structured light to avoid interfering with other computer vision [11].

Stereo vision profilometry techniques simulates human vision through two camera setups angled with each other, which aims to identifying and match common features of an object images from multiple allowing it to be reconstructed through triangulation techniques [11]. Stereo vision normally is a passive 3-D sensing system but there are new camera setups which also uses a projected structured light in the object that turns them into active stereo vision [7].

Another active vision techniques are through time of flight light measurement. This technique uses light pulses with a known camera range so the time for the emitted light to travel from the camera and hits the object and it reflected to the camera is measured, based a fixed and known light speed the distance can be calculated [7].

Light coding imaging is also an active 3-D sensing system but instead of using light pulses it keeps light source constantly turned on. It also uses an infrared spectrum emitter and receiver, which analyses lens distortion, the emitted light patter and the distance between object, emitter and receiver and the deformation of the light over the inspected object [7].

2.5 MVS Industrial Evaluation

Pérez et al. [7] compared several 3-D machine vision techniques applied to industrial environments emphasizing which factors need to be considered in order to select the most adequate vision, considering, system accuracy, working distance, image output, system advantages and limitations. An overview of this evaluation is shown in Fig. 4 along with the current status of machine vision system in the automotive industry.

MVS TYPE	TYPE	PRECISION	WORKING DISTANCE	ADVANTAGES	CURRENT LIMITATIONS	AUTOMOTIVE INDUSTRY PERSPECTIVE
Traditional Camera System	2D	up to 0,1mm (*1)	18 mm up to 2m (*1)	Solutions are commercially available with customizable lenses and lighting accessories	Influenced by environment light conditions Object and Camera must be static Fewer image processing features which limits some defect type and object detection	Already in use (*3). AI applications under technical viability evalution
Photoeletric or Laser System	2D	(*2)	60mm up to 5m		Influenced by environment light conditions Object and Camera must be static	Already in use (*4)
Laser Triangulation	3D	(*2)	-		Influenced by environment light conditions	Under technical viability evalution
Time of Flight Triang.	3D	10mm	0,25m up to 3m	Independent of ambient light Static Object and Camera are not necessary	Low acurracy	Under technical viability evalution
Light Coding Imaging	3D	10mm	1m up to 3m	Static Object and Camera are not necessary	Low acurracy	Technology not evaluated yet
Structured Light	3D	34 µm up to 0,12mm	157mm up to 480mm	High Accuracy	Short working distance / Sensor can be quite large It may be influenced by ambient light depending on structured light type Static Object and Camera are needed	Technology not evaluated yet
Stereo Vision and Photogrammetry	3D	up to 50 µm	0,25m up to 3m	High Accuracy	Influenced by environment light conditions Physical marks necessary Point cloud density can be low Object and Camera must be static Intensive image processing required and it mat be time consuming	Under technical viability evalution
Projected Texture Stero Vision	3D	up to 0,1mm	0,25m up to 3m	No physical marks necess	Influenced by environment light conditions Object and Camera must be static Intensive image processing required and it mat be time consuming	Technology not evaluated yet
(*1) - Depend on Lens Selection, Camera Resolution, Working distance, object size and object tolerances						
(*2) - Increasing working distance decreses inspection accuracy.						
(*3) - Used for part detection, poka yoke - New process or process modification greatly affects its performance. New products may no be detected with the current						
(*4) - Used for part detection and precision measurement						

Fig. 4. MVS system assessment. Adapted from [7].

Environment light influence is one of the major problem to MVS, only a few systems are not subject to external light conditions. Another constraint that may affect your MVS selection is the necessity of both the camera and the object to remain static which, in some cases, are an exception in the industry. Accuracy and working distances are variables that must be taken in account, because depending on the precision needed the MVS solutions options narrows down.

2.6 MVS Applications to Industry 4.0

The fourth industrial revolution or Industry 4.0 aims to develop intelligent factories with upgraded manufacturing technologies through new features such as cyber-physical systems (CPSs), the Internet of Things (IoT), Big Data and cloud computing. New manufacturing systems propose simultaneous monitoring of physical processes with being controlled by digital technologies, being able to make smart decision through real-time communication and interaction between humans, machines, or any smart device [12].

Figure 5 contains a simplified 4.0 Industry diagram, adapted from more complex diagrams available in the literature. Machine vision is located in an IoT layer. Its function is to provide image data through a connected network to a big data cloud server. This data will be subject to mining and cleaning procedures, removing unnecessary information. This information can be used as an input for machine learning techniques, allowing an integrated system to detect and describe what happened to the product, determining why that happened, predict what may happen and prescribe which actions must be taken.

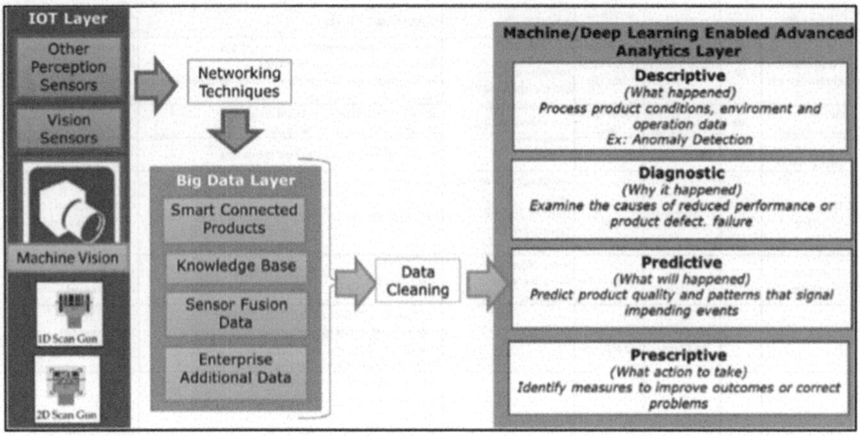

Fig. 5. MVS integrated with a simplified 4.0 Industry diagram. Adapted from [8, 13].

MVS future solutions, such as knowledge-driven decision-making, real time control, online advanced analytics and artificial intelligence in CPS, are considered as challenging implementation process. It may take from 3 to 10 years for industries to achieve a concrete degree of maturity and obtain a fully operational system with these functionalities [14].

3 Methodological Approach

In order obtain a detailed comprehension of the theme and to direct future studies, a systematic review is proposed. Based on the keywords identified in the theoretical foundation, they were grouped in in three fields of study: Industrial Quality Control (IQC), AI and Machine Vision (MV). Papers available through Scopus database were chosen, covering the period between 2007 to 2017.

Figure 6 shows each keyword used for each group. Keywords combinations from same group were not used in this paper, in order to increase the likelihood of significant search results.

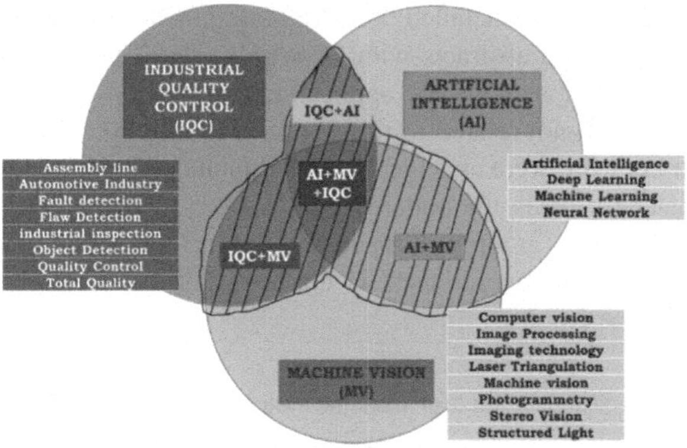

Fig. 6. Proposed field groups with each composing keyword.

The primary search results totalized 60.176 articles but they contained duplicate values. Before removing duplicate values, results which belonged of at least more than one search group were labelled as 'AI + MV + IQC'. After that duplicates were removed, 42.858 articles remained.

Figure 7 shows these non duplicated publications distributed over the analysed years. The graphic results indicates an increased number of publications for each group. Artificial intelligence and machine vision keywords combination presented the most relevant increase, mainly after 2012. It can be observed that vision systems applied to industrial quality through AI technologies tend to be revelant in the following years.

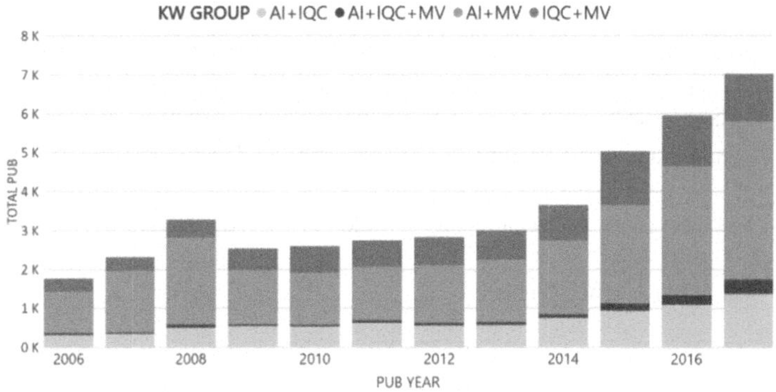

Fig. 7. Publications in each field of application over the years.

We filtered our search results to article labelled by SCOPUS as Journals, reducing to 16760 articles. Through ISSN information of each journal and the database extracted from SCIMAGO, a link between database could be established with the remaining search results. With SCIMAGO information another filter was applyied, selecting journals that has been evaluated by SCIMAGO, totalizing 8549 articles.

A content analysis with detailed keyword identification was made using the remaing articles. Titles and abstracts with keywords related to medicine, human features identification and non industrial applications were used to create an exclusion filter, because they were not related to this paper, resulting in 3350 articles.

New relevant keyword were also identified and included in initial keywords used to create the first database. With the updated groups, a filter with articles considering at least one keyword of each group was made and 289 results were found.

Table 1 contains the keywords used in the last filter and Table 2 summarizes all filtering steps database results.

Table 1. Search results for machine vision applications and trends.

Vision		Industrial/industrial quality			AI
Image	Feature matching	Assembly line	Flaw	Product analisys	Artificial intelligence
Object recognition	SURF	Assembl	Flaw detection	Anomaly detection	Deep learning
Shape recognition	ORB	Industrial	Fault detection	Anomaly	Machine learning
Computer vision	3D	Manufac	Fault	Measurement	Neural network
Machine vision	3-D	Product	Product quality	Quality prediction	
Part recognition	Scanning	Production	Quality control	Visual quality	
2D	Image processing	Industrial applications	Quality assessment	Measure	
2-D	Imaging technology	Industry	Defect detection	Automated quality control	
Tracking object	Laser triangulation	Factories	Quality testing	Industrial inspection	
Track object	Photogrammetry	Facility	Inspection	Total quality	
SIFT	Stereo vision	Manufactory	weld	Automotive industry	
Feature detection	Structured light	Vehicle			

Table 2. Search results for machine vision applications and AI and IQC trends.

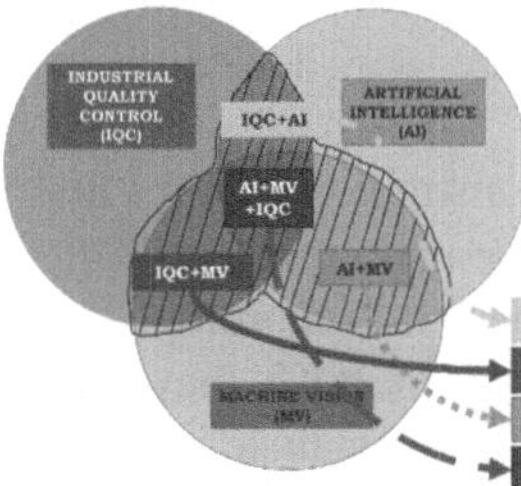

					Title Reading and Abstract Keywords Identification		Abstract Reading
	Keyword Search Combinations	Search Results	Non Duplicate Results	Scopus Journal Results	Scimago Journal Results	Non Related keywords Removal	Relevant Key Words *2
IQC+AI	32	9.539	8.110	3.615	1.861	899	34
IQC+MV	64	11.566	9.275	3.657	2.066	823	0
AI+MV	32	34.087	24.099	9.016	4.394	1.533	226
AI+MV+IQC	*1	5.524	1.374	472	228	95	29
Total	128	60.176	42.858	16.760	8.549	3.350	289

3.1 Initial Results

During abstract reading step, solutions which integrates AI and IQC applied to MVS were found. One proposed solution used genetic programming with machine learning to develop and modify preprocessing programs. It has the ability to adapt to new production parameters and light conditions changes with an automated preprocessing framework. This solution has a potential to solve common MVS problems [15].

One common aspect of most of the articles is that they only provide a solutions according to a specific type of industry, such as welding systems, PCB fault detection, and sometimes in does not have the potential to be applyied to other scenarios. One important factor detected in the articles is the absence of a common key performance indicators (KPI) in order to evaluate how accurate is each MVS solution. Another point identified is the absence of a method for selecting the best AI solution framework for each kind of solution. Figure 8 shows that from 289 results, only a few articles provides a framework or method as an important part of the abstract.

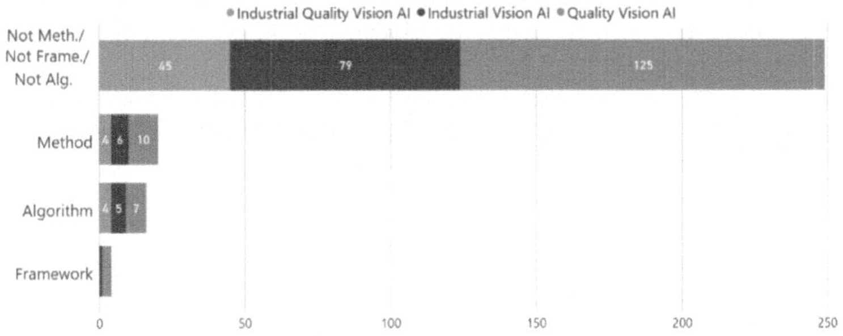

Fig. 8. Publications in each field of application over the years.

4 Conclusion

MVS solutions applied to quality inspection for the industry can be improved thorugh existing and new technologies such as AI, increase inspection detection processing speed and the capacity detect new types of defects.

There are many project restrictions and technical constraints in MVS implementation, which must be consider during selection, implementation and validation steps for industrial solutions, otherwise the system may not perform accordingly.

Despite of existing MVS solutions with AI applied to IQC, they tend to be exclusive for each scenario and they lack of a common KPI to evaluate its performance or the ability the replicated in other industrial scenarios. A method to select the most appropriate type of AI technique and how to integrate with existing or new MVS systems it is still lacking.

5 Future Work

A detailed review initial of the current research is necessary, in order to indentify which are main adopted AI frameworks and techniques to MVS and IQC, which are the KPI's to evaluate MVS performance, how much MVS with AI are improving industrial KPIs and which are the main researches.

Acknowledgments. This work was supported by Araucaria Foundation for Science and Technology/ FA-PR under Grant 40/2017 and Renault Brazil.

References

1. Vergara-Villegas, O.O., Cruz-Sánchez, V.G., de Jesús Ochoa-Domínguez, H., de Jesús Nandayapa-Alfaro, M., Flores-Abad, Á.: Automatic product quality inspection using computer vision systems. In: García-Alcaraz, J.L., Maldonado-Macías, A.A., Cortes-Robles, G. (eds.) Lean Manufacturing in the Developing World, pp. 135–156. Springer, Cham (2014). https://doi.org/10.1007/978-3-319-04951-9_7
2. Satorres, S., Gómez, J., Gámez, J., Sánchez, A.: A machine vision system for defect characterization on transparent parts with non-plane surfaces. Mach. Vis. Appl. **23**(1), 1–13 (2012). https://doi.org/10.1007/s00138-010-0281-0
3. Szkilnyk, G.: Vision-based fault detection in assembly automation, Thesis, Queen's University, Canada (2012)
4. Golnabi, H., Asadpour, A.: Design and application of industrial machine vision systems. Robot. Comput.-Integr. Manuf. **23**(6), 630–637 (2007). https://doi.org/10.1016/j.rcim.2007.02.005
5. Labudzki, R., Legutko, S., Raos, P.: The essence and applications of machine vision. Tehnicki Vjesnik **21**(4), 903–909 (2014)
6. Lerones, P., Fernández, J., García-Bermejo, J., Zalama, E.: Total quality control for automotive raw foundry brake disks. Int. J. Adv. Manuf. Technol. **27**(3–4), 359–371 (2005). https://doi.org/10.1007/s00170-004-2165-9

7. Pérez, L., Rodríguez, Í., Rodríguez, N., Usamentiaga, R., García, D.F.: Robot guidance using machine vision techniques in industrial environments: a comparative review. Sensors **16**(3), 335 (2016). https://doi.org/10.3390/s16030335
8. Wang, J., Ma, Y., Zhang, L., Gao, R. X., Wu, D.: Deep learning for smart manufacturing: methods and applications. J. Manuf. Syst. (2018). https://doi.org/10.1016/j.jmsy.2018.01.003. In-press
9. Chauhan, V., Surgenor, B.: A comparative study of machine vision based methods for fault detection in an automated assembly machine. Procedia Manuf. **1**, 416–428 (2015). https://doi.org/10.1016/j.promfg.2015.09.051
10. Su, X., Zhang, Q.: Dynamic 3-D shape measurement method: a review. Opt. Lasers Eng. **48** (2), 191–204 (2010). https://doi.org/10.1016/j.optlaseng.2009.03.012
11. Van der Jeught, S., Dirckx, J.J.: Real-time structured light profilometry: a review. Opt. Lasers Eng. **87**, 18–31 (2016). https://doi.org/10.1016/j.optlaseng.2016.01.011
12. Zhong, R.Y., Xu, X., Klotz, E., Newman, S.T.: Intelligent manufacturing in the context of Industry 4.0: a review. Engineering **3**(5), 616–630 (2017). https://doi.org/10.1016/J.ENG.2017.05.015
13. Pal, A., Dasgupta, R., Saha, A., Nandi, B.: Human-like sensing for robotic remote inspection and analytics. Wirel. Pers. Commun. **88**(1), 23–38 (2016). https://doi.org/10.1007/s11277-016-3239-3
14. Leitão, P., Colombo, A.W., Karnouskos, S.: Industrial automation based on cyber-physical systems technologies: prototype implementations and challenges. Comput. Ind. **81**, 11–25 (2016). https://doi.org/10.1016/j.compind.2015.08.004
15. Nagato, T., Koezuka, T.: Automatic generation of image-processing programs for production lines. Fujitsu Sci. Tech. J. **52**(1), 27–33 (2016)

Improving the Innovation Process by Harnessing the Usage of Content Management Tools Coupled with Visualization Tools

Houcine Dammak[1] and Mickaël Gardoni[1,2(✉)]

[1] École de technologie Supérieure, Montreal, Canada
Houcine.dammak.1@ens.etsmtl.ca,
Mickael.gardoni@etsmtl.ca

[2] Institut National des Sciences Appliquées, Strasbourg, France

Abstract. Having an intelligent and a creative workplace in which employees, machines and stakeholders are more productive by accessing easily to the information and making better decisions is becoming one of the main areas that organizations are investing in nowadays in order to stay competitive in the market.

Today, organizations have access to multiple information that contains valuable data from internal and external sources. These information are present everywhere in the workplace and represent a huge amount of data. Content Management tools appeared to manage this huge amount of information. It was proved that Big Data has a contribution to creativity, the next step would be to show how Content Management solutions could be used to improve innovation process.

We believe that using Big Data and Content Management tools will make a positive difference in the first steps of the innovation process, that is to say the creativity/ideation part. We will be also coupling Content Management tools and visualization tools to support our approach. Indeed, having a framework that integrates these tools, Big Data, Content Management and visualization tools, in the day to day, should improve the workplace innovation process to make it more "intelligent" and "creative".

Keywords: Content management · Big data · Innovation process
Ideation · Creativity · Knowledge management · Graph · Visualization

1 Introduction

The majority of organizations today are investing in having an intelligent and creative work-place. These investment decisions are due to multiple changes that are affecting the market. The main changes are the new technologies and its important advancement that increased the competition and made it global and also the apparition of small players that disrupted the market and are presenting a threat to organizations that are not following the wave of technology. Recent studies show that corporate life expectancy is decreasing. Professor Richard N. Foster shows in a study published by

Published by Springer Nature Switzerland AG 2018.
P. Chiabert et al. (Eds.): PLM 2018, IFIP AICT 540, pp. 642–655, 2018.
https://doi.org/10.1007/978-3-030-01614-2_59

Innosight that corporate life expectancy was 61-year tenure in 1958 then decreased to 25 years in 1980 and to 18 years in 2012. This study is based on the S&P 500 index (Standard & Poor's) [1].

The market is changing rapidly and every organization is trying to do its best to stay alive. They should follow an agile methodology in their offer in order to be flexible with the market. Many organizations like Kodak, Nokia, Blockbusters and Blackberry for example disappeared or are struggling because they did not innovate in their products and offerings. Other companies, they are excelling very well and innovating every day like Apple that did a successful shift in its offer to follow the new technologies. Innovation may differ from one company to another and it is not necessarily related to the product. It may be related to a process, a market... The question that every each executive should ask is: Do I want my organization to be Apple or Black berry?

So, how those organizations will be able to innovate?

Many people may think that by implementing an innovation program they will become innovative. They will capture ideas and then evaluate them but not necessarily those ideas are with high added value. And usually the ideation step is one the most critical step in an innovation process. The ideation step require the access to valuable information. The majority of the existing methodologies encourage organizations to collect ideas from employees, suppliers, clients... Those insights have shown interesting added value in many organization due to the proactive behavior that is developed with stakeholders. The fact that organizations today have access to multiple information from different sources, this may led to a competitive advantage. Availability of information is one of the critical success factors for organizations to survive. While trying to overcome this critical success factor, organizations are facing different challenges like the huge volume of data and information that exist in different formats and that is not easy to use. So, organizations today are facing a significant amount of uncontrolled content that needs to be managed efficiently.

To cope with this challenge, Content Management Tools appeared. Content Management tools has different names but the most common one is ECM (Enterprise Content Management). It is defined as the technologies, tools, and methods used to capture, manage, store, preserve, and deliver content across an enterprise (AIIM) [2]. It is also defined as a collection of strategic resources and capabilities that provides an automated enabling framework for efficient lifecycle management of valuable organization asset, i.e. contents and processes, to carry out required business operations in a collaborative fashion, supports governance and compliance, provides integration within and outside the business boundaries to achieve business intelligence, knowledge management and decision support capabilities with focus on fulfillment of business goals and objectives for competitive advantage [3].

In the literature, we find that the majority of researchers focused on the operational and tactical benefits of ECM and very few of them focused on the strategic benefits. From the operational benefits, using ECM will allow saving costs and reducing workload by streamlining tasks, and improving search and retrieval [4]. Concerning the tactical benefits, ECM improves internal and external collaboration, enhances content quality and maintain consistency and standardizes workflows. From a strategic level, it includes increasing decision making capabilities and facilitating creativity [4].

In this work, we are exploring different ways to add other layers to the innovation program like the use of Content Management tools in a way that helps us to optimize this process. We are proposing a framework showing how Content Management tools could be beneficial in the ideation step of an innovation process.

2 Problem Statement

The ideation step in an innovation process is a critical step. Providing tools to participants in ideation sessions may enhance the creativity. As mentioned above, ECM is a tool that will be provided to participants of ideation sessions in order to see its impact on the creativity of an organization. ECM users will have access to valuable information that are structured and easily accessible. This access to information will allow to enhance the creativity of users to create new knowledge. The gap is present and the benefits expected are really promising but unfortunately until today, in the ECM research, Creativity, Innovation and Knowledge Management has played a minor role.

With the Content Management tool, we are planning to use indexes (Metadata) related to each content in order to do searches. By using this metadata layer, the participant will receive a list of contents as a search result. The majority of commercial ECM tools present the search results as a list of contents (documents) grouped by the category of the content (Example: Thesis, Article, Product Catalog, Invoices…) and details with all the metadata related (Date, field, author, location, university…). The metadata depends on the category of documents and it is configured at the implementation stage of an ECM solution. So, the participants of an ideation session, depending on the criteria that they will select, will receive a list of content as a search results. This list of content may inspire them in their ideation session to come up with innovative ideas.

Here is a presentation of the use of content management tools in an innovation process (Fig. 1):

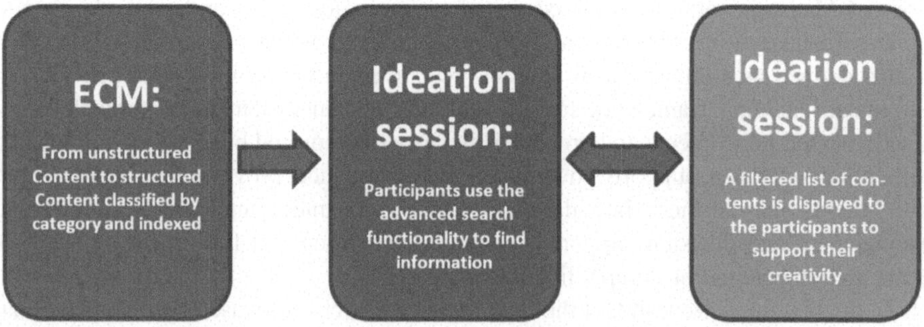

Fig. 1. Modelling the use of content management tools in an innovation process

As a result, the search result is presented as a list of contents grouped by category. But within a specific category we don't have any grouping, the only information is the content name, description and all the metadata related.

Some researchers proved that access to large database of information can overwhelm users, in their innovation process, and tend them to return to known solutions which will decrease the creativity. To avoid this situation, instead of presenting the search results to participants as a list of contents with the metadata related, we will be proposing a relational analysis between these contents in order to display them in a graph which may help them.

In this context, we are planning to explore the use of content management tools to support the creativity. As mentioned previously, ECM is the platform that stores content and make it available to users when then need it. So, we will be proposing a framework that couples the ECM output and the innovation process at the ideation stage. And this by proposing a relational analysis of the list of contents displayed by the ECM and representing them in a graph. The difficulty here is about the important number of analysis properties to identify the right graphs and all the combinations between these analysis properties.

So, this work will focus on identifying the most pertinent graphs from all the possible set of graphs that will allow to exploit content management tools in the innovation process.

How the use of Content Management tools coupled with visualization tools support the ideation step in the innovation process?

3 State of the Art

3.1 The Innovation Process

With new technologies and the ease of access to information, organizations today need to innovate continuously. Different approaches are used to manage the Innovation program and the majority of the existing methodologies encourage organizations to collect ideas from employees, suppliers, clients… Those insights have shown interesting added value in many organization due to the proactive behavior that is developed with stakeholders. In this section, we will present the Innovation system as described by Cooper and Edgett [5].

The authors state that many companies have already a solid innovation process or a Stage-Gate system implemented. So the process is in place to launch new product or process. This Stage-Gate system starts from Stage 1: ideas to Stage 5: Launch. Senior executives considers that the process is not enough if we don't have the right input which is strong and high value ideas (Fig. 2).

Different approaches appeared to solve this problem like organizing: Brainstorming sessions, Jam sessions, Innovation days, challenge-driven events, Shark Tank competitions… and these events proved their results by providing a huge number of ideas and then following an evaluation process we could reach the expected strong and high value ideas.

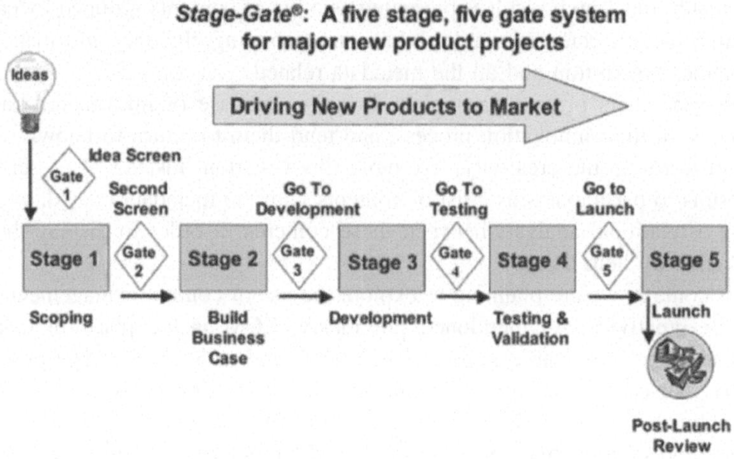

Fig. 2. A typical stage-gate product innovation system [5]

The ideation process which is the first step in the innovation process is the most critical step. We believe that companies can leverage their knowledge throughout the organization, expand their knowledge further based on existing expertise, appropriate knowledge from partners and other organizations, and develop completely new expertise by probing new technologies or markets [6].

Some authors propose that to generate radical innovations, it is necessary to combine already existing knowledge but in an unexpected fashion [7].

The combination of teams existing technical knowledge and limited domain-specific knowledge provokes more original and diverse ideas, which confirms there is creative value in the combination of KDD (knowledge discovery from databases) with teams' existing knowledge [8].

So, existing knowledge is very important for the ideation step. This existing knowledge may come from internal or external data that an organization holds or has access to. In the following section, we will present the importance of data in this context and researchers positioned it in the innovation process.

3.2 Importance of Data

For all organizations regardless their size, their market or their market share, they all have to deal with data in different forms. This data represents a valuable source of knowledge. We start here by defining some key terms that will be used in this work.

- Data: Are symbols that represent the properties of objects and events [9].
- BIG Data: the volume of the data is too large. Secondly, it is impossible to analyze it using conventional technologies [10].
- Knowledge: Can be defined as information that is validated, contextual, relevant and actionable [11]. Jacobs et al [12] defined it as a massive pool of data that allows creating insights and values that are not possible to generate from smaller scale of same data.

- Tacit Knowledge: is subjective and informal [13, 14]. It is usually hard to express, transfer or share using common ways.

The data that any organization has comes from different sources and in different forms. Kabir and Carayannis [15] present knowledge into two forms: Explicit and Tacit. It is usually impossible to analyse it using conventional technologies especially if we add to this data the information available on the internet. That's why and as mentioned above, it called Big Data.

Several researchers studied the importance of Big Data and the knowledge that it has for organizations.

Provost and Fawcett [18] mention that insights and knowledge from big data boost management's ability to take well-informed decisions.

According to Kabir and Carayannis [15], knowledge has all the potential of creating economic value for an organization and bolster innovation, productivity and growth. Thus, it is also a possible major source of competitive advantage.

Knowledge and the capability to create and utilize knowledge are considered to be the most important source of a firm's sustainable competitive advantage [14, 16, 17]. In a nutshell, Big data:

- Is a source of innovation that can enable development of new products, processes and services.
- Using various analytics data can generate knowledge and insights that can support and improve organizational decision making significantly [18].
    - Offers the promise of unlocking novel insights and accelerating breakthroughs [19].

3.3 Content Management Tools

As mentioned previously, access to digital data is becoming much easier and cheaper that's why we believe that Big Data will make a huge difference in the quality of innovation in an organization. Some researchers have already worked on this and proved that Big Data may result a positive impact on the generated ideas [8].

Today, organizations has a huge amount of data from different sources. These data is in different formats: documents, management platforms, databases… that is not easy to use and that represent a huge amount of uncontrolled content that needs to be managed efficiently. Content management tools has appeared to cope with these challenges. Content Management tools could become the system of record of all these data and knowledge.

Enterprise Content Management (ECM) has been defined as "the strategies, tools, processes, and skills an organization needs to manage all its information assets (regardless of type) over their lifecycle" [20].

ECM is different from other management platforms. It manages the entirely of an organization's assets like: reports, spreadsheets, web pages, presentations, emails, office documents, images, audio or video files… [21]. Figure 3 models the ECM system.

efficiency, availability, traceability, and consistency

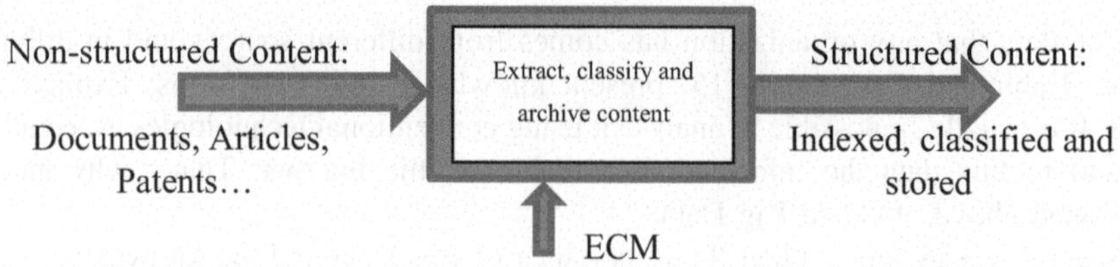

Fig. 3. Modelling the ECM system

An ECM implementation should follow the following content stewardship activities presented in the following Fig. 4 [14]:

- Capture: It contains all the activities related with collecting content. It is usually about identifying the content that it wants to capture and all its dimensions. This content could be captured from internal to external databases.
- Organize: It involves indexing, classifying and linking databases together. This step utilize different techniques like: OCR (Optical Character Recognition) and smart templates for indexing, workflows for classification based on business rules and ODBC connections to link content with other databases.
- Process: Analyze the content already classified in order inform decision makers and other existing management systems.
- Maintain: It is mainly related to the maintenance of the content. How to keep it accessible? How to link it with new content? And for how much time we should keep it?

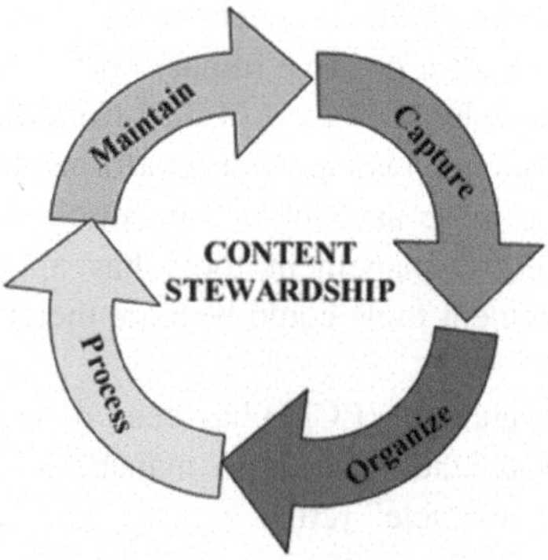

Fig. 4. Content stewardship are at the heart of an ECM strategy [14]

ECM solutions are mainly used for daily and operational tasks. Usually, the main reasons to implement ECMs are: reducing searching times, unifying the presentation or adhering to reporting obligations [21].

After organizing and structuring the content, ECM will deliver it to users in the format of a list. We will be using visualization tools to change this output to a graph format that highlights the relationships between contents.

4 Methodology

Content management tools could support the innovation process in different stages. In this work, we are considering the Content Management tool as a system of record for all the company's content. Users of this tool will be provided access to all the company's content in one single location linked to all other existing management platforms. This may reduce search times and access to information will be easier. Then, we will be exploring how this tool could support the innovation process at the ideation stage.

As mentioned above, we will be working on the output of the ECM, which is a list of contents structured and classified, to represent it in a graph and provide it to participants in an ideation session. So, we will see the impact of using a graph of contents versus not using it at the ideation stage. The evaluation of the ideas will be done by an independent evaluation team who will rank the ideas.

Here is a presentation of the use of content management tools coupled with visualization tools (Fig 5):

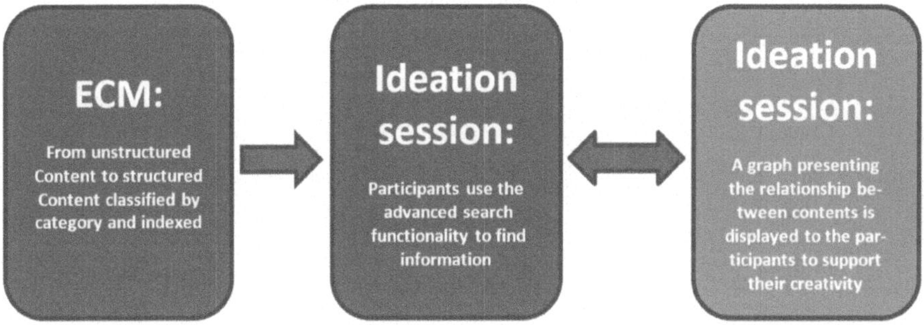

Fig. 5. ECM coupled with visualization tools in an innovation process

Using a visualization tool will present a second layer of filtering content – To group them together based on certain parameters. The search result will be presented in a Graph with links and weights. So, we are propose a relational analysis of the list of contents displayed by the ECM and representing them in a graph. The difficulty here is about the important number of analysis properties to identify the right graphs and all the combinations between these analysis properties.

Here is an example showing a list of contents (search result). This example considers that we have two categories of contents (the first one is Thesis) and the first category has three indexes (University, Field and Year) (Table 1).

Table 1. Contents stored within the example and related indexes

category				Category 1			Category 2		
				Index	Index	Index	Index	Index	Index
				University (a)	Field (b)	Year (c)	d	e	f
1	Content	c1	Thesis 1	ETS (x)	Innovation (s)	2012 (u)			
1	Content	c2	Thesis 2	McGill (y)	Innovation (s)	2012 (u)			
1	Content	c3	Thesis 3	Concordia (z)	Innovation (s)	2012 (u)			
1	Content	c4	Thesis 4	ETS (x)	Innovation (s)	2012 (u)			
1	Content	c5	Thesis 5	ETS (x)	Innovation (s)	2015 (j)			
1	Content	c6	Thesis 6	ETS (x)	Electrical (r)	2015 (j)			
1	Content	c7	Thesis 7	McGill (y)	Electrical (r)	2012 (u)			
1	Content	c8	Thesis 8	Concordia (z)	Electrical (r)	2012 (u)			
2	Content	c9					q	t	p
2	Content	c10					q	t	p
2	Content	c11					q	t	p
2	Content	c12					q	t	p
2	Content	c13					w	i	l
2	Content	c14					w	o	l
2	Content	c15					w	o	l
2	Content	c16					q	o	k

The goal here is to study the links between all the contents presented in the search result and to present them in a graph. To do this, we need to present the Content/Index matrix and then the Content/Content Matrix.

Once we present the Content/Content matrix, a graph presenting the links between contents based on indexes can be presented. Different graphs tools are available.

In this example, we can consider the indexes to link the contents. Different other parameters could be considered and also different graphs are possible to draw. So, this work is focusing on identifying the most pertinent graphs from all the possible set of graphs that will allow to exploit content management tools in the innovation process.

The range of possible graphs is wide and depends on different parameters. Some researchers already did the exercise of analyzing the different software tools (software) [23] and found their number is important and in general, the overall architecture of these software tools is structured according to a reference model provided by Card [24]. This reference model will be used as a guideline to our methodology.

Card [24] presents visualization (graph) as a mapping from data to a visual form that the human perceives. The following Fig. 6 presents this reference model that shows how the flow of data goes through a series of transformations. The human may interfere at different steps to make adjustments to these transformations.

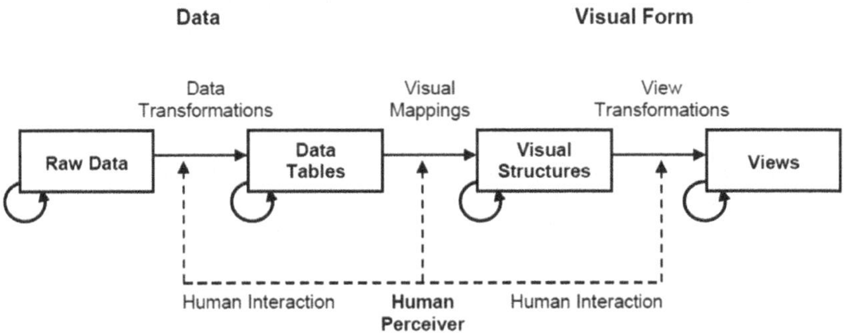

Fig. 6. Reference model for visualization [24]

Using an analogy to this reference model to apply it in our context, the following Fig. 7 presents the modelling of our methodology that will be explained later step by step:

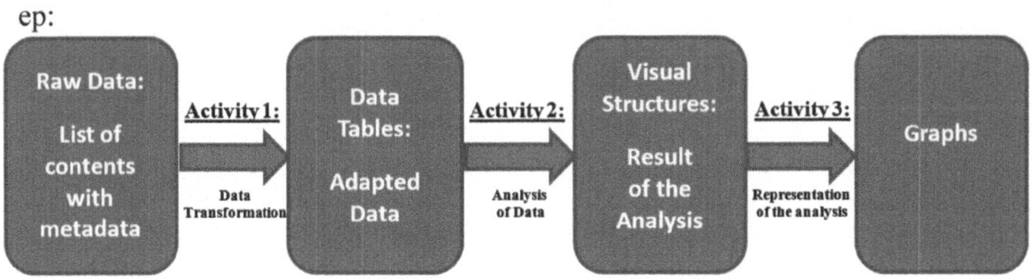

Fig. 7. Methodology to convert the output of the ECM to a graph

– Activity 1

As mentioned above, the output of the ECM is considered our input in the innovation process. In our methodology, it is considered as raw data. Activity 1 which is data transformation converts raw data into more usable data tables. In our context, the raw data is a list of contents with metadata and is difficult to use by participants in ideation sessions since it could overwhelm them and have negative impact on their creativity. This activity will transform the list of contents to an adapted state of data which is easier to analyze. The adapted data is usually presented in a table format and shows the relationship between data. The example that we presented above is a sample of data transformation.

- Activity 2

This activity will analyze the adapted data and present its result in different format. The core of the reference model is the mapping of adapted data to results of the analysis. Data tables are based on mathematical relationships whereas the results of the analysis are based on graphical properties processed by human vision. In the reference model, this is the most difficult activity. To manage it, we are planning to follow these steps:

• Contextual filter

From the adapted data, we have different data in tables. Different analysis properties are possible to analyze the relationship between contents. In this step, we are planning to enumerate them based on the literature then doing a contextual filter related the context of ECM and innovation process. So, we identify what are the properties that could be applied and that make sense to use them.

• Statistical verification

Once we identify the most pertinent properties that applies to our context, we will validate them by doing tests on small sample. We are planning to do the tests with patents. So, uploading them to the ECM, extracting metadata, analyzing the relationship between them and displaying the most appropriate graph then using those graphs in small brainstorming session at the research lab level.

From this activity, we are able to analyze all the relationship between contents and identifying the most important analysis properties.

- Activity 3

The aim of this activity is to transform the result of the analysis to graphs. It is about representing in a comprehensive way to users.

Once we converted the output of the ECM to graph, we are planning make this approach available to participants of ideation sessions. We will be testing this approach in an industrial environment and in the 24 h Innovation event organized by ETS. Then, we will be comparing the impact of proving of graphical tool representing the contents to participants versus not using it and presenting to users to list of contents in a list format.

So, we will be using an independent evaluation team to evaluate the ideas from both approaches (with the graphical tool and without) to observe its impact on the creativity.

Actually, for the coming edition of 24 h innovation that will be held at ÉTS, we will be testing the following scenario:

1. We will identify a complex challenge that requires a lot of reading (in the 24 h event, challenges are submitted by businesses)
2. From the teams that will participate in this challenge, we will selected 2 teams. We will try to find two similar teams (background, age, gender percentage, …)
3. The first team will have access to an ECM that has already thousands of contents (documents) uploaded into it and indexed. The team will use the advanced search functionality to search for relevant fields. A list of contents will be displayed depending on their search criteria and then they have to consult each one of them to get inspiration.
4. The second team will have access to the same ECM as team one with the same content. While doing their search for relevant content, instead of displaying the search result as a list of content, it will be displayed as a graph grouping contents depending on certain parameters and relating them with links. Then, participants will consult those contents.
5. Once the 24 h is over, both teams will submit their solutions to the jury in a 2 min video (this is the current format used in the 24 h event). Then, a local and international jury will evaluate the proposed solutions (ideas) and rank them.
6. Depending on the ranking giving by the independent jury, we will assess the results to see if there is an impact of providing a graph to users while they are doing their ideation session.
7. This scenario will be tested with at least 10 teams and 5 challenges so at least statistically we can confirm the obtained results.

Once we confirm the expected results with the 24 h event, we will do the same scenario in an industrial environment.

5 Conclusion

The amount of content and information is increasing every day in a very fast pace. And organization has to look to this amount as an opportunity and use it in their innovation process in order to become more creative. In this work, we presented a framework on how content management tools coupled with visualization tools may participate in the innovation process within an organization.

The purpose of using content management tools is to benefit from the huge amount of information which is considered as a wealth of knowledge. As explained, the content itself is present in different sources and it is unstructured but with using the proposed tools, we will be able to structure this content and use it in the innovation process.

The next work is expected to test the different approaches presented in this paper and to discuss the obtained results.

References

1. https://www.innosight.com/wp-content/uploads/2016/08/creative-destruction-whips-through-corporate-america_final2015.pdf
2. AIIM: Association for Information and Image Management. www.aiim.org
3. Usman, M., Muzaffar, A.W., Rauf, A.: Enterprise content management (ECM): needs, challenges and recommendations. In: 2009 2nd IEEE International Conference on Computer Science and Information Technology, ICCSIT 2009, pp. 283–289. IEEE, August 2009. https://doi.org/10.1109/ICCSIT.2009.5234541
4. Alalwan, J.A., Thomas, M.A., Weistroffer, H.R.: Decision support capabilities of enterprise content management systems: an empirical investigation. Decis. Support Syst. **68**, 39–48 (2014). https://doi.org/10.1016/j.dss.2014.09.002
5. Cooper, R.G., Edgett, S.J.: Generating Breakthrough New Product Ideas: Feeding the Innovation Funnel. Product Development Institute (2009)
6. Von Krogh, G., Nonaka, I., Aben, M.: Making the most of your company's knowledge: a strategic framework. Long Range Plann. **34**(4), 421–439 (2001). https://doi.org/10.1016/S0024-6301(01)00059-0
7. Fleming, L., Szigety, M.: Exploring the tail of creativity: an evolutionary model of breakthrough invention. In: Ecology and Strategy, pp. 335–359. Emerald Group Publishing Limited (2006)
8. Escandon-Quintanilla, M.L.: Effects of data exploration and use of data mining tools to extract knowledge from databases (KDD) in early stages of the Engineering design process (EDP). Doctoral dissertation, École de technologie supérieure (2017)
9. Ackoff, R.L.: From data to wisdom. J. Appl. Syst. Anal. **16**(1), 3–9 (1989)
10. Manyika, J., et al.: Big data: The Next Frontier for Innovation, Competition, and Productivity. McKinsey, New York (2011)
11. Soliman, F., Youssef, M.: The role of critical information in enterprise knowledge management. Ind. Manag. Data Syst. **103**(7), 484–490 (2003)
12. Jacobs, A.: The pathologies of big data. Commun. ACM **52**(8), 36–44 (2009)
13. Polanyi, M.: Personal Knowledge: Toward a Post-critical Philosophy. University of Chicago, Chicago (1958)
14. Nonaka, I.: The Knowledge-Creating Company Harvard Business Review, November–December, pp. 96–104 (1991)
15. Kabir, N., Carayannis, E.: Big data, tacit knowledge and organizational competitiveness. In: Proceedings of the 10th International Conference on Intellectual Capital, Knowledge Management and Organisational Learning, ICICKM, p. 220, January 2013
16. Nonaka, I.: Chishiki-Souzou no Keiei (A Theory of Organizational Knowledge Creation). Nihon Keizai Shimbun-sha, Tokyo (1990). (in Japanese)
17. Nonaka, I., Byosiere, P., Borucki, C.C., Konno, N.: Organizational knowledge creation theory: a first comprehensive test. Int. Bus. Rev. **3**(4), 337–351 (1994)
18. Provost, F., Fawcett, T.: Data science and its relationship to big data and data-driven decision making. Big Data **1**(1), 51–59 (2013)
19. Chen, Y., Argentinis, J.E., Weber, G.: IBM Watson: how cognitive computing can be applied to big data challenges in life sciences research. Clin. Ther. **38**(4), 688–701 (2016)
20. Smith, H.A., McKeen, J.D.: Developments in practice VIII: enterprise content management. Commun. Assoc. Inf. Syst. **11**(1), 41 (2003)
21. Vom Brocke, J., Seidel, S., Simons, A.: Bridging the gap between enterprise content management and creativity: a research framework. In: 2010 43rd Hawaii International Conference on System Sciences (HICSS), pp. 1–10. IEEE, January 2010

22. Gregory, R.L.: L'oeil et le cerveau: la psychologie de la vision. De Boeck Supérieur (2000)
23. Dkhil, A.: Identification systématique de structures visuelles de flux physique de production. Doctoral dissertation, Strasbourg (2011)
24. Card, S.K., Mackinlay, J.D., Shneiderman, B. (eds.): Readings in Information Visualization: Using Vision to Think. Morgan Kaufmann, London (1999)

PLM Maturity, Implementation and Adoption

Product Lifecycle Management Maturity Models in Industry 4.0

Kássio Cabral Pereira dos Santos[1,2(✉)],
Eduardo de Freitas Rocha Loures[1], Osíris Canciglieri Junior[1],
and Eduardo Alves Portela Santos[1]

[1] Pontifical Catholic University of Paraná, Curitiba, Brazil
kassio.santos@pucpr.edu.br
[2] Positivo University, Curitiba, Brazil
kassio.santos@up.edu.br

Abstract. Today's manufacturers face ever-increasing demands of variability, greater customization of the products, smaller lot sizes, sudden supply-chain changes, and disruptions. With intelligent factories and products, changes will happen in the way the products will be manufactured, impacting on various market sectors. PLM holds the promise of seamlessly integrating and making available all of the information produced throughout all phases of a product's life cycle to everyone in an organization, along with the key suppliers. Industry 4.0 will make it possible to gather and analyze data across machines, enabling faster, more flexible, and more efficient processes to produce higher-quality goods at reduced costs. A research question then arises: What are the opportunities found between the Product Lifecycle Management Maturity Models and the Industry 4.0? Thus, this research proposes a literature review to identify the main researches related to Product Lifecycle Management Maturity Models, adopting the Knowledge Development Process Construtivist (ProKnow-C) method. For that, the AHP method was conducted to verify the adherence of the PLM maturity models having as reference the Industry 4.0 criterias (RAMI 4.0 and perspectives), allowing a diagnostic view about the existing maturity models. As a result, future research opportunities concerning PLM maturity models through Industry 4.0 perspectives are highlighted.

Keywords: Industry 4.0 · Product Lifecycle Management · Maturity models
Multicriteria decision making/analysis

1 Introduction

The world is amidst a revolution in the way products and services are created and delivered, comparable in effect to mechanization, mass production, and automation. The agents of that shift are new technologies in data capture, transmission, storage, and processing. The development towards the fourth industrial revolution has presently a substantial influence on the manufacturing industry. It is based on the establishment of smart factories, smart products and smart services embedded in internet of things. The main principles of Industry 4.0 have been firstly published by [1] and have built the foundation for the Industry 4.0 manifesto published in 2013 by the German National

Published by Springer Nature Switzerland AG 2018.
P. Chiabert et al. (Eds.): PLM 2018, IFIP AICT 540, pp. 659–669, 2018.
https://doi.org/10.1007/978-3-030-01614-2_60

Academy of Science and Engineering. According to Kagermann [2] the "Industrie 4.0 is a new level of value chain organization and management across the lifecycle of products". One of the differentials of the companies are the early launch of the products and the ability to the develop them, with the objectives to meet the growing needs and expectations of the customers. The product lifecycle is getting shorter, which encourages the continued flow of new product development projects in the industry. Increasing competition is forcing companies to enhance their information systems, decision-making techniques, and processes. One of the opportunities is to seek help from Product Lifecycle Management (PLM). As defined by Stark, 'PLM is the business activity of managing, in the most effective way, a company's products all the way across their lifecycles; from the very first idea for a product all the way through until it's retired and disposed of [3]. In this emerging scenario of Industry 4.0 there is an interest in evaluating the PLM domain under the influence of this new industrial revolution. In this scenario, the review of present maturity models in PLM represents a promising opportunity in this investigation. So, a research question then arises: How is the relation between the Product Lifecycle Management Maturity Models and the Industry 4.0?

In the remaining part of this paper, a literature review based on the ProKnow-C method is presented, in order to identify Product Lifecycle Management Maturity Models and their main concerns and assessment criteria. The Product Lifecycle Management Maturity Models are presented in Sect. 3 following by the concepts of RAMI 4.0 in Sect. 4. Section 5 is devoted to discuss the results from the conceptual adherence analysis of PLM Maturity Models to the Industry 4.0 perspectives. At the end, the conclusion and future work is given in Sect. 6.

2 Research Methodology

The first phase of the work consisted in the implementation of a well-defined method to structure the systematic review. Review of the literature precedes the development of a research project and aims to highlight the already widespread scientific knowledge on the subject. The literature review allows to the researcher: (1) consolidate the knowledge about the subject that you want to investigate; (2) evaluate the scientific relevant and the uniqueness of the proposed work; (3) establish the scientific basis used to highlight the frontier of the knowledge on the topic; (4) evaluate the worldview adopted, the potential and opportunities to contribute to the subject. In order to accomplish this research, the structured process Knowledge Development Process Constructivist (ProKnow-C) was chosen [4]. The process ProKnow-C is composed of four macro stages: (1) to select a bibliographic portfolio on the theme, (2) to conduct a bibliometric analysis of the articles of the selected bibliographic portfolio and its references in order to identify the main periodicals, authors, articles and keywords, (3) to perform a systemic analysis of the articles of the selected bibliographic portfolio, based on the theoretical views of performance evaluation, (4) to identify the gaps in the literature and suggest opportunities for future research.

According to the references, it is necessary to define the main question around to the systematic review. The main question addressed in this paper is: What are the main maturity models in Product Lifecycle Management? The research question was essential for the survey keywords definition as well as for the papers evaluation. The initial keywords were defined for the two axes of research previously described: (i) Axis 1 – Product Lifecycle Management. (ii) Axis 2 – Maturity. The parameters for identifying the articles are essential in order to answer the research questions and to reduce the likelihood of bias. These criteria made it possible to include or exclude case studies emerging from the research databases.

The criteria used in the selection of the database is that should be in the CAPES (Coordination of Improvement of Higher Education Personal) portal. This portal provides search tools that are compatible with Boolean expressions, as well as tools that allow the search of the title, abstract and keyword fields. To obtain a comprehensive set of papers, the search string was constructed through the combination of the operator 'and', were published in journals, conference proceedings book series, and were written in the English language. The survey was carried out through the following search engines: Science Direct, Springer, IEEE, SCOUPS and Web of Science, accessed by the Pontifical Catholic University of Parana.

The alignments of the keywords in the database were verified through the amount of papers for the combination of the keywords. The selection of the database occurred from the verification of the basis that allows entire access through the CAPES portal. As the results of this first research, 262 publications, conference proceedings and book series were found. In the phase of filtering the batch of rough articles, the 262 publications of the batch of rough articles were evaluated according to the following aspects: (i) if the articles are not repeated (redundancy); (ii) if the titles of the articles are aligned with the theme of the research; if the articles possess scientific knowledge; (iii) if the abstracts of the articles are aligned with the theme of the research; (iv) if the entire text of the article is aligned with the theme of the research. As a result, 41 repeated papers were excluded and 221 original papers remained.

In the analysis of the alignment of the title with the theme of the research, it was noticed that some of the selected papers focused on the areas of construction industry, medicine and enterprise communication, and were thus beyond the focus of the research, so 113 papers were removed. A total of 108 original papers, the titles of which were aligned with the theme of the research, were retained. It must be pointed out that the removed articles did not present total alignment with the theme of the research and were nonetheless kept for more detailed analysis in the following phases.

The next phase consisted of the verification of scientific recognition of the papers; in this phase 22 papers were removed. The next step consisted of reading the 86 abstracts of the papers, aiming to verify the alignment of the article with the theme of the research, so 49 were removed. Finalizing the step of filtering the batch of rough articles, the 37 selected papers were analyzed according to the availability and alignment of the whole text with the theme of the research. It's important to describe that this research didn't have only the objective to identifying the main maturity models, but also the perspectives and criterias involved in the analysis and dimension of Industry 4.0.

3 Product Lifecycle Management Maturity Models

In this section, the 37 selected papers were analyzed having the objective of identifying the Product Lifecycle Management Maturity Models. The Product lifecycle management (PLM) is the process of managing the entire lifecycle of a product from its first concept, through design and manufacture, to service and disposal. PLM integrates people, data, processes and business systems and provides a product information backbone for companies and their extended enterprises [5].

According to [6], basic elements of all maturity models are number of dimensions (such as the 'process areas' in Classification of Maturity Models (CMM's)), number of levels (typically three to six), and a descriptor for each level (such as the CMM's differentiation between initial, repeatable, defined, managed, and optimizing processes). Maturity can be defined as "the state of being complete, perfect or ready" [7]. The main Product Lifecycle Management Maturity Models extracted from the systematic literature review are described below:

Batenburg Proposal: is designed to assess the PLM achievements of individual companies or business units of a company [8]. Applies four maturity levels: (1) ad hoc (where there is no vision available for PLM and there are no consistent PLM processes and supporting systems), (2) departmental (where PLM is seen as data management problem that should be dealt with on departmental level that starts to implement PLM systems), (3) organizational (where PLM is interpreted as a business problem that requires a corporate vision and an integral approach and PLM systems are integrated with other major enterprise systems, such as ERP) and (4) inter-organizational (where PLM is seen as a business problem that spans the complete product lifecycle and PLM systems are integrated with those of the suppliers to enable collaboration).

Saaksvuori and Immonen Proposal: Identifies five stages: (1) unstructured (where there are no defined approaches concerning lifecycle management; all lifecycle and product management issues are resolved by individuals on a case-by-case basis), (2) repeatable but intuitive (where lifecycle and product management processes have left to individuals, there is not any formal development, definition, training or communication of standard processes), (3) defined (where the PLM processes or basic PLM concepts are not best-of-the-breed, nor are they uniform throughout the corporation, however they are formalized), (4) managed and measurable (where PLM processes and concepts are under constant improvement and provide best practices) and (5) optimal (PLM processes and concepts have been refined to the level of best practice, based on continuous improvement and benchmarking with other organizations).

Schuh et al.: have implemented a framework that comprehends seven maturity elements of PLM: (1) the PLM definition (that provides the boundaries within which the reference models are detailed), (2) the PLM foundation (based on the specification of the fundamental concepts for the PLM implementation), (3) the set of process reference models (that vary according to a group of features of a company, sector, size, order type, which coherently define typical industrial enterprises), (4) the vendor neutral software description (that lists the software requirements needed to support process activities), (5) the PLM software support (that identify the profiles of specific Software solutions), (6) the knowledge base (that supplies the necessary material to support training), (7) the PLM benefits (like reducing time-to-market, improving product functionality and increasing ability of customizing resulting from changes within the company's processes after PLM implementation).

Stark Proposal: defined a maturity model for PDM, which is an important component of PLM. The model is composed of six maturity stages: (1) Traditional, (2) Archipelago of PLM Islands, (3) Frontier-crossing PLM, (4) Enterprise-wide, (5) Enterprise-wide, (6) Enterprise-deep. For each of these stages he described particular features from three different viewpoints: the company, the product development process and PDM. He also developed a questionnaire based on this model on basis of which a company can be assessed with respect to PDM maturity. The assessment is used to determine the current situation of a company.

Kärkkäinen et al. Proposal: examined how organizational maturity should be assessed in order to successfully implement and develop a PLM scheme. They define the maturity of customer dimension, and they provide preliminary maturity level descriptions for this dimension. In the level descriptions of maturity in customer dimension, they discern the following main levels, namely (1) Chaotic, (2) Conscientious, (3) Managed, (4) Advanced and (5) Integration stages.

Terzi S.: defines a model of assessment for the new product development process that provides a snapshot of the company in order to offer a starting point for further analysis and the definition of a strategy for improvement in its processes of engineering and innovation [9]. The proposed model identifies three aspects of investigation: Organization, Process and Knowledge Management, divided into nine subareas totals. The model elaborates the five levels of maturity usually defined in the literature, identified by the acronym Climb: (1) Chaos, (2) Low, (3) Intermediate, (4) Mature, (5) Best Practice.

4 Rami 4.0

To provide a common base around the Industry 4.0, a group of collaborators from different European enterprises and R&D institutions suggested a "reference architectural model" for Industry 4.0 (RAMI 4.0, Fig. 1), which purpose is the grouping and representation of different aspects of the industry in a common model, vertical integration, end-to-end engineering and horizontal integration [10]. The horizontal integration refers to the integration of the various IT systems used in the different stages of the manufacturing and business planning processes that involve an exchange of materials, energy and information both within a company. The vertical integration refers to the integration of the various IT systems at the different hierarchical levels. In general, the RAMI 4.0 provides "basic reference architecture" for an Industry 4.0 [10]. The architecture model requires a three-dimensional representation. The three axes of RAMI 4.0 describe the hierarchical levels of a manufacturing system networked via the Internet, the lifecycle of systems and products, and the IT structure of an Industrie 4.0 component.

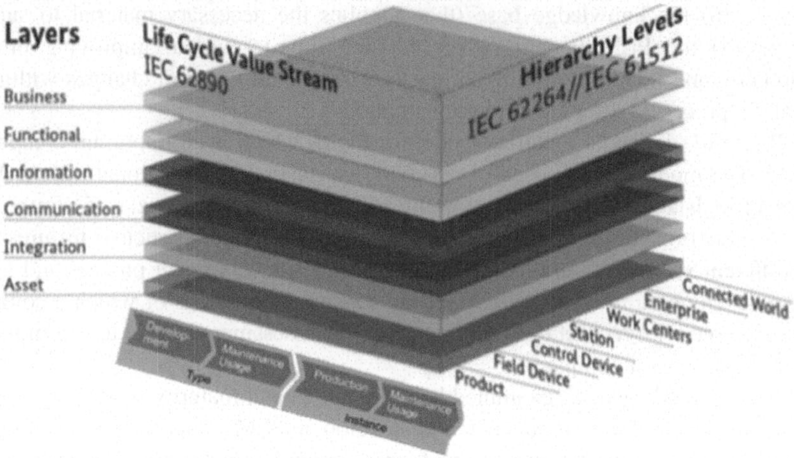

Fig. 1. Overview RAMI 4.0 (Plattform Industrie 4.0 e ZVEI, 2015).

The description of the lifecycle of systems and products with the corresponding value-added chains is based on the draft of IEC 62890, which makes a distinction between type and instance. The type of a product appears in several phases during the development process. Based on the type released for series production, the system then manufactures products that are instances of the type. Component discontinuations or improvements may require changes to products. These changes are made to the type and are introduced into the manufacturing process as a new product version once the change has been finalized and released. The data generated in the process chains is already largely available in digital form. It is then processed in PLM and ERP systems. In order to manufacture individual products, it must be possible to store the data provided by customers to producers for the manufacture of their instances electronically in a suitable, instance-related format in IT systems. This data must be available throughout the entire lifecycle of the instance and linked to the associated type.

Hierarchy Levels: a horizontal axis that is based on the IEC 62264, an international standard for enterprise control system integration, that presents four layers called ‘Enterprise’, ‘Work Centers’, ‘Station’, and ‘Control Device’ (from top to bottom). In the RAMI 4.0 were added three layers to support the smart factory. At the bottom are the ‘Field Device’ (to enable the control of machines or systems in an intelligent way, e.g., smart sensors) and ‘Product or Workpieces’. At top was added the ‘Connected World’ layer, whereby the factory can go beyond its boundaries and reach external partners by collaborative service networks. These layers represent the fundamental aspects for the Industry 4.0 organization.

Life Cycle and Value Stream: this axis describes assets in the value stream from idea, development and maintenance with respect to an asset type and the production, usage and maintenance of the concrete instances of the asset type, which is based on IEC 62890, a draft standard for guideline life cycle management.

Layers: a vertical axis to describe the decomposition of machines and physical entities in a way to enable its virtual mapping. The layers are used to represent perspectives, such as data maps, functional descriptions, communications behavior, hardware/assets or business processes, they define a structure of ICT representing the Industry 4.0. The corresponding layers of this axis from top to bottom are 'Business', 'Functional', 'Information', 'Communication', 'Integration', and 'Asset".

5 Relational Analysis Approach

In the next subsections, are devoted to discuss the results from the conceptual adherence analysis of PLM Maturity Models to the Industry 4.0 perspectives.

In order to get an overview about the maturity models in PLM domain, the research grouped the attributes into five aggregated categories, following the structure proposed in [11] and shown in Table 1. In the category of *Detail Level* are describe the "Business Dimensions" and "Maturity levels". The aggregate category named *Testing* groups attributes such as "Number of questions" and "Total number of respondents". *Effectiveness* groups attributes such as "Practicality of evidence" and "Guidelines for the PLM implementation". The category named *Application* groups attributes such as "Support of application", "Method of application" and "Mutability. The last category, *Addressed Domain* groups the attribute "Concept of maturity". The weights of this table were used as a reference to do the pair-wise comparison in the AHP method.

Table 1. PLM maturity models

Maturity Models	Batenburg	Schuh	Saaksvuori	Stark	Kärkkäinen	Terzi
Detail Level	1.72	1.11	1.51	1.75	3.33	2.29
Testing	1.87	0.00	0.00	0.00	0.00	2.00
Effectiveness	1.00	0.50	1.50	1.00	0.50	0.50
Application	2.33	1.17	1.17	1.17	1.17	1.67
Addressed Domain	0.75	0.75	0.75	0.75	1.00	1.00
Total Score	7.67	3.53	4.93	4.67	6.00	7.46

The second analyze (Table 2), describe the relation between the Rami 4.0 axes with the PLM maturity models. The signals (+), (++), (+++) are used to weight a weak, medium and strong relationship between the concepts, respectively. In the axis described as *Layers,* the *"Assets"* are the physical elements (sensors, actuators) that make up the real world and provide timely information on particular equipment. The Batenburg and Kärkkäinen has the biggest relationship because has the part of Control well defined in their process. The level of *"Integration"* is the form that this data will be transmitted from the real world to the digital world, that is, they are protocols and communication interfaces (OPC-UA, etc.). In this level all the PLM maturity models has the structured data. The *"Communication"* layer is where the information will be available to be accessed the way it is collected in the physical environment. The Schuh model has the knowledge base as a strong characteristic and receives the highest weighting in the table. The *"Information"* layer is the structuring of the acquired data that allows it to become clear to the users. In this layer, the Stark Model has a fragile relanthioship, because the main objective is the product data management. The *"Functional"* level holds the set of elements that make up the assets functions, allowing the entire factory floor to be integrated and its shared information guaranteeing the complete integration of the process. In this layer the highest values were weighted to the Batenburg and Kärkkäinen models, because both models working with real information from the factory floor. And finally, the *"Business"* layer, which evaluates all the data generated so that important decisions are made to improve production where several business areas are directly involved. The concepts of Batenburg, Schuh and Kärkkäinen are the models that best working with data to support a decision making. To the axis *Life Cycle Value Stream* all the requirements has a strong relationship, because all the Maturity Models has the product phase information as an application. In the axis *Hierarchy Levels,* the layer *"Product"* has a strong relation with all the PLM maturity models. The layer *"Field Device"* consists of standard terminology and object models that are used to define which information to exchange. In this case, the Saaksvuori model has the best performance, because has a good reference guideline for implementation. The third layer *"Control Device"* consists of attributes for each objective defined in layer 02. Objects and attributes can be used to provide and exchange information between different systems, but can also be composed as a relational database base. As in the second layer, the Saaksvuori model still has the best relation. The fourth level *"Station"* concentrates on the functions and activities of the production layer. It provides guidelines for describing and comparing the production levels of different websites in a standardized way. The Batenburg, Schuh, Saaksvuori and Kärkkäinen models are the reference to compare data of the production. The fifth level *"Work Centers"* the technical specification defines object models that determine what information is exchanged between the MES activities. The models and attributes are the basis for the design and implementation of interface standards that ensure the flexibility and exchange of information between different requests. All models have in evidence these characteristics, with the exception of the Stark and Terzi models paying less attention to these concerns. The layer *"Enterprise"*, operations connects and organizes production and activities through the definitions from previous levels. The main models followed the reference of the last layer. *"Connected World"* has external platforms that are capturing data from your internal processes. One of the most traditional technologies is Cloud Computing. The Batenburg and Kärkkäinen model has the Information technology as an important characteristic.

In order to prioritize the selection criteria, and to distinguish in general the more important criteria from the less important ones, further investigation was conducted by employing the AHP approach [12]. The AHP method helped to specify numerical weights representing the relative importance of each individual criteria (Maturity Models, Layers, Life Cycle Value Stream and Hierarchy Levels) as well as their associated selection criteria with respect to the goal. In the level 1 is showed the selection of the criteria. Level 2 is realized the analyze of the categories, with concepts of PLM Maturity Models and Industry 4.0, that has the RAMI 4.0 with a reference. In the next level, is realized the analyze of the attributes, that have criterias with concepts from the literature of PLM Maturity Models and I 4.0 (Rami 4.0) The last level, is

Table 2. PLM maturity models x RAMI 4.0

	Batenburg	Schuh	Saaksvuori	Stark	Kärkkäinen	Terzi
Layers	**Axis 1**	**Axis 1**	**Axis 1**	**Axis 1**	**Axis 1**	**Axis 1**
Business	++	++	+	-	++	-
Functional	+++	+	++	-	+++	-
Information	++	+	+	-	+	++
Communication	-	+++	-	+	-	+
Integration	+	+	+	+	+	+
Asset	+++	-	-	+	+++	+
Life Cycle Value Stream	**Axis 2**	**Axis 2**	**Axis 2**	**Axis 2**	**Axis 2**	**Axis 2**
Development	+++	+++	+++	+++	+++	+++
Maintenance Usage (Type)	+++	+++	+++	+++	+++	+++
Production	+++	+++	+++	+++	+++	+++
Maintenance Usage (Instance)	+++	+++	+++	+++	+++	+++
Hierarchy Levels	**Axis 3**	**Axis 3**	**Axis 3**	**Axis 3**	**Axis 3**	**Axis 3**
Product	+++	+++	+++	+++	+++	+++
Field Device	++	+	+++	++	+	++
Control Device	++	+	+++	++	+	++
Station	++	-	++	-	++	++
Work Centers	+++	+++	+++	-	+++	-
Enterprise	++	++	++	-	++	-
Connected World	+	-	-	-	+	-

demonstrated the alternatives. The pair-wise comparison judgments were made with respect to the attributes of one level of hierarchy given the attribute of the next higher level of hierarchy (from the main criteria to the sub-criteria). For designing the paired comparison matrices, the decision hierarchies were formed as visualized in Fig. 2.

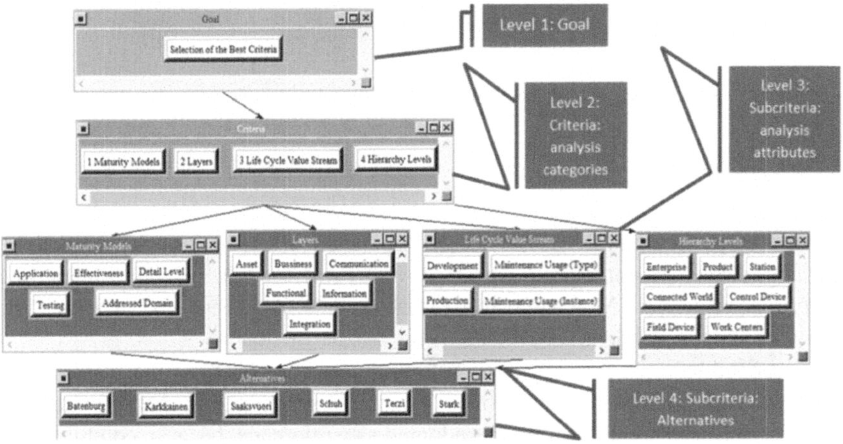

Fig. 2. The decision hierarchy for selecting PLM maturity models.

Figure 3 shows the final result of the AHP analysis comparing the axis Maturity Models, Layers, Life Cycle Value Stream, Hierarchy Levels and following the weighting of the Tables 1 and 2. Is evidenced that the Batenburg maturity model had the highest score (18.83%) between the models. The Kärkkäinen model (17.71%) is the second that presented the greatest score, followed by the Terzi model (17.47%).

Name	Graphic	Ideals	Normals	Raw
Batenburg		1.000000	0.188394	0.062798
Karkkainen		0.940359	0.177158	0.059053
Saaksvuori		0.878351	0.165476	0.055159
Schuh		0.826439	0.155697	0.051899
Stark		0.735120	0.138493	0.046164
Terzi		0.927743	0.174782	0.058261

Fig. 3. Analysis of result.

From AHP method a sensitive analysis was conducted in order to determine the stability of the outcome to wide perturbations in the judgments. In Fig. 4, it is represented, for instance, the Asset node (attribute) with a 0.80 weighting factor. In this parameter, represented on the y-axis (percent) the Batenburg method still have the highest weight (19.1%) but now the Terzi method has the second weight (18.3%). Each one attributes relating in each category (criteria and Subcriteria) are objects of the sensitivity analysis, allowing a refined research on the adherence of PLM MMs on the scope of evaluation in Industry 4.0 domain.

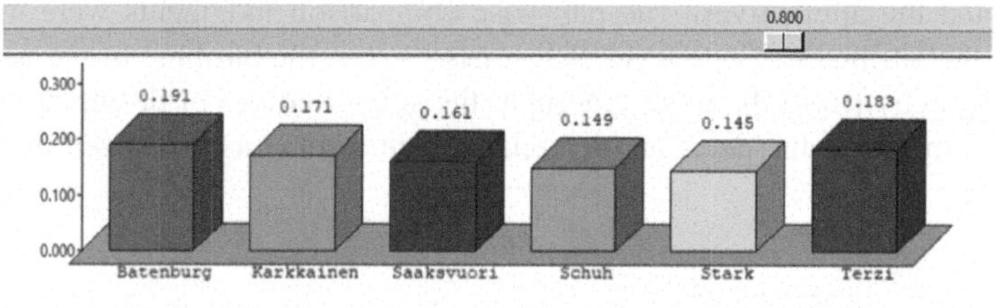

Fig. 4. PLM comparative models – asset node.

6 Conclusions

In a first step, a literature review was conducted founded on the methodology Knowledge Development Process Constructivist (ProKnow-C), in order to identify the main Product Lifecycle Management maturity models. As a result, six relevant PLM maturity models were identified.

In a second step, an investigation on how the relation between the PLM maturity models and Industry 4.0 is characterized. For this research the RAMI 4.0 (Reference Architectural Model Industrie 4.0) was adopted as a reference, because combines all IT elements of Industry 4.0 in a layer with a product lifecycle model. Through an AHP analysis, a comparison (weighting) on the maturity models characteristics with the layers of the RAMI 4.0 was carried out. In the research, it was identified that the PLM maturity model with greater adherence to industry 4.0 dimensions was the Batenburg maturity model highlighting highest final score.

It's fact that the Industry 4.0 concepts involve the integration of the physical and digital technologies with the phases of the Product. When this integration happens in the right way, many opportunities are found: the company can allocates efficiently the machines, identify problems quickly, reduce the production bottleneck, optimize process, reduce defects in products and prevent problems before manufacturing the prototype. The integration between these areas provides more customization to the production and to the product, reducing the product development time and the time required to market the finished product.

References

1. Kagermann, H., Wahlster, W., Helbig, J.: Recommendations for Implementing the Strategic Initiative INDUSTRIE 4.0. Industrie 4.0 Working Group of Acatech, Berlin (2013)
2. Kagermann, H., et al.: Industrie 4.0 Mit dem Internet der Dinge auf dem Industrially Revolution (2011)
3. Stark, J.: Opportunities and PLM. In: Stark, J. (ed.) Product Lifecycle Management: Paradigm for 21st Century Product Realization, pp. 81–92. Springer, London (2011). https://doi.org/10.1007/978-0-85729-546-0_5
4. Silva da Rosa, F., Rolim Ensslin, S., Ensslin, L.: Environmental disclosure management a constructivist case. Manag. Dec. **50**(2), 47–62 (2013). https://doi.org/10.1590/0103-37862015000300004
5. Saaksvuori, A., Immonen, A.: Integration of the PLM system with other applications. In: Saaksvuori, A., Immonen, A. (eds.) Product Lifecycle Management, pp. 53–65. Springer, Berlin (2008). https://doi.org/10.1007/978-3-540-78172-1_5
6. Mettler, T.: A design science research perspective on maturity models in information systems. Technical Report, Universität St. Gallen, St. Gallen, Switzerland (2009)
7. Kärkkäinen, H., Silventoinen, A.: Different approaches of the PLM maturity concept and their use domains – analysis of the state of the art. In: Bouras, A., Eynard, B., Foufou, S., Thoben, K.-D. (eds.) PLM 2015. IAICT, vol. 467, pp. 89–102. Springer, Cham (2016). https://doi.org/10.1007/978-3-319-33111-9_9
8. Batenburg, R., Versendaal, J.: Maturity matters: performance determinants of the procurement business function. Paper presented at the Proceeding at the 16th European Conference on Information Systems, Galway, Ireland (2008)
9. Terzi, S.: Elements of Product Lifecycle Management: Definitions, Open Issues and Reference Models. domain_stic.inge. Université Henri Poincaré - Nancy I (2005). English
10. Platform Industrie 4.0. Referencial Architectural Model Industrie 4.0 (RAMI 4.0) (2016)
11. Vezzetti, E., Violante, M.G., Marcolin, F.: A benchmarking framework for product lifecycle management (PLM) maturity models. Int. J. Adv. Manuf. Technol. **71**, 899–918 (2013). https://doi.org/10.1007/s00170-013-5529-1
12. Al-Harbi, K.M.A.S.: Application of the AHP in project management. Int. J. Proj. Manag. **19**, 19–27 (2001). https://doi.org/10.1016/s0263-7863(99)00038-1

Understanding PLM and PLM Customizing: A Theoretical Fundament for a Conceptual Approach

Ezgi Venghaus (Sucuoglu)[1,3](✉) and Rainer Stark[2,3]

[1] Volkswagen AG, Wolfsburg, Germany
ezgi.venghaus@volkswagen.de
[2] Fraunhofer Institute for Production Systems and Design Technology, Berlin, Germany
rainer.stark@ipk.fraunhofer.de
[3] Technische Universität Berlin, Berlin, Germany

Abstract. The continuous development of product lifecycle management (PLM) technology depicts many needs for clarification and action especially in PLM understanding and PLM implementation. The adaptation and customizing of PLM technologies become unavoidable and implicate high expenditure in form of costs, time and effort which is often underestimated by organizations. Despite of the importance of PLM adaptation and PLM customizing and its influence on the success of a PLM implementation project, there is no clear basis for an understanding of what PLM adaptation and customizing really is. Furthermore a lack of solution approaches exists that can guide companies during the process of PLM adaptation and customizing. The aim of this paper is to build a foundation for understanding PLM and the customizing of PLM. Furthermore a solution area beyond the software driven focus will be suggested.

Keywords: Product lifecycle management · PLM adaptation
PLM customizing · PLM realization · PLM change management
PLM adoption

1 Introduction

Product lifecycle management (PLM) has become essential for companies in order to deal with the challenges of the era of digitalization, net economy or in other words the internet of things. For reducing costs, shortening innovation cycle and development schedules [1], acting and collaborating globally by increasing complexity in products and processes, companies require innovative approaches which accompany their products through the entire lifecycle. These approaches built the core idea of PLM. For the purpose of realizing this idea and enabling the management of the company's products all the way across their lifecycle [2], PDM/PLM vendors offer PDM/PLM solutions that represent a combined set of IT application frameworks and a PDM backbone [3].

The implementation of such solutions however requires a cost and time intensive adaptation in special customizing, since the PDM/PLM solution itself as well as the

Published by Springer Nature Switzerland AG 2018.
P. Chiabert et al. (Eds.): PLM 2018, IFIP AICT 540, pp. 670–680, 2018.
https://doi.org/10.1007/978-3-030-01614-2_61

enterprise (company), which is implementing the PDM/PLM, has to deal with various challenges, as summarized in Fig. 1.

Firstly, companies have diversified processes which are mostly historically grown and a heterogeneous IT landscape that is fragmented through the entire enterprise [4]. Only inside the product development are diverse domains with different requirements. For instance, in the automotive industry the development of electronic components requires other information, data, knowledge and accordingly tools and methods than the development of sheet metal components. In some extent the requirements are extremely domain or task-specific, so an in-house solution is generated or a third-party solution is integrated to fulfill these requirements. Unfortunately PDM/PLM vendors can still not offer simple opportunities to integrate third-party task-specific solutions except their own applications [3]. Secondly, PDM/PLM solutions do still not have the capability or functionality to cover the broad base of product development practices that companies execute among different even global product markets [5]. Additionally, companies need intelligent solutions that assist, anticipate and automate engineering activities. However, PDM/PLM solutions as know of today are not capable of generating such intelligence [3]. Thirdly, with the aim of complying with many PLM functionalities, PDM/PLM vendors merged different applications, components or modules in their existing platform and hence increased the technical complexity but on the other hand reduced the flexibility of their products [5]. The companies though need user-centered solutions with a higher level of usability and thus flexibility.

The above specified problems induce a long PLM adaptation process and an expensive PLM customizing procedure. However, also due to the marketing concept of PDM/PLM vendors, companies are not aware of the impact of PLM adaptation and customizing on the success of PLM implementation. Moreover, they are vastly underestimated. Such misalignment can have disastrous results such as a significant extension in project time (double or triple of the originally estimated timeline), vastly increasing costs for PLM implementation as well as unsatisfied, unmotivated PLM project teams and even shut down of the entire PLM implementation.

Due to the importance of PLM adaptation and PLM customizing, this paper primarily aims to give a broad understanding of PLM itself and its adaptation and customizing. After clarifying the research approach in Sect. 2, a conceptional framework is presented in Sect. 3 for better understanding the scope of PLM. In order to describe PLM customizing as a part of PLM adaptation (Sect. 4) the terminology of customizing is given in Sect. 5. A conceptional framework for PLM customizing is suggested in Sect. 6. Finally in Sect. 7 an outlook for further researches and work is discussed.

2 Research Approach

The research approach is based on the Design Research Methodology (DRM) [6] and covers a comprehensive research plan, as shown as in Fig. 2.

The theoretical framework (step 1) and a qualitative study with experts to represent the state of the art in industry (step 2) were given in [7]. Constitutively, this paper focuses on the state of the art in theory (step 3) and suggests a conceptional framework for the PLM and PLM adaptation (step 4). A model for a successful PLM customizing

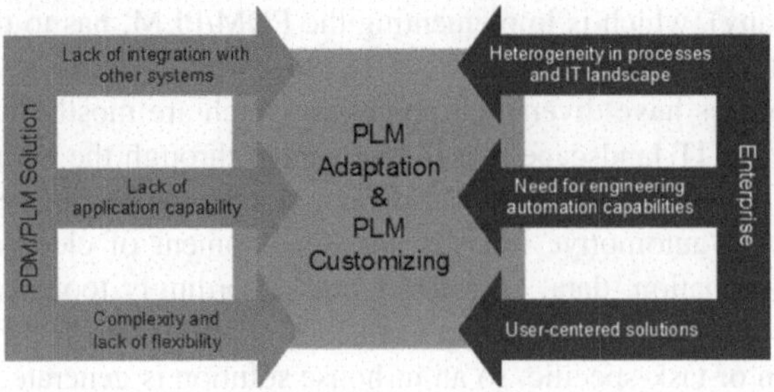

Fig. 1. Challenges and drivers for PLM adaptation and PLM customizing

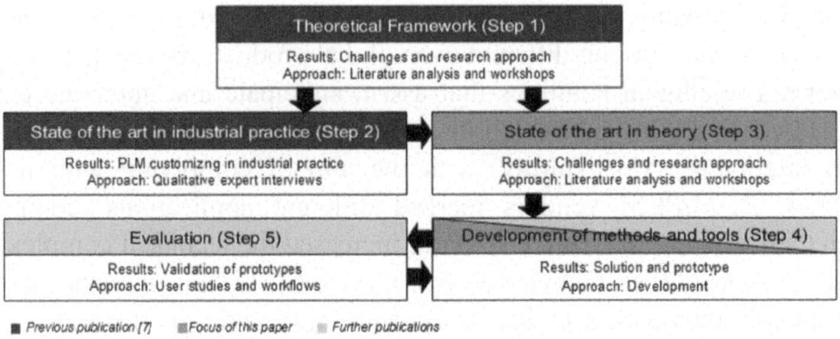

Fig. 2. Research approach

procedure is being developed and validated (step 5) and will subsequently presented in further publications.

3 Conceptional Framework for Understanding PLM

The basic idea of PLM arose with the evolution of computer-based solutions and applications in engineering design (e.g. computer aided design (CAD)) and manufacturing (e.g. computer integrated manufacturing (CIM)) in the 1970s. In the 1980s the necessity of managing all the engineering data produced by the tools led to the development of engineering data management (EDM) and furthermore product data management (PDM), which represents the backbone for a PLM solution [8]. In the 1990s simultaneously to the advancement of PDM the first generation of enterprise applications was introduced (e.g. enterprise resource planning (ERP), customer relationship management (CRM), supply chain management (SCM)). Each of these applications emphasizes a particular lifecycle phase of a product and does not consider its' whole lifecycle. Consequently, at the end of the 1990s, the PLM approach was born: to enable a platform for creating, organizing and disseminating all product related information, data, knowledge through all stages of a product lifecycle from the ideation to the point of disposal/recycling [2, 9].

Since PLM has its roots in computer-based solutions, it is mainly considered as an IT solution and still defined in many industries as a synonym for PDM [10].

However PLM is more than that, it is "*an integrated, information-driven approach comprised ... all aspects of a product's life, from its design through manufacture, deployment and maintenance - culminating in the product's removal from service and final disposal*" [8].

In order to realize the main idea of PLM it is essential to understand the scope of PLM in a holistic approach. Hence based on literature, the state of the art and our industrial experience we purposed a conceptual framework for PLM, concerning all relevant aspects of a product lifecycle (Fig. 3). Mainly the following models provided input for our framework:

- MTO[1] Approach [11]: The success of implementing computer-aided systems depends on a comprehensive approach taking into consideration the technique, the organization as well as its design but also the employee and his/her qualification. STROHM and ULICH came to this conclusion after many years of analyzing designing computer aided systems (here GRIPS[2]) and developed the MTO-Approach. The approach does not only highlight the importance of organization but also comprises the aspects of work psychology in a technical environment. In our framework we expand this approach on further depending aspects in the context of PLM.
- The Engineering Operation System (EOS) [3, 12]: In 2013 Fraunhofer IPK and TU Berlin proposed the integrative EOS model with the aim of depicting a holistic approach for product and manufacturing engineering and the associated development environments. The main focus of EOS is the interaction of four different levels or areas: (1) process and organization, (2) engineering activities, (3) data and information and (4) (IT)-tools and applications. Their interaction is key for engineering and this can be used as a foundation to unfold the complete potential of PLM. In addition to product and manufacturing engineering we consider in our framework also the phases of production, after sales management and end of life management, with their related processes and activities.

In the following the components of our framework will be explained.

3.1 Organization

Many studies define the organization as an essential component of PLM. Still, a detailed description of the scope of organization in PLM context is not given. In this study organization comprises the structural organization as well as the operation execution. The enterprise size, type and value, the operation level (e.g. global) and the organizational culture all represent important criteria which have to be considered in order to successfully realize PLM. The function of organization covers all management activities (e.g. decision-taking, setting of objectives [2], defining the strategy and

---

[1] MTO stands for the german acronyms: M for "Mensch" (human), T for Technik (technique), O for "Organisation" (organization).

[2] GRIPS illustrares the german concept "**G**estaltung **r**echnerunterstützter **i**ntegrierter **P**roductionssysteme" (eng: desging of computer aided integrated production systems).

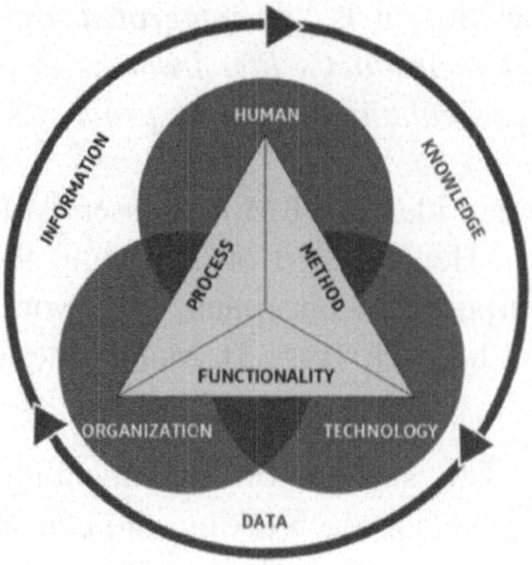

Fig. 3. Conceptional framework for PLM

vision) and management functions (e.g. governance and compliance, analytics and reporting, economics calculation [13]).

3.2 Human

The human factor in PLM context is mentioned in studies concerning the resource aspect, the importance of skills with its relevant facets, as well as in engineering and its activities (e.g. [12]). Beyond these aspects we consider in our concept the approach of information ergonomics and the science of work psychology in PLM context.

3.3 Technology

The dimension of information and communication technology (ICT) is very commonly assessed to describe PLM in a most specific way. This aspect is also defined as PLM system to highlight (generally one singular) software system. Furthermore, to describe a whole environment of IT infrastructure which enables PLM, the terminus PLM solution is used. In our study we use the term technology to comprise all "mechanical art" [14] components that purpose the realization of PLM. Additionally to the common PDM/PLM solutions (software & applications) we also consider technologies such as augmented reality or even enterprise social media[3].

3.4 Process

The processes are usually considered as a part of the organization within the scope of business process in many studies analyzing PLM components. Supplementary

[3] Enterprise social media is defined as: "*Web-based platforms that allow workers to (1) communicate ... or broadcast messages to everyone in the organization; (2) explicitly indicate or implicitly reveal particular coworkers as communication partners; (3) post, edit, and sort text and files linked to themselves or others; and (4) view the messages, connections, text, and files communicated, posted, edited and sorted by anyone else in the organization at any time of their choosing.*" [15].

regarding the lifecycle processes of a product a process oriented focus on PLM also exists. In our study, additionally to existing approach, we consider process as an organizational specification and moreover as framework which is agile and flexible since it is "lived" and formed by people in order to fulfill activities in the lifecycle of the product. Therefore, processes are represented in our framework in combination with organization and the human factor.

3.5 Method

A method is defined as "*a particular procedure for accomplishing or approaching something*" [16]. In the context of PLM such procedure is usually mentioned as a component for company-specific PLM solutions and used as a synonym for tools, techniques or equipment which support the management of information through the product lifecycle. Similarly we characterize methods as procedure for performing the activities or tasks by people in a technological environment. Thus, methods are illustrated with the focus of human factor and the technology.

3.6 Functionality

In the scope of PLM functionalities are mentioned in order to define capabilities of PDM/PLM solutions. Beyond that we consider the functionality as a technological framework which supports the mapping of processes defined by the organization. Therefore we represent the functionality of PLM in the context with organization and technology.

3.7 Information/Knowledge/Data

The main idea of PLM involves all facets of knowledge management, since PLM supports the gaining, organization and reusing of knowledge through the lifecycle of a product [9]. Beyond the approach of information management in the scope of PLM, which is also presented as closed-loop PLM (e.g. [17]), in our concept, we also consider the vision of knowledge. While information is defined as data "that is organized to describe a particular situation or condition", knowledge additionally includes perspectives, concepts, truths, beliefs, judgments, expectations, and know-how in the scope of human factor [18].

4 PLM Adaptation and PLM Customizing

The realization of PLM in companies implies an alteration in the whole enterprise, since PLM concerns the entire company environment. Based on our conceptional framework we illustrate the three types of PLM adaptation as PLM change management, PLM adoption and PLM customizing (Fig. 4).

We describe the organizational adaptation as PLM change management. The main focus of the adaptation in the context of PLM change management is the organizational environment but it affects all PLM components such as human and technology through

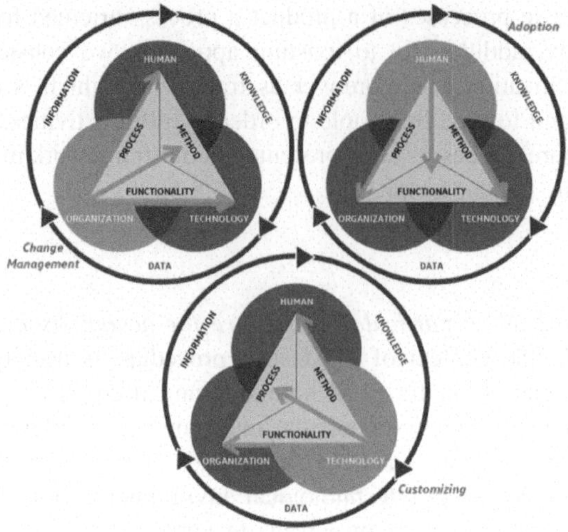

Fig. 4. Scope of PLM adaptation

the adaptation of processes, methods and functionalities. PLM change management contains the approaches of cultural change management, business reengineering and others. On the other hand PLM adoption is described as the human specific adaptation of PLM and includes aspects such as software ergonomics or human–computer interaction. Although the human factor is at the center, the implication of PLM adoption broadens all aspects of PLM with the adaptation of methods, processes and functionalities. In this paper, we concentrate on PLM customizing, which can be described as the technological adaptation of PLM with an impact of the entire PLM scope including the human factor and the technology as well as the processes, the functionalities and the methods.

5 Understanding Customizing

In industry PLM customizing is interpreted very differently (e.g. [7]) even within the same PLM project. Hence a homogeneous understanding of customizing is essential for a successful realization of PLM.

Customizing or customization is defined in literature as "the action of modifying something to suit a particular individual or task" [16]. In the context of business and management customizing is the "design and development of a product to meet the specific requirements of a single customer" [19]. Besides the view of business management, economics or academic, in detail the definition of customizing strongly differs from the product itself which is customized and from the producer of the product. In the field of information and communication technology especially enterprise software terms such as configuration, modification, parametrization, in house development or out of the box (OOTB) are used to describe customization. The business area of SAP describes customizing as a tool-assisted parametrization and adaptation of the software to the company-specific requirements without any programming [20], whereas the PLM vendor Siemens PLM characterizes customizing as any adaption, extension and change in the software by using several different applications and toolkits including code generation and programming [21]. We define customizing, as shown in Fig. 5, as any change and individualization in the context of PDM/PLM solution or rather PLM technology. For instance, in the scope of a PDM/PLM solution PLM customizing comprises workflow generation, a new object in data modelling or an added attribute as well as an extension programming for task-specific functionalities.

The raise in change of the PLM technology leads to more expenditure in programming, but usually also to more functionality. Additionally the release ability is getting reduced. On the other hand more individualization induces larger process mapping but also less flexibility. Supplementary the dependencies and mutual reactions of the PLM technology increase. Therefore it is very important to understand PLM customizing towards defining a strategy for PLM adaptation.

6 Solution Space for PLM Customizing

As mentioned in Sect. 1, for the purpose of enabling a better fit of the PLM technology with the company-specific requirements PLM customizing is inevitable. After defining the comprehension of PLM customizing we suggest a solution space for PLM customizing as shown in Fig. 6 aiming to support the decision of how to customize in the scope of PLM technology. In our concept companies which implement the PLM technology, are defined as PLM user whereas the provider of the PLM technology is defined as PLM vendor.

The goal of both PLM user and PLM vendor should be Area I. In this space, any changes in the PLM technology are conducted by the vendor and hence included in the standard technology; the support is also done by the vendor. The collaboration between vendor and user both on the strategic and on the operative level is very high. This leads to a "win-win situation", especially for innovative business segments. For instance many industry specific modules offered by PDM/PLM vendors are based on special requirements from PDM/PLM users or even more from their "in-house solutions" which are then converted in the out of box solution. Area II comprises all kinds of configuration and is usually performed by using the applications or toolkits suggested and supported by the vendor. Although this area is also considered as "good customizing" it is associated with many costs concerning performing and testing (including regression tests). Beyond that the toolkits and applications which are offered by the vendor to perform the configuration can change or even become obsolete. In this case the maintenance of the scope of customizing has then to be supported by the PLM user and hence will move in Area IV. Area III comprises commonly the integration and interoperability subjects, with other words the PLM extensibility. The initial customizing is performed by the vendor and the support and operation is done by the user. The integration of PDM/PLM solutions with CAD solutions or ERP solutions are typical examples of this area. It is also possible that the vendor develops certain interfaces for the user, which will then be placed in Area I. In that case it is very important to have verified regulations and agreements regarding the collaboration and

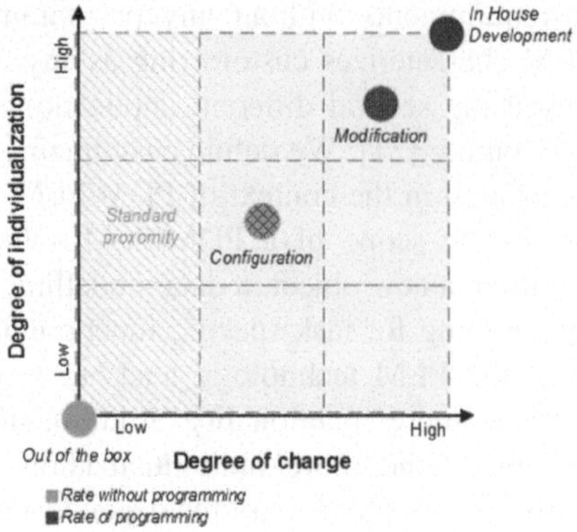

Fig. 5. The scope of customizing

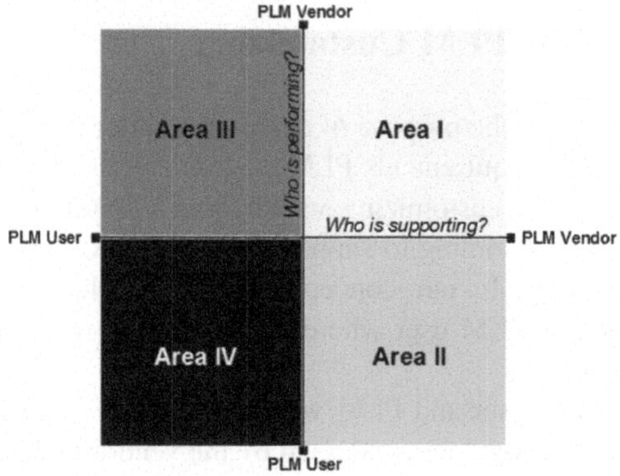

Fig. 6. Solution area for PLM customizing

cooperation between vendor and user. Area IV comprises all kind of modification and extension programming and should be avoided by the user. Not only that the performing, testing and supporting of customizing causes very high costs and extensions of the implementation time but also the ability to release a new PLM technology is vulnerable. However, in practice, many companies are located in Area IV and imperatively need to develop strategies to change in a different area.

7 Conclusion and Outlook

The realization of PLM poses many challenges for companies that are implementing PLM technologies as well as for the vendor of the PLM technology itself. Especially customizing, as a part of PLM adaptation, has a broad and varied impact of PLM implementation. In this paper, we primarily provided a comprehensive framework for understanding the main idea of PLM. Adapted from the proposed PLM framework we described PLM customizing as a part of PLM adaptation and suggested a solution area for companies to deal with the challenges concerning PLM customizing.

Since PLM customizing in the state of the art is unavoidable, studies that suggest a detailed framework for executing PLM customizing would be very valuable. Such studies should give a deep understanding of the PLM customizing process by considering not only the input and output parameters, but also the drivers and the stakeholders. For instance a stakeholder analysis under consideration the customer-supplier relationship would help organizations to define the suitable collaboration model and method within the PLM implementation project, not only on the operative and tactical level, but also on the strategic level. Furthermore, there is a lack of usable, expedient KPIs for PLM customizing. Studies that define such parameters and propose a suitable valuation model would draw great attention not only in the industrial, but also in the academic field.

Acknowledge. The results, opinions and conclusions expressed in this thesis are not necessarily those of Volkswagen Aktiengesellschaft.

References

1. Jackson, C.: The CIO's Role in PLM: Facilitation "Great Product" Development to Drive Economic Recovery (2010)
2. Stark, J.: Product Lifecycle Management (Volume 3): The Executive Summary. DE. Springer, Cham (2018). https://doi.org/10.1007/978-3-319-72236-8
3. Stark, R., Damerau, T., Hayka, H., Neumeyer, S., Woll, R.: Intelligent information technologies to enable next generation PLM. In: Fukuda, S., Bernard, A., Gurumoorthy, B., Bouras, A. (eds.) PLM 2014. IAICT, vol. 442, pp. 485–495. Springer, Heidelberg (2014). https://doi.org/10.1007/978-3-662-45937-9_48
4. Holler, M., Dremel, C., Herterich, M., Uebernickel, F., Brenner, W.: Product lifecycle management im konzernumfeld: herausforderungen, lösungsansätze und handlungsempfehlungen. HMD - Praxis der Wirtschaftsinformatik **55**, 1–18 (2017)
5. Hewett, A.: Product lifecycle management (PLM): critical issues and challenges in implementation. In: Nambisan, S. (ed.) Information Technology and Product Development. AOIS, vol. 5, pp. 81–105. Springer, New York (2010)
6. Blessing, L.T.M., Chakrabarti, A.: DRM, A Design Research Methodology. Springer, Dordrecht (2009). https://doi.org/10.1007/978-1-84882-587-1
7. Sucuoglu, E., Exner, K., Stark, R.: PLM customizing: results of a qualitative study with industrial experts. In: Ríos, J., Bernard, A., Bouras, A., Foufou, S. (eds.) PLM 2017. IAICT, vol. 517, pp. 49–58. Springer, Cham (2017). https://doi.org/10.1007/978-3-319-72905-3_5
8. Grieves, M.: Product Lifecycle Management: Driving the Next Generation of Lean Thinking. McGraw-Hill, New York (2006)
9. Ameri, F., Dutta, D.: Product lifecycle management: closing the knowledge loops. Comput.-Aided Des. Appl. **2**(5), 557–590 (2005)
10. Abramovici, M.: PLM – Best Practice Einführungsstrategien, Rapperswil (2010)
11. Strohm, O., Ulich, E. (eds.): Unternehmen arbeitspsychologisch bewerten: Ein Mehr-Ebenen-Ansatz unter besonderer Berücksichtigung von Mensch, Technik und Organisation. vdf Hochschulverlag, Zürich (1997)

12. Lünnemann, P., Wang, W.M., Stark, R., Manteca, P.I.: Engineering activities: considering value creation from a holistic perspective. In: Jardim-Gonçalves, R., Mendonça, J.P., Pallot, M., Zarli, A., Martins, J., Marques, M., (eds.) Engineering, Technology and Innovation Management Beyond 2020: New Challenges, New Approaches, pp. 315–323. IEEE, Danvers (2017)
13. Eigner, M., Stelzer, R.: Product Lifecycle Management: Ein Leitfaden für Product Development und Life Cycle Management, 2nd edn. Springer, Dordrecht (2009). https://doi.org/10.1007/b93672
14. Arthur, W.B.: The Nature of Technology: What It Is and How It Evolves. Free Press, New York (2009)
15. Leonardi, P.M., Husman, M., Steinfield, C.: Enterprise social media: definition, history, and prospects for the study of social technologies in organizations. J. Comput.-Mediat. Commun. **19**, 1–9 (2013)
16. Oxford Dictionary: Englisch Oxford Living Dictionaries. https://en.oxforddictionaries.com/
17. Kiritsis, D.: Closed-loop PLM for intelligent products in the era of the Internet of things. Comput.-Aided Des. **43**, 479–501 (2011)
18. Baskerville, R., Alina, D.: The theoretical foundations of knowledge management. In: Edwards, J.S. (ed.) The Essentials of Knowledge Management, pp. 47–91. Palgrave Macmillan, Hampshire (2015)
19. Law, J. (ed.): A Dictionary of Business and Management, 6th edn. Oxford University Press, Oxford (2016)
20. Thomas, O., Scheer, A.-W.: Referenzmodell-basiertes (Reverse-) Customizing von Dienstleistungsinformationssystemen: Heft 173. Institutsveröffentlichung, Saarbrücken, Deutschen Forschungszentrum für Künstliche Intelligenz, Institut für Wirtschaftsinformatik (2003). ISSN 1438 5678
21. S-PLM: Getting started with Customization. In: Siemens Product Lifecycle Management Software Inc. Teamcenter 8.3 HTML Help Collection (2008)

PLM in SME, What Are We Missing? An Alternative View on PLM Implementation for SME

Bas Koomen[1,2](✉)

[1] University of Twente, Enschede, The Netherlands
s.p.koomen@utwente.nl
[2] Cadmes b.v., 's-Hertogenbosch, The Netherlands
bas@cadmes.com

Abstract. Today, the concept of Product Lifecycle Management (PLM) is widely accepted as strategically important. It is used to manage the increasing complexity of products, processes and organizations. The need to adopt PLM is growing rapidly for Small to Medium-sized Enterprises (SME). PLM implementations are costly and require a lot of effort. The business impact and financial risks are high for SME. Also, SMEs seem to have relatively more difficulties to benefit from PLM. The study at hand addresses the question, based on literature research, why these difficulties exist and how they can be overcome. To answer that question, three sub questions are discussed in this paper. (1) A generic PLM implementation process structure. (2) A list of identified PLM implementation challenges, specific for SME. (3) A classification of PLM research for SME, related to the common PLM implementation process structure. A hypothesis for a PLM implementation failure mechanism in SMEs is formulated, based on the findings. Also, a potential research gap on operational implementation knowledge in SMEs is identified.

Keywords: PLM · SME · Implementation

1 Introduction

Product Lifecycle Management (PLM) is defined as a business activity or strategy. It manages products from their conception to their end-of-life disposal or recycling. This definition is used by industrial institutions like CimData [1] and Gartner Group [2], but also by academic authors like Stark [3, 4], Eigner [5] and Grieves [6, 7]. PLM should not be confused with *PLM software* that supports processes within PLM. Examples of PLM software are *Product Data Management* (PDM), *Computer Aided Design and Manufacturing* (CAD/CAM), *Project Management*, *Workflow Management* and *Production Planning*.

Nowadays, many *Small to Medium-sized Enterprises* (SME) start to adopt PLM. An SME, as defined by the European Commission [8], is a company with less than 250 employees with an annual turnover up to EUR 50 Million. For PLM implementations, SME specific challenges could also apply to larger companies.

Published by Springer Nature Switzerland AG 2018.
P. Chiabert et al. (Eds.): PLM 2018, IFIP AICT 540, pp. 681–691, 2018.
https://doi.org/10.1007/978-3-030-01614-2_62

The importance of PLM for companies grows with the increasing complexity of products, processes and organizations [5], also in SMEs. The introduction of the concept of *The Fourth Industrial Revolution* or *Industry 4.0* intensifies this increase in complexity [9]. Organizations have to work differently than before, if they want to make use of developments like *Internet of Things* (IoT), *Product Service Systems* (PSS) or *Mass Customization.*

Industry and academia have made efforts to improve the methods of PLM implementation. Nevertheless, industry surveys [10–13] show that companies are still struggling to implement PLM successfully. Some authors [4, 14, 15] claim that 50% of PLM implementations do not achieve their initial project goals. Unfortunately, no specific definition of project failure or project goals is giving in these references.

For this paper, we analyzed published research about PLM in SME. We searched for PLM challenges and for methods to overcome these challenges. To organize the results, we reviewed publications about PLM implementation and derived a suitable classification structure. The research method is explained in Sect. 2 and the result can be found in Sect. 3. In Sect. 4, we formulate a hypothesis for an SME specific failure mechanism, identify a potential research gap and propose future research.

2 Research Method

2.1 Research Questions

The key question in this paper is: "Why do SMEs struggle to implement PLM and what are the proposed solutions in academic literature?". To answer this question we have defined three sub-questions:

1. Which implementation methods are described in literature?
2. What are the challenges in PLM implementation, specific for SMEs?
3. Which improvements are proposed in literature?

2.2 Literature Research for PLM Implementation Guidelines

A search was done for concepts *PLM* and *Implementation,* using Scopus, Web of Science, Google Scholar. We selected papers, specifically on the implementation process, holistically or partially. This selection was based on title, keywords and abstracts. Furthermore, we did a secondary search, using the references in the selected papers. This resulted in an additional number of books, articles, dissertations and industry reports. We derived a *generic PLM implementation process structure* from this literature to classify the results from the systematic literature review on PLM and SME.

2.3 Systematic Literature Review PLM and SME

We searched in Scopus, Web of Sciences and Google Scholar for both concepts (*PLM* and *SME*). Results were left out when SME or PLM had a different meaning than our purpose or when the terms were found only in the references section (Google). We were able to obtain full texts for approximately 50% of the resulting papers (Table 1).

Table 1. Literature research results by database.

Database	Hits	Viewed	Relevant	Full text
Web of science	23	23	16	10
Scopus	66	66	48	23
Google scholar	5970	250	120	71
Total (overlapping)			**148**	**75**

We analyzed the retrieved papers in two ways. Firstly, we identified SME-specific challenges that influence the implementation and adoption of PLM.

Secondly, we related the main research topic (contribution) of each paper to one or more steps in the aforementioned generic PLM implementation process structure.

3 Results

3.1 Implementation Guidelines

We selected the following publications that contain a holistic description of a PLM implementation process: Stark [3, 4], Eigner et al. [5], Grieves [6, 7], Feldhusen et al. [16, 17], Schuh et al. [18], Bitzer [19] and Arnold et al. [20]. There is a clear structure of preparation, analysis, design and implementation that can be found in all of these publications. We derived a simplified 4-phase structure from these publications, as shown in Table 3 in Sect. 3.3.

3.2 SME Challenges

We identified SME specific challenges in the full-text papers and organized them in 12 categories. The results are listed in Table 2, ranked by occurrence.

Table 2. SME specific PLM challenges, found in literature.

SME Challenge	Sources	References
High cost of implementation	16	[21–36]
Lack of skilled resources	11	[22, 25, 27–31, 33, 37–39]
Network dependency	10	[26, 29, 33, 38, 40–45]
Limited understanding of PLM	9	[18, 22, 31, 40, 43, 46–49]
Informal processes	9	[33–35, 40, 44, 50–53]
Informal organizations	8	[27, 33, 50, 52–55]
Lack of suitable PLM solutions	7	[29, 33, 35, 36, 38, 47, 48]
Unstructured information (flow)	6	[23, 52, 55–58]
Business risk	5	[33, 42, 44, 50, 59]
PLM complexity	5	[23, 31, 33, 36, 46]
Unstructured knowledge management	4	[21, 40, 50, 60]
Lack of strategic business planning	1	[43]

3.3 Proposed Solutions in Literature

After reviewing the papers, we related the research to subphases in our generic PLM implementation process structure. Classification is based on our interpretation of the main contribution of the papers. This interpretation is intrinsically subjective, also because of variations in structure of the reviewed papers (e.g. case studies, theories, reviews, etc.)

Table 3. Research on PLM in SME, categorized by implementation phase.

Phase/sub phase	Sources	References
1. Prepare and define		
1.1. PLM Awareness	5	[42, 47, 48, 61, 62]
1.2. PLM Vision	2	[18, 63]
1.3. Maturity level	4	[31, 49, 61, 64]
1.4. Goals	2	[18, 49]
1.5. Strategy	3	[30, 63, 65]
2. Analyze and measure		
2.1. Product structure	2	[37, 54]
2.2. Processes	7	[22, 38, 47, 50, 52, 54, 66]
2.3. Organization	4	[52, 67]
2.4. Infrastructure and ICT	0	
2.5. Requirements documentation	3	[38, 47, 54]
3. Design		
3.1. Data model	17	[23, 25, 26, 28, 30, 36–38, 41, 45, 46, 60, 68–72]
3.2. Processes	18	[21, 26, 30, 36–38, 40, 46, 53, 54, 58, 67, 69–74]
3.3. Organization	3	[41, 46, 53]
3.4. Infrastructure and ICT	7	[24, 25, 27, 37, 39, 57, 59]
3.5. Specification documentation	2	[54, 65]
4. Implement and maintain		
4.1. Project management	2	[54, 75]
4.2. Vendor selection	4	[25, 32, 76, 77]
4.3. Realization	2	[37, 69]
4.4. Customization	8	[26, 35, 38, 54, 62, 69, 72, 74]
4.5. Verification	1	[27]
4.6. Deployment	0	
4.7. Training	0	
4.8. Evaluation	3	[33, 56, 62]

3.4 Interpretation of the Results

Prepare Phase. Solutions and challenges are clearly related in the papers related to this phase. Awareness creation aims to overcome the challenge of limited understanding of PLM. With insight into the potential of PLM, organizations can build a vision for the future.

Maturity assessment enables organizations to describe the gap that needs to be bridged. Furthermore, better strategic planning and reduction of business risk is possible when the gap is known to the organization. Priorities can be set rationally.

Some papers emphasize the importance of vision, strategy and goals. Nevertheless, little has been written about how an SME can define them practically.

Analysis Phase. Analyzing the current state processes and organization of an SME is difficult. This is related to the SME challenge of informal processes and organization.

Generally, SMEs are rigid on a macro level and flexible on an operational level [67]. To overcome this, several new approaches have been proposed to assess these ad-hoc processes, for example by focusing on information flow and collaboration methods.

Design Phase. The largest number of papers has been published on the design of process models, data models or on both (ontology). With these process and data models, researchers aim to solve the issue of lacking availability of suitable solutions. They propose industry specific alternatives to the existing models.

Case studies have been done with new PLM models for specific situations. No evidence for a successful universal SME-approach has been presented in the reviewed papers.

Implementation Phase. Customization gets most attention in this phase for two reasons. Some papers propose to lower the cost of software by developing a new platform for SME. It is questionable if this is a valid approach, since only 20% of implementation costs is software cost [16, 20, 26] and software development is also a cost.

Others see a need for adoption of commercial software to overcome functional deficits for SMEs. This has been studied in specific cases.

In contrast to the high interest in customization, there is less interest in operational aspects of implementation (realization, verification, deployment, training), which has also been observed in a research by Bokinge et al. [78].

4 Conclusions and Future Research

In this paper we discuss answers to the sub-questions in Sect. 2.1 and we formulate a hypothesis for an answer to the main research question.

4.1 Sub Questions

Sub Question 1, Implementation Methods. We found a common structure for a generic PLM implementation process in various publications. This process can be very elaborate if all steps are followed consistently, even for large enterprises.
This method also implies that SMEs need to formalize their processes and organization drastically, sacrificing flexibility. Flexibility is a valuable asset of SMEs.

Sub Question 2, Challenges. We have identified 12 SME specific challenges in PLM implementation. This comprehensive list of challenges helps to understand reasons for possible PLM implementation failure in SMEs. Organizations can take these challenges into account in future PLM implementations and manage project risks better.

Sub Question 3, Solutions in Literature. We have seen a variety of approaches to PLM for SME in the papers we reviewed. Our classification in the PLM implementation process structure uncovered *hotspots* and *white spaces* in published research. The largest hot spot is *data and process modeling*, the largest white space, or research gap, is *operational implementation knowledge*.

4.2 Main Research Question

Commercial PLM systems seem to be developed for reference process models, derived from large enterprises. These reference models often do not fit SMEs (Lack of suitable PLM solutions). Also implementation partners do not have clear answers on how to implement PLM for SME [33].

Every SME specific PLM challenge could cause failure, if it is not taken into account during an implementation. Most challenges can be overcome by good project management, following generic PLM implementation guidelines.

The exception is the dilemma between flexibility and formalization. We conclude from our literature research that this challenge needs an alternative approach, compared to large enterprises.

Our hypothesis is that if organizations (companies and implementation partners) are not conscious enough about the aforementioned dilemma between formalization and flexibility, they are at risk. They will start PLM implementations in the "large enterprise style" in expectation that good project management will ensure success. At some point the organization will run into problems with flexibility, leading to increased overhead costs (application management, new administrative work, waiting times, etc.), extensive customization to overcome functional deficits and/or massive rejection by users.

4.3 Future Research

As a next step, we plan to analyze implementation projects from the past. This qualitative empirical research should give more insight into the influence of the identified PLM implementation challenges in the implementation process in practice. This research can also provide more quantitative data on failure rates of PLM projects, under the condition that a neutral definition of failure can be defined.

Also more research is needed on operational PLM implementation knowledge.

References

1. CIMdata: About PLM (2017). https://www.cimdata.com/en/resources/about-plm. Accessed 16 Jan 2018
2. Gartner: IT Glossary - Product Lifecycle Management (2018). https://www.gartner.com/it-glossary/product-lifecycle-management-plm. Accessed 25 Jan 2018

3. Stark, J.: Product lifecycle management. Product Lifecycle Management. DE, pp. 1–29. Springer, Cham (2015). https://doi.org/10.1007/978-3-319-17440-2_1
4. Stark, J.: Product lifecycle management. Product Lifecycle Management (Volume 2). DE, pp. 1–35. Springer, Cham (2016). https://doi.org/10.1007/978-3-319-24436-5_1
5. Eigner, M., Stelzer, R.: Product Lifecycle Management; Ein Leitfaden für Product Development und Life Cycle Management [Product Lifecycle Management; a Guideline for Product Development and Lifecycle Management]. Springer, Heidelberg (2009). https://doi.org/10.1007/b93672
6. Grieves, M.: Product Lifecycle Management: Driving the Next Generation of Lean Thinking. McGraw-Hilll Education, New York (2005)
7. Grieves, M.: Virtually Perfect: Driving Innovative and Lean Products through Product Lifecycle Management. Space Coast Press, Merritt Island (2011)
8. EuroStat (2018). http://ec.europa.eu/eurostat/web/structural-business-statistics/structural-business-statistics/sme. Accessed 1 Mar 2018
9. The Fourth Industrial Revolution: what it means, how to respond (2016). Accessed 05 Mar 2018
10. AberdeenGroup: The PLM for Small to Medium-Sized Manufacturers Benchmark Report - Enabling Profitable Growth for SMEs. Aberdeen Group, Waltham (2006)
11. Woo, T.: Data Management in PLM: Optimize Your Business Performance. AberdeenGroup, Boston (2016)
12. CIMdata, Cloud PLM: Understanding Adoption Prospects. CIMData, Ann Arbor (2018)
13. Leeder, N.: PLMPulse Survey - Edition 2017. i42R, Utrecht (2018)
14. Wognum, P.M., Kerssens-van Drongelen, I.C.: Process and impact of product data management implementation. Int. J. Prod. Dev. **2**(1), 5–23 (2005)
15. Siddiqui, Q.A., Burns, N.D., Backhouse, C.J.: Implementing product data management the first time. Int. J. Comput. Integr. Manuf. **17**(6), 520–533 (2004)
16. Feldhusen, J., Gebhardt, B.: Product Lifecycle Management für die Praxis: Ein Leitfaden zur modularen Einführung, Umsetzung und Anwendung [Product Lifecycle Management for Practitioners: a Guideline for Modular Implementation and Application]. Springer, Heidelberg (2008). https://doi.org/10.1007/978-3-540-34009-6
17. Feldhusen, J., et al.: Development of methods to support the implementation of a PDMS. In: Brissaud, D., Tichkiewitch, S., Zwolinski, P. (eds.) Innovation in Life Cycle Engineering and Sustainable Development, pp. 381–395. Springer, Dordrecht (2006). https://doi.org/10.1007/1-4020-4617-0_26
18. Schuh, G., et al.: Process oriented framework to support PLM implementation. Comput. Ind. **59**(2), 210–218 (2008)
19. Bitzer, M.A.: Entwicklung einer Methode zur prozessorientierten Planung und Optimierung von Product-lifecycle-Management-Lösungen: am Beispiel der Automobilindustrie (Development of a Method for Process Oriented Planning and Optimization of PLM Solutions: by Example of the Automotive Industry). TU Kaiserslautern, Kaiserslautern. p. 165 (2008)
20. Arnold, V., et al.: Product Lifecycle Management Beherrschen: Ein Anwenderhandbuch für den Mittelstand [Mastering Product Lifecycle Management: a User Manual for Medium Enterprises]. Springer, Berlin (2011). https://doi.org/10.1007/978-3-642-21813-2
21. Arrieta, J.A., Azkarate, A., Aranguren, N.: Advanced business intelligence system adapted to SMEs, within a defined product life-cycle management frame. In: ICE Conference (2004)
22. Bedolla, J.S., et al.: Fostering PLM implementation in SMEs: modelling and managing verification processes. IFAC Proc. **46**(9), 1762–1767 (2013)
23. Bruno, G., Taurino, T., Villa, A.: MAKO: manufacturing knowledge organization system to support SME. IFAC Pap. **48**(3), 1559–1564 (2015)

24. Cheung, W.M., et al.: A framework for distributed workflows, peer-to-peer and PLM/PDM collaborations to support OEMs and SMEs (2004)
25. David, M., Rowe, F.: What does PLMS (product lifecycle management systems) manage: data or documents? Complementarity and contingency for SMEs. Comput. Ind. **75**, 140–150 (2016)
26. Eigner, M., Nem, F.M.: On the development of new modeling concepts for product lifecycle management in engineering enterprises. Comput.-Aided Des. Appl. **7**(2), 203–212 (2010)
27. Germani, M., Mengoni, M., Peruzzini, M.: A QFD-based method to support SMEs in benchmarking co-design tools. Comput. Ind. **63**(1), 12–29 (2012)
28. Jardim-Goncalves, R., et al.: SMART-fm: setting interoperability in SME-based industrial environments. In: Advanced Manufacturing. An ICT and Systems Perspective, pp. 57–69. CRC Press (2007)
29. Litvikova, J., Rafaj, M., Valcuha, S.: Product lifecycle in small and medium-sized enterprises. Ann. Oradea Univ. (1), 171–174 (2013). https://doi.org/10.15660/AUOFMTE.2013-1.2805. ISSN 1583-0691
30. Löwer, M., Heller, J.E.: PLM reference model for integrated idea and innovation management. In: Fukuda, S., Bernard, A., Gurumoorthy, B., Bouras, A. (eds.) PLM 2014. IAICT, vol. 442, pp. 257–266. Springer, Heidelberg (2014). https://doi.org/10.1007/978-3-662-45937-9_26
31. Messaadia, M., et al.: PLM adoption in SMEs context. Comput.-Aided Des. Appl. **13**(5), 618–627 (2016)
32. Ristova, E., Gecevska, V.: AHP methodology and selection of an advanced information technology due to PLM software adoption. In: Proceedings of the 15th International Scientific Conference on Industrial Systems (2011)
33. Saaksvuori, A.: PLM Vision 2016 and Beyond. Sirrus Capital Ltd., Helsinki (2011)
34. Silventoinen, A., Papinniemi, J., Lampela, H.: A roadmap for product lifecycle management implementation in SMEs. In: ISPIM Conference (2009)
35. Soto-Acosta, P., Placer-Maruri, E., Perez-Gonzalez, D.: A case analysis of a product lifecycle information management framework for SMEs. Int. J. Inf. Manag. **36**(2), 240–244 (2016)
36. Yildiz, O., Pernelle, P., Gzara, L., Tollenaere, M.: A framework for PLM model design. In: Bernard, A., Rivest, L., Dutta, D. (eds.) PLM 2013. IAICT, vol. 409, pp. 159–169. Springer, Heidelberg (2013). https://doi.org/10.1007/978-3-642-41501-2_17
37. Colombo, G., Pugliese, D., Rizzi, C.: Developing DA applications in SMEs industrial context. In: Cascini, G. (ed.) CAI 2008. TIFIP, vol. 277, pp. 69–82. Springer, Boston, MA (2008). https://doi.org/10.1007/978-0-387-09697-1_6
38. Le Duigou, J., et al.: Generic PLM system for SMEs: application to an equipment manufacturer. Int. J. Product Lifecycle Manag. **6**(1), 51–64 (2012)
39. Silcher, S., et al.: A holistic management model for manufacturing companies and related IT support. In: Cunha, P.F. (ed.) Forty Sixth Cirp Conference on Manufacturing Systems 2013, pp. 175–180. Elsevier Science Bv, Amsterdam (2013)
40. Denkena, B., et al.: Knowledge management in process planning. Cirp Ann.-Manuf. Technol. **56**(1), 175–180 (2007)
41. Kadiri, S.E., et al.: Collaborative process control: observation of tracks generated by PLM system arXiv preprint arXiv:0811.1950 (2008)
42. Goto, S., Yoshie, O., Fujimura, S., Tamaki, K.: Preliminary study on workshop facilitation for IoT innovation as industry-university collaboration PLM program for small and medium sized enterprises. In: Ríos, J., Bernard, A., Bouras, A., Foufou, S. (eds.) PLM 2017. IAICT, vol. 517, pp. 285–296. Springer, Cham (2017). https://doi.org/10.1007/978-3-319-72905-3_26

43. Nupap, S., et al.: A framework to lead Thai SMEs to fit international business requirement: case study of Solution Ceramic Co., Ltd., Thailand. In: 2011 4th International Conference on Logistics, LOGISTIQUA 2011. Hammamet (2011)
44. Pol, G., et al.: Implementation of collaborative design processes into PLM systems. Int. J. Prod. Lifecycle Manag. **3**(4), 279–294 (2008)
45. Subrahmanian, E., et al.: Challenges in supporting product design and manufacturing in a networked economy: a PLM perspective. In: Proceedings of the International Conference on Product Lifecycle Management (2005)
46. Bruno, G., Antonelli, D., Villa, A.: A reference ontology to support product lifecycle management. Procedia CIRP **33**, 41–46 (2015)
47. Plo, L., Robin, V., Girard, P.: Understanding PLM system concepts to facilitate its implementation in SME: the real case study of POULT. In: Harik, R., Rivest, L., Bernard, A., Eynard, B., Bouras, A. (eds.) PLM 2016. IAICT, vol. 492, pp. 512–522. Springer, Cham (2016). https://doi.org/10.1007/978-3-319-54660-5_46
48. Pinna, C., et al.: An approach to improve implementation of PLM solution in food industry - case study of poult group. Int. J. Prod. Lifecycle Manag. **10**(2), 151–170 (2017)
49. Savino, M.M., Mazza, A., Ouzrout, Y.: PLM maturity model: a multi-criteria assessment in southern Italy companies. Int. J. Oper. Quant. Manag. **18**(3), 159–180 (2012)
50. Antonelli, D., Chiabert, P., Villa, A.: Introducing product lifecycle management to small medium enterprises: discussion and analysis. In: IFAC Proceedings Volumes, pp. 1059–1064 (2012)
51. Germani, M., Mengoni, M., Peruzzini, M.: A method to define a co-design platform to support cooperative work in SMEs. In Proceedings of the PLM09 Conference, Bath, UK (2009)
52. Pol, G.: Improving design coordination in computer supported environments in SMEs: implementation of a tool for capturing and analysing collaboration between actors. Cranfield University (2008)
53. Kadiri, S.E., et al.: An approach to control collaborative processes in PLM systems arXiv preprint arXiv:0803.0666 (2008)
54. Eynard, B., Merlo, C., Pol, G.: Towards PLM implementation method in SME. In: DS 35, Proceedings ICED 2005, The 15th International Conference on Engineering Design, Melbourne, Australia, 15–18 August 2005 (2005)
55. Medina-Barbosa, D.A., Siller, H.R.: Product lifecycle management model for new technology based enterprises. In: Luo, Y. (ed.) CDVE 2013. LNCS, vol. 8091, pp. 93–100. Springer, Heidelberg (2013). https://doi.org/10.1007/978-3-642-40840-3_15
56. Kaganski, S., Paavel, M., Lavin, J.: Selecting key performance indicators with support of enterprise analyze model. In: 9th International Conference of DAAAM Baltic: Industrial Engineering, DAAAM-Baltic 2014, DAAAM International (2014)
57. Basselot, V., Berger, T., Sallez, Y.: Active monitoring of a product: a way to solve the "lack of information" issue in the use phase. In: Borangiu, T., Trentesaux, D., Thomas, A., Leitão, P., Barata Oliveira, J. (eds.) Service Orientation in Holonic and Multi-Agent Manufacturing. SCI, vol. 694, pp. 337–346. Springer, Cham (2017). https://doi.org/10.1007/978-3-319-51100-9_30
58. Mahdikhah, S., et al.: A business process modelling approach to improve OEM and supplier collaboration. J. Adv. Manag. Sci. **2**(3), 246–253 (2014)
59. Tähemaa, T., Karjust, K., Pohlak, M.: ERP and PLM resources in estonian SMES. In: 7th International DAAAM Baltic Conference: Industrial Engineering. DAAAM International (2010)

60. Bernard, A., Laroche, F., Da Cunha, C.: Models and methods for knowledge formalisation in a PLM context. In: 3rd International Congress Design and Modelling of Mechanical Systems CMSM 2009 (2009)
61. Paavel, M., Karjust, K., Majak, J.: PLM maturity model development and implementation in SME. In: 50th CIRP Conference on Manufacturing Systems, vol. 63, pp. 651–657 (2017)
62. Peruzzini, M., Mengoni, M. and Germani, M.: PLM benefits for networked SMEs. In: Pels, J.H., et al. (eds.) The Proceedings of 11th International Conference on Product Lifecycle Management, PLM 2011, 11–13 July 2011. Eindhoven University of Technology. 14 pp. (2011)
63. Paavel, M., et al.: Optimizing PLM implementation from vision to real implementation in Estonian SMEs. Benefits **14**, 15 (2014)
64. Batenburg, R., Helms, R.W., Versendaal, J.: PLM roadmap: stepwise PLM implementation based on the concepts of maturity and alignment. Int. J. Prod. Lifecycle Manag. **1**(4), 333–351 (2006)
65. Kienbaum, G.S., et al.: A transdisciplinary process oriented framework to support generic PLM implementation for use by small and medium enterprises. In: 23rd ISPE Inc. International Conference on Transdisciplinary Engineering, TE 2016. IOS Press BV (2016)
66. Le Duigou, J., et al.: Specification of a generic PLM system dedicated to SMEs based on a PPRO meta-model. In: 16 th CIRP International Conference on Life Cycle Engineering (2009)
67. Pol, G., et al.: Prerequisites for the implementation of a product data and process management tool in SME. In: ICED 05, 15th International Conference on Engineering Design: Engineering Design and the Global Economy. Engineers Australia (2005)
68. Bruno, G., Antonelli, D., Korf, R., Lentes, J., Zimmermann, N.: Exploitation of a semantic platform to store and reuse PLM knowledge. In: Grabot, B., Vallespir, B., Gomes, S., Bouras, A., Kiritsis, D. (eds.) APMS 2014. IAICT, vol. 438, pp. 59–66. Springer, Heidelberg (2014). https://doi.org/10.1007/978-3-662-44739-0_8
69. Le Duigou, J., et al.: Application of PLM processes to respond to mechanical SMEs needs. In: Bernard, A. (ed.) Global Product Development. Springer, Heidelberg, pp. 319–326 (2011)
70. Le Duigou, J., et al.: Generic model for the implementation of PLM systems in mechanical SMEs. In: Thoben, K., et al. (eds.) International Confereence on Product Lifecycle Management 2010, Inderscience, Geneva, Bremen, Germany, pp. 439–448 (2010)
71. Pol, G., et al.: From PDM systems to integrated project management systems: a case study. In: Proceedings of the International Conference on Product Lifecycle Management, Lyon, France (2005)
72. Sakao, T., Liu, Y., Gustafsson, R., Thörnblad, G.: A method for lifecycle design of product/service systems using PLM software. In: Ríos, J., Bernard, A., Bouras, A., Foufou, S. (eds.) PLM 2017. IAICT, vol. 517, pp. 710–718. Springer, Cham (2017). https://doi.org/10.1007/978-3-319-72905-3_63
73. Cheballah, K., Bissay, A.: Change management and PLM implementation. In: Bernard, A., Rivest, L., Dutta, D. (eds.) PLM 2013. IAICT, vol. 409, pp. 695–701. Springer, Heidelberg (2013). https://doi.org/10.1007/978-3-642-41501-2_68
74. Le Duigou, J., et al.: Global approach for technical data management. Application to ship equipment part families. CIRP J. Manuf. Sci. Technol. **1**(3), 185–190 (2009)
75. Wynn, M.G.: Managing IS projects in SMEs–Tailoring the PRINCE2 TM1 methodology (2008)

76. Maranzana, N., Segonds, F., Lesage, F., Nelson, J.: Collaborative design tools: a comparison between free software and PLM solutions in engineering education. In: Rivest, L., Bouras, A., Louhichi, B. (eds.) PLM 2012. IAICT, vol. 388, pp. 547–558. Springer, Heidelberg (2012). https://doi.org/10.1007/978-3-642-35758-9_49
77. Rocha, L., et al.: Cloud management tools for sustainable SMEs. Procedia CIRP **40**, 220–224 (2016)
78. Bokinge, M. Malmqvist, J.: PLM implementation guidelines relevance and application in practice: a discussion of findings from a retrospective case study. Int. J. Prod. Lifecycle Manag. **6**(1), 79 (2012)

PLM Competencies Analysis Based on Industry Demand

Mourad Messaadia[1(✉)], Samir Ouchani[2], and Anne Louis[1]

[1] CESI/LINEACT, Rouen, France
{mmessaadia, alouis}@cesi.fr
[2] CESI/LINEACT, Aix En Provence, France
souchani@cesi.fr

Abstract. Last decade recognizes a high job demand, more specialized trainings with very oriented jobs offers. This situation makes hiring and recruitments officers in the difficulty to select and find easily the appropriate candidate as well for candidates to choose the best practices and trainings to find later a respectable position. This work aims to help all actors in the job sector by modeling the Product Lifecycle Management (PLM) competencies and analyzing the demands especially in industry 4.0. First, the enterprises needs, in terms of skills, are identified through various job offers distributed on online media. Job offers are structured according to profile, geolocation and required competencies, etc. Then, the analysis is based on information retrieval and text mining through a statistical measure used to evaluate how important a competence to a job offer in a given collection. This contribution applies the Term Frequency Inverse Document Frequency (TF-IDF) to determine what skills in a corpus of job offers is the most requested in PLM jobs. This contribution addresses more than 1300 job offers, written in French, and posted in France during the period of (2015–2016). The offers cover more than 388 K words, from which 20 types of PLM job titles and 106 terms are related to the job competencies. The obtained results allow us to identify the most requested jobs, skills and classifying jobs and competencies for a better guidance of PLM job actors.

Keywords: PLM competencies · PLM job offers · TF-IDF · Clustering

1 Introduction

The industry sector, which is part of a globalized economy with high competitiveness requirements, is currently undergoing deep structural changes in its business model that is related principally to scientific, economic, demographic and societal factors. This change will, in the short or medium term requires new skills able to understand and to face the jobs searching and hiring challenges.

The roadmap for manufacturing 2.0 places human at the center of the organization [1]. Thereby, the development of the necessary human resources concerns the whole process of small and large industrial enterprises. For that, an enterprise should carry out a complete diagnosis of its business lines and the skills held by its employees [2], as well as tools (GPEC, eRH, etc.) already deployed in the context of human resources

Published by Springer Nature Switzerland AG 2018.
P. Chiabert et al. (Eds.): PLM 2018, IFIP AICT 540, pp. 692–701, 2018.
https://doi.org/10.1007/978-3-030-01614-2_63

management (job repositories, job descriptions, interview schedules, etc.). Depending on its medium and long-term strategy and the context (economic, social, technological, regulatory, etc.), the enterprise projects future jobs and skills in order to measure the gaps with the existing one [1]. At this stage, the external support (specialized consultant) is often recommended to handle a part of this stage's tasks.

With the arrival of Industry 4.0, manufacturing processes will evolve and generate an increased technical and organizational complexity [3], which will involve significant challenges for manufacturing companies (SMEs). This issue will go beyond the financial investment needed to acquire new technologies to reach the human aspects. Effectively, one of major aspects facing the company is the skilled workforce at all levels, that are able to face the growing complexity of Industry 4.0 [4].

According to "Global Industry Analysts" prediction, the global market for PLM will reach 65.8 billion $ by 2022. Further, PLM software market will grow to 20.41 billion $ during 2019, with 7.4% of annual Growth Rate [5]. However, it is announced that more than 25,000 PLM specialists are missing in Europe [6]. PLM adoption includes very extensive changes in organizational practices and requires new types of persons' skills and capabilities [7]. Investigations show that size of enterprise and human capital of the workforce, have an impact on PLM adoption [8]. As a consequence, it is mandatory to analyse PLM job offers and PLM competencies needed for industry.

The job offers analysis means analysing the content of the job offers and the competencies sought behind. For example the system proposed in [9] that is based on competence model permit to recommend potential candidates for an offer emitted by a recruiter. It relies on extracting the job title, skills and experience required for the posted position. Further, work in [10] focuses on job offer recommendation process based on user and job offer modeling.

PLM competencies mean developing a model based on a description of the competence concept. Erol et al. [4] developed a problem-competency framework based on three-dimensional: management, production process and type of competency. The competencies addressed in this model are personal, social, action and domain. Wittorsky [11] located a competence at the intersection of 3 fields: socialization and biography of the individual and the professional experience and training.

This paper is composed of four main sections. After introducing PLM problems and sketching our contribution, we provide an analysis of PLM competencies, a job offer structure and competencies extraction method. Then, Sect. 3 presents job offers analysis based on the developed model. Finally, we conclude the paper and hint the future directions.

2 PLM Competencies Analysis

PLM adoption implies more collaboration between people in the same department, between the different departments of a company and between companies and their partners (supplier for example). PLM competencies (engineers, consultants etc.) will have a key role to play in Industry 4.0 evolution. The French employment association for executives (APEC) carried out a study according PLM job offers where it shows an increasing of PLM skills by 36% in only one year [12]. The work analysis 'PLM jobs' and its related competencies are grouped in three major steps as shown in Fig. 1. Herein, we develop each of steps: job offers preparation, competencies extraction, and competencies evaluation.

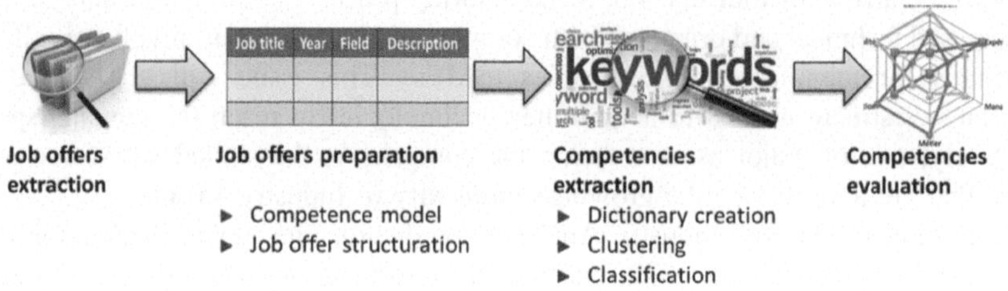

Fig. 1. Proposed approach

Initially, the jobs offers are presented in a textual form describing, the title, the jobs description, etc. To enhance the processing of the considered offer, we parse first step, the textual document, to extract a set of keywords following three steps [13]:

- Tokenisation: words are separated, by splitting the text at each whitespace and removing the special characters (punctuations, accents…). In this step we defined unique word for same words written in different ways. e.g. 3DExperience, 3D-Experience and 3D Experience become 3DExperience.
- Words filtering: words that don't convey any information are removed, such as the determinants, or if it belongs to a list set beforehand [14]. This step allows us to only keep the needed words (tokens issued from tokenization phase) and then generate the dictionary.
- Words processing: reduce the word's list by excluding words having the same/close meaning (e.g. competence/competencies) [15].

2.1 Proposed Model

To model the PLM competencies and their system management, we align within the existing modeling standards, especially UML. The proposed model is developed according to two main parts the competencies and job offers. Competencies modeling is addressed according to internal aspects such (to-know-how, to-know and to-know-whom) presented in [16]. Job offers modeling is proposed according to online job postings analysis.

Figure 2 shows the class diagram describing the competences and job offers model. We explain each class related to the competencies as follows.

- "Knowledge" represents everything that is learned by an initial or specific training which addresses: theoretical knowledge, knowledge about the existing on the environment in which a skill is fulfilled the procedural knowledge (procedures and operating methods related to the activity).

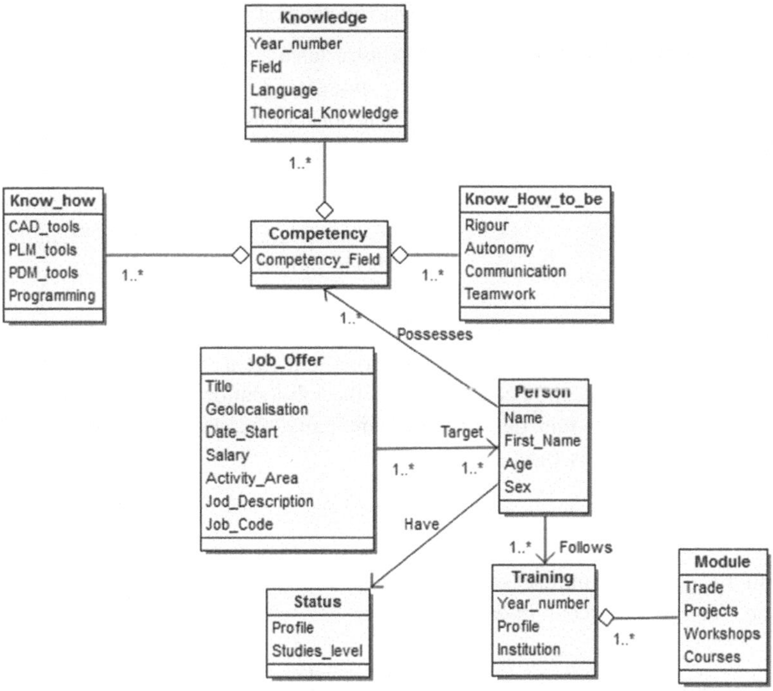

Fig. 2. Competencies class diagram model

- "Know_how" is related to experience and operational capabilities and that means I know how to do it, I know how to do it and I can teach someone else to do it.
- "Know-How_to_be" represents an individual characteristic that allow adopting a particular behavior in a given situation. They combine relational skills (associated with cooperative behaviors), cognitive skills (intellectual operations of problem solving) and behaviors (personal qualities).

Each job offer targets one or more person with specific competences. Each person follows training, composed of one or more modules, and has a status describing his profile and study level (Fig. 2).

2.2 Job Offer Structuration

Job offer is a description of a vacant position in a job offer described in a textual document. This document is presented as a text and posted on recruitment websites (APEC, Indeed, Monster, etc.) in order to attract the appropriate candidate. The job offer is separated into several textual fields such title, company description, location, contract, study, experience, sector, and job category. The job adverts is described according two types of fields, unstructured which is purely textual and written in natural language, or structured with numbers such experience (Table 1).

Table 1. Data structuration.

Title	Structured	Unstructured
PLM Functional Consultant	Enterprise field; year; Position; Job Code; Salary; Place	… Position and missions: Enovia/CATIA V6 Functional Consultant: To participate in workshops and functional document specifications for digital models. Profile: 2 years of experience minimum, Bilingual English required (French oral/written) to begin for mid-March, early April …

In the structured data we have the enterprise field, year of job offer apparition, the position of the candidate, the occupation and the job location. The non-structured data contains the textual job offer description. Principally, the structured data will be used for the job offers analysis (non-structured).

2.3 Competencies Extraction

A job offer is seen as a multiset of terms called "Bag of words", which is a set in which the same element can occur several times.

$$T = \{T_1, T_2, \ldots, T_n\} \tag{1}$$

A collection of "n" documents and "m" distinct terms can be represented as a matrix, which represents the document database.

$$W = \begin{bmatrix} & T_1 & \cdots & T_m \\ D_1 & w_{11} & \cdots & w_{1m} \\ \vdots & \vdots & \ddots & \vdots \\ D_n & w_{n1} & \cdots & w_{nm} \end{bmatrix} \tag{2}$$

Most of the methods of transforming text into Bag of Words can be divided into three main approaches. The first is a purely statistical approach based on the occurrence of terms like Term Frequency (TF) and Term Frequency-Inverse Document Frequency (TF-IDF) [17]. The second is a semantic based approach, which includes both Latent Semantic Analysis (LSA) and Latent Dirichlet Allocation (LDA) [18] methods. The third one is an alternative approach between both (all the methods of the N-gram family) [19].

The N-gram family is more adapted to word sequence analysis and LSA requires the order of words appearance and used for the semantic aspect of the sentence such synonyms detection. The TF-IDF is the most used method because it helps to weight the importance of a term within a document and its importance in a corpus, but requires the use of "bag of words". It also, allows avoiding the word filtering step.

In this work, TF-IDF is used for determining the relative frequency of competencies in job offers compared to the inverse proportion of that word over the entire document corpus. The calculation determines how relevant a given term is in a particular document. Terms that are common in a single or a small group of documents tend to have higher $w_{i,j}$ weight than common words such as articles and prepositions [17].

$$w_{i,j} = tf_{i,ji} \times idf_i = \frac{n_{i,j}}{\left\|d_j\right\|} \times \log\left(\frac{N}{df_i}\right) \tag{3}$$

Where (according to each job):

$tf_{i,j}$ = frequency of apparition of i (term) in j (document)
$n_{i,j}$ = the number of occurrences of i (term) in j (document)
$\left\|d_j\right\|$ = the length of the document
df_i = number of job offers containing i *term*
N = number of corpus (documents)

For our case study, we replace the length of the document $\left\|d_j\right\|$ by the length of the total competencies identified and N is replaced by number job offers with same title. Thus, the tf leads to a weighting proportional to the number of occurrences of a competence according to the set of competencies.

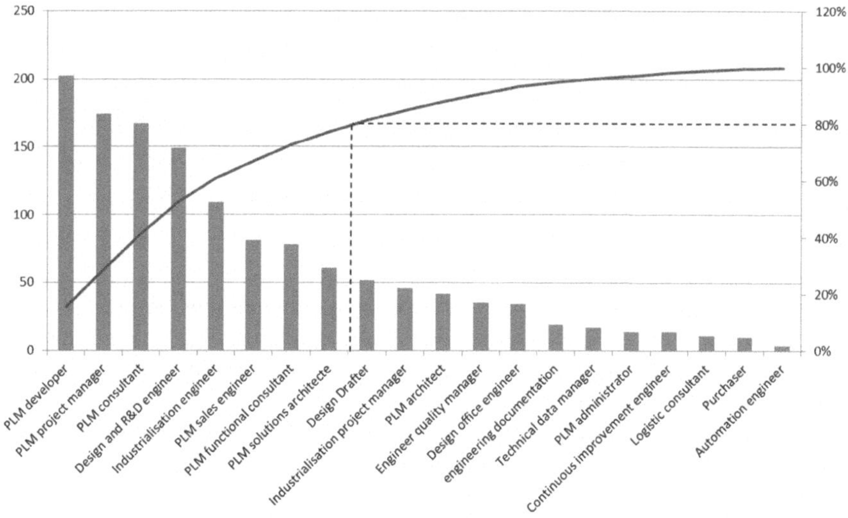

Fig. 3. Types of PLM job offer.

3 Job Offers Analysis

Based on (1300) job offers collected from APEC database for the period between (2015–2016), we extract the PLM job types from offers titles and then classified into 20 job categories (Fig. 3).

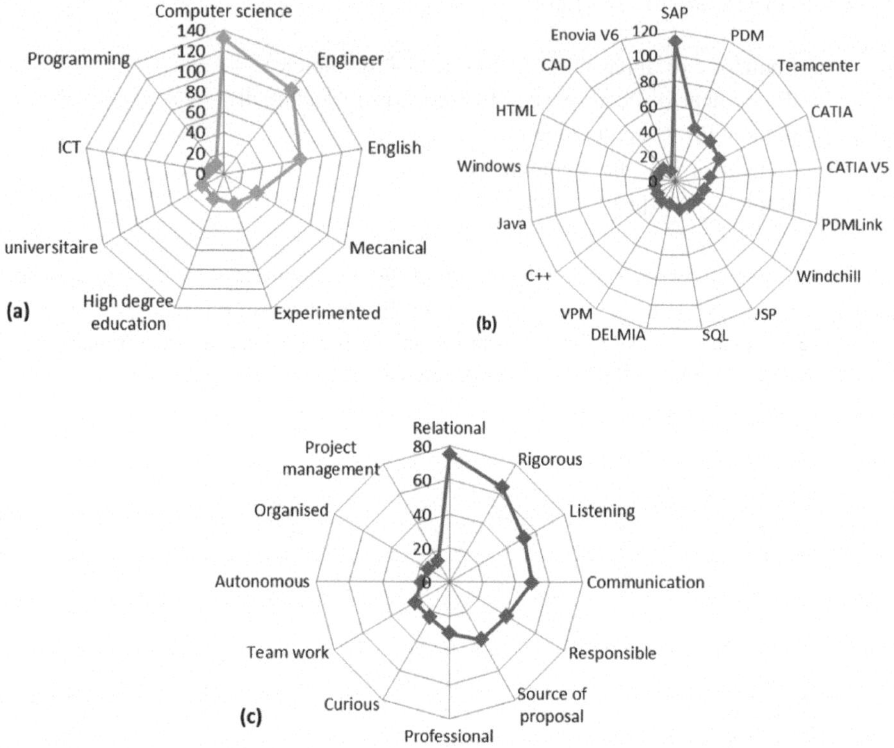

Fig. 4. Frequently required competencies for PLM consultant job: (a) knowledge, (b) know how, and (c) know how to be.

The pareto diagram (Fig. 3) shows the frequently required jobs. We can see that 8 PLM jobs account for 80% of required job: PLM developer, PLM project manager, PLM consultant, design and R&D engineer, industrialisation engineer, PLM functional consultant, and PLM solution architect.

The radar diagrams in (Fig. 4) give an overview of the frequently required competencies according to the PLM consultant job:

(a) Shows knowledge where computer science education competence is the most required then we find the level of engineer without requirement on the field of specialty. English seems important for this kind of job.

(b) Shows know how, where SAP is the most needed competence. This diagram is usefull if we need to classify PLM tools or PLM software owners. With CATIA, Dassault Systems Company is just after Teamcenter then Windchill of PTC. For PLM consultant the computer science level is characterized by JSP, SQL, C++ and java competencies.
(c) Shows the how know to be, where relational and rigorous for PLM consultant job and for the eight PLM jobs identified in (Fig. 3). Listening, communication and responsible are also required for this kind of job.

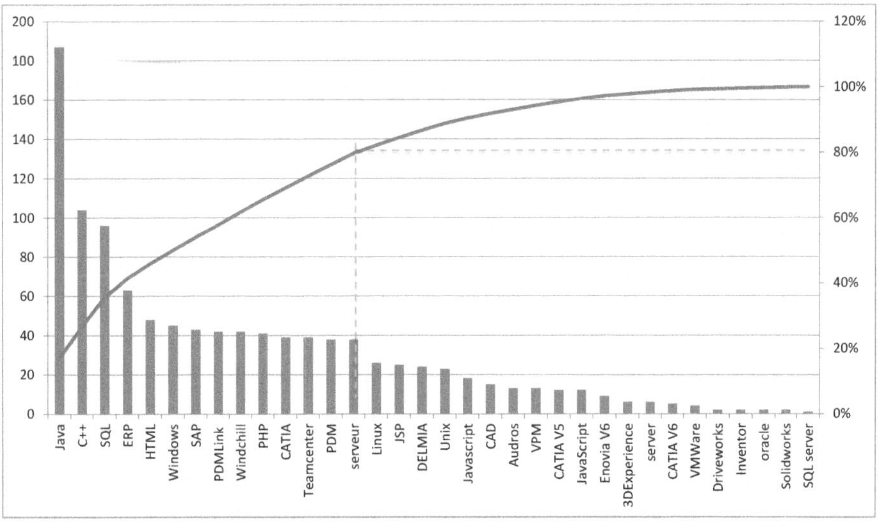

Fig. 5. Required competencies for developer job

The same analysis is conducted for each PLM job, where we analysed the competence required frequency. (Figure 5) shows the pareto diagram of PLM developer job. Among the most requested competencies (80%) we find programming competencies (Java, C++, PHP), Database (SQL, Server), product data management (PDM and PDMLink), PLM software (SAP, windchill and team center) and CAD (CATIA).

During our analysis, the ERP often appeared in job offers. As showed in (Fig. 5) the ERP frequency appears before PLM tools. This can be explained by the lack of maturity of the PLM, which pushes the recruiters to begin by introducing the ERP which seems an alternative for PLM. This can be also seen as a need to train people to PLM solutions.

The TF-IDF deployment gives a great vision of competencies needed. However this method is based on an existing dictionary of existing competencies. If we want to identify new competencies (don't existing in the dictionary) in automatic way, we will have to go to other methods such as N-gram family.

4 Conclusion

To help job actors in Industry 4.0, we developed a PLM modeling and analysis framework. The latter model describes enterprises needs where job offers are structured according to profile, geolocation and required competencies, etc. Further, the analysis of the model relies to the information retrieval and text mining to evaluate how important a competence to a job offer in a given collection. The framework enhances TF-IDF to determine what skills in a corpus of job offers. The effectiveness of the framework has been shown on more than 1300 job offer. The obtained results allowed us to identify the most requested jobs, skills and classifying jobs and competencies for a better guidance of PLM job actors.

We would like to extend our work in different directions. First, we will include the level of experience needed in order to guide the level of deepening of knowledge during training. Methods such N-gram family will be explored. Then, we will evaluate distances between different types of PLM jobs across skill types. Further, experiment the framework with different sectors and datasets.

Acknowledgement. This work is supported by the French Government's Program "Investments for the Future". Acknowledgement is made to APEC for the job offers database.

References

1. ICT for Manufacturing The ActionPlanT Roadmap for Manufacturing 2.0. https://setis.ec.europa.eu/energy-research/sites/default/files/static-projects/files/roadmap.pdf
2. Thoben, K.D., Wiesner, S., Wuest, T.: Industrie 4.0" and smart manufacturing–a review of research issues and application examples. Int. J. Autom. Technol. **11**(1), 4–16 (2017)
3. Schuh, G., Potente, T., Varandani, R., Schmitz, T.: Global footprint design based on genetic algorithms–an "Industry 4.0" perspective. CIRP Ann.-Manuf. Technol. **63**(1), 433–436 (2014)
4. Erol, S., Jäger, A., Hold, P., Ott, K., Sihn, W.: Tangible industry 4.0: a scenario-based approach to learning for the future of production. Procedia CIRP **54**, 13–18 (2016)
5. https://www.marketsandmarkets.com/PressReleases/quality-lifecycle-management-software.asp. Accessed 29 Jan 2018
6. Jacques Raud. http://www.jacquesraud-consulting.com/fr/industrie-4-0-un-defi-pour-trouver-les-competences-plm/
7. Kärkkäinen, H., Pels, H.J., Silventoinen, A.: Defining the customer dimension of PLM maturity. In: Rivest, L., Bouras, A., Louhichi, B. (eds.) PLM 2012. IAICT, vol. 388, pp. 623–634. Springer, Heidelberg (2012). https://doi.org/10.1007/978-3-642-35758-9_56
8. Messaadia, M., Benatia, F., Baudry, D., Louis, A.: PLM adoption model for SMEs. In: Ríos, J., Bernard, A., Bouras, A., Foufou, S. (eds.) PLM 2017. IAICT, vol. 517, pp. 13–22. Springer, Cham (2017). https://doi.org/10.1007/978-3-319-72905-3_2
9. Casagrande, A., Gotti, F., Lapalme, G.: Cerebra, un système de recommandation de candidats pour l'e-recrutement. In: AISR2017 (2017)
10. Diaby, M.: Méthodes pour la recommandation d'offres d'emploi dans les réseaux sociaux. Doctoral dissertation, Sorbonne Paris Cité (2015)
11. Wittorski, R.: De la fabrication des compétences. Education Permanente, no. 135 La compétence au travail, pp. 57–70 (1998)

12. APEC – Tendance métiers dans l'industrie: Le PLM (2017). ISBN 978-2-7336-1030-5
13. Sebastiani, F.: Machine learning in automated text categorization. ACM Comput. Surv. (CSUR) **34**(1), 1–47 (2002)
14. Leskovec, J., Rajaraman, A., Ullman, J.D.: Mining of Massive Datasets. Cambridge University Press, Cambridge (2014)
15. Liu, H., Christiansen, T., Baumgartner, W.A., Verspoor, K.: BioLemmatizer: a lemmatization tool for morphological processing of biomedical text. J. Biomed. Semant. **3**(1), 3 (2012)
16. Girodon, J.: Proposition d'une approche d'amélioration des performances des organisations par le management opérationnel de leurs connaissances et compétences. Ph.D. thesis, Université de Lorraine (2015)
17. Ramos, J.: Using TF-IDF to determine word relevance in document queries. In: Proceedings of the First Instructional Conference on Machine Learning, vol. 242, pp. 133–142 (2003)
18. Blei, D.M., Ng, A.Y., Jordan, M.I.: Latent Dirichlet allocation. J. Mach. Learn. Res. **3**(Jan), 993–1022 (2003)
19. Kešelj, V., Peng, F., Cercone, N., Thomas, C.: N-gram-based author profiles for authorship attribution. In: Proceedings of the Conference Pacific Association for Computational Linguistics, PACLING, vol. 3, pp. 255–264 (2003)

3D Printing and Additive Manufacturing

A New Methodology of Constructing Products Using Additive Manufacturing Technology: Case Study of a Push Button

Konstantinos Bailas(✉) and Paraskevas Papanikos

Department of Product and Systems Design Engineering, University of the Aegean, Ermoupolis, Syros, Greece
kbail@aegean.gr

Abstract. The effective construction of innovative and customized products using Additive Manufacturing Technology remains a challenging task when dealing with mass production in industry. This paper describes a new methodology for solving various problems of constructing a product using Additive Manufacturing technology. The objective is to minimize the number of parts of the final product by embedding those parts to the main geometry while simultaneously increasing the lifecycle of the product. This can be achieved by integrating one or more parts to the main structure of the product with the proper use of a parametric CAD system that generates parts with parameterization and constraints. The developed methodology has been applied to the manufacturing of a push button as an integrated product consisting only of one part. Finite element simulation and mechanical testing was used to verify the approach based on design requirements related to fatigue strength and distance to stroke. The results demonstrate the effectiveness of the proposed approach.

Keywords: Additive manufacturing technology · Product lifecycle Design intent · Finite element analysis · Push button

1 Introduction

Additive manufacturing (AM), also referred to as 3D printing [1], is a technology that draws attention of academics and manufacturing industries over the last 20 years and has been dynamically entered the field of low volume production in industry [2, 3]. AM contribution to the manufacturing industries is believed to be revolutionary [4] and recent applications of this technology as the manufacturing of metallic components, show that this revolution has become more realistic than ever [5]. One of the most important advantages of AM technology in industry is the ability to fabricate complex geometries, customized, sustainable and flexible products that are impossible to build with traditional methods such as tools or molds, during the manufacturing process [6]. The processes and a wide variety of materials that AM uses can build complex geometries that in many cases, reduce the assembly work needed to accomplish a final product and can be further optimized according to functionality with no need of restrictions set from production technology or supply chain constraints [3]. However, the capabilities of AM in industry have a numerous of limitation that need to be

Published by Springer Nature Switzerland AG 2018.
P. Chiabert et al. (Eds.): PLM 2018, IFIP AICT 540, pp. 705–714, 2018.
https://doi.org/10.1007/978-3-030-01614-2_64

consider when dealing with mass production. Specifically, low production speed compared to conventional production methods and many individual moving parts that make up a product, makes the integration of AM technology into mass production a difficult issue [2, 3]. Nevertheless, design for manufacturing and assembly (DFM) gave the designers the opportunity to solve serious problems in manufacturing using AM and many companies are now having successful production lines, such as Siemens, Boeing and others with customized products [7]. Products made of AM processes are models from various CAD systems [8]. Each model contains information such as geometric properties and relations between edges, faces, vertices and sub-parts that determines its design intent. A shape of a model determines most of the time its function and is important for controlling the effectiveness of above parameters during the Finite Element Analysis (FEA). This is proven to be crucial for estimating the lifecycle of the product [9]. The reduction of the number of parts that consist a final product without affecting its function and durability can reduce the production time since no extra time is required for its assembly [8]. In this paper, a methodology for the reduction of the number of parts is developed and applied by embedding a push-button to the main geometry of a product during the design process. A push-button is a simple switch mechanism for controlling some aspect of a machine and having rectilinearly-movable operating part or parts adapted for pushing or pulling in one direction only [10].

2 Design Intent

Using a state of the art parametric CAD system, three different products were created, i.e., Specimens A, B and C (Fig. 1). Each specimen simulates a push button and consists of three different geometries, Geometry A (Chassis), Geometry B (Two Ribs) and Geometry C (Push Button) that were all embedded into one solid (Fig. 2).

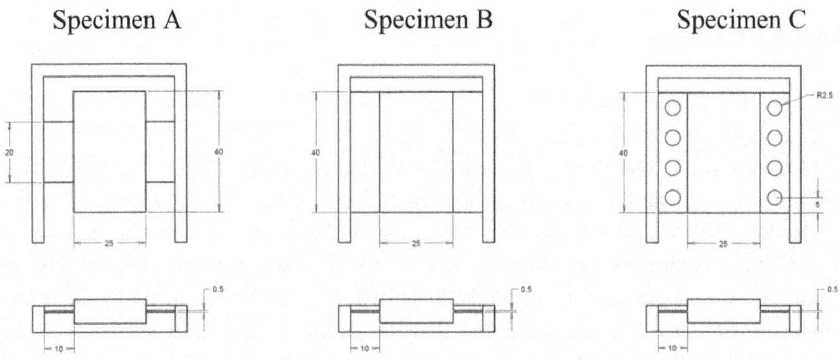

Fig. 1. Specimens geometry.

Design intent played an important role during the design process of those specimens and included all the necessary product information, such as parameters and constrains to easy manipulate the geometry of each specimen. These parameters were the "Length", "Width" and "Thickness" for each rib of Geometry B (Fig. 3), the value of radius for each hole for Specimen C and the definition of constant parameters for Geometry C (Fig. 1).

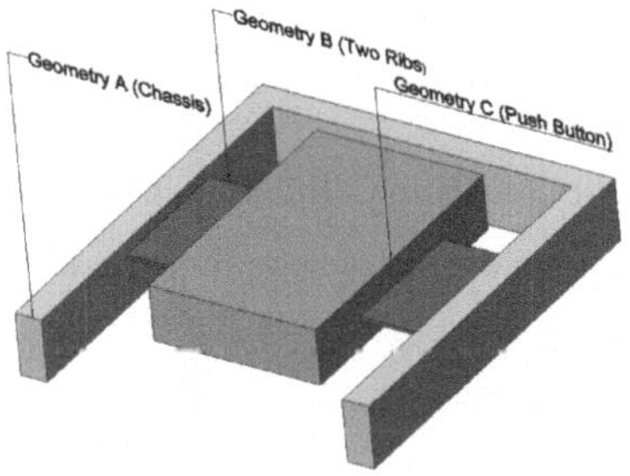

Fig. 2. Geometries that consist the push button.

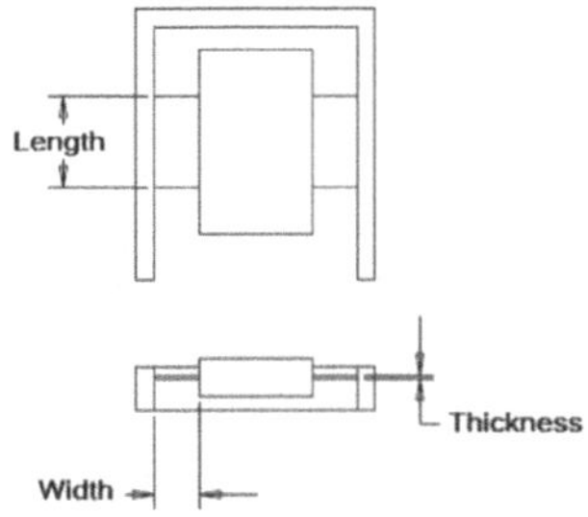

Fig. 3. Parameters of geometry B.

Design intent also helped to control the effectiveness of those specific parameters during the Finite Element Analysis (FEA) in a targeting manner without affecting, e.g. geometries A and C. It should be noted that rib thickness was set to 0.5 mm to be within the tolerances of structural stability of the additive machines, which were used for manufacturing the prototypes.

3 Analysis and Optimization

Using Creo Simulate platform, mechanical analyses of specimens A, B and C were carried out to evaluate the relationship between equivalent stress (von Mises) and displacement for each push button (Table 1). The applied force at the top plane of each push button was set to 5 N, a common force value for triggering a push button (Fig. 4) [10]. We use three different materials that are widely used in additive manufacturing machines. These are ABS with Young's Modulus 2 GPa and density 1100 kg/m^3, PLA with Young's modulus 2.1 GPa and density 1250 kg/m^3 and PA6 with Polycarbonate (PC) blend material with Young's modulus 0.48 GPa and density 350 kg/m^3. The values of the Young's moduli were measured from simple three-point bend tests of flat specimens made from the three materials and corresponding additive manufacturing techniques. This was important for the correct analyses using CreoSimulate platform and for the comparison between the simulation and testing results related to the mechanical behavior of the push buttons that follows in another section of this paper. Figures 5 and 6 show the stress distribution and the deformation of specimen C. The maximum displacement value for each of the above material specimens (Tables 1, 2, 3) determines which geometry is appropriate to activate a button at a force of 5 N.

Table 1. Analyses results for ABS, using Creo Simulate platform.

Specimen	Maximum displacement (mm)	Maximum stress (MPa)
A	0.468	14.4
B	0.231	6.5
C	0.252	8.0

Table 2. Analyses results for PLA, using Creo Simulate platform.

Specimen	Maximum displacement (mm)	Maximum stress (MPa)
A	0.445	14.4
B	0.220	6.5
C	0.263	8.0

Table 3. Analyses results for PA6-PC, using Creo Simulate platform.

Specimen	Maximum displacement (mm)	Maximum stress (MPa)
A	1.949	14.4
B	0.961	6.5
C	1.050	8.0

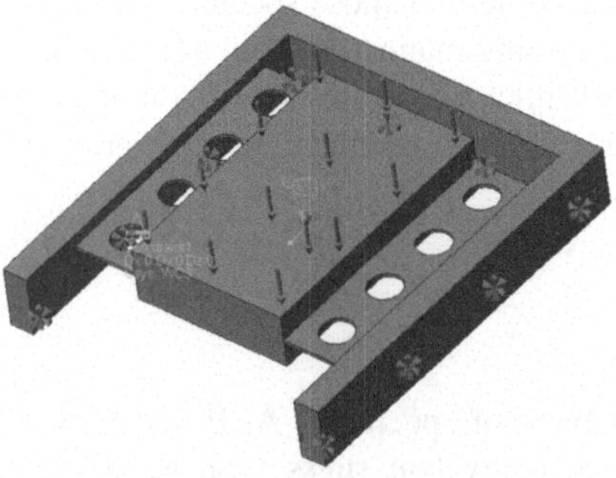

Fig. 4. Applied force on specimen C.

Fig. 5. Stress distribution of specimen C.

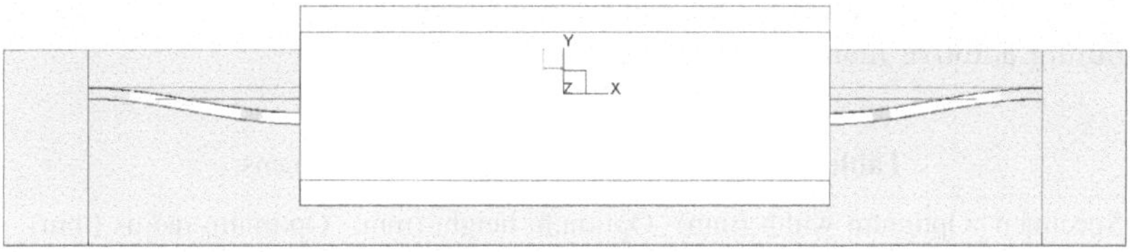

Fig. 6. Maximum displacement for specimen C.

The results of the analyses for ABS material for each of three specimens showed that the maximum stress developed in specimens B and C was lower than the minimum reported fatigue strength of the material, which is 11 MPa [11]. For specimen A the maximum stress is larger than the lower fatigue strength but well within the allowable range of 11–24 MPa [11]. Since the maximum stress value of specimens B and C are much lower than the fatigue strength, we can conclude that their geometry can be further optimized. The results of the analyses for PLA material for each of the three specimens showed that the maximum stress developed in all specimens was much lower than the minimum fatigue strength of the material, which is 45 MPa [12]. This means that their geometry can be change much more drastically than the geometry of ABS specimens. On the contrary the results of the analyses for PA6-PC material for each of three specimens showed that the maximum stress developed in specimens A, B and C was above the minimum fatigue strength of the material, which is 5 MPa [12], meaning a short life cycle of a product. The analyses for all materials (ABS, PLA, PA6-PC) also demonstrated that geometry B (ribs) and its parameters (Figs. 2 and 3) strongly influences the maximum stress values, whereas virtually no influence was found for the other two parts.

Considering the effectiveness of Geometry B (ribs) to the mechanical behavior of each specimen an optimization study was carried out. The design limits considered related to specific values for the maximum displacement (= 0.5 mm) and depend on the material fatigue strength, i.e. 11 MPa, 45 MPa and 5 MPa, respectively. The design parameters were the width and thickness values for all specimens and the radius value for specimen C. Width was set to a range of 10 to 20 mm due to constraints we have during the design process in relation to other neighboring objects, such as electronic boards, batteries, etc. The thickness of each rib was set to a range of 0.5 to 1 mm, which helps staying within the tolerance of structural stability of the additive manufacturing machines. Radius was set to a range of 5 to 8 mm, a value indicating how dense the netting to be created on the ribs of specimen C would be.

The value of the maximum displacement for push buttons is also called "Displacement to Stroke" and means the displacement of the button, from its initial position until it reaches the activation point, and its value varies according the technical specifications of its button [13]. The results of the optimization study for each of three materials (Tables 4, 5, 6) showed that we had the ability to control the "Displacement to Stroke" value of each button under certain design limits without exceeding the fatigue strength for a specific material while maintained the geometry at the desired limits. It was also noticed that mechanical optimization analyses helped to find and predict an optimum geometry that can be functional when integrating it into a final solid during additive manufacturing process.

Table 4. Optimization study for ABS specimens.

Specimen	Optimum width (mm)	Optimum height (mm)	Optimum radius (mm)
A	13.85	0.68	-
B	13.07	0.50	-
C	12.26	0.50	5.67

Table 5. Optimization study for PLA specimens.

Specimen	Optimum width (mm)	Optimum height (mm)	Optimum radius (mm)
A	10.1	0.50	-
B	10.2	0.50	-
C	10.1	0.50	8.0

Table 6. Optimization study for PA6-PC specimens.

Specimen	Optimum width (mm)	Optimum height (mm)	Optimum radius (mm)
A	10	0.92	-
B	10	0.57	-
C	10	0.64	5.12

Due to the large fatigue strength of PLA, and the manufacturing related limit of minimum thickness of 0.5 mm, the optimized geometry for specimens A and B relates to the minimum values of thickness and width. In this case, the maximum stress obtained is only 15 MPa, which is much smaller than the fatigue strength, meaning that for the PLA material and the optimized geometry the life cycle of the product is almost infinite. For the PA6-PC material, due to its low strength, the optimized geometry corresponds to high thickness values (e.g. from 0.57 to 0.92 mm).

4 Experimental Investigation

All experiments were carried out at the Integrated Industrial Design Lab (INDEL) of the Aegean University at the Department of Product and Systems Design Engineering. We used two different technologies of Additive manufacturing machines and three kinds of materials to produce a total of nine physical products for our experiment. Fused Deposition Modelling (FDM) Technology was used to produce three ABS and PLA specimens using Dimension STRATASYS and Davinci PRO XYZPrinting model machine, respectively. Using Selective Heat Sintering (SHS) technology with Blue-printer M02 model machine, we produced three more Polyamide 6 (PA6) –

Polycarbonate (PC) specimen prototypes needed for our experiment. A mechanical testing machine, SHIMADZU AGS-X Series was used to measure the applied force in relation to displacement of each of nine products (Fig. 7). Displacement was applied at a speed of 2 mm/s and the corresponding force was measured up to a maximum force of 6 N.

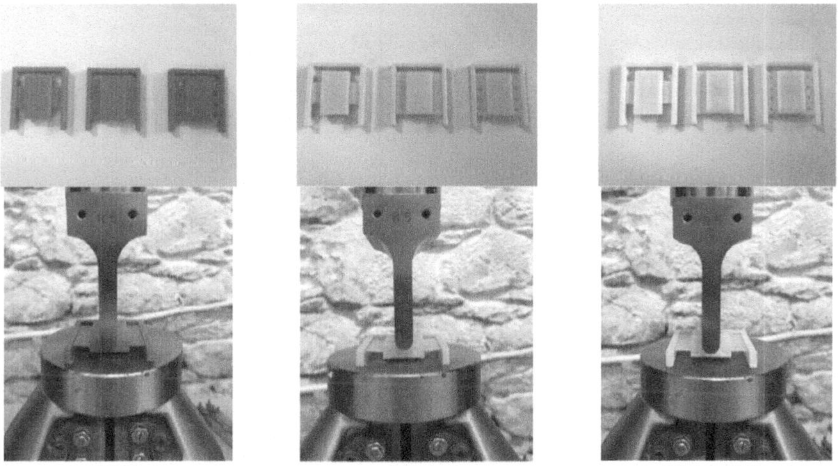

ABS PLA PA6-PC

Fig. 7. Specimens and testing procedure.

The above nine specimens were also modelled using Creo Simulate platform to compare the experimental and predicted mechanical behavior. Apart from the geometrical features, the inputs to the models were the mechanical and physical material properties described above.

The results are presented in Fig. 8 in the form of force-displacement curves. All simulation results are straight lines as the materials behavior was assumed perfectly linear-elastic for the small loads considered (up to 6 N). The experimental results showed similar behavior with very small deviation from a straight line. Careful examination showed that this is due to small slips (e.g. chassis) during testing and not due to non-linear material behavior. This was also verified by measuring residual deformations of the specimens after load removal, which were found to be less than 0.005 mm.

Figure 8 shows that for all cases examined, specimen B shows larger stiffness followed by C and A. As expected from the stiffness of the materials, specimens made from PLA showed the larger stiffness, followed closely by ABS, both having a stiffness of about 20 N/mm. Push buttons made of PA6-PC showed very small stiffness of about 4 N/mm. Testing results are very close to simulation results with maximum deviation less than 5% for the stiff materials (ABS and PLA) and larger for the soft material (PA6-PC) up to 15%.

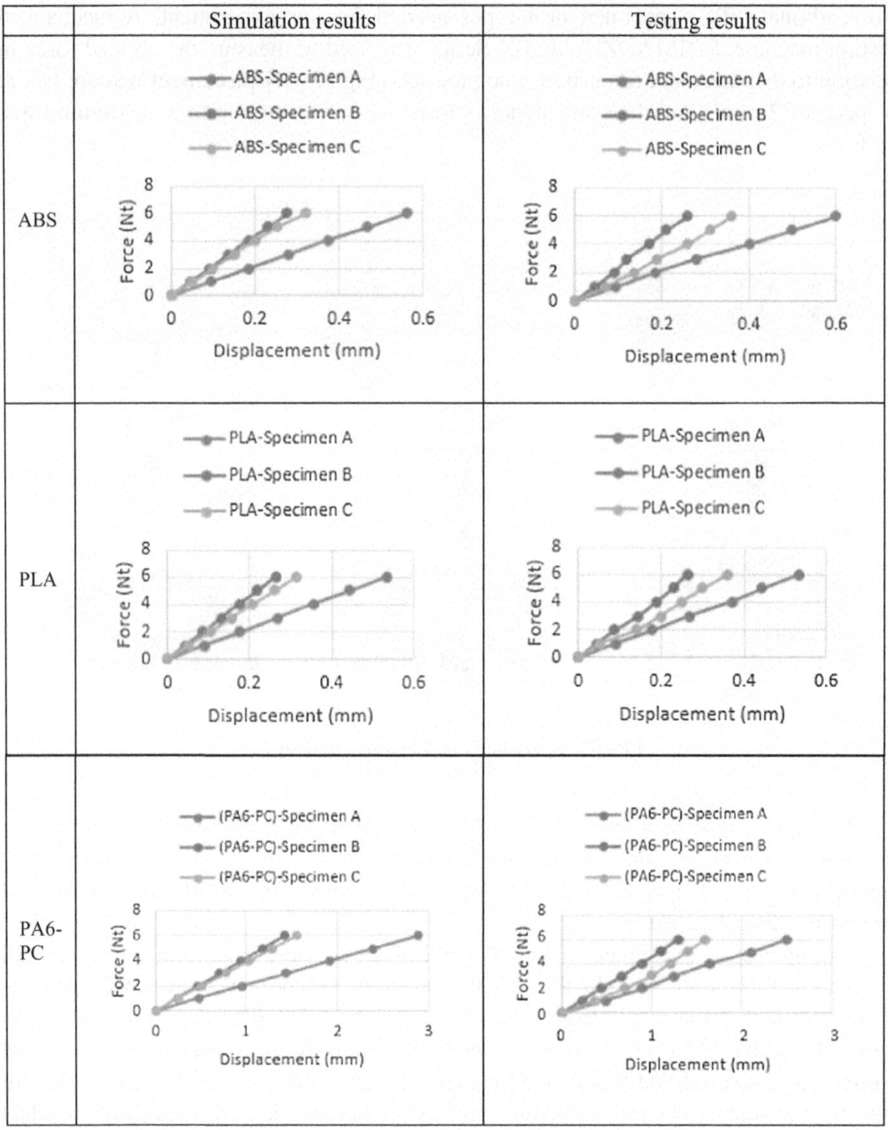

Fig. 8. Comparison between simulation and testing results.

5 Conclusions

Using AM technology, we can produce industrial products made up of individual parts in a small-scale industry. In this paper, it has been demonstrated that if some of these parts are incorporated into the main geometry of a product, during the design process, by using a CAD system and by introducing appropriately the concept of design intent, we have the possibility to produce equally functional products where embedded moving parts perform the same function and exhibit the same or even greater durability than being separate parts. This has the effect of reducing the production time since fewer sub-products of an assembly will have to be produced using less manufacturing technologies, while at the same time removing the cost of the extra moving parts, thereby significantly reducing its total production cost. In the example of the push button using design intent, all the information and constraints to achieve the integration of geometry were incorporated into a CAD model. It has been shown that those information's significantly influences the production of an assembly that used AM technology to be manufacture. In this way, the following were achieved:

No moving parts (e.g. chassis) can be designed so they are not affected during the operation of the moving parts. This is important because it was demonstrated that we can control which geometry will or may not be affected by the moving parts incorporated into it.

It has been shown that we can evaluate, using FEA which material (used by AM technology) is the most suitable and meets the requirements of the built-in geometry.

It has been demonstrated that we can estimate the optimal geometry to achieve a long product life cycle of a product before its production, considering the fatigue strength.

It has been shown that the use of netting and the density of it, affects the function of an integrated geometry, leading to lower mass and cost, without altering the function of a product.

References

1. Lipson, H., Kurman, M.: The new world of 3D printing, 1st edn. Wiley, Indianapolis (2013)
2. Gao, W., et al.: The status, challenges, and future of additive manufacturing in Engineering. Comput.-Aided Des. **69**, 65–89 (2015). https://doi.org/10.1016/j.cad.2015.04.001
3. Weller, C., Kleer, R., Piller, F.T.: Economic implications of 3D printing: market structure models in light of additive manufacturing revisited. Int. Prod. Econ. **164**, 43–56 (2015). https://doi.org/10.1016/j/ijpe.2015.02.020
4. Liu, P.W., et al.: Investigation on evolution mechanisms of site-specific grain structures during metal additive manufacturing. J. Mater. Process. Technol. (2018). https://doi.org/10.1016/j.jmatprotec.2018.02.042
5. Gustavo, T., Elwany, A.: A review on process monitoring and control in metal-based additive manufacturing. J. Manuf. Sci. Eng (2014). https://doi.org/10.1115/1.4028540
6. Rodrigue, H., Rivette, M.: An assembly – level design for additive manufacturing methodology. Hal. Archives-ouvertes (2015). https://doi.org/10.1007/978-2-8178-0169-8
7. Gibson, I., Rosen, D.W., Stucker, B.: Design for additive manufacturing. Additive Manufacturing Technologies, pp. 299–332. Springer, Boston, MA (2010). https://doi.org/10.1007/978-1-4419-1120-9_11
8. Guo, N., Leu, M.C.: Additive manufacturing: technology, applications and research needs. Front. Mech. Eng. **8**, 215–243 (2013). https://doi.org/10.1007/s11465-013-0248-8
9. Li, M., Langbein, F.C., Martin, R.: Detecting design intent in approximate CAD models using symmetry. Comput.-Aided Des. **42**, 183–201 (2010). https://doi.org/10.1016/j.cad.2009.10.001

10. Doerrer, C., Werthschuetzky, R.: Simulating push-buttons using a haptic display: requirements on force resolution and force-displacement curve. ResearchGate (2002)
11. Kunwoo, L.: Principles of CAD/CAM/CAE Systems, 1st edn. Addison Wesley Longman Inc., Reading (1999)
12. Jerez-Mesa, R., Travieso-Rodriguez, J.A., Liuma-Fuentes, J., Gomez-Gras, G., Puig, D.: Fatigue lifespan study of PLA parts obtained by additive manufacturing. Procedia Manuf. **13**, 872–879 (2017). https://doi.org/10.1016/j.promfg.2017.09.146
13. Malliaros, I.: An approach to identify the appropriate design requirements and specifications to define the target percept of an in-car interface: case of non-visual senses. Instituto Superior Técnico (2013)

Linkographic Analysis of Design Ideation Session: Idea Graph Representation and Additional Tools for Analysis

Abdellatif Dkhil[1], Mickael Gardoni[1](✉), Lamine Belgacem[2], and Remy Houssin[3]

[1] ETS Montréal, 1100 Notre-Dame West, Montreal, QC H3C 1K3, Canada
abdellatif.dkhil.1@ens.etsmtl.ca,
mickael.gardoni@etsmtl.ca

[2] Bombardier Canada, 500 Boulevard Côte-Vertu Outest, Dorval, QC H4S 1Y9, Canada
lamine.belgacem@aero.bombardier.com

[3] INSA Strasbourg, 24 Boulevard de la Victoire, 67000 Strasbourg, France
remy.houssin@unistra.fr

Abstract. Linkography is a method for analysis of ideation process in the conceptual design stage. This method has been used to provide information about the ideation session, to investigate the structure of idea generation process and to compare idea session productivity. The progress of an ideation session is made observable through the analysis of connection between ideas. The main goal of this paper is to improve the analysis of idea generation session. Through the use of graph theory for visualizing and analyzing the connection between ideas.

Keywords: Linkography · Conceptual design · Ideation · Graph Analysis tools

1 Introduction

The ability to invent, create, and innovate is the center of engineering and product development. The conceptual design stage is an interactive endeavor involving the evolution of ideas between two or more participants in discussion. The ideation process has the most significant impact to generate innovative products and this is essential for any organization to maintain its competitive position [1]. To better understand dynamics that take place in the ideation, the Linkography research approach proposes a method for recording, visualizing and analyzing connections between actions, ideas or events. The proposed method is seen as a system of notation and design analysis process that focuses on links between design moves, design ideas or decisions developed by Goldschmidt: [2–7] and extended by others [8–14]. Van-der-Lugt [15], adapted Linkography approach was further developed as a method for assessing the idea generation process by means of investigating the connections between ideas produced in the ideation. The Van-der-Lugt research work aims to understand the black box of the ideation process to better understand the inner processes under which ideas

P. Chiabert et al. (Eds.): PLM 2018, IFIP AICT 540, pp. 715–725, 2018.
https://doi.org/10.1007/978-3-030-01614-2_65

are elaborated. This process starts with the selection of design ideation team and the definition of the design problem. Then, the application of particular ideation method to permit ideating. Finally, the protocol of the ideation or the record of design team's ideation meeting will be analyzed. In the last step, the Linkography approach are used to analysis and understanding the ideation session. Figure 1 gives a description of application of Linkography approach steps. The first step permits the identification of ideas listed by segmentation of protocol. Then the link between ideas will be generated in matrix form. Ideas link matrix permit the generation of Linkography representation, called linkograph. This representation enters links among ideas as an input and displays structural idea reasoning patterns as an output. The ideation process can then be looked in terms of the patterns in the linkograph, which display the ideation reasoning and the structure of process. Finally, in the third step, the connections between ideas are analyzed to provide information, investigate the structure and compare productivity [7, 16]. The linkograph pattern of productive ideation team will be different from that of less productive group. Productive team will elicit ideas that have a high potential for connectivity to other ideas, while less productive team will have more random trails with ideas that did not have a high potential contribution.

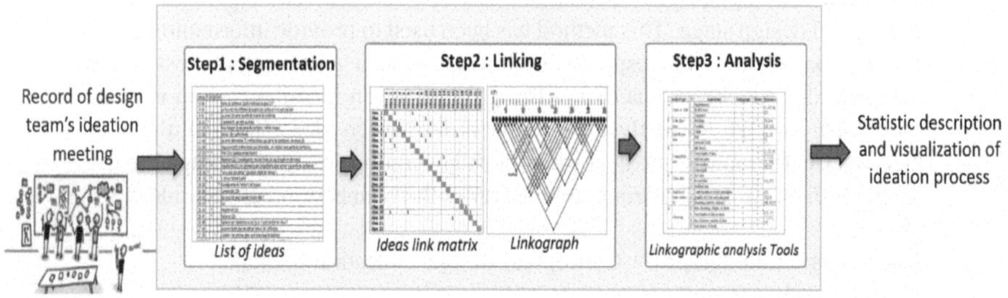

Fig. 1. Steps for application of Linkography approach

Several authors discussed the limits of the Linkography approach as developed by Goldschmidt's, in particular its subjectivity [15, 17, 18]. The interpretations of a linkograph lack objectivity. The authors studied the possibility of using objective methods to acquire information from the Linkography. They proposed different metrics for linkographic analysis. Some are studies used sophisticated mathematical tools to improve linkographic analysis, such as Kan et al. [18] and Cai et al. [19]. Our work is a part of the improving linkographic analysis perspective. In this study, we propose to use graph theory for visualizing and analyzing the ideation session. We will define an idea graph as a graph in with the nodes represent ideas and the lines represent the relation between them. Idea graph has several noticeable benefits compared to linko-graph. The great advantage of this representation is the possibility to use a large number of analysis tool proposed by the Graph theory. In addition, on its pictorial representation, graph theory offers a wide range of structural analysis tools. These tools allow a quantitative analysis of connectivity and relationships between ideas.

Following this introduction, the next section present a bibliographic review of the linkographic analysis tools. In the third section, we strat by given the advantages of using ideas graph representation in linkographic analysis. Then, we present a methodology for obtaining references graph based tools for idea graph analysis. After, we put the finger on the application of some analysis tools in order to illustrate the utility of graph-based tools in linkographic analysis applied in real case study.

2 A Bibliographic Review of Linkographic Analysis Tools

According to the literature, different tools of linkographic analysis has been proposed. These tools can be adapted and used to study the ideation session. In Table 1 we present a bibliographic review of linkographic analysis tools. These identified Tools are classified by type of analysis and the type of data: Linkograph and link matrix (Fig. 1).

A. Analysis of link types indicate the nature of the connections between ideas. Categorizing the links permits to see the possible transformation between two or more ideas. Van-der-Lugt [15] proposed three links categories. For a modification link, the existing line of thought is kept, but structural changes in the idea are provided. This link indicates direct variations. Supplementary correspond to a small and auxiliary changes: relationship between ideas is based on minor improvements on the same general idea. Tangential is based on free association and indicate the big leaps between ideas into a different direction.
B. Each link can have two directions: Backlinks and Forelinks [9]. Backlinks are links that has a specific idea with each of the previously generated ideas. Backlinks tend to signify analysis, verification, evaluation, assessment, and refinement. Forelinks, on the other hand, signify the specific ideas impact on idea generation to come and are marked in the row next to the idea. Goldschmidt [9] pointed out the Forelinks indicate new ideas, proposals, prospects, even breakthroughs.
C. Ideas Links distributions reflects the structure of ideation session and the status of ideation reasoning. When the reasoning is productive, the distribution acquires particular patterns, which are geometrically discernable in the Linkograph [9]. Low productivity yields unstructured Linkographs in which no patterns are discernable. Goldschmidt [9] identifies three geometrical patterns: chunk, Web and Sawtooth.
D. Link density (LD) of an ideation process or a portion of it is the ratio between the number of links and the number of ideas that form them [15]. High LD indicates that the ideas have many connections with earlier ideas, which means that participants have been building on earlier ideas. Low L.D's were found in the cases of inexperienced teams and those the experiencing difficulties in dealing with a particular design problem. The Self-link index is the ratio of the links that participants make with their own prior ideas, in relation to the total number of links made. Thus, an ideation team with a low self-link index is a team that generates ideas by building on each participant's ideas. This index indicates to what extent participants interact when generating ideas. According to Goldschmidt, ideas that generate a notably higher number of links, in one or both directions (backlinks, Forelinks), are particular interest: she calls them CI and she postulates that they are

Table 1. Bibliographic review of linkographic analysis tools

Analysis type		N	Analysis tool	Linkograph	Matrix	References
A	Types of Link	1	Supplementary	*	*	[9, 15, 16, 20]
		2	Modification	*	*	
		3	Tangential	*	*	
B	Links directions	4	Backlinks	*	*	[2, 7, 8, 21]
		5	Forelinks	*	*	
C	Specific patterns	6	Chunk	*		[4, 15, 21]
		7	Web	*		
		8	Sawtooth Track	*		
D	Connectedness	9	Link Density (LD)		*	[4, 5, 7–9, 14–16, 21]
		10	Total number of ideas		*	
		11	Self-link index		*	
		12	Critical Ideas (CI)	*		
		13	Critical path	*		
E	Types ideas	14	New idea	*	*	[8, 14]
		15	Revised idea	*	*	
		16	Modified idea	*	*	
F	Analysis of teams creativity	17	Creativity indices of each participants		*	[4–6, 10, 22, 23]
		18	Quantity of CI for each participant		*	
		19	Measuring creativity (entropy)		*	
G	Clustering	20	Ideas clustering, Number of cluster	*	*	[8, 10, 12, 14]
		21	Total number of link in cluster	*	*	
		24	Size of cluster (number of idea)	*	*	
		25	Link density of cluster	*	*	

more important than the other ideas in terms of advancing the ideation [3]. There is relationship between CI and the number of links that maintain. Core ideas could be CI, in the sense that they generate a large number of links, and very good ideas are those that spin the largest number of links among themselves and other ideas. The sequence of all CI in a process is defined as its critical path. Goldschmidt used these numbers and the critical path to benchmark the productivity of a design session. The critical path reflects the essence of the reasoning process and exhibits the issues and the notions, which are foremost on the designer's mind.

E. An idea is a form that emerged from the consciousness through the ideation process. Contemplating ideas is associated with the ability of reasoning, self-reflection, of the ability to acquire, apply intellect, intuition and inspiration, etc. In Wu et al. [8] analysis of ideas are identified by three different types of ideas: new, revised and modified. The idea that team discussed it for the first time in the ideation session is called new idea. Revised idea is to observing the repetition of the idea, and then it is revisited. Modified idea occurred when a revisited idea is modified or elaborated.

F. The Creativity indices and the quantity of CI calculate, what could be called, the creativity indices of participants using the number of ideas proposed by each participants [22]. Kan and Gero [23] suggested using entropy for measuring creativity. The higher entropy reflects a richer idea generation process in the sense that degree of uncertainty has similar meaning to the design creativity. A dense links merely implies high participations and are not requirements for the generation of creativity.

G. According to Goldschmidt [2, 21] a cluster is a series of successive ideas that explore same specific issues. Different ways to cluster ideas has been proposed [10, 14]. For example, Link cluster can be determined by visual inspecting of the Linkograph. The 'cluster size' is the number of ideas in the cluster. For further details, we refers to this research work; Bilda and Gero [14] and in Wu et al. [8].

- **Limits of linkographic analysis tools**

Several authors discussed the limits of the linkographic analysis tools as developed by Goldschmidt's, and studied the possibility of using objective methods to acquire information from the linkographic analysis [12, 17]. The availability of tools and metric for the structural ideation process analysis is biggest limitation of Linkography approach: this is due to the representation way. According to Goldshmith [2], some specific patterns in linkograph have a low frequency of occurrence. This decreases the utility and the use of some proposed tools in analysis. In addition, using linkograph has some communicative limitations due to the relationships between ideas, which are sometimes difficult to interpret by novice users. The most difficulty concern the representation and the analysis of a linkograph with a big number of ideas and a large variety of relations between themes. Hence, the description often lost the complexity and richness of the idea process. Linkograph has a limitation in describing the entire structure of ideas with multiple relationships. In the linkograph, the sequence of ideas generation is not clearly apparent compared to the graph representation. With linkograph it is difficult to retrace the path of ideas construction. Van-der- Lugth used only the link matrix to represent ideas and their relationships [16, 20]. He did not use the linkograph and only link matrix as input data are used.

3 Graph Based Tools for Linkographic Analysis

The proposed approach is based on the use graph for visualizing and improving the analysis of the ideation session. In this section, we highlight advantage of using graph representation compared to linkograph. Then we present our methodology to identify a reference graphs based tools to linkographic analysis. Finally, we put the finger on the application of some analysis tools in order to illustrate the utility of graph-based tools in linkographic analysis applied in real case study.

3.1 Advantages of Using Ideas Graph Representation

Idea graph has several noticeable benefits compared to linkograph representation. It simplify the representation and the relations between ideas by using standard representation allowing a comprehensive structure of ideation processes. This representation provides a more lucid representation to understand the characteristics of each ideations process and identify the differences intuitively. Graph has long provided visual languages and have been widely used in many different disciplines as formal representation system. The ideas graph described in the best ways the richness and complexity of the ideation process. It can be seen as a graphical representation of the ideation process and aimed at representing the comprehensive structure of a cognitive process while describing the relationships and ideation flows.

Ideas graph seems to be a particularly good way of organizing the ideas generated. Thus the graph of idea has a long idea flow which represents progressive development of an idea because it provides a view of the entire structure of the ideas elements in a ideation process. Ideas graph display describes the diversity and the depth of the entire ideation process as well: this provide accurate and highly structural information then linkograph representation. Ideas graphs are effective tool for making the structure of ideas generation process explicit because this is essential for the ideation team to clarifying their thinking and verifying the establish links. Graph can serve the ideation team in understanding their own ideas better and simplify the representation and the relations between ideas. Organizing and prioritizing new ideas permit stimulating creative thinking allowing for understanding. This representation showed notifiable differences in exploration of precedents, and generation and development of ideas. Graph can also be used in other ideation meeting to stimulate the process of ideas generation. In new ideation session, the ideas graph can be used for serval purposes such as to generate ideas or brainstorming, to develop complex structures, to communicate complex ideas. Visual learning as identified for the ideation team.

The other great advantage of this presentation way is the possibility to use a large number of structural analysis tools proposed by the theory of graphs. These tools allow a qualitative and a quantitative analysis of connectivity and relationships between ideas.

3.2 References Graph Based Tools for Linkographic Analysis

In the literature, a large wide of graph based analysis tools have been proposed. It is evident that not all these tools are useful or applicable in our study context. For this reason, we propose to select and identify the most important tools and we called them References graph based tools. The Methodology to identify a reference graphs based tools to linkographic analysis is given by Fig. 2. The first step correspond to a bibliographic review of graph analysis tools. In order to identify the most useful tools for analysing idea graph we propose a contextual analysis in the step 2. After, we propose in step 3 a statistical analysis. The goal of this second analysis is to evaluate the relevance of the selected tools applied to a real data. The measure indicators for each tools must be defined. The selected tools corresponds to the referential tools and will be used to linkographic analysis.

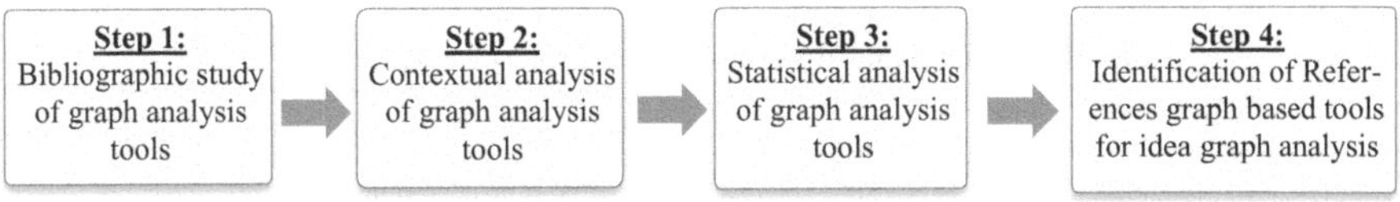

Fig. 2. Methodology for obtaining References graph based tools for idea graph analysis

3.3 Example of Using Graph Based Tools for Linkographic Analysis

This section aimed to present some example of analysis tools issues from graph theory and their utility in the analysis of ideas graphs. We use a real case study for this illustration. The used case study correspond to a brainstorming session to resolve a specific design problem kept anonymous for confidentiality reasons. The duration of the session is one hour. The experiment employed a ideation design team composed of four designers. The Linkography approach, given by Fig. 1, is used to analyse the brainstorming session. The application of step 1 (segmentation) and step 2 (linking) permit the obtaining of ideas links matrix. This ideation session allowed the generation of 22 ideas. Figure 3 present the Application of brainstorming method and the obtained ideas link matrix.

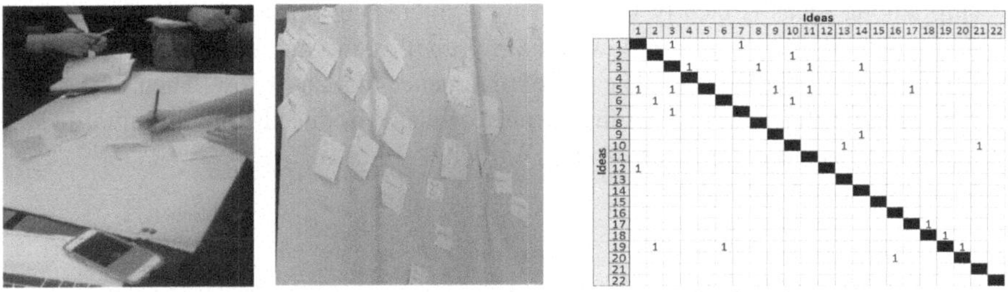

(a) Application of brainstorming method *(b)Ideas link Matrix*

Fig. 3. Application of brainstorming method and the obtained ideas link matrix

1. ***Linear Order:*** consists in sorting the ideas set in order to minimize the Feedback Arc Set (FAS). This concept is an extension of the level concept, to cyclic graphs and it permits the identification of the main flow in the studied system. The Fig. 4 shows the linear ordering of ideas before the application of linear ordering tool: this correspond to chronological ordering of the ideas generation. The FAS rate correspond to 32% (Number of FAS (8) devised per the total number of link (25)). We Use the Tabu search algorithm developed by Zhou et al. [24] to identify the optimal linear ordering given by Fig. 5.

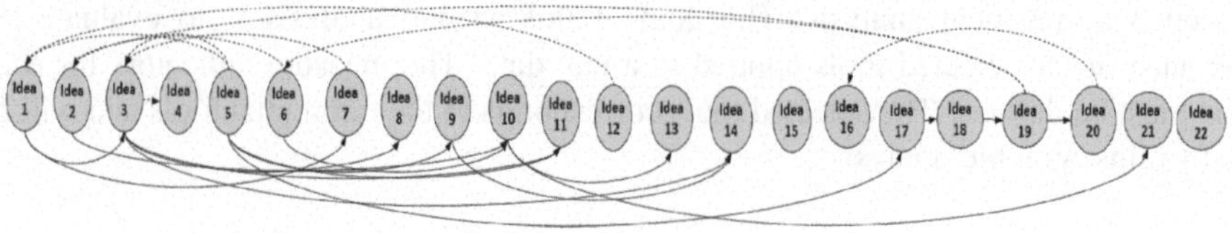

Fig. 4. Initial Total ordering of idea (rate of FAS = 32%)

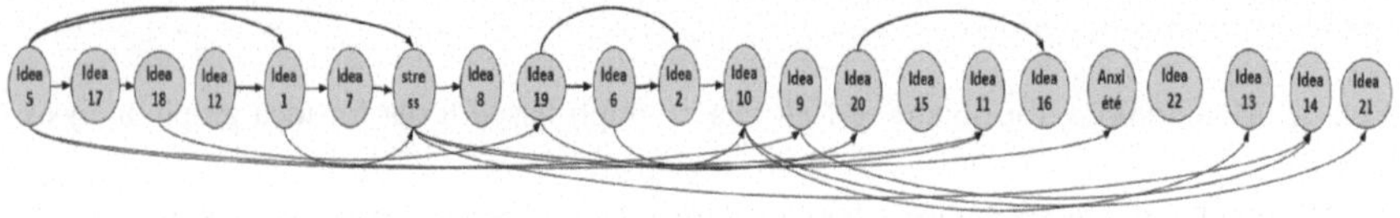

Fig. 5. Optimal total ordering of ideas (rate of FAS = 0)

2. ***Levels:*** The linear ordering allows to identify the minimum FAS. A graph without FAS is a directed acyclic graph (DAG). Vertices of a DAG can be partially ordered. Each vertex is assigned with a rank such that the initial vertex of an edge which has a lower rank than the terminal vertex of this edge. The set containing vertices with the same rank defines a level. This concept can be measured by the number of vertexes per level corresponding to the rate of level. In this study the Level rate: 36.36% (Nb of level (8)/Nb of ideas (22)). The level decomposition given by Fig. 6 is very useful for understating the structure of ideas generation session. It highlights a "main" flow in the idea generation session. In addition, the precedence relationship among ideas is clearly visible. This is interesting during the ideation session analysis. If the level ratio is low: this informs that the number of ideas produced from an initial idea is small. The rate of divergence of ideas is low. Then, If the level ratio is high: this informs that the number of ideas produced from an initial idea is high. The rate of divergence of ideas is high.

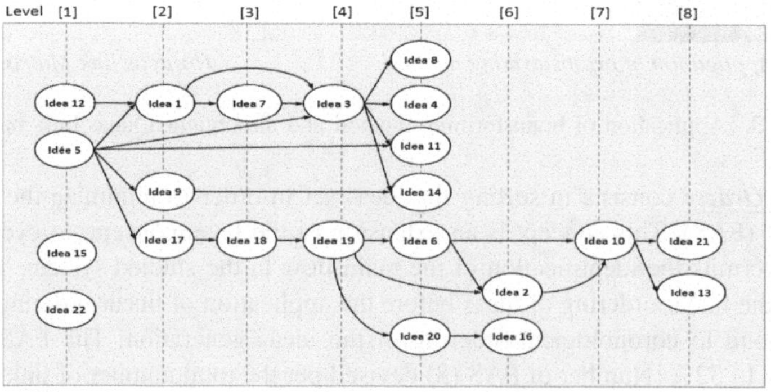

Fig. 6. Decomposition of ideas graph by level

3. **Degree of vertex:** The adjacency list of vertices is used for degree of vertex analysis. The INdegree of a vertex v or the half degree of entry of a vertex v is the number of edges incoming to v and is denoted by $d^{-}(\mathrm{v})$. The OUTdegree of a vertex v or the half degree of exit from a vertex v is the number of arcs outgoing from v and is denoted by $d^{+}(\mathrm{v})$. The degree of a vertex v denoted by d (v) is the sum of the INdegree and the OUT degree $\mathrm{d(v)} = d^{-}(\mathrm{v}) + d^{+}(\mathrm{v})$. The degree of vertex inform the Criticality of ideas. Critical ideas are those that have a significant number of links to other ideas. The Fig. 7(a) show the graph representation with the degree of ideas.

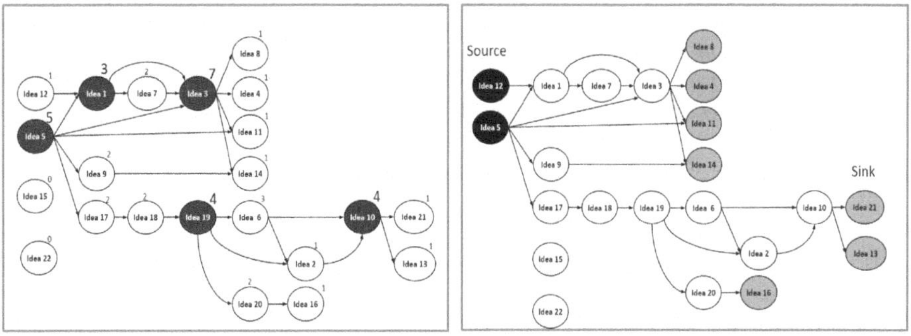

(a) Degree of Vertex (b) sink and source in ideas graph

Fig. 7. Application of the degree of vertex and Source/Sink Tool

4. **Sources/sink:** A vertex is called as a source vertex if no incoming edge exists (see Fig. 7(b)). Thus a vertex v is a source if $d^{-}(\mathrm{v}) = 0$. A vertex is called as a sink vertex if no outgoing edge exists. Thus a vertex v is a sink if $d^{+}(\mathrm{v}) = 0$. In general, we have only one source called the root of graph correspond to the initial generated idea. The sink give a measure of the opportunity for new creations or initiations. Pointed out the sink indicate new ideas, proposals, prospects, even breakthroughs.

4 Conclusion

Our work intent to improving linkographic analysis. We shed the light on the usefulness of graph theory in analysing and representing of idea generation session. We started with an overview of Linkography approach and followed by a bibliographic review of linkographic analysis tools. Then, the advantages of using ideas graph representation are given. Ideas graph display describes the diversity and the depth of the entire ideation process perfectly: this provides an accurate and high structural information better than with linkograph. Another important advantage of this representation is the possibility to use a large number of structural analysis tools proposed by the theory of graphs. To illustrate the utility of graph-based tools in linkographic analysis we put the finger on the application of some analysis tools applied in real case study.

These tools allow quantitative analysis of connectivity between ideas. In addition, we proposed a methodology to identify a reference graphs based tools to do linkographic analysis. This methodology will be applied in our future work. Firstly, we will elaborate a bibliographic review of graph analysis tools. Secondly, we will propose a contextual analysis to identify the most useful tools. Finally, we will propose a statistical analysis to evaluate the relevance of the selected tools applied to a real data. The selected tools correspond to the referential tools will be used to linkographic analysis.

References

1. Escandón-Quintanilla, M.-L., Gardoni, M., Cohendet, P.: Big data analytics as input for problem definition and idea generation in technological design. In: Harik, R., Rivest, L., Bernard, A., Eynard, B., Bouras, A. (eds.) PLM 2016. IAICT, vol. 492, pp. 468–477. Springer, Cham (2016). https://doi.org/10.1007/978-3-319-54660-5_42
2. Goldschmidt, G.: Linkography: assessing design productivity, pp. 291–298 (1990)
3. Goldschmidt, G., Weil, M.: Contents and structure in design reasoning. Des. Issues **14**(3), 85–100 (1998). https://doi.org/10.2307/1511899
4. Goldschmidt, G.: Cognitive economy in design reasoning. In: Lindemann, U. (ed.) Human Behaviour in Design, pp. 53–62. Springer, Heidelberg (2003). https://doi.org/10.1007/978-3-662-07811-2_6
5. Goldschmidt, G., Tatsa, D.: How good are good ideas? Correlates of design creativity. Des. Stud. **26**(6), 593–611 (2005). https://doi.org/10.1016/j.destud.2005.02.004
6. Goldschmidt, G., Hochman, H., Dafni, I.: The design studio “crit”: teacher–student communication. Artif. Intell. Eng. Des. Anal. Manuf. **24**(3), 285–302 (2010). https://doi.org/10.1017/S089006041000020X
7. Goldschmidt, G.: Linkographic evidence for concurrent divergent and convergent thinking in creative design. Creat. Res. J. **28**, 115–122 (2016). https://doi.org/10.1080/10400419.2016.1162497
8. Wu, P.-F., Yen, J., Fan, K.-Y.: Investigating the design behavior of animation expert-the difference of idea links mode on story ideation. Bull. Jpn. Soc. Sci. Des. **57**(5), 27–36 (2011). https://doi.org/10.11247/jssdj.57.27_2
9. van der Lugt, R.: How sketching can affect the idea generation process in design group meetings. Des. Stud. **26**(2), 101–122 (2005). https://doi.org/10.1016/j.destud.2004.08.003
10. Kan, J., Gero, J.: Design behaviour measurement by quantifying linkography in protocol studies of designing. In: Human Behaviour in Design 2005, Key Centre of Design Computing and Cognition, University of Sydney (2005)
11. Kan, J., Gero, J.: Quantitative methods for studying design protocols (2017)
12. Kan, J.W., Bilda, Z., Gero, J.S.: Comparing entropy measures of idea links in design protocols. In: Gero, J.S. (ed.) Design Computing and Cognition 2006, pp. 265–284. Springer, Dordrecht (2006). https://doi.org/10.1007/978-1-4020-5131-9_14
13. Bilda, Z., Gero, J.S., Purcell, T.: To sketch or not to sketch? That is the question. Des. Stud. **27**(5), 587–613 (2006)
14. Bilda, Z., Gero, J.S.: Idea development can occur using imagery only. In: Gero, J.S., Goel, A.K. (eds.) Design Computing and Cognition 2008, pp. 303–320. Springer, Dordrecht (2008). https://doi.org/10.1007/978-1-4020-8728-8_16
15. Van der Lugt, R.: Sketching in design idea generation meetings. In: Industrial Design Engineering. Delft University of Technology, Netherlands (2001)

16. Van der Lugt, R.: Functions of sketching in design idea generation meetings. In: Proceedings of the 4th Conference on Creativity & Cognition, Loughborough, UK, pp. 72–79. ACM (2002). https://doi.org/10.1145/581710.581723
17. Perry, G.T., Krippendorff, K.: On the reliability of identifying design moves in protocol analysis. Des. Stud. **34**(5), 612–635 (2013)
18. Kan, J.W.T., Gero, J.S.: Acquiring information from linkography in protocol studies of designing. Des. Stud. **29**(4), 315–337 (2008)
19. Cai, H., Do, E.Y.-L., Zimring, C.M.: Extended linkography and distance graph in design evaluation: an empirical study of the dual effects of inspiration sources in creative design. Des. Stud. **31**(2), 146–168 (2010). https://doi.org/10.1016/j.destud.2009.12.003
20. van der Lugt, R., van der Graaf, A.: Context indicators for determining links between design ideas. In: Dubrovnik, M.D. (ed.) DS 30: Proceedings of DESIGN 2002, the 7th International Design Conference, Dubrovnik, pp. 261–266 (2002)
21. Goldschmidt, G.: Criteria for design evaluation: a process-oriented paradigm. In: Kalay, Y.E. (ed.) Principles of Computer-Aided Design: Evaluating and Predicting Design Performance, pp. 67–79. Wiley, New York (1992)
22. Ardaiz-Villanueva, O., et al.: Evaluation of computer tools for idea generation and team formation in project-based learning. Comput. Educ. **56**(3), 700–711 (2011). https://doi.org/10.1016/j.compedu.2010.10.012
23. Kan, J., Gero, J.S.: Can entropy indicate the richness of idea generation in team designing? In: Digital Opportunities: Proceedings of the 10th International Conference on Computer-Aided Architectural Design Research in Asia, vol. 1, pp. 451–457. Architexturez Imprints, New Delhi (2005)
24. Jiand, Z., Marc, B., Roland, D.G.: Quasi-source heuristic for the production line formation of manufacturing system. J. Integr. Des. Process. Sci. **7**(1), 25–58 (2003)

Development of a Concept for a Holistic Knowledge-Based Additive Manufacturing over the Entire Lifecycle

Cordula Auth(✉), Alexander Arndt, and Reiner Anderl

Department of Computer Integrated Design, TU Darmstadt, Otto-Berndt-Str. 2, 64287 Darmstadt, Germany
auth@dik.tu-darmstadt.de

Abstract. Based on the increasing digitalization, collecting data and using it for process optimization gets more important nowadays. In the field of additive manufacturing (AM), data are neither collected nor analyzed standardly over the entire lifecycle. Nevertheless, the optimization of the process of AM with the help of process information is one possibility to increase the quality of manufactured components. Thus, the data handling and usage in the field of AM forms a huge research gap. Therefore, the main aim of this paper is the development of a concept for a holistic knowledge-based AM over the entire lifecycle starting at material production, following by product development, production process with pre-, in- and post-processing, use phase of the product and ending with recycling or disposal.

The introduction deals with the definition of and the motivation for a knowledge-based AM. The following part explains the AM process chain and the lifecycle of a product. The next part contains the concept for the development of a knowledge-based AM. Therefore, the AM process chain needs to be connected with the lifecycle and all steps of the new created process need to be defined. Aims of the concept are the collection of process data and the efficient use and storage of the collected data. With the help of the data, an optimization of the quality and process reliability is possible. The last part of the paper covers an outlook on the implementation of the concept. The outlook and conclusion highlight potential benefits of the knowledge-based AM.

Keywords: Additive manufacturing · Process chain · Lifecycle
Data management · Process optimization

1 Introduction

The importance and the industrial usage of AM grew over the last years. The Wohlers Report 2017 shows an increase of the AM patent applications from 1996 to 2016, with a surprising 7.7 times grow from 2013 to 2016 [1]. Besides, the number of AM system manufacturer nearly tripled from 2013 to 2016 [2]. Furthermore, there exist some examples of the serial use of AM parts in different industries. Since 2014, Airbus integrated printed parts in the airplane A350 XWB [3, 4]. Another example is a

Published by Springer Nature Switzerland AG 2018.
P. Chiabert et al. (Eds.): PLM 2018, IFIP AICT 540, pp. 726–735, 2018.
https://doi.org/10.1007/978-3-030-01614-2_66

German supplier for automobile industry, who produces over 40.000 plastic parts for costumers [5]. The examples emphasize the increasing acceptance and the benefits of AM methods.

The increasing usage of AM methods results from the improvement of the manufacturing methods and special requirements of the costumers. In some cases, the economic efficiency of AM methods exceeds the economic efficiency of conventional manufacturing methods. AM methods help to produce small lot sizes or individualized and complex geometries in an economic efficient way. The benefits of AM methods result from the short and mostly digital process chain. A complex programming do not take place compared to a milling process chain [6].

In addition to the trend of AM, there is an increasing trend of digitalization. New use cases grow through the benefits of Industrie 4.0 and digitalization. Examples are the formation of dynamic value networks as horizontal integration or the linkage of production systems as vertical integration [7]. Through Industrie 4.0, new business models occur. A precondition for the efficient implementation of Industrie 4.0 strategies is the availability of relevant information and data in real time. Therefore, productions are equipped with sensors and incoming data are saved and used. The connection and linkage of humans, systems and objects foster the formation of value networks. These can be optimized on their costs, quality or even sustainability [8].

The aim of the holistic knowledge-based AM is the efficient use of the benefits of digitalization and Industrie 4.0 for the optimization of the process of AM and the quality of every manufactured component. Therefore, the process chain of AM is integrated in the product lifecycle. Thus, the following part deals with the AM process chain and the product lifecycle. After this, the next section contains the concept for the holistic knowledge-based AM over the entire lifecycle. The first step is the integration of the AM process chain into the lifecycle. An explanation of the new phases follows. The main part of the concept is the collection of data for the process optimization. Therefore, it follows a description which data needs to be collected. An outlook on the implementation of this concept follows in the next part. The last part deals with an outlook and a conclusion of the paper.

2 AM Process Chain and Product Lifecycle

This chapter deals with a definition of the AM process chain and a definition of the product lifecycle with different views. The AM process chain stands out for a flexible, direct and rapid fabrication of parts based on 3D CAD data. Compared to conventional manufacturing methods, AM methods do not need intermediate stages as for example tool manufacturing [9, 10]. The AM process chain is described in different ways by various authors, but the tasks are more or less the same following any process chain [for example 10]. In the official VDI standard, the AM process chain has three process steps on the first level of abstraction: the pre-processing, the in-processing and the post-processing [9].

During the pre-processing, the machine preparation, the creation and transformation of the data, orientation and positioning of the part, generating of support structures and the slicing process take place. After these steps, the in-processing starts. The in-processing means the manufacturing process of the part. The laser or nozzle build the part layer-on-layer through following the path of the sliced geometry. After finishing the building process, all actions for unloading and part removal take place in this step. The last step is the post-processing. One task of the post-processing is the removing of the powder or the support structures. Another task can be the improvement of the characteristics of the manufactured component, for example a surface treatment.

The three phases of pre-, in- and post-processing with the depending activities are shown in Fig. 1.

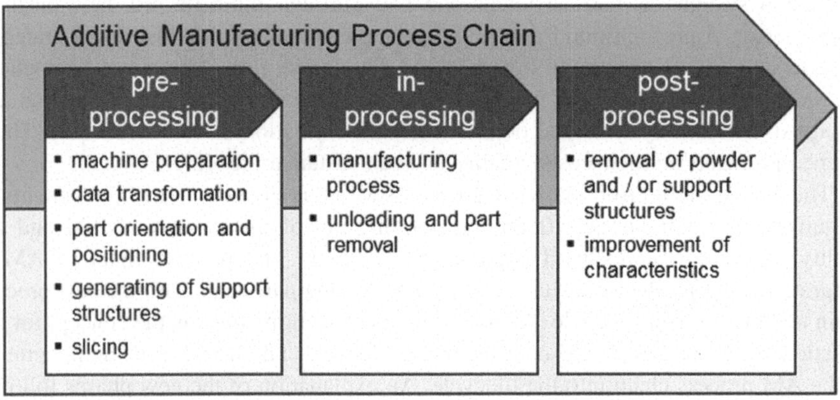

Fig. 1. The AM process chain with the three phases pre-, in- and post-processing

After explaining the AM process chain, this chapter deals with the product lifecycle. There exist different directions of the product lifecycle: an economical view, an ecological view and an information technological view [11]. The economical view deals with the relation of sales, earnings and costs. The ecological view describes the material and information flow. There exist four phases: material production, manufacturing, product use and recycling or disposal. The information technological view comprises seven phases, which are represented in a loop. The first four form the product development. These are product planning, construction, work preparation and product manufacturing. The phases product distribution, product use and product recycling or disposal follow the product development [11, 12].

Like explained, this is the actual state of the art for the AM process chain and the lifecycle. This state of the art is not sufficient to realize a holistic knowledge-based AM. Therefore, the AM process chain needs to be integrated into the lifecycle as one fundamental step in the following chapter.

3 Concept for a Holistic Knowledge-Based AM Over the Entire Lifecycle

After explaining the AM process chain and different views of the product lifecycle, the concept for a knowledge-based AM is generated. To develop a method for a holistic knowledge-based AM, the ecological and the information technical views of the product lifecycle are important. The first step is the connection between the AM process chain and the product lifecycle. Therefore, in a first step, the ecological and the information technological view of the product lifecycle are connected. Following, the AM process chain is integrated into the overall product lifecycle in the phases product development and manufacturing. Figure 2 shows the overall view of the product lifecycle connected with the AM process chain, called the holistic AM lifecycle.

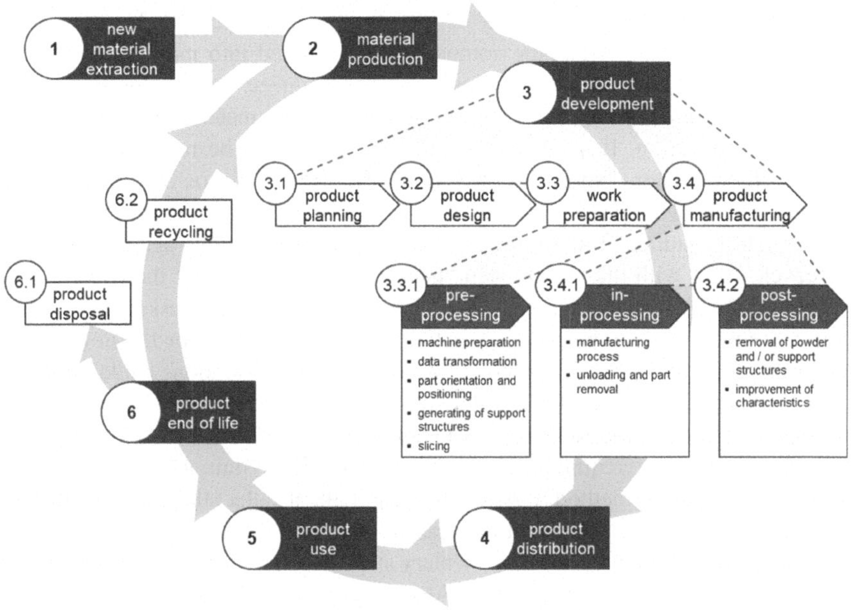

Fig. 2. The holistic AM lifecycle

The holistic AM lifecycle starts the first step of "new material extraction" (1). In this step, new raw material gets into the holistic AM lifecycle. In the beginning, this step is the starting point for the holistic AM lifecycle. The second step is the "material production" (2). In this step, the raw material is transformed into a usable form, for example powder or filament. The raw material and the usable form are depending on the selected AM method. The third step is the "product development" (3). This step can be divided in four minor steps, starting with the "product planning" (3.1). This step serves to establish the requirements for the desired product. The 3D CAD geometry of the desired component is developed in the step "product design" (3.2). The next step is the "work preparation" (3.3). In this step, the "pre-processing" (3.3.1) of the AM process chain is integrated. In this step, the machine is prepared, data is transformed, the part is oriented and positioned, support structures are generated and part and support structures are sliced in the end. The need of support structures depend on the chosen AM method. After the work preparation, the "product manufacturing" (3.4) follows. In this step, the "in-processing" (3.4.1) and the "post-processing" (3.4.2) are integrated. In the in-processing, the manufacturing process and the unloading and part removal take place. The post-processing serves for the removal of the powder or the support structures. Besides, the characteristics of the component can be improved in this step. An important improvement can be a surface treatment. After the step of product development, the "product distribution" (4) follows. In this step, the produced component becomes the property of the costumer. The fifth step is the "product use" (5). The component is still property of the costumer. Thus, the costumer decides on the time and way of usage. The sixth and last step is the "product end of life" (6). There are two possibilities for the product end of life, the "product recycling" (6.1) and the "product disposal" (6.2). Thus, the component is separated into individual parts. The parts can be recycled or disposed. If a component is produced with the fused deposition modeling for example, it can be shredded and the resulting material can be used again for material production. If materials are used, which cannot be recycled easily, they escape the lifecycle for disposal. It is possible that either both or only one step take effect for a component. Once the material flow is activated, the recycled material from step six might be sufficient to go through the holistic AM lifecycle again. In this case, the lifecycle starts with the second step "material production" after the recycling.

Figure 2 shows a sequential sequence. This describes the process chain to manufacture a component. The initial point is the material production or the new material extraction starting at the cradle. Some of the phases and the decisions made during one phase can affect other phases. For the holistic AM lifecycle, decisions for the design of the component and for the suitable AM manufacturing method need to be made. The decisions depend on the requirements for the product. The requirements of the product filter the manufacturing method. Besides, the requirements affect the choice of material, the product development in general and the product end of life.

The holistic AM lifecycle is an elementary step for a successful development of the concept for a holistic knowledge-based AM. To achieve a holistic knowledge-based AM, data has to be collected in the different process steps. There exist four primary requirements for the concept and its implementation:

- Important process and lifecycle parameters need to be identified
- Data need to be collected for every important process parameter
- Collected data need to be analyzed and stored
- There has to be an additional benefit besides the storage of the data

The first requirement of the identification of important process parameters serves to create a benefit in the end. Only if the right parameters are identified, they can be collected, analyzed and optimized. Important process parameters have an impact on the quality of the part, process reliability, process time, process costs and process sustainability. The process parameters can concern the original AM process chain, the holistic AM lifecycle or the AM part itself. Besides the factors cost, quality, time and sustainability, they can contain information concerning the interaction of process steps.

The decision, which process parameters have an impact on the factors, is depending on the AM method and the depending process characteristics. In general, information about the following topics have to be collected concerning the holistic AM lifecycle:

Choice of Material
The AM method effects the choice of material. The material has an impact on the component behavior, besides the component design for example. Furthermore, the mechanical rigidity or material characteristics can change with material replacement. The choice of the material effects the material production, the product development and the product end of life with recycling or disposal of the component.

Manufacturing Information of the Material
The material has an impact on the quality of the component. To achieve good quality, the material has to be faultless. Therefore, manufacturing information of the new material as particle size or filament diameter (depending on the manufacturing method) need to be collected. Process parameters as nozzle temperature help to monitor the process. Besides, environmental influences can have an impact and have to be documented. Significant environmental influences are humidity, ambient temperature and vibrations.

Relation of New Material to Recycled Material
To conserve high quality, the effect of recycled material on the behavior of the component has to be observed. For example, plastic powder changes the characteristics because of the heat through an AM process, even it is not sintered in the selective laser sintering process. Therefore, the relation of used or recycled material to new material is an important information.

Information Through Product Planning
Requirements concerning the behavior of the component have an impact on potential process parameters, for example layer sizes or manufacturing speeds. The planned usage of a part effects the design of the part and in the end, the manufacturing process. The requirements do not only address the product use, it can concern various phases of the lifecycle as the product development and the product recycling. Therefore, information of the product planning need to be conserved and connected.

Product Design
The design of the component results from the requirements on the product, the technical possibilities of the chosen manufacturing method and the characteristics of the material. The design effects the product characteristics, the reasonable orientation of the part and the economic efficiency. Moreover, the strived quality has an impact on the design. Potential improvements of the part characteristics have to be included in the design phase. Furthermore, desired functions of the component can be considered in the design phase and integrated directly.

Data Transformation
Through the change of the data format mistakes can be occur. Common data format is the Standard Tessellation Language (STL). The transformation contains an

approximation of the original geometry with the help of triangles. The approximation of the native CAD-geometry of the part has to take place in an appropriate way, as a trade of between data volume and approximation accuracy.

Nesting, Support and Slicing

The nesting of the part has an impact on the quality of the whole part and the surface. With a false orientation of the part, the staircase effect can occur in the printing area and minor the quality of the part. Furthermore, the orientation has an impact on the mechanical resistance and residual stresses. With an unfavorably mechanical stress, delamination can be the result for example. Therefore, information about the nesting need be collected and included in quality control. Besides, the place and amount of support structures can have an impact on the part quality, the building time, surface qualities, process temperatures, and the costs. Therefore, information about the installing of support structures are collected. For the slicing, the layer thickness has to be decided as a trade of between building speed and component quality.

Manufacturing Information of the Part

The collection of manufacturing information serves the process monitoring and the process optimization through analyses of the data. Important information are traverses, building speeds, temperatures of the nozzle or intensity of the laser, temperatures of the building space, vibrations and information about the used material. Abnormalities during the manufacturing process can affect the mechanical resistance of the component and the surface quality.

Environmental Influences During the Manufacturing Process

As for the material, the environmental influences during the manufacturing of the part can have an impact on the quality of the part and the manufacturing process. Important environmental influences are the temperature and the humidity. Furthermore, vibrations during the manufacturing process influence the accuracy of the building process and in the end, the quality of the component. The influences are documented to explain downstream effects as early failure of the part.

Information of Product Distribution

Time and place are important, when the component changes from the property of the manufacturer to the user. The handling of the component during the distribution can have an impact on the quality and the function. With the product distribution, the warranty starts.

Time and Way of the Use of the Manufactured Part

Time and way of the usage of the manufactured part can have an impact on the component lifetime. New findings about the effects may help to extend the lifetime. Information of this phase can help to develop a suitable component design depending on the usage and optimize the pre-processing with data transformation, part orientation and positioning.

Environmental Influences During Usage

Influences as for example temperature or humidity can have an impact on the component lifetime. The geographic place of usage has a significant impact. If the impact can be quantified, it can be factored in the component design.

Recycling of Disposal of the Part

Based on the shortage of natural resources, recycling gets more important. Knowledge of recycling processes can affect future designs of components. Suitable designs for recycling are determined through the generation of a database. The requirements of the recycling process and the knowledge of suitable designs are integrated into the product design phase. Information concerning the material and the corresponding material behavior during and after a recycling process are relevant information for the material production phase. Besides an effect on the environment, a reasonable recycling concept reduces costs of material purchasing. To create a suitable recycling concept, information are needed.

Return of Information from Phases into Other Phases

The kind and amount of information, which are fed back, can only be optimized, if these are documented. The benefit of returned information is controlled to optimize the data flows. The return of information is important for the efficient optimization of every phase of the AM lifecycle. Findings of the product use phase need to be included in the improvement process of the component design. Information of the recycling phase are important for the development of the component design and the material production.

An elementary approach is the data exchange through a database. Information are not only collected, they are analyzed to optimize the process stability. Furthermore, they are stored for long term analyses in case of an early component failure. Additionally, information are transferred to different phases of the overall AM lifecycle. The result of the implementation of a database is the creation of a holistic knowledge-based AM over the entire life cycle. With the help of the holistic approach, the overall AM lifecycle and the resulting products can be optimized comprehensively. To realize a holistic knowledge-based AM, a communication concept with a data management concept needs to be developed and implemented. To show the installation and the benefit of a holistic knowledge-based AM, the following chapter deals with an outlook on the implementation of the holistic approach.

4 Outlook on the Implementation of a Holistic Knowledge-Based AM over the Entire Lifecycle

The AM lifecycle phases have to be realized in the real or the virtual world. Therefore, the use case of a holistic knowledge-based fused deposition modeling (FDM) is chosen and described in the following. The main aim of the holistic knowledge-based AM is the collection and analyses of interesting process parameters. The parameters are collected through the installation of additional sensors in the whole AM lifecycle. An important task is the identification of components and their measured values. This is necessary to gain information concerning part quality and process reliability.

In the phase "new material extraction", new material from outside the life cycle gets in. Therefore, new raw material is ordered and used in the second step, the "material production". For material production, a material extruder has been developed and build. Material in the form of granulate or shredded scrapped parts serve as raw material for the extruder. The material extruder produces new filament, which is collected on a spool and used in a following AM job. In the phase of the material production, data concerning the quality of the new filament are collected. With the help of sensors, the availability of new raw material is proved, the temperature of the extruder nozzle, the temperature of the water-cooling basin, the diameter of the new produced filament and the length of the produced filament are measured. The third phase of product development is realized through a working station for the product planning and design. Furthermore, a FDM printer represents the work preparation and the product manufacturing. To monitor the product manufacturing, a sensor to measure the temperature of the nozzle, a thermal imaging camera for the temperature distribution on the building platform and the manufactured layers, four piezo sensors to measure the vibrations of the whole machine, acceleration sensors to track the movement of the building platform and a sensor to track the amount of the used filament are installed. During the "product distribution", the component moves to the costumer for the following "product use" phase. For the "product end of life", the component is separated into individual parts and the decision of recycling or disposal is made. This decision depends on the used material. PLA used in the fused deposition modeling process can be shredded and used again in the second phase of material production. At the actual state, a shredder for components is developed to produce recycled raw material for the material production.

With the help of automated data analyses, the management system can inform if a measured parameter is outside the approvable range. This is a first step to develop and implement a quality control concept. To realize data collection, the implementation of the communication concept is necessary. In terms of Industrie 4.0, the communication is realized with the Message Queue Telemetry Transfer (MQTT) protocol. Therefore, all machines are enhanced to cyber physical systems. In case of the FDM lifecycle demonstrator, microcontroller are integrated into the machines to enable communication.

5 Conclusion and Outlook

In the field of AM, data are rarely collected and analyzed for process optimization or quality improvement. To maximize the benefit of the data management, a holistic approach is necessary. Therefore, the original AM process chain is integrated into the ecological and the information technological view of the product lifecycle. This new holistic AM lifecycle starts at the new material extraction. The material production follows as second phase. The third phase is the product development. This contains the four smaller phases product planning, product design, work preparation and product manufacturing, where the pre-processing of the AM process is integrated into the work preparation and the in- and post-processing into the product manufacturing. The fourth phase is the product distribution. As fifth phase follows the product use. Finally, the product end of life is the sixth and last phase. This phase slits into the two possibilities of product recycling and product disposal. The realization of the phases is described shortly as an outlook on the implementation for the use case of fused deposition modeling. Next steps are the detailed explanation of the use case and the development of an installation plan for the sensors. The sensors have to be integrated into the holistic

AM lifecycle. The communication between the sensors and a database as well as the storage of the data have to be examined. To collect sufficient data for process and quality optimization, the process needs to be automated.

References

1. Wohlers, T.T.: Wohlers Report - 3D Printing and Additive Manufacturing - State of the Industry - Annual Worldwide Progress Report (2017). ISBN 978-0-9913332-3-3
2. Wohlers, T.: Wohlers Talk – AM System Manufacturer Growth (2018). http://wohlersassociates.com/blog/. Accessed 27 Jan 2018
3. Korner, R.: Mit dem Titanbauteil aus dem 3D-Drucker befindet sich nun erstmals ein additiv gefertigtes Bauteil in der Serienproduktion einer Airbus 350 XWB Passagiermaschine (2017). https://www.3d-grenzenlos.de/magazin/3d-objekte/airbus-a350-xwb-3d-gedrucktes-bauteil-27303023/
4. Krämer, A.: Stratasys Direct Manufacturing druckt Teile des Airbus A350 XWB (2017). https://www.3d-grenzenlos.de/magazin/kurznachrichten/stratasys-direct-manufacturing-airbus-a350-xwb-27288483/
5. Krämer, A.: Automobilzulieferer Thomas Pazulla setzt auf 3D-Druck in der Serienproduktion (2017). https://www.3d-grenzenlos.de/magazin/kurznachrichten/thomas-pazulla-3d-druck-fuer-serienproduktion-automobilteile-27261893/
6. Auth, C., Arndt, A., Anderl, R.: Method for the evaluation of economic efficiency of additive and conventional manufacturing. In: 28th Solid Freeform Fabrication Symposium 2017, Austin, Texas, 07 August–09 August 2017 (2017). https://sffsymposium.engr.utexas.edu/sites/default/files/2017/Manuscripts/MethodfortheEvaluationofEconomicEfficiencyo.pdf
7. Promotorengruppe Kommunikation der Forschungsunion Wirtschaft – Wissenschaft: Umsetzungsempfehlungen für das Zukunftsprojekt Industrie 4.0. (2013). https://www.bmbf.de/files/Umsetzungsempfehlungen_Industrie4_0.pdf
8. Plattform Industrie 4.0: Umsetzungsstrategie Industrie 4.0 – Ergebnisbericht der Plattform Industrie 4.0 (2015). https://www.bitkom.org/noindex/Publikationen/2015/Leitfaden/Umsetzungsstrategie-Industrie-40/150410-Umsetzungsstrategie-0.pdf
9. Verein Deutscher Ingenieure: VDI 3405 – Additive Fertigungsverfahren – Grundlagen, Begriffe, Verfahrensbeschreibung (2014)
10. Gibson, I., Rosen, D., Stucker, B.: Additive Manufacturing Technologies – 3D Printing, Rapid Prototyping, and Direct Digital Manufacturing. Springer, New York (2015). https://doi.org/10.1007/978-1-4939-2113-3
11. Grote, K.-H., Engelmann, F., Beitz, W., Syrbe, M., Beyerer, J., Spur, G.: Das Ingenieurwissen: Entwicklung, Konstruktion und Produktion. Springer, Heidelberg (2014). https://doi.org/10.1007/978-3-662-44393-4
12. Anderl, R., Trippner, D.: STEP – Standard for the Exchange of Product Model Data. Eine Einführung in die Entwicklung, Implementierung und industrielle Nutzung der Normenreihe ISO 10303 (STEP). Springer, Wiesbaden (2000). https://doi.org/10.1007/978-3-322-89096-2

TEAM: A Tool for Eco Additive Manufacturing to Optimize Environmental Impact in Early Design Stages

Laverne Floriane[1(✉)], Bottacini Enrico[2], Segonds Frédéric[1], Perry Nicolas[3], D'Antonio Gianluca[2], and Chiabert Paolo[2]

[1] LCPI, ENSAM Paris, 151 bd de l'Hôpital, 75013 Paris, France
floriane.laverne@ensam.eu

[2] DIGEP, Politecnico di Torino, Corso Duca degli Abruzzi 24, 10129 Turin, Italy

[3] I2M, ENSAM Bordeaux, Esplanade des Arts & Métiers, 33405, Talence, France

Abstract. Nowadays, the environmental impact of a product is a major factor for the design team and for the end customer. To decrease the environmental impact of a product during its whole lifecycle, many design methods are available focusing on the multitude of data from the product once it is fully designed (Lifecycle Analysis etc.). However, the design choices made in the early design stages have a crucial importance on the environmental impact of the chosen solution. It is therefore necessary to propose to the multidisciplinary design team a tool to help them choosing the best concept and the best way to produce it as early as possible. The emphasis in this paper is on Additive Manufacturing technologies, which are widely used in concept development. A design tool prototype is presented and evaluated in order to foster early eco-additive manufacturing of concepts.

Keywords: Additive Manufacturing · Sustainability · Early design stages

1 Introduction

Additive Manufacturing (AM), one of the pillars of Industry 4.0 listed by the Boston Consulting Group (Scalabre 2018), is considered as a promising manufacturing process that enables rapid manufacturing of fully functional products. It appears as a technical lever for product innovation and sustainability, because it brings opportunities both by enabling to create complex products but also by consuming less resources than traditional processes for their production. This research is focusing on the design stage of the product lifecycle where AM is used to obtain physical representations of the product and where the design team have to manage knowledge coming both from this new technology but also from the growing considerations of the Design for Environment approach.

In this contextual framework, AM is used for rapid prototyping. The aim of the research presented in this paper is to study the opportunity of assisting the design team with a tool that enable a sustainable use of AM machines compatible with the need of

Published by Springer Nature Switzerland AG 2018.
P. Chiabert et al. (Eds.): PLM 2018, IFIP AICT 540, pp. 736–746, 2018.
https://doi.org/10.1007/978-3-030-01614-2_67

creating product representation for the design assessment. The proposed solution which is presented and assessed through user tests is a tool dedicated for the improvement of (1) the environmental efficiency of the prototypes production with AM machines through the specification of adequate machine settings minimizing the resources consumption; (2) the environmental effectiveness of the prototype design through design rules that enable to convert the concept CAD into a new lean CAD where essential features are available for the validation of the concept and with the simplest material distribution. After a description of the context of the research, the global structure of the tool is described and then results about user tests are presented and discussed.

2 State of the Art

2.1 Additive Manufacturing Use in the Product Lifecycle

Nowadays AM is considered as a promising manufacturing technology because it allows making objects "from 3D model data, layer upon layer, as opposed to traditional manufacturing technologies" (F2792-12a 2012; ISO 2015). Thus, its role for the near future inside the industrial environment is crucial because it upsets traditional manufacturing practices. The reasons for this craze is the high design freedom due to four possible complexities available in a same product: material, functional, geometrical and hierarchical complexity (Gibson et al. 2015). AM enable to produce shapes impossible to be manufactured by traditional machines. The possibility of enclosing voids, inserting components or employing different materials at the same time enable reducing the number of components, thus the assembly time and the scraps for parts out of tolerances. Moreover, customization of products is easy and time to market of small batches is decreased because no tools are required. These new design opportunities have been strengthened with the huge efforts in both increasing the type of available machines and making lower their purchase price on the marketplace (Wohlers 2014).

If AM upsets the design paradigm and offers wide possibilities for product innovation (Laverne et al. 2015), we must not forget its original use i.e. rapid prototyping for the production of physical representations of products; more precisely conceptual and functional prototypes (Mellor et al. 2014). Indeed, the adoption of AM, especially polymer technologies, provides the designer with the opportunity to quickly figure out any idea during the early design stage. Discussing about the creative potential of a concept proposed during a creative workshop or analyzing its technical feasibility has been eased by the adoption of AM during the early design stages (Segonds et al. 2014) and delays in the manufacture of prototypes have also deeply. Thus, AM has brought a significant advantage at these early design stages because design decisions about the product are taken and validated with tangible objects; consequently, the number of costly design modifications during the detail design stages are reduced.

2.2 Sustainability Considerations

The problem of environmental sustainability is one of the main objectives of the fourth industrial revolution (Stock and Seliger 2016). Companies have to develop sustainable products not only because of ethical reasons but also for market requirements since customers are becoming more aware of their impact on the environment.

One approach for improving the sustainability of a product is eco-design i.e. "the development of products by applying environmental criteria aimed at the reduction of the environmental impacts along the stages of the product life cycle" (Bakker 1995). Eco-design here means analyzing the product "from cradle to grave" in order to conserve energy and natural resources (water and material) and to reduce waste and emissions. Another definition of eco-design is given by Manzini (1999) who considers that eco-design indicates a "design activity aimed at connecting what is technically possible to what is ecologically necessary in order to arouse socially and culturally acceptable new proposal." This definition outlines the importance of matching the technological possibilities to the necessity of environmental saving. This also conduct to think about sustainable manufacturing. According to Mani et al. (2014), sustainable manufacturing is the "creation of manufactured products that use processes that minimize negative environmental impacts, conserve energy and natural resources". Among Despeisse and Ford (2015), AM is promising for sustainable manufacturing and sustainable design because it brings some significant advantages:

- Reduction of the raw material consumption and of the waste because of the nature of the AM process and of development the lightweight parts,
- Reduction or elimination of the stock due to the ability to manufacture on-demand the products,
- Shorter supply chains by enabling localized production or maintenance.

However, all the benefits stated above are mainly impacting sustainability during the manufacturing and the distribution stages of the product lifecycle. It also raises the following question: how does the use of AM during the early design stages through the rapid prototyping approach impacts the sustainability of a new product?

2.3 AM Dilemma Between Creativity and Sustainability

AM machines, which are now available in every fablab of companies to foster the creative approach of a design team, have encouraged action-research methods (Coghlan and Brannick 2005) widely used in early design. Design that consists in an inductive work where stakeholders are involved in a two stages cyclic work called action and critical reflection (Mejía et al. 2007), encourages product representations. Thus, the achievement of prototypes with AM (i.e. action) and its assessment (i.e. critical reflection) bring knowledge about the product and enable at each cycle a design improvement of the concepts. Technical barriers limiting the materialization of concepts have disappeared.

Unfortunately, the designers who have to consider eco design rules in order to offer a product with reduced environmental impact during its whole lifecycle, are not aware about their contribution resulting from their prototyping activities on the product lifecycle (da Silva Barros and Zwolinski 2016). Hence, there is a real need for a method and a tool to help designers to decrease the environmental impact that will be generated during the prototyping phases. Two ways are available to help designers taking into account AM paradigm for developing new products: involving AM experts during the early design stages, or supporting design work with specific tools dedicated to their creative work (Laverne et al. 2016). The design tool which is presented in the next section aims to compensate the lack of knowledge about the consequences of a heavy use of AM. It also enhances the environmental efficiency of designers by enabling them to make prototypes right i.e. with AM parameters that ensure the characteristics of the prototype and minimize the resources consumption of the AM machines.

3 A Proposal of Tool for Eco Additive Manufacturing

3.1 Objectives

The goal of developing a Tool for Eco Additive Manufacturing (TEAM) is to provide the designers with AM recommendations in order to help them having the lowest environmental impact when they produce tangible representation of concepts; without compromising the essential characteristics or properties needed for its use. TEAM is applicable in early design stages, while the first CAD drawing is still under development. This article presents the environmental efficiency improvement allowed with TEAM. This improvement is based on a set of optimal manufacturing parameters depending on:

- AM machines/technologies available in the company.
- Materials desired for the prototype
- The desired strategies for minimizing the resources consumption (material, energy or flow saving and best environmental compromise for the three resources).

The optimal parameters used in TEAM were determined after a prototype lifecycle analysis based on lifecycle assessment (LCA) principles (ISO 2006). This LCA evaluated environmental performance by considering the potential impacts from all stages of manufacture, prototype use and end-of-life. The relevant inputs and outputs measurement useful for the inventory analysis, have been measured after an experimental campaign achieved on three AM technologies commonly used for prototyping (FDM, material jetting and binder jetting) and four different machines (professional and consumer). Results were then analyzed with OpenLCA databases. Then the impact assessment was calculated considering midterms impacts such as climate change, ozone depletion, … Thus, indicators were available for manufacturing strategies comparisons and AM machine selection regarding consumption.

3.2 Tool Development

Tool Platform. To study, through users' tests, the relevance of assisting designers for an efficient use of AM during early design stages, we aimed at developing a tool capable to be intuitive and with the lowest possible constraints.

Two different platforms commonly used for software development were selected: POP and Axure RP. On the one hand, POP is an open source software available for all kinds of devices. It allows to create basic applications, is very easy to handle and user friendly but gives limited options concerning the interface ergonomics. On the other hand, Axure is a professional software mainly used for dynamically model a web interface. It gives more possibilities for developing the environment to the programmer (due to several libraries). For the development of the tool a tablet and a mobile phone were chosen to be the support of the tool interface, respectively for Axure and POP.

A three clicks rule (Boucher 2013) was chosen for the data entry: to define his input data, the user should click maximum three times on the screen. However, the rule was sometimes not followed in order to include a confirmation check.

Tool Flowchart/Logic. A common problem appeared with the two software: the difficulties in managing the information given by the user. Indeed, the resulting mobile application created with POP or Axure is only able to achieve one point. Thus, the inputs of the user have to converge to only one solution. This issue has driven the optimization of the logical flowchart, described on Fig. 1, during all the steps of the concept definition. This flowchart is common to the two TEAM prototypes: the user must fulfil data about two different items before getting the results: process and product.

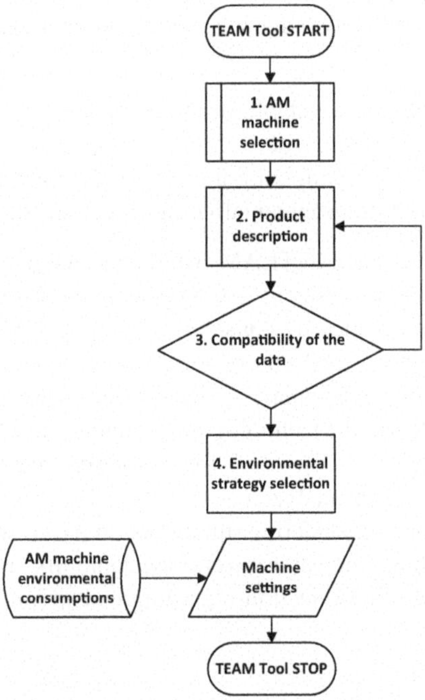

Fig. 1. Flowchart for TEAM tool

The first step is the AM machine selection: TEAM needs to collect information about AM technologies and/or machines. To do this, the user chooses the AM technologies available in his company among the seven ones described in the ASTM standard; then he selects in a list the machine(s) that he wants to use in order to prototype the concept.

In the second step called product description, the designer must fulfil data concerning the main attributes of the concept: CAD of the prototype must be uploaded (as a STL file), and information concerning the desired material and the batch size are required.

Once the process and product data are set, a control loop is activated (step 3 on Fig. 1) in order to ensure the compatibility of the data; in particular if the dimensions (through the calculation from the CAD file of the part's bounding box) and the material of the prototype are in adequacy with the building volume and the material's availability of the selected machines. If an adequacy problem is found, the user is informed through a message and has two possibilities: modify the given data (such as splitting the CAD design into two parts) or modify the required material. If data are validated, the user chooses an environmental strategy (step 4), between the four offered possibilities:

- Decreased use of a specific resource, i.e. minimization of energy, flow or material consumption
- Best compromise for the use of the three resources.

At least, based on the machine consumption and the given data, the machine settings for an eco-manufacturing of prototype are provided to the designer.

Tool Outputs. After the eco-manufacturing strategy selection, the user gets the adequate settings to be introduced on the AM machine in order to produce the prototype. These settings are specific to an AM machine. Indeed, production software vary according to the technology or the brand of the machine: AM machine are more or less open; thus, parameters that can be modified by user are different. the output data have been put in the app, dividing them in two sections: the parameters for the machine and the modifications in the CAD part design. Figures 2 and 3 present some screenshots of the two versions of the tool. Figure 2 deals with a TEAM version developed with POP software and devoted for fitting on Android-based devices, in particular on Sony Xperia. Figure 3 is about the TEAM version resulting from Axure and developed for tablets (iPad). In both the figures, the synthesis of the product description obtained at the end of the step 2 are here about the prototyping of a new lightened bracket dedicated for aircrafts studied and the recommended machine settings which are shown are dedicated for a manufacturing on the Stratasys Dimension Elite machine.

First Comparison of the Two Versions. One difference between the two developed versions of TEAM was the feedback of the data fulfilment on the navigation page. With POP, it was represented by two lines summary in the bottom of the page. With Axure, the user went back to a summary page called "your prototype" every time he defined a preference. This decision of implementation has been supported by considering the already existing apps and noticing that the use of the line for showing the preferences defined concerns mainly the web site design.

The second main difference relied on the appearance. TEAM version developed on POP appeared poorer than those on Axure. One reason is the extended possibilities of Axure that do not exist with POP to create a neat interface.

Finally, the chosen interface size revealed that handling TEAM on mobile phone (i.e. with POP) is uneasy due to the screen size and consequently, the data fulfilment

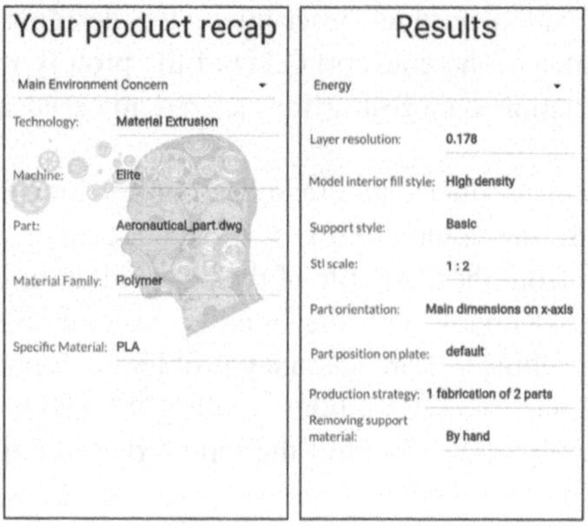

Fig. 2. Data synthesis and results pages with POP

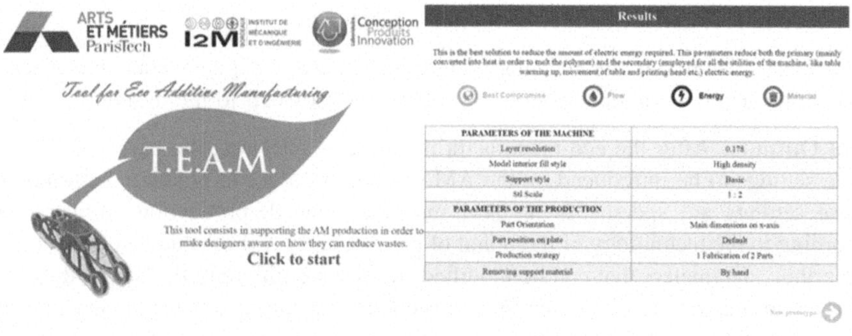

Fig. 3. Welcome page and results pages with Axure

become complicated. For these reasons the Axure version has been selected as the best one for performing trials with users.

3.3 Tool Evaluation

A test of the tool was performed in order to collect their feedback about the use of TEAM tool and its potential added value during early design.

Panel. The tool has been tested with 28 participants. The sample included professionals and Master students specialized in product development and innovation. They were aged from 20 to 35 (M = 24). Different backgrounds were represented in the panel (engineers, designers and ergonomists) in order to consider the pluri-disciplinary aspect of the early design stages.

Protocol. Each participant was provided with an iPad where an Axure version of TEAM was available. They had to handle TEAM as if they wanted to get the best environmental settings for prototyping a proof of concept of a new lightened bracket dedicated for aircrafts. At the end of the test, participants were invited to fill in a questionnaire subdivided into three parts. The first part focused on the participant, more specifically on his/her knowledge about AM and eco-design. The second part was oriented towards the user experience of the tool using three criteria defined by Nielsen (Nielsen 1994): usability of the tool focusing more precisely on learnability and on satisfaction, utility of the provided recommendations and acceptability. The last one gathers the opinion of the users on the opportunity to develop the TEAM part related to the environmental effectiveness of the early design of product.

For each question, answers were prepared with 6 points Likert scale where the first and last points were the two semantics descriptors about the agreement of the assumption. An even Likert scale was chosen in order to ensure that users can balance their response without the possibility of giving a neutral opinion. A non-mandatory open answer was placed following each question in order to enable the participants to precise their opinion.

Results Analysis and Discussion. Results were first analyzed focusing on the global feedback of the TEAM tool user experience and then comparing the influence of the AM knowledge and the eco-design knowledge on the answers.

Results showed for the entire panel of users an intermediate-to-high level of acceptability (M = 5,05, SD = 1,03); learnability (M = 4.14, SD = 0,93), satisfaction (M = 4,71, SD = 0,91) and utility (M = 4.53, SD = 0,92) which is encouraging for a first prototype. The prospect of using TEAM tool therefore seems to be beneficial for designers involved in early design stages.

Open answers were analyzed in order better understand the users' opinion and to identify the improvements that could be made. Most of them were about usability. The trials feedback emphasized the wide difference of expectations on the tool from the users. For instance, concerning the selection sequence of the data, some people preferred to double click to define a choice while others wanted a check button or even preferred that the decision would be taken at the first click. Another point in which the requirements of the users diverged were the button position on the screen. Most of the participants are used to have the backward button on the left and the forward on the right, but since the app recalls the same page after every decision the button's position for checking the decision cannot be defined objectively.

After this first analyze, a comparison of the influence of AM Knowledge (AMK) and Eco-Design Knowledge (EDK) on the answers collected during the survey, an analysis was performed to assess if TEAM could be used as a vehicular tool i.e. independent from the knowledge level of the users. For each kind of knowledge (AMK and EDK), participants were separated into two groups:

- The first group included the designers who reported having little or no knowledge about the subject (score 1 to 3 on the Likert scale)
- The second group consisted of participants who declared they had an advanced level of knowledge (score 4 to 6)

A Shapiro–Wilk test was performed and showed that all the variables studied in the survey (learnability, satisfaction, utility and acceptability) were not normally distributed. Hence, to compare the results of the two groups, we used nonparametric Mann–Whitney U test. Results, presented in Tables 1 and 2 below, showed that none of the variables get significant difference between the two conditions (with or without AMK or EDK). The knowledge users had on eco-design or on AM did not influence their opinion of TEAM.

Table 1. Mann–Whitney U test for the grouping criterion "AM knowledge level"

	Usability learnability	Usability satisfaction	Utility	Acceptability
U de Mann-Whitney	76,5	48,5	80,5	63
W de Wilcoxon	266,5	93,5	270,5	253
Z	−,474	−1,912	−,259	−1,186
Asymptotic significance (bilateral)	,635	,056	,796	,236
Exact significance	,664	,068	,809	,285

Table 2. Mann–Whitney U test for the grouping criterion "Eco-design knowledge level"

	Usability learnability	Usability satisfaction	Utility	Acceptability
U de Mann-Whitney	47,5	63	45	75,5
W de Wilcoxon	257,5	273	255	111,5
Z	−1,77	−0,911	−1,87	−0,245
Asymptotic significance (bilateral)	,077	,363	,062	,806
Exact significance	,099	,409	,079	,823

Results on the TEAM user experience revealed that within the scope of our study, designers are willing to use such a tool in their early design activities. It allows them to compensate for their lack of AMK and EDK with easily obtained and ready to use recommendations for eco-parameters of AM machines and thus devote more specifically to their creative activities by easily usable recommendations and thus devote themselves more specifically to their creative activities.

4 Conclusions

To reduce the contributions on a new product lifecycle of the rapid prototyping activities eased by the adoption of AM machines during the early design stages, this paper deals with the opportunity of increasing the designers' knowledge about the sustainability of their creative work with a new design tool.

The proposed tool that is presented and tested is intended to improve the environment efficiency of the designers involved. It suggests an adequate AM machine and the set of parameters ready to introduce in the selected machine so that prototypes are manufactured with the least consumption of resources possible. Results, obtained at the end of user-experience tests, showed that TEAM use can de promising to help designers reduce their environmental impact when they materialize their ideas or concepts. However, results also suggest making some changes on the interface. Thus, TEAM new version is currently evolving toward a more suitable support (i.e. a website), in order to allow an easier and more robust development of the flowchart. Another ongoing work involves changes for extending the tool functionalities especially including the environmental effectiveness of the prototypes' design. Furthermore, an extended experimental campaign will start in order to quantify the savings resulting from TEAM use. Moreover, if the technology adopted during industrialization is AM, an extension of this tool will make it possible to quantify the total environmental impact related to the product.

References

Bakker, C.A.: Environmental Information for Industrial Designers (1995). http://resolver.tudelft.nl/uuid:35b9dbef-3718-40fc-b64a-178b1cd0fed8

da Silva Barros, K., Zwolinski, P.: Influence of the use/user profile in the LCA of 3d printed products. Procedia CIRP **50**, 318–323 (2016). https://doi.org/10.1016/j.procir.2016.05.005

Coghlan, D., Brannick, T.: Doing Action Research in Your Own Organization, 2nd edn. SAGE Publications, London (2005)

Despeisse, M., Ford, S.: The role of additive manufacturing in improving resource efficiency and sustainability. Paper presented at the Advances in Production Management Systems: Innovative Production Management Towards Sustainable Growth, Tokyo, Japan (2015)

F2792-12a, ASTM: Standard terminology for Additive Manufacturing Technologies. ASTM International, West Conshohocken, PA (2012)

Gibson, I., Rosen, D.R., Stucker, B.: Additive Manufacturing Technologies, 2nd edn. Springer, New York (2015). https://doi.org/10.1007/978-1-4939-2113-3

ISO: ISO 14040:2006 Environmental management – Life cycle assessment – Principles and framework, p. 20 (2006)

ISO: ISO/ASTM 52900:2015 Additive manufacturing – General principles – Terminology, p. 19 (2015)

Laverne, F., Segonds, F., Anwer, N., Le Coq, M.: Assembly-based methods to support product innovation in design for additive manufacturing: an exploratory case study. ASME J. Mech. Des. **137**(12), 121701–121708 (2015). https://doi.org/10.1115/1.4031589

Laverne, F., Segonds, F., D'Antonio, G., Le Coq, M.: Enriching design with X through tailored additive manufacturing knowledge: a methodological proposal. Int. J. Interact. Des. Manuf. **11**(2), 279–288 (2016). https://doi.org/10.1007/s12008-016-0314-7

Mani, M., Lyons, K.W., Gupta, S.K.: Sustainability characterization for additive manufacturing. J. Res. Natl. Inst. Stand. Technol. **119**, 419–428 (2014). https://doi.org/10.6028/jres.119.016

Manzini, E.: Strategic design for sustainability: towards a new mix of products and services. Paper Presented at the Proceedings of the First International Conference on Environmentally Conscious Design and Inverse Manufacturing, Tokyo, Japan (1999)

Mejía, R., López, A., Molina, A.: Experiences in developing collaborative engineering environments: an action research approach. Comput. Ind. **58**(4), 329–346 (2007). https://doi.org/10.1016/j.compind.2006.07.009

Mellor, S., Hao, L., Zhang, D.: Additive manufacturing: a framework for implementation. Int. J. Prod. Econ. **149**, 194–201 (2014). https://doi.org/10.1016/j.ijpe.2013.07.008

Nielsen, J.: Usability Engineering, 362nd edn. Morgan Kaufmann Publishers Inc., San Francisco (1994)

Scalabre, O.: Embracing Industry 4.0 and Rediscovering Growth (2018). https://www.bcg.com/capabilities/operations/embracing-industry-4.0-rediscovering-growth.aspx

Segonds, F., Cohen, G., Véron, P., Peyceré, J.: PLM and early stages collaboration in interactive design, a case study in the glass industry. Int. J. Interact. Des. Manuf. **10**(2), 10 (2014). https://doi.org/10.1007/s12008-014-0217-4

Stock, T., Seliger, G.: Opportunities of sustainable manufacturing in Industry 4.0. Procedia CIRP **40**, 536–541 (2016). https://doi.org/10.1016/j.procir.2016.01.129

Wohlers, T.T.: Wohlers Report 2014: 3D Printing and Additive Manufacturing State of the Industry Annual Worldwide Progress Report (2014)

A Review of Integrated Approaches for Material, Design and Process Selection and a Proposal for the AM Processes

Manuela Galati(✉), Flaviana Calignano, and Luca Iuliano

Politecnico di Torino, Corso Duca Degli Abruzzi 24, 10129 Turin, Italy
{manuela.galati,flaviana.calignano,
luca.iuliano}@polito.it

Abstract. The comprehensive approach to the development of a product should analysis all of the phases, from the design to the manufacturing for the selection of a good combination of materials, designs and manufacturing processes. Due to the complexity of addressing an all-inclusive problem, the decision is usually entrusted to the manufacturing engineers for which products that have producible features easily and simple geometries are desirable, even if sacrificing the component performances. However, today, Additive Manufacturing (AM) processes offer a wide degree of design freedom that allows overcoming the traditional manufacturing limitations.

The aim of this paper is to provide a thorough review of the process selection (PS) approaches by taking into account manufacturing technologies in conjunction with the material and design performance. The paper attempts to provide as result a basic and generic methodology, which provides guidelines for the effective introduction of the AM processes in the process selection problem.

1 Introduction

A designer has the responsibility of ensuring the conformity of a product according to the specifications indicated by the customers and ensuring the quality of the product from manufacturing to assembly while limiting time and costs [1–3]. From this point of view, sets of design rules have been drawn up to guide designers on the feasibility of their designs [4], such as the Design for Manufacture (DfM). DfM states that designers must adapt their designs taking into account manufacturing problems [5, 6], in order to eliminate any manufacturing difficulties, and minimize the manufacturing operations, assembly and costs [7, 8]. That integrated approach, known as concurrent or simultaneous engineering (CE), can aid industrial engineers in the success of this issue. CE is a methodology of designing and developing products, in which the different stages run simultaneously, rather than consecutively. On example of the practical application of CE is the development of the process selection (PS) tools, which work by allowing the designer to select the best manufacturing resource to produce a specific part. However, decisions become difficult when the design stage is affected by numerous uncertainties as for the definition of the manufacturing process as well as specifications of the mechanical and functional requirements. In fact, due to DfM rules, the end of design

Published by Springer Nature Switzerland AG 2018.
P. Chiabert et al. (Eds.): PLM 2018, IFIP AICT 540, pp. 747–756, 2018.
https://doi.org/10.1007/978-3-030-01614-2_68

stage can be established once the manufacturing process is defined. In addition, at the beginning of the design stage, some specification could be evaluated only approximately [9]. For example, several materials could be excluded from the process selection because the production unfeasibility even if they satisfied the performance requirements. Therefore, potentially the decision-making activity about the selection of material and manufacturing processes should precede design stage. On the other hand, the design of the part should be the first input in order to select at least one manufacturing process and explore its feasibility [3]. As a consequence, a complex relationship results between designs, materials and manufacturing processes [9]. Therefore, the choice is often entrusted to the manufacturing engineers which modify the initial design according to their personal knowledge and background [9, 10] in order to producible features even sacrificing the part performances. Recently, Additive Manufacturing (AM) has revolutionised the manufacturing approach, because it offers the possibility of manufacturing parts of any geometric complexity without using additional tools or machines [11]. The advantage of AM over conventional subtractive or formative methods is clearly illustrated by the great design freedom that can be achieved [12], such as the possibility of producing customised geometries or topologically optimized geometries for lightweight components. AM processes allow increased flexibility, compared to the production costs and lead-times of traditional manufacturing [13]. Particularly for the metal components, current AM technologies permit the manufacturing of complex end-usable parts [13–15].

The aim of this paper is to provide a thorough review of PS approaches by taking into account manufacturing technologies in conjunction with the material and design performance. A basic, generic methodology is also proposed in light of the developing of a PS tool for the selection of the better manufacturing resource to produce a component that includes the AM processes. This led to a PS tool based on an all-inclusive methodology. The tool thus considers the combination of three elements: material, design and manufacturing process to determine the better alternative to produce the part.

2 Literature Review

The first approaches of developing a PS tool based on an integrated approach between design, materials and manufacturing processes [16, 17] used reference parts as an example of the optimal part to be produced with a specific manufacturing system. Ishii, Adler [16] presented the simplest selection in which the best technology resource was selected by comparing the part to be produced with the database of the reference parts. Boothroyd [17] introduced the importance to take into account manufacturing processes already at the design stage. He provided a review of published and successful case studies in which quite geometry modifications have been applied in order to improve the match between the design and the process constraints. However, since this kind of PS tools were developed on the base of real case studies [16, 17], they can be helpful only when a small range of geometries, materials [18] and manufacturing processes [10] can be considered. In fact, while this approach allows to trade off some process from the selection problem, it does not give a quantitative comparison among the remained alternatives and a unique solution of selection problem [9]. Swift and Booker [3] introduced the first structured approach based on several matrixes in which the capability of 65 manufacturing processes have been included. The method was called PS maps (PRIMAs) and it worked by selecting the process that satisfies the design specifications. Practically, in each matrix, the processes are classified according to the satisfaction of a specific requirement such as processable materials. The selection is obtained by matching the requirements of the design against the capability of the process. However, due to the uncertainty of the design at the design stage, the authors highlighted that the intention of this methodology have been just proving a guide for the selection of some processes which could the most appropriate candidates to produce that component. Poli [19] compared polymer processing, metal casting, and sheet metal forming not only from a design point of view but also considering the manufacturing costs. Pursuing this line of work, Boothroyd, Dewhurst [20] also included machining, casting and injection moulding processes into the PS analysis. Both books [19, 20] reported a detailed review of the DfM rules in order to analyses an integrated material and manufacturing process problem. DfM rules have been collected for each process. The selection were performed by matching the design and its requirements with the constraints of the manufacturing process. Boothroyd, Dewhurst [20] addressed the comparison between all processes using a production rule and pattern matching and Poli [19] provided a methodology for the selection of materials and processes for special purpose parts using tables and charts that would aid the designer throughout the design process and during the evaluation of the manufacturing alternatives. Because all of these approaches considered a qualitative assessment of the design specification, a ranking between alternatives appears difficult. Giachetti [9] presented an integrated multi-criteria decision (MAMPS) where the fuzzy logic has been applied to address the uncertainties of the requirements. In this case, a quantitative scale has been considered in order to convert the qualitative assessment given to each criterion. Precompiled databases have provided in order to avoid the effect of personal background and the final evaluations have been aggregated using a weighted geometric mean. A similar approach was adopted by Yu, Krizan [10] in which several variables have been considered. Those variables have been grouped into three categories: material, design features, and manufacturing variables. Each category has an independent classification. The three obtained classifications have been aggregated in order to obtain a unique ranking. Both of the studies [9, 10] neglected the effects of correlated variables that could contribute with redundant information when the variables are aggregated into a unique score. Among the used variables, processing cost for each part would appear strongly correlated with the material as well as the weight of the part with the density and the material cost. In addition, the qualitative indicators have been used by entrusting the evaluation to the individual's background. Therefore, that evaluation could result filtered through the personal experiences of the evaluator in a specific manufacturing process.

Until now, AM processes have been excluded from the comparison with other manufacturing processes because the rapid prototyping has been considered their only application for many years [21]. Deglin and Bernard [22] dealt a knowledge-based system for the selection of a most proper process to prototype components rapidly. Wilson and Rosen [23] and successively Gibson, Rosen [24] addressed the process selection for metal AM processes using a quantitative approach. The considered variables have been aggregated by using a weighted sum formulation. The alternatives have been ranked according to the achieved score. Since no guideline was provided about how to weight the variables, the authors suggested running a sensitivity analysis to determine how different values of the weights impact the final ranking. Samperi [25] dealt the comparison between metal AM processes following the classical approach where the design rules are matched with the design specifications. However, variables as the build time or cost estimations have been neglected. In order to extend the decision problem to the AM processes, uz Zaman, Siadat [26] suggested a first methodology that allowed to compare different AM and traditional manufacturing processes using three design criteria: function, cost and environment. Even in this case, a single value was used to aggregate the variables. Some comparison for the selection of the best technology resource in the case of AM processes was presented as a case study. Some of these showed the effectiveness of AM process for low production volume if compared with high pressure die casting [27], an improving of the supply chain in the reduction of lead time and the total cost [28], a reduction buy-to-fly ratio for the aero engine if compared with machining [29]. However, those approaches cannot constitute an effective guideline for the process selection because of the lack of general guidelines.

All of the review models utilised the same geometry as input for each analyzed process, and no design optimisation has been considered. Instead, the redesign of the part [30] is today recognized as a mandatory step to exploit the advantages of AM processes. The applications of AM processes without change the classical approach could be lead to erroneous solutions that in turn results in the abandonment of the technology due to, for instance, excessive pricing. Therefore, at the state of the art, no all-inclusive PS tool compares the AM with the other manufacturing systems while the proper characteristics introduced by AM in the manufacturing/design world are considered.

3 Proposed PS Tool

AM was recently recognized as manufacturing processes with exclusive benefits [31] especially to produce metal parts. For this reason, there is the need to develop of a proper decision model that can consider the benefits of the AM process in the comparison with the others manufacturing processes and can be helpful already in the design stage. When the AM processes are considered in a PS problem, there is some aspect that must be addressed with particular attention. One of these concerns the manufacturing cost per part, which was used as the only factor that drives the process selection in the existing literature models. However, currently, the parts produced by AM processes are often not competitive in terms of manufacturing costs. This should be explained because the geometry is not performed for AM process, the high price of the powder compared the ingot, and/or the high machine cost.

In the light of the in-depth literature survey and the current development of the metal AM processes, the proposed PS tool (Fig. 1) compares different manufacturing processes, including AM processes by:

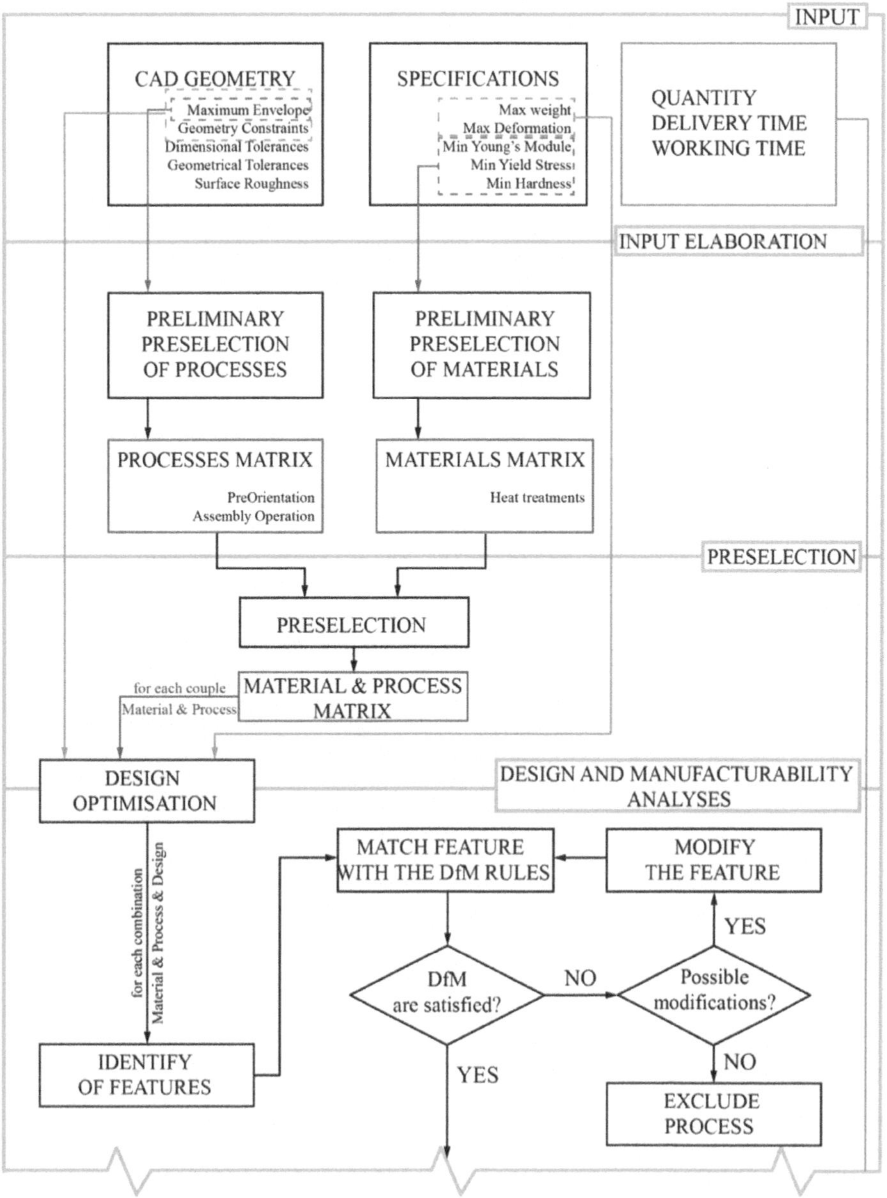

Fig. 1. Proposed PS tool

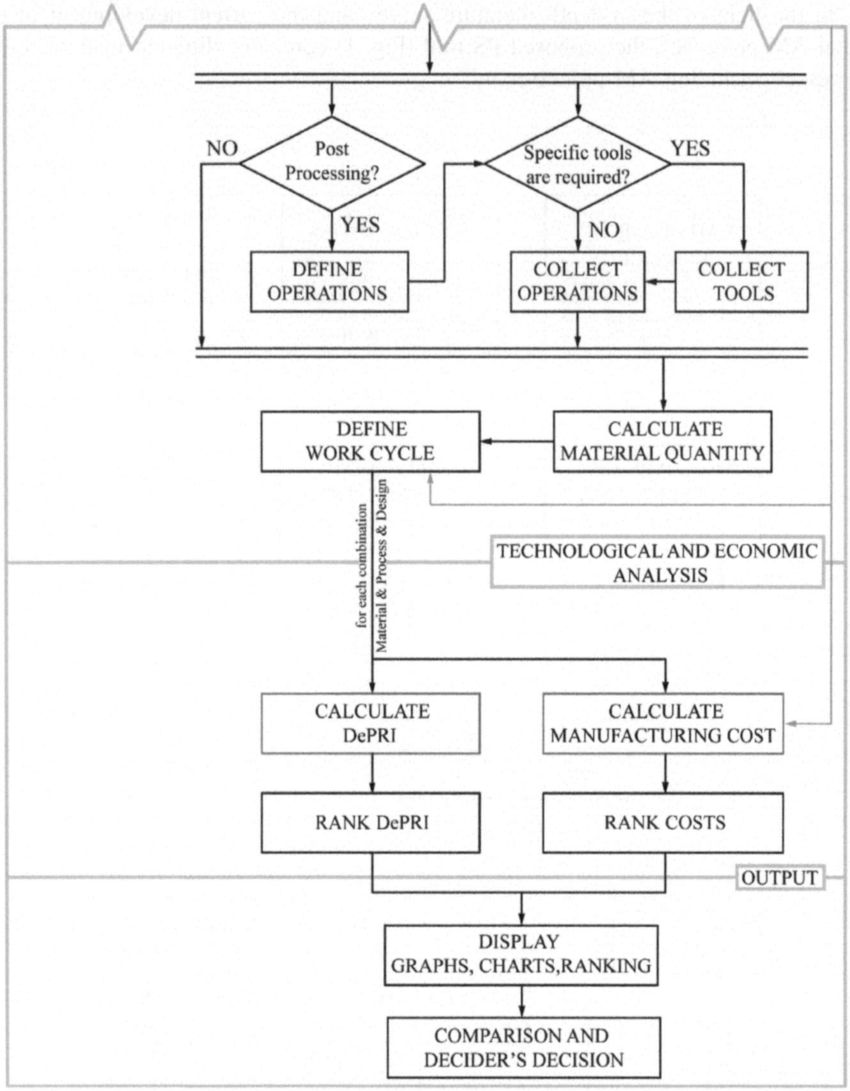

Fig. 1. (*continued*)

- Taking into account the design for the part performance and the design for manufacturing
- Considering a quantitative evaluation in order to exclude personal assessments
- Considering a broader analysis of the effectiveness of the design and its specification not only limited to the part but toward the effects on the whole system

Considering two independent ranks: one for the technical aspects and one for the manufacturing costs, in order to avoid redundant information and give a comprehensive description of the decision problem. The tool operates using panel and subpanels based on the consideration of three key factors: the material, the design of the component, and the ranking of the alternatives. The basic requirements to implement this suggested procedure are two databases: one that contains the manufacturing processes and the machines that are available (or to be evaluated) for a specific manufacturing process and one that contains the materials that are available (or to be evaluated) for a specific manufacturing process.

The *Input* panel collects the data and specification of the component such as information about the basic geometry, the minimum requirements for the material and for the design and the estimated quantity to be produced.

The *Elaboration of input data* panel extracts the information from the *Input* panel about the maximum envelope of the part, the tolerances, the roughness and heat treatments required for the components. In this step, a preliminary screening is run. The build volume of each available machine is compared with the maximum envelope of the part. The machine and the manufacturing process is collected is they match the requirement. On the contrary, it is possible to evaluate other orientations of the part in the build volume and/or the splitting of the part into two or more components. As far as the material is concerned the properties of each material are compared with the technical specifications for minimum elastic module, hardness and yield stress. Post heat treatment operations on the material are considered to improve the material proprieties and collected. From this step, two new databases are compiled. The first one contains the processes for which at least one machine is able to produce the part geometry. This database also includes information about the assembly, if it is necessary. The second database contains the materials that matched the requirements and heat treatments if they are needed.

The *Preselection* panel works to establish the process/material couples that can be proper to produce the part. Each material is compared with the capabilities of each process. In addition, because the information that derived from preliminary process preselection could contain assembly operations, the compatibility of the material with the assembly operations is checked.

The *Design and Manufacturability analysis* panel is the stage of the process selection that represents the core of the feasibility analysis. The material and the manufacturing specification converge to the first process selection in which the geometry is matched with the DfM rules. The basic operations to obtain the part are defined. This phase involves considering a design stage in which design methodologies, such as topology optimisation (TO), are applied to search the best performance of the component. This step is the most important to the success of the AM processes. Generally, the designer provides geometries already simplified in order to avoid high manufacturing costs or features that are obviously unfeasible. These considerations are almost fully irrelevant for AM processes because the increasing geometry complexity is not strongly correlated to an increasing of tge cost for an additive production.

The *Technical and Economic analysis* panel provides the technical index and the manufacturing cost per part. This two information are kept expressly independent in order to avoid redundant information and to provide a general overview and clearer results of the process selection phase. The technical or Design and Process Performance Index index (DePrI) is aimed to the comparison the manufacturing processes from a technical point of view. The index evaluates attributes grouped into three categories: material performances, design performances and process capabilities. An example of the evaluable attributes is given in Table 1. Each attribute should be weighted according to the design requirements. Therefore, DePrI can be computed using the weighted sum formulation. The rank in descending order will collect the alternatives from the most favourable to the least. The attempt is to obtain an indicator that not only can suggest what is the proper manufacturing process to produce the part but also what manufacturing process could allow the production of a part with the best performance.

Table 1. Example of evaluable attributes by using DePrI

	Attributes
Material performances	Strength of the material
	Stiffness of the material
	Hardness of the material
Design performances	Geometric complexity of the design
	Capabilities of the design to satisfy the required weight of the part
	Capabilities of the design to satisfy the required constraint on the maximum displacement of the part in all load conditions weight of the part
Process capabilities	Capabilities of the process to produce the required holes without finishing operations
	Capabilities of the process to produce surfaces with the prescribed roughness without finishing operations
	Capabilities of the process to produce features with the prescribed tolerances without finishing operations
	Capabilities of the process to produce the part in the delivery time

For this reason, DePrI can be used for several purposes not least for as to "weight" the cost per part. In fact, that definition takes into account the hidden effect of considering a combination of material, design and manufacturing process. Therefore, this value is also a "measure" of the benefits that could be achieved by adopting the new geometry (material and process).

The last one is the *Output* panel that should provide the decider a quantitative analysis together with chart and graphs in order to support decisions.

4 Conclusion

A literature review was made in the field of the PS tools in order to identify the shortcoming and limits of applicability when the AM processes are included in the PS strategy. It was concluded that there is no PS tool that can consider properly the advantages of the adopting of the AM processes. The main weaknesses of the literature approaches were found on the using the same geometry as main input for the process selection and the use of costs-driven methods for the process selection. In light of that, a new framework was introduced in order to provide an index to compare the alternatives, considering not only the manufacturing cost but also the features and the specification of the best design that can be obtained using the manufacturing process. The proposed PS tool is, therefore, an all-inclusive methodology between material, process and design that considers the combination of these elements to determine the best alternative to produce the part. The evaluation must be carried out by using DePrI and the manufacturing cost. DePrI is able to quantitative evaluate the performance of the design, material and process and it can be used as a weight for the information provides by of the manufacturing cost analysis in order to justify, for instance, an increase of cost manufacturing cost from the traditional to additive manufacturing. The proposed tool aims to facilitate the introduction of AM processes in the metal industry giving more sensibility of the peculiarity of the AM processes as regards the design optimisation.

References

1. Anderson, D.M.: Design for Manufacturability: Optimizing Cost, Quality, and Time to Market. CIM Press, New York (2001)
2. O'Driscoll, M.: Design for manufacture. J. Mater. Process. Technol. **122**(2), 318–321 (2002). https://doi.org/10.1016/S0924-0136(01)01132-3
3. Swift, K.G., Booker, J.D.: Process selection: from design to manufacture. Butterworth-Heinemann, Oxford (2003)
4. Edwards, K.: Towards more strategic product design for manufacture and assembly: priorities for concurrent engineering. Mater. Des. **23**(7), 651–656 (2002). https://doi.org/10.1016/S0261-3069(02)00050-X
5. Kerbrat, O., Mognol, P., Hascoët, J.-Y.: A new DFM approach to combine machining and additive manufacturing. Comput. Ind. **62**(7), 684–692 (2011). https://doi.org/10.1016/j.compind.2011.04.003
6. Shukor, S.A., Axinte, D.: Manufacturability analysis system: issues and future trends. Int. J. Prod. Res. **47**(5), 1369–1390 (2009). https://doi.org/10.1080/00207540701589398
7. Gibson, I., Rosen, D.W., Stucker, B.: Design for additive manufacturing. In: Additive Manufacturing Technologies: Rapid Prototyping to Direct Digital Manufacturing, pp. 299–332. Springer, Boston (2010). https://doi.org/10.1007/978-1-4419-1120-9_11
8. Zhou, M., Fleury, R., Shyy, Y.-K., Thomas, H., Brennan, J.: Progress in topology optimization with manufacturing constraints. In: Proceedings of the 9th AIAA MDO Conference AIAA-2002-4901 (2002)
9. Giachetti, R.E.: A decision support system for material and manufacturing process selection. J. Intell. Manuf. **9**(3), 265–276 (1998). https://doi.org/10.1023/A:1008866732609
10. Yu, J.-C., Krizan, S., Ishii, K.: Computer-aided design for manufacturing process selection. J. Intell. Manuf. **4**(3), 199–208 (1993). https://doi.org/10.1007/BF00123964
11. Galati, M., Iuliano, L.: A literature review of powder-based electron beam melting focusing on numerical simulations. Addit. Manuf. (2017) https://doi.org/10.1016/j.addma.2017.11.001
12. Gibson, I., Rosen, D.W., Stucker, B.: Additive Manufacturing Technologies: Rapid Prototyping to Direct Digital Manufacturing. Springer, Boston (2010). https://doi.org/10.1007/978-1-4419-1120-9

13. Wohlers, T.: Additive Manufacturing State of the Industry in Wohlers Report 2014, Fort Collins, USA
14. Das, S.: Physical aspects of process control in selective laser sintering of metals. Adv. Eng. Mater. **5**(10), 701–711 (2003). https://doi.org/10.1002/adem.200310099
15. Larsson Morgan, L.U., Ola, H.: Rapid manufacturing with electron beam melting (EBM)—a manufacturing revolution? In: Solid Freeform Fabrication Symposium, Austin, TX (2003)
16. Ishii, K., Adler, R., Barkan, P.: Application of design compatibility analysis to simultaneous engineering. Artif. Intell. Eng. Des. Anal. Manuf. **2**(1), 53–65 (1988). https://doi.org/10.1017/S0890060400000548
17. Boothroyd, G.: Product design for manufacture and assembly. Comput. Aided Des. **26**(7), 505–520 (1994). https://doi.org/10.1016/0010-4485(94)90082-5
18. Beiter, K., Krizan, S., Ishii, K., Hornberger, L.: HyperQ/Plastics: an intelligent design aid for plastic material selection. Adv. Eng. Softw. **16**(1), 53–60 (1993). https://doi.org/10.1016/0965-9978(93)90029-S
19. Poli, C.: Design for Manufacturing: A Structured Approach, vol. 1. Butterworth-Heinemann, Boston (2001)
20. Boothroyd, G., Dewhurst, P., Knight, W.A.: Product Design for Manufacture and Assembly. CRC Press, Boca Raton (2010)
21. Campbell, I., Bourell, D., Gibson, I.: Additive manufacturing: rapid prototyping comes of age. Rapid Prototyp. J. **18**(4), 255–258 (2012). https://doi.org/10.1108/13552541211231563
22. Deglin, A., Bernard, A.: A knowledge-based environment for modelling and computer-aided process planning of rapid manufacturing processes. In: Chedmail, P., Cognet, G., Fortin, C., Mascle, C., Pegna, J. (eds.) Integrated Design and Manufacturing in Mechanical Engineering, pp. 85–92. Springer, Dordrecht (2002). https://doi.org/10.1007/978-94-015-9966-5_11
23. Wilson, J.O., Rosen, D.: Selection for rapid manufacturing under epistemic uncertainty. In: ASME 2005 International Design Engineering Technical Conferences and Computers and Information in Engineering Conference. American Society of Mechanical Engineers (2005)
24. Gibson, I., Rosen, D., Stucker, B.: Guidelines for process selection. Additive Manufacturing Technologies: 3D Printing, Rapid Prototyping, and Direct Digital Manufacturing, pp. 303–327. Springer, New York (2015). https://doi.org/10.1007/978-1-4939-2113-3_13
25. Samperi, M.T.: Development of design guidelines for metal additive manufacturing and process selection. The Pennsylvania State University (2014)
26. Uz Zaman, U.K., Siadat, A., Rivette, M., Baqai, A.A., Qiao, L.: Integrated product-process design to suggest appropriate manufacturing technology: a review. Int. J. Adv. Manuf. Technol., 1–22 (2017)
27. Atzeni, E., Salmi, A.: Economics of additive manufacturing for end-usable metal parts. Int. J. Adv. Manuf. Technol. **62**(9–12), 1147–1155 (2012). https://doi.org/10.1007/s00170-011-3878-1
28. Chiu, M.-C., Lin, Y.-H.: Simulation based method considering design for additive manufacturing and supply chain: an empirical study of lamp industry. Ind. Manag. Data Syst. **116**(2), 322–348 (2016). https://doi.org/10.1108/IMDS-07-2015-0266
29. Allen, J.: An investigation into the comparative costs of additive manufacture vs. machine from solid for aero engine parts. DTIC Document (2006)
30. Salmi, A., Calignano, F., Galati, M., Atzeni, E.: An integrated design methodology for components produced by laser powder bed fusion (L-PBF) process. Virtual Phys. Prototyp., 1–12 (2018). https://doi.org/10.1080/17452759.2018.1442229
31. Gibson, I., Rosen, D.W., Stucker, B.: Additive Manufacturing Technologies, vol. 238. Springer, Boston (2010)

Modular Design and Products and Configuration and Change Management

A Dynamic Contextual Change Management Application for Real Time Decision-Making Support

Widad Es-Soufi(✉), Esma Yahia, and Lionel Roucoules

Arts et Métiers ParisTech, CNRS, LSIS, 2 cours des Arts et Métiers, 13617 Aix en Provence, France
{Widad.ES-SOUFI,Esma.YAHIA,Lionel.ROUCOULES}@ensam.eu

Abstract. Decision making is a fundamental process within organizations for many reasons. It is indeed involved at all levels (new product decisions, management and marketing decisions, etc.) and has a direct impact on companies' efficiency and effectiveness. Many researches are conducted to enhance the decision-making process by proposing decision support systems where the most frequent challenge is the change management. Indeed, all businesses operate within an environment that is subject to constant changes (like new customers' needs and requirements, organisational and technological changes, changes in key information used to derive decisions, etc.). These changes have a major impact on the quality and accuracy of the proposed decision if they are not detected and propagated, at the right time, during the decision-making process. The present work attempts to resolve this challenge by proposing a dynamic change management technique that allows three tasks to be automatically performed. First, continuously detect changes and note them. Second, retrieve from the detected changes those that are related to the decision rules. Finally, propagate them by computing the new value of the decision rule. The proposal has been fully implemented and tested in the supervision process of gas network exploitation.

Keywords: Change management · Dynamic change propagation
Decision making · Process patterns · Business process

1 Introduction

The 21st century is characterized by rapid changes that are due to the technological progress, as well as the economic, political and social changes. In this context, it becomes critical that organizations perform two tasks. The first one is to develop capabilities to implement changes in order to improve their competitiveness and sustain their business growth. The second task consists in informing the decision-making process of these changes. Indeed, the latter is considered as one of the most complex and critical processes in an organization for three reasons among others. First, it is the key function to a company's success where any decision made, no matter how simple it may be, has a significant impact on the other processes and thus on the business performance [1]. Second, it is highly constrained by the decision context, that is often

Published by Springer Nature Switzerland AG 2018.
P. Chiabert et al. (Eds.): PLM 2018, IFIP AICT 540, pp. 759–767, 2018.
https://doi.org/10.1007/978-3-030-01614-2_69

subject to several changes which need to be considered to make the right decision. Third, it sometimes involves several teams (subject matter experts, business analysts, engineers, etc.) that collectively analyse problems, evaluate alternatives and decide.

Many researches focus on supporting engineers by developing decision supports systems (DSS), which are computational tools that enable decision makers to select, at each time, the best alternative among a set of alternatives that are sometimes contradictory. After the appearance of artificial intelligence and learning techniques, the concept of intelligent decision support system (IDSS) arose. It is a DSS that provides direct access to expertise by supporting learning in the decision-making process [2]. In [3], authors propose a process mining based IDSS that performs two tasks. First, it analyses the past process executions, using process mining techniques, to identify and generate the different process patterns as well as the decision points and the rules that control them (cf. Fig. 1). Second, it filters the detected patterns and propose a ranking of the ones that fit the decision context.

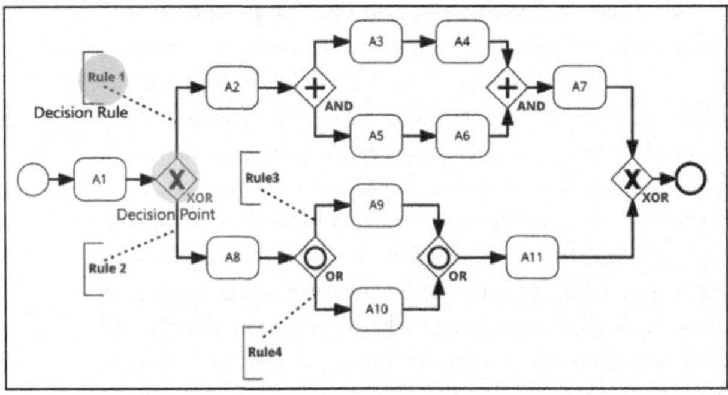

Process patterns:

P_1: $A_1A_2A_3A_4A_5A_6A_7$
P_2: $A_1A_2A_3A_5A_4A_6A_7$
P_3: $A_1A_2A_3A_5A_6A_4A_7$
P_4: $A_1A_2A_5A_6A_3A_4A_7$
P_5: $A_1A_2A_5A_3A_6A_4A_7$
P_6: $A_1A_2A_5A_3A_4A_6A_7$
P_7: $A_1A_8A_9A_{11}$
P_8: $A_1A_8A_{10}A_{11}$
P_9: $A_1A_8A_9A_{10}A_{11}$

Fig. 1. The identified process patterns, decision points and decision rules

In the present paper, authors focus on developing an executable application whose objective is to inform process mining based IDSSs of the changes that dynamically occur during the decision-making process. It updates the decision context whenever a change is detected and automatically filters the patterns that are generated from the IDSS based on the decision rules, also generated from the IDSS. Authors assume that, no matter how many changes occur, the developed application helps to make the right decision given a context at time t_i, where i goes from 0 (start of the decision-making process) to n (end of the process). Furthermore, authors assume that the application enables innovation by discovering new patterns from the already existing ones.

This paper is organized as follows. In Sect. 2, a literature review on change management during the decision-making process is presented and discussed. In Sect. 3, the proposed application is presented, then tested and verified in an industrial case study in Sect. 4. Finally, the future work is discussed before concluding the paper.

2 Contextual Change Management During Decision Making

Change management is the process in which a change is identified, analysed, evaluated, planned and propagated [4]. Three major types of change are identified in literature. First, the change that comes before making a decision such as an organisational change, technological change, etc. [5]. This type of change helps companies to remain relevant by keeping up with technological advances and changes in the marketplace and is generally planned and evaluated before deciding to successfully implement it. The second type is the product change management also called engineering design change [6]. This type concerns the modifications that are applied to products to meet the clients' needs among others and is, thus, linked to the first change type. The product change management consists in propagating the changed (i.e. new) product data throughout the product lifecycle. The third type is the contextual change management [7]. It consists in predicting, identifying or managing the context changes for successfully addressing dynamic (also called real time) decision making support. Indeed, in dynamic environments, only real time contextual data can provide decision makers with the accurate knowledge that is necessary to make decisions [8]. In the present paper, authors are interested in the contextual change management since it responds to their objective, which is to inform the IDSS of the changes that affect the decision-making context. Therefore, only the last type of change is explored and discussed in the following sub-sections.

2.1 Literature Review

A decision is defined by [9] as an irreversible commitment to a proposition or a plan of action based on evidence, the expected metrics associated with the outcome and the context in which the decision is being made. The context is an essential and powerful concept for effective real time decision-making. The context definition that is adopted by most researchers is that it is "any information that can be used to characterise the situation of an entity" [10]. This context information can be imported from sensors, derived from other information, reasoned, computed or explicitly entered by users [7]. There are two categories of context [11]. The dynamic context that consists of dynamic information such as heart rate, pressure data streams and the static context where information are static such as decision makers names, etc. [7].

There are many approaches in literature that focus in understanding the behaviour of the decision-making context. Some approaches intend to model the context and are based on Bayesian reasoning techniques [12], fuzzy logic [11], graphical modelling [13] and some other ontology-based modelling approaches that allow a formal representation of concepts and their relationships that is used for knowledge reasoning about context [14]. In [15], authors propose an overview of the context using the user behavior modelling. In addition to the modelling based approaches, there are other approaches that intend to predict the future context, in order to improve the contextual change management, by using data mining techniques such as classification, neural networks, and statistics-based techniques [7]. Other approaches use expert systems and rule engines for context prediction [7].

2.2 Discussion

Most of the approaches explored in the precedent sub section are related to the context modelling or prediction. these techniques face some challenges that concern, among others, the prediction of human actions that may be part of the real time decision context [16]. The latter, as defined in [7], is a representation of the environment as a set of contextual data which provide the decision maker with the necessary knowledge to decide as soon as these data are obtained. In authors' context, these contextual data are both static and dynamic and are not always pre-defined or inferred since some of them change constantly, will be known only in real time or interfere with other contexts (e.g. A station's pressure may depend on the other surrounding stations behaviour, as well as on its lifetime and/or the climate change). In addition, authors need to express the context in a deterministic way, since it is used to filter the end-to-end patterns based on some decision rules in the form "if (pressure >25) then send an emergency technician", here, a precise value of the pressure (i.e. 25) is needed rather than the distribution or prediction of pressure values. To achieve their objective, authors need continuous insights on the environmental changes and explicit knowledge of the current context. Therefore, they assume that the explored approaches cannot be used to achieve their objective and propose in the next section an application that, based on the contextual data that are obtained on the move, aims at supporting real time decision making in an informed way.

3 Proposal: The Dynamic Change Management Application

The workflow presented in Fig. 2 is the overview of the proposal that enables the current objective to be achieved.

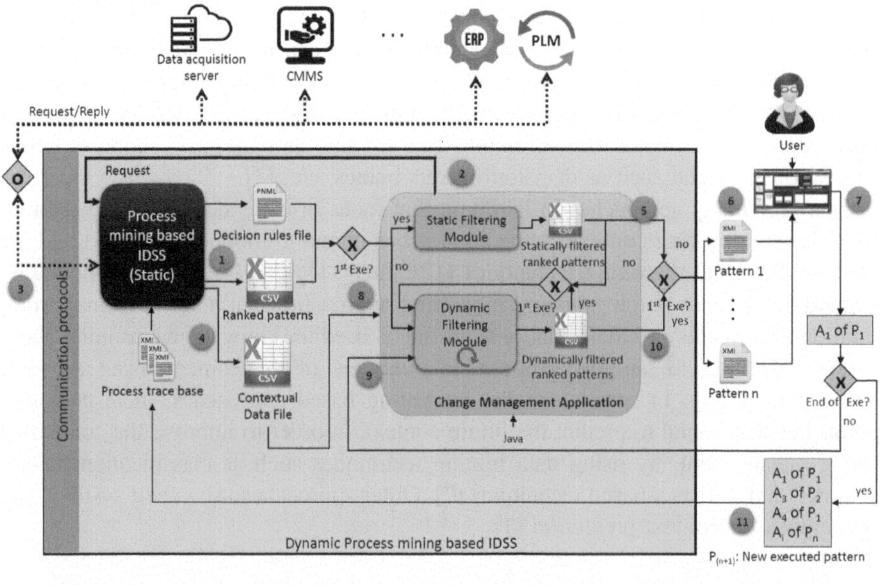

Fig. 2. Workflow of the proposal (Expressed in BPMN(http://www.bpmn.org/))

The first step consists in executing the static IDSS to generate the "decision rules" and the "ranked patterns" files from the process trace base as explained in [3]. This base contains the past process executions, also called traces, that were generated with respect to the trace metamodel identified in [17]. The "decision rules" file contains the rules that control how the process flows and is expressed in PNML (Petri Net Markup Language) format. The latter is an XML based standardized interchange format for Petri nets that allows the decision rules to be expressed as guards, this means that the transition from a place (i.e. activity) to another, can fire only if the guard, and thus the rule, evaluates to true. For instance, rule 1 in Fig. 1 is the decision rule that enables the transition from A_1 to A_2. The second document, generated by the static IDSS, is the "ranked patterns file". It contains the distinct end-to-end process patterns (e.g. patterns P_1 to P_9 in Fig. 1), that were identified in the process trace base and sorted by frequency.

Once the two files are generated by the IDSS, and if it is its first execution for a given decision problem, the static filtering module is invoked. This latter requests the current context from the IDSS (step 2) which transmits the request to the connected systems via the communication layer (step3). This layer is beyond the scope of the present paper, authors aspire to present it in detail in another article. Among the systems that are connected to the IDSS, authors cite the data acquisition server that collects data from the different field devices (e.g. pressure sensors), the CMMS (Computerized Maintenance Management System) that delivers maintenance data such as the date of failure/repair, the ERP (Enterprise Resource Planning) that delivers the operational processes information (e.g. delivery date) and PLM software (Product Lifecycle Management) that contains all the product/process information throughout the product lifecycle (e.g. design data).

Once the IDSS receives the context from the connected systems, it copies it in a "contextual data" file which is sent to the static filtering module (step 8). The execution of this module generates the "statically filtered ranked patterns" file (step5) that associates to each pattern, of the "ranked patterns" file, a decision rule flag whose value is either 1 or 0. 1 means that the pattern satisfies the decision rules in the current context's conditions and is, thus, ready to be proposed to the user (step 6) via the IDSS graphical user interface presented in [18].

The user chooses one of the proposed patterns and starts to execute its first activity (step 7). If the executed activity does not refer to the end of the process (i.e. "activityEvent $\neq$ end" as explained in [17]), then both the activity and the pattern to which it belongs are sent to the dynamic filtering module (step 9). The latter requests the context at time t (execution of the steps 2, 3, 4, 8), and takes as inputs the "contextual data" and the "statically filtered ranked patterns" files as well as the last executed activity and its pattern in order to update the statically filtered ranked patterns to a new file called "Dynamically filtered ranked patterns", where the decision rule flag is updated according to whether the decision rules are satisfied by the new current context. If the latter satisfies the rule 1 (cf. Fig. 1) for example, the activity A_2, and all the patterns that contain it (P_1 to P_6) are updated to 1 while the patterns (P_7 to P_9) are updated to 0.

The patterns whose decision rule flag equals to 1 are proposed to the user based on their frequency order (step 6). Then the steps 7, 9, 2, 3, 4, 8 are repeated in a loop until the last executed activity refers to the end of the process (i.e. "activityEvent = end" as explained in [17]). In this case, the new pattern that contains all the executed activities is sent to the process trace base to enrich it (step 11). Note that the new executed pattern is sent to the base even if it is one of the existing patterns, since the component that generates the "ranked patterns" selects only the distinct patterns and associates to each one the number of its occurrence (frequency).

The proposed change management application enables the IDSS, developed in [3], to be dynamically aware of context changes. It is fully implemented using the Java programming language.

4 Case Study: Supervision of Gas Network Exploitation

As discussed in [3], systems supervision is a business process that consists of complex decision based activities. During this process, supervisors have to take actions (i.e. decisions) depending on both the supervision result and the set-point (i.e. target value for the supervised system) in order to maintain the well-functioning of an industrial process, in case an alarm is received or when the performance target is seeming far from being met. The authors prefer to reuse the same supervision case study, presented in [3], where the supervisor of an industrial process should take, in the shortest time, the right decision in case an alarm is received. The IDSS is intended to support this supervisor during his problem-solving process by proposing the right decision even if the context (that can be described by the field sensors values, season, supervisor's name, etc.), changes considerably and quickly (e.g. the pressure of a gas station at time t_i may be very different from the pressure at time t_{i+1}).

The problem-solving process starts by receiving the malfunction alarm. The IDSS identifies the decision points and rules (c.f. Fig. 3) as well as the different end-to-end patterns and export them to two files: The decision points/rules file in pnml format and the ranked patterns file in csv format [3].

After encountering the first gateway, the IDSS asks the connected systems for the context at time t_1 (step 2,3 in Fig. 2) based on which it statically filters the ranked patterns by filling the decision rule column to 1 if the pattern satisfies the rule, 0 otherwise (step 5 in Fig. 2). All the patterns are then displayed in the IDSS interface, based on their frequency, where those whose decision rules flags equal to 1 are printed in dark black and can be selectable while the other patterns are displayed in grey but can also be selectable as the IDSS aims at supporting the user, not restricting his choices. Therefore, as depicted in Fig. 4(a), the pattern "P4T1John" is the only one that satisfies the context at time t_1 (cf. Table 1 and rules in Fig. 3) and is selected by the user. The latter starts to execute the next proposed patterns activities, namely, "Send an emergency technician" and "Measure the flow rate". Before proposing these activities, the IDSS does not ask for any context information since it does not encounter any gateway, where one choice among others must be made. After the activity "Measure the flow rate" is executed, the IDSS asks for the context at time t_2, according to which it filters the patterns. In this case, the pattern that satisfies the new context is still the same (P4T1John) and the IDSS continues proposing its next activity "Simulate the pressure setpoint decrease". Once this latter is executed, the IDSS asks for the context at time t_3, based on which it filters the patterns. The new pattern that satisfies the rules is henceforth "P3T1John" as depicted in Fig. 4(b).

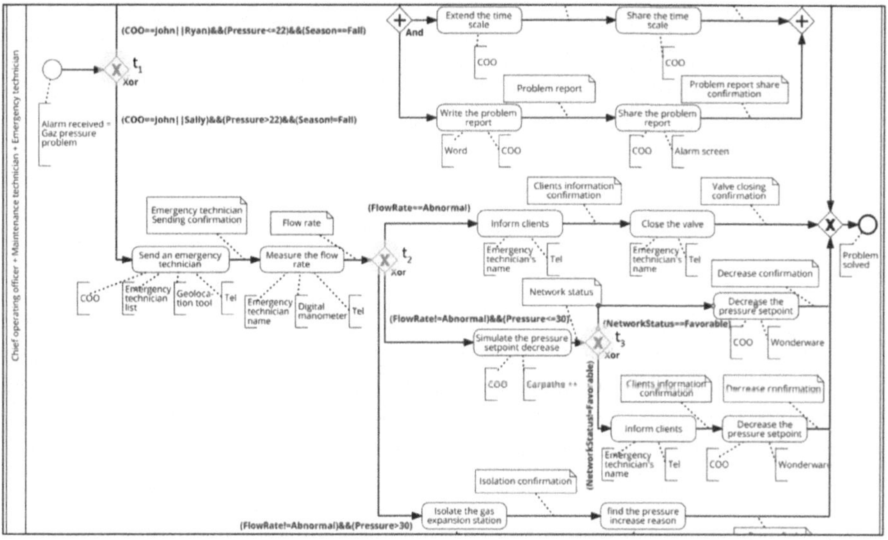

Fig. 3. Part of the supervision process with the identified decision points and rules

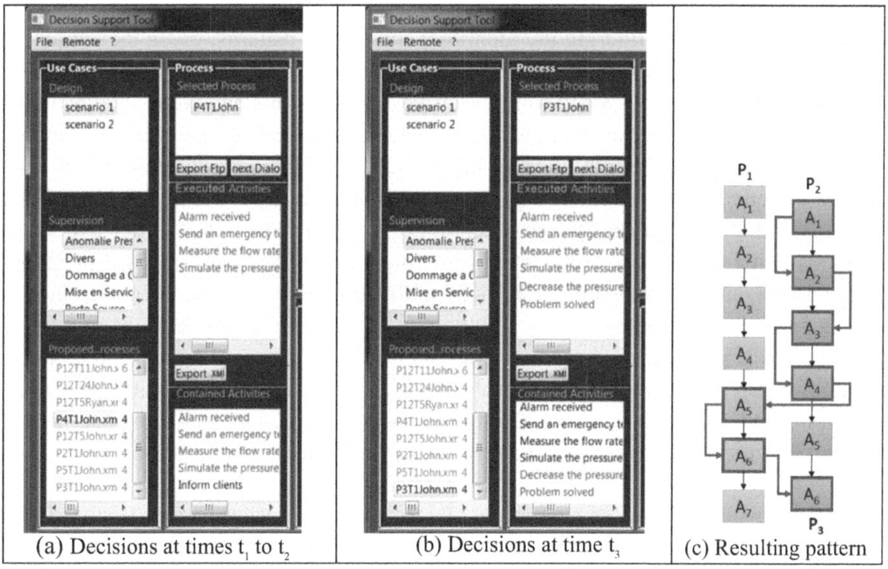

Fig. 4. Real time switching from one pattern to another while supporting decision making

Table 1. Contextual data at times t_1, t_2 and t_3

	t_1	t_2	t_3
Supervisor	John	John	John
Season	Winter	Winter	Winter
Pressure	25	28	28
Flow rate	Abnormal	Normal	Normal
Network status	Unfavourable	Unfavourable	Favourable

The IDSS proposes the activity "inform clients" and repeats all the steps until the activity "Problem solved", that refers to the end of the process (activityEvent=end), is met. Note that the user may refuse to execute the proposed pattern and start to execute new activities. In this case the IDSS listens and traces the full executed pattern in order to send it to its process trace base to enrich it.

5 Conclusion and Future Work

The objective of this paper is to inform process mining based IDSSs (Intelligent Decision Support Systems) of the changes that dynamically occur when supporting engineers during their decision-making processes. Through the proposed technique, the IDSS starts by statically filtering the identified end-to-end patterns, given the context at the beginning of the decision-making process, to fit the identified decision rules. Then the filtered patterns are proposed to the user who chooses one and starts to execute its activities. The IDSS requests the new context whenever a decision point is encountered to make sure that the patterns filtering takes account of the correct context, and thus propose the effective decision. The proposed technique is generic and can be used by every IDSS that uses process mining techniques to learn from data to infer decisions. Authors assume that the use of the process mining based IDSS along with the proposed change management application, promote innovation within organizations, since it helps to create new patterns (way of thinking or solving a problem) from several existing ones (Fig. 4(c)). Future work consists in testing this assumption and evaluate the IDSS using a real-world design problem. It also consists in continuing the development of the IDSS' interface to make it more interactive and to enable the user to add his own activities to the proposed pattern and/or trace his new executions.

Acknowledgments. This research takes part of a national collaborative project (Gontrand) that aims at supervising a smart gas grid. Authors would like to thank the companies REGAZ, GDS and GRDF for their collaboration.

References

1. Blenko, M., Mankins, M., Rogers, P.: Decision Insights: The Five Steps to Better Decisions. Bain & Company, Boston (2013)
2. Arnott, D., Pervan, G.: Eight key issues for the decision support systems discipline. Decis. Support Syst. **44**(3), 657–672 (2008)
3. Es-Soufi, W., Yahia, E., Roucoules, L.: A process mining based approach to support decision making. In: Ríos, J., Bernard, A., Bouras, A., Foufou, S. (eds.) PLM 2017. IAICT, vol. 517, pp. 264–274. Springer, Cham (2017). https://doi.org/10.1007/978-3-319-72905-3_24
4. Crnkovic, I., Asklund, U., Dahlqvist, A.P.: Implementing and Integrating Product Data Management and Software Configuration Management. Artech House, Norwood (2003)
5. Helfat, C.E., et al.: Dynamic Capabilities: Understanding Strategic Change in Organizations. Wiley, New York (2009)
6. Ullah, I., Tang, D., Yin, L.: Engineering product and process design changes: a literature overview. Procedia CIRP **56**, 25–33 (2016)
7. Burstein, F., Brézillon, P., Zaslavsky, A.: Supporting real-time decision making: the role of context in decision support on the move, vol. 13. Springer, Boston (2011)
8. Delic, K.A., Douillet, L., Dayal, U.: Towards an architecture for real-time decision support systems: challenges and solutions. In: Proceedings 2001 International Database Engineering and Applications Symposium, pp. 303–311 (2001)
9. Resulaj, A., Kiani, R., Wolpert, D.M., Shadlen, M.N.: Changes of mind in decision-making. Nature **461**, 263 (2009)
10. Dey, A.K.: Understanding and using context. Personal Ubiquitous Comput. **5**(1), 4–7 (2001)
11. Delir Haghighi, P., Krishnaswamy, S., Zaslavsky, A., Gaber, M.M.: Reasoning about context in uncertain pervasive computing environments. In: Roggen, D., Lombriser, C., Tröster, G., Kortuem, G., Havinga, P. (eds.) EuroSSC 2008. LNCS, vol. 5279, pp. 112–125. Springer, Heidelberg (2008). https://doi.org/10.1007/978-3-540-88793-5_9
12. Fox, V., Hightower, J., Liao, L., Schulz, D., Borriello, G.: Bayesian filtering for location estimation. IEEE Pervasive Comput. **2**(3), 24–33 (2003)
13. Henricksen, K., Indulska, J., Rakotonirainy, A.: Modeling context information in pervasive computing systems. In: Mattern, F., Naghshineh, M. (eds.) Pervasive 2002. LNCS, vol. 2414, pp. 167–180. Springer, Heidelberg (2002). https://doi.org/10.1007/3-540-45866-2_14
14. Truong, B.A., Lee, Y.-K., Lee, S.-Y.: Modeling uncertainty in context-aware computing. In: Fourth Annual ACIS International Conference on Computer and Information Science (ICIS 2005), pp. 676–681 (2005)
15. Ziebart, B.D., Maas, A.L., Dey, A.K., Bagnell, J.A.: Navigate like a cabbie: probabilistic reasoning from observed context-aware behavior. In: Proceedings of the 10th International Conference on Ubiquitous Computing, Seoul, Korea, pp. 322–331 (2008)
16. Nurmi, P., Martin, M., Flanagan, J.A., et al.: Enabling proactiveness through context prediction. In: Proceedings of the Workshop on Context Awareness for Proactive Systems, Helsinki, vol. 53 (2005)
17. Es-Soufi, W., Yahia, E., Roucoules, L.: Collaborative design and supervision processes meta-model for rationale capitalization. In: Eynard, B., Nigrelli, V., Oliveri, M.S., Peris-Fajarnes, G., Rizzuti, S. (eds.) Advances on Mechanics, Design Engineering and Manufacturing. Lecture Notes in Mechanical Engineering, pp. 1123–1130. Springer, Cham (2017) https://doi.org/10.1007/978-3-319-45781-9_112
18. Roucoules, L., Yahia, E., Es-Soufi, W., Tichkiewitch, S.: Engineering design memory for design rationale and change management toward innovation. CIRP Ann. Manuf. Technol. **65**(1), 193–196 (2016)

An Integrated Tool for the Optimization and Simulation of Hybrid Product-Process Layouts

Gianluca D'Antonio(✉) and Paolo Chiabert

Politecnico di Torino, Corso Duca degli Abruzzi 24, 10129 Turin, Italy
{gianluca.dantonio,paolo.chiabert}@polito.it

Abstract. The design of a manufacturing process is a crucial phase for ensuring a profitable production. In particular, an appropriate layout for the facilities must be identified to minimize the impact of transporting manufacturing units throughout the shop-floor on both process performance and production cost. In a former work, a mathematical model capable to define process, product and hybrid layouts has been defined by minimizing the average distance travelled by each manufacturing unit. The present paper aims to present an integrated tool able to: (i) deploy the optimization model to autonomously evaluate the optimal layout proposal that fits with a set of input provided by the designer; (ii) evaluate a set of KPIs to assess the layout; (iii) compile a discrete event simulation model on FlexSim to enable the designer to evaluate layout performance in a multiplicity of operating scenarios.

Keywords: Facility layout problem · Facilities planning and design
Optimal facility layout · Hybrid facility · Discrete event simulation

1 Introduction

The operating cost of a manufacturing process as well as its overall productivity is significantly affected by the position of the facilities within the shop-floor [1]. Tompkins et al. [2] found that 20–50% of the manufacturing costs are due to the handling of parts: a poor layout and flow design results in excessive work-in-process, high lead times, low or unbalanced equipment utilization and high costs for material handling and logistics equipment [3]. In other words, a weak arrangement of resources is a main source of wastes, according to the lean manufacturing classification.

The optimization of the facilities position is known as the Facility Layout Problem (FLP) and has been studied since the 1960s [4]: the problem aims to make layouts more efficient by considering various interactions between facilities and material-handling systems while designing layouts [5]. Nonetheless, FLP solution generally exhibits a NP-hard complexity [6] and is thus decomposed in simpler problems [7]. Various efforts have been made to systematize the knowledge about this class of problems: literature surveys have been proposed by Kusiak and Heragu [8], Meller and Gau [9], Singh and

Published by Springer Nature Switzerland AG 2018.
P. Chiabert et al. (Eds.): PLM 2018, IFIP AICT 540, pp. 768–777, 2018.
https://doi.org/10.1007/978-3-030-01614-2_70

Sharma [10], Drira et al. [1], Anjos and Vieira [6]. Drira et al. [1] defined a classification for the organization of manufacturing systems that is now well-acknowledged:

- **Fixed product layouts:** the facilities circulate around the product (which is not moved) to perform the necessary operations;
- **Process layouts:** the facilities with similar functions are grouped together in cells, enabling to deal with a large variety of products;
- **Product layouts:** the facilities are organized to match with the sequence of manufacturing operations to be performed for obtaining a specific product;
- **Cellular layout:** heterogeneous resources are grouped into cells, and each cell is in charge of manufacturing a particular product family.

To choose the appropriate manufacturing layout for a given process, both the variety of involved products and the material handling system (MHS) must be considered. Most of the approaches available in literature take into account the rigidities due to the MHS. Nonetheless, the significant technical efforts spent in the last decades led to the availability of Automated Guided Vehicles (AGVs) capable to freely navigate into a given space and safely interact with other vehicles and with humans. This capability opens unprecedented possibilities for the FLP. Further, manufacturers increasingly require facilities capable to quickly shift from one product to another without huge investments for major retooling, resource reconfiguration, or replacement of equipment [11].

This paper aims to present a novel tool capable to define and simulate a layout proposal based on a hybrid product-process layout. The term hybrid is used because the tool is able to formulate product layouts, process layouts, and intermediate solutions in which process cells – with a proper number of machines – may be conveniently duplicated.

The remainder of the paper is organized as follows. In Sect. 2 the existing methodologies to deal with the FLP are reviewed. The integrated tool for layout optimization and discrete event simulation (DES) is described in Sect. 3 and the results of some case-studies are presented in Sect. 4. Conclusive remarks and improvement perspectives are presented in Sect. 5.

2 State of the Art

The unequal areas FLP (UA-FLP) has been first stated in 1963 by Armour and Buffa [4]. In literature, this problem is mainly dealt with a two-steps approach: (i) a given (rectangular) area is divided into a finite number of regions, each of them representing a different department, and a method to minimize the overall distance travelled by each manufacturing unit is used; (ii) the internal layout of each cell is then defined [6, 10]. Usually, the facilities can be placed anywhere within the planar domain, provided that they must not overlap with each other [1].

Different methods have been proposed. First, researchers tried to solve exactly the FLP. A branch and bound approach was used by Kouvelis and Kim [12] to solve the unidirectional loop layout problem, while Xie and Sahinidis [13] solved a minimum-cost network flow problem to obtain a feasible layout from the sequence-pair representation of the relative position layout. However, obtaining a reliable solution requires too much time for dealing with huge problems and alternative heuristics have been developed.

In 1991, Montreuil [14] began to use the Mixed-Integer Linear Programming (MILP): rectangular departments are arranged orthogonally in a rectangular facility, using binary variables to specify the relative location of each department pair and prevent their overlapping, on both the horizontal and the vertical directions. However, even problems with 5 or 6 departments exhibited big challenges. Thus, Meller et al. [15] redefined the binary variables in the MILP model and studied the structure of acyclic subgraphs. Sherali et al. [16] improved this formulation and solved a problem with 9 departments in less than 10 h. Bukchin and Tzur [17] further improved the performance: they solved many problems made of 10 departments in less than 6 h. Their algorithm was also able to simultaneously define the layout of the departments and their internal layout, including both departments rectangular and L/T department shapes.

An approach alternative to MILP consists in genetic algorithms (GA), which systematically search for a solution but do not guarantee optimality. Mak et al. [18] used GAs to minimize the cost of material handling cost in case all the departments have equal areas. Azadivar and Wang [19] developed an approach that integrates GAs and simulation, to both optimize the layout and evaluate its performance; they aimed to minimize the cycle time and maximize productivity. Nonetheless, GAs exhibit a non-linear computational cost, which is an issue for big FLPs. Thus, Dunker et al. [20] developed a coevolutionary algorithm: the huge problem is split into smaller ones linked with each other. Galaxe Paes et al. [21] used a strategy for problem decomposition and reconstruction to handle problems with big dimensions: they have been able to solve layouts with 150 facilities in a few minutes.

Other metaheuristics inspired to natural phenomena have also been developed. Komarudin [22] used an ant system, a discrete optimization technique that resembles the behaviour of an ant colony in finding the shortest path to reach its food source. Niroomand et al. [23] used the migrating birds optimization method. An approach based on collision detection and force exertion heuristics has been presented by Sikaroudi and Shahanaghi [24]. Each department is modeled as a centroid and a surrounding area: the centroids interact with each other through forces that avoid cells overlapping. Departments are placed randomly to set an initial solution; then, the algorithm iteratively converges towards the optimal solution. The authors were able to solve a layout made of 100 departments in 230–250 s.

In former work [25] a mathematical model to define hybrid product-process layouts has been presented. In the present work, we aim to introduce an integrated tool for exploiting this model and automatically compile a DES model to evaluate the performance of such layout in a multiplicity of operative scenarios.

3 The Optimization and Simulation Tool

3.1 Layout Optimization

The tool for layout optimization acquires in input a set of parameters provided by the user and a table containing the bill of process (BoP). Then, the following tasks are performed:

1. **Definition of the process cells.** This task aims to find a suitable grouping of the machines into cells to guarantee the fulfillment of the BoP. In order to implement the hybrid product-process approach, a parameter named *Closeness* is introduced. It represents the maximum, normalized distance in the BoP between two operations for which grouping in the same cell is admissible. So, the tool scans the BoP and for each operation reads the next *Closeness* percent of the list, searching for possible operations to be grouped with the one at stake. The value of *Closeness* is set by the user; in particular, setting this parameter to 0 or to 1 result in product or process layout, respectively; intermediate values lead to hybrid solutions and, hence, different cells performing operations technologically similar can be defined. This step leads to the creation of *C* cells. Then, the duration of each operation (taken from the BoP) and the desired takt time for the line (provided by the user) are considered to evaluate the number of machines necessary to keep stable each cell, i.e. to have an average utilization lower than 1.
2. **Definition of the layout within the cells.** As a second step, the tool assigns the position of the machines within the above-defined cells. Each cell is made of identical machines, and no internal flow of manufacturing units (MUs) has to be considered. Therefore, a finite set of standardized cells designs can be defined a priori. At this stage, for each cell defined in the first step, the design corresponding to the number of machines to be contained is selected. This solution enables to solve the intra-cellular layout in a short time keeping a high quality of the design.
3. **Definition of the cells position within the available area.** In this task, the position of the cells is defined with the aim of minimizing the average distance travelled by each manufactured unit (MU). This is the trickiest task and relies on a mathematical algorithm that models the manufacturing process as a mechanical system of bodies connected with each other through a set of springs. The connected bodies represent the *C* cells defined in the previous step, and the points where they enter and leave the process (for example, the warehouses for raw materials and finished products). The springs model the inter-cellular travels to be performed according to the BoP. The aim of the algorithm is to identify an equilibrium condition for the bodies, which corresponds to the minimum residual energy, that in turn provides the optimal position for the manufacturing cells. The complete description of the mathematical model can be found in [25].
4. **Evaluation of KPIs for layout assessment.** To objectively evaluate the layout proposal, a set of performance indicators is evaluated, including the number of machines and cells necessary to perform the process, an estimation of the area

occupied by the machines, the overall average distance travelled by each MU. Also, the number of intersections among paths connecting different cells is evaluated: the higher is this number, the higher is the probability of traffic jams that may lower the performance of the line.

The tool has been implemented in Matlab, version R2017a. A graphical interface has been implemented to enable the user to quickly input data and consult the performance indicator; it is shown in Fig. 1, left panel. A snapshot of the layout is also generated. The data necessary for compiling the DES model are stored into an Excel spreadsheet, readable by both the simulation software and by the user.

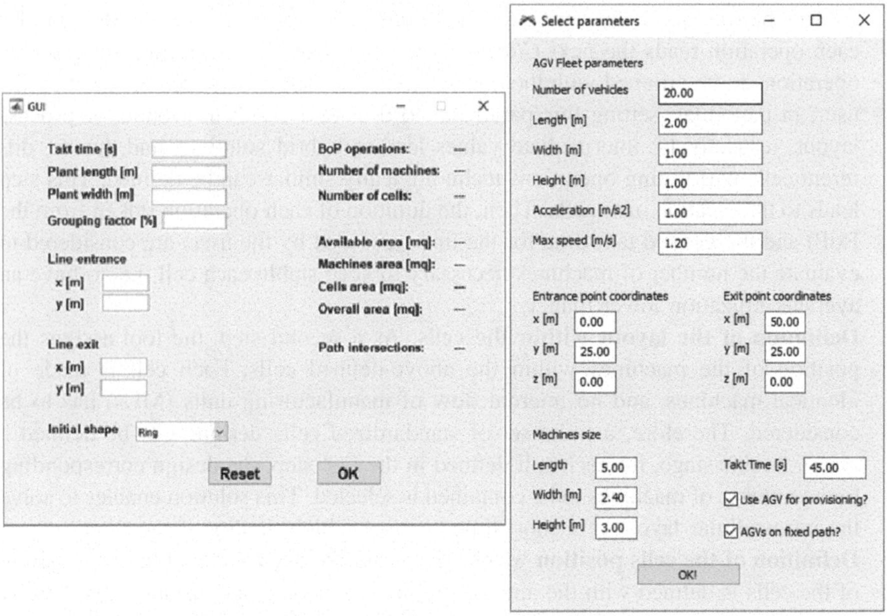

Fig. 1. Left. Graphical interface for the layout optimization tool. The input required by the user are collected on the left side; the performance indicators are shown on the right side. Right. Graphical interface for the DES tool.

3.2 Discrete Event Simulation

In order to compile the simulation model, several objects have to be considered for each machine included in the layout proposal: (i) a processor, modeling the machine; (ii) a queue and a bay, to model the interface between the machine and the material handling system; (iii) a container for the components to be added to the product. Therefore, given M machines to be included in the model, $O(M^4)$ objects are to be added, connected and customized in the model. Then, all the criteria to manage the flow of manufacturing units and the fleet of AGVs must be implemented. As the number of objects to be added in the model increases, this preparatory activity may become time consuming and error prone, although the added value provided to the designer is quite low.

Therefore, a higher-level approach has been undertaken. A meta-model containing the rules for providing the DES model with the objects and the flow rules has been developed. In this way, the model user just has to insert a few input; the model is ready for simulation or for fine tuning within a few seconds. In particular, the meta-model is able to:

1. Insert the entrance and exit points according to the coordinates input by the user;
2. Insert processors, queues, bays, components containers in the positions provided by the optimization model;
3. Insert the fleet of AGVs in charge of transporting both the MUs with the proper features for speed and acceleration;
4. Connect all of these objects in agreement with the BoP;
5. Set the rules for determining the setup and processing times, and the destination of the MU: each processor may load MUs at different stages of development, with different processing duration and different destinations.

The model can also take into account the consumption of components necessary for the manufacturing process. Therefore, the criteria for components deployment are taken by reading the BoP and rules for provisioning are implemented: when a given threshold (e.g. 20% of the refill lot size) is achieved, an alert is run, and a vehicle transports the lot from the proper warehouse to the container. Moreover, the meta-model is able to deal with AGVs used in free navigation as well as on constrained paths.

The meta-model has been implemented in Flexsim, version 2017. Also in this case, a graphical interface has been implemented to support the user to quickly compile and deploy the model; it is shown in Fig. 1, right panel.

4 Case Study

A case study taken from the automotive industry is shown in this section. The test process aims to assembly engine heads and is made of 19 operations belonging to 11 different technological families. All the machines to be used are assumed to have the same size, namely a length equal to 4 m and a width equal to 1.8 m. Further, the minimum distance to be kept among cells is set to 5 m, in order to enable material handling. The test room is a square with edge length equal to 50 m. The plots in Fig. 2 show three alternative layout proposals obtained by varying the magnitude of the parameter *Closeness*. The entrance and exit points are on the left and right edges, respectively. As the value of *Closeness* increases, as expected, the number of machines decreases while the average distance travelled by each MU increases.

The layout proposal is then loaded into the discrete event simulation meta-model for the evaluation of dynamic scenarios: a screenshot of the model obtained for *Closeness* equal to 0.25 is shown in Fig. 3.

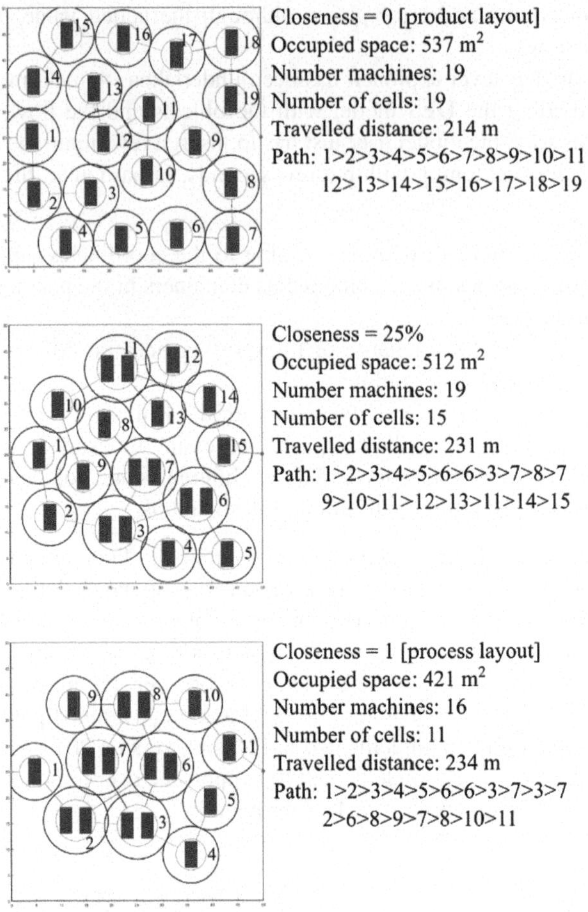

Fig. 2. Examples of layout obtained with the optimization tool. Blue rectangles represent the machines; the concentric circles represent the area occupied by the cell and the surrounding space to enable AGV transit. (Color figure online)

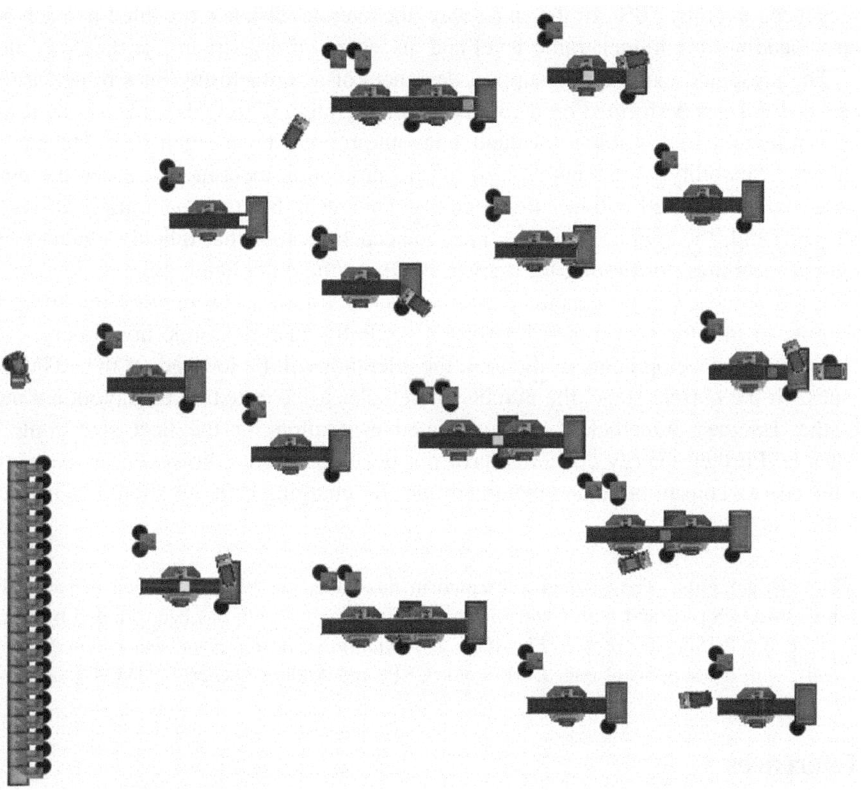

Fig. 3. Example of DES model obtained through the integrated tool. The green/black elements represent the workstations; the grey rectangles represent the bays for dropping off and picking up MUs. The yellow vehicles represent the AGVs, which interact with the production system through the black points. The red rectangles represent the containers of components close to the machines, while the warehouses are placed on left side of the layout. (Color figure online)

5 Conclusions

In the present paper, an integrated tool to support automated optimization and simulation of a hybrid product-process layout has been presented. This research is motivated by the availability – for a moderate price – of autonomous vehicles (such as the AGVs) capable to freely navigate throughout a given area. On the one side, the deployment of this technology enables to depict layouts with a reduced number of constraints; on the other side, a careful optimization must be made to achieve the best compromise between the quantity of machines to be used, the fleet of AGVs to be integrated, and the path to be travelled by each manufacturing unit. The latter factor, in turn, affects the work in process and the cycle time of the line, as well as possible safety issues due to traffic. An extended campaign to validate the mathematical model is discussed in [25]. It was found that by varying the grouping factor, the number of machines necessary to set a layout – and, in turn, the economic investment in manufacturing machines – may be reduced even by 50%. In the same way, the average distance travelled by each MU arises, leading to a higher traffic level and an increased investment for the AGV fleet.

The presented tool aims to support designers of manufacturing lines in performing their tasks. Tests performed on a common laptop (Intel i5 2.6 GHz CPU, 3 GB RAM) showed that the tool is able to evaluate a layout proposal in less than 10 s. The almost-real-time capability is maintained also by the simulation meta-model: given the input, the model is compiled within a few seconds. This result has two main implications: on the one hand, the routine activities are replaced by a tool that quickly evaluates the optimal machines positioning for a given input; on the other hand, different layouts for the same process can be generated and compared within a few minutes, enabling the designer to find the best trade-off between flexibility and economic investment.

In further developments of the tool, the attention will be focused on the AGV fleet issues. At the current stage, the number of vehicles to be tested on the layout are input by the designer; nonetheless, an automated estimation for the fleet size could be valuable. Further, energy concerns have not been considered; however, an estimation of the energy consumption and the downtimes for charging batteries should be included in the tool.

Acknowledgements. The research presented in this paper has been developed in partnership with COMAU S.p.A. and with Centro Ricerche Fiat. The research has been funded by Centro Ricerche Fiat within the project *FlexAGV: Exploitation of flexibility in smart manufacturing systems*, with the support of eng. J. Mascolo (CRF) and Andrea Ascheri (COMAU).

References

1. Drira, A., Pierreval, H., Hajri-Gabouj, S.: Facility layout problems: a survey. Annu. Rev. Control **31**(2), 255–267 (2007). https://doi.org/10.1016/j.arcontrol.2007.04.001
2. Tompkins, J., White, J., Bozer, Y., Tanchoco, J.: Facilities Planning. Wiley, New York (2010)
3. Heragu, S.S.: Facilities Design, 4th edn. CRC Press, Clermont (2016)
4. Armour, G.C., Buffa, E.S.: A heuristic algorithm and simulation approach to relative location of facilities. Manag. Sci. **9**(2), 294–309 (1963). https://doi.org/10.1287/mnsc.9.2.294
5. Shayan, E., Chittilappilly, A.: Genetic algorithm for facilities layout problems based on slicing tree structure. Int. J. Prod. Res. **42**(19), 4055–4067 (2004). https://doi.org/10.1080/00207540410001716471
6. Anjos, M.F., Vieira, M.V.: Mathematical optimization approaches for facility layout problems: the state-of-the-art and future research directions. Eur. J. Oper. Res. **261**(1), 1–16 (2017). https://doi.org/10.1016/j.ejor.2017.01.049
7. Hassan, M.M.D.: Machine layout problem in modern manufacturing facilities. Int. J. Prod. Res. **32**(11), 2559–2584 (1994). https://doi.org/10.1080/00207549408957084
8. Kusiak, A., Heragu, S.S.: The facility layout problem. Eur. J. Oper. Res. **29**(3), 229–251 (1987). https://doi.org/10.1016/0377-2217(87)90238-4
9. Meller, R.D., Gau, K.-Y.: The facility layout problem: recent and emerging trends and perspectives. J. Manuf. Syst. **15**(5), 351–366 (1996). https://doi.org/10.1016/0278-6125(96)84198-7

10. Singh, S.P., Sharma, R.R.K.: A review of different approaches to the facility layout problems. Int. J. Adv. Manuf. Technol. **30**(5), 425–433 (2006). https://doi.org/10.1007/s00170-005-0087-9
11. Benjaafar, S., Sheikhzadeh, M.: Design of flexible plant layouts. IIE Trans. **32**, 309–322 (2000). https://doi.org/10.1080/07408170008963909
12. Kouvelis, P., Kim, M.W.: Unidirectional loop network layout problem in automated manufacturing systems. Oper. Res. **40**(3), 533–550 (1992). https://doi.org/10.1287/opre.40.3.533
13. Xie, W., Sahinidis, N.V.: A branch-and-bound algorithm for the continuous facility layout problem. Comput. Chem. Eng. **32**(4), 1016–1028 (2008). https://doi.org/10.1016/j.compchemeng.2007.05.003
14. Montreuil, B.: A modelling framework for integrating layout design and flow network design. In: Progress in Material Handling and Logistics, vol. 2, pp. 95–115. Springer, Berlin (1991). http://dx.doi.org/10.1007/978-3-642-84356-3_8
15. Meller, R.D., Narayanan, V., Vance, P.H.: Optimal facility layout design. Oper. Res. Lett. **23**(3), 117–127 (1998). https://doi.org/10.1016/S0167-6377(98)00024-8
16. Sherali, H.D., Fraticelli, B.M.P., Meller, R.D.: Enhanced model formulations for optimal facility layout. Oper. Res. **51**(4), 629–644 (2003). https://doi.org/10.1287/opre.51.4.629.16096
17. Bukchin, Y., Tzur, M.: A new MILP approach for the facility process-layout design problem with rectangular and L/T shape departments. Int. J. Prod. Res. **52**(24), 7339–7359 (2014). https://doi.org/10.1080/00207543.2014.930534
18. Mak, K., Wong, Y., Chan, F.: A genetic algorithm for facility layout problems. Comput. Integr. Manuf. Syst. **11**(1), 113–127 (1998). https://doi.org/10.1016/S0951-5240(98)00018-4
19. Azadivar, F., Wang, J.: Facility layout optimization using simulation and genetic algorithms. Int. J. Prod. Res. **38**(17), 4369–4383 (2000). https://doi.org/10.1080/00207540050205154
20. Dunker, T., Radons, G., Westkämper, E.: A coevolutionary algorithm for a facility layout problem. Int. J. Prod. Res. **41**(15), 3479–3500 (2003). https://doi.org/10.1080/0020754031000118125
21. Galaxe-Paes, F., Alves-Pessoa, A., Vidal, T.: A hybrid genetic algorithm with decomposition phases for the unequal area facility layout problem. Eur. J. Oper. Res. **256**(3), 742–756 (2017). https://doi.org/10.1016/j.ejor.2016.07.022
22. Komarudin, K.Y.W.: Applying ant system for solving unequal area facility layout problems. Eur. J. Oper. Res. **202**(3), 730–746 (2010). https://doi.org/10.1016/j.ejor.2009.06.016
23. Niroomand, S., Hadi-Vencheh, A., Shahanaghi, R., Vizvári, B.: Modified migrating birds optimization algorithm for closed loop layout with exact distances in flexible manufacturing systems. Expert Syst. Appl. **42**(19), 6586–6597 (2015). https://doi.org/10.1016/j.eswa.2015.04.040
24. Sikaroudi, A.M.E., Shahanaghi, K.: Facility layout by collision detection and force exertion heuristics. J. Manuf. Syst. **41**, 21–30 (2016). https://doi.org/10.1016/j.jmsy.2016.07.001
25. D'Antonio, G., Saja, A., Ascheri, A., Mascolo, J., Chiabert, P.: An integrated mathematical model for the optimization of hybrid product-process layouts. J. Manuf. Syst. **46**, 179–192 (2018). https://doi.org/10.1016/j.jmsy.2017.12.003

A Causal Dependencies Identification and Modelling Approach for Redesign Process

Thierno M. L. Diallo(✉) and Marc Zolghadri

Quartz Laboratory, Supmeca-Superior Engineering Institute of Paris, Saint-Ouen, France
{thierno.diallo,marc.zolghadri}@supmeca.fr

Abstract. Systems and products are changed throughout their lifecycle to adapt to users' needs changes or to technological advances, among other reasons. The redesign process consists in modifying one or several parameters to reach the awaited redesign targets (better performance for instance). However, due to dependencies among parameters, changing one parameter may have unintended impacts on others. The problem we study in the redesign process concerns its underlying process of change propagation through the so called dependency model. The dependencies among parameters are correlation or causal. As a first contribution, the paper argues that the most interesting links to identify, model and work on are causalities. Therefore, the challenge to overcome is to identify the existing causal links among parameters using data exploration or expert knowledge mappings. The second contribution discusses a Causal dependencies identification and modelling approach for Redesign process, CaRe in short, which uses the Bayesian Network theory. CaRe is made to generate a causal Bayesian Network that allows evidential and causal inferences, supporting redesign decision-makings. The steps of CaRe are discussed in detail and future research works are presented at the end of the paper.

Keywords: Redesign · Dependency model · Change propagation
Causality · Bayesian Networks

1 Introduction

This research deals with change propagation during the redesign process. Throughout its lifecycle, a system or product undergoes many redesign or renewal and upgrade operations [1]. Redesign or upgrade consists in partial or total redesign of the system triggered by causes such as user needs, obsolescence of some functions or components, etc., see [2, 3].

A system consists of a set of physical and functional interdependent elements. Furthermore, the system and its environment influence on each other. Changes propagation is the fact that an engineering change to one component (physical or functional) of the system or its environment results in one or more additional changes to other components, when those changes would not otherwise have been required or observed [4, 5].

Published by Springer Nature Switzerland AG 2018.
P. Chiabert et al. (Eds.): PLM 2018, IFIP AICT 540, pp. 778–788, 2018.
https://doi.org/10.1007/978-3-030-01614-2_71

The redesign consists of changing one or more of system parameters. However, due to their (explicit or implicit) dependencies, changing one parameter would generate others. The prediction and management of the impacts of these undesired changes represent a great challenge for complex systems [2]. The aim of this research work is to contribute to the better identification of these impacts through identifying, appropriately modelling and exploiting causal dependencies among the system parameters. Having a better understanding of the possible (wanted and unwanted) consequences allows a better (re-)design decision-making. The unwanted consequences should be controlled far in advance before any real change in the system; they do not have to violate the system constraints.

As far as we were able to find out, in the engineering change management literature, no study does focus on the very nature of dependency links. This paper studies both causal and correlation dependency links used in a redesign process as a fundamental element of the dependency model. Nevertheless, the main target is put on the causal dependencies that provide more capabilities to designers.

To obtain such causal dependency model, we propose an approach based on the system architecture. The system architecture is defined as a physical structure, the functional structure and the mapping between these two structures [6]. Determining by this way, the architecture facilitates the identification of the causal dependencies model. In some cases, the correlation links may persist in the model depending on the quality of used data or expert knowledge. Once, in hands, such causal dependencies model, if modelled by an appropriate dependency language, may be used for redesign decision-makings. In our research we use the Bayesian Network as the dependency theory for modelling, mainly due to the various reasoning possibilities it offers.

The remainder of this paper is organized as follows. First, some main change management concepts and change propagation methods are presented in Sect. 2. This section will end up with a summary conclusion about the dependency modelling and engineering change management. The main motivations of our research are explained there. The Bayesian approach is then explained very briefly to allow the understanding of the approach (Sect. 3). In Sect. 4, we present in detail the proposed approach, called "Causal dependencies identification and modelling approach for Redesign process", "CaRe" in short. The paper ends with a summary of our findings and discusses the future works in Sect. 5.

2 Literature Review

An engineering change is any change or modification made in the form, fit, material, dimension and function of a product or a component [7]. Change management is defined by [8] as "the comprehensive evaluation and approval or disapproval of a change that takes into consideration all effects of the change". Change management is studied by lots of authors, see [2–5]. The change propagation is studied using various tools. For instance, Clarkson and his colleagues [2, 4, 5] use DSM (Design Structure

Matrix) and other similar matrix-based tools (MDM-Multiple-Domain Matrix, DMM-Domain Mapping Matrix, HoQ - House of Quality). However, no DSM-derived approach studies the nature of the links that could be correlation and causality.

Other proposed methods are specialized for geometrical change propagation. Cohen et al. [3] propose the C-FAR (Change Favourable Representation) methodology to trace and predict change propagation in computer-aided mechanical design. Most of the CAD (Computer-Aided Design) tools has a kind of change propagation features. Their main drawback is the fact that they propagate only a specific type de change.

The relationships between parameters may be a correlation or causality. However, “Correlation does not imply causation” [9]. When there is a correlation link between 2 parameters, this means that if a value of one of the parameters is observed, it is also expected to observe a given value of the second. The existence of causal link between 2 parameters implies that the modification of the cause will have an impact on the effect.

Correlation relationships express what we know or believe about the world, while causal relationships describe physical constraints. Correlation relationships characterize static conditions while the causal analysis deals with dynamic situations [10].

Relying on these distinctions, we postulate that the most interesting links to identify for changes propagation during the redesign process are causal. The redesign process involves actions or interventions on the system (change of the architecture or the functions, replacement of a component, etc.). Intervention (surgery on mechanisms) is one of the fundamental characteristics of causality [11]. The identification of the causality makes it possible to predict the consequences on the effects while acting on their cause parameter. Therefore, the first challenge is to identify the existing causal link among parameters. The research we presented here is focused on determination of causalities and assess their consequences during the redesign or upgrade process.

3 main approaches have been proposed to model causal relationships and to make causal inferences namely: the Neyman–Rubin causal model, the Structural Equation Model and Directed Acyclic Graphs also called Bayesian Networks (BN). It has been demonstrated that BN is the most commonly used tool to represent causal relationships and to make causal inferences [11].

3 Bayesian Network

A Bayesian Network (BN) is a Directed Acyclic Graph (DAG) represented by the pair (V, E) where V is a set of vertices and E a set of directed edges connecting vertices [12]. A marginal or conditional probability distribution table is associated to each vertex. The set of probabilities of the network, also called the network parameters, is denoted by P. The couple (G, P), with G = (V, E) a DAG, is a Bayesian network if it satisfies the Markov condition.

Edges in a BN do not necessary represent causal relationships among variables [11]. There are causal and belief (non-causal) networks. Non-causal networks express only the conditional independences between the nodes of the graph induced by the Bayes' theorem and the Markov condition. Causal networks, in addition to independence relations, express cause-effect relationships between the nodes.

3.1 Causal Discovery from Observational Data

The BN can be obtained thanks to expert knowledge. But, this becomes hard or unfeasible for large systems for practical reasons. However, it is also possible to make causal inference from the observation data [11, 13, 14]. This possibility is of great interest for complex systems. Performing causal inference based on observational data requires some assumptions [14, 15]:

- We must assert explicit causal assumptions about the process that generated the observed data.
- Compliance with Causal Markov Condition. To fulfill Causal Markov Condition:
  - There must be no hidden common causes. No two variables in the set of observed variables V can have a hidden common cause, or, if they do, it must have the same unknown value for every unit in the population under consideration.
  - Absence of selection bias which is dependency created between two variables having a common effect when this common effect is instantiated.
  - Absence of causal feedback loops: if X has a causal influence on Y, Y does must not have a causal influence X.

Several causal BN construction algorithms are proposed in the literature. This involves either constraint-based learning algorithm (e.g. PC algorithm [13]) or hybrid learning algorithms such as Min-Max Hill Climbing algorithm [16]. Since most of these construction algorithms are heuristics, their use often requires the validation by experts of the constructed network.

3.2 Evidential Reasoning and Causal Reasoning

The difference between a causal and a non-causal Bayesian network can also be observed in the inference process. To illustrate the difference between evidential (observational) and causal reasoning, let us consider the causal Bayesian network represented in Fig. 1 [17]. The full joint distribution of the left-side BN (Fig. 1(a)) is:

$$P(X_1, X_2, X_3, X_4, X_5) = P(X_1) \,.\, P(X_2|X_1) \,.\, P(X_3|X_1) \,.\, P(X_4|X_2, X_3) \,.\, P(X_5|X_4) \quad (1)$$

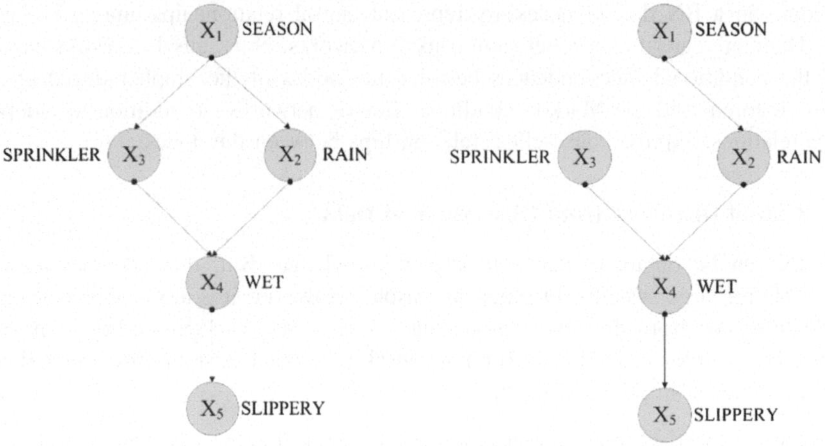

(a) BN representing causal relationship among season (X1), it is raining or not (X2), the sprinkler is on or not (X3), the pavement is wet or not (X4), and the pavement is slippery or not (X5)

(b) Modified Bayesian network (removal of the causal link between the season X1 and the sprinkler X3) following an intervention on the sprinkler (turned on)

Fig. 1. Evidential and causal reasoning (adapted from [17]).

Evidential Reasoning

From the graph presented in Fig. 1 and the joint distribution probability, it is possible to determine any conditional probability given some evidences. For example, the probability that the sprinkler is on, after observing that the pavement is slippery, is:

$$P(X_3 = on | X_5 = true) = \frac{P(X_3 = on,\ X_5 = true)}{P(X_5 = true)} \tag{2}$$

$$= \frac{\sum_{X_1,X_2,X_4} P(X_1, X_2, X_3 = on,\ X_4, X_5 = true)}{\sum_{X_1,X_2,X_3,X_4} P(X_1, X_2, X_3, X_4, X_5 = true)}$$

$$= \frac{\sum_{X_1,X_2,X_4} P(X_1)P(X_2|X_1)P(X_3 = on|X_1)P(X_4|X_2, X_3 = on)P(X_5 = true|X_4)}{\sum_{X_1,X_2,X_3,X_4} P(X_1)P(X_2|X_1)P(X_3|X_1)P(X_4|X_2, X_3)P(X_5 = true|X_4)}$$

Causal Reasoning

The causal reasoning is the reasoning process that takes place when a certain intervention occurs on one of the model parameters. For example, what happens if one turn on the sprinkler? Contrary to the observation phenomenon, the intervention will have two effects: 1) modification of the value of the parameter that undergoes the action (X3 = on) and 2) modification of the structure of the graph (removal of the causal link between the season X1 and the sprinkler X3 (see Fig. 1(b)). The joint probability distribution becomes:

$$P(X_1, X_2, X_3, X_4, X_5) = P(X_1).P(X_2|X_1).P(X_4|X_2, X_3 = on).P(X_5|X_4) \quad (3)$$

4 Proposed Approach for Change Propagation Analysis Model Construction

The causal dependencies identification and modelling approach for redesign process, CaRe, is based on the determination of causal links among the system parameters. We use the BN formalism to model the causal dependencies exploiting expert knowledge and data exploitation. The CaRe approach is composed of five steps (see Fig. 2):

Step 1. Definition of the system boundary
Step 2. System architecture identification
Step 3. Determination of interfaces and exchanges between components via these interfaces
Step 4. Quantification of exchanges between components and construction of the causal model
Step 5. Exploitation of the change propagation model

4.1 Step 1 - Definition of the System Boundary

The goal is to identify the system elements to consider. In particular, one must ensure that the causal Markov condition is fulfilled, that is, there are no hidden common causes (left-side situation in Fig. 2) or selection bias or causal feedback loops (right-side situation in Fig. 2). This step is critical for the reliability of the model. Its realization requires the participation of experts in the different areas covered by the system parameters.

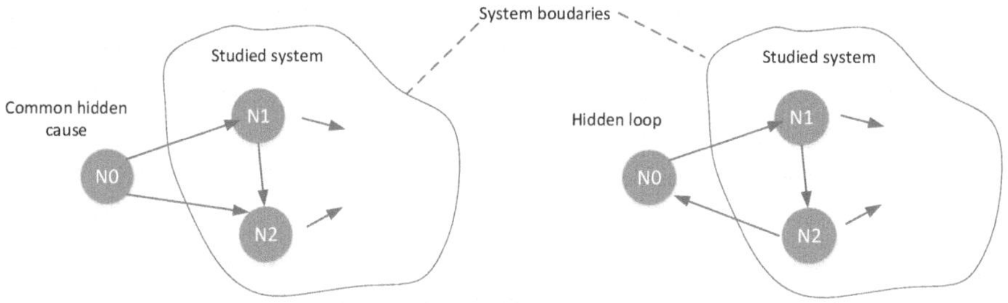

Fig. 2. System boundary

4.2 Step 2 - System Architecture Identification

Product architecture is the scheme by which the function of a product is allocated to physical components [6]. Here, we define first the functions of the system. The system physical components are then identified. Finally, their mapping is established. This step allows to determine components involved in the realization of each of the functions. Functions should be characterized by quantitative indicators.

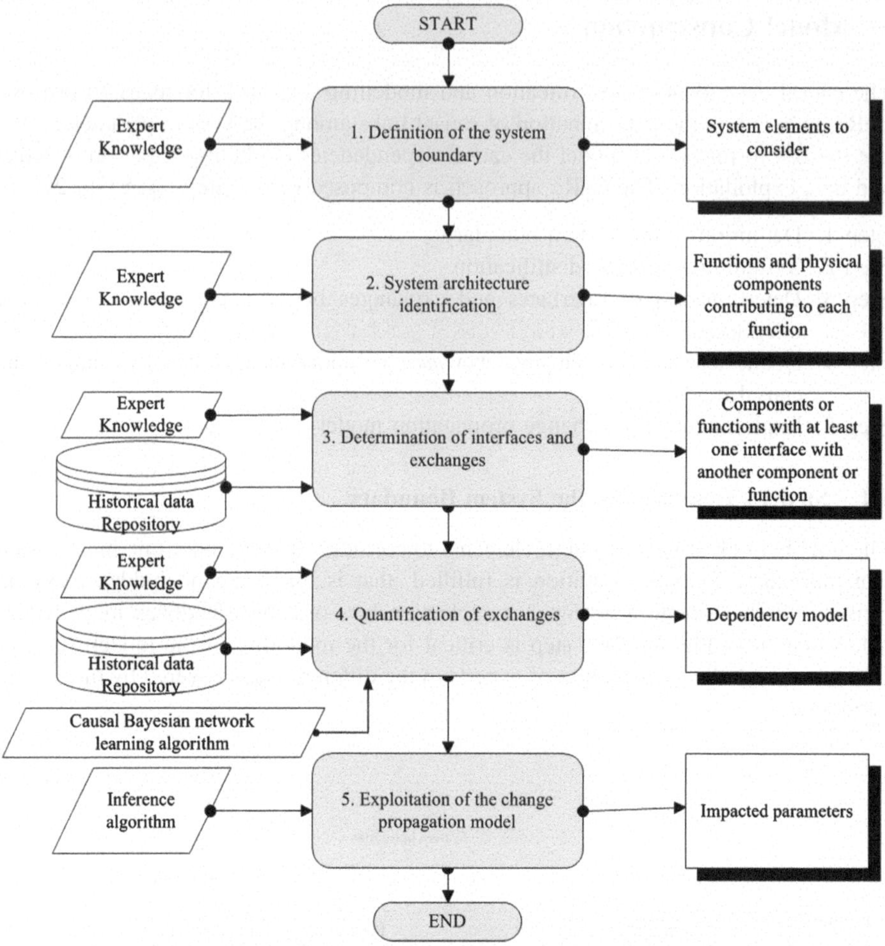

Fig. 3. CaRe: the proposed approach for the causal dependency modelling

4.3 Step 3 - Determination of Interfaces and Exchanges Between Components and Functions via These Interfaces

We then determine the relationship among components and functions. Two components or functions are linked when they share an interface. Four types of exchanges can be done through an interface [18]: Material, Information, Spatial, Energy (MISE in short) exchanges. The interfaces define the change propagation channels (see Fig. 3).

It is also necessary to identify the exchanges between the functions of the system using functional DSM. This step allows to select the relevant parameters for the rest of the approach. Indeed, only components or functions with at least one interface with another component or function will be retained.

The components and their MISE exchanges, the functional model and their inter-depencies, and finally the components-functions mapping allow to complete the architecture of the system (Fig. 4).

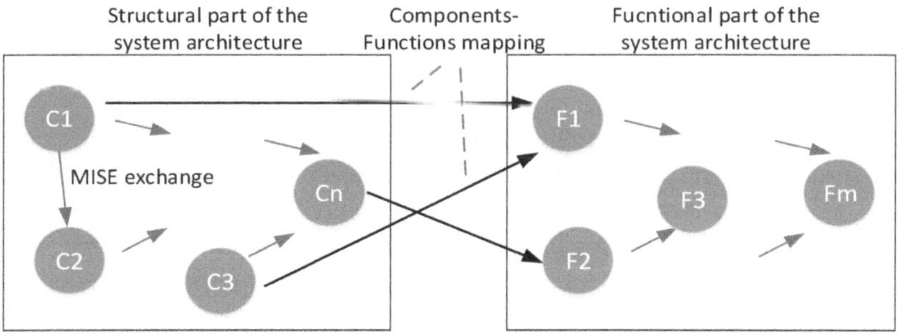

Fig. 4. Architecture and exchanges among components and functions and their mapping

4.4 Step 4 - Quantification of Exchanges Between Components and Construction of the Causal Model

The goal is to quantitatively assess the identified links and to build the causal model by exploiting the data representing the exchanges between functions/components.

Data Collection

In order to facilitate understanding of the data collection process, we consider the trailer exposed in Fig. 2 of [6]. This trailer is composed of 6 components (Box, Hitch, Fairing, Bed, etc.) and realize 6 functions ("Protect cargo from weather", "Connect to vehicle", "Minimize air drag", "Support cargo load", etc.). All parameters characterizing a function or a component or shared with other function/component are identified:

- Function: Fx_MISE_xy (Parameter y characterizing or shared by function x). For example, "Connect to vehicle" function (identified by x) might be characterized by the dimensions of the contact surface and the maximum force it is expected to sustain. Each of these parameters will be identified by a specific y (y_1 and y_2).
- Component: Cx_MISE_xy (Parameter y characterizing or shared by component x). We proceed in the same way as previously replacing functions by components.

Observed values of each parameter are then collected for different periods of time. The historical data table takes the form of Table 1.

Table 1. Historical data for causal model construction

	Functions							Components						
	F1			F2			...	C1			C2			...
Exchanged parameters	F1 MISE 11	F1 MISE 12	...	F2 MISE 21	F2 MISE 22	...		C1 MISE 11	C2 MISE 12	...	C2 MISE 21	C2 MISE 22	...	
Observed values														

Causal Model Building

The causal Bayesian network representing causal relationships among parameters is learned from historical data using a causal Bayesian network learning algorithm. Building a Bayesian model requires the determination of its structure (vertices and edges) and the marginal and conditional probabilities distributions. But first, a choice has to be made on how to model vertices or nodes. Two choices may be made:

- A node represent the state (changed or not) of the corresponding parameter following a change. In this case, nodes are discrete (binary random variable) and the network parameters are conditional probability tables. In this configuration, it is relatively easy to convert a likelihood DSM into a Bayesian model, see [19]. However, this presupposes that a certain number of conditions are met, including: (1) Being able to define the states (changed or not) of each parameter; and (2) The possibility to an expert to quantifies all change propagation probability from one component to the other.
- A node represent the value of the correspond parameter. If we suppose that functions and components parameter are continuous, then nodes are continuous too. In most cases, these parameters are also expected to follow a normal distribution. In this case, root nodes parameters are marginal distributions and the other nodes parameters are expressed as a Gaussian linear function of parent nodes [20]. This approach requires only sufficient data. As parameters are supposed to follow a normal distribution, one can define a normal fluctuation interval $[\mu \pm k\sigma]$ for each parameter, μ being the mean and σ standard deviation.

We recommend to proceed by the second modeling approach. Considered parameters are supposed to be continuous and the researched BN is a Gaussian BN. Each node represents a random variable corresponding to the value of the corresponding parameter. The structure of the causal Bayesian network representing the change propagation model can then be learned using one constraint-based [13] or hybrid learning algorithm [16]. In addition to historical data, most of these learning algorithms allow to exploit expertise in order to reduce the learning process and/or to improve the quality of the built network. The result of this learning process is a network with nodes representing value of functions and components parameters and arcs corresponding to the causal link existing between the connected nodes.

4.5 Step 5 - Exploitation of the Change Propagation Model

For this step, an inference process taking into account the causal aspect of the network is defined (cf. Sect. 3.2. Evidential reasoning and causal reasoning). For a given change made on a parameter, the inference algorithm update the parameters' value and identify all other impacted parameters following this change. These impacted parameters are identified by the calculation of the conditional probabilities after having modified the structure of the network and updated the value of the modified parameter (see example in Sect. 3.2.). Those parameters for which the updated value is outside the normal fluctuation interval $[\mu \pm k\sigma]$ are considered to be the impacted parameters. It is also possible to quantify this impact by calculating the difference between the updated value and the initial value.

5 Conclusion and Future Work

Existing systems are more and more subject to redesign process because of the rapid advances in technology and the constantly evolution of users' needs, among other reasons. Changes propagation management and the control of their consequences on the system functionalities and performances are a major challenge in many industrial sectors.

Change propagates along existing links between components or parameters of the system being redesigned. In this research, we analyze the two types of links that may exist among components or parameters, namely correlation and causality relationships. Based on this analysis, we postulate that the privileged changes propagation links during the redesign process are the causal links. We then review main existing methods for causal relationships identification and causal inferences. The findings suggest that Bayesian Networks are the most appropriate framework to represent causal relationships and to make causal inferences. An approach for change propagation analysis model construction, CaRe (for Causal dependencies identification and modelling approach for Redesign process) is proposed. This approach is based on Bayesian Network theory and uses DSM (Design Structure Matrix).

Some assumptions made in our approach require further research. All the parameters necessary to build the model are supposed known and their historical data available. However, this is not always the case for real system. Therefore, incomplete and missing data should be considered in the learning process. Parameter are supposed continuous variables and the researched BN is a Gaussian Bayesian network. Hybrid Bayesian network containing both discrete and continuous variables could be the most flexible solution for complex systems.

References

1. Zolghadri, M., et al.: Complex systems renewal: positioning, concepts and architectural issues. IFAC Proc. **47**(3), 8731–8736 (2014). https://doi.org/10.3182/20140824-6-ZA-1003.01771
2. Clarkson, P.J., Simons, C., Eckert, C.: Predicting change propagation in complex design. J. Mech. Des. (Trans. ASME) **126**(5), 788–797 (2004). https://doi.org/10.1115/1.1765117

3. Cohen, T., Navathe, S.B., Fulton, R.E.: C-FAR, change favorable representation. Comput. Aided Des. **32**(5), 321–338 (2000). https://doi.org/10.1016/S0010-4485(00)00015-4
4. Koh, E.C., Caldwell, N.H., Clarkson, P.J.: A method to assess the effects of engineering change propagation. Res. Eng. Des. **23**(4), 329–351 (2012). https://doi.org/10.1007/s00163-012-0131-3
5. Giffin, M., et al.: Change propagation analysis in complex technical systems. J. Mech. Des. **131**(8), 081001 (2009). https://doi.org/10.1115/1.3149847
6. Ulrich, K.: The role of product architecture in the manufacturing firm. Res. Policy **24**(3), 419–440 (1995). https://doi.org/10.1016/0048-7333(94)00775-3
7. Huang, G.Q., Mak, K.L.: Current practices of engineering change management in UK manufacturing industries. Int. J. Oper. Prod. Manag. **19**(1), 21–37 (1999). https://doi.org/10.1108/01443579910244205
8. Mooz, H., Forsberg, K., Cotterman, H.: Communicating Project Management: The Integrated Vocabulary of Project Management and Systems Engineering. John Wiley & Sons, Hoboken (2003)
9. Aldrich, J.: Correlations genuine and spurious in Pearson and Yule. Stat. Sci. **10**, 364–376 (1995)
10. Holland, P.W.: Statistics and causal inference. J. Am. Stat. Assoc. **81**(396), 945–960 (1986). https://doi.org/10.2307/2289064
11. Pearl, J.: Causality. Cambridge University Press, Cambridge (2009)
12. Pearl, J.: Probabilistic Reasoning in Intelligent Systems: Networks of Plausible Inference. Morgan Kaufmann Publishers, San Franciso (1988). http://books.google.fr/books?id=k9VsqN24pNYC
13. Spirtes, P., Glymour, C.N., Scheines, R.: Causation, Prediction, and Search. MIT Press, Cambridge (2000). http://books.google.fr/books?id=vV-U09kCdRwC
14. Neapolitan, R.E.: Learning Bayesian Networks. Prentice-Hall, Inc., Upper Saddle River (2003). https://www.researchgate.net/profile/Richard_Neapolitan/publication/235410247_Learning_Bayesian_Networks/links/02e7e52dcf3617aa9c000000.pdf
15. Conrady, S., Jouffe, L.: Bayesian Networks and BayesiaLab: A Practical Introduction for Researchers. Bayesia, USA (2015). https://books.google.fr/books?id=etXXsgEACAAJ
16. Tsamardinos, I., Brown, L., Aliferis, C.: The max-min hill-climbing Bayesian network structure learning algorithm. Mach. Learn. **65**(1), 31–78 (2006). https://doi.org/10.1007/s10994-006-6889-7
17. Pearl, J.: Bayesian networks. Department of Statistics, UCLA (2011). https://escholarship.org/uc/item/53n4f34m
18. Engel, A., Reich, Y.: Advancing architecture options theory: six industrial case studies. Syst. Eng. **18**(4), 396–414 (2015). https://doi.org/10.1002/sys.21312
19. Lee, J., Hong, Y.S.: Bayesian network approach to change propagation analysis. Res. Eng. Des. **28**(4), 437–455 (2017). https://doi.org/10.1007/s00163-017-0252-9
20. Scutari, M., Denis, J.B.: Bayesian Networks: With Examples in R. Taylor & Francis, Boca Raton (2014). http://books.google.fr/books?id=v-XMAwAAQBAJ

Information Systems Simulation for Performance Evaluation - Application in Aircraft Maintenance

Yinling Liu[1(✉)], Tao Wang[2], Haiqing Zhang[3], and Vincent Cheutet[1]

[1] Université de Lyon, INSA Lyon, Laboratoire DISP (EA4570), Villeurbanne, France
{yinling.liu,vincent.cheutet}@insa-lyon.fr

[2] Université de Lyon, Université Jean Monnet, Laboratoire DISP (EA4570), Villeurbanne, France
tao.wang@univ-st-etienne.fr

[3] School of Software Engineering, Chengdu University Information Technology, Chengdu, China
zhanghq@cuit.edu.cn

Abstract. In the design phase, an effective performance evaluation on the information system model for aircraft maintenance helps better iteratively refine the system design. Although many works have emerged to achieve this aim, complex systems are hard to be completely described and the consideration of real-world processes is missing. Thus, how to investigate the system performance with consideration of the real-world aircraft maintenance is our focus. From our point of view, an agent-based simulation modeling is a promising approach to overcome such problem. In this paper, we develop an agent-based simulation model for the whole maintenance process, focusing on cooperation among sub business processes. This model describes the flight process, cooperation between stakeholders and failure repairs, where scheduled/unscheduled maintenance and with/without uncertain event scenarios have been addressed. The performance evaluation of this model is based on the analysis of impacts of key factors on the airline's service level and maintenance cost.

Keywords: Agent-based simulation modeling · Information system
Business process · Civil aircraft maintenance

1 Introduction

The unified business process for aircraft maintenance has been proposed as an AMSS (Aircraft Maintenance Service System) model [1], which is capable of providing a platform where all the relevant information can be collected and a decision can be made from the global point of view. This architecture of the AMSS explains the aircraft maintenance from the business point of view [2]. Seven components, including Customer Requirement Component (CRC), Service Strategy Component (SSC), Service Task Component (STC), Workshop

Published by Springer Nature Switzerland AG 2018.
P. Chiabert et al. (Eds.): PLM 2018, IFIP AICT 540, pp. 789–799, 2018.
https://doi.org/10.1007/978-3-030-01614-2_72

Component (WC), Supply Chain Component (SCC), Quality Control Component (QCC) and Service Decision Component (SDS), have been involved. The CRC determines maintenance requirements. The SSC is to provide strategies for maintenance issues. How to carry out maintenance work and keep aircraft serviceable are illustrated in the STC, WC, SCC. Moreover, the improvement of maintenance is implemented with the help of the QCC and SDC.

In this paper, **we focus on the performance evaluation of the AMSS with a consideration of real-world maintenance processes**. The AMSS model emphasizes the individuality of stakeholders and the cooperation between them. Performance evaluation is a tedious task since it is almost impossible to quantitatively estimate it a priori (i.e. before the implementation). Simulation is known as a powerful approach to meet this objective in other contexts [3].

More precisely, an agent-based modeling can be defined simply as essentially decentralized, individual-centric approach to model design [4]. The real-world maintenance process and decentralized stakeholders provide this method with the possibility of detecting unknown (or unexpected) behaviors of complex system [5]. The agent is autonomous [6], which is just sensible to present stakeholders. For example, the agent may refuse the request from another agent. Because inside agents, they own their own internal states. Specific states receive specific signals. If the signal is sent at an inappropriate time, it will be neglected. Therefore, **the agent-based modeling simulation method is a good choice for modeling the AMSS and evaluating a priori its performance**.

In this paper, Sect. 2 discusses the application of simulation methods in aircraft maintenance domain and information system performance evaluation approaches. Section 3 provides an approach to realize the agent-based simulation modeling. The experiments are conducted to analyze the impacts of key factors on airline's maintenance cost and service level in the Sect. 4. Finally, Sect. 5 concludes the paper with future perspectives.

2 Literature Review

2.1 Aircraft Maintenance Simulation

Simulation approaches have been widely used in the both civil and military aircraft maintenance. In the military domain, some earlier works [7,8] involve the military logistic application analysis, but these do not consider the whole maintenance process. Although Mattila's work [9] tends to describe the whole maintenance process, his work lacks the consideration for the importance of impacts of individuality on the performance of the model. Recently, MacKenzie et al. proposes an agent-based simulation for application to the sortie generation process, focusing on a single fighter aircraft unit [10], and Datta et al. develop a discrete-event simulation model representing an end-to-end repair line for jet aircraft to evaluate different manpower resource utilization decisions [11]. However, the evaluation of manpower utilization decisions is just based on the utilization rate of manpower and neglects other factors like maintenance cost, service level, etc.

In the civil aircraft domain, the simulation method for aircraft maintenance tends to be prevailing. Most of the works [12–14] attempt to combine simulation methods with optimization objectives. Simulation methods are principally used for estimating the performance of optimal model. However, these works either only underline some specific phases of maintenance like spare parts allocation, personal scheduling, etc., or are inadequate to the stress of behaviors of individual objects. Therefore, the evaluation indicators for proposed models appear to be insufficient. In addition, the combination of multi-agent system modeling and interdisciplinary approach is proposed to model the safety culture, in order to evaluate workers' commitment to safety [15]. The agent-based model was implemented in Java instead of any agent modeling tools, because they thought that conceptual models of agents and specification languages limited their purposes. Thus, that work is contributed more to the theory development of safety culture.

To conclude, on the one hand, most works are dedicated to the solving of formulated problems rather than to the methodological details; on the other hand, little description of the complexity of the aircraft maintenance such as cooperation between stakeholders is addressed.

2.2 Information System Evaluation

The evaluation of information systems is utterly difficult, as its multidimensionality, quantitative and qualitative aspects, and conflicts among evaluator viewpoints [16]. Most of works [17–19] contribute to providing more complete indicators for evaluating the existing information systems, in order to investigate their performances. From our point of view, the evaluation is principally relied on developed information systems. They are evaluated either intrinsically with informatics indicators or a posteriori observations once they are deployed inside the organization. Nevertheless, very few works try to evaluate a priori impacts of their deployment and the performance of the new organization.

Maintenance systems for aircraft are kinds of complex systems, which concentrate on individuality of stakeholders, distributed and ephemeral cooperation between stakeholders. Jennings [6] points out the flexible, high-level interactions of agents make the engineering of complex system easier. The author recalls that complex systems are always distributed and agent decomposition is very important to manage complexity. Agent-based systems are essentially decentralized and individual-centric. Moyaux et al. [20] explains that the system complexity makes it difficult to know every possible interaction in the system, because the system only has partial control and observability over its environment, and thus, this environment is highly unpredictable. Agent-based decentralization takes this into account by letting each agent continuously coordinate its actions with other agents, instead of making this agent apply a behavior prescribed at design-time.

As for our simulation model, the distributed and ephemeral characteristics are captured by agents. For example, the flight agent schedules the plane agent to service, while the service task agent maybe is requesting a specific part. Two agents accomplish their tasks independently. If the signal from the flight agent reaches the plane agent at an inappropriate moment, this signal will be neglected by the plane agent. Because agents are autonomous. Thus, in this case, the cooperation between agents is ephemeral. Thanks to the simulation tool *Anylogic*, we can build our agent-based simulation model easily dealing with distributed and ephemeral issues. Additionally, since agents own high level of individuality, the cooperation of them may make the system produce some unknown behaviors.

The major contributions of our work are: **(1) effectively describing the behaviors of the AMSS; (2) enabling maintenance designers to fully investigate the system performance.** Therefore, the simulation analysis allows maintenance designers to have enough flexibility in the phrase of model design. Additionally, this analysis is automatic and has improved the traditionally manual analysis process to be more accurate, more rapid and less error-prone.

3 The Agent-Based Simulation Framework

Aiming at investigating the performance of the AMSS, an agent-based simulation model is developed, which is shown in Fig. 1. This model is capable of dealing with four kinds of maintenance scenarios: scheduled/unscheduled maintenance and with/without uncertain events. The unscheduled maintenance and uncertain events are determined by fault events and uncertain events respectively. In this model, we have created nine agents: Flight Agent (FA), Plane Agent (PA), Equipment Agent (EA), Customer Requirement Agent (CRA), Service Strategy Agent (SSA), Service Task Agent (STA), Supply Chain Agent (SCA), Quality Control Agent (QCA) and Service Decision Agent (SDA). The maintenance logic is completely from the AMSS model. Therefore, we derive agents from components of the model. In addition, we add the FA, PA and EA to run the simulation more smoothly. FA is dedicated to scheduling plane. PA is created to just simulate a plane. EA allows us to get a better insight of repairing issues. In the following, the development of PA, EA and STA is discussed in details.

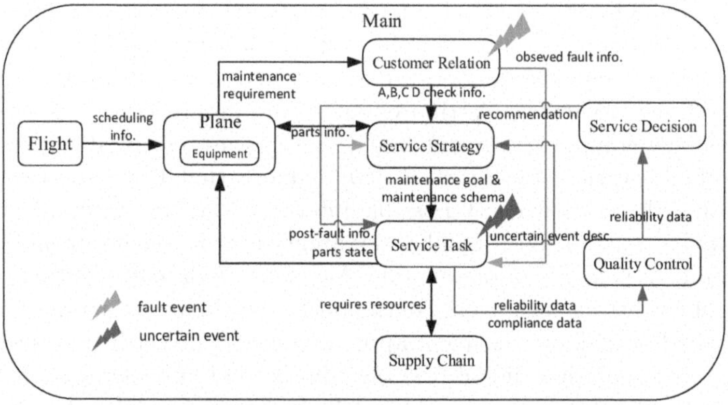

Fig. 1. Agent-based simulation model for AMSS

3.1 Plane and Equipment Agent

The plane agent is a kind of composite agents, which contains the equipment agents. The data for this agent consist of aircraft data (*aircraftNumber, aircraftType, aircraftState*), the flight data (*flightNumber, flightHours, city*), scheduled maintenance data (*ACheckTime, BCheckTime, CCheckTime, DCheckTime*) and parts data (*type, changeoverTime, repairTime, repairingTime, serialNumber, price, equipmentState*).

When all the aircraft are loaded from the database, they are in the state "Ready". They are scheduled by *departure* and *arrival* events, which are defined in the FA. In the state "SidedTransitCheck", we assume that fault events occur with a specific probability. This state is the only place where the CRA may be triggered. When one aircraft needs to do the scheduled maintenance like "TransitCheck", "ACheck", "BCheck", "CCheck" or "DCheck", the EA will be called to check states of relevant parts.

In terms of the EA, the major objectives of this agent are to check the states of parts and determine the repairing strategies for faulty parts. As for the unscheduled maintenance, one faulty parts list will be delivered to the EA. The repairing strategies for them are determined by decision rules shown in Table 1. When receiving the scheduled maintenance, the parts will be checked just to see whether it needs to be replaced. It should be noted that the *repairTime* refers to the overhaul time of parts. The *repairingTime* implies the repairing time of part is short.

Table 1. The decision rules for repairing strategies

```
if (currentUseTime ≥ changeoverTime)        repairType = "replace";
else{
    if (repairingTime ≥ plane.interval)         repairType = "replace&repair";
    else {
        if (changeoverTime − currentUseTime ≥ plane.interval)
            repairType = "repair";
        else
            repairType = "replace";
    }
}
```

3.2 Service Task Agent

The data of the STA are the *aircraftNumber, aircraftType, interval, state, faultDesc, detailedFaultDesc, parts, partsChecking* and *aircraftTechnicians*. The state chart of the STA is shown in Fig. 2. This agent is capable of dealing with issues like fault identification, maintenance planning (resource request and labor assignment) and uncertain events. When receiving signals from CRA, it will trigger fault identification process. When receiving signals from SSA, it means the set of

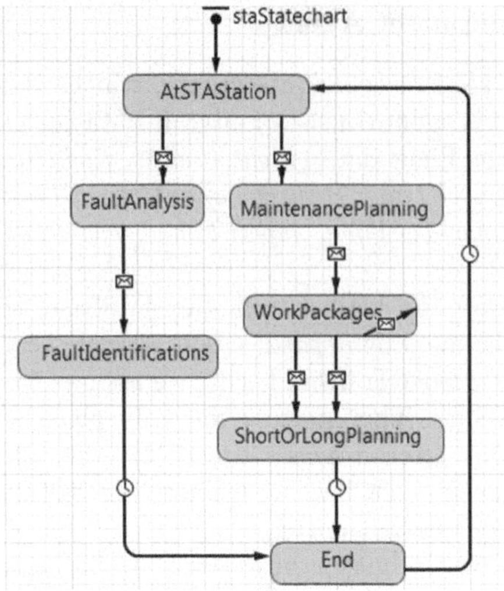

Fig. 2. The state chart of the STA

possible faulty components has been determined by SSA. Thus, it starts to make maintenance plans. During the process of repairing ("WorkPackages" state), uncertain events maybe happen. Then, it will trigger agents like SSA, QCA and SDA, in order to find better solutions. The logic of dealing uncertain events is shown as blue arrows in Fig. 1.

It should be noted that we recognize unknown events occurring during the process of repairing of dysfunctional components as uncertain events.

4 Case Study

4.1 Experiment Design and Data

The performance evaluation of the AMSS is conducted via examining the impacts of the number of aircraft (experiment 1) and technicians (experiment 2) on service level (sl) and maintenance cost. In this model, the key factors are: the probabilities of the occurrence of fault events and uncertain events, and the numbers of aircraft and technicians. We expect to create a severe simulation environment to see the responses of the system. Thus, the probabilities of the occurrence of fault events and uncertain events are amplified, which are assigned as 0.5 and 1 respectively.

In terms of cost analysis, the downtime cost, labor cost, stock cost and parts purchase cost are taken into consideration. The definitions of costs are shown below in equation (1)–(4), where the *totalRepairTime* (shown in Table 2) and interval are counted by seconds, the salary (i) and time (i) represent the ith aircraft technician's salary counted by hours and the corresponding working time, the number (i) implies the number of the ith kind of parts and the *days* means the number of storing days, and the cost (j) means the cost of the jth kind of parts. In addition, all the costs are counted by dollars. It should be noted that the *scheduledTime* in Table 2 means the total repair time of scheduled maintenance.

$$DowntimeCost = (totalRepairTime - interval) * 2.8; \tag{1}$$

$$LaborCosts = \sum_{(i=1)}^{n} salary(i) * time(i); \tag{2}$$

$$StockCosts = \sum_{(i=1)}^{n} number(i) * 10 * days; \tag{3}$$

$$PartsPurchaseCosts = \sum_{(j=1)}^{n} cost(j); \tag{4}$$

The industrial relevance of values for data is explained in the following. The data *interval*(around 1 h), *inventoryPrepare*(1–3 h), *repairingTime*(20–120 mins) (the faulty parts that can be repaired on site) and *repairTime*(5–30 h) (the faulty parts that have to be repaired at workshops) are of a certain level of industrial relevance. The value for data *inventoryPrepare* is given by the random distribution $uniform\_discr(min, max)$. The rest are determined by the data stored in the database. However, in terms of the data *informationDelivery* and *maintenancePlanning*, the values for them are assumed as 2 s and 10 min respectively, which are of less of industrial relevance. The data of the *faultIdentification*, *exceptionalEventSSA* and *exceptionalEventSTA* are determined depending on knowledge stored in the database. If the solution has been stored in the database, they will take 0 min. If not, they will take either 30 min or one hour.

Table 2. The definitions of total repair time on maintenance scenarios

Maintenance scenario	Total repair time
Scheduled	informationDelivery, maintenancePlanning, inventoryPrepare, repairing
Scheduled+ Uncertain event	**exceptionalEventSTA(eSTA)**, **exceptionalEventSSA(eSSA)**, scheduledTime
Unscheduled	**faultIdentification, faultAnalysis**, scheduledTime
Unscheduled+ Uncertain event	**faultIdentification, faultAnalysis**, **eSTA**, **eSSA**, scheduledTime

The definition of service level is shown as follow:

$$servicelevel = totalRepairTime - interval. \tag{5}$$

The relation between the delayed time and service level is shown in Table 3. When analyzing the service level for aircraft maintenance, the first two important indicators are the "sl = 10" and "sl = 0". The indicators of "sl = 9 to 6" are the second most important indicators.

Table 3. The relation between delayed time(minute) and service level

Delayed time	0	(0, 30]	(30, 60]	(60, 120]	(120, 240]	(240, $+\infty$)
Service level(0–10)	10	9	8	7	6	0

4.2 Experiment Hypothesis

The major experiment hypotheses consist of:

- all the aircraft fly from London to the other cities around the world. Then, they will fly back to London;
- fault events can happen only when aircraft reach the "SidedTransitCheck" state in the PA. Uncertain events always take place in the STA;
- each faulty part only occupies one technician who is randomly distributed and has matched skills;
- all maintenance business processes are included in the combination of scheduled/unscheduled maintenance and with/without uncertain events;
- for the *departure* event, if there is no available aircraft for the departure of one flight, this flight will be canceled. For the *arrival* event, if the downtime for departure is over 4 h, this flight will be canceled neither;
- fixed parts are as good as news after maintenance actions.

4.3 Experiment Results and Analysis

This simulation experiment is implemented in Anylogic PLE 8.2.3. The configurations of running laptop are 8G memory and 4 processors (i7-6500U CPU). The simulation is set as two weeks, which takes around 4.5 h. The experiment results are divided into two parts: impacts of the number of aircraft (Fig. 3) and the number of technicians (Fig. 4) on airline's service level and maintenance cost.

The result of the first experiment is very interesting. With the increase of the number of aircraft, the number of on-time flights (sl = 10) goes up steadily.

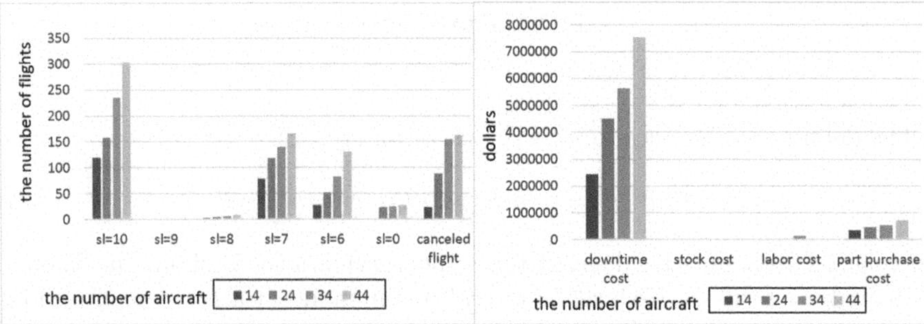

Fig. 3. The impacts of the number of aircraft on airline's service level and maintenance cost

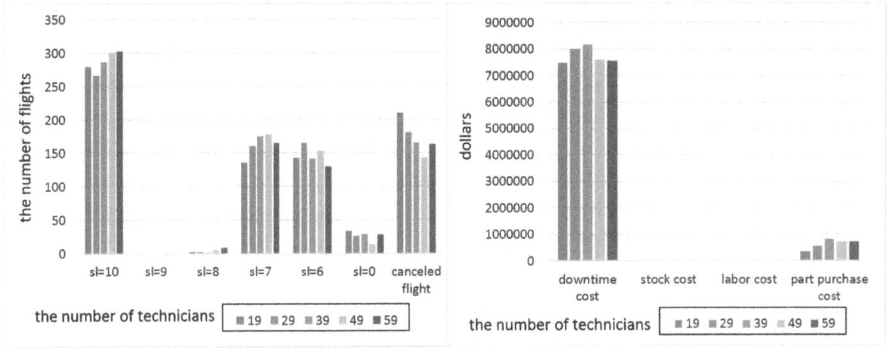

Fig. 4. The impacts of the number of technicians on airline's service level and maintenance cost

But the number of the canceled flight represents variability. For instance, when the number of aircraft rises from 14 to 34, the canceled flight increases regularly. While when the number of aircraft equals to 44, the number of canceled flights just shows a slight increase. Thus, based on the result of the service level, we have found 44 is the most appropriate sum for the number of aircraft for airlines. For the maintenance cost, the downtime costs increase regularly and the part purchase costs rise slowly, with the increase of the number of aircraft. However, the stock cost and labor cost are less significant.

The second experiment is very significant as well. The major trend for all the indicators remain stable. Comparing with the impacts of the number of technicians on the number of flights, we find that 49 is the most suitable sum for the number of technicians. If the number of technicians equals to or less than 49, the number of flights increases gradually despite a slight fluctuation when the number of technicians ranges from 19 to 39. When comparing the cases of the number of technician equaling to 49 and 59, they almost share the same level of the number of flights, but the former shows better in the indicators of "sl = 0" and canceled flight. As for "sl = 7 and 6", they are much less important than the indicators of "sl = 0" and canceled flight. At the same time, they almost share the same changing trend. As a result, we suggest that 49 is better for the number of technicians. As for the maintenance cost, the downtime cost firstly increases then decreases, with the increase of the number of technicians. When the number of technicians equals to 39, the values of the downtime cost and part purchase cost both reach the peak. Above all, the maintenance cost does not experience any remarkable change with the increase of the number of technicians.

Even though we just conduct two experiments on the evaluation of the system, this agent-based model simulation allows us to evaluate almost all the aspects of the system. In fact, the impacts of each significant factor and maintenance strategies on system performance can be explored via changing their values and strategies respectively. As a result, in this paper, we provide the basic simulation model for aircraft maintenance, which enables maintenance designers to fully examine the system.

5 Conclusion

In this paper, the agent-based simulation model describes the AMSS behavior via combining flight scheduling, cooperation between stakeholders, and failure repairs as a whole maintenance process, concentrating on scenarios of the combination of scheduled/unscheduled maintenance and with/without uncertain events. The experiment results show this method not only has the strong capability of describing complex information systems but enables us to investigate the system performance from the global point of view. When maintenance designers need to investigate the impacts of some environment variables and maintenance strategies on maintenance efficiency and cost, our approach can provide a qualitative and quantitative analysis on this problem. The authenticity of initial data is a big issue in our work. In order to realize this experiment, some key data is still based on our hypothesis. Thus, one of our perspectives is to apply more realistic data to the proposed simulation model for better evaluation and improvement. Moreover, the theoretical verification of this model is still missing. In the future, the formal method will be employed to verify the feasibility of the AMSS model.

Acknowledgments. This research work is supported by the China Scholarship Council.

References

1. Liu, Y., Wang T., Cheutet V., Zhang H.: An architecture modeling methodology for aircraft maintenance service system. In: The 24th STP Conference (2017)
2. Liu, Y., Wang T., Cheutet V., Zhang H.: Towards standards analysis and application in process of aircraft maintenance repair overhaul. In: IFAC World Congress, Toulouse, France (2017)
3. Alrabghi, A., Tiwari, A.: A novel approach for modeling complex maintenance systems using discrete event simulation. Reliab. Eng. Syst. Saf. **154**, 160–170 (2016). https://doi.org/10.1016/j.ress.2016.06.003
4. Anylogic. https://en.wikipedia.org/wiki/AnyLogic
5. Bonabeau, E.: Predicting the unpredictable. Harv. Bus. Rev. **80**, 109–116 (2002)
6. Jennings, N.R.: On agent-based software engineering. Artif. Intell. **117**(2), 277–296 (2000). https://doi.org/10.1016/S0004-3702(99)00107-1
7. Kang, K., Gue, K., Eaton, D.R.: Cycletime reduction for naval aviation deports. In: Proceedings of the 30th Conference on Winter Simulation, pp. 907–914 (1998)
8. Balaban, H.S., Brigantic, R.T., Wright, S.A., Papatyi, A.F.: A simulation approach to estimating aircraft mission capable rates for the United States air force. In: Proceedings of the 2000 Winter Simulation Conference (2000)
9. Mattila, V., Virtanen, K., Raivio, T.: A simulation model for aircraft maintenance in an uncertain operational environment. In: Proceedings of 17th European Simulation Multiconference, Nottingham, England, pp. 456–461 (2003)
10. MacKenzie, A., Miller, J.O., Hill, R.R.: Application of agent based modelling to aircraft maintenance manning and sortie generation. Simul. Model. Pract. Theory **20**, 89–98 (2012). https://doi.org/10.1016/j.simpat.2011.09.001

11. Datta, P.P., Srivastava, A., Roy, R.: A simulation study on maintainer resource utilization of a fast jet aircraft maintenance line under availability contract. Comput. Ind. **64**, 543–555 (2013). https://doi.org/10.1016/j.compind.2013.02.011
12. Lee, L.H., Chew, E.P., Teng, S., Chen, Y.: Multi-objective simulation-based evolutionary algorithm for an aircraft spare parts allocation problem. Eur. J. Oper. Res. **189**, 476–491 (2008). https://doi.org/10.1016/j.ejor.2007.05.036
13. Van den Bergh, J., De Bruecker, P., Belien, J., De Boeck, L., Demeulemeester, E.: A three-stage approach for aircraft line maintenance personnel rostering using MIP, discrete event simulation and DEA. Expert. Syst. Appl. **40**(7), 2659–2668 (2013). https://doi.org/10.1016/j.eswa.2012.11.009
14. Regattieri, A., Giazzi, A., Gamberi, M., Gamberini, R.: An innovative method to optimize the maintenance policies in an aircraft: general framework and case study. J. Air Transp. Manag. **44**, 8–20 (2015). https://doi.org/10.1016/j.jairtraman.2015.02.001
15. Passenier, D., Mols, C., Bím, J., Sharpanskykh, A.: Modeling safety culture as a socially emergent phenomenon: a case study in aircraft maintenance. Comput. Math. Organ. Theory **22**, 487–520 (2016). https://doi.org/10.1007/s10588-016-9212-6
16. Hamilton, S., Chervany, N.L.: Evaluating information system effectiveness-Part I: comparing evaluation approaches. MIS Q. **5**, 55–69 (1981)
17. Petter, S., DeLone, W., McLean, E.: Measuring information systems success: models, dimensions, measures, and interrelationships. Eur. J. Inf. Syst. **17**(3), 236–263 (2008)
18. Petter, S., DeLone, W., McLean, E.R.: The past, present, and future of "IS Success". Eur. J. Inf. Syst. **13**(5), 341 (2012)
19. Khodakarami, F., Chan, Y.E.: Exploring the role of customer relationship management (CRM) systems in customer knowledge creation. Inf. Manag. **51**(1), 27–42 (2014). https://doi.org/10.1016/j.im.2013.09.001
20. Moyaux, T., Chaib-draa, B., D'Amours, S.: Supply chain management and multiagent systems: an overview. In: Chaib-draa, B., Müller, J.P. (eds.) Multiagent Based Supply Chain Management, pp. 1–27. Springer, Berlin (2006). https://doi.org/10.1007/978-3-540-33876-5_1

Author Index

The manufacturer's authorised representative in the EU is Springer Nature Customer Service Centre GmbH, Europaplatz 3, 69115 Heidelberg, Germany. If you have any concerns regarding our products, please contact ProductSafety@springernature.com

Printed and bound by CPI Group (UK) Ltd, Croydon, CR0 4YY

05/10/2026

02228143-0007